Chronology of Civilization *to 1648*

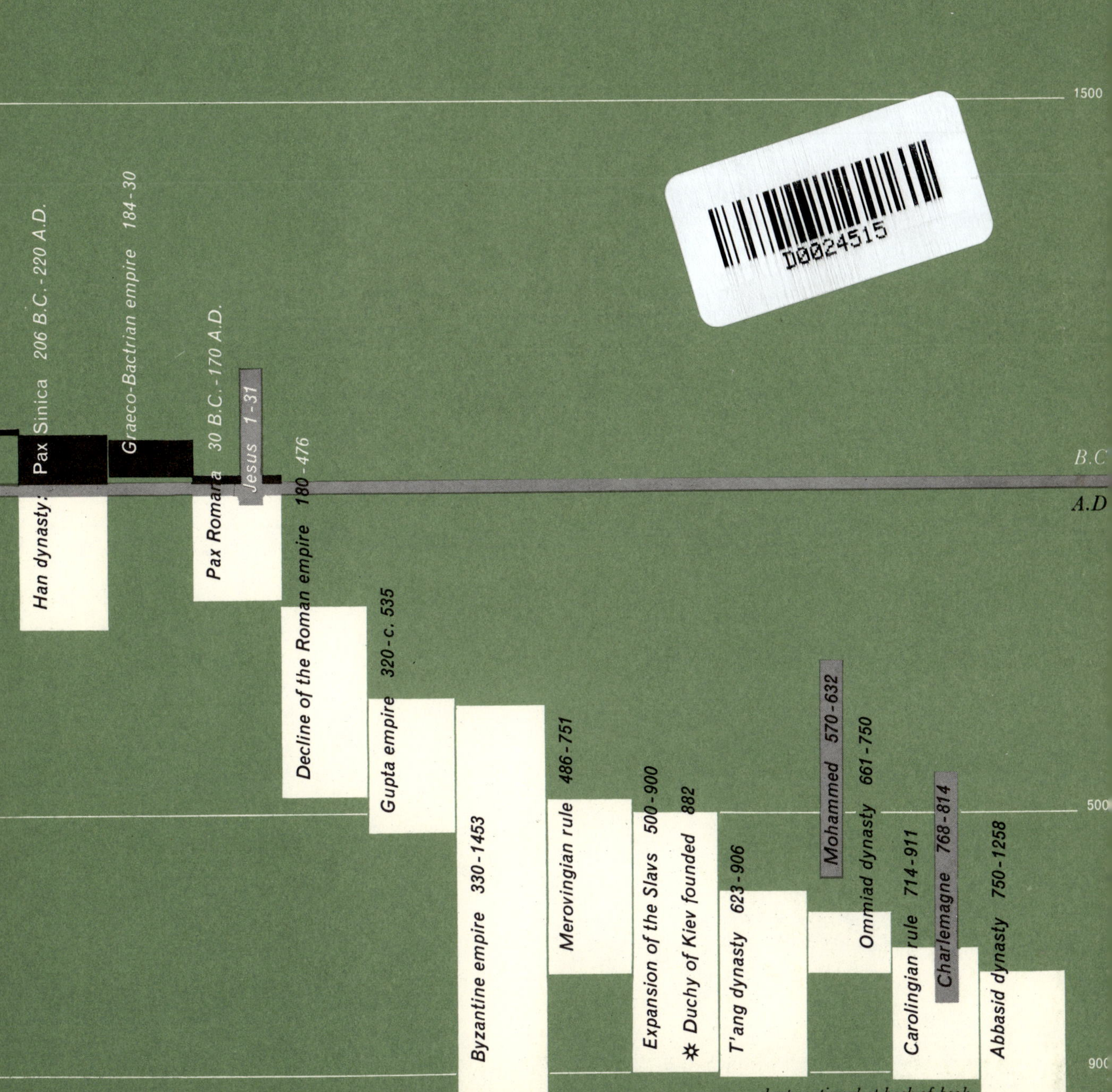

chart continued at back of book

Civilization *past and present*

A survey of the history of man—his governmental, economic, social, religious, intellectual, and esthetic activities—from the earliest times to the present, in Europe, in Asia, and in the Americas

Volume one **From the beginnings of civilization through the discovery and conquest of the New World. Paleolithic Era to 1650 A.D.**

T. Walter Wallbank *Professor of History, University of Southern California*

Alastair M. Taylor *Formerly of the University of Southern California, now in research, Balliol College, Oxford*

Scott, Foresman and Company *Chicago, Atlanta, Dallas, New York, San Francisco*

Third edition

Civilization *past and present*

Preface to the third edition

This volume was first planned on the eve of the Second World War when the majority of the American people were still endeavoring to insulate themselves from participating in, or accepting the consequences of, world events. Many citizens still believed it possible to rely on the geographic protection of oceans, on the Monroe Doctrine, and on the tradition of "no foreign entanglements." A reflection of this widespread attitude was the limitation to western culture of most college survey courses in "civilization" and "world history." The consequent neglect of the Middle East, China and Japan, south and southeast Asia, and Latin America—areas which constituted the vast majority of the planet's population and culture—was repaired only by more specialized courses.

In the face of this historical egocentrism, the authors then believed that the United States was about to embark on a new role of world leadership, which would necessitate an informed citizenry for its successful execution. This meant that students should be given the opportunity of familiarizing themselves with the nature of the great culture systems of the world, their historical antecedents, and their current trends and problems, shaping the course of contemporary world affairs. To meet this need *Civilization Past and Present* not only endeavored at that time to present the salient facts in the evolution of European civilization but for the Middle East, south Asia, China, Japan, and Latin America.

The events of the past fifteen years have done much to justify the original purposes of this text. The changing pattern of power in the nation-state system, together with the incredible developments in science and technology, have compressed men and their affairs into one close mold. As a result a revolution has taken place in the relationship of the average American to the "outside world." Tremendous quantities of his money are being spent in foreign lands; even larger amounts are being expended for defense because of the menace of a rival system of culture. Furthermore, his country functions as one of the most influential forces in a relatively new international organization, the United Nations. Concurrently, practically every young man is expected to serve in his country's armed forces, often overseas; and in another sphere hundreds of Americans, as technical experts, teachers, and scholars, travel abroad under the auspices of Point Four and Fulbright funds. As the problems, attitudes, and aspirations of people all over the globe have become its business, the United States has assumed world leadership; for the well-informed citizen it demands an understanding of the implications contained in such items as N.A.T.O., neutralism, thirty-eighth parallel, Apartheid, Mao's *New Democracy,* chain reaction, Mau Mau, and the Arab League. Since the days when the pursuit of Clio, the Muse of history, was part of the preparatory education of lawyers, doctors, and clergymen, not to speak of the dilettante needs of gentlemen, the purposes and form of general history have radically changed. Now history must meet the needs of a large and diversified university population; it has to offer to all students, regardless of their future vocation, some idea of how the world in which they live came to be.

This kind of broad offering has its limitations. Emphasis necessarily must be upon wide movements and trends rather than in the intensive analysis and study of limited periods. The historical specialist is always tempted to scoff at its "superficiality"; but his alternative, a thorough understanding of some epoch in some specific area, would seem to the average person to constitute a much less useful and functional body of information. In general the authors believe that the parlous nature of existing human affairs, the obviously arrested development of the social sciences in contrast to technological advances, and the complexity of even the minimum historical background essential for understanding our contemporary world culture, necessitates a greater investment in time and effort than is usually the case with world history in the existing pattern of general education. Four semesters of study would be more nearly the time required by the average college student to gain insight into the genesis, nature, and direction of twentieth-century civilization. This is not only an affirmation of the importance of a broad treatment of the unfolding of world history in all its manifold and connected aspects of politics, economics, the arts, thought and religion; but also a plea for recognizing the validity of general education in whatever discipline of learning.

In this, the third edition of *Civilization,* the authors have sought to profit by the many helpful suggestions that have come from the classroom, to utilize the latest results of historical research, and to extend the historical narrative down to the present date. Generally speaking, the following areas have been given additional space and emphasis: eastern Europe, Russia, the Middle and Far East. Expert assistance has been obtained in a number of fields: astronomy, geological history, early man, the anthropology of primitive cultures, ancient Egypt, and modern Africa and the Middle East. Volume I has been revised in three key areas. First, the chapters on ancient India and China have been rewritten to make use of important new materials. Second, the three chapters dealing with the classical world have been reorganized for a double purpose: experience has borne out that students obtained a more coherent grasp of the Greek and Roman contributions when these civilizations were assigned separate chapters; the authors have attempted a valuable new approach by providing an interrelated view of three major contemporary societies—the Graeco-Roman world-state, India, and China—stressing culture impact and exchange among those great civilizations. Third, this volume has been augmented in the field of political history by the addition of Chapter 12 on political developments in the early Middle Ages, with special emphasis on the genesis of Russia and the evolution of the Slavic world; and by a second chapter, sixteen, which discusses political trends in Europe in the late Middle Ages and the Renaissance. In Volume II the post-1945 domestic trends in the most important areas of the world have been brought up to date, with emphasis on developments in Soviet Russia. The narrative of international affairs likewise has been carried down to the armistice in Korea and the rise of serious unrest in the Russian satellites. The chapters on nineteenth- and twentieth-century art, thought, and science have been revised to point up basic tendencies. The original topical treatment of nationalism and democracy in the nineteenth century has been altered in the direction of a more chronological approach; new historical material on the pivotal year, 1848, was utilized. In keeping with the rapid tempo of events in the Middle East and south Asia, new sections have been added on the Arab Revival and the general liquidation of the colonial system. The student is directed briefly to the rapid development of nationalism in Africa and to the disturbing deterioration of race relations.

To improve the visual and graphic features of the text the chronological tables have been redesigned, new illustrations introduced, and a number of interpretive spot maps added. Included in each volume is a sixteen-page historical map section in color for reference purposes.

As in the first edition, the present text consciously tries to direct the student's thought in the direction of history as process as well as fact. Attention is called to the importance of ideas, the problem of the rise and fall of civilizations, and the importance of culture diffusion. Finality and positiveness, of course, can never be achieved in studying Form, Movement, Cause, and Effect in human affairs. But the pursuit of the "why" and the "how" is stimulating to most students and is often the motivation for a careful and precise study of historical facts. Most important, encouraging the student to ruminate about the past will give him the desire and some ability to evaluate the stream of history in which he lives.

T.W.W.
A.M.T.

Julian, California
Oxford, England
January 1954

Acknowledgments

In revising this survey of world history, as in preparing the original edition, the authors could not, of course, depend solely upon their own resources, except in a few fields where they have developed special interests. Strong reliance, therefore, has been placed upon a host of scholars whose monographs span from Java Man to regionalism in American art. In every known instance where the phraseology of these helpful scholars has been used, a citation is included to indicate our indebtedness. These citations are indicated by superior figures (sources for which are listed by chapters at the end of the volume). Further, for each chapter there has been compiled a list of authorities whose works have been of particular value in planning and shaping the material, and to whom we are also indebted. Any lapses from this policy (of which we hope there are none) may be explained by the fact that one is not always conscious of the exact derivation of phrases or particulars of fact that turn up on the far side of the typewriter ribbon. But like S. MacGillvary Brown in his *Medieval History,* we quote the words of Lessing that he "should be poor, cold, shortsighted indeed, if he had not to some extent learned humbly to borrow foreign treasure, to warm himself at the others' fire and to reinforce his vision by the glasses of art."

The authors wish to express their gratitude for the valuable advice and criticism of Dr. Mustapha Ziada, chairman of the Department of History, Fuad I University, Cairo, Egypt—the Islamic material; and of Dr. Ahmid Fakhry, Director of Pyramid Studies for the Egyptian government—ancient Egypt.

At the University of Southern California, the authors are especially indebted to Dr. A. S. Raubenheimer, Education Vice-President, and Dr. Tracy E. Strevey, Dean of Letters, Arts, and Sciences, for making it possible to offer a vital and comprehensive history of world civilization at the University, and for advice and encouragement during the writing of this book. Also at the University of Southern California the authors wish to acknowledge the able suggestions of Dr. Thomas Clements, head of the Department of Geology—historical geology of the earth; of Dr. Joseph E. Weckler, head of the Department of Anthropology—prehistoric man and cultural anthropology; and of Dr. John A. Russell, head of the Department of Astronomy, and Dr. Gibson Reaves—the latest research in the field of astronomy, especially the significance of the discoveries made by the Palomar Telescope. And to the teachers and students who have used *Civilization,* we are indeed grateful for their help in making this a more useful book.

Since this is a revision, substantial portions of the earlier editions have been retained. Therefore, it is fitting once more to record our gratitude for the help of the following persons: Professor Louis Gottschalk for criticisms and suggestions, both general and detailed; the late Professor H. F. MacNair of the University of Chicago—the material on China, Japan, and the Pacific islands; Professor G. V. Bobrinskoy of the University of Chicago—the material on India; Professor Fay-Cooper Cole of the University of Chicago—Chapter 1; Professor W. E. Caldwell of the University of North Carolina—Chapters 2, 5, and 6; Professor James Lea Cate of the University of Chicago—Chapters 8, 9, 10, 13, 14, 15, and 16; Professor Francis H. Herrick of Mills College—Chapters 17 and 18; Mr. Hugh M. Cole of the University of Chicago—Chapter 20; Mr. Francis J. O'Malley of Notre Dame University—the history of the Church.

We express our thanks to the following persons whose work enlivens the pages of the text: to Mr. R. M. Chapin, Jr., who besides drawing many of the maps, gave discriminating attention to the best possible ways to dramatize and clarify certain important geographical impressions; to Mr. Wallace Dierickx, who planned and integrated with the text the new reference and spot maps in this revision; to Marilyn Knudson for the design of the reference map section; to Mr. George Armstrong and Mr. James M. Goodman, who drew certain of the new maps; to Franz Altschuler for drawings in the interparts and in the Prologue; to Miss Charlotte Speight, for assistance in selecting art illustrations; to Dr. Otto Bettmann for further assistance in selecting illustrations.

Finally, we express our appreciation to the publishers from whose books quotations have been made, and to those persons who have permitted us to reproduce various illustrations. (The quotations and illustrations are credited in detail under "List of Illustrations" and "Bibliography and Acknowledgments.")

Contents *volume one*

Part two Around the Mediterranean 118

Part three Along the Caravan Routes 250

Reference map section

List of Maps

1. Toward civilization

2. The Nile, the Tigris, and the Euphrates

3. The Indus and the Ganges

4. The Wei and the Hwang Ho

5. The Greek achievement

6. The ascendancy of Rome

7. The world in classical times

8. Interval in the West

9. Crossroads of the world

10. The triumph of Islam

11. The Guptas and the T'angs: two golden ages

12. The dawn of a new Europe

13. Castle, manor, and town

14. Bishop, priest, and monk

15. University and cathedral

16. Nations in the making

17. Man is the measure

Note on Reference Maps

Since the first edition, *Civilization, Past and Present* has carried as an integral part of the text a series of spot maps intended to show dynamically the impact of various cultural developments in the history of civilization. To supplement these spot maps, the special section of eleven reference maps beginning on the following page has been added. The reference maps are designed primarily to acquaint the student with the location of as many as possible of the cities, political subdivisions, and geographic features with which this book deals.

To accomplish that purpose, the authors and editors have elected to show certain of the major civilizations within the scope of this book which have existed in various parts of the world. As a result, it has been possible to include in the reference maps practically every place name of importance which is mentioned in the text. On some of the maps, it has been possible to show two or three civilizations, and although some of these may have flourished at different times, discrepancies in time will be apparent to the careful reader.

Where the areas of two civilizations overlap, the colors have been superimposed by the use of special transparent inks. While only the major topographic features with which the book is concerned are shown, mountains are represented by triangles of black and deserts by fields of black dots. The names appearing on the maps are indexed following the regular text entries in the "Index" on page 623.

Atlantic Ocean
North Sea
Baltic Sea
BRITAIN
CELTS
London
SLAVS
GERMANS
Rhine River
Danube River
CARPATHIANS
Volga River
Dneiper River
SCYTHIANS AND SARMATIANS
URAL MTS
Ural River
GAUL
Lyons
ALPS
Massilia
PYRENEES
CORSICA
SPAIN
Rome
MACEDONIA
Black Sea
CAUCASUS MTS.
Caspian Sea
Byzantium
SARDINIA
Pergamum
GREECE
Corinth
Athens
Ephesus
Sparta
SICILY
Mediterranean Sea
Carthage
CRETE
CYPRUS
Antioch
Tyre
Damascus
Jerusalem
MESOPOTAMIA
Tigris River
Euphrates River
Ecbatana
Ctesiphon
Seleucia
Babylon
PARTHIA
PERSIA
Persepolis
Persian Gulf
Cyrene
Alexandria
Memphis
EGYPT
Nile River
Thebes
DESERT TRIBES
SAHARA DESERT
ETHIOPIA
Red Sea
SEMITIC TRIBES
Roman Empire in 14 A.D.
Provinces added after 14 A.D.
Temporary conquests
Parthian Empire 200 B.C.-600 A.D.
Maurya Empire 320 B.C.-190 B.C.
Han Empire 200 B.C.-200 A.D.

1. The Ancient World

Ob River
Yeneser River
Lake Baikal
TATARS
Lake Balkash
Axartes River
GOBI DESERT
CHINA
WALL
A River
Bactra
HINDU KUSH
Taxila
GANDHARA
Indus
River
HIMALAYA MTS
Brahmaputra River
Yangtze
Salween
Wei River
Hwang Ho
Loyang
Changan
River
Si River
KOSALA
Ganges R.
Pataliputra
Champa
MAGADHA
Narbada River
Godavari River
KALINGA
ANDHRA
DECCAN
Kistna River
Irrawaddy River
River
Mekong River
i a n
a
Bay of Bengal
JAPAN
40°
20°
0°
80°
100°
Prepared by Rand McNally & Co., Chicago.

Black Sea
Adrianople
MACEDON
Sea of Marmara
Hellespont
Troy (ruins)
Nicaea
PONTUS
Delphi
Thebes
Corinth
Mycenae
Athens
Olympia
Tiryns
Piraeus
Sparta
DELOS
Epidaurus
Pergamum
LYDIA
Ephesus
ASIA MINOR
COS
CRETE
Cnossus
Phaestus
ISLE OF RHODES
Mediterranean Sea
CYPRUS
Seleucia
Antioch
Edessa
MESOPO
Euphrates
Palmyra
PHOENICIA
Damascus
Acre
Nazareth
PALESTINE
Jerusalem
Bethlehem
Alexandria
Rosetta
Damietta
Heliopolis
Gizeh
Memphis
Petra
Nile River
HEJAZ
AR
Red Sea
Karnak
Thebes
Jiddah
Mecca
1st Cataract
Aswan
2nd Cataract
3rd Cataract
NUBIA
4th Cataract
5th Cataract
30°
35°
40°
Prepared by
Rand McNally & Co., Chicago

2. Early Civilizations in the Middle East

Prepared by
Rand McNally & Co., Chicago.

3. The Roman Empire c. 117 A.D.

HUNS
HS
SARMATIA
Aral Sea
Caspian Sea
THIAN MTS.
IA
Black Sea
CAUCASUS MTS
THRACE
NIA
Byzantium
Sea of Marmara
Hellespont
Pergamum
Aegean
ebes
thens
Sea
Ephesus
MESOPOTAMIA
Tigris
Euphrates
Ctesiphon
River
River
ETE
Cnossus
RHODES
CYPRUS
Sea
Damascus
Tyre
Jerusalem
Alexandria
Memphis
EGYPT
River
Nile
Persian Gulf
Red Sea

4. Medieval Far East

T'ang Empire 618-906
Mongol China 1280
MANCHURIA
MONGOLIA
TURKESTAN
FERGHANA
Yarkand
TAKLA MAKAN DESERT
PAMIR MTS.
Tashkurgan
KANSU
NAN-SHAN MTS.
TIBET
HIMALAYAS
Hwang Ho (Yellow) River
HOPEI
Peking
Anyang
SHENSI
Wei R
Sian (Sianfu) (Changan)
Loyang
Huai R
Nanking
SZECHWAN
Yangtze River
FUKIEN
KUANGSI
KUANGTUNG
Canton
Macao
BURMA
Mekong
TONGKING
HAINAN ISLAND
Menan R
River
SIAM
Angkor Wat
CHAMPA
Champa
Gulf of Siam
MALAYA
Malacca
Strait of Malacca
SUMATRA
BORNEO
CELEBES
JAVA
Batavia
Borobodor
BALI
TIMOR
PHILIPPINE ISLANDS
South China Sea
FORMOSA
Pacific Ocean
East China Sea
Yellow Sea
KOREA
Seoul
Sea of Japan
HOKKAIDO ISLAND
HONSHU ISLAND
Fujiyama
Mt. Tokyo
Kyoto
Nara
SHIKOKU ISLAND
Nagasaki
KYUSHU ISLAND
150°
40°
30°
20°
130°
10°
0°
80°
90°
100°
Prepared by Rand McNally & Co., Chicago.

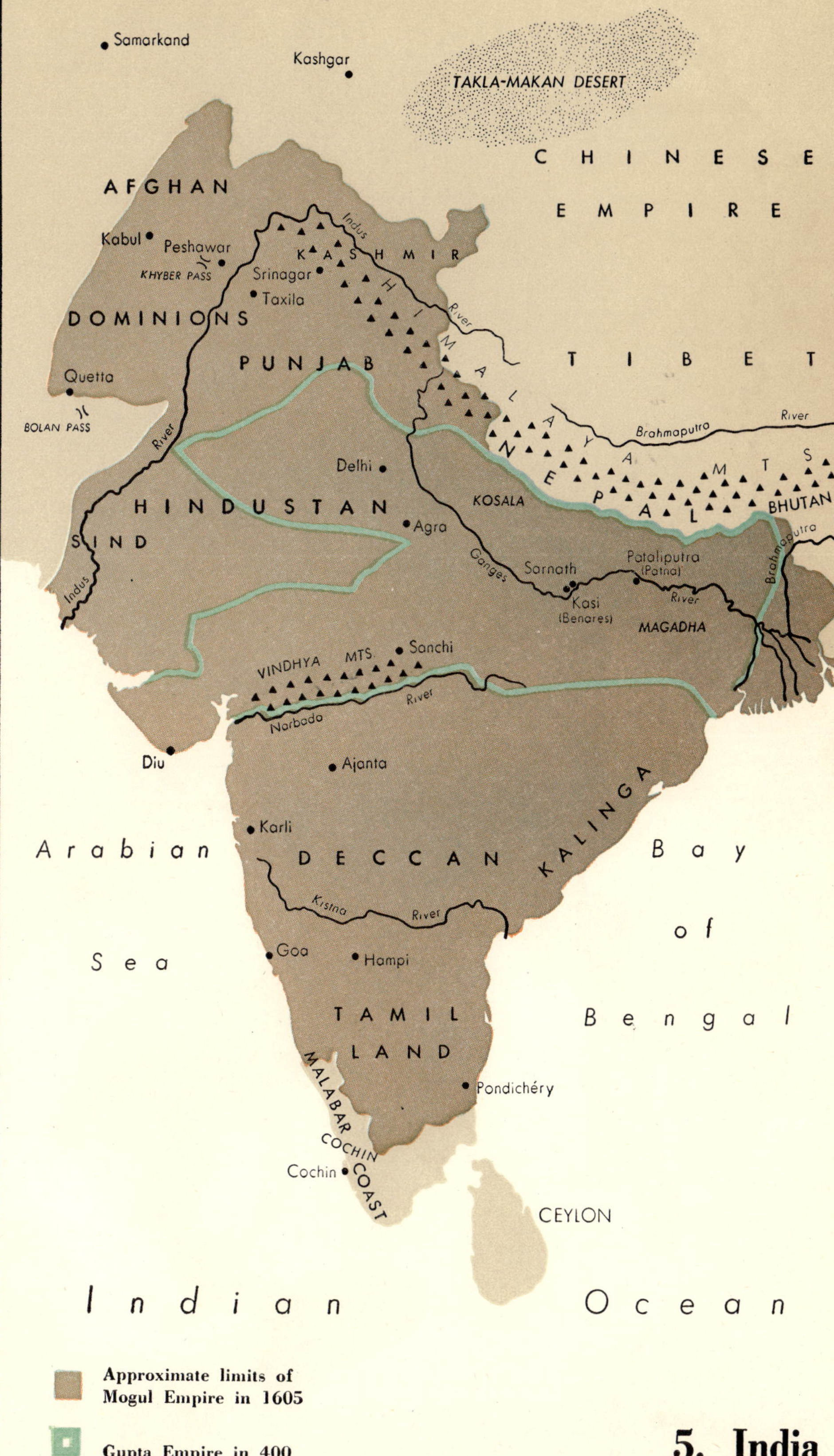

Approximate limits of Mogul Empire in 1605

Gupta Empire in 400

5. India

Prepared by Rand McNally & Co., Chicago.

6. Hohenstaufen Empire 1138-1254

7. Central and Eastern Europe 1350

8. Medieval France, Spain, and Low Countries in 1328

England and possessions
France
Kingdom of Navarre
Kingdom of Castile and Leon and dependencies
Kingdom of Aragon and dependencies
Kingdom of Granada
Portugal
Atlantic Ocean
North Sea
English Channel
Bay of Biscay
Mediterranean Sea
Haarlem
Amsterdam
Rotterdam
GERMANY
Bruges
FLANDERS
Ghent
Agincourt
Ypres
Louvain
Crecy
Lille
Brussels
Cateau-Cambresis
Cambrai
ARDENNES
Amiens
Rouen
Vervins
Rocroy
LUXEMBURG
MONT ST MICHEL
NORMANDY
Compiegne
Soissons
Brest
BRITTANY
Champeaux
Chartres
Paris
Seine
Verdun
LORRAINE
CHAMPAGNE
Toul
Rhine River
ANJOU
Orleans
Carnac
Loire
River
Clairvaux
Molesme
ALSACE
Tours
Vezelay
Luxueil
POITOU
Poitiers
BURGUNDY
Cluny
SWITZERLAND
ALPS
Cognac
Lyon
Bordeaux
AQUITAINE
MASSIF CENTRAL MTS.
ITALY
ASTURIAS
Oviedo
Covadonga
GASCONY
Santiago de Compostela
CANTABRIAN MTS.
PASS OF RONCEVALLES
Toulouse
Nimes
Rhone
Leon
PYRENEES
Carcassonne
THE CORNICHE
Marseilles
Narbonne
Toulon
Porto
Ebro
SPANISH MARCH
Salamanca
Saragossa
Segovia
CORSICA
Madrid
Barcelono
Tagus River
Lisbon
Toledo
Valencia
BALEARIC ISLANDS
SARDINIA
Cordova
Guadalquivir R.
Seville
Cadiz
Granada
Strait of Gibraltar
PILLARS OF HERCULES
Tangier
Prepared by Rand McNally & Co., Chicago.

9. The British Isles in 1536

Prepared by
Rand McNally & Co., Chicago.

Spanish Hapsburgs
Austrian Hapsburgs
Holy Roman Empire
FAROE IS.
SHETLAND IS.
ORKNEY IS.
SCOTLAND
Edinburgh
ULSTER
IRELAND
Dublin
PENNINES
ENGLAND
Bristol
London
Southampton
NORWAY
Oslo
Stockh
DENMARK
Copenhagen
North Sea
Atlantic Ocean
HOLLAND
Antwerp
SPANISH NETHERLANDS
Brussels
SP. NETH.
Osnabruck
Munster
Rhine
Elbe
BRANDENBURG
Berlin
Oder
River
SAXONY
GERMAN STATES
BOHEMIA
Prague
Brest
Seine
Paris
River
Verdun
Metz
PALATINATE
Toul
Nantes
Loire
Orleans
River
FRANCE
Augsburg
Danube
BAVARIA
Munich
AUSTRIA
Vienna
Basel
SWITZERLAND
ALPS
Bordeaux
Toulouse
PYRENEES
Avignon
Rhone River
Marseilles
Turin
Po
Milan
Venice
River
Genoa
ITALIAN STATES
APENNINES
Adriatic
Oviedo
CANTABRIAN MTS.
Ebro
River
PORTUGAL
Duero
River
SPAIN
Saragossa
Madrid
Tagus
Lisbon
Barcelona
CORSICA
Rome
NAPLES
Naples
BALEARIC IS.
SARDINIA
Cordova
Guadalquivir
R
Seville
Cadiz
Granada
Tangier
Mediterranean Sea
Algiers
Tunis
Palermo
Messina
SICILY
Prepared by Rand McNally & Co., Chicago.

10. Europe in 1648

25°
35°
DEN
Novgorod
Volga
River
Volga
ic
Riga
Konigsberg
Vilna
EAST PRUSSIA
OLAND
Dnieper
arsaw
River
Kiev
River
Don
River
River
Caspian
Sea
45°
ARY
CARPATHIANS
Dniester
River
CAUCASUS MTS.
Danube
Bucharest
River
Black Sea
OTTOMAN EMPIRE
Adrianople
Constantinople
Salonika
Aegean
Sea
LEPANTO 1571
Athens
20°
25°
RHODES
30°
CYPRUS
35°

GREENLAND
(To Denmark)
ICELA
(To Den
Hudson
Bay
LABRADOR
NEWFOUNDLAND
NEW FRANCE
Quebec
NOVA SCOTIA
LOUISIANA
VIRGINIA
AZO
BERMUDAS
MEXICO
CANARY IS
BAHAMAS
WEST INDIES
CUBA
Mexico City
Belize
JAMAICA
CAPE VERDE IS.
DARIEN
SIERRA
GUIANA
PERU
Lima
BRAZIL
Rio de Janeiro
Santiago
CHILE
Buenos Aires
Strait of Magellan
British
French
Spanish
Dutch
Portuguese

11. European Empires about 1700

Prepared by
Rand McNally & Co., Chicago.

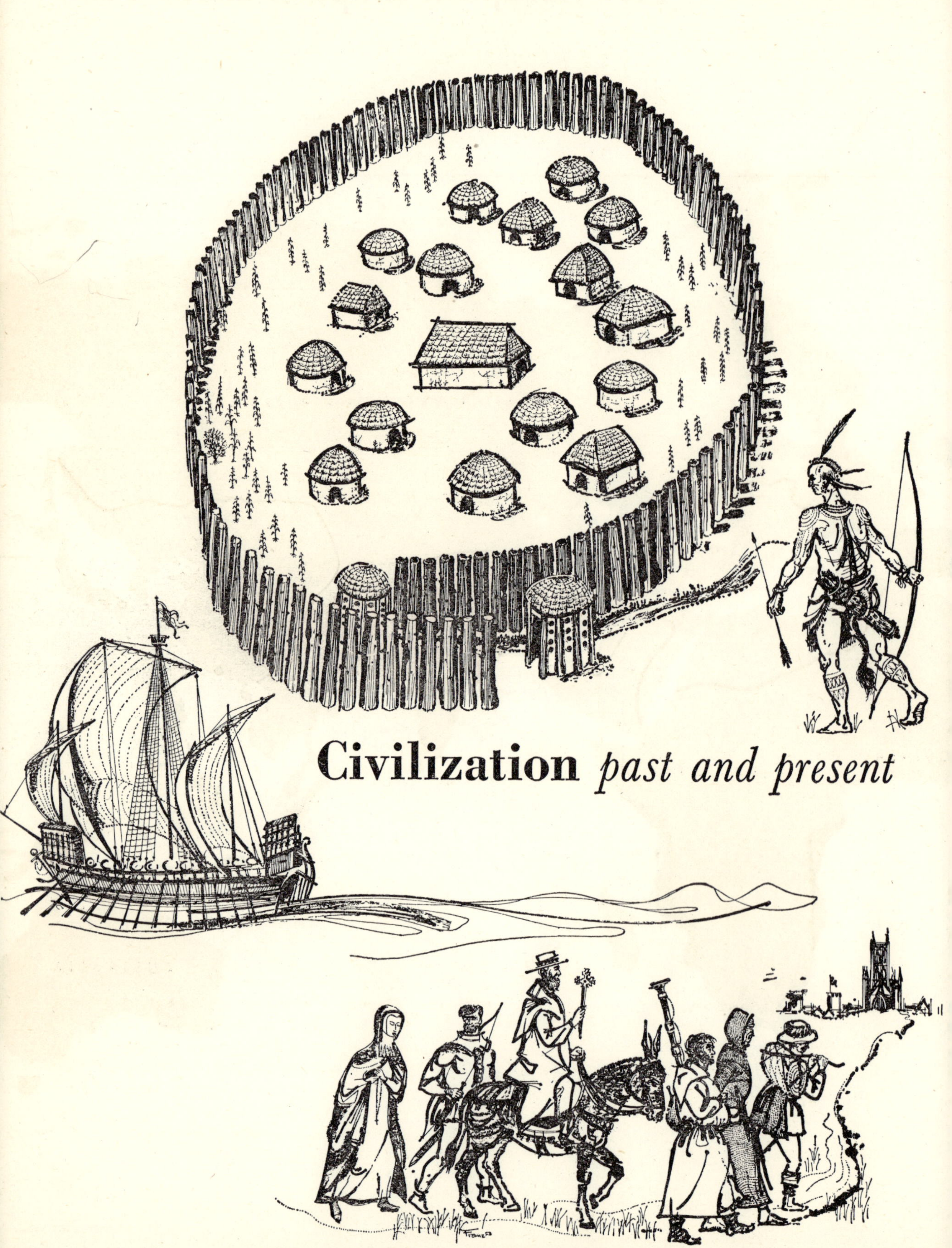

Civilization *past and present*

A Prologue: Perspective on Man

America in Mid-Century

On December 17, 1903, on the coast of North Carolina, two young brothers named Wright managed to get a frail-looking contraption into the air. That first flight of a heavier-than-air machine lasted twelve seconds. Fifty years later this airplane's swept-winged, jet-propelled descendants were breaking the sonic barrier, crossing the earth's oceans and continents daily, and exploring the stratosphere at heights two and three times that of Everest—which in turn had succumbed at last to man's courage and resourcefulness. That the next fifty years might see the conquest of still other "Everests"—perhaps even outside this planet's atmosphere—was no longer a comic-strip fantasy, so swiftly had the tempo of discovery and change been accelerating. Tomorrow is anybody's guess.

That our journey through the second half of the twentieth century should be at least equally momentous can be judged by the dizzy pace at which contemporary civilization has been transformed in the past fifty years. For example, a veritable revolution in transportation has taken place. Whereas in 1900 there were only 13,824 automobiles registered in the United States, and these were almost exclusively the property of the wealthy, half a century later there were over 44 million cars jammed in city streets or cruising along thousands of miles of turnpike and six-lane highways—designed to keep pace with a population about double that of 1900, and many more times as mobile. The motorcar in turn made possible a decentralization of industry and the development of suburbs which were considerably removed from a man's place of work, while it also put an end to the age-old isolation of the farmer and broadened the geographical horizons and social awareness of an entire nation.

The automobile, however, could not have helped transform our way of life had there not also occurred a technological revolution. After Henry Ford had perfected his assembly-line technique, the automobile industry began to turn out cars by the millions, and in a short time the entire American economy was stepping up the mass production of life's necessities as well as of numerous items which had hitherto been considered luxuries.

But mass production requires a mass consumer market, and here we find a clue to an unprecedented economic transformation which occurred during the first half of the century. In 1900 the average American family could not have afforded a car—even assuming that the automobile industry had been able to turn out a mass-produced unit—nor did it enjoy a forty-hour working week, vacations with pay, or the education of its children at least through the high-school level. Working conditions and the national income have steadily improved since then, not only because of organized labor's efforts and the effects of social legislation, but also because increasing numbers of industrialists (like Ford as early as 1914) became convinced that it was to their own interest to give employees wages high enough to buy the products coming off their assembly lines. As more was produced, the lower became the cost of the individual item; this in turn created more consumer demand and still further increased production.

This dynamic expansion of the American economy, which was stepped up by two world wars, experienced various stresses and maladjustments. The most serious of these was the great depression of the 1930's, in which the national income seriously slumped, the products of factory and farm piled high as unbought surpluses, and millions were thrown out of work. The depression left as its legacy memories of bread lines and insecurity. The government increased its participation in the economic field in order to assist the less fortunate and help restore equilibrium to the national economy. Just as important was the new social consciousness that took root among the American people—there was a growing realization that in a complex technological age, when the individual has become part of a giant industrial machine governed largely by factors beyond his control, his well-being is linked intimately with that of every other member of the community.

Even as developments at home made Americans conscious of their interdependence and mutual responsibilities, so the impact of world affairs—abetted by science's progressive shrinking of distances—brought them a new awareness of their inescapable relationship with events on the other side of the Atlantic and Pacific. In 1900 the afternoon newspaper thrown on the veranda facing Main Street was filled almost entirely with local news, together with a few dispatches from Washington or New York. Half a century later, the principal stories on the front page possibly included the "Cold War," the convening of the United Nations General Assembly, NATO, Point Four programs for southeast Asia, or other subjects equally incomprehensible to the newspaper reader of 1900.

By virtually any standard of measurement that might have been employed in 1900, then, the United States had become scarcely recognizable by the middle of the present century. It was twice as populous and many more times as productive and wealthy. There had been an important shift of population to the cities, but meanwhile the farmer had acquired a station wagon and his wife a deep freeze, while his daughter majored in International Relations at "State." The American woman now had the vote, was likely to be some two inches taller than her grandmother (wore shoes at least two sizes larger!), and could expect to live well into the twenty-first century. The average American enjoyed the best health and longest life-span in his country's history and the highest living standard ever recorded. The sizable economic and social gap which in 1900 had existed between groups born on different "sides of the track" had been strikingly narrowed, and the status of minority groups had as strikingly improved. Matching these material advances, the American people had acquired more mature cultural values and social attitudes, and—perhaps largely as a result of the painful impact of two world wars—had accepted the heavy and often thankless responsibilities of international leadership.

These have been remarkable advances, in some instances as magnificent as the development of the airplane since its first flight at Kittyhawk. With the advent of atomic energy and its all but limitless potentialities, it requires little imagination to forecast that the decades ahead will continue to transform western civilization, perhaps at an ever accelerating tempo. Surely the prospect for tomorrow is as exciting as training the great two-hundred-inch telescope at Mount Palomar upon a particular area of the heavens and finding evidence of new island universes hitherto unrevealed.

But there is another way of looking at the world in mid-century: it is a world of tensions, of ideological "cold wars" competing for men's souls, of atomic missiles and the largest appropriations in history for armaments. It is this picture which has led some to describe our times as an "age of crisis" and as "civilization on trial." In this regard it has been said that contemporary man is involved in three kinds of conflict: with nature, with his fellow men, and with himself.

The first of these conflicts may be the most fundamental, and can in fact be richly rewarding. For, as we have already seen, our century bears testimony to man's progressive conquest of his environment and the forces of nature, while his unlocking of her innermost secret, atomic energy, holds out hope of almost unlimited possibilities for human advancement in the future. But in other respects, man's conflict with nature has not yet been fully resolved in his favor. One critical problem facing him is the continuing depletion of natural resources, including irreplaceable mineral wealth and land lost by erosion. Another relates to the increase of the world's population, an increase of some 70,000 more births than deaths every day; India's population, to take one example at random, has jumped by 50 million in a single decade. Experts disagree whether the basic question here is overpopulation or rather underproduction of food. Many take the optimistic view that science and an improved use and distribution of land may make it possible to support a much greater population than now exists on the planet. However this may be, there are in the present era two inescapable realities: per capita food consumption is less now than it was 15 years ago, and the planet's population is increasing faster than its food production.[1]

These still unresolved conflicts between man and nature tend to intensify his conflicts with his fellow men. Hundreds of millions of people in underdeveloped areas live in a "geography of hunger" (to use yet another term employed to describe this aspect of the contemporary crisis), in which social unrest and political conflict breed rapidly. Because many of these underdeveloped regions have in the past been part of the overseas empires of various European states, our century has witnessed a great "colonial ferment" in Asia and Africa. In large measure, this has taken the form of demands for freedom from external political controls and from racial inequality. The years immediately following the Second World War saw an unprecedented number of colonies acquire self-government or outright independence. Seen in broad outline, these developments mark the West's recognition of the claim of other areas to a partnership in world affairs. But freedom itself does not automatically ensure more food or education, and though various new political states obtained their independence on the maxim that "good government is no substitute for self-government," some of them have been learning by the painful process of administrative inefficiency and even corruption that the converse of this maxim must also hold true.

In any case, political independence may well prove illusory unless it is backed up with economic development capable of raising the living standards of the broad masses. The benefits of modern science must be utilized to create better balanced economies and to narrow the gap separating underdeveloped areas from the highly industrialized, and therefore economically stronger, countries. Unfortunately, current evidence shows that this gap is, on the contrary, still being widened; the advanced economies are progressing more rapidly than the underdeveloped countries, with the result that the standards of living of the two groups are getting increasingly out of balance. A hopeful sign of the times is the recognition by the United States and members of the British Commonwealth that practical measures must be taken to aid the underdeveloped countries. As a result, large sums of money and valuable technical assistance are being provided under both the American Point Four Program and the Colombo Plan, which is financed by the developed economies in the Commonwealth.

Earlier we had occasion to observe how technological advances in our century have had the effect of integrating the main segments of the national economy and of making the American people increasingly aware of the interdependence of all classes and groups. Similarly, at a time when the newly established states are enshrining the doctrine of national sovereignty, the economic and political realities of the postwar era have forced the countries of the West to move progressively toward closer association. Consequently, a number of significant groupings have come into existence, chief of which are the North Atlantic Treaty Organization, the Council of Europe, and the European Coal and Steel Community, based on the Schuman Plan. The emergence of these political, economic, and military entities eloquently attests to the international tension of the mid-century.

The chief reason for such tension is not hard to find. In 1945 the United Nations was established on the premise that the wartime alliance of big powers would continue and so ensure the maintenance of global peace and security. But this hope was almost immediately shattered by fundamental disagreements between the Soviet Union on one hand and the western powers on the other. The result, as everyone knows, has been the splitting of the world into two great hostile camps, bringing mankind at moments close to the brink of a third world war. Without assessing at this point the positions of the protagonists in the "Cold War," it can be said that this struggle represents the supreme crisis of our age. It is not only political, economic, and strategic in character, but stems from fundamentally opposed philosophies of life which have their roots deeply implanted in history. And at stake is nothing less than the basic pattern of human existence in the decades ahead.

When man's conflict with his fellow men reaches such peaks of intensity, it would be impossible for him not to expect repercussions within himself. Of course the present situation must not be exaggerated to give the impression either that men have not had to contend with, and overcome, critical situations in the past or that contemporary times afford nothing constructive from which we may derive satisfaction and strength. We have already noted the phenomenal advances of our century in health and education and in raising standards of living in the West. Furthermore, technology has gone far to free us from the physical drudgery which at one time consumed most of man's energy simply that he might exist. Nor should we overlook society's increasing solicitude for the halt, lame, blind, and others in unfortunate circumstances, or the extensive growth of public services which citizens enjoy in common.

Yet when all this is said, the prevailing mood of the average man and woman is surely tinged with feelings of insecurity. In this regard, our life today is appreciably different from that of our grandparents, who of course had their share of problems but nevertheless lived in an environment apparently built on unshakable foundations. What has happened to disturb, if not destroy, this feeling of basic security? According to one observer of the contemporary scene, the majority of Americans in 1900 "lived among familiar people and familiar things—individuals and families and fellow townsmen much of their own sort, with ideas intelligible to them. A man's success or failure seemed more likely than in later years to depend upon forces and events within his own range of vision. Less often than his sons and grandsons did he feel that his fortune, indeed his life, might hang upon some decision made in Washington or Berlin or Moscow, for reasons utterly strange to his experience. The world at which he looked over the dashboard of the family carriage might not be friendly, but at least most of it looked understandable."[2]

If our analysis seems correct, and man *is* in conflict with nature, his fellow man, and himself, the mid-century does indeed confront us with a crisis—but also with a challenge which we cannot refuse. How shall we meet it? There is no clear-cut solution, but if our problems both in the national and international spheres call for remedial action, we must first of all gain some understanding of the processes by which those problems came to exist. Consequently, a study of history becomes essential at this point if we are to comprehend the significance of our times, for as has been said, "the value of history... is that it teaches us what man has done and thus what man is."[3]

The word "history" is capable of numerous definitions. We may consider it as a particular type of research: it inquires into human actions in the past, and does so by using as nearly as possible a scientific method to discover and analyze existing evidence. In this way, the historian attempts to understand man's tumultuous journey through the ages: his emergence out of the mists of antiquity, the triumphs and failures of his struggle against environment and ignorance, the decline and fall of numbers of his civilizations, and the significance of his past actions in fashioning the kind of world in which we live today. History shows that all patterns and problems in human affairs are the end-product of a long and generally complex process of development. By throwing light on that process, it provides the means by which alone it is possible to profit from human experience, whether we are concerned with the universal problems of mankind or the minute but intimate world of the individual. There would be no landmarks, no points of reference, no foundations on which to build if the individual were bereft of his past. The system of government under which he lives, the frontiers of the country in which he resides, the type of economy in which he works, the novels he reads, the viewpoints to which he is exposed—all these factors of immediate concern to a person's existence take on meaning only in terms of history.

The Cultural Approach to History

From the beginning of human history to the present day, man has had to contend with many recurrent problems which, though never identical in all respects, yet retain certain fundamental characteristics. For example, primitive man was forced to work at great length to kindle in his cave a simple fire, a situation vastly different from that of the Minneapolis housewife enjoying thermostatically controlled central heating in her home. The obvious differences, however, should not obscure the presence of a common factor in the two situations: the continuing need of man to protect himself against the elements in order to maintain life.

The universal culture pattern. True, the problems faced by our primitive ancestors were largely concerned with physical survival. Such intricate questions as technological adjustments, ideological conflicts, and balances of political power have developed out of the complexities of modern life. Yet it is a cardinal principle that, irrespective of time and place, history is compounded of the interplay of man with his environment and of man with his fellow man—and that in consequence, historical development has tended to be both gradual and increasingly complex. This principle leads us to examine in turn another concept: in coping with the problems of his environment, man has expressed himself in terms of certain fundamental needs. These form the basis of a "universal culture pattern" and deserve to be enumerated.

The need to make a living. Man must have food, shelter, clothing, and the means to provide for the survival of the next generation. These needs have forced him to wrest a living from nature. In earliest times he was a nomad who hunted animals for their meat and skins. Later, he learned to domesticate cereals and animals and became a farmer. He began to engage in trade, and developed industry from the making of tools and utensils. But a more complex economy forced man to develop business techniques and devise laws on the ownership of property and the employment of labor. The economic life of today and of ancient Mesopotamia, Egypt, India, and China are linked by the same basic need to make a living.

The need for law and order. The earliest communities had to keep the peace among their individual members, protect property, and ensure defense against the attacks of outside enemies. It is an old, and undecided, argument whether any primitive societies had a democratic form of government, but the fact remains that men have necessarily required some sort of governmental machinery. This has taken many forms in history—patriarchy, matriarchy, monarchy, oligarchy, tyranny, democracy, fascism, communism. History has shown the gradual, though by no means constant, trend from minute political units to larger governmental formations. The first were little more than family units, which gave way in time to the clan. Then larger units, such as the tribe, developed. Finally, and much later, what we call the nation appeared. Sometimes these nations were welded into larger governmental units called empires. Today, the world is organized on the basis of some eighty or so sovereign national states, each claiming independence of status and action, yet attempting to carry out programs of international cooperation through bodies like the United Nations. We seem to have advanced a long way politically from the days of ancient cultures, but we still have problems familiar to their peoples: for example, the extent to which smaller political units should be subordinated to a centralized authority and the degree of control which government in general should properly exercise over the individual.

The need for social organization. The problems of raising families, making a living, and keeping law and order have demanded in turn some form of community organization which could allocate tasks and duties. In ancient India, for example, society was based on four classes, or castes, each of which had certain social responsibilities and privileges. The highest, or Brahman, caste was composed of priests, who were the religious authorities of the community. The second caste was that of the warriors, who owned the land and ruled and defended the territory. The third caste was composed of merchants, while the fourth and lowest caste was made up of the hewers of wood and the drawers of water. Despite profound changes in the history of the Indian subcontinent, the caste system has survived into contemporary times, thus attesting to the strength of certain forms of social organization. At different times and in different places, varying importance has been assigned to members of the major social groups. In China, for example, the soldier was long placed at the bottom of the social ladder. In modern times the merchant, or businessman, has tended to hold a privileged place in a society where the expression "How much is he worth?" reveals an emphasis on wealth as a measure of social prestige.

This need for social organization has created some fundamental problems which have not yet been solved. In ancient Mesopotamia—and the example could easily be multiplied—the people suffered from social inequality and rigid stratification, and from the unimportance of the average man in the general scheme of things. The developments of the past century have certainly been in the direction of doing away with social stratification and other barriers and raising the status, and political and economic power, of the so-called "common man." Yet today the proponents of Anglo-American democracy and Soviet Marxism differ radically in their concepts of the relative importance of man and the social organization in which he lives. We have still to answer the vital question, which takes precedence, the individual or society.

The need for knowledge and learning. From his earliest days, man has had to pit his intelligence against the forces of nature. He has had to fight hunger and disease, to adapt to climate and topography. Slowly and painfully he has acquired greater knowledge and mastery of the forces of nature and has made himself increasingly proficient in the theoretical and practical sciences. With this science he has transformed his entire life and has added to his own span of years on earth. But knowledge results from the accumulation of endless experiences, and it can best be transmitted by speech and writing. Therefore men have had to develop languages and to pass on their knowledge and skills by verbal or written methods. Primitive societies spent comparatively little time in passing on their knowledge, of which but a small amount existed. However, in the modern age there has been a growing emphasis upon the necessity for preserving knowledge and making it available through education to as many people as possible.

The need for self-expression. Man has always been a creator, and he has responded to the beauty and grandeur of his environment from earliest times. As proof of this, the walls of the caves where primitive men lived have been found decorated with paintings—generally of the animals which they hunted—showing the finest skill and imagination. The tombs of the pharaohs in Egypt and the excavated sites of ancient Mesopotamia, India, and China abound in examples of unexcelled pottery and jewelry, while sculpture has perhaps never been fashioned by more sensitive hands than those of the early Greeks. Poetry, too, is an ancient art, and great epics have come down to us from ancient India, Greece, Rome, and Scandinavia. Music, drama, and the dance also are of ancient lineage, having been commonly associated with civic and religious rites. And, as we shall see, architecture, which developed out of man's need for protection against the elements and to meet economic and social conditions, had many periods as creative and exciting as our own.

The need for religious expression. As ancient as man is his attempt to answer the "why" of life. Primitive peoples responded to their environment, of which they were almost completely ignorant, by attempting to propitiate what they feared. The ancient gods were vengeful deities who demanded blood sacrifices, and the rules of religious conduct were cast in negative form, as taboos. As man progressed in his understanding of the universe, fear of the unknown has gradually given way to a spirit of reverence for life in its many aspects. All peoples of history have had religious beliefs, for the desire to explain the purpose of existence appears to be universal. Much that was once deemed supernatural has been explained by science in terms of natural phenomena. Yet even today, as in ancient Mesopotamia, men find a fascination in gazing upon the great constellations of the sky and seeking there an answer to the riddle of the universe. Science helps to provide explanations for the "how," but for the "why" of life man must turn to religion and philosophy.

The concept of "culture." We are saying, in effect, that, irrespective of time and place, the activities by which men have met the basic problems of environment and human association have followed a pattern which contains certain common elements. As we have just seen, these elements include social organization, political institutions, economic activities, law, science, art, religion, and philosophy. The total pattern, common to all groups or societies, may be termed the "universal culture pattern." When a group of people behave similarly and share the same institutions and ways of life—that is, the same traits—they can be said to have the same "culture."

"The concept of culture implies that any given society is an integral . . . whole, in which basic processes of living and characteristic social relationships constitute a pattern of social behavior. The pattern of culture conditions individuals, providing their basic assumptions and their tools of observation and thought, and setting the frame of reference for their living."[4] This is an important concept to remember for an understanding of this volume's approach to history. Culture in this sense refers to *all* the traits of a people in a society—not simply to their artistic achievements or social graces.

All peoples, then, have cultures, and it follows that the fundamental differences between peoples are essentially differences in their cultures. It requires no great stretch of the imagination to see that the basic differences between the farmers of ancient China and those of Kansas lie mainly in the fact that their culture traits are in disparate stages of development, even though the two share a basic culture pattern that is universal. But even among contemporary peoples we find a wealth of different cultures. Primitive groups such as the

Australian bushmen and African pygmies have cultures far different from those possessing more highly developed political, social, economic, and intellectual traits—groups which we call "civilized."

"Civilization" defined. Although civilizations differ from one another in many respects—and indeed usually contain extensive variations within themselves—some generalizations can be made. Most civilizations are characterized by a relatively advanced state of physical and social well-being, by the importance of urban influences, and by an involved pattern of both material and nonmaterial activities. In other words, a people possess civilization when they have developed a highly complex culture pattern which rests upon an intricate social organization and wide control over nature. Civilization is merely an advanced, in contrast to a primitive, form of culture. How culture first developed into "civilization" in various areas will be the theme of our second chapter.

Scope of the cultural approach to history. As we progress with our story of man through the ages, our primary concern will be to grasp the main content and significance of cultures and civilizations. This cultural approach to the history of mankind has, we believe, much to offer. It deals with whole societies and all major aspects of life. Consequently, this book is at least as concerned with such fields of human endeavor as religion, economics, and art as with more traditional subject-matter like military campaigns, dynastic alliances, and secret diplomacy. In other words, we agree with Milton that "peace hath her victories no less renowned than war"—and we intend to pay our respects to the accomplishments of Aristotle, Confucius, Euclid, Abelard, Leonardo da Vinci, Bach, Newton, and Einstein fully as much as to those of Hannibal, Caesar, Charlemagne, and Napoleon. Because of its emphasis upon the universal culture pattern, this book also attempts to point out the fundamental relationships between past and present cultures. It is concerned with culture change—with the growth of institutions and the evolution of ideas and attitudes. And it analyzes the relationships between men and their society—a question which has always been important, and never more so than today.

Diffusion as a factor in culture change. Cultures are not static. Nor are they ever wholly isolated. True, a particular culture will have an individuality which sets it off from other cultures, but invariably it is influenced by the other cultures with which it comes into contact. The history of man is largely the story of the contact of cultures and the spread of culture traits. Items of culture belonging to one people are constantly being adopted by another, as a few examples will demonstrate. The Europeans brought back from the New World the use of the potato, tobacco, and chocolate. The Industrial Revolution began in England, but in a short time machines were being put into operation all over the world. Today, such mass information media as the newspapers, movies, and radio are daily disseminating the American "way of life" to every continent—just as the typical American "institutions" of gum, baseball, Coca Cola, and slang accompany the armed forces wherever they are posted abroad.

Culture traits are freely interchanged whenever direct contact is established between peoples. The colonists took from the North American Indians the use of maize, while the latter in turn obtained the horse from the white settlers. In ancient times travel was extremely difficult and often dangerous, and we tend to think that there could not have been much contact between such widely separated areas as the Mediterranean Basin and China. Yet, from the days of Rome down through the Middle Ages, there was a steady give and take of culture traits. China's contributions to the West included among other things the peach and the apricot, silk and tea, porcelain and paper, playing cards, and probably gunpowder and the compass. The West reciprocated by sending East such diversified things as carrots, grapes, alfalfa, the process of manufacturing glass, Graeco-Roman art, Nestorian Christianity, and Islam.

Culture contacts between peoples may be peaceful or warlike. Nazi Germany tried to force its culture upon the Czechs and Poles, and Japan attempted the same process with the peoples of the Far East. These attempts met with active resistance. Following the Second World War the Communists sought by force to impose their ideology as well as their political control on the peoples of eastern Europe and parts of Asia—as in Poland, the Republic of Korea, Indo-China, and Malaya. Here again, such attempts met with varying degrees of resistance. To take another example, two great culture groups, both inhabiting the Indian subcontinent and sharing many cultural traits, nevertheless split, largely because of differences involving one of the major segments of the universal culture pattern—religion. As a result, they set up two separate states, India and Pakistan.

Geography as a factor in culture change. The growth and modifications of culture are also influenced by geography. Climate, natural resources, and land formations are important influences on the life of people anywhere. We shall note early in our study that the first civilizations originated in protected and fertile river valleys. During classical times, when western civilization was focussed upon the Mediterranean, the British Isles were far removed from the center of things and were culturally backward. Britain long remained a marginal fragment of Europe, and it was not until the discovery of the New World and the development of oceanic trade that England began to rise rapidly as a powerful national state.

Some scholars have been so impressed with the importance of geographical factors that they consider physical environment the most important influence in shaping the development of culture. But these geographical determinists have been challenged by other scholars. One of these dissenters, Toynbee, has pointed out that while fluvial civilizations developed along the Nile and the Tigris-Euphrates, none emerged in the physically comparable valleys of the Jordan and the Rio Grande.[5] However, we can safely say that physical environment shapes in varying degrees the character of a culture's development. It may also be maintained that, however important environmental influences may have been in the past, their effect is likely to become less marked as time goes on. The development of irrigation schemes for transforming deserts in the southwestern United States into rich citrus belts and the discovery of methods for growing fruit north of the Arctic circle are but random examples of man's growing mastery over his physical environment.

Invention as a factor in culture change. Invention is another important source of culture change. As we have already seen, such an invention as the automobile has revolutionized transportation, the growth and planning of cities, and even the home life of the American people. But such revolutionary inventions do not come full-blown. Rather, they are built gradually upon achievements of the past. An invention like the automobile is highly complex and could not have been realized without earlier discoveries in electricity, internal-combustion principles, the vulcanization of rubber, and that most indispensable and ancient of inventions, the wheel itself. Similarly, the development of atomic energy resulted from a "chain reaction" of scientific inventions which go back for centuries. Significantly enough, the invention of the atomic bomb—which was hastened by still another culture trait, war—was the result of ideas pooled by a number of scientists from a variety of cultural backgrounds—American, British, Canadian, French, German, Italian, Jewish, and others.

Race as a factor in culture change. As we have already observed, there is no such thing as a "pure" culture, developed in isolation by one particular group. Similarly, there is no "pure" race of people, because as cultures have been diffused the different groups which make up mankind have intermixed. Yet at various times an unscientific, and vicious, theory has been put forward that cultural advancement is due to the efforts of certain "superior" or "pure" races.

"Race" is a much misused term, and its only value is to denote one of several great divisions of mankind that can be recognized on the basis of certain distinctive physical characteristics. For example, we speak of the Caucasoid (white), Mongoloid (yellow), and the Negroid (black) races. Is any one of these "races" superior to the others? Scientists tell us there is no such thing as a superior race, and a study of history shows conclusively that no so-called race has ever possessed a monopoly of culture. All that can be said is that for a specific and relatively brief period in mankind's history, one race may enjoy technical and political supremacy and produce an impressive record of cultural creativeness. The Caucasoid peoples have held such a position in modern times, although present-day events show unmistakably that the Mongoloid and Negroid races are insisting upon a new partnership of equality in the world's affairs. Lest those of the West attach undue

importance to their racial and cultural origins, this question may be pertinent: What were their ancestors in western Europe doing in the days when the great pyramids were rising in Egypt, when the peoples of Mesopotamia were living under the first law code in history, or when Confucius and the Buddha were presenting new ethical and moral systems to peoples whose cultures were already refined by thousands of years of creative living?

Uniqueness of each culture. We have now seen that all peoples have a culture, which in turn is marked by the interaction of its physical and nonphysical traits. Also, we have noted that the addition (or deletion) of a particular trait can modify the entire character of a culture. It is this difference in the number and variety of traits, and in the emphasis given to each, which distinguishes each culture from all others and thus makes it unique. For example, the number and variety of inventions resulting from the Industrial Revolution, and the emphasis placed upon the need for organizing our economic and social life in the light of modern science and technology, help to differentiate twentieth-century American culture from that of ancient Rome.

Culture lag. It is apparent that the institutions of society are continually undergoing change. Some parts of a culture pattern will change more rapidly than others, so that one institution becomes outmoded in terms of other institutions in a society. When such a situation develops, different parts of a society fail to mesh harmoniously. This condition is often referred to as "culture lag."

Examples of culture lag in our modern society are not difficult to find. Despite our advances in science and education, primitive thinking still motivates great numbers of people. For example, many continue to rely upon such ancient pseudo-sciences as palmistry, astrology, and numerology. Nor is society devoid of persons who hold the number 13 in special awe, refuse to walk under ladders (apart from the fear of wet paint), or manifest a primitive belief in luck and chance. Until very recently, the subject of sex was largely taboo, and a dangerous prudery prevented many people from obtaining the necessary guidance and aid which medical science and psychology had made available.

The social and economic status of women has also been a flagrant example of culture lag. For centuries men believed that women were the less intelligent of the sexes, and even after women had demonstrated their ability to write novels, minister to the sick, teach, conduct business, and fill other professions capably, they were not given political and economic equality. Only since the last decade of the nineteenth century have women been enfranchised in various countries. Different standards for men and women still exist in many phases of social, economic, and political life, even in socially progressive countries.

Some observers believe that the most dangerous culture lag in modern society is the great disparity existing between material and scientific advancement, on the one hand, and our social attitudes and institutions on the other. Machinery, they point out, has completely revolutionized agriculture and industry as these were known even half a century ago. In America there is no longer any problem of material production, but as the depression days of the 1930's attest, it is apparently still possible to have unemployment and hunger-in-the-midst-of-plenty. In other words, our economic institutions may not yet be adjusted sufficiently to cope with a technology that is advancing at dizzy speed.

This culture lag in the domestic field has been accompanied by one in contemporary international relations. Science and the Industrial Revolution have made the countries of the world interdependent both in war and in peace, yet old political boundaries often act as obstacles to world cooperation. The virtual impotence of the United Nations in maintaining peace and security can be traced largely to the fact that although the problems with which it has been concerned must be approached on an international basis, many of the member nations have been reluctant—or have refused—to subordinate their prerogatives of national sovereignty. This has been notably true of the Soviet Union, which consistently has used its veto power in the Security Council (as well as its strong influence in the General Assembly) to block any action which might limit its power. This kind of culture lag could prove fatal to world civilization. Nations which fail to internationalize the control of the atomic bomb, for instance, may one day find it out of control. We might mention one further example of culture lag which has limited the effectiveness of the United Nations and its program. Although this organization and its specialized agencies recognize the necessity of bringing the world's food resources into general equilibrium with its mounting population, some of the most populous member states nevertheless are hampered by traditional practices which prove inadequate either for increasing food production or for limiting population growth.

As we follow the story of man through the ages, we shall be in a position to note how culture lags develop, and how the drag of tradition and inertia on the part of well-meaning persons can be sometimes as dangerous as the overt acts of tyrants and dictators.

The "Why" of History

So far, we have shown that culture is universal and that it is in a constant state of development and modification. But here a problem arises: although all societies possess a culture, some of them have remained in a relatively static or "primitive" condition, while others have gone on to create great civilizations. What accounts for this phenomenon? Furthermore, why have most of the great civilizations of the past perished, and what were the significant factors contributing to their decline and fall? And, in view of the contemporary crisis, what are the chances of survival for our own civilization?

At this point we are dealing with the philosophical question of historical causation, the attempt to understand the "why" of history. Later, in our chapter on the "fall" of the Roman empire, we shall return to this fascinating search for causes of the growth and decay of civilizations.

We have already dismissed race as a fallacious theory for explaining historical developments. We have also pointed out that physical environment, while important in the shaping of cultures, cannot be considered the sole cause of the rise and fall of human societies. Let us look briefly at some other theories which have been advanced from time to time.

Theories of history. A large number of persons, among them theologians and philosophers, have held what is called the teleological view of history. That is, they have discerned in its movements the guidance of a Divine Will directing human destinies in conformity with a cosmic plan or purpose. This "providential" theory also prevailed much earlier among the Jews and the medieval Christians, but lost ground in modern times with the spread of rationalist doctrines and the nineteenth century's belief in the ability of man to progress indefinitely by his own efforts. It is interesting to note, however, that in the present day, which has seen a reaction against such easy assumptions about the inevitability of human betterment, at least one historian considers that "a religious interpretation of the whole drama of human life is the only one that is tenable for a moment..."[6]

Another school has emphasized the role played by outstanding individuals—such as Mohammed, Dante, Shakespeare, Luther, and Napoleon—in determining the course of human events. This Great Man school is associated particularly with Thomas Carlyle, who stated: "... Universal History, the history of what man has accomplished in this world, is at bottom the history of the Great Men who have worked here. They were the leaders of men, these great ones; the modellers, patterns, and in a wide sense creators, of whatsoever the general mass of men contrived to do or to attain.... the soul of the whole world's history, it may justly be considered, [was] the history of these."[7]

Carlyle's theory was far different in character from the economic determinism of Karl Marx. The foundations of human history, according to this philosopher, are to be found in the methods of economic production. Men adapt their political, legal, and other institutions to fit in with this all-important aspect of life. For example, the feudal system was the most effective way at one time for exploiting the use of land, but it decayed as new methods of production displaced the localized position of feudalism. Marx also believed that the change from one economic stage to another—such as from feudalism to capitalism—carried with it inevitably political, juridical, and social changes. It was one of his cardinal views that changes in the powers of production do not come by peaceful or gradual means, but by sporadic jumps, which are "revolutions." These occur because the class which comes to economic and political power, although originally progressive, after remodeling the state in its own image resists further progress in order to keep its vested position secure. As a result, society is made up of the "exploiters" and the "exploited." The "proletariat" will be the last exploited class in this struggle, Marx wrote, and it is destined to overthrow the exploiting capitalist class as soon as the powers of modern production and the conflicts inherent in the capitalist system provide it with the necessary strength. The end result of this last revolution would be a classless society and a gradual withering away of the state.

Theories of civilization. After the First World War, in the period of disillusionment which followed that conflict, great popularity was won by the work of Oswald Spengler, a German who had written a massive analysis of civilization called *The Decline of the West* (1918). Spengler interpreted history in terms of a morphological theory. He saw world history as the "collective biography" of a number of cultures, "each springing with primitive strength from the soil of a mother-region to which it remains firmly bound throughout its whole life-cycle;" and each with "its own new possibilities of self-expression which arise, ripen, decay, and never return."[8] These cultures—including the Indian, Graeco-Roman, Arabic, and our own western—grow as organisms, with the same "superb aimlessness" as the flowers, obeying laws of causation which Spengler calls Destiny. Each is fated to pass through a four-period cycle of spring, summer, autumn, and winter. Pessimistically, Spengler declared that western civilization was in its winter period and had passed into a state of rapid decline.

Oswald Spengler, criticized as responsible for starting the "fashionable current thesis of historical decadence," for a time at least exercised considerable influence. One historian to acknowledge his indebtedness has been Arnold J. Toynbee, whose impressive *A Study of History* became a "best seller" following the Second World War. Professor Toynbee contends that man achieves civilization "as a response to a challenge in a situation of special difficulty which rouses him to make a hitherto unprecedented effort." For example, the evolution of the ancient Egyptian civilization could thus be attributed to the challenge which the marshes of the Nile Delta presented to the inhabitants, and to their response in draining and building upon it. Proceeding with his hypothesis of Challenge-and-Response, Professor Toynbee has presented a number of examples to show that men have generally made a better response to adversity and difficult environmental conditions than to "easy" situations. But he also maintains that challenges can be too severe. Thus, Massachusetts presented European colonists with a severe challenge which evoked a successful response, but Labrador, presenting a still more severe challenge, proved too much for them.

A civilization continues to grow, Toynbee believes, as long as it is motivated by creative individuals or by creative minorities. When, because its creative power fails, this minority can no longer inspire the majority and can maintain its dominant position only by coercion, there is a consequent loss of social unity in the society as a whole. This results in the failure of that society to determine its own path of action—and the civilization breaks down. Unlike Spengler, Professor Toynbee does not believe that a civilization is similar to an animal organism, "condemned by an inexorable destiny to die after traversing a predetermined life-curve." However, his study of history has led him to the conclusion that of some twenty-six civilizations which he has identified, no less than sixteen are now dead and buried; of the remaining ten, all but modern western society have already broken down. And the West itself, he maintains, is in a perilous position.

The role of the unforeseen. It cannot be emphasized too strongly that all philosophies of history—whether those of Carlyle, Marx, Spengler, Toynbee, or others—must remain highly controversial because the final word on this subject cannot be written. Individual events occur at unique points in time and place, and historical prognostications based on some special system have a habit of suffering the same fate as the prognostications of betting "systems" at the race track: the unforeseeable element all too often upsets the calculations, and the "dark horse" runs off with the prize money. Whether broad historical patterns can be discerned beyond the variables of individual events is a question which will probably continue to call new philosophies of history into existence—and one for which there will just as probably never be a definitive answer.

As a matter of fact, to balance our presentation of some of those theories professing to find a recurring pattern in history, we wish to point out that some thinkers find no pattern at all. One eminent Oxford historian had this to say: "Men wiser and more learned than I have discerned in history a plot, a rhythm, a predetermined pattern. These harmonies are concealed from me. I can see only one emergency following upon another as wave follows wave, only one great fact with respect to which, since it is unique, there can be no generalizations, only one safe rule for the historian: that he should recognize in the development of human destinies the play of the contingent and the unforeseen. This is not a doctrine of cynicism and despair. The fact of progress is written plain and large on the page of history: but progress is not a law of nature. The ground gained by one generation may be lost by the next. The thoughts of men may flow into the channels which lead to disaster and barbarism."[9]

"Faith of a Historian." In his presidential address to the American Historical Association in 1950, the Harvard historian, Samuel Eliot Morison, said, ". . . I have cultivated the vast garden of human experience which is history, without troubling myself overmuch about laws, essential first causes, or how it is all coming out." He added that his creed was probably no different from that of the great majority of historians in the western world. Professor Morison maintained that the historian must be intellectually honest and subordinate his own views of what ought to have been in order to set forth what really happened. "The historian's professional duty is primarily to illuminate the past for his hearers or readers; only secondarily and derivatively should he be concerned with influencing the future."[10]

Professor Morison warned what can happen when a historian consciously writes to shape the future instead of to illuminate the past—when a man becomes the victim or prisoner of his "frame of reference." The results of this approach, he maintained, are not history in the accepted, traditional sense. Professor Morison added that "frame of reference" history "is of course the only kind that historians are allowed to write under a dictatorship, but under

such circumstances they are not allowed to construct the frame."

The eclectic approach to history. This book does not present any single thesis to explain the "why" of history. Rather, it tends to be eclectic in its approach, since we see merit in a number of concepts put forward at one time or another. These include: the importance placed by the geographical school on the interrelationship of physical environment and man's institutions; the necessity of accounting for the powerful role played by economic as well as political factors; the unique position in history of certain outstanding figures and the impact of personality upon events; and the necessity of being as scientific and objective as possible in our handling of historical evidence. Finally, we believe that by stressing the cultural approach we are in a better position to examine whole societies and the multitudinous aspects of human existence; and we feel that this approach, which cuts across political and racial barriers, best serves our present purpose—to find a global historical perspective.

The problem of progress. But whatever approach may be used to interpret history, the student is likely sooner or later to ask himself: Are we making any progress? This is a question which has been on the minds of philosophers and historians ever since the Marquis de Condorcet, while in prison awaiting the guillotine during the French Revolution, had the courage and capacity to write *The Outline of a Table of Progress of the Human Spirit,* which envisaged the progressive advance of man toward an ideal future. In the nineteenth century, men confidently believed that mankind was inevitably progressing, just as the evolutionary theory showed progress in the natural world.

But the crises of our own century have shattered such easy optimism and, as we saw earlier, have instead encouraged the formation of various gloomy, if not despairing, theories on the decline of civilization. In the first section of this essay, we examined some of the reasons for the existence of our present state of mind. In effect, we saw that never have men been so secure in their control of the forces of nature—and never have they been more haunted by the insecurity of the future. If this is the case, then surely the multiplication of material comforts, for example, cannot in itself be an adequate criterion of progress. The Athens that produced Socrates and an unsurpassed galaxy of artists and thinkers managed somehow to get along without airplanes, plastics, motels, and color television. Progress—and indeed survival itself—must depend upon other factors besides mechanical inventions.

It might be argued that people have tended to confuse progress with "progression," or mere movement. To get into an airplane at Chicago and fly westward for four hours is in fact the reverse of progress if we find at the end of that time that our destination should have been New York. In other words, progress would seem to imply a goal, and the question arises whether, as a society, we know where we want to go. Certainly a capitalist's concept of progress implies vastly different goals from those of a communist. Moreover, standards vary from century to century and from decade to decade, and we are already far enough removed from our Victorian forebears to perceive that the social goals which they considered desirable differ in many respects from those we value now.

We might, however, find at least a partial solution to our dilemma by keeping in mind the yardstick of "progress" adopted by one English historian, Professor Collingwood. His yardstick works as follows: progress in science, for example, "would consist in the supersession of one theory by another which served to explain all that the first theory explained, and also types or classes of events or 'phenomena' which the first ought to have explained but could not."[11] Instances of progress in these terms would be Darwin's theory of the origin of species and Einstein's advances over Newton's theory of gravitation. In other words, progress can take place when a person (or theory or institution) solves the same problems as those solved by his predecessor and, in addition, goes on to answer other problems for which his predecessor had been able to find no solution. "Progress," Professor Collingwood points out, can take place only where there is gain without any corresponding loss.

Standards of progress. Whether or not it is possible to set up an all-inclusive standard of what constitutes "progress," we can at least suggest some factors which we believe might profitably be applied in any test of man's progress in history. Progress should include *material advancement*: that is, the improvement of living and health standards, increased efficiency in agricultural and industrial production, and the distribution of goods so as to provide the greatest possible benefit to the greatest number of people.

Another important factor would be *intellectual and spiritual activity*. The increase in literacy and the availability of educational opportunities irrespective of economic status might be among the criteria for judging educational progress. Although difficult to measure because of the subjective factors involved, intellectual progress should also be reflected in achievements in religion, science, literature, philosophy, and the arts.

Social progress might cover the development of the "good life" for all—the adjustment and general happiness of the individual within the group—and might include such matters as the abolition of slavery and conditions of servitude, the emancipation of women, the establishment of laws based on religious, national, and racial tolerance, a reduction in lawlessness and crime, and the treatment of prisoners and the insane from the standpoint of medical and social therapy.

Students of political science maintain that another factor in progress is the *improvement of political organization*. Admittedly, any standard set up here will reflect a particular political philosophy. From a democratic viewpoint, a test of progress should include the number of opportunities for the individual to participate in government and assume public responsibilities. The efficiency and integrity of government officials provide another test of a society's state of political health. Still another yardstick might be the protection of the individual's right to hold views at variance with those held by others. And, what is always important, such protection should extend to the civil rights of racial, religious, and political minorities.

One of the great obstacles to the improvement of civilization has been warfare. This all too popular institution has flourished as the result of clashes either within a given culture or between two or more different cultures. Modern history has seen the rise of national states and the prevalent use of warfare to settle differences between these political entities. Man's attempts to avoid warfare are a test of progress, and today, when trade and economic interdependence make every major war a global affair, the growth of *international cooperation* becomes basic in any discussion of progress. This involves the maintenance of peace and security, the international arbitration or other peaceful settlement of national disputes, and the promotion on an international basis of improved economic and social standards.

Finally, as a corollary of the above, one test of progress which has come increasingly to the foreground involves the *treatment of dependent peoples.* A great many nations at one time or another have controlled dependent or so-called "backward" peoples. More than 200 million people still live in territories which do not govern themselves but are the colonies of various countries. And within many of the most technically advanced countries are groups—often large ones—of people with different racial or cultural ancestries. One of the tests of progress, surely, must be the amount of opportunity such people are given to develop their potentialities.

The Challenge

A striking phenomenon of the postwar era has been the upsurge of nationalism, as a result of which hundreds of millions of people in Asia have acquired independence, while scores of millions more in Africa are demanding the right to be master in their own house. The proliferation of national states in the former colonial areas has, to take one example, markedly affected both the membership and decisions of the United Nations. As a result, the influence of Europe in international bodies is today far less than it was before the Second World War. This shift in political power marks the end of centuries of unrivaled supremacy enjoyed by a number of imperial powers, and the manifold consequences of this vast development have yet to be seen. Meanwhile, the events transpiring in Asia and Africa are perhaps the most spectacular contemporary confirmations of this book's thesis that history is largely compounded of culture contacts and the constant spread of culture traits.

The national state developed originally in Europe under conditions which generally corresponded to linguistic frontiers. But neither Asia nor Africa possesses those homogeneous, compact conditions under which the national state originally developed. Therefore, we may expect to see nationalism in these two areas take different forms and encounter different problems from those experienced by Europe. It may be asked why the non-western peoples have been so eager to adopt a political concept like the national state when it is not part of their original culture. The answer lies in the extraordinary force with which cultures can sometimes come into contact. According to one historian, the national state as an institution "was deliberately imported from the West, not because it had been found by experimentation to be suitable to the local conditions of these non-Western worlds, but simply because the West's political power had given the West's political institutions an irrational yet irresistible prestige in non-Western eyes."[12] The sudden introduction of such an important trait from one culture into another may have unforeseeable consequences.

We have singled out the above example, not only because of its potential political consequences in the years ahead, but also because it underscores the functional value of the study of history. We shall find the world in which we live and the variegated pattern of its historical evolution much more meaningful if we try to keep in mind some of the basic concepts with which this Prologue has dealt. For example, we should be on the lookout for the multitudinous ways in which cultures have come into contact and affected one another, borrowing traits, ideas, customs, and inventions. We can often find a valuable clue to a people's economic and social organization by recognizing the unique role of environment and climate. Every civilization studied, including our own, will be better understood if we can discover to what extent it satisfied basic human wants as set forth in the universal culture pattern. And as we witness the procession of great eras passing across the stage of time like a mighty pageant compounded indissolubly of comedy and tragedy, our understanding of man's journey out of the cave and up into the stratosphere will be enriched if we refer from time to time to the question of "progress" and the tests that have been devised to measure it.

This Prologue, we believe, indicates the manner in which history can be used to understand our present challenge, and thus it provides a key to the fundamental approach used in the chapters ahead. It might be well, therefore, to summarize some of the concepts with which we have now dealt:

History is the result of the interplay of man with his environment and of man with his fellow man, and historical development tends to be both gradual and increasingly complex.

Man has always expressed himself in terms of certain basic needs such as those for physical livelihood, political and social organization, knowledge of his environment and transmission of such knowledge, self-expression, and religious or philosophical beliefs. These activities together make up the "universal culture pattern."

When groups of people share the same institutions and ways of life, they possess the same "culture"—a pattern of behavior which conditions every member of that society and provides him with his basic assumptions and attitudes. Fundamental differences between groups are essentially differences in their cultures.

When a people have a highly complex culture pattern, resting upon an intricate social organization and exerting wide control over nature, they gradually achieve what is called "civilization," which represents a relatively advanced state of physical and social wellbeing.

Cultures are never wholly static or isolated, and the history of man is largely the story of the contact of cultures and the spread of culture traits. These contacts, which may be peaceful or warlike, affect—and are in turn affected by—the various other traits within the culture pattern.

No one race or group has ever possessed a monopoly of culture, but each culture pattern has a variety of traits which makes it unique. In any culture pattern some parts may change more rapidly than others, with the result that different parts of a society fail to mesh harmoniously, thus creating "culture lag."

The study of civilizations has led to extensive theorizing on the philosophy, or "why," of history. This book does not advocate any single doctrine to explain historical development, but sees merit in a number of views which have been put forward at different times. It recognizes the importance of environmental factors, the role of economic forces, the impact of outstanding personalities, and of course the value of the cultural approach in studying societies as a whole and in a universal perspective.

Inherent in the study of history is the question of what constitutes progress and how it can best be measured. Again, while not attempting to dogmatize, we think that certain factors might be usefully included in any test of man's advancement—factors relating to his material progress, political organization, intellectual and spiritual activity, his ability to cooperate with other cultural entities, and his treatment of people outside his own group.

Certainly this question of progress is of particular concern to our own period in history. As we saw at the beginning of the Prologue, the last fifty years, when measured by various material and social yardsticks, can be accounted phenomenally fruitful and beneficial. On the other hand, when they are seen from a different perspective—especially from the psychological and spiritual points of view —we must admit that our century has been fraught with conflict. Man is in conflict with nature, with his fellow man, and with himself. In an era which has become progressively global in its culture pattern, we see that man's technological innovations have outstripped his ability to make commensurate moral and spiritual advances. Here, then, may be the supreme culture lag of our times.

To numbers of people, it appears almost hopeless to try to rectify a world which, in Hamlet's words, seems so "out of joint." We disagree heartily with these prophets of doom. In the chapters ahead, we shall come across many situations where the outlook was gloomy in the extreme—and made gloomier by the faint-hearted. We are optimistic, perhaps incorrigibly so, about the ability of this troubled twentieth century to "muddle through." In any case, we are convinced that this is no time for defeatism. History teaches us that man has never yet given up his struggle for survival and the betterment of life. We agree with that scholar who wrote: "Others claim man will destroy himself, which is of course a political prediction. This seems to me a fate as unlikely as committing suicide by holding your breath. Man, for all his frailties, is now one of the toughest, most adaptable animals in the kingdom...and I am sure that he is here to stay."[13]

Part One

Along the banks of rivers

Along the banks of rivers

What is usually known as history is a comparatively short period in the story of man, extending back from today about 7000 years. Early man, however, was on this planet nearly one million years ago. The span from that remote date down to 5000 B.C. is usually referred to as preliterate or prehistoric times. Man as yet had not perfected the art of writing, so that no written records were left with which historians can re-create his past. But our primitive ancestors did leave traces of their way of life which have enabled us to understand fairly accurately how they lived. In the first chapter, therefore, we will see how in the immense span of preliterate times man slowly created for himself and for his teeming descendants the fundamentals of civilization, such indispensable beginnings as tools, weapons, dwellings, and the domestication of plants and animals.

About 5000 B.C. the records of history become more readily understandable. The invention of writing, the use of metals, the advance of arts and crafts, and the organization of large political units signified that man was entering a new era of existence. Life became more complex and rich. Man extended his control over nature and began to use it for his own purposes. That momentous advance was not general all over the earth but was concentrated in a few great river valleys. This was no mere historical accident. The great rivers annually overflowed their banks, depositing a film of rich soil on the floors of their valleys. The well-watered soil produced abundant harvests. These in turn made possible a large increase in population. Cities and villages emerged. Artificial irrigation of crops, with the accompanying construction of dams and canals, necessitated group effort and cooperation among the people. In some localities everybody was required to help build the dikes and keep open the canals. Furthermore, dependence upon a wide network of interrelated canals demanded that all people within the area they served accept certain rules for the repair and defense of the works and the use of water. This naturally stimulated the development of governments to enforce what became known as law.

The rich surplus of crops produced in the river valleys encouraged trade and commerce. The merchant set up his stand, and ships began to carry wares from one area to another. Rivers have always been one of the best means of transportation, but they were especially important in primitive days when no good roads existed anywhere. From commerce came the exchange of ideas and inventions between people of different regions, a potent force in the shaping of human destiny. It was to become increasingly potent later when men built ships strong enough to skirt the shores of the Mediterranean, and ultimately to sail the seven seas to every far corner of the earth.

Along the banks of rivers, then, we look for our first great civilizations. When we find them, we see that they are widely scattered: Egypt grows beside the Nile; Mesopotamia sprawls between the Tigris and the Euphrates; India arises along the Indus and the Ganges; and China expands from the region of the Wei and Hwang Ho. These civilizations—all prolific in their gifts to mankind and so dynamic that two of them are still very much alive—evolved more or less independently of one another. Yet their similarities are at least as arresting as their differences. In all four areas, political systems were developed. The crafts flourished and commerce expanded. Striking intellectual developments were achieved. Alphabets and calendars were invented. Art and literature of extraordinary effectiveness were created. Religions and philosophies came into being to satisfy the inner yearnings of the people.

It is true that there were differences among these four early civilizations. They differed in their languages, literatures, and political and religious philosophies, though not nearly so much as we might expect, considering their almost complete isolation. These differences did not spring from variations in biological and psychological make-up. Fundamentally, in his mentality, his emotions, his continuing struggle against natural forces, his hopes and fears, man is very much the same kind of person no matter when or where we find him. We appreciate and sympathize with our primitive ancestors because we feel instinctively that we would have acted much the same as they did had we been living in their world. The differences that set one civilization off from another come not so much from human nature as from social and physical environment. We shall understand this better as we compare and contrast the four civilizations that lie immediately ahead.

We are at the beginning, then, of man's travels through the ages. White, black, and yellow, he developed in many parts of the earth, and we today are his inheritors. The account of his journey cannot be limited to Europe or any other single continent. At the outset we find him in Egypt, Mesopotamia, India, and China. In time we shall discover him pitting his puny strength and boundless audacity against the forces of every portion of the globe's surface. When we first find him, he is content to live along the banks of rivers; one day he will master the poles and the stratosphere.

Chapter 1

Chronology of events and developments discussed in this chapter

Approximate age of Earth	2 billion years
Archeozoic Era	500 million years duration
No geologic record of the existence of life	
Probably one-celled forms	
Proterozoic Era	925
Fossils indicate existence of simple life, i.e., algae, protozoa, sponges	
Paleozoic Era	350
Marine plants and animals, amphibian vertebrates, reptiles	
Development of land plants and animals in the latter part of the era	
Mesozoic Era	125
Age of giant reptiles, i.e., the dinosaur	
First birds, insects	
Cenozoic Era	60
Increase of mammals and the decline of reptiles	
Flowering plants, grass	
Paleocene Epoch	
General resemblance to the Mesozoic Era; mainly reptiles	
Eocene Epoch	
Disappearance of dinosaurs. Great development of mammals	
Forerunners of the horse, rhinoceros, pig, and ruminants	
Fish of modern character	
Birds more numerous and highly developed	
Oligocene Epoch	
Great variety of mammals, distinguished as carnivores, insectivores, rodents, and ruminants. Mammals were of mixed types, forerunners, and representatives of modern groups	
Miocene Epoch	
Development of insects, seals, giraffes, elephants, pigs, moles, hedgehogs, and cats	
Pliocene Epoch	
Animal and plant life similar to modern times	
Possibly the earliest appearance of forerunners of man	
Ape-Men of South Africa: combination of ape and human characteristics; lived in the late Pliocene or early Pleistocene Epoch	
Pleistocene Epoch (Divided into four Glacial Ages)	
Java Man: small brain capacity, thick skull with heavy brow ridges	1 million years ago
Peking Man used fire and made tools	Less than 1 million years ago
Heidelberg Man existed in the first or second Interglacial Age	
Neanderthal Man: skilled in the use of flint implements and fire, and lived by hunting; existed in the Old Stone Age (Lower Paleolithic), characterized by unpolished chipped flint tools	
Holocene Epoch	25,000 years including contemporary period
Cro-Magnon Man: Homo sapiens, *the direct ancestor of modern man, lived in the Upper Paleolithic*	40,000 to 25,000 years ago
New Stone Age (Neolithic): characterized by domesticated animals, cultivation of crops, spinning, weaving, and pottery	10,000 B.C.
Lake huts built on piles served as dwellings	
The Metal Age: subdivided into the Copper, Bronze, and Iron ages during which sailing ships, the wheel, anvils, and sickles were developed	4000 B.C.

Toward civilization

The beginnings

About one million years ago our earth, even then perhaps two billion years old, was the scene of a momentous event—the appearance of human creatures. Shuffling, ungainly, as yet without speech or tools, these ancient ancestors of ours gave little indication of their great potentialities. The many living creatures around them paid scant respect and attention to the newcomers whose descendants one day would build wings to speed them through the air, wheels to increase their gait a hundredfold, and deadly weapons to hurl against anyone foolhardy enough to stand in their way.

Since for hundreds of thousands of years early men could not write, they left no written records to chronicle their progress from savagery to partial civilization. But the geologist and archaeologist have come to the rescue. Unearthing fossilized remains of early man and also his tools and weapons, the scientists have succeeded remarkably in reconstructing the story of early man's development. The geologist in particular pushes his investigations even farther back than the one million years ago when the first man made his appearance. By a minute examination of plant and animal fossils preserved in the rock strata, the geologist penetrates to the very dawn of life—about two billion years ago.

In the twentieth century we are prone to overemphasize the superiority of modern man and scoff at the barbarous characteristics of our ancient ancestors, for we have invented radios, dynamos, and automobiles. We take for granted agriculture, speech, writing, and fire, and many other basic facts in our civilization that were initiated by early man thousands of years ago. Yet these are of much more fundamental importance than many of our modern inventions. They are so important that life would be inconceivable without them. It was a series of momentous events when early man first fashioned the fist hatchet, the sire of all man's later instruments, when he succeeded in producing fire artificially, cultivating the first garden, and inscribing the first written message on a boulder for a friend to read.

Prelude to History

M***an and immensity.*** Before commencing our story of man's progress from barbarism to civilization, it will be desirable to have some comprehension of the character of the road and the nature of the land on which the journey has been made.

The spinning planet earth, both home and prison of mankind, seems to us a rather huge affair, with its diameter of nearly 8000 miles. But our sun, 93 million miles away, has a diameter of 864,000 miles and is thus well over a million times as large as the earth. This flaming body plus the nine planets and multitude of lesser objects that revolve about it constitute what we call the solar system. If we were to imagine the earth as a small ball, one third of an inch in diameter, located on one goal line of a football gridiron, the sun would be about 108 yards away—in the opposite end zone—and would have a diameter of one yard. The outermost planet of the solar system would, on this scale, encircle the stadium at a distance of about two and one-half miles.

Huge as it is by terrestial standards, the solar system is but a tiny part of a vast celestial system that astronomers call the Galaxy. Our Galaxy is a mammoth disk strewn with 100 billion stars, many of which are far larger than our sun. The dimensions of this disk, in fact even the various separations between its individual stars, are so enormous that mere miles are inconvenient units of measurement. The nearest known star, for example, is 25,000,000,000,000 miles from our earth! The common unit of interstellar distance used by astronomers in their calculations is the light-year, that is, the distance traveled by a beam of light in one year at the rate of 186,000 miles per second. One light-year is thus nearly 6000 billion miles in length. Even the solar system's nearest stellar neighbor is over four light-years away; to span our Galaxy a light beam requires about 100,000 years. If we return to our model earth on the gridiron goal line and calculate where this neighboring star should be located in the same model, we find that the surface of the earth is not large enough to allow its inclusion. In point of size the orbit of the earth about the sun bears the same relation to our Galaxy that the head of a common pin bears to the continent of Asia! It is the composite light of this great wheel of stars that produces that band of light across the heavens that we term the Milky Way.

It has been firmly established by the greatest modern telescopes that our Galaxy, immense as it is, by no means represents the sum total of matter in the universe. Only in recent years have scientists begun to grasp the staggering immensity of the universe, and in contrast the microscopic insignificance of our home, the earth. This is mainly the result of the discoveries and celestial explorations of the giant two-hundred-inch reflecting Hale telescope on Palomar Mountain in southern California. The instrument is a marvelous product of scientific knowledge and engineering skill, for its mirror—weighing fourteen and one-half tons—gathers 640,000 times as much light as the human eye and for accuracy has been polished to within a few millionths of an inch of its calculated curve. The Hale telescope began observations in 1948, probing out to find new galaxies at distances of 500 million light-years. It has been estimated that this partially explored region contains upwards of 100 million galaxies, each of which consists of billions of stars similar to our sun. Fragmentary observations have been made with the two-hundred-inch telescope of galaxies as far as 1000 million light-years away. In miles it would be 1,000,000,000 times 6,000,000,000,000. The astronomers of Palomar, in order to give the layman some conception of the size of what has become an expanding universe, explain the matter this way. If a man could travel at the speed of light, he could go from Los Angeles to New York in less than one sixteenth of one second. It would take him just a second and a quarter to reach the moon and eight minutes to get to the sun. Continuing his terrestial flight he could cross the solar system in eleven hours. Reaching toward the Milky Way our traveler would arrive at its outermost star in four and one-half years and in 100,000 years he would have crossed it from one edge to the other. Proceeding at the speed of light it would now take one billion years for our hypothetical space tourist to reach the outer limit of the Palomar telescope's range.[1]

When we reflect upon the immensity of the universe, the spatial dimensions of our earth appear infinitesimal by comparison. But we must contract even farther the stage on which man's history has been enacted, for of the total surface area of the world 71 per cent is covered by water and much of the 29 per cent remaining for land is barren and unsuited for human habitation.

As we commence our history of human civilization, a realization of the relatively infinitesimal size of man's domain on earth might tend to make human affairs seem insignificant and dwarfed. But we can be reassured by remembering that man has really taken the universe captive by unraveling its secrets. The most staggering aspect of the universe—its immensity—is being progressively conquered by puny man's telescopes and powers of reasoning. And as the noted astronomer F. R. Moulton observes, it is not so much the tremendous size of the cosmos that is significant to man, "but that which holds him awe-struck is the perfect orderliness of the universe and the majestic succession of the celestial phenomena. From the tiny satellites in the solar system to the globular clusters, the Galaxy, and exterior galaxies there is no chaos, there is nothing haphazard, and there is nothing capricious."[2]

The why and how of earth's creation. Now that we have some idea of the huge dimensions of our universe, the question arises, how did it originate? There is evidence to indicate that the earth, our Galaxy, and even the remote galaxies, may have started the process of development toward their present states two billion or so years ago. Whether there actually was a "beginning" at this epoch or whether the universe has existed much as it is today for an indefinitely long time is a matter on which cosmogonists differ. Taking the universe as a whole, the why and how of creation may forever remain an unsolved riddle.

But progress is being made in attempts to explain how and when the sun and its nine planets came into being. The study of the solar system gives us at least a clue to the origin of that part of the universe most important to us—the earth.

The explanation most commonly accepted during the first few decades of this century is called the Hypothesis of Dynamic Encounter, formulated about 1900 by T. C. Chamberlain and F. R. Moulton of the University of Chicago. In brief it suggests that our solar system had its birth when the sun was approached by another huge star. The latter, through the operation of the law of gravitation, detached from the sun great masses of flaming gas. The orphan masses from the parent sun gradually cooled and crystallized to become the nucleii of planets. These continued to revolve around the sun, held in their orbits by the gravitational pull of the

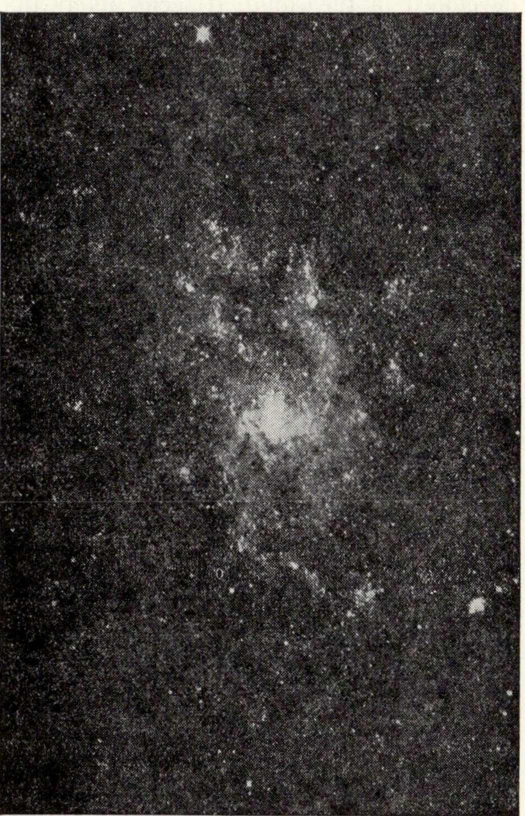

Our universe would look like this if seen from a point a million light-years distant; earth's position would be about a half inch off center. This photograph is of Spiral Nebula Messier 33, Mt. Wilson observatory.

parent body. This theory has become untenable in the light of two more recent investigations. First, it has been shown that masses of hot gas extracted from the sun would not condense into planets, but would dissipate into space. Second, in order to extract the necessary gas with the requisite velocity from the sun, the passing star would have required a velocity far in excess of the known velocities of stars.

Recent advances in our knowledge of the theory of turbulence and the physical chemistry of the sun and planets have resulted in the revival and extension of a theory of origin for the planets that was published by Immanuel Kant, a famous German scholar, in 1755. Kant assumed that the sun and planets developed out of a great primordial cloud of material. We now know that the mass of dust and gas which moved about the embryonic sun probably possessed physical properties that would have rendered impossible a smooth flow. Vortices or turbulent eddies would have developed in the cloud. It seems likely that the planets evolved by accretion in the major eddies or vortices of this matter that swirled about the sun. The whirling and turbulence that transformed the primordial dust cloud into planets has been poetically described:

> Big whirls have little whirls,
> That feed on their velocity;
> And little whirls have lesser whirls,
> And so on to viscosity.[3]

As the protoplanet earth grew, it increased its gravitational pull and was thus able to maintain a gaseous atmosphere around its surface, providing a favorable circumstance for the development of life. Its growing gravitational pull also enabled it to hold water vapor, which, condensing as rain, gradually filled in the lower parts of its uneven surface to form our oceans and divide our continents. The surface of the earth changed slowly, over millions of years, through processes of weathering, shifts in the bedrock, and volcanic action, producing mountain ranges and other distinctive irregularities of surface.

Earth's age revealed. Thinkers in all ages have speculated upon the age of the earth. Some ancient thinkers, for example, considered it as eternal, as having always existed. Another widely held view was that the world was created, complete with all its myriad forms of life, at a given date in the distant past. But during the past century the findings of the geologists have thrown new light on the age-old problem. In 1795 a Scottish scientist named James Hutton published his *Theory of the Earth,* proposing the hypothesis that the making of the earth had necessitated an immense period of time. Sir Charles Lyell in his famous treatise *The Principles of Geology* (1830), building on the investigations of Hutton, collected evidence showing that the earth is the product of a long period of evolution, which can be demonstrated by examining the stratified rocks of the earth's surface.

These strata, or layers of rock, constitute what is known as the geologic timetable. Geologists in the nineteenth century proved that the uppermost strata were much more recent in origin than the lower rock formations. This made possible an understanding of the sequence of geological events.

No one area in the world presents a continuous and uninterrupted sequence of geologic formations from the oldest to the most recent. The record of the rocks in any one region is incomplete, as some strata have always been disturbed or obliterated. But by exhaustive study, by fitting a layer from one area upon a formation from another locality, a complete record of geologic time has been pieced together. Geologists now have an all-embracing succession of strata, the so-called geologic column, properly identified and fitted into a time sequence, which has a thickness of ninety-five miles. As a result of this work scientists now hold that the earth was born at least two billion years ago.

Geologic eras of earth's history. The history of the earth is represented geologically by five great eras, corresponding to definite stratified rock formations in the earth's crust:

Era	Estimated Duration
Archeozoic	500 million years
Proterozoic	925 million years
Paleozoic	350 million years
Mesozoic	125 million years
Cenozoic	60 million years

The names of these eras indicate the general nature of life found in each. Archeozoic, for example, means the age of the most ancient life (Greek *archaios,* ancient + *zoe,* life) and Cenozoic refers to life of a recent type (Greek *kainos,* recent). The five eras are in turn divided into lesser geologic time spans called epochs (see chronological chart, p. 20).

An Evolving Pattern of Life

O*rigin of living species.* Scientists tell us that there are 250,000 distinct species of plants and twice this number of species of animals alive on the earth today. When did these myriad life forms first appear, and have they all had a continuous existence from the time when life first appeared on our planet?

As late as the mid-nineteenth century it was generally held that all the plant and animal species now in existence had been simultaneously created and that the thousands of species we know today had come down to us absolutely unchanged in form. During the past hundred years, as we have seen, geologists have found that the rock formations of the earth's crust go back millions of years in their origin. During that tremendously long time span no written records were kept, of course, but the rock formations reveal when life first made its appearance on our planet and how it evolved. That story has been told by scientists who have made an intensive study of the many fossils which have been unearthed from the strata.

Development of fossil study. The word *fossil* comes from the Latin *fossilis,* from *fodere,* to dig, and is used by geologists to refer to any trace or remains in the rocks of organisms from the past. Fossils usually consist of the bony part of an organism, such as the skeleton of the now extinct saber-toothed tiger. But the imprint of a leaf which exists as a "carbon copy" in coal shale, the footprint of an animal on a soft lake bottom which has been exposed and turned to sandstone, and the borings left by worms are all fossils of a kind. A knowledge of these fossils goes back nearly two thousand years. They were known to the ancient Greeks, discussed by Roman poets, and commented upon by Arabic writers of the tenth century. However, Leonardo da Vinci, the famous fifteenth-century Italian artist and scientist, was the first person who had an inkling of the real significance of fossils. For several hundred years after his time a fossil controversy raged in which many ridiculous ideas were aired. Some people maintained that fossils were the grown products of a magical kind of egg that had somehow been buried in the earth.

The seventeenth and eighteenth centuries saw fossil hunting become a popular hobby with scientists, but as yet no one realized that some of the fossils represented species that were extinct. With the accumulation of a great mass of fossil remains a new science called paleontology, the study of the remains of animals and plants buried in rocks, made its appearance in the latter part of the eighteenth century. There are many important names connected with the rise of the new science, but the French scientist Georges Cuvier is especially memorable. Cuvier in 1800 received some bones that had been discovered in a quarry near Paris. Assembling the fossil remains, he discovered that they belonged to an elephant larger than or different from the existing species—an animal, therefore, that must have become extinct.

About this time an Englishman named William Smith made a valuable contribution

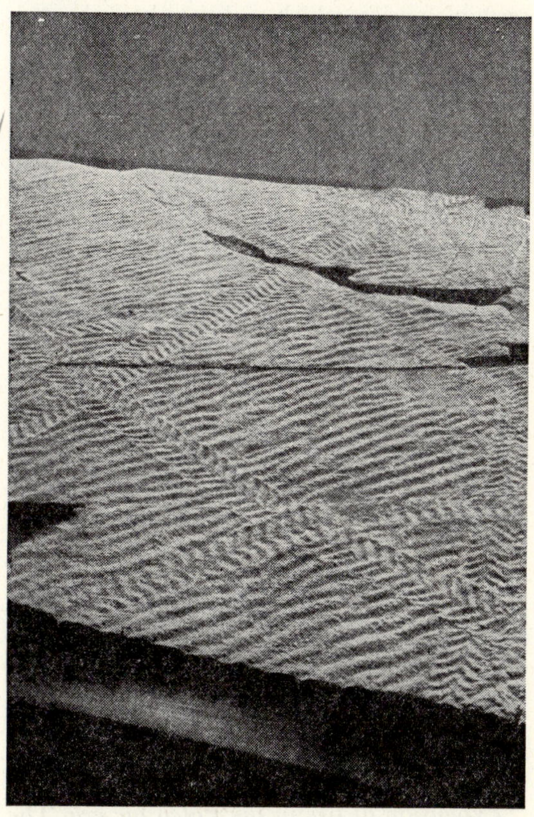

This slab of Potsdam sandstone was cut from a rock formed by the solidifying of a sea beach of early Paleozoic time. The ripple marks are crisscrossed by the trails of some wormlike animal.

to the science of paleontology. As a surveyor he had managed to make an extensive collection of fossils. One day in 1798 as he was classifying his treasures, it dawned on him that given strata always yield the same kind of fossils, while all other strata have different fossil remains—"the law of faunal succession."

During the nineteenth century paleontology made amazing progress. In the face of its findings the theory that all forms of life had been simultaneously created in their modern forms gave way to a new explanation of the origin of life. The unearthing and classification of thousands of fossils demonstrated that an unmistakable evolving pattern of life could be traced from the most ancient to the most recent rock formations. In the older strata, life, as revealed by fossils, is comparatively simple and elementary in form, and each successive stratum exhibits more complex and advanced forms of life. And further, while the older strata contain no fossil evidence of certain species which exist today, there is abundant evidence of the remains of plant and animal organisms which have now become extinct.

Earliest forms of life. We will recall that geologists have determined upon five great eras corresponding to definite strata of the earth. The first of these strata, the Archeozoic, contains no evidence of the existence of life. Many scientists, however, assume that life did exist, since in all probability the first life forms were soft and had no shells or skeletons which could be perpetuated as fossils. Life probably first began along the edge of the oceans. There the elements of which living matter is composed—carbon, hydrogen, oxygen, nitrogen, sulfur, and phosphorus—existed in unstable compounds most favorable to new combinations. The earliest forms of life were probably one-celled organisms.

From the next era, the Proterozoic, we have fossils of the simplest kind. There is evidence of simple plants called Algae, of tracks left by worms, and of skeletons of microscopic creatures called Radiolaria. This era has been designated as the age of primitive marine invertebrates (sea animals without backbones).

Expansion of life in the Paleozoic era. The third era, the Paleozoic, gives evidence from its fossils of the rapid expansion of plant and animal life. Not only were there increasing numbers of species but there were more highly developed and complex forms of life. During the greater part of this era, there was as yet no land life. Life had its home in the seas. At first the water teemed with shellfish, crabs, and worms, while seaweeds grew in profusion. Fish were rare but increased until they became the most important forms of animal life. In the latter periods of the era, plants and animals began their struggle to live on the land and to breathe the air. Creatures with legs and lungs developed, as did species of plants adapted to survive without being surrounded by water. Amphibians appeared, vertebrates able to live both in the water and on land. Land life in the Paleozoic era was meager and struggling for existence. Away from the edge of the water the land was lifeless. As yet there were no flowers or birds. But more and more life moved in the direction of the land away from the water, which had seen its genesis and been its home for millions of years.

The age of great reptiles. The Mesozoic era was the age of great reptiles. The earliest of these beasts were not unlike our crocodiles, with large bellies and short, weak legs. The Mesozoic reptiles gradually ceased their wallowing existence and began to walk rapidly on all fours. Some took to walking on their hind legs like a kangaroo. The largest and the most diverse of these beasts was the group known as the dinosaurs. One of these, called *Gigantosaurus*, was more than fifty feet long. *Tyrannosaurus* is another example of dinosaur size and frightfulness. Walking like a kangaroo, the huge beast had an immense head which towered more than twenty feet above the ground. There were even flying reptiles. Also in this era the first birds made their appearance. Reptilian life completely dominated the earth during Mesozoic times, but it later became almost completely extinct. Only a few lizards, crocodiles, and tortoises exist today as reminders of that time. The sudden termination of the master creatures of the Mesozoic era, the reptiles, is one of the most significant happenings in the history of life before the advent of man.

The Cenozoic era. At the beginning of the fifth and most recent geologic era, the Cenozoic, the world was pretty much as it is today in appearance. Flowers, bees, and butterflies had made their appearance, and grass, which plays such an important part in our modern life, was beginning to clothe great stretches of land in vivid green. This era saw the appearance of modern mammals. The predecessors of the modern horse, pig, camel, monkey, and elephant appeared. At first these mammals were puny and weak, but they grew rapidly in size, and, more important, in brain power, so that they completely eclipsed the formerly all-powerful dynasty of reptiles.

Geologic background of man's development. There are seven geologic epochs of the Cenozoic era, the most recent being the Holocene, in which we are now living. Compared with the other six Cenozoic epochs it is very brief indeed, only 25,000 years at the most. Preceding the Holocene was the Pleistocene, or Glacial, epoch, perhaps one million years long. During this time great ice sheets from the polar regions pushed down over much of Europe, Siberia, and the northern portion of the Near East. On the North American continent the most advanced march of the ice is still marked in New England and in the valleys of the Ohio and the Missouri by a line of boulders which were pushed in front of the ice. Much of northern Europe and North America were ice-covered, as Greenland is today. There were four great advances of ice, each separated by an interglacial age. During their existence and the intervening iceless ages early man developed. Partly because the ice sheets never reached the Mediterranean, civilization first began in the Nile valley and Mesopotamia. In Europe the icy cold of the Pleistocene epoch forced man to live in caves. There he left utensils and weapons, to be discovered in modern times.

The Development of Man

Java Man. Thus far we have seen from fossil remains in the earth's crust how plants and animals have evolved. In addition to these traces of plant and animal life, scientists have found numerous traces of early man. In 1891-1892 Dr. Eugene Dubois, a surgeon in the Dutch colonial army service, discovered in Java several fragments of the skeleton of a manlike creature. These were the top of a skull, part of a jawbone, three teeth, and a left thighbone. Numerous other finds of *Pithecanthropus* and related forms have been made in Java since 1936. From the geological formation in which the fossils were found, it was estimated that the creature lived in early Pleistocene times, nearly one million years ago. Paleontologists have developed amazing skill in reconstructing from minute and often broken remains the skeletons of primitive man. From the fossil fragments found in Java, therefore, scientists were able to reconstruct the skull of Java Man or, as he was named by Dr. Dubois, *Pithecanthropus erectus.* The skull as restored had a brain capacity varying from 750 to 914 cubic centimeters, smaller than that of the most primitive living race today. The forehead of Java Man receded, there were very heavy ridges over the brow, and the bone of the skull was very thick. He decidedly belonged to the human family but not to the genus *Homo,* man as we know him.

Piltdown Man. In 1908, while searching for specimens of early man, Charles Dawson, an amateur scientist, became interested in a gravel pit near Piltdown Manor in southeastern England. During the next four years he acquired portions of a skull, from which the whole skull was reconstructed. The skeleton was first judged to be that of a female creature who lived in the first interglacial age, more than 600,000 years ago. Dawson's fossil woman was called *Eoanthropus dawsoni,* or Dawson's Dawn Man (Greek *eos,* dawn + *anthropos,* man). In the fall of 1953 the scientific world was astounded when the Geology Department of Oxford University, using the latest methods for determining the antiquity of fossils, asserted that this famous human fossil was an elaborate forgery. It was shown that while the skull fragment was that of a primitive man, it was only 50,000 years old. The other fragments were those of a modern chimpanzee or orangutan, cleverly treated with chemicals to show extreme age. Who was responsible for this "paleontological hoax" is not known. The fraud was uncovered by a new technique, the fluorine test, which determines age by estimating the amount of fluorine absorbed by any fossil from the soil. Other new tests, such as the radioactivity of carbon, will aid scientists in reconstructing the story of early man.

Peking Man. In China between 1927 and 1938 more than forty skeletal fragments of an ancient race were unearthed about thirty-seven miles from Peking. These remains established the existence of another genus of primi-

NEANDERTHAL MAN USES FIRE

tive man called *Sinanthropus* (*Sin* from the Greek name for China) *pekinensis.* Like Java Man these early men had low, receding foreheads and massive brow ridges, but their brains were bigger. The age of Peking Man has been the cause of much dispute. The American paleontologist Roy Chapman Andrews maintains that the Peking skulls go back one million years and are as old as Java Man. Authorities now agree that Peking Man, while roughly contemporary with Java Man, should be classed as slightly younger. The Peking type, however, was more advanced than his contemporary in Java. We know that Peking Man was a maker of tools and a user of fire. More than two thousand of his bone and stone implements have been found. We know too that he was able to hunt with both craft and skill, to fashion crude but usable tools, and to organize his life so that nature in some degree was tamed and compelled to do his bidding.

Heidelberg Man. A sandpit more than sixty feet deep near Heidelberg, Germany, was the scene of another important discovery in 1907. Here a professor from Heidelberg University discovered a well-preserved human jaw eighty-two feet below the earth's surface. From fossil remains of the woolly rhinoceros and other animal mammoths now extinct which were found with the Heidelberg jaw, the specimen has been identified as belonging in the first or second interglacial age.

Neanderthal Man. The best known of all extinct species of early man is the Neanderthal race. During the middle and latter part of the Pleistocene, or Glacial, epoch Europe and western Asia were populated mainly by these men. Toward the end of their span of existence, which was perhaps 100,000 years, the fourth great Glacial Age came on and forced them to seek shelter in caves. This explains why so many Neanderthal remains have been preserved. Skeletons of the Neanderthal man have been found in France, the Balkans, Gibraltar, Palestine—in fact, all around the Mediterranean and east Africa, in Russia and even Java.

Neanderthal Man was short and stocky, about five feet, four inches. Although he stood upright, his posture was not fully erect, and as he walked he gave a slouching appearance. He possessed a large brain, but certain of its centers were not yet fully developed. Nevertheless, the brain was for all intents and purposes like that of a modern man. With it Neanderthal Man became skilled in making flint implements and in using fire, and he had some kind of conception of life after death, for he buried his dead. Dominating Europe during the last interglacial age and the early part of the last glacial stage, Neanderthal men were suddenly replaced or absorbed by a modern species of man known as Cro-Magnon. Abruptly the Neanderthal race disappeared, although some anthropologists think certain modern European types show traces of Neanderthal ancestry.

CRO-MAGNON MAN AS HUNTER AND ARTIST

Ape-Men of south Africa. In 1925 Professor Raymond Dart found in the Transvaal province of south Africa a fragmentary skull, face, and jaw that exhibited a puzzling mixture of ape and human characteristics. He named it *Australopithecus africanus* (South African Ape). Since 1936 a bewildering abundance of skeletal remains has been discovered in Transvaal caves by Dart and a colleague, Dr. Robert Broom. These fossil remains, as a group, are usually referred to as the Australopithecids. As the geology of Africa is not sufficiently well known to certify exactly the antiquity of these Ape-Men, their discoverers, while without complete proof, tentatively date the Australopithecids as early Pleistocene or even Pliocene, thus possibly several million years old. These primitive Ape-Men had small brains and snoutlike faces, but many features of their teeth and face were more humanlike than any known apes. In addition their stance was upright; they knew the use of fire; and they used stones—the first tools—to crack the heads of baboons. Authorities disagree whether these creatures should be called human. If they prove to be old enough, they might turn out to be representatives of a stage of evolution just prior to the appearance of Java Man.

Cro-Magnon Man. The first skeleton of the Cro-Magnon race was found in Wales in 1823, but its importance was not appreciated until the discovery of five skeletons in 1868 in a rock shelter in France. Of that group of remains, those of the Old Man of Cro-Magnon were the most important. His stature was just under six feet, his brain capacity was larger than the average modern European's, his forehead was broad and fairly high, and his brow ridges were of moderate size. Gone were the chinless head, the receding skull, and the slouching gait of the various races of earlier man. Here at last was *Homo sapiens.* Making his first appearance some 25,000 to 40,000 years ago, Cro-Magnon Man had many tools and ornaments and had already begun to express his artistic sense in wall paintings and in sculpture. The race was not exterminated like other stocks of early man and thus can be considered the direct ancestor of the modern races of man.

TEMPLE BUILDERS IN UPPER NEOLITHIC PERIOD

GOD MAKERS IN THE NEW STONE AGE

Man's origin and evolution. Any discussion of man's origin and development is a delicate matter, touching as it often does upon a person's philosophical and spiritual convictions. Be this as it may, although the theory of evolution does not yet enjoy the full stature of a scientific law, it has gained the support of such a mass of evidence and the defense of so much expert opinion that no student of the development of man's civilization can afford to be ignorant of its claims. At the same time it is every person's unchallenged right either to accept or reject the theory as he sees fit. Many thinkers maintain that knowledge of the fact that man has succeeded in the face of tremendous obstacles in elevating himself from his once lowly estate to a position of at least partial civilization today is a thrilling and romantic story, which should in no way detract from our belief in the nobility and dignity of man. On the contrary, this knowledge should renew our faith that man in the future will likewise prove competent to solve his difficulties.

A contemporary anthropologist writes:

"One cannot conclude a volume of facts, reflections, and speculations concerning the course of human evolution without asking himself if there is any place for a guiding intelligence in this marvelous progression of organic events. However you look at him, man is a miracle, whether he be a miracle of chance, of nature, or of God. . . . That evolution has occurred I have not the slightest doubt. That it is an accidental or chance occurrence I do not believe, although chance probably has often intervened and is an important contributing factor. But if evolution is not mainly a chance process, it must be an intelligent or purposeful process."[4]

In reviewing our discussion of man's evolution, we should keep in mind that not a single authority maintains that man has descended from any species of monkeys. Rather it is asserted that man and other primates descended from a common ancestor, a primitive primate which long ago became extinct. For a long time all primates were one species, but at a crucial stage in the evolutionary process a split occurred in the common stem. From then on the primate which was eventually to become man went one way in his upward climb; the other primates, another. There is still much debate as to whether human fossil types such as Java Man and Peking Man should be regarded as direct ancestors of man as we know him, that is, as stages in the direct line of man's development, or as collateral relatives, manlike stocks which split off from the main line of human development but became extinct without issue. Cro-Magnon Man is one of the earliest forms universally accepted as one of our ancestors. Practically every year paleontologists and anthropologists in various parts of the world uncover evidences of ancient human life and skeletal remains of primitive man. Many of the missing pages in the fascinating story of the long and upward march of man still remain to be discovered. For example, recent discoveries in the United States of ancient tools and human remains have revolutionized the entire chronology of the American Indian (see Chapter 20).

Special attributes of man. It must be admitted that in many respects man is eclipsed in his endowments by the animals. He cannot compete with the strength of the elephant or the gorilla, the speed of the antelope, the bite of a shark, or the vision of a hawk. But despite these disadvantages man is in certain fundamental respects biologically superior to the animals. This explains his present position of overlord over all plants and animals which must serve his needs. Man has an upright stature that frees his arms from the task of locomotion. His hands are tool-making hands; they are much more agile and dexterous than those possessed by the apes. This is largely explained by the existence of the opposable thumb on man's hands. His vocal powers are also unique. Man's voice box has a much wider range of sounds than that of the animals, making speech possible. Finally, he is fortunate in possessing unique mental powers. His brain capacity is twice as large as that of his nearest animal competitor, the ape. Even more important than quantitative superiority is the qualitative ability to reason and apply imagination. So important is the human brain as a factor differentiating us from the animals that it has been termed "the organ of civilization."

The importance of culture. In addition to biological superiority man possesses a cultural heritage which is passed from one generation to another. If this heritage were to be lost, man, despite his superior nature, would have a status little better than that of an animal. In fact, man is probably too weak to survive without tools and culture. If, for example, a group of small children were taken to an uninhabited island, given a sufficient store of food to ensure their survival, and left undisturbed for about thirty years, at the end of that time they could hardly be described as modern human beings. An explorer finding them would think them the lowest of all savages. These creatures would have grown up without any of the knowledge, customs, literature, and traditions of their parents. If abandoned early enough, they would have no speech. Being civilized, then, is based not only upon the possession of unique mental powers and tool-making hands but also upon the opportunity to utilize man's cultural heritage.

The development of culture. The pattern of man's culture in any age develops, as we have seen (Introduction), in answer to certain basic needs, both physical and spiritual. Like the animals, man has always been very strongly influenced by such primal needs and instincts as food, shelter, and sex. But man is much more than an animal. He is the one living creature who has developed art, religion, principles, and idealistic sentiments. Human history is a confusion of physical urges and spiritual aspirations. Man has always been concerned with certain basic physical problems revolving around self-preservation, but he has always found time to be a martyr, a saint, a creative artist—and sometimes a fiend and a destroyer.

The many-faceted culture pattern arising from man's needs and aspirations evolved along with man himself. Among our earliest ancestors the culture pattern was undoubtedly one-sided, heavily weighted in favor of the satisfaction of physical needs. As he grew in intelligence and as his cultural heritage increased, man began to evolve religious notions, social relationships, laws and customs, and forms of artistic expression. He provided the first crude beginnings of our own cultural heritage.

Evidence of early man's culture is of two sorts. We have direct evidence in the form of "fossils of the mind," the implements or tools that early man invented and the drawings and carvings with which he decorated his caves and tools. These "fossils of the mind" reveal much about primitive man's material achievements. Almost nothing survives which tells of his social organization, the nature of his religion, his laws and customs, and his attitudes. But we have indirect evidence of these aspects of his culture in present-day primitive societies in the same stage of development. We shall now examine in turn these two types of evidence and endeavor to reconstruct as completely as possible the culture pattern of pre civilized man.

Tools and Art of Early Man

"***Fossils of the mind.***" The fossils of the body of primitive man add up to an interesting and important story, but they are not so generally significant as the "fossils of the mind," the implements or tools that early man invented. Thousands of these implements, or

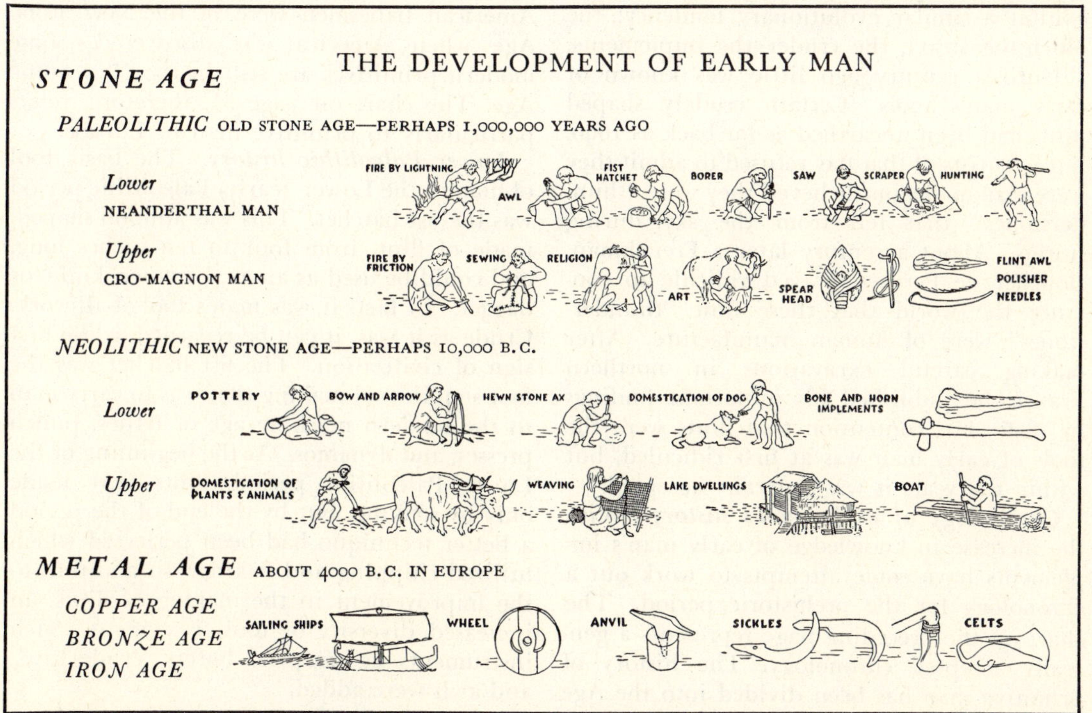

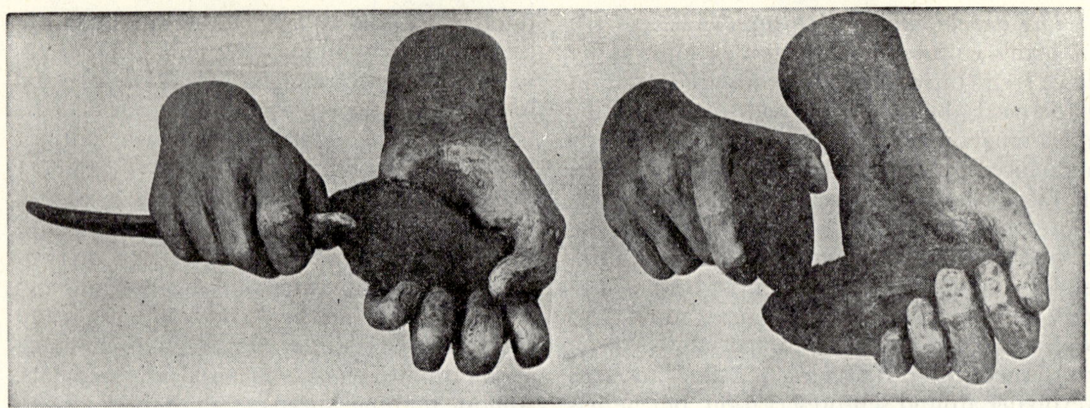

The fist hatchet was man's earliest tool. The primitive striking, or percussion, method of making the fist hatchet is illustrated at the right. The later flaking method, allowing more refinements, is shown at the left.

artifacts, have been discovered in the earth. The places where early men lived and where their debris collected are known technically as stations. The greatest number of stations so far uncovered have been in western Europe, and at some of these as many as 20,000 specimens of early man's tools have been found. Scientists have shown that the oldest strata in which fossils of man are found contain the most primitive skeletal remains and that subsequent geologic formations afford increasing evidence of the progressive development of man's physical make-up. Early man's artifacts exhibit a similar evolutionary tendency; the older the strata, the cruder the implements.

Until a century ago little was known of early man's tools. Certain crudely shaped flints had been unearthed as far back as 1690, but scientists of that day refused to admit they were man-made, but believed they were "thunderstones" that fell from the sky during storms. About a century later a Frenchman, Boucher de Perthes, braved ridicule to convince the world that these flint "thunderstones" were of human manufacture. After making careful excavations in northern France, he published his important findings in 1846. His contention that flints were the tools of early man was at first ridiculed, but within ten years it was generally accepted.

Chronology of early man's history. With the increase in knowledge of early man's implements have come attempts to work out a chronology for the prehistoric period. The chart on the preceding page represents a generally accepted chronology. The history of primitive man has been divided into the Age of Stone and the Age of Metals. The Stone Age has been further divided into the Paleolithic and Neolithic periods (literally the Old Stone Age and New Stone Age). Introduction of the bow and pottery, and above all the invention of agriculture and domestication of animals, in the Neolithic period mark it sharply from the Paleolithic. Scientists have disagreed greatly about the duration of these periods. Actually no general scheme of dates can be applied to primitive man all over the world. For example, Europe was entering the Age of Metals about 4000 B.C., but most American tribesmen were in the New Stone Age when America was discovered. Some modern primitives are still in the New Stone Age. The chart on page 31, therefore, refers particularly to primitive man in Europe.

Lower Paleolithic history. The basic tool of man in the Lower (early) Paleolithic period was the fist hatchet. This was almond-shaped, made of flint, from four to ten inches long, and could be used as an ax, hammer, knife, or dagger. In fact, it was man's tool-of-all-work. Crude as it was, it can be regarded as the first sign of civilization. The fist hatchet was the first step in tool making that was to carry man to the modern machine age of lathes, punch presses, and dynamos. At the beginning of the Lower Paleolithic period, flints were made only by striking, but by the end of the period a better technique had been perfected which utilized chipping and flaking. In addition to the improvement in the making of flints, an increased diversity of tools is evident. Such instruments as scrapers, borers, crude saws, and awls were added.

During the Paleolithic period man was a hunter and a wanderer, heavily dependent upon the caprice of nature. He was able to exert almost no control over his environment. For food he had to follow the migrations of herds of game and the fowls of the air, supplementing such fare with plants, berries, and nuts. He had already learned about the use of fire for warmth. At first the climate was warm, but in the latter part of the period the advent of the fourth great ice sheet in Europe forced him to seek the shelter of caves. The protection from the elements which an enclosed, roofed space furnished, crude though it was, can be considered the first step toward the development of architecture. Architecture has been the outgrowth of one of man's most basic needs, shelter, and to a great extent climate has influenced its development.

Neanderthal Man dominated Europe. Looking back over 150,000 years we can visualize a group of our ancestors squatting at the entrance of their cave. We may be sure there was a stream nearby, for the lack of pottery demanded that Neanderthal Man be within easy reach of water. Not far away was a cliff, a source of flint, which was as important to these Old Stone Age men as oil wells, coal and iron mines, and forests combined are to us. Fire was all-important. We do not know whether early Paleolithic man could kindle fire, but once having procured it, from lightning or elsewhere, he kept the precious embers bright all the time. Fire was the best protection against surprise attack by wild animals. Clothing was a formless one-piece affair made of skins. Style and comfort had to await the invention of the eyed needle, though nearly all cave men wore ornaments made of teeth and shells.

Primitive and uncouth as the early people may seem, they were as intrepid and courageous as any modern race. The presence of many cracked bear skulls in their caves tells us that they were mighty hunters. Food was varied, but its supply was always uncertain. Neanderthal Man had a diet made up of acorns, chestnuts, honey, snails, cherries, game, birds' eggs, and fish. To this was added bones smashed into a paste. Much of the food was eaten half-spoiled.

Upper Paleolithic history. With the coming of the Upper Paleolithic period, Cro-Magnon Man, the first race of modern man, appeared. The intense cold forced him to live most of the time in caves. This did not slow up his development; on the contrary, greater leisure apparently resulted in the invention of more and more tools, for many new artifacts were devised. In addition to flint awls and polishers, eyed needles and spearheads were made of bone. Also made of the same material were whistles and flutes. Better weapons, especially the harpoon and the spear, gave Cro-Magnon Man superiority over the animal world. The shape of many flints from this period indicates that they were mounted on wooden handles as knives or spears, but the true ax was not used until Neolithic times. A most important discovery was made—the making of fire by rubbing two sticks together.

The first trace of religious feeling evidently appeared in the Middle Paleolithic period; there is evidence of human burial and funerary practices. The concepts of the soul and life after death were in the making. No one knows when speech began, but it probably originated about the time the first man-made artifacts were devised in early Paleolithic days. Cro-Magnon Man possessed a rudimentary system of vocal communication and perhaps experimented with written signs.

Early art. One of the highest achievements of the men of the Old Stone Age was their art. Art is one of man's most ancient activities. He was an artist endeavoring to give expression to his creative imagination long before he could write or fashion a metal knife. Ancient art furnishes an invaluable clue to many features of prehistoric life, for it constitutes the oldest form of record.

There is little or no trace of art in the Lower Paleolithic period. Neanderthal Man evidently was not much of an artist, but his successor, Cro-Magnon Man, showed considerable ability. In the Upper Paleolithic period the cave man became a prolific artist. He carved in ivory, horn, and bone, engraved on the flattened surface of these materials, modeled in clay, and covered the walls of his caves with carved and painted designs.

Among the things the cave man left behind him were decorated tools, weapons, and ceremonial objects. His tools, though often decorated, were made for use, and the decoration remained within the dictates of function. For example, tools and weapons with animals carved on the handles have been found in

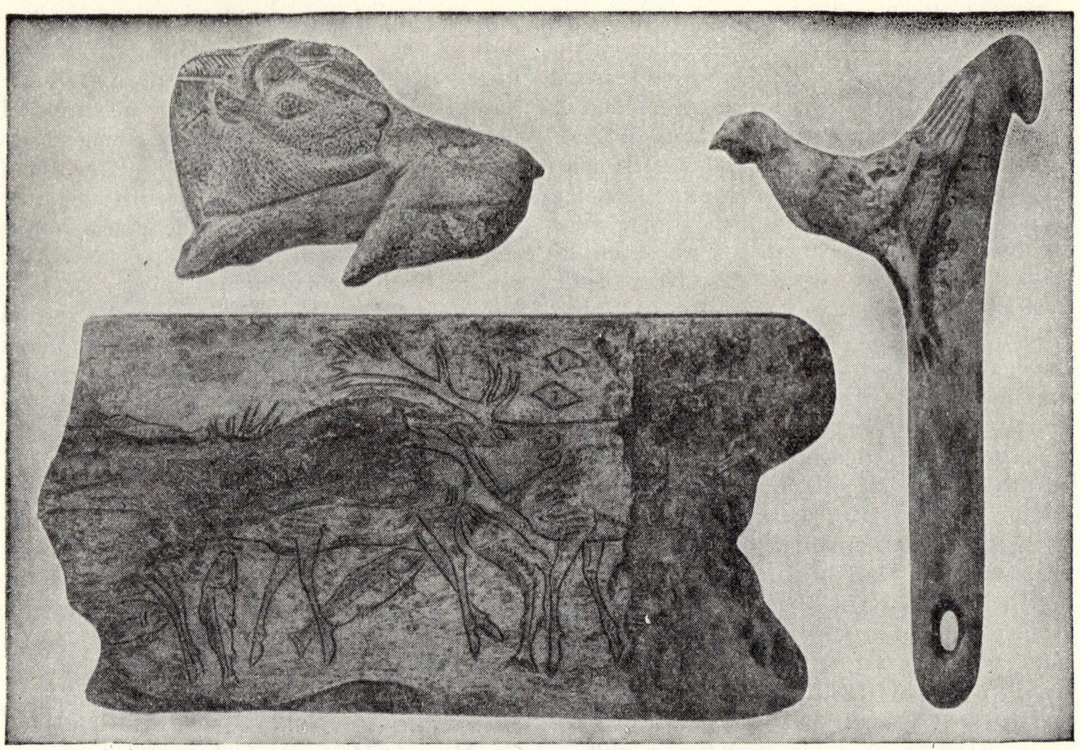

CARVED TOOLS OF EARLY MAN, DECORATED WITH BIRDS, FISH, AND ANIMALS

which the animal shape is sensitively adapted to the shape of the user's hand. The bird decoration above shows such adaptation. Fragments of ivory tools have also been found in which line drawings have been scratched into the tool with a sharp instrument. This technique allowed decorations without projections to spoil the handling surface. The group of reindeer and fish above is an example of such line engraving. The carver had obviously observed the animals around him. With simple line and the suppression of non-essential details, the artist represented reindeer and fish in characteristic poses.

A few carved figurines have come down to us. They are usually of the female body, very primitive in design, and they were undoubtedly used in connection with fertility rites.

Early man's first attempts to paint and carve on the walls of his caves were halting and rather grotesque and consisted of simple contours of animals. He was also prone to copy the outline of his hand pressed against the walls of his caves. His next step was the enrichment of painted outlines of animals by the use of shading. The final development of Paleolithic painting was polychrome art, when the painter used red, black, and yellow instead of limiting himself to one color.

In 1879 Sautuola, a Spanish nobleman, was exploring a cave on his Altamira estate in northern Spain. His little daughter, who had accompanied him, suddenly cried, "Toros! toros!" ("Bulls! bulls!") The father turned around and saw his little girl pointing to the ceiling. He perceived a thrilling sight, a long procession of magnificently drawn bison. The following year Sautuola published his discovery in a little pamphlet, but archaeologists scoffed. The paintings were "too modern" and "too realistic." In a few years other caves in northern Spain and southern France yielded many additional examples of prehistoric art, and Sautuola was vindicated.

In the Altamira murals the outline of the animals was usually traced in black and then shaded with a mixture of red, black, and yellow colors. These paintings of animals, with their actions, attitudes, and skillfully drawn anatomy, show that man was observing keenly the world around him. Careful observation and an intelligent selection of impressions were needed to produce pictures showing essential movements of the animals rather than mere static details. To call this art primitive and crude would be a great mistake. Such a picture as the "Charging Bison" at Altamira eliminates all nonessential lines and shapes; the artist has used only those lines and shapes which emphasize the forward, charging movement of the animal.

Cro-Magnon Man concentrated his efforts upon painting animals of all kinds—wolves, reindeer, horses, mammoths, and bison. Scant attention was paid to the human body. Perhaps the concentration upon animals can be explained by assuming a relationship between the art of the cave man and his belief in the supernatural. In making visual representations of animals in his caves, Cro-Magnon Man probably believed he could bring them under his control and thus make his food supply more certain. Occasionally he drew arrows piercing the sides of animals he hoped to bring home.

Neolithic achievements. The Paleolithic period was one of the most important eras of achievement in the history of mankind. It bequeathed to us fire, clothing, and some of the arts, basic elements in our modern civilization. But the life of Paleolithic man was still very limited. He had no cooking utensils, axes with handles, buildings, bows and arrows, cultivated grain or vegetables, or domestic animals. These important things, essential for man's well-being, appeared in the Neolithic period.

The chief European sites of Neolithic history are in Scandinavia, Switzerland, England, and France. The early Neolithic period was characterized by the introduction of pottery, an innovation which made possible the storing of water and the cooking of such new dishes as soups and stews. To pottery were added the bow and arrow, making possible long-range fighting and greatly increasing man's effectiveness in hunting wild game. The hewn stone ax was a valuable addition to early man's tools, and the number of new bone and horn implements increased rapidly. The dog was domesticated in the early Neolithic period. In all probability he was not captured and then tamed but at some time voluntarily attached himself to man as an easy means of securing shelter and food. Man's earliest "pooch" was "a parasitic hanger-on, a shy, tolerated, uncared-for scavenger."

The beginning of agriculture. Important as such advances were, the really striking achievements of Neolithic man came in the latter half of the New Stone Age. Grinding and polishing of flints produced fine daggers, poniards, and graceful axes. All-important was the domestication of plants, the beginning of agriculture. To develop such crops as barley, wheat, millet, peas, lentils, and flax, painstaking selection and slow cultivation of wild grasses and other natural plants were first necessary. Along with planting came the domestication of animals, which were "no longer victims so much as property."[5] At first animals were tamed; then a long time had to elapse before they could be trained to work in a harness. The final step in the process was controlled breeding, which produced breeds best adapted to serve the needs of man. The possession of cattle and crops gave man a stake to fight for, possessions that he must protect. At the same time the accumulation of goods encouraged attack. In case a neighbor suffered bad crops

"CHARGING BISON," CAVE PAINTING AT ALTAMIRA

NEOLITHIC BOWL WITH GEOMETRIC PATTERN

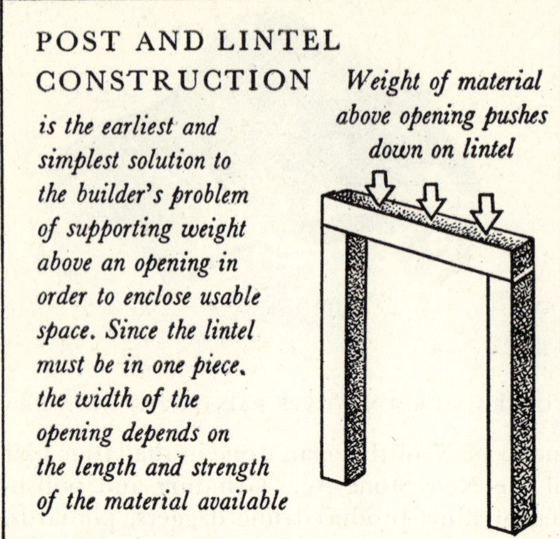

or his food supply was destroyed by fire, there was an incentive for him to use force to obtain the food he lacked.

POST AND LINTEL
CONSTRUCTION
is the earliest and simplest solution to the builder's problem of supporting weight above an opening in order to enclose usable space. Since the lintel must be in one piece, the width of the opening depends on the length and strength of the material available
Weight of material above opening pushes down on lintel

With the practice of agriculture, man ceased to be a hunter or collector roaming over the countryside. A settled existence became possible. This resulted in the development of small villages, in which the first real houses appeared. Sedentary group living now came into existence. Men had to learn to cooperate with one another and to obey certain rules or laws which the group decided were essential to its safety and comfort; more attention had to be paid to the group leadership and organization which were to develop into what we now know as government. J. T. Shotwell, in evaluating the importance of the advent of agriculture, says, "The greatest social revolution of primitive mankind came about when man, settling on the soil instead of wandering, and so accumulating goods which involved foresight, began to calculate for a future."[6] So significant a trend in man's control over nature was the advent of agriculture that a famous British anthropologist has popularized this development as the "Neolithic Revolution."

Neolithic art and building. The earliest houses built by man were outside Europe, probably in the Near East. In Europe the first dwellings seem to have been built in the Danube Valley, Spain, and France. Perhaps the most famous and interesting early wooden houses of which we have any evidence were dwellings in Neolithic lake villages in Switzerland. These villages were built on piles that were driven into the lake floor or into marshy ground. In one instance remains of fifty thousand piles driven at great effort to support one village have been uncovered. In the debris around the piles, tools of all kinds, house furnishings, wheat, barley, fish nets, and small boats attest to the advanced civilization of the lake dwellers.

STONEHENGE: MONUMENTAL SETTING FOR EARLY MAN'S RELIGIOUS RITES

MYSTERIOUS MEGALITHIC MONUMENTS FOUND AT CARNAC, FRANCE

The houses of the lake dwellers are the earliest known architecture in the world. When man had lived in caves, he was unable to locate his home as he wished, near a water supply or in a place easy to defend from animals. With the discovery of fire, caves undoubtedly became smoky and stuffy. There could be only one entrance, little ventilation, and certainly no natural light. So Neolithic man constructed his own shelter, giving it a roof, walls, holes in the roof for smoke to escape, and more openings for ventilation. In the lake dwelling was found for the first time the important post and lintel construction (see page 36). These basic problems of enclosed space, roofing, entrance and exit, ventilation, and lighting have always occupied architects.

Neolithic art is less brilliant than the Cro-Magnon creations. Neolithic man produced tools, but decoration was confined mostly to geometric patterns, often of great beauty and well suited to the shape of the decorated object. His lack of interest in animal representation can perhaps be explained by his greater control over nature. The shapes of his pottery are simple and pleasing. One of the basic determinants of any art form is the nature of the material. Clay is an extremely pliable material before it is hardened by heat, and clay vessels must be made so that the lower part can hold the weight of the top without warping or buckling. Neolithic pottery was probably made by the coil method—by building a series of clay coils one on top of another and then smoothing them together.

Although he was not much of a painter or carver, New Stone Age man was a great builder in stone. After the need for shelter, religion provided an early incentive for building. In connection with his religious rites he erected huge monuments called megaliths, meaning "large stones," often arranged in rows or circles. The most famous monument is Stone-

Pictured above is a museum diorama, developed through the studies of scholars, which shows the megalithic monuments at Carnac, France. Here is a priest of primitive time looking down the long avenue of stones to welcome a new day.

henge in England (page 36). Others have been found at Carnac, France (see page 37).

Other Neolithic achievements. In addition to the new technique of making flint tools by grinding, the domestication of plants and animals, and the building of huge stone monuments, the later Neolithic period is important for the introduction of weaving, the making of the first rude boats, the start of surgery and of specialized vocations, and the rise of commerce which centered around the bartering of such precious commodities as flint and jade.

Primitive Thought and Custom

Early man's nonmaterial tools. Tools, monuments, art, and other visible remains give the historian a good deal of data from which to reconstruct the material aspects of early man's life. But the nonmaterial aspects of his culture are fully as important as his material achievements. Such things as his beliefs, religious observances, family life, and system of law and government are just as much tools designed to answer human needs as a fist hatchet or canoe. Unfortunately these nonmaterial tools of culture leave no fossils, and it is therefore exceedingly difficult to re-create early man's beliefs and social organization. The only thing the historian can do is assume that the various primitive peoples living today possess many of the customs and beliefs of our early ancestors.

If we find a native tribe today using what could be described as Neolithic tools, we infer that its legal system, religious beliefs, system of land tenure, and so on, are similar to those used by our ancestors in the Neolithic period several thousand years ago. Of course this inference may not be wholly correct. The culture of present primitives may have much in it that has been borrowed from superior civilizations. But notwithstanding this possibility it can be assumed that, in the main, the thoughts and institutions of primitive people today are similar to those of primitive man of the past.

The anthropologist has a great amount of material to work from. There are large numbers of contemporary primitive people in the western hemisphere living in much the same way as when Cortes and Pizarro came to the New World. There are also many such people in inner Asia. The anthropologist also finds the native population of islands in the Pacific a valuable storehouse for information about primitive customs. The same holds true for large sections of Africa. Of course many of the primitive people of the world have been killed off or displaced as a result of the expansion of western culture. The last native in Tasmania died about fifty years ago, the Newfoundland primitive disappeared a century ago, and most of the Indians in our own land east of the Mississippi were uprooted and scattered before the middle of the nineteenth century.

Complexity of primitive society. It is natural for people living in a sophisticated machine age to assume that primitive people possess little in the shape of law, government, education, codes of conduct—the paraphernalia of social organization. This is far from true. In many ways the organization of primitive society is as complex as our own. Rules regarding the role of parents, the treatment of children, the punishment of the evildoer, the conduct of business, the worship of the gods, the education of the younger generation, the conventions of eating, recreation, and the like, have been carefully worked out, and effective methods exist to compel the individual, if necessary, to observe the correct usages.

The elementary family. Among primitive people the elementary family is a basic unit. As far as we know, no people exist who do not in some way formalize marriage. Family organization may take several forms. In monogamy, the usual family system, there is just one husband and one wife. In polygamy one man has two or more wives, and in polyandry one woman has several husbands. In many respects family relations among primitive people would seem to us very modern and reasonable. The wife is usually not the chattel of her husband, and the tribal law lays down carefully the respective duties, obligations, and rights of both parents. As in most societies, including our own, the male is apt to think of himself as the more important. We find this condescending note in many of the proverbs of primitive people: "Woman is a mat which must be beaten." "If a woman looks nice it is through her husband." (He had to foot the bill.) "Women like to be where there is money."

Many tribes give the husband the right to chastise his spouse, but if this is done without cause the wife can appeal to her relatives or to the tribal council for redress.

The economic duties of wife and husband are also regulated by custom. The wife has the usual household duties and in addition may be expected to take care of the growing crops. The husband does the heavy labor of breaking and preparing the ground for sowing; he hunts, participates in the tribal council, and takes care of whatever cattle he may have. Among some primitive people, the wife has the exclusive use of some of the family land. She can barter or sell its produce and the return is her own. This "pin money" can even be loaned to her husband, who must pay it back according to tribal custom. There is nothing "savage" about the treatment of children. Anthropologists say that frequently children are spoiled by doting parents. At an early age the boys and girls are given some duties to perform; in Africa, for example, the boys usually are given the task of herding the family cattle.

The extended family. In addition to the elementary family there often exists among primitives what is termed the extended family. This is a circle of related people who usually trace their descent through their mothers. In the extended family, children call their mother's brother "father" and his sons and daughters their "brothers" and "sisters." The related people in this extended family are bound together by strong ties of mutual loyalty and helpfulness. It is said that in certain tribes the strongest bond between man and woman is not the marriage relationship but that which exists between brother and sister. Even after a woman is married she looks for protection, if necessary, to her brothers.

The clan. A third primitive social unit is the clan—a group of individuals who believe that they have a common ancestor and therefore are "of one blood, or of one soul." Although English scholars refer to father or mother clans, in America it has been the practice to use the term *clan* when usage is made by the group of female descent, and *gens* when descent is traced through the male line. All members of a clan or gens are blood brothers bound to avenge any wrong inflicted on one of their number and to offer aid whenever it is needed by a member of the group.

Like ourselves, primitive people generally do not sanction marriage between close relatives. Nevertheless, instances may also be found where the opposite is true, that is, where marriage within the restricted group is actually required. Many clans and gens are characterized by a totem. The totem is an animal or some other natural object which gives the group its name and emblem. The members sometimes believe that originally they sprang from the totem, which is revered by a complex pattern of taboos and ceremonies. Totemism, while not universal, is found in many parts of the world. Nearly everyone is acquainted with the totem poles and totem masks of British Columbia and Alaska. Totemism of a sort is far from dead in modern society. An anthropologist—Ralph Linton—made a study of arm-patch symbols in the American army as totems around which unit loyalty gathered. Fraternal organizations such as the Elks, Moose, Eagles, etc., also have their insignia of totemism, and numerous colleges have their mascots, symbolic axes, and victory bells as symbols around which the group rallies when "danger" threatens—on the football field or elsewhere.

The tribe. The fourth circle in which primitive people live is the tribe, which may be thought of as a collection of clans or gens. Each tribe has a definite name, such as the Masai, Zulu, Kikuyu. Each has a common speech or distinctive dialect and a specific land area in which it dwells. Members of a tribe are just as proud of their own group's accomplishments as is the citizen of a modern state. It is said, for example, that Eskimos refer to other Indians as "children of a louse's egg," and the Lakotapi, a North American tribe, have a saying to the effect, "We are the original people, better than any other group, and it is a matter of our goodness to grant rights of any kind to other people."

Frequently a tribe's name for itself is its word for "man" or "human being," implying something less than human status for other people. As the growth of civilization is traced in the chapters that follow, an important part of the story of progress will be seen to be the broadening of man's social horizons to include more and more diverse peoples in the concept of "fully human." The modern nation includes many more diverse people than ever did the ancient tribe, but as modern man struggles to create a harmonious world community we are still far short of seeing all people as fully human.

Primitive government. As a general rule, in primitive societies the political unit—the village or tribe—is usually small and is in essence a miniature nation independent of all other villages or tribes. This exemplifies the restricted social horizons of primitives. In practice, the details and machinery of the governmental system of primitive people vary widely. In New Guinea there is little political machinery. Each group, or tribe, merely has a designated leader who is the mouthpiece of his fellows. In the islands of the mid-Pacific a form of central government exists which provides for gradations of rank such as noble, commoner, and slave. In Australia political organization includes a group of elders who wield governmental power. As for Africa, the usual form of government consists of a chief who rules by the consent and advice of the wise men. In certain areas there are large governmental political units under a ruler who maintains a standing army. Although many different governmental forms prevail among primitives, there seems generally to be an absence of what we might term political despotism. The chief must rule according to the unwritten law and custom of his tribe, and in the event of very serious decisions he must consult his council of elders. This strong representative element in the political machinery of backward people has led some observers to assert that political despotism runs counter to a deep-seated instinct in mankind.

This Masai girl belongs to a magnificent tribe of contemporary "primitives." They are the great warriors of east Africa. In hunting lions, they are armed only with spears.

Primitive law. Among primitive people a definite code of law exists which has as its purpose the protection of society and, for certain crimes, the punishment of the evildoer. Unlike modern law codes most primitive law is civil rather than criminal. Many acts we regard as crimes are not considered by primitives as offenses against society. The basic idea of primitive law, especially in Africa, is maintaining an equilibrium. If a man steals some property from another, the economic equilibrium has been unjustly disturbed. The victim is satisfied, however, if the thief restores what he stole or its equivalent. When equilibrium has been restored everybody is satisfied. The thief according to our modern legal ideas goes unpunished. Even in the case of a killing the tribal authorities do not intervene, but the culprit must make adequate restitution to the relatives of his victim. There are, however, certain acts which constitute such a danger to the social group that they are thought of as crimes and thereby merit some penalty from the tribal government. Some examples are treason, witchcraft, and incest. Such acts cannot be settled by the payment of compensation. They come under what we would term public law, and the punishment meted out by the authorities for these crimes is usually death.

If such misdemeanors as stealing do not result in punishment as long as restitution is made by the culprit, how is law and order maintained among primitive people? Behind the rules of the tribe stand the religious beliefs of the group. It is believed that anyone who continually breaks the law will be haunted by the annoyed spirits of his ancestors and will also suffer the curses of the tribal gods. Equally potent as a deterrent to antisocial behavior is the existence of collective responsibility. When an offense has been committed the culprit's kinsfolk must accept the responsibility of seeing that proper restitution is made. If a member of a clan gets into trouble too often, his fellows will regard him as a social nuisance and a downright economic liability; they will accordingly outlaw him from the group or execute him. For minor offenses primitive people use with great effectiveness the weapons of ridicule and ostracism. Fear of the supernatural, the force of collective responsibility, and the weapon of ridicule insure respect for the customs and laws of the tribe.

Primitive religion. Perhaps the strongest single force in the life of primitive people is religion. It colors every aspect of their activity: the birth of children, rain making, initiation into the tribe, seedtime and harvest, marriage, death, and war. Religion goes back to the dawn of history. Man has always been filled with awe and wonder of nature. Among primitives, with little knowledge of science, there has always been a deep feeling of helplessness and of weakness in the face of such inexplicable phenomena as drought, a plague of insects, disease, and death. The urge to associate oneself with and to reverence the mysterious forces dominating human affairs led to what we call religion.

In general, religion fills the gap between a society's technical knowledge and the control he desires over nature. The hunter musters all his skill and his best weapons but prays his quarry may be rendered docile and unsuspicious; the farmer plants and tends his fields the best he knows how but prays for adequate rain or for no unseasonable cold. Although primitive people often possess the concept of a supreme good God and a supreme evil spirit, these exist in a supernatural world of many lesser deities. Monotheism, the belief in one god, was developed by civilized peoples, although primitives often believed in a single supernatural force.

Religion and magic. Closely associated with primitive religion is the practice of magic. Magic may be defined as a technique directed at obtaining the aid of supernatural forces to control nature and time. Professional rain makers, for example, are said to have the secret of appealing to the spirits who command the weather; diviners are in touch with spirits which give them the clue to the future; medicine men can supply charms which give immunity from disease or protect one from accidents. Witches and wizards practice the magic most feared by primitives—witchcraft. The witch can throw a spell upon a victim which will bring about his quick death or inflict upon him a calamity such as the loss of his crops or the death of his cattle. If the victim learns that he has been bewitched he will immediately repair to a witch doctor, who will give him an antidote to cope with the malevolent forces in league with the witch. The primitive unquestioningly believes that witchcraft exists. Even today in many parts of Africa there are reported cases in which a native believes himself to be bewitched, resigns himself to his fate, and dies.

Basic attitudes. An examination of primitive society reveals several basic characteristics. The first is the extreme conservatism of the group. There is little sympathy for new ideas, and effective deterrents—such as ostracism or ridicule—are utilized against any individual who broaches new beliefs or criticizes the gods. There are numerous prohibitive rules called taboos whereby certain actions are absolutely forbidden. Taboos are sanctioned by the gods, and few individuals ever dare go against them. This subordination of the individual mind to the group mind results in a social solidarity which enables the tribe to survive but at the same time makes primitive society static, with little opportunity for social development. This attitude is by no means completely absent in modern societies. While we welcome technological changes, we strongly resist changes in family organization and social institutions generally, though these must inevitably be modified by the very technological changes we welcome.

In addition to the extreme conservatism of primitive peoples, the group rather than the individual is emphasized. In many tribes land is held in trust by the elders, who allocate it to the various families. This land cannot be privately owned. In the event a member of the tribe returns from a long absence away from the group he still can claim his rightful share of the land. Unlike our highly atomized society, with every individual seeking to advance his own interests (often at the expense of the group), the primitive man must always think of group and family interests rather than of his own. If a man runs short of food he can appeal to his many blood brothers in his extended family or in his clan for assistance. It has been said that one would never find a tribesman starving; if the village had any food at all, everyone would get his share. This strong feeling of mutual helpfulness is one of the most admirable features of primitive society.

Primitive economy. Economic activity is primarily oriented about production for subsistence, and family and kin produce and share their labor as a cooperative group. Surpluses are more likely to be produced for ceremonial purposes or prestige—for feasts rather than for trade. Where trade does exist it is likely to be specialized: one village making pots to trade with another for salt or baskets. Barter is the rule, and often the law of supply and demand does not operate because values are determined by tradition. For example, unlike the situation in most modern societies, the mere accumulation of goods is not of itself praiseworthy and the clinging to such wealth is distinctly frowned upon. High prestige and praise comes when the goods a family has produced by industriousness are dispersed in a socially approved manner. A Plains Indian Warrior who stole many horses from the enemy was publicly acclaimed when he gave them all away; he would have been severely censured had he kept them for himself. A "big man" in Oceania is one who provides vastly more food at a feast than the assembled multitude can eat. In economics, as in all else, primitive societies are more unified than ours; everyone believes in the same social mechanisms, values, and ends.

Education. Primitive education is not the conscious, even artificial, process that it is with us. Children learn by doing—their games and play and family responsibilities all teach them the techniques of society. Social values may be taught by instilling fear of supernatural punishment, or by stressing the family's expectation that all its members will contribute to its good name. The gradual induction into ritual mysteries impresses on the child the importance of conformity and the desirability of becoming an accepted adult. The end product is an individual who is oriented toward serving the welfare of his kin group and deeply observant of the social needs of his society. Anthropologists observe that perhaps modern education could benefit from a careful study of aboriginal educational processes.

In a crude but effective manner African society imparts to its young people the skills and information deemed essential for proficient adulthood. There is no classroom. A group of boys squat on the ground in a clearing between the huts and listen to advice from a mighty hunter or sober words from a dignified elder. Graduation time comes when the young boys and girls go through their initiation ceremonies. For several weeks the young people are given intensive instruction and finally are inducted into the adult membership of the tribe. This last "class" in African education is accompanied by many strenuous exercises reminiscent of college fraternity rites, designed to impress upon the young people what their elders think they should know.

Disappearance of primitive culture. Generally speaking, the primitive peoples of the world today are emerging rather rapidly from the crude culture of their ancestors. The mission and governmental school, the advice of the medical and agricultural officer are all doing their part in this work. Perhaps the day will come when it will be impossible to find human reminders of a remote Stone Age.

Meanwhile our contemporary primitive peoples are living in a culture not far different from that of early man. It is thus possible for us to reconstruct the life of our early ancestors. Blood relationship, then and now, was the basis of human organization. Such organization consisted of several social groupings, notably the elementary family, the clan, and the tribe. Little political machinery existed among primitive tribes. Government was simple and law enforcement was not usually the concern of society. Injuries were taken care of by the payment of compensation to aggrieved parties. Extreme conservatism dominated the primitive group. Men had to tread perpetually in an accepted circle of custom.

The Dawn of Civilization

The Age of Metals. The Neolithic period slowly came to an end about 5000 B.C. in the Near East and merged into a new period, the Age of Metals. The use of copper began in Egypt perhaps as far back as 5000 B.C. Copper needles have been found in the valley of the Nile dating back at least to 4000 B.C. These were probably the earliest metal tools fash-

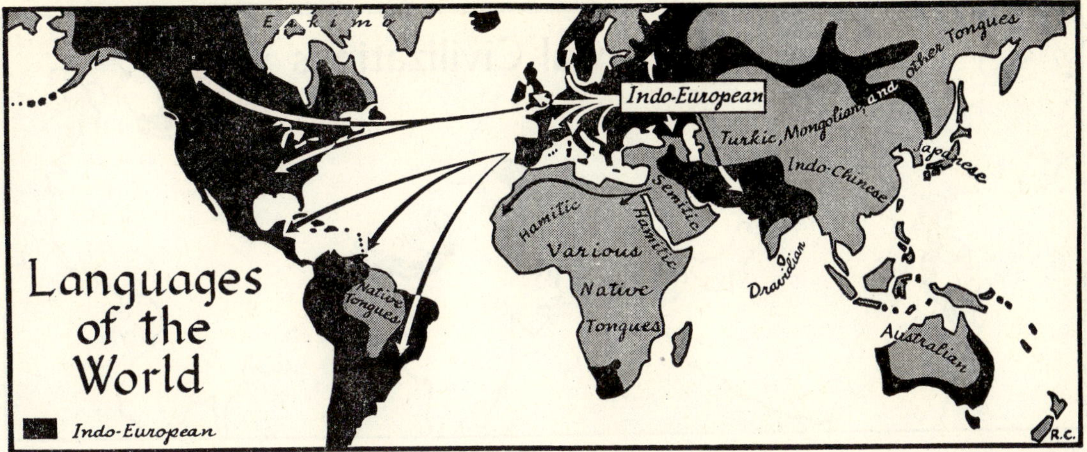

ioned by man. About the same time metal began to be used in Mesopotamia, a valley region lying between the Euphrates and Tigris rivers. As copper implements were soft and dull, a harder metal was desirable. It was eventually obtained by making an alloy of copper and tin. Bronze, as the new alloy was called, was introduced into Egypt about 3000 B.C. The use of metals spread from Egypt and Asia Minor to Europe, where, in the southeastern areas adjacent to the Near East, copper began to supersede stone about 2500 B.C. Bronze was first used in Europe around 2000 B.C. The use of iron apparently had its origin in Asia Minor about 1300 B.C., whence it spread to Egypt and the general Mediterranean area. Just as the Stone Age is divided into two periods (Paleolithic, Neolithic), so the Age of Metals can be thought of as comprising the Copper, Bronze, and Iron ages. The date for the termination of one early period (such as the Neolithic) and the start of a new period (such as the Copper) depends upon what geographical area is considered. The Age of Metals began in the Near East at least 1500 years before its advent in western Europe. And even today, while we think of the Stone Age as being as dead as the fossils of Neanderthal Man, there are still many primitive people in various parts of the world who live in much the same way as the Neolithic cave man lived in Europe thousands and thousands of years ago.

Stone Age man in western Europe by 5000 B.C. had succeeded in making several splendid advances. We recall his introduction of agriculture, his domestication of animals, and his achievements in art. But Stone Age man everywhere was without the important skill of writing, the wheel, so indispensable to travel and transport, large sailing ships, large-scale government, and the use of metals. These very important fundamentals of civilization were first developed in Mesopotamia and in the valley of the Nile. The story of their development by peoples in the Near East will be told in the next chapter.

Peoples of the ancient world. The first really human being to live on this earth has been described as Cro-Magnon Man. Discovered first in France, the remains of Paleolithic cultures identical with the Cro-Magnon have been found all over Europe. While modern man was emerging in Europe, an equally advanced human type was developing in north Africa, the Near East, and Asia (not in the Americas, as man came to these continents relatively late in history). These various detached representatives of the human family, because of their separation from each other and the different physical environments, developed distinctive mental, social, and physical characteristics. So by the time man had discovered how to use metals in the more advanced cultures of the ancient world, there were different peoples destined to play an important part in history.

Before recorded history a large group of nomadic peoples had their home north of the Black and Caspian seas (we noted them in our discussion of the Aryan myth in the Introduction). These people, speaking an Indo-European, or "Aryan," language and hence called Indo-Europeans (and sometimes "Aryans"), began a series of great migrations about 2500 B.C. One wing moved westward and passed

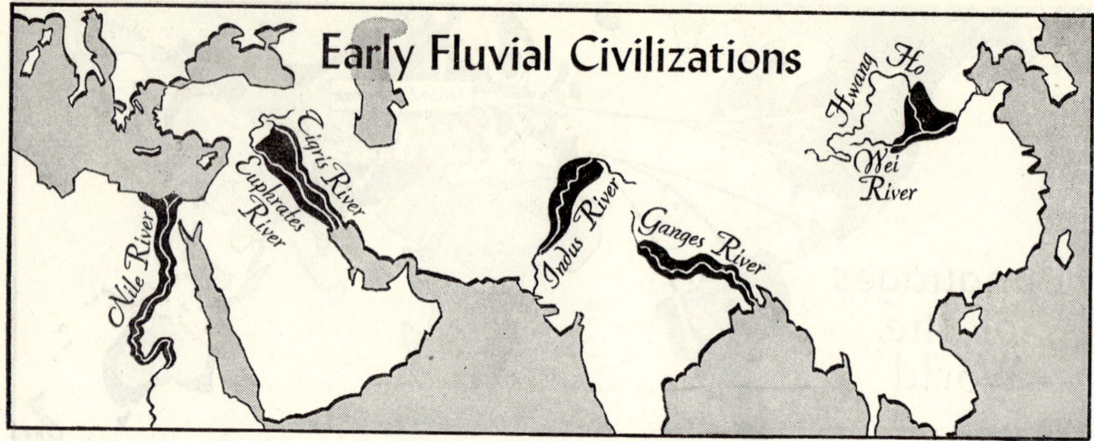

into northern Asia Minor, Greece, and Italy. These nomads were the ancestors of the later Celts, Romans, Greeks, and Armenians. Another Indo-European group, the eastern branch, split about 1800 B.C. One migration made its way toward Mesopotamia and became the famous Medes and Persians; the other group moved to the east and settled in northern India. The last group is commonly known as Indo-Aryan.

Another great body of people, called the Semites because they spoke a Semitic tongue, occupied the territory immediately to the south of the Indo-Europeans, stretching from Mesopotamia along the African coast to the western end of the Mediterranean. The most important Semites were the Phoenicians, Hebrews, Arameans, Assyrians, and Babylonians. In ancient times Indo-Europeans and Semites were rivals for lands in the Mediterranean and Near-Eastern regions. A third, much smaller, language group is the Hamitic. It includes the Egyptians and other people who live in northeastern Africa.

The Indo-Europeans, we noted carefully, were not a single master-race responsible for all the great achievements in history. But the Indo-European language comes near to being a master-tongue. Today, as the map on the preceding page shows, most of the world speaks Indo-European tongues. These have been spoken in Europe and India for many centuries. In early modern times European languages were carried by explorers to the New World, where they rapidly replaced native Indian tongues.

A moment in history. The peoples of the ancient world, some of whom were to develop the civilizations to be discussed in the next chapter, had already a venerable history of cultural development before the dawn of recorded history. Behind their culture stretched the vast eras, measured in millions of centuries, of the development of the world, of life, and of man. In the light of these vast stretches of time the traditional divisions of ancient, medieval, and modern history, including altogether some sixty centuries, seem somewhat out of date. According to the traditional scheme ancient history begins at 4000 B.C., the approximate date of the first written records left by man. Medieval history is initiated by the fall of Rome in 476 A.D. Modern history, having its birth in the fifteenth century, is associated either with the fall of Constantinople in 1453 or with the discovery of America in 1492. Perhaps in the future there will be some alteration in our scheme of historical chronology taking into account the vast stretches of time uncovered by the geologist. The traditional dates for ancient, medieval, and modern history remain most useful, however, in studying the development of civilization.

Summary

The horizons of history go back into the infinite past. The earth, scene of the history of man, was violently born about two billion years ago, a tiny particle of a universe whose vast size and age are unknown and almost incomprehensible. Yet the earth is perhaps unique in all the universe as the scene of the evolution of life and the achievement of civilization.

In the rocks of the earth the miraculous story of the unfolding of life is revealed. By studying fossils we know approximately when life first arose and how it evolved from simple and undifferentiated varieties to complex and advanced life forms. Man too is a part of this evolving stream of life. Fossils have been discovered showing that man was in the process of evolution for about one million years and that he finally appeared as we know him some forty thousand years ago.

More important than these fossils of the body are the fossils of the mind, the tools early man created to satisfy his many wants. The first artifact, the fist hatchet, was a crude implement, but during the Stone Age there was a steady improvement in man's tools, indicating an advancing culture. Organic evolution was thus paralleled by cultural evolution.

The first great period of man's cultural evolution was the Paleolithic. It saw the invention of numerous tools, such as the harpoon and spear, and the manufacture of fire. Above all it was the period in which the first art was created, an art far from being crude, as carved tools and mural paintings show. Building on these foundations, men of the Neolithic period created the first houses, boats, and great stone monuments called megaliths, and introduced weaving, agriculture, and the domestication of animals.

The non-material aspects of early man's culture left no fossil remains, but they may be deduced from the study of contemporary primitive peoples. From these we learn that society was probably organized into families, clans, and tribes. A complex set of customs and taboos took the place of formal law and justice, and the group rather than the individual was supreme. Religion and magic were perhaps the most potent forces in the life of early man.

In more advanced regions the Neolithic era gave way about 5000 B.C. to the Age of Metals and the dawn of civilization. So ended the first great stage in human progress. In its way it was just as important as the Age of Pericles in ancient Greece, the Renaissance at the close of the Middle Ages, and the Industrial Revolution in modern times. It provided the beginnings of the cultural heritage of modern man.

Chronology of events and developments discussed in this chapter

Chapter 2

Egypt	c. 5000-525 B.C.
Pre-Dynastic period: *skilled techniques in agriculture and pottery*	c. 5000-3100
Formation of the Upper and Lower kingdoms; earliest nations	5000
First calendar	4241
Dynastic period: *Egypt ruled by one pharoah*	3100-2600
Old Kingdom: construction of pyramids	2700-2200
Feudal Age: breakdown of central government	2200-2050
Middle Kingdom: restoration of national unity	2050-1800
Hyksos invasion: regression under Asiatic conquerors	1800-1570
The Empire: a territorial state; theocratic despotism	1570-525
Alien rule: *(Persians, Greeks, Romans, Arabs, Turks, French, and British)*	525 B.C.-1922 A.D.
Old Babylonia	4000-1750 B.C.
Sumerian city-states: *cuneiform writing; legendary epics*	Pre-4000-2500
Akkadians: *Sargon, founder of first Semitic empire*	2500-2300
Amorites: *second Semitic empire under Hammurabi; written code of laws*	2050-1750
Hittite empire: *introduced the use of iron to the Near East*	2000-1200
Age of transition and small nations	1750-700
Lydia: *originated coined money; zenith under Croesus*	800-546
Phoenicians: *navigators, colonizers, and traders; developed an alphabet*	1200-854
Arameans: *Phoenician alphabet dispersed by overland trading*	2000-732
Hebrews: *glory under Solomon; greatest contribution in religion*	1025-586
Assyrian empire *greatest in West before 500 B.C.*	910-612
New Babylonia Chaldean empire: *able imperial administrators*	604-539
Persian empire *tolerant imperial system under Cyrus and Darius*	549-331

The Nile, the Tigris, and the Euphrates

Egypt and the Fertile Crescent: 5000 B.C. *to 333* B.C.

All peoples, whether they are savage Masai in east Africa or sophisticated city dwellers in metropolitan New York, have a more or less complex culture. We have already seen on page 6 that the term culture used in this sense describes the sum total, or pattern, of any people's governmental, economic, social, religious, and intellectual institutions, no matter whether its people are primitive or advanced. But though culture is a characteristic of all peoples, the same cannot be said of civilization. People are civilized only when they have succeeded in evolving an advanced and complex culture pattern which rests upon a complicated social organization and extensive control over nature. Civilization has been defined as "that stage of life in which there takes place the organization of sedentary folk into towns and cities, in order that life may become safer, more cultured, happier, and more productive of those elements which induce what is optimistically called progress."[1] The growth of civilization has been mainly associated with the rise of town and city life, as the above definition indicates. In fact the term civilization is derived from the Latin word *civilis,* which refers to *civis,* meaning citizen. Complex social organization has developed not among nomadic peoples but rather among dwellers in cities, where the circumstances of people living close together and depending on one another for fulfillment of needs require cooperation and a high degree of organization.

More specifically, civilization necessitates the existence of a device whereby the experience and the accomplishments of one generation can be passed on to the next. This becomes possible to a significant degree only with the development of writing, which enables the cultural heritage to become cumulative. There must also exist an advanced material culture guaranteeing people some degree of physical comfort and security from famine and want. Freed in this way from anxiety over uncertainty of food supply, man is given the necessary leisure and tranquillity of mind to turn to artistic and intellectual achievement. Thus art, architecture, literature, philosophy, and science are developed.

While Paleolithic and Neolithic man had been making striking advances in the direction of civilization in western Europe, parallel progress was being made in the Near East, near the Nile, in Mesopotamia, in India, and probably in China. Our discussion, however, has been concentrated upon the advances made in Europe, for there we have more evidence of early man's progress than in any other area in the world. The rate of advance of Paleolithic and Neolithic man apparently was about the same in Europe and in the Near East until about 5000 B.C., when progress was accelerated in the latter area and Europe was left far behind.

In Egypt, the land of the pharaohs and the pyramids, we will see how man succeeded in creating a flourishing civilization along the banks of the Nile. Then we will turn east, leave north Africa, cross the great desert of Arabia to another ancient river valley, the Tigris and Euphrates, extending north from the Persian Gulf. Here a succession of important peoples rose and fell, and each made important contributions to civilization. This was the home of the Sumerians, Assyrians, Babylonians, and Persians.

A narrow band of fertile land connects this second great river home of ancient civilizations with the coast of the eastern Mediterranean. The connecting corridor, called the Fertile Crescent, played an important part in ancient history. It was the highway for trade and for the mass migrations of peoples. In this area such peoples as the Phoenicians, Hebrews, and Arameans played their parts in history.

Cradles of Civilization

Advent of civilization. It can be said that culture becomes civilization and recorded history dawns between 4000 and 3000 B.C. in what is known as the Ancient Near East (see map, page 50). As we shall see in later chapters, civilization had several cradles, for in addition to the Ancient Near East mankind made early and notable progress in India and China. Archaeologists have spent much time in arguing about which of these areas really can claim the honor of originating civilization, and the argument has not been definitely settled. Much earth still has to be moved by the archaeologist's spade, but at the present there is rather general agreement that the Nile valley has the better claim.

Early civilization a river product. In the origin of civilization geography played an important part. Significantly, all early known civilizations—Egypt, Mesopotamia, India, and China—developed in river valleys. This was no historical accident, especially in Egypt and Mesopotamia. The great rivers annually overflowed their banks, depositing a film of rich alluvial soil on the floors of their valleys. In regions where rainfall was sparse, great pools were created in order to provide irrigation facilities. The well-watered soil produced abundant harvests. These in turn made possible a large increase in the population, and small cities and villages arose. Artificial irrigation of crops with the accompanying construction of dams and canals necessitated group effort and cooperation among the people. For this reason, everybody was required to help build the dikes and keep open the canals. Furthermore, dependence upon a wide network of interrelated canals demanded that all people within the area they served accept certain rules concerning the repair and defense of the works and the use of the water. Of necessity there developed a government whose word was law for the entire area served by the canals.

The rich surplus of crops encouraged trade and commerce. The profession of merchant was born, and caravans and merchant vessels began to carry wares from one area to another. Contact between peoples led to the exchange of ideas and inventions. Culture diffusion, discussed in the Prologue, became an instrument of progress. We can understand, then, the importance of rivers in the growth of civilization.

Water has always exerted an important influence upon human affairs. Scholars sometimes refer to it in dividing civilization into three great epochs: (1) the fluvial, centered along the banks of rivers and in fertile river valleys, (2) the thalassic, focused in great inland seas such as the Mediterranean, and (3) the oceanic, in which man utilizes the great oceanic stretches of water as bonds of contact making the world one unit. Until the time of Greece, civilization can be regarded as essentially fluvial. European civilization then became thalassic, centering in the Mediterranean, and remained so until the fifteenth century. Finally, with the age of exploration and the voyages of Columbus and his successors, civilization became oceanic.

Civilization Dawns along the Nile

Egyptian culture and history. The life span of ancient Egypt extended from about 5000 B.C. to 525 B.C. During that period the Egyptian pattern of life evolved from a rather primitive Neolithic culture to a flourishing civilization in which pharaohs ruled with absolute sway, agriculture and commerce throve, a noble art flourished, and mighty temples and monuments were constructed. Then decay set in, and the once proud land of the pharaohs passed under the rule of the Persians in 525 B.C. For more than two thousand years a succession of alien peoples—Romans, Greeks, Arabs, and Turks—ruled over Egypt. The most recent foreign rule was that of the British, whose direct control ended only in 1922.

The dates of Egyptian history have not been definitely established, but the following chronology is roughly accurate. Egyptian history before 3100 B.C. is called the Pre-Dynastic period. The era after this date, when the land was ruled by one pharaoh, is known as the Dynastic period. This includes three periods of greatness and two interludes of retrogression: the Old Kingdom (2700-2200 B.C.), followed by the transitional Feudal or First Intermediate Age (2200-2050 B.C.); the Middle Kingdom (2050-1800 B.C.), ended by the foreign Hyksos domination known as the Second Intermediate period (1800-1570 B.C.); and the Empire (1570-525 B.C.).

Pre-Dynastic Egypt. Artifacts have been discovered in Egyptian tombs that go back as far as 10,000 B.C. These remains show that the early Egyptians passed through the main divisions of the Old and New Stone Ages and had even begun to use copper for tools before the time of the Old Kingdom. Progress was apparently rapid, and soon the people lived in crude houses, had weapons of flint and copper, and engaged in agriculture. Examination of grain and husks found in vases placed in tombs shows that as early as 6000 B.C. the Egyptians had developed superior strains of barley seed which could be easily cultivated and which produced heavy yields. The early Egyptians, whose race has not yet been conclusively ascertained, wore linen garments and were especially remarkable for their artistic skill, particularly in pottery. Their polished red and black ware was never surpassed by their descendants, even in the periods of highest Egyptian accomplishment.

During the long Pre-Dynastic period, largely because of the necessity for cooperation in building canals and irrigation works, the small political units gradually merged into larger ones, until finally two kingdoms, Upper Egypt in the south and Lower Egypt in the north, were created. These date back perhaps to about 5000 B.C. and were probably the earliest nations.

Several noteworthy accomplishments were made in the Egypt of this time. The introduction of the plow increased the acreage a man could cultivate, and the first national irrigation system was evolved. Progress was made in writing and in the invention of papyrus and ink. Another important achievement was the creation of the first calendar, which, it has been claimed, goes back as far as 4241 B.C. If true, the date for the beginning of the Egyptian calendar is the oldest in history.

The Dynastic period. About 3100 B.C. Menes, a strong leader in Upper Egypt, effected the union of the two kingdoms and established his capital at Memphis, at the head of the Nile delta. This event marks the beginning of the Dynastic period, which in the space of 400 years saw the birth of the Old Kingdom. This period endured for almost 500 years and can be regarded as the first great epoch in Egyptian civilization.

The Old Kingdom. During the period of the Old Kingdom the Age of Metals was definitely inaugurated in Egypt. Mining expeditions were sent to the nearby peninsula of Sinai to obtain copper. Trade was also developed. Boats were sent to the coast of Syria to obtain timber which was needed in Egypt for the construction of boats, houses, and furniture. Important advances were also made in industry, for papyrus-making was begun, the potter's wheel was perfected, glass was manufactured, and beautiful jewelry was made by expert craftsmen.

One indication of the advance in civilization during the period of the Old Kingdom is its pyramids. The first of these gigantic monuments was constructed by the architect Imhotep for a pharaoh of the Third Dynasty. The tomb, which is the oldest existing building of stone masonry in the world, was a terraced structure, with each successive layer smaller than the previous one. Today it is known as the Step Pyramid.

Of the six dynasties of the Old Kingdom, the fourth was the most powerful and prosperous, and consequently its pyramids were the most impressive, according to the Greek historian Herodotus. The largest of them, the tomb of Pharaoh Khufu, also known as Cheops, required the labor of 100,000 men for thirty years. The building of these great tomb fortresses, designed to protect the dead pharaoh's body so that, as the representative of his race, he might become immortal, required a

knowledge of geometry, knowledge of the principle of the inclined plane, and the use of bronze saws to cut the great stone blocks.

The Feudal or First Intermediate Age. During the rule of the Sixth Dynasty of pharaohs of the Old Kingdom, strong centralized government was undermined by the rise of independent provincial governors. Civil war broke out and the authority of the pharaohs collapsed. For more than a century petty governors fought each other while the lot of the common people became almost unbearable, as they faced famine, robbery, and oppression by petty tyrants. This period is known as the Feudal or First Intermediate Age (2200-2050 B.C.) and marks the transition to Egypt's second great epoch of civilization, the Middle Kingdom.

The Middle Kingdom. After more than a century of disunity and declining civilization, the princes of Thebes, a city on the upper Nile, succeeded in establishing national unity and progress recommenced. Under pharaohs of the Twelfth Dynasty, like Amenemhet, the Middle Kingdom (2050-1800 B.C.) flourished under law and order and economic prosperity. If the Old Kingdom is famous for its pyramids, the Middle Kingdom is especially noted for its literature and general excellence in the arts. As is so frequent in history, however, this greatness was followed by decline, as the country again lapsed into civil war and in 1800 B.C. was conquered by an alien Asiatic people known as the Hyksos. For more than two hundred years the Egyptians groaned under the cruel and rapacious rule of their conquerors, but finally the princes of the south, led by the great emancipator Aahmes of Thebes, restored independence to the unhappy land.

The period of the Empire. The reign of Aahmes (1570-1545 B.C.) can be thought of as the beginning of the third and last magnificent period in Egyptian history, the Empire. The new dynasty, the Eighteenth, founded by Aahmes, successfully carried out the policy of establishing naval supremacy in the eastern Mediterranean and conquering strategic areas in the Fertile Crescent. The greatest pharaoh of the period was Thutmosis III (1490-1436 B.C.), who is often called the Napoleon of Egypt. This redoubtable warrior conquered Syria, Phoenicia, and Palestine, even crossing the Euphrates and receiving gifts from distant Babylonia. Nubia and the northern Sudan

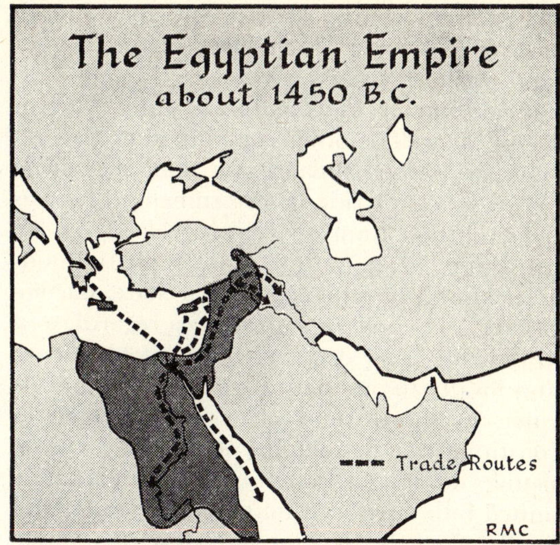

were also brought under his sway. In the Sudan, a statue of his son has been found not far from the modern city of Khartoum.

Under Amenhotep III (1413-1377 B.C.) the Empire reached a dazzling height. Law and order flourished along the Nile valley, vast wealth in the form of tribute flowed in from conquered lands, and Thebes—the imperial capital—became the most magnificent city in the world. After Amenhotep III, imperial power began to decline. His son Amenhotep IV, best known as Ikhnaton, weakened Egypt by unpopular religious innovations and enemies from without began to nibble away bits of the Empire. Ramses III (1301-1234 B.C.) tried to restore the glory of the Empire and had partial success, but it was Egypt's last demonstration of national vigor. In this period of decline reigned the weak emperor Tutankhamen, who has received an undeserved immortality and fame as a result of the discovery of his magnificent tomb in 1922.

As the Empire declined rapidly, Egypt ceased to be a factor in international affairs and thus became a puppet of a long line of conquerors from Cambyses, the Persian emperor in the sixth century B.C., to Lord Cromer, the British ruler of Egypt in the late nineteenth century. All over the Near East new peoples were rising to power—Hittites, Arameans, Hebrews, and Greeks. Finally, after a period of Assyrian occupation in the seventh century B.C., Egypt was conquered by the Persians and the cycle of national life that had begun in 3100 B.C. came to an end. The valley of the Nile henceforth was to know many conquerors, as Greeks, Romans, Arabs, Turks, French, and British each in turn established themselves in the ancient land of the pharaohs.

Evolution of the territorial state. Ancient Egypt (as well as other contemporary civilizations in Mesopotamia, as we shall see) made one significant stride in government. This was the evolution from a primitive social system, consisting of miniature and multitudinous rival kinship groups, to a great state, encompassing all people in a given area regardless of kinship ties and exacting from all obedience and loyalty to one central government and its ruler. In short, many clans were merged to constitute one nation. Egyptian villages, consisting of related families, were gradually united into territorial units called nomes, and finally these became united into one single kingdom. The development of the territorial state was the major contribution of Egypt and the other oriental countries to the political evolution of civilized man.

Egyptian government. The governmental system of the territorial state, as it finally evolved in Egypt during the Old Kingdom, was an extreme absolutism. All power resided in the ruler, who was called Pharaoh, meaning Great House. The powers exercised by modern totalitarian rulers look almost meager when compared with those of the ancient Egyptian despot. The pharaohs owned all the land; they decided when the crops should be sown, controlled the irrigation system, and exacted a share of the crops produced by the semiservile laborers who toiled on the huge royal estates. With none to question his powers, which the Egyptians believed were sanctified by the gods, in regal splendor, surrounded by elaborate court etiquette, the pharaoh dictated every aspect of the life of his subjects. Egyptian government was theocratic, that is, the pharaoh combined both religious and political functions. He was both an earthly king and a god, the chief priest of the land and the spiritual symbol of the nation in all its important religious rites.

It is interesting to note that the ancient Egyptians had succeeded as early as the time of the Old Kingdom in creating a complex and efficient administrative system which alone made possible the centralized absolutism of the pharaoh. By this time, too, there apparently existed a law code. Although under the government of the pharaoh the people were at the mercy of their ruler and had nothing approaching the self-government later developed by the Greeks, Egyptian government was paternal. Most pharoahs endeavored to protect their subjects and to rule in their own way with kindness and justice.

Life and Work in Ancient Egypt

Home and social life. In the days of the Empire, Egypt proper, not including the subject peoples in Syria, had a population of about seven million. The great bulk of the people were semislaves who lived in squalid villages made up of little mud and thatch houses in which the only furniture was a few crude jars, boxes, and a stool. These people lived in constant dread of the royal tax collector. They were subject to forced labor—work on the roads or tilling the royal fields, or worse, hauling huge stones for great temples and obelisks. The merchants and skilled craftsmen of the middle class had more comfortable and pretentious dwellings, and those of the nobility were palatial. Here furniture and draperies were luxurious, while extensive and beautiful gardens surrounded the house.

During the passing of more than two thousand years since the Pre-Dynastic period of primitive Egypt, substantial changes had taken place in the social grouping of the people. Among primitive people all individuals are, in general, members of the same social and economic class. There may be a small ruling clique, and at the bottom captured enemies may form a slave class, but the great bulk of people perform the same economic tasks, live in similar houses, and possess about the same worldly goods. But with civilization come gradations in society. Some men remain laborers, others become skilled artisans, and others become wealthy merchant princes. In Egypt, as elsewhere, the growth of population, the tendency toward specialized vocations, and the increase of wealth soon resulted in the creation of distinct classes in society. Three main social divisions can be distinguished: (1) the court nobility, royalty, priests, and the landed aristocracy, (2) the middle class, composed of merchants and craftsmen, (3) the bulk of the population, who were servile laborers. Although such grouping existed in Egyptian society, it was not rigid. People of merit could elevate themselves into higher social ranks.

The status of the Egyptian woman was exceptionally favorable. Besides being the equal of man, she dominated many aspects of society. Sons inherited property through their mothers, and there are several instances where a woman actually ruled as queen of the land. Even in courtship women often took the initiative. Many love poems were written by women. The following is a good example of one of these poems:

I am thy first sister,
And thou art to me as the garden
Which I have planted with flowers
And all sweet-smelling herbs.
I directed a canal into it,
That thou mightest dip thy hand into it
When the north wind blows cool
. . . .
It is intoxicating to me to hear thy voice,
And my life depends upon hearing thee.
Whenever I see thee
It is better to me than food or drink.[2]

Economic life. Throughout Egyptian history agriculture has remained the basic economic activity, but industry began in the early days of the Old Kingdom and developed rapidly. In addition to extensive copper mining in the Sinai peninsula, stone quarrying became highly organized to meet the demands of pyramid building, and huge quantities of sun-dried bricks were made. Cabinetmakers fashioned handsome furniture out of the famous cedars of Lebanon. Tanning became a specialized craft, the process of fusing copper and tin to make bronze became known, glass blowing and

An Egyptian lady is having her hair set in tight curls. In one hand she holds a mirror, in the other a beverage. A servant is fixing her another.

Duck hunting for this Egyptian is a matter of decoying the ducks from his papyrus boat and hitting them with his boomerang, while his wife and daughters gather lotus blossoms. To the right of the papyrus hedge the same man spears fish, steadied by his wife and daughter. The grown-ups wear thin, cool clothes, while the youngest wears none at all.

Osiris sits in judgment as his dog-headed god, Anubis, weighs the heart of a lady temple musician against a feather. Isis stands behind the musician. The scene was inscribed on papyrus and buried with the mummy of the woman.

enameling were developed by skilled artisans, and weavers were highly proficient. Egyptian craftsmen exhibited a degree of technical efficiency that was seldom surpassed in western Europe until the Industrial Revolution. During the period of the Empire the products of the craftsmen were exceptionally fine. Beautifully glazed jars, delicate stone dishes, and exquisite brooches attest their skill.

During the Old Kingdom much commerce plied up and down the Nile, expeditions were sent southwest to the interior for ebony and ivory, and the pharaohs sent ships down the Red Sea. The Egyptians can claim to have developed the first sea-going ships for use on the Mediterranean. As early as 2750 B.C. Egyptian ships were sailing the eastern Mediterranean bound for Phoenicia, and by 2000 B.C. extensive trade relations existed with Crete. Egyptian commerce never developed so extensively as that of Syria and Mesopotamia; it was not until the invasion of the Hyksos that it became very important. Apparently the Hyksos were great traders, and their contact with the Egyptians was a strong stimulus to commerce. Trade reached its height during the Empire, when Egypt controlled the trade routes of the Near East.

Empire commerce was conducted along four main routes (see map, page 51): (1) To expedite merchant voyages, a canal was constructed which connected the Red Sea with the eastern part of the delta (shown on the map on page 50); (2) along the Nile numerous ships brought goods from the south; (3) a busy caravan route maintained contact with Mesopotamia and southern Syria; and (4) shipping from northern Syria, the mainland of Greece, Crete, and other islands came to a focus at the delta of the Nile. The main exports were wheat, linens, scarabs (charms), and gold wares. The most important Egyptian imports were ostrich feathers, metal weapons, spices, tapestries, woods, gold, and silver.

Religion in Egypt. Egyptians were called by the Greeks the most religious of all men. And so they were, for religion saturated their viewpoint and influenced every aspect of society.

"The kings of Egypt were gods; its pyramids were an 'act of faith'; its art was rooted in religious symbolism; its literature began as religious decoration of tombs, temples, and pyramids; its science centered in the temple; its gods were conceived to be in intimate touch with men and alive as men; a vast part of its wealth and energy was spent in the effort to secure the continuance of the physical life after death."[3]

The great obsession of all people was to achieve immortality for their souls. In the days of the Old Kingdom, the lower classes felt aggrieved because they could not have their bodies mummified after death, as the pharaoh and the rich nobles did, nor could they obtain full funeral rites. These were serious handicaps in securing immortality. So strong was the desire for the afterlife that the common people agitated not for political but for religious equality. This was obtained in the second half of the Middle Kingdom, and thenceforth all people could claim full funeral rites.

Osiris. Their all-pervading emphasis upon immortality was largely due to the influence of the god Osiris. He was the god of the Nile, and the rise and fall of the river symbolized his death and resurrection, which were celebrated each year. Then an interesting myth developed. It was recounted that Osiris was murdered by Seth, his evil brother, who cut the victim's body into many pieces and scattered them over the land. Isis, the bereaved widow, collected all the remnants of the corpse. These were then put together, Osiris was resurrected, and became immortal. Finally Horus, the son of Osiris, avenged his father against Seth.

The Egyptians saw in the myth a way to escape death. Osiris was the first mummy. Only by the recovery of the many parts of his body had he achieved immortality. Every dead Egyptian, therefore, was regarded as a second Osiris. The way to give him immortality was to preserve the corpse. This was achieved by mummifying and placing the body in a tomb which would give it the maximum of protection. As befitted the first man of the land, a pharaoh was given a massive tomb-fortress, a pyramid, to protect and preserve his body until judgment day.

If the soul came to Osiris cleansed of sin, it would be permitted to live forever in the Happy Field of Food. At the time of soul-testing, Osiris weighed the candidate's heart against the feather of truth. If the ordeal was not passed, a horrible creature devoured the rejected heart. The priesthood, which exercised a very strong influence in the Egyptian state, often to the detriment of the state, claimed that it alone knew clever methods of surviving the soul-testing. For a consideration, charms and rolls of papyrus containing magical prayers and formulas were sold to the living as insurance policies guaranteeing them a happy immortality after death. That it was a lucrative business is seen by the fact that some 2000 papyrus rolls containing such magical formulas have been taken from ancient tombs. They constitute collectively what is known as the *Book of the Dead.* Pictured on page 54 is a scene from one of these rolls.

Characteristics of Egyptian religion. Egyptian religion for many hundreds of years had no strong ethical character. Immortality was not regarded as a reward for goodness while a person was alive. That idea, however, developed gradually until eternal life was regarded as a reward merited only by those who were just and good while alive. In praising Egyptian ethical standards, the late Professor Breasted, America's first great Egyptologist, pointed out that their main sins were "murder, stealing, especially robbing minors, lying, deceit, false witness and slander, reviling, eavesdropping, sexual impurity, adultery, and trespass against the gods or the dead...."[4]

Religion was of paramount concern to the Egyptian people, and it was also extremely complex in character. It concerned the worship of many gods, such as Ra, the sun deity, Osiris, the god of water, Isis, the Great Mother, and many animal-headed gods. At first Ra was the most important, but with the rise of Thebes in political importance a place had to be found for its deity, Amun. The supreme god, therefore, became Amun-Ra. A famous pharaoh and reformer in the time of the Empire, Amenhotep IV, who adopted the name of Ikhnaton, tried unsuccessfully to supplant Amun-Ra and the confusing multiplicity of minor gods by substituting a religion based on one deity, a sun god called Aton. Amenhotep developed an advanced conception of one all-prevailing and kindly god (monotheism). This was given beautiful expression in his famous *Hymn to the Sun* (see page 57). Amenhotep's efforts tragically failed, and in arousing religious factionalism among his subjects, he only weakened the Empire. Ancient Egypt retained its polytheism to the end.

Literature, Science, and Learning

Evolution of writing. One of the most important Egyptian contributions to civilization was the development of the art of writing, especially the introduction of an alphabet. Writing originated through the use of picturelike signs to represent objects first and then ideas. The next advance was to use the same signs to represent the sounds of the words expressing those ideas. Once the signs were identified with sounds, some were conventionalized to represent the sounds of syllables, the stage called syllabic writing. With syllabic

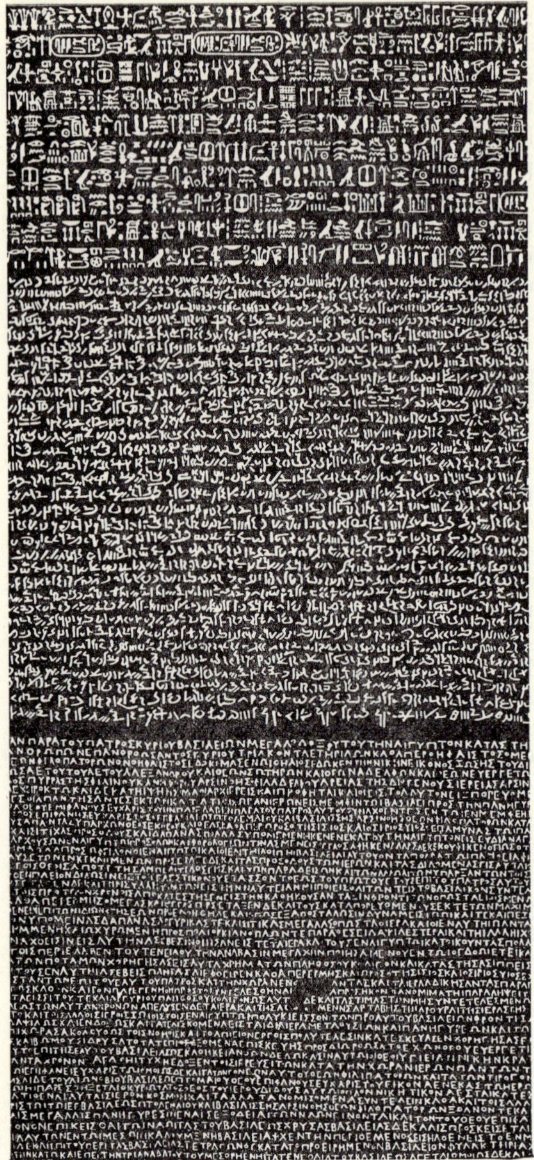

The Rosetta Stone, discovered in Egypt in 1799 by an officer in Napoleon's army, supplied the means by which Jean Champollion was able in 1822 to decipher Egyptian writing, thus founding the study known as Egyptology and laying open a whole new field for research. The stone is now in the British Museum, and contains a decree inscribed in three different languages, as is shown by the section reproduced here. The lowest layer of writing is Greek, which Champollion could read. Working from the Greek he was able to figure out the other inscriptions. The middle layer is Egyptian demotic, or popular writing. The top layer is the more formal system of hieroglyphic writing.

signs an indefinite number of words could now be written phonetically—with symbols representing their sounds.

About 3000 B.C. the Egyptians had reached the point of using special characters for certain vowels and consonants. They were actually on the verge of attaining a real alphabet. But there were too many symbols (about twenty for *A*, about thirty for *H*, and so on). They also continued to use their syllabic signs and ideographs (symbols for ideas). Thus in several thousands of years they never succeeded in developing a purely alphabetic system of writing.

The ancient Egyptians had what we might call the first books. Libraries have been discovered dating from 2000 B.C., consisting of rolls of papyrus in earthen jars. Papyrus was the forerunner of paper. It was made by splitting the papyrus reed into strips and pasting these strips together to make long rolls of durable writing surface, much more practical than the heavy clay tablets used, as we shall see shortly, in Mesopotamia. Ink was prepared by mixing vegetable gum with lamp black.

The invention of writing represents one of the great milestones of human progress. Now man could accumulate knowledge, record it, and pass it on to his descendants. Writing also made possible the preservation of literature.

Literature. We can hardly speak of a literature in the days of the Old Kingdom because none has survived. The oldest inscriptions we have are the pyramid texts, which have been called the oldest chapter of human thought extant. They were mainly religious and are found on the walls of tombs and pyramids of the Fifth and Sixth dynasties. Their purpose was to assist the deceased to obtain immortality, and they consisted of a jumble of magical incantations, myths, and religious hymns.

During the Middle Kingdom, especially in the period of the Twelfth Dynasty, literature became much richer, more varied, and more secular. Many folk tales and collections of proverbs were now set down in writing. The period of the Twelfth Dynasty is called the classical age of Egyptian literature. One popular story told of the romantic adventures of a noble who wandered all over Syria but at last made his way back to his native land. Another story recounted the perils of a shipwrecked sailor, a narrative which is a prototype of Sindbad the Sailor. Other narratives of importance were the *Tale of the Two Brothers,* which has striking resemblances to the Biblical story of Joseph and his brethren; the *Tale of the Eloquent Peasant;* and *A Dialogue Between a Man Weary of Life and His Soul.* The last work, poetical in form, is philosophical in tone and demonstrates profound thought. It is one of the most important of the Egyptian poems which have been preserved. Most of the literature was expressed in poetical language, though much of it was in prose form.

The most beautiful surviving piece of Egyptian literature is Ikhnaton's *Hymn to the Sun.* A few lines will suffice to give some idea of its poetic beauty and its conception of one all-powerful and beneficent Creator and Heavenly Father.

Thy dawning is beautiful in the horizon of
 the sky,
O living Aton, beginning of life!
When thou risest in the eastern horizon,
Thou fillest every land with thy beauty.
Thou art beautiful, great, glittering, high
 above every land,
Thy rays, they encompass the lands, even all
 that thou hast made....
How manifold are thy works!
They are hidden from before us,
O sole god, whose powers no other possesseth.
Thou didst create the earth according to thy
 heart
While thou wast alone.[5]

The calendar. We moderns accept our calendar as a commonplace detail of everyday life and do not realize that it is an indispensable tool of civilized existence. Like fire-making, knives, and pottery, the calendar had to be invented, a process taking several thousand years. In fact, the final step in the evolution of our present calendar took place as late as 1582 A.D. Neolithic man was the first to realize how essential a calendar was to fix the dates of his holy days and accurately ascertain the time for planting crops. He therefore devised a lunar calendar of twelve months, each twenty-nine and a half days in length, giving in all a year of 354 days. In order to harmonize his reckoning with the seasons, it was necessary from time to time to add a thirteenth month.

After the lunar calendar, the next major step was the development of a calendar based

At modern Luxor on the Nile stood ancient Thebes, capital of the imperial pharaohs. These are the remains of a beautiful temple unearthed at Karnak. Note the graceful column with its spreading papyrus capital.

on the solar year. The Egyptians developed a system of twelve months, each of thirty days, totaling 360 days in all, and at the end of each year they added five days. This calendar year was just six hours short of the solar year, which forged ahead of the calendar one day in every four years. The Egyptians realized that something was wrong but never corrected the difficulty. It was not until Julius Caesar added the Julian intercalary day every four years that the next major improvement in the calendar was achieved.

Science. In their learning the Egyptians were a practical rather than a speculative people. Philosophy was not their forte; learning had to serve practical needs. That was why the Egyptians were the first people to develop a real science of mathematics. Precise measurements were needed to build the pyramids, and the constant obliteration of field boundaries by the inundations of the Nile necessitated frequent land measurement. To meet these needs the Egyptians learned to add and subtract. They also could multiply and divide by two and three. In surveying they utilized the rudiments of geometry, and they had some knowledge of algebraic equations. They developed a primitive decimal system, but it was never perfected; twenty-seven signs, for example, were needed to write the number 999. They computed the area of a circle by giving π the value of 3.16. In addition to important advances in astronomy and chemistry, amazing accomplishments were made by the Egyptians in medicine.

Art and Architecture: Culmination of Egyptian Culture

Architecture. Important as were the accomplishments of the Egyptians in government, religion, literature, and science, they cannot compare with their gains in art and architecture, which were the most distinctive elements in Egyptian civilization. The Egyptians have been called the greatest builders in history. As far back as we know them they were advanced engineers, able to build in stone. The problems of shelter, light, and circulation (entrance and exit) had been solved. The structure of their society called for no houses above the merest mud huts for the common population, and evidently the palaces were not built well enough to last. The preoccupation with life after death meant that the kings did not spend their energies building great palaces but concentrated on tombs to preserve their bodies eternally. Thus the two great types of architectural expression which have lasted and into which went the greatest effort were the tombs for the kings and the temples for the rich, priestly class. These temples also glorified the kings, who were themselves identified with religion.

As already noted, the pyramids were commanded by the pharaohs of the Old and Middle Kingdoms. Today after four thousand years, many of these monuments still remain, scattered along the Nile south from the delta for a distance of fifty miles. At Gizeh the pyramid of Cheops, covering a base of thirteen acres, seems unbelievably huge. It was constructed of over two million limestone blocks, each averaging about two and a half tons, and is 481 feet high. It was built without mortar, and some of the stones were so perfectly fitted that a knife cannot be inserted in the joint. The pyramids are the best single expression of Egyptian civilization. In their quiet repose, dignity, and massiveness, they reflect the religion-saturated character of Egyptian society.

If the Old Kingdom achieved immortality through its pyramids, the power and the glory of the days of the Empire still live in the ruins of the pharaohs' temples at Thebes. Booty and tribute from conquest made Thebes, with its great temples and palaces, a lavish capital city. Today there still remain the magnificent ruins of the Temple of Karnak and the Temple of Luxor on the east side of the Nile, and on the west the great cemetery with its rock cliff tombs of the pharaohs, together with numerous temple and palace remains.

The builders of the temple at Karnak, like the early lake dwellers, employed the structural system which was to be used almost exclusively until the Roman period—the post and lintel construction. This system enabled the builders to span openings for windows and doors and to roof over spaces. The size of the window or door and the width of the roofed space were limited, of course, by the size of the stone slabs. Post and lintel construction demands heavy stone work and partly explains the massive appearance of the buildings. Columns were used throughout the interiors of buildings in order to provide supports for roofing of larger areas. The Temple of Karnak is an expression of the mystery of the Egyptian religion, just as the pyramids are an expression of the desire to hide the tombs for eternity.

The Temple of Karnak contains a huge colonnaded, or hypostyle, hall, the largest ever built. The tallest columns are seventy feet high. The two central rows of columns are taller than the others and have a separate roof, allowing wall space above the lower roofs of the two side aisles. This space was pierced with windows called clerestory windows. The higher middle aisle and the clerestory windows were later used in the Roman basilica and the Gothic cathedral.

Sculpture. Egyptian sculpture, like Egyptian architecture, was simple and formal. The Egyptians' tools and their ability to use them were far superior to the technical equipment of the Stone Age artists. In sculpture, as in architecture, their work shows an advance in technical skill. Sculpture was used as decoration for entrances to tombs and temples, and line carving and low relief were used as wall decoration. The latter types of sculpture are almost two-dimensional in themselves and are therefore particularly adapted to a two-dimensional surface. Everyday subjects decorated the walls of the tombs, presumably to equip the dead with all that had surrounded them in life. The picture at the top of page 53 is an example of decorative line-carving illustrating an everyday scene.

In Egypt appears for the first time an advanced sculpture in the round. Statues which stand free from the wall on all sides naturally have to be designed in a three-dimensional manner, differing from reliefs, which are more nearly two-dimensional. The sculptors of the Old Kingdom had a great feeling for simplicity and conventionalized the bodies to conform to the blocks of stone. In these block statues the human figure is always shown, sitting or standing, looking squarely in front, which produces a certain rigidity. But when it is remembered that the statues were used in connection with a massive architectural setting, this rigidity is highly fitting.

Many statues were colossi, such as the Sphinx, which was carved out of the natural rock. This immense statue conveys a remarkable impression of the dignity and power of the pharaoh. Many carved figures were religious symbols, strange combinations of men and birds and animals. The representation of divinities was usually effected by placing an animal's head on a human body.

One of the most significant developments in the Empire period was the personalization of statuary. Sculptors were trying to get away from the abstract and symbolic, which had dominated their work in the Old Kingdom. In so doing they became excellent portraitists, but sculpture lost the fine architectural use of earlier days. The head of Ramses II shows a typical piece of Egyptian realism. Notice the sensitivity and individuality of the features which show Ramses more as a person rather than as a symbol of imperial power and dignity.

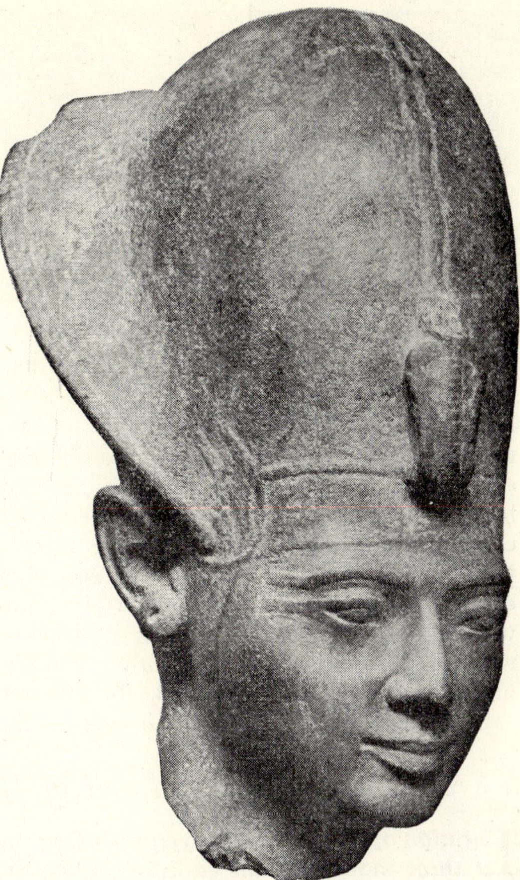

PORTRAIT OF PHARAOH RAMSES II

This is the great pyramid of Khufu (Cheops) at Gizeh near Cairo, built by a pharaoh of the Fourth Dynasty. A labor force of 100,000 men brought 2,300,000 blocks of limestone, averaging two and a half tons, from quarries forty miles away and then floated them across the Nile on barges. At the shore's edge, they were placed on a huge ramp and dragged to the pyramid.

In portrait sculpture, the ancient Egyptians displayed extraordinary skill in their manipulation of hard stone. However, the sculptors of Ikhnaton's time (c. 1375 B.C.) sometimes used limestone, a softer stone than diorite or the quartzite of the Ramses head, which allowed greater freedom for realistic treatment. Ikhnaton and his queen Nefretete are known to us through such true-to-life portraits.

Painting. Painting in Egypt was used to decorate the walls of tombs and palaces. There was no attempt to show objects receding in perspective, but sometimes it was shown that one object was behind another by overlapping objects in a series, or by putting one object above another. As painting was used as a mural decoration, these particular conventions of perspective

EGYPTIAN DANCING GIRLS (WALL PAINTING)

and flat treatment were very successful. The ruler or god was shown as larger than the other figures to emphasize his importance. These religious pictures with their many symbols may seem lifeless and uninteresting, since they are hard to understand without a complete knowledge of the meaning of the symbols. From a purely decorative point of view, however, they can certainly be enjoyed today. Certain colors were generally used in all these paintings—rich reds and yellows made from the earth pigments, and black and green-blue for contrast.

More appealing perhaps to our eyes are the murals which depict everyday scenes. The painting of the dancers, although still following the conventions, is completely human and understandable, even in the twentieth century.

Throughout the ancient world (Egypt, Crete, and Greece) different types of binding materials were mixed with paint. To ensure that pigment will stay attached to a surface it must be mixed with a material such as wax, gum, or egg. These mixtures produce surface paintings which do not withstand all weather conditions. Fresco, on the other hand, is permanent when properly done. The painting is executed on wet plaster, and a chemical reaction makes it part of the wall. But it is not definitely known that wet-plaster fresco was used before the time of Rome.

Minor arts. In the minor arts the Egyptians exhibited the same decorative sense. Jewelry was made of gold, semiprecious stones, and beads (see the collar illustrated below). Egyptian gold jewelry reveals the wealth of merchants, priests, and pharaohs. The Egyptians also made beautiful glass and pottery vessels.

The Land of the Fertile Crescent

Location of the Fertile Crescent. During the three thousand years and more when the Egyptians were building pyramids, perfecting writing and the calendar, and developing commerce, equally important advances in civilization were being made in an area not far removed from the land of the pharaohs, a belt of territory now called the Fertile Crescent. Bounding the great Arabian desert on the north, east, and west, this narrow band of fertile land starts at the Persian Gulf and extends to the north, skirting the desert through Babylonia and Mesopotamia, then turns west and bows south through Syria and Palestine along the Mediterranean to the desert of Sinai on the borders of Egypt (see map, page 50).

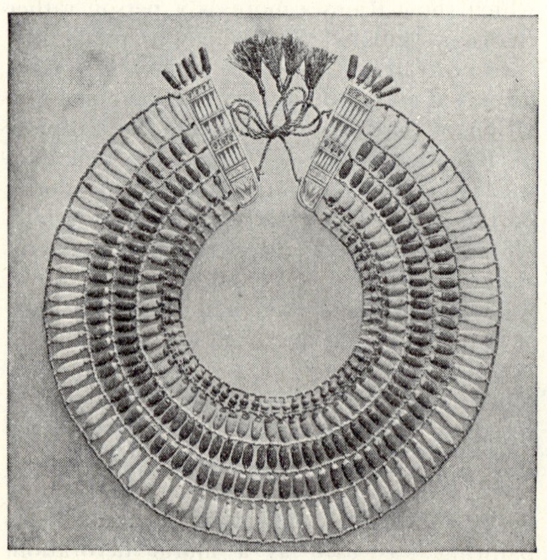

AN EGYPTIAN COLLAR OF BEADS

Mountains and high plateaus serve as boundaries of the Fertile Crescent on the north and east. In this elevated region lived restless Indo-European peoples who persistently pushed their way into the inviting narrow crescent of fertile land. Within the arc of the crescent were another people, desert nomads called Semites, mainly Arabs and Hebrews, who, driven by hunger and a desire for easier living, were continually fighting their way into the Fertile Crescent. Unlike Egypt, which was protected by the natural barriers of desert on the east and west, the Nile's cataracts to the south, and the sea to the north, and hence suffered few invasions and interruptions to the continuity of her civilization, the Fertile Crescent was the scene of constant warfare. This took the form of continual struggle between the Indo-European hill folk and the Semitic desert people for control of the fertile land belt that edged the desert. Although at times promising civilizations were cut short by the shock of war, this was perhaps more than amply compensated for by the stimulating effects of the culture impacts of the movements and transplantations of peoples. Despite much warfare, therefore, the achievements in civilization made by the inhabitants of the Fertile Crescent do not suffer in comparison with those made along the Nile. The rise and fall of numerous nations, however, make the history of the Fertile Crescent rather complex. In order to simplify the story, the development of civilization in the Fertile Crescent may be divided into the following periods:

Old Babylonia, the second cradle of western civilization (4000-1750 B.C.)

The Age of Transition and the Era of Small Nations (1750-700 B.C.)

The period of Assyrian dominance (700-600 B.C.)

New Babylonia, the empire of the Chaldeans (600-539 B.C.)

The Persian empire (539-333 B.C.)

Old Babylonia: The Second Cradle of Western Civilization

The plain of Shinar. The first great civilization in the Fertile Crescent, like that of Egypt, was fluvial. It had its origin in a rich plain which extended about one hundred seventy miles north of the Persian Gulf between the Tigris and Euphrates rivers. These two rivers rise in the mountains of eastern Asia Minor and flow southeast in a roughly parallel direction. Just less than two hundred miles from the gulf, they emerge from the desert, approach each other very closely, and flow through a flat valley of alluvial soil that was brought down from the north and deposited by the rivers. This plain was early called Shinar, and later it came to be known as Babylonia. Although the term Mesopotamia was originally used to refer only to the land between the two rivers north of Shinar, today it includes all the territory between the rivers from Asia Minor to the Persian Gulf. Since 1918 the latter area, with its capital at Bagdad, has been known as Iraq.

It was no accident that civilization should appear early in the plain of Shinar. There the soil was very rich, the summers warm, and the winters mild. There was little rainfall, but, as in Egypt, there was an annual flood of the rivers. Dependence upon flood waters led, as along the Nile, to the development of irrigation, which in turn encouraged cooperation between the various groups of people living in the valley.

Early Sumerian culture. The people in western Asia who first inaugurated a civilization superior to the Neolithic stage were the Sumerians. Details of their racial origin are meager, but they probably migrated from hilly country to the northeast into the plain of Shinar sometime before 4000 B.C. Overwhelming the Semitic inhabitants they found there, the Sumerians began to reclaim the marshes, build irrigation projects, and develop a settled community life. By 3500 B.C. they had achieved an advanced civilization with flourishing cities, well-organized city-state government, the use of metal, and the perfection of a system of writing called cuneiform. The latter, like the Egyptian system, started with a pictographic stage and by 4000 B.C. had evolved into a phonetic scheme of writing, in which each of 350 signs represented a complete word or a syllable. In writing, the Sumerians used a square-tipped reed to make impressions in soft clay tablets. The impressions took on a characteristic wedge shape; hence the term cuneiform (Latin *cuneus,* wedge). Many other people, such as the Hittites, the Babylonians, and Persians, adapted this same system of writing to their own languages, and cuneiform continued in use until the Phoenician alphabet superseded it just before the time of the birth of Christ.

The southern portion of Shinar, which now became known as Sumer, saw the development of several independent Sumerian city-states, each of which was under a ruler who served as the war leader, the supervisor of the irrigation system, and the high priest. No strong centralized government was evolved by the Sumerians, and their history is mainly a chronicle of continual fighting between Ur and rival cities. The most prosperous period of the diminutive city-kingdoms was from 2900 to 2500 B.C. Ur was the earliest city to obtain the

leadership of Sumer, and its first ruler, Mesannipadda, is one of the earliest-known kings in western Asia. The inability of the Sumerians to unite proved their undoing, for in the twenty-sixth century B.C. Semitic people from Akkad, on the plain of Shinar, invaded Sumer and became masters of the entire plain.

Advent of the Akkadians. For two hundred years, from 2500 to 2300 B.C., the Semitic Akkadians ruled over an empire which extended from the Persian Gulf far up into Mesopotamia. Its founder was the great warrior Sargon, whose conquests made a profound impression on the peoples of the Near East. Although the Sumerian cities were subjugated, their culture was not destroyed. The hardy but primitive Semites led by Sargon readily adopted Sumerian writing, for they had none of their own, accepted the Sumerian calendar, and borrowed the business methods and city habits of their late adversaries. In short, there was a general mingling of peoples and cultures.

Renewal of Sumerian supremacy. The absence of the rigors of nomadic life on the desert and the new-found luxuries of sedentary life in the Sumerian cities weakened the descendents of Sargon and his fellow conquerors and ended the first Semitic empire after barely two centuries of existence. In its place again rose the old Sumerian cities. The city of Ur about 2300 B.C. successfully imposed its rule over the entire plain of Shinar, and its ruler called himself the King of Sumer and Akkad. Its supremacy, however, was short lived, ending after a century. The rule of Ur was followed by even shorter periods of dominance by other Sumerian cities.

Hammurabi's second Semitic empire. Just before the end of the third millennium, two streams of invaders completely crushed the old Sumero-Akkadian power. The Semitic Amorites from Syria, under the leadership of their capable king Hammurabi (1948-1905 B.C.), finally brought all Sumer and Akkad under one rule. They even extended their sway to Assyria, a region in the northeast corner of the Fertile Crescent. Babylon, heretofore an obscure village on the Euphrates, was made their capital and became so important that the plain of Shinar was known from then on as Babylonia. After the founding of the second Semitic empire the Sumerians never again figured politically in history. Their civilization, however, persisted as the foundation for all subsequent civilizations in Syria and the Tigris-Euphrates valley.

Sumerian cities. The Sumerians were city dwellers and lived in small cities situated on artificial mounds around which were erected walls for defense purposes. Within were the dwellings of the inhabitants, constructed of sun-baked bricks. Houses were usually rectangular in shape, and each had a court on its north side. In the middle of every town, constituting the center of its activities and its most sacred and important edifice, was the temple.

Economic and social life. Agriculture was the basic economic activity. Outside the Sumerian towns extended well-tilled fields, whose fertile soil was skillfully watered by irrigation ditches. We have the word of Herodotus that "the whole land of Babylonia is, like Egypt, cut up by canals."[6] Barley, oats, and dates were produced in huge quantities, and domesticated cattle and goats made possible a flourishing dairy industry. The use of the plow was common, and here the first sowing machine was invented. Wheeled carts and chariots were in use. The Sumerians are given credit for introducing wheeled vehicles. The use of the wheel facilitated transportation enormously. Heretofore it had been necessary to carry things or drag them, which limited the size of the load. The Egyptians used the wheel but probably borrowed it from their Fertile Crescent neighbors.

Although industry lagged behind agriculture, there were numerous distinct crafts, with skilled artisans and their apprentices turning out beautiful metalwork and exquisite textile goods. Raw materials for manufacturing were obtained from the north, made into finished products, and then exported to pay for imported wares. Active trade was carried on by the Sumerians over a wide area. Caravans journeyed north and west via the Fertile Crescent to the eastern Mediterranean and Egypt. Contact between Egypt and Sumer explains the similarity of several items of their culture. Both used the pear-shaped war mace and balanced animal figures in decorative art. Reliable evidence has recently been found indicating Sumerian trade connections with India. The Sumerians were, above all, a practical business people. Credits and loans were carefully regulated; a mass of contractual business records has survived.

Social organization followed the same general pattern as that in Egypt. There was a close connection between government and religion. Rulers were considered divine and absolute. Social gradations based on wealth were the rule, as in Egypt, but in Sumer the lines between classes were drawn more rigidly, and the principle of social inequality was enshrined in law.

Architecture and art. The monuments and sculptures of Egypt have resisted the ravages of time surprisingly well, but not so in Sumer. An absence of stone there forced builders and architects to use sun-dried bricks. Before fierce sandstorms and destructive floods the Sumerian cities, common dwellings and temples alike, soon disintegrated into shapeless mounds of refuse.

But the artistic and architectural achievements of Sumer have not been lost entirely. For a century archaeologists have been burrowing into many such mounds and have exposed the delineaments of temples and recovered priceless art objects. We know, for example, that one royal palace (3500 B.C.) was constructed on an elaborate plan, that it utilized great stairs, and that its walls were decorated with human and animal figures. We know that the Sumerians were familiar with the arch, vault, and dome. The lack of large stones meant that the post and lintel construction characteristically used in Egypt was impossible in Sumeria. Solid brick walls with roofs presumably of wood were the general rule. Although these builders experimented with the arch and vault, such devices were not used on a large scale until the time of the Romans.

The most important buildings of the Sumerians were the temple towers, or ziggurats. Every town had such an edifice, dedicated to its patron deity. The typical ziggurat consisted of several stories, or levels, each stepped back and smaller than its predecessor. On one side was a great triple stairway, like a ramp, converging upon the entrance into the shrine of the god. Each story was given a different symbolic color. One might be black to represent the underworld, another red to indicate this world, and a third blue to symbolize the sky and the heavens. Profuse use was made of trees and gardens on the stepped-back terraces. Rising high above the flat valley floor, the vari-colored temples with their rows of terraced verdure shimmering under the brilliant sun must have presented a spectacle of great beauty.

The Egyptians, on the whole, surpassed the Sumerians in art. Scarcity of stone was a serious handicap to Sumerian sculpture. As a result, portrait sculpture never attained the excellence achieved by the Egyptians during the Old Kingdom. Generally speaking, Sumerian sculpture consisted of reliefs used for decorative and narrative purposes and small figures, or figurines. Strong, muscular people were typical subjects of Sumerian sculpture.

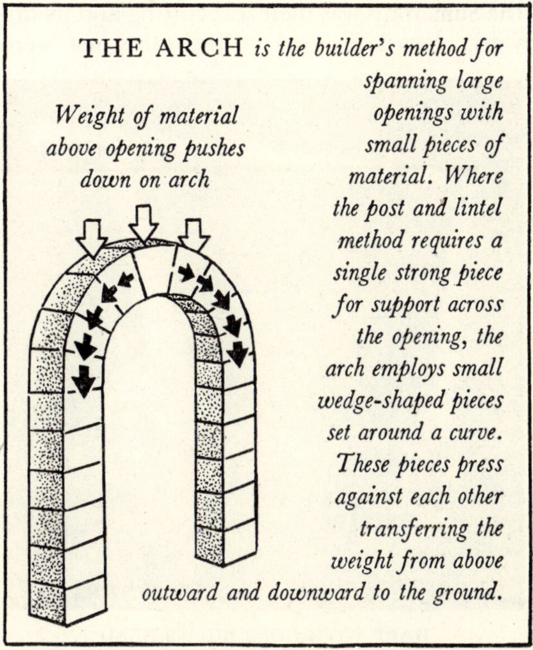
Weight of material above opening pushes down on arch
THE ARCH *is the builder's method for spanning large openings with small pieces of material. Where the post and lintel method requires a single strong piece for support across the opening, the arch employs small wedge-shaped pieces set around a curve. These pieces press against each other transferring the weight from above outward and downward to the ground.*

A signature seal and its impression, showing a Sumerian ruler in audience with his local god. Seated on his throne, a dragon snake springing from each shoulder, the bearded god gestures impressively, while behind the ruler his protective goddess raises her hands to intercede. The sun and moon are symbols which guide the ruler's destiny.

The figures were squat and heavy and their features were depicted simply. Figurines of animals were, however, more skillfully executed.

Heraldic devices originated with the Sumerians. Ultimately such symbolic devices became widely copied by rulers and governments for their insignias and coats of arms. Our American eagle, for example, is an adaptation of the Sumerian eagle of five thousand years ago.

Perhaps the most delicate artistic work of the Sumerians was their seal cutting and metalwork. Small seals of cylindrical stone were carved in low relief in ornamental pictorial designs of great beauty involving infinite patience and expert technique. Every important citizen had his seal, which he constantly used to "sign" letters and documents written on clay tablets. The seal shown in the picture above belonged to a wealthy Sumerian, possibly a ruler of one of the cities. The interesting wedge-shaped relief patterns on the clay impression are cuneiform characters in reverse, having been impressed on the seal itself in the usual manner. Metal ornaments, vessels, and weapons found when the royal tombs at Ur were uncovered show a high degree of artistic ability. The harp with the golden bull's head shows Sumerian skill in handling the medium of gold. The mosaics decorating its base are patterned of shell and lapis lazuli, and the bull has a delicate beard of lapis lazuli.

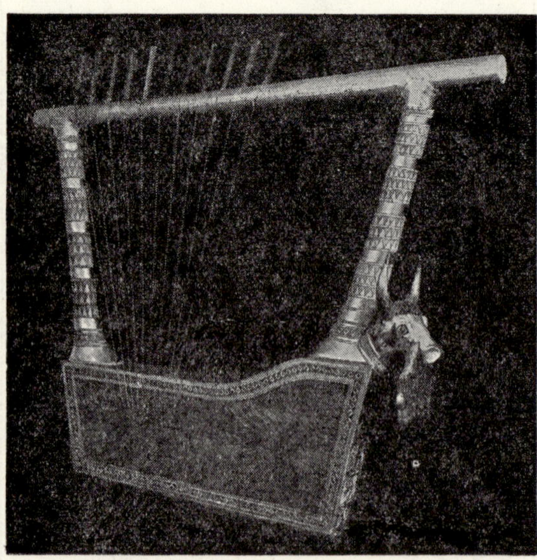

HARP WITH GOLD BULL'S HEAD

Religion. Religion occupied almost as important a place in Sumerian life as it did in Egyptian. But there were significant differences. The Sumerians were little concerned with the future life. They had no conception of heaven or hell and placed little emphasis upon the ethical aspects of human behavior. Religion was for them primarily an instrument to guide and control man's activities on earth, a belief in keeping with the practical nature of the Sumerian people. Each Sumerian city had its favorite god.

Literature. The literature of the Sumerians, and that of the later Babylonians and Assyri-

Sumerian

ans, which was based upon it, was largely religious in origin and content. Two great epics are outstanding, one relating the story of creation and the other the story of the flood. Their legends are also notable: the stories of Etana, the shepherd who searched the heavens for the herb which was the source of life; of the fisherman Adapa, the first man, who like Adam lost the treasure of immortal life; and of Tammuz, who came back from the lower world.

Sumerian literature is more significant than that of Egypt, for it included the first great historical and mythological epics. The two Sumerian epics of the flood and the creation are similar to the later Hebrew stories of those events, as found in the Old Testament. The flood epic was adopted by the later Semitic Babylonians and incorporated in the longest and most beautiful of their epics, *Gilgamesh*. In it are recounted the adventures of Gilgamesh, a Sumerian Ulysses who sought to gain immortal life but failed and who heard the story of the flood from the Noah of Babylon, Ut-napishtim. The remarkable resemblances between the Babylonian epic and the later flood story as found in Genesis can be seen in the following lines from *Gilgamesh:*

What I had, I loaded thereon, the whole harvest of life
I caused to embark within the vessel; all my family and relations,
The beasts of the field, the cattle of the field, the craftsmen, I made them all embark.
I entered the vessel and closed the door....

I sent forth a dove, I released it;
It went, the dove, it came back,
As there was no place it came back. . . .

I sent forth a crow, I released it;
It went, the crow, and beheld the subsidence of the waters;
It eats, it splashes about, it claws, it comes not back.[7]

Other Sumerian contributions. The Sumerians made numerous other contributions to civilization. They invented certain techniques of warfare. The military phalanx, in its elementary form, was probably their invention. In mathematics they made important progress. They originated a number system based upon the unit 60, which today is the basis for dividing a circle into 360 degrees (60 x 6) and an hour into 60 minutes. They devised geometric formulas to compute the areas of triangles and irregular four-sided figures and also formulated the earliest known cubic equation. Additional gifts to civilization were the beginnings of city-state government and the foundations of business organization. Sumer also furnishes the earliest documents relating to international law, the most ancient international compacts, and the earliest known example of an attempt to settle a dispute by arbitration.

Semitic culture. In the land of Sumer and Akkad the Sumerians did not enjoy a monopoly of significant contributions. The rude Semitic tribes from the desert and from far-off Syria which invaded Shinar simply copied Sumerian culture at the outset, but soon they were making contributions of their own. Sargon's empire was progressive, but the second period of Semite dominance was especially rich in original contributions. We have already seen that Semitic people named Amorites established themselves in Sumer and Akkad about 2050 B.C., making Babylon their capital, and that Hammurabi, the sixth king of his line, subjugated the entire plain. So important did the new capital become that we usually lump together all the various peoples who figure in the history of the plain from the earliest time to about 1750 B.C.—Sumerians, Amorites, and all others—and refer to them as Babylonians and the period as Old Babylonia.

Hammurabi was one of the greatest rulers of the ancient world. We are fortunate to possess fifty-five of his letters, which give a vivid picture of the Babylon of his day and reveal how the king's eagle eye supervised every phase of governmental activity. In these ancient burnt clay tablets we can see Hammurabi sending orders to his subordinates in the local districts, checking delinquent taxes, and ordering the dredging of the Euphrates and the canals.

Hammurabi's code. Valuable as his letters are, Hammurabi's law code is infinitely more important. It is written in cuneiform on a black diorite monument nearly eight feet high. The code of Hammurabi is notable for the harshness of its punishments, which invoke the *lex talionis* principle, "an eye for an eye." For example it stipulated: "If a man destroy the eye of another man, they shall destroy his eye." Implicit obedience to their father was demanded from children, for we read: "If a son strike his father, they shall cut off his fingers."

Hammurabi receives his code from the sun god in the scene which heads the monument on which the code is carved.

Medical quacks and corrupt building contractors were punished also: "If a physician operate on a man for a severe wound with a bronze lancet and cause the man's death; or open an abscess (in the eye) of a man . . . and destroy the man's eye, they shall cut off his fingers." And again: "If a builder build a house for a man and do not make its construction firm, and the house which he has built collapse and cause the death of the owner of the house, that builder shall be put to death." But while punishments were stern, on the whole, the code attempted to secure a crude form of justice. Punishments were graded in their severity so that the higher the culprit in the social scale, the more severe the penalty. The status of women was fairly high, but in the main the code was designed for a man's world. The following clause refers to an erring wife: "If she has not been economical, but a gadder-about, has neglected her house and belittled her husband, they shall throw that woman into the street."[8] Punishment for offenses was no longer in private hands by recourse to the blood feud between families but that justice had become a function of the state.

Hammurabi's code is the most complete and famous ancient body of laws, but recently older codes have been discovered in Mesopotamia. In 1947 and again in 1948 such codes were found, and in 1953 an American archaeologist published an account of yet another that had been deciphered. This had been promulgated by a Sumerian king, Ur-nammu, three hundred years before Hammurabi's code, and its laws were very humane. Their prologue declares it is the king's purpose to see that "the orphan did not fall a prey to the powerful," "that the man of one shekel did not fall a prey to the man of one mina (sixty shekels)."[9]

Achievements under Hammurabi. The age of Hammurabi, when compared to the Sumerian period, is not especially notable for advances in civilization. It is particularly lacking in art. During the first Semitic period, under Sargon, there had been some artistic advance, especially in sculpture. But during the age of Hammurabi seal cutting and sculpture declined.

The Semites of Old Babylonia made their mark in law and government. They also adapted the old Sumerian legends into such great epics as *Gilgamesh.* Of very great significance was the development of business procedures during the age of Hammurabi. During his time wills, promissory notes, and all kinds of witnessed and sealed documents were being used. Here was the invention of what we now call commercial paper. It was not until about 1500 A.D., with the rise of modern capitalism, that western Europe utilized a more advanced variety of contractual instruments in business.

The Age of Transition and the Era of Small Nations

Eclipse of civilization in Babylonia. The empire of Hammurabi was of short duration. Soon after his death hostile mountaineers from the east invaded the plain of Shinar. By 1750 B.C. they had become its masters and remained so for six hundred years. The Old Babylonian civilization described in the previous section, so brilliantly inaugurated by the Sumerians and carried forward by the Semites under Hammurabi and his house, went into an eclipse from which it did not emerge for more than a thousand years.

The Hittite empire. The center of emphasis now shifts to the lands of the Near East bordering the Mediterranean—to Asia Minor, Syria, and Palestine. During the Hyksos domination in Egypt (1780-1580 B.C.), a powerful new empire arose in the north central part of Asia Minor. The Hittites, who inhabited this area, rapidly extended their influence after 2000 B.C. and reached their height of power about 1500 B.C., when they controlled much of Asia Minor and Syria. The rapid expansion of the Hittites down the western band of the Fertile Crescent aroused the fear of the Egyptians, and a long and desperate struggle ensued between the two powers. This so weakened the antagonists that the Hittite empire fell apart about 1200 B.C., and Egyptian power collapsed in the following century.

We may note in passing that during this period of turmoil and transition the Aegean world was also in confusion. As we shall see in our discussion of Greece, during the period from 2000 to 1400 B.C. a highly cultivated civilization had developed in the eastern Mediterranean with its center at Cnossus on the island of Crete. But shortly after the beginning of the second millennium, streams of northern invaders—Indo-European tribes whom we now call Greeks—invaded the Aegean world and by 1400 B.C. had destroyed Aegean culture. Another such Indo-European attack overwhelmed the Hittite empire.

What part did the Hittites play in the history of civilization? Until a few years ago they were a people of mystery, neglected by most historians. Recent discoveries, however, are demonstrating that such neglect was hardly justified. Imposing ruins of a once-great city have been uncovered in modern Turkey together with over 20,000 clay tablets. Hittite civilization was not equal to that in Babylonia or Egypt. The Hittite empire was a group of semi-independent clans acknowledging one king rather than a strongly organized and autocratic state. But it had considerable influence on contemporary civilizations. Its use of guardian lions and sculptured reliefs in architecture was copied by the Assyrians, and it influenced the diffusion of the art of writing. Babylonian clay tablets probably came to Crete through the Hittites. Most important is the fact that they were among the earliest people to work iron, and through them that metal was distributed throughout the Near East.

An era of small nations. Following the collapse of the Hittites about 1200 B.C., the peoples of the Fertile Crescent were without a master power. Egypt was weak, Babylonia was impotent, and Assyria was just beginning to be powerful. The Near East as yet did not need to fear the Greeks, since from about 1200 to 800 B.C. the newcomers in the Aegean world were experiencing the "middle ages" of their history, a period of little advance in civilization or power. For nearly five hundred years a number of small states flourished in the Fertile Crescent. Many individual cultures had an opportunity to develop, because no one state could impose uniformity.

As we have seen, Babylonia was subject to constant infiltration of Semitic peoples from the adjacent desert. Similarly, droves of nomadic Semites had pushed west into Syria-Palestine, the narrow band of land fronting the eastern Mediterranean. Most important of these peoples were the Phoenicians, the Arameans, and the Hebrews. The country in which they settled was a narrow avenue of land four hundred miles long and from eighty to a hundred miles wide. It was admirably located for trade. In north Syria were splendid harbors. But Syria-Palestine was not fitted to support the rise of a great power; its natural resources and its area were too limited. It has always been the prey of strong powers, and only the absence of such powers in the period from 1200 to 700 explains why small independent monarchies were permitted to develop there and make a brief bid for historical fame.

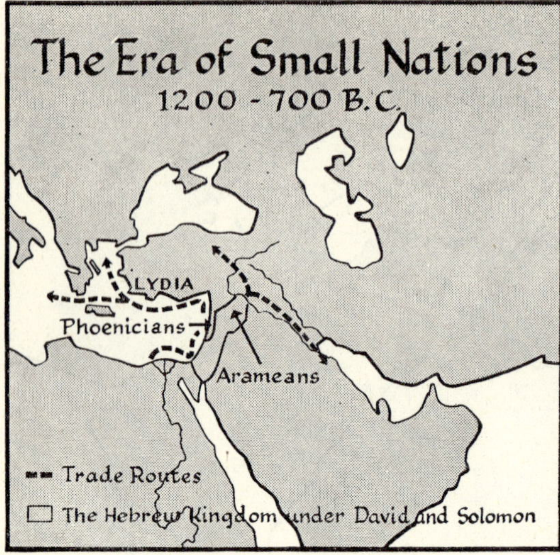

The Lydians. The most powerful state to arise in Asia Minor following the end of the Hittite empire was Lydia. Under their king Croesus the Lydians reached the height of their power in the early sixth century B.C. The wealth derived from valuable gold-bearing streams and prosperous commerce made Lydia the envy of its neighbors, and even today the phrase "rich as Croesus" is a reminder of Lydian opulence. As early as the ninth century B.C. Lydia originated coined money, a most important invention. Unlike the several small states in Syria, such as those of the Phoenicians, Hebrews, and Arameans, Lydia was able to maintain its independence against the Assyrians but finally fell a victim to the Persian army in the sixth century B.C.

The Phoenicians. Little is known of the early history of the Phoenicians. It is believed that this Semitic people entered the western band of the Fertile Crescent during the third millennium B.C. They founded a number of coastal settlements, the mountain ranges protecting them from attack on the land side. Their cities were all seaports, the most important being Tyre and Sidon. The Phoenicians were successively conquered by Sargon and Hammurabi, and about 1600 B.C. the Egyptian pharaoh brought them under his influence. For another four hundred years they remained under foreign rule until about 1200 B. C., when the decline of Crete, of the Hittite empire, and of Egyptian power gave them an opportunity to play an independent role. In a remarkably short period they became the greatest traders, navigators, and colonizers before the Greeks (see map, page 129) and were rivals of the Greeks for many years. Their settlements could be found in the Mediterranean area, of which the greatest colony was Carthage. Passing through the Strait of Gibraltar, intrepid Phoenician sailors founded a settlement on the Atlantic coast of Spain and even ventured down the west coast of Africa.

The Phoenicians were skilled manufacturers. Their purple dye became famous, and their textiles, metal goods, and glassware had a wide market. They learned most of their industrial skill from Egypt. As the preëminent middlemen and great international traders of their age they acted as the intermediaries between the west and the east. These Phoenician traders brought to the Greeks a desire for the luxuries of the Near East, as well as some knowledge of oriental art.

There was little originality in Phoenician civilization, except perhaps for their skill in navigation and their business methods. The Phoenicians were not creative. They have left behind no literature, and their art is negligible. Yet as imitators they made their most important contribution, the perfection of the alphabet. The origin of the alphabet is still a moot question. Perhaps between 1800 and 1600 B.C. certain western Semitic peoples, influenced by the Egyptian semi-alphabetic writing, started to evolve a simplified method of writing. The Phoenicians, seeing the value of this, carried on the experiment and developed a system made up of individual consonants. Their alphabet consisted of twenty-two consonant signs (the vowel signs were later introduced by the Greeks). The Phoenicians arranged their signs in a definite order, their first two symbols being *aleph* and *beth.* Our word alphabet reminds us that the Phoenicians are primarily responsible for alphabetic writing.

The Phoenicians never became a politically united people. They were evidently not interested in conquest or fighting. Rather they influenced the advance of civilization through peace, colonization, and trade.

The Arameans. Another Semitic people, similar to the Phoenicians, were the Arameans. Entering the fertile region around Damascus during the latter half of the second millennium B.C., the Arameans established a group of prosperous little kingdoms, the most important of which was Damascus. Situated at the head of the caravan route to Babylonia, the Arameans served the caravans just as the Phoenician harbors served Mediterranean shipping (see map, page 68). The Arameans have therefore been called the Phoenicians of inner Asia. For several hundred years the Aramean cities acted as a buffer against Assyrian expansion into Syria and Palestine, enabling the Hebrew kingdoms to enjoy national independence much longer than would otherwise have been possible. In 732 B.C., however, the Arameans fell before the might of Assyria, just as the Phoenicians had lost their independence to the same power a century earlier, in 854 B.C.

Political domination by the Assyrians, however, did not terminate the influence of the Arameans. Energetic Aramean merchants still took their trade caravans all over western Asia. They were excellent scribes and businessmen and often found employment in Babylonia, Assyria, and Persia. The Arameans, realizing the advantages of the Phoenician alphabet, used it in preference to the Babylonian cuneiform. Aramean merchants in their caravans carried bills and receipts in the simplified writing all over the Fertile Crescent. The alphabet was thus widely diffused and rapidly displaced the use of cuneiform. Its use then spread to Babylonia, Persia, Assyria, and even to India.

In the centuries just before the time of Christ, Aramaic became the general language of the entire Fertile Crescent. It even displaced Hebrew in Palestine. On this point M. I. Rostovtzeff says: "It is still a puzzle how they were able to drive out of general use the Babylonian language and cuneiform writing, which had been to some extent international in the second millennium, and to have their own speech and character accepted instead."[10] Whatever the reason, the Arameans serve as an early example of trade as a carrier of civilization, a frequent phenomenon in history.

The Hebrews. Accompanying the Arameans into the Fertile Crescent was another Semitic people who are called Hebrews, Israelites, or Jews. Racially these people were probably a mingling of several types. Their mixing with the Hittites may have given the Hebrews their characteristic aquiline nose, for it is not originally Semitic. In war, diplomacy, architecture, and art the Hebrews made little splash in the stream of history, but in the fields of ethics and religion their contributions to world civilization were tremendous. It has been said that no other people in history so few in number and so weak in political power, except the Greeks, have so influenced civilization.

Tradition has it that the Hebrews originally made their home in the lower Euphrates valley and that Abraham was their patriarchal founder. Nomads for hundreds of years, they wandered in search of a homeland that offered a reasonable chance to develop a prosperous and contented society. From 1400 to 1200 B.C. they filtered into the land of Canaan, later to be called Palestine, a small region tucked between the desert and the sea. It was only 150 miles long, about the size of the state of Vermont. Another group of tribes had, according to tradition, been enslaved by the Egyptians. They were led out of bondage by the great national hero Moses, who gave his people the Ten Commandments and a new conception of God. Nearly all of Palestine was at that time in the hands of the Canaanites, a mixed Semitic and Hittite people. The conquest of these people by the Hebrews took a long time, for the various tribes were slow to unite against their common enemy.

When the Canaanites had been subjugated, another and far more dangerous foe appeared. The Philistines (from whom we get the word Palestine) came originally from southern Asia Minor and from certain Mediterranean islands, chiefly Crete. Capable and warlike, they drove the Hebrews to the hill country.

About 1025 B.C., however, the Hebrews, led by Saul, a popular leader who was made king, began a series of revolts against the Philistines. Saul was defeated and thereupon committed suicide, but his place was taken by David, who, like Saul, was a military man. He was in addition endowed with religious fervor and a strong capacity for political leadership. King David (1000-960 B.C.) made Jerusalem, an impregnable stronghold, the center of his power and speedily subjugated the Philistines. A promising kingdom was now established, the strongest in the region of Palestine-Syria.

Palestine reached the height of its influence and power during the reign of Solomon, David's son (see map, page 68). Solomon became one of the leading patrons of trade in the Near East. He owned a fleet in partnership with the king of Tyre. Living in oriental luxury, he loved display and built a magnificent temple at Jerusalem. His influence and power enabled him to claim a daughter of a pharaoh as his wife. But his kingdom was short-lived. Solomon taxed his people so heavily that discontent was aroused, which led in his son's reign to the secession of the northern part of Palestine. There were now two Hebrew kingdoms, Israel in the north and Judah in the south. Thus weakened, the Hebrews were in no position to defend themselves. In 722 B.C. the Assyrians captured the capital of Israel, and the northern kingdom came to an end. The Assyrian king Sennacherib then attacked Jerusalem, but a mysterious plague decimated his army, and for the time being Judah was saved (see II Kings 19:32-37). But in 586 B.C. Nebuchadnezzar, the Chaldean from Babylonia, destroyed Jerusalem and carried the inhabitants into exile. The Hebrew nation had been conquered after only some 450 years of existence. Following the defeat of the Chaldeans by the Persians about fifty years later, however, the Hebrews were permitted to return to Jerusalem, where they restored the temple destroyed by Nebuchadnezzar.

After Persian rule came that of the Greeks and the Romans. The Jews rebelled against the rule of the Roman Caesars. For four years savage fighting desolated the Holy Land, and in 70 A.D. Jerusalem was totally destroyed and her population massacred or scattered. The Jews were driven to all parts of the earth, and the Diaspora—the "scattering"—was at its height.

The story of the past nineteen centuries is replete with sorrow and tragedy for the Jewish people. To the miseries of the medieval ghetto (the residence quarter to which the Jew was restricted) was added the horror of the pogrom (organized massacre) in early modern times, and during recent years there has been brutal persecution in many lands, especially Nazi Germany and Soviet Russia. Only with this background in mind can one understand present day Jewish Zionism, the effort to create a new homeland in modern Israel.

The Hebrew religion. In the beginning, Hebrew religion was a primitive polytheism, or worship of many gods. Gradually there was developed the concept of one tribal god, Yahveh (Jehovah), who was a stern, warlike deity. After their entrance into Palestine many of the Hebrews adopted the religious customs of the Canaanites as well as their more sophisticated and luxurious manner of living. This was especially true of the northern Hebrews. In the south there was much resentment against the renunciation of Hebrew traditions. Many people chafed against the growth of wealth and consequent social injustice in the north and idealized the simplicity and purity of the old folk traditions, the adventures of the patriarchs such as Abraham, Isaac, and Joseph.

About 750 B.C. a succession of great spiritual leaders, the Hebrew Prophets, began to try to purge Hebrew thought and religion of all corrupting influence in order to elevate and dignify the concept of Yahveh. In inspired messages such Prophets as Amos, Isaiah, and Ezekiel taught that the Hebrew God was a loving Father, that He alone was the only and the true God of the universe. During the Babylonian captivity the Hebrew exiles at first seemed crushed by their misfortune, but a great unknown Prophet again emphasized in a series of soul-stirring speeches that Yahveh was the sole God and that the tribulations of the Hebrews were according to God's design, for only through suffering could a people be prepared for true greatness. When Cyrus the Persian defeated the Chaldeans, and the Hebrews were permitted to return to Palestine, they came back with renewed faith in their destiny and a new comprehension of their religion. They had now attained a monotheistic religion, that is, a belief in one God. Coupled with this was their belief that a Messiah would arise among them to establish an ideal order on earth.

Upon the return to Jerusalem the old writings of the Law, the Prophets, and the Psalms were arranged and collected. It was not until Christian times that these were put into one book, which we call the Old Testament. Its influence upon western civilization is incalculable. The phraseology of the Bible has become an integral part of nearly all European languages. We unconsciously use such Biblical expressions as "a land flowing with milk and honey," "eat, drink, and be merry," "a still, small voice," "an apple of one's eye," and such suggestions as "Put not thy trust in princes," "Go to the ant, thou sluggard," and "Righteousness exalteth a nation." An example of the great literature to be found in the Old Testament is this famous passage from the Book of Ecclesiastes, at the top of the next page:

Remember now thy Creator in the days of thy youth, while the evil days come not, nor the years draw nigh, when thou shalt say, I have no pleasure in them;

While the sun, or the light, or the moon, or the stars, be not darkened, nor the clouds return after the rain:

In the day when the keepers of the house shall tremble, and the strong men shall bow themselves, and the grinders cease because they are few, and those that look out of the windows be darkened,

And the doors shall be shut in the streets; when the sound of the grinding is low, and he shall rise up at the voice of the bird, and all the daughters of music shall be brought low;

Also when they shall be afraid of that which is high, and fears shall be in the way, and the almond tree shall flourish, and the grasshopper shall be a burden, and desire shall fail: because man goeth to his long home, and the mourners go about the streets:

Or ever the silver cord be loosed, or the golden bowl be broken, or the pitcher be broken at the fountain, or the wheel broken at the cistern.

Then shall the dust return to the earth as it was: and the spirit shall return unto God who gave it.[11]

The Period of Assyrian Dominance

Assyrian expansion. By 700 B.C., although Lydia and the Hebrew kingdom of Judah still retained their independence, the era of such small states as those of the Arameans, Phoenicians, and Hebrews was ended. A new power, Assyria, was ready to make a bid for empire which was to give her complete mastery of the Fertile Crescent in just three generations. The secret of her meteoric rise lies in the nature of her people and in her geographical position. Assyria was a highland region overlooking the Tigris River north of Nineveh. Unlike Egypt which was favored with protective barriers along most of her frontier, this country lay open on all sides to attack and invasion. For a thousand years the Assyrians were forced to struggle for survival, especially against the Babylonians and the Hittites. In the face of constant menace from invasion, Assyria had to conquer or be destroyed. Racially the Assyrians were a mixed stock, predominantly Semitic. Cradled in the invigorating climate of a highland region and schooled for a thousand years by constant war, the Assyrians, mostly peasants, became redoubtable soldiers.

After several short periods of expansion, the Assyrians began their course of imperial conquest just before the close of the tenth century B.C. In 910 Babylon was conquered. A generation later Asurnasirpal II (884-860 B.C.) conducted a series of brilliant campaigns against the Arameans and marched to the Mediterranean. After a brief period of decline, the process of expansion was again taken up by the Assyrian emperor Tiglath-Pileser, who again subdued Babylonia and recovered control over Syria. In 722 B.C. a new dynasty took over the government of Assyria. Its first emperor was Sargon II, who inaugurated a program of conquest which was to make Assyria the complete master of the Fertile Crescent by 700 B.C. The great Assyrian conqueror took the name of Sargon after the ruler of the first Semitic empire in the Tigris-Euphrates valley, some eighteen hundred years previously.

Assyrian methods of warfare. Sargon II and his descendants were the architects of the greatest empire in the western world before the sixth century B.C. What was the secret of its creation? The answer is threefold: a matchless army, the terrorization of all people who resisted As-

Two Assyrian generals, making camp for the night, talk things over and perhaps exchange a toast. At the right a servant is making the bed for them. Outside the tent the camels and goats are settling down for the night on the desert.

syrian rule, and the most advanced system of provincial administration thus far developed by any people. The Assyrian empire existed by and for its army, which was the most highly trained and most efficient of its day. It was the first to be completely equipped with iron weapons. The bow, with vicious iron-tipped arrows, was its principal weapon. After a stream of well-directed arrows had weakened the enemy, the Assyrian heavy cavalry and chariots would smash with relentless fury the ranks of their foes, driving them headlong from the field. All the ancient world dreaded these fighters, "whose arrows were sharp and all their bows bent; the horses' hooves were like flint and their wheels like a whirlwind."[12]

These four Assyrians seem to be rowing their boat in opposite directions. At the right is a man fishing from a goatskin filled with air. The fancy stream is the Tigris.

After victory came great feasts and celebrations of triumph. Huge parades were held in which the conquering soldiers showed off their booty and long lines of miserable prisoners who were soon to suffer cruel deaths of torture. The climax came in an orgy of feasting and drinking in which the whole populace participated.

The second factor explaining the success of the Assyrians in making their empire was their use of systematic terrorization. Perhaps no people in history have been so frankly cruel and heartless. Following a battle the Assyrian soldiers would search the field for wounded foes, whose heads would be cut off and brought back to camp. Assyrian military history is a dreadful chronicle of massacres, the burning of cities, and barbarous cruelties to captives. In boasting of his exploits, one Assyrian emperor inscribed on a monument, "Their booty and possessions, cattle, sheep, I carried away; many captives I burned with fire. I reared a column of the living and a column of heads. I hung up on high their heads on trees in the vicinity of their city. Their boys and girls I burned up in flame. I devastated the city, dug it up, in fire burned it; I annihilated it."[13]

Assyrian political administration. The third factor in the success of the Assyrian empire was the well coordinated system of political administration developed by its rulers. Here the Assyrians made their one valuable contribution. Within the empire a closely knit cosmopolitan civilization developed, for now there was peaceful contact and trade among heretofore warring peoples. The forcible transplantation of people from their homeland after conquest by the Assyrians, although an inhuman act, in the long run served to make civilization more cosmopolitan, to bring the inventions and customs of one people to the attention of others. The advent of the Assyrians brought a new epoch in political history. By using new agencies of internal organization and centralization, they created a better coordinated state than the Egyptian empire. Royal messengers continually traversed the empire, carrying the dictates of the emperor to his provincial governors. Communication between the ruler and his governors required roads, and thus the earliest system of nation-wide highways was inaugurated. The Assyrians also developed the first postal system.

Art and architecture. In order to glorify themselves and enhance their prestige, Assyrian rulers built imposing and luxurious palaces. Sargon's palace at Khorsabad, built into the wall of the city, was on a high platform, and its walls were thick and heavy, like a fortress. It contained not only the king's living quarters and the royal stables but also a temple and a ziggurat. The arch, borrowed from Babylonia, became an impressive feature in Assyrian palace gates.

To guard the palace gateways, the Assyrians installed huge human-headed winged bulls carved from imported stone (page 74). In these and other Assyrian motifs can be seen combinations of beasts later used in European heraldry. These impressive creatures were carved with five legs so that they would not seem to be lacking a leg when seen from the front or the side. The Assyrians knew a great deal about the anatomy of men and animals. They exaggerated and stylized muscles, suggesting strength and brutality. Beards and hair were also treated in conventionalized fashion.

The inside brick walls of the royal palaces were masked below with stone reliefs and painted above in bright colors. Assyrian cruelty and ferocity are reflected in the vigorous reliefs, especially in battle and hunting scenes. Although the men's beards and hair and the lions' muscles, manes, and claws in the above relief are all stylized, the figures are remarkably real, in contrast to the static and monumental winged bull. The winged bulls functioned primarily as symbolic architectural decoration, while the reliefs depicted action or told a story.

LION HUNT FROM ASSURBANIPAL'S PALACE

Assurbanipal's library. Assyrian kings were apparently interested in preserving the past.

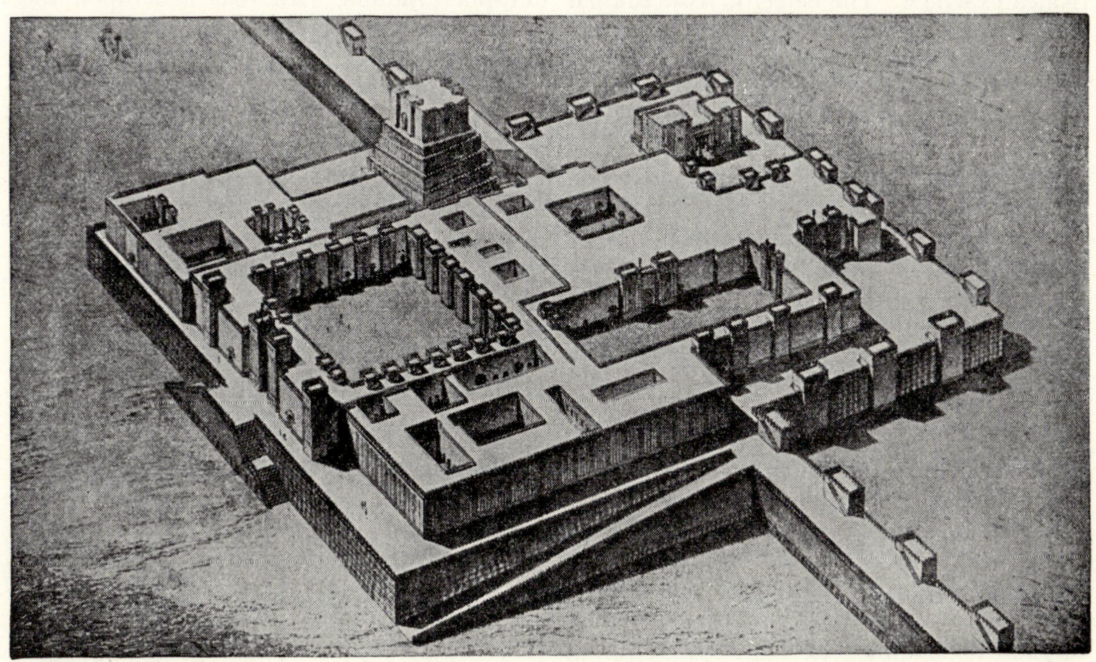

SARGON II'S FORTRESS-PALACE AT KHORSABAD (RECONSTRUCTION)

WINGED BULL FROM SARGON'S PALACE

The annals of the kings were kept with unrivaled exactness. The emperor Assurbanipal collected over 22,000 clay tablets, comprising the first great library. At immense cost and effort the knowledge of the Fertile Crescent was gathered for the royal bibliophile. Sumerian hymns, temple rituals, myths of creation and the deluge, grammars, and medical texts found their way to his library. On each tablet was the emperor's mark of ownership, and just as a modern library stamps a warning on its books against surreptitious removal, Assurbanipal had inscribed on his tablets: "Whosoever shall carry off this tablet... may Assur and Belit overthrow him in wrath and anger, and destroy his home and posterity in the land."[14]

Decline of Assyria. The Assyrian empire obtained its main resources from booty and conquest. The failure of such a system was inevitable in the long run. About the middle of the seventh century B.C. evidences of decline became apparent. The sturdy Assyrian stock had been decimated by the long series of wars, the task of ruling such a huge empire was proving too difficult for the ruling class, and finally the cruelties of the Assyrians had made implacable foes intent on their downfall. To the south, Babylonia had come under the control of a new group of Semites, the Chaldeans, who revolted against Assyrian rule. Wild tribes roamed north of the Fertile Crescent, constantly threatening Assyrian frontiers. Also to the north and northeast, the Indo-European Medes and Persians were on the march. By 616 B.C. the Chaldeans had captured Babylonia, and in 612 these people, joining the Medes, attacked Nineveh, the Assyrian capital, which was captured and totally destroyed. Not one building was left standing. From one end of the Fertile Crescent to the other there was rejoicing over the extermination of Assyria. In the words of the Hebrew Prophet Nahum, "All that look upon thee shall flee from thee and say, 'Nineveh is laid waste.' "

With the exception of their animal sculpture, their innovations in military science, and their ability as imperial administrators, the Assyrians made few original contributions to civilization. Their role was rather one of borrowing from the cultures of other peoples, unifying the best elements into a new product, and assisting in its dissemination over the Fertile Crescent.

New Babylonia: The Empire of the Chaldeans

The kingdom of the Medes. The destruction of the Assyrian empire in 612 B.C. left four powers to struggle over its legacy, the Medes and Persians, the Chaldeans, Egypt, and Lydia. The Medes were an Indo-European people who by 1000 B.C. had established themselves just east of Assyria. In the eighth century B.C. they had managed to create a strong kingdom with Ecbatana as capital. Under King Cyaxaras the Medes had extended their overlordship to the Persians, who lived east of the Tigris. The Persians were of the same racial ancestry as the Medes and for a time were content to be their vassals.

New Babylonia. While the Median kingdom controlled the highland region, the Chaldeans, with their capital at Babylon, were masters of the Fertile Crescent. Nebuchadnezzar, becoming Chaldean king in 604 B.C., raised Babylonia to another epoch of brilliance after over 1000 years of weakness following the reign of Hammurabi. Nebuchadnezzar routed the Egyptians from Syria, thus terminating Egyptian aspiration to re-create another empire. When the little Hebrew kingdom of Judah rebelled against his rule, the Chaldean king destroyed Jerusalem (586 B.C.) and carried several thousand Hebrew captives to Babylon.

Babylon was now rebuilt and became one of the greatest cities of its day. Herodotus, the Greek historian, has left us a graphic description of its huge size and the tremendous walls that were wide enough at the top to have rows of small houses on each side with a space between them large enough for the passage of a chariot. In the center of the city ran the famous Procession Street, which passed through Ishtar Gate. This great arch, still standing, is the best example of Chaldean architecture. In the city there were also several imposing temples, the grandest of which was dedicated to the Chaldean deity Marduk. There was also the immense palace of Nebuchadnezzar. Inclosed by walls, the palace towered terrace upon terrace, each resplendent with masses of fernery, flowers, and trees. These roof gardens, the famous Hanging Gardens, were so beautiful that they were selected by the Greeks as one of the seven wonders of the ancient world.

Chaldean astronomy. New Babylonia made few original contributions to civilization apart from the field of science, but in astronomy her influence was profound. The Babylonians were interested in the stars as a means of foretelling the future. The observation of the stars with the view of showing their influence upon human affairs is called astrology, a pseudoscience which still persists today. A reminder of its influence exists in our language idiom when we refer to our "lucky star" or to an "ill-starred venture." The interest of the Chaldeans in the heavens led to the identification of the twelve groups of stars identified under the twelve signs of the zodiac. Five planets were considered especially fateful in controlling the destinies of men. The names of the five most important Chaldean gods were applied to the five fateful stars. Later the Romans substituted the names of their gods. Thus the planet Marduk became Jupiter, Nabu was changed to Mercury, Ishtar to Venus, and so on.

Even though astronomy was primitive and illogical, it encouraged the systematic observation of the heavens. Astrology had been practiced in Old Babylon, but Chaldean observations were much more accurate and complete. The prediction of eclipses was common, and continuous observations of the heavens were made for over three hundred years. One of the foremost Chaldean astronomers computed the length of the year to within twenty-six minutes.

The Persian Empire

Persian expansion. During the long reign of Nebuchadnezzar, some forty years, Babylon flourished, but at his death the power he had evolved rapidly crumbled. In the latter years of his reign a new people, the Persians, began to assume the offensive. They threw off the Median yoke and captured Ecbatana in 549 B.C. The Medes apparently readily accepted their new ruler, the redoubtable Cyrus the Great. Within twenty years the Persian leader had created a great empire. His first opponent was wealthy King Croesus of Lydia, who met defeat in 546 B.C. At the same time Cyrus assumed control of the Greek Ionian cities and then turned east, establishing his power as far as the frontier of India. Babylon

These old men are subjects from Syria on the other side of the Fertile Crescent, bringing gifts to the emperor at Persepolis—gold vessels, bracelets, horses, even a chariot. This relief decorated a wall of Xerxes' palace at Persepolis.

was next on his list, for in 539 B.C. without resistance the city capitulated to the Persian host. Following the death of Cyrus, his son Cambyses conquered Egypt. The next ruler, Darius, crossed the Hellespont and annexed Macedonia and Thrace to his empire.

It now appeared as if the promising Greek city-states would also be crushed by the Persian steam roller. In 493 B.C. Darius began his first campaigns against Greece. They precipitated a bitter struggle in which the Greeks, fighting heroically, not only repelled the invasion but ultimately, under Alexander the Great, carried the war into the enemy's territory and crushed the great Persian army. All of this will be told in Chapter 5.

Persian imperial administration. The governmental structure designed by the Persian rulers to administer their extensive dominions was built upon the Assyrian model but was far more efficient than its predecessor. The Persian imperial system was first devised by Cyrus the Great and carried to completion by Darius. The empire was divided into twenty-one provinces, or satrapies, each under a provincial governor called a satrap. To check the satraps, a secretary and a military official representing the king were also installed in every province. Special inspectors, "the Eyes and Ears of the King," were also sent to the satrapies to report on the administrative methods of the satraps.

A great empire must possess good communications. Realizing that need, the Persians built great imperial post roads, which in the thoroughness of their construction rivaled the later Roman roads. The main highways connected the four capitals, Susa, Ecbatana, Babylon, and Persepolis, which had been established in various parts of the empire. Along the Royal Road between Sardis and Susa there was a post station every fourteen miles, where fresh horses could be obtained by the king's messengers. By means of this first "pony express," royal messengers could cover a distance of 1500 miles in a little more than seven days, while ordinary travelers took three months.

Persian rulers demonstrated a high sense of responsibility toward all their subjects, alien or Persian. In fact, the Persian empire was the first attempt at governing many different racial groups on the principle of equal rights and responsibilities for all peoples. In their treatment of subject peoples there was a humaneness and spirit of consideration which had been absent in the Assyrian empire. The Persians respected the gods of all conquered people. The king made the prosperity of every part of the empire his concern, in order that all provinces would be enabled to provide the tribute levied against them. The tax burden, however, was not excessive. The introduction of a uniform system of coinage also did much to weld the empire together.

Zoroastrianism. The religion of the Persians was founded by a prophet named Zarathustra (called Zoroaster by the ancient Greeks). The date of his birth is a matter of dispute. Tradition places it about 1000 B.C., but the most recent scholarship puts his birth at 660

B.C. Zoroaster taught that there was a continuous struggle in the world between two great cosmic forces. Mazda, or Ahura Mazda, symbolized righteousness; Ahriman was the summation of everything evil. The sayings and legends concerning Zoroaster were collected early in the Christian era and made into a sacred book called the *Zend-Avesta*. In it the principle of good is referred to as "Ahura Mazda, the creator, radiant, glorious, greatest and best, most beautiful, most firm, wisest, most perfect, the most bounteous spirit." The *Avesta* contained significant ideas on how the world would come to an end. The last days were conceived as involving a mighty battle between Mazda and Ahriman in which the forces of good should prevail. Then would come a last judgment involving a heaven for some and a hell for others. The word paradise is Persian in its origin.

The wise toleration of the Persian rulers was perhaps a result of their religion. In describing some of his victories, Darius, on the famous Behistun monument, declares:

"On this account Ahura Mazda brought me help . . . because I was not wicked, nor was I a liar, nor was I a tyrant, neither I nor any of my line. I have ruled according to righteousness."[15]

The followers of Zoroaster are sometimes called fire worshipers, because they regard fire as a symbol of the deity of light and purity. Their religion still persists among a group of about 100,000 people called Parsees, who live in and around the city of Bombay in India.

Art. The art of the Persians is not very original. They borrowed from their predecessors in the Fertile Crescent, especially the Assyrians. Their most important work was in palace architecture. The royal residences at Persepolis are the best remaining evidence of Persian building. Here a high terrace, or platform, was constructed, reached by a grand stairway, the face of which was covered with beautiful relief sculptures. The practice of raising the palace on a platform originated as a protection against disease from the swamps. Other features were brilliantly colored enameled bricks, entrances flanked by huge human-headed bulls, and numerous columns to support the roof. The columns were topped by

THE RUINED PALACE OF XERXES AT PERSEPOLIS, SHOWING COLUMNS AND TYPICAL PALACE PLATFORM

large heads of bulls, used for capitals as the Egyptians had used lotus motifs. Upon the terrace stood a number of palaces and halls used for audience chambers. The walls of the buildings were covered with brilliant enameled tiles. The arch was not copied from Babylonia; doors were capped with horizontal blocks of stone in the Egyptian fashion.

Summary

The evolution of human affairs in the Ancient Near East from primitive culture to civilization has now been recounted. The principal areas concerned were Egypt at the western terminus of the Fertile Crescent, Syria-Palestine, forming the western band of the Crescent, and Assyria and Babylonia, constituting the eastern bow. Civilization rose about the same time in the western and eastern ends of the Fertile Crescent, that is, in Egypt and in the plain of Shinar, later to be called Babylonia. Both those civilizations were river-made, one by the Nile, the other by the Tigris and Euphrates rivers. Natural barriers forming a defense for Egypt explain the almost uninterrupted continuity of its civilization. Along the Fertile Crescent, however, there were constant fighting and movements of people, owing to the absence of any such barriers. The history of that region, then, is a rather complex account of the rise and fall of numerous nations.

The story of Old Babylonia is primarily concerned with the significant achievements of the Sumerians and the later adoption of their civilization by Semitic invaders. The most important of the Semitic states was Babylon, created by the great Semitic leader Hammurabi. Following an era of brilliant civilization in Old Babylonia, attention was focused on Syria-Palestine. There the duel between Egypt and the Hittite empire, which weakened both contestants, gave small nations, Phoenicia, the Arameans, and the Hebrews, a chance to enjoy a brief period of independence. Political diversity was ended by the rise of the Assyrian empire, which had a span of about three hundred years (900-600 B.C.). The fall of Assyria left four peoples to contest for the crumbs of empire: the Egyptians, the Lydians, the Medes and Persians, and the Chaldeans. At the outset New Babylonia, or Chaldea, under the great Nebuchadnezzar was the center of a brilliant and powerful civilization, but the expansion of Persia quickly terminated its independence. Persia became the greatest empire the world had yet seen; it even endeavored to extend its power over ancient Greece.

If the Paleolithic and Neolithic periods represent the first great chapter of progress in human history, the accomplishments in the Ancient Near East represent a second. There metals were first used on an extensive scale and the wheeled vehicle, the plow, and irrigation introduced. Seagoing ships were built first by the Egyptians, the use of coinage was spread by the Lydians, and business contractual instruments were developed by the Babylonians. In engineering, the Egyptians demonstrated remarkable skill in transporting tremendously heavy blocks of stone over long distances and then elevating them to great heights. During this early period in the history of man, warfare was put on a firm basis by the Sumerians and then developed to a high degree of efficiency by the Assyrians. Great political states were created in which there were remarkable centralization and coordination in administration. Writing was evolved as early as 4000 B.C.; later the Phoenicians made a notable contribution in devising an alphabet. In architecture the Egyptians evolved many of the basic features which were later developed to perfection by the Greeks. Sculpture was used with regard to its architectural setting, and Egyptian mural painters were highly skilled.

In the Tigris and Euphrates valley the outstanding artistic contributions were in palace building and sculpture. In the building of palaces some of the Mesopotamian peoples used the arch and narrow vault successfully though not extensively. The Assyrian use of the arch may have influenced the Romans, and certainly some of their decorative animal motifs influenced later heraldry. In sculpture there were some beautiful wall decorations, especially in the Assyrian period. The greatest gift in literature was the Hebrew Bible, but mention should also be made of the Mesopotamian epics of the flood and creation and the Persian holy *Zend-Avesta*. Finally in religion, the Ancient Near East contributed some notable religious concepts.

Such is the role of the Ancient Near East in world history. But after several thousand years of advance, progress seemed to level off and almost entirely cease. One great bar to progress was that in all the countries of the Near East there was no thought of political liberty or the right of the individual to have a part in the affairs of government. Coupled with the despotism of kings was the tyranny of priests. The old gods had to be obeyed, old customs and mores implicitly accepted. There was little opportunity for speculation, and society tended to become more and more static.

Finally, it must unfortunately be noted that civilization brought with it not only many blessings in the form of more elevated religions, great cities, higher standards of living, and noble art, but also the urge and the means for more frequent and deadlier wars. Before cities and territorial states grew up, sparseness of settlement, poverty of life, nomadic existence, and the absence of efficient weapons limited the extent and duration of fighting between human groups. The rise of civilization, however, brought more wealth and property, increased population, settled government, and fixed frontiers. As a result, more advanced societies sought to extend their control of markets and sources of raw materials; poorer peoples attempted, through force, to obtain wealth by conquering their richer neighbors. Advanced nations for their part not only conquered "barbarian lands," but as bitter rivals also contended one against the other for territories in the building of empires. This evil of war becomes more deadly and extensive as mankind advances. Referring to this tragic and ironic fact, an eminent British scholar observes, "Every one of the factors contributing to the rise of civilization . . . served to increase the possibility of conflict. . . ."[16]

Chronology of events and developments discussed in this chapter

Chapter 3

Indus valley civilization: *on a level with contemporary Egypt and the Fertile Crescent as revealed by the excavations at Mohenjo-Daro and Harappa*	4000-2500 B.C.
Downfall of the Indus valley civilization probably by disaster	2500
Indo-Aryan invasions: *forced the Dravidians south; beginning of the caste system on a color basis*	2000-1000
Vedic times: *rural economy; no political unification*	2000-1000
Vedas: *sacred Sanskrit literature handed down by word of mouth by the Brahmans; a composite of philosophy, religion, and magic along with sociological information*	
Heroic or Epic Age: *city-states ruled by rajahs; solidification of the caste system on a social basis with four classes and the pariahs*	1000-500
Mahabarata: *warrior epic: included the* Bhagavadgita, *sacred Hindu work*	
Ramayana: *epic showing the growth of chivalric ideals among the Indo-Aryans*	
Upanishads: *chief philosophical basis for Hinduism and Buddhism; more sophisticated than the earlier Vedic beliefs*	800-600
Gautama Buddha: founded Buddhism, a religion based on the individual's quest for nirvana; *basic belief in the essential oneness of everything; embodies an ethical code; opposed to the Hindu caste system*	563-483

The Indus and the Ganges

Ancient India: Paleolithic Times to 483 B.C.

A street in the modern flourishing city of Bombay presents a varied sight. Streetcars clang down the center. Taxis and automobiles draw up to the curb before fine shops displaying English clothes, Parisian perfumes, and American household appliances. Along the sidewalks saunter English businessmen, talking perhaps with a rich Parsee merchant or rajah from one of the provinces to the northwest. At an intersection where a Sikh policeman is directing traffic, a great mass of people push their way in all directions: tall, fair-skinned herdsmen down from the hills of the north, dark-skinned laborers out of the rice plantations, workers hurrying to the jute mills of the city, beggars in rags crying for alms, holy men and fakirs, bazaar-keepers, underfed children eyeing the sweetmeats of the hawkers, and heavily bespangled women with caste marks visible on their foreheads. It is a motley scene. The streetcars and taxis, freighters unloading at the busy docks, and handsome public buildings and railway stations combining English and Indian architecture proclaim the impact of western culture upon this Indian metropolis. But the bazaars, caste marks, religious temples, strange costumes, and the endless variety of languages spoken on every side reveal an indigenous culture which has resisted the West.

Civilization had flourished in India for at least five thousand years. This is shown by the fairly recent discovery in the Indus valley of a culture whose antiquity, Pandit Nehru recalls, thrilled him as he stood among the ruins of one of its great cities. The Indian sub-continent has often been subjected to invasions—and indeed one of them eventually resulted in the creation of a large modern Moslem state, Pakistan. (The sub-continent was partitioned in 1947. Until the text deals with that event, the word India will refer to the entire sub-continent.) Yet in the course of a long and tortuous past,

Indian civilization has maintained a striking continuity of thought and outlook. Early in her history an intricate religious philosophy developed together with a unique pattern of social organization. Thus the focal point of Indian thought has been religion, and the focal point of Indian society has been caste. As a result, one of her scholars maintains: "All that India can offer to the world proceeds from her philosophy."[1]

Geography and Early Times

I*ndian geography.* The geography of India gives us many important clues to an understanding of her civilization. A sub-continent of about 1,575,000 square miles, situated largely in the tropics, with a seacoast of some 3400 miles, India has a population of about 390 million. Thus India has an area about one half that of the United States, a seacoast approximately the length of the overland distance from New York to San Francisco, and a population between two and three times that of America. We can think of India as a gigantic triangle, with two sides bounded by ocean and the third by the great mountain-wall of the Himalayas, which runs along India's northern frontier for 1600 miles. In ancient times India was inaccessible from the sea, and the only approach lay through the mountain passes to the northwest. That fact has colored all Indian history, for down the passes have swarmed armed conquerors, restless tribes, and merchants from the west. In modern times Great

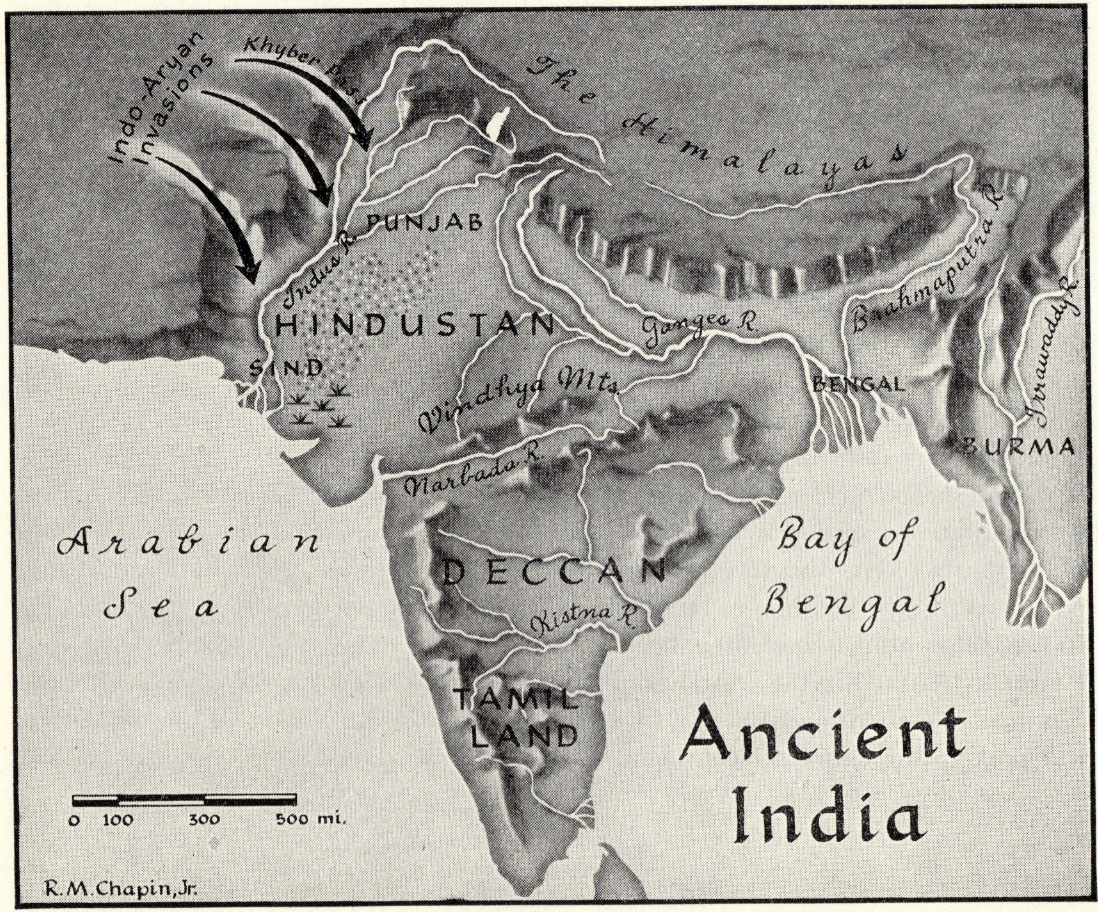

Britain, by gaining control of the seas, was able to conquer and dominate India without having to enter through the mountain passes.

India can be conveniently separated into three principal divisions. The area north of the Narbada River is called Hindustan; the area as far south as the Kistna River is known as the Deccan, and the remaining territory down to the southern tip of India is called the Far South, or Tamil Land. Northern India is separated clearly from the Deccan and Tamil Land by the Vindhya Mountains, a sandstone range about 3000 feet in height, once covered with an impenetrable jungle. This barrier prevented early northern invaders from penetrating successfully into the Deccan plateau and Tamil Land. Our interest lies principally in the events that took place in Hindustan and, especially during the earliest historical period, in the basin of the Indus. For in the alluvial plain watered by the Indus and four of its tributaries (called the Punjab, or Land of the Five Rivers) and in the territory to the south of that plain (called Sind, the land of the Sindhus, the ancient name for the Indus) India developed its first real civilization. Although the Indus was the initial home of Indian civilization, we shall find that after the Indo-Aryan people invaded India, they spread eastward until in the Epic Age (1000-500 B.C.) they were creating kingdoms along the Ganges valley. In Hindustan, India developed the culture of her present.

The earliest cultures. The earliest inhabitants of India had a culture at least as primitive as that of other Paleolithic peoples. Both Paleolithic and Neolithic remains have been found scattered throughout the entire peninsula. In southern India Neolithic man became fairly civilized, making use of the potter's wheel, domesticating the dog, goat, and ox, fashioning ornaments out of conches, pearls, and gold, hollowing out timber, dressing skins, and cultivating crops. Later, stone tools were replaced by iron in the south and copper in the north. There appears to have been no Bronze Age in India, but probably long before 5000 B.C. iron tools had become common.

The early cultures of India were mainly fluvial. Large numbers of inhabitants congregated along the river banks. We have seen that early Near Eastern cultures were fluvial mainly because of the fertility of the soil in the river valleys. Since nearly all Indian soil is fertile in

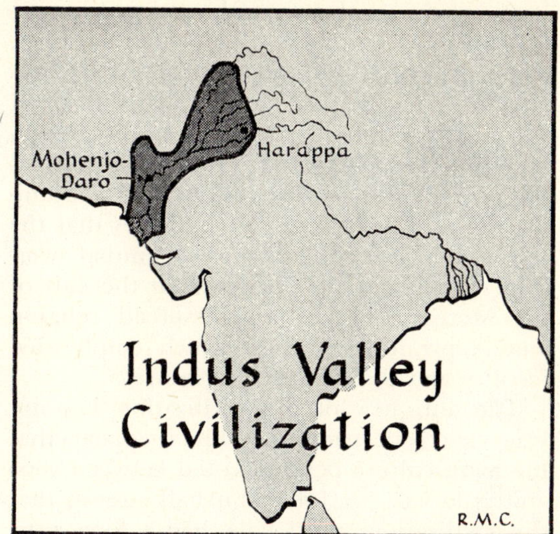

comparison with the semidesert conditions of Egypt and Mesopotamia, the rivers in India were important primarily as means of water supply and communication.

The Indus valley civilization. Since 1922, archaeological studies under Sir John H. Marshall have revealed the existence in the Indus valley of an ancient civilization (c. 4000-2500 B.C.). From the location of excavated cities such as Harappa and Mohenjo-Daro, it appears that the Indus valley civilization embraced all of Sind and the Punjab, a part of the coastal region, the valleys of the North-West Frontier Province, and perhaps part of the Gangetic basin (see map above).

Excavations at Mohenjo-Daro show a well-laid-out town with straight streets, an elaborate drainage system consisting of horizontal and vertical drains with the houses possessing private wells and baths—so that the city was far in advance of European towns thousands of years later—industrial and commercial quarters, and flat-roofed buildings of burnt brick. Evidence shows that the people maintained close contact with the outside world, such as southern and eastern India, Central Asia, Sumeria, Egypt, and Crete. With its easy land and water communications, this civilization was evidently the meeting ground of peoples from diverse regions. The cosmopolitan character of the population has been proved by craniological tests of Mohenjo-Daro skeletons, which reveal four racial types: Proto-Australoid, Mediterranean, Mongoloid, and Alpine.

That the citizens of Mohenjo-Daro and Harappa were artistic is apparent from the large collection of seals and amulets (charms) which have been found, ornamented by tigers, elephants, crocodiles, and other animals. Statuettes of a dancing girl and a male torso, of splendid execution, have also been discovered, as well as exquisite pottery of highly burnished red ochre and ingenious toys in bird and animal forms. Much of the art indicates that the Indus valley inhabitants were animal worshipers and that they believed in the cult of the Mother Goddess—a widespread religion among primitive peoples which emphasized fertility and the divinity of Nature.

The antiquity of this civilization has not been exactly determined. While it appears that the main culture period existed between 2800 and 2500 B.C., Sir John Marshall stresses that this civilization "must have had a long antecedent history on the soil of India, taking us back to an age that at present can only be dimly surmised."[2] The reason for the downfall of this flourishing civilization—apparently as rich and varied as any in contemporary Egypt or the Fertile Crescent—is not known. That some tragedy—perhaps a great flood or plague—befell the populace seems evident from the fact that groups of skeletons have been found in some of the rooms, as if the victims had met a common fate. Sir John Marshall believes that by the time the Indo-Aryans entered the Punjab (see below), the Indus valley civilization could have been "but a mere shadow of its former self."[3]

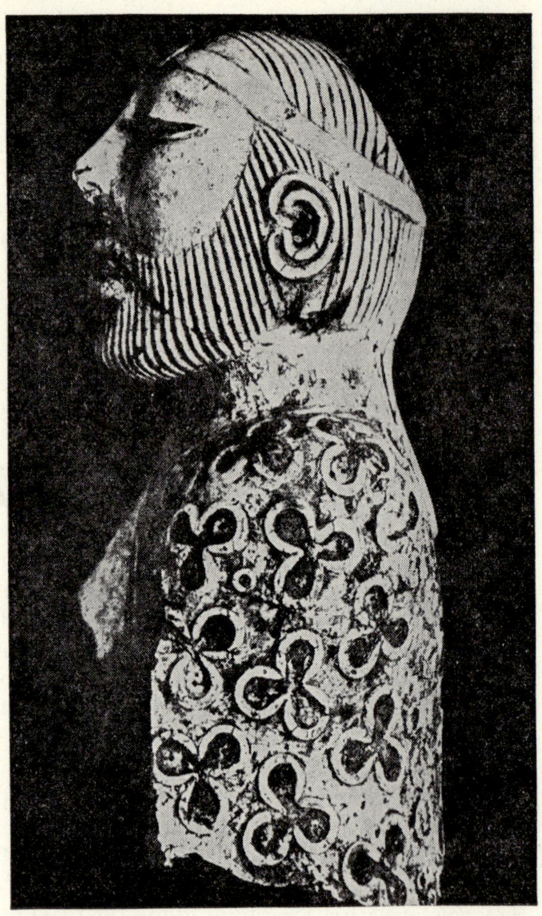

Aloofness and hauteur mark a precisely ornamented Indian statue found at Mohenjo-Daro.

Vedic and Epic India

Indo-Aryan invasions (2000-1000 B.C.). We are ignorant of the history of India for a period of some five hundred years following the fall of the Indus valley civilization. About 2000 B.C., however, tribes began to enter the land from the northwest. Where did these marauding immigrants come from, and of what race were they? Again the answer is far from certain. Possibly they came originally from central Asia or an area bordering on the shores of the Caspian Sea. Language resemblances as well as religious similarities indicate that they were related to the peoples of the Near East. We may conclude that the Hittites, Medes, Persians, and Aryan-speaking tribes (called Indo-Aryans) which invaded India were branches of the great Indo-European family which probably had its original home somewhere near the Caspian Sea. The Indo-Aryans began to invade India about the same time that their relatives overran the country of Babylonia.

The Indo-Aryans were a fair-skinned, tall people of strong physique, with long heads, straight noses, and finely developed features. They ate heartily, drank copiously, fought readily, and boasted noisily. At the time of their arrival in India they lived a simple life. Wealth was measured in terms of cattle, and the word for war meant "a desire for more cows." Milk, butter, and grain were the staple foods, although meat was not forbidden. The father of the family was its head, and his sons and grandsons dwelt with their families beneath his roof. The father was also the priest of the family, lighting the sacred fire and making sacrifices to the gods. At that time there were no castes. The king, or rajah, at the head of the tribe (made up of numerous families) administered justice or led his people into war. There were also the family priests and the warriors—males of fighting age who formed a council to aid the king. Women occupied a high social status and administered their households. Marriage was monogamous and was forbidden both outside the racial group and between people too closely related.

The Dravidians. The Indo-Aryans did not conquer northern India without a struggle. As they pushed slowly eastward along the Indus and Ganges valleys until they occupied all of Hindustan, they came into conflict with the people who had already settled there, also of unknown origin. The entire racial history of India is obscure. The oldest remains go back to an early post-glacial period and seem to indicate a Negroid stock akin to those of Africa. Various invasions into India of primitive Negroid stocks probably took place from time to time, and despite later invasions by Aryan-speaking groups from the north, the south lands of India even today possess remains of the ancient Indo-Negroid races. They have been called Dravidian because Dravida was the old name of the Tamil country. It has also been suggested that they were descended from the people who had once inhabited Mohenjo-Daro and Harappa.

At any rate, they appear to have been shorter and darker than the Indo-Aryans and were considered by the latter to be ugly, coarse, and uncivilized. The Aryan-speaking tribesmen looked askance at these "noseless" people who spoke a vulgar tongue so that they seemed to be "yelling hideously like dogs," who ate raw flesh, worshiped strange gods and trees and snakes, and practiced polygamy. Yet, despite such Indo-Aryan opinion of the dark-skinned natives, the Dravidians possessed a civilization superior to that which their conquerors brought from the northwest. They had built castles and large, luxurious cities, were excellent mariners, and had commercial contacts with Babylon and the Sumerians. The Indo-Aryans borrowed many customs and ideas from the Dravidians, including, apparently, their systems of land tenure and taxation and their village community.

The triumph of the Indo-Aryans. The Indo-Aryans proved masters of the Dravidians in warfare, however, and the Dravidians were enslaved or driven southward in much the same manner as the North American Indian was pushed back by the American pioneers.

The Indo-Aryans looked upon driving back the Dravidians as a primary duty, and the poems they wrote tell much about the wars between the two peoples. However, many of the invaders intermarried with the Dravidians and began to adopt some of their customs. The Indo-Aryans soon saw that they would be absorbed completely by the more numerous Dravidians, whom they considered inferior, unless they took steps to prevent such intermarriage. This racial restriction was directed mainly at preserving the fair color of the Indo-Aryans. Thus the caste system began to be used not to preserve social status but to preserve, if possible, purity of race. The early word for caste was *varna*, meaning color (it was translated by later Portuguese travelers as *casta*, from the Latin *castus*, meaning pure). The Indo-Aryans as yet placed no caste restrictions upon marriage within their own group.

Vedic times (2000-1000 B.C.). Our knowledge of early India is derived largely from the literature of the times. As the first writings of the Indo-Aryans are to be found in the *Vedas*, we call the period which they describe the Vedic Age (about 2000-1000 B.C.). Later, great epic poems—the *Mahabharata* and *Ramayana* especially—were composed to commemorate the heroic deeds of early warriors. We therefore call their period the Heroic, or Epic, Age (about 1000-500 B.C.). The epics throw much light upon contemporary conditions.

When the Indo-Aryan invaders had once conquered the land they began to settle down to a rural existence. They tilled and irrigated the soil, raised barley, millet, wheat, lentils, and sesame. They used oxen for plowing and drawing wagons, raised cattle and ate cow's meat at festivals, and made out of grain an intoxicating drink called *sura*.

Village life was similar to that of modern India. At the head of the village (*grama*) was the headsman (*gramani*), sometimes elected and at other times holding his position by hereditary right. The village was composed of a group of families, and villages were scattered over the country at varying distances, connected by roads and tracks. Most of the village occupations were agricultural—dairying, tanning, spinning wool and weaving cloth, fashioning hoes and plowshares, and making household utensils. The Indo-Aryans owned the lands nearby and considered it a disgrace to work for someone else.

The houses were made with mud walls, clay floors, and thatched roofs. Clothing consisted principally of a skirt and a shawl worn over the shoulder. Ornaments such as earrings and necklaces were fashionable. There were three modes of marriage: consent, purchase, and abduction of the bride. The last method was considered a great compliment by the women. Among the rich, polygamy was sometimes practiced; however most Indo-Aryans were monogamists. During Vedic times the status of women was high. They mingled freely with the rest of society at public occasions, joined in religious sacrifices, and were free to engage in intellectual pursuits. The practices of *purdah* (seclusion of women) and the *suttee* (self-destruction of a widow on her husband's funeral pyre) were rare until later ages. Among the popular amusements were gambling, dancing, chariot racing (for the upper classes), music, and listening to tribal bards.

The Epic Age (1000-500 B.C.). Society in the Epic, or Heroic, Age was quite similar to that of the Homeric Age of Greece, as we shall see in Chapter 5. The Indo-Aryans had been expanding eastward and creating kingdoms along the Ganges valley. These kingdoms were small, isolated city-states. There was no central authority; each kingdom was a unit in itself. The epics tell of constant warfare among the kingdoms, with occasional alliances between some of them in order to wage war against others.

The cities of the Epic Age were surrounded by moats and walls, and their streets were well planned, lighted, and even cleaned. In the center stood the palace of the king, or rajah. His powers were greater than those of the village headsman of Vedic times. Like the later Germanic chieftains he was surrounded with a faithful retinue of followers who pledged to him their personal loyalty and followed him into battle, receiving in return weapons, food, and honors. While the king's political powers were very great, he was responsible for the protection of his subjects and the administration of justice. To advise and help him, he had a royal council, composed of his relatives and nobles. He received taxes from the people and probably was the owner (in theory at least) of all land. He made foreign alliances personally and often cemented political agreements with marriage ties.

Besides the king and the warrior class, other groups were coming into prominence. The priest still occupied a subordinate place in society, as there was yet no definite, formalized religion. The family priest persisted from Vedic times and officiated at the numerous and expensive sacrifices. In the cities a kind of middle class was rising. The variety of occupations indicates the advanced development of Epic life: metalworkers, wood-workers, stone-workers, leather-workers, glass-makers, ivory-workers, basket-makers, house-painters, potters, dyers, fishermen, sailors, butchers, barbers, shampooers, florists, cooks, confectioners, physicians, armorers, incense sellers, tailors, goldsmiths, actors, and washermen. The menial tasks were performed by slaves—captives, debtors, and members of the Dravidian group. Although the slaves possessed no legal privileges, they were apparently well treated.

The epics indicate that as in Vedic times women were socially well-off, although *suttee* was increasing. Polygamy was also much more common now than during the Vedic Age, but polyandry was exceptional. Favorite pastimes of the privileged were hunting, gambling, fighting, and watching the performances of dancing girls. The cow was now considered sacred (for reasons which we shall discuss later), but other forms of flesh were eaten. A strong alcoholic beverage called *soma* was in use.

Economic developments of Epic times. Trade was steadily advancing. Two-wheeled wagons carried produce overland, but the bad roads and numerous taxes which had to be paid at every frontier must have proved discouraging. River and ocean commerce increased, thanks particularly to the Dravidians, who were skilled in navigation. About 860 B.C. ships carrying Indian perfumes, silks, spices, muslins, and precious stones made their way to Egypt, Arabia, and Mesopotamia. In early times there was no coinage, and trade was carried on by barter. Then cattle became the currency (brides were often purchased with cows), giving way later to a copper coinage. By the time of Buddha (about the close of the Epic Age) a credit system had been evolved. Merchants in various cities made use of letters of credit, and loans were being made at eighteen-per-cent interest.

Growth of the caste system. We saw earlier that the first caste division dealt not with social stratification within the Indo-Aryan group but with the separation (along color lines) of the Aryan-speaking invaders and the native Dravidians. During the Epic Age caste became more sharply defined. The division into social groups was not a new phenomenon with the Indo-Europeans. The early Iranians, an Indo-European people, were divided into three classes: priests, warriors, and agriculturists; later the artisans became a fourth class. The four castes evolved by Indo-Aryan society were, in order of their rank, (1) the Brahmans, or priests, (2) the Kshatriyas, or warriors, (3) the Vaisyas, or agriculturists and traders, and (4) the Sudras, or serfs. During the Epic Age the Kshatriyas, or warriors, had a higher social rank than the Brahmans; but as warfare declined in intensity, religion grew in complexity and importance. The priests, as the educators of youth, oral historians of the people, and intermediaries between the gods and men, had assumed a dominant position in Indian society by the close of Epic times, a position which they have successfully maintained down to the present century.

Meanwhile, there had appeared a small group of people who lay outside the four castes. Because they had been captured in warfare or reduced to slavery for some reason, these unfortunates lost all right to caste. Hence they were called outcastes, or pariahs. Their numbers multiplied, until today there are almost 50,000,000 "untouchables" at the very base of Hindu society, whose touch and very shadow are believed to be defiling to a Brahman.

We have noted that the caste system became more sharply defined during the Epic Age than it had been in Vedic times. In the centuries following the Epic Age the caste system grew more and more complex until it came to have racial, social, political, economic, and religious implications and was split up into thousands of sub-castes.

Theories of caste history. Scholars are by no means agreed as to the origin and development of the caste system. Stanley Rice suggests the following plausible view: (1) The Indo-Aryans on their arrival in the country found that the Dravidians already had a sort of caste institution which was designed to keep them apart from the older aborigines; (2) the Indo-Aryans saw that by adopting this custom they might in turn keep themselves apart from the Dravidians, and as the obvious distinction was between the fair and dark-skinned, they named the institution *varna*, or color; (3) the Indo-Aryans probably recalled that their kinsfolk, the Iranians, also possessed a caste division, based on occupations, and this precedent helped confirm their own action; (4) the caste system received religious sanction until as time went on it crystallized into a religious prohibition; and (5) the caste system was bound up with occupational problems, so that it became natural for each task, from that of the lowly flayer of cattle to the powerful Brahman priest, to be assigned a definite social status and religious purpose.[4]

Caste, as it exists in India today, is the combination of all these factors in varying degrees. If we have dwelt at some length upon the subject, it is because the problems of modern India cannot be understood without a grasp of the complexities of this unique institution.

Language, Literature, and Art

Indian languages. India has five or six distinct families of languages, of which the Indo-Aryan is but one. The Dravidian languages have been affected by Indo-Aryan but nevertheless are independent in structure. In recent times, the richness of the early literature of the Dravidians has been brought to light. However, we are concerned primarily with the speech and writings of the Indo-Aryans. When these fair-skinned tribes came through the northwest passes, they spoke a variant language of the mother tongue of the Indo-European family which in its general features was more or less the same as the earliest Greek. The different tribes, however, spoke a variety of dialects. Within a thousand years of their arrival the Indo-Aryan language had evolved into the tongue known as Sanskrit. This language belongs to the same family as Persian, Greek, Latin, and English. The early Indo-Aryan speech became the mother of such languages of northern India as Marathi,

Hindi, and Bengali, all of which evolved over a period of centuries.

By the time of the rise of the Magadha empire in the fourth century B.C. Sanskrit existed in three forms: the strict Sanskrit of the Brahmans, who were interested in scriptural exactness, the language of the poets and court bards as found in the great epics, and the less literary Sanskrit, which was used in treatises on politics, law, and the arts. There is evidence in the *Rig-Veda* that even in Vedic times vernacular dialects which differed from Sanskrit were arising in various localities. Sanskrit has always been the language of the learned people.

The Vedas. Sanskrit literature is probably the oldest, the most diversified, and the most voluminous of all Indian literatures. Moreover, it is the most representative of Indian thought. The *Vedas,* from which our knowledge of primitive India is gleaned, were written in Sanskrit. The word *veda* means knowledge, and a *Veda* is really a compilation of knowledge regarding religion, philosophy, and magic. Of the four *Vedas* which have survived to present times, the oldest and most famous is the *Rig-Veda.* Consisting of 1028 hymns in praise of different gods, it is a peculiar combination of childlike questions such as why white milk should come from red cows, petitions to the gods for good crops or longer life, and (sometimes) religious concepts of deep beauty.

Rival tribes lock in mortal combat in this rich manuscript illustration for the Ramayana. *The poem has interested artists ever since Epic times.*

The *Vedas* were considered too sacred to be revealed to a Sudra, or serf; hence they were not written down but were transmitted orally from father to son among the Brahmans. A Chinese traveler, visiting India in the late seventh century A.D., tells us that "in every generation there exist some intelligent Brahmans who can recite 100,000 verses."[5]

The Upanishads. After the *Vedas* ceased to be composed, various treatises were produced, including the famous *Upanishads.* Written about 800-600 B.C., the *Upanishads* reflect that age's growing distrust of the old Vedic concepts and their replacement by profound philosophical speculations about the ultimate truth that lies behind the process of creation. Recurring throughout the *Upanishads* is the famous dictum *"Tat tvam asi"*—"That art thou"—which underscores the fundamental concept of the oneness of life. "That" stands for *Brahman,* the cosmic principle and eternal power "which creates, sustains, preserves, and receives back into itself again all the worlds," while "thou" stands for *Atman,* the individual self or soul. In other words, as one *Upanishad* states: "The universe is *Brahman,* but the *Brahman* is the *Atman*"; while a Upanishadic philosopher tells us:

"This my *Atman* in my inmost heart is smaller than a grain of rice, or a barley corn, or a mustard seed, or a millet grain.... This my *Atman* in my inmost heart is greater than the earth, greater than the sky, greater than the heavens, greater than all the spheres. In him are all actions, all wishes, all smells, all tastes; he holds this All enclosed within himself; he speaks not, he troubles about nothing; —this my Atman in my inmost heart, is this Brahman. With him, when I depart out of this life, shall I be united. For him to whom this knowledge has come, for him, indeed, there exists no doubt."[6]

Scholars have pointed out that the later philosophical systems and religions of India have developed in one way or another out of the *Upanishads.* Nor has their influence been confined to India. In the nineteenth century, the German philosopher Schopenhauer was moved to say, "In the whole world there is no study so beneficial and so elevating as that of the *Upanishads.* It has been the solace of my life—it will be the solace of my death."

Epic poetry. The literature of ancient India was not confined merely to priestly teachings. The great epic poems, the *Mahabharata* and the *Ramayana,* tell of heroic deeds of the early Indo-Aryans. They describe events from about 1000 to 500 B.C. The *Mahabharata,* like the Greek *Iliad,* deals with a great war and is undoubtedly the product of many poets who added fragments over a long period. In its present form the *Mahabharata* contains 107,000 octameter couplets and is seven times the length of the *Iliad* and *Odyssey* together. The poem glorifies the Kshatriyan caste, as it tells of warfare between two Indo-Aryan tribes. The main story is interrupted by myths, genealogies, love stories, lives of saintly persons, and discourses on such topics as religion and the duties of kings.

The most famous part of this epic is the philosophical poem called the *Bhagavadgita* (*The Lord's Song*), familiarly known as the *Gita.* Of some 700 verses, the *Gita* is an anonymous work whose date "may be assigned to the fifth century B.C., though the text may have received many alterations in subsequent times."[7] This, the most treasured piece in Hindu literature, derives its main inspiration from the *Upanishads* and is at once superb poetry and profound philosophy, combined with a message of action. The *Gita* sets forth a problem of extreme subtlety. The warrior Arjuna is about to commence battle in defense of his people, but in so doing will have to fight his own relatives. At first he espouses the doctrine of nonresistance, but his teacher, Krishna, makes it clear that Arjuna must first follow his duty as a member of the warrior caste. However, when engaging in this, or any other kind of action, Arjuna must do so in a spirit of complete detachment (that is, without passion or anger), since it is by developing such detachment and faith in the Absolute that one frees himself from the bondage of action. And Krishna tells Arjuna that even if death should result from his actions, his soul is indestructible and eternal.

"Never was there a time when I was not, nor thou, nor these lords of men, nor will there ever be a time hereafter when we shall cease to be. . . . Just as a person casts off worn-out garments and puts on others that are new, even so does the embodied soul cast off worn-out bodies and take on others that are new."[8]

The second epic, the *Ramayana,* is much shorter than the *Mahabharata.* It has been likened to the Greek *Odyssey* because it also tells of a hero's wanderings and his faithful wife's long vigil. Where the *Mahabharata* is a vigorous glorification of war and adventure, the *Ramayana* shows the growth of chivalric ideals among the Indo-Aryans. The chief characters possess a flawless nobility, marked by compassion, gentleness, and generosity. Both epics have provided all subsequent Indian literature with untold numbers of stories.

Art. It is unfortunate that there is a gap in our knowledge of Indian art and architecture from the time of Mohenjo-Daro to about 250 B.C. The buildings of the Indus valley culture were built of brick, while those of the Vedic and Epic Indo-Aryans seem to have been constructed of wood. Stone was not used until later. Decorative use was frequently made of the Buddhist symbols of the Wheel of Life and the lotus or water lily. The Wheel of Life was especially important because it symbolized the revolving of human souls in the great cycle of reincarnation.

Painting was in evidence as far back as Neolithic times. Drawings of animals have been discovered in prehistoric caves. Again gaps occur in our knowledge, due largely to the corruptive influences of climate upon paints and the disruptive work of the idol-smashing Moslems in medieval times. A group of Buddhist frescoes found on the walls of a cave in central India is the first datable painting (about 100 B.C.). It is a pity that our appreciation of the early Indian arts has been limited by the incompleteness of our knowledge, but we can safely attribute to these people a high state of artistic expression and skill.

Religion and Philosophy

Influence of religion. The power of religion is extraordinarily strong in India. Every aspect of Indian life has always had religious significance. It is commonly found in literature, art, economics, philosophy, sociology, politics, or even science. This phenomenon perhaps accounts for the recent leadership in Indian national affairs of a man who was not a statesman but a religious figure—Mahatma Gandhi. We may expect, then, to discover two major facts: first, that the history of religion in India is long and complex and, second, that Indian religious thought has evolved ideas which are among the most novel and most intricately worked out in all the history of the human race.

Religion in early India. The vanished people of Mohenjo-Daro appear to have been members of the cult of the Mother Goddess, a religion common throughout the Near East. It was natural that early man should have soon realized that his existence depended upon the fertility of the earth. Therefore he came to look upon it as a great mother which nourished him and was forever creating fresh life.

When the Indo-Aryans swarmed into India long after the days of Mohenjo-Daro, they found the Dravidian inhabitants following an animistic and totemic worship. Good and bad spirits who dwelled in trees, stones, streams, and mountains had to be placated by magic spells and incantations to keep the worshiper safe. The Dravidians worshiped snakes, especially the cobra.

Vedic religion. Dravidian practices differed profoundly from those of the Indo-Aryans, who had brought with them into India their own religious theories. The Indo-Aryans worshiped the Devas, or Shining Ones, the gods who dwelled in the firmament. The most popular of all the gods was Indra, the Indian Thor, who wielded the thunderbolt and helped the Indo-Aryans against their Dravidian foes. Indra, the mighty warrior, was depicted as eating bulls by the hundreds and quaffing lakes of wine. The Vedic religion required no temples or images, but sacrificial rites, including the offering of *soma* juice and the pouring of liquid butter into the fire, were performed by the Brahmans. Vedic philosophy was not complicated. After death the human soul simply entered into eternal punishment or everlasting happiness. There was as yet no thought of reincarnation of the soul. However, in the later *Vedas* there grew slowly the idea that there is Something beyond the everyday acts of both gods and men, Something which underlies all life, a Moral Law which governs even the gods themselves. The *Vedas* demonstrate the evolution of early Indian religion and philosophy from a simple belief in many gods toward a deep pantheism, a conception of the entire universe and everything in it as God. We have already pointed out that the most famous of the *Vedas* is the *Rig-Veda*. And the loftiest of all the religious poems in the *Rig-Veda* is the oft-quoted "Creation Hymn." The Hymn tries to discover the beginning of universal life, even before the gods themselves were created. In reading the majestic lines we can perceive at once the pantheistic note that dominates the poem:

Nor Aught nor Naught existed; yon bright sky
Was not, nor heaven's broad woof outstretched above.
What covered all? What sheltered? What concealed?
Was it the water's fathomless abyss?
There was not death—yet was there naught immortal;
There was no confine betwixt day and night;
The only One breathed breathless by itself,
Other than It there nothing since has been.
Darkness there was, and all at first was veiled
In gloom profound—an ocean without light—
The germ that still lay covered in the husk
Burst forth, one nature, from the fervent heat.
Who knows the secret? Who proclaimed it here?
Whence, whence this manifold creation sprang?
The gods themselves came later into being—
Who knows from whence this great creation sprang?
He from whom this great creation came,
Whether His will created or was mute, The
Most High Seer that is in highest heaven, He
knows it—or perchance even He knows not.[9]

The philosophy of the Upanishads. By the time of the *Upanishads* (about 800-600 B.C.) the old Vedic religious beliefs had been largely discarded. Like their Greek kinsmen, the Indo-Aryans now interested themselves in cosmology (the attempt to find a rational explanation of the processes of the universe). While the *Upanishads* do not present a logically worked out system of thought (for they were composed over a period of centuries), the following main points, from which all subsequent Indian philosophy has developed, can be found:

(1) The one essence which permeates every aspect of the universe is an impersonal, immaterial, unborn and undying spirit or force called *Brahman*. It is the essence of all things, the "Real of the Real," the "World-stuff."

(2) There is a universal Soul of which all individual souls are an unbreakable and eter-

nal part; this Soul of all souls is called *Atman.*

(3) *Brahman* and *Atman* are one and indivisible. Therefore we as individual souls and God as the essence of all things are one. The unity of all life is the only reality. The *Upanishads* repeat over and over again the fundamental fact that no matter what we see about us, "That art thou."

(4) As individual souls living in a world of the senses, we think that each of us and the world itself must exist apart from the one all-pervading Soul or essence; but that belief is *maya,* or illusion. The world of the senses is transitory and exists only as part of the one unchanging *Brahman.* The illusion of separateness must be completely abandoned before we perceive the truth.

(5) While we are living in a state of illusion, we place our faith solely in those things which are transitory, and therefore their effect upon us is transitory and unsatisfying. Hence we are afflicted with sorrow and pain. We shall never be free from the world's sorrow until we achieve *moksha*—deliverance. *Moksha,* which comes through our awareness of the reality only of the one, eternal life, insures our re-absorption into the *Brahman.*

(6) Only through long experience can the individual soul learn the lesson of the illusion of separateness, a lesson which can never be learned except in the world of the senses. Therefore each soul must receive many experiences. Experiences are received only by the incarnation of the soul into many physical bodies. Thus the doctrine of *transmigration,* or *reincarnation,* is an essential feature of the *Upanishad* philosophy.

(7) The actions of all aspects of life are governed by an immutable, eternal moral law called *karma.* It can be roughly summed up as the law of action and reaction, or, as it is stated among Christians, "For whatsoever a man sows, that shall he reap." By *karma* the Indians explain the conditions of men. The environment into which a person is born, together with his attending fortune and misfortune, is due not to the whimsy of a capricious God but to the acts of the individual himself in past lives. The Indian says there is no favoritism in the universe but only immutable law and justice.

The philosophy of the *Upanishads* is still the basis of most Hindu thought. The late Indian poet, Rabindranath Tagore, and the famous leader of India, the late Mahatma Gandhi, have both been indebted to the *Upanishads* for many of their beliefs. The *Upanishads* have had an effect outside India also. We noticed the praise which the nineteenth-century German philosopher Schopenhauer bestowed upon the ancient teachings. Several nineteenth-century Americans, among them Ralph Waldo Emerson, were likewise influenced by the *Upanishads.*

Hinduism. So far we have discussed the essentials of the philosophy of the *Upanishads.* Yet we read today about Hinduism and Buddhism. Where do these faiths fit into such a philosophy?

The *Upanishads* are the basis of both religions. Hinduism developed out of *Upanishad* philosophy, largely through the efforts of the Brahman caste. Hinduism grew for the reason that the people do not respond so readily to philosophy as they do to religion. Therefore, Hinduism, while accepting the *Upanishads,* has added certain features of its own. It gave the caste system a religious significance by linking it up with the theory of reincarnation. The Hindus maintain that each of the four major castes is for the purpose of learning unique experiences. Thus, the Sudra is only starting his cycle of human reincarnation and has many lessons to learn, whereas the Brahman is approaching the attainment of *moksha* and therefore will not have to be re-incarnated in the world of the senses again.

To the philosophy of the *Upanishads* Hinduism has also added ceremonies and rituals. Further, Hinduism is polytheistic; that is, it worships many gods. The three most important deities are Brahma the Creator, Vishnu the Preserver, and Shiva the Destroyer. The Hindu worships this trinity because he sees everywhere in life three great processes: creation, preservation, and destruction. The common people divide their popular devotion between Vishnu and Shiva, and festivals are annually held in honor of each. Superstition early entered Hinduism, and because that faith teaches the sacredness of all life as belonging to the one universal "World-stuff," deities were made of such creatures as cobras, crocodiles, and parrots. The cow is held in special veneration by the Hindus. Today sixty-six per cent of India's population is Hindu.

Modern Hindu customs. After having examined the more important religious and social beliefs of ancient India, we can apply them to our own understanding of that land today, because these concepts have persisted with amazing vitality down to present times. The Hindu looks upon all living things as part of the one Life. Therefore nothing must be slain, whether it be man, cow, or even poisonous snake. Similarly, because of his attitude toward the taking of life, the conscientious Hindu eats no meat of any kind. The strictness of his diet is also accounted for by his belief that the physical body has a direct bearing upon the spiritual life and that therefore to degrade his body with impure food is to impair his soul's purity.

We can now see, too, the religious significance of the caste system. The devout Hindu believes firmly that the caste idea is of divine origin. According to a man's actions in his past life, he is assigned to an appropriate caste where he has to work out duties to himself and his caste which help his spiritual nature unfold. These codes of duty are attributed to the legendary Laws of Manu (Manu was considered by Hindus the father of mankind) and cover such matters as government, economics, domestic life, morality, diet, travel, and caste eugenics. Whereas in Vedic times caste was largely of racial significance, in medieval and modern times it became a matter of religious importance. And it is the religious aspect which has kept the caste system all-powerful up to present times. The priestly Brahman today still maintains his supremacy in Hindu religious and social life and feels that his soul has been defiled if he comes in contact with even the shadow of a pariah, or outcaste. And because the present-day outcastes, the "untouchables," are still religiously taboo, they are confined to the most menial and unpleasant occupations in the Indian economy, such as those arising from lack of modern sanitation.

Gautama Buddha

Brahman dogma. The *Upanishads* had developed a philosophy which stressed the necessity of individual effort to win freedom from the illusion of the physical world. We remember that, from Vedic times on, the religious rites were in the hands of the Brahmans. While they had worked out the philosophy of the *Upanishads*, nevertheless they continued to keep their hold over the people by stressing the necessity of religious ceremonies and costly sacrifices. Salvation was to be won not so much by individual effort as by accepting wholeheartedly the dogmas of the Brahman priestcraft. The more profound minds of the day saw the discrepancy clearly and revolted against the system.

Though Gautama forbade the practice of idolatry, numberless statues like the giant Buddha at Kamakura, Japan, were later erected to him throughout the east.

Likewise, as we have noticed, the *Upanishads* came to be written largely out of the growing disbelief in the older Vedic gods and theology. India stood in need of religious reform so that the beliefs of the people would be more in keeping with the ideals and spirit of the *Upanishads.*

The life of the Buddha. The great religious reformer who now appeared was Gautama Buddha (563?-483 B.C.). He stands out in history as one of the profoundest influences in the life of mankind. This influence is due to two principal factors: the beauty and simplicity of his own life and the philosophical depth and ethical nobility of his teaching.

Gautama was born about 563 B.C., the son of the king of Kapilavastu, at the foot of the Himalayas. He led a happy life as a youth and received training both in arms and in philosophy. He married his beautiful cousin and had a son. But according to tradition, Gautama one day became profoundly aware of the misery, pain, disease, and sorrow that he saw as he walked through the streets of the city, and the sight of death moved him to speculate about its cause. Palace life offered him no solution, and the very happiness which he had found in his wife and son only made the world's suffering more unbearable by contrast. He determined to leave everything and seek in the world for an answer to his problem. With pious joy the devout Buddhist recounts the tale of the Great Renunciation, the forsaking of pleasure by the young prince and his departure from the palace in a simple yellow robe. For seven years he dwelled in the forest, practicing the self-mortification rites of the yogis whom he found there. Yogis are men who follow the practice of yoga, a philosophy having as its object union with the Supreme Spirit. To accomplish such a union, the yogi leads an ascetic life, gaining mastery over his body through the strictest discipline and purity of action and meditating constantly so that he may realize, consciously and completely, his unity with all that lives.

Gautama nearly died from his yoga fastings and self-tortures, and he came at last to the conclusion that these practices never lead to wisdom. He was meditating on the problem of human suffering beneath a large tree when he received "enlightenment." From it he was able to construct a religious philosophy which has affected the lives of literally thousands of millions for nearly twenty-five hundred years. Soon he had attracted disciples, of whom the Buddha's most beloved was the faithful Ananda, who occupies the same position in Buddhist stories as the disciple John in the New Testament. Dressed always in his simple yellow robe, with begging bowl in hand, the Buddha, the "Enlightened One," wandered through the plains of the Ganges, constantly preaching to the villagers who flocked to hear him in the shade of evening. He spoke with everyone, irrespective of caste, and, like Jesus, who congregated with sinners and publicans instead of the "respectable" Pharisees, he would decline the sumptuous banquets of nobles to partake of the simple hospitality of peasants and even social outcasts.

Scenes from the life of Buddha are depicted on gateways of the great stupa at Sanchi, India, which were carved around 100 B.C.

Death of the Buddha. At last, when eighty years old and worn out by his constant travels and labor, the Buddha was invited by a poor smith to a meal. The food was tainted, but Gautama ate it rather than offend his host, although he forbade his disciples to follow his example. Later in the day the Buddha was taken with severe pains, and he knew death to be near. Calling his disciples together, he bade them, "Be ye lamps unto yourselves. Be a refuge to yourselves. Hold fast to the truth as to a lamp. Look not for refuge to anyone beside yourselves." The legend tells us that at that point the faithful Ananda could not restrain himself but went aside and burst into tears. The master gently reproved him, saying, "Enough, Ananda! Do not let yourself be troubled; do not weep! Have I not already, on former occasions, told you that it is in the very nature of all things most near and dear unto us, that we must divide ourselves from them, leave them, sever ourselves from them? What ever is born must be dissolved." After telling his disciples to inform the poor smith that he should not reproach himself for the food, the Buddha addressed the group: "Behold now, brethren, I exhort you saying, 'Decay is inherent in all component things! Work out your salvation with diligence!' "[10] This was the last word of the Blessed One.

Buddhist teachings. What is the fundamental teaching of the Buddha? Briefly stated, it consists of the Four Noble Truths, which were revealed to Buddha in the "great enlightenment," and the Eightfold Path, which is the fourth Noble Truth:

"1. 'the truth of pain,' as manifest in 'birth, old age, sickness, death, sorrow...'

2. 'the truth of the cause of pain,' craving for existence, passion, pleasures, leading to rebirth;

3. 'the truth of cessation of pain,' by the ceasing of craving, by renunciation;

4. 'the truth of the way that leads to the cessation of pain,' vis. the Middle Path, which is the Eight-fold Path consisting of: 'right views, intention, speech, action, livelihood, effort, mindfulness, and concentration.' "[11]

In addition to the above teachings, the Buddha set forth certain moral injunctions: not to kill, not to steal, not to speak falsely, not to be unchaste, and not to drink intoxicating liquors.

A definite relationship existed between Buddhist and *Upanishad* philosophies, although they differ in many important aspects. The Buddha sought to strip the *Upanishad* teachings of the encumbrances and superstitions which had enveloped them with the passage of time. Gautama had no use for the caste system but said that whether a man is born a Brahman or a Sudra has no bearing on his spiritual stature. Only by living the philosophy could one win deliverance from illusion (*maya*). Nor was he interested in rituals or ceremonies or priestly mediators. "Buddhism is personal and individual to the end. One holds fast to one's own personality until one's final beatitude is attained."[12] As a consequence, Buddhism has no trinity (unlike Hinduism) nor does it even posit the existence of a God or First Cause. "Buddhism holds that nothing was created singly or individually. All things in the universe—matter and mind—arose simultaneously, all things in it depending upon one another, the influence of all mutually permeating each, thereby making a universal symphony of spiritual totality. One item lacking, the universe is not complete; without the rest, one item cannot be."[13] When the whole cosmos attains its ideal state, all beings will be in perfect harmony.

Meanwhile, according to the Buddha, the individual cannot hope to attain an ideal state so long as he remains attached by transitory desires to the wheel of Birth and Rebirth. Reincarnation is a necessary doctrine in Buddhism, for only by repeated lives can the individual come to realize that the world of the senses is but a spiritual illusion. Once this is learned, the path by which sorrow is removed opens to the seeker. The strict rules of the Eightfold Path will free him from the bondage of rebirth and make possible a reabsorption into the Universal Life, the "slipping of the dewdrop into the Silent Sea"—the entry into *nirvana.* What is *nirvana,* and does it represent extinction of the individual or rather the annihilation of the illusion of separateness from the One Life? According to one Indian scholar, *nirvana* "is incommunicable, for the Infinite cannot be described by finite words. The utmost that we can do is to throw some light on it by recourse to negative terms. Nirvana is the final result of the extinction of the desire or thirst for rebirth. . . . it is the incomparable and highest goal. . . . Buddha purposely discouraged questions about the reabsorption of the individual soul, as being of no practical value in the quest for salvation."[14]

Buddha as a reformer. There is much justification for considering the Buddha as a reformer of contemporary Indian philosophy and religion. He fought against the rites and dogmas of the Brahmans, broke the iron-bound rules of caste, considered all men equal, and gave the world a code of morals and ethics whose purity is universally recognized. His doctrine of the Middle Path of action shunned fanaticism and extremism of all kinds. Perhaps it was the reasonableness and gentleness of Buddhism which later made it so acceptable to the Chinese.

During the Buddha's lifetime, his teachings spread over the central belt of India to various tribes inhabiting the Himalayan foothills. The Buddha founded orders of monks, with the result that monastic institutions gradually developed into important academic centers for training missionaries and for bringing together students and scholars. Their present-day ruins give some idea of the magnificence of these institutions, which have been termed "the most remarkable contribution of Buddhism to Indian culture."[15]

Although the Buddha himself was a reforming element, many of the evils which he had inveighed against crept into Buddhism in turn after his death. He had demanded that each man work out his own destiny and forbade the worship of gods, yet in time men were praying to him as a deity who could assure their salvation. Later we shall see how his teachings were elaborated into rival metaphysical schools—and how Buddhism in its new form was to spread throughout eastern and southeastern Asia.

Summary

During the formative period in India occurred the foundation of Indus valley civilization, the gradual infiltration of the Indo-Aryans through Hindustan, and the rise of certain highly important institutions. The philosophy and religion of modern India were developed in the *Vedas* and *Upanishads.* Likewise, the all-important caste system with its religious, social, and economic ramifications was gradually elaborated. Buddhism not only gave India and the world new philosophical concepts but later became the great religion of the common people in Ceylon, Tibet, Burma, China, and Japan. Sanskrit developed as the rich literary language of poets who wondered at the ways of the gods and the universe in the *Vedas* and sang the praises of Indo-Aryan warriors in magnificent epics, the *Mahabharata* and the *Ramayana.* Music, painting, sculpture, and architecture progressed during pre-Buddhistic history, as did agriculture and the crafts of the rising cities. Indian social life was thus well rounded and progressive in its pattern.

If we accept the definition that civilization is that stage of life in which society becomes sedentary, creates towns and cities, and so orders its life that its people are made safer and happier, then we can state with positive proof that the Indians not only created a civilization but created one that was flourishing and advanced. The Indo-Aryans ceased their nomadic existence, settled upon the lands that fell to them as conquerors, and built innumerable villages and cities there. From the Dravidians they gained many cultural advantages. These, added to their own heritage, made Indo-Aryan civilization at once unique and enduring. They made definite political advances. Their government evolved from a tribal existence to established political units. They sang rude songs which gradually assumed artistic form and became mighty epics. They used their hands to fashion beautiful sculptured objects and their minds to fashion even more impressive philosophical concepts. Flocks and herds fattened; lands became more extensive and fertile. They expanded eastward until all Hindustan was theirs, and the day was to come when all India also would be their possession.

Chronology of events and developments discussed in this chapter

Chapter 4

Yang Shao culture: *red, black, and white pottery*	2000 B.C.
Lung Shan culture: *thin black pottery; agriculture; social organization*	2000-1700
Shang dynasty: *agrarian society; first "historic dynasty"; excelled in bronze art*	1450-c. 1000
Chou dynasty: *feudalism; village social organization; chivalry*	1027-256
Early Chou: ruler had political control	1027-771
Middle Chou: puppet monarchs; Pa *controlled the power*	771-474
Confucius: social and moral codes; linked heaven, the state, and the family; reverence for the past	551-479
Contending States: incessant warfare; new military techniques	474-256
Mencius: democratic doctrine of the place of the individual in government and his right to rebel	372-289
Lao-Tzu: revolt against the limits of the intellect	4th century

The Wei and the Hwang Ho

Ancient China: Paleolithic times to 256 B.C.

THE TWENTIETH CENTURY has witnessed immense upheaval in the most populous country of the world. In the early years of our century, China underwent a revolution that established a republic after more than two thousand years of monarchical rule. In the succeeding decades, the young republic had to cope with the multitudinous problems of at least 400 million people whose grinding poverty and virtual social inertia stood in striking contrast to the swift moving technological developments of the West, and of their westernized neighbor across the Yellow Sea, Japan. From 1931 to 1945, Japan sought by force to dismember China both politically and economically, and even threatened its very existence as a sovereign state. Emerging from the Second World War, the Chinese Republic enjoyed international status as one of the Big Five—yet internally it was all but prostrate, and exposed to fierce ideological tempests. In the civil war that followed, the government which had successfully withstood the Japanese aggressor was forced to retreat to the island of Formosa, and the mainland passed to the control of a Communist regime.

Whatever may be China's future role, it must be ever increasingly related to the course of global events. No longer will China be able—or indeed allowed—to enjoy that relative isolation created largely by its geographical situation and fostered by an indigenous culture so rich that it prompted the Chinese for centuries to look upon the outside world as barbarian. Certainly the impact of twentieth-century technology and ideology alike is bound to create far-reaching problems and changes in Chinese institutions and attitudes. The extent of these changes cannot readily be surmised at present, but any attempted estimate should take cognizance of the history of the Chinese people.

This history is worth examining for its own sake. For untold centuries the Chinese have been refining the art of living and creating institutions which will endure. Their approach may betray a conservatism at times irritating to the speed-conditioned westerner, but its humanistic emphasis must also excite his respect, and its poise perhaps his envy. The history of China explains the temperament of the people, their reasonableness, realism, urbanity, and fundamental good nature. Likewise, it explains the splendid cultural and intellectual contributions made during an unbroken period of at least three thousand years. The Chinese created an art which did not seek to be pretentious and awe-inspiring, but instead succeeded in being natural and exquisite. Their poetry is likewise concise and restrained, their philosophy less concerned with the cosmos than with providing workable rules of ethical and moral conduct. Their science in turn has been characteristically practical and progressive. They made advances in sericulture so that the raising of silkworms would give them more beautiful clothes, found out about tea so they could enjoy a pleasant beverage and then created the world's finest porcelains in which to drink it, invented paper and block printing in order to multiply the learning which they so dearly love, discovered the value of the magnetic compass so they might travel more safely from one place to another, invented folding fans to keep themselves cool in summer and umbrellas to keep themselves dry in winter, and finally hit upon gunpowder, which, because they pride themselves upon being reasonable people, they used for fireworks in celebrations and not for war.

China: Its Earliest Civilization

Geography of China. We have seen the importance of geography in Indian civilization. In China too the physical features of the land are inseparably linked with the civilization of the people. This huge country has a total area of over four million square miles (larger than that of the United States), while its population, estimated in excess of 450 million, is three times as great as ours. On the east China is bounded by the Pacific Ocean, whose expanse made attack from that direction wellnigh impossible until modern times. On the west, northwest, and southwest great mountain chains, vast desert stretches, and semiarid plateaus isolate and protect the middle regions.

There is a difference of thirty-five degrees in China's latitudes, ensuring a variety of climate. The south is subtropical, with monsoons and typhoons, while the north experiences extremes of heat and cold. There is a corresponding variety of vegetation, aided by the natural fertility of great sections of the country. The north possesses the loess, a type of soil which was perhaps built up of dust carried by winds eastward from the plains of central Asia. It is exceedingly fertile. The central and northeast areas contain a large alluvial plain formed by deposits from the muddy waters of the Yangtze and Hwang Ho, in which agriculture flourishes.

China proper (roughly the area of the map on the opposite page) comprises three major regions: the valley of the Hwang Ho, the Yangtze valley, and southern China. Through the first region flows the sluggish Hwang Ho (or the Yellow River), depositing great amounts of silt so that the bottom of the river is sometimes higher than the surrounding land, necessitating the use of dikes to keep the water in the proper channel. In times of flood the river may break through the dikes, sweeping away crops and farms and destroying untold numbers of lives. With good reason the Chinese have termed the Hwang Ho "China's Sorrow."

Farther south is the valley of the Yangtze Kiang, one of the greatest rivers in the world. Thirty-two hundred miles in length, it allows ocean-going vessels up its channel for six hundred miles, while smaller steamships can travel upstream still another nine hundred miles.

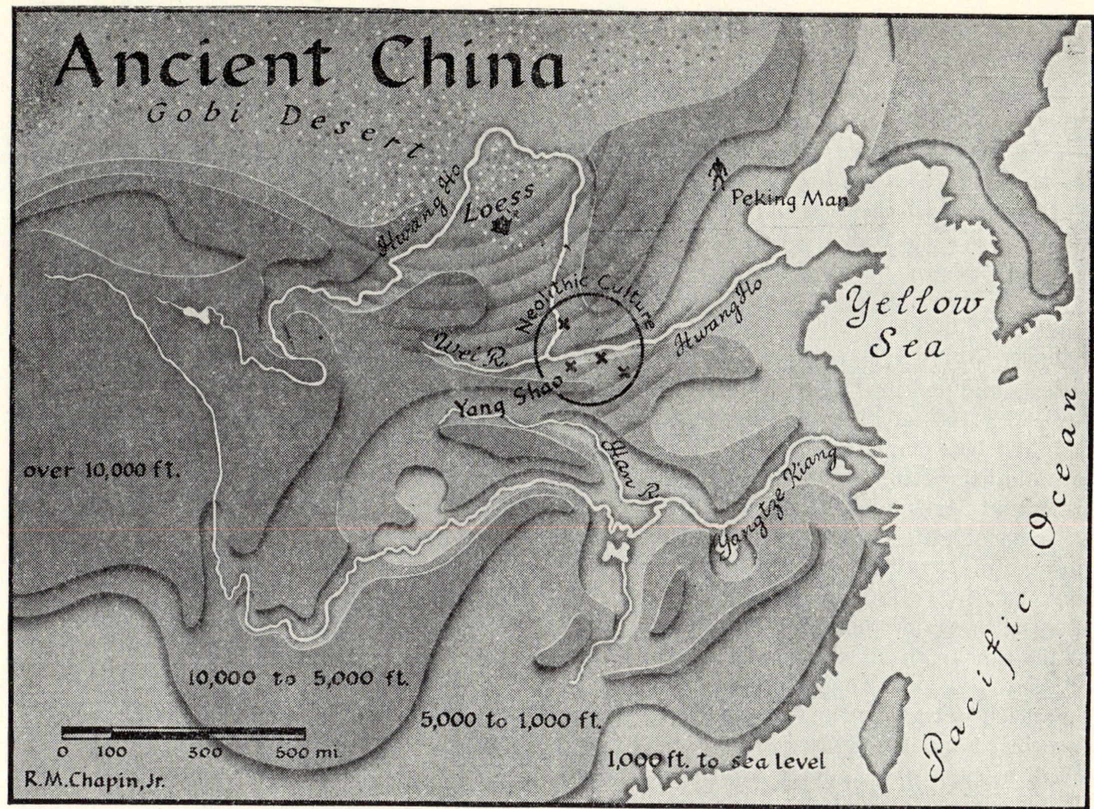

The Yangtze valley today contains many large cities. The fertile soil and reliable rainfall produce an abundance of crops. Southern China is very mountainous and is rich in mineral resources and citrous products. This southern region also has a large aboriginal population.

"The history of the Chinese is the story of the gradual peopling of the great river valleys and plains of China, and of this people's expansion and development in their own part of Asia and beyond, on both the mainland and the coastal islands."[1] As we shall see, important culture sites have been excavated, for example, in central China at the confluence of the Hwang Ho and its tributary, the Wei. Like Egypt, Mesopotamia, and India, China first developed a fluvial civilization. Water was at once the cheapest and most efficient means of transportation and communication. The major rivers have many tributaries which act as waterways. China is even today largely fluvial in its civilization. China has long been more homogeneous politically, racially, and culturally than many other areas of comparable size, because the presence of so many important rivers has made communication a relatively simple matter.

Early historical fables. China is the historian's paradise, for there he has always been honored and his works prized. For this reason perhaps, China has the most nearly complete historical records left by any civilization. When, however, we push back the centuries far enough, we come to accounts which are no longer history but mythology. In those fabulous legends, the arts of civilization are credited to a succession of splendid and wise emperors. Thus the emperor Yü, for example, was supposed to have controlled the floods of nine rivers by cutting through nine mountains and creating nine lakes. "But for Yü we should all have been fishes," the story goes.

Origins of the Chinese people. Yet if the ancient accounts abound in fables, scholarship and a scientific sifting of available evidence have contributed a growing body of facts which is scarcely less fascinating for being authentic. The origins of the Chinese people are ancient indeed—for man made his appearance in the Far East perhaps as early as one million years ago. Working in caves south of

Peking, paleontologists in 1929 discovered the bones of *Sinanthropus pekinensis* (see Chapter 1, page 27), the Peking Man. Of an age and type somewhat similar to *Pithecanthropus erectus,* the Peking Man possessed certain characteristics—such as conformation of jawbones and teeth—which are peculiar to the Mongoloid race. Peking Man represents an early Paleolithic culture; he lived in caves, made use of crude stone implements and knew how to make fire.

There are great gaps in our knowledge of human and cultural development in China. Around 50,000 B.C., lived a Stone Age hunting people whose remains have been found in communities scattered over north China, Mongolia, and Manchuria.

Archaeologists have been able to trace a number of Neolithic cultures appearing after 4000 B.C. in various parts of China. About 2000 B.C. certain important cultures evolved, which can be classified as late Neolithic. One of these, the Yang Shao culture—named from an ancient settlement in western Honan province in central China—was discovered by the Swedish scientist J. Gunnar Andersson. These people had acquired outstanding skill in the fashioning of pottery; they may in fact have made use of a potter's wheel. Consequently, their culture is identified by splendid examples of their pottery. Of different shapes and strikingly designed with motifs in red, black, and white, this pottery bears certain resemblances to Neolithic vases and vessels found in Turkestan and western Asia, but scholars are inclined to doubt that the Yang Shao people derived their culture from the Near East. Rather, it is believed they developed their culture in north and western China, though they possibly included Turkish and Tibetan elements. These people were for the most part cattle breeders and agriculturists.

Pottery vase of the Yang Shao culture about 3000 B.C., *decorated with a rhythmic spiral pattern in black and purple. A similarity to Cretan pottery may be noticed (see page 126).*

Meanwhile, in about 2000 B.C. appeared in eastern China, in what is now Shantung province, another culture, the Lung Shan (named after the site where the principal discoveries were made). Here again, the Neolithic culture was distinguished by the production of exceptionally fine pottery, this time black in color and often thin, unpainted, and lustrous in appearance. The people of the Lung Shan culture were farmers, although they also hunted and kept herds. They lived in mud houses in villages commonly surrounded by walls of pounded earth. "There are unmistakable signs that their society was already divided into classes, and that they had a state organization at the head of affairs."[2] The Lung Shan culture plays an important role in the history of Chinese civilization, for all evidence points to its being the "missing link" between the earlier Neolithic cultures and the Shang period (see below) which originated somewhere about 1500 B.C.

The Lung Shan culture existed in eastern China until about 1700 B.C., and possibly somewhat longer in the south. According to traditional Chinese history, this is also supposed to have been the period of the Hsia, which the Chinese considered to have been the first of their ruling dynasties. The traditional genealogy of the Hsia rulers may well have been a falsification of later times, for actually we have no tangible evidence that they existed. On the other hand, despite the semilegendary character of this dynasty, there is some likelihood that between 1800 and 1500 B.C. a small state of Hsia made its appearance in what is now the province of Shansi near the last bend of the Yellow River. Because of the outstanding excellence of bronze vessels in the next great period—the Shang—it is quite possible that proficiency in the use of metal had developed at this time in centers along the Yellow River.

The Shang Dynasty

F*irst of the "historic" dynasties.* To this point we have been dealing with basically Stone Age cultures which did not possess writing. As we enter the second half of the second millennium B.C. (c. 1500-1450), we leave the mists of preliterate China, in which archaeological fact alone provides us with a guidepost to find our way through a morass of legends and fables, and we come onto terrain where the historian finds his footing increasingly secure. For here he enters the civilization of the Shang dynasty, of whose origins we know little, but of whose existence there is no doubt.

Some historians prefer to call the Shang period "pre-Chinese" because it lacks some of the characteristics to be found in Chinese civilization at a later stage. For example, during the Shang period, religion was basically concerned with fertility rites connected with soil and vegetation; society had matriarchal elements of family life in distinction to the patriarchal pattern which later evolved, and the feudal system was primitive. On the other hand, the people of the Shang civilization led an agrarian life familiar to later times, practiced sericulture, developed a form of writing upon which subsequent Chinese script was to build, and made use of bronze in forms which we associate with Chinese artistic canons.

While we know little of the origins of this Bronze Age culture, the theory most accepted today is that the Shang people came from the same racial stock as the Neolithic inhabitants of north China. In fact, as stated earlier, the Shang culture probably descended from the Lung Shan. There are indications that the Shang inhabited the plains of what is now northern Honan, southern Hopeh, and southwestern Shantung and that the most remote of the Shang sites was not much more than one hundred miles from the Hwang Ho.

The excavation of the capital city has revealed much about Shang culture. Like the Lung Shan settlements, it was surrounded by a mud wall and included the ruler's palace and rectangular houses, possibly used by the artisan class. The excavation also unearthed a large number of objects inscribed with writing. For example, inscriptions have been found on bronze pieces, ceremonial daggers, jade, and pottery. However, the largest number of inscriptions were made on "oracle bones"—fragments of animal bones and also tortoise shells. These fragments, which have provided much new information on conditions prior to the twelfth century B.C., contain records of questions put to the people's ancestors and gods on numerous matters. "The divination itself probably took place in the ancestral temple. The diviner asked a question, such as 'So-and-so is ill; if this fact is announced to the spirit of Grandfather Ting (will he aid him to recover)?' Heat was applied to the back of the shell or bone, and this caused a T-shaped crack to appear on its face. From this crack the diviner decided whether the answer of the spirits was favourable or unfavourable, and announced the result to the king or other person for whom he was divining."[3] From such practices may have developed the cult of ancestor worship in China, which some historians believe originated at this time.

These inscriptions show the art of writing was well advanced in Shang times. Some of the

Bronze lei of the Anyang type from the Shang dynasty. Bronze vessels, used in religious ceremonials, contained nourishment for the dead.

pictographs appear similar to those found in Egypt and elsewhere, but there is also much to be said in favor of the view that Chinese writing developed independently. Like modern Chinese script, Shang writing was pictorial in character, though more rudimentary. The Shang Chinese possessed over 2000 written words—compared with some 10,000 words in the vocabulary of an average person—and were consequently in a position to express themselves with facility. We know much less about the spoken language. Likely the Chinese had a larger vocabulary than can be enumerated on the basis of the written language and undoubtedly they spoke a number of dialects. Our present knowledge of Shang writing shows, therefore, that China had already advanced to a high intellectual level.

Description of the Shang state. At the head of the state was the ruler, who commanded the armies in battle but whose political power evidently was not extensive, since the more distant parts of the kingdom were under the control of strong nobles. The ruler's most important function seems to have been that of high priest, assisted by other priests. The official religion of this period was the worship of a supreme deity, Shang-ti, a god of vegetation, while the earth was worshiped as a mother goddess "who bore the plants and animals procreated by Shang-ti." The sun and stars were also given reverence for their effect upon the earth and its inhabitants. To stimulate the earth's fertility, recourse was made to human sacrifices. It thus becomes apparent that religion at this period had a dual role—to offer sacrifices to various deities and elements to insure fertility and abundance, and to pay homage to the royal ancestors in order not to offend the spiritual world and to seek their advice by means of divination already described.

Religion made use of ritual, which in turn fostered sacred dancing and music, the latter apparently held in special favor. Various instruments evolved in these early centuries are still in use, including drums, cymbals, bells, ocarinas, and stringed instruments. The musical system was pentatonic (five-toned) and highly mathematical in its principles.

The most famous artistic expression of the Shang period is its magnificent bronzes. The process of making and casting bronze was probably imported into China from the West at a time perhaps antedating the Shang dynasty. During the Shang period advances were made in technique which raised the bronzes to new levels of beauty. The bronzes unearthed in recent years at Anyang disclose full mastery of this art. These examples display architectural massiveness and equilibrium, elegance of form, and decorative splendor. Among the bronze pieces are the pot tripods, known as *li*, and various ceremonial vessels (see page 101). Added to these bronzes, excavations have also brought to light marble sculptures, jade ritual objects, wrought ivory, dagger axes, harness ornaments, and chariot fittings.

All of these discoveries prove that the Shang civilization was one of considerable material advancement, at least in the capital. Urban life was marked by economic specialization. But the major part of the population was composed of peasants who grew wheat, millet, and rice, and bred cattle, sheep, pigs, dogs, and horses. "They do not seem to have had a real plough, but only a sort of hoe and a spade that was held by one person and dragged through the soil by a second person by means of a rope."[4]

Warfare was frequent in Shang times; it was during this period that the Chinese adopted a new military technique—the two-wheeled chariot, which was probably imported from nomadic neighbors. The chariot, used by the ruling house and upper class, facilitated the expansion of Shang domination and colonization.

In the eleventh century the Shang state was confronted with a new, warlike power which had developed in the northwest—the Chou. In that same century, as the result of a successful rebellion, these Chou from the rugged western marches overthrew the Shang ruling house, which had evidently become effete, and established a great new dynasty.

The Chou Dynasty (c. 1027-256 B.C.)

Beginnings of the Chou. Prior to their assumption of power, the Chou had been dwelling west of the Shang state, where their culture was related to the Yang Shao (red and black painted pottery culture). Their conquest of China was accomplished with the aid of other peoples, with the result that once established, the Chou rulers distributed different regions as fiefs to their relatives and to the chieftains of those tribes which had helped make victory possible. As a consequence, over a thousand feudal states were created. The imperial authority was installed in Shensi near modern Sian. As the map on this page shows, the Chou kingdom at its height extended from the southern part of Manchuria to a small section south of the Yangtze River and from the seacoast westward to Kansu.

While it is difficult to give precise dates for the Chou dynasty—whose unrivaled length of time upon the imperial throne amounted to some seven and three-quarter centuries—it is possible to divide the Chou age into three convenient periods: Early Chou: c. 1027-771 B.C., when the Chou monarchs actually could claim to rule their kingdom; Middle Chou: c. 771-474 B.C., which was marked by the transfer of the royal capital eastward, and the loss of royal power; Late Chou: c. 474-256 B.C., which is known as the era of Contending States, when continuous warfare prevailed.

The last Chou ruler abdicated in 256 B.C. The struggle between rival states continued for another thirty-five years, however, and culminated finally in the triumph of the Ch'in in 221 B.C.

Early Chou. During the first centuries of their rule, the Chou monarchs enjoyed considerable prestige and were able to keep their position fairly secure. Their retention of control, however, depended upon the support of the feudal nobles since the Chou themselves were numerically small and, as we have seen, had acquired power with the help of others.

The empire was large and its administration cumbersome. The subjugated nomadic tribes of Turks and Mongols, who were situated close to the capital, kept rebelling because the Chou garrison settlements diminished their pasturage. The feudal lords at first had demonstrated their loyalty by providing their king with auxiliary forces to maintain order. As time went on, however, they became progressively immersed in local affairs and in strengthening their own position. As a consequence, the burden of holding the nomadic tribes in check and of administering the empire fell increasingly upon the inadequate resources of the Chou rulers themselves. These rulers found it difficult to cope with the ambitions of dissident nobles, especially those bent on consolidating their own strength in areas removed from the capital.

By about 800 B.C., imperial authority had declined sufficiently to permit principalities to act pretty much as they pleased. At last the time came when certain nobles, who had been gaining power at the expense of weaker neighbors, felt sufficiently strong to instigate a revolt. In 771 B.C. an alliance among them resulted in a successful attack upon the capital and the slaying of the ruler.

Middle Chou. One of the royal family, however, managed to escape eastward to Loyang, where the Chou dynasty established another capital at which it resided for another five centuries. Yet the period when the Chou could claim to rule as well as to reign was over. Henceforth, they were fated to an impotent existence with their functions limited to those of a religious nature and to arbitrating differences among feudal lords. So weak, indeed, did the Chou monarchs become that eventually the most powerful of the princes exercised a hegemony known as the *Pa*. "The functions of the *Pa* were to repulse the increasingly troublesome barbarians and to enforce respect for the Chou sovereign. The institution of the *Pa* prevented another strong state from setting itself up as ruler in place of the Chou. This delicate balancing of power and the traditional respect for kingship kept a member of the Chou on the throne."[5]

The Middle Chou period was also marked by the immigration of peoples into the rich Yangtze valley, a diminution in the number of feudal states, and the emergence of powerful princely states.

Late Chou. We now enter the period often referred to as that of the Contending States. It was marked not only by merciless conflict in contrast to the chivalrous warfare of the past, but by the introduction of new military techniques. Previously, armies had been made up principally of nobles fighting from chariots; now one of the northern states copied its Turkish and Mongol neighbors and equipped itself with companies of archers mounted on horseback. Other states adopted this new technique. In addition, the art of siege developed with the invention of catapults.

The savage and almost incessant warfare of this period culminated in a struggle between two states. One of these, the Ch'u, had gained control over the Yangtze valley, while the other state, the Ch'in, had grown to power in the northwest of China. In 256, the last of the Chou dynasty abdicated in favor of the ruler of Ch'in. Although this marked the end of the royal house of Chou, the struggle for power to reunite China did not cease for another thirty-five years.

In this struggle, the Ch'in state was favored in certain respects. Geographically, it was protected by mountains, deserts, and steppes which rendered attack difficult. Its inhabitants were hardy and although the Chinese considered them barbarous because of Turkish and Tibetan elements in their blood, they proved themselves adept in the arts of both peace and war. The Ch'in rulers encouraged immigration and trade, built roads which could at once serve military and commercial needs, and engaged in an ambitious irrigation program to assure ample food production. A military machine superior to that of any other state was carefully organized with particular attention being paid to the use of cavalry. In addition, the state was strengthened by the acceptance of the views of the Legalists, an important philosophical school of this period which championed the theory of absolutism on the part of the ruler and obedience on that of his subjects. Such a theory was admirably suited to a military state such as the Ch'in, and it provided the social cohesion necessary for the conquest of the other states in China. Finally, in 221 B.C. the last of the rival states was conquered. China had been reunited by the Ch'in under the leadership of one of history's most remarkable men, who took the title of Shih Huang Ti—the First Emperor. In Chapter 7 we shall discuss the further exploits of this "Chinese Caesar."

Political organization under the Chou. We have reviewed briefly the chronological history of the Chou dynasty. But this period is also notable for its political, social, and economic institutions, many of which have endured to modern times.

During the Chou period, the king was called the Son of Heaven, a title retained by later rulers. Theoretically, he ruled because of the decree or mandate of heaven. Thus he

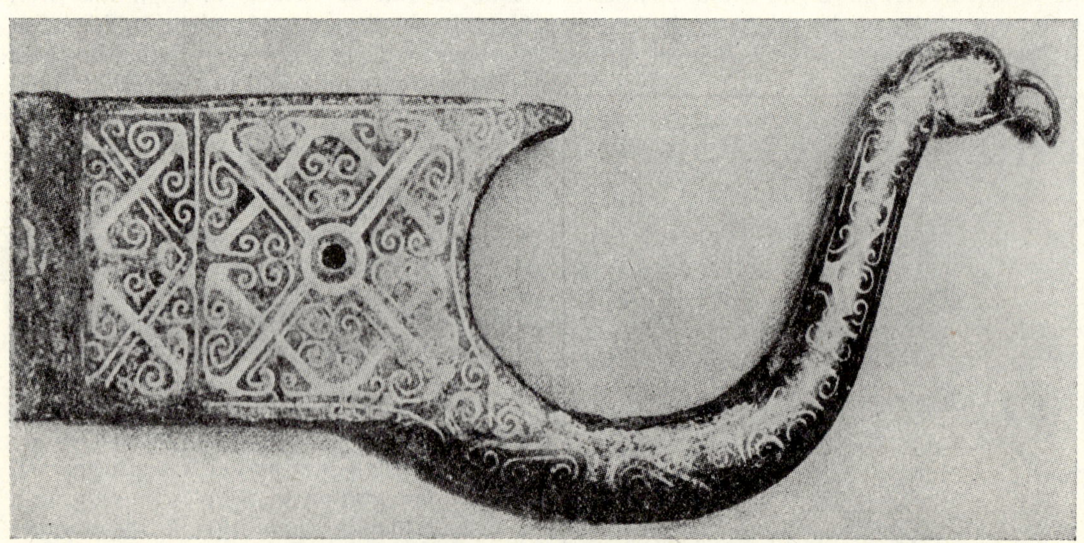

BRONZE CHAIR OR CHARIOT MOUNT INLAID WITH SILVER, 5TH TO 3RD CENTURIES, B.C.

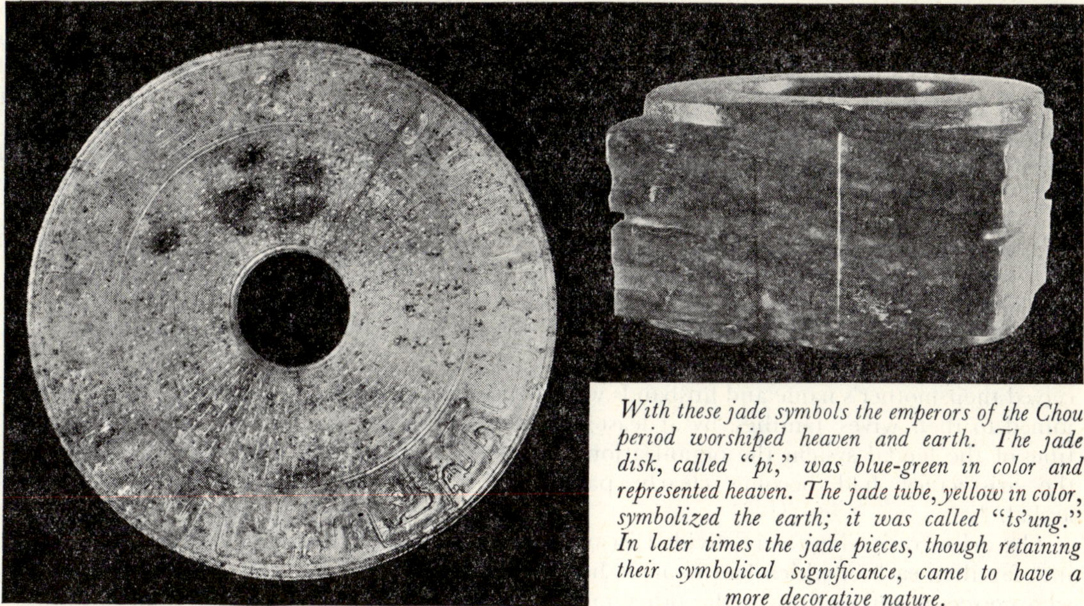

With these jade symbols the emperors of the Chou period worshiped heaven and earth. The jade disk, called "pi," was blue-green in color and represented heaven. The jade tube, yellow in color, symbolized the earth; it was called "ts'ung." In later times the jade pieces, though retaining their symbolical significance, came to have a more decorative nature.

bore the title of *Wang*—Ruler. The ruler had a chief minister and other officials who attended to such matters as agriculture, public works, religious rites, the army, and the monarch's personal affairs. They also administered the royal domains which the *Wang* ruled directly.

The country was organized on a feudal basis; lands not directly controled by the monarch were parceled out as fiefs to his many vassals. The feudal princes and lords owed the ruler homage and had to pay him tribute in kind as well as provide auxiliary forces for the maintenance of law and order. They were received at court with a strict ritual designed to exalt the position of the Son of Heaven. The feudal hierarchy was organized in grades "distinguished by the titles which have been translated as equivalent to the European, Duke, Marquis, Count, Viscount, and Baron."[6] In the early part of the Chou period, the title of Duke *(kung)* was restricted to the rulers of the greater states or those connected with the royal house. In later times, however, rulers of other states "assumed such titles as they considered suited to their dignity, until in 325 B.C. all the surviving rulers usurped the royal title itself."[7] As we have seen this was the time when the territorial lords had become virtually independent of their royal ruler and China had actually developed into a confederacy of powerful princes.

Although the ruler was now politically impotent, the feudal system rendered him indispensable for two reasons. First, the Son of Heaven was required to make the title of a lord legitimate, to mediate between the rival claims of nobles, and to formalize the existence of a new state. Secondly, from the religious standpoint, he was to China as the pharaoh had been to Egypt. He alone could act as the great mediator between heaven and earth. He performed the sacred sacrifices to ensure that a proper harmony and balance would continue to exist between the spirit of heaven and the spirit of earth, that the fertility of the soil might be assured, and that the four seasons continue to bless China.

The political history of later China was affected by certain developments during the era of Contending States. For example, the state of Ch'in established two classes of administrative units—*chun* (commandery) and *hsien* (district), administered by paid officials of the crown and not, as formerly, by the actual owners of the land. As a result, a man with ability could now enter the service of a ruler as an administrator. "This brought about other developments. The scholars of the time began private teaching and thereby opened the way for the common people to receive an education and enter government service. This soon gave rise to a class of professional statesmen. Occasionally, a state would hire from the frontier areas a non-Chinese who was skilled in military matters and would put him in charge of army affairs. Thus was created a class of professional soldiers."[8]

Social organization. The *Wang* and aristocracy were sharply separated from the mass of the people on the basis of ownership of land and family descent. The nobility were members of a widespread clan system, with each clan professing to trace its descent through the male line to a common ancestor, such as a monarch, hero, or god. "If, as seems possible, in primitive times the children received their mother's name and husbands were joined to their wives' families, by at least the time of the feudal system the organization of the aristocracy had become clearly patriarchal."[9]

The aristocratic clans were divided in turn into families, each of which had its male head who possessed authority over the other members. Until the later stages of Chou rule, the nobility held the chief posts in the army and occupied the important administrative offices. Naturally, because of the importance attached by the aristocracy to its genealogy, great emphasis was placed upon the elaborate rituals connected with ancestor worship. Such observances appear to have been "the privilege of the land-owning clans, just as the higher rites of sacrifice to the gods of the soil and crops were reserved for a prince who had absolute power over some territory, however small. Princely rank depended on such lordship, and was intimately bound up with these religious observances."[10]

Underlying this feudal structure was the code of chivalry. The quarrels of the nobles have been described as being as tedious as those which disturbed the political life of medieval Europe. Yet like the Middle Ages in Europe, they were marked by a strict code of behavior. Whereas the medieval knight fought and jousted on horseback, the Chinese nobles waged war riding in chariots and arrayed in breastplates, while carrying bows, lances, and standards bearing symbolic devices. The chivalric code decreed that the life of a vanquished adversary must be spared if he had borne himself bravely, not only because to do otherwise would be ungenerous but because extreme measures ran counter to a code which emphasized the virtues of moderation.

The conduct of the feudal lord in peacetime was also governed by the chivalric code. "His belts ornamented with jade trinkets which made 'a harmonious tinkling sound', he would come to the court of his seigneur to take part in tournaments of the noble sport of archery which was accompanied by musical airs and interspersed with elegant salutations, the whole regulated like a ballet."[11] Likewise, strict etiquette regulated behavior at the royal audiences, the holding of which was to continue for some two and a half thousand years and end only with the fall of the Manchu dynasty in 1912 A.D.

In contrast to the privileged position of the feudal nobility was the lot of the masses. They possessed no political rights of their own, nor did they own the land on which they passed their lives, although peasant proprietorship may have begun toward the end of the period. Rather, they cultivated the fields for their masters, paid taxes to the prince, and served as common soldiers in his armies. Families lived together in villages, which derived their names from the group that had founded them. These villages, perhaps on heights overlooking the fields and out of the reach of floods, would usually be walled and clustered about the residence of a local noble or official, while village life would revolve around the market place. As time elapsed, the village community came to include members who were not related by blood to the original family groups. Thus the village became an economic and political entity, whose leaders were chosen by common assent instead of along kinship lines. This arrangement still exists; we see, then, the formation in Chou times of one of the most fundamental of Chinese institutions, the village social structure.

The Chou period also saw the spread of urban life, concomitantly with the growth of trade. Centers developed at the capitals of the *Wang* and the feudal princes. It was also at this time that urban society began to evolve beyond the family pattern of organization. Craftsmen and merchants would group themselves into associations—guilds—according to the type of industry or commerce in which they were engaged. While these guilds may have come into existence primarily for economic reasons, they seem—like the medieval guilds in Europe—to have been concerned with protecting and advancing the social interests of their members. Thus a merchant or artisan undertook certain personal as well as business responsibilities for his apprentices. We are told that by about 600 B.C., industry had become specialized along craft lines, while trade was divided into mercantile associations.

Economic organization. Whether we speak of China of the Chou period or of the twentieth century, agriculture has been the occupation of the overwhelming proportion of the population. "How to keep farmers well fed, well clothed, and contented has been the chief concern of Chinese statesmen. As rainfall in northern China is irregular and usually inadequate, irrigation works were developed as early as the Chou period...to insure reliable crops. Irrigation works were first developed on the plains of northern China in the states of Han and Wei. In the third century B.C. irrigation was begun in the state of Ch'in (modern Shensi)."[12] It is interesting to note that some of the immense irrigation systems of this period are still contributing to China's economic life.

The farmers raised millet, rice, wheat, and barley as well as fruits and vegetables; pigs and chickens appear to have been as omnipresent in Chou as in subsequent periods. According to tradition, land was originally laid out in plots which could be cultivated in common by eight families; this ancient system, however, seems to have passed away by the time the era of Contending States was reached. Developments in that era were to revolutionize both the cultivation and the ownership of land. According to one authority, "the beginning of the iron age, the use of oxen to pull the plough, and the increasing application of animal fertilizer to cultivation and the consequent revolutionary growth in the productivity of labor in agriculture, played havoc with the ancient land system and gradually brought about private land ownership."[13]

A central problem in Chinese economics has been the small size of the fields of the majority of workers, so that they cannot produce a crop surplus to tide them over during periods of scarcity. That the small farm was in existence in Chou times is shown by the "first family-budget study in China," made about 400 B.C. by a minister of the state of Wei: "A farmer having a family of five usually cultivates a farm of 100 *mou* [a *mou* of the Chou dynasty was smaller than the modern *mou* which is approximately one-sixth of an acre]. From every *mou* he can get one and a half piculs of millet, making a total of 150 piculs of millet. From this total, one-tenth is taken as tax. So what remains amounts to 135 piculs. A person usually consumes one and a half piculs per month. A family of five will consume 90 piculs for the whole year. Subtracting this amount, the remainder will be only 45 piculs. At the price of 30 cash per picul, 45 piculs can be sold for a sum of 1350 cash. On religious services 300 cash must be spent, leaving only 1050 cash. For clothing one must spend 300 cash on every person, making 1500 cash per family of five. Therefore the deficit at the end of a year is 450 cash. Nothing is put aside for such emergencies as sickness, funeral expenses, and extra taxes. Consequently the farmers are always in a state of poverty."[14] It may well be that the deficit was sometimes made up in other ways, but the fact that two-thirds of the farmer's crop was consumed in feeding his family alone is indicative of the low standard on which he had to subsist—a situation similar to that revealed by twentieth-century studies of Chinese family budgets.

Although agriculture was the chief occupation of the majority of the population, trade and industry undoubtedly flourished during Chou times. Merchants sold beautiful linens and silks; tailors made brocaded gowns for the rich. Leatherworkers fashioned gaiters, and jewelers and their assistants carefully cut exquisite jades and made earrings or highly ornamented ivory combs and pins for the coiffures of noble ladies.

Furniture played an important role in making the abodes of the rich comfortable and luxurious. Skilled craftsmen made screens of embroidered silk and curtained couches. Woodcarvers designed beautiful panels for the lower portions of home partitions. Kitchen utensils of pottery and iron occupied the efforts of still more skilled laborers, while one guild of workers devoted its attention to the creation of bronze vessels.

Custom and fashion in ancient China. In the feudal courts a strict code of manners developed. The code became so important to the nobility as a symbol of gentle breeding and so complex in its ramifications that the nobles devoted years to its mastery. The status of women was evidently high; the literature of the Chou dynasty indicates the relatively great freedom which they enjoyed. The history of China, in fact, is replete with incidents where a woman wielded even royal power.

Marriage, then as now, was arranged by the parents of the youth and the girl, but often the choice was disregarded by either the man or woman. As a rule, a man might have but one wife, although a husband was permitted to possess concubines. Often the bride of a young noble would take along as a gift for her husband a younger sister and perhaps a cousin. It was the wife, nevertheless, who was the mistress of the household and who worshiped the ancestral spirit with her husband. It was likewise the rule that her oldest son should be the heir.

Life was becoming increasingly refined and luxurious among the wealthy classes, while poverty among the peasants and unskilled laborers was prevalent. The houses of the poor were hovels of earth and thatched roofs, whereas the abodes of the rich were constructed of brick with tiled roofs and laid out in groups of buildings separated by courts and gardens.

Food was served in dishes which might be made of bamboo, bronze, or earthenware and was eaten with chopsticks sometimes fashioned of ivory. The peasants raised swine and poultry and lived largely on millet in the north and rice in the south. The rich had sumptuous banquets involving the "five flavors," the sweet and sour, the salty and spicy, and the bitter.

The costume of the period was not unlike that worn in the Manchu dynasty of a later period. Over a long gown a shorter coat was worn. Ornaments of gold and jade and precious stones decorated women's ears and fingers, and some ladies of the seventh century B.C. wore wigs.

Many of our present-day amusements were to be found among the leisure occupations of Chou courtiers. They would while away their time playing chess, perfecting their horsemanship, hunting, training horses and dogs, gambling on dice and cockfights, and fencing.

Progress despite social upheaval. The long Chou dynasty and the short period following its demise, which ended with the reuniting of China in 221 B.C., were times of political and social upheaval. Yet these centuries were also full of tremendous intellectual activity and of evolutionary progress. "The Chinese consider this their classical age—when some of the most memorable poetry and prose were composed; when the laws were written down for everyone to see; when market places increased and a money economy appeared; when advances in craftsmanship and methods of production, notably fertilizers, irrigation, and the traction plow, were made; when iron began to displace bronze in common tools and weapons; when science and thinking took great leaps forward, and increasing numbers of new ideas began to seep through the land barriers to the west and southwest to stimulate their own native genius."[15] Communication improved with the construction of roads and canals. In science, astronomy was making good progress so that by the fifth century it was known that the year contained 365¼ days, while Halley's comet was observed at least as far back as 240 B.C. These advances were to affect the course of Chinese civilization.

Yet far-reaching as these were, they may still be overshadowed by another phenomenon: in the three centuries beginning with the sixth century B.C., China's most important philosophical teachings were formulated by a group of men destined to influence intimately all subsequent Chinese thought down to our own century.

Early Philosophy

Chinese emphasis on moral philosophy. Chinese philosophy has from the outset emphasized the moral qualities of man, rather than his intellectual and material capacities. Unlike the Indians the Chinese have not been overly interested in metaphysics, nor have they paid particular attention to questions relating to the nature of the universe, as did the early Greeks, for example. "Chinese philosophy, on the other hand, because of its emphasis upon the way of the 'Inner Sage,' has delved deeply into the methods of self-cultivation.... And in this respect China truly has a great contribution to offer."[16] Self-cultivation in Chinese philosophy manifested itself in a deep preoccupation with two subjects: the problems of man as an individual, his actions as a private citizen, and his obligations as a member of the state; and the establishment of satisfactory codes of morals and ethics.

The later Chou period saw the fruition of Chinese philosophy. As we have noted, the period of the Contending States was highly unstable, consequently political institutions, social organization, and the economic structure all underwent fundamental changes. Men asked themselves how an end might be put to the prevailing discord and war, and whether some principle of moral authority could be discovered which would unite society under an ideal government. In their efforts to work out a rational solution, it was not so much the form of political organization which troubled the Chinese philosophers (as, we shall see, was the case with other peoples, such as the Greeks). The ancient Chinese accepted monarchy as natural. The problem to them was the creation of moral principles which should instill in ruler and subject alike the highest expressions of virtue and benevolence.

Confucius. The most famous and influential of all Chinese philosophers was Confucius, who was born in 551 B.C. somewhere near the present town of Chüfu in Shantung. Born into a family descended from priests of the Shang dynasty, Confucius received a scholarly education and then began teaching others. He also engaged for a period in public life and is said to have become an official of the state of Lu in 501 B.C., but later resigned because of opposition to certain actions of the feudal ruler. He spent the last years of his life wandering with his disciples and died in 479 B.C. One scholar calls Confucius "a punctilious gentleman of the old school," basing this observation on the sentence from the tenth book of the *Analects* which states of Confucius that "If his mat were not straight he would not sit on it."[17] He was evidently gracious and kindly, urbane and courteous, and of unblemished personal character.

Confucius' teachings. Confucius was not concerned with formulating theories to explain the nature of the universe or of knowledge. Rather, he laid down moral and social codes to govern the relationships of individuals with one another and with society as a whole. Confucius retained the basis of the old Cult of Heaven by stressing that the universe was governed by law which regulated the stars and planets in the heaven. Likewise, it was the duty of men to govern themselves in harmony with this universal principle.

In the universe, heaven and earth are

Proverbially ugly, Confucius gazes good-naturedly from this silk painting (from a later period).

the bases; husband and wife have similar roles in society. Consequently, the family must be the foundation of social organization. Since the state is a part of society, the family is also the foundation of the state. At this point, Confucius added the patriarchal concept which the Chou had emphasized when they conquered China. "In the universe, heaven is the directing force; and in the family, father is the directing authority. In the State the position of the sovereign corresponds to that of heaven in the universe, and of father in the family....He is the directing authority of the State. In order to preserve the family virtues in political organization, Confucius became an ardent advocate of the doctrine of filial piety and of the institution of ancestor worship."[18]

From the above it can be seen that Confucius linked heaven, the state, and the family together in a system of close relationships. He believed harmony could be maintained if people understood and acted according to the ramifications of this system. Instead of such harmony, there existed in Confucius' day only political chaos, in which the imperial ruler displayed little strength or control. Confucius, therefore, sought his models in the earlier traditional history of China, in order to make clear his concepts as to how a true ruler should act and thus bring about the desired harmonious relationships in the state. There is no doubt that Confucius was not above falsifying these accounts to serve his purposes. It is also true that Confucianism fostered the forces of traditionalism and conservatism as a result of this glorification of China's past.

The ideal government, according to Confucius, would be based upon virtue and benevolence. It would work for the greatest welfare of the people, improve the productivity of the nation, and assure a richer life for the population. Confucius was evidently an advocate of governmental regulation, and laid down as a rule in this respect: "Find what is profitable to the people and profit them." Policies were to be established in accordance with the principles of human nature and the changing conditions of time and place.

The philosopher taught that proper education would bring out the natural sympathy and good will latent in all men. The purpose of his educational scheme, in which piety and sincerity were stressed, was to help develop the "superior man," who aims at nine things: " 'In the use of his eyes, his object is to see clearly. In the use of his ears, his object is to listen distinctly. In expression, his object is to be gracious. In manners, his object is to be respectful. In speech, his object is to be sincere. In business, his object is to be earnest. In doubt he seeks clarification. In anger, he thinks of consequences. In the face of gain, he thinks of righteousness.'...He does not do to others what he does not want others to do to him, 'repays evil with justice (uprightness) and repays kindness with kindness,' exercises filial loyalty, [and] is respectful to his superiors."[19]

Influence of Confucius. Like the Buddha, Confucius looked upon himself as a reformer of existing abuses rather than as a prophet. Yet just as Gautama was later glorified into a religious master, so Confucius was elevated to that exalted position. The complete transformation took place in 195 B.C. under the Han dynasty (see page 211), when an emperor paid a visit to the tomb of Confucius and offered a sacrifice to his spirit. This innovation began the national cult of the worship and veneration of Confucius.

It is difficult to overestimate the influence of Confucius on the later history of China. For centuries his texts were the subject matter in the official schools, his conservatism and reverence for the past were inculcated into the national character, and his code of morals and ethics permeated Chinese thought. Unfortunately, Confucianism often sterilized Chinese thinking, because scholars rehashed ancient Confucian texts instead of embarking upon original ideas. Likewise, it proved a useful tool in the hands of rulers who were able to take advantage of its emphasis upon organized, traditional authority to advance their own interests at the expense of those of the people.

Nevertheless, it should be pointed out that according to his lights, Confucius was justified in hammering home traditions and obligations in an age when society had lost its political and moral bearings and required fresh moorings. And as one scholar has pointed out, Confucianism solved the problem of enabling the population of an overcrowded country to live in peace and cooperation. "Everyone knew his position in the family, and so, in a broader sense, in the State; and this prescribed his rights and duties. We may feel that the rules to which he was subjected were pedantic; but there was no limit to their effectiveness: they reduced to a minimum the friction that always occurs when great masses of people live close together; they gave Chinese society the strength through which it has endured to this day."[20]

Mencius (372-289 B.C.). A famous successor of Confucius was Meng Tzu or, as his name has been Latinized, Mencius. Living toward the close of the Chou period, Mencius was concerned, among other problems, with the role of the people in government and with the question of when a ruler could be replaced. His doctrine proved extremely democratic. Like Plato in Greece, Mencius stressed the desirability of states being administered by rulers who were also philosophers. At the same time, he pointed out that all political and economic institutions have been created on behalf of the people. This being so, "even the ruler himself is a man who has been put in office only that he may serve them."[21] Like Thomas Jefferson two thousand years afterwards, Mencius bravely contended that the people had the right to rebel and depose their rulers if their welfare was not safeguarded.

A Sung dynasty artist produced in bronze this beaming portrait of Lao-Tzu, sitting comfortably atop a water buffalo. The figure, a statuette, belongs to a period much later than the supposed lifetime of the little philosopher.

Lao-Tzu. While, on one hand, philosophers like Confucius and Mencius were developing humanistic theories, there were others who emphasized an intuitive, mystical interpretation of the life processes. Of the most famous person associated with this school, Lao-Tzu, we know very little. Traditionally, he is supposed to have been an older contemporary of Confucius, but a number of modern scholars believe that Lao-Tzu properly belongs to the fourth century B.C. or even later. He may, as the oldest biography states, have been a court official in one of the states until he retired to lead a life of reflection. The views of Lao-Tzu are to be found in the *Tao Te King,* a book which has gained wide currency in many modern translations, and whose philosophy has profoundly influenced Chinese thought and art.

The *Tao Te King* is couched in vague language—perhaps deliberately so—and hence it is not easy to give a precise formulation of its philosophical tenets. Inherent in any understanding of Lao-Tzu's teachings is the key word *Tao*. The primary meaning of this word is "road" or "way." With Lao-Tzu, however, *Tao* has been given a metaphysical meaning—it represents a universal first principle of existence. As the *Tao Te King* puts it:

"There is a thing, formless yet complete. Before Heaven and Earth it existed. Without sound, without substance, it stands alone without changing. It is all pervading and unfailing. One may think of it as the mother of all beneath Heaven. We do not know its name, but we term it *Tao*."[22]

It has been said that whereas the goal of

Confucianism is the fully developed life in society, that of Taoism is to bring men into simple harmony with the laws and rhythms of the universe. This could best be done, according to Lao-Tzu, by retirement from the chaos and moral decadence which he saw about him in contemporary feudal society, and by adherence to the doctrine of *wu wei,* which has been defined as "passive achievement." This doctrine advocates a way of behavior which, like nature itself, is nonassertive and spontaneous. Lao-Tzu points out that in nature all things work silently; they fulfill their function and, after they reach their bloom, each returns to its origin. "The Tao undertakes no activity, and yet there is nothing left undone."

In effect, Taoism advocated a philosophical anarchism. Somewhat like Rousseau in eighteenth-century France, who preached the necessity of returning to a primitive state of nature, the Taoists maintained that the less people are governed, the better off they are. Laws are created by intellectuals, for example, yet laws do not stop crime. Why? Because the secrets of the universe are gained not by the mind but only through an intuitive contemplation of the vast, silent, ceaseless flow of nature in every atom of life. The sage does not cram his mind with facts but learns to appreciate the laws of the universe and to dwell in harmony with them. In the Taoists' insistence on the need to understand the vital impulse of nature which motivates evolution ceaselessly, we catch a foreshadowing of the philosophy of Bergson and other twentieth-century thinkers. Taoism is a revolt against the intellect's limitations, and indeed one of the most famous Taoist philosophers, Chuang-tzu, even questioned the reality of the world of the senses, as we learn from the following oft-quoted anecdote:

"Once Chuang-tzu dreamed that he was a butterfly, flying about enjoying itself. It did not know that it was Chuang-tzu. Suddenly he awoke, and veritably was Chuang-tzu again. I do not know whether it was Chuang-tzu dreaming that he was a butterfly, or whether now I am a butterfly dreaming that I am Chuang-tzu."[23]

When Taoism and Chinese art are studied together, one is at once struck by their similarity of attitude. Both shy away from the baldly realistic aspects of life. Neither one places much trust in an intellectualized interpretation of nature. On the contrary, both are deeply introspective and intuitive. The Chinese artist is a Taoist at heart. He wanders off alone to some quiet grove where there is a view of a waterfall with forested peaks beyond. Instead of painting at once, as the western artist might do, the eastern painter is more likely to contemplate the scene, musing upon its beauty and letting the serenity of the landscape sift into his feelings. Then he will return home to paint his picture. The result is not an exact replica of what he has seen; rather it is an impressionistic reaction to what he has felt. The Chinese artist and the Taoist philosopher alike seek to understand the processes of nature that created the landscape; the landscape in itself is not all-important.

Art and Literature under the Shang and the Chou

Characteristics of Chinese artistic expression. The Chinese have a deep-rooted love of nature which affects their artistic expression to a marked degree. Not only do they possess a sensitivity to beauty which demands that the most common household utensils be esthetically acceptable, but they insist that their arts be completely appropriate. Their buildings are dignified and sober yet are marked by a rhythm of line that fits in with the trees among which they are carefully situated. The landscapes are depicted on scrolls with a technique which, through relatively few simple lines, suggests tremendous feeling and insight. The psychological richness of Chinese painting comes from the practice of Chinese artists of spending whole months in contemplating and meditating upon some natural scene which they love. The Chinese arts are in general marked by restraint and a sense of poise. These qualities probably come from their attitude of conservatism and serenity. A poem, for example, seldom gushes but in a line or two quietly sums up the most poignant human emotions, such as those of a woman who has lost her soldier husband:

By building a dam one may stop the flow of
 the Yellow River,
But who can assuage the grief of her heart
 when it snows, and the north wind
 blows?

BRONZE CEREMONIAL VESSEL OF THE SHANG DYNASTY

Jade art. We associate jade with China, and rightly so, for jade ornaments have been found in the earliest Chinese graves. Perhaps as early as 2500 B.C. the Chinese were cutting jade into forms of fishes as "sound-stones" which, when struck, could emit an exceedingly clear sound for a considerable length of time. Early jade work was stimulated by religious uses, and the symbolism of the amulets found in graves has prompted much speculation as to the precise meaning of these artistic masterpieces.

The ancient Chinese considered jade the most precious of stones, so sacred and so imbued with the spirit of virtue that it should be used only in the fashioning of ritualistic objects. The Son of Heaven used to give his lords jade tokens as a symbol that he recognized them, because, as we recall, the king was at once a political and a religious leader, and his ceremonies always possessed religious significance. Jade was cut into shapes of a symbolic nature, pertaining to heaven, earth, and the four points of the compass.[24]

Bronze art. By about the second millennium B.C. beautiful ceremonial bronzes were being fashioned and continued to be made for the next 1500 years. We have already alluded to the splendid bronze pieces which were a product of the Shang period. The illustration above shows one of these early vessels, decorated with characteristic interlacing motifs which emphasize its angularity. Many Shang bronzes are huge sacrificial jars with mythological decorations, and libation cups, used by the ruler in the rites of heaven and earth and more commonly by each Chinese family in ancestor worship.

Ceramics. Unquestionably the Chinese take first place among all peoples in the art of ceramics. We shall see that it attained its most perfect forms in later dynasties, but during the early, formative centuries the Chinese were already skillful technicians and sensitive artists. Where we in the West value china mainly for its household utility, the Chinese combined in pottery both utility and the highest expression of beauty. That Chinese pottery is very ancient can be realized by recalling our discussion of Neolithic times in China, when beautiful red and black pieces were created by skillful artists at least five thousand years ago. Other pieces have been found which have been ascribed to the Shang dynasty, but we have to wait for the productive Han dynasty

(206 B.C.-220 A.D.) before we find Chinese pottery again assuming artistic proportions.

Architecture. There are several arts of which we have little evidence from the Chou period. One is architecture. It was never considered a major art in China, as it always has been in the West. One type of building, characterized by an overhanging, steep-pitched roof and upturned corners, was made to serve secular and religious, public and private purposes. Because the building material was principally wood, there are today no examples remaining from the earliest periods.

Painting and sculpture. Painting has been called the most characteristic art of China, because it embodies the Chinese spirit of restraint and poise. More can be said about the rich contributions of Chinese painting to world art when we examine later periods. Unfortunately no examples survive of the earliest Chinese painting. But literature tells us that it was an established and skilled art centuries before the birth of Christ. Even of Chou painting we have no remnants, but Confucius speaks of certain temple frescoes and of the strong effect they had on him.

Sculpture is yet another art which did not become important until the Han dynasty. Legend tells of the huge bronze statues cast before this time, but, if they existed, they were probably melted up by later dynasties for making coins.

Language. The Chinese language is monosyllabic. Difference in meaning is achieved through the use of tones, of which there are from four to nine for each word sound. The written language is composed of about forty thousand characters, each of which expresses a distinct idea. Whereas the spoken language of China has split into a hundred dialects so that a Cantonese usually cannot understand a man from the north, the written language has remained comparatively unchanged. Under the Chou dynasty it took on the form which it possesses (with some modifications) today. There has probably been more change in English since the days of Chaucer in the fourteenth century than there has been in written Chinese during the two thousand and more years since Chou times.

Chinese is noted for its terseness and brevity and, at the same time, for its subtlety and complexity. Its long, changeless continuity has its advantages, for it means that a literate Chinese living today can read the literature which was written twenty centuries ago, even though he would be totally at a loss to say how the characters he is reading were formerly pronounced. The Chinese script and pictures symbolize in some ways the character of China's civilization. Despite all changes and departures they remain constant and conservative.

Poetry. During China's formative centuries literature flourished richly. Unfortunately, most poetry written prior to the age of Confucius has been lost, but three hundred five poems have been preserved in the *Shih Ching*, or *Book of Odes*. The odes vary in age from those of the Shang dynasty a thousand years prior to Confucius down to those of his own day. From the *Shih Ching* we gather unmistakably that human nature has changed little, that the problems of war, famine, disease, and solitude, together with the joys of love and domestic life, affected the ancient Chinese in just the same fashion as they affect us. In our own age we can sympathize deeply with soldiers engaged in a conflict which they did not create:

How free are the wild geese on their wings,
And the rest they find on the bushy Yu trees!
But we, ceaseless toilers in the king's services,
Cannot even plant our millet and rice.

What will our parents have to rely on?
O thou distant and azure Heaven!
When shall all this end?...
What leaves have not turned purple?
What man is not torn from his wife?
Mercy be on us soldiers:—
Are we not also men?[25]

And here is a love poem which is timeless in spirit and typically Chinese in its restraint and tenderness of expression:

The morning glory climbs above my head,
Pale flowers of white and purple, blue and red.
I am disquieted.

Down in the withered grasses something stirred;
I thought it was his footfall that I heard.
Then a grasshopper chirred.

I climbed the hill just as the new moon showed,
I saw him coming on the southern road,
My heart lays down its load.[26]

Summary

Beginning as a fluvial culture, China became through diversified climate and fertile soil primarily a country of agriculture and peasant farmers. The individuality of Chinese culture came in great measure from the comparative geographical exclusiveness of the country. We do not know anything definitive about the origin of the Chinese people though present evidence shows that human life has existed in China for an extremely long time, perhaps since the early Pleistocene era. Probably almost all China proper possessed a Neolithic culture, while the second millennium B.C. witnessed the evolution of a Bronze Age with advanced techniques.

The early history of China is shrouded in the mists of legend and fable. Although scholars are not yet sure whether or not a Hsia dynasty existed, there is no doubt as to the existence of the Shang with its strong formative effects upon later Chinese civilization. The Chou dynasty had the longest existence—and one of the stormiest—in the history of the country. The formative importance of this period deserves to be emphasized, for it gave to China those unique characteristics of its social customs, economic organization, government, philosophy, literature, and art which have endured to our own day. Among the social institutions developed during these centuries were the village pattern of government, the town guild system, and the beginning of a civil administrative system.

Chinese art can be appreciated and understood best if one remembers that it strives to depict the creative essence of life and hence is relatively more subjective, abstract, and mystical than most western art. We must reserve for another chapter the highest achievements in ceramics, painting, and sculpture, but even during the formative centuries China's artists wrought beautiful ornaments and vessels in jade, bronze, and pottery. Chinese literature also contains the same subjective spirit which we find in the country's art.

The glory of the Chou dynasty was its roster of great philosophers. While the Indians created metaphysical systems which explained the workings of the gods and of nature, the Chinese sought only a means of showing men how to live rational and ethical lives here on earth. The ideas of Lao-Tzu, Confucius, Mencius, and the many other philosophers of the day have exerted an important influence upon Chinese culture for more than two thousand years. In fact, their influence has in modern times often proved more of a curse than a blessing, since it has kept many of China's intellectuals in the bondage of tradition at a time when they might have been grappling with modern problems and using modern ideas.

The common people of course were not concerned with the abstruse points of the ethics of Confucius and Mencius. They satisfied their consciences by fulfilling their traditional religious rites. They knew and approved of the sacred rites of heaven and earth, which the ruler performed on behalf of the country and its inhabitants. Of a more personal nature was the family ceremony of offering tribute at the ancestral hearth to the spirits of the family dead.

An eminent Sinologist, writing of the origins of Chinese culture, leaves us with a concept applicable not only to this but also to all subsequent chapters relating to China's rich civilization. "Chinese culture is unique in its continuity. Its most striking characteristic is a capacity for change without disruption. It would appear that that characteristic goes back even to the Neolithic cultures which preceded the Shang in northeast China. Shang culture, like all great cultures, was eclectic, fertilized by influences from many quarters. But these influences and techniques, when they were accepted, met the same fate which has overtaken every people, every religion, every philosophy which has invaded China. They were taken up, developed to accord with Chinese conditions, and transmuted into organic parts of a culture which remained fundamentally and characteristically Chinese."[27]

Part Two

Around the Mediterranean

Around the Mediterranean

THE FIRST PHASE in the evolution of civilization was almost unbelievably long. It took about one million years to bridge the gap between *Pithecanthropus erectus* and Cro-Magnon, the first modern man. But then the tempo of progress picked up, and in less than five thousand years man added more refinements to his way of living than he had during the preceding million years.

During this period, beginning around 5000 B.C., men in seemingly isolated parts of the world began to develop civilizations along the banks of rivers. As we have seen, it was then that people living in the Indus and Ganges valleys evolved a high state of culture, marked by a caste system, original philosophical concepts, great epic poems, and the appearance of one of the world's outstanding religious teachers, Gautama Buddha. Meanwhile, people living by the Wei and Yellow rivers, in that period of legendary history lasting to the twelfth century B.C., were forging the tools of culture. Then, during the rule of the notable Chou dynasty, which lasted for nearly nine centuries, the basic characteristics of Chinese government, art, and philosophy were established.

In the Near East, in the regions affected by the Tigris-Euphrates and Nile rivers, civilization after civilization rose and fell during this period. Out of the medley of many cultures—Sumerian, Babylonian, Egyptian, Assyrian, Hebraic, and Persian—came numerous enrichments for the life of mankind. From this area Europe received its alphabet, its temple architecture, its first great literature, and the rudiments of science. But the creative genius of the Near East was ultimately sterilized by royal autocracy and the despotic conformity imposed by priests. For the next period of important cultural advance in the West, we must shift our focus from the Near East and the banks of rivers to the shores and hinterland of the Mediterranean basin.

THIS NEW PHASE in the history of civilization was mainly the achievement of two peoples, the Greeks and the Romans. The civilization which the Greeks brought to fruition in the fifth century B.C. was to endure for over a thousand years. This is often referred to as the classical age—and so powerful was its influence that its philosophy, literature, and thought in general have remained the "classic" studies of the western world.

Yet we should not give these peoples indiscriminate credit for their remarkable achievements. The Greeks, for example, borrowed from the Near East many basic ideas which came to them by way of the coast of Asia Minor and numerous small islands in the Aegean Sea, where a splendid civilization had earlier been established. This Aegean culture was in some measure destroyed, in other ways adopted, by the Greek newcomers, who in the first millennium B.C. proved themselves brilliant innovators in art, government, and thought.

Meanwhile, a new power—Rome—was developing in Italy. After some five centuries of modest growth, it embarked about 500 B.C. upon a career of unexampled conquest. In time the rule of Rome was extended throughout the entire Mediterranean area and into the hinterland beyond. This political unification of the western world made possible in turn the diffusion of Greek civilization which the Romans admired. Until the fifth century A.D. a mighty Graeco-Roman world-state flourished in the West.

The civilization of the Greeks and Romans "was essentially a product of the Mediterranean area, and the Mediterranean Sea which was *'mare nostrum'* to them in a double sense—a political possession but also a great formative influence."* Yet the very impetus of their expanding civilization carried them far to the east, where traders, following the trails blazed by Alexander the Great and others, braved the vast stretches separating the Graeco-Roman empire from the two other massive civilizations of the age, India and China. These, as we shall see, had continued to develop their indigenous cultures with notable success. And now, in the first centuries of the Christian era, we enter a brief but fascinating period, where the principal civilizations of West and East were in contact and there was a fruitful exchange of both wares and ideas.

But this process of culture contact and diffusion, which might have had incalculable effects on world history had it been able to continue and expand, was brought to an untimely halt, largely because of crisis in the West. The Graeco-Roman world was subjected to a series of shattering invasions by Germanic tribes, and once again our attention reverts to the Mediterranean basin to witness the political and social upheavals which ensued. In 476 A.D. Rome itself was sacked, and the crucial question arose whether the Graeco-Roman cultural legacy would be destroyed. For a century or two the issue stood in doubt, but a new and powerful agency—the Christian Church—was on the side of preservation. Perhaps more than any other institution, it was to blend the Roman, Greek, and German elements into a new pattern of civilization that finally emerged as the foundation of modern Europe.

*M. Cary, *The Geographic Background of Greek and Roman History,* Oxford, Clarendon Press, 1949, p. 1.

Chapter 5

Chronology of events and developments discussed in this chapter

Aegean civilization *Crete, Asia Minor, and Greek mainland*	3200-1200 B.C.
Golden age in Crete: extensive trade	2400-1450
Height of Aegean culture in Greece: commerce and piracy	After 1500
Destruction of Cnossus	1450
Aegean civilization overrun by barbaric invaders	1200
Indo-European invasions: Aeolian, Achaean, Ionian, Doric	2000-1000
Hellenic Age *Cultural foundations for western civilization*	1200-338
Homeric Age: pastoral economy; tribal units based on kinship	1200-800
Homer: credited with the Iliad *and the* Odyssey	800
Age of Nobles: class system; colonization; economic development	750-500
Formative period of the city-states: Athens and Sparta	700-500
Draconian code: criminal punishment under state jurisdiction	621
Spartan League: autocratic military state	600
Solon: encouraged democracy and industry; reformed the law code	594
Age of Tyrants: power usurped for public good	550-500
Apex of Athenian democracy: freedom under pure democracy	500-400
Persian wars: threat of eastern dominance quelled	499-479
Delian League: naval alliance of the city-states under Athens	478
Socrates: question method of analysis	469-399
Age of Pericles: glory of Greek culture	460-429
Phidias: zenith of fifth-century sculpture	440
Peloponnesian War	431-405
Plato: theory of external and unchanging "Ideas"; the Republic	427-347
Aristotle: reality in Form and Matter: the syllogism	384-322
Hellenistic period *Diffusion of Greek culture: center in Alexandria*	338-146
Alexander: Macedonian conqueror; theory of divine kingship	356-323
Empire broken up: Ptolemaic, Seleucid, Macedonian	After 323
Euclid: geometric theory	c. 300
Archimedes: contributions in math and physics	287-212
Eratosthenes: calculated the circumference of the globe	276-195

The Greek achievement

The Hellenic and Hellenistic world: 3000 B.C. to 146 B.C.

SCARRED AND WEATHER-BEATEN, the ruins on the Athenian Acropolis stand against a vivid blue Aegean sky, overlooking the trees and buildings of a modern city sprawled beneath. Their columns shattered by time and foreign hands, their roofs no longer resisting the elements, and their steps strewn with the wreckage of the ages, these ruins are mute symbols of a departed civilization. The highest achievements of the Greek world —in government, thought, and art—stemmed from the Athenian democracy at its height, the symbol of which is the Acropolis.

The Acropolis in its prime must have presented a striking picture. The temples and statuary then were not pock-marked and dingy, but gleaming and new, the achievements of great and original artists. Standing on the west brow of the Acropolis was a giant statue in bronze of Athena herself, the warrior goddess of the proud Athenians. Her helmet and spear tip gleamed in the sunlight and flashed to Athenian sailors far at sea the welcome signal that soon they would be safely home. In the perfectly proportioned Parthenon stood another statue of the goddess, fashioned of gold and ivory by the renowned Phidias and judged a marvel by all who looked at it.

Today the Acropolis is a ruin; but even in the twentieth century there is an imperishable spirit about it that can give us the clue to the civilization which created its grandeur. The Parthenon, despite its broken columns, remains a masterpiece of proportion and symmetry.

Here, then, are our clues to the glory of Greek civilization. Throughout the history of the Greek people we shall repeatedly see their love of proportion and symmetry, not only in their architecture but in everything they attempted. Despite this quality, however, the Greeks proved unable to achieve the necessary balance or harmony of their political relations. They quarreled continually, and that fervid individualism which moved them to matchless creative effort blinded them to the necessity of cooperation. That is why we shall find the political and economic life of the Greeks marked by fratricidal conflict—until the inevitable happens and they are subjugated by powerful conquerors from the north and west.

Yet, because those conquerors had a sincere admiration for Greek cultural achievements, the western world has inherited such a magnificent legacy of knowledge and art from ancient Athens and Alexandria that Shelley, the English poet, could say with justification that "We are all Greeks." The cultural heritage of the West and to a lesser extent of the East then, is derived from two sources. The first is Hellas (Greece) itself, where outstanding works of art, philosophy, and science were created. The second is the successful diffusion of Greek culture throughout a world-state by the conquerors of the city-states.

Because of their emphasis upon naturalism and humanism, their use of critical inquiry and their respect for truth, the Greeks of classical times were unhindered by the bondage of oriental tradition and absolutism. As a result of their unique approach to their environment, a relative handful of Greeks were able to create the basic pattern of cultural development for the entire western world. Few other people, if any, can claim to have made as permanent an impress upon the course of history.

The Aegean Civilization: Transition from Asia to Europe

Archaeological discoveries. An erroneous view was once held by scholars that Greek culture developed independently of any oriental influence. Thanks to the efforts of archaeologists we know now that a rich civilization existed in and about the Aegean Sea as far back as the fourth millenium B.C. The evidence for this culture is found in three main centers: Cnossus and Phaestus on the island of Crete, Troy on the coast of Asia Minor, and Mycenae and Tiryns on the Greek mainland.

The story of the discovery and excavation of Troy reads like a romance. That this city existed only in the epic poems attributed to Homer, the *Iliad* and *Odyssey,* had long been the accepted view, but a German named Heinrich Schliemann believed otherwise. After having accumulated a private fortune, Schliemann put his theory to the test by excavating in 1870 at the legendary site of Troy near the Hellespont. Within four years he had unearthed nine cities built one on top of another. Later, this enthusiastic though somewhat amateurish student of classical civilizations excavated the cities of Mycenae and Tiryns, thereby proving in turn that centers of Aegean culture had also existed on the Greek peninsula. But possibly the most valuable archaeological research was performed under the direction of Sir Arthur Evans, who began his excavations at Cnossus on Crete in 1899.

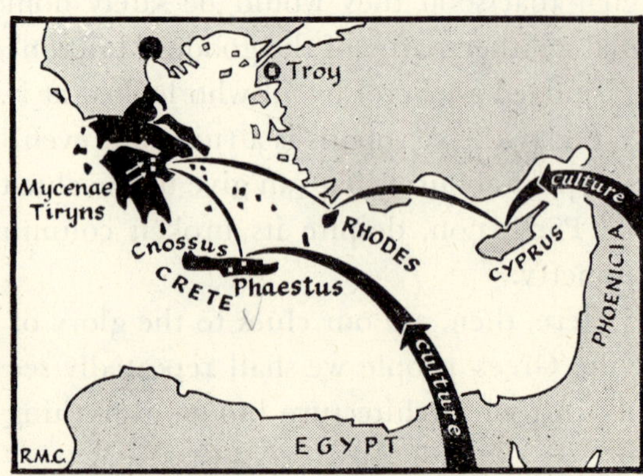

Along the trade routes to Rhodes and Crete, and thence to Mycenae and Tiryns in Greece and Troy in Asia Minor, spread the culture of Phoenicians and Egyptians.

THE CORBELED ARCH *spans an opening with layers of material that overhang from each side until they meet. The detail below shows how the lever action of each overhanging piece is balanced by the heavy material above pushing down on its supported end. With stone as the building material this method of making an opening requires massive walls for support.*

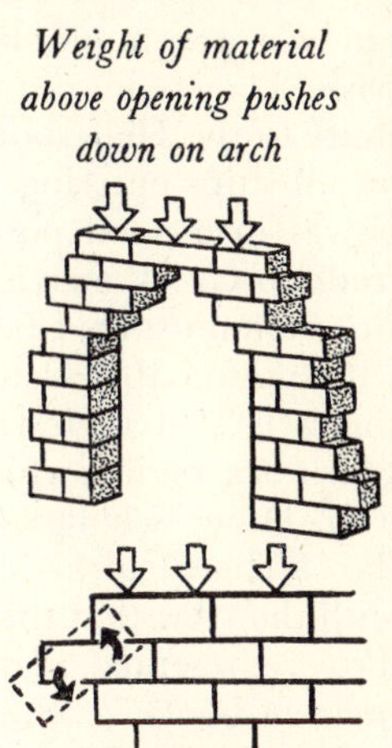
Weight of material
above opening pushes
down on arch

Aegean civilization. We know little or nothing of the origins of the people inhabiting the Aegean cities, nor is it certain when they came into this region, although they may have migrated there about 8000 B.C. during the Neolithic Age. Probably about 3200 B.C., before the end of the Pre-Dynastic period in Egypt, these Aegean people began to make use of copper, and subsequently learned to work extensively in bronze. Some scholars believe that the bronze culture of Europe originated in the Aegean area, where people were not acquainted with iron.

A continuous development of Aegean civilization took place during the Middle Bronze Age, approximately between 2400 and 1800 B.C., which was marked by the building of splendid palaces at Cnossus and Phaestus in Crete and the establishment of a complete Aegean culture on the Greek mainland. The next four centuries have been termed the greatest and most flourishing period of the Greek Bronze Age culture, for Crete then enjoyed its Golden Age. The excellent geographical and strategic location of the island offered both profitable commercial possibilities and comparative protection from outside warring forces. The Cretans dominated Aegean commerce and for centuries traded actively with Egypt, exporting their staple, olive oil, as well as wine, honey, and their celebrated pottery. Egypt in turn probably sent back gold, fine stones, grain, linen fabrics, and even, according to one source, negro soldiers. Clay tablets found at Cnossus (whose script has not yet been fully deciphered) would seem to indicate the prominent role that business played in the island's life. Then some time after 1450 B.C., Cnossus was destroyed, as a result of either internal revolution or invasion, and the center of Aegean culture shifted from Crete to the mainland and the eastern islands of the Mediterranean.

Meanwhile, Aegean civilization had also been flourishing on the coast of Asia Minor. In the late Neolithic period, a small village called Troy had been established near the Hellespont, which links the Mediterranean and the Sea of Marmora. At this strategic point, the Trojans could command the traffic between Europe and Asia at the entrance into the Black Sea, and by 2500 B.C. the city's rulers had become wealthy. Troy was then rebuilt more sumptuously, and the treasure of golden earrings, hairpins, and bracelets discovered by Schliemann in this second city (about 2500-2000 B.C.) led him to believe that he had excavated Homeric Troy. However, it was later shown that the city of the great epics had probably been the sixth of the nine towns erected

LION GATEWAY AT MYCENAE

over a period of some 2500 years, the last being built by the Romans.

Some historians believe that the famous Trojan war recounted by Homer has a factual basis. They point out that because of the proximity to the Hellespont, Troy could exact toll on all ships entering the Hellespont and that it was in a good position to close Black Sea trade to Greek merchants. If this were so, the situation must have been galling to the Greeks, who presumably determined on war to rid themselves of their rival and to conquer the Black Sea region which was rich in gold and iron. Other scholars, however, maintain that the archaeological evidence accords better with the view that the siege and destruction of Troy represented "a mere Viking adventure in quest of booty."[1]

The third principal center of Aegean civilization was found in the two cities of Mycenae and Tiryns on the Greek mainland, inhabited by people perhaps of the same race as the later Greeks. Again it was Schliemann who brought these towns to the attention of the world. Excavating the prehistoric fortress of Mycenae, he discovered beneath the pavement of the market place a number of stone chambers containing many gold ornaments, of which the most interesting was a splendid royal crown. Aegean culture on the Greek peninsula reached its height after 1500 B.C., coming to fruition later than that of Crete or Troy. Mycenae and Tiryns were protected by walls against inland attack and in this way differed from the cities on Crete. Besides Mycenae and Tiryns there were several other Aegean centers on the Greek peninsula, all of which existed on their commerce and piratical practices, with Egypt, Crete, Cyprus, and the regions to the north offering profitable returns.

The civilization on the mainland of Greece had advanced from the tribal stage to an early urban stage in which the people congregated in small cities to carry on maritime pursuits. In Egypt, Mesopotamia, India, and China we have noticed the eventual breakdown of initial

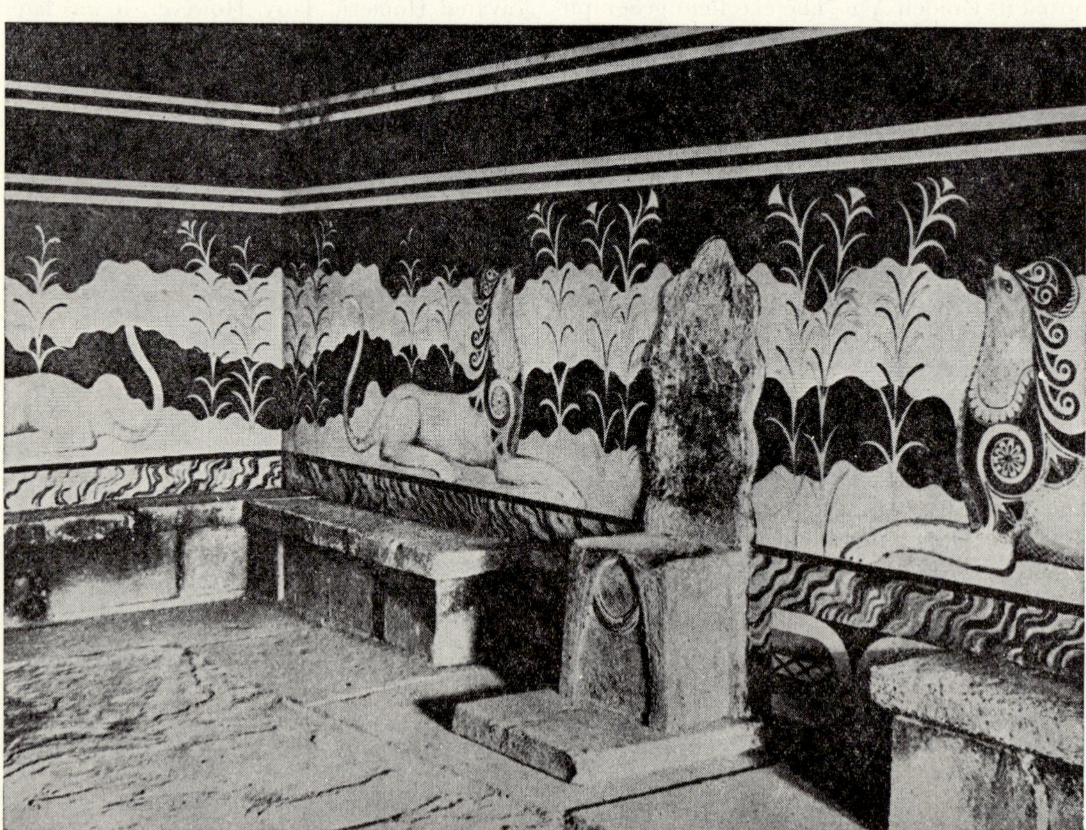

Perhaps King Minos, in whose fabulous labyrinth Theseus slew the Minotaur, held court from this throne in the council room of the Palace at Cnossus, under the aegis of two haughty griffins.

biological groupings and the realignment of people into political groups for the purpose of coping more effectively with new political and economic situations. The small Aegean city with its fortifications was a forerunner of both the later Greek city-state and the medieval feudal castle.

Aegean life. One authority has described the Aegean culture as "the most human civilization of the more ancient world, the world before 1000 B.C."[2] Certainly the palaces, chamber-tombs, and art treasures which have been excavated bear eloquent testimony to the fact that these maritime and commercial people succeeded in combining their practical bent of mind with a splendid sense of artistic appropriateness, and they enjoyed a society which was sophisticated as well as largely secular in character. The Aegean culture impresses us with its distinctly modern note. Thus, the palace at Cnossus seems to have been furnished with hot and cold water and possessed a scientific sanitation system surpassing anything in ancient times until Roman days, or even in modern times until nineteenth-century England. It is believed also, judging from the evidence found in frescoes, that the social status of Aegean women may have been on a par with that of men and, at any rate, was superior to the position of women in Greek and Roman times. This feminist aspect may be partly accounted for by the fact that the highest Aegean deity was a goddess, the Earth Mother, for whose cult a chapel was set aside in the palace at Cnossus.

The Aegeans possessed the secular and practical outlook that tends to go with an urban civilization engaged in extensive commerce with other peoples. We have already mentioned their important contacts with Egypt, from which they imported both commercial wares and various art techniques. But the Aegeans also profited by their many culture contacts with other contemporary cultures. Thus, the importation of amber from Baltic shores to Mycenae attests to trade with northern Europe, while the fascinating discovery in the oldest settlement at Troy of an ax head of white jade shows that trade must have existed between the Far East and the Mediterranean as far back as the third millenium B.C., for white jade was in use only in China.

Aegean art. We have already seen that the Aegean people were supremely esthetic. Cretan architecture was of post and lintel construction like the Egyptian, but in its reflection of secular life it was very different. Thus the palace at Cnossus had comparatively little space set aside for religious purposes, whereas in Egypt the buildings designed to endure were either temples or tombs. The columns supporting the stone structure of the palace were of wood with bases smaller than the capitals, thereby giving a certain sophistication quite in keeping with the spirit of Cretan society. Today it is possible to mount the palace's grand staircase of three flights on its original steps of low tread, magnificently conceived and splendidly executed. The terraced palace, with its tiers of flat roofs towering above the town, possessed innumerable rooms and courts and beautifully frescoed walls showing ceremonial bull fights as well as animals and birds.

CRETAN SNAKE GODDESS IN IVORY AND GOLD

The paintings of the Aegean peoples in cities of the mainland as well as in Crete again reflected the sophistication of their life. Aegean art at its best period was highly unconventional and in many ways akin to our own

CRETAN OCTOPUS VASE

artistic concepts. Frescoes were extremely decorative and executed in flat brilliant colors with strong black outlines. The figures in the paintings were purposely distorted, with pinched-in waists and elaborate costumes and hairdresses, in order to give them an air of opulence and elegance.

We find no large-sized sculpture in Crete, but there were many small wooden figurines, probably used in religious rites. The most famous of these is the Snake Goddess (see page 125). Still another artistic triumph of the Aegean people was their pottery. Taught by the Egyptians to use pottery wheels, the Cretan craftsmen found much of their inspiration in nature. Flowers and animals were stylized to fit the shape of the pots. One of the finest examples of such decorative pottery shows an octopus (see this page) "that seems to be swimming at us from off the vase."

The Greek invasions. For a short time, the Aegean civilization "was probably the most beautiful and most esthetic, though possibly not the most luxurious culture of the world."[3] Cretan culture reached its apex about 1800 B.C. and the fourteenth and thirteenth centuries B.C. still witnessed the flourishing of the Mycenean culture. However, Indo-European invaders were gradually seeping into Greece from the north all this time, and by 1200 B.C. the Aegean civilization was almost completely swamped by the barbaric invaders. Yet enough of the old culture survived to serve as a foundation for the Greek civilization that was to emerge later. Those Aegeans who did not perish or flee intermarried with the invaders, and consequently the Greek, or Hellenic, people of whom we shall be speaking were really a mixture of Aegean and Indo-European types. Perhaps it was from their Aegean, rather than Indo-European, ancestors that the Greeks inherited their esthetic characteristics and love of beauty.

The Geography and the Racial History of Hellenic Greece

The Hellenic civilization. The Indo-European invaders from the north supplanted the Aegean civilization on the Greek peninsula with a new civilization, the Hellenic. The name Hellenic is derived from Hellas, which is the Greek word for Greece. The "Hellenic" Age refers to that period in which the Greeks created a civilization whose principal center was on the Greek peninsula and whose chief city was Athens. This Hellenic period endured until 338 B.C., when the Greek city-states were conquered by Macedon.

Geography. The Hellenic world included the hundreds of fair-sized and small islands dotting the Aegean Sea, the Greek colonies founded on the coast of Asia Minor, and, most important, the jagged Greek peninsula of some 25,000 square miles of mountain ranges and narrow plains, roughly the area of the map on page 127. Special attention deserves to be paid to certain geographical factors which not only determined the basic thalassic character of the civilization we are about to examine—as contrasted with the fluvial civilizations previously studied —but also played a considerable role in shaping major developments in Greek history. First of all, the numerous islands and the heavily indented coastlines of the Greek peninsula and of Asia Minor stimulated maritime commerce and the founding of protected cities and ports. In this regard, it might be noted that while the west coast of the Greek peninsula is rugged with few good anchorages, the east coast is rich in bays and harbors, and consequently, from the outset, Greek activities and interests tended to be directed toward the east. This fact helps account in turn for the fairly long period of time which elapsed before the Greeks had much contact with another Indo-European people who were also engaged in building up a thalassic culture, but whose capital and principal harbors were on the west coast of the Italian peninsula.

There was every incentive for the Greeks to go down to the sea in ships. The climate was warm and the winds favorable to sailing vessels. Furthermore, the rocky soil and poor natural resources of the peninsula (save for excellent marble and granite quarries which were to make a valuable contribution to Greek sculpture and architecture) incited the Greeks to seek their fortune on the sea and to establish colonies abroad. In addition, the fact that the peninsula is crisscrossed with numerous mountain ranges made internal communications extremely difficult and, as we shall see, encouraged the development of a number of belligerently independent political communities known as city-states. Topography in turn was a determining factor in the location, size, and structure of the typical Greek city-state, which generally stood back from the sea and on a slope rising abruptly from the plain, surmounted by an outcrop of rock. Here was built the citadel, while dwelling houses and the market place occupied the shelving ground.

Thus, the city-state was located on a site providing security, access to the sea, and, in addition, proximity to a pocket of cultivable land.

In conclusion, while guarding against any exaggerated estimate of the effects of geography upon Greek civilization, we might agree with one authority that the history of ancient Greece "is largely a record of successive thalassocracies, and Greek civilization was mainly the product of cities with a seafaring tradition." Furthermore, "the most outstanding feature of ancient Greek politics was the invincible separatism of its several cities and cantons, which was in part at least a result of the geographic fragmentation of the country."[4]

The Greek peoples. Perhaps as early as 3000 B.C. barbarian tribes of Indo-European-speaking pastoral people began to drift into the Aegean world from the grasslands of the Danube valley. These tribes were related biologically to the Indo-European people who swept through the mountain passes of northwest India between 2000 and 1000 B.C. As we learned in our chapter on early India, the Indo-Europeans probably came originally from an area bordering the shores of the Caspian Sea. One branch (including the barbarian tribes later known as Greeks) surged westward, and another branch (the Indo-Aryans) conquered Hindustan. These two branches were closely tied not only biologically but also philologically. Consider, for example, the similarities of the following words. In Sanskrit we find *pitâ,* in Greek *pater,* in Latin *pater,* in German *vater,* and in English *father*—all have the same meaning.

We have no precise information regarding the number of Indo-European invasions of the Aegean world, which seem to have begun in earnest around 2000 B.C. and to have continued for a thousand years. There were possibly three successive waves of conquerors, the oldest being the Aeolian and Achaean, followed by the Ionian and Dorian in that order. These three groups took up positions in Greece and the coast of Asia Minor as shown by the map on page 127. The Achaeans, a Bronze Age people, sacked various Aegean cities, but, compared with the Dorians, theirs was a relatively peaceful infiltration. Invading the region around 1150 to 1000 B.C., and bringing both their herds and the Iron Age to Greece, these Dorian conquerors defeated the Achaeans, occupied most of the Peloponnesus, and later settled also in Crete and the southwestern portion of Asia Minor. Many of the people whom they dispersed migrated to Asia Minor, especially Ionia, carrying with them those aspects of the earlier Aegean civilization that they had absorbed.

With the destruction of the Aegean culture, the migration of peoples, and the prevalence of violence and piracy, Greece endured what has been called a Dark Age. However, following the Dorian invasions and the general settling down of the region, the Greek states as we know them began to emerge, and Greek civilization to develop. This cultural quickening first took place in the coastal cities of Ionia, which had escaped the Dorian onslaught and where Greek elements and the remnants of the older Aegean culture were able to intermix. Furthermore, the Ionian Greeks mingled with Near Eastern peoples and communicated with Sardis, the capital of Lydia. From the Lydians the Ionians learned weaving, embroidery, purple dyeing, metallurgy, and the use of coined money (perhaps a Lydian invention). The civilization which was to culminate in the glory of Athenian culture was thus born in Ionia. Pioneers in exploration and trade, in science and philosophy, the Ionians "first kindled the torch of Hellenism," whose flame was later to be fanned into a fierce splendor by their kinsmen of Attica, the Athenians.

The Political Evolution of Greece

Early developments. The period from about 1200 to 800 B.C. is called the Homeric Age because the epics of Homer give a vivid picture of contemporary life. Much of that period, as we have noted above, was also a Dark Age for the Greek world until the forces of political stability and economic activity reasserted themselves. During the Homeric Age people lived by a simple agricultural and pastoral economy. Political organization was tribal, with the members of the small states united by kinship of blood and ruled over by a king, who in turn found his advisers in the heads of aristocratic families.

By the middle of the eighth century the nobles had taken over control of government

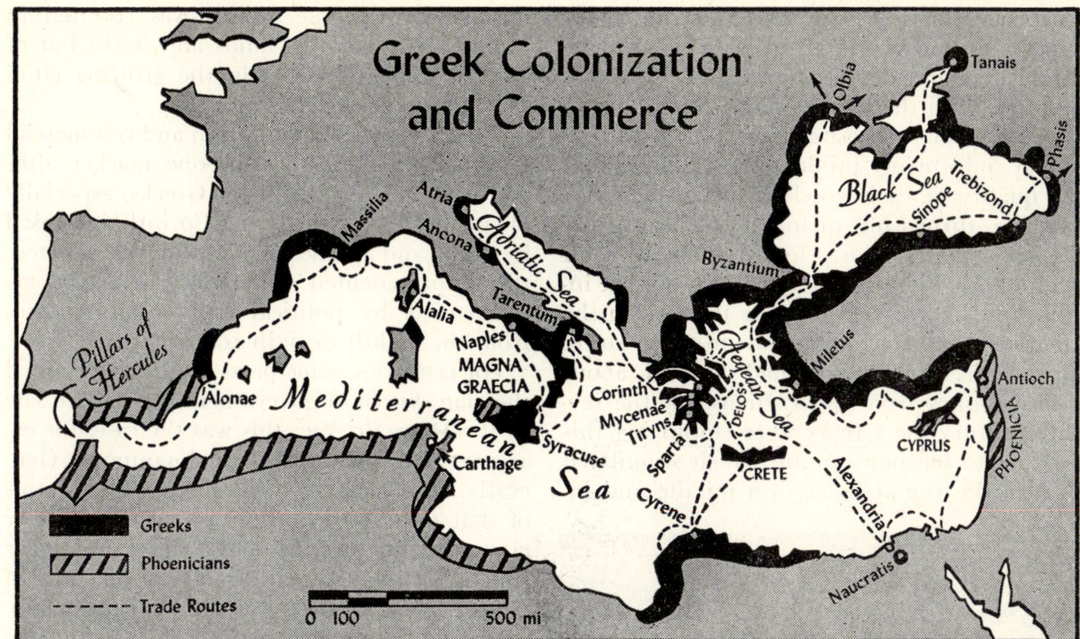

from the tribal kings. This transfer of power from hereditary rulers to aristocratic families marked a departure from the old kinship organization of the state; the territorial state based on law had become the unit of government. Politics was henceforth governed by class interests, and the tribal ownership of land was transferred to private control. The nobles, together with the rising class of wealthy merchants, were in a favorable position to further their own interests, and the common people had little or no say in government, which was in the hands of an all-powerful council of nobles.

Greek colonization. During the age of nobles two developments of far-reaching importance began—colonization and economic growth, continuing from 750 to about 500 B.C. Why did many Greeks wish to emigrate at this time? First of all, the land in Ionia and the Greek peninsula was poor and scarce, and since the population was growing in size, the problem of an adequate food supply became increasingly acute. Secondly, the rising cities required new markets for the disposal of their products. Thirdly, the political and social unrest resulting from the ruthless policies of the nobles incited many less fortunate Greeks to emigrate. Lastly, numerous Greeks must have been prompted by love of adventure and the desire to seek new fields and new fortunes.

The new Greek colonies were planned out in detail before the emigrants left the mother city. The colony was politically independent, but sentimental and economic ties usually persisted, and the success of the new city generally resulted in increased trade for the mother city (*metropolis*). And so an unprecedented colonial expansion took place, with Greek settlements springing up in the east on the banks of the Dardanelles and the Sea of Marmora and around the Black Sea. Meanwhile, a similar process went on in the west; eastern Sicily and southern Italy were so extensively colonized that the region became known as Magna Graecia, while in southern Gaul the Greeks established an important settlement at Massilia (Marseilles) and even settled towns on the south coast of Spain.

The Greeks, however, met with keen competition in their attempts to exploit all profitable colonial sites around the Mediterranean. Their chief competitors were the Phoenicians, who had seized western Sicily and colonized a large part of the coast of North Africa. There they established such important settlements as Carthage, destined one day to be engaged in a gigantic contest with Rome for control of the entire Mediterranean.

All these colonizing activities were accompanied by a veritable economic revolution. The Greeks changed over from mixed farming for local subsistence to specialized farming for export. The new agriculture was matched by complementary developments in trade and industry, with the various cities competing to produce specialized wares for export, and constantly improving production methods and the quality of their goods. Thus Athens, for example, turned out quantities of beautifully decorated vases which found their way all over the Mediterranean. There was a great increase in the number of slaves to work in the vineyards and factories and to row ships. Meanwhile, the Ionians had learned about coined money from the Lydians. By the seventh century the Greeks were employing this new aid to business—an aid which stimulated in turn the rise at home of a middle and industrial class whose wealth was counted in the ownership not of lands and flocks but of currency, indispensable in the growing cities as a means of exchange.

This caryatid, a sculptured draped figure used as a column, is from the Erechtheum on the Acropolis.

The city-state. Colonization and commercial enterprise had opened up one market after another, and the wealth of Greeks, especially of such cities as Athens and Corinth, increased by leaps and bounds. As would be expected, this unprecedented economic growth was accompanied by political and social changes from the eighth to sixth centuries B.C.

For centuries, some parts of Greece retained the clan system of government such as we saw in the Homeric Age; this was the case, for example, with Arcadia in the Peloponnesus. Generally, however, the Greeks developed in terms of that unique institution, called the *polis* or city-state. The origins of the city-state appear to go back to Aegean times in the Ionian cities of Asia Minor, and the institution subsequently developed on the Greek peninsula. Originally, the *polis* was the elevated, fortified site, or *acropolis,* which served as a citadel where inhabitants of the neighborhood might take refuge in times of attack. This elevated area also contained the temple. As time went on and commerce grew, there developed below the *polis* another center, the *asty,* where people lived and traded. When the two parts amalgamated and the neighboring territory was taken into the *polis'* jurisdiction, the final stage in the evolution of the Greek city-state had been reached.

The city-state was at once the political, economic, social, and religious center of the district united around it. All the inhabitants of this territory were classed as citizens, and they jointly organized the life of the community. Only foreigners, serfs, and slaves were excluded from citizenship. The Greek citizen was deeply attached to his *polis* by blood and civic ties; he shared in its triumphs and defeats and in the parochial attitude of a community that scorned as inferior—although only because they were different—the customs, religious practices, and dialects of other city-states. The *polis* was large neither in population nor area; generally it ranged from fifty to five-hundred square miles. But its small size made it possible for the citizens to participate directly in the community's political life, which in turn developed and sustained strong patriotic emotions. The keynote of the *polis* was thus absolute independence, and here we find a clue to the inability of the Greek city-states to unite into a permanent confederacy and so transcend their parochial limitations. This weakness was one day to prove fatal.

The city-states tended to follow a general political pattern in their evolution, though with numerous variations. Power passed by stages from the hands of the clan king to those of leading families, and finally to the citizens as a whole. The first of these stages is known as "aristocracy," the last as "democracy." So far we have quickly reviewed the evolution of Greek political life down to the period when the nobles were in control. It is now appropriate to examine in some greater detail the subsequent development of those two city-states "which gradually step to the front of political life, and in whose history, as in a mirror, the whole history of Greece is reflected."[5] These are Athens in central Greece and Sparta in the Peloponnesian peninsula.

The City-States: Athens and Sparta

Growth of Athenian democracy. In the seventh century B.C., the Athenian king lost all political importance and retained only certain religious functions in his capacity as chief priest. There was a popular assembly, but the real power was concentrated in the hands of a council of nobles, while the most important public office was held now by the archon, an official chosen from the aristocracy and elected annually. The power of the aristocracy of birth was weakened, however, by the necessity of creating a larger army. The land-owning aristocracy, which originally had to bear the whole burden of defense, was inclined to shift some of this burden to other rich citizens and in return to grant certain political concessions. As a result, military duties and political rights came eventually to be counted on an economic rather than a hereditary basis.

Here we see an important political transition: Athens had begun the process of sweeping away its old institutions founded on clans and families and of creating a democratic system based on a codified legal system. Meanwhile, the economic changes of the seventh century, examined above, induced further change. In the new economy, many small landowners were ruined and forced to become tenant farmers on lands owned by the aristocracy, who treated them harshly and thereby added to the growing discontent of the lower classes. These possessed no political rights and they began to seek strong leaders who would redivide the land and abolish debts. Stability had to be achieved among the Athenian population.

The Draconian code. In 621 B.C. an attempt toward achieving that stability was made by the codification of oral law, a work attributed to a noble named Draco. Little is known of the Draconian laws except that they were so harsh that one critic complained that the code had been written not in ink but in blood. However, two points of interest emerge here: the Draconian code attests to the severity of criminal legislation under aristocracy-dominated Athens and it put crime under state jurisdiction rather than at the disposition of clan or family action.

Solon. Economic unrest continued to harass Athens, and the cry of the common people for reform was answered in 594 B.C. by the appointment of Solon as archon. Numerous reforms have made his name a metaphor for wise statesmanship. Solon abolished serfdom and slavery in connection with debt, limited the amount of land which any one person might own, developed Athens as an industrial center by encouraging skilled artisans to reside there through the promise of citizenship, stimulated exports and industry in general, and reformed the law code. In the political field, Solon made it possible for the lowest class of Athenians to vote in the popular assembly, which elected the magistrates and passed on state measures. Another of his innovations was the creation of the *Heliaea,* a law-court in which any citizen could be a judge and which heard appeals from decisions made by the archons and tried magistrates for misdeeds. Although he maintained the privileges of the highest classes, by broadening the franchise to include the least wealthy in the state and by establishing the new court, Solon prepared much of the ground for Athens' later democracy.

The tyrants. Solon's archonship was followed, however, by civil strife until order was restored by a military leader named Pisistratus, who came forward as the champion of the

DORIC ORDER: THE PARTHENON

small landowners and common people against the aristocracy. Pisistratus was a tyrant (the word did not originally have the same unfavorable meaning it now possesses) in that he had usurped power and ruled by unconstitutional means. However, tyrants such as Pisistratus—a not uncommon phenomenon in Greek political development at this time—were public benefactors in that they advanced the interests of the citizens as a whole instead of perpetuating the rule of the nobles. Pisistratus destroyed none of the democratic foundations set down by Solon. He fostered commerce and a progressive foreign policy in order to extend Athens' prestige and, more important from our present standpoint, he weakened the aristocracy still further by banishing many of the families and distributing their confiscated estates among the poorer citizens.

The next important tyrant to contribute to the development of Athenian democracy was Cleisthenes, who gained control in 508 B.C. By introducing a new system for classifying citizens—a system made up of ten electoral units—Cleisthenes destroyed the political importance of the old tribal divisions based on kinship and clan, and with it the dominant power of the noble families. In addition, he created a Council of Five Hundred, to which each of the ten electoral units contributed fifty members chosen annually by lot. The discussion and passage of laws remained the prerogative of the popular assembly, while the Council of Five Hundred was responsible for handling such matters as finance, war, and foreign policy. Cleisthenes thus brought into operation a workable governmental system based on the political equality of citizens and on universal participation in the functioning of that system. In the period following Cleisthenes, a new device was introduced, known as *ostracism* (public banishment of persons considered dangerous to the public welfare). By this means the Athenian populace acquired a potent weapon (at times abused) against those leaders who became too powerful.

The culmination of Athenian democracy. Athens was to become even more democratic during the fifth century. In the years following Greece's triumphant repulse of Persia's attempted conquest (page 134), the Athenians brought their democratic system to its peak. The government was then vested in three main bodies: the popular assembly, in which all male citizens over eighteen could participate; the Council of Five Hundred, whose members received a daily stipend and were entrusted, as Aristotle puts it, with "the guardianship of the constitution"; and the *Heliaea,* or popular court, which was composed of six thousand jurors (six hundred drawn by lot from each of the ten units). A juror was required to be over thirty years old and was paid for his services. The amazing size of the jury was calculated to prevent bribery and intimidation, and decisions were reached by majority vote.

The archonship was by this time of little consequence, and the most important posts in the government were filled by the ten generals (*strategi*) who were the commanders of the army and navy and also formed a kind of cabinet, a development going back to the Persian wars. Foreign and domestic policy was now under their control, and the success or failure of that policy determined whether the generals would be re-elected at the end of their year's term or else be sentenced to exile or even death. The great statesman Pericles, with whose name the most splendid age of Athenian culture is linked, was voted into office some fifteen times. In addition, there were numerous executive officials, all appointed by lot annually. "When we consider the jurors, soldiers, and sailors, we have at the very least 20,000 Athenians who were on the pay roll of their city."[6]

Athens was a limited democracy in that the foreigners and slaves in its population had no voice in the government. But within those limits, Athenian democracy made noteworthy contributions. The ideal prevailed that all citizens could participate fruitfully in the public life of the city-state. In the words ascribed to Pericles:

"Our form of government does not enter into rivalry with the institutions of others. We do not copy our neighbors, but are an example to them. It is true that we are called a democracy, for the administration is in the hands of the many and not of the few. But while the law secures equal justice to all alike in their private disputes, the claim of excellence is also recognized; and when a citizen is in any way distinguished, he is preferred to the public service, not as a matter of privilege, but as the reward of merit. Neither is poverty a bar, but a man may benefit his country whatever be the obscurity of his condition."[7]

We have now examined briefly the evolution in the Athenian government of "pure" democracy, where the entire citizen body gathered to participate in government—as contrasted with the "representative" form of democracy which our own society requires because of its much greater size and more complex structure. Athenian democracy, superior to the government of any other Greek city-state, created that climate of political freedom essential for true self-expression. It was this freedom which made possible those remarkable intellectual and artistic outpourings of Athens in the fourth century. However, this particular political system bred at once strong civic consciousness and a fierce patriotic attachment to the *polis*. Unfortunately, it also set limitations on the ability of the Athenians later to submerge parochial interests and to federate with other Greek cities for the sake of common survival. This is a crucial problem to which we must return shortly.

Sparta. All during this period, the rival city-state of Sparta had been evolving in a far different fashion. The warlike Dorians had early conquered a large portion of the Peloponnesian peninsula and by the sixth century had created a Spartan League which controlled nearly all that peninsula. While Sparta was perhaps the most powerful state in Greece at this time, its actual citizens numbered not more than 25,000, who dominated a population some twenty times as large. The government retained two kings as its nominal heads and also a Council of Elders, but more important was the popular assembly, made up of all adult Spartans who possessed full citizenship rights and served in the army. This assembly elected the Council and also the five overseers (*Ephors*) who in reality controlled the state.

"The peculiarity of Sparta was not the constitution: it was the creation of an absolutely unique social organization, intended to increase the military strength of the country. All social and economic relations were based on absolute subordination of the individual to the state, and on the conversion of all the dominating class into a standing army, ready at any moment to take the field."[8] In this totalitarian state, every Spartan was first of all a soldier, and his training from birth was directed accordingly. Government officials examined every child at birth, and each that was found sickly or deformed was exposed to die. At seven a boy was taken from his family and put in a group where he was given a rigorous course of military discipline lasting for years. The girls in turn were given rigorous physical training to prepare them to be healthy mothers of warrior sons. At the age of thirty, the male Spartan was considered mature and permitted to attend the assembly and hold political office. He was forbidden to engage in trade or industry. Iron coinage was retained since the unwieldy iron bars discouraged easy commerce and, of course, were not recognized as a medium of exchange outside Sparta. Likewise travel was prohibited because ideas from the outside might disturb the status quo within Sparta itself. The lot of the serfs (*helots*) was wretched. Forced to produce the necessities of life for their masters, these *helots* were kept under constant surveillance, with secret agents moving about in their midst and liquidating without trial the most intelligent among them. This was done to prevent *helot* uprisings. Another group of subject inhabitants, the *perioeci,* fared better. They controlled the industry and commerce of the country and, while never attaining full Spartan citizenship, the *perioeci* often reached posts of importance.

While Sparta developed the physical fitness of its chosen few and possessed the finest military machine in Greece, it remained intellectually and culturally backward. Its self-imposed isolation forbade those culture contacts without which no balanced civilization can develop. Sparta is a classic example of rigid regimentation accompanied by intellectual stagnation.

Unity and Separation in the Hellenic World

The Persian wars. By 500 B.C. the more important Greek states had passed through the Age of Tyrants. A new series of events now confronted the populace of Greece. During the sixth century Lydia had grown in power and conquered all the Greek cities in Asia Minor excepting Miletus. Lydia in turn was conquered by Cyrus and his Persians in 546 B.C. (Chapter 2). The Asia Minor Greeks, feeling the loss of their old independence and resenting subjection by oriental despots, revolted. From 499 to 494 B.C. the Ionian cities held out against Darius and his Persian hosts. Athens contributed twenty ships to the Ionians. The odds were too great, however, and the Persians finally suppressed the revolt, burning Miletus in revenge. Darius realized that the Ionians would be incited to revolt again by their cousins, the Athenians, unless the latter were also brought into subjection. That reason, together with the desire to punish the Athenians for their aid to the rebels, influenced Darius in 492 B.C. to send an expedition through Thrace to conquer the Greek upstarts. But a storm partially destroyed the accompanying fleet, and the Persians returned home.

In 490 B.C. a second expedition set forth from Persia and sailed across the Aegean, disembarking finally in the Bay of Marathon. The Athenians, finding the dreaded foe only twenty-six miles from their city, dispatched messengers to Sparta to beg aid and then marched off to try to repel the invader. The Persians numbered probably twenty thousand men; the Athenians had no more than half that number. But under the skillful generalship of their leader Miltiades the Athenians won an overwhelming victory at the battle of Marathon, killing perhaps six thousand of their foe, with a loss of only one hundred ninety-two of their own forces. The Greeks had won the first encounter.

Ten years later (480 B.C.) the Persians again set sail for Greece. But Athens was not unprepared this time, for under the advice of the astute statesman Themistocles, the city had built a powerful fleet with which to repel Xerxes, the Persian king (Darius had died in the meantime). The enemy came by land and sea. To meet the first danger the Spartans guarded the mountain passes, finally encountering the huge Persian host at Thermopylae. Although the Spartans under King Leonidas put up a magnificent struggle, the Greeks were annihilated by treachery and the weight of overwhelming numbers. The enemy now advanced and burned Athens. But the tide of victory was turned as the Greek fleet destroyed the ships of Xerxes in the Bay of Salamis. With their lines of communication thus cut off, the Persians had no alternative but to retreat to Asia, especially when they were decisively defeated at the battle of Plataea in 479 B.C. Greece was safe from any future invasion from the east. It was free to work out its own destiny and thereby to influence all subsequent European history.

The ascendancy of Athens. The great victory over Persia had been made possible by the unity of Hellenic arms, to which Athens, Sparta, and Corinth had been the chief contributors. But this unity was unfortunately only temporary, for with the danger at an end, Sparta retired to its territory south of the isthmus of Corinth. Instead, the next half century, from the battle of Plataea to the outbreak of the Peloponnesian War in 431 B.C., was made memorable by the ascendancy of Athens, marked at home by the brilliant Age of Pericles and in foreign relations by the creation of a maritime empire.

The Persians had destroyed both Athens and its port of Piraeus, but these were speedily rebuilt and the area strongly fortified by two long walls connecting the city and port. With such fortifications and with the largest naval fleet in the region, Athens had now become an important military power as well as the most active commercial center in Greece. However, a future invasion by Persia was still feared by

Athens and certain other Greek cities on the peninsula and the coast of Asia Minor, and so in 478 B.C. they took a logical step—they formed a defensive alliance. Known as the Delian League because its treasury was kept on the island of Delos, this maritime confederacy was supported by contributions of ships and men from the large cities, while the smaller members provided money. As the most powerful member, Athens had the dominant voice and vote in the League's affairs; thus it was made permanent head and given charge of the fleet, and was empowered to collect the money. Through the League's action, the Aegean was gradually cleared of the Persians, and communities on the Hellespont and the Sea of Marmora joined the alliance.

With the Persian threat removed, at least for the time being, various members of the Delian League grew restive and felt it unnecessary to continue the confederacy, especially since a number of cities resented Athens' dominant position and feared its motives. The decision rested with the latter, and instead of reverting to the political situation which had existed prior to the Persian wars, Athens took a momentous step: it proceeded to convert the confederacy into an Athenian maritime empire. The decision may have been taken partly because the Athenian leaders believed the danger from the east not yet at an end, but undoubtedly it was also dictated by economic considerations, such as the need to maintain lucrative markets in the Mediterranean and to destroy such dangerous commercial rivals as the Phoenicians. At any rate, Athens began to use force to prevent the withdrawal of members from the League. Then, in 454 B.C. the treasury was removed from Delos to Athens, and it soon became clear that some three hundred city-states, each of whose citizens possessed a fierce civic pride, were no longer the allies but the subjects of Athens. In effect, an empire had been acquired during the Age of Pericles, when Athenian democracy was in full swing at home. But that empire was destined to be short-lived, for Athens' political and economic triumphs were bitterly resented by its two chief rivals, Sparta and Corinth. In 431 B.C. the Peloponnesian War broke out between Athens and the other city-states, and as a result of this catastrophe the Greeks forever lost that strength and unity which alone could repel foreign invasion. This fatal inability of the Greeks to profit from the lesson of unity, which alone had defeated the Persians, deserves comment.

In our survey of the political evolution of the Greeks, we noted that they developed a unique institution, the city-state, which admirably suited the growth of "pure" democracy and of civic consciousness and pride, but which was also extremely parochial—we might say "isolationist"—in its attitudes and loyalties. We also saw that whereas in the beginning the simple subsistence economy of the city-state was a logical counterpart to its political structure. But during the seventh and sixth centuries an economic revolution took place in the form of colonization and production of specialized wares for export. In other words, in the economic field city-states such as Athens and Corinth gave up concepts of self-sufficiency and became interdependent. But as some historians have pointed out, this new economic system, to work effectively, required a political framework that also transcended city-state parochialism. The Delian League might have provided the necessary international political order but, as we have just seen, some of the city-states at the first opportunity demanded a return to their age-old local independence of action, while Athens, instead of attempting to develop the federal idea of government, became a tyrant city and established an empire by force. Arnold J. Toynbee and some other scholars are of the view that the failure of the Greeks to solve this political problem, a result of their economic revolution, was responsible for the breakdown of Greek civilization. "Having defeated Xerxes in the years 480 and 479 B.C., they were defeated between 478 and 431 B.C. by themselves."[9] Later, we shall have occasion to examine how this same political problem—namely, resolving the conflict between the political concept of the city-state and the need for a larger political organization—was handled in the Hellenistic and Roman periods. It is a question which, in amended form, is also of prime importance to us in the twentieth century.

The Peloponnesian War. The devastating conflict that broke out between the Greek states in 431 B.C. has been described by that great historian, Thucydides, as follows: "...The Peloponnesian War was a protracted struggle and attended by calamities such as Hellas had never known within a like period of time. Never were so many cities captured and depopulated.... Never were exile and slaughter more frequent, whether in the war or brought about by civil strife....The real though unavowed cause I believe to have been the growth of Athenian power, which terrified the Lacedaemonians (Spartans) and forced them into war...."[10]

At the beginning of the war Athens possessed a large empire, an unrivaled navy, and a rich treasury. Against this power Sparta and Corinth mustered a strong army which kept invading and pillaging Attica. Despite her strength, Athens lost the bitter struggle for a number of reasons. For one thing, revolts among her subject states proved a source of trouble; then, in 429 B.C. a plague carried off a third of the Athenian population. "The dead lay as they had died, one upon another, while others hardly alive wallowed in the streets and crawled about every fountain craving for water."[11] Pericles himself died a victim of the plague. After ten years of war and the conclusion of peace, Athens began the struggle again with a disastrous expedition in 415 B.C. against Syracuse in Sicily. By 413 two great fleets and a huge army had been destroyed and the remnants of the Athenian forces had mostly been sold into slavery by the Syracusans. Still the war dragged on, but the last Athenian fleet was defeated in 405 near the Hellespont and the next year saw Athens forced to capitulate. The walls connecting Athens and its port of Piraeus were torn down, all but twelve ships were destroyed, every foreign possession was stripped away, and Athens was made a subject ally of Sparta.

But the latter's rule was short-lived. The next fifty years saw constant clashes among the various city-states and the manipulations of Persia to gain control of Asia Minor. The city-state of Thebes triumphed temporarily over Sparta in 371 B.C., but its power in turn collapsed by 362, and the final chapter was soon to be written to the political history of the Hellenic world.

A history of the Hellenic world would be incomplete without an account of the remarkable achievements of the Greeks in philosophy, science, and the arts. Although the conquest of Greece by Macedon in 338 B.C. ended the Hellenic period and the political supremacy of the Greek city-states, the cultural accomplishments of that period have endured.

Hellenic Social and Economic Life

Economic growth. We have already seen how the political development of Greek city-states was intimately bound up with their economic evolution. Thus, during the age of nobles the ownership of land was transferred from a tribal to private basis, which in turn created serious landowner-peasant problems and incited many Greeks to emigrate to the colonies then springing up around the Mediterranean. Such colonization was accompanied by a rapid increase in commerce and shipbuilding and the change-over to specialized manufactures. The introduction of a coinage system into the Greek world by the seventh century B.C. facilitated these changes and at the same time made possible the rise of a new and powerful class whose wealth was measured not in lands but in money. This class helped to wrest political power from the landed aristocracy.

Meanwhile, the growing city populations could not adequately be supported by the land because of the poor quality of the Greek soil and the primitive methods of cultivation; not until the fourth century B.C. was the inefficient two-field system replaced by a three-field method, which finally reduced the amount of fallow land by employing improved rotation of crops. Perhaps as early as 800 B.C. certain urban centers found it necessary to import food supplies, and the fact that Athens depended for its existence upon such supplies helps to explain its foreign policy. As we have seen, by the fifth century Athens had geared its commercial and industrial activities to mesh with—and in turn accelerate—the ever-developing economic life of the Mediterranean basin. Then as a natural, but thoroughly unwise, corollary, the Athenians in the Age of Pericles decided to protect and increase their overseas interests by establishing a maritime empire, a policy destined to ruin Athens and indeed all Greece.

Athens in the Age of Pericles. In the fifth century, Athens was the busiest industrial region in the Hellenic world. Athens' economic prosperity was complemented by its possession of the largest naval and mercantile fleets and by its virtual monopoly of trade throughout the eastern Mediterranean and Black Sea areas. Industrial activity was intense in the port of Piraeus and certain quarters of Athens; here were carried on many different manufactures, such as metalworking, the making of arms, shipbuilding, and pottery-making. Characteristic of the period was the highly developed division of labor. Xenophon, for example, could speak about shoemakers who made only men's shoes and others who made only women's, while one shoemaker would not cut the leather and another would not sew the shoes.[12] Likewise the textile industries and the building, pottery, and metal trades were highly specialized. The usual day's wage for a workman was a drachma (about 24 cents), which enabled him to raise a family and even retain a fair margin. The craftsmen generally worked in groups not much larger than twenty, and many performed their tasks at home. They were affiliated in craft associations which had religious and social purposes, and because the social status of skilled craftsmen was relatively high, the industrial life of Athens in the fifth century tended to be both prosperous and contented. On the other hand, the unskilled laborers worked long hours and had a low social status. The lot of the slaves varied. Those in wealthy homes were often treated like members of the family, but those in the silver mines, for example, were chained in gangs and subjected to wretched conditions.

With economic prosperity went political and cultural advancement in Athens. The Age of Pericles (460-429 B.C.) has been well termed the Golden Age of Greece. Athens was at this time the chief economic and political power in the Greek world and the physical changes wrought in the years following the Persian wars attested to its accepted role as the capital of Hellenic civilization. The ruins left by the Persians in 480 B.C. quickly gave way to a new city, whose lower town retained its dusty, tortuous streets and unpretentious brick houses, but whose Acropolis was now crowned with a group of magnificent public buildings. Here stood the gleaming symbols of Athenian might and of its intellectual and artistic splendor. About a thousand feet in length, the Acropolis was adorned with great staircases, temples, and statues erected to Athena, the patron and protector of the city.

But if they were sumptuous in their expression of civic pride, the Athenians led a daily existence which frowned on extravagant display. "For we are lovers of the beautiful, yet simple in our tastes, and we cultivate the mind without loss of manliness," wrote Pericles. "Wealth we employ, not for talk and ostentation, but when there is a real use for it. To avow poverty with us is no disgrace; the true disgrace is in doing nothing to avoid it. An Athenian citizen does not neglect the state because he takes care of his own household; and even those of us who are engaged in business have a very fair idea of politics."[13]

A Greek shoemaker is fitting a customer in this vase painting (fourth century B.C.*). Other shoes hang on the wall.*

The democratic processes demanded active citizen participation, and an Athenian was not likely to evade jury service or escape attending the assembly. During their leisure hours, all classes frequented the numerous gymnasia and wrestling schools to exercise and play games for the sake of health. The Athenians also attended the festivals of drama held twice a year and participated in banquets, where long discussions would be held on such subjects as politics, art, or philosophy. Or they might, if so inclined, drop into a gambling house or seek the company of some courtesan. Athens' culture was predominantly masculine, and women no longer played the role which had been theirs when Greece and Ionia were ruled by aristocracies. Now their sphere was reduced to the kitchen, nursery, and *gynaeceum,* a special part of the house reserved for women and children.

Weakening of the social fabric. The Peloponnesian War ruined the power of Athens, and brought about the social and economic decline of all the Greek cities. Even the victor,

Music and poetry (note the four lyres and the flute) seem to be the principal subjects taught in this Greek academy. The figures in this painting on the Duris vase are red.

Sparta, was little better off than the vanquished, for wealth and power did much to destroy the old Spartan virtues of frugality and simplicity. Luxury was prevalent among the upper classes, while the poverty of the masses became more marked by contrast. It is not surprising that Sparta was subsequently defeated by Thebes and thenceforth relinquished any claim to power and influence.

The Athenian countryside had been harried all through the Peloponnesian conflict, and the city had suffered a terrible loss of life. The cost of living nearly doubled. Yet despite these difficulties, Athens continued to be the business center of the Aegean, and the lot of the workers remained better there than in other cities. Furthermore, as we shall see, the creative power of its citizens expressed itself as strongly in the fourth century as during the great Periclean Age. Indeed, for a long time to come, Athens was to remain one of the great cities of the world.

The Glory That Was Greece

The Greek spirit. In our own age we consider the Greek intellectual and artistic contributions among the most vigorous and enduring achievements of mankind. The Greeks were the first to formulate many of the western world's most fundamental concepts in philosophy, science, and art. That a relative handful of individuals could bequeath such a magnificent legacy raises the question of how this originality can be explained.

Probably the definitive answer will always elude the historian, but we might at least set forth some possible explanations. We have seen that geographical factors made for political individualism and separation from the Orient with its emphasis on absolutism, social compulsion through tradition, priestcraft, and supernaturalism. The Hellenes were thus given a priceless opportunity to break from the bondage of the past, and to develop new and fundamental ideas of democracy. This freedom from authoritarianism was unique in the ancient world.

Furthermore, the successful wars with Persia, against overwhelming odds, secured Greek independence and freedom of the seas. With the resulting increase of commerce and travel, intellectual and scientific exploration followed as a matter of course. The victory over the Persians also stimulated the pride and self-confidence of the Greeks, for they had learned to trust their own resources. The Greek at his best reflected this spirit by relying on his own reason and artistic judgment, beginning a tradition of humanism which continues to influence modern life profoundly. The spirit of inquiry which characterized the Greek as he explored the ancient world, enabled him not only to promote knowledge but indeed to formulate the main foundations of western civilization.

It is said that an Egyptian priest once told Solon that the Greeks were perennially children. That they were woefully immature in their political relationships has already been demonstrated. But in a deeper sense we can say that the Greeks possessed certain childlike qualities which never quite deserted them: boundless curiosity concerning the universe and their own part in it; a basic simplicity of approach to new situations; and an instinctive response to nature and the natural. The Greeks could be suspicious, vindictive, and even merciless to their enemies, but at its best their spirit was fresh, rational, audacious. And that spirit, which seems to permeate their intellectual and artistic legacy, was guided by an underlying ideal of harmony which, for them, was the basis of life and of all forms of expression.

The puzzle of creation and existence. The freedom of thought which the Greeks enjoyed together with their insatiable curiosity led to a search after the facts and laws of nature; and their sense of harmony and proportion led to a belief in a cosmos governed by order and intelligence. As a result, science and philosophy were interactive from the Greek standpoint, and it is therefore not surprising to learn that some of the greatest philosophers—such as Pythagoras, Plato, and Aristotle—were at the same time men of science.

The study of philosophy was also encouraged in part by questions arising out of various religious beliefs. In primitive times, the Greek religion had been local and animistic, with each region possessing its particular friendly and hostile spirits. Gradually a mythology about specific gods developed; and from the immortal but often immoral gods of the old myths there evolved the idea of deities or fates controlling the universe and man's destiny. Some thinkers came to believe, furthermore, that there must be a reckoning for all mortals in a life after death. More important to the mass of people than the afterlife, however, were the means of ascertaining the divine will in this life. As a result, oracles, omens, and divination were prominent in Greek religion. Throughout the entire classical period these forms of superstition were common, except among a relatively few educated persons, whose religious views were less crudely anthropomorphic (i.e., patterned after man and his activities) and more concerned with the puzzles of creation and existence.

Nature of the universe. Early in the sixth century B.C., in the cultured city-state of Miletus in Asia Minor, certain individuals began to speculate about the physical construction of the universe. The results of these initial studies in cosmology—that branch of philosophy which treats of the universe as an orderly system, or cosmos—were momentous for western philosophy and science.

"The Father of Philosophy" is the title given to a statesman of Miletus named Thales. A traveler who had learned from the Babylonians the secret of calculating eclipses, Thales came to the conclusion that such phenomena in the skies were not the results of the whims of gods but of natural, fixed laws. Looking for a basic substance from which all else in the universe is composed, Thales came to the belief that it was water, which exists in different states and is indispensable to the maintenance and growth of organisms. That we disagree with him today is quite unimportant to our discussion; the important point is that Thales was the first western philosopher to offer an explanation of life in terms of naturalistic causes.

Miletus produced successors to Thales, and they concerned themselves also with cosmological speculations. These pioneers in philosophy had different theories as to what was the true "earth-substance." Their conclusions were scarcely in accord with modern scientific knowledge, but they started men on a fascinating quest to understand the nature of the universe.

Mathematics has always been closely allied with both science and philosophy, and many of the world's greatest philosophers have been also outstanding mathematicians. The relationship between these two fields of thought was clearly seen by another early Greek philosopher, Pythagoras (born about 582 B.C.). Pythagoras, whose theorem in geometry is known (presumably) by every schoolboy, believed that the universe was founded on mathematical principles. He went so far as to maintain that all things were really numbers, and "to get its number" was to obtain the

A statue of Socrates (Vatican museum, Rome) is from all accounts a good likeness of the great man.

principal characteristics of an object. In music, Pythagoras discovered by experimenting with a vibrating cord that musical harmony is based on arithmetical proportions.

By the beginning of the fifth century B.C., Greek philosophy was flourishing. Men were now more sophisticated and they criticized the views of the Milesians. Water, they reasoned, could not change into a multitude of things absolutely unlike water in every way. The problem of change thus came to the fore.

Some men reasoned that existence alone was real and that it was impossible for it to be other than eternal, immovable, and indivisible. Therefore, they said, movement and change were logically impossible, and were only illusions of the mind. But the contrary view was held by the brilliant Heraclitus (about 540-475 B.C.). To him life was change and change alone. The entire universe is in flux; life is forever "on the go." Our bodies and minds are always changing, and life is a constant transition. "Everything changes except change," declared Heraclitus, who was the first to expound the doctrine of relativity, an important doctrine in present-day mathematical, scientific, and philosophical theories.

Despairing that a single earth substance would be found to explain the nature of the universe, some thinkers concluded that it was composed of a number of substances, such as earth, water, fire, and air. One philosopher, Democritus (460?-370? B.C.), at length developed the theory that the universe was composed of atoms, which could not be seen and which differed not in quality but only in shape, size, position, and arrangement. Democritus argued that these atoms move about continuously and combine to create objects. To him reality was the mechanical motion of atoms. The mechanical atomic theory is one which scientists have used to the present day, although the atom is no longer believed to be indivisible and indestructible.

With their limited knowledge of science, yet having managed to deduce brilliant theories relating to change and the atomic structure of the universe, the Greeks had now gone as far as they could in their study of cosmology. A new field of inquiry presented itself. With the development of ideas about the universe, questions had arisen about the place of man in the scheme of things. Therefore, we find an increasing number of Greek philosophers interesting themselves in problems of ethics, logic, knowledge, and political theory.

Socrates. We now come to three Hellenic philosophers who during the century beginning about 425 B.C. laid down the main lines of Greek thought, and whose intellectual and moral contributions were of such a magnitude that the entire course of western culture has been affected by them.

At this time there were some thinkers who denied the existence of any universal standards to guide man in his principles and actions. Such were the Sophists, who became famous as teachers of rhetoric and gained reputations for "sophistry" by their tendency to emphasize the relativity of truth. The outstanding opponent of this school of thought was the Athenian-born Socrates (469?-399 B.C.), a snub-nosed, ugly man who proved his courage on the battlefield and in death as a martyr to his convictions. This fascinating conversationalist was, in the words of Cicero, "the first to call philosophy down from the heavens and to set her in the cities of men, bringing her into their homes and compelling her to ask questions about life and morality and things good and evil."[14] He believed that by asking such questions and by subjecting the answers to logical analysis, it was possible to come to agreement upon ethical standards and rules of conduct. And so he would question passers-by in his function—to use his own figure of speech—of midwife assisting in the birth of correct ideas. Socrates, who linked virtue and knowledge together and who took as his motto the famous inscription on the temple of Apollo at Delphi, "Know thyself," was tireless in his quest after truth. This quest in time led to his undoing, for a suspicious generation charged him with corrupting Athenian youth and carrying on political intrigue. Socrates was condemned to die, and although given ample chance to escape execution, he calmly accepted his fate, contending that a citizen should not disobey even an unjust sentence.

Plato and his doctrine of Ideas. The greatest of Socrates' many disciples was the aristocratic Athenian, Plato (427?-347? B.C.). At the death of Socrates, Plato found Athens unsafe and traveled abroad for some ten years. Upon his return he founded a famous school called the Academy, which lasted almost nine centuries until closed by order of the Roman emperor Justinian in 529 A.D. Many prominent youths were educated in the Academy, including Aristotle.

Plato's philosophy centers about his famous "Theory of Ideas." Like Socrates, Plato believed that truth exists and, furthermore, that truth is eternal and fixed. Yet Plato saw that nothing is permanent in the world of physical senses. Therefore permanence can be found only in the realm of thought, of Ideas or Forms. In this other world are certain universal Ideas, such as Beauty, Truth, and Justice, the greatest of all Ideas being Good. Many of us believe now that an Idea exists only in the human mind, but to Plato it had a real existence apart from our intellects. Furthermore, he believed, our concepts of justice, beauty, or truth in the world of the senses are only reflections—and very imperfect reflections at that—of the eternal and changeless Ideas. The world of Ideas is spiritual and not physical; and because man's soul is linked with the spiritual "Idea" world, it follows that the human soul is also spiritual and immortal.

Plato expounded his concepts of an ideal state in his *Republic,* which is the first systematic treatise on political science and constitutes the first "utopia," or ideal human society. Founded on the Idea of Justice, this state has as its function the satisfaction of the common good. In it, Plato provided for three classes: the workers, who would produce the necessities of life; the warriors, who would guard the state; and the philosophers, who would rule in the best interests of all the people. Plato's society was a "spiritualized Sparta" in which the state rigorously regulated virtually every aspect of the individual's life, so that even marriage was controlled in order that children might be produced eugenically. The family and private property were to be abolished on the grounds that both institutions bred selfishness. Much of the *Republic* has been unpalatable to ancient and present-day readers alike, but it does represent the first attempt to conceive a planned social order involving such "modern" ideas as division of labor and eugenics.

Aristotle, the first technical philosopher. Plato's greatest pupil was Aristotle (384-322 B.C.), who journeyed to Athens when eighteen to attend the Academy. Later, Aristotle tutored young Alexander of Macedonia and subsequently set up his own school, the Lyceum, at Athens. There he would walk up and down while lecturing to his pupils and thus the group came to be called "Peripatetic" (Greek *peripatein,* to walk), a term afterwards applied to the Aristotelian system.

In all human history there has probably never been another brain so encyclopedic as Aristotle's. He investigated all known fields of knowledge, and wrote brilliantly on mathematics, physics, astronomy, biology, physiology, anatomy, botany, natural history, psychology, politics, ethics, logic, rhetoric, art, theology, and metaphysics.

Although deeply appreciative of the contributions of Plato, Aristotle differed from Plato on the question of Ideas. Real Being for Aristotle was found not in universal Ideas but in the particular, the individual, and the concrete. Furthermore, every concrete object is composed of Form and Matter. Thus, in a marble statue, the marble is the Matter, while the shape conferred by the sculptor is the Form. Neither form nor matter has any real existence apart from the other, says Aristotle, though Plato separated his Ideal forms from matter.

In writing on ethics, Aristotle stressed that man's function is to live in conformity with reason and that happiness comes from an unobstructed pursuit of a rational life. He realized that normal human desires should not be repressed, and he stressed the virtue of moderation, warning against excess in any form.

Aristotle is also famous for having developed deductive reasoning. One of his many logical devices, that of the syllogism, is valuable in pointing out fallacies in human reasoning. This process of proof consists of a trio of propositions. The first two propositions (the major and minor premises) must be patently valid and so logically related that the third proposition, the conclusion, inevitably follows. For example, (1) all Greeks are human; (2) all humans are mortal; (3) therefore all Greeks are mortal.

Like his teacher, Aristotle was very much interested in politics, maintaining that man is a political being who achieves the fullest life only with other individuals. But he differed with many of Plato's political theories, contending that property and family life are valuable incentives. Because democracy had degenerated in Greece during his lifetime, Aristotle favored the rule of a single strong man. He also favored slavery, for he thought that some men are fit by nature only to wait upon their biological superiors. He had no concept of the present national state system, and he wrote only about the small *polis* of his own age.

Where Plato had condemned poetry, Aristotle in theories on esthetic problems saw the value of the poet and artist in sublimating or refining human passions. His theory of Unity of Action remains today a standard for the construction and criticism of the drama. On virtually every subject on which he wrote, Aristotle was considered secondary to Plato in ancient times. It was not until the medieval revival of Aristotle that he took precedence over Plato.

Hellenic scientific developments. Because of the close relationship which existed between Greek philosophy and science, we could expect the study of scientific problems to make use of much the same methods as those employed in philosophical speculations. The philosophers had for the most part proceeded on the basis of deduction; that is, they reasoned from general principles to more particular principles. Experimental science, on the other hand, is an inductive process which reasons from specific facts to principles about those facts. In the Hellenic period, as a result of the emphasis placed upon the speculative deductive method, the Greeks made notable advances in mathematics, in logic, in theories of matter, and in the classification of physical forms and types. On the other hand, theoretical conclusions were often made without sufficient proof based on experimentation in such fields as medicine, physics, and zoology. Unfortunately, the resulting errors, because they had been accepted by such authorities as Aristotle, were in turn uncritically accepted for the succeeding millennium or even longer.

We have already noted that two philosophers, Pythagoras and Democritus, made notable contributions to mathematics and the atomic theory respectively, while Heraclitus' brilliant deduction concerning the nature of change is today an accepted principle in science. Another philosopher in the sixth century B.C. anticipated the nineteenth-century evolutionary hypothesis of the struggle for existence when he surmised that the earlier animal species had lived in the water and had worn bony protective covering (such as the upper shell of the turtle) when they first ventured on land.

Perhaps the most successful Hellenic example of the use of inductive methods is to be found in Aristotle's advances in biology. Aristotle defined life as "the power of self-nourishment and of independent growth and decay." His conclusions were based upon keen personal observation, the use of dissection, and a wealth of data gathered by travelers, scholars, fishermen, and others. From his observations he concluded that there is an evolutionary process by which an organism develops from a simple to a more complex form, and that as the organism grows more complex there is a corresponding increase in intelligence. Aristotle also performed outstanding work in the field of embryology.

Although preconceived and false ideas about the human body often influenced Greek healing methods, the use of experiment appeared in the school founded at Cos about 420 B.C. by Hippocrates, who is often referred to as the Father of Medicine. This school approached the problem of disease with the idea that it resulted from natural and not supernatural causes. Writing of epilepsy, considered at the time a "sacred" malady, one Hippocratic writer observed: "It seems to me that this disease is no more divine than any other. It has a natural cause just as other diseases have. Men think it supernatural because they do not understand it. But if they called everything supernatural which they do not understand, why, there would be no end of such things!"[15] Hippocrates emphasized the value of observation and the careful interpretation of symptoms, and he set forth a high code of professional ethics—doctors today still pledge to adhere to this code in their daily practice, when they take the "Hippocratic oath" at the time of receiving their medical degrees.

Writing of history. With the Greeks, history (which itself is a Greek word, meaning an investigation or inquiry) was not legend nor was it attributed to the acts of a deity. Rather it was a humanistic study which sought to learn about the actions of men at determinate times. Often called the Father of History, Herodotus of Halicarnassus (484?-425? B.C.) in his history of the Persian wars pointed out the clash of two distinct civilizations, the Hellenic and the oriental. His portrayal of both the Greeks and the Persians was eminently fair, and he emphasized the effect of climate and geography upon social customs. Herodotus was not always accurate, however, because his fondness for a good story often led him to include it in his work regardless of its historical merits.

Thucydides (460?-400 B.C.) was the first great scientific historian. He was careful in weighing the value of his evidence, divorced history from supernaturalism, and even paid considerable attention to such factors as the psychological. Thucydides wrote about the Peloponnesian War (we have already quoted from his work on several occasions in this chapter), and in his account of the conflict laudably subordinated his Athenian sympathies in order to achieve objectivity.

Greek poetry and drama. All Greek poetry is marked by clarity and brevity of expression. It cannot be called bare or lacking in emotion, however; rather we see in it an expression of the Greek emphasis on proportion, form, and order. The epic poems and the philosophical drama are concerned with eternal themes of the fate of man in the universe, and these are portrayed vividly but with simplicity and pro-

THE THEATER AT EPIDAURUS

RED-FIGURED LECYTHUS, OR OIL JAR

portion—therefore without excessive emotion. The resulting literature is thus typical of the Greek concern with harmony and the larger philosophical issues of life.

The poetry of Greece goes back to the epic poems of Homer, the *Iliad* and the *Odyssey*. There is some question whether these poems were written by one man and whether Homer was actually a historical figure. At any rate, the epics were set down in their present form around the ninth century B.C. All scholars agree that any translation of Greek poetry must suffer badly; the sound of the language cannot be duplicated. But the artistry of the *Iliad* and *Odyssey* is not confined to sound. The descriptions of character, disaster, and human emotion are models of the simple epic forms that have influenced many subsequent literary efforts.

The immortality of Greek poetic literature is ensured by the compelling majesty of the Hellenic drama. Not only did the Greeks develop drama from primitive beginnings to complex forms which have scarcely been surpassed as models of dramatic imagination to the present day; they also portrayed vividly through the drama their own psychology and culture. The theater filled a civic-religious function in Greek society; and the plays which were written for this theater often show man in conflict with destiny, expressing again the Greek concern with universal law and the necessity for harmony. The Greek dramatists followed rigorous canons of form which were designed to achieve proportion and harmony. The Greeks wrote and enjoyed both tragedies, which were grave and religious, and comedies, which were secular, often bawdy, but always spirited.

Old, familiar legends of gods and heroes were used as plots for the tragedies, which thus retain a timelessness and dignity. Many Greek plays have been lost, so that only three tragedians survive through their works today; but these men are giants. The first of them was Aeschylus (525-456 B.C.), whose simple but profound plays convey a deeply religious spirit. He used actors and chorus with intense dramatic effect to depict such problems as sin, moral responsibility, and the purpose of existence. His successor, Sophocles (about 495-406 B.C.), advanced the techniques of characterization, suspense, climax, and the use of dialogue among several actors. His *Oedipus Rex* is still performed as a masterpiece of psychological study of man against fate. Greek drama was at its height in the Periclean Age. Toward the close of the fifth century the works of the playwright Euripides (480?-406? B.C.) began to reveal the growing unorthodoxy and critical attitude of Greek thinkers. Where Aeschylus was deeply religious, Euripides rationalized about the gods, leaving many questions of fate open to doubt.

Fortunately, among the extant comedies are those of the brilliant Aristophanes, master of satire and comic situations. He typifies the riotous Greek comedy in his satires on social customs, institutions, and famous Athenians.

The spirit of Greek art. The most striking expressions of the Greek ideals of moderation, proportion, and naturalism are to be found in their art. As Pericles said, "We love beauty without extravagance." Later, in Hellenistic times, such extravagance often did manifest itself, and Greek art declined. But at its finest, it was unsurpassed and exerted a profound influence on the art of Rome, India, and the western world—as can be seen, to take a random example, in the predominant architecture of our own capital, Washington.

CORINTHIAN ORDER: THE OLYMPIUM

IONIC ORDER: THE ERECHTHEUM

Greek art succeeded in fusing the natural with the universal. Whether in small utilitarian objects like the oil jar shown on page 144, the perfectly proportioned Parthenon, or one of their many statues in which the human form takes on godlike attributes, the Greeks expressed their belief in the existence of a fundamental harmony throughout the cosmos.

The Greeks as builders. Greek art reached its zenith in Athens in the fifth century B.C. In the previous century architecture had flourished in Miletus and other Ionian towns with the construction of large temples of stone, whose form developed from early wooden structures. The Persian invasion made Athens a heap of smoking ruins; but the repulse of the oriental invaders left the Athenians free to reconstruct the Acropolis, or sacred hill, into a treasury of temples and statues.

The Parthenon, the Erechtheum, and the other temples on the Acropolis show the perfection of the characteristic features of Greek architecture. These were the post and lintel construction, the gable roof, and the marble colonnade. All these structural features were

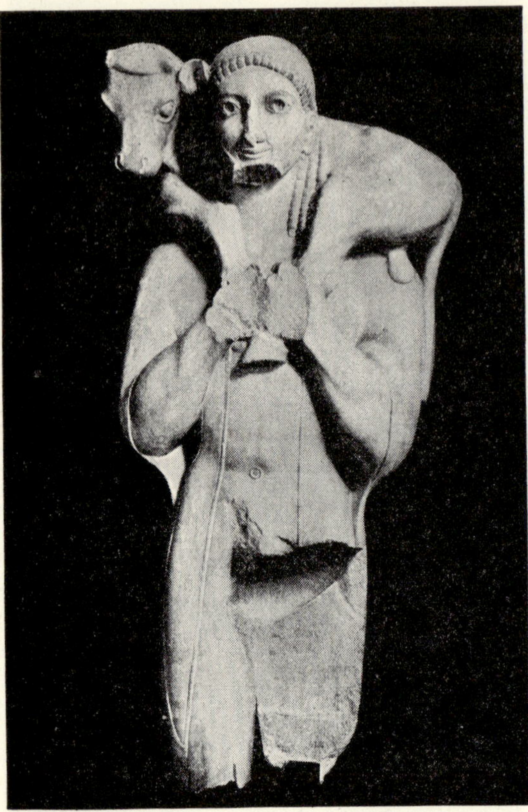

ARCHON: THE CALF-BEARER

used with the subtle precision that makes Greek structures so harmonious to the eye. The spacing of the columns, the curvature of the floor and roof, and the proportions of all elements were mathematically plotted and executed to achieve perfect balance. This tradition of perfection, as well as the perfected elements of construction which the Greeks made their own, have been imitated but not surpassed since their time. We often see modern examples of the three orders, or styles, of Greek columns—the simple Doric, which was used in the Parthenon (illustrated on page 132), the Ionic, seen in the Erechtheum (page 145), and the later Corinthian (page 145). The last style was usually too ornate for the simplicity-loving Greeks. However, the more ostentatious Romans used it widely in their massive public buildings, for example in the Pantheon and, centuries later, its influence persisted in medieval churches such as that of St. Gilles. (page 432).

The Acropolis buildings, as well as the Athenian treasury built at the shrine of Delphi, show a strong sense of civic pride. Put where all men could see and enjoy them, the Greek temple buildings afford interesting comparisons with those of Egypt. Whereas the temple of Egypt was enclosed and mysterious, the Greek temple was open for all, with a colonnaded porch and single statue hall inside. In fact there were often outside altars.

Other types of buildings also express the Greek way of life. Notable among these are the theaters, stadiums, and temples. In these gathering places Greek artists studied the human body and learned to express its forms in sculpture. The Greek love of drama has been described. The theater at Epidaurus, (see page 143) shows the plan of the typical outdoor Greek theater. The circular shape of the spectators' sections and the plan of the orchestra and stage were the ancestors of the modern theater.

Greek sculpture. Early Greek sculptors were influenced by Egyptian models, and their statues have one foot advanced and the arms hang with clenched fists like Egyptian figures. The "archaic" statues such as "The Calf-Bearer" shown on this page are also stiff and lacking in technical subtlety, but they are extremely vigorous. The fifth century B.C., however, witnessed a rapid technical improvement,

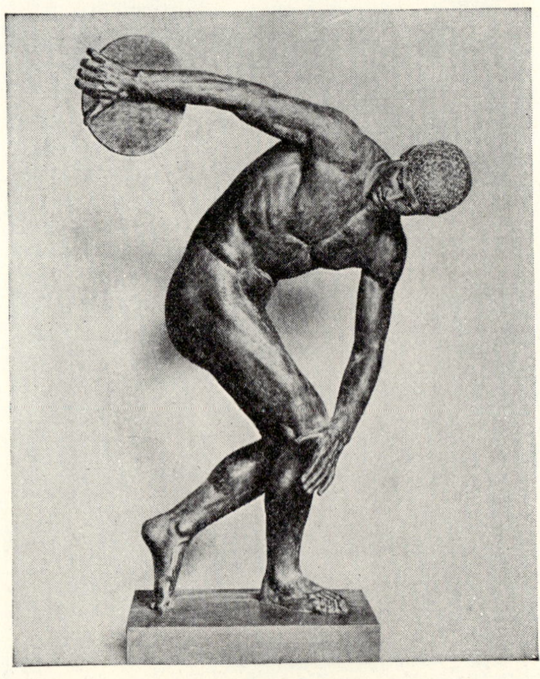

THE DISCUS THROWER

HORSEMEN ON THE PARTHENON FRIEZE

and a group of excellent sculptors now came to the fore in Athens. Two of these may be singled out for special mention.

Advancing far beyond the early stiff sculpture, Myron (about 450 B.C.) shows us, in his "Discus Thrower" (page 146) an athlete in motion, but at the same time he retains balance and restraint in the action. In this statue can also be seen the splendid carving and the idealization of the human form typical of Greek art in the Periclean Age. Myron was a master at portraying muscles and athletic poses, but has been described as lacking the ability to endow his figures with corresponding intellectual vigor.

Fifth-century sculpture reached its zenith in the work of Phidias and his school (about 440 B.C.). Phidias supervised the decoration of the Parthenon and fashioned the gold and ivory statue of Athena for the temple. That masterpiece and his Zeus at Olympia—also of gold and ivory—are known to us only by tradition, which speaks of their magnificence. But the art of Phidias' school may still be studied in the Elgin Marbles (in the British Museum) and the friezes of the Parthenon (a detail of which is illustrated on this page). Those friezes have been carved with a restraint and "calm exaltation" which makes them a perfect com-

HERMES, OF PRAXITELES

plement for the architectural elements of the temple.

Of the great sculptors of the fourth century, Praxiteles was the most famous. His "Hermes with the Infant Dionysus" is the only undisputed extant original of antique sculpture. Although it lacked some of the godlike characteristics associated with the art of the previous century, it was gracefully posed and governed by a strong sense of restraint.

The New Hellenistic World

Hellenistic civilization follows the Hellenic. We left the political history of the Hellenic world (page 136) during the aftermath of the Peloponnesian War, which saw the Greek city-states weakened as a result of internecine strife during a period of some 65 years. Although Hellenic culture was menaced by fratricidal conflict, it did not perish. These conflicts were stamped out by mighty conquerors, Philip and Alexander the Great of Macedon, who admired Hellenic culture and spread it over a large part of the Middle East, thus creating the second phase in Greek civilization, the Hellenistic.

This bronze head of a youth, "Speusippus," shows both idealization and stylization in the treatment of the hair and features.

When Alexander the Great diffused Hellenic culture throughout his empire, he inaugurated the "Hellenistic" period—that is, the extension of Greek civilization to non-Greeks, the counter influence of non-Greek cultures upon Greece, and the transfer of the intellectual capital of the pre-Roman world from Athens to Alexandria in Egypt. The Hellenistic Age ended in approximately 146 B.C.

Philip of Macedon. To the north of Greece lay Macedon, a region inhabited by hardy peasants and fighters who spoke an Indo-European dialect but were culturally inferior to their southern cousins. Under Philip II, who had secured a Greek education and ascended their throne in 359 B.C., the Macedonians began to advance rapidly. Philip was a master strategist. He created a permanent infantry which deployed eight men deep—the famous phalanx formation. After uniting Macedon, Philip turned his attention to the disunited Greek city-states, defeating the Athenians and Thebans in 338 B.C. The following year he founded the Hellenic League consisting of all the states in Greece except Sparta, which refused to become a member. The League members were allowed to retain self-government. Philip was head of the League, and it was his intention thus to unite the forces of Greece and Macedon in waging war against Persia. In 336 B.C., however, Philip was assassinated, and the rule of the League fell to his gifted twenty-year-old son, Alexander.

Alexander the Great. The youth Alexander, educated under the tutorship of Aristotle himself, was alive to the glories of Hellenic culture and, reveling in the heroic deeds of the *Iliad*, determined to spread Greek civilization throughout the world. Having stamped out rebellion at home, he set out in 334 B.C. at the head of an army of 35,000 soldiers to conquer the despotisms of the Orient. In quick succession Alexander conquered Asia Minor, Syria, Palestine, and Egypt, where he founded the city of Alexandria, destined to become the capital of the Hellenistic world. Then he turned eastward, marching over the Fertile Crescent, and near the ruined city of Nineveh defeated the overwhelmingly larger forces of the Persian Darius III at the battle of Arbela in 331 B.C. Within a few days Alexander entered the ancient city of Babylon in triumph. He was now master of a proud empire that had once held sway over the entire Near East but had nevertheless been unable to conquer a small, stubborn band of hostile Greek cities.

Alexander now campaigned from 330 to 324 B.C. in the Far East, venturing as far as the rich valleys of the Ganges in India before his travel-weary army forced him to turn back from world dominion. Though he was not given the opportunity of conquering India, the Hellenic culture which he introduced there later influenced the art of that country, as we shall see in Chapter 7. Alexander's journey was therefore not without effect.

In 323 B.C. the youthful monarch, who had made himself master wherever he marched, who never had to taste the gall of defeat in battle, and who was still planning new conquests in the western Mediterranean, died at the age of thirty-three at Babylon, the victim of fever and excessive drinking. This phenomenal young man has staggered the world with the daring of his actions and the scope of his imagination. Although his successes were due in no small measure to the great military machine which his father had created and to the disorganized internal conditions of the crumbling Persian empire, Alexander himself was a master at military pursuits. Had he lived longer, his empire might still have perished like those which he himself destroyed.

One of Alexander's most important legacies to later political thought was the theory of divine kingship. He saw in such a philosophy the sanctification of royal policies and commands. As we shall see later, the theory of divine kingship occurs again and again in history.

Hellenistic political developments. The suddenness of Alexander's death destroyed any plans he may have had for realizing his dream of bringing about the "marriage of Europe and Asia." Since he had left no heirs of sufficient age or ability to carry on his work, a struggle for power among his generals was virtually inevitable. In time the empire was roughly divided into three main parts: Egypt, ruled by the Ptolemy family; Syria and Persia, governed by Seleucus and his descendants; and Macedon and Greece, which had been reconstituted as a separate power, by Antigonus Gonatus. Meanwhile, other parts of Alexander's empire had broken free, including India, Bactria, Mesopotamia, and the northern part of Asia Minor.

Alexander the Great, carved in sardonyx in the Vienna cameo, is shown with Roxane, his queen. His helmet is decorated with the symbols of the god who was reputed to be his father.

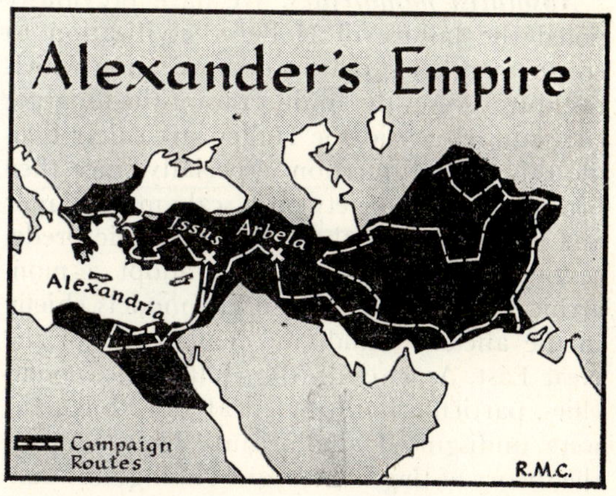

In the wake of Alexander's conquests, the Greeks had embarked upon a new movement of colonial expansion, which resulted in the establishment of a large number of cities and the diffusion of Greek culture to the east. The new rulers were Greek kings surrounded by Greek advisers, and even the chief administrators of the Seleucid and Ptolemaic empires were Greek. The cities not only took over much of the civic consciousness and pride of the Hellenic *polis,* but were similar even in town planning and had the same types of buildings and public institutions—such as the ever popular *gymnasia.* It is therefore possible to say that the Hellenistic world possessed a social and, to some extent, a political unity, maintained by a network of Greek settlements. On the other hand, this unity never penetrated deeply. The vast mass of the native peoples did not become hellenized, but maintained their traditional way of life. Greek culture and influence was to be found in the cities, while the indigenous way of life persisted in the countryside.

Absolutist monarchies. We have previously noted the failure of Hellenic civilization to create a workable political organization which could transcend the limitations of the separate city-state. How did the Hellenistic rulers handle this crucial question, especially since they had to organize society on a scale much larger and more complex than their Hellenic predecessors? Their answer was to adopt a monarchical system which found its models chiefly in the ancient semidivine monarchies of the Near East. As a result, the Hellenistic monarchies, particularly the Seleucid and Ptolemaic, were undisguised absolutisms. They adopted the theory of the divine right of kings and centralized the administration in the hands of a permanent Greek bureaucracy, thus creating an unbridgeable gulf between ruler and subject and making impossible the development of responsible government. From a practical standpoint, the Hellenistic monarchies succeeded in governing large areas, particularly where absolute monarchies were traditional. Furthermore, they conceded a fairly large measure of self-government to both the old and the new Greek city-states. This tempering of absolutism was particularly noticeable in the Antigonid empire. Later, this pattern of government was to influence the Romans in large measure when they came to organize their domination over the Mediterranean.

These developments in political organization, however, did not secure the Hellenistic monarchies against destruction by internal dissension and external aggression. The Hellenistic world continued to be plagued by separatist tendencies within the monarchies, dynastic troubles, and wars between the kingdoms. With these troubles came moral and physical decay. In 212 B.C., Rome entered into Hellenistic affairs and, taking over the various remnants of Alexander's domains, finally swallowed up the last morsel, Egypt, in 30 B.C. Yet, in spite of being relatively short-lived, the Hellenistic world had a far-reaching influence on the spread of Greek culture, particularly in the fields of literature, art, philosophy, science, and learning. Some historians point out that the Hellenistic genius might have created still more than it did had its development not been cut short. While Roman aggrandizement is in some measure responsible for the untimely demise of the Hellenistic world, Rome's intervention only accelerated a process of destruction already initiated by internal dissension among the Greeks themselves.

The Hellenistic world. The conquests of Alexander had far-reaching economic as well as political effects. The establishment of Greek colonies throughout his empire created new commercial ties and markets between Greece and the East, and brought about a type of economic union hitherto unknown in the ancient world. Alexander's designs for unification were further aided by his introduction of a uniform and abundant coinage. As a result of these factors, the Hellenistic Age was preeminently a commercial one. This was also due in no small measure to the fact that the period was marked by rapid urban development, for cities provide bigger and more varied markets than do farms.

Far larger than any of the Hellenic cities were the great Seleucid centers of the Hellenistic period, Antioch and Seleucia-on-the-Tigris, and of course Alexandria in Egypt. Foremost among Hellenistic cities and boasting a population of perhaps a million, Alexandria had two wide boulevards laid out at right angles and leading to its four gates, whose porticoes were illuminated at night. Conspicuous also was the great lighthouse—rising to an estimated height of 370 feet and judged one of the wonders of classical times—which guided ships into a double harbor. Nearby stood the magnificent royal palace with its spacious gardens, the famous library containing some 750,000 works, the museum, the great zoo, the tombs of the Ptolemies, and a mausoleum built for Alexander's body by Ptolemy II. The city also possessed concert halls, stadia, a hippodrome for chariot races, theaters and temples, shops and bazaars, private houses several stories high, and parks and squares. A canal brought in Nile water which was distributed through conduits into underground cisterns. The busy streets were filled with a mixture of peoples—Greeks, Macedonians, Egyptians, Semites, Persians, and other nationalities. "That this vast agglomeration of humanity could ever be a 'city' in the strict Greek sense was a physical impossibility. Alexandria was a collection of *politeumata* based on nationalities, the Greek *politeuma* being much the most important; outside these stood a few privileged Macedonians at one end and the mass of Egyptians at the other."[16] Cosmopolitanism, based on Greek culture and the use of a modified form of Greek in official circles, was the keynote of Hellenistic life.

All the existing arts, sciences, and speculations of the human mind could be found in Alexandria. At the height of her greatness her streets were filled with as many famous figures as climbed the steps of the Acropolis in the Age of Pericles. It was largely from the Hellenistic world that the Romans learned of the cultural and intellectual wealth of the past.

The Hellenistic world grew wealthy from the trade which streamed from India to the Persian Gulf, up the Tigris and over the Fertile Crescent to Damascus and Antioch, or south through Arabia to Alexandria. In the third century the center of trade shifted from Greece to Egypt, Rhodes, and the coast of Asia Minor. Thus Alexandria imported metals, wools, marble, wines, spices, and horses, while at the same time she controlled the export of grain, supplied the world with linen, and enjoyed a large trade in paper (papyrus), glass, and jewelry. Hand in hand with this rich trade went the development of industry and the organization of labor. A number of industries were royal monopolies, both in extraction of natural products and in manufacture, while the existence of detailed governmental regulations shows that the state exercised close control over Hellenistic economic life. Industrial development was accompanied by increased division of labor and specialization of workers. With such specialization went improvement in technical methods, including the organization of the apprentice system. At the same time, slaves were frequently employed in both industry and agriculture, while criminals in chain

THE BRONZE BOXER, BY APOLLONIOS

gangs (and sometimes prisoners of war) toiled in the mines and quarries.

Despite the wealth of such cities as Alexandria and Antioch, discontent was rife because of the excessive social and economic differences separating the rich and poor. The development of industry apparently did little to improve the material condition of the free worker, who all too often was exploited and pauperized. Political power, lands, money, and trading privileges were allowed to fall into the hands of the favorites of the rulers, while a large percentage of the people had no political rights and no economic security. For these reasons, various cities were obliged to furnish the unemployed with cheap or free grain to keep them from revolting, a practice resorted to in Rome.

The Hellenistic Contribution

Cultural diffusion. The admiration which Alexander the Great held for Greek culture resulted in a momentous journey to the East, on which he was accompanied by scientists and scholars. Thus a new influence was exerted on the peoples of the extensive Hellenistic empire. Although the Hellenistic Greeks made great strides in the fields of science, commerce, and city life, their importance in this field lies primarily in the diffusion of Hellenic culture throughout the empire. By this means Hellenic knowledge in the arts, philosophy, and science became the basis for Roman civilization and hence later western and to some extent eastern culture.

Hellenistic philosophy. By the time of Aristotle's death, the Greek city-states had been subjugated by the Macedonians, Alexander had conquered the east, and the Hellenistic era had commenced. Developments in philosophy reflect the profound political and psychological changes which had transpired. With the loss of freedom by the city-states and the prevalence of internal disorder, there was no longer an incentive for philosophers to formulate theories designed for an ideal society operating in a harmoniously designed cosmos. Rather, in the Hellenistic Age, there was a growing concern for the problems of individual ethics and salvation. This change to introspection and subjectivity in a world of increasing political chaos led to the rise of three principal schools of thought—Epicureanism, Stoicism, and Skepticism.

Epicurus (342?-270 B.C.) taught that the highest good was pleasure of body and mind and that there was no afterlife. He also maintained that the finest pleasures were intellectual, but many of his followers later debased his teachings into the pursuit of sensual satisfactions. In opposition to Epicureanism, Zeno of Cyprus (336?-264? B.C.) maintained that there should be but one aim in the world, freedom from the desires of life. To be tranquil of soul and indifferent to pain and pleasure, joy and sorrow, were ideal virtues to the Stoics. These two philosophies, as we shall see later, were to have a marked effect upon the Romans.

Meanwhile, the Skeptics reflected most clearly, perhaps, the doubts and misgivings of the age. According to this school, not only is it impossible to know anything outside the physical senses, but these do not agree: thus pleasure for one is pain for another; one person feels cold when another feels warm, and so on. Who can say, then, what is truth? Therefore a wise man, the Skeptics argued, does not pretend to hold any opinions of his own but follows the customs and traditions of the locality in which he happens to live.

Hellenistic science. As we have seen, the geographical and political frontiers of the Greeks greatly expanded during Hellenistic times and the culture was strongly commercial and cosmopolitan in character. The intellectual approach became in turn more "down-to-earth" and critical than had been the case in the Hellenic Age. It was therefore natural that Hellenistic scientists should be essentially "practical" in their aims—such as by putting geography on a scientific foundation—and that in their methodology they should emphasize as never before specialization and experimentation. The Greek element remained predominant in Hellenistic learning, but Babylonian astronomy was important and Egyptian influences were not inconsiderable in such sciences as geometry. As a result, Hellenistic science exemplifies the fusion of Greek and oriental elements—and, incidentally, the perennial value of keeping science on the broadest possible international basis. The results were brilliant to the extent that only in modern times have men advanced as far in scientific exploration as their Hellenistic predecessors.

The great expansion of geographical knowledge incited scientists to make accurate maps and to plot the size of the earth, which was known to be a globe by virtue of the earth's shadow having been observed in a lunar eclipse. The most noteworthy name connected with the founding of scientific geography is Eratosthenes of Alexandria (276?-195? B.C.), who used a brilliant method in calculating the circumference of the globe. Measuring the difference in the angles of the noonday sun during the summer solstice at Aswan and Alexandria and estimating the distance between the two places, Eratosthenes computed the circumference at 252,000 *stades*. A *stade* is equal today to 581½ English feet. Assuming that the geographer had in mind a short *stade,* he had succeeded in calculating the earth's circumference at 24,662 miles, or less than 200 miles short of the actual figure. If Eratosthenes had in mind a *stade* of slightly greater length, his result has an 11-12 per cent error. In any case this was the only really sound attempt to measure the globe in the classical period, and it remained the most scientific measurement until early modern times. Eratosthenes also drew a map of the world which was both more accurate and more extensive than anything done previously.

Astronomy also made rapid advances in this period, so that one Alexandrian astronomer was able to compute the solar year correctly to within five minutes and the lunar month to within one second. In the third century B.C. a radical theory was put forward by Aristarchus that the earth rotates on its axis and moves in an orbit around the sun. However, few if any of his contemporaries were willing to give up the geocentric theory—that the world was stationary and the sun revolved around it—because, as it has been observed, men have preferred to believe themselves the center of all things. It was not until the sixteenth century that scientists were again to espouse the views of Aristarchus.

The most famous mathematician of Alexandria was Euclid (about 300 B.C.), who developed plane geometry into its present forms and theorems. Contributions were also made to higher mathematics by Archimedes of Syracuse (287?-212 B.C.)—perhaps the best-known name in Hellenistic science—who calculated the limits for the value of π, invented a terminology for expressing numbers up to any magnitude, and laid the foundations of calculus of the infinite. But it was in physics that Archimedes especially excelled. He invented a compound pulley, the windlass, an endless screw for pumping out ships and draining flooded fields, and such military weapons as catapults, burning-glasses, and grapnels—with which he is said to have kept the Romans for three years from capturing his native Syracuse.

The advances made earlier in medicine by Hippocrates and his school were now added to by the Hellenistic Greeks, who based their learning on intensified methods of observation. At Alexandria they practiced dissection of the human body and thereby were able to trace the main outlines of the nervous system, to master the main principles of the circulation of blood, and to ascertain that the brain, not the heart, was the true center of consciousness. It is remarkable how in medicine, as in other scientific fields, so many of the fundamental discoveries of early modern times—and even of the nineteenth century—were anticipated by the Greeks.

Architecture and Sculpture. Architecture was given a tremendous impetus in Hellenistic times as a host of new cities sprang up. The Greek colonnade and architrave invaded the interior of Asia, while the arch and vault (long known in Babylonia) and the cupola made their appearance in the West. Many temples were erected, with Sicily possessing the five largest, including the temple of Zeus at Acragas, which measured 363 by 182 feet. But the Hellenistic world was particularly concerned with putting up massive palaces and governmental buildings, colonnaded market places, docks and lighthouses. In the new cities, which had the benefit of town planning and whose streets were laid out in rectangular form, the great public edifices were elaborately constructed and stressed ornamentation; this was an age which, like the Roman civilization, preferred the Corinthian to the Doric order.

Some of the finest and most familiar ancient sculpture was composed during the Hellenistic period, the last great phase of Greek art. Hellenistic sculpture is characterized by brilliant technique coupled with lack of self-control. The sculptor's mastery over the technical aspects of his medium incited him to display his skill by depicting the violent and dramatic.

DETAIL FROM THE LAOCOÖN GROUP

Thus, he was able to twist the stone into writhing forms, as in the detail from the Laocoön group on this page. Hellenistic sculpture displays a realism which could make stone simulate flesh, but it leaves little to the imagination and lacks that self-discipline and balance which is the hallmark of Hellenic sculpture. However, it was also the Hellenistic Age which fashioned the superb Nike (Goddess of Victory) of Samothrace, shown at the right, which is today one of the treasures of the Louvre—as is another Hellenistic creation, the world-famous "Venus de Milo."

Hellenistic writings. In literature the Hellenistic Age proved generally inferior to the preceding Hellenic. No great epics or dramas were produced, for the old harmonies and unities were gone from both public life and literary forms. Paradoxically, that sophisticated age witnessed the production of superb pastoral poetry—but the popularity of these bucolic poems may be due to their special appeal to the city-dwellers of Alexandria, who had long since forgotten what the countryside and its life meant. The chief Hellenistic contributions to literature were probably the invention of textual criticism, by the comparison of manuscripts and the study of philology; the production of books on a scale hitherto unknown; and the establishment of great libraries, of which the greatest was that at Alexandria—which existed until broken up and partly destroyed in 272 A.D. It is difficult, however, for us to assess Hellenistic literature. "Including science and philosophy, over 1100 Hellenistic writers are known, but most are little but names; for the great bulk of Hellenistic literature has entirely perished. We possess only wreckage, though the sands of Egypt are steadily increasing the amount."[17]

The Nike of Samothrace, on the prow of a warship, was carved by Pythocritus to celebrate naval victories.

Summary

All of us know the story of Achilles, the hero of Homer's *Iliad* and a youth of surpassing valor and beauty, who must have remained immortal had not Paris' arrow pierced him fatally in the heel, the only vulnerable part of his body. Achilles was a hero of the Greeks, and with good reason, for as a people they shared his virtues. But like Achilles, the Hellenes had one great defect—the incapacity to submerge individual differences for the sake of common survival—and with their own arrows they destroyed themselves.

We have traced the growth of the city-state system and watched how it failed to adapt itself to changing political realities in the fifth century B.C., especially following the colonial and economic revolutions which had occurred earlier and had linked the destinies of Athens and other cities with those of a larger Mediterranean community. We noted too that instead of developing the Delian League into a true Greek federation, Athens placed her individual interests first and converted it into a maritime empire—thus bringing on the fatal Peloponnesian War.

But if the city-state system failed to meet the challenge of external cooperation, it stimulated the growth of democracy—albeit in a limited form—within the state itself. As a result, one of the great Greek contributions to western thought was the development of a body of political theory which had been nonexistent in the Orient. We owe to the Greeks the concepts of a democratic government responsible to the governed, of trial by jury, and of civil liberties. They further gave us some valuable political ideals: those of public service and of the responsibility and privilege of citizen participation.

In the nonpolitical fields, our debt to the Greeks is almost unlimited. They were the first to search after a rational explanation of the universe. So far did they advance in speculative thought that many of the philosophical problems they posed are still the questions for which we are seeking answers. Especially important among Greek contributions were the atomic, relativity, and evolutionary theories, while Plato's theory of Ideas and Aristotle's logic have had incalculable effect upon later systems of thought.

We are indebted to Aristotle for classifying the main divisions of scientific knowledge as well as for his contributions to biology. Thanks to Hippocrates and his school, medicine was placed on a rational and more ethical basis. In physics the work of Archimedes proved invaluable, as did that of Pythagoras and Euclid in geometry, Aristarchus in astronomy, and Eratosthenes in geography.

We still find delight in the epic poems of Homer, the tragedies of Aeschylus, Sophocles, and Euripides, and the brilliant comedies of Aristophanes. The basis of modern historical writing was established by Herodotus, while Thucydides took as his ideal the recording of data that was both accurate and rational. In architecture and sculpture the same spirit of fidelity to ideals is apparent. Likewise, the architectural contributions of the Greeks—their three orders of columns, their principle of proportion, and their building forms, such as the temple of the Parthenon—still influence modern design.

What is it about Greece that makes us, over two thousand years removed from Plato and Phidias, speak in words of admiration? The secret lies in the originality with which the Greeks met every situation. Free of oriental tradition and superstition, they saw each problem in an entirely new light. They examined it in a spirit of critical inquiry, and they sought for an explanation that accorded with natural rather than supernatural law. Their view of life was thus something entirely new in the world's history; it tended to be secular and rational instead of religious and credulous. This psychological change in human thinking may have been the greatest contribution of the Greeks.

Chapter 6

Chronology of events and developments discussed in this chapter

Indo-European invasions *Later Italic tribes: Umbrians, Samnites, Latins*	2000 B.C.
Etruscan dominance *Influence in northern Italy and Rome*	900-400
Elected king replaced by aristocratic republic with two consuls	509
Plebeians safeguarded their rights and extended political privileges	509-300
All magistracies and one consulship opened to the plebeians	367
Romans gained control over the Mediterranean	509-133
Latin League allied with Rome	493
Rome at war with the Gauls	390
Rome quelled the Latin League	338
Rome defeated the Samnites	296
Magna Graecia conquered by the Romans	270
First Punic War: Carthaginians defeated	264-241
Plautus: forerunner of modern dramatic comedy	254-184
End of the Second Punic War: Hannibal defeated	201
Macedonians defeated	197
Terence: sophisticated comedy	190-159
Egypt allied herself with Rome	168
Third Punic War: Romans destroyed Carthage	149-147
King of Pergamum willed his territory to the Roman empire	133
Civil war *Senatorial oligarchy controlled the government*	133-33
Tiberius and Gaius Gracchus unsuccessfully attempted reform	133-121
Sulla (Senatorial support) defeated Marius (backed by popular assembly)	111-78
Golden age of literature: Cicero, Virgil, Livy	80 B.C.-14 A.D.
Caesar overcame Pompey: dictatorial reforms	49-44 B.C.
Rule of Augustus: power concentrated in imperator	30 B.C.-14 A.D.
Pax Romana *Preservation of Greek and Latin culture; spread of Christianity; important developments in government and law*	30 B.C.-170 A.D.
Julian Caesars: ineffectual rule under Nero, Caligula	14 A.D.-69 A.D.
Silver Age of literature: Juvenal, Pliny the Elder	14-138
Flavian emperors	69-96
Antonine Age: "Five good emperors"; height of Roman power	96-180
German invasions: beginning of the decline of the empire	170

The ascendancy of Rome

The Roman world: 2000 B.C. *to 180* A.D.

EVEN AS THE ATHENIAN saw in the rock-jutting Acropolis above him the symbol of his city-state's democracy and culture, so the Roman found in his Forum the material evidence of an imperial capital. Where the Acropolis was crowned with statues to Athena, here were the triumphal arches and columns commemorating victories and conquests and the extension of the frontiers of empire from the Rhine to the Euphrates. Here, too, were to be found temples, but in contrast to the Acropolis, the Forum was dominated rather by immense secular buildings—basilicas, the Colosseum, and the great palace of the emperors rising on the nearby Palatine Hill. Long vistas provided an effect of massiveness and opulence. Rome was the capital of a world-state, and its citizens were proud of their imperial mission.

Yet if we look more closely at the buildings in the Roman Forum, we see that they appear fundamentally Greek in conception and style, but at the same time are more monumental and sumptuous. Where the Greek artist, for example, has employed the simple Doric order in his columns, the Roman has preferred the ornate Corinthian. Here, then, are two clues to our study of Roman culture: it borrowed profusely from the Greek and in large measure was imitative rather than original, but it modified Greek concepts and forms to meet Rome's own practical purposes. Adoption and adaptation are key words in the study of Roman civilization.

Rome was the great intermediary—the bridge over which passed the rich contributions of the Fertile Crescent, Egypt, and especially of Greece to form the basis of modern civilization. Into the political vacuum caused by the anarchy and civil war which threatened to destroy Hellenistic civilization stepped the Romans. They restored law and order and, having little philosophy, literature, and art of their own, enthusiastically adopted those of the conquered Greeks. With the extension of the Roman empire, Hellenistic civilization was spread from Britain to India.

Yet Rome was more than an intermediary. It had greatness in its own right. Throughout a history which led from a simple farming civilization in the plain of Latium to the assumption of mastery of the Mediterranean community, and finally of the entire known western world, the Romans met every challenge with practicality and efficiency. They linked their distant provinces with an unrivaled network of roads and constructed great public works, so that today the remains of baths, amphitheaters, and aqueducts are scattered throughout countries once part of the Roman empire. They developed and modified their administrative institutions to meet changing needs. Most permanent and far-reaching of all, their institutions in government and law have served as the framework of western political life to this day. Roman law forms the basis for much of the contemporary civil code, while the *jus gentium,* the law developed originally for the outlying parts of the empire, became incorporated to a great extent in our commercial law.

Early Rome

I*taly's origins.* From a chronological standpoint, it is convenient to discuss Greek history before that of the Romans, for Hellenic culture reached its zenith prior to Latin civilization, while the latter in turn outlived—after having incorporated—Hellenistic culture. However, we might remember that the Greeks and Romans were offshoots of a common Indo-European stock, and that in the earlier centuries the Greek and Italian peninsulas followed broadly parallel stages in their historical evolution.

Thus, about 2000 B.C. when Indo-European speaking peoples were invading the Aegean world, a western wing of the same invaders entered Italy, where they encountered an apparently indigenous folk whose culture, unlike that of the Aegean peoples with whom the early Greeks came in contact, was primitive. The newcomers brought copper and bronze with them to their new settlements in the Po valley, where they developed what has been termed the Terramara culture—because the ruins of this culture lie in a rich black soil (*terra mara* or *marna*).

At a much later date, they were followed by other Indo-European peoples who came from the Danube region equipped with iron weapons and implements. In time these newcomers intermingled with the older settlers and spread throughout the peninsula in three groups: the Umbrians, who occupied the northern part of the peninsula and a section of the center; the Samnites, who took lands

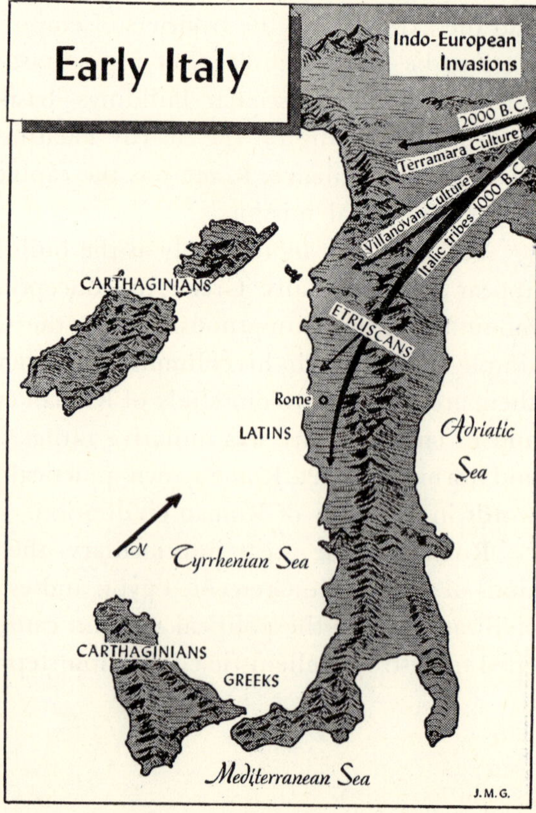

in the south; and the Latins, who settled in the lower valley of the Tiber, a region which became known after them as the plain of Latium.

These Italic tribesmen in turn came into contact with more advanced cultures when Greek settlers after the eighth century occupied the south coasts of the peninsula and the island of Sicily, where, we will recall, they established flourishing settlements known as Magna Graecia. These colonies were important centers for the diffusion of Hellenic culture and in addition acted as a buffer against the spread of Carthaginian power until the Italic tribes were ready to wage battle on their own behalf.

Still earlier, about 900 B.C., an immigrant people from Asia Minor, speaking a language which has not yet been interpreted, settled on the west coast of central Italy. These people, the Etruscans, possessed a fairly highly developed culture and the highest civilization in Italy before the rise of Rome. Once settled, they then proceeded to expand their dominion. After having subjugated a large portion of northern Italy, they conquered parts of Latium and Campania. By the middle of the sixth century it appeared that the Etruscans might extend their sway over the entire peninsula. However, this movement to the south was stopped, partly by Greek opposition and partly by the efforts of the Samnites and the Latins. Meanwhile the Etruscans' hold on northern Italy had been weakened by the pressure of Celtic invaders into the Po valley. Thereafter Etruscan power declined until absorbed by Rome during the fourth century.

However, while their own history is of secondary importance, the Etruscans were intimately bound up with the formative years of Rome, about whose origins we have little precise data. It seems likely that during the eighth and subsequent centuries small settlements which had been established on the Palatine, Esquiline, Quirinal, and Capitoline hills were united, with a common meeting place—the Forum—established in the valley between. The situation of this community at a place convenient for fording the Tiber and at the center of road communications in Italy undoubtedly had economic importance—which was to increase with time—but scholars feel that the town's chief importance then lay in its value as a military outpost against the encroaching

An interesting study in armor is to be found in this bronze statuette of an Etruscan warrior.

Etruscans. Nevertheless, it seems quite certain that the Etruscans, as a result of their penetration into Latium, established their predominance over Rome, where the half-Etruscan dynasty of the Tarquins ruled for some time. Consequently, the Latin inhabitants adopted much of the Greek-inspired culture of the Etruscans and some of their customs. These included various political symbols, such as the two-headed ax enclosed in a bundle of rods (*fasces*)—the symbol of the absolute authority of the king. From the Etruscans also the Latins may have learned the use of the arch and other building methods, as well as certain religious traditions pertaining to Jupiter, Minerva, and Juno. Almost certainly they acquired from them the practice of prophesying by examination of animal entrails (*haruspicium*). It has been suggested that the Etruscans may have contributed even the name of the city itself—for *Roma* appears to be derived

Originally a market and meeting place, the Roman Forum later became the center of the political activity in the government basilicas.

from the Etruscan *ruma.* Of greater importance to Rome's future, however, was the fact that it ceased to be a settlement of armed herdsmen and merchants and became a city like the neighboring Etruscan and Latin communities. "As the chief centre of Etruscan predominance in Latium, Rome now for the first time aspired to be the controlling power not only over the plain of Latium but over the whole country."[1]

In such an ambition, Rome was favored by geography. While the Italian peninsula has a great mountainous backbone, the Apennines, running down most of its length, the country is not so rugged as Greece, and consequently mountains did not constitute such a barrier to political unification. Furthermore, the plain of Latium and its chief city, Rome, occupied a strategic position. The city and surrounding area were therefore easy to defend, and once the Latins had begun a career of conquest, they occupied a central position which made it difficult for their enemies to unite successfully against them. "Thus Rome was marked out by Nature to be the capital of a unified Italy, just as Italy, by virtue of its large manpower and relatively central situation within the Mediterranean lands, was the natural seat of a Mediterranean empire. Rome's lordship over the ancient Mediterranean world was in accordance with the basic facts of Mediterranean geography."[2]

The Roman republic. In our examination of Greek political development, we will recall that in the earliest stage authority was vested in the king, but next, as the city-state developed, power was transferred into the hands of the nobles. The third stage was represented by the struggle of the nonaristocratic elements of the citizenry to gain adequate representation in the control and direction of government. While too close a parallel should not be drawn here, it will be seen that Rome's political development underwent similar stages of growth.

During the period of Etruscan dominance, the Roman city-state had at its head an elected king whose *imperium*—that is, his power of life and death over the citizens—was conferred by a popular assembly known as the *Comitia Curiata,* comprising all citizens, grouped according to the *curiae,* or districts, where they lived. This popular assembly actually possessed little real power, however; it passed on the nomination of high officials and such matters as war and peace, but it could not initiate laws. In fact it did little more than give assent to the decisions of the *Senate,* an advisory council whose membership was restricted to the *patricians,* a landed aristocracy. The other class in Roman society, the *plebeians,* the nonnoble freemen who were usually small farmers and artisans, exercised little influence in government at this time.

The despotic rule of one of the Etruscan line of kings gave the nobles their chance, and in a revolt staged in 509 B.C. they established Rome as an aristocratic republic. The *imperium* was now transfered to two new officials, *consuls,* elected annually but chosen from the patrician class and invariably exercising their power in the interests of that class. The power of the consuls when first established was very broad: they were commanders of the army and high priests, and they possessed police powers at home. In the event of war or serious domestic emergency, a dictator could be substituted for the two consuls, but he was given supreme power for a term of six months only.

We can say, then, that the expulsion of the Etruscan dynasty and the substitution of the republic for a monarchy had brought one major change in the political evolution of Rome: the aristocracy was now in control, exercising its power through the consuls and the Senate. But just as in the analogous case of the evolution of the Greek city-states, Rome was at this time increasing in commercial importance, a factor bound to create a growing demand on the part of the business, nonlandowning elements of the population for greater political recognition. Also, the wars of conquest in which Rome presently found itself engaged gave the plebeians, indispensable in filling the ranks of the Roman army, greater bargaining power. We are now to trace the struggle of the plebeians for political and social equality, a struggle which lasted for some two centuries following the establishment of the republic. The conflict between the two classes was bitter and attended by outbreaks of violence, but it never degenerated into outright civil war. Nor was it necessary for the plebeians to have recourse to tyrants to assist them in gaining their political goals, as happened in the Greek city-states.

Growth of democracy. Much of the success of the plebeians in this struggle was due to their tactics of collective action and to their having organized a corporate group within the state. This unofficial group was known as the *Concilium Plebis,* presided over by its own officials called *tribunes* (eventually ten in number), who had the job of safeguarding the interests of the plebeians and of negotiating with the consuls. (Later another popular assembly, the *Comitia Tributa,* was established to include all the people, but in practice the difference between the two bodies was merely technical.) Meanwhile, still another popular assembly had evolved, known as the *Comitia Centuriata.* This body, the origins of which are obscure, was an assembly of arms-bearing men, later expanded to include all citizens. In time it took over various functions formerly held by the older *Comitia Curiata,* which in turn lost most of its power and influence. For our purposes, we can say that the plebeians were to acquire greater participation in political affairs by increasing the strength of two popular assemblies, the *Concilium Plebis* and the *Comitia Centuriata,* whose respective powers were not always clearly defined.

The advancement of the plebeians in this period—that is, from the founding of the republic to about 300 B.C.—took two main lines: the safeguarding of their fundamental rights and the progressive enlargement of their share of political power. As in Athens, the common

The master shakes his fist at an impudent late comer in a Roman school, and the other pupils snicker.

people resented the fact that the law was unwritten and that it was being interpreted to suit the interests of the patricians. Agitation to codify the law so as to curb arbitrary decisions by patrician magistrates led, according to tradition, to the sending of a committee to Athens in 454 to study the Draconian code and the work of Solon. Soon after, the Laws of the Twelve Tables were adopted. Roman law was now in written form and the average citizen knew just where he stood in this regard. The plebeians also acquired fundamental safeguards in the following ways: they secured the right to appeal from a severe judicial sentence imposed by a consul and of retrial before a popular assembly; the tribunes gained in time a veto power over any legislation or executive act that threatened the rights of the plebeians; and the latter acquired a new social and political status by the passage of a law permitting their marriage with patricians.

These legal and social gains were matched by the acquisition of a more dominant role in the direction of government itself. Thus, the *Concilium Plebis* gained the right of legislation, while the *Comitia Centuriata*, the other main popular assembly, acquired the right of electing the consuls and other higher magistrates. Then in 367 B.C., one consulship was made open to the plebs and by the end of that century they were admitted to all magistracies. These included such important offices as those of *quaestors,* charged with financial functions; *censors,* who took care of the census and guarded the people's morals; and the *praetors,* who held a rank next to the consuls and performed various judicial and civil duties. Furthermore, the holding of these higher political offices constituted a stepping stone to the Senate itself and, as a result, plebeians were now in a position to enter that august body, whose membership had earlier been restricted to the patrician class.

We can now see that by the beginning of the third century B.C. a series of piecemeal reforms had robbed the old patriciate of its former privileged position. Instead, a new class, recruited from patricians and plebeians alike, was to come to the fore; this was a class composed of families whose members held important offices and who would make it difficult for newcomers to break into their ranks. This new development made many of the gains of the past two centuries more illusory than real, as did various problems arising from Rome's numerous wars, as we shall see. However, these facts should not detract from the plebeians' example of the value of political development by means of peaceful, constitutional reform.

Life in the early republic. We know little of Roman civilization in the early days of the republic. It would appear that wealth was reckoned in flocks and that industry was confined to the making of crude pottery and a few bronze weapons and tools. Before 500 B.C.

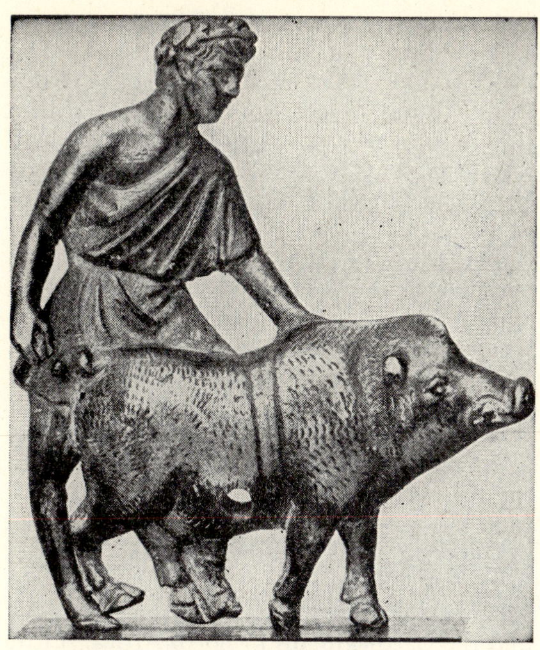

A bronze statuette shows the Roman sacrificial butcher about to kill the boar chosen for sacrifice.

iron was little used for implements. The average Roman was a small landholder who produced crops chiefly for his own household use. These early Romans were an industrious, hardy, and unsophisticated folk.

The fundamental unit of early Roman society was the family, where the father's power was absolute and discipline was strongly imposed upon the offspring from the outset in order to instill those virtues to which the Romans attached particular importance, such as loyalty, courage, and self-control. What education was imparted at this time was received at home, where the father taught his children what would amount to the "three R's." Young Romans were not exposed to the intellectual stimuli enjoyed by Greek youth in the same period, but the strong influence of home and family undoubtedly provided the early Romans with their greatest personal attribute, strength of character. There is a danger, of course, that the Roman character of the early republic has been overromanticized, but it remains true that the social forces conditioning the young Romans produced citizens who took their civic duties seriously and were loyal and courageous in their conduct.

This simple mode of early republican life was reflected in the Romans' uncomplicated and practical approach to the larger issues of man and the universe. Here were no philosophers concerning themselves with cosmological mysteries or the nature of human existence and knowledge. The average Roman appeared to be interested only in abundant crops, his family, and civic life. His religious views were quite unsophisticated. Ideas about the future life remained very vague, and religion was largely concerned with placating supernatural powers and enlisting the support of the gods on behalf of the family and the state. To protect his family, the father as *pater familias* made offerings to Vesta, whose realm was the hearth, to Janus, who watched over the doorway, and to the spirits guarding the house stores. It was also believed that certain deities protected the state, and a kind of public religion developed which emphasized the citizen's duty to the state and at the same time endeavored to secure the gods' favor and assistance on its behalf. The most important of these were Jupiter, who controlled the universe; Mars, the god of war; Janus, the guardian of the gateway to Rome, and the female deities Juno and Minerva, who with Jupiter had been introduced into Rome by the Etruscans. The worship of this triad was observed in a temple built on the Capitol, which thus became the religious center of Rome, akin in this respect to the Acropolis of Athens. In their religion then, the Romans were indebted to the Etruscans—and directly or indirectly to the Greeks—for much of their ritual, the practice of divination, and even for some of their most important gods.

From City-State to World Conqueror

The background of Roman expansion. Now that we have traced the genesis of the Roman republic and seen how the early Romans lived, we are ready to recount one of the most remarkable stories of conquest in world history. We shall see how a diminutive city-state in a little less than four hundred years (509-133 B.C.) became the master of the Mediterranean world.

We have seen how early Rome was surrounded by powerful neighbors and how for a time she was ruled by one of them. In the preliminary rounds fought for supremacy in Italy the Romans were not participants. The main contenders were Carthage, the Greeks, and the Etruscans. At first the Greeks were victorious. They defeated a Carthaginian army that had invaded Sicily (480 B.C., the same year as the battle of Salamis), and a little later the Greeks defeated a large Etruscan fleet. By 400 B.C. it seemed inevitable that the Greek colonies would develop into a single nation that would dominate Italy and the western Mediterranean.

This likely event, however, did not materialize. The intermittent warfare that was waged among the Etruscans, Greeks, and Carthaginians ultimately eliminated two of the trio and left only Carthage in the field against Rome.

Roman expansion in Italy. Rome had meantime been slowly growing in power. After the expulsion of the Etruscan kings, Rome was on the defensive for nearly a century. Under the Etruscans Rome had been recognized as supreme over the plain of Latium. After the decline of Etruscan influence, however, the Latin peoples on the outskirts of Rome declared their independence and established a Latin League of defense. After some fighting with Rome, the other Latin tribes realized that a truce with Rome was essential in order for them to combine against their mutual enemies, the Etruscans and certain unfriendly Italic tribes. In 493 B.C., therefore, the Latin League and Rome entered into a loose league of defense.

The new combination was so successful that by the beginning of the fourth century B.C. it had become the chief power in central Italy. About that time (390 B.C.) a temporary disaster fell upon Rome. Fierce blond warriors from the Po valley, the Gauls, fell upon the city and burned it to the ground. The citadel on Capitol Hill, however, was not taken, and after a long siege the Gauls finally left Rome. Her citizens, undaunted by its destruction, rebuilt the city and constructed a new wall of fortifications.

Rome's expansion over her neighbors was now resumed. The allies of Rome, the members of the Latin League, became alarmed at her growing power, and war followed. The conflict was ended in 338 B.C. with the victory of Rome. The Latin League was dissolved, and each city or tribe was forced to sign a separate treaty of alliance with Rome. The date for the victory of Rome over the Latin League is important. Not only did it signalize the rise of a new power in the western Mediterranean, but in the same year the Greek city-states fell into the hands of Philip of Macedon.

The Etruscan cities were now rapidly succumbing to the Roman advance. A new foe appeared, however, who for a time menaced Rome. The Samnites, a strong Italic tribe, had established themselves in the highlands of the Apennines in central Italy. War broke out between them and Rome. After severe fighting in which the Romans lost several early battles, the Samnites, though assisted by both Etruscans and Gauls, were overwhelmed in 296 B.C.

Only two rivals remained to contest Rome's meteoric rise to supremacy in the western Mediterranean, the Greeks in southern Italy and the Carthaginians in north Africa. Little more than ten years after the defeat of the Samnites, the Romans moved down on Magna Graecia. The Greeks, with their fondness for luxury and their tendency to factionalism, were a poor match for their adversaries. However, Tarentum, the leading Greek city, succeeded in obtaining the assistance of Pyrrhus, a capable and ambitious Greek king. It was his aim to defeat the Romans and carve out for himself a great empire like Alexander's in the west. Bringing 20,000 foot soldiers, 3000 cavalry, and a force of elephants, Pyrrhus was a dangerous foe. He defeated the Romans in the first encounter but at so heavy a cost that a dearly bought triumph has ever since been termed a Pyrrhic victory.

The hard-pressed Romans at this juncture were assisted by the Carthaginians, who mistakenly thought that the Greeks were their greatest danger. They sought to maintain what diplomats call today "the balance of power" by assisting the Romans. Later they were to pay dearly for their mistake. Pyrrhus was finally defeated by the Romans on land, his fleet was scattered by the Carthaginians, and he returned to Greece. With no one to bar their way, the Roman legions now proceeded to conquer southern Italy, and by 270 B.C. all of Magna Graecia had passed into Roman hands.

In a space of about 225 years, Rome, the primitive little city on the banks of the Tiber, had become master of Italy from the toe and heel of the peninsula in the south to the valley of the Po in the north. There had been no definite or preconceived plan in the expansion. Surrounded by enemies, Rome had been forced to fight for her existence, and as she disposed of rivals near at home, her success caused more remote powers to attempt to crush her. In meeting these threats Rome became supreme in Italy.

Treatment of conquered peoples. In general the Romans, rather than enslaving their conquered foes, treated them with tact and justice. This policy made possible the development of a common patriotism, based on loyalty to Rome, throughout the Italian peninsula. The former adversaries of Rome were divided into three groups: (1) Roman citizens proper: those who lived in the vicinity of Rome and had full rights of citizenship, and others living in old Latin towns that had been conquered by Rome who were citizens but could not vote and hold office in Rome, (2) Latin allies, related peoples, who were given much local self-government, (3) and the Italian allies, comprising the bulk of the conquered people. Bound to Rome by treaty, the Italian allies had to supply troops and adhere to Rome's foreign policy. The peninsula was now under the protectorate of one power. The name *Italia* was coming into use, showing the beginning of national unity. Real political and cultural unity, however, was as yet a long way off. The language and customs of Rome did not triumph fully in Italy for another two centuries.

The Roman legions. The efficiency of the Roman military forces was a significant factor in the conquest of Italy. The sturdy, patriotic peasantry from which the legions were recruited made superb soldiers. Whether on attack or defense the early Romans exhibited great bravery, physical stamina, and iron discipline. The basic military unit of the Romans was the legion, composed of three thousand heavily armed men, supplemented by a cavalry squadron of three hundred and an army of twelve hundred light-armed foot soldiers. The phalanx, used by the Greeks, had tremendous crushing power. Like a mastodon it moved slowly forward with irresistible force. The Roman legion, on the other hand, was like a pack of lions, incredibly swift and powerful in attack. The Roman army obtained its maneuverability by the perfection of "joints" in its formation. In other words, the legion was broken up into smaller units, each capable of independent and rapid action. A Roman army was divided into three parallel divisions. In the event that any part of the front line gave way, a section of the rear divisions moved to the front. Each of the three divisions was in turn broken up into maniples of 120 men. Each maniple could move backward or forward without disturbing the formations on either side.

The Carthaginians. With the extermination of Greek power in Magna Graecia only Carthage remained as Rome's rival in the west. The great trading city situated on the African coast just southwest of the island of Sicily had been founded as a Phoenician colony about 875 B.C. The Carthaginians, like other early Phoenicians, became famous as sailors and traders. Their ships went into the Atlantic and as far north as the Baltic. The western Mediterranean was essentially Carthaginian water, and Carthaginian trade restrictions greatly hampered the commerce of all other traders in the region.

The primary concern of the people of Carthage was business. Little else mattered. The state was controlled by a wealthy clique of businessmen. There was no large body of freemen. The army was made up of hired mercenaries. Much more wealthy and populous than Rome, Carthage seemed powerful enough to halt Roman expansion, but the selfishness of her commercial oligarchy and the lack of a loyal body of free citizenry proved a source of fatal weakness.

The First Punic War. War broke out in 264 B.C. over a trivial incident in Sicily, which both Rome and Carthage wished to control. At first Rome could make little headway, for her citizens were a nation of landlubbers, and she had never possessed a large fleet. Undaunted by this drawback, the Romans built one hundred ships and meanwhile trained crews of oarsmen on land. During the First Punic War (the Latin word for Carthaginian was *punicus*) several naval disasters overtook the Romans, costing the lives of 200,000 men. But by great sacrifices the citizens of Rome raised additional money for new fleets, which finally defeated those of Carthage, and in 241 B.C. the Carthaginians had to sue for peace. As a result of the encounter Rome annexed

Sicily and gained naval supremacy in the western Mediterranean.

Hannibal. Thwarted in the Mediterranean, Carthage now busied herself in trying to build an empire in Spain. Rome, however, was determined that she should not recoup her might. While both powers jockeyed for position, a young Carthaginian general precipitated war by attacking a town in Spain that was allied to Rome. The young commander was Hannibal, who had sworn to his father lifelong enmity to Rome. Taking the initiative, Hannibal with an army of about 60,000 men crossed the Alps. His campaign was based on the hope that the Gauls would aid him and that Rome's allies would desert to his side. After terrible privations Hannibal and his men, barely thirty thousand, reached the fertile Po valley. His little army, however, soon proved its mettle. Within three years the Romans had suffered three serious defeats. In one battle, Cannae, nearly fifty thousand Romans were killed.

Hannibal's forces never matched those of the Romans in numbers. At Cannae, for example, 80,000 Romans were almost completely destroyed by barely 40,000 Carthaginians. From time to time Hannibal obtained additional recruits from across the Alps, from Spain and Gaul, but these were less than 10,000 in all and untrained. Hannibal also received some help from the Greek cities and even some Italian cities that forsook their alliance with Rome, but help from these sources was never dependable. Although outnumbered he usually was able to outwit the Roman commanders by his rapid marches. He showed amazing skill in living off the land in an unfriendly country.

Hannibal was above all an inspiring leader. He was never too tired to mingle with his men after a tiring march or bloody battle, cheering the wounded or disconsolate and keeping up an amazing morale that carried the Carthaginian army successfully through many ordeals. Hannibal was never defeated in Italy, but his inadequate resources did not enable him to inflict a knockout blow upon the Romans, who tenaciously kept up the struggle despite a long string of defeats. This Second Punic War has been described as a "colossal contest between the nation Rome and the man Hannibal."[3] Hannibal's military genius and inspiring leadership received inadequate support from home, while a united Roman people refused to despair in the face of disastrous defeats. Under such conditions no individual, however brilliant, could triumph over the will of a united nation.

At last the Romans obtained a general, Scipio, who was a match in military strategy for the great Hannibal. Forced to return home after fifteen years spent on Italian soil, Hannibal met the legions of Scipio in the decisive battle of Zama. The Carthaginians suffered a complete defeat and in 201 B.C. were forced to accept a harsh treaty. Spain was taken by Rome, while Carthage was disarmed and forced to pay an indemnity.

Carthage was now little more than a protectorate of Rome, and there was therefore no justification for waging further war against her. But the lust of conquest was becoming apparent in Rome as her citizens sensed their destiny as world conquerors. Acting as their spokesman the influential Cato, a censor, ended all his speeches with "*Delenda est Carthago*"—"Carthage must be destroyed."

The Third Punic War. Treacherously provoking a war in 149 B.C., the Romans besieged Carthage for two years. In spite of heroic resistance the defenders were unable to prevent the scaling of the walls of the city. For six days the inhabitants fought with the fury of despair in the city streets but were finally overpowered. Most of the people were sold into slavery, the city was fired, and the ground on which it had stood was plowed and salt flung into the furrows to destroy the soil's fertility.

A kind fate prevented Hannibal from witnessing the destruction of Carthage. Following the Second Punic War he had become an exile in the east, where he tried to enlist support for a coalition against Rome. Failing in his plans, he became a fugitive and finally obtained asylum with the king of a small region in Asia Minor. His host, however, betrayed him, and to escape capture by an armed band of Romans Hannibal committed suicide (about 183 B.C.). His last words are reputed to have been, "Let us release the Romans from their long anxiety, since they think it too long to wait for the death of an old man." The story of Hannibal has been called "history's most glorious failure."

Roman intervention in the east. During the many conflicts which enhanced Rome's

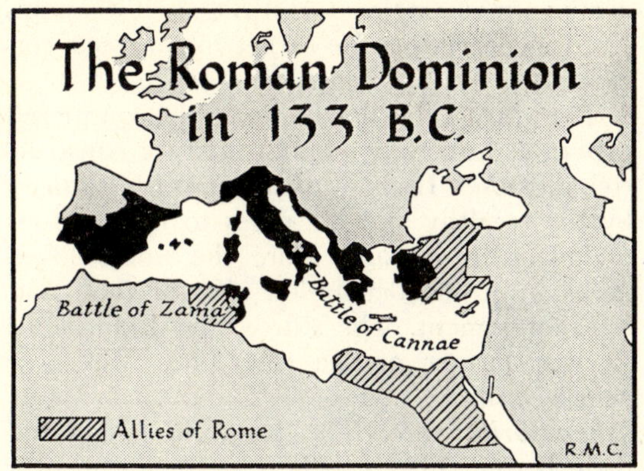

power, the heirs of Alexander's great empire were carrying on ceaseless feuds among themselves. In Rome's struggle with Hannibal, the latter had obtained the assistance of Philip v of Macedon. The Roman Senate greatly resented Philip's action and also feared that Philip might endeavor to create a coalition which would menace Rome. The Romans therefore felt obliged to turn eastward and wage war on Philip of Macedon. In a decisive battle in 197 B.C. the heavy Macedonian phalanx proved no match for the swift and mobile Roman legion.

A few years later, in a quarrel over Greece and Asia Minor, Roman armies humbled the powerful Syrian Seleucid king. Although they annexed no territory from his domains, they enhanced Roman prestige in the eastern Mediterranean and made it plain to the Seleucid ruler that he was to stay out of the Roman sphere of influence. In 168 B.C. Egypt, another large division of Alexander's empire, allied herself to Rome. Most of the Mediterranean region was now under the influence of the Roman empire.

Following the defeat of Philip of Macedon, Rome permitted the Greek city-states to rule themselves subject to Roman protection. The next fifty years, however, brought little peace and order to the Greek peninsula. Two more wars were fought between Macedon and Rome, while the Greeks themselves, though free from Macedonian rule, continually quarreled among themselves and plotted against Rome. An end came to that state of affairs when, in 146 B.C., the exasperated Romans burned down the city of Corinth. After this the Greek city-states came under close Roman rule.

In 133 B.C. another important extension of Roman power occurred. In that year the king of Pergamum in Asia Minor died leaving no heir. Realizing perhaps that Roman conquest was inevitable, he willed his territory to Rome. Using this bequest as a start, Rome eventually took over Asia Minor and other territories in the Near East.

By 100 B.C. the power of Rome extended all round the Mediterranean. Subsequently, we shall trace the further expansion of Roman supremacy in the first century B.C. and also during the period of the empire itself. However, it has been pointed out that except for advances northward into Europe, the later wars of Rome were to be waged not so much to enlarge as to consolidate her dominions. The maps on these pages show the continued expansion of Roman power.

From Republic to Empire

Changes in government. As we glance back over the political history of Rome thus far, it is apparent that it consists of two dominant themes: (1) the democratization of the government, which was achieved by 287 B.C., and (2) the expansion of Rome. With the extermination of Carthage and the defeat of the rulers who inherited Alexander's empire in the eastern Mediterranean, Rome became the mistress of the western world. But the next century (133-33 B.C.) was to see Rome convulsed with civil war and threatened with extinction. Her conquests created many social and economic problems which the Senate was unable to solve. The inability of the republic to rule efficiently finally led to dictatorship

and the extinction of constitutional government. Let us see what the problems were which followed in the train of the Roman conquests.

The decline of small farming. When Sicily was conquered, her inhabitants were forced to pay a huge tribute in wheat. In addition cheap cereals were imported into Italy from Africa. The small farmers in Italy soon found it impossible to compete with the imported produce. Improved farming methods copied from Sicily encouraged wealthy aristocrats to buy up tracts of land and introduce large-scale farming. The latter trend was especially profitable because thousands of slaves from the conquered areas were available to work on the estates. The large slave plantations were called *latifundia*, and by 200 B.C. they had become the rule in Italy, while small farms were the exception.

The disappearance of the small landowner was the basic cause of the degeneration of the Roman common people. Thousands of sturdy farmer peasants returned from the wars to find farming unprofitable. Many peasant lads came back from their adventures abroad with the legions quite unwilling to settle down to a humdrum life on the farm. The decay of small farming sent a large army of these unemployed laborers flocking to the city of Rome.

Profiteering and luxury. Roman officials in the provinces seized opportunities for graft and became a wealthy class of aristocrats. Opportunities for profit in large-scale farming and war contracts had resulted in the growth of an opulent class of businessmen called *equites*. Nearly everyone among the upper classes tried to get his hands on the war contracts, which had to do with supplying the army with wheat, meat, clothing, and weapons. Even in peacetime the racket in contracts corrupted the government.

The vast wealth flowing from the conquered provinces into Italy was not used for constructive purposes. Instead it was spent for luxuries by the wealthy and for doles to the landless plebeians. More and more the unemployed mobs in Rome demanded gifts of food and free amusement. The sturdy and industrious Roman farmer of the early days was now nearly extinct.

Senatorial rule. The republic had fared little better. The plebeians, as we have seen, had gained political equality after a long struggle, but the many wars nullified their gains. During the terrible war against Hannibal the people had allowed the Senate to run the state. Although the government remained in theory a democracy, in practice it was now an oligarchy. The tribunes, guardians of the people's rights, became mere "yes men" of the Senate. The landless populace lost all interest in good government just so long as the politicians supplied food and circuses in return for their votes.

The influence of Greece. One of the most important results of the conquest of the Mediterranean was the hellenization of Roman culture. Contact with the superior and more sophisticated culture of Greece had its beneficial results. A new refinement appeared among certain classes in Rome. Greek teachers were imported to enrich the educational cur-

A small farmer brings his wares to the public market in this relief from Augustan Rome.

riculum, and Roman writers were inspired to imitate Greek literary models. The crude buildings of Rome took on a new elegance as her architects strove to imitate the models of Athens.

Such innovations were all to the good, but in the main the Romans imitated Greek vices rather than Greek virtues. The philosophy of Epicureanism was misinterpreted as an excuse for self-indulgence. Greek individualism, when adopted by the Romans, led to a decay of the old Roman traits of discipline, simplicity, and respect for authority. Rome became thronged with returned war veterans convinced that the state owed them a living. The city swarmed with fortune hunters, dandies, and fops, with thousands of imported domestic slaves, and with discontented, unemployed farmers.

Roman weaknesses. Such were the problems that faced the Romans as they entered a century (133-33 B.C.) that was to see the streets of Rome red with the blood of thousands of her citizens killed in civil strife, a succession of dictators, and the end of the republic. Thus as Rome neared the end of the second century B.C., the bulk of the population in Italy was impoverished and landless, government was controlled by a wealthy, selfish clique, and the old city-state system of government in the hands of the Senate had proved itself unable to cope with the problems of governing a great world-state. The need of solving internal weaknesses was made more urgent by disquieting rumors of savage Germanic tribes north of Italy whose hordes of wild soldiery now threatened the frontier of the empire.

The beginning of revolution. While a majority of the ruling class, that is, the senators, opposed any basic reforms, there were among the aristocracy those who perceived the need for drastic action, especially in regard to the land problem. One of these young reformers was Tiberius Gracchus, a scion of one of Rome's finest families. Well aware that his reform program would not be endorsed by the Senate, Tiberius campaigned and was elected tribune in 133 B.C. At once he proposed to the popular assembly an agrarian law limiting the holdings of public land to 500 *iugera* (312 acres) per person, with an additional 250 for each of two grown-up sons. All other public land—at this time in the hands of great landlords—would be confiscated and allotted to landless Roman citizens. It was known that these proposals would be adopted by a wide majority, but at this point one of the tribunes sided with the Senate and vetoed the measure. Tiberius now took a fateful—and unconstitutional—step by having the assembly depose the tribune in question, after which the agrarian bill was passed. Tiberius again violated custom in standing for reëlection as tribune, and he did so on a still more radical platform. During the election, he and some 300 of his followers were murdered by partisans of the Senate, which subsequently executed still others of his followers as public enemies on the grounds that Tiberius was attempting rebellion.

His work was taken up by his younger brother, Gaius Gracchus, who was elected tribune in 123 B.C. Gaius went even further than his brother in proposing reforms. His program included an extension of the policy of confiscating and reallocating public land; the foundation of new commercial colonies in south Italy and Carthage; and the proposal that the Roman franchise be extended to the Latin cities and perhaps to the Italian allies. Gaius is perhaps best remembered for his law obliging the government to buy grain at a fair price to protect the poor against speculation, but what may have been intended as a temporary measure outlived him and with unfortunate results. In time, this system was expanded into a "dole," whereby free food was distributed—all too often for the advancement of astute politicians—to the entire urban proletariat. Like his brother Tiberius, Gaius was trying to weaken the power of the senatorial class, and the latter again retaliated. In 121 B.C. Gaius fell a victim of assassination in a riot.

The Gracchi were inspired by idealistic motives, but it is doubtful whether their policies, even if fully implemented, could have solved Rome's dilemma. For, as in the case of Athens before her, Rome had now developed into a world-wide power, and new forms of government were required to cope with her far-flung political commitments and the drastic changes that had taken place in her economic life. In any case, the Senate had shown that it had no intention of initiating the necessary legislation, and the Gracchi's deaths were ominous portents of the manner in which the Romans were to decide their internal disputes.

Civil war—first stage: Marius and Sulla. Starting about 111 B.C., Rome had to engage in a number of wars which lasted many decades and which involved campaigns against enemies in north Africa, Asia Minor, southern France and, still closer to home, in the heart of Italy itself. One of the important results of these conflicts was the extension of Roman citizenship to peoples in the Italian provinces. But although the enfranchisement of Italy was to prove of long-range political value, it had no immediate effect upon the course of Roman politics, where conditions were working up to civil war.

In 88 B.C., the ambitious king of Pontus declared war on Rome and the question arose about the choice of a general to oppose the enemy. It was customary in such cases to choose by lot one of the two consuls then in office, and the choice fell on Cornelius Sulla, an able general and a staunch supporter of the Senate's position. However, the democratic forces, making use of the political concept that important decisions in foreign affairs rested with the popular assembly, chose Gaius Marius, another able general and popular hero, who had reformed the army by enlisting volunteers on terms of long service—a reform which was retained, for these volunteers fought well, but which in turn was to create a professional soldiery ready to follow any leader with profitable prospects. The rivalry between Sulla and Marius had exposed a fundamental weakness in the existing governmental machinery: in effect both the Senate and the popular assembly claimed to be the ultimate authority in the state. The results of this conflict were disastrous; civil war broke out between the rival generals, each of whom with his personal army captured Rome, and thousands of persons on either side were slain in the attending reigns of terror. This first stage of civil war ended in a complete victory for Sulla, who restored and even increased the powers of the Senate, while drastically curtailing those of the tribunes and the popular assembly. Sulla was in effect dictator, and he could have abolished the republic had he so desired. Instead, having accomplished his ends, he voluntarily resigned his office, and died in 78 B.C.

Civil war—second stage: Pompey and Caesar. Most of Sulla's innovations were to be short-lived. Ten years of civil war had but increased factionalism and the numbers of those discontented, and meanwhile the Senate proved its incompetence to cope with disturbances either abroad or at home. The populace was looking for new strong men, and these presently came forward. The first of them was a rich and ambitious general, Gnaeus Pompeius (Pompey), who made a name for himself with his successful campaigns in Italy, Africa, and Spain. In 70 B.C. Pompey was elected a consul and, although a former partisan of Sulla, the ambitious general now found it opportune to obtain the repeal of Sulla's laws against the assembly. Subsequently, Pompey added to his reputation by his widespread conquests in the East, which carried Roman influence and power to the Euphrates and even beyond. "Not since the days of the Scipios had a Roman general contributed so greatly to the extension of the far-flung Empire, exacting the toll of blood and suffering which the glory won for Rome by a policy of imperialism demanded from enemy and citizen alike."[4]

Still another strong man made his appearance when, in 59 B.C., Julius Caesar was elected consul. At this time in alliance with Pompey, Caesar put through various land laws, confirmed Pompey's eastern settlement, and secured for himself command of forces with which he proceeded to conquer Gaul. Caesar's brilliance as a general succeeded by 50 B.C. in extending Roman frontiers to the Rhine—and his lucidly written *Commentaries on the Gallic War* succeeded, in turn, in propagating his personal fame. Caesar's conquest of Gaul was to have tremendous consequences for the course of western civilization, for its inhabitants quickly assimilated Roman culture. Consequently, when the Roman empire collapsed in the west in the fifth century A.D., the Gauls were able to preserve—and transmit—some elements of classical civilization despite the impact of barbarian invasions.

Jealous of Caesar's achievements in Gaul, Pompey turned against his former colleague and combined with the Senate to discredit and ruin him. When the Senate demanded in 49 B.C. that Caesar disband his army on pain of being declared a public enemy, the latter crossed the Rubicon—a stream south of Ravenna marking the limit of Caesar's province—and marched with his forces to Rome. Pompey and most of the Senate fled eastward, but within a short time the senatorial opposition had been crushed, Pompey was dead, and Caesar was absolute master of Rome.

During his brief period of rule (49-44 B.C.), Caesar assumed a dictatorship, under which he carried through various far-reaching reforms. He weakened the power of the Senate, improved the administration of the provinces, and reduced the number of those receiving free grain. One of his major acts was to reform the solar calendar in the light of Egyptian knowledge; with minor changes, this is still the calendar in use today. Still another major innovation was his extension of Roman citizenship to various free communities outside Italy.

Caesar was one of the few leaders of his day who realized that the old republic was in fact dead, and he believed that benevolent despotism was the only way of saving Rome from continued civil war and preventing its great empire from falling apart. We do not know whether he intended to accept the title of king, as his enemies charged, but he seems to have regarded his power as hereditary, and in a will by which he adopted his grandnephew, Gaius Octavius, he made it clear that he regarded the latter as the heir of his position. Meanwhile, Caesar had incurred the enmity of those who had sought wealth at the expense of the state and also of those who still believed that the old republic should be retained and saw in him only a dangerous tyrant. On the Ides (15th) of March, 44 B.C., Caesar was stabbed to death in the Senate house by a group of conspirators. This act plunged Rome once more into conflict.

Civil war—third stage: Antony and Octavian. Who was to be Caesar's successor? His eighteen-year-old heir, who upon adoption had taken the name Gaius Julius Caesar Octavianus (Octavian), made an alliance with one of Caesar's colleagues, Marcus Antonius (Mark Antony), against the armies of the conspirators. This alliance then went on to suppress other political opposition—including the famous orator and champion of the Senate party, Cicero, who was put to death—and for more than a decade these leaders exercised a complete autocracy, thanks to their control over the armed forces. However, the ambitions of each proved too great for the alliance to endure. In the east, Antony had become infatuated with Egypt's ruler, Cleopatra, and had even transferred Roman territories to her dominions, and Octavian took advantage of this high-handedness to arouse Rome and Italy against him. In 31 B.C., Octavian's fleet met Antony's at Actium; details of the battle are not certain, but in any case Antony and Cleopatra fled to Egypt where Antony committed suicide, as did his mistress soon afterwards when Alexandria was taken in 30 B.C. After a little over a century of civil violence, in which the republic had given way to the empire, Rome was at last united under one ruler—Octavian—and two centuries of imperial greatness were to follow.

Augustus and the empire. Following his return to Rome in triumph Octavian (on whom the Senate bestowed the title Augustus in 27 B.C.) announced that he would "restore the republic." It is true that, instead of establishing an outright monarchy, Augustus provided the Senate with considerable authority; consulted it on important issues, and gave it the legislative functions of the popular assembly which had now fallen into abeyance. Furthermore, after Augustus' death the Senate appointed his successor, though in later practice it had to accept nominations made by the emperor or, in many cases, the army heads. At the same time, Augustus broadened the membership of the Senate to include picked representatives of the Italian municipalities.

After 23 B.C., Augustus held the consulship only twice and then for but a short part of the year. Where, then, did his strength lie? He kept a proconsular power which gave him control over a group of provinces (about half of the total number), an overriding control over the governors of the remaining provinces, and a tribunician power (as a patrician he could not be a tribune himself) over the magistrates at Rome. Augustus summed up his position as that of princeps, or first among equals, and his form of government is therefore known as the principate. But perhaps the chief source of Augustus' strength lay in the fact that he controlled all the armed forces, who had to pay allegiance to him personally. As supreme leader of the army he was called *imperator*—from which we derive our modern term emperor and which, it has been pointed out, "correctly conveys the essence of his position."

Later, when we examine the contributions of the Romans to political theory and the art of government, we will have occasion to evaluate the contribution made by Augustus. Meanwhile we can agree that he effected a compromise "between the need for a monarchical head of the empire and the sentiment which enshrined Rome's republican constitution in the minds of his contemporaries."[5] Yet this compromise was only of a transitional nature in the evolution of the Roman empire—an absolute monarchy was eventually to make itself supreme.

Reconstruction under Augustus. Augustus was faced at the outset with the problem of removing the many evils and scars that had resulted from a century of civil strife. The job of reconstruction was a task that demanded great statesmanship. The general run of Roman citizens had just about lost confidence in their government and in the destiny of their country. Many of the provinces were depopulated and had been ravaged by war. The aristocracy was in many respects selfish and unpatriotic. In the cities an unemployed mob had been kept on free bread and circuses and had long ago lost any interest in work. On the frontiers were large armies, many quite undisciplined, some of which were toying with the idea of setting their candidates on the imperial throne.

Augustus wisely concentrated on these internal problems and did not try to extend the empire's territories. He did, however, extend Roman control to the Danube as a defensive measure against the danger of barbarian invasion. During the long reign of Rome's first princeps, administration was improved in the provinces, law and order were revived throughout the land, and a trained and loyal body of civil servants was established. Taxation was made more efficient and just, and the finances of the empire were placed on a sound basis.

The Julian Caesars. When Augustus died in 14 A.D. after a glorious and successful reign, he was followed by four descendants of his family, the line of the Julian Caesars. Of these emperors Tiberius and Claudius were reasonably efficient and devoted rulers. But of the other two, one, Caligula, was a madman who, among other whimsies made his horse a consul. The other, Nero, was a monster infamous for his persecution of the Christians, his immoralities, and the murder of his wife and his mother.

The Flavian emperors. The Julian Caesars ended their rule in 69 A.D. and were followed by the Flavian emperors. For thirty years that imperial line gave the empire reasonably good, if not brilliant, rule. Vespasian saw to it that the provinces were administered justly and improved the defenses of the Rhine-Danube frontier. Domitian, the last of the Flavians, paid special attention to the defenses of the northern frontier. By the time of his rule the subterfuge of the principate, in which the Senate enjoyed the empty forms of authority and the princeps the real essence of power, was becoming more and more a meaningless fiction. Domitian was a thorough autocrat. He demanded, for example, that he be addressed as lord and god. Roman government now was, for all intents and purposes, a monarchy passed from father to son, in which the worship of the emperor was carried out as a part of the duties of citizenship.

The "five good emperors." The Flavian period was followed by that of the "five good emperors." Although strictly speaking only the last two of the "five good emperors" were Antonines, the period of their rule (96-180 A.D.) is commonly know as the age of the Antonines. In this period the Roman empire reached the height of its prosperity and power. Few lines of rulers in history, if any, showed more devotion to duty and strength of character than the "five good emperors."

Three of these emperors are especially worthy of notice. Trajan (98-117 A.D.) was famous for his military exploits and for his ambitious building program in Rome. Trajan conquered territory north of the lower Danube and made it a Roman province. Held by Roman legions for little more than a century and a half, this area nevertheless was strongly influenced by its brief contact with Roman culture. Even today, the inhabitants of the region call themselves Rumanians.

Trajan was succeeded by Hadrian, one of the ablest of all Roman emperors. His reign extended from 117 to 138 A.D. During this time no attempt was made to extend the boundaries, the main emphasis being on the improvement of the governmental machinery.

Marcus Aurelius, who better than most rulers approached Plato's ideal of the "philosopher-king," ascended the throne in 161 A.D. The last ruler of the Antonine Age was faced, six years after becoming emperor, with the peril of German barbarian tribes breaking through the northern frontier. The invasion was met successfully, but Marcus Aurelius was forced to continue fighting against the German tribes until his death in 180 A.D. The scholar-emperor would have preferred the quiet contemplation of his books rather than the blood and brutality of the battlefield. Marcus Aurelius was of saintly character, devoted to the state, and a lover of philosophy. While on his campaigns against the Germans, he wrote his *Meditations,* a little volume of philosophical musings notable for its lofty idealism and love of humanity. No successor to the imperial throne was so fine a man or so devoted to the service of the state.

Decline of the empire. The overthrow of the nonfunctioning republic and the advent of one-man rule had brought the Roman world two centuries of peace, the *Pax Romana,* which lasted from the establishment of the principate by Augustus in 30 B.C. to the invasions of the German hordes about 170 A.D., in the reign of Marcus Aurelius. Following the death of Marcus Aurelius the empire quickly declined. For a century after the rule of the "philosopher-king" the empire was rent by internal revolution and increasing pressure from the barbarians on the frontiers. Then followed a brief period of restoration and reorganization, from 284 to 337 A.D., under the emperors Diocletian and Constantine. Their efforts, however, only slowed down the process of collapse. The next one hundred fifty years witnessed the disintegration of governmental authority, the defeat of Roman armies, and the tramp of German barbarian invaders in the Roman capital city.

Life in the Antonine Age

Roman prosperity. Under the five good emperors of the Antonine Age (96-180 A.D.), the Roman empire reached the height of its prosperity and power. Never before had such a large part of Europe, Asia, and Africa been so prosperous, contented, and well governed. Industry expanded, cities increased in population, and commerce flourished. The famous eighteenth-century historian Edward Gibbon even contended that in this period the human race reached the acme of happiness. At the beginning of the next chapter, which presents a larger view of "The World in Classical Times" and traces the development of early contacts between the civilizations of East and West, we shall study the administrative organization and economic interdependence of the Roman world-state during this period. The present section examines its social fabric.

Social life. The best place to observe the social conditions of the age was in the capital, Rome itself. At the pinnacle of its power and prosperity, Rome had over one million inhabitants living in an area about three miles square. Rome presented a striking contrast of magnificence and tawdriness—splendid public buildings, forums, baths, and parks, and crowded narrow streets lined with tenements. The streets in turn swarmed with all manner of people jostling one another: unemployed in rags, high governmental officials in immaculate togas, blond Germans, Ethiopians, soldiers of the Praetorian Guard, hucksters selling their wares, slaves from Britain, and scientists from Alexandria. Rome was, in fact, "the common center and crucible for everything good and bad in the huge, teeming Mediterranean world."[6]

Rome possessed a large police force to keep

A Roman apothecary fills a prescription in this ancient drug store, while his wife keeps store.

order. Nevertheless, at night few honest citizens dared venture down the winding streets without proper guard. In the poor sections of the city the walls of the buildings were covered with scribblings—messages for a friend, insults for an enemy, romantic sentiments for one's lady love. The wooden tenements on these streets, where the great majority of the populace lived, were overcrowded firetraps whose flimsy construction often caused them to collapse. It was little wonder that the plebeians seemed always to be searching for better quarters.

While a large proportion of the populace was dependent upon state support in whole or in part, many plebeians made a fairly good living as artisans. These workers usually belonged to *collegia,* or guilds, of which there were some eighty, each comprising the workers of one trade. The *collegia* were social rather than economic in purpose, providing a hall for their members, caring for the sick, and arranging for feasts and celebrations. There was no thought of collective bargaining, of controlling the training of apprentices, or of such matters as wages and conditions of work.

An estimated fifty per cent of Rome's population was made up of slaves, whose conditions of living varied a great deal. Those in domestic service, for example, were often treated humanely and their years of efficient service might even be rewarded by emancipation. Furthermore it was not uncommon for freed slaves to rise to places of eminence in business and letters. On the other hand, conditions among slaves on the large plantations could be indescribably harsh, with the lash of the whip all too often their lot.

At the top of the social order were the old senatorial families who owned large estates in the country. With the coming of the empire, the aristocracy tended to lose its power and influence to the wealthy business class, which was composed often of newly rich families who spent much of their time—and money—in showing that they "had arrived." In contrast to the tenements of the poor, the homes of the rich were palatial, containing courts and gardens with elaborate fountains, rooms furnished with marble walls, mosaics on the floors, and numerous works of art and frescoes. These furnishings were often in excellent taste, as the excavations at Pompeii have revealed. An interesting aspect of Roman furniture was the abundance of couches and absence of chairs. The people usually reclined, even at meals—a custom which may have had its value during the long and sometimes mammoth dinners served by the wealthy gourmands, who were not above administering emetics to permit their starting afresh on more viands and wines.

Public entertainment. No picture of the social life of the empire would be complete without mention of its recreation and sports. The Romans liked their public baths, of which they had a great many, the largest being the Baths of Caracalla and of Diocletian. Such athletic activities as racing, boxing, and wrestling were engaged in informally, but the chief sport was chariot racing. So popular was this pastime that under the emperors the Circus Maximus had to be enlarged to hold at least 150,000 spectators, who excitedly followed, often with wagers, the fortunes of their favorite teams. By the fourth century chariot races took up sixty-four days in the year.

Scarcely less popular, but infinitely less civilized, were the gladiatorial contests which had been organized under the emperors as a regular feature on the amusement calendar. These

The peristyle or inner court of the restored house of the Vettii in Pompeii shows the splendor of the homes of wealthy Romans.

AN AERIAL VIEW OF THE COLOSSEUM, ROME, SCENE OF GLADIATORIAL COMBAT

cruel spectacles, which have no exact counterpart in any other civilization, were held in arenas, the largest and most famous of which was the Colosseum. The contests took various forms. Different animals were pitted sometimes against one another and sometimes against armed combatants; occasionally they were even matched against unarmed men and women who had been condemned to death. Another type of contest was the fight to the death between gladiators, who were generally equipped with different types of weapons but matched on equal terms. Some of the gladiators lived to win fame and fortune in these bloody encounters, nor was it uncommon for the life of a defeated gladiator who had fought courageously to be spared at the request of the spectators. It should also be pointed out that many Romans, like Seneca, decried these bloodletting contests. Nevertheless, this streak of cruelty in Roman public amusements can scarcely be comprehended, far less condoned. It was entirely absent, for example, from the sports of the Greeks.

Social life in Rome was duplicated by the towns in the provinces, in proportion to their individual means. They too had their circuses and chariot races, their arenas and gladiatorial contests. And as in Rome, their citizens patronized the theaters and baths and in general enjoyed the amenities which an imperial economy provided. "One may say without exaggeration that never in the history of mankind (except during the nineteenth and twentieth centuries in Europe and America) has a larger number of people enjoyed so much comfort; and that never, not even in the nineteenth century, did men live in such a surrounding of beautiful buildings and monuments as in the first two centuries of the Roman Empire."[7]

The Roman Contribution

The Roman world-state. As we have seen, this sprawling Roman empire—which at the pinnacle of its power under the Antonine Caesars was organized into forty-five provinces containing some seventy-five million people—had been created by force of arms over a period of centuries. Roman militarism and the subjugation of other peoples has often been justifiably criticized on moral and other grounds, but this should not lead us to minimize certain positive contributions which were made to civilization as a result of this era of empire building. For the first time in history a great world-state was created in which many varied races and nationalities lived in peace and harmony with one another, unmolested from attack beyond the frontiers. Let us now turn to those developments in government, political theory, and law which made possible the centuries-long existence of the Roman empire and which represent some of Rome's most important contributions to world culture.

Graeco-Roman culture diffusion. The Romans did not establish a narrow national empire. Instead, as we have seen, it was customary for the conquerors to treat their former enemies generously and permit them to retain their own customs, creeds, and even a considerable amount of local self-government. In fact, it has been pointed out that the harmonious maintenance of a diversity of cultures and religions within a political unity was the greatest achievement of Rome.

The Roman world-state was basically a synthesis of two principal cultures: Greek and Latin. At the outset we noted that the Greeks and Romans were offshoots of a common Indo-European stock and that the early Romans were exposed to various Greek influences. But the full and permanent impact came after the Punic Wars when the Hellenistic world was overrun by the Romans, who became strong admirers of everything Greek. Thus they learned the Greek language, copied Greek architecture, employed Greek sculptors, and identified their gods with those of Greece. Latin poets in general adopted Greek meters, and the poet Virgil related the Trojan origin

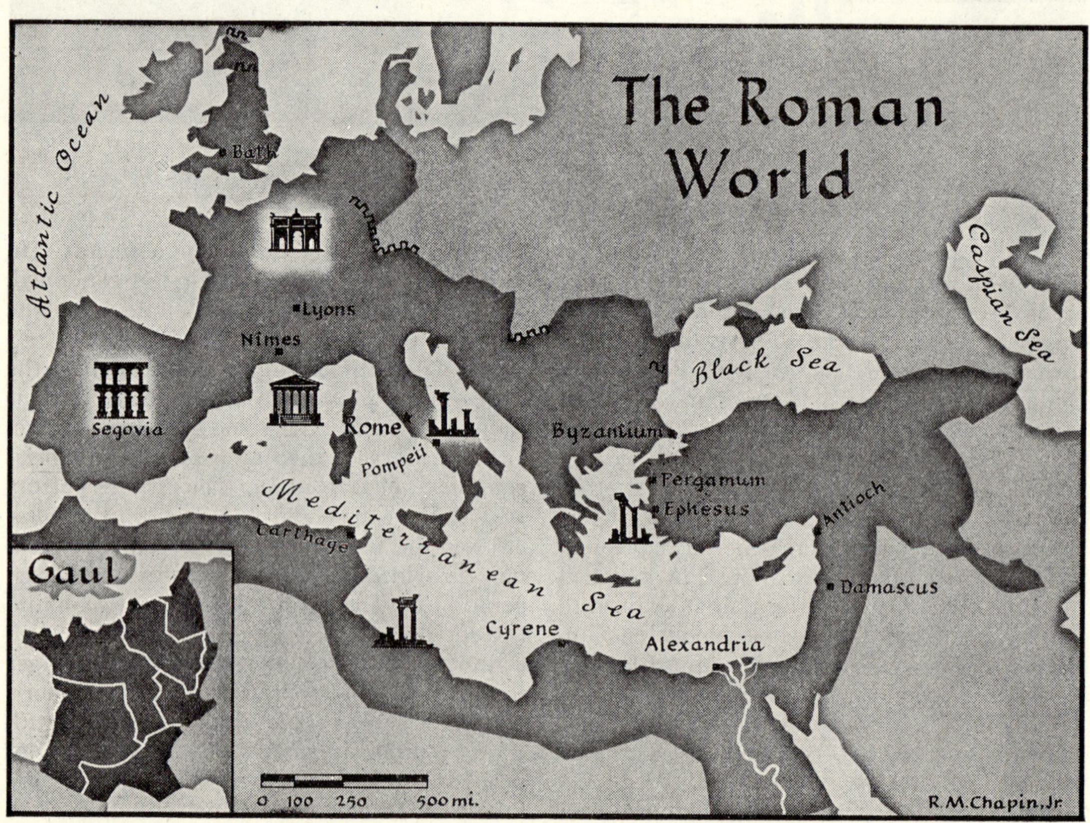

of the Romans in the *Aeneid* in order to demonstrate the Latin connection with the Homeric myths. In short, to use the well-known phrase of Horace: *Graecia capta ferum victorem cepit, et artes intulit agresti Latio*—"Conquered Greece took her savage conqueror captive, and introduced the arts into rustic Latium." In our brief examination of the major contributions of Rome to history, we shall have occasion to point out the extent of its indebtedness to this brilliant "captive."

Yet, as we have had occasion to witness, the hellenization of Rome was not always for the best. The early Romans had been instilled with the simple virtues of self-reliance, personal integrity, family cohesion, and discipline. The Greek influence softened the ways of the Romans, making them less harsh and insensitive, but it also inculcated habits of sophistication which were often corrupting and even decadent. Furthermore, the Roman conquest of the Hellenistic world paved the way for the spread to the West of various oriental cults, often based on superstition, divination, and other-worldly antidotes. From the east was also introduced the cult of the divinity of the monarch, which in turn reinforced the doctrine of absolutism, a theory repugnant to the Romans of the early republic.

Perpetuation of Greek culture and Christianity. Nevertheless, it was fortunate for all concerned—which includes the contemporary western world—that the conquering Romans did not destroy but incorporated Greek culture in their own and that, by establishing the first great world-state, they then made permanent the Hellenic and Hellenistic contribution. Without the *Pax Romana,* much or all of Greek culture would have perished, as did earlier civilizations which had been followed by times of trouble.

One of the most permanent and profound effects of the long Roman diffusion was the adoption in the western world of a hellenized Christianity. We shall see that the universality of the Greek language as a cultural medium and the breaking down of Greek philosophy into a quest for individual salvation made possible the extension throughout the eastern Hellenistic world of what might otherwise have been an obscure Jewish sect. The Romans in turn, by accepting and spreading Christianity to the farthest confines of their empire, ensured the Christianization of Europe, and the universality of Christianity.

Furthermore, the Roman world-state, by embracing through its brilliant administrative machinery the goal of unity-in-diversity, gave men a conception of one universal culture based on peace and order which they had never had before, and which remained with them for some fifteen hundred years. This conception passed into the Catholic Church (the literal meaning of the word *catholic* is "universal") and later to the medieval Holy Roman Empire. The forcible conquest by the Romans of northern Italy, Spain, England, Belgium, France, and parts of Austria, Hungary, Rumania, and western Germany was of incalculable importance in the spread of culture and of Christianity.

The Roman world-state also made possible a number of cultural and commercial contacts with India and China (as we shall see in Chapter 7), and enabled Graeco-Roman knowledge, especially that of the Greeks, to be transmitted to the Arabs. They in turn preserved it during the medieval period when culture in Europe was at low ebb and eventually transmitted it back to the western world. Here, then, is another example of the interdependence of peoples and cultures.

The Roman spirit. What were the characteristics of the Roman conquerors that permitted this peaceful adoption and diffusion of culture? Their background as a nation of farmers provided the tradition of plain living and serious thinking. The Roman spirit was compounded of many factors. It was stimulated by favorable geographical conditions. The Romans were in the middle of a peninsula, and Italy itself was in the middle of the Mediterranean. This put them in the most favorable position to expand to the south of Italy, or Magna Graecia, and to the whole Mediterranean world. The Romans met the challenge of geography, and with it the challenge of rival powers, especially the Carthaginians. For centuries Romans were faced with the need to conquer or be conquered, and they had to encourage national discipline and duty to the state. Their geographical and political growth in turn demanded the practical solution of new administrative and legal problems. The Romans provided a practical response to a complex and ceaseless challenge; and the result was not only a workable world-state but the development of a strong sense of duty and a skill in administration, law, and practical affairs.

But the Roman spirit also had another side. It could be arrogant and cruel, and its deep-rooted sense of justice was too often untempered with mercy. Where the Greeks had worshiped reason, the Romans enshrined authority; where the former had demanded self-expression and personal freedom to the point of anarchy, the latter emphasized self-control and discipline.

Although the Romans lacked the brilliance of the Greeks as theorists and creative artists, they excelled in the arts of government and administration. If it is said that the Romans constructed no original system of philosophy, invented no new art forms, and made no outstanding scientific discoveries, it should be added that they made unique and lasting contributions in the fields of jurisprudence and political theory. By and large, the Romans lacked the creative fire of the Greeks, but they knew superbly well how to preserve, adapt, and disseminate a new civilization. Therefore we might characterize the Romans as synthesists rather than innovators—and at the same time pay respect to their recognition of cultural indebtedness. There is shown here a certain magnanimity of attitude characteristic of the Roman spirit at its best. For all their limitations, the Romans had greatness as a people, even in defeat and decline—unlike the Greeks, who in their political relationships all too often showed themselves to be petty and irresponsible. The *Pax Romana* could have been fashioned and maintained only by a people mature in judgment and conscious of their responsibilities to others.

Contributions in government. The Romans created the political framework of modern Europe. Many administrative divisions now found in that continent, such as the parish, county, and province, are derived from Roman practice, and in some instances the boundaries of the divisions are little changed from those existing in the days of the Caesars. And as we shall see the medieval Church modeled its organization after the empire. (Compare the Roman organization of Gaul, map page 176, with the ecclesiastical organization of the same area shown on the map on page 389.) The lasting influence of the Romans in government is further illustrated by such political terms in present-day use as fiscal, senate, consul, plebiscite, citizen, municipal, and census.

Early Rome was simply a city-state, but with its assimilation of other regions and peoples it was faced with new problems of government. As we have seen, it evolved the system of progressively extending citizenship to non-Roman peoples, first in Italy and later in the provinces beyond and, as occurred in the days of the empire, of broadening the composition of the Senate to include elements from all sections of the Roman world. The utmost possible autonomy was conceded to the individual self-governing town—though in the later days of the empire the central government increased its power at the expense of the local unit. "The fact remains that the city-state, as developed by Rome, raised the Greek model to educative and civilizing heights from which have derived the conceptions of political autonomy and political federation. A man's duties lay, above all, in the political sphere, as a member of a self-governing unit; to be a *civis*—'citizen'—was to be a fellow citizen: the word enjoyed both meanings."[8]

Although Roman political theory succeeded admirably in enabling citizens to participate in the political life of the local city-state, no means was worked out for permitting active participation by the ordinary citizenry in the affairs of the empire. Despite his reforms and innovations, Augustus "failed to bridge the gulf between the government and governed in the Roman empire." Today, of course, representative democracy has bridged this gulf, but one authority warns: "The lesson which the ultimate failure of classical civilization in its phase of a world-state teaches is that stagnation is inevitable when orthodox political theory fails to progress in response to changed political conditions. Today national sovereignty dominates political thought as firmly as did the orthodox theory of the city-state . . . in the classical world."[9]

Yet though they may have failed to solve the supreme political problem of history's first world-state, Roman political thinkers such as Cicero and Seneca contributed the germs of many theories of government popular in later centuries: the social-contract theory (that government originated as a voluntary agreement among citizens); the idea of popular sovereignty (that all power ultimately resides with the people); the principle of the separation of powers (that the legislative, executive, and judicial branches of the government should be kept separate—an idea that was incorporated in our Constitution); and the concept that law must be the paramount rule in government. The despotism of the Roman emperors in the last phase of the empire vitiated many of these splendid theories and in their place substituted the theory of the divine right of kings which had been promulgated by Alexander the Great. Yet these concepts were never lost sight of, but were transmitted to early modern times to form the theoretical basis of contemporary western constitutional governments.

Roman law. Of the contributions made by the Romans in government and politics, Roman law is pre-eminent. Abundant evidence of the fact exists today. Two great legal systems, Roman law and English common law, enjoy a monopoly in most modern civilized nations. The Roman law is the basis for the law codes of Italy, France, Spain, Japan, Scotland, and the Latin American countries. In addition, it has strongly affected the development of Moslem law, and the legal systems in Holland and South Africa show Roman influence. It also strongly influenced the law of the medieval Church, called canon law. Many legal terms in the English common law are taken from the Latin, such as *posse, habeas corpus, juror, mandamus,* and *stare decisis.* The law of equity was especially based on Roman maxims. International law has borrowed many principles inherent in Roman law. Roman influence in international law is attested by the common use of such Latin terms as *de facto, status quo, casus belli,* and *jus soli.*

Roman law evolved slowly over a period of about one thousand years. At first, when Rome was a struggling little city-state, the law was unwritten, mixed with religious custom, narrow in its point of view and harsh in its judgments. As Rome became more prosperous and life consequently became more complex, the law was gradually separated from religion. In other words, the law was secularized, and the *jus divinum* (divine law) became the *jus civile* (the civil code, or the law of the city). In 449 B.C. upon the demand of the plebeians, the law was written in the Laws of the Twelve Tables.

The next step in Roman judicial development was the expansion of judicial machinery. In the fourth century B.C. a special official, the *praetor urbanus,* was established to conduct trials. Under the guidance of the praetors, the Roman law was expanded to meet new conditions and problems. Upon assuming office every praetor drew up his edict, which stated the maxims of law he would adhere to during the term of his office. The edicts were based on the old law, but in addition new principles and usages were introduced if the praetor thought them necessary.

The acquisition of an empire brought under Roman rule many different kinds of people, each with its distinct customs and laws. To meet the situation, a new official, called the *praetor peregrinus,* was created in 242 B.C. This officer had charge of courts where non-Romans were concerned. The new praetor had to take into consideration many different kinds of custom. In a word, he had to range far outside the *jus civile* in seeing that justice was meted out to non-Romans. As a result a new kind of law, the *jus gentium* (law of nations) developed that could be applied to all foreigners. It soon became recognized that the law of nations was much more elastic and comprehensive than the old Roman civil law, whether the case concerned Romans or foreigners. Consequently the civil law became denationalized. Enriched by the *jus gentium* it developed into a system of law that was applicable to the whole empire. The *jus gentium* had conquered the *jus civile.*

Codification of the law. By the fourth century A.D. a great mass of law had accumulated, and it was getting increasingly hard to use. The logical answer was codification—a systematized legal system reduced to fundamental principles. During the first two centuries of the empire a remarkable series of jurists carried on the work of systematizing the law. These men were greatly influenced by Stoic philosophy with its conception of a humane, rational, and natural law applicable to all mankind. The law was humanized, and the test of any law, wherever it might exist, was considered to be "what a man of common sense and good faith would deem to be right." The process of codification saw the adoption of many legal principles borrowed from the *jus naturale* (natural law). Thus the once primitive and narrow law of the small city-state of Rome evolved into a humane and

Paved street leading into the Forum in Pompeii shows the two triumphal arches, which also protected merchants in inclement weather.

comprehensive legal system that filled the needs of a world-state.

After several attempts to achieve a complete codification of the law, the emperor Justinian, between the years 528 and 534, made a compilation of Roman law from all sources (see page 266). This work of codification and systematization enabled the Roman law to be condensed in a few volumes and thus easily preserved for posterity.

The Romans as builders. Government and law were but two essential aspects of the management of an empire. The physical problems of communication and city life had also to be met. The administrative needs of an extensive empire necessitated the building of road systems, bridges, sewers, and aqueducts. Moreover, the imperial capital with its numerous governmental agencies called for the erection of huge and pretentious public buildings. Pride of empire also led to the erection of ostentatious monuments that symbolized the dignity and the might of the Roman state.

As road builders the Romans surpassed all previous peoples. Their roads were carefully planned for strategic and administrative purposes, constructed according to sound engineering principles, and kept in constant repair.

One of the earliest main Roman highways was the Appian Way, built to connect Rome with cities to the south. Later the Flaminian Way was built running northeast from Rome to the Adriatic, connecting with other roads to the northern provinces.

In bridges and aqueducts built throughout the empire, the Romans put a series of arches next to each other so that they could support each other and finally carry the thrusts to the ground. "Devil's Bridge," built to supply the city of Segovia with water, shows the tremendous size of the typical Roman aqueduct (compare it with the figures standing at the foot) and illustrates the construction and function of the arch. This famous aqueduct is still in use today. In addition to their achievements as aqueduct, bridge, and road builders, the Romans showed great skill and daring in constructing dams, reservoirs, and harbors. The practical, utilitarian nature of Roman building is underlined in these magnificent achievements of her engineers.

A distinctive Roman architecture. In architecture the Romans at first copied Greek models slavishly, but gradually a distinctive Roman architecture developed which perpetuated basic Greek forms and elements but transformed them into works essentially Roman. For spanning openings Roman builders used the arch extensively and daringly. For roofing large areas they extended the arch into a vault (see diagram at the right). This extension of the arches, a barrel vault, required thick walls. It had been used in Mesopotamia, but the Romans used it more extensively. Later the Romans discovered that the vaults could be intersected with arched openings. This discovery led to the development of the intersecting vault, which required support at only a few places instead of all along the walls (as the diagram shows). This development allowed windows, which the massive solid walls of the barrel vault did not permit. It remained for the builders of the medieval period to develop vaulting to its greatest height and delicacy.

Types of buildings. The Greeks evolved the temple, theater, and stadium as basic architectural forms. The Romans contributed the triumphal arch, bath, basilica, amphitheater, and storied apartment house. The triumphal arch symbolized the glory and might of the empire. The two arches near the Colosseum

A BARREL VAULT *is a continuous series of arches forming a tunnel-like structure. Its walls must be thick and strong to support the sidewise and downward pressure of the material above.*

AN INTERSECTING VAULT *occurs where two barrel vaults meet at right angles, permitting openings in the supporting walls for windows. These openings may be filled with rubble since they need not support weight from above.*

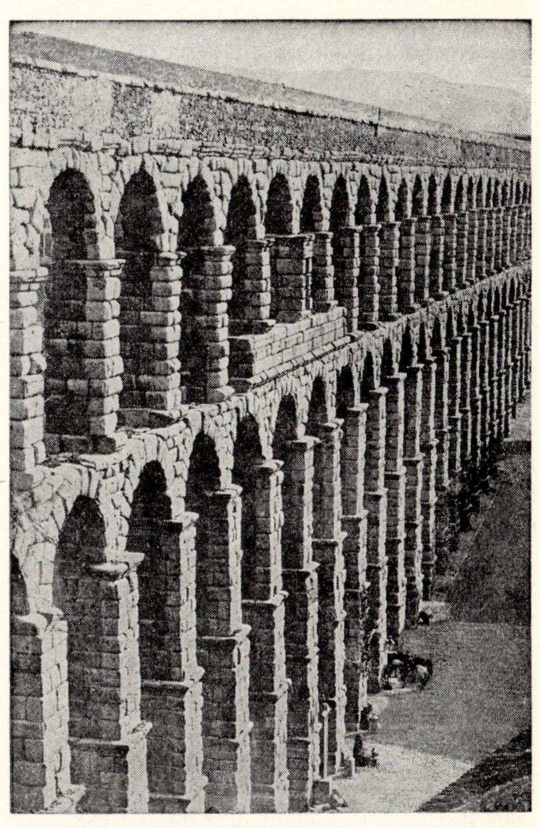

"DEVIL'S BRIDGE"—ROMAN AQUEDUCT AT SEGOVIA, SPAIN

BASILICA OF CONSTANTINE, ROMAN FORUM

shown in the picture on page 175 are typical Roman triumphal arches. The Romans also used columns to commemorate their imperial heroes and their national achievements. These were customarily single shafts set on pedestals.

Every large Roman city possessed its baths. They were huge, showy buildings containing many rooms and high, wide halls, giving an impression of spaciousness and splendor. The baths were the counterpart of our modern clubs. They were patronized by both rich and poor. An old Roman inscription states "The bath, wine, and love ruin one's health but make life worth living."

The basilica was an important Roman civic building, utilized for many purposes. A colonnaded building, it had a main central nave with barrel vaulting in the ceiling, and aisles on the sides. The central roof was elevated above the side walls to permit clerestory windows, like those of some Egyptian temples. Remains of these walls and windows can be seen above the central vault in the illustration of the Basilica of Constantine on this page. The influence of the Roman basilica on later architecture was very marked. In plan it contained the germ of the Gothic cathedral.

Another method applied by the Romans to roof over large areas without intermediate support was the construction of immense concrete domes. The weight of a domed roof was carried down the dome directly to the walls, and since there was no sidewise thrust, no other support was necessary. The largest of the domed structures was the Roman temple called the Pantheon, which is still in existence. Domes have been used in many later periods. They tend to give a monumental effect to public buildings—the state capitols, for example.

Perhaps the most famous Roman edifice is the Colosseum, built late in the first century A.D. The exterior is about one quarter of a mile around, and the seating capacity is estimated to have been at least 45,000. The Colosseum utilized three stories of arches, a typical Roman feature, and for ornamental effect inserted a column between the arches. These columns are engaged—applied flat to the wall with only about a quarter of the diameter protruding. The engaged column is no longer a structural element but becomes merely decorative. In the Colosseum the three orders, Doric, Ionic, and Corinthian, have been arranged sensitively, with the heaviest at the bottom and the most ornate and delicate, the Corinthian, at the top.

Two characteristics of Roman construction were solidity and magnificence of conception. Roman buildings were built to last, and their vastness, grandeur, and decorative richness aptly symbolized the proud imperial spirit of Rome. Sumptuousness, splendor, and complexity of plan were also characteristic of Roman architecture. The severe Greek structures were too simple for the Romans, who loved elaborate ornamentation. The Greek column was extensively used both for support and for decoration, but the Romans preferred the ornate Corinthian rather than the Doric or the Ionic column. Many of our modern public buildings are copied very largely from Roman models.

Decorative sculpture and realistic painting. After the conquest of Greece thousands of statues and other art pieces were brought to Rome. People seemed to have a passion for art, and the homes of the wealthy were filled with all kinds of Greek art. Yet, although Roman sculpture never achieved the distinction attained by Roman architecture, a truly Roman art did develop.

Roman artists excelled in portraiture, both in sculpture and in painting. The earlier Etruscan culture probably exerted a strong influence in this regard. Two salient features of Etruscan life and thought were a firm belief in a future life and a reverence for ancestors.

Accordingly, their native art was devoted chiefly to the embellishment of the abodes of their dead, and the custom of preserving lifelike memorials of them became universal. Fine cinerary urns and ancestral busts still exist. The Romans found this realistic approach to sculpture to their liking, and their sculpture and painting, while also influenced strongly by Greek models, were realistic, secular, and individualistic. Whereas the Greeks idealized their subject matter and portrayed types rather than individuals, the Romans were at their best when portraying lifelike busts of administrators, soldiers, and emperors. The bust of Caracalla at the bottom of the page shows the distinctly realistic treatment characteristic of Roman portraiture.

The historical relief sculpture found on Roman imperial monuments is also exceptionally fine. The Romans were skilled in using reliefs to tell a story or to recount the victories of their emperors. Again we see the contrast between the idealized art of the Greeks, which was often religious in purpose, and the realistic, secular art of the Romans, which glorified the empire and its heroes.

MARBLE BUST OF THE EMPEROR CARACALLA

ORNAMENTAL FRAGMENT FROM TRAJAN'S FORUM

Other important artistic achievements of the Romans were their decorative sculpture and scrollwork, their coins, their equestrian statues, and their sculptured coffins or sarcophagi. The Romans developed a great fund of decorative motifs such as cupids, garlands of flowers, and scrolls of various patterns. These were very popular during the Renaissance and have persisted until today. The illustration above shows a group of these motifs worked in stone. The Romans also used stucco wall decoration in distinctive fashion, and were much more realistic in their decoration than the Greeks. Roman coins with relief portraits of emperors permitted another art which served to glorify the Roman empire. The Augustan penny illustrated on page 184 shows one of these portraits, which because of the small size of the coin had to be less realistic than the marble busts.

In painting, the Romans were far advanced in technical achievement, although they probably used Greek models almost exclusively. They were more interested in realism in their paintings than were earlier peoples. Compare the painting of Perseus and Andromeda (page 184) with the Cretan Snake Goddess (page 125) and the Egyptian dancers (page 60). Note the three-dimensional rounded treatment in the Roman painting as contrasted with the flatness of earlier work. From the Romans we can get some idea of what Greek painting must have been like. The frescoes still to be seen in Pompeii and elsewhere show that the artists knew how to draw the human figure accurately and to show objects in correct perspective. Their whole approach was too realistic to allow them to take any artistic liberties with nature. Roman influence on later art can be seen in the early catacomb paintings,

AN AUGUSTAN PENNY

such as the one on page 438, but it was superseded in the Middle Ages by the influence of Byzantium.

The Romans as writers. In literature as in art the Romans turned to the Greeks for their models. In poetry, for example, Roman epic, didactic, dramatic, and lyric forms were usually written in conscious imitation of Greek masterpieces. Compared with Greek literature, Latin literature boasts few really outstanding writers. Notwithstanding this, it is one of the world's greatest literatures. And in certain fields of literary activity, such as the didactic poem, historical writing, and satire, the Romans made substantial and original contributions.

In one respect, at least, Latin literature had greater historical significance than the Greek, because the political power of Rome made Latin the vehicle of thought for the western world, and consequently its literature was the dominant influence in the development of vernacular literature in Europe. Furthermore, the West received much of its knowledge of Greek literature through Latin translations. These factors attest to an influence so strong upon western thought and letters that educated men kept writing in Latin continuously for more than a thousand years after the expiration of the Roman empire.

Roman drama. The most important development in early Latin literature was the drama, derived in great measure from Greek sources, and which is interesting for its plots rather than for style or intellectual content. The writer Plautus (about 254-184 B.C.) has left us twenty plays which shed interesting light upon the customs and manners of Rome in the third century B.C. The style of Plautus was ribald and vigorously humorous. He wrote for the common man, who greatly enjoyed his rollicking plots of illicit love, the shrewish wife, or the lovelorn youth. Plautus suggested many of the types that modern comedy has assumed, such as the farce, burlesque, and comedy of manners. From him Shakespeare got the ideas for his *Comedy of Errors* and *Merry Wives of Windsor;* and Molière, the famous seventeenth-century French dramatist, was undoubtedly influenced by Plautus. Terence (about 190-159 B.C.) has given us six polished and elegant plays. Unlike Plautus, his comedies are restrained and sophisticated and sparkle with subtle wit. Terence was too intellectual for the common people, who never accepted nor enjoyed his plays as they did those written by Plautus.

The Golden Age of Latin literature. Although Latin literature had its beginnings in the Punic Wars, it was in the first century B.C. that it entered its first great period of creative activity. Prior to about 80 B.C. Roman writers for the most part had been steeping them-

PERSEUS AND ANDROMEDA, POMPEIAN FRESCO

selves in the treasures of Greek thought (as Plautus and Terence had done), and perfecting the Latin language as a literary medium. Then followed an outpouring of splendid intellectual effort at the very time when the republic was in its last stages. This marks the first half of what has been called the Golden Age of Latin Literature, and is known as the Ciceronian period because of the stature of its greatest literary figure, Marcus Tullius Cicero (106-43 B.C.).

This Ciceronian period was marked by exuberance and spontaneity in its lyrical poetry, the best of which was written by Catullus (84-54 B.C.), described as a young man-about-town who wrote intensely of his loves and hates—and of his unsuccessful infatuation for a beauty of his day. At the other end of the personality spectrum was Catullus' contemporary, Lucretius (99-55 B.C.) a poet immersed in Greek philosophy. In his epic poem, *On the Nature of Things (De Rerum Natura),* Lucretius brought to Rome Epicurus' philosophy of hedonism, at the same time linking it with the atomic theory of Democritus which explained the physical world in mechanistic terms. In addition, Lucretius anticipated Darwin by setting forth the theory of the survival of the fittest. It has been said that "no other Roman ever made a like effort of sustained scientific imagination, and his artistry in language and metre gave attractive form to his severe reasoning."[10]

In the field of prose, this period was marked by the excellent historical narrative of Caesar, whose versatility, we are told, extended even to poetry and astronomy. But the greatest master of Latin prose and perhaps the outstanding intellectual influence in Roman history was Cicero. Acclaimed as the greatest orator of his day, he found time during his busy public life to write extensively on philosophy, political theory, rhetoric, and literary criticism. Some nine hundred of his letters still exist and these, together with his other numerous writings, give us unrivaled insight into Cicero as a personality as well as into the problems and manners of republican Rome. Cicero also made a rich contribution by passing on to later ages much of Greek thought—especially from Plato and the Stoics—and at the same time interpreting it from the standpoint of a Roman intellectual and practical man of affairs. Finally, Cicero did more than any other Roman to make Latin a great literary language, and his influence in this regard extended through the Italian Renaissance and the "classical" period of English thought and literature.

Augustus brought to the new empire political stability and a social and intellectual climate conducive to a further outpouring of poetry and prose. As a result, we enter now upon the second—or Augustan—period of the Golden Age of Latin Literature, noted particularly for the greatness of its poetry. Famous for his lyrical odes was Horace (65-8 B.C.), who also wrote satirical verse. His urban outlook and polished style help explain the hold which Horace has maintained on succeeding generations of educated people, who have turned to him both for enjoyment and for quotable phrases. Quite a different sort was Ovid (43 B.C.-17 A.D.), a poet akin to Catullus in spirit and personal life, who nevertheless combined a predilection for themes on love with first-rate storytelling. It is, in fact, largely through his *Metamorphoses* that classical mythology was transmitted to the modern world.

Virgil (70-19 B.C.) was probably the greatest of all Roman poets. Virgil's masterpiece was the *Aeneid,* a great national epic which glorifies the Julian family of emperors and eloquently asserts Rome's destiny to conquer and rule the world. Using Homer's *Odyssey* and *Iliad* as his models, Virgil recounted the fortunes of Aeneas, the legendary founder of the Latin people, who came from his home in Troy to Italy. (Thus the Romans were given a paternity equal to that enjoyed by the Homer-endowed Greeks.) The *Aeneid* breathes Virgil's deep and enthusiastic patriotism and is just as much a piece of imperial symbolism as are the triumphal arches of Titus and Constantine.

The Silver Age. The period following Augustus' death in 14 A.D. was one of continuing prosperity and stability. Interest in literature remained high, the theater flourished, and numbers of writers both in Rome and the provinces produced a large volume of original work in poetry and prose. Although the quality of this production did not in the main measure up to the superlative standard set during the Augustan period, yet it was of sufficient excellence to merit the application of the term "Silver Age of Latin Literature" to the century and a quarter from Augustus to the death of Hadrian (14-138 A.D.). This Silver Age was marked by a more critical and negative spirit than that of its predecessor, so that whereas the Augustan period had evoked lyrical odes and a majestic epic, the Silver Age was memorable for its brilliant literary satire, a form of writing probably originating with the Romans. With Juvenal (55?-138? A.D.), satire in Latin poetry reached its height. This master of poetic invective flayed the shortcomings of contemporary Roman society and his brilliant epigrammatic phrases were destined to influence the writings of the famous neoclassical English satirists Dryden, Swift, and Pope.

The Golden and Silver Ages also witnessed advancement in the work of historians, three of whom deserve mention. The first of these, Livy (59 B.C.-17 A.D.), was a contemporary of Virgil and his immense *History of Rome,* like the latter's *Aeneid,* is of epic proportions and in effect glorifies Rome's conquests and achievements. Livy assembled the traditional records of early Roman history and welded them into a single continuous narrative—"the first time that anything of the sort had been done."[11] But while this was a contribution, and while in its epic proportions the *History* is worthy to stand alongside the other achievements of the Augustan Age, Livy lacks the scientific approach and techniques of the Greek historian Thucydides.

In the Silver Age, historians did not attempt to emulate Livy but confined their efforts to shorter and more contemporary periods. Tacitus (c. 55-c. 117 A.D.), like Juvenal, was concerned with improving contemporary society, but used history rather than poetry to serve his ends. In his *Germania,* Tacitus contrasted the life of the idealized, simple German tribes with the corrupt and immoral existence of the Roman upper classes. In the *Annals,* a history of Rome from the death of Augustus to that of Nero, he used his vivid prose to depict the shortcomings of the emperors and their courts. Tacitus was a master stylist whose historical narratives sparkled, and he was critical in his use of source materials. Unfortunately, he suffered from personal prejudices which warped his better judgment and seriously detracted from the value of his otherwise great writings.

The most famous Greek author of Roman civilization was Plutarch (46?-120? A.D.). Holding a governmental office for the Roman authority in his local city, he utilized his leisure to carry out research on the great figures in Roman and Greek history. Plutarch was interested in what we might call personality analysis; he was anxious to discover what qualities make men great or ignoble. His *Lives* contains forty-six biographies of famous Greeks and Romans. Usually these character sketches are presented in pairs for the purpose of comparison. Plutarch's *Lives* is a mine of invaluable information for the classical historian and is great literature as well.

The language of literature. From about the second century A.D. until the collapse of the empire in the west in the latter part of the fifth century, chaotic political conditions and general unrest prevented the creation of any great works, either in art or in literature. But the fall of Rome did not mean oblivion for the language of the Romans. The Latin language was one of Rome's most permanent contributions. During the period of the empire it provided a universal language for church, law, medicine, literature, and learning. For one thousand years, until the late Middle Ages, Latin remained almost exclusively the language of literature, and it was used by scholars until the eighteenth century. Out of the Latin spoken by the common people in the Roman empire there gradually evolved during the Middle Ages the Romance languages, Italian, Spanish, Portuguese, Catalan, Provençal, French, and Rumanian. It is estimated that more than half of our English words are of Latin origin.

The vernacular languages largely displaced Latin as the common literary medium in early modern times. But down to the twentieth century—and even today in some European countries such as England—Ciceronian Latin remained a regular part of the educational curriculum. Latin also lives in the ritual of the Roman Catholic Church. Rome is justly famous for its law and governmental administration, but not the least of its contributions to civilization is the logical, lucid, and sonorous language which today forms the basis for languages used by more than 200,000,000 people.

Stoicism and Epicureanism. Neither in science nor in philosophy did the Romans approach the Greeks. They contributed no original philosophical theory but preferred to adopt and reshape existing Greek systems of thought to suit their needs. As men of action with grave governmental responsibilities, the Romans paid scant attention to such abstract problems as the nature of the universe and of human knowledge, but instead concentrated on Greek ethics, which had an obvious bearing on questions of politics and personal behavior. As a consequence, the two main Greek ethical systems, Epicureanism and Stoicism, attracted far more interest in Rome than the speculations of Plato and Aristotle.

Epicureanism made its greatest impact during the last days of the republic, since men found its tenets comforting in a period of political upheaval when no one knew what the morrow would bring. Virgil and Horace as young men embraced Epicureanism, of which the poet-philosopher Lucretius was perhaps the most important Roman interpreter. *On the Nature of Things* has already been cited as a brilliant piece of literature, combining poetry, science, and philosophy. In setting forth his philosophical doctrine, Lucretius bases his explanation of the "nature of things" on materialism and atomism, and calls on men to free themselves from superstition and to rely instead upon their own resources—since the gods have nothing to do with the fate of human beings. Basing his views on the philosophy of his Greek master, Epicurus, the Roman poet calls on men to "make the most of today," to seek pleasure—not in sensuous gratifications but in philosophical serenity—and to have no fear of death.

More enduring, especially in the days of the empire, was the appeal of Stoicism as modified to suit the Roman temperament. It has been said that the Romans gave Stoicism "a dose of common sense," for they aimed at controlling rather than stifling their emotions. The goal of the Roman stoic was right conduct—that is, to remain poised in a world full of uncertainty, pain, and sorrow. The solution advanced by Stoic thought was resignation and self-sufficiency. Man must not question the operation of natural law but, if wise, will accept whatever fate nature has in store for him, remaining in full control of his emotions and impervious to pleasure and pain alike.

Stoicism was too intellectual and austere to appeal to the Roman populace, but its influence was far-reaching. Thus, it had a humanizing effect on Roman law in the third century, stressed the dignity and worth of men irrespective of their social status, and advocated a way of life embracing service to humanity, constancy to duty, and courage in adversity. Stoicism also produced some outstanding followers, one of whom was the thinker and writer Seneca (c. 3 B.C.-65 A.D.). He was regarded with high favor by the leaders of the early Christian Church for, more than most Romans, Seneca came near the concept of monotheism and the doctrine of immortality, and he emphasized the virtues of service to mankind and human brotherhood. This philosopher occupies an important place in the development of moral theory in Europe, for his essays enjoyed a wide reputation in the Middle Ages and Renaissance and influenced some of their greatest thinkers.

Science in the Roman empire. The Romans themselves had little scientific curiosity to impel them to use their critical faculties and formulate hypotheses. Being basically utilitarian in their approach, they preferred to borrow Hellenistic science and apply it to their daily problems. Here they were masters, excelling primarily in applied medicine, public health, engineering, and map-making.

The Romans instituted the first real hospitals and medical schools. They also organized one of the first systems of socialized medicine. In the early empire a public medical service was started, with a large army of public doctors. Infirmaries were also established where the poor could obtain free medical care. Additional examples of the Roman concern for public health were the great aqueducts that supplied 300,000,000 gallons of water to Rome daily, the well-ventilated houses in Roman cities, admirable drainage systems, and the development of hydrotherapy, that is, the extensive use of mineral baths for healing.

Characteristic of their utilitarian—and uncritical—approach to science was the Romans' predilection for amassing immense encyclopedias. The most important of these was the *Natural History* compiled by Pliny the Elder (23-79 A.D.), an enthusiastic collector of all kinds of scientific odds and ends. In writing his massive work, Pliny is reputed to have read more than two thousand books, and the result is a marvelous mixture of fact and fable thrown together with scarcely any method of classification. The encyclopedia describes, for example, men whose feet point the wrong way, tribes with heads directly on their shoulders, and one man whose keen sight enabled him to see objects more than a hundred miles distant. It should be pointed out, however, that the *Natural History* did contain much factual material on science, geography, and various other subjects. It was the most widely read book on science during the empire and much of the Middle Ages.

If the Romans themselves were seldom preoccupied with scientific investigation, there were others in the empire who were engaged in serious research. During the *Pax Romana*, the Greeks at Alexandria continued to demonstrate considerable vitality in their mathematical studies and also in the field of geography. This was a period when Roman legions in Europe and the Greeks in their quest of trade in the east were extending the frontiers of knowledge continuously, thus providing geographers with important data with which to construct new maps of the world. The most famous of these geographers was an Alexandrian scholar named Ptolemy (Claudius Ptolemaeus), who lived in the middle of the second century A.D. Ptolemy drew many maps, for which he used an excellent projection system, but they contained some serious errors. One of these was his exaggeration of the length and width of the known world and this, as we shall see later, had a direct influence on Columbus' decision to set sail from Spain in search of Asia. Ptolemy also wrote the *Almagest*, or *Great System of Astronomy*, which provides the usual Hellenistic proofs of the globe, but accepts the world as at rest in the middle of the universe. Thus Ptolemy championed the geocentric theory (unlike Aristarchus before him), and this view was generally accepted in western Europe until the sixteenth century.

Still another Greek in the Roman empire should be noted for his research, this time in the field of medicine. Galen (130?-200?) was born in Pergamum in Asia Minor, but his fame led to his being called to Rome where in time he became physician to Marcus Aurelius. Galen made notable advances in physiology and anatomy, but it is his medical encyclopedia, summarizing existing knowledge, by which he is best known. This work, in fact, was considered authoritative until well into the Renaissance.

Summary

The story of how Rome rose from the insignificant status of a muddy village along the banks of the river Tiber to the mighty position of master of the Mediterranean world will always remain one of the most fascinating epics in world history. Emerging from obscurity about the middle of the eighth century before Christ, the Latin people, clustered about Rome and its seven hills, succeeded in 509 B.C. in ousting their Etruscan overlords from power and establishing a republic. The next four hundred years of Roman history concerned two dominant themes: the democratization of the government and the conquest of the Mediterranean.

Following the expulsion of the Etruscan kings, the aristocratic Senate took charge of the state. Only the nobles exercised political rights, and the people—the plebeians—had no voice in the affairs of government. During the next two centuries, however, the plebeians succeeded in breaking down the privileged position of the patricians by obtaining recognition of their fundamental rights as citizens and by acquiring a progressively more important share of political power. Yet these gains, significant as they were, proved largely illusory, for the rank and file of citizens never gained actual control of the government of the republic—and the latter eventually was transformed into a principate and then a monarchy.

However, the tradition of a representative democracy is seen in the development of Roman law and political theory. Under the Antonines, the extension and reform of the legal system made the most progress, and under Justinian the law was codified to become an influence upon all subsequent legal thought. The Romans gave us the concepts of the supremacy of the law, of social contract, the sovereignty of the people, and the separation of governmental powers.

The other theme in the early history of Rome was the conquest of the Mediterranean. Between the years 509 and 270 B.C. the Romans managed to crush all resistance in Italy. They then turned their attention to Carthage, Rome's only remaining rival in the western Mediterranean, and after a herculean struggle marked by the brilliant tactics but final defeat of Hannibal, Carthage was completely destroyed in 146 B.C. Having conquered the west, the Romans now became involved in disputes in the east, and in short order the petty and inefficient successors of Alexander the Great were defeated, and their territory came under the rule of the Roman republic. But when the western world was conquered, it soon became evident that Rome herself faced civil war and degeneration. The wars of conquest had resulted in the disappearance of the sturdy Roman farmers, the cities were filled with parasites and loungers who demanded free bread, and the government was corrupt.

Several patriotic reformers, such as the Gracchi brothers, tried to get the Senate to enact necessary reforms, but to no avail. After the Gracchi a series of military heroes came to the fore in Roman history. Marius, Sulla, Pompey, and Julius Caesar mark the appearance of one man rule and the end of the republic. Augustus, the heir of Caesar, ruled Rome wisely and well. On the surface the old republican characteristics of government, such as the Senate, were preserved, but Augustus wielded the real power in the new government, which was thenceforth called the principate. For two hundred years, during the *Pax Romana,* the people of Italy and the many other millions of subjects in the empire's provinces enjoyed peace and prosperity.

Through the Roman achievement of a single empire and a cosmopolitan culture, the Greek legacy was preserved, synthesized, and disseminated—and the Romans were able in their own right to make important contributions. For the first time in the western world, secular architecture on a monumental scale evolved with the erection throughout the empire of baths, government buildings, stadia, and triumphal arches. In other arts, the Romans contributed realistic portrait sculpture, historical reliefs, stone and stucco decoration, and realistic painting.

The Romans accomplished little in abstract thought and pure science, because they had slight interest in scientific speculation or experimentation. Borrowing Hellenistic science wholesale, they applied it to meet their practical needs. They were the first to have hospitals, public medical service, efficient sewage systems, and a workable calendar. In philosophy the Romans got their thought ready-made from Greece. Epicureanism and Stoicism appealed most to the Romans; in their hands the latter was given new force and dignity. In literature the Romans evolved few new forms except the satire, but their sonorous prose set a standard for later centuries. The Latin language, throughout the Middle Ages the vehicle of literature, law, and the Church, is the foundation of the modern languages spoken by more than 200,000,000 people.

Chapter 7

Chronology of events and developments discussed in this chapter

Classical world linked from the Atlantic to the Pacific	334 B.C.-220 A.D.
Alexander's journey east: dispersed Greek culture	334 B.C.
Alexander's penetration into Punjab	326 B.C.
Alexander's empire broken up: Seleucid, Ptolemaic, Macedonian	323 B.C.
Maurya dynasty in India: founded by Chandragupta Maurya	322-184 B.C.
Pergamum gained independence from the Seleucids	282 B.C.
Asoka: made Buddhism a powerful religion by missionary activity	273-232 B.C.
Andhras dynasty in central India	225 B.C.-225 A.D.
Ch'in rule: basis of Chinese rule up to 1912	221-206 B.C.
Shih Huang Ti: administrative changes: Confucian feudal system attacked	221-210 B.C.
Han dynasty: period of the Pax Sinica	202 B.C.-220 A.D.
Graeco-Bactrian empire established in India by Demetrius	184-30 B.C.
Wu Ti: greatest of the Han emperors; repulsed the Huns	140-87 B.C.
Conquest of Ferghana: established link with western Asia and Europe	102 B.C.
Babylonia and Damascus linked by desert route through Palmyra	100 B.C.
Later Han period: Rome-China silk trade carried on by middlemen	25 A.D.-220 A.D.
Drain of specie in trade to the East	31-192 A.D.
Sea route between India and Egypt made use of monsoon winds	50 A.D.
Official recognition of Buddhism in China; Graeco-Indian artistic influence	58-76 A.D.
Reign of Hadrian: Greeks took sea route to China	117-138 A.D.
Kanishka ruled Kushan empire: encouraged spread of Mahayana *Buddhism*	120 A.D.
Roman decline: political conflict; economic decline; loss of prestige	180 A.D.
End of the Kushan empire: Greek influence on Indian art at Gandhara	220

The world in classical times

The West, India, China: 334 B.C. *to 220* A.D.

HOW CAN WE VISUALIZE the world in classical times? It is immense, and we shall have to take up a position some distance from the planet if we are to view it all—in fact, sufficiently far off to see in one glance that great land mass, Eurasia, which together with north Africa constituted the classical world. In the west, we perceive a political agglomeration of diverse peoples—the Graeco-Roman empire—living for the most part around the Mediterranean Sea. It is a vast culture, basically thalassic, but one which has penetrated the hinterland as far north as Britain and the Baltic and as far south as equatorial Africa. Eastward this empire gives way to the deserts and mountains of the Middle East, but we can see ships ploughing through the Arabian Sea and taking advantage of the monsoon from the west to reach a second great center of civilization in India. Or we can go still further east across the Eurasian land mass—either by striking through the mountain passes of northeast India or by taking the caravan routes that trek across the vastness of Asia into Turkestan—and so into the outer provinces of the mighty Han empire. Nor is our journey ended even here, for the Hans have been extending their power and civilization down to the Yellow Sea, where ships can carry us across to the island culture of Nippon.

Each of these three great areas of civilization—Graeco-Roman, Indian, and Chinese—was for the most part developing its own way of life at this time, yet they were connected by tenuous, sprawling ganglia which were stimulated irregularly by commercial and cultural impulses. Let us visualize three scenes that were possible in any decade of the second century A.D.: in the palace on the Palatine Hill, an empress arrayed in priceless silks from China; in a seaport in southern India, Greek sailors paying out Roman coins for cinnamon; and near a stone tower in the wastes of Turkestan, traders from West and East silently exchanging the wares of two empires.

The first of these three great civilizations, the Graeco-Roman world-state, has already been studied. Nurtured by centuries of peace and prosperity, this civilization must always be considered one of the crests of human endeavor. We have already indicated something of its tremendous impact upon the course of western history. We shall now trace the penetration of Graeco-Roman culture into Asia, pausing first to examine briefly the administrative unity and economic growth of the empire at its height. This diffusion of Graeco-Roman civilization to the East initiated in turn a counter, though weaker, movement of cultural penetration from East to West. This chapter, in presenting the results of these reciprocal impacts, gives us our first global cross-section of historical development.

It will be our task also to take up here the historical development of India and China, the other great contemporary centers of civilization, during the centuries when Rome was evolving into a world-state. As we shall see, the centuries immediately preceding and following the birth of Christ were marked by cultural developments in India and China which paralleled to a striking degree those in the West. It is possible that the thousand years ending in the fifth century A.D. were the great formative years of our modern world. They spanned the evolution of a Graeco-Roman culture upon which our own was founded, and they witnessed the development of the religious and philosophical systems, together with the intellectual and artistic achievements, upon which so much of contemporary Indian and Chinese culture rests.

We shall see that although the contact between East and West was eventually cut off, it endured long enough to establish a lasting tradition that beyond the mountains and deserts to the east or to the west lay great civilizations. This tradition incited adventurous spirits many centuries later to bring the great "halves" of world civilization together once again.

Graeco-Roman Civilization at Its Height

The **Pax Romana.** For two centuries following the accession of Augustus in 30 B.C., the world of which the Mediterranean was the center enjoyed peace, prosperity, and stability such as it had never known before. After decades of civil strife, the victory of Augustus had established the *Pax Romana* from Britain to Egypt. There was a progressive increase in commerce and standards of living, the forces of law and order had largely stamped out brigandage and piracy, and the legions protected the far-flung frontiers. There was a great intermingling of races and cultures, and a growing belief in the eternal existence of this world-state. The spirit of the times is caught for us in the proud words of Pliny the Elder: "Now diverse products from many places are carried to and fro throughout the world for the welfare of mankind, since the boundless majesty of the Roman peace acquaints men of different lands and races not only with one another but with mountain ranges that rise to the clouds and with plants and animals hitherto unknown. May the gods continue this grace forever! For indeed they seem to have sent Rome as a second sun to prosper the affairs of men by her light."[1]

The empire rested upon the foundation of diversity within unity, for the goal was to maintain peace and harmony among its myriad different nationalities and ethnic groups. Furthermore, we will recall (Chapter 6), the empire was composed of two major cultures—Hellenistic and Latin—whose intermingling developed naturally after the eastern and western segments of the empire were unified politically and economically. Yet no attempt was made by the West to latinize the East, as the Romans might understandably have wished. Thus, while Latin was used in official circles, Greek and Aramaic were the commonly employed tongues in the former Hellenistic territories. As a result both of the assimilation of Hellenic elements into its own culture and of the preservation of Hellenistic culture in the eastern provinces, Rome was perpetuating the Greek legacy. It is therefore proper to look upon the world-state of the *Pax Romana* as the acme of Graeco-Roman civilization.

Administration of the Roman empire. At the head of this world-state stood the emperor, at once the chief defender and symbol of unity, and therefore an object of veneration. The empire, populated by some seventy or eighty millions, was divided in Hadrian's time (117-138 A.D.) into forty-five provinces, some of which were governed by the Senate, acting through proconsuls appointed annually, while others were under the administration of the emperor, who delegated powers to legates and procurators serving at his pleasure.

The provinces possessed their own councils of deputies from towns and districts, who usually convened once a year to discuss questions of general import. By reporting back to Rome on the activities of the provincial governors, these councils helped materially in providing a better administration than had existed under the republic. A strong feature of imperial administration was the large measure of local self-government enjoyed by both provinces and cities. As a result, the empire became a congeries of self-governing communities, and at least 312 cities were even issuing their own coins by the first half of the third century. It was generally believed that such autonomy contributed to imperial unity. This view was expressed by an orator from Asia who told his listeners in Rome that, "no longer are the cities at variance, hearkening, some to one man and others to another, while to one city guards are sent and by another are expelled, but . . . the whole inhabited world, in more complete accord than any chorus of singers, prays that this Empire, welded together under its single leader, may endure for all time."[2]

Roman cities. The premier city of the empire was of course Rome, which by the end of Hadrian's reign was the most magnificent center in the world. Augustus had set about to make Rome a capital worthy of a world empire, and he boasted that he had found it built of brick and left it of marble. Augustus and his successors created an imperial city possessing impressive civic buildings, temples, stadia, forums, and triumphal arches. Officials responsible for the administration and defense of the empire worked in dozens of governmental buildings, into which poured a constant stream of reports and messages from all corners of the world-state.

In the provinces were such thriving cities as Alexandria, Ephesus, Antioch, Pergamum, and Lyons. On the edge of the desert in Syria and in north Africa still other centers flourished, while in southern France, for example, numerous cities were founded, such as Nîmes, where one can still see a great Roman amphitheater, a splendid temple, and a famous bridge-aqueduct. Roman city-states were also created in northern France, Spain, and Britain. The names of such English towns as Chester and Cirencester betray their Roman origin, for *chester* comes from the Latin *castra,* meaning a military camp. Nearly all the provincial cities did their best to emulate Rome by installing water systems (often fed by aqueducts), by laying down paved streets, and by building baths, stadia, and forums.

Roman roads. One of the greatest achievements of the Romans was their network of solidly built trunk roads, which connected all parts of the empire with Rome. It is said that the speed of travel possible on the highways was not surpassed until about 1800. If one

Roman settlers in the Rhine valley in the time of Caesar pay their taxes to a collector.

traveled along one of the great imperial trunk roads of Rome, one would see regiments of soldiers marching to their posts on the frontier, numerous peddlers making their way from village to village with their wares, caravans of goods bringing luxuries to Rome from Alexandria, horse-drawn coaches of wealthy travelers, and mounted imperial messengers bringing dispatches to the emperor from distant provincial governors.

Economic unity and expansion. The Roman empire was the economic as well as political successor to the old Hellenistic monarchies, and the unification by Rome of the eastern and western segments of the empire had in turn a far-reaching result. The unification of the entire Mediterranean world and the creation of new tastes in the west, the elimination of tolls and other artificial barriers, the suppression of piracy and brigandage, and the establishment of good communications and a reliable coinage are all factors which help to explain the vast economic expansion that occurred during the first and second centuries A.D., probably reaching its height during the reign of Hadrian.

Farming. Although the city constituted the dominant influence in Roman life, agriculture remained the basic economic activity in the empire. The small farmer was disappearing. The general drift, which later was to become so serious, was toward absentee ownership of huge estates. On these tracts large numbers of *coloni,* free tenants, tilled the soil. The *coloni* were gradually superseding the slaves, who were becoming increasingly hard to secure.

Commerce. Commerce at this time was not marked by any new forms of organization; its expansion was due to the favorable economic and political factors then prevailing. Yet the scale which imperial commerce attained is shown by an account of one of the largest ships of the age. It was built to carry to Italy a column of stone which still stands by one of Rome's city-gates, and transported in addition 1200 passengers, 200 sailors, 4000 Roman bushels of wheat, and mixed cargo of glass, spices, and linen.[3] Commerce was now more diversified, a development assisted by the improvement of banking and credit machinery which facilitated trading ventures.

The most important commercial center of the empire was Alexandria, which among other matters handled the rich trade with the East. Rome for its part exported comparatively little, but so much revenue poured into the capital from the provinces that its citizens had the necessary purchasing power to buy immense quantities of goods from other parts of the empire and also from regions far to the east of the imperial frontiers. Grain was one of the most important Roman imports, which in addition included textiles, papyrus, and a variety of luxury goods for the wealthy.

Industry. The growth of industry went hand in hand with the expansion of trade. Extensive mining operations were carried on north of the Danube, in Spain, and in Britain. In Gaul the development of industry was of notable importance, especially in the making of pottery. Industry also flourished in the eastern Mediterranean. While Greece seemed to lag behind, Asia Minor enjoyed a profitable trade in purple dyes, carpets, and tents. Syria exported its glassware and leather goods, and Alexandria dealt in perfumes, embroideries, gems, and cosmetics.

As with commerce, the advances made by industry were due to such general factors as the expansion of imperial markets and demands rather than to any fundamental improvements in its organization or technology. Machinery never supplanted handicrafts, and

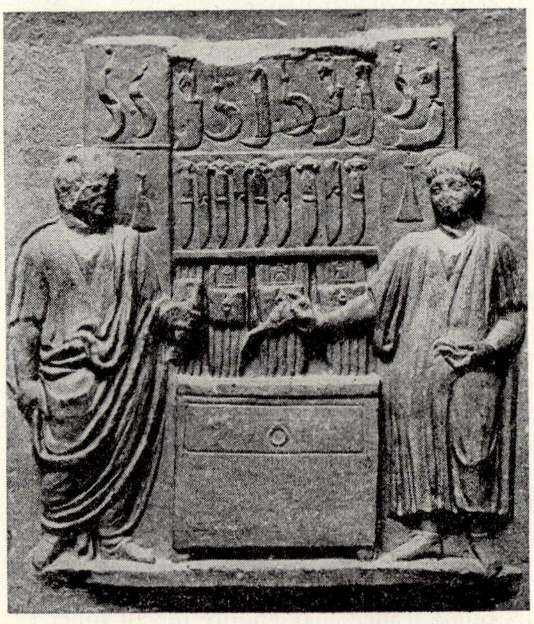

Two merchants exhibit their stock—a variety of knives and sickles—in this relief study.

the development of large-scale production—and with it standardization of commodities—made little progress. Industry in the Roman empire was organized on a small shop basis. Decentralization was another important characteristic, due in measure to the difficulties and costs of distributing goods over long distances.

The Meeting of East and West

New frontiers opened. During the period of its greatest prosperity, the Graeco-Roman world-state was in contact, directly or indirectly, with two other great civilizations: those of India and China. One of the principal media of contact was trade. For example, the Vicus Tuscus, a market quarter of imperial Rome, sold Chinese silk—and did a thriving business. Merchants from India could be seen on the streets of Alexandria, and Strabo, a Greek historian, was told that 120 vessels sailed to India every year from Egyptian ports. It was said by Philo, a Jewish philosopher, that "at the present day in our search for wealth we ransack every corner of the earth" and by the Roman Seneca that the "desire of trafficking drags a man headlong over every land and sea in the hope of making gain."[4] All of this evidence indicates a broadening of contacts between East and West.

The study of Graeco-Roman civilization has often been too restricted in the past. It has concentrated upon the development of three principal centers, Athens, Alexandria, and Rome, in that order, and has then concerned itself with the diffusion of Graeco-Roman culture around the Mediterranean basin and into western Europe. This approach has tended to neglect the richness and vitality of the diffusion of Graeco-Roman culture to the east of the Mediterranean. As a result, many important and interesting developments have been overlooked, such as the importance of Greek culture in the spread of Christianity, its influence on the later development of Islamic and Byzantine thought, and the numerous contacts made between the western world and India and China during classical times. In the four centuries beginning around 330 B.C., the frontiers of civilization were progressively enlarged until finally a continuous zone of intercommunicating states extended from the Atlantic Ocean to the Pacific Ocean.

The Hellenistic impact. The story of this linking up of the world in classical times properly begins with Alexander the Great. Setting out in 334 B.C. with a few thousand loyal Macedonians to conquer the mightiest power of the day, the Persian empire, Alexander in the space of three years subjugated Asia Minor, Syria, Egypt, and Persia. He defeated Darius in three pitched battles and made himself master of the western world. It has been said that Alexander's outstanding contribution to cultural history was "to shift the centre of gravity of Greek culture from Greece to Asia." By means of the conquests enumerated above, he succeeded in spreading Greek influence as far east as the Indus River. He later pushed still farther east, into India itself (a story which we shall take up shortly).

As a great city builder, Alexander founded some seventeen "Alexandrias" (including that in Egypt), and his successors in turn built many more city-states. As a result, these new centers, where Greek and oriental elements intermingled, became the chief agents for the spread of Hellenistic culture from the Aegean to India and from the Caspian to the cataracts of the Nile. Though this cultural impact never penetrated very deeply among the indigenous peoples, Alexander's conquests were nevertheless to have far-reaching consequences in several ways. Thus, in western Asia, Greek culture radiated out from the cities, with the result that untold numbers of Asians learned Greek and used it for business and to read Hellenic classics. "Greek law was also a strong Hellenizing influence, for all the native populations in the cities were subject to the city law, which was Greek; in Syria, for example, there ultimately grew up a mixed Graeco-Syrian law."[5] And, as we shall see, Greek art and thought made a permanent impact farther east upon Indian civilization itself.

Greek culture and Christianity. This Hellenistic "culture-sphere" in the Near and Middle East had profound implications in the religious field. The universality of the Greek language and culture was important in the growth and spread of Christianity, while Greek thought was influential in shaping early

Christian thought. The conquests of Alexander brought the language of Greece to Asia Minor. After his victory over Judea, hellenization of that land followed quickly, accelerated by Alexander's favorable disposition toward the Jews. As part of the Seleucid empire, Jerusalem found itself with gymnasia, temples, Greek amusements, and even with ordinances for the hellenization of Jews. Later, the Jews freed themselves of Seleucid control, but Greek influences did not disappear. "St. Paul required no gift of tongues to preach to the civilized world. He wrote in Greek to Jews, Galatians, Macedonians, and Romans. . . ."[6]

The Gospel according to Saint John, with its identification of the Christ Incarnate with the Logos, or Divine Intelligence, shows the impact of Greek philosophical thought upon Christianity. The universality of Greek culture in the Near and Middle East and the administrative unity of the Roman empire made possible the rapid growth of Christianity into a mighty world religion, and its eventual acceptance as the official religion of the Graeco-Roman world. It also facilitated at a still later date the establishment of a new hellenized empire having its capital at Byzantium (Constantinople), an empire destined to play a splendid role in transmitting the cultural legacy of the classical world to modern times, and to lay the cultural foundations of Russia.

Hellenistic kingdoms in the East. The death of Alexander the Great precipitated political changes in the area of his conquests. The empire lost its political unity, and a number of independent kingdoms developed. After his death, the Egyptian part of his empire fell to the Ptolemies, while Seleucus acquired domains extending in Asia from the Mediterranean to the borders of India. (See map, page 150.) The Seleucid empire for a time provided the comparative peace and economic stability necessary to ensure the partial hellenization of a vast area. One result was the introduction of a calendar in which for the first time chronology was reckoned from a fixed era, as today, instead of from the beginning of a king's reign. Another was the establishment of important cities, such as Seleucia-on-the-Tigris, a wealthy center for East-West trade. Alexander had dreamed of a complete fusion of races and cultures, and had encouraged marriages between his Macedonian soldiers and women of the Near and Middle East. But there were insufficient Greeks to begin to colonize Asia; they were only islands in an

THE ALTAR AT PERGAMUM, AN EXAMPLE OF HELLENISTIC ARCHITECTURE

oriental ocean, and this ocean encroached more and more as time elapsed.

The gradual weakening of the loosely knit Seleucid empire under this dominant pressure of Asia eventually resulted in the creation of independent kingdoms on the edge of the Hellenistic world. One of these was Pergamum in Asia Minor (see reference map 1), which became independent in 282 B.C. Small but wealthy, Pergamum had an ornate capital possessing luxurious palaces and baths, a theater, and a library which ranked next to Alexandria in size, while its scholars enjoyed a deserved reputation. The fame of Pergamum for scholarship has been perpetuated in the word *parchment,* derived from its name.

In 248 B.C. a tribe of nomads who had thrust south from beyond the Caspian founded the kingdom of Parthia, situated between Seleucid territory to the west and Bactria, a Greek outpost still farther east. In time, the Parthian rulers wrested Babylonia and Media from the Seleucids, and then added Persia and parts of Bactria to form the Parthian empire. For a long period, Parthia was to be the scarcely assailable enemy of Rome and, because of her strategic position, was to dominate the rich trans-Asian caravan trade.

Meanwhile, in the latter part of the third century, the Seleucid satrapy of Bactria—situated high on the western watershed of the great Pamir divide in what would now be northern Afghanistan and Soviet Turkestan—achieved independence. Its third king extended Bactrian power, while his son Demetrius in turn proceeded to conquer northern India in 184 B.C. Demetrius, who is appropriately shown on Bactrian coins wearing the elephant-scalp, the symbol of power (see the illustration on page 198), for a few years ruled from the Persian Gulf to the middle of the Ganges valley. We shall have occasion later in the chapter to say more about this Graeco-Bactrian empire in Punjab, which was destroyed in the first century B.C. Meanwhile, Bactria itself—whose high state of culture is attested by its coins, which have been called "the most noble examples of Greek art as applied to portraiture"—was itself overwhelmed by Scythian tribes sweeping out of Central Asia.

Commercial expansion. So far, we have briefly traced the eastward drive of Hellenism by successive steps from the Mediterranean into India. A natural concomitant of these political and cultural developments was a marked increase in economic activity throughout western Asia and in the exchange of goods between East and West. A result of this flourishing international trade, which has been described as a "dominant factor" throughout the period, was the advance made in geographical knowledge.

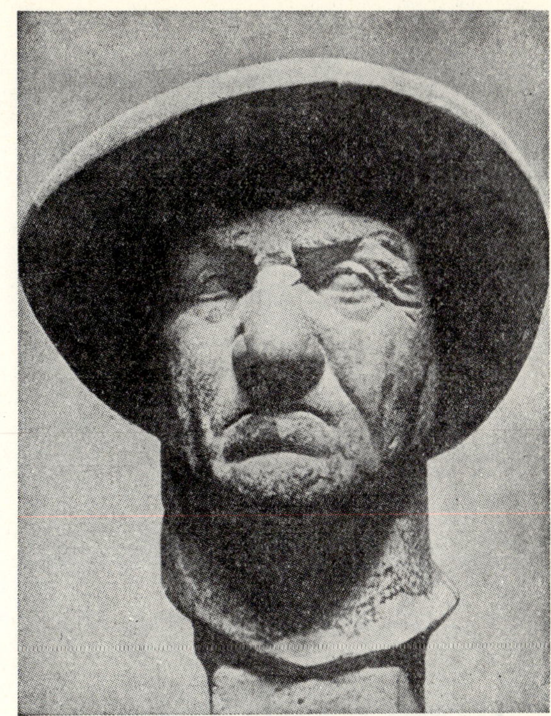

A Greek portrait in marble of the Bactrian king, Euthydemus, displays intense realism, a striking contrast to the idealism of most Greek sculpture in the Age of Pericles.

The trade between India and the West took several routes (see map, pages 202-203). During the third century, the important route led by sea from Indian west coast ports to the Persian Gulf, then up the Tigris to Seleucia. This was supplemented by an overland caravan road, which started from Pataliputra in the Ganges valley, ran northwest to Taxila and up to Bactra (the capital of Bactria), then west by south across long stretches of Persian and Median territory until Seleucia had been reached. By either route, then, trade funneled into Seleucia, which became one of the wealthiest cities of antiquity. From there, some caravans would move up the Euphrates and over to Antioch, while others preferred following the

COIN OF DEMETRIUS, KING OF BACTRIA (c. 190 B.C.)

course of the Tigris and then crossing west to Edessa and from there to the Mediterranean region at ports in Syria or Asia Minor. Later on, as we have noted, the Parthians captured control of lands extending from the Caspian to the Persian Gulf, but they found it profitable to maintain the flow of East-West trade through their territories. Meanwhile, around 100 B.C., chaotic conditions in the western section of the route brought about the establishment of a short-cut across the desert from Babylonia to Damascus by way of a fascinating "caravan city" called Palmyra, which afforded protection against nomadic attacks.

There was, in addition, an important southern route linking India with the West during Hellenistic times. This led from India by sea to depots in south and southeastern Arabia, where goods were transferred to the hands of Arabs—who, in the third century B.C., enjoyed a monopoly of this trade. Arab caravans would then carry the goods to another caravan city, Petra in northern Arabia, from where the goods would either continue north to Damascus or Antioch, or west to Alexandria in Egypt. In time, however, the Ptolemies took measures to share this profitable commerce by developing the carrying-trade up the Red Sea and thence to Alexandria.

Maritime developments. When Rome gained control of Egypt and other Hellenistic areas it also took over the rich trade with the East. From the government's standpoint, the overland route to India had a serious disadvantage: it led through Parthian territory, which Rome could not control, and it was subject to heavy tolls by the Parthian government. As a result, Augustus and his successors began to encourage the use of the southern or sea route to India. Among steps taken were expeditions against the Arabs of the Red Sea coast in order to check their raiding.

Meanwhile, a most important maritime discovery occurred. Scholars are not agreed as to its exact date or the name of the discoverer (although Hippalus is often given the credit), but mariners had learned by about 50 A.D. that it was possible to take advantage of the monsoon winds, which blow across the Arabian Sea from May to October from the southwest, and so to sail by the open sea directly from the Gulf of Aden to the west coast of India. Furthermore, ships could return from India by making use of the counter monsoon blowing from the northeast between November and March. This discovery opened the way for a rich new commerce, since round trip voyages from Egypt to India could now be made within the twelve months or less; the open-sea route lessened the danger of pirates who were lurking along the coasts of Arabia; and the costs of shipping were materially reduced by the swifter voyages and the saving of tolls paid out to Arab officials.

This increase of sea trade in turn stimulated European merchants to strike still farther east by ship, and the southern point of India and Ceylon were subsequently circumnavigated. During the reign of Hadrian (117-138 A.D.), Greeks crossed the Bay of Bengal. Eventually they reached the coast of Indo-China, and a few pioneers even sailed some distance up the coast of China and brought back the earliest first-hand information of that country.

Early silk routes to China. Meanwhile, China had also been the object of trade by overland routes. The first move to pierce the land barrier separating China from the West came from the Chinese rather than the Europeans. In 128 B.C., the Chinese emperor, Wu Ti, dispatched an ambassador with a mission into west central Asia. This ambassador returned to China, bringing with him a great store of carefully gathered geographical knowledge of lands beyond the Pamirs. He had visited such Hellenistic outposts as Bactria, and had returned to China bringing seeds of the grapevine. As a result the emperor resolved to open up permanent relations with the lands beyond the Pamirs.

As a result of Chinese initiative in this case, the Pamir divide had been penetrated by the end of the second century B.C. and regular trade established with western Asia, so that the use of silk spread during the early years of the first century B.C. to the Mediterranean. Silk was brought to the West by a route which began in northwest China and ran along the northern rim of the Nan Shan mountain range to Kashgar by alternative roads designed to escape the terrible Takla-Makan desert. The route then again divided into roads leading past Samarkand and Bactra and converged at Antiochia Margiana (Merv), after which it ran west-south-west through Parthian country to Seleucia-on-the-Tigris, thence into the Roman world by roads already described (see page 197).

As might be expected, this long and tortuous land route linking China and Rome over the roof of Asia passed through the territories of different authorities whose interference adversely affected the flow of silk. The Parthians, for example, derived much revenue from the trade by exacting toll from caravans in transit. This tended to increase the cost of transporting silk, as did the high profits which caravan merchants made as middlemen. The price of silk was reduced, however, by diverting part of the commodity onto roads that branched off the main trans-Asian route and went south to ports in Burma, Bengal, and northwest India, and thence by Roman shipping to the Red Sea and Egypt. As a result of this sea-borne competition, the silk trade became so highly developed—with a progressive lowering of price—that its use eventually spread to all social classes.

Intercommunicating states. To this point, we have seen that a series of cultural impacts took place during classical times, affecting in some degree the three major civilizations. These impacts were political, cultural, and economic. In some instances they were direct, such as the consequences of Alexander's conquests upon western Asia and northern India. On the other hand, the contact established between China and the West was both tenuous and indirect; its maintenance depended upon intermediaries distinct from either civilization, so that we do not know whether any Roman subject actually visited China or if any Chinese ever reached the Roman empire by means of the overland route. Nevertheless, the classical world was linked by intercommunicating states, and for the most part the meeting of East and West had been due to the latter's initiative. So far we have examined the western impetus as it spread across the stretches of Asia; it is now appropriate to study the contemporary histories of India and China and see, among other matters, to what extent that impetus influenced their basic culture patterns.

India under Asoka and Kanishka (322 B.C.–220 A.D.)

Rise of the Magadha empire. Early Buddhist literature tells us that there were some sixteen states or tribal territories in northern India at the time of the rise of Buddhism. The two most important were Magadha in the eastern corner of India and Kosala northwest of Magadha. About 540 B.C. the Magadhas began to take control, finally absorbing completely the kingdom of Kosala. In 413 B.C. there arose a dynasty known as the Nine Nandas, and one of the nine was reigning over Magadha when Alexander the Great descended upon India in 326 B.C. Alexander was told that the Nanda had an army of 200,000 infantry, 20,000 cavalry, 2000 chariots, and 3000 war elephants, but no battle ever developed, because Alexander's soldiers refused to march so far east into unknown territory.

Alexander's march to India. In February, 326 B.C., Alexander crossed the Indus and was hospitably received by the ruler of the region. His Indian journey is traced on the map at the bottom of this page. There Alexander was amazed at such novel customs as the throwing of the dead to vultures and the offering of young girls for sale in the market place by fathers too poor to provide a dowry. The naked ascetics whom he saw in the outskirts of the city practicing strange penances perhaps reminded Alexander of the famous Cynic philosopher whom he had encountered in Athens—Diogenes, who, dedicated to the search for an honest man, lived and meditated in a wooden tub.

Continuing eastward, the young Macedonian general encountered a great Indian army. Through brilliant strategy Alexander won the day and was able to push on to the east. He hoped to reach the empire of Magadha in order that he might subjugate it also, but his weary, homesick soldiers refused.

Before retracing his steps Alexander built twelve altars to commemorate his most easterly site. He had prepared a fleet of some 2000 vessels, and he now embarked his army with the purpose of sailing down the Indus, annexing the country through which he passed. After much fighting on the way, he reached the head of the Indus delta. A portion of the army had been sent home earlier. Another part under Alexander's own command marched along the coast to the Persian Gulf, and a third with the fleet returned home by water.

BACTRIA
Taxila
MAGADHA
KOSALA
Alexander's Route
Alexander in India
R.M.C.

The land trip was difficult because of the terrible deserts which had to be crossed, while the tidal bore of the Indus River wrought havoc among the ships. The spectacle of a school of whales brought fear and trembling to iron-nerved Macedonian soldiers, who infinitely preferred the terrors of the battlefield to those of unknown waters. Dissuaded from further Indian conquests, the army arrived at Susa in April-May, 324 B.C.

Within thirteen months Alexander died, and the empire he had built in such meteoric fashion quickly disintegrated—so that by 321 B.C. his domain in the Punjab had completely disappeared. Alexander's conquest had been so ephemeral that his invasion is not mentioned in any contemporary Indian literature. The long range effects of his episode were yet to become apparent.

Chandragupta Maurya. In 322 B.C. a new era dawned for India, for in that year a great empire sprang up. Magadha at that time was ruled by an unpopular Nanda king. Chandragupta Maurya, a young man who is said to have met Alexander, gathered a robber force from the north and seized the kingdom, aided by a wily Brahman adviser. In the next twenty-four years Chandragupta established his rule over all northern India. He may be called the first emperor of India, although his power did not extend into the far south. He began the Maurya dynasty, which endured until about 184 B.C.

India as seen by Megasthenes. About 305 B.C. Seleucus, the general who inherited Alexander's eastern empire, crossed the Indus in an effort to regain Alexander's Indian conquests, but Chandragupta proved too strong for him, and he had to retreat. Seleucus ceded to the Indian emperor lands which he held west of the Indus. A few years later Seleucus sent an envoy called Megasthenes to the court of Chandragupta at Pataliputra. Thanks to the detailed and scholarly reports of Megasthenes, we have a very clear picture of these early Indian times.

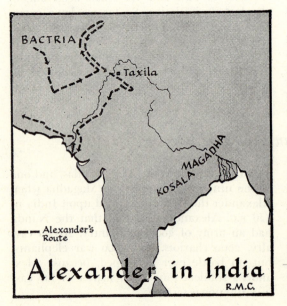

Pataliputra, the capital city, was a splendid center of about eighteen square miles, with massive wooden city walls containing sixty-four gates and 570 towers. The streets were laid out according to plan, and there were inns, theaters, gaming houses, bazaars, and two- and three-story houses. In the center of the city stood the royal palace surrounded by a walled park containing tame peacocks, fish, and ornamental trees.

In the midst of this wealth the emperor tended eagerly to his state duties. The army of perhaps 600,000 men was under the supervision of a well-organized war office of six boards. The government was ably administered. The empire was divided into three provinces, each of which was governed by a viceroy who had at his side a civil service of commissioners and officials.

All land belonged to the state, and agriculture was the main source of wealth. Irrigation was important, and a special department in charge of it levied water rates upon all irrigated lands. Crop rotation was practiced, and Megasthenes tells us that famines were almost unknown. There were officers in charge of forests and mines, and others whose duty it was to collect taxes on crops and on goods sold.

There were many towns, all connected by excellent roads, which included milestones and rest houses and over which royal couriers maintained a postal service. Trade was cosmopolitan, and the bazaars of Pataliputra displayed goods from southern India, China, Mesopotamia, and the Greek cities of Asia Minor. Indian ships sailed the Indian Ocean to the Tigris and to Arabia, and Indian goods were carried overland to Europe.

Manufacturing was important in the Mauryan empire. Greek writers refer to the manufacture of arms and agricultural implements and the building of ships. The northwest was famous for its cotton cloth and silk yarn, and fine muslins were exported in large quantities to the Roman empire in the first century A.D. Weavers and other craftsmen were often organized into guilds, which were very common at this time and often served the purpose of modern banks.

Megasthenes was struck by the similarity of the Brahman philosophy to that taught by the Greeks:

"In many points their teaching agrees with that of the Greeks—for instance that the world has a beginning and an end in time, and that its shape is spherical; that the Deity, who is its Governor and Maker, interpenetrates the whole; that the first principles of the universe are different, but that water is the principle from which the order of the world has come to be; that besides the four elements, there is a fifth substance (*akasa,* ether) of which the heavens and the stars are made; that the earth is the center of the universe. About generation of the soul, their teaching shows parallels to the Greek doctrines, and on many other matters. Like Plato, too, they interweave fables about the immortality of the Soul and the judgments inflicted in the other world and so on."[8]

Justice was administered fairly but sternly in both civil and criminal cases. In the social field, the caste system appears to have reached a definite stage in the Mauryan empire, for no one was allowed to marry out of his own caste or exercise any calling or art except his own. In the days of Megasthenes there appear to have been seven castes, including philosophers, soldiers, husbandmen, herdsmen and hunters, traders and artisans, overseers, and councilors. People lived frugally and observed good order. Slavery existed but was mild, and slaves could purchase their freedom. Dancing, wrestling, and chariot races were popular, and the royal family enjoyed hunting. "Dice play afforded pleasure to many though its baneful effects are frequently alluded to. Buddhist writers refer to games on boards with eight or ten rows of squares from which chess play ultimately evolved."[9] State feasts, caste festivals, strolling players, acting entertainments, and gay processions through the illuminated streets of the capital all added to the excitement and pleasure of living in the Maurya dynasty.

Life of the emperor. Chandragupta was a splendid general and administrator, an alert thinker, and a colorful figure. He allied his empire with the fortunes of the Seleucus family, appears to have married one of its princesses, and fostered a friendly exchange of information between the two empires. He lived in great state, surrounded by Greek intimates, and his court was run according to Persian ceremonial, factors which by no means endeared the monarch to his Indian subjects. So great was the danger of conspiracy, in fact, that Chandragupta had to dwell in strict seclusion. He was surrounded by a bodyguard of women who cooked his food, served his wine, and in the evening carried him to his apartment where he was lulled to sleep by music. He would even change bedrooms at night to thwart possible attempts on his life

Atlantic Ocean
LEAD TIN
LEAD, TIN
AMBER COUNTRY
FUR, TIMBER
Tanais
Black Sea
Caspian Sea
Byzantium
MACE-DONIA
Phasis
Cyrus
Oxus
Rome
GREECE
Athens
Pergamum
Corinth
Edessa
Merv
Mediterranean Sea
Antioch
Palmyra
Ecbatana
HYRCAN
RHODES
Dura
Ctesiphon
PARTHIA
Damascus
Seleucia
Alexandria
Petra
Persian Gu
IVORY, GOLD AND OSTRICH COUNTRY
Tema
Gerrha
SAHARA DESERT
ARABIA
Red Sea
IVORY AND GOLD
CINNAMON AND INCENSE COUNTRY
Arabia
SUDAN
Aden
SOCOTRA
MONSOON—MAY

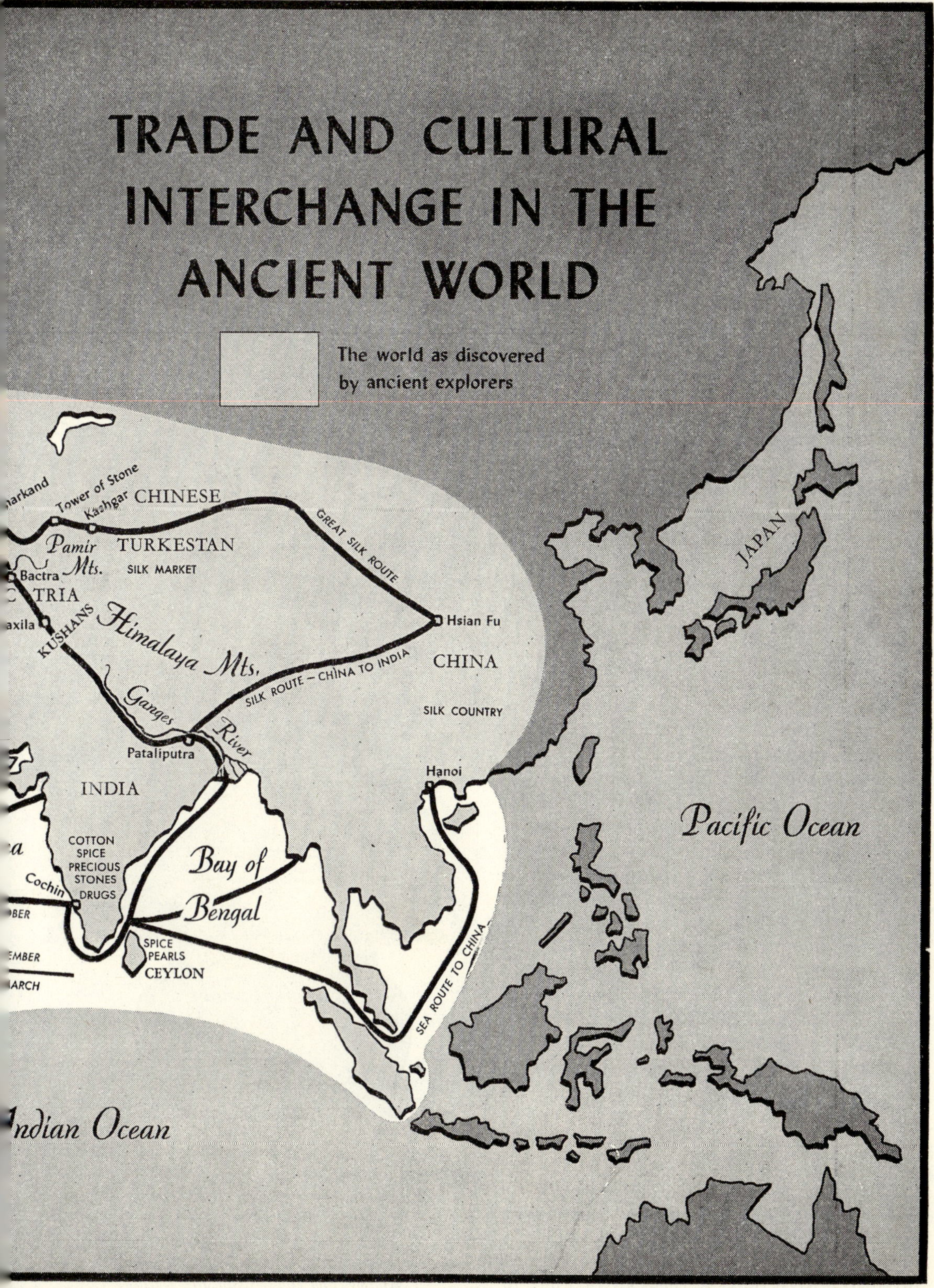
TRADE AND CULTURAL INTERCHANGE IN THE ANCIENT WORLD
The world as discovered by ancient explorers
Tower of Stone
Kashgar
CHINESE
TURKESTAN
SILK MARKET
Pamir Mts.
Bactra
GREAT SILK ROUTE
Hsian Fu
KUSHANS
Himalaya Mts.
CHINA
SILK ROUTE – CHINA TO INDIA
SILK COUNTRY
Ganges River
Pataliputra
INDIA
Hanoi
COTTON SPICE PRECIOUS STONES DRUGS
Cochin
Bay of Bengal
SPICE PEARLS
CEYLON
SEA ROUTE TO CHINA
JAPAN
Pacific Ocean
Indian Ocean

by Indian conspirators who are said to have dug tunnels under the palace walls.

Bindusara. In 298 B.C. Chandragupta was succeeded by his son Bindusara, of whom we know very little. However, we have a charming story about Bindusara's youth, which indicates the close cultural relations which existed between the Maurya and Seleucid rulers to the west at this time. Bindusara, writing to Seleucus in Syria, asked for a sample of Greek wine, some raisins, and a Sophist. In his reply Seleucus says he sends the wine with pleasure, but that "it isn't good form among the Greeks to trade in philosophers."[10]

Asoka. Bindusara in turn was succeeded by his son Asoka in 273 B.C. Asoka is one of the outstanding rulers in history. He was one of the few early kings who pursued the arts of peace more diligently than the arts of war; his first military campaign was also his last. In 261 B.C. Asoka went to war with Kalinga, one of the last independent states, situated to the south on the Bay of Bengal. The Kalinga inhabitants stubbornly resisted his invasion, and a war of extermination followed, culminating in a victory for Asoka. Hundreds of thousands were either killed or carried away captive. Asoka's empire now included nearly all of India to the edge of Tamil Land (see map). But the cruelty of the campaign horrified the king, and he resolved never again to commit such acts of butchery. About this time Asoka was converted to Buddhism, and his conversion may well have helped turn him away from warfare. From that time forward he resolved to govern only by the Law of Piety or Duty (*dharma*), for "the conquest of the Law," he said, "is alone a conquest full of delight."

Asoka and religion. As the years elapsed, Asoka became more deeply religious. Everywhere throughout his empire he had edicts carved upon stone pillars, some of which still stand today. These edicts were a practical application of the teachings of Buddha, and stressed compassion, kindness to all living things, truth, purity, and liberality. Asoka believed in complete religious toleration, and although he himself was a devout Buddhist,

The lion-crowned capital of one of Asoka's pillars illustrates culture diffusion in its blending of Near-Eastern and Indian conventions. Assyrian lion subjects with stylized manes and claws (compare with page 73) were transmitted to Indians of the Punjab through the Persians. The bell-shaped capital, wheel symbol, and composition are Indian.

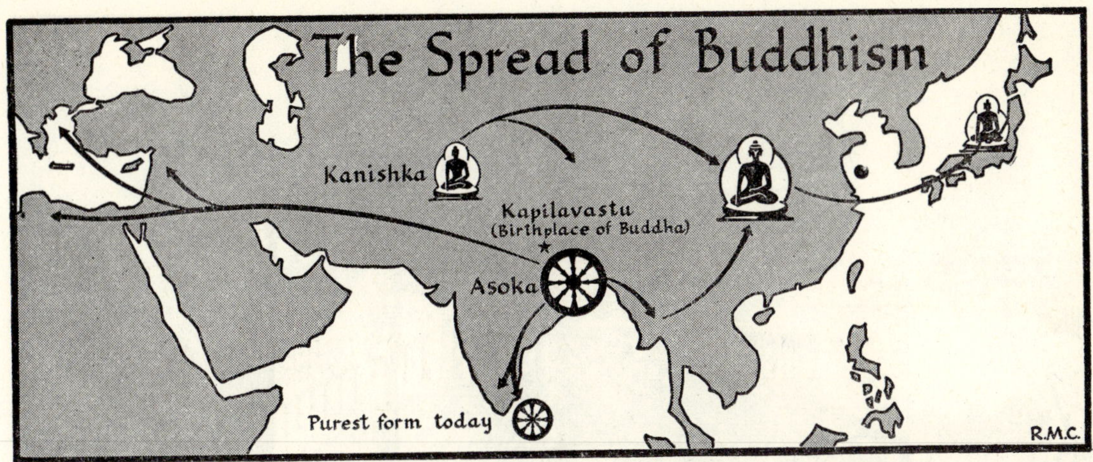

The above depicts the Buddhist symbol of the "Wheel of Birth and Rebirth" to which man remains attached until he wins release from the bondage of illusion. The large wheel shows the origin of Buddhism. The smaller wheel, in Ceylon, indicates the home of Hinayana *Buddhism, while the seated figures show the spread of* Mahayana *Buddhism with its emphasis upon Gautama as a savior.*

he liberally aided the Brahmans, Jains, and other sects. He relaxed the harsh laws of his grandfather, Chandragupta, and gave his governors wide powers in pardoning prisoners. He abolished royal hunting, forbade animal sacrifices, and ate no meat himself.

Asoka sent Buddhist missionaries into distant lands to teach the gospel of salvation and equality. The effect of their missionary work still endures. He sent teachers to the Himalayan regions, the Tamil kingdoms, Ceylon, Burma, and the Greek monarchies of Syria, Egypt, Cyrene, and Macedonia. Thus he transformed Buddhism from a small Indian sect to a powerful religion and made its influence felt on three continents (see map above). His missionary work was especially successful in Ceylon (where he sent his brother), and in Ceylon today we find Buddhism in its purest form. Asoka was to Buddhism what Paul was to Christianity—the great propagator of religion.

Asoka's pillar edicts. The inscriptions on Asoka's pillars not only show that the art of calligraphy was highly developed but indicate that writing was commonly used for practical purposes throughout the empire. The inscriptions (written in the vernacular, not in Sanskrit) would have been useless unless reading and writing were quite common, at any rate among the officials instructed to make known to every citizen the edicts of the monarch.

It is known that Asoka was highly practical in his charities, that he desired all his subjects to possess the attribute of charity, to him one of the highest forms of morality. By the promulgation of an edict such as the following, Asoka hoped to emphasize for his subjects the value of charity:

"Everywhere has His Sacred and Gracious Majesty the King made two kinds of curative arrangements, to wit, curative arrangements for men and curative arrangements for beasts. Medicinal herbs also, medicinal for man and . . . beast, wherever they were lacking, have been imported and planted; roots also and fruits, wherever they are lacking, everywhere have been imported and planted. On the roads both wells have been dug and trees planted for the enjoyment of man and beast."[11]

Architecture in the time of Asoka. Undoubtedly Indian art had a rich history prior to the days of Asoka, for the remains of the artistic works produced in his reign show maturity everywhere. But knowledge is lacking of pre-Asokan art, and so our history of Indian art really begins with his reign. In Asoka's reign stone was used for building instead of wood. These stone buildings retained the wood type of construction, however, translated into stone. The stone roofs were carved to look like wooden beams.

Of particular interest are his *stupas* (pictured on the following page), which were used to enshrine the relics of Buddhist saints or to mark a holy spot. They were domes, originally made of earth but later of earth faced with brick. They were surrounded by a rail and

A BUDDHIST STUPA, SHOWING CARVED GATEWAYS, AT SANCHI, INDIA

four gateways of stone, covered with carving like the one in the picture above. On the top of the dome was a boxlike structure surmounted by an umbrella, the Indian emblem of sovereignty symbolizing Buddha's princely birth. Later, when Buddhism spread to other countries, the *stupa* type of architecture went along, and its gateway was widely copied.

Dating from this period are rock-cut temples, whose form was also developed from earlier wood construction. The temple at Karli shows the typical copying of wood construction. Although the temples were cut from solid rock and needed no structural elements, they were made to look like earlier free-standing wooden structures. At the end of the nave can be seen the *chaitya,* the early symbol of Buddha. (Note its similarity to the *stupa.*) On the entrance wall was placed a large horseshoe window which provided dramatic lighting for the *chaitya.* These buildings as well as the *stupas* were richly carved with decorations.

Early Indian sculpture. Sculpture in early India decorated the *stupas* and cave temples. Popular subjects were Buddhist scenes, like those on the Sanchi *stupa* gates above, and animals, such as those on the capitals in the Karli temple and on Asoka's pillars. Love of decoration was evident, and although later periods showed great technical advance, early Indian artists did excellent work. The capitals in several civilizations reveal interesting differences. The columns at Karli and Asoka's lion pillar show bell-shaped capitals surmounted by animals. Compare these with the papyrus capitals of Karnak (page 57), the intricately decorated Byzantine capital (page 266), and the classic orders of Greece (pages 132 and 145). Given the same problem in architectural decoration, sculptors of different civilizations treated it in distinctive fashion.

End of the Mauryan dynasty. About 232 B.C. Asoka died, and his empire began almost immediately to disintegrate. In 184 B.C. the last Mauryan emperor was assassinated, and the empire was at once invaded by a ruler from the south—and by Demetrius, who, we will recall, swept into northwest India from Bactria, quickly overrunning the Punjab (page 197).

The Mauryan dynasty had been powerful, and Asoka can be considered one of the truly great rulers of world history. Yet his empire crumbled almost overnight, a development so dramatic and with such grave consequences that, like the decline and fall of the Roman empire, it has provoked scholars to speculate on a satisfactory explanation. Some have felt that the turn of events was due to Asoka's religious policy and the reaction of hostile Brahmans; however, it has been pointed out that there is no evidence of such hostility and that Asoka treated the Brahmans with marked respect. Other scholars have sought an explanation in Asoka's doctrine of nonviolence as a policy of state, which caused the military ardor of the empire to vanish. Still other possible explanations take into account the communications problems facing this wide-spread empire, the growth of a spirit of local autonomy in outlying provinces, and intrigue and oppression by various members of the royal family—all of which contributed to a weakening of central control. One Indian scholar has pointed out, however, that the Mauryan empire would have fallen to pieces sooner or later even if Asoka had followed his grandfather's policy of conquest. "But the moral ascendancy of Indian culture over a large part of the civilized world, which Asoka was mainly instrumental in bringing about, remained for centuries as a monument to her glory and has not altogether vanished even now after a lapse of more than two thousand years."[12]

The Graeco-Bactrian empire. When Demetrius subjugated northern India and captured the Mauryan capital of Pataliputra (184 B.C.), he organized the country along the lines of a Seleucid kingdom. In keeping with Alexander's ideal of taking other peoples into partnership, Demetrius issued a bilingual coinage which had Greek legends on one side and Indian (Kharosthi) on the other, and he made an Indian city, Taxila, his capital.[13] His policies were in turn carried on by Menander, his general and successor, who according to a legend even became a Buddhist. In the middle of the first century B.C., Menander died and Greek rule steadily declined until its last remnants were extinguished about 30 B.C.

This was a period when nomadic tribes sweeping south and east out of central Asia took possession of Bactria and seized the Kabul valley and adjoining regions. By the first century A.D. the chief of the most important clan, the Kushans, had established himself as master of a large part of northwestern India, and another important Indian empire arose, the Kushan empire.

Kanishka's Kushan empire. The most outstanding Kushan king was Kanishka, who came to the throne about 120 A.D. He ruled all northwest India, perhaps as far south as the Narbada River, and certain mountain kingdoms to the north (see page 208). Under him the arts and sciences flourished. Fine buildings were built at Taxila and the capital, Peshawar, and great advances were made in medicine.

Mahayana Buddhism. King Kanishka was converted to Buddhism, an important event in the development of the religion. He called a council of five hundred monks from which arose the *Mahayana* (Greater Vehicle) school of Buddhism. *Mahayana* Buddhism is not an

THE CHAITYA HALL OF THE KARLI CAVE TEMPLE, NEAR BOMBAY, INDIA

A masterpiece of Gandharan art is this image of Kuvera, Buddhist god of riches.

individualistic philosophy like that taught by Buddha but an emotional religion full of myth and ceremony. Buddha is made into a Bodhisattva, an exalted being who renounced *nirvana* to save mankind. *Mahayana,* or northern, Buddhism spread along the trade routes of the north and became the Buddhism of China, Tibet, and Japan (see map, page 205). *Hinayana,* or southern, Buddhism has persisted in Ceylon. Kanishka, like Asoka, was instrumental in making Buddhism a world-wide faith.

While the adoption of Buddhism by Kanishka had very beneficial effects in the matter of its spread to other countries, in the long run it probably served to lessen its popularity in the land of its birth. Buddhism had accepted the Greeks and Kushans and allowed itself to be associated with them. Hinduism, on the other hand, rejected foreigners as outcasts and hence came to be regarded as more truly Indian than Buddhism.

Graeco-Buddhist art. It was in the Kushan empire that Greek artistic forms were blended with indigenous art to create a rich and prolific Graeco-Buddhist school of art at Gandhara. Prior to this time, the Buddhists had refrained from depicting their master in human form. But in this area, which had been exposed to Greek invasion and cultural impacts, the Buddhists had turned to Greek artists to depict scenes from Gautama's life. As a result, the westerners had sculpted the Buddha in the likeness of a Hellenic god, so that he appears even in the guise of Apollo. Through Gandhara many western art formulas were absorbed into Indian art, though some Indian art critics feel that the actual Gandhara sculptures "are mainly the work of western craftsmen employed . . . to interpret Buddhist ideas, rather than Indian workmen under western guidance; and if some of the workmen were Indian by birth, they nevertheless did not give expression to Indian feeling."[14]

The Kushan empire touched upon the Chinese empire to the north, and through this channel Hellenistic art penetrated into the heart of central Asia. In this way, the Greek influence was extended in the form of Graeco-Buddhist art first to Chinese Turkestan, then to China proper, and finally to Japan. Thus, Graeco-Buddhist art and the *Mahayana* school of Buddhism—both developing in the Kushan empire—spread together through eastern Asia.

Kushan drama and literature. The origin of Indian drama is obscure, but it seems to have

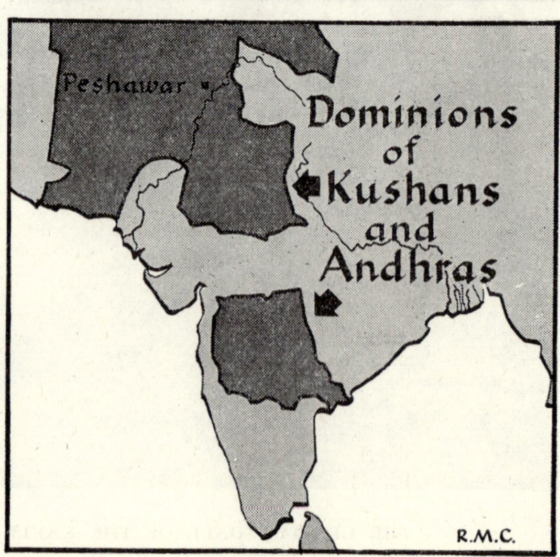

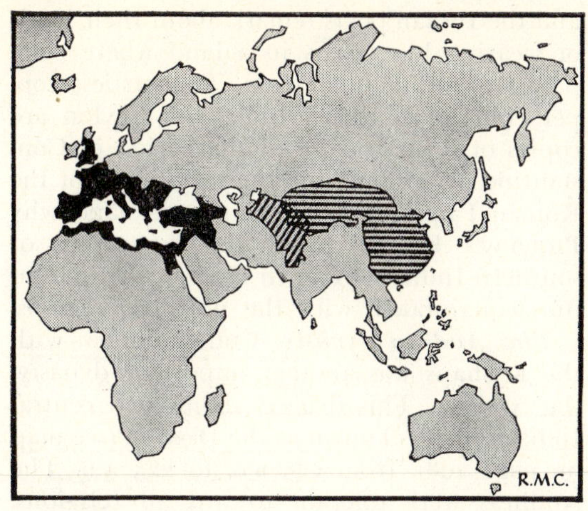

The Roman empire (black), the Kushan dominions in India (diagonal stripe), and the Han empire in China (horizontal stripe) are shown here about the year 100 A.D.

developed considerably during the Kushan period. It may have been derived from the coalescence of epic legends and pantomimic art. The Sanskrit drama differed in many respects from that of the Greeks. It was never tragic, and all problems of grief, sorrow, and terror were dispelled by a happy ending. Indian drama had very little action. Another peculiar feature was its employment of different dialects according to the social status of the characters. Kings, Brahmans, and nobles spoke in Sanskrit, while women and social inferiors, according to unbreakable custom, had to converse in the vernacular.

Kushan culture declined with the break-up of the Kushan empire in 220 A.D. It had been one of the richest periods in Indian civilization. It was an age of intense literary and artistic output, due largely to Hellenistic influence, in which the drama, the court epic, and classical Sanskrit evolved.

Indian trade with the West. The Kushan empire existed during the early centuries of our era when the Graeco-Roman empire's trade with the East was at its height. It is known that the Kushan rulers were on friendly terms with the Romans, and an Alexandrian sea captain who visited India tells of the trade between the two peoples; spices and silks left the Indian ports to be exchanged for Roman gold coins, Greek wines, and "choice girls for the royal harems."

Although Kushan trade with the West was extensive, the greatest part of Indian trade was carried on by Tamil kingdoms in the extreme southern part of India. We know little of the political history of these Tamil kingdoms prior to the ninth century A.D. But it is certain that they developed a high state of civilization independent of that of the Indo-Aryans and carried on a rich trade with the Roman empire in the early centuries of the Christian era. Even before the advent of the Roman empire, these Tamil kingdoms had engaged in prosperous commercial relations with Egypt and Arabia to the west, as well as the Malay archipelago and China to the east. The widespread nature of their commerce is proved by some interesting examples. The Hebrew word for peacock is a Tamil word, while the Greek words for ginger, cinnamon, and rice come from the same language.

All during the Hellenistic period, the Greeks engaged in profitable trade with the Tamil kingdoms, and the Romans developed the commerce still further. When Augustus became head of the Roman world, the rulers of one Tamil kingdom sent a congratulatory embassy, an honor never before paid any western prince. Starting from India about 25 B.C., it took about four years en route, and bore such gifts as a "gigantic python, huge tor-

SIX GOOD SPECIMENS OF MODIFIED CORINTHIAN CAPITALS FROM GANDHARA

toises, and an armless boy who could shoot arrows and throw darts with his feet."[15] Yet we should not allow these diverting details to obscure the fact that such embassies—at least nine from India visited the Roman emperors in the period up to Constantine—must have had a diplomatic purpose, namely to arrange for the protection and well-being of the natives of those states involved in this rich trade.

Large hoards of coins discovered in southern India attest to the magnitude of this trade. The paucity of Hellenistic coins as compared with those of the Roman empire show that commercial intercourse reached its height in the first two centuries of our era. During the first century, whole colonies of Roman merchants dwelt in Tamil seaports, importing precious metals and coins, pottery, glassware, wine, silverware, and even such human cargo as craftsmen and masons. Meanwhile, India was exporting pepper, cinnamon and other spices, drugs, pearls, silks, and muslins. That works of art also sometimes left India is proved by excavations at Pompeii, which in 1939 brought to light a fine ivory statuette of Indian workmanship portraying the Indian goddess of luck, Lakshmi. "Some merchant before 79 A.D. (when Pompeii was overwhelmed) must have brought back from his Indian ventures this delicate piece of work."[16]

Tamil poets have left for us descriptions of Roman ships which were guarded by archers against pirates. In fact, the Tamil kings themselves employed bodyguards of Roman soldiers, and the Indian poets remark about their habit of wearing long coats in a land where comparative nudity is the rule. The earliest copper coins of southern India and Ceylon are copies of Roman coins of the period of Constantine. After realizing the magnitude of the Roman-Tamil trade, we can understand why Ptolemy's knowledge of the geography of southern India is so much more accurate than his acquaintance with the northern regions.

The Andhra dynasty. Contemporary with the Kushans was another important dynasty, the Andhra. This dynasty dominated central India, which is known as the Deccan (see map on page 208), from 225 B.C. to 225 A.D. The Andhras were tolerant toward all religions, though the Brahmans occupied a special place of honor with them. The Buddhist *stupa* of Amaravati shows in its sculptures a blending of traditional Hindu style with Graeco-Buddhist motifs originating at Gandhara.

Like the Kushan empire, the Andhra domains broke up in the early part of the third century, and India entered into a chaotic period, from which it was to emerge with a splendid Hindu civilization under the Guptas. But this lies beyond the confines of the present chapter, in which we are concentrating upon the first centuries of our era. Let us now follow the direction of *Mahayana* Buddhism—or the silk routes running east from Parthia—and examine the cultural evolution of the third great civilization of classical times, that of China.

The Ch'in and Han Dynasties (221 B.C.—220 A.D.)

Ch'in rule (221-206 B.C.). Confucius lived during the turbulent years of the long declining Chou dynasty, a period which was marked politically by the division of China into innumerable petty states (page 104). In fact, the years 841-221 B.C. have been described as the feudal age of China, so utterly was the country divided and the monarchy decentralized. The last monarch of the Chou dynasty died in 256 B.C., and the principal states of China spent the next thirty-five years in struggling for supreme power. One of them was the state of Ch'in, a large area to the northwest, which was composed of a mixture of Chinese and non-Chinese peoples and was looked down upon by the older states as quite barbarian. But the kings of Ch'in triumphed over their rivals, annexing one state after another, so that by 221 B.C. the Middle Flowery Kingdom was once more ruled by a single monarch.

Shih Huang Ti. The king of Ch'in assumed the august title *Shih Huang Ti*, or First Emperor, and by creating the Chinese empire he established a form of government which was to endure, under various dynasties, for over 2000 years, until 1912. The founder of this empire was an extraordinary man, one of the most extraordinary in all history. He organized the country into thirty-six military areas, each with its military governor, who was also a civil administrator and supervisory official. He destroyed the conflicting law systems of the feudal states and substituted the code of Ch'in. Weights and measures were also made

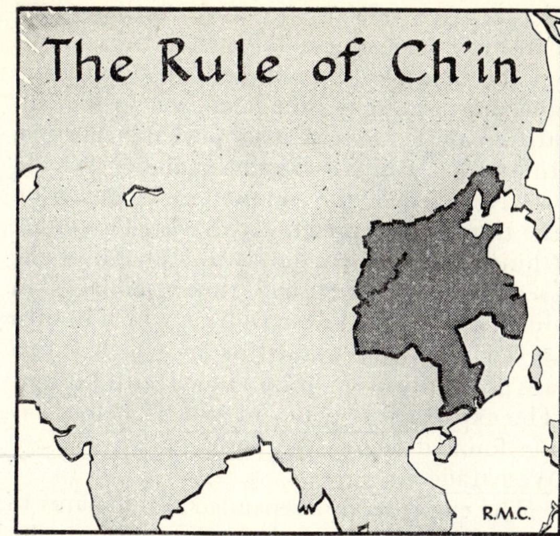

uniform, and even the carriage axles had to be the same length. Shih Huang Ti built an imperial network of tree-lined highways, fifty paces broad. To protect the empire from incursions by nomadic marauders, the Huns (Hsiung-nu), he added to, and joined together, sectional walls that had previously been erected on the northern marches. When Shih Huang Ti was finished with this task, a Great Wall ran some 1400 miles from the northwest frontier of Ch'in eastward to the sea. This huge fortification, built partly of stone and partly of brick and earth, was some twenty-five feet high and fifteen feet thick and was erected by forced labor at such an effort that it was said that "every stone cost a human life." In addition, Shih Huang Ti enlarged the empire's territory by conquests in the south which added the regions of Fukien, Kuangtung, Kuangsi, and Tongking.

This "Chinese Caesar," as one historian calls him, was not content to institute sweeping political and administrative changes throughout his empire; he also took drastic measures to destroy both the old feudal system and the literature of the Confucian school, which lauded the early feudal age as an era of virtue and justice. The emperor perceived the danger of allowing hostile scholars to spread reactionary doctrines, so he ordered the *Shu Ching*, or *Canon of History*, and the *Shih Ching*, or *Book of Poetry* to be burned, and forbade discussion or teaching of these outlawed classics. It is said that on one occasion he had 460 scholars executed for violating his decrees, but some scholars deny the validity of this allegation. In any case, although the outlawed literature was subsequently pieced together for the most part, Shih Huang Ti accomplished his purpose: the ancient institutions lost their claim upon the popular mind.

Shih Huang Ti's achievements. Naturally, many Chinese scholars have been harsh in their estimate of Shih Huang Ti, who was admittedly often cruel and shortsighted in his methods. On the other hand, the first empire which he established initiated the important ideal of a unified China governed by a responsible centralized government. Mustafa Kemal Ataturk, the twentieth-century dictator of Turkey, was in some respects analogous to this "Chinese Caesar." Both men rescued their countries from internal disintegration and external attack. Both encouraged drastic changes in the written languages of their countries, both instituted important domestic reforms, and both broke old political and religious traditions despite bitter resistance.

The Han dynasty (202 B.C.–220 A.D.). When Shih Huang Ti died in 210 B.C., he was succeeded by his inept son, who committed suicide within three years. The empire quickly fell into a condition of anarchy and violence. In 202 B.C. a general who had risen from humble origins won control and, establishing his new capital in Sianfu, founded one of China's most illustrious dynasties. Deriving its name from the fact that the new emperor had once been stationed for four years on the Han River, a tributary of the Yangtze, the Han dynasty was to endure for four centuries.

THE GREAT WALL OF CHINA

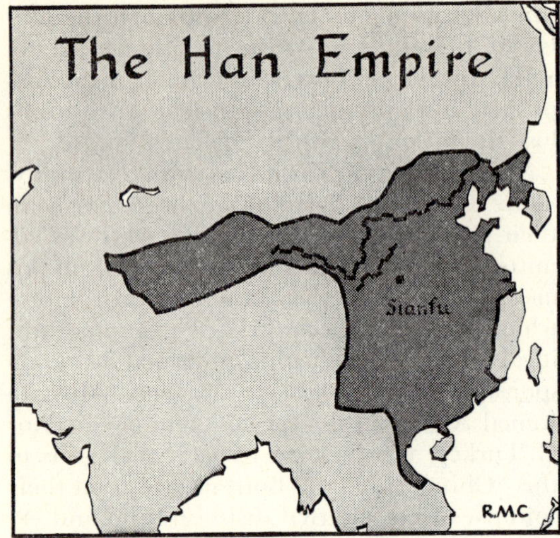

Certain important events occurred in the early years of the new dynasty. In 195 B.C. the emperor paid a visit to the tomb of Confucius and there offered a sacrifice to the sage's spirit. From that time on, an ever-increasing reverence began to be paid the philosopher, until the time came when the worship of Confucius was established as a great national cult which later dynasties were to glorify to dizzy heights. However, as one scholar points out, the first mention of such a cult is in 59 A.D., when the emperor decreed that sacrifices should be paid the scholar in the government schools.[17]

Expansion under Wu Ti. During this early period, the empire had to contend on the other side of the Great Wall with fierce nomadic Huns, who were in control of the stretches of upper Asia. In consolidating their position, the Huns had driven other non-Chinese nomads, apparently Scythians, west and south, and the latter had in turn invaded Bactria and taken possession there. It was now the plan of the greatest of Han rulers, Wu Ti (140-87 B.C.), the Warrior Emperor, to bring the Huns under control.

As a first step, Wu Ti sent an envoy by the name of Chang Ch'ien to the new occupants of Bactria with a proposal that they join in a war against the Huns. But the Scythians were well content with their position in Bactria and had no desire to resume fighting. Chang Ch'ien returned with a negative answer, but he brought with him the seeds of the grape and a great store of valuable geographical and other information, on the basis of which Wu Ti decided to take action in central Asia. Between 121 and 119 B.C., under brilliant generalship, the Chinese inflicted heavy defeats on the Huns and established their authority and prestige. Some time later Wu Ti sent his first envoy to western Asia, probably Parthia. In 102 B.C. China's expansion under Wu Ti was climaxed by the conquest of Ferghana on the threshold of present-day Soviet Turkestan. Chinese military conquests by the end of the second century B.C. had thus established a direct contact with western Asia, which in turn served as an important link by which China was gradually brought into touch with Europe. The expansionist policy of Wu Ti helped lay the foundation for the development of East-West trade.

The emperor also expanded his domains to part of Korea and lands in the southeast, including a region whose center was Canton. At the time when the armies of Marius and Sulla were strengthening Roman domination over the Mediterranean world, those of Wu Ti "established a *Pax Sinica* in Central and Eastern Asia, the Far Eastern equivalent of the *Pax Romana*."[18] It is because this dynastic period was marked by the expansion of Chinese power and influence, as well as by a splendid flowering of thought and the arts, that even today the Chinese have a favorite name for themselves, "Sons of Han."

Animal motifs, of which this brownish-yellow jade Elk is representative, formed an important segment of Han art. From the West was derived a tendency to elongate the animal, thus giving the impression of movement and suppressed energy.

The period of the later Han. When Wu Ti died in 87 B.C. he had no one competent to succeed him. The later decades of the first century B.C. were marked by a progressive weakening of the dynasty, climaxed by a brief interregnum, during which power fell into the hands of a usurper. The fortunes of both the dynasty and the country improved greatly, however, by the beginning of the second century A.D., in the period of the later Han (25-220 A.D.). Thus the area south of Canton, which had rebelled, was now incorporated into China as a province, while in central and western Asia, where the Chinese had lost a good deal of ground during the period of internal troubles, a protectorate was re-established during the first century A.D. This had been made possible by the brilliant military feats of one general, Pan Ch'ao, who was honored with the title "Protector of the Western Regions" and of whom it was said, "He kept order as far as the Pamirs and the Hanging Passes," which means to the entrances of Persia and India.

The silk trade. The Roman empire's trade with the East was at its greatest during the first and second centuries of our era. While Roman subjects were able to trade directly with India, the silk trade between Rome and China, as we have seen, was carried on through middlemen, including the Parthians, who in 94 A.D. sent an embassy with gifts to the Han court. Meanwhile the Chinese were interested in learning more about the West, especially of the Graeco-Roman world about which they had heard. Consequently, in 97 A.D. the envoy Kan Ying was dispatched west with instructions to proceed to the Roman empire. Actually, Kan Ying did not get beyond Babylonia, for the Parthians discouraged him from embarking on a sea voyage to Rome by exaggerating its dangers, probably because they did not want the Romans and Chinese to enter into direct touch with one another to their own possible disadvantage.

There is also the fascinating account of the attempt by a Graeco-Roman merchant, Maes Titianus, to explore the silk route from Syria eastward. His agents traveled past Bactria and over the Pamirs as far as a place called the "Stone Tower," which may have been located near Tashkurgan. "Here was the meeting place of two worlds; a lonely rock among the mountains, towering above the waters of the Yarkand river. To this . . . came caravans from China and the countries of the farthest East. No word was spoken, but the merchants from east and west set down their wares in silence, and added or took away from the heap until the bargain was struck, after which the caravans made their way back across mountains, rivers, and deserts."[19] The knowledge brought back by Maes' agents contributed greatly to Ptolemy's geography of the East.

The overland trade route was expensive and beset with political and physical hazards, so that, as we have seen, much of the silk commerce was diverted down to ports in the Persian Gulf and elsewhere and picked up by Roman shipping. Toward the end of the second century, there were even all-sea contacts with China by Roman merchants—but unfortunately the succeeding centuries witnessed the political and economic decline of the Graeco-Roman world.

Before concluding this brief account of the rich silk trade that crossed thousands of miles of the Eurasian land mass, we might draw attention to a study by one scholar who has examined in detail the recurrence of barbarian

A Tibetan lama holds his rosary and the prayer wheel whose turning wafts his prayers heavenward. He belongs to one of a multiplicity of complex sects which grew out of mingled Buddhism and Christianity.

The Buddhist-inspired pagoda is seen in square form on this decorated pottery model of a Han-dynasty building. Notice the cleverly built sliding doors.

invasions of the Roman empire from 58 B.C. to 107 A.D. Professor Frederick J. Teggart found a direct relationship between disturbances in the western regions of China and the barbarian invasions of the eastern frontiers of the Roman world. This relationship Professor Teggart decided, was due to interruptions occurring in the profitable trade along the vital silk route linking the two civilizations. If so, it shows that even in those days of relative isolation, peoples of the classical world were nevertheless interdependent in ways which have hitherto not been sufficiently understood. From this, he concludes that the knowledge "which is indispensable for an historical account of Roman affairs, for an understanding of the situation on the northern frontiers...can be obtained in no other way than by the comparison of events throughout Eurasia."[20]

The spread of Buddhism into China. The Kushan empire in northwest India was on friendly terms with the Hans. This fact, together with the pacification of central Asia by the Chinese, facilitated the spread of *Mahayana* Buddhism from northwest India across eastern Asia during the later Han dynasty. The Buddhist missionaries traveled the same routes as the silk caravans. In the Tarim basin has been found a Buddhist sanctuary of about the third century A.D. containing frescoes which are Buddhist in theme but Graeco-Roman in treatment.

Emperor Ming Ti (58-76 A.D.) gave Buddhism official recognition, and so it began to spread through China. At first its progress was hindered by the suspicion on the part of the Chinese that Buddhist monasticism (similar to Christian monasticism) did not fit into the country's family tradition. But much of its mysticism was like that of Taoism and this slowly became adaptable to the Chinese mind. Again, the Buddhism which made so many converts in China was quite unlike the faith taught by Buddha in India. The Chinese version was *Mahayana* Buddhism, with its acceptance of Bodhisattvas, Buddhas, and even local Chinese gods. Today there are about ten separate Buddhist sects in China, and scarcely any is similar in its teachings to the doctrines taught by the Buddha.

Yet the influence of Buddhism on China has been extensive and enduring. Not only did Buddhism bring to the Chinese a new spiritual horizon in which salvation was held out to all classes, rich or poor, in contrast to the more aristocratic Confucianism and the much more abstruse Taoism, but it had a tremendous effect on the intellectual and artis-

Grecian influence in art reached China by missionaries and traders from Gandhara, where Alexander the Great had planted the western tradition. These stucco Bodhisattvas from the Tunhwang caves shows marked Greek influence.

tic life of the people. Its philosophy was sufficiently complex and far-reaching to engage the mind of the cleverest philosopher, while the cloisters of the Buddhist monastery provided a safe haven for those gentle or weary souls who wished to escape the chaos of the outer world and seek a life of contemplation.

Buddhist influence in art and literature. In the realm of art fresh ideas were created by the presence of Buddhism. In northwest India, although Buddha had forbidden it, the first statues of him were made. We have seen the influence of Greek art on Indian sculpture and the resulting development of a Graeco-Indian technique (see page 208). This style soon found its way to China, where statues have been found which show apparent Greek influence in their faces and draping.

The pagoda came with Buddhism—undoubtedly inspired, in part at least, by the Indian *stupa.* Made of wood, brick, or stone, the pagodas vary greatly in shape, being round, square, or polygonal. As time went on, the pagoda lost its connection with Buddhism and was considered a means of bringing good luck to the city in which it was built.

In spite of the prohibitions against idolatry, Buddhism stimulated sculpture in stone, bronze, and clay. Painting, too, was presumably influenced by the new subject matter. The only surviving examples of Han painting are a few bricks with painted figures, but the excellence of later painting shows that highly developed art must have preceded it.

Han literature and scholarship. The peace brought to China by the Han dynasty endured long enough to encourage literature and the arts. The invention of paper in the first century A.D. proved of tremendous aid to literature, its superiority to pottery, bones, and bamboo slips being obvious. The Hans were responsible for recovering a great portion of the Confucian literature which Shih Huang Ti had ordered destroyed. We will recall that Confucianism had been established at this time as the official philosophy and religion, and this influenced in turn the development of scholarship, for Confucius' followers carefully studied the ancient literature. As a result, commentaries on the classics were written in the imperial university.

More important, perhaps, from our standpoint was the production of the first great Chinese history, written by a contemporary of Wu Ti named Ssu-ma Ch'ien. This "Chinese Herodotus" wrote a universal history treating Chinese society from its origins to the historian's own age, and called the *Shih Chi,* or *Historical Memoirs.* This work, equivalent in length to about one and a quarter million words in English, has been praised highly for its freedom from superstition, its careful weighing of evidence, and its inclusion of a vast amount of information about ancient China. A second important history was also written at this time, by Ban Gu, who wrote of the entire world then known by the Chinese. Ban Gu's *History of the Former Han Dynasty* (Tsien-Han-shu) concentrated on the last two centuries B.C. and thus originated the practice in China of devoting a whole history to a single epoch.

The Han dynasty performed a valuable service for later scholars when the *Shuo Wen,* a study of the meanings of some ten thousand Chinese characters, was compiled. The book, published in 100 A.D., is probably the oldest dictionary in the world.

Many brilliant poets flourished under the Han dynasty. There is a saying that "the *Shih Ching* represents the roots of the Chinese poetical tree, the Han poetry its bursting into leaf, and the T'ang poets its full fruition."[21]

Notable advancement was also made in the sciences during the Han period. We are told that one scholar reckoned the year at 365 385/1539 solar days, that the Chinese had observed sunspots as early as 28 B.C., and that even a primitive seismograph was invented. Popular belief held that eclipses, comets, and such catastrophes as earthquakes and floods were manifestations of heaven's displeasure.

An earthenware group of Figures Playing a Game, with a green lead glaze which is similar to that found on certain Roman and Parthian pottery.

But a rational attitude was displayed by the scholar Wang Ch'ung (ca. 27-100 A.D.), who pointed out: "On an average, there is one moon eclipse in about 180 days, and a solar eclipse in about every 41 or 42 months. Eclipses are regular occurrences and are not caused by political action. All anomalies and catastrophes are of the same class and are never dependent upon political events."[22]

The decline of the Han dynasty. The *Pax Sinica* of the Han period had brought to China new lands, a new religion, and new developments in the arts, sciences, and scholarship. But this happy state of affairs was destined not to last, for the Han dynasty relapsed into decadence, and abuses in the economic and social life of the people all combined to foster political discontent. An agrarian uprising in Szechuan in 184 A.D. was suppressed, but the suffering of the people continued. Meanwhile, various warlords took to the field in an effort to usurp the power from the crumbling dynasty. At length, in 220 A.D., the last of the Hans was deposed—and while Chinese civilization was again to rise to cultural levels at least as high, it had first to endure a long period of transition and strife. The centuries that followed were filled with civil wars, the division of China into numerous kingdoms which rose only to perish in short order, and external wars with such invaders as the Tatars and Turks. China was to become a melting pot of races, customs, creeds, and tongues. But what appeared on the surface to be a civilization in collapse was in reality one in transition and assimilation.

The End of an Epoch

Severance of East-West contacts. Unfortunately for the cause of international relations, commercial and cultural intercourse among the three great civilizations of classical times was progressively interrupted from the third century A.D. We have just seen how in 220 A.D. the great Han dynasty was overthrown and China entered upon a period of internal strife and upheaval, accompanied in turn by a decline in power and prestige in central Asia. In the same year, coincidentally, the Kushan empire in northwest India succumbed and Indian civilization also underwent a process of change and transition. Nevertheless, both China and India remained in a position to continue their commercial and other ties with the West. The causes for the disruption in Eurasian relations must rather be sought in the West itself.

From the third century onwards, the Graeco-Roman world underwent profound changes. These changes radically altered conditions in the West and played a large role in western civilization's transition from a basically classical culture pattern to a medieval one.

Following the death of Marcus Aurelius in 180 A.D., the Roman empire was beset by bitter conflict, with claimants for the throne warring upon one another and emperors being murdered. In this political confusion the empire also underwent a sharp economic decline. The high cost of continuous warfare and general dislocation were accompanied by the loss of revenue from lost provinces and a progressive depreciation of currency, with its ever-ruinous effects. The decline of Roman strength and prestige was accompanied not only by a diminution of Roman purchasing power—so that the volume of trade with the East would inevitably suffer—but by an increasing inability either to carry on energetic commerce with the East or to safeguard the trade routes. A crowning blow came when Red Sea commerce was intercepted by Abyssinians and Arabs, who were then in a position to dominate the all-important sea trade with the East. The Emperor Constantine in the fourth century established his capital, Constantinople, in the eastern part of the empire; this city was ideally located for carrying on trade with India and China by way of the Persian Gulf-Euphrates and trans-Asian routes. But unfortunately a now-powerful Persian empire established a strangle hold over the supply of silk, which by this time had become more of a necessity than luxury to the West. The prospect of little or no silk was met, however, by the smuggling of silk-moth eggs—probably by two monks, who around 552 carried them from the East to Europe in a hollow stick. This event ultimately rendered Europe free of the Orient for its silk supply.

The traditional date for the collapse of the Roman empire is 476 A.D. It is true that by this time much of the empire's prosperity had disappeared. But a large amount of economic activity, based on Mediterranean sea routes, persisted until the Arab conquests of the seventh and eighth centuries. The Arabs' conquests made any intercourse between the peoples of the East and West virtually impossible.

Drain of specie. The volume of the Graeco-Roman world's oriental trade had been exceedingly great. Because Roman exports to the East could never match in quantity or value the empire's imports of silk, spices, perfumes, gems, and other luxuries, the West suffered seriously from an adverse balance of trade. This situation forced the continual export of precious metals to Asia. Pliny declares that India, China, and Arabia drained away at least 100,000,000 *sesterces* (around $5,000,000 at a time when dollars had more purchase value than today) annually, "so dearly do we pay for our luxuries and our women." The discovery of vast hoards of Roman coins in India and the mention in old Indian poems of Yavana (Roman Greek) vessels coming to Malabar with gold and leaving with pepper support Pliny's statement. Few Roman coins have been found in China, but this was probably because the Romans purchased the silk produced in China from Parthians, Kushans, and other middlemen in western Asia.

One competent scholar has estimated that between the years 31 B.C. and 192 A.D. alone, Rome's trade with the Orient cost her a net money loss of some £175,000,000 ($500,000,000).[23] This serious drain took place at a time when the known sources of gold and silver supply within the empire were being exhausted, and must be reckoned as a major factor in the economic decline of the Roman world.

The geographical consequences. So far we have noticed the chief factors which brought about the severance of East-West relations in classical times. Now, in conclusion, we might summarize some of the important and permanent contributions which this epoch of classical expansion contributed. First of all, there was a vast increase in man's knowledge of his physical world. Ancient travelers succeeded in exploring the entire Mediterranean area; the seaboards of western Europe, of Asia from Suez to Canton, of west Africa almost as far as the equator and of east Africa even beyond the equator; all Europe south of the Rhine and Danube, together with parts of Germany and southern Russia; Asia Minor; the Caspian lands; the plateau of Iran; the Indus River system; a silk route to China; the Nile basin to the region of the Sudan; a route from the east African coast to Lake Victoria Nyanza; and two or three tracks across the Sahara to Sudan and Nigeria.[24]

FROM A RELIEF PANEL REPRESENTING THE VISIT OF THE GOD SAKRA (INDIA) TO BUDDHA

These ancient explorations had a profound effect upon medieval and early modern times. The most influential of all classical geographers, Claudius Ptolemy, gathered all available data and constructed a map of the world. Ptolemy was inaccurate in many respects, yet two of his errors actually facilitated exploration in early modern times. He greatly miscalculated the distance between western Europe and eastern Asia, making it look much smaller than it actually was. Centuries later, Columbus accepted those calculations and was encouraged—as he never would have been had he known the true distance—to sail westward in an effort to reach Asia. Ptolemy had also drawn a strip of land extending from Africa to Asia. This fiction encouraged explorers to look for this "terra australis incognita." By chance they stumbled upon the continent which we know as Australia.

The influence of West upon East. The Roman impact on the East was made largely through Roman trade with India and China. These commercial relations were not only profitable in themselves but substantially increased the knowledge of both sections of the world about each other. In addition, we know that commercial relations encouraged considerable numbers of Roman and Indian subjects to travel between the two empires over a considerable period of time.

However, the principal impact came as a result of Greek and Indian cultural, and counter-cultural, influences. There is little doubt that the strongest Greek influence on Indian civilization was in the field of sculpture, as demonstrated by the results of the Graeco-Buddhist school at Gandhara, which in turn affected art forms in China and even in Japan. Indian coinage also bears the strong imprint of Hellenistic influence.

It seems certain that Indian astronomy, which made significant advances in its own right, had the benefit of Greek assistance. "The Yavanas [Roman Greeks] are barbarians," said the author of one Sanskrit astronomical work, "yet the science of astronomy originated with them, and for this they must be reverenced as gods."[25] On the other hand, it is doubtful that Indian medical science was influenced by western thought. Likewise the claim that the Greeks influenced Indian drama is very debatable. In the field of religion, there is no doubt that a large number of Greek and Roman deities were known to the Indians but there is nothing to prove that they influenced the trend of Indian religious thought.

The influence of East upon West. There has been adequate opportunity to notice the impact which both India and China made upon the economy and social habits of the Graeco-Roman world. The conditions of life became more comfortable by the import of a variety of spices, muslins, and silks, as well as other objects of trade. On the other hand, it is difficult to estimate the intangible imports from the East. We have already set forth western influences on the East as evaluated by western scholars. It will now be interesting to see what an Indian scholar believes was the influence of his civilization upon the West.

Dr. R. C. Majumdar is of the view that the ideas of Pythagoras and other Greek philosophers show numerous coincidences between Indian and Greek philosophy. "Whether the doctrines of these Greek thinkers were derived from Indian philosophy, or were independently evolved, cannot, of course, be definitely decided." However, he points out, the fact that these coincidences exist, plus the Greek tradition that so many of the Hellenic philosophers visited oriental countries to study, "render the first alternative at least highly probable." This scholar also states that when Christianity arose, Indian culture and "religion was already an important factor in the region of its early activity," the eastern Mediterranean, and that undoubtedly some of the early Christian mystics were profoundly influenced by Indian ideas.[26]

Other influences. In concluding this summary of cultural impacts, we might recall that during this period of East-West relations, each great segment of the Eurasian "axis" was being permanently affected by the interplay of cultural forces within its own confines. We have traced earlier the tremendous impact made by Greek thought and art upon the Romans. In this chapter, we saw how in turn the Graeco-Roman culture influenced the life of western Asia. Likewise, Indian culture, primarily in its religious and artistic elements, traveled northward to leave a lasting impress upon the civilization of China, and subsequently on that of Japan as well. In the later chapters we shall study the Graeco-Roman cultural radiation which prepared the way for the growth and eventual triumph of Christianity in the West, and the great Indian-Chinese cultural radiation which made possible in turn the evolution of Buddhism into another major world religion.

Summary

The hackneyed statement that "East is East and West is West, and never the twain shall meet" certainly is being disproved in our own day, but not in our day alone. It was disproved by centuries of contacts made during classical times. Yet in fairness to Rudyard Kipling, the author of that statement, we should recall that East and West *could* meet when "strong men" stood face to face, "though they come from the ends of the earth." And this is precisely what happened in the centuries immediately preceding and following the Christian era. The soldiers of Alexander followed their leader through uncharted wastelands surrounded by enemies, until they reached the Indus. Mariners such as Hippalus braved the Arabian Sea in frail craft to reach the ports of southern India. Chinese envoys and generals struck westward across forbidding deserts and mountain ranges to make contact with other peoples. As a result, East and West were brought together in the mountain kingdom of Bactria and along the northwest frontiers of India; they met on the silk routes of Turkestan and in the market places of Rome and Alexandria. And not only sailors and merchants met, but artists, scientists, and philosophers exchanged views and theories.

These were the truly formative centuries of our modern world, for the Graeco-Roman civilization established the basic intellectual, political, economic, and artistic forms of expression for the West. At the same time, as we have seen, the Mauryan dynasty, and especially the pious Asoka, stimulated the progressive evolution of Indian culture and the dissemination throughout southern and eastern Asia of the civilizing tenets of Buddhism—a development supported and strengthened in turn by the great Kushan monarch, Kanishka. China was fortunate in possessing one of its greatest dynasties in the Hans, under whom the bounds of the empire were enlarged and a *Pax Sinica* established. This encouraged the development of the arts and scholarship on a scale never known in Chinese history before and perhaps to be known only once again.

That "peace hath her victories no less renowned than war" is attested to eloquently by the civilization which flourished within the territories patrolled by the Roman legions, or that safeguarded by the Great Wall, or that ruled by the king—Asoka—to whom "conquest of the Law is alone a conquest full of delight." As a result, it has not been difficult to find parallels in the cultural development of East and West during these centuries.

But the parallel breaks down when we examine the subsequent history of these three civilizations. In the East, violence assails both India and China, but their indigenous cultures retain their fundamental forms and so, by a process of transition and assimilation, these civilizations endure and grow. In the West, the Graeco-Roman world-state is in turn subjected to ruthless attack, but here the political framework and economic and social structure disintegrate, so that a different form of western civilization eventually emerges, as we shall see presently.

With the decline of the Graeco-Roman world and the severance of all direct contacts between East and West, the only unity which the world had known to that time disappeared. Men were to wait for another thousand years before Marco Polo and his successors braved the dangers of the unknown and penetrated the East, thus refuting medieval fable with geographic fact.

Chronology of events and developments discussed in this chapter

Chapter 8

Death of Commodus ushered in a century of civil war	192-284 A.D.
Dominate replaced principate; army controlled emperor	193
Diocletian: despotic stable government; ended civil war	284-305
Constantine: sole ruler after victory over rivals; built Constantinople	324-337
Caste system imposed: coloni bound to land and guildsmen to trade	332
Rise of Christianity	1-350
Lifetime of Jesus	1-31
Paul's ministry: spread Christianity throughout ancient world	35-65
Reign of Marcus Aurelius: Christianity was the dominant religion	161-180
Edict of toleration of Christianity issued by Galerius	311
Edict of Milan: Constantine raised Christianity to legal status	313
Council of Nicaea: doctrinal schism: Athanasius upheld against Arius	325
Ulfilas: missionary to the Germans; translated the Bible into Gothic	311-383
St. Augustine: successful missionary in England	354-430
St. Patrick: missionary to Ireland: Celtic abbeys preserved culture	389
Gregory the Great: increase in political power of papacy	590-604
Gradual decline of Rome	161-476
Attempted invasions and gradual infiltration by the barbarians	161-300
German invasions: caused by land hunger, adventure, the Huns	375-500
Battle of Adrianople: German conquest; Rome no longer invincible	378
Division of the Roman empire: Constantinople and Rome	395
Sack of Rome by the Visigoths under Alaric	410
Battle of Châlons: Germans and Romans defeated the Huns under Attila	451
Vandals looted Rome: civilization survived but power destroyed	455
Clovis I: Franks converted to Christianity; extensive conquests	466-511
Boethius: philosopher and preserver of knowledge	c. 475-525
Fall of Rome: end of Augustan emperors; control by the Germans	476
Theodoric's Ostrogothic kingdom in Italy	488-554
Lombard rule in Italy	568-774
Venerable Bede: English historian	673-735

Interval in the West

Fall of Rome; rise of the Church: 180 A.D. to 650 A.D.

Although the Roman world-state endured into the fifth century, its existence was soon to be threatened by the incursion of barbarian hordes. The barbarians, called Germans by the Romans, were not merely the ancient inhabitants of modern Germany. The Germans known by the Romans included people living in an area reaching from the Black Sea to the mouth of the Rhine and from the Scandinavian peninsula to the boundaries of the Roman empire along the Danube. The barbarians exercised a tremendous influence on the course of European history.

In a sense the Roman empire had been undergoing "barbarization" for a long time before its fall. German soldiers were encouraged to enlist with the legions, Germans were settled on vacant lands, and many blue-eyed tribesmen from north of the Danube went south into the Roman provinces to seek their fortune. If this peaceful contact had been permitted to continue, in all probability a huge number of Germans would have been assimilated in the empire. The devastating invasions of the fifth century ended peaceful infiltration, and the Roman political structure collapsed. In the ensuing confusion, however, a powerful agency moved into the gap left by the Caesars. The place of the Roman emperors was taken by the Popes, and the Christian Church played the dominant role in the five hundred years following the waning of the classical world.

Although we speak of the fall of Rome or the end of the Graeco-Roman world, the phrase is not strictly accurate, for only the western half of the empire with its capital at Rome was inundated by Germanic invaders. In the East, Constantinople perpetuated the glory of the Caesars, and for one thousand years her civilization was superior to that of western Europe. Her Byzantine culture will be described at length in Chapter 9.

People often refer to the period of the Germanic invasions as the Dark Ages. But it was a significant period, during which the civilization of the classical world, mainly Greek and Roman, which in turn had been based on the civilization of the Near East, was blended with Germanic institutions to produce our modern world. In the process of blending the various elements into a new historical compound, the catalytic agent, as chemists would say, was the Christian Church. It preserved knowledge until men in the western world were ready again to appreciate it, took over some of the neglected functions of government, restrained the bellicose Germanic tribes, and protected the weak and helpless. It is a fascinating story—how elements from the ancient Near East, Greece, Rome, and the Germanic tribes were fashioned into a new product which, as we shall see, began about 1100 to produce outstanding literary, intellectual, and artistic achievements for the enrichment of world civilization.

The Last Phase of the Roman Empire

A century of civil war. The death of Marcus Aurelius (page 173) brought to an end two centuries of imperial prosperity. His son, Commodus, who succeeded him in 180 A.D., proved to be a cruel tyrant who emptied the imperial treasury by his voluptuous living and shocked the Romans with his dissipations and cruelties. After he had reigned twelve years, a group of conspirators bribed Commodus' athletic trainer to strangle his royal master. The death of the tyrant ushered in a century of civil war which was terminated in 284 only by the accession of the strong and efficient Diocletian to the imperial throne.

Following the murder of Commodus civil war broke out among the military leaders, who fought among themselves for the privilege of naming the next emperor. After much bloodshed Septimius Severus became emperor in 193. His accession marks the end of the principate. From now on the emperor made no attempt to hide the fact that he was "army-made" and would not tolerate the senate's interference. Septimius Severus was the first real absolute ruler of Rome. He called himself *dominus* (lord), and the principate was replaced by absolute rule known as the dominate. The new emperor was a good soldier and defeated some of the barbarian invaders who had managed to cross the Roman frontier.

The army now became the real power in the empire, and many of the high government offices were filled with uncouth soldiers to whom the emperor was indebted for his support. On his deathbed, Septimius Severus is reputed to have told his sons, "Make the soldiers rich and don't trouble about the rest." This toadying to the soldiery was to have dire effects on the empire.

The line of Septimius Severus held the imperial office until 235. After its extinction a period of virtual anarchy ensued. In the next fifty years there were twenty-two emperors, twenty of whom were murdered. The latter part of the third century was a terrible period for the Roman empire, for it was lashed from without by foreign invaders and rent from within by bloody civil wars revolving around disputed elections of the emperors.

Imperial decline explained. The most obvious factor in the rapid decline of the empire was the virtual collapse of the authority of the central government. No effective system of constitutional succession to the imperial throne had been worked out, and no one was ever certain who was to be the next emperor. This gave the army its opportunity. The imperial scepter was dragged in the gutter by the generals of the various armies, who murdered emperors with no compunction, intimidated the senate, placed their puppets on the imperial throne, and then unhesitatingly murdered them on the slightest excuse, to make way for other puppets. "The empire," declares M. I. Rostovtzeff, "became the chattel of the soldiers."[1] Often the legions marched through the countryside, pillaging as they went. Irresponsible soldiery destroyed vast amounts of wealth.

Another factor explaining the decline of Rome in the third century was the attack of

The Saalburg is a reconstructed Roman castellum which was part of the Limes fortifications, built against the barbarians. Notice the arched gateways and the ditch along the wall.

foes from without. Lack of discipline in the army and its neglect of duty gave the enemies of Rome their opportunity. Numerous barbarian tribes, especially Goths, attacked the frontier. All of the territory held by Rome north of the Danube and east of the Rhine was lost. In the east a new menace appeared, a reinvigorated Persia under the rule of the brilliant Sassanid dynasty (226-641 A.D.), under whom the Persians conquered the Fertile Crescent. In the face of the inability of the central government to cope with these attacks, the people on the frontier began to establish independent states and take measures for their own defense. One senator ruled not only Gaul but also Britain and north Spain, independently of Rome. The loss of territory was a serious matter for a time, but the unity of the empire was again restored by the heroic efforts of two third-century emperors, who pushed back the barbarian tribes on the north and reconquered Asia Minor and Gaul.

Economic decline. Less obvious than governmental chaos and foreign invasions, but more deadly in the long run to the well-being of the empire, was economic decline. The trend toward the concentration of land ownership in a few hands, which we noted at the time of the Gracchi, had gone on in spite of all efforts at control. In Nero's reign, for example, the whole province of Africa consisted of a half-dozen estates owned by six wealthy landlords. By the third century land monopoly was so widespread that nearly all land in the empire was controlled by a small aristocratic clique.

The small farmers could not compete with the large farms, or *latifundia*, and were consequently forced to give up their little parcels of land. The small farmer became a *colonus*, that is, he obtained a plot of land from a large landholder. By arrangement with the landholder the farmer was free to cultivate his small patch of land, but in return he had to agree to render many manual services in the fields of his landlord. As time went on, the *colonus* became nothing more than a semi-slave, technically a freeman but bound to the soil, passing with the land if it changed owners. It was the first step toward serfdom, a form of livelihood which was to play such an important role during the Middle Ages. Many sturdy farmers forced off their land refused to become *coloni* and fled to the cities where they often became an unemployed rabble living off the dole.

To make matters worse, confusion reigned in the monetary system. The currency was debased by reducing the content of precious metal in the Roman coins, which of course made them less valuable. It therefore took more coins than before to buy the same quantity of goods, or, to put it another way, the prices of commodities tended to rise out of all reason.

Civil war decreased purchasing power and disturbed trade, which had never rested on a satisfactory basis. Rome had never developed a sufficiently vigorous export trade, and too much of her glittering prosperity in the days of her glory was made possible by the tribute exacted from the provinces. Fundamentally, too much of Roman commercial activity was unproductive. The French historian Victor Duruy admirably sums up the matter when he declares, "Rome, which made the provinces send her everything, never reimbursed them except with the money from the taxes, that is to say, with the very sums with which these provinces had provided her. Her so-called commerce was thus only indirect robbery. The capital, being an unproductive city, was truly an octopus.' "[2]

Economists also point out that the Roman empire never developed large-scale industry. Each locality tended to be self-sufficient. The decline in commerce spelled ruin for the cities, which were dependent upon trade for their very existence. The empire, we recall, was basically a collection of numerous city-states which were to the empire what cells are to the human body. When they lost their vigor, the great imperial structure became afflicted by an incurable disease.

The empire in the east. During the third century, when evidences of serious decline began to manifest themselves in the Roman state, it began to appear that the western half of the empire, especially Italy, was going downhill much faster than the provinces in the eastern part of the empire. Commerce and trade in the Balkan peninsula more than held their own, while the rapid expansion of the *latifundia* system in Italy was degrading the populace and filling Rome with unemployed farmers. From that time on, emperors turned their attention more and more to the east, until one of them, as we shall see shortly, actually created a new imperial capital, coequal with Rome, in the eastern part of the empire.

Diocletian. The Roman world was given a much needed respite from decline when Diocletian became emperor in 284. With his accession civil war ended. The new ruler was a strong and capable administrator who immediately set about trying by drastic measures to restore the efficiency of the government, defend the frontiers, and stop the steady economic decline. Although they arrested the decline, in the long run his efforts only strengthened the factors causing the downfall of the empire.

The first task was to strengthen the government. Diocletian completed the trend toward despotism initiated by Septimius Severus. The Roman senate was relegated to the status of a mere city council. The emperor adorned himself with robes sparkling with jewels and was addressed as "the most sacred lord." Furthermore, he assumed the title of Sun God, surrounding himself with all the glitter of an oriental despot, in frank imitation of oriental ways. An imperial etiquette, similar to that introduced in the French court by the monarch Louis XIV in the seventeenth century, was established, which made of the emperor a veritable god.

The administration of the empire was reorganized. Twelve dioceses were formed and into these were grouped some hundred provinces. Over each diocese was a vicar, over each province a governor. The new diocesan units in turn were grouped into four prefectures, ruled by prefects. There was little room in the new system for local government. We remember that the menace of the Persian autocratic way of life had been successfully repelled by the Greeks in the fifth century B.C. But the once sturdy individualism of Greece and Rome had now at last been conquered by a rigid despotism.

The new administrative reforms necessitated a huge civil service. Then, in order to detect graft in the ranks of the government servants, a large secret service was created. But the evil of corruption apparently was so deeply rooted that the spies seemed to make little improvement. As someone said, "Who is to watch the watchers?"

Diocletian also introduced what he hoped would be a better method of succession to the throne. He chose an assistant named Maximian and made him co-emperor in the west, while he controlled the eastern half of the empire. These two Augusti then each chose another assistant, called a Caesar. There were now four rulers responsible for the government of the empire. The idea was to found a new dynasty, so that there would be no question but that the Caesars would take over the reins of government when the Augusti retired from office.

Constantine. Following the retirement of Diocletian in 305 his grandiose system collapsed. Civil war broke out. Diocletian's system of imperial succession did not work in practice, and in 310 there were five rival emperors, or Augusti, but no Caesars. In a few years one of the contestants for the throne forged to the front. He was Constantine, who had himself been converted to the new religious sect called Christianity. After a victory over one of his rivals, Constantine issued an edict of toleration for Christianity in 313. This was, as we shall see, one of the most momentous acts of the new emperor. After sharing his rule for a few years with another emperor, Constantine became sole ruler in 324.

The division of the empire. It was now becoming more and more apparent that the eastern part of the empire was much stronger and in less danger of collapsing than the western part. Constantine accordingly built a new capital on the site of the Greek town of Byzantium, an excellent strategic location. It was surrounded on three sides by water and could be reached only through a long narrow channel that could be made practically impregnable. Byzantium also possessed a splendid harbor. Constantine named his eastern capital New Rome, but it soon became known as Constantinople. The erection of the eastern capital put the seal on the division of the empire into two halves, the east and the west. For about half a century following the death of Constantine in 337, the unity of the empire was preserved by the rule of two joint emperors, one in the east and the other in the west. But after the emperorship of Theodosius the empire was permanently divided (395), governed as two separate units and never again united.

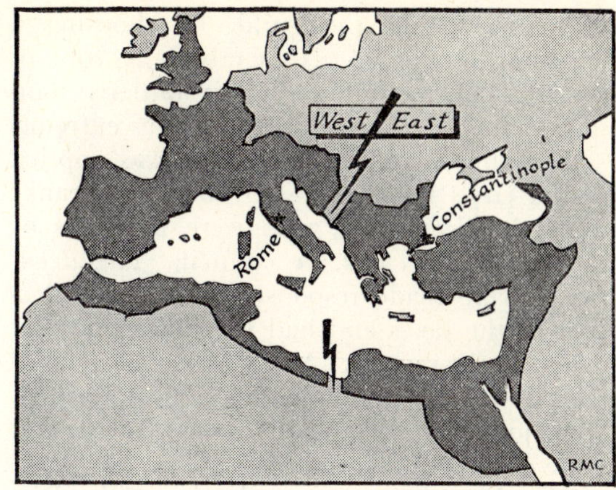

Economic absolutism. Both Diocletian and Constantine made strenuous attempts to arrest economic decay in the empire. They tried to control economic life with the same absolute authority they had introduced in government. The fluctuation of the price level caused Diocletian in 301 to issue an edict which set the maximum price for goods. The law was impractical and unenforceable. The net result was injustice and even more misery for certain classes.

Social regimentation, a veritable caste system, was also introduced to serve the economic interests of the state. In 332 Constantine decreed that thenceforth no *colonus* could leave the soil and that his children had to accept the same status as that of their father. His economic absolutism went further. Everyone was "chained to his post." In the cities the same caste system was applied to members of the corporations, or guilds (*collegia*). All guilds whose activities—such as supplying grain, baking, transportation, and entertaining the city mobs—were essential to the state, were made hereditary organizations. The members were bound to their occupations and even had to marry within the guild, by choosing a daughter of one of its members. A son, of course, had to follow in his father's footsteps. Thus, social regimentation was extreme.

The same hereditary principle was applied to the city's middle class, from whose ranks came the *decuriones,* who were members of the municipal *curia,* or council. The *decuriones* were made responsible for the collection of the taxes and had to make good any deficit in the revenue. Many of the *decuriones* tried desperately to evade the crushing burden. Some joined the army, others the Church, and some even became *coloni.*

The desperate measures instituted by Diocletian and Constantine were to no avail. In the long run the remedy was as bad as the disease from which the empire suffered. A famous historian has described conditions in the latter part of the fourth century thus: "The Roman Empire . . . was based on ignorance, on compulsion and violence, on slavery and servility, on bribery and dishonesty."[3] The principate had given way to the dominate, a vast bureaucracy had been created, and economic regimentation chained men to the soil and to their guilds. But there was no stopping the progressive sapping of the empire's strength.

Popularity of new religions. In the face of these conditions, a disillusioned people sought solace in new types of religion. The old Roman faith was too cold and formal to meet the needs of the unhappy population. Many of the educated classes turned to Stoicism for comfort and fortitude. Neo-Platonism also appealed to many intellectuals. It taught that real happiness was to be realized only by the union of the soul with God through contemplation and ecstasy. The Neo-Platonists believed the only reality is spirit; the material world is unreal and non-existent. The soul can never be happy on earth. Its main objective, therefore, is to escape from the material world and get back to its spiritual home. With such a belief the Neo-Platonists had little interest in the problems of this world. The most noted teacher of Neo-Platonism was Plotinus (204-270), an Alexandrian.

Stoicism and Neo-Platonism had little appeal for the common people, who turned to many religions that had been imported from the east. Among the most popular of the oriental religions were the worship of the Egyptian Isis and Osiris, the Phrygian Cybele (Magna Mater), the Greek Dionysus, and the Persian Mithras, god of light, a cult which was especially popular among the soldiers. The Roman people were attracted to the oriental religions because they presented the comforting idea of a divine protector and the hope of everlasting life, and also because they appealed to the emotions. In brief, these religions gave a new sense of hope and power to their devotees. The people were also attracted by the pomp, the mysterious rites, and the intoxicating songs, which helped them forget the worries of this world. In most of the oriental religions there was the promise of remission of sins, and purification rites invited the worried sinner to repent and begin life anew.

The greatest of the religions coming from the Near East has not yet been mentioned. It was Christianity.

The Rise of Christianity

The life of Jesus. Christianity was founded by Jesus Christ. He was born in Bethlehem of very lowly parents, Joseph and Mary, who lived in Nazareth. Here Jesus spent the first thirty years of His life in the obscure village in Galilee, following the trade of a carpenter. Although He had little formal education, Jesus studied the sacred writings of His people and, while only a boy, astonished the learned men in the temple at Jerusalem by His grasp of the Scriptures and His profound wisdom.

The Jews at this time were finding Roman rule intolerable and longed for the advent of a great national leader, the Messiah, who would drive the Roman masters from their land and reëstablish an independent and prosperous Jewish state.

About 28 A.D. Jesus emerged from obscurity and began to preach the coming of a new order in which suffering and injustice would be no more. Mingling among the poor and lowly classes of society, Jesus carried on His mission, using graphic and simple words and explaining His doctrines by homely parables based upon the everyday experiences of His listeners. Jesus preached a gospel based upon love of one's fellow man. He stressed humility and urged service and helpfulness to one's neighbors rather than the selfish pursuit of wealth and power. Violence was to be shunned, for evil could always be overcome with good. The selfishness of the rich and the self-righteousness of the Jewish priests He denounced with burning eloquence.

During His ministry, which lasted perhaps three years, Jesus obtained many friends and followers among the poorer classes. The fame of His teachings, His holiness, and His miracles spread throughout the land. When He came to Jerusalem to attend the Feast of the Passover, He was welcomed triumphantly by huge crowds who regarded Him as the promised Messiah who would lead the Jews to a glorious victory against their oppressive Roman masters.

But Jesus apparently had no interest in creating an earthly kingdom. He was no conquering hero. The kingdom about which He spoke so eloquently to His followers was a spiritual one based on peace and righteousness enshrined in the hearts of men. When the people realized that Jesus had no intention of leading a nationalistic movement against the Romans, they turned against the young leader. As His followers melted away, other antagonistic groups that had been waiting their opportunity joined in open opposition against Jesus. During His short ministry He had alienated the businessmen by His denunciation of wealth and His scourging of the money changers and merchants in the temple at Jerusalem. The Jewish priests resented the popularity of Jesus and feared that the movement He sponsored might deprive them of their privileged position. Many Jews regarded Jesus as a radical underminer of the foundations of society, a disturber of the status quo, and a blasphemer of Jehovah.

Betrayed by one of His followers, Jesus was condemned by the Jewish Sanhedrin, a religious court, and then was turned over to the Roman authorities. For the crucifixion that followed some hold that the local upper classes were in effect responsible—some argue that Pilate was eager to be rid of Jesus as a threat to Roman rule. In any case, Jesus died a common criminal and it seemed as though His cause had been exterminated. Apparently nothing remained of His work; no written message had been left behind for His few loyal followers, who were now scattered and disheartened.

Early Christianity. The martyrdom of Jesus, however, soon had momentous consequences. Rumors soon spread that Jesus had been seen after His crucifixion, that He had spoken to His disciples and urged them to carry on His mission and thus make way for the second Coming of Christ. Quickly a little group of devoted followers concentrated at Jerusalem, where they reverently reminisced about the teachings of their Master and began quietly to try to convert other Jews to their cause.

At first there were few new converts, but about 45 A.D. the movement was expanded by the inauguration of missionary work among the numerous Jews who were scattered throughout the Mediterranean world. Whereas the Jews in their homeland were inclined to be narrow and intolerant in their religious views, Jews living in foreign lands, in contact with new ideas and modes of living, were less hidebound in their outlook, less firmly committed to traditionalism. Among Jewish communities in such great cities as Athens, Antioch, Corinth, and Rome, the new religion first made real headway.

Paul. As long as the followers of Jesus regarded Him exclusively as the Jewish Messiah who had no interest in the salvation of non-Jews, or gentiles, the growth of the new religion was seriously impeded. The obstacle was removed by St. Paul, the great missionary of early Christianity, who made it a universal religion. Paul was born in a flourishing city in Asia Minor. After following the trade of tentmaker for a time, Paul carried on advanced studies in the best schools of his country. Endowed with a keen mind, he soon became a fine Greek and Hebrew scholar well versed in the Jewish law, which he may have taught for a time at Jerusalem. While a contemporary of Jesus, he never met Him, but was aroused by His teachings, which he regarded as undermining Roman authority. Paul assisted in the persecution of the Christians until, about 35 A.D., he experienced a profound spiritual conversion, which revealed to him the error of his ways. Immediately afterward he became a zealous and loyal follower of Jesus.

Paul's missionary work. Paul quickly appreciated that Christianity could grow only very slowly in Palestine. He perceived that the most fertile soil for converts was in other areas of the Roman empire, where hundreds of thousands of gentiles, dissatisfied with the state religion and with the many pagan cults, were seeking new truth that would give them hope and serenity in a world filled with injustice and economic misery. The Jews outside of their homeland, as we have already noted, were also more receptive to Christianity than those in Palestine steeped in the orthodox beliefs of Judaism.

Paul eliminated many of the narrow characteristics from Christianity and made it a universal religion. No longer was there to be a distinction between Jew and gentile. Paul shrewdly concentrated his missionary work in the great urban centers of the eastern Mediterranean. He preached the gospel at Salonika, Athens, Antioch, Corinth, and Rome. One of the techniques Paul used in strengthening and encouraging the many little Christian communities he had founded was the frequent dispatch of letters to his converts. Some of his letters now form the Epistles of the New Testament. Besides his missionary activity, Paul exercised great influence upon the development and shaping of Christian doctrine. Jesus was recognized as the Christ, the Son of God who had died to atone for the sins of mankind, and acceptance of this belief guaranteed life after death to all.

During his many missionary journeys Paul underwent privation, opposition, and even physical violence. Finally he went to Rome to stand trial for his religious views. Our knowledge concerning the last few years of his life is meager, but apparently, after spending several years in the Roman capital busily engaging in Christian evangelism, he was beheaded about 65 A.D., during the reign of Nero.

The growth of Christianity. After the death of Jesus, Christianity grew slowly, as we have seen, finding its adherents chiefly among the humble classes. The Jews were generally despised, and people were inclined to be contemptuous of what they considered the latest manifestation of the religious fanaticism of God's "chosen people." As a result of the missionary efforts of Paul and his followers, however, the new sect made phenomenal progress, and when the great evangelist died, there were Christian communities in all the important cities of the empire. By the reign of Marcus Aurelius (161-180), Christianity had become the dominant religion in the eastern part of the empire and was challenging the most important pagan cult, Mithraism, for supremacy in the western provinces of the empire. By 300 it was well on its way to becoming the dominant religion throughout the Roman world.

Reasons for the spread of Christianity. What factors can the historian advance to explain this remarkable growth? As the empire declined, men strove to find solace in some religion that would turn their thoughts away from the turbulence and misery of their day. In Christianity they found the comradeship and solace which they sought. The doctrine of the equality of all men, the doctrine of a loving Father who had sent His only Son to atone for men's sins, the vision of blessed immortality, and the idea that regardless of how base man had been, it was possible to be "born again" and be cleansed of sin—these doctrines uniquely met the fundamental spiritual longing of the age. In a word, Christianity better than any other religion gave men a feeling of hope and spiritual assurance which helped compensate and offset the uncertainty and insecurity now plainly apparent in the world about them.

Christianity was a dynamic, aggressive religion. It created a church organization which was far more united and efficient than any possessed by its competitors. Other elements which influenced the growth of Christianity were the definiteness of its teachings, the enthusiasm and zeal of its converts, and the courage with which they faced death and persecution.

The New Testament. A unique Christian literature was developed—the New Testament. Not long after the death of Christ the need arose for a history of His life and an account of His teachings and sayings. Gradually a number of documents, written mainly by certain outstanding disciples of Christ, emerged. There were originally many writings other than those now contained in the twenty-seven books of our New Testament. This resulted in a great amount of discussion as to what writings should be included in the Christian canon, but the process of selection was finally achieved by the seventh century. None of the original copies of the books of the New Testament has come down to us. Written on papyrus, they were very perishable. The oldest known manuscripts of the New Testament date from the fourth century.

In the dim, eerie passageways of the catacombs the Christians held their first timid meetings. The martyr Maximus is buried in this chapel in the catacombs of St. Sebastian, Rome.

Government persecution of Christians. Practically everyone has heard about the terrible persecutions of the Christians at the hands of Roman officials. The Roman government tolerated any religion which did not threaten the safety or tranquillity of the state or interfere with the worship of the emperor. Roman officials had no quarrel with a person's religious preference as long as he was willing to take part in the ceremonies of state cults. The worship of the emperor was a patriotic rite uniting all Roman subjects in common loyalty to the Roman government. The Christians, however, would have nothing to do with the state religious ceremonies. To them there was only one God; no other could share their loyalty to Him. In the eyes of the Roman officials this attitude branded the Christians as unpatriotic.

In addition, the Christians would not engage in military service and refused to accept political office. They also were criticized because of their fierce intolerance of other religious sects, which often led to religious riots. They would not associate with their pagan relatives and refused to participate in social functions, which they thought sinful or degrading.

In the face of these facts the emperors inaugurated persecution against the Christians, not because of intolerance of belief but because they seemed to threaten the very existence of the state. Marcus Aurelius was one of the most determined foes of the new religion. In the third century a series of severe persecutions was carried out. The first widespread campaign against the Christians was carried out by the emperor Decius in 249, and the last by Diocletian in 303.

Official recognition and acceptance. It soon became apparent that there was to be no stamping out of the new religion by force. In fact, the Christians seemed to welcome martyrdom, and the "blood of the martyrs became the seed of the church." In 311 the emperor Galerius issued an edict of toleration, and two years later, by the Edict of Milan, Constantine raised Christianity to the status of a legalized religion, on a par with all pagan cults. In his struggle for the imperial crown, Constantine had had to engage in a desperate battle with his rival Maxentius. At the height of the conflict, tradition has it that Constantine saw emblazoned across the sky a cross with the words "*In Hoc Vince*" ("By this sign conquer"). The edict of legalization followed his victory, and henceforth Constantine favored Christianity.

Constantine's successors, with the notable exception of Julian, carried out a pro-Christian policy. During the reigns of the emperors Gratian and Theodosius in the latter part of the fourth century the government ceased to support the pagan temples and transferred state support to the Christian Church. In 395 the emperor Theodosius made Christianity the sole and official religion of the state. In little more than three hundred years, Christianity, in spite of all obstacles, had become the official religion of a world empire. The first decades of the fifth century saw the destruction of pagan altars, and by the middle of the century the pagan cults were being extirpated by force.

Early church organization. For a half century after the death of Christ there was little organization in the Christian movement. The earliest converts saw no necessity for organization, for they regarded their present world as only a temporary thing which would speedily end with the Second Coming of their Lord. But Christ did not appear, and the Christians gradually had to adjust themselves to the practical fact that since hundreds of years might elapse before the Second Coming it was essential to develop a definite church organization.

Development of church offices. At first there was little or no distinction between laity and clergy. Soon a number of famous teachers appeared, who traveled about visiting far-flung Christian communities, to which they then preached and gave advice when it was needed. This system soon proved quite inadequate. The tremendous increase in the ranks of the Christians demanded that special church officials be created who would devote all their time to church work, who could keep abreast of the rapidly developing Christian dogma, take care of the funds, and conduct the church services and rituals efficiently. At first the officials were called elders, or presbyters; they were also referred to as bishops, or overseers. By the second century the offices of bishop and presbyter had become distinct. The bishop now had the right to enforce obedience from his presbyters and from other subordinates such as stewards and recorders. New churches organized in the country adjacent to the mother church, which was usually located in a city, were administered by presbyters responsible to the bishop. Thus an administrative division evolved, called a diocese, under the jurisdiction of a bishop.

The office of bishop was the most important in the Church. The bishop had charge of all church property in his diocese, and was the official interpreter of Christian dogma. The bishop of the most important city in each province (made up of a number of dioceses) enjoyed more prestige than his fellows and became known as the archbishop or metropolitan. The provinces were grouped into another administrative division called a patriarchate. The title of patriarch was applied to the bishop of such great cities as Rome and Alexandria. In a city like Constantinople, for example, a man could be a bishop, archbishop, and patriarch at the same time.

In the evolution of an organized hierarchy the Church was indebted to Roman governmental models. In building their organization the Christian officials took over the administrative divisions of the Roman empire and borrowed much of its law. The title of bishop, for example, came from an important office of the Roman municipality.

The papacy. A development of outstanding importance in the organization of the Christian Church was the rise of the bishop of Rome to a position of preëminence in the hierarchy of the Church. At first Rome was only one of several patriarchates, no more important than Alexandria, Jerusalem, Antioch, or Constantinople. But gradually the bishop at Rome was recognized as the leader of the Church and assumed the title of Pope.

There were many factors explaining the development of the papacy at Rome. Rome was the capital of the political world. It had a proud tradition. Why should it not be regarded as the spiritual capital of Christianity? Rome was also the largest city in the west, and its church the most important. It was the center of a strong missionary movement, and the Christian churches, which it founded, naturally turned to the mother church and its bishop for help and guidance. The Church at Rome was not rent by disputes concerning doctrine, which weakened and divided the Christians in the east. Its reputation for purity of doctrine often caused other churches engaged in theological disputes to bring their problems to the bishop at Rome for settlement, a practice which redounded to the prestige of Rome.

Perhaps the most important factor in the rise of the papacy was the Petrine doctrine. The doctrine taught that the Roman Church had been founded by Peter, the leader of Christ's disciples. It stated that the Savior had appointed Peter as His successor, that Peter went to Rome and established a church. He thus became the foremost bishop, and before his death he passed on his leadership to another bishop at Rome.

The fact that Rome had been the center of Christian persecution sanctified its Church with the aura of martyrdom. The weakening of political power in the west and the transfer of the capital from Rome, causing the bishop at Constantinople to be overshadowed by strong emperors, also helps explain the great powers which came to be associated with the Popes at Rome. Finally, the higher offices of the Church in the west were in the main filled by a remarkable series of outstanding administrators and constructive theologians, whose efforts tended to strengthen the power and authority of the bishop of Rome. By the year 600 the bishop at Rome had become the spiritual emperor of the western world. His supremacy in that area was undisputed.

The eastern Church. In the eastern part of the old empire, however, the Pope's claim to supremacy was disputed by the patriarch at Constantinople. In the latter part of the fourth century a bitter dispute arose between church leaders in Rome and in Constantinople. This controversy was carried on with little interruption until 1054, when the two branches of the Christian Church definitely split. The Christian Church in the west—now known as the Catholic Church—acknowledged the primacy of the Pope; the Greek Orthodox Church in the east admitted loyalty to no other official than the patriarch at Constantinople. Thus the Christian Church was sundered into two rival divisions, undoubtedly reducing its effectiveness and decreasing the possibility of cooperation between western and eastern Europe in the event of an emergency.

Growth of Christian doctrine. We have just seen how the early Christian communities, possessing little organization to start with, became slowly welded into a unified system with a numerous army of graded officials culminating in the all-powerful Pope. The clergy was now a distinct class set apart from the laymen, acting as an indispensable intermediary between God and man. While the administrative structure was being erected, the beliefs of the Church were being unified and organized.

Jesus in His day gave little heed to the development of an intellectualized creed for His followers. His religion was eminently simple. It was a way of life based on humility, love, and service to others. There were many converts, however, who brought to Christianity a training in, and a love for, Greek thought. Paul was one such convert. The converted Greek scholars wanted the teachings of Christ explained and systematized.

This process began with Paul, who stressed the divinity of Christ and interpreted His death as a miraculous atonement for man's sins. As the doctrine of the Trinity was gradually formulated, Christ was regarded as one of three persons in what was called the Godhead, consisting of God the Father, God the Son, and God the Holy Ghost. The creed of Christianity thus became more complex and subtle, and, in keeping with the trend toward closer unity in church organization, there was a tendency to develop one authoritative creed which all Christians had to accept.

While the process of creed-making was going on and dogma was in a fluid state, there were many differences of opinion over doctrinal matters. It will be impossible to discuss the many schools of thought (heresies) which differed from that of the Popes at Rome. One of the most important heresies was Arianism. The basic question at issue in the Arian controversy was the relative position of the three members of the Trinity. As expounded by Arius (256-336), a presbyter of Alexandria, Christ was not of a substance identical with God and was not coeternal with Him. So serious became the controversy between Arius and the followers of Athanasius, who espoused the more common view of the equality of God and the Son, that the emperor Constantine convened the famous Council of Nicaea in 325. Here the view of Athanasius was upheld. Christ was declared to be consubstantial with God the Father and coeternal. The beliefs upheld at the Council of Nicaea were formulated into the Nicene Creed. Some churches use this creed today, substantially unchanged although more than sixteen hundred years old.

The Church Fathers. Both the development of the Church's administrative hierarchy, which led to the formation of the papacy, and the creation of a body of authoritative dogma owed much to the great Church Fathers, who lived mainly in the fourth and fifth centuries. They were influential in shaping theology, which dealt in the main with the nature of Christ, the role the Church should play in this world, and what man had to do to obtain salvation. In the east the Greek Church owed much to the ability of such Fathers as Origen (185-254), who was a stern foe of heresy; Athanasius, whose views were accepted at the Council of Nicaea; and St. Basil (329?-379), who also combated various heresies. In the west the three greatest Church Fathers were St. Ambrose (340?-397), bishop of Milan; St. Jerome (340?-420), one of the greatest scholars of his day, most famous for his Latin translation of the Bible, called the Vulgate, which is still the official translation of the Catholic Church; and St. Augustine (354-430), the most important of all the Fathers. St. Augustine's book *The City of God* had tremendous influence upon the thought of the Middle Ages, and the views expounded in it became the foundation of much of the Church's theology.

Ritual. The service of worship in the early churches was plain and simple, consisting of prayer, the reading of the Scriptures, hymns, and preaching. Gradually, however, the service was transformed into beautiful and significant ceremonial. The simple commemoration of the Last Supper became a liturgical rite suffused with spiritual symbolism and central in the life of the Church: the Mass. Baptism became an important sacrament of purification. Other elements added to the ritual were the veneration of the saints, penance, and confession.

In the early period of Christianity the believer worshiped God and sought salvation largely through his own efforts. Following the growth of church organization and the crystallization of its dogma, the Church now constituted the indispensable intermediary between God and man. Without the Church the individual could not hope to approach God.

The "Fall of Rome"

Reasons for the collapse of the empire. It has been pointed out that beginning with the reign of the emperor Marcus Aurelius (161-180 A.D.) the empire began to decline rapidly in strength and prosperity. Some of the factors mentioned to explain this process were (1) an unsatisfactory system of imperial succession that made the emperorship the football of irresponsible army leaders, (2) the collapse of commerce, (3) the disappearance of the small-farmer class, and (4) the creation of a system of imperial despotism designed by such rulers as Diocletian to retard Rome's decline, which in the long run only served to accelerate the process of disintegration.

In her long history Rome had shown that it was possible for her to solve serious weaknesses. Faced with civil war in the first century B.C., she averted a catastrophe by substituting the principate for the republic. Again the century of revolution which followed the rule of the Antonine emperors was ended by the oriental despotism of Diocletian. It appeared for a time that Diocletian and Constantine would be able to reëstablish strong government and economic prosperity and that Rome would again be able to ride out the storm that threatened to destroy her. But it was not to be. Left to her own devices, perhaps imperial Rome could have attained a new period of tranquillity and power, but a new menace arose which shattered all attempts at Roman imperial reconstruction. This was the impact of barbarian invasions.

The Celts. Between 500 B.C. and the birth of Christ a blond, blue-eyed people called the Celts, forced westward by restless Germanic tribes, crossed the Rhine and Danube rivers, poured into Gaul, crossed the English Channel, and took possession of the British Isles. When the Romans conquered Gaul, its Celtic inhabitants became part of the Roman empire. In certain parts of France, such as Brittany, and in Wales, Ireland, and northern Scotland the Celtic language has been perpetuated with little change, because the Germanic tribes who followed the Celts into Europe never succeeded in establishing themselves in those areas as they did elsewhere. One of the traits of the Celts has been perpetuated down to this day—the use of mistletoe. The Celtic priests, called Druids, used it as a sacred symbol; today mistletoe plays a part in many people's Christmas festivities.

The Germanic tribes. The original homeland of the German people is a matter of conjecture. Some authorities have traced their wanderings back to the great steppes of Russia, which they inhabited about 2000 B.C. They early wandered from their homeland and pushed westward. Behind the retreating Celts the Germans spread out over a large area and gradually split into two great divisions, the Teutons and the Goths. The western group (the Teutons) was made up of such tribal peoples as the Franks, the Alamanni, and the Saxons, living in the main between the Rhine and Elbe and the Baltic Sea and upper Danube region. The eastern group consisted of the Ostrogoths, the Visigoths, and the Vandals. They settled for a time along the lower Danube and the Black Sea.

Germanic life and customs. Our earliest accounts of Germanic institutions are those written by Julius Caesar and by the Roman historian Tacitus in his *Germania.* The Germanic people were not savages. They were seminomads, midway between a pastoral and an agricultural economy. The early Roman accounts of the Germans tend to idealize them. Much praise is given for their physical strength and courage, their respect for women, and their freedom from the vices of sophisticated Roman society. Praise was to some extent warranted, but the Germans had their faults too. Their gluttony and heavy drinking were notorious, and their love of gambling caused many a German to wager even his freedom on the throw of the dice. Their respect for women did not prevent the men from having their wives do most of the menial work.

The form of marriage practiced by the Germans was usually monogamy. Adultery seems to have been rare. Tacitus, manlike, omits mention of faithful wives and refers only to what happened when the husband found out that his spouse was faithless. "Its punishment is instant, and at the pleasure of the husband. He cuts off the hair of the offender, strips her, and in the presence of her relations expels her from his house, and pursues her with stripes through the whole village."[4]

Another interesting custom of the Germans was that of listening to bards. On important feast days great storytellers would appear before the assembled warriors and begin to chant old tales handed down by word of mouth for hundreds of years. As the day wore on and night overtook the host, the atmosphere became more and more electric and dramatic as the bards gesticulated and shouted before the leaping flames of the great fire that cast an eerie glow over the audience. Such entertainments were held especially on the eve of battle, when they were designed to instill the old traditions of courage and fortitude into the warriors. The German people detested cowardice above all else. It was expected that no soldier would ever abandon his shield in flight.

The Germans took great care not to spoil their children. As Tacitus says, "No indulgence distinguishes the young master from the slave. They lie together amidst the same cattle, upon the same ground, till age separates, and valor marks out, the freeborn."[5]

The Germans had little money in the usual sense; cattle were used as a measure of value. They had little commerce and practically no manufacturing. In their pattern of culture they were probably about as far advanced as some of the more advanced North American Indian tribes. They worshiped a hierarchy of good and evil gods and goddesses, whom they supplicated and tried to appease. Among their deities were Wotan, the chief of the gods, Thiu and Thor, the gods of war and power respectively, and Freya, the goddess of fertility. The names of these ancient Germanic deities have been perpetuated in the names of four of our days of the week (Tuesday, Wednesday, Thursday, Friday).

German political practices. The Germans were sturdy individualists who enjoyed much personal freedom. This trait was reflected in their political institutions, for their kingships were not hereditary, nor were their kings despotic. The rulers were elected by the tribal assembly, a body composed of all the freemen of the tribe. The assembly also had a voice in determining such basic policies as peace and war.

Every great warrior leader had a retinue of followers, or *comites,* who were tied to him by personal loyalty. In return for their fighting services the chief gave his *comites* food, weapons, and shelter. The band was called the *comitatus*, or *gefolge*. The institution, placing strong emphasis upon personal loyalty, had an important bearing on the rise of feudalism, the characteristic political system of the Middle Ages.

Germanic law customs. Perhaps most interesting of all their original customs was the German system of law and justice. There were no written laws. Instead justice was meted out according to the immemorial custom of the tribe. This practice is at the bottom of the development of English common law, which is based not so much on laws passed by legislatures but rather upon a body of developing custom.

Most crimes and grievances were taken care of by the German people themselves, not by the king and his officials. If the injured party was paid compensation by the offender, everybody was satisfied. The principle of compensation was the basis for the whole system of justice. It was rather handy, too. If you entered a free-for-all fight, you could keep in mind a schedule of just how much injury you could afford to inflict on your foes. There was a stipulated payment if you bit someone's ear off, so much for twisting off his nose, and a certain sum for breaking his leg. These payments were called *bots*. In the event that you should lose your temper and actually kill your opponent, you would be called on to pay *wergeld*, a large sum. Incidentally, it cost forty times as much to kill a noble as a common man.

On certain rare occasions the state, that is, the king and his officials, would intervene because the crime was *botless*, that is, it was of such a grave nature that compensation could not be paid. If someone were charged with this crime, a trial would be held, at which the defendant had to produce oath helpers who would swear to his good character. This was called compurgation, a practice also used in settling *bots* in private quarrels. In the event that the defendant was a hardened criminal and could not obtain oath helpers, he had to stand the ordeal. There was little chance of escaping scot free. Three ordeals were used: hot water, hot iron, and cold water. In the first, the defendant had to plunge his arm into a vessel of boiling water and lift out a small stone. A few days were given for his scalded hand to heal; if it had not done so, he was guilty. In the second, the culprit had to walk blindfolded with bare feet across a floor on which had been placed pieces of red-hot metal. If he succeeded in avoiding the hot metal he was innocent. In the third type of ordeal, the culprit was tightly bound and thrown into a stream. If he floated he was innocent; if he sank he was guilty. No person was given any of these ordeals if there was not a strong presumption of his guilt.

The early Germanic invasions. As early as 113 B.C. Germanic tribes had endeavored to break through Rome's frontiers but were turned back. Again in the time of Julius Caesar a group of Germanic tribes tried to conquer eastern Gaul, but their invasion was frustrated by the military genius of Caesar. For a time the Roman rulers planned to conquer and incorporate in their empire all the Germans living between the Rhine and the Elbe rivers, but in the reign of Augustus the design collapsed when a Roman army suffered a serious defeat at the hands of the Germans in 9 A.D. From that time on, the Romans were generally content to hold their frontier at the Rhine-Danube line.

For a century and a half the Germanic tribes caused little trouble, but during the reign of Marcus Aurelius (161-180) the Germans began making determined efforts to get into the empire. Their attempts continued for one hundred fifty years. The Franks invaded Gaul, and the Goths forced the Romans to cede them territory to the northeast of the empire. Few of the invaders, however, were allowed to remain south of the Rhine-Danube frontier, and after the year 300 the Germans remained quiescent for seventy-five years.

But though marauding German bands were ejected from the empire, thousands of German people found a new home among the Romans. During the many centuries in which the Romans and Germans faced each other across the northern frontier, there was much peaceful contact between the two peoples. Many Germans found employment in the Roman legions, large numbers captured in battle were brought to Rome as servants and slaves, and thousands were allowed to settle in the vacant lands of the empire. So far the Romans had been able to keep the Germanic people under control by force of arms, by great walls along the frontiers, by practicing a "divide and rule" policy, utilizing one German tribe to fight against other tribes, by paying the Germans tribute when they got restless, and by over-

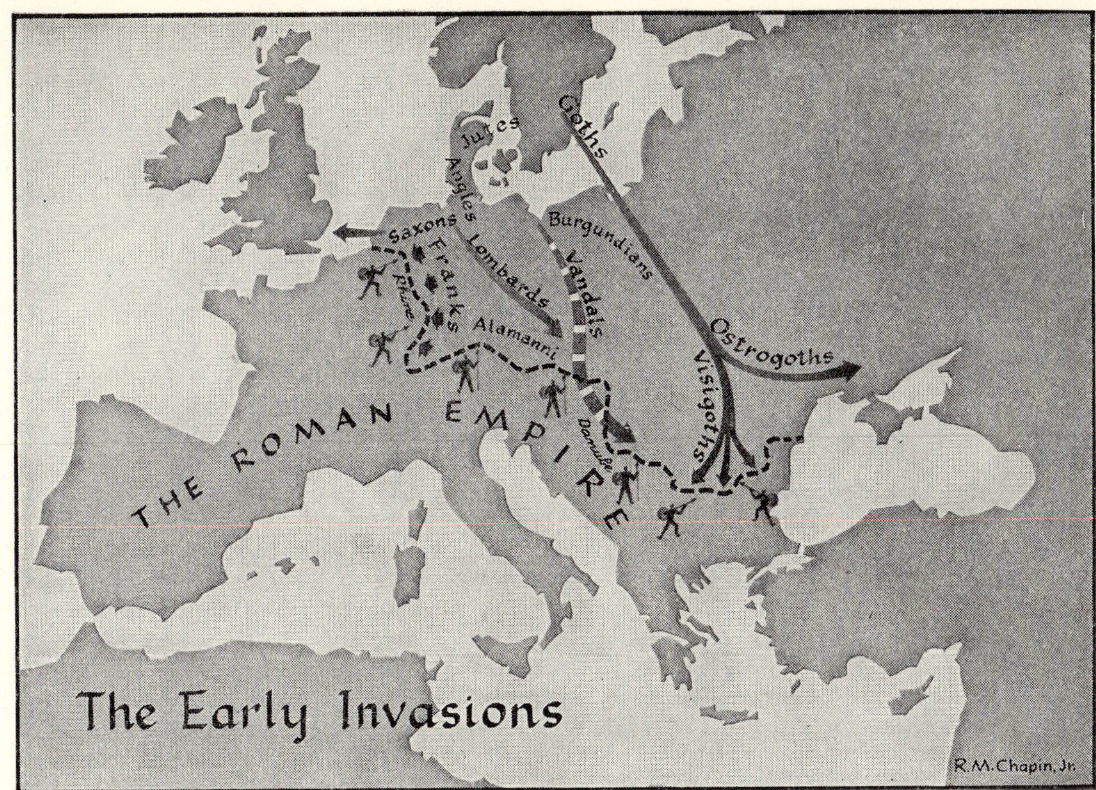

awing them by the magnificence and prestige of Roman culture.

In the last decades of the fourth century, however, these methods proved ineffectual. The period of the great invasions commenced (375-500). The basic factor behind the restlessness of the Germans seems to have been their land hunger. Their numbers were increasing, much of their land consisted of forest and swamp, and their methods of tillage were not efficient. Another impelling cause of the invasions was the German love of adventure and the call of the southern lands of the empire where riches and booty were plentiful.

The Huns. In addition to the German tribes, there was another restless people, the Huns. They were mounted nomads from central Asia, who on many occasions throughout history swept into eastern Europe on marauding expeditions. We know very little about these Huns, where they originated, or what prompted them to move westward relentlessly. Reaching Europe in the fourth century they struck terror into the German people, who stood between the Huns and the Roman empire. Old chronicles tell us of the terrible savagery and repulsive appearance of the Huns. They are described as having thick bodies, legs bowed from living in the saddle, flat noses, and small pig-like eyes. Mounted on wiry ponies, the Huns were able to cover great distances in an amazingly short time. "They lived on horseback, and so well did they ride and so much of a piece did they seem with their horses, that all who saw them were reminded at once of Centaurs. Even in their food they did not get away from horses, for they subsisted largely on mare's milk and horseflesh, which they 'cooked' by placing it beneath the cloth that served as a saddle and relying upon the natural results of friction—a method to be recommended only by its simplicity."[6]

Adrianople. In the year 372 the Huns crossed the Volga and soon subjugated the Ostrogoths. Terrified at the prospect of being conquered by the savage Hun horsemen, the Visigoths begged the Roman officials to allow them to seek safety in the empire. Permission was granted, and in 376 a large concourse of people crossed the Danube into Roman territory. The Visigoths had been promised food and lands, but these were not given

This Hunnish wagon (reconstructed) was ample for moving supplies and provided a home for the nomads at the same time.

in sufficient quantities, and further, the Roman officials irritated the newcomers by imposing many petty restrictions upon them. In desperation the Visigoths turned upon the Roman officials and began to pillage the land. To meet the threat, the emperor Valens led an army to give battle to the rebellious Germans. In the ensuing battle at Adrianople (378) the legions were totally defeated and the emperor Valens was killed.

Wholesale barbarian invasions. Adrianople was a momentous event. The legend of the invincibility of the Roman legions had now been destroyed. The battle marks the beginning of a terrible period of chaos lasting one hundred fifty years, in which barbarian tribes moved almost at will on the empire and completely destroyed the old governmental system in the western part of the empire. For a few years, under the strong rule of the emperor Theodosius, the victorious Visigoths remained quiescent, but following his death in 395 they began to migrate and pillage under their leader Alaric. After much fighting and wandering Alaric invaded Italy, and in 410 his followers sacked Rome. In the same year Alaric died. His successor made peace with the Roman officials and was assigned a large tract of territory in southern Gaul. Here the Visigoths created a powerful kingdom, which at its height covered all of southern Gaul and most of Spain.

The march of the Visigoths under Alaric was the signal for wholesale invasion by the Germans all along the northern frontier. In 406 Roman defenses collapsed in the Rhine area, and a flood of Germans crossed into Gaul. Vandals, Alamanni, Franks, and Burgundians pushed aside all resistance and settled in the empire. The Vandals first made their way through Gaul to Spain, but pressure from Visigoths who also entered the peninsula caused them to cross to Africa, where they established a strong kingdom under their leader Gaiseric (see map, page 241). The high point of their power came in 455 when the Vandals crossed over from Africa and sacked Rome. Their kingdom was not destined to endure, for the great Justinian, sixth-century Roman emperor in the east, later crushed it with his armies.

The Burgundians settled in the Rhone valley, but their kingdom, like those of the Vandals and the Visigoths, did not last. Reaching a high degree of prosperity in the early fifth century (see map, page 241), it soon passed under the rule of another Germanic people, the Franks, who gradually conquered all of northern Gaul. We shall see later how the Franks were, with the exception of the Angles and Saxons in England, the only Germanic tribe entering the confines of the Roman empire to perpetuate their kingdom into the early Middle Ages.

Defeat of the Huns. While the Germanic peoples were relentlessly moving and cutting their way through the western part of the empire, a new danger arose which for a time menaced both the Germans and the Roman provincial people alike. The Huns under their leader Attila left their homes along the lower Danube and marched through Germany and crossed the Rhine in 451. In the great battle of Châlons Germans and Romans fought side by side to stem the Hunnish invaders (see map opposite). Attila was forced to withdraw from Gaul. For a brief time he menaced Italy, but in 453 his death lessened the power of the Huns. Leaderless, the nomad bands broke up, and their power quickly evaporated.

Rome during the invasions. During the period of turbulence, what was happening to the imperial authority at Rome? Following the death of the capable Theodosius (395), the empire was divided between his two sons, Arcadius in the east and Honorius in the west. The sack of Rome in 410 by Alaric and again in 455 by Gaiseric did not destroy Roman civilization (although the city was plundered), but Roman rule grew increasingly decadent and powerless. Honorius, who ruled as emperor in Italy from 395 to 423, was utterly incompetent, and his successors were mere puppet em-

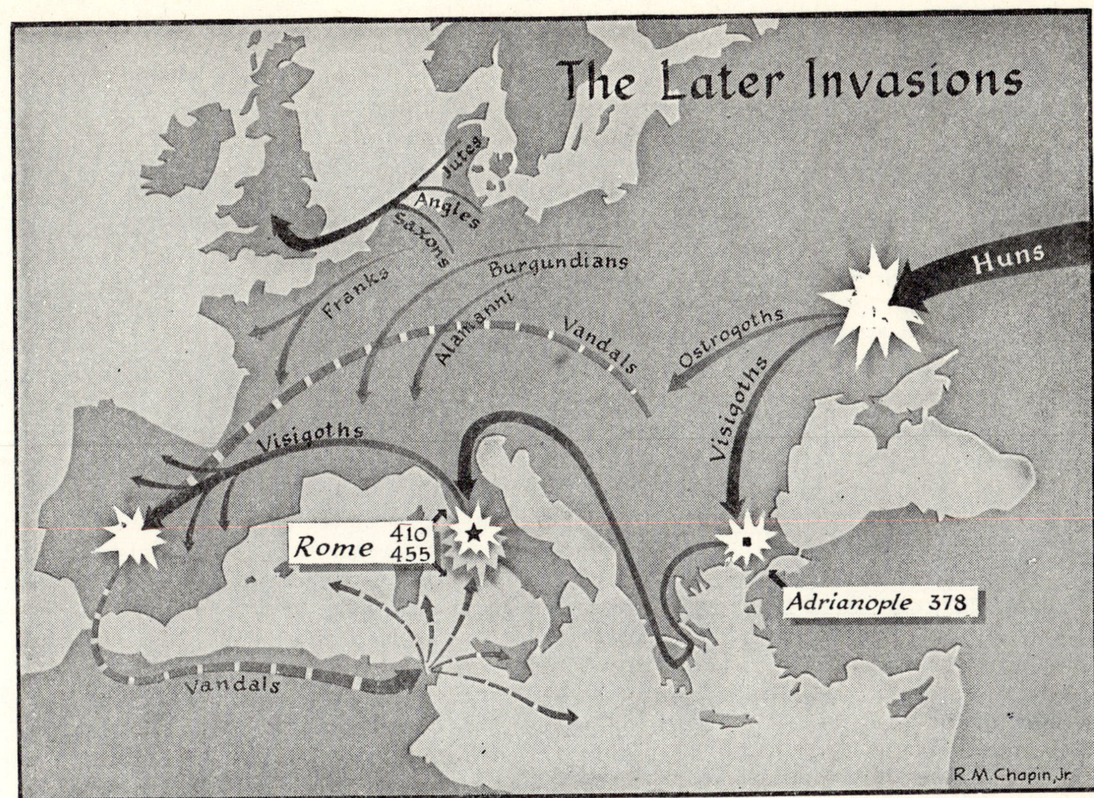

perors. The real power was exercised by leaders of the mercenary soldiers, whose ranks were now mainly German.

For seventeen years following the second gutting of Rome in 455 by the Vandals the choice of the emperor was dictated by a German general in the imperial army. After his death the role of political boss in Italy was assumed by Orestes, a former officer in Attila's army, who placed his small son on the throne. Put there by the consent of the ruffianly soldiery, the new emperor was satirically dubbed Romulus Augustulus (Little Augustus).

476 A.D. Three years later Orestes lost favor with the army, and another leader of the soldiers, a German named Odoacer (or Odovacar) came to the fore. Odoacer, seeing no reason for carrying on the sham of emperors, deposed little Augustus and proclaimed himself head of the government. His action, taken in 476 A.D., just short of a century after the battle of Adrianople, is usually regarded as the most convenient event to mark the fall of Rome. In reality this date is no more important than several others that might be selected, such as 410 or 455. No single date for the fall of Rome is really accurate, since the fall was a long and gradual process. Notwithstanding such considerations, the date 476 A.D. is perhaps the one best date to represent the end of the Roman empire in the west, for it marks the end of the long line of emperors inaugurated by Augustus and the outright control of Italian politics by Germanic

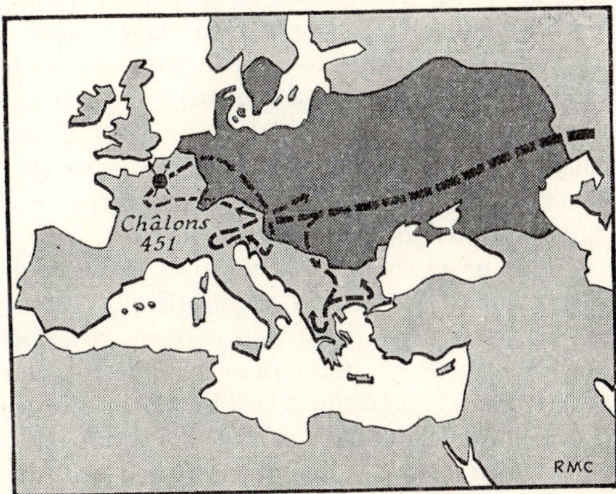

The Huns under Attila created a large if ephemeral empire which threatened to engulf all Europe before they were turned back at Châlons.

leaders. It is true that Odoacer did accept in theory the overlordship of the eastern emperor in Constantinople, who, now that the emperors in Rome were no more, considered Italy as one of his administrative divisions. But in reality Constantinople had little power in the west, which was now in the hands of the Germans.

Theodoric's kingdom in Italy. We have seen how the Visigoths created a strong kingdom in Spain while their kinfolk, the Ostrogoths, were under the harsh rule of the Huns. Following the defeat of Attila at Châlons the Ostrogoths were free to follow their own inclinations. For twenty years after their freedom from the Huns the Ostrogoths seemed uncertain what to do, but in 476 a young Ostrogothic noble named Theodoric became their leader and in no time galvanized his people into action. Theodoric is one of the most important of all the early German leaders. At the age of seven he was sent to Constantinople as a hostage. There he learned to admire and appreciate the learning and splendor of the great city. After receiving a good education, he went back to his people at the age of eighteen and became their leader. It was Theodoric's desire to lead his people so that they could get some of the good things he himself had learned to enjoy while a captive in Constantinople.

Zeno, emperor in the east, feared the ambitious Theodoric and was glad to offer him the commission of reconquering for the imperial authority the province of Italy, now in the hands of the German leader Odoacer. Accepting the offer, Theodoric in 488 led more than 100,000 of his people into Italy. Three years of hard fighting followed. Odoacer sued for peace and was treacherously murdered. Theodoric now established a strong Gothic kingdom in Italy, which lasted until its destruction in 554 by Narses, one of Justinian's generals from the eastern empire.

Under its Ostrogothic king Italy enjoyed a generation of peace and tranquillity. There was little change in the structure of the Roman government. Every attempt was made to preserve Roman civilization. At Theodoric's court at Ravenna Latin was used, the Roman law was retained, and coins were issued in the name of the eastern emperor, for Theodoric regarded himself as an imperial official. This wise statesman maintained schools and tried to repair the Roman aqueducts. Following the death of Theodoric in 526, civil war and factionalism broke out in Italy, paving the way for its conquest by Justinian.

The Lombards. A few years after the destruction of the Ostrogothic kingdom by Justinian's armies, a new wave of Germanic invaders, the Lombards, poured into northern Italy. They are reputed to have been the most brutal and fierce of all the Germans. A history written in the eighth century relates the story of one Lombard king, Alboin, who had a drinking cup fashioned from the skull of one of the enemies he had killed with his own hand. It is also claimed that Alboin forced his dead rival's daughter to marry him and compelled her to drink from her father's skull. The insult had a sequel, for later the wife of Alboin got revenge upon her brutal husband by artistically arranging for his murder. Entering Italy in 568, the fierce Lombards overran most of Italy and established a powerful kingdom which endured until 774.

The barbarians in England. When the great German invasions began, Roman authorities began withdrawing the legions from the outposts of their empire. The last Roman troops left England in 407. They left the island defenseless, and within a generation swarms of Angles, Saxons, and Jutes from the base of the Danish peninsula and the German lowlands invaded Britain and took possession of most of the country (see map, page 237). The Germanic conquest in England seems to have been more devastating than in any other area of the empire. Roman civilization seems to have been almost completely obliterated. Life in England during the fifth and sixth centuries was a tragic experience for its Celtic inhabitants, who were often butchered or driven to the western highlands of the island. Not only was there fighting between the German invaders and the Celts, but the Germanic tribes also struggled among themselves.

The demise of the Roman empire. In less than one hundred years after the Germanic tribes had swarmed over the Rhine-Danube frontier in 406, the western Roman world saw a Visigothic kingdom created in Spain, Vandal tribes established in north Africa, the Burgundians in possession of southeastern Gaul, the Franks settled in the northern half of that country, and a Gothic kingdom flourishing in Italy, first under Odoacer, then under Theodoric (see map, page 241). The historian may have difficulty in deciding just what event, if any, should be singled out as the fall of Rome, but by 500 A.D. there can be no question that the Roman empire in the west was no more.

Fundamental causes of Roman collapse. There have been many explanations advanced to explain the great catastrophe. Some historians rely mainly upon political factors as the key to the problem, such as the graft of an entrenched bureaucracy, the unsatisfactory system of imperial succession, and the decline in Roman patriotism. Some also emphasize that the empire was doomed to extinction because its civilization—its art, wealth, villas, education, security—belonged to the upper classes, not to the people. A reasonably good standard of living and an effective influence in government were denied the common people. Corruption and final collapse is the usual fate of governments run by bureaucrats whose actions are not tempered by the power of the common people, under a system of self-government, to remove from office and even punish corrupt officials. Perhaps it is no exaggeration to assert that the entire history of mankind can be interpreted as a struggle for liberty. Again and again, as we follow man through time, that theme dominates history.

Historians with an economic outlook present us with a long list of causes for the fall of Rome, among them currency debasement, soil exhaustion, and the disappearance of a free peasantry. Other students seem to prefer a biological explanation which stresses the evils of race mixture. They maintain that the Romans were a superior people and that their mixing with "inferior races" weakened their physical virility and destroyed their intellectual creativeness. There are few authorities who accept the thesis that mixture of peoples results in a weak racial product.

Another common view is that Rome declined because of its immorality, a view held especially by the early Christians. However, the period when vice was most rampant in Rome was from 50 to 100 A.D., and with the exception of that period the Romans can hardly be regarded as more immoral than any other people of their time. It was hardly immorality that brought about the collapse of Rome; rather it was a weakening of morale, or, as Sir Gilbert Murray puts it, the Romans "lost their nerve." One of the most competent students of Roman history believes that the ultimate failure of Rome must be attributed to her too complete success. She conquered all rivals, easily acquired wealth and power, and imported a ready-made culture from conquered peoples. Indolence and self-satisfaction resulted. "Thus . . . in the case of the Roman empire, a steady decline of civilization is not to be traced to physical degeneration, or to any debasement of blood in the higher races due to slavery, or to political and economic conditions, but rather to a changed attitude of men's minds."[7]

Causation in history. As we look back on one thousand years of Roman history, questions must arise: Why did Rome rise and fall? What started her on her career of expansion and imperial destiny? What initiated her decline and final collapse? Already in the Prologue to this volume we have asked the same questions in our study of the development of civilizations and their decline. Civilizations seem to follow an organic parallel: infancy, youth, vigorous manhood, old age, senility, and oblivion. In connection with this chapter on the fall of Rome it seems wise to ponder these facts and to ask again—is there a cyclical movement inherent in the history of civilizations?

Theories of historical cycles. Much thought has been expended on this interesting problem, with the result that some scholars maintain that the story of civilization is made up of a series of civilizations with "life analogies." Perhaps the most significant of these thinkers is Oswald Spengler, whose work we discussed in the Prologue (page 11). In *Decline of the West,* which he wrote during the First World War, he paints the whole panorama of human experience and sees it as the manifestation of eight super-cycles of civilization: the Chinese, the Babylonian, the East Indian, the Graeco-Roman, the Arabian, the Mayan of Mexico, and the western of our own day. In a pessimistic vein Spengler declares that our civilization reached its zenith about 1800 and during the past 150 years has been rapidly declining. Another important interpreter of the historical process is the English scholar Arnold J. Toynbee. In his profound analysis of twenty-six great civilizations in *A Study of History,* he concludes that civilizations break down through a failure of creative power in the creative minority. Losing that power the minority can no longer inspire the lethargic majority, which consequently brings about a loss of social unity.

The linear theory. The linear theory accepted by some historians is much more optimistic. In brief, the linear theory envisages human experience as a stream of water that begins its journey as a small rivulet. As it flows on through the ages many peoples and civilizations enrich and increase its waters. The important thing is not that civilizations come and go but that all of them contribute to the stream of history, which gets broader and richer as time goes on.

Schools of historical thought. The problem of historical causation is a fascinating one. The beginning student, however, must content himself at first with becoming conversant with the basic facts of history. Only then can he commence the much more difficult task of seeking to understand the forces and processes which explain, or at least throw light upon, the unfolding of history. But there are a few general concepts or schools that the beginning student of history can sometimes find useful in understanding what he reads.

The political school, for example, maintains that history is past politics, that its most important theme and its most significant facts relate to wars, alliances, treaties, and diplomatic intrigue. In studying the collapse of Rome, the historians of this school would emphasize the part the military commanders played in dictating the succession of the emperors and the gradual development of a despotic oriental rule.

The great-man school, associated particularly with the British historian Thomas Carlyle, stresses the part that outstanding leaders have played in determining the course of human events. Adherents of this viewpoint believe that personality is all-important in history. They would maintain that Rome ceased to produce the right kind of leadership, that soft living and graft destroyed the class which had once given the state incomparable generals, administrators, and lawgivers.

The economic, or materialistic, conception of history maintains that man's imperative need for food and clothing, his zealousness for economic gain, and the many resulting institutions associated with the production, distribution, and consumption of goods constitute the mainspring of historical events. The economic historians can find much in the history of Rome to back their theories. The collapse of the sturdy peasant class and the advent of the *latifundia* with their servile cultivators, the destruction of the middle class (or, as we would say today, the white-collar class) because of high taxation, the unfortunate tinkering with the currency which led to violent and unpredictable fluctuations in prices, the inability of Rome to work out a satisfactory economic system after the wiping out of its small farm population—all these were significant economic causes for the end of Roman supremacy.

The geographical school, commented upon in the Introduction, stresses the interrelation between natural resources and physical environment on the one hand and man's institutions and activities on the other. It would point to the possible importance of the diminution in rainfall in the Roman empire and its effect upon crop yields. Then again it would direct attention to the problem of erosion, which apparently became quite serious in certain areas and influenced the imperial economic structure.

Other schools focus their attention upon the influence of ideas, which may be called the intellectual interpretation of history; or upon the development of pure science and technology, the scientific school of history; or upon the anthropological approach, which stresses the importance of such cultural processes as diffusion (see page 7 in the Prologue), in the development of civilization. And the spiritual, or teleological, school believes that behind the movements of history is the guidance of a Divine Will, which directs human destinies to conform with some great cosmic plan or goal.

Trends in interpretation of history. In reviewing historical schools or various interpretations of history, we can say that most historians agree that in the past political facts in history have received too much emphasis. That type can be called "drum and trumpet history." Many historians also agree that in any one period of history one or more factors—economic or religious or geographic, and so on—will be predominant and will then in the next period give way to another set of factors. More and more, historians today are recognizing that the historical process is a complex product resulting from the interaction of all the various factors we have mentioned.

Reference to the various schools of history has given us a glance into the field of historical causation. History may be made more interesting and perhaps more meaningful if we try occasionally to appraise and analyze events in terms of the various schools of history and to see which sets of factors operate to bring about certain events.

The Fusion of Cultures

T*he nature of the invasions.* Now that we have traced the various streams of German invaders that broke through the frontiers and established themselves in the Roman empire, it is essential that something be said about the character of these invasions. Did the Germans annihilate large sections of the Roman population? Was there much pillaging and looting? Was the powerful civilization that Rome had created destroyed?

In answering such questions it is important to understand that infiltration of Germans into the empire had been going on several hundred years before the great invasions of the fifth century. Thousands of Germans had been permitted to settle on vacant lands or serve in the legions. Before the terrible chaos of the fifth century a process of culture fusion, or blending, was taking place peacefully and imperceptibly. The Germans living in the empire were taking on the culture of the more civilized Romans around them. If the pressure of the Huns on the Gothic tribes had not become so acute in the fourth century, it is probable that the infiltration of the Germans would have continued to be peaceful. But the menace of the Huns accelerated the movement of the German tribes, and what had formerly been a rather gradual and peaceful activity soon became a pell-mell attack on the frontiers.

Although superficially the great invasions seemed entirely different from the former peaceful infiltration of the Germans, they were not fundamentally different in character. It is true that there was at times ruthless pillaging by the invaders, and in certain sections of the

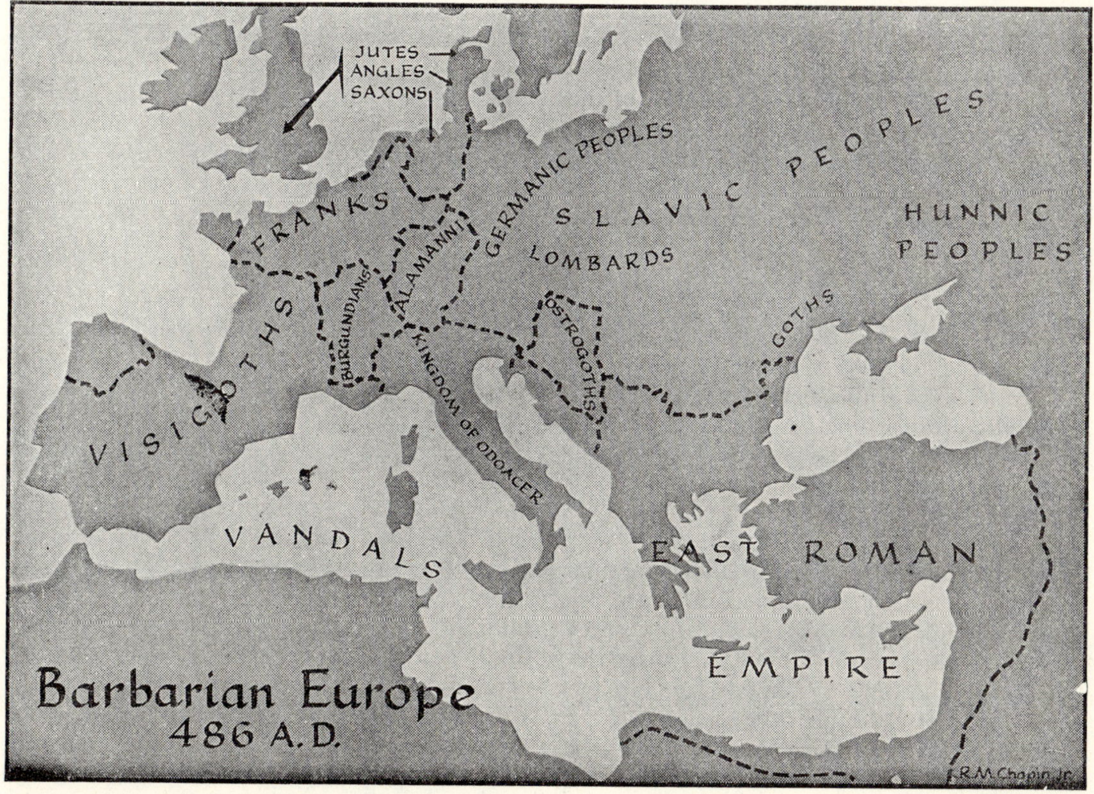

empire, especially in Britain, Roman civilization was entirely wiped out. The Germans seized much of Roman land; perhaps as much as two thirds exchanged ownership. In the main, however, the blending and fusing of the two peoples, which had been going on before the period of the great invasions, continued without serious interruption. The barbarian invasions, in other words, must not be regarded as cataclysmic.

In most of the areas of the empire the invaders represented a minority of the population. Although they were the political enemies of the Roman government, they admired Roman civilization and tried to assimilate it. This explains why the invader soon began to lose his Germanic speech, customs, and religion. Most of the Germanic leaders continued to use Roman administrative agencies, employed members of the old civil service, and perpetuated the use of Latin in governmental affairs. That is why there is hardly a trace of the Germanic languages in Italy, Gaul, and Spain. While the invader was assimilating Roman civilization, life for the people of the empire went on much as usual.

Civilization during the Dark Ages. While the new and the old were being blended, there was a decline in civilization, and trade and commerce suffered a setback. For nearly five hundred years after the great invasions of the fifth century European civilization was unsettled. It retrogressed rather than advanced. But the period of the so-called Dark Ages was one of preparation, in which a new civilization, even more fruitful than the old, compounded of both Germanic and Roman elements, was being evolved.

The immediate effect, however, was the decline of city life. Abandoned Roman cities soon collapsed in ruins. There was also a serious decline in learning, art, and architecture. Soon there were few scholars who knew how to write good Latin. The Bishop of Tours, writing in the sixth century, lamented, "In these times when the practice of letters declines, nay, rather perishes in the cities of Gaul, there has been found no scholar trained in the art of ordered composition to present in prose or verse a picture of the things that have befallen. . . ."[8] Along with the decline of literary Latin went a decline of the knowledge of Greek, as contact with Constantinople and the eastern part of the empire was broken off.

Scholars of the transition period. Enlightenment and learning, of course, did not entirely die out in western Europe. The most important scholar in the west in the early sixth century was Boethius, who lived in Italy and was a member of a noble Roman family. Having received an excellent education, he entered the government service of the Ostrogothic king Theodoric, when the latter established his kingdom in Italy. In his spare time Boethius busied himself making Latin translations of Greek works. His translations were the only source of Greek learning available to medieval scholars until, six hundred years later, as we shall see, more complete accounts were obtained through Arabic sources. Boethius' importance is as a transmitter of classical thought to the Middle Ages. Unjustly accused of treachery by Theodoric, Boethius was thrown into prison and while awaiting execution wrote the famous *Consolations of Philosophy*. The work deals with the basic questions of man's existence and was one of the most popular philosophical treatises during the Middle Ages. It is still being read by students of philosophy today.

Another important scholar, a contemporary of Boethius, was Cassiodorus. He too served Theodoric for a time, retiring to found two monasteries. He devoted the remainder of his long life (he lived to be over ninety) to the preservation and collection of learning. He was not what we call a productive scholar, but he preserved a vast amount of classical learning. Cassiodorus did much to make monasteries centers of learning, for he encouraged the monks to copy and transcribe valuable manuscripts. Soon practically all monasteries had scriptoriums, departments concerned exclusively with the copying of manuscripts.

Another scholar of some importance was Isidore of Seville, who was bishop of Seville from 600 to 636. His most important work was his *Etymologies*, a fascinating encyclopedia that included a jumble of queer odds and ends taken from classical sources. It reminds one of Pliny's *Natural History*. Isidore was an important preserver of knowledge, and for three hundred years his *Etymologies* was a standard work of reference in the western world.

In the early Middle Ages there was a dearth of good historians. The only worthy predecessor of the Venerable Bede, who will be discussed shortly, was Gregory of Tours. Living in the sixth century, this bishop has left us the only good source material for the early history of the Franks, one of the most important of the Germanic tribes which broke through the Roman frontiers and poured into the empire in the chaotic fifth century.

The role of the Church. As the Roman world-state declined and finally collapsed, it seemed to many people in the fifth century as though the end of the world had come. A great empire with its law, its roads and commerce, its cities and culture was dissolving; civilization as men knew it was being drowned in the barbarian flood that had broken through the defensive dikes. One observer in far off Bethlehem in the Holy Land lamented: "A remnant of us survives not by our merits, but by the mercy of God. Innumerable savage peoples have occupied the whole of Gaul. All that lies between the Alps and the Pyrenees, the Rhine and the Ocean is devastated by the barbarian. . . . Who could believe that Rome, on her own soil, fights no longer for glory, but for her existence; and no longer even fights, but purchases her life with gold and precious things."[9]

That this melancholy observation was exaggerated has been made clear in our refutation of the catastrophic explanation of the so-called fall of Rome. The process of infiltration had been going on for a long time, and to many Germans the empire was "not an enemy but a career."[10] The willingness of most of the barbarian invaders to respect and even imitate the culture they had seized helps explain the preservation of much that was Roman. But in addition there was at work a powerful and positive force assisting the fusion between conqueror and conquered and cushioning the shock of the impact between German and Roman. This was the Christian Church.

When the Roman empire fell in the West before the barbarians, the Church in a large measure was not part of the disaster. During the past two centuries, side by side with the Roman governmental structure, it had built up its own organization and developed its distinctive official hierarchy. It was an autonomous organization possessing great land holdings which gave it sustaining economic power. Furthermore, it had the best trained minds of the time, provided by the best and often the only schools available. And lastly, the Church lived on because of the power of its ideology. This spiritual force was all the stronger because it was immaterial and psychological, capable of unobtrusively capturing and directing the simple and uneducated minds of the Germanic invaders. As the uncouth Germans were converted, therefore, they became less warlike and more amenable to Roman culture, and they came to be supporters of law and order.

In the field of government, the Church assumed many secular responsibilities when the Roman empire collapsed. This is illustrated in the famous incident of Pope Leo I and Attila the Hun. Attila was dissuaded by the Pope from attacking Rome. The political power of the papacy was especially increased during the pontificate of Gregory the Great (590-604), who assumed the responsibility of defending Rome from the Lombards. Gregory, it is said, "ordered the police, regulated markets, coined money, maintained civil and criminal courts, repaired the walls and aqueducts, supported schools and hospitals, commanded the militia, and defended the city in case of attack."[11]

The Church's missionary activity. Another great contribution of the early Church was its missionary activity, which was not only a Christianizing movement but one which disseminated civilization. One of the earliest Christian missionaries to the Germans was Ulfilas (about 311-383), who spent forty years among the Visigoths. He translated the Bible into Gothic, an important event, for heretofore the Germans had had no satisfactory system of writing. The labors of Ulfilas were the beginning of the spread of Christianity among many of the German tribes. The type of faith propagated, however, was of the Arian variety. As we have already noted, this was an heretical creed and came to be the religion of all the Germanic tribes in the empire with the notable exception of the Franks. The adoption by this powerful tribe of the official Roman Catholic Christianity espoused by the Pope was to have momentous consequences during the period of critical transition from ancient to medieval Europe.

Another great figure in early missionary work was St. Patrick, who was born in Britain about 389. He became a monk in Gaul and later went to Ireland as a missionary. As a result of his activities Christianity obtained a strong foothold in Ireland, centering around

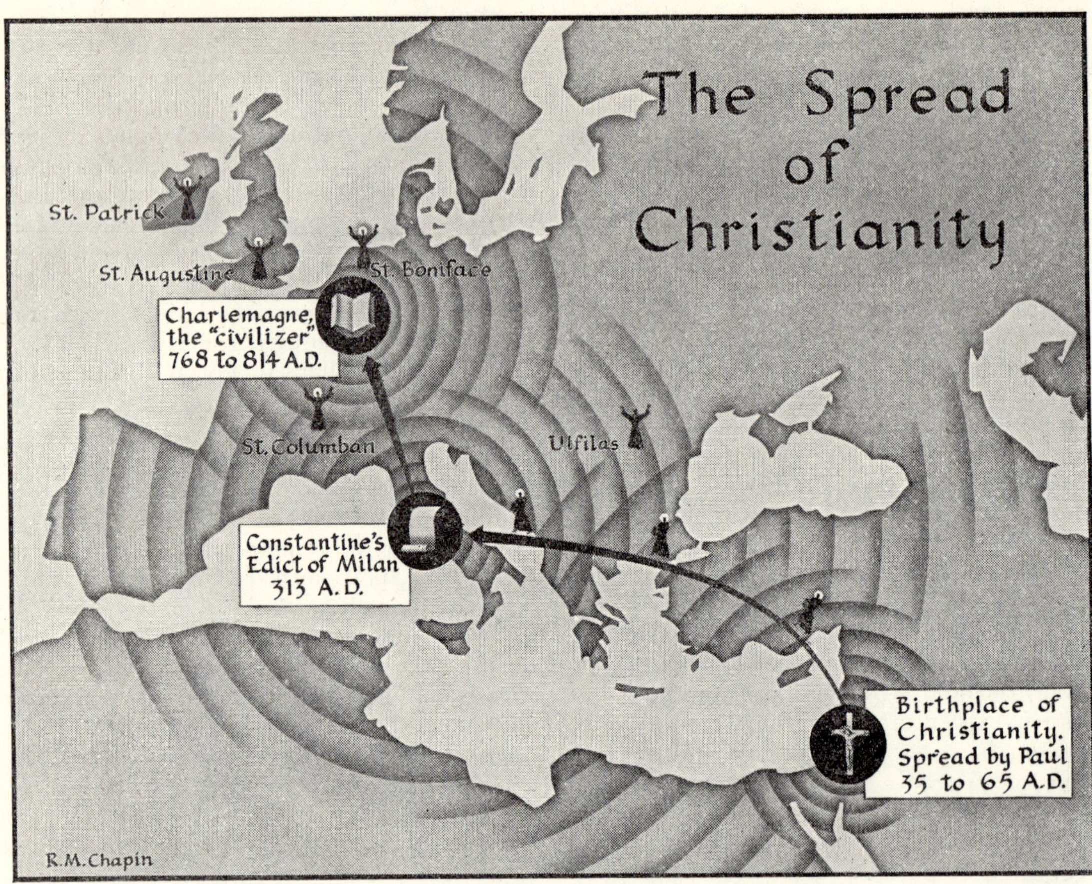

the monasteries. From these institutions went a stream of monks to Scotland, north England, the kingdom of the Franks, and Italy. These Celtic missionaries were of vital importance in spreading civilization among the Germanic tribes and assisting the revival of culture. Among the most important was St. Columba (521-597), who went from Ireland to Scotland, where in 563 he established a monastery on the island of Iona off the west coast. A center for the diffusion of piety and learning, this institution for two hundred years well deserved the title of the Nursery of Saints. It was from Iona that there came the monks who founded the famous monastery of Lindisfarne on Holy Island off the northern coast of England, and it, too, was for many years a vigorous center of civilization.

Irish missionaries were active on the European continent in the late sixth and seventh centuries. About 585 A.D. St. Columban (c. 540-615) and twelve other Irish monks went to the kingdom of the Franks and settled in Burgundy. There they were granted a site for an abbey which was built at Luxeuil. This monastery with its 600 workers became one of the great monastic centers of western Europe, from which at least fifty new monasteries were founded. St. Columban was also active in his missionary labors in what is now Switzerland, and he finally crossed the Alps into Italy, where he established the last of his monasteries, Bobbio, in the Apennines. As we will note shortly, these Irish monks eagerly pursued scholarship and their monasteries were repositories of priceless manuscripts.

These carriers of Celtic Christianity from Ireland were not the only missionaries, for the Church at Rome was also very active. One of its most significant and successful missions was that of St. Augustine to England. In 596 Pope Gregory the Great, who was active in furthering missionary work, sent a mission to the small kingdom of Kent. St. Augustine converted its king, and thus Kent became the first Anglo-Saxon state officially to accept Christianity. From its center at Canterbury, Roman Christianity eventually spread all over

England, and finally the Celtic Church that had been founded by St. Patrick acknowledged the primacy of Rome.

The English Church prospered. In a sense it paid back its debt to Pope Gregory by taking an important part in the expansion of Christianity on the continent. The greatest missionary figure from England in the eighth century was a Benedictine monk named St. Boniface, who spent thirty-five years among the German tribes. Starting his missionary labors first in Frisia in 715, he went to Rome in 718 to receive instructions for his mission in Germany. St. Boniface became known as "the Apostle of Germany" establishing many new abbeys and bishoprics and crowning his labors by the establishment of the monastery of Fulda in Thuringia. This establishment was patterned after Monte Cassino, the great Benedictine monastery in Italy, and was to become the center of learning and the model for most of the other monasteries in Germany. As we shall see in Chapter 12—in connection with our discussion of the rise of the Frankish empire—St. Boniface also played an important role in politics. Finally, feeling that his work had been done in Germany, he returned to Frisia, the scene of his first missionary work, where he suffered a martyr's death in 755 at the hands of pagan pirates.

Roman Catholic missionaries were also active in Scandinavia and among the Slavic peoples of eastern Europe. And as will be shown in the following chapter, the eastern or Orthodox Church under its Patriarch in Constantinople was no less active in its missionary endeavors. It was the pioneer in Christianizing the Hungarians and Bohemians and above all those people among the East Slavs who came to be known as Russians.

Monasteries. Besides the Church's assumption of political obligations and its missionary work, the founding of monasteries was another very important activity in furthering the fusion of cultures and the preservation of learning in the early Middle Ages. We have already seen how Cassiodorus helped make the monasteries centers of learning, so let us go back for a moment and examine the nature of the monasteries and their growth.

The monastic way of life originated long before the birth of Christianity. Some men in all ages have believed that the world around them was sinful and that the routine of life detracted from one's ability to serve his God and achieve spiritual serenity. The only solution they saw was to isolate themselves from materialistic preoccupations of the world. Christian monasticism originated in the East in the third century and was influenced in its development by such monastic leaders as St. Anthony and Basil the Great.

The monasteries were agricultural pioneers in Europe. In the early Middle Ages much of the land was forest or swamp. Monks drained the swamps and felled the forests. Of the Cistercian monks in England it was said, "They turned the waste land into good land; they planted the trees; they improved the streams; they made corn grow where thistles had sprung unchecked; they filled the meadows with cattle and stocked the uplands with sheep."[12]

Perhaps the most significant contribution of monasticism was the preservation of learning. In this respect the monks in Ireland were outstanding. At a time when the continent was reeling from the shock of the barbarian incursions and when its intellectual life was in rapid decline, the Irish monasteries were the nuclei of a remarkable civilization. In fact, in the late sixth and seventh centuries Ireland was the intellectual leader of Europe and the preserver of civilization. In Irish mon-

This is the carved ivory cover of a medieval religious book, now in the Church of Hildesheim, Germany.

asteries Greek and Latin were studied, manuscripts copied and preserved, and art masterpieces produced in the illumination of manuscripts. *The Book of Kels,* which can be seen in the Library of Trinity College, Dublin, is a masterpiece of its kind; so, too, is the manuscript art of the magnificent *Book of Gospels* found at the monastery of Lindisfarne.

The influence of the monasteries was diffused throughout Ireland, stimulating an outburst of art, learning, and literature. There was a rich production of poetry in the Gaelic vernacular which still constitutes one of the richest legacies of legend and folklore possessed by any people. It is interesting to see how the glories of the past furnish inspiration for the present. In our own twentieth century, Irish nationalists seeking independence from Great Britain for their island have rediscovered their country's Golden Age.

On the continent of Europe most of the schools existing in the early Middle Ages were in the monasteries. Here also the monks in the scriptoriums labored at copying and preserving the few remaining precious works of classical antiquity. In such a monastery at Jarrow in the north of England the Venerable Bede (673-735), one of the few great scholars of his day, pursued his studies. Bede is most famous for his *Ecclesiastical History of the English Nation,* the best account we have for almost two hundred years of English history, notable for its excellent historical writing and its fine prose style.

The Franks. In the amalgamation of the Roman and Germanic peoples and cultures, the part played by a group of German tribes called the Franks was especially significant. As we shall see, the Franks became the first pillar of a new civilization in Europe. Of several tribes of Franks, the Salians and Ripuarians were the most important. The former lived in the valley of the Rhine close to the sea, while the latter settled along the right bank of the Rhine River.

Clovis and the Merovingians. In the fifth century the Franks began to move into northern Gaul. Under the Salian king Clovis I (466?-511) the Franks began a remarkable career of conquest that was to make them the most powerful and influential people in the west and, at the same time, the ally and the instrument of the papacy at Rome. Clovis became ruler of the House of Merovingians at sixteen. In character he was a thorough barbarian. He knew what he wanted—power and territory—and from his arsenal of weapons he used marriage alliances, treachery, assassination, and religious conversion. In 486, with the help of allies, Clovis first disposed of Syagrius, a Roman general, who represented the last foothold of Roman authority in central Gaul. The victor then turned against his friends and subdued them.

Clovis had married a Christian Burgundian princess named Clotilda, and perhaps largely through her influence he became converted to Christianity in 496. The sixth-century historian, Gregory of Tours, gives the story that the actual conversion came about as a result of a battle fought by Clovis at Strasbourg against the Alemanni. On the eve of the conflict, according to Gregory's account, Clovis declared: "If thou wilt give me victory over my enemies and I prove that power which thy followers say they have proved concerning this, I will believe in this and will be baptized in thy name." The victory was won and Clovis was baptized together with his warriors. His conversion made him the only orthodox Christian ruler in the West, for the other Germanic tribes either were pagans or embraced some heretical form of Christianity, such as Arianism. Clovis had little interest in dogma or religion; what was important to him was the political significance of his religion. He realized that most of the Roman inhabitants of Gaul were Catholic in faith and he knew that the people of Burgundy and of southern France and Spain would welcome deliverance from their Arian German rulers.

The conversion of the Franks must be considered a decisive event in European history. The great obstacle to co-operation between the Christian Church in the West and the Germanic tribes had been one of doctrine. Furthermore, this act not only gained for the Franks the all important support of the Church, but it assured them of the loyalty of their large Roman, and Catholic, population. Most important to Clovis, he could carry out military conquests and expand his realm in the name of piety and the Christian religion. His southern neighbor was the Germanic kingdom of the Visigoths, which included all of Spain, lapped over the Pyrenees into southern France, and extended north to the Loire River. In 507 Clovis attacked this kingdom declar-

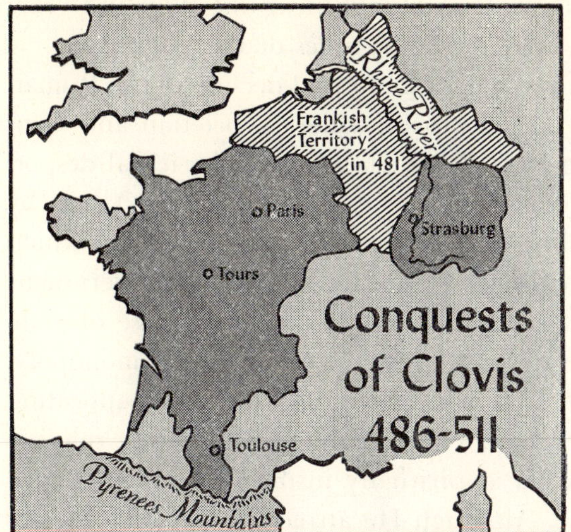

ing: "Verily it grieves my soul that these Arians should hold a part of Gaul; with God's help let us go and conquer them and take their territories."[13] In the great battle that followed the Visigothic king was killed and his people had to flee from their capital at Toulouse, cross the Pyrenees, and set up a new capital in Spain at Toledo.

Content with his conquests, Clovis spent the last years of his reign at Paris, now the Frankish capital. Following his death, in spite of much civil war and bloodshed, his quarrelsome sons and grandsons expanded the Merovingian state. All of Gaul was firmly united, Burgundy was annexed, and Frankish power was extended across the Rhine into Bavaria and Thuringia. This expansion of the aggressive Franks meant that the papal missionary activities were expanded. Civilization was thus disseminated, as monasteries, churches, and schools followed in the wake of the victorious Franks. Clovis' conversion meant that the one active disseminator and preserver of civilization—the Catholic Church—was able to use the king for its own purpose.

Germans and Romans. In the middle of the seventh century, Europe still displayed the essential character of Roman civilization, despite the perilous times that have been surveyed in this chapter. Politically, the new German rulers carried on the imperial tradition in court ceremonial, the routine of the old administration, and the system of tax registry. In theory the new German kings accepted the emperor in Constantinople as their legal sovereign; he in turn described them as allies. Theodoric had governed in the name of the emperor and Clovis accepted the title of consul from him. In the field of politics the Germanic kingdoms, though in practice quite independent, were at the same time overawed by the imperial traditions and authority which had originated in ancient Rome and now resided in Constantinople.

In the economic field as well as in politics the basic pattern had been preserved. To understand this fact, it is essential to recall the thalassic character of Roman civilization. The great inland sea of the Mediterranean was the pathway for the exchange and movement of ideas, culture, and commerce. Trade in particular flowed easily in a single-currency area based on the gold *solidus* that had been introduced by Constantine. It is significant that nearly all the empire's great cities were near or on the sea: witness Carthage, Alexandria, Naples, Rome, Antioch, and Constantinople. As one moved back from the coasts of this thalassic civilization, the less active was commerce and the less prevalent was city life.

After the first shock of the Germanic incursions and after some balance had been restored, trade recovered and there was considerable exchange of goods and money. A great authority in this field, Henri Pirenne, points out that actually all of the features of the old economic life persisted: the importation of oriental products, the minting and circulation of money, and the continuation of commercial activity in the cities. Commerce, like other aspects of Roman civilization, suffered a severe setback from the barbaric invasions, but there was no definite break from the economic pattern of the old Roman world.[14]

Summary

The events discussed in this chapter cover, roughly, the period from 180 to 650. This was the great era of transition from classical to medieval civilization. The conventional date, 476, for the fall of Rome is usually accepted as the termination of ancient, or classical, history. Western European history for approximately the next one thousand years is described as medieval. This chapter covers early medieval times or the Dark Ages.

The latter part of the second century A.D. was a period of rapid decline in the Roman empire. The downward trend was arrested by the capable rulers Diocletian and Constantine. The principate was now quite forgotten. In its place were an oriental despotism and a centralized bureaucracy. In the long run the extreme measures taken by Diocletian and Constantine to arrest the decline only exaggerated the evils from which the Roman world was suffering. The chief evils were interference in the government by the irresponsible soldiery, the destruction of the middle class, the decrease of commerce, the consequent decline of the prosperity of the city-states, and land monopoly.

In the face of such conditions men were sick at heart. They turned to appealing oriental religions for escape. It soon became apparent that the most satisfactory religion was Christianity, whose founder, Jesus, preached a spiritually inspiring message of love and helpfulness and a better world to come. Although He attracted relatively few adherents during His short ministry, His followers rapidly increased after His martyrdom. In the spread of Christianity the work of Paul was particularly important.

The fall of Rome started a widespread process of culture fusion in Europe, a process which blended Roman and Teuton into a new people. The Germans were the political enemies of Rome, but they admired Roman civilization and were eager to assimilate it. The Christian Church assisted materially in the fusion of barbarian and Roman. It converted and transformed the wild Teuton into an agent of law, order, and civilization. In fact the whole history of western Europe from the fifth to the sixth centuries is a reminder of the importance of spiritual factors in history. The Church assumed great political power, preserved learning, and co-operated with the most promising Germanic nation, the Franks. The conversion of Clovis, the founder of Frankish greatness, must be regarded as a decisive event in European history.

Much has been written about the nature of the fall of Rome. That it was gradual and not catastrophic is now generally understood. In spite of a decline in both commerce and cultural activities, and a decrease in urban population, the new Germanic kingdoms did not destroy the basic political and economic features of the thalassic Roman world. This change was to come late in the seventh century, when Islam expanded through North Africa and the Mediterranean became a Moslem lake.

The assimilation of Roman culture by the German tribes meant much more than the mere perpetuation of a purely Roman civilization. Roman civilization, it will be recalled, had borrowed in a large measure from the Greeks who were in turn obligated to the peoples of Egypt and Mesopotamia. Thus the successful fusion of Roman and Teuton meant not only the preservation of much of the Roman way of life; it meant, too, the passing on of cultures founded along the Nile and beside the Tigris and the Euphrates, in the hills of Palestine and the city-states of Greece.

It should be pointed out that we have been concerned only with the events following the end of Roman authority in the West. The eastern, or Byzantine, empire, continued to flourish for a thousand years and made many contributions to civilization.

Part Three

Along the caravan routes

Chapter 9 **Crossroads of the world**

Chapter 10 **The triumph of Islam**

Chapter 11 **The Guptas and the T'angs**

Along the Caravan Routes

THE OUTLOOK FOR civilization in western Europe as presented in the last chapter looked none too encouraging. The culture of the classical world was now threatened with extinction by the Germanic invasions. There was, however, one dynamic and constructive force working to preserve classical culture, the Christian Church. We have noted how it came into being, how it brought a new feeling of hope and spiritual serenity to a distraught western world, how its teachings were spread through an impressive church organization headed by the papacy, and finally, how Christianity succeeded in converting some of the most important German chieftains, such as Clovis the Frank.

That conversion had momentous consequences, for it meant that in the work of building a new order in Europe the new German rulers were to cooperate with the Church. In the latter part of the eighth century, the Church and a great Frankish leader, Charlemagne, actually succeeded in working together to bring law and order, political unity, and advances in letters and thought to western Europe. The Carolingian Renaissance, as it is called, was a brilliant achievement, but it was premature. Following the death of Charlemagne, the great Frankish empire disintegrated, and a new series of invasions from the north, carried on by fierce and uncouth Vikings, again plunged Europe into disorder.

While Europe was reeling from the collapse of the Carolingian empire and the invasion of the Northmen in the ninth century, civilization was flourishing in other parts of the world. It would have indeed been a calamity if, after the collapse of classical civilization in the west, civilization had also retrogressed everywhere else. But in the history of the world, while civilization may have declined in one or more areas, it has maintained its capacity for growth in others.

The fact is well illustrated by the thriving civilization in the Near and Far East during the "Dark Ages" of Europe. The ensuing chapters will show that India was enjoying its golden age. Chandragupta II, a great ruler, established a stable government. Sculpture and poetry flourished, and striking advances were made in astronomy, mathematics, and medicine.

China during the European chaos enjoyed a golden age even more magnificent than that in India. Political unity, law, security, and a magnificent outpouring of art and thought were achieved under the T'ang Dynasty. China became the largest and most powerful state in the world, reaching west as far as Persia and the Caspian Sea and south to Burma and the Himalaya mountains.

Nearer to western Europe, in the Near East, civilization was also maintained on a high plane. When we speak of the fall of Rome, we sometimes forget that only the western portion of the Roman empire succumbed to the German invader, that in the east Constantinople carried on the classical tradition. This vigorous remnant of the Roman empire, known as the Byzantine empire, from the fifth century to the fifteenth, acted as a buffer for western Europe, staving off attacks from the Turks and other invaders, thus allowing Europe to recuperate and reorganize its strength without serious interference.

The only rival of Byzantine civilization outside of the Far East was that developed by the followers of Mohammed in Asia Minor and along the north African coast to Spain. The story of Mohammedanism relates the rise of a great prophet who inculcated in the hearts of the people of Arabia a vital sense of their destiny to conquer and rule the earth in the name of Allah. With unbelievable swiftness and success the followers of the Prophet swept across North Africa and surged into Spain in the west, up through Syria and Palestine, and eastward until they could one day claim suzerainty over the distant Philippines. Along their caravan routes passed the merchants of the world, converging on Bagdad with ivory from Africa, spices from India, and silks from China.

But more than trade flowed back and forth along these routes, for the Islamic world was the great preserver, adapter, and spreader of culture. The style of the numerals which number this page was brought from India by the followers of Islam and later given the title "Arabic." One of man's greatest accomplishments—the making of paper—was learned by Arabs from Chinese prisoners in Samarkand in the eighth century and transported to the western world, while the knowledge of block printing was transmitted westward by Turkish people.

Porcelain had arrived in the Near East from China by the twelfth century. New medical discoveries and drugs circulated along the caravan routes, as did the all-but-lost Greek learning with which the Moslem savants came in contact in the Near East.

We can lay aside the tribulations of western Europe as we pursue a more hopeful theme. Ahead lie some of the most vivid and illustrious pages of mankind's history—the colorful, cosmopolitan refinements of the Byzantine empire, the fervor and vitality of a sprawling Mohammedan world, and the golden ages of medieval India and China.

Chronology of events and developments discussed in this chapter

Chapter 9

Dedication of Constantinople	330 A.D.
Visigoths triumph at Adrianople	378
Empire divided into eastern and western segments under Theodosius	395
Constantinople threatened by the Huns under Attila	441
Ostrogoths pillaged Macedonia and threatened Constantinople	487
Justinian's rule: tried to restore Roman grandeur	527-565
Justinian's codification of Roman civil law	529
Nika Revolt: failure of attempt to dethrone Justinian	532
Belisarius conquered the Vandals in north Africa	533-534
St. Sophia dedicated: innovations in architecture	537
Narses recovered Italy from the Ostrogoths	554
Dark years: Byzantines menaced by the Moslems	565-715
Moslems controlled north Africa, Syria, parts of Asia Minor	600
Hellenization of the empire: resulted in an oriental outlook	600-700
Leo III: defeated the Moslems; internal economic and political reforms	717-740
Leo III forbade image worship: precipitated the iconoclastic controversy	725
Scholarship limited largely to recovering and classifying Greek learning	800-1200
Images restored to the churches	843
Eastern branch of Catholic Church gained converts by missionary activity	863
Basil II: crushed the Bulgarians	976-1025
Byzantine decline: threatened by Turks, Normans, and aggressive aristocracy	1000-1100
Psellus: philosopher from the principal school in Constantinople	1018-1079
Separation of Roman Catholic and Greek Orthodox churches	1054
Alexius Comnenus: checked Turks, Serbs, Bulgarians; restored order	1081
Constantinople sacked and ruled by Fourth Crusade and Venetians	1204-1261
Ottoman Turks captured Constantinople	1453

Crossroads of the world

The Byzantine empire: 330 to 1453

On May 11, 330 A.D., the emperor Constantine formally dedicated his magnificent new eastern capital of the Roman empire. He named it Nova Roma, but it soon became known as Constantinople. And on May 29, 1453, another emperor, the last of the scores of rulers who had governed the great capital for 1123 years, met his death in battle as the victorious Turks put an end to an empire that had stood as the successor of Roman sovereignty and Greek culture. This is at once a dramatic and tragic story, the story of a civilization that stood as an isolated outpost of Europe, facing a hostile and barbarous East and protecting an unappreciative West that was itself slowly arising out of barbarism to new cultural heights.

During the thousand years that it survived the western empire, there were occasions when the eastern empire came perilously near collapsing, but these periods were followed invariably by splendid revivals in power and civilization. The empire had its weaknesses —revolts and intrigues, overemphasis upon circuses and upon theological disputes, and customs which were quite often barbarous and cruel. But on the other hand, it made some magnificent contributions which more than compensate for its negative characteristics. It preserved for later civilizations the Greek language and learning; it perpetuated the Roman imperial system and codified Roman law; it introduced into Europe many of the finest features of Moslem culture through the contacts which it made with the East. The Byzantine empire fused Greek and oriental art and dedicated the new creations to the glorification of the Christian religion. Because of its splendid situation at the crossroads of the East and West, the empire of Constantinople could act as the culture disseminator for all peoples who came in contact with it. And its contacts were many, owing chiefly to the far-reaching trade which it so successfully carried on in the Mediterranean and Black Sea areas and the entire Near East.

For over a thousand years the eastern empire, with its center at Constantinople, was the most splendid civilization the Middle Ages knew. Its wealth excited the envy and greed of all other peoples, especially the Turks in the east and Italians in the west, and made inevitable the destruction of the empire when its military and naval power became sufficiently weakened. But during the height of its power the greatness of Constantinople was known throughout the world. That rich and turbulent metropolis was to the early Middle Ages what Athens was to Greece, and Rome to the Mediterranean world. Well has it been called "The City," for it was known and envied in three continents.

The History of the Eastern Empire

The beginning of the eastern empire. On the peninsula that juts out from Europe to Asia, on the magnificent harbor of the Golden Horn stood the ancient Greek city of Byzantium. On this site in 327 A.D. Constantine began the building of a new capital for the Roman empire. His purpose was not illogical, for the empire had lately been undergoing definite changes. Oriental cults were spreading throughout the west, replacing the old Roman faith in popularity. From Egypt had come the worship of Isis and Osiris, from Asia Minor the Magna Mater cult, from Persia the worship of Mithras, the god of light, and from Palestine Christianity. The Goths were periling the empire on the Danube, and the Persians were a menace in Asia; Rome's location in the west made effective resistance more difficult. Again, while Italy was declining economically, the east was becoming more and more important in trade and manufacturing.

Lastly, significant changes had taken place in the nature of Roman monarchy. Gone were the days when the princeps of the early empire mixed freely with his subjects. The empire had been turning more and more toward the east. Diocletian and his successors borrowed from the brilliant Sassanid court in Persia its oriental conceptions of divine sovereignty, wherein the subject must prostrate himself before the heaven-appointed emperor, who surrounded himself with lavish rituals, costumes, and ceremonials. These various changes made logical a shift of capitals. The new city, Nova Roma, or Constantinople, was dedicated in 330 and soon became the most spectacular in Christendom.

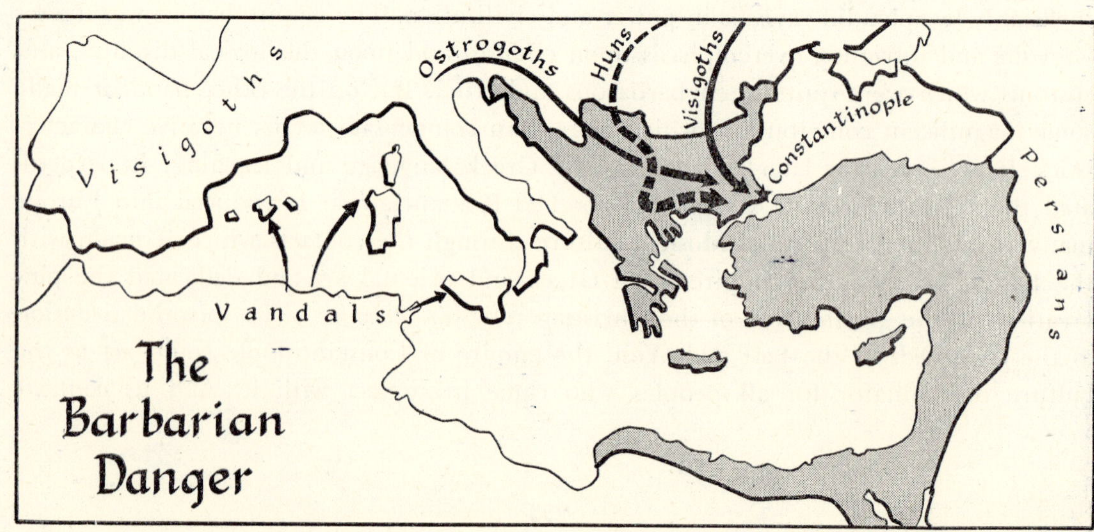

Theoretically Rome and New Rome were the double capitals of a unified empire, but in the year 395 Theodosius divided the empire between his two sons, one to rule over the east, the other over the west. From this time on, there was a definite separation between the two sections, and we can now talk about "a Roman empire of the east." It is true that the fiction of imperial unity continued for years afterward, and Justinian's splendid though brief conquests in the west actually made the entire Mediterranean once more a Roman sphere. But his project of political reunification was a lost cause, and after his death the west declined completely, while the eastern empire endured for almost a thousand years. Thus the eastern Roman empire with its original Roman traditions was transformed by geography, time, and circumstances into a civilization that was unique. It was the fusion of Roman, Greek, and oriental elements.

Gothic invasions. From the outset the eastern empire was beset with dangers. In 378 the Emperor Valens was killed at the battle of Adrianople while unsuccessfully attempting to hurl back the Visigoths. The latter were all-powerful; then their leader, Alaric, led them west into Italy in search of fresh lands and booty. With the Visigoths gone, the empire was safe for a time. In 441 Attila and his hordes of Huns crossed the Danube and threatened Constantinople; but he, too, turned to the west in search of new conquests. Then came the Ostrogoths, who forced the eastern emperors to allot them lands in 462, pillaged Macedonia, and threatened Constantinople in 487. But Theodoric the Ostrogoth was also tempted to win Italy, and New Rome was once more saved. Thus New Rome emerged more independent and intact than ancient Rome at this time, and New Rome naturally turned to the east for its culture and livelihood.

Justinian. The sixth century is marked by the reign of the famous emperor Justinian (527-565). His ambition was to restore the Roman empire to its ancient grandeur and at the same time to place the power of Constantinople, as the true heir of Rome, over the now barbarized lands of the west. Justinian owed much of his success to his beautiful and gifted wife, the empress Theodora, and to his brilliant general Belisarius. His military policies were defensive in the east and offensive in the west. He bought off the Persians, who had been threatening in the Near East, and devoted his attention to conquering the west. In 533-534 Belisarius destroyed the Vandal nation and took over northern Africa. From 535 to 548 the doughty general tried to reconquer Italy from the Ostrogoths. However, it remained for another excellent Byzantine general, Narses, to accomplish this difficult assignment about 554 A.D.

In the meantime, Justinian's forces gained the southeastern portion of Spain from the Visigoths, and incorporated it with neighboring islands into the empire (see the map above). But Justinian's empire was only half the Roman empire at its height. He possessed but little of Spain and nothing of Gaul, Britain, or Germany. Furthermore, the reconquest had been accomplished only by exhausting the empire, both militarily and financially.

Justinian's reign was remarkable for its domestic advances. Such scholars as the historian Procopius continued the Greek literary tradition. The imperial administration was reorganized, while that great monument to legal scholarship and Justinian's far-sightedness, the codification of Roman law, was completed under the emperor's orders. Art was stimulated by the patronage given to sculptors and workers in mosaics, and the greatest of all Byzantine architectural triumphs, the cathedral of St. Sophia, was raised to the glory of God and the everlasting fame of Justinian.

Dark years. The hundred fifty years following the death of Justinian were dark indeed for the eastern empire. In 568 the Lombards established a new kingdom in Italy, so that the emperor now controlled only the southern tip of the peninsula and the territory around Ravenna. Fierce Slavic tribes invaded the Balkan region, among them the Avars, who failed to capture Constantinople (626) and later migrated to Italy. The emperor Heraclius (610-641), after a bitter struggle, managed to hold back the growing incursions of the Persians into the empire, but a new and more terrible danger now arose. The early part of the seventh century saw the birth of Islam, the union of the tribes of Arabia under a new and warlike religious faith, Islam, about which we shall read in the next chapter. Inspired by a fanatical zeal to conquer in the name of their Prophet, the Moslems by the end of the seventh century had taken over north Africa and Syria and even parts of Asia Minor. The eastern empire stood on the brink of disintegration, especially since the Balkan region was now in the hands of the Bulgars (a semi-oriental people) and various Slav peoples. The power of the emperor extended no farther than Constantinople and its environs, and a fringe of ports in the eastern Mediterranean. Elsewhere their hold was precarious indeed.

The empire becomes "Byzantine." In the seventh century the eastern Roman empire was transformed into the "Byzantine" empire. The name comes from the Greek settlement of Byzantium, on the site of which Nova Roma was built. When, as we are to see immediately, the eastern Roman empire was transformed into a Hellenized civilization, an appropriate title for it was the Greek name for its capital.

First of all, a merging of peoples took place. Croats, Serbs, and Bulgars penetrated the empire and mingled with the Greek peoples. The blending of races helped rejuvenate the empire by the infusion of new blood. Even more important, the Byzantine empire became Hellenized. In the seventh century Greek replaced Latin as the official language. The governmental edicts were drawn up in that tongue, Greek titles instead of Latin were bestowed on administrative officers, and Greek was used in giving commands in the army, besides remaining the language of the Church in the east. Until 1453 the Byzantine empire called itself the empire of the Romans, but

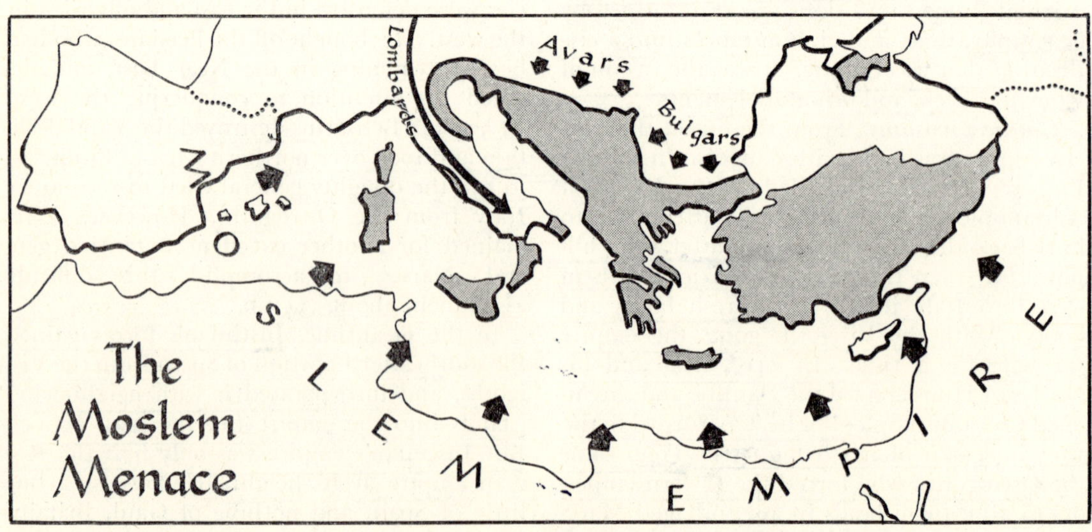

this was a fiction, for it was now in reality a separate, independent, Hellenized monarchy having its center at Constantinople and possessing a decidedly oriental outlook.

Leo III. The eighth century opened unhappily for the Byzantines, but the rule of Leo III (717-741) brought order back to the hard-pressed monarchy. Leo defeated the Moslems on the sea in several engagements and repulsed them in their siege of Constantinople in 717-718. This Moslem defeat occurred some fifteen years before Charles Martel won over their forces in the battle of Tours in 732 (see page 278), and it clearly shows how determined was the Islamic attack on Christendom in the eighth century. Leo's internal reforms were extensive. He reformed the criminal and civil law and reorganized the administration of the empire by dividing huge areas into smaller districts that could be governed more efficiently. He prevented the growth of huge estates at the expense of the peasantry, promulgated a nautical code which encouraged the development of a merchant marine, and attacked monastic abuses and the worship of images in the eastern Church. This started a quarrel known as the iconoclastic controversy, which later brought about a schism between the eastern and Roman churches.

Ninth- and tenth-century disorders. But the death of Leo III ushered in more decades of disorder and dangers. In the ninth and tenth centuries the Byzantine empire rode out the storm of external attack because of its strong naval position. The Moslems were defeated in the Aegean, and by capable armies the Byzantines held back the powerful Bulgarians who aimed at possessing all the Balkans. Under the dynamic leadership of Basil II (976-1025), the Byzantine forces finally crushed their foes with great severity. On one occasion 15,000 Bulgars were blinded and only 150 were left a single eye each to guide the rest home. This cruel treatment of the Bulgars caused Basil II to be known thereafter as *Bulgaroctonos*—"slayer of the Bulgars." Basil II fought the Moslems also but was only intermittently successful against them and gained no important territories. Thus Syria, Palestine, Egypt, and lands to the west, over which Justinian had once ruled, remained in Moslem hands during Basil's reign.

Basil II brought strength and prosperity to his empire. After restoring Byzantine control over the Balkan peninsula and southern Italy, the *Basileus* (for such was the Greek title of the emperor) tried to placate his new subjects by allowing them to retain their own governments. He was friendly, too, with the powerful prince of Kiev in southern Russia and was instrumental in bringing about that ruler's conversion in 989. Thenceforth Russians around Kiev adopted Christianity and began to accept some Byzantine customs and learning. Basil II fostered commerce and industry and died leaving a large surplus in the imperial treasury. Unfortunately, a decline in Byzantine resources and initiative took place afterward.

Eleventh-century decay. Internally the emperors had to contend with an aggressive aristocracy which was gaining too much power in the provinces, and with a Church that was constantly absorbing lands for monastic purposes. Land so held no longer paid taxes to the state. But the external danger was even more pressing. Venice became stronger in the west and took over control of the Adriatic region. In the east there appeared the formidable and barbarous Seljuk Turks, whose Mohammedan fanaticism incited them to make continuous attacks on the weakening empire. In the eleventh century these invaders captured Jerusalem and even gained the shore opposite Constantinople in 1079. The Byzantine empire suffered a terrible blow in this victorious campaign of the Seljuk Turks. Defeated at the battle of Manzikert (1071), it lost the eastern portions of Asia Minor to the Turks (see map, page 258). These rich territories the empire never regained.

Another great threat to Byzantine power was the pressure of the Normans in Italy. During the eleventh century under Robert Guiscard, Norman adventurers began to carve out possessions for themselves in southern Italy at the expense of the Byzantine empire. By 1080 Byzantine power on the mainland and in Sicily was smashed and its prestige in the west seriously weakened. But then, when the empire was torn by anarchy and apparently completely exhausted, its most able general, Alexius Comnenus, gained the throne by a *coup d'etat* in 1081. He restored order and imperial prestige, and he and his successors kept the Turks in check for almost 125 years. Serbia and Bulgaria came under Byzantine control in the twelfth century, and the empire waxed wealthy in trade.

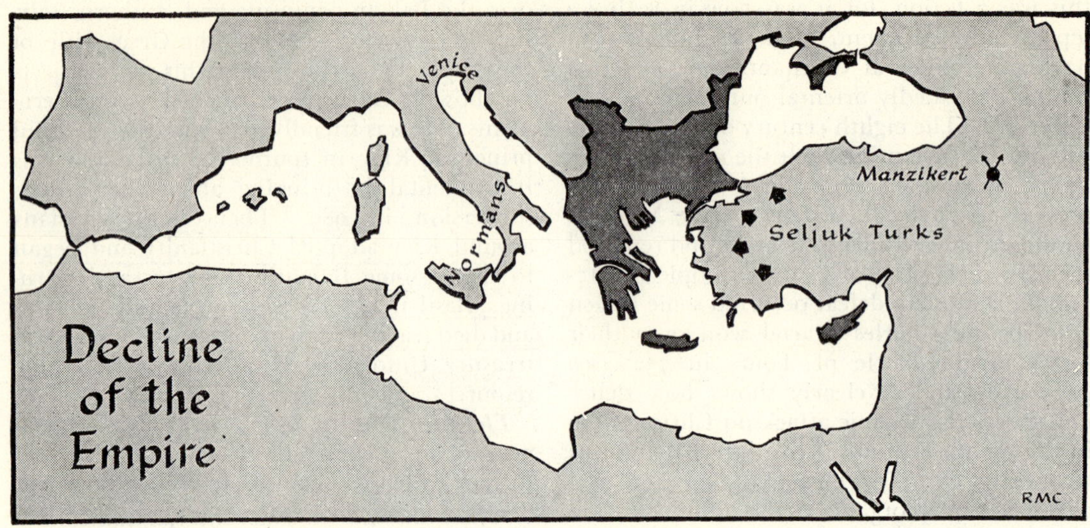

Italian control. The most serious blow fell in 1204. Up to that year the emperors had succeeded in preventing the Turks from capturing Constantinople. Since the eleventh century the western world had been engaged intermittently in great conflicts with the Moslem world over possession of the Holy Land. These campaigns, known as crusades, had been of value to the Byzantine emperors in helping stave off the onrush of the Moslems. But the Fourth Crusade furnished a pretext for semibarbarous crusaders and rapacious Venetian merchants to sack the great capital and found an empire which endured until 1261 and contained a multitude of feudal lordships on the western pattern. Thus the Byzantine commercial wealth fell to the Venetians and the empire was ruined economically. The catastrophe of 1204 proved a mortal wound to the Byzantine empire, even though the empire kept a semblance of its former might for another two centuries.

Reasons for Byzantine decline. After 1261 various Greek emperors succeeded in regaining control, but their rule was of short duration. They tried to curb Venetian power by making trading treaties with Genoa, but their action only confused matters and filled the eastern Mediterranean with more Italian fleets and colonies. The Byzantine empire was on the downgrade all through the fourteenth century. One authority cites three important internal and three external causes for this decadence. The empire was disturbed internally by civil wars in which conflicting factions weakened the empire and gave enemies opportunities to come in; by social and religious disputes during which the lower classes revolted and the eastern clergy quarreled bitterly with the Latin Church; by financial and military disorder through which taxes and customs duties diminished, coinage was debased, and the military and naval forces grew too weak to protect the empire. On the outside, Serbs and Bulgarians weakened the empire by prolonged warfare; a new group of Turks, the Ottomans, were growing in power and finally captured even Constantinople itself in 1453; the Latins, especially the Venetians and Genoese, did not help the Byzantine empire in its hour of need but made the most of every opportunity to take advantage of its distress and hasten its end for their own interests.[1]

The destruction of the Byzantine empire was now only a matter of time; the end came in 1453. After a magnificent defense in which the emperor Constantine XIII had to confront the Turkish army of nearly 160,000 soldiers with only 9000 men (half of whom were foreigners), the great eastern bulwark of Christian civilization crumbled before the might of Islam, and the thousand-year-old Byzantine empire fell forever.

Reasons for endurance of Byzantine empire. We can see from the preceding résumé of Byzantine political developments that the empire suffered from endless internal and external attacks. Yet despite the outbreak of some sixty-five revolutions in a little over a thousand years and the abdication or murder of more than sixty emperors, the empire endured as a definite political entity for a long period. What enabled it to surmount these difficulties? One reason lies in the continuous use of a money economy, in contrast to the primitive economy then characteristic in the west. This money system facilitated trade and the payment of taxes and enabled the empire to provide military and naval forces more easily in times of stress. Another reason for the prolonged existence of the state lies in its political system. Where the west was broken up into innumerable feudal groups and thus had no single institution which centralized power, the opposite situation existed in the east. Here there was an absolute monarchy surrounded by a well-trained and centralized bureaucracy. The control of the emperor was absolute. Only a successful revolution could depose him, and, because he was consecrated with holy oil by the patriarch and hence was a priest-king who claimed the divine right to rule, he had complete power in civil, religious, and military affairs.

History is replete with examples of the absolute jurisdiction achieved by rulers who united in themselves both political and religious offices. We will recall the power of the Egyptian pharaoh, at once a priest and ruler. Likewise the emperor of China was both a monarch and the officiator of the sacred rites of heaven and earth. He was supposed to rule by the mandate of heaven. The worship of the Roman emperor was an attempt to gain the loyalty of all subjects by the deification of the ruler. Later on we shall see how exalted a position the ruler of the Incas held as a priest-king, while in seventeenth-century Europe such monarchs as James I of England and Louis XIV of France justified their despotism by maintaining they had divine right to rule their subjects as they pleased.

The emperor of Byzantium was another such ruler. He stood at the top of an intricate official hierarchy and bureaucracy, a dazzling manifestation of a government which held the entire empire firmly in its grasp. However, while the emperor was able to act as autocratically as he desired, he was dependent upon a well-trained civil service for administration, and this group served to check somewhat the absolutism of the ruler. The most important civil servant was the master of offices. This post had been created by the Roman emperors by the fourth century A.D. and endured into Byzantine times. Duties devolving upon the master of offices varied from time to time, and there was eventually more than one master.

The prestige attached to the position of master of offices was greater than that of any other save that of the emperor, for the master of offices was in charge of foreign affairs, the royal correspondence, court ceremonial, and the introduction of embassies from abroad. Financial affairs were handled by various officials, of whom the most important was the count of the sacred largesses. The chief police official in Constantinople was known as the city prefect.

By the beginning of the eighth century the empire had been divided into seven or eight *themes.* This word at one time signified an army corps, and later came to mean the territory which the corps occupied. The head of each *theme* was known as the *strategis,* or military commander. The *strategis* was not only commander of affairs relating to warfare and the army but came to control all civil administration as well. This system was brought to completion in the eighth century (when each *theme* had its particular army corps), and as such it continued to exist while the empire itself endured.

Religious and Social Life

Iconoclasm and the break with Rome. Justinian attempted without success to hold the Church together as one body throughout the Roman empire. The churchmen at Constantinople and Rome constantly quarreled over ecclesiastical problems, and in 1054 there was a final separation, so that to this day, despite many attempts at reunification, the Roman Catholics and the Greek Catholics have been distinct and independent of one another. The Roman Church became a great international body with jurisdiction throughout western Europe. The eastern, or Orthodox, Church became a great state church whose interests were interfused with those of the empire.

The bishop of Constantinople came in time to occupy much the same administrative position as the bishop of Rome. He became the

patriarch of Constantinople with jurisdiction over twenty-eight provinces, just as the bishop of Rome became, as Pope, the head of western Christendom. The patriarch was chosen by the emperor, who made his appointment from a list of three candidates drawn up by an ecclesiastical council of archbishops. If the monarch so wished, he appointed a patriarch of his choice. Naturally, the policies of empire and Church were inseparably linked in Byzantine times.

Unhappy relations between the eastern and western churches were of long standing. The strong Leo III (717-740) instituted many reforms in the Byzantine empire, after having defeated the Moslems. While Leo had no use for their religion, he seems to have agreed with its contention that the use of images and pictures in worship led eventually to idolatry. In 725, therefore, Leo issued his famous edict forbidding image-worship as superstitious and irreverent, and he ordered the whitewashing of the pictures of the saints upon church walls as well as the removal of all statues. At once rioting broke out in Constantinople, and the officials who were taking down the large figure of "Christ Crucified" from the main palace gate were cudgeled to death by a fanatical mob. The demonstration was put down by troops, who killed some of the rioters. Leo then had a plain cross put above the palace gate and explained that symbols of the Christian faith were to be substituted for pictures and statues.

The patriarch of Constantinople objected to Leo's course of action. He was replaced by another man more agreeable to the emperor's will. Riots broke out in Greece and Italy, while the Pope at Rome, Gregory II, protested vehemently, and the succeeding Pope called a council of ninety-three bishops who read out of the Church all those who had accepted the program of iconoclasm (image-breaking). In 843 the schism was temporarily healed by the restoration of images in the eastern Church, but other sources of friction made any permanent reunion impossible. The Latins were accused by some of the eastern ecclesiastics of acting irregularly by eating eggs in Lent, making use of unleavened bread in the Mass, and permitting priests to shave their faces. The rivalry between Latin and Greek churchmen over the conversion of the Slavic peoples in eastern Europe proved to be still another source of irritation and complaint. Finally, in 1054 the breaking point was reached, and henceforth the papacy in the west and the Orthodox Church in the east maintained separate existences, filled with mutual suspicion and intolerance.

Importance of the eastern Church. The Orthodox Church played an important role in the daily life of the people. Linked as it was to the state, it received automatically the loyalty of the people, and it gratified their love of pomp and pageantry by the splendor of its ritual and services. Undoubtedly there was a great deal of superstition of a gross kind among the Byzantines, centered around magic, witchcraft, fortune-telling, charms, and various secret ceremonies, some of them obscene, which the Church did little to prevent. On the other hand, the Church was the center of keen theological speculation, and it stimulated the arts profoundly.

The Orthodox Church converted the Slav world. About 863 A.D. the brothers Cyril and Methodius set out from Constantinople for Hungary and Bohemia to bring these people the gospel. They devised an alphabet of modified Greek characters in which to write the Slavic language; then they translated portions of the Bible and the divine service. Although the peoples of this region eventually came under Roman jurisdiction, the work of the two brothers (afterward made saints) triumphed to the east and south, so that ultimately the Greek Orthodox Church extended from Constantinople to the Baltic Sea (see map above). From the Byzantine Church also sprang the Russian Church, whose dogma, worship, and discipline were molded on the pattern of the former. With the extension of the Greek Church went an extension of Byzantine culture, so that today the semi-Greek alphabet of the Russians is a modification of Cyril's invention, while Greek art, commerce, and intellectual life have permeated most of the Slav world. The literature of the Slavs has been conditioned by Byzantine models. From the empire went architects and painters to build and ornament churches and public edifices, such as existed in Russia's old capital, Kiev, until recently. From Constantinople came both the proper style of dress and the correct ritual for court life in the Slavic kingdoms. Russia, Rumania, Bulgaria, Yugoslavia were all made the richer for Byzantine culture diffusion.[2]

Social life. Social life in the empire was colorful. The center of the empire was Constantinople, and the center of Constantinople consisted of the royal palace, the cathedral of St. Sophia, and the giant Hippodrome. The palace had groves of trees, gardens, banqueting halls, fountains, school, barracks, and stables filled with costly race horses. When the emperor sat down to dine, he ate from gold plate. One banqueting hall had doors of silver and tables of gold and silver and rich enamel, while the floors were strewn with roses, rosemary, and myrtle. So magnificent was the imperial palace that visitors from the drab and poverty-stricken west were awestruck at the wealth which they saw so lavishly displayed on all sides, and prostrated themselves at the feet of the emperor.[3] Constantinople was the largest and wealthiest European city in the Middle Ages. The most notable characteristic of the capital was its urbanity. Constantinople's trade, crafts, and industries made it the hub of the empire, and it could not help becoming the intellectual and social capital.

Byzantine social life was marked by tremendous contrasts. The religious attitude was deeply ingrained in the popular mind. Asceticism and monasticism were widespread throughout the empire, and to an extraordinary degree even the most commonplace individual seemed to take a vital interest in the deepest theological discussions, while all the people were much affected by a religious mysticism in their daily lives. But in contrast, the same people were exceptionally fond of all types of amusements. The great Hippodrome, seating 80,000 wide-eyed spectators, was the scene of hotly disputed chariot races which split the entire populace into rival factions of "Blue" and "Green." One authority has graphically pictured for us the color and importance of these Hippodrome races.

"Every reader will picture the scene for himself: the serried ranks of Greens and Blues in their thousands, the patricians and senators in their gorgeous robes of silk and flashing jewels seated on the terrace reserved for them; high above the course, connected with the palace and cut off from the Circus itself, the boxes of Empress and Emperor. The long suspense; then the arrival of the imperial guard; a movement: the Emperor enters his box; he raises his mantle, and makes the sign of the Cross. The choirs sing, and strangely mingled with praises to the Christ and the Virgin pour the passionate supplications for the victory of this or that charioteer. Then the cars burst away: Triumph! Defeat!—and later under cover of night in the dark passageway of the narrow street a knife gleams for an instant, and a body falls; a splash in the sea and the current sweeps something away. A 'Green' has had his revenge on a victorious 'Blue.' "[4]

Byzantine women. Women played an important part in Byzantine society. The empresses Theodora and Irene and many other prominent women exercised great influence. Byzantine women had a more equitable status than women anywhere else in Europe.

Many contradictory and libelous statements have been made about the Empress Theodora, wife of Justinian, but even the meager facts on which we can rely mark her out as an interesting and dynamic historical figure. While Justinian was yet only the heir to the throne,

A sixth-century Byzantine mosaic pictures the Empress Theodora with two of her attendants.

he announced to the world that he intended to marry this woman. Court society was shocked, for Theodora was a dancer on the comic stage and was reputed to be the daughter of an animal trainer at the circus. But in all the years which she was married to the great lawgiver, Theodora never caused a breath of scandal to be raised about her conduct. Of brilliant mind and poise, the empress gave invaluable help to her husband, counseling him wisely.

The climax of her career came in the famous Nika Revolt of 532. We have noticed the rivalry that existed between the Green and Blue factions at the Hippodrome. These antagonistic groups differed on religious and political grounds as well, and in 532 much rioting occurred. Justinian ordered the leaders of both factions to be executed. But two of the ringleaders escaped, one a Blue and the other a Green. They united their respective followers into one rebellious throng, and six days of desperate rioting ensued. Finally the mob shouted for the deposition of Justinian himself. It happened that the main portion of the emperor's army was away fighting the Persians, and his ministers counseled Justinian to flee by sea. He was about to follow their advice when Theodora spoke up before the council with these words, which Procopius (the chronicler of Justinian's court) has preserved for us:

"May I never be separated from this purple, and may I not live that day on which those who meet me shall not address me as mistress. If, now, it is your wish to save yourself, O Emperor, there is no difficulty. For we have much money, and there is the sea, here the boats . . . as for myself, I approve a certain ancient saying that royalty is a good burial-shroud."[5]

Justinian and his ministers took heart at this brave declaration, a final assault routed the mob, and the emperor kept his throne, thanks to his low-born but high-spirited wife.

Slavery. Slavery was a characteristic feature of Byzantine life. That slavery had nearly always existed among the ancient peoples, we can realize by thinking back upon the civilizations we have already studied. Even enlightened Athens had her full share of slaves. Christianity had much to do with lightening the burden of this wretched class of human beings by teaching that every man was equally endowed with a divine soul. By the time of Justinian's reign public opinion was condemning the worst features of ancient slavery. Justinian's legislation allowed slaves and free persons to intermarry and stipulated that the children of such unions would be free. Furthermore, he made it a criminal offense for a master to make a prostitute of a slave. Hereditary slavery diminished, although the arrival of heathen captives prolonged it unduly in the Byzantine empire.

Byzantine lack of balance. The Byzantines possessed both a love of beauty and a streak of cruelty and viciousness. Their sports were often bloody and sadistic, their tortures were horrible, and the lives of their aristocracy were a mixture of luxury, intrigue, and studied vice. Some historians have described Byzantine immorality with grim joy. While they have exaggerated this aspect of Byzantine life, it is true that the Byzantines were promiscuous.

Where the Greek ideal had been one of moderation in conduct, the Byzantines never achieved that balance. They tended toward excess in almost everything they did, a phenomenon that may be partly explained by their political situation. The empire was never free from the fear of invasion, and its inhabitants were constantly aware of their imminent danger. Because Byzantine civilization was a fusion of the oriental and Greek, perhaps we can ascribe to the former the Byzantine love of splendor and indulgence and to the latter its keen appreciation of intellect and art.[6]

Industry, Commerce, and Wealth

Industry. The splendor of Byzantine civilization was derived from wealth amassed from its extensive industry and commerce. Constantinople's geographical situation made it the crossroads of the East and West (see map, page 376), which helps explain why it was the wealthiest Christian city of the Middle Ages. But Constantinople was not merely a trading center. It was the home of a teeming industrial life which supplied Christendom with innumerable products. Other industrial centers besides Constantinople existed throughout the empire and added to its prosperity: Antioch, Damascus, and Salonika, to

The near-divine status of Justinian is apparent in this mosaic which represents the haloed emperor flanked on the right by men of the Church—a church official bears the cross—and on the left by courtiers and a bodyguard of his soldiers. Note the elegance and richness of the costumes.

mention but a few. But when we talk of Byzantine commerce and industry, we can think of its center as the huge metropolis-capital of about a million inhabitants.

To this city of wealth and activity, once-proud Rome was a contrast indeed. Rome by this time had declined to only a shadow of its imperial glory, and its chief claim to fame now lay in being the home of the Pope.

Constantinople specialized in luxury goods. Metalwork flourished with the manufacture of armor, weapons, hardware, and bronze pieces. The goldsmith became a popular and expert craftsman, owing to the ecclesiastical demand for altars, crosses, censers, and gold reliquaries. Gold caskets and cups were beautifully decorated by jewelers. Religious needs also encouraged a large wax and tallow candle industry. Tapestries and hangings of unexcelled workmanship found a ready market outside the empire. Filigreed and enameled glasswork, porcelain, and mosaics were prized wherever they were exported. Perfumes, manuscripts, carpets, leather goods, and a variety of jeweled, engraved, and enameled ornaments were likewise a part of the highly profitable luxury trade in Constantinople.[7]

It was the textile industry, however, upon which the fame of Byzantine industry chiefly rested. Until the time of Justinian all raw silk necessary for the manufacture of precious fabrics had to be imported from China by way of the Persian Gulf. Then about 550, according to the story, Nestorian missionaries, a group of heretics who had fled from Europe, smuggled silkworms out of the Middle Flowery Kingdom and brought them to the eastern empire. It was not long before the silk industry was flourishing around Constantinople, and it soon became the most fostered industry in the empire, and, in fact, a state monopoly. Silken stuffs of purple, violet, yellow, and green, embroidered with gold and silver thread and fashioned into costly vestments for church services or regal court attire, were eagerly sought after all over Europe.

Government regulation. The Byzantine government exerted a strict control over all manufacturing and trading. Private ownership was subjected to governmental regulation regarding wages, prices, and labor conditions. At Constantinople the trades and professions were in the charge of hereditary guilds, which resembled in some aspects the *collegia* of the Roman republic. The nature of governmental control over the trade guilds has been described in the tenth-century *Book of the Prefect.* Capital could not ruthlessly exploit labor, but the craftsmen had to continue working in their guilds. Prices for the buying of raw materials and the selling of foods were alike fixed by governmental decree. The state also designated when and where goods made by guilds were to be sold, and punished violators severely. Thus the government kept a close watch over industry.[8]

The empire regulated its economic life in much the same fashion as modern totalitarian states. Commerce and even agriculture, which, unlike the situation in the west, seems to have been of less economic importance than industry, had governmental regulation in some respects. Many great estates were supervised by the state and cultivated by *coloni* and serfs. But large private estates still existed, run in much the same way as the manorial system in the west, which will be treated in Chapter 13. The land tax was an important aspect of Byzantine finance, and so heavy did taxation become that poor farmers tended to transfer their parcels of land to large landowners. As a result, serfdom increased throughout the empire and thereby created a problem reminiscent of the agricultural difficulties of Rome.

Commerce and wealth. Commerce gave the empire its chief source of wealth. At the crossroads of the east and west and protected by a powerful navy that combed the sea-routes for pirates and Moslem enemies, Byzantium grew wealthy from its export and import trade. As time elapsed, however, foreigners began to monopolize the business, so that the shrewd merchants of Venice and other states received a lion's share of the profits.

Constantinople had two main types of exports: the products manufactured within the empire itself, such as textiles, metal, leather, and luxury goods; and the products which came from the east and were re-exported from the empire's trading centers, such as spices, drugs, aromatics, and precious stones. Two-way commerce was carried on in the following manner: Constantinople exported to Russia its luxury goods, wines, spices, and silks, and imported furs, fish, caviar, beeswax, honey, and amber. To the east went the products manufactured in the empire, while back to Constantinople came those precious spices, jewels, costly woods, and essences which made the orient a synonym for fabulous luxury among the peoples of western Europe.[9]

We can catch a vivid picture of the wealth and bustle of Constantinople from the pen of a twelfth-century traveler, Benjamin of Tudela: "From every part of the Empire of Greece tribute is brought here every year, and strongholds are filled with garments of silk, purple, and gold. Like unto these storehouses and this wealth, there is nothing in the whole world to be found. It is said that the tribute of the city amounts every year to 20,000 gold pieces, derived both from the rents of shops and markets, and from the tribute of merchants who enter by sea or land. The Greek inhabitants are very rich in gold and precious stones, and they go clothed in garments of silk with gold embroidery, and they ride horses, and look like princes. Indeed, the land is very rich in all cloth stuffs, and in bread, meat, and wine. Wealth like that of Constantinople is not to be found in the whole world. Here also are men learned in all the books of the Greeks, and they eat and drink every man under his vine and his fig tree."[10]

This keen-eyed traveler also informs us that the streets are filled with merchants from Babylon, Mesopotamia, Persia, Egypt, Russia, Hungary, Italy, Spain, and elsewhere. The merchants come by sea and land, and "there is none like it in the world except Bagdad, the great city of Islam."

Another Mohammedan traveler visited the metropolis about the same time and reported, "Constantinople is a city larger than its renown proclaims. May God, in His grace and generosity, deign to make of it the capital of Islam!"[11]

But one writer has reason to complain of the strange mixture of races that congregated daily in the trading center: "The men are very thievish who dwell in the capital of Constantine; they belong neither to one language nor to one people; there are minglings of strange tongues and there are very thievish men, Cretans and Turks, Alans, Rhodians and Chians . . . all of them being very thievish and corrupt are considered as saints in Constantinople."[12]

The wealth of the Byzantine empire was enormous. Its currency, the gold bezant, could be found throughout the entire Mediterranean basin and was the standard money of the area. The Byzantines with pardonable exaggeration maintained that three quarters of the world's wealth lay within their city's confines. Little wonder, then, that the eyes of the rest of the world were turned with greedy anticipation on an empire whose disintegration finally became obvious to all. Crusader and Moslem alike acted upon the old adage—"to the victor belong the spoils."

Cultural Contributions

The preservation of Greek tradition. As we have seen already, the eastern empire had been founded with Latin as the official language of both state and Church. But from the time of Justinian onward, the language of everyday life, Greek, became also the language of scholarship, government, and the ecclesiastics. The official adoption of Greek (which had been spoken in the region since Hellenic times) in Justinian's reign was a blessing for later generations, since it meant the preservation of the Greek classics in philosophy, literature, and science.

Scholarship. The scholars who perpetuated the Greek tradition were not ecclesiastics as in the west but rather members of that educated governmental bureaucracy, or civil service, which we have mentioned previously. The reopening of the principal school of higher learning in Constantinople in 863 enlarged the intellectual horizon of the empire. There "eminent teachers, under the solicitous patronage of the sovereign, taught philosophy, rhetoric, and the sciences; and around their chairs students crowded, coming from all points of the Byzantine and Arabian Orient."[13]

This school appears to have been founded as early as 425 A.D. by Theodosius II, but its life was a most uncertain one in succeeding centuries because of foreign wars and civil struggles. Furthermore, like other institutions of the empire, it was dependent upon the initiative of the emperor. At various times it became inactive and was then revived by a new ruler. In 1045 the institution was organized with two faculties, Law and Philosophy.

The most famous teacher of philosophy was Michael Psellus (1018-1079). Psellus has left us some addresses which he gave to his students. He pleaded for a more active pursuit of learning, "for you do not rouse your souls, neither do you devour the fire of my zeal, but you lay hold of knowledge as though you were one of those in the market place." He would then contrast his laggard students with the ancient Greeks, maintaining that the latter never had to be goaded into seeking knowledge. Psellus was undoubtedly the greatest of Byzantine scholars. His mind was inquisitive and all-embracing, while his love of philosophy, especially Platonic, did much to encourage the study of that subject.

Byzantine scholarship flourished particularly between the ninth and twelfth centuries. It was concerned almost entirely with recovering and classifying Hellenic and Hellenistic learning. Greek medicine was preserved and added to by such eminent Byzantine physicians as Aëtius, the court doctor of Justinian, and others. The contributions of the Greeks in mathematics, biology, and physical sciences were likewise recovered in large measure by Byzantine scholars, and from them in turn the Moslem scientists derived much of their knowledge. The discussion of Greek philosophy and literature created that interest in classical culture which was to be known centuries later in Italy as Humanism.

Byzantine scholarship had one great weakness—it was not creative but imitative. Scholars were dazzled by the glories of Hellenic and Hellenistic thought, and they spent their lives in compiling, classifying, and discussing the classics. They were great encyclopedists, and for their persevering labors we are grateful, but their own contributions lack vitality because they are simply a rehash of the works of ancient scholars. Byzantine education was the privilege of only a few wealthy people, and this fact in part accounts for the lifelessness and narrow sophistication surrounding the scholarship of the empire.

Justinian's law code. One of the most important contributions of Byzantine scholarship was written partly in Latin, partly in Greek. It was the famous codification of Roman civil law under the orders of Justinian, which was discussed in Chapter 6. In 528 Justinian convoked a commission to gather and classify the imperial constitutions promulgated since Hadrian's time. This was the Justinian Code, published first in 529 and reissued in 534. In 533 appeared the *Digest*, or *Pandects*, dealing with the writings of the earlier great jurists, which reduced some three million lines of legal literature to one hundred fifty thousand. The *Institutes* was published for the benefit of students, and summarized in a single manual the principles of the Code. Lastly, the *Novels*, or laws promulgated by Justinian between 534 and 565, were appended to the famous *Corpus Juris Civilis* (the Code, the *Digest*, and the *Institutes*).

The Code and commentaries were edited in haste, and they contain some errors, but they comprise a very great work, one which contributed a good deal to human society. Not only did this work keep alive for the west the idea of the state and the fundamentals of social organization, but "by permeating the rigor of the old Roman law with the new spirit of Christianity, it introduced into the law a regard, hitherto unknown, for social justice, public morality, and humanity."[14]

Sculpture and painting. Byzantine artists combined influences from the orient with the Christian spirit, producing a brilliant and luxurious art. Their art was used to glorify the Christian religion. They portrayed Christian saints, but foreign indeed to the simplicity of Jesus' teachings were the ornate, elegant, and formalized figures of their mosaics and paintings. The icon on this page is Christian, but the oriental influences are evident in the

BYZANTINE ICON (RELIGIOUS PAINTING)

BYZANTINE CAPITAL, CHURCH OF SAN VITALE

BYZANTINE MADONNA (MOSAIC) IN SAINT SOPHIA CATHEDRAL, CONSTANTINOPLE

luxurious robe and the beautiful gold decoration of the halo. Love of bright colors and rich orientalism combined with Christian religious concepts is one of the outstanding features of Byzantine art. The iconoclastic controversy resulted in the substitution of flat representations for statues. Decorative patterns very oriental in feeling, such as those on the capital on the opposite page, were used instead of figures. Note how much more successful the artist was in working out interlaced decorative patterns than in carving the animals.

Byzantine artists used beautiful mosaics for church decoration. Mosaics are made with small pieces of glass or stone set in cement in patterns, providing decorations of brilliant colors, usually with gold backgrounds. The church patterns depict scenes from Christian legends and are often highly symbolic. In the mosaic above, the figure on the left carries a model of a church and the one on the right, a model of a city, symbolizing the religious and the secular dedicating themselves to the Virgin and Child. The Madonna shows the stylized treatment typical of Byzantine mosaic work. The medium, consisting of rows of stones, would not allow realistic or subtle representation.

Byzantine painting was generally flat and sometimes stereotyped, yet such early Italian masters as Cimabue and Giotto received inspiration from its religious subject matter, its color, and its beautiful patterns. Painted religious images, called icons, were used in daily worship. The icons were stiff and conventionalized, and many of their conventions, such as the hook-like lines to suggest folds in drapery (notice particularly those on the knee in the illustration), were learned by rote. However, Byzantine artists had an important influence on later painting. They kept alive the technique of tempera on wood. Tempera painting uses egg as a binding material. It is a permanent and very exact medium, excellent for work with lines and hard edges. Although it gives a brilliancy of color, it does not adapt itself readily to soft shading and realistic light and shade. The icons reveal certain beauties such as sensitive oriental line, equally oriental patterning of flat colors, and backgrounds of brilliant color and gold. The painter did not care for realistic representation, designing his work instead so that its lines were very rhythmic. He cared most about a pleasant pattern of line and color, often distorting his subject to compose as he wished.

THE CATHEDRAL OF ST. SOPHIA

IVORY THRONE IN THE PALACE AT RAVENNA

Minor arts. Byzantine artists excelled in illuminating manuscripts. Their work is noted for its elaborate detail and brilliant coloring. Carvings in ivory were a distinctly Byzantine achievement, as were decorated book covers, caskets, thrones, and altars. The throne below shows the richness of detail typical of this work, with decorative animals, plants, and stylized human figures. We owe much to the rich inventiveness of the Byzantines. Their decorative motifs and ivory carvings were later translated almost literally into stone in early Romanesque sculpture. Enamel working was also highly developed; it too was used for ornamental purposes, such as enriching crowns, icon frames, and altar fronts. Byzantine jewelers made themselves famous with their skill in creating designs in precious metals and jewels.

Architecture. The most outstanding Byzantine artistic achievement was in church architecture. The church of St. Sophia at Constantinople, built by order of Justinian and formally opened by him in 537, is a huge edifice designed like a great Greek cross and crowned with an immense dome. The effect of the radiance from the light catching the mosaics has been related by one Byzantine writer:

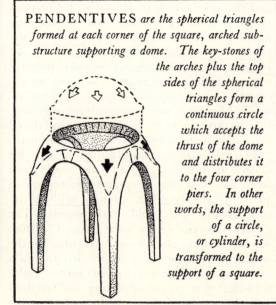

PENDENTIVES *are the spherical triangles formed at each corner of the square, arched substructure supporting a dome. The key-stones of the arches plus the top sides of the spherical triangles form a continuous circle which accepts the thrust of the dome and distributes it to the four corner piers. In other words, the support of a circle, or cylinder, is transformed to the support of a square.*

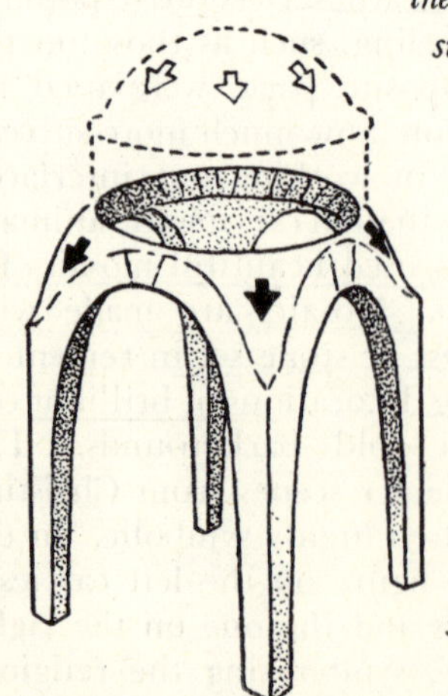

"The dome of Saint Sophia seems to float in the air. . . . You would say that sunlight grew in it."[15] Procopius describes his impressions: "Who can tell of the splendour of the columns and marbles with which the church is adorned? One would think that one had come upon a flowery meadow; one marvels at the purple hues of some and the green of others. . . ."[16] Ironically, the church today is dedicated to God in the name of Allah. Extra chapels and minarets have been added since it has become a mosque, and its magnificent mosaics were whitewashed by a people whose faith forbids the use of pictures in a mosque. However, the present Turkish government has permitted large portions of the walls to be cleansed of whitewash.

The principle upon which St. Sophia is built represents an important Byzantine contribution to the science of architecture. The Romans had made use of the dome in the Pantheon, but their dome had been erected upon a flat, circular wall. The dome of St. Sophia is raised above the roof of the remaining portions of the building and rests on the keystones of four arches that spring from four large piers at each corner of a square. The problem of raising a dome over a square area is solved by means of pendentives, illustrated in the diagram on page 268. St. Sophia is a particularly fine example of the influence of the Orient. It follows the oriental idea of simple, plain exteriors and ornate, luxurious interiors. The pendentive, brilliantly evolved by Byzantine architects, was copied by western builders occasionally in Romanesque buildings, and notably in the cathedral of St. Mark's at Venice.

Summary

The ornate civilization that centered for a thousand years about Constantinople, crossroads of the world, was fascinatingly cosmopolitan, for its inhabitants came from diverse regions of Europe and Asia, enriching the city on the Golden Horn with a multitude of new customs and ideas. The variegated social life of those who flocked to St. Sophia and the Hippodrome, the costly wares and the lively bickerings of merchants who touched even distant Russia, the bejeweled splendor of Byzantine art and the stately strength of Constantinople's buildings—all these, together with the nervous energy exhibited by a people conditioned through historical and geographical circumstance to "live dangerously," mark this civilization as peculiarly kaleidoscopic.

But Constantinople was much more than a cultural *potpourri.* When western Europe declined after the waning of the classical world, and learning was all but lost, the Byzantine world remained the custodian of classical knowledge and ideals, until a resurgent west was able to assume its guardianship. For a thousand years Constantinople acted as a buffer state, repulsing the attacks of Persians, Arabs, Turks, and Mongols, while the weak, divided west grew in strength.

And Constantinople did much more than all this. In "The City," Roman, Greek, and oriental elements were fused into a distinct and original culture. A proof of this is found in Byzantine art, where the lavish riches of the orient united in the glorification of Christianity. Many other contributions of lasting value came from Byzantine society: the codification of Roman law, liturgical verse which enriched church ceremony, and commercial practices such as a standardized currency. Lastly, the Byzantine empire spread the message of Christianity to the Slavic peoples and brought to Russia and neighboring lands the benefits of a modified Greek alphabet and literature.

Chronology of events and developments discussed in this chapter

Chapter 10

Mohammed: founder of Islam	570?-632
The Hegira: Mohammed fled from Mecca to Medina	622
Mohammed conquered Mecca: Arabs accepted Islam	630
Abu Bakr: first caliph; preserved and extended the faith	632-634
Othman: issued official text of the Koran, guide for Moslem actions	644-656
Civil war among claimants to the caliphate	656-661
Ommiads: ruled Asia Minor, north Africa, Spain, central Asia	661-750
Moawiyah: Byzantine pattern of administration; capital at Damascus	661-680
Moslems turned back at the battle of Tours by Charles Martel	732
al-Walid: period of greatest Ommiad dominion	705-715
Abbasids: capital at Bagdad; peak of empire until its disintegration	750-1258
Translation of Greek and Hindu treatises: synthesis, not innovation	762-900
Rhazes: medical treatises	865-925
Death of Hunain Ibn Ishaq: translated Greek works into Arabic	877
Moslem learning reached its peak	900-1100
Alhazen: developed optics; source for medieval writers	960-1039
Avicenna: physicist, philosopher, and physician	980-1037
Omar Khayyam: author of the Rubáiyát	d. 1123
Seljuk Turks gained control of the caliphs	1055-1258
Mongols destroyed Bagdad and ended the Abbasid dynasty	1258
Constantinople captured by the Moslem Ottoman Turks	1453

The triumph of Islam

Moslem expansion: 570 to 1453

Medieval Christian literature is filled with the word "Mahound," a name given to the devil himself. Because the name is a corruption of Mohammed, one can easily see with what horror our pious ancestors of the Middle Ages looked upon the founder of the great and warlike faith which for centuries seemed to threaten to engulf all Europe. In this spirit the crusaders set forth to gain spiritual blessing—and earthly booty—by ridding the Holy Land of the Prophet's followers, the infidels, as they were called. They failed to achieve their purpose, however, a sore point which must have rankled in the minds of more than one devout theologian who could not understand how Mahound was able to triumph over the forces of Christianity. But it must have been even harder for the average crusader to understand that his Moslem foe was the product of an infinitely more highly developed and sophisticated civilization than any in Christendom. We know today that the crusades were mainly a military fiasco and failed to attain their desired goal but were a success in a way which the crusaders could scarcely have imagined and would have been shocked to discover. They established invaluable points of contact between Christendom and the Islamic world and aided the infiltration of the achievements of Islamic civilization into the West.

The civilization we are about to analyze is religious in its origin, for it springs from the teachings of a Prophet who lived in what had been until his time an obscure and out-of-the-way corner of the world—Arabia. That Prophet, Mohammed, united the Arabian peninsula with his fundamental teaching of monotheism and Islam (submission to God). This faith is commonly refered to by people in the western world as Mohammedanism and its converts as Mohammedans. The disciples of Mohammed the Prophet, however, frown upon these terms, which to them imply the worship and deification of Mohammed, who was only the servant and messenger of God (Allah). The name given by Mohammed and that preferred by his followers is "Islam." This term, meaning submission or surrender, is derived from the Islamic holy book, the Koran, in the passage in which Mohammed describes the submission (*aslama*) of Abraham and his son Isaac to the supreme test of sacrificing the latter according to God's command. Followers of Islam are known as Moslems.

The dynamic faith of Mohammed spread so rapidly that within a hundred years after the Prophet's death his followers had sped westward along the northern coast of Africa, crossed into Spain and beyond the Pyrenees. They pushed northeast along the shores of Asia Minor and almost captured Constantinople itself, migrated eastward past the Tigris and Euphrates, overran Persia, extended their power into Turkestan, and even penetrated the valley of the Indus. The breath-taking religious and political expansion was followed by a flowering of Islamic culture which rivaled the achievements of the Byzantine empire and far surpassed those of western Europe. It is becoming more and more apparent that no people contributed so much to learning in the Middle Ages as did the scholars and scientists of the Moslem world. The importance of Moslem achievements, together with the significance of Islamic culture diffusion and its effects upon the West, make it imperative that we give full appreciation to this rich medieval civilization.

Mohammed and His Faith

Arabia and the Arabs. Arabia is a quadrangular peninsula with an area of about 1,200,000 square miles. It is surrounded by water except to the north and northeast, where it is bounded by Syria and Mesopotamia, the valley of the Tigris and Euphrates. At least a third of Arabia is a desert, while rainfall is scarce in the remainder of the peninsula. Thus vegetation is scant and there is little incentive for active agricultural life. The inhabitants are largely nomadic "sons of the desert." Their racial origins are uncertain. They are of the Semitic language group, which includes the Assyrians, Chaldeans, Hebrews, Phoenicians, and Arameans.

Nomad life. The roving desert Arabs, the Bedouins, had not attained in the sixth century the same degree of civilization which their distant kinsmen, the Hebrews, had long before enjoyed. The Arabs led a wandering life. They were driven by climate and the seasons from place to place in search of vegetation sufficient to keep alive their flocks of sheep and goats. Their economic life was thus precarious and simple, augmented, however, by the persistent practice of raiding caravans. Their social and political organization was, and is today, patriarchal in character. The family is controlled by a head man, while families join together into a tribe ruled over by a leader called the sheik. In the sixth century, the Arabs were emerging from barbarism, a transition marked by their slow acceptance of a written language. They were given to such practices as blood feuds, excessive drunkenness and brawling, and the burying alive of unwanted female infants. They were also intensely superstitious, strongly addicted to storytelling, and sincere lovers of poetry.

Mecca. Although the majority of Arabs were nomads, some important communities grew up along the coasts, whence sea trading developed. The most important region lay along the Red Sea and was known as Hejaz (see reference map 2). It was the commercial center of Arabia. The most important towns were Medina, a date-growing community, and Mecca, fifty miles inland from the port of Jiddah and the terminus of the caravan route across the desert to Syria. Moreover, Mecca was important as a holy place and possessed the Kaaba (the cube), a square temple of uncut stones which contained the sacred Black Stone, by legend brought to Abraham and his son Ishmael by Gabriel. The stone had once been white, according to tradition, but the sins of those who touched it had changed it to black. The Kaaba housed the images of some three hundred sixty local deities and fetishes (material objects believed to be dwelling places of spirits and capable of protecting the worshipers from harm and disease), for idol worship was popular among the people of the sixth century. Credence was also given to the existence of a vague and little understood deity who was the ruler of the universe. He was called Allah-Taala (God Almighty), but he did not figure actively in popular religion, because he was not supposed to be particularly interested in human affairs.

Mohammed (570?-632). Into this environment at Mecca there was born about 570 A.D. a person destined to transform completely the religious, political, and social organization of his people. Mohammed came from a family that belonged to the powerful Kuraish tribe, but he was brought up a poor boy who had to tend sheep much of his time and hence never obtained a formal education. When about twenty years of age he entered the service of the wealthy widow Khadijah, whose caravans traded with Syria. Young Mohammed appears to have been an excellent profit-maker for the widow. In his twenty-ninth year he married Khadijah, who was some eleven years his elder. Through his marriage Mohammed attained economic security and a social position of importance in Mecca. Yet throughout his interesting life, the future Prophet lived simply, remained abstemious in all his habits, and was particularly fond of children. In appearance Mohammed is said to have been of medium height, with an oval face, large eyes, long dark hair, and a dignified mien.

Mohammed was in the habit of retiring to a small cave among nearby foothills to wrestle with the philosophical problems that beset his mind. One day in the cave Mohammed is supposed to have heard a voice commanding,

> Recite in the name of the Lord who created—
> Created Man from nought but congealed blood;—
> Recite! For thy Lord is beneficent....

The heavenly speaker then told Mohammed, "Thou art God's Prophet, and I am Gabriel," and, giving the astonished mortal the blessing of Allah, departed. Revelations appeared to him frequently in the years that followed (the first was in 611), and from them he conceived his religious views. We shall not concern ourselves with the validity of his revelations; it is the effect of his experiences which concerns us. Mohammed was utterly sincere in believing them valid, and his own sincerity acted as a tremendous driving power in creating a dynamic religion which affected three continents. Mohammed quickly converted his wife and his cousin Ali, as well as Abu Bakr, who became prominent later as Mohammed's most trusted adviser. But the new teachings proved unpopular with most Meccans, who saw in Mohammed's monotheism a distinct threat to the city's lucrative pilgrimage trade centering about the many-idoled Kaaba.

The Hegira. Khadijah died in 619. At the same time the popularity of Mohammed reached its lowest point. Finally in 622 he fled his native city and journeyed northward to Medina. That year, which marks at once the lowest ebb in Mohammed's fortunes and the start of his phenomenal success as a religious leader, is reckoned by the Moslems (followers of Mohammed) as the year one. The epoch-making flight is called the Hegira. It represents the end of Mohammed's persecution and the creation of a conquering religious organization. Where his kinsmen at Mecca had rejected him, the townsmen of Medina accepted Mohammed as their leader. He built there his first mosque and set forth new codes of conduct regarding social, religious, and political problems. Allah was worshiped as the only real God and Mohammed was his chosen spokesman, or Prophet. Medina became a theocracy. Its government recognized the immediate sovereignty of God, and government leaders considered themselves His spokesmen.

Arabian adoption of the faith. The religion spread, as did the fame of Mohammed. Various raids and skirmishes between the Meccans and the men of Medina during the years 624-630 resulted in victory for the Medinans, added to Mohammed's popularity, and gave weight to his claim that Allah would aid his followers on the field of battle. At last, in 630 A.D., having won converts far and wide and deeming his forces irresistible, Mohammed marched on his native city, and his old enemies had to surrender Mecca to Allah and His

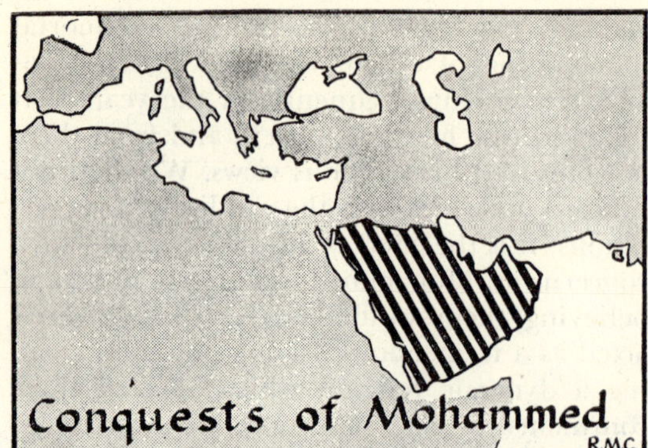

Prophet. Mohammed cast out of the Kaaba its multitude of idols and stone fetishes, but the temple itself, together with the sacred Black Stone, was preserved as the supreme center of Islam, the holy place or "mecca" to which each devout Moslem should make a pilgrimage.

With Mecca and Medina both under his absolute control, Mohammed became the undisputed master of the Arabian peninsula. Tribe after tribe of Bedouins offered him their submission and loyalty. In 632 the Prophet died, after having created a faith which had at last united Arabia and would astound the world with its proselytizing power.

The Koran. The new religion the Prophet taught is to be found in the Moslem Bible, the Koran (*Quran,* Reading or Recitation). One of its cardinal features is that God Himself is regarded as the principal speaker in the Koran. It gives the book an infallible authority in the eyes of its followers, and when they carry out its precepts they feel that they are God's own messengers.[1] Mohammed himself evidently did not write down any part of the Koran. After he had been dead about a year, his close friend Abu Bakr ordered the Prophet's teachings to be compiled as accurately as memory permitted. Disputes arose over the words of the Prophet, and the third successor of Mohammed, Othman, issued an official text.

The Koran contains 114 chapters, or Suras, arranged according to their length, with the longest chapter placed first. Thus there is no logical sequence to the material in the book, and in reading it one must appreciate that each chapter represents a separate message set forth at some particular event. The Koran in its original form is made up of irregular lines containing definite cadences. It is highly poetic in its use of imagery. Here is the opening prayer, rendered into free verse:

Praise be to Allah, Lord of the worlds,
Merciful and compassionate,
King of the Day of Judgment!
Thee do we serve, and of Thee do we beg assistance.
Guide us in the right way—
The way of them who are pleasing in Thy sight,
Not of them who bear Thy wrath; not of them who are astray.[2]

The next selection might almost be found in the Old Testament, where the orthodox Jew or Christian would welcome its sentiment and majesty of thought:

Praise the name of thy Lord, the most High,
Who created and designed all things,
Who preordained them and directs them;
Who makes the grass to grow in the pastures,
And then burns it brown like straw....
Happy is he who purifies himself
And remembers the name of his Lord in prayer.
But ye prefer the life of this world,
Though that to come is better, and is everlasting.
For this of a truth was in the books of old,
The books of Abraham and Moses.[3]

Mohammed never ceased describing the coming Day of Judgment and the pleasures or pains which were to accrue therefrom. No one reading the lines below can fail to catch the vivid quality of their message. This passage is reminiscent of that selection from *Ecclesiastes* which we read in connection with Hebrew literature (page 71).

When the sun shall be folded up,
And when the stars shall shoot downwards,
And when the mountains shall be set in motion,
And when the camels ten months gone with foal shall be abandoned,
And when the wild beasts shall be gathered together,
And when the seas shall be swollen,
And when the damsel that had been buried alive shall be asked
For what crime she was put to death,
And when the leaves of the Book shall be unrolled,
And when the heaven shall be stripped away,
And when hell shall be made to blaze,

And when paradise shall be brought near,
Every soul shall know what it hath produced.[4]

Arabic as a language has unusual force and beauty of sound, and the Arabs as a people have always been especially moved by the spoken word. Thus it was that the Koran was written particularly to be recited and heard. And anyone who has listened to its chant can attest to the Koran's cadence, power, and melody. It has been said, "The triumph of Islam was to a certain extent the triumph of a language, more particularly of a book."[5] The Koran is probably the most widely used book in the world, constituting as it does the basic primer from which nearly all Moslems learn their Arabic, no matter what part of the world they live in, so that they may recite the holy creed. And as the Koran was the earliest important work in Arabic prose, it has remained the stylistic model and standard for Arabic writers, even down to modern times. Furthermore, this book of the seventh century A.D. remains the last word on Moslem theology, law, and social institutions and is still the most important textbook used in Moslem universities, such as the famous El Azhar in Cairo. Because of the Koran, the diverse people of the Arab world in the Middle East and north Africa have preserved their linguistic unity. While Egyptians, Iraqis, Moroccans, and Saudi Arabians use a different form of spoken Arabic, none of these followers of Islam would have difficulty in reading Arabic in written form.

Origins of Islam. We have seen that Arabia was the common ground of many different religions, especially Persian, Hebrew, and Christian. From such a wealth of religious ideas, brought largely to Arabia by traders from neighboring countries, Mohammed added many features to his new religion. The Prophet relied especially upon the Old Testament, praising the Jewish patriarchs and leaders. That Mohammed was acquainted with Christianity is proved by his acknowledgment of Christ as one of the major prophets preceding Mohammed, but the New Testament is not cited specifically as is the Old.

The Islamic faith. What was the new religion that the Prophet taught? The six main beliefs to which every good Moslem adheres implicitly are:

1. Belief in one God, Allah.
2. Belief in angels who intercede for men.
3. Belief in the Koran.
4. Belief in the prophets of Allah.
5. Belief in judgment, paradise, and hell.
6. Belief in the divine decrees.[6]

The central tenet of Islam is monotheism. There is only one God, Allah. Mohammed may have arrived at an independent conclusion that the universe must have been the creation of one supreme being, although it appears likely that he was also influenced by the monotheistic concepts of the Jews and Christians, with whom he came in contact during his trading missions as a young man. But Mohammed rejected the trinitarian belief of the Christians that God was somehow divided into Three Persons, distinct yet indivisible. Ninety-nine names are used in the Koran to describe the majesty of the Creator: the One, the Mighty, the Powerful, the King, the Overcomer, the Avenger, the Dominator, the Slayer, the Provider, the Compassionate, the Forgiving. God rewards men who act according to His laws and punishes those who transgress them. Salvation is attained by all who submit to God, that is, live according to His rule as revealed by Mohammed. Hence Mohammed used the word "Islam" (submission to God) to characterize his faith.

There are angels who intercede for men. Eight angels guard God's throne, nineteen guard Hell, and Gabriel is the archangel. There also exist *jinn,* or genii, who are spirits midway between men and angels. Some genii are good and some are wicked. The most powerful of the latter is the devil, called *shaitin* in the Koran, from the Hebrew Satan.

The Koran is accepted as a direct revelation from Allah to Mohammed and hence forms the basis of all Moslem teaching. The Koran lists twenty-eight prophets, twenty-two of them from the Old Testament, three from the New Testament (including Jesus), and three from outside the Bible (one of whom is Alexander the Great). But to Moslems the greatest of the prophets is, of course, Mohammed.

Mohammed used 852 verses to foretell the fateful Day of Judgment when Allah would reward all men with either eternal bliss or punishment. Geography played an important role in the Prophet's concepts of Heaven and Hell, even as it did with the Hebrew theologians. Paradise is pictured as a great garden filled with fountains, rivers, shade trees, and a balmy climate, while Hell is hotter than the most torturous desert which the Arabs might imagine, and abounds in "burning wind and scalding water." What could be more logical than for a son of the desert to picture Paradise as a glorified oasis set apart from a desert Hell with its torments of burning thirst and broiling sun? Here is one description of the life which the inheritors of Paradise shall pass in "the gardens of delight":

Upon inwrought couches,
Reclining thereon, face to face.
Youths ever-young shall go unto them round about
With goblets and ewers and a cup of flowing wine,
Their [heads] shall ache not with it, neither shall they be drunken;
And with fruits of the [sorts] which they shall choose,
And the flesh of birds of the [kinds] which they shall desire.
And damsels with eyes like pearls laid up
We will give them as a reward for that which they have done.
Therein shall they hear no vain discourse nor accusation of sin,
But [only] the saying, "Peace! Peace!"[7]

But the inmates of the lower world shall drink boiling water, "And ye shall drink as thirsty camels drink!" For in this Hell the sinner "shall not die therein, and he shall not live."

In addition to the six main tenets of Islam there are five essential duties which a loyal Moslem must perform:

1. Repetition of the creed every day in the original Arabic, "There is no God but Allah, and Mohammed is his Prophet." This is the most frequently used and heard phrase in the lifetime of a Moslem. They are the first words he hears when he comes into the world, the phrase he intones every day, and the last benediction uttered at his funeral.
2. Prayer. The Koran demands this five times a day. The praying person must bow toward Mecca.
3. Almsgiving.
4. Fasting during the days of the month of Ramadan.
5. The pilgrimage to Mecca at least once in a lifetime if at all possible.[8] A constant stream of pilgrims travels across Central Africa toward Mecca and is joined in Arabia by other bands from India, China, Malaya, and Indonesia. Between 1918 and 1940 the official estimate of Moslems visiting Mecca averaged 172,000 a year.

Influence of Mohammedan teachings. The teachings of the Prophet had an elevating effect upon his followers. He attacked idolatry and gave the Arabs the much more refined concept of monotheism. His ethical injunctions forbade acts of revenge, counseling instead the practice of forgiveness. He banned infanticide, discouraged the drinking of alcoholic liquor, and attempted to have women treated more humanely than formerly, although sanctioning the maintenance of four wives and an unspecified number of concubines. Mohammed stressed the essential unity of all true believers and thus prevented dangerous class distinctions and ensured equality of all Moslems before the law. In this way Islam was spared the priestly tyranny which arose in India, where the Brahmans considered themselves superior to all other classes in the rigid caste system.

Mohammed taught that all men within the confines of Islam were brothers. In one of his famous sermons he urged: "O ye men! harken unto my words and take ye them to heart! Know ye that every Moslem is a brother to every other Moslem, and that ye are now one brotherhood. It is not legitimate for any one of you, therefore, to appropriate unto himself anything that belongs to his brother unless it is willingly given him by that brother."[9] And so it was that the quarrelsome and diverse Arab tribes were bound together by the new unity of a common faith; and from Arabia, as we shall see in the next section, the new religion expanded to convert and embrace people of many colors and cultures. Islam is among the most important religions in minimizing and demolishing the obstacles of race and nationality. In Africa, for example, where it has grown rapidly in the past century, "... Islam recognized no race discrimination. The converted negro was willingly admitted into Islamic society, and to him the Moslem was a brother not only in name but throughout the sphere of social life."[10]

Christians have criticized much in Islam.

They say that it recommends the use of the sword to convert the unbeliever, it appeals to the sensuous in man with its promises of reward, and it is often naïve in its philosophy. The belief in fatalism (*kismet*) among so many Moslems is frankly negative and unhealthy, while the social and moral status to which Moslem women have been subjected in the past is low by western standards. But despite these weaknesses, Islam has been, and is, a great religion. It emphasizes kindness to servants and animals, respect for parents, moderation and hygiene in personal habits, protection of the weak and ill, and charity toward the poor and unfortunate. It united masses of people who, prior to the time of Mohammed, had never known social solidarity or a civilization higher than that of the desert. With the expansion of the faith from continent to continent in the years immediately following the Prophet's death, a rich and varied civilization was born, probably the richest in the medieval West. It is remarkable how one man—a camel-driver in a remote caravan terminus in the desert—could have so affected the course of world history.

The Spread of Islam

Reasons for Islam's spread. The phenomenal success of the spread of the new faith was based on several significant facts. First of all, the Prophet had taught that any Moslem dying in battle for the faith was assured certain entrance into Paradise. The sanctification of warfare bred in the Moslem Arabs, who already possessed a fierce love of fighting, a fanaticism that proved well-nigh irresistible. The fierce, proud, and tenacious Bedouins, who have been described as a "bundle of nerves, bones, and sinews," were magnificent warriors. The armies made up of these desert nomads also utilized new military techniques; especially notable is their use of the camel as cavalry, which gave the Arabs greater mobility and striking power than their foes. Secondly, the Prophet had promised his followers world domination if they should carry Islam to the ends of the earth, and the prospect of gaining rich and fertile territory must have proved a strong incentive to a people who had been forced to eke out a bare existence from a barren desert. Lastly, the policy adopted by the Moslem conquerors toward their subject peoples worked to their advantage. In comparison with the stern government of the Byzantine emperors, that of the Moslems was tolerant. Jews and Christians discovered that if they submitted to the new rule they would be allowed to pursue their former way of living and retain their religion. Islam's tolerant attitude, together with the simplicity of its creed, attracted numerous converts from among Christians, Jews, and Zoroastrians.

The tradition has persisted from medieval times that Islam was a faith inflicted upon defenseless, peaceful people by sword-flourishing fanatics. The opposite is much nearer the truth. The Moslem leaders were interested in extending their political control, and they knew that to interfere forcibly with another people's faith is the surest means of bringing about revolt. Furthermore, the Moslems needed the economic support of the people of other religions, and so they chose to tolerate their different views.[11] An English scholar of Arabic history maintains: "Some destruction there must have been during the years of warfare, but by and large the Arabs, so far from leaving a trail of ruin, led the way to a new integration of peoples and cultures."[12]

Mohammed's ruling successors. Mohammed died in 632, with a great portion of Arabia converted to Islam. On his death the question arose as to who should direct the fortunes of the faith. The Prophet had but one child, a

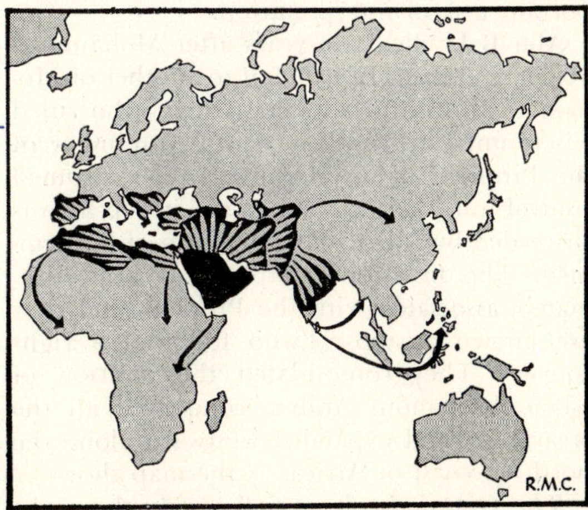

Islam was spread by conquest from Spain to India, while missionaries carried the faith even farther throughout the Old World.

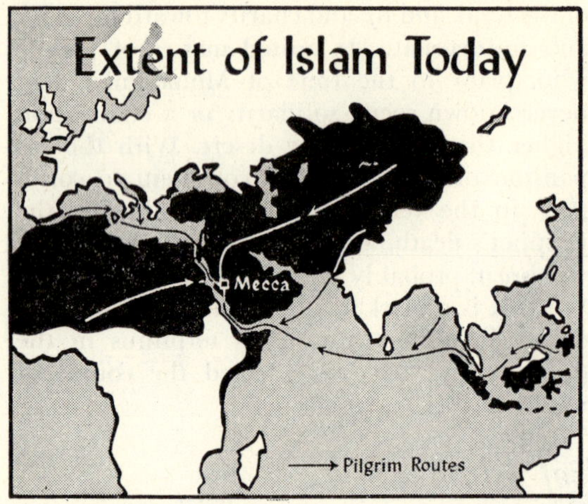

daughter called Fatima. The rule passed instead to Mohammed's most trusted friend and adviser, Abu Bakr, who thus became the first caliph (*Khalifa,* successor of the Prophet).

The caliph, who was "Successor of the Prophet" and "Commander of the Faithful," had to preserve and extend the faith, and because of the inseparable tie-up of the religious, social, and political aspects of Islam, he was the most important figure in the Moslem world. He also had some judicial power but almost no power to legislate. This peculiar situation arose from the doctrine that the only valid law was Divine Law, which had been given by God to the world through the agency of Mohammed. Therefore there could be no new law but only the reinterpretation of the one and only Divine Law. It was the special function of the *ulema,* or doctors of law, to perform the important task of interpretation.

Abu Bakr died two years after Mohammed (634), and the caliphate fell to another of Mohammed's faithful advisers, Omar, who ruled wisely until his death in 644. A son-in-law of the Prophet, named Othman, then assumed control until he was slain in 656, when he was succeeded by Ali, a younger cousin of Mohammed. The first four caliphs had been intimately associated with the Prophet, and they are known as those "who followed a right course." They consolidated the position of Islam throughout Arabia, conquered all the Near East, and expanded westward along the northern coast of Africa, as the map shows.

The Ommiads. From 656 to 661 there was a period of civil war among various claimants to the caliphate. Finally an able leader named Moawiyah triumphed and founded a new dynasty known as the Ommiad, which ruled from 661 to 750. Because the new caliph was supported most strongly in Syria, he shifted the capital of the empire from Medina to Damascus and set up an administrative organization based largely on Byzantine principles. A powerful Moslem fleet constructed by Moawiyah proved victorious over the Byzantine fleet and gained for the Ommiads some islands in the eastern Mediterranean. The forces of Islam now swept through Asia Minor and from the south and east converged on Constantinople. However, that city was able to repel all Moslem attacks for many centuries, until the fatal year 1453. The Moslems next began the conquest of the whole of northern Africa. At first they encountered stubborn resistance from the Moors, but they eventually won out, and the warlike Moors were converted by the thousands to the strength of Islam.

In Spain lay the weak kingdom of the Visigoths, and in 711 an army of Moors led by Tarik (the word Gibraltar comes from "Jebel-al-Tarik"—"Mount of Tarik") landed on the coast of Spain and within seven years had forced its way beyond the Pyrenees (though not under Tarik, who had been recalled). They swept across what is now south and central France and were turned back only by Charles Martel at the battle of Tours in 732, a century after Mohammed's death.

The Moslems also expanded into central Asia, raiding and seizing lands held by the Turks, Afghans, Chinese, Tibetans, and Hindus. Before the eighth century was half over the Moslem warriors could claim for the caliph lands in Turkestan and in the Indus valley. Still later they entered India, to conquer it and control its people until the British came in the eighteenth century.

The Ommiads held their greatest dominion

This is a model of an Arab dhow. In frail ships like this one—150 to 200 tons—the Arabs sailed the Mediterranean, invaded Spain and the African coast, and threatened Constantinople.

during the caliphate of al-Walid (705-715), when they controlled an empire extending from the Pyrenees and the Atlantic to India and central Asia (map right). Their empire was governed according to local customs, for the Arabs were not themselves organizers like the Romans. They made few radical changes in government administration in the lands they conquered but took care to place their own officers in the posts of greatest importance.

The Abbasids. But the Ommiads were falling into disrepute throughout the empire, especially among the Moslems of Persia, who resented the hegemony exercised by Syrian interests at Damascus. After various unsuccessful insurrections, a new dynasty, the Abbasid (which traced its descent from Abbas, the uncle of Mohammed), rose to power in 750 and established its capital at Bagdad. The Abbasid dynasty ruled from 750 to 1258 and marks the high tide of Islamic civilization. For the first time the Persian element, which was the most intellectual in the Moslem world, gained ascendancy. The Abbasid caliphs reduced the old Arabic aristocracy and set themselves up as oriental autocrats, surrounded by a lavish court life that would have distressed the simple-living Mohammed.

During the rule of Harun al-Rashid especially, from 786 to 809, Moslem civilization attained that dazzling state described in the *Arabian Nights*. The caliphs were generous patrons of the arts and sciences, and scholars were welcomed to their courts irrespective of their racial or religious backgrounds. The large city which sprang up—Bagdad—was seething with strangers from all corners of the known world. Around the bazaars could be seen merchants who had brought fabulous carpets from Persia, delicate silks from China, tempered steel from Damascus, cottons from Egypt, red and yellow Moroccan leather, together with the tasseled fez, and jewelry and fabrics from Bagdad, whence came also the new paper fashioned out of rags, an art copied from the Chinese. In the great capital there could be found swarming past the bazaars and up the twisting alleys a motley population: guardsmen of the caliph, beggars, Ethiopians, gesticulating traders, veiled harem girls under escort of eunuchs, Hindu philosophers, Byzantine merchants, poets, painters, ruffians, desert tribesmen, and a host of others, clad in every color.

Life flourished under Harun al-Rashid because the Moslems drew on the entire known world for customs, culture, and inventions. The high state of their civilization can be appreciated when one contrasts it with the barren life pursued by the Frankish subjects of Harun al-Rashid's famous western contemporary, Charlemagne (Chapter 12).

Under these Abbasid caliphs the Islamic empire reached its widest extent. At this time it was greater in area than the imperial domain of the Roman Caesars, extending as it did from Spain to northwest India and from central Asia to the Sudan in middle Africa. And it should be kept in mind that during their expansion the Moslem Arabs "assimilated to their creed, speech, and even physical type, more aliens than any stock before or since, not excepting the Hellenic, the Roman, the Anglo-Saxon, or the Russian."[13]

THIRTEENTH-CENTURY PERSIAN ILLUMINATION

Political disintegration of the empire. But the Abbasids, like the Ommiads before them, declined in power. Owing to internal weaknesses, including a breakdown in the administrative system, the political solidarity of Islam disintegrated. An Ommiad emir (prince or commander) broke away from Abbasid control in 756 and set up his own dynasty at Cordova in Spain, which became a caliphate in 929. Another caliphate, the Fatimid, was established in 909 in north Africa, and in 969 its capital was set up in Cairo. The Abbasids in Bagdad could do nothing to stem the disintegration of the empire into autonomous states. They themselves, in fact, had become victims of rival political factions in Bagdad.

The Seljuk Turks. The eleventh century saw the Abbasids fall under the control of the Seljuk Turks, a Tatar or Mongol people, who had been employed originally as mercenary troops by the Abbasids but had proved so powerful that in 1055 they began to rule the caliphs. They subdued all Persia and defeated the Byzantine emperor in 1071, crippling his power. It was the great advance by the Turks through Asia Minor that prompted Pope Urban II in 1095 to set western Christendom the holy task of wresting from the Moslems the Lord's Sepulcher in Jerusalem.

The Seljuks continued to dominate the puppet Abbasids until 1258, when the Mongol forces of a nephew of the dreaded Genghis Khan (d. 1227) devastated Bagdad and put an end to the Abbasid dynasty. Then came a new group of rulers, the Ottoman Turks. Like the Seljuks, they came from central Asia originally. The Ottomans adopted Islam with a fanaticism that made their might almost invincible, and, gaining control of the Abbasid dominions, the new Moslems pitted their strength against the crumbling power of the Byzantine empire. Constantinople fell at last in 1453, and the Ottomans pressed on in southeastern Europe, driving as far as Vienna, where they were turned back with difficulty in 1529 and again in 1683.

Although the great Abbasid empire had crumbled politically under the hammer blows of the Turks, Islam continued to expand as a missionary faith, holding and extending its strength in central Asia, Malaya, and the great islands (such as Java, Sumatra, and Borneo, in Indonesia). In the nineteenth century it pushed south and east into equatorial Africa. The universal appeal of the Islamic faith has attracted numerous converts, aside from those who were affected by the political activity of the early expansion. Many people were attracted by the specific promises and by the comparatively simple rules of conduct which Islam set down. Since the late nineteenth century a spiritual and political plan of uniting the Moslems has achieved some popularity, even though no concrete ramifications are evident, showing the strong kindredship which remains among the Moslems. The Ottoman Turks in adopting the religion of the government they replaced perpetuated the Islamic faith. Thus, although political unity was not maintained by a single Moslem empire, a form of unity was perpetuated by a common faith and way of life. The world of Islam emerged in modern times as a solid ribbon of peoples stretching east-west from Morocco to Indonesia and north-south from the fringe of Siberia to Zanzibar. About one-seventh of the world's population is rated to be Moslem, making a total of over 300 million adherents.

Political, Economic, and Social Life

Mohammed's changes in government. Before Mohammed the social organization of the Arabs had been based on blood kinship. Like all other primitive societies, the Arabs were united by ties of blood. Groups claimed descent from a common ancestor and possessed a common worship and a common set of mores. The individual counted for little by himself but for much as an integral member of the group. The family interpreted the social and legal actions of its members. Mohammed substituted for blood kinship "the community of faith." The Prophet looked upon all Moslems as equal before Allah and the civil law. But after his death an aristocracy grew up, composed in theory of the descendants of Mohammed and his advisers.

The caliph and his administration. The one real ruler of society was Allah; therefore Islam was a theocratic state. "The object of government is to lead men to prosperity in this world and to salvation in the next."[14] Allah was believed to rule through an earthly representative, the caliph, and the latter governed all Islam according to Moslem law as prescribed in the Koran and according to the interpretation of the law by the learned legal doctors called the *ulema.* But the caliph did not administer his vast domains himself. Machinery was set up similar to that of the Byzantine empire. The Abbasids had ten governmental departments: finance, war, expenditures, registry, correspondence, seals, court of appeals, office of posts, bureau of freedmen and slaves, and bureau of state property. They also divided their empire into thirteen provinces, each ruled by a prefect responsible to the caliph.

At the royal palace of the Abbasids were various subordinate officials who were always

"Punishment of a Criminal," a Persian manuscript illumination, showing Chinese influence.

at the beck and call of the caliph. They included the chamberlain, who introduced envoys and visiting dignitaries, the executioner, who was famed for his proficiency at torture, and the astrologer, without whose advice some caliphs would not act. The most powerful person next to the caliph was the vizier, who carried out the highest functions of government on behalf of his superior (and, in fact, was often the real power when the caliph was weak-willed). He appointed and deposed governors of provinces and judges, and presided over the council which was made up of the heads of different departments.

The most important department was the bureau of finance. The Moslems paid no poll tax, but the state levied a tax (the *zakah*) on arable lands, herds, wares, and gold and silver. All money collected from Moslems was given to such believers as the poor, the orphans, and slaves and captives who were to be ransomed. The unbelievers, on the other hand, were required to pay a land tax (the most important source of revenue), a poll tax, and tithes levied upon their merchandise. The caliph used the revenue from these taxes for the payment of troops, the upkeep of mosques, and the building of roads and bridges.

The government employed police, among whose duties was the regulation of public morality (such as chastising all men who dyed their gray beards black). There was also a postal system which used pigeons as letter carriers. An intelligence service employed men and women as spies to ferret out information of value to the government.

Weaknesses of the governing system. The caliph might nominate as his successor any one of his sons he favored, or even some kinsman whom he considered worthy. Needless to say, such a loose policy of succession proved a constant source of weakness and irritation. But the chief weakness of the entire administrative system was the extraordinary power given to the caliph in military, political, and religious matters, which under the later Abbasids proved distinctly unfortunate. Because many of the caliphs became more interested in harem delights than in governmental duties, more and more power was delegated to the vizier, who thus saw it to his advantage to foment harem intrigues in order to gain his own way. An inevitable decline in governmental efficiency resulted.

In time some of the provincial officials rebelled against the caliph and had to be recognized as sultans, or sovereigns in their own right.

The life of a provincial ruler. An interesting description of life in Cairo in the eleventh century has been left us by a Persian writer. The caliphal palace actually housed 30,000 people, including 1000 horse and foot guards and 12,000 servants. At festivals the young caliph could be seen, pleasant looking, clean-shaven, and simply dressed in white, riding on a mule with an attendant holding over him a parasol embroidered with precious stones. The caliph in Cairo possessed thousands of houses, generally constructed of brick, and often rising five or six stories above the lamp-lighted streets. He also owned an immense number of shops, which he rented out. The shopkeepers who sold their wares there had to sell at a fixed price. Any one of them found guilty of cheating was paraded on a camel through the streets, ringing a bell and confessing his sin to the bystanders.

The Fatimid caliph al-Mustansir was the most lavishly inclined of all the rulers. From his predecessors he inherited millions. His riches included jewels, crystal vases, inlaid gold plates, ivory and ebony inkstands, musk phials, steel mirrors, amber cups, chessboards of gold with gold and silver pieces, jeweled daggers and swords, and rich embroidered fabrics from Damascus. He is supposed to have had erected in his palace a pavilion shaped like the sacred Kaaba in Mecca. There he would drink to the accompaniment of stringed music and sweet singers, and maintain (in perfect truth), "This is pleasanter than staring at a black stone, listening to the drone of the muezzin, and drinking bad water."[15] Gone was the Prophet's ideal of simple living here.

Harun al-Rashid (786-809). Just as the Abbasid was the most brilliant of all Moslem dynasties, so the reign of Harun al-Rashid was the most spectacular of the Abbasid rule. He was the contemporary of the great Charlemagne, and there can be no doubt that Harun was the more powerful ruler and the symbol of the more highly advanced culture. The two monarchs were on the most friendly terms, even though their friendship arose out of self-interest. Charlemagne wanted Harun as a possible ally against the Byzantine emperors. (As we will see in Chapter 12, Charlemagne was the first ruler in western Europe to establish an extensive empire after Rome's fall). Harun wanted to use Charlemagne against the powerful Ommiad caliphs of Cordova, who had broken away from Abbasid domination. Numerous embassies and presents were exchanged between Charlemagne and Harun. For example, the Moslems sent the Christian rich fabrics, aromatics, and even an elephant. An intricate clock from Bagdad seems to have been treated in the barbaric west as a miracle.

Relations between the Abbasid caliphate and the Byzantine empire were never very cordial, for conflicts often broke out over the constantly shifting boundary lines that separated Christian and Moslem territories. In 782 Harun (while yet only the future successor to the throne) commanded an expedition that reached the Bosporus and forced the Byzantine leaders to conclude a humiliating peace which involved the payment of a huge tribute. Later the Byzantine emperor repudiated the terms of the treaty and even sent a letter asking for the return of the tribute money already paid. Harun al-Rashid, in magnificent anger and scorn, sent back the letter with the following penned on the back:

"In the name of God, the Merciful, the Compassionate. From Haroun, Commander of the Faithful, to Nicephorus, the dog of the Greeks. I have read your letter, you son of a she-infidel, and you shall see the answer before you hear it."[16]

Whereupon the irate caliph sent forth expeditions to ravage Asia Minor, captured several Byzantine cities, and even imposed a humiliating tax on the emperor himself and on each member of the royal household.

The capital city. Bagdad in the days of Harun al-Rashid was indeed a city worthy of description. Its wealth and splendor equaled that of Constantinople, and its chief glory was the royal palace. With its annexes for harem, eunuchs, and officials, the caliph's residence occupied one third of Bagdad, and its gorgeously appointed audience chamber, furnished with the richest rugs, cushions, and curtains which the orient could create, must have been breath-taking in its effect.

On ceremonial occasions the extent of the caliph's riches could be better realized. At the marriage of the daughter of one of Harun's viziers, the caliph had a thousand pearls of extraordinary size rained upon the couple, who stood upon a golden mat studded with sapphires and pearls. The royal princes and guests were showered with balls of musk, each containing a ticket claiming an estate or splendid slave. It is said that at one reception some Byzantine envoys mistook first the chief chamberlain's office and then the vizier's office for the royal audience hall. In the Hall of the Tree they saw an artificial tree of gold and silver which had on its branches birds of the same metals made to chirp by means of automatic devices. These tales could be multiplied, and it is little wonder that the magnificence and lavishness of the Abbasid court created a legend of oriental romance and splendor which has existed to our own times, chiefly through the *Arabian Nights*.[17]

Elsewhere we noticed the cosmopolitan nature of Bagdad, with its bazaars containing goods from all over the known world. There we would find spices, minerals, and dyes from India; rubies, fabrics, and slaves from central Asia; honey, wax, and white slaves from Scandinavia and Russia; ivory, gold dust, and black slaves from Africa. One bazaar in the city specialized in goods from China, including silks, musk, and porcelain. The merchants were a wealthy and respected group, as were the professional men and scholars. We have an account of one scholar's routine: He took a daily ride, then went to a public bath where attendants poured water over him. Then he put on a lounging robe, sipped a cool drink, and took a siesta. This concluded, he burned perfume to give himself a soothing aroma, and ordered a dinner which often consisted of soup, chicken, and bread. Then he went back to sleep, and upon awakening drank some choice old wine. To this repast he added quinces and Syrian apples whenever he desired fresh fruits.

Moslem society. The upper level of Abbasid society consisted of the caliph and his family, government officials, and prominent members of the army. The upper portion of the common people included literary men, scholars, artists, merchants, and professional men, while below them were ranked the farmers, herdsmen, and the country population. Slavery was prevalent, its members coming from non-Moslem groups who had in all likelihood been captured in war. Slaves were often Greeks, Slavs, and Armenians, while many blacks were recruited from Africa. Some of the slaves were eunuchs attached to the harems, while slave girls were often employed as dancers, singers, and concubines. At first only Arabians occupied important posts, but intermarriage with non-Arabs changed the situation, so that eventually there came a time when the officials were mostly Persian or Turkish.

Fashions and amusements. The clothes of men included a black high-peaked hat of felt or wool, wide trousers, a shirt, vest, and jacket. Among the furnishings of the home were cushions, hand-woven carpets, tables of wood inlaid with ebony and mother-of-pearl, and a *diwan*, a sofa running around three sides of the room. The gastronomic delights of the prosperous included chicken, shelled nuts, and sherbets flavored with extracts of violets, bananas, roses, and mulberries. Although the Koran distinctly forbade the drinking of alcoholic beverages, the wealthy, the scholars, the poets, and high government officials were quite willing to forget the prohibition. One of the most popular drinks was *khamr*, made of fermented dates. Bagdad had many public baths, because a Moslem tradition states, "Cleanliness is a part of faith." Men used these baths not only for hygienic purposes but also as resorts of amusement, while women were allowed to visit the baths on special days.

Men indulged in such favorite indoor games as dice, backgammon, and chess. Or they might prefer outdoor pastimes such as archery, polo, fencing, javelin throwing, horse racing, and hunting. Many of the Abbasid caliphs were particularly fond of hunting lions and wild boars. Travelers to Persia brought back with them falconry and hawking.

Etiquette. The social conduct of the Moslems has been conditioned by the dictates of the Koran and the accounts of the Prophet's own life. Sayyid al-Bekri wrote a book on etiquette, in which statements attributed to Mohammed regarding conduct were reproduced. Concerning the code D. S. Margoliouth has written:

"When friends meet and salute, they should not bow, nor should they kiss, but it is right for them to embrace, i. e., put their arms round each other's shoulders; if a man sneezes, those who are present should wish him well, and they are justified in doing so even should he sneeze while saying his prayers. Many pious men will not use fork or knife, because the Prophet is not known to have employed those instruments; if they use them, they will at least hold the fork in the right hand, because it is known that the Prophet ate with his right."[18]

Moslem women. Islamic people have been much criticized in literature in the West for the low social and moral status assigned to women. It is true that the Prophet's permission of polygamy (a Moslem might have four legitimate wives) did not make for equality between the sexes. While it was considered a duty in Islam for men to marry, women were held in a low social state, for a woman's prime duty consisted in obeying her husband's commands, caring for his children, and managing his household.

However, in judging Moslem standards, we must at all times remember the task which Mohammed faced in dealing with very illiterate, fetish-worshiping nomads who used to abandon unwanted female infants. While Islam places women in an inferior position and forbids them to lead prayer when men are present, it assigns them a definite religious role. There is a general impression among Christians that the Moslems believe that women have no souls. Such an impression is without foundation. True enough, the delights of Paradise are painted with a view to capturing the imagination of the male, but the fact that women are allowed (and even supposed) to take part in Islamic religious ceremonies should prove beyond a doubt that their reward for so acting will be the gaining of Paradise for their souls.

Under Mustapha Kemal Ataturk, Turkey after the First World War raised the status of women immeasurably by granting them the right to vote and the right to enter professions and by removing certain religious restrictions, such as the wearing of the veil. This last is a real departure from the custom of centuries, for the good Moslem regarded the woman who did not cover her face with a veil as highly immodest and brazen, and always considered Christian women, for example, as quite shameless for that reason.

Moslem economic advantages. We have already noted the manufacturing and commercial prosperity enjoyed by the Moslem empire, a prosperity that endured from the seventh throughout the twelfth centuries and did not come to Europe to a similar degree until the sixteenth and seventeenth centuries. Added to the natural ability of the Moslems as traders were the size and wealth of Islam's territories and the far-sighted economic policies set forth by the Prophet himself, who had always encouraged commerce among his people. Certain other factors were also very important in the economic success of Islam. First of all, the empire was in a most suitable geographical position, being in close contact with three continents and thus able to shuttle goods back and forth from China to Spain and from Russia to central Africa. Another reason for its economic well-being was the tolerance of its rulers, who allowed non-Moslem merchants and craftsmen to reside in their territories and carry on mutually profitable commerce with their home countries. Again, the fact that the Moslems were skilled both in industry and agriculture gave them products which enriched their commercial activities and made for a well-balanced economy. Lastly, the presence of such splendid urban centers as Cairo, Bagdad, and Cordova tended to stimulate trade and industry throughout the Moslem world.

Industry. The textile industries of the Moslems were particularly prosperous and produced silk, cotton, muslin (the word comes from Mosul in Mesopotamia), and linen goods. Metal, leather, enamel, pottery, and the variety of luxury goods which we have enumerated in connection with Byzantine manufacturing life were also produced in abundance. As in the Byzantine empire, the workers in the great manufacturing cities of Islam were organized into guilds and crafts supervised by the government. A merchant or craftsman guilty of fraud was denounced publicly. However, despite the limitations imposed by governmental supervision, the guilds enjoyed a large measure of freedom of action.

Trade. Commerce was extensive and exceedingly profitable because of the daring and navigating skill of the Arab shipmasters. Their vessels could be found in the ports of India, the seas of China, the river mouths of the Black Sea, the Persian Gulf, and throughout the Mediterranean. Most of the trade was between various countries of the Moslem empire, but commerce sprang up also with Christian lands, especially after the ninth century. There can be no doubt that Islamic trade was extensive, for even in such out-of-the-way countries of northern Europe as Finland, Sweden, Russia, Norway, the British Isles, and Iceland Islamic coins in considerable numbers have been unearthed.[19] Besides trade by ships there was trade by "ships of the desert"—camels. Overland from Bagdad journeyed the great caravans to India and China or northward to Syria and Asia Minor.

The only real competitor of the Moslems was the Byzantine empire, but the commercial activities of the latter were confined to a much smaller area—the eastern Mediterranean, the Black Sea, the lands extending to the Baltic and including Russia, and Asia Minor. Furthermore, as the Middle Ages wore on, the Byzantine empire disintegrated while the Moslems managed to retain control of what they had won.

Farming. Moslem economic wealth was increased by the innovations made in agriculture. Mesopotamia flourished because of its extensive system of irrigation, and large quantities of fruits and cereals were grown. Wheat came from the regions of the Nile, cotton from north Africa, olives and wines from Moorish Spain, and wool from eastern Asia Minor, while Persia was noted for its horse raising. The farming system was analogous to that of the Middle Ages in Europe in that estates were worked by free peasants, slaves, and serfs.

Cultural Contributions

Arabic words in the English language. The large number of words in the English language coming directly from Arabic will prove conclusively our debt to Moslem civilization. Some of the commoner words are algebra, zero, bazaar, traffic, lilac, admiral, magazine, cheque, tariff, douane, caravan, coffee, arabesque, lute, alkali, alchemy, attar, cipher. Words derived from Moslem proper nouns such as muslin, mecca, damask, fez, ottoman, morris (from Moorish) are further indicative of the extent to which we have borrowed from another civilization.

The high attainment of the Moslems in the intellectual and artistic fields cannot be attributed to the Arabs, who as a group remained quite unprogressive, but rather to those peoples who had embraced Islam in Syria, Egypt, Persia, Mesopotamia, north Africa, and Spain. Diverse peoples, they were nevertheless united by a common language, Arabic. The supremacy of that tongue was kept unchallenged by the command that the Koran must not be used in translation.

Translations from Greek and Indian. The amazing brilliance of Moslem learning was due not so much to indigenous genius as to Islam's ability to synthesize the best in other cultures. The cosmopolitan spirit which permeated the Abbasid dynasty supplied the tolerance necessary for new ideas, so that the philosophy and science of ancient Greece, India, and even China found a welcome in Bagdad. Under Harun al-Rashid and his successors translations of the Greek classics were made in Arabic. One of the most outstanding translators was Hunain Ibn Ishaq (d. 877), a Nestorian Christian. He and his associates translated works by Galen and Hippocrates on medicine and collected manuscripts to give Bagdad a magnificent library. The search after Greek writings at last made available for Arabic scholars a complete knowledge of such Hellenistic intellects as Aristotle, Euclid, Ptolemy, and Archimedes. Between the ninth and the twelfth centuries, more works were produced in Arabic than in any other language.

The period from 762 to 900 was an era of translation not only of Greek treatises but also of those from India, whence came the Moslems' knowledge of Hindu mathematics, including the use of "Arabic" numerals and algebra. Thus from Greece, Persia, and India came the basis of Moslem learning, and from Islam an augmented knowledge was in turn later transmitted to Jewish and Christian scholars in western Europe.[20] In Chapter 16 we will see that this learning entered Europe mainly by way of Spain. These new ideas did much to end the so-called Dark Ages in western Europe and to pave the way for the awakening known as the Renaissance.

Advances in medicine. The next two hundred years (900-1100) can be called the golden age of Moslem learning. This period was particularly significant for advances made in medicine. The first and perhaps greatest Moslem physician was al-Razi (about 860-925), better known to the West as Rhazes. One of the great doctors of all time, Rhazes wrote more than two hundred works, of which one of the most famous is *On Smallpox and Measles,* the first clear description of the symptoms and treatment of these diseases. His most monumental writing was the *Comprehensive Book,* a huge encyclopedia. In it he cites for each disease all Greek, Syrian, Arabian, Persian, and Indian authors and includes his own personal experiences and opinions as well. Many translations of the encyclopedia were later used by European physicians, and by 1542 five separate editions had been printed in Europe. Rhazes also wrote copiously on theology, mathematics, astronomy, physics, meteorology, optics, and alchemy.

The most familiar name in Moslem medicine is that of Avicenna (980-1037), a great physicist, philosopher, and physician. Into his million-word *Canon of Medicine* he packed all the legacy of Greek knowledge together with Arabic medical learning. The *Canon* was translated into Latin by Gerard of Cremona in the twelfth century and was so much in demand that it was issued sixteen times in the last half of the fifteenth century and more than twenty times in the sixteenth. It is still read and used in the Orient today.

Not only did medical theory flourish at this time; hospitals were in use throughout the empire. They were divided into sections for men and women and had their own wards and dispensaries and sometimes even a library. The qualifications of physicians, druggists, and barbers were subject to inspection.

In spite of the limitations imposed on the Arabs by their religion (such as their being forbidden to study anatomy), they were in some ways superior to their European contemporaries. Whereas the Moslems were skilled practitioners whose technique was at least sane, the Christian doctors, especially during the Middle Ages, were plagued with superstition. For proof we have an account of the time of the Crusades taken from the narrative of a Syrian physician called Thabit:

"They brought before me a knight in whose leg an abscess had grown; and a woman afflicted with imbecility. To the knight I applied a small poultice until the abscess opened and became well; and the woman I put on diet and made her humor wet. Then a Frankish physician came to them and said, 'This man knows nothing about treating them.' He then said to the knight, 'Which wouldst thou prefer, living with one leg or dying with two?' The latter replied, 'Living with one leg.' The physician said, 'Bring me a strong knight and a sharp ax.' A knight came with the ax. And I was standing by. Then the physician laid the leg of the patient on a block of wood and bade the knight strike his leg with the ax and chop it off at one blow. Accordingly he struck it—while I was looking on—one blow, but the leg was not severed. He dealt another blow, upon which the marrow of the leg flowed out and the patient died on the spot. He then examined the woman and said, 'This is a woman in whose head there is a devil which has possessed her. Shave off her hair.' Accordingly they shaved it off and the woman began once more to eat their ordinary diet—garlic and mustard. Her imbecility took a turn for the worse. The physician then said, 'The devil has penetrated through her head.' He therefore took a razor, made a deep cruciform incision on it, peeled off the skin at the middle of the incision until the bone of the skull was exposed and rubbed it with salt. The woman also expired instantly. Thereupon I asked them whether my services were needed any longer, and when they replied in the negative I returned home, having learned of their medicine what I knew not before."[21]

Physics and chemistry. Other branches of science besides medicine progressed during the golden age. Physics continued the paths of inquiry laid down by Hellenistic leaders, but Moslem scientists arose who were no mere copyists. Alhazen (965-1039?) developed optics to a remarkable degree and wrote a treatise on the subject. He challenged the view of Ptolemy and Euclid that the eye sends out visual rays to its object, interested himself in optic reflections and illusions, and examined the refraction of light rays through air and water. He was the chief source of all medieval western writers on optics.[22]

Chemistry started out as alchemy, the attempt to transmute base metals into precious ones and to find a magic elixir for the preservation of human life. The Moslem alchemists produced many new drugs and chemicals, including alum, borax, cream of tartar, sal ammoniac, carbonate of soda, and corrosive sublimate.

Astronomy and mathematics. In astronomy the Moslems followed primarily the views of Ptolemy. They developed good astronomical instruments and built observatories in some of the largest cities. But they fell into the error of the Chaldeans and Persians, mixing up astronomy with astrology, a practice that continued to plague the progress of true science for many centuries.

In mathematics the Moslems were particularly indebted to the Greeks and Hindus, from whom they learned most of their arithmetic, geometry, and algebra. From the Greeks came the geometry of Euclid and the fundamentals of trigonometry, which Ptolemy had worked out. From the Hindus came the nine signs now known as the Arabic numerals. However, it may well be that the Arabs invented the all-important zero, although some scholars would assign this honor also to the Indians. Two names deserve special mention when we speak of Moslem algebra: Al-Khwarizmi (d. about 840) wrote treatises on astronomy, the Hindu method of calculation, algebra, and arithmetic, while the famous poet Omar Khayyam (d. 1123?) advanced even beyond Al-Khwarizmi in regard to equations. Where the latter dealt only with quadratics, Omar Khayyam devoted much of his treatise on algebra to cubic equations.

Moslem geography. Although the Moslems were synthesists rather than originators in science as a whole, they did make some important contributions of their own to the science of geography. Trade and the administration of a far-flung empire made imperative an accurate knowledge of lands. From the ninth to the fourteenth century a voluminous geographical literature was written in Arabic. In the first half of the ninth century Greek treatises were translated. Maps of the world were made during the tenth century, the first of them showing Mecca in the center, just as early medieval Christian cartographers were inclined to allot this position of honor to Jerusalem.

The tenth and eleventh centuries witnessed studies by scholars on climate, while a vogue of descriptive geography arose. In the eleventh century the mathematical aspect of geography was stressed when one scientist began to make tables of latitudes and longitudes. Al-Idrisi (1099-1154) was a geographer at the court of the Christian ruler Roger II of Sicily. He tried to synthesize preceding geographical knowledge, to reconcile descriptive and astronomical geography, and to formulate principles of a scientific nature. He may possibly have conceived of the earth as a sphere. Yaqut (1175-1229) is noted for having compiled a large geographical dictionary (1228), in which all names are listed in alphabetical order. Certainly the geographical knowledge of the Moslems was far superior to that of any people in Christendom during the Middle Ages.

Arabic poetry. Arabic literature is prolific, yet it is little read by westerners as a rule, perhaps because of the traditional difference between westerners and easterners in matters of style and subject matter. Long before Mohammed was born, Arabia had produced hundreds of genuine poets with an original gift for story-telling. The Prophet himself was an excellent bard. To us, Omar Khayyam is the most familiar Persian poet. His *Rubáiyát* is world-famous because of the musical (though not over-accurate) translation by Edward Fitz-Gerald. Here are some stanzas from the poem which will indicate its beautiful imagery, gentle pessimism, and frank hedonism:

O threats of Hell and Hopes of Paradise!
One thing at least is certain—*This* Life flies;
  One thing is certain and the rest is Lies;
The Flower that once has blown for ever dies.

Strange, is it not? that of the myriads who
Before us pass'd the door of Darkness through,
  Not one returns to tell us of the Road,
Which to discover we must travel too.

. . . .

We are no other than a moving row
Of Magic Shadow-shapes that come and go
  Round with the Sun-illumined Lantern held
In Midnight by the Master of the Show;

But helpless Pieces of the Game He plays
Upon his Chequer-board of Nights and Days;
  Hither and thither moves, and checks, and slays,
And one by one back in the Closet lays.

. . . .

The Moving Finger writes; and, having writ,
Moves on: nor all your Piety nor Wit
  Shall lure it back to cancel half a Line,
Nor all your Tears wash out a Word of it.

And that inverted Bowl they call the Sky,
Whereunder crawling coop'd we live and die,
  Lift not your hands to *It* for help—for It
As impotently moves as you or I.[23]

Moslem prose. The piece of Moslem prose literature most familiar to western readers is the *Arabian Nights.* It is a collection of vivid tales, supposedly recounted by a vizier's daughter to a king as a means of preventing him from slaying Moslem brides the morning following their marriage. Altogether the story-teller takes a thousand and one nights to relate her engrossing stories, each tale filled with suspense. The collection covers many aspects of Moslem social life. While often frankly erotic, these tales are at once fascinating and brilliant and have influenced later literary patterns. As a matter of record, when the lovely story-teller was through, the king not only decided to forego the custom of putting Moslem brides to death, but made her his wife and queen.

Almost unknown to westerners are the Moslems' histories. Within the first eleven hundred years of Islam about six hundred historians had delved into the past and written accounts. Some of their treatises are indeed outstanding, such as the *Chronicle of Tabari* which runs to the year A.H. 302 (that is, 924 A.D., because the Mohammedans begin their calendar with 622, the year of the Hegira). The *Chronicle* occupies almost eight thousand pages, of which over a thousand deal with pre-Islamic events. Historical criticism was a strong point with the Moslems, because they were so keenly interested in the accuracy of the Koran and all other writings concerning the Prophet. They specialized in three main fields: biographies of Mohammed and other Islamic figures of importance, accounts of the spread of Islam, and world histories. Besides histories, Moslem scholars wrote dictionaries, grammars, and studies on philology, while in the fourteenth century they compiled a dictionary of national biography in twenty-five volumes.

Philosophy. Philosophy was also a favorite Moslem subject, although it was borrowed from the civilizations which the Moslems overran or was influenced in large measure by Greek ideas. Like the medieval Christian philosophers, Moslem thinkers largely concerned themselves with applying Aristotelian principles to religious problems as a means of bolstering up orthodox creeds, and we find many prominent philosophers attempting to reconcile reason with faith.

Avicenna, the physician, wrote commentaries

THE MOSQUE OF KAZENNAIN, BAGDAD

on Aristotle and his own Moslem predecessors, which were translated into Latin and had a far-reaching influence upon European thought. Moses Maimonides (1135-1204) was a Spanish Jew living under Moorish rule whose learning made him perhaps the greatest Jewish philosopher of the Middle Ages. Another Spaniard, Ibn Rushd, better known as Averroës (about 1126-1198), was the most profound commentator on Aristotle in the Moslem world and had the greatest effect of any Moslem philosopher upon European thought. His theology was based on the belief that conflict between philosophy and revealed truth as enshrined in the Koran was unthinkable.

Art. The place of art in Moslem civilization was not particularly strong, owing to certain religious restrictions. Because the Prophet feared the return of idol worship, sculpture and pictorial art were absolutely forbidden, although manuscript illumination developed profusely in later periods. Music likewise received scant favor, because its only religious use was in chanting the Koran. Dancing was discouraged. But the Moslem love of splendor was gratified by the lavish use of ornament in their architecture and the adornment of private dwellings with sumptuous silks, jewels, fine rugs, and vessels inlaid with gold and silver.

Persian influence in art. Moslem art owed what originality it had mostly to Persia. The brilliant Sassanid era in Persia (226-641) had produced architecture, sculpture, and richly decorative minor arts. The Sassanid love of decorative animal figures remained an influence throughout Moslem art.

It is interesting to note the extent of Persian influence on non-Moslem peoples. The Japanese have in a shrine at Nara a silken banner of Persian design which dates back to the ninth century. It is said that Charlemagne himself was buried in a Persian shroud, and Tamerlane's tomb was designed by a Persian architect. Rugs on the floors of many homes today are Persian in motif.

Architecture. The two fields in which the Moslems excelled were architecture and the decorative arts, the latter developing as a compensation for the religious ban on pictorial art. As time went on, an original style of architecture evolved, so that the great mosques have such typical Moslem features as domes, horseshoe arches and minarets, slender towers from which the faithful are summoned to prayer. The Mosque of Kazennain, illustrated above, shows these features. Note the arcade of horseshoe arches to the far right, the domes, and the minarets. Different stylistic features can be observed in various parts of Islam. In Persia the mosques were usually built of brick and had high, round minarets and large domes, while those of the Moors usually had a flat roof.

The Moslems generally did not build on a monumental scale, but with the usual orien-

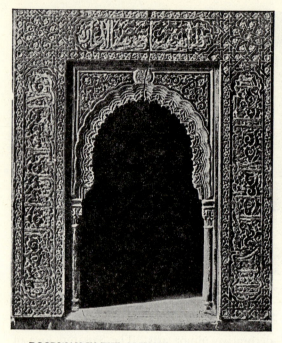

MESOPOTAMIAN POTTERY

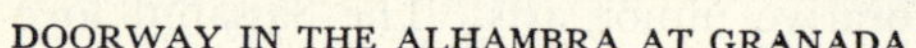

DOORWAY IN THE ALHAMBRA AT GRANADA

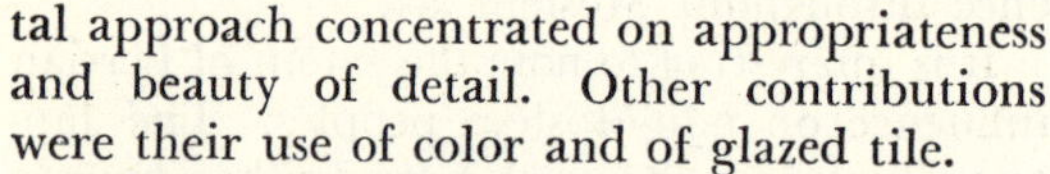

tal approach concentrated on appropriateness and beauty of detail. Other contributions were their use of color and of glazed tile.

Besides the mosques, the Moslems built large palaces, of which the most famous is the Alhambra at Granada in Spain. It is a fine example of Moslem architecture in a conquered country. The Spanish interpretation of the Moslem tradition was particularly delicate and elegant. Intricate details, like those of the doorway illustrated, were used throughout, always with restraint. Other examples of Moslem architecture, such as the Taj Mahal (page 595), based largely on Persian motifs, are to be found in India.

Decoration. The decorative skill of the Moslem artists was highly developed. Being restricted in their subject matter, craftsmen conceived beautiful patterns from flowers, while geometrical figures were used to develop graceful, curving patterns. An outstanding feature of ornamentation was the use of Arabic inscriptions. The beauty of the letters of this language made it adaptable to intricate ornamentation on mosque walls and the sides of urns. Tiles and mosaics were used with becoming effect to produce the lavish and conventionalized Moslem patterns. This reveals oriental concentration on the more abstract elements of art, such as line and pattern, rather than on western interests such as the scientific and realistic use of modeled forms, perspective, and atmosphere.

Moslem decorative skill found expression also in such other fields as carpet and rug making, brass work, and the famous steel products with gold inlays. Persian pottery has simple design and beautiful decoration. The dish above shows plant and animal motifs which were commonly used instead of the human figure. Note the manner in which the design is stylized and the figure distorted to fit the circular pattern. In the arts that the Moslems found open to them they improved upon their predecessors; their work is not large or grand but has a pleasing delicacy. Islamic art has modified western art, especially by richness of design.

Summary

We have now briefly traced the development of Islam as a world religion and the rise of this belief as a great religious, social, political, and economic system that spread to three continents and innumerable people. In addition to noting the phenomenal growth of the empire, we have witnessed the richness of Islam's cultural contributions. The Moslems were especially gifted in medicine, mathematics, and geography among the sciences, in poetry and historical writing in the field of literature, in commentaries on Aristotle in philosophy, and in architecture and the decorative arts. The unity of Moslem thought was preserved by the universal use of Arabic as the one medium of expression, a medium which was at once clear, concise, poetic, and adaptable to the most technical scientific terminology. But we should not forget that Moslem intellectual life was the product of a genius for synthesis of varying cultures rather than one of original contributions.

The influence of Islamic civilization upon the culture of Europe was significant. Although the Byzantine empire, Syria, and Sicily were important, the great intermediary was Spain, situated in Europe yet possessing outstanding Moorish and Jewish scholars. Learned Jews translated Arabic treatises on Greek and Moslem science into Latin. Beginning about the eleventh century and continuing for the next 150 years, scholars gathered at Narbonne, Marseilles, and Toledo for the all-important task of translation. During these years they made available to Europe the scholarship and scientific writings of the Moslems. Aristotle was introduced to Europe in Latin through Spain. The great diffusion of Greek and Arabic knowledge, more or less completed by 1300, was a tremendous factor in the revival of classical learning and the coming of the Renaissance.

Why, one may ask, has Islamic civilization in modern times failed to retain its cultural supremacy? One reason was the influx of semibarbarous peoples into Islamic lands during the Middle Ages. Another was the stagnation that accrued from a too rigid interpretation of the Koran, so that a ban was placed on material change and progress. Still another reason was the corrupt and despotic rule of such Moslem dynasties as the Ottomans in Turkey, who destroyed all progressive political and economic movements. But a new day is at hand for modern Islam. The Moslems have amply proved that they have the intellectual and administrative gifts to make themselves a great people, and the rejuvenation of Turkey after the First World War under the able guidance of the late Mustafa Kemal Ataturk has indicated a possible road for the modern descendants of Mohammed the Prophet. In addition to the Turks, other Moslem people have been on the march in recent times. The Arab peoples of the Middle East and north Africa—Tunisians, Moroccans, Egyptians, Iraqis, and Syrians—not to mention other Moslem peoples such as the Iranians, Pakistanis, and Indonesians have experienced a remarkable and dynamic awakening. These people have resurrected the memories of their glorious past; they are determined to enjoy complete political independence and to see to it that the Moslem world will play an important part in international affairs. This Moslem revival will constitute one of the major themes dealt with in our narrative of the twentieth-century world.

Chapter 11

Chronology of events and developments discussed in this chapter

India	300-1526
Panchatantra: *Indian fables*	300-500
Gupta dynasty: epitome of Hindu culture; spread of Hinduism	320-535
Kalidasa: lyric and epic poet; author of Shakuntala	c. 400-455
Chalukya dynasty in the Deccan: resisted Harsha	550-750
Harsha: rajah who united the northern warring states	606-647
Rajput clan rule in northern India	647-850
Sailendra dynasty: kingdom in Malay and the Indonesian archipelago	700-800
Turks under Mahmud annexed northwest India	1022
Moslem conquest of India	1175-1450
Delhi sultanate in northern India	1206-1526
Timur: looted Delhi; destroyed the northern Indian government until 1450	1398
China	220-1368
Fall of the Han dynasty	220
Huns captured Loyang, the capital, and the emperor	317
Eastern Chin dynasty established: refined civilization	317
Sui dynasty: united China; constructed canals	580-618
T'ang dynasty: land and tax reforms; fine culture; official histories	618-906
T'ai Tsung: great T'ang emperor; administrative reform; increased commerce	627-650
Li Po: lyric poet; showed Chinese life	701?-762
Tu Fu: greatest Chinese poet; combined artistry and realism	712-770
Turkestan lost to the Arabs: beginning of the T'ang decline	751
First known block print found in Japan; process developed in China	770
Province governors declared their independence: end of the T'ang dynasty	906
Sung dynasty: threatened by the Khitan and Jurchen; Neo-Confucianism	960-1368
Wang An-shih: statesman; devised concepts of a welfare state	1021-1086
China divided into Chin and Sung empires	1126
Genghis Khan: Mongolian leader; empire extended from Danube to Pacific	1162?-1227
Remnants of the Chin empire vanquished by Mongols	1234
Marco Polo arrived in Peking; wrote travelogue describing China	1275
Yuan dynasty: Kublai Khan, first ruler; capital at Peking	1279-1368
Japan	552-1198
Buddhism brought to Japan and became a dominant religion	552
Great Reform: document, giving emperor formal authority	645
Tai-ho: law code	702
Nara period: strengthening of Buddhism	710-794
Heian period: two new types of phonetic writing invented	794-1156
Yoritomo: shogun, *had effective controlling governmental power*	1146-1198

The Guptas and the T'angs: two golden ages

Medieval India, China, and Japan: 220-1450 A.D.

Previously, we traced the development in India and China of splendid indigenous cultures, marked by certain outstanding dynastic periods such as the Mauryan and the Han. When we left them, however, both India and China were engulfed in political upheavals and about to plunge into centuries of disunity and transition. Yet, whereas the contemporary troubles which beset the Graeco-Roman world in the West eventually brought an end to a thousand years of classical rule and culture, in India and China this era of conflict proved but the interlude to new and even more splendid flowerings of indigenous civilization. As a result, at the very time when the West found itself immersed in the so-called Dark Ages of the early medieval period, the East was reaching new heights of human attainment. First, India with the creation of the Gupta empire experienced its golden age of Hindu culture. Later, China entered upon what has also been described as a golden age with the accession to the imperial throne of the mighty T'ang dynasty, to be followed in turn by still other rich cultural epochs.

The medieval period in Asia is memorable in still other ways. There was an expansion of Indian civilization throughout southeast Asia, with a consequent enrichment of indigenous societies in what are now Burma, Indo-China, the Malay peninsula, and Indonesia. Similarly, there was a continuous impact of Chinese culture eastward upon the peoples of the Korean peninsula and the islands off the Asian mainland. As a result, there emerged the largely derivative culture of Japan, which at this time began its long road under an unbroken dynasty toward a position of preëminence in the modern world.

It might be said that the earlier sections on India and China described the formative period of their indigenous civilizations, while the present chapter relates to great eras of cultural consolidation. Yet this statement should be qualified. Both civilizations suffered periodically from internal conflict and external aggression and, in the case of India, Hindu society was appreciably changed by the impact of its Moslem conquerors. China in turn was subjected to repeated invasions by Mongol and other nomadic peoples who wrought important political and social changes. But whereas India became the synthesis —though not altogether successful or complete—of two opposing cultures, China was able to assimilate foreign elements to its basic native culture. In the case of both countries, however, historical development permitted the accretion of numberless customs and intellectual and artistic contributions, and the establishment of culture patterns destined to endure down to modern times.

India: The Imperial Guptas (c. 320-535)

The Gupta empire. We will recall that the Kushan empire, which had been one of the richest periods in Indian civilization and had witnessed the rise of Mahayana Buddhism, broke up after 220 A.D. Thereupon events in northern India followed a pattern that recurs time and again in Indian history: an epoch of distinction followed by a period of political disintegration and comparative cultural darkness.

In the fourth century, however, northern India entered upon the golden age of Hindu culture with the advent of the Gupta empire. The first of the Gupta dynasty established himself as ruler of the Ganges valley about 320 A.D. The next ruler, Samudragupta, who reigned some fifty years (c. 335-c. 385), was an outstanding warrior who sent his armies in all directions until at the time of his death his empire stretched across northern India from the Himalayas to the Narbada River, thus making it the greatest in extent and power since the days of Asoka six centuries earlier. His son, Chandragupta II (no relation to Chandragupta Maurya whom we have met before, page 200), extended the empire still farther west. It was during Chandragupta's reign (c. 385-c. 413) that the Gupta empire reached its zenith of power and splendor (see map, left). In fact, India probably achieved its closest approximation to national unity during the reigns of Asoka, Chandragupta II, and Akbar, whom we shall meet later.

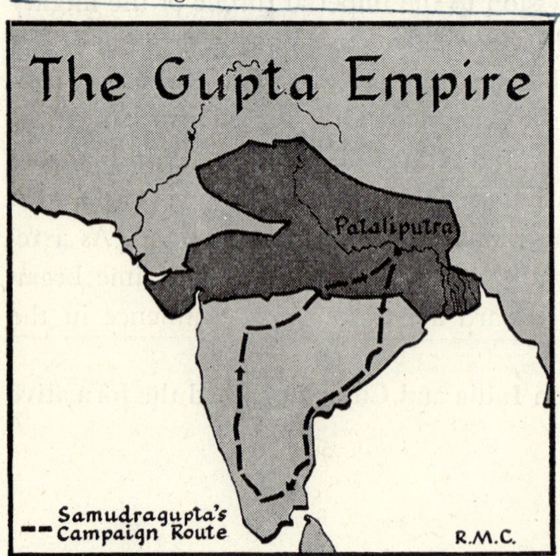

The Gupta monarchs normally "held all the levers and handles which worked the governmental machinery," and the king often administered justice himself. His principal revenues came from taking one-sixth of the land's produce, from duties levied at ports and ferries, and as income from crown lands and mines. We are told that women of the upper classes took a prominent share in the administration of certain areas, and that several of them even acted as governors as well as the heads of villages. Polygamy was widely prevalent and *suttee*—"the custom of burning widows on the funeral pyres of their husbands was coming into general use, at least among the ruling clans." Our most graphic account of conditions in the reign of Chandragupta II has been handed down in the journal of Fa Hien, a Chinese Buddhist pilgrim to India. He informs us that the empire was peaceful, prosperous, and well governed. "The people

The figure of Shiva in his "Dance of Destruction" is almost womanly in this fourteenth-century bronze.

are numerous and happy. They have not to register their households, or attend to any magistrates and their rules. The king governs without decapitation or other capital punishments. People of various sects set up houses of charity where rooms, couches, beds, food and drink are supplied to travellers."[1]

Religious developments. The Gupta age witnessed important religious developments. Buddhism, which had received its greatest impetus from Asoka and Kanishka, still had powerful exponents in various sages and philosophers. However, in the succeeding centuries it lost ground, owing in part at least to Hun invasions which must have destroyed great numbers of Buddhist monasteries in the northwest and eastern parts of India, so that in time Buddhism almost vanished from the land of its birth. Hinduism not only revived and became the dominant religion but it was during the period from about 185 B.C. to 750 A.D. that this faith gradually crystallized into the form it has today. This was in no small measure due to the imperial patronage enjoyed by the Brahman caste and the personal preference of the Gupta rulers for Hinduism. Yet in spite of the increasing influence of that faith, religious tolerance was an outstanding characteristic of the Gupta period, aided by the growing importance at this time of *bhakti* (devotion to a personal deity) with its love of fellow-beings and toleration of the opinions of others.

As we stated in Chapter 3, Hinduism adheres to the philosophical tenets of the *Upanishads,* so that it "recognizes the unity of all life—one source, one essence, and one goal—and regards the realization of this unity as the highest good, bliss, salvation, freedom, the final purpose of life. This is for Hindu thinkers eternal life; not an eternity in time, but the recognition here and now of All Things in the Self and the Self in all."[2] During the medieval period, various philosophical schools arose to expound the tenets of Hinduism, while popular devotion was shared between the cults of the Hindu Trinity, embodying the three great life processes of creation or Brahman, preservation or Vishnu, and destruction,

Vishnu the Preserver, in contrast to the dancing Shiva, is all calmness and veneration.

Shiva. Superstition had early crept into Hinduism, however, so that numberless other deities were also worshiped. Then as now, the cow was considered an object of veneration because she was gentle, was the giver of milk, and was a symbol of the sacredness of life.

Gupta scholarship and science. Students from all over Asia came to India's foremost university, situated at Nalanda, which had eight colleges and three libraries. Certainly, scholarship and science were of a very high caliber during this period. The most famous scientist was the astronomer and mathematician, Aryabhata. He discussed, in verse, quadratic equations, the value of π, solstices and equinoxes, the spherical shape of the earth and its rotation. Other Indian astronomers were able to predict eclipses accurately, to calculate the moon's diameter, and to expound the theory of gravitation.

Indian astronomy and mathematics were unequaled (except in geometry) by those of any ancient western people. Our Arabic numerals and the decimal system appear to have come originally from India. The numerals can be found on the rock edicts of Asoka (256 B.C.), while Aryabhata and Brahmagupta were using decimals long before the Arabs, Syrians, and Chinese had a chance to borrow them. Even the zero may have come from Indian sources. The mathematicians created the concept of a negative quantity (without which algebra could not exist), found the square root of 2, and solved complicated equations.

The Hindus were remarkably advanced in industrial chemistry, for they had discovered the secrets of calcination, distillation, and sublimation, the preparation of metallic salts and alloys, and the making of soap, glass, and cement. They were the finest temperers of steel in the world.

In medicine, the Gupta doctors were continuing the splendid tradition set down by Susruta. Susruta was surprisingly modern in his techniques, such as sterilizing a wound by fumigation, preparing for an operation, and stressing the need of dissection of dead bodies as essential in the training of surgeons. Like Hippocrates, Susruta had a high moral standard. He maintained that the poor, widows, neighbors, travelers, friends, and priests should be treated without charge by the physician, who should look upon them as if they were his own relatives.

In concluding our estimate of Indian science, it would be well to state that scholars have not yet satisfactorily estimated how much Indian science was influenced by its contacts with Greek and Arabic contributions, especially in mathematics and medicine.

Gupta literature. This period has been called the golden age of Sanskrit, the classical language of India. Court poetry was zealously pursued and the kings were generous patrons of a number of writers, the most famous of whom was Kalidasa (c. 400-455). While excelling as both a lyric and an epic poet, Kalidasa in addition has been termed the Indian Shakespeare because of his superb dramas, of which *Shakuntala* is the most outstanding. This drama created a great stir in Europe in 1789, when it was first presented in translated form. Despite its lack of action, to which western audiences are not accustomed, *Shakuntala* abounds in beautiful imagery which won the unstinted admiration of Goethe, the German literary master. It is not surprising that the play is still very popular in India. Another drama, written after Kalidasa's masterpiece and attributed to a king named Sudraka, is *The Little Clay Cart.* Distinctive for its vigor and action, the plot is urban in scene and concerns the lives of a rich courtesan and a Brahman merchant brought to ruin by overgenerosity. The two eventually marry after many comic experiences. That *The Little Clay Cart* is rich in satirical passages is illustrated here by the cynical words of one of the characters in the play:

Those men are fools, it seems to me,
  Who trust to women or to gold;
For gold and girls, 'tis plain to see,
  Are false as virgin snakes and cold.

. . . .

As fickle as the billows of the sea,
  Glowing no longer than the evening sky,
A woman takes your gold, then leaves you free;
  You're worthless, like cosmetics, when you're dry.[3]

Indian fairy tales and fables—with their depiction of such interesting characters as thieves, courtesans, procuresses, and hypocritical monks caught in extraordinary situations involving feats of magic, strange beasts, and exotic worlds—constitute the most original element in that country's literature. The oldest fables are found in the *Mahabharata* (see page 89), while the most famous storybook is the *Panchatantra,* composed in Sanskrit between 300 and 500. Like other storybooks, the *Panchatantra* consists of a group of tales set within the pattern of a single narrative. These secular fables were translated in time into Syriac and Arabic and from there into the languages of Europe.

Other collections of fairy tales and fables grew up in India, and from them came the world-famous story of Sindbad, which eventually found its way into the *Arabian Nights.* Some of the most outstanding European storytellers have been indebted to Indian folklore, including Boccaccio, Chaucer, La Fontaine, Grimm, and Kipling, while many fables and stories have passed into our western oral tradition. India presented an unusually fertile soil for the creation of fables and folklore. Its religions stressed the unity of all life and the cycle of transmigration. Therefore, it was not difficult to reverse the positions of the animal and human kingdoms, for example, and to conceive of beasts acting like men and vice versa. Again, the tropical environment of the country presented a wealth of birds, animals, trees, fish, and flora, and abounded—as it does today—in a multitude of races, languages, and customs.

Gupta art. We will recall that in our previous section on India, we examined Gandhara sculptures, which were a fusion of Greek and Buddhist influences both in subject matter and in execution. Gupta art was by contrast national and non-Hellenistic. As befitting a great classical period, its sculpture and painting were restrained and dignified in expression. It has been stated that while the earliest impulses of Indian art appear to have been more or less secular, the dominant motifs governing its evolution from the third century B.C. onwards have been religious. In keeping with these fundamental esthetic canons, the Indian artist held the concept of Art as Yoga (union). In other words, he sought to create a state of mind whereby he could identify himself with the object of his work. His purpose was neither self-expression nor the realization of beauty for itself. Like the Gothic sculptor in the Middle Ages of the West, the Indian artist was content to be a pious artisan for whom "the theme was all in all, and if there is beauty in his work, this did not arise from aesthetic intention, but from a state of mind which found unconscious expression."[4] Because Indian art was essentially religious and sought to depict superphysical values, the artist would choose subject matter which had a continuous pertinence, irrespective of changes in time and place. For example, he would depict the Buddha attaining Enlightenment, a subject of supreme and lasting importance to every follower of that teacher. And in his work he tended toward the use of formalized techniques.

The finest Gupta sculpture is to be found in the Buddha images of Sarnath, near Benares. Placed in an elaborately carved setting, the simple figures show the restraint and grace characteristic of Gupta art. Here the sculptor

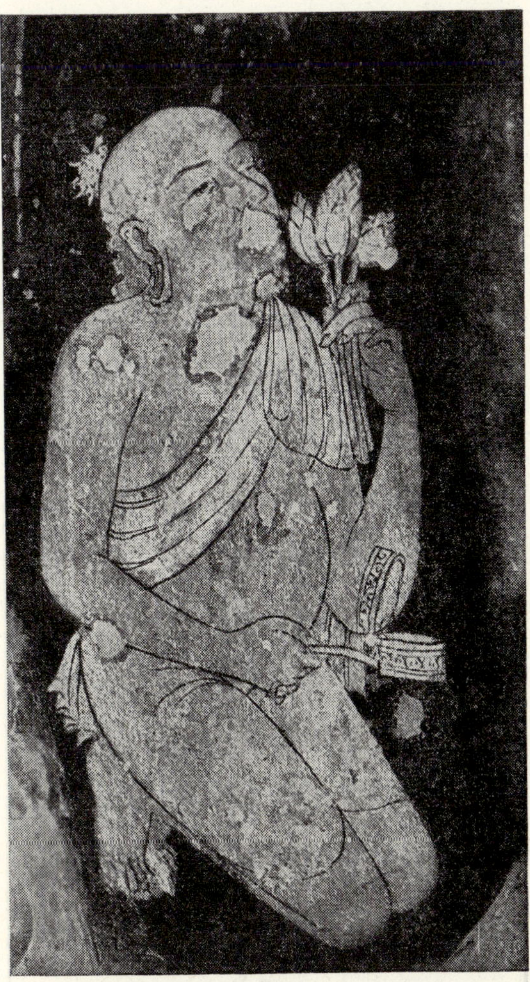

DETAIL FROM AN AJANTA FRESCO

was concerned not with realistic portraiture but with expressing religious values. A comparison with early Gothic sculpture (page 437) shows the same lack of interest in realism and a similar effect of dignity, less graceful in the European work. It is worth noting that Gupta sculpture formed the basis of the splendid later developments of colonial Buddhist and Hindu art in southeast Asia, especially in Cambodia and Java.

Few examples of Gupta painting survive. However, the caves at Ajanta are decorated with famous frescoes depicting scenes from the life of the Buddha and from Indian court and domestic life. These paintings are impressive in scale and possess great beauty of line as well as a sensitive portrayal of nature. The Ajanta fresco (see page 297) is a detail from one of these frescoes and, although damaged, it still conveys an impression of rhythmic curving lines. The Ajanta frescoes were painted over a period of many centuries, with even the earliest of them possessing technical excellence. Apart from their artistic merits, these paintings provide a valuable picture of Indian social life some fifteen hundred years ago.

Unlike the Sarnath sculpture or the Ajanta frescoes, almost nothing of Gupta architecture survives, though we know that imposing palaces and public buildings were erected at this time. Their loss can be attributed to the ravages of Hun and Moslem invaders in later centuries.

India to the Moslem Invasion

Hun invasion of northern India. With the death of Chandragupta II in 413, the Gupta empire began to break up. Huns invaded the Punjab at the end of the fifth century, just as their relatives were ravaging Europe under Attila, "The Scourge." Although they were prevented from advancing through eastern India by a confederacy of Hindu princes, they held control of northwestern India and intermarried with the natives.

Harsha. In the seventh century there were various states in the Ganges valley, all constantly at war with one another. Then a strong man arose, Harsha, rajah of one of the northern kingdoms, who in the short space of six years (606-612) made himself master of much of the territory formerly ruled by the Guptas (see map on this page). He was unable, however, to penetrate into the Deccan.

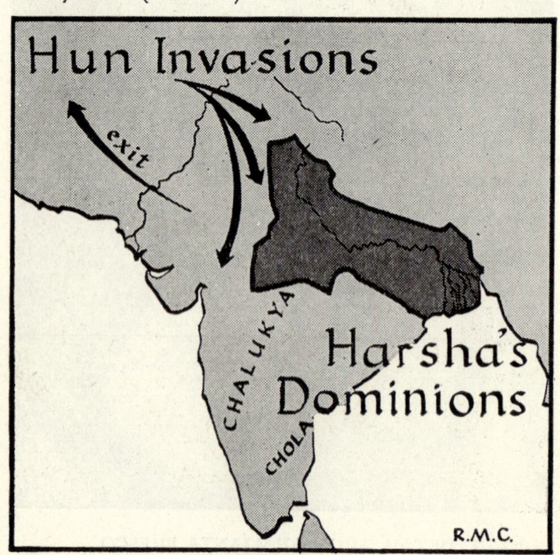

We are again indebted to a Chinese Buddhist pilgrim, this time Hiuen Tsang, for our clear knowledge of the reign of Harsha. The learned foreign scholar spent eight of his fifteen years (630-645) in India within Harsha's dominions. He found the caste system well established. He reported the people as well behaved and law abiding, the taxes light, the standard of living high, learning in high esteem, with thousands of students receiving instruction in grammar, mechanics, medicine, logic, and metaphysics, and the government excellently administered by the tireless Harsha. The king was a splendid example of the benevolent despot—a soldier and administrator, a patron of the arts, and himself a skilled poet and dramatist. Unfortunately Harsha left no heirs to continue his beneficent rule.

The Rajputs. With the death of Harsha in 647, northern India once more underwent an age of political confusion and change. During the next two centuries a new order or society arose, headed by clans of a people who called themselves Rajputs, or Sons of Kings. Today there are thirty-six Rajput clans, who claim to be descended from the Kshatriyas (the warrior caste) of the ancient epics, but they are in reality the descendants of central Asian tribes who migrated into the northwest areas of India in the fifth and sixth centuries. The newcomers married with the Hindus, promptly

A hunting scene of running deer, a charging lion, and frisky horses is represented in this bas-relief which decorates the sides of the stairway to an emperor's throne at Hampi in southern India.

forgot their origins, and assumed the haughty privileges of the "blueblood" Hindus.

The Rajputs spent their time in patronizing the arts, especially the poetry of the court bards, and in exterminating one another. They had a code of chivalry not unlike that in medieval Europe. Youths were educated by means of epic stories, initiated at puberty into knighthood, and taught to live according to a code which respected women, spared the fallen, and permitted no foul play.

The Deccan. We must remember that our study of Indian history has been confined so far to northern India (Hindustan). The geography of the country made intercourse with the Deccan and the kingdoms of the Far South (Tamil Land) nearly impossible (see map, page 82). Penetration of the Deccan from the north began about the seventh century B.C., but our earliest date in Deccan history is 256 B.C., when Asoka dispatched a Buddhist mission to the south.

The southern areas had developed a remarkable culture. From 225 B.C. to 225 A.D. the Deccan was ruled by the Andhras dynasty, which governed it almost from sea to sea at the height of its power (see map, page 208). The kingdom was divided into three provinces. Trade flourished in the hands of guilds similar to those of medieval Europe, and a regular coinage system was in existence. Literature was written in Prakrit, a language related to Sanskrit.

The next famous dynasty was the Chalukya (550-750 A.D.), and the most outstanding king of this line was Pulakesin II (608-642). We are indebted once more to the Chinese traveler, Hiuen Tsang, for our knowledge of Pulakesin, who prized equally the arts of war and learning. Hiuen Tsang described Pulakesin's subjects as well behaved and submissive. Before the king sent his soldiers into battle, he would have wine given them so as to make them much braver and their charge against the enemy more irresistible. Wine was also given to the war elephants for the same purpose. That the armies of Pulakesin II were well trained and capable is suggested by the fact that, aided by natural barriers, they were able to withstand the armies of Harsha, who dominated northern India (see map, page 298). The Chalukyas fell about 750, and various other dynasties came to power in turn until in 1318 the invading Moslems put an end to Hindu rule in the Deccan.

The people in the Deccan never took wholeheartedly to Buddhism, and there is scarcely any mention of it after the twelfth century. Orthodox Hinduism eventually won control of the Deccan prior to the Moslem invasion.

Outstanding artistic achievements of the region were the monasteries hewn out of the rock hillsides. The Kailasa temple, built in the latter half of the eighth century, is completely cut out of solid rock so that it stands free from the hillside.

Tamil Land. The Far South, or Tamil Land, was from ancient days divided into various Dravidian kingdoms. Their political history is unrecorded prior to the ninth century A.D. It will be recalled, however (Chapter 7), that these kingdoms conducted an extensive trade with the Roman empire during the early centuries of the Christian era.

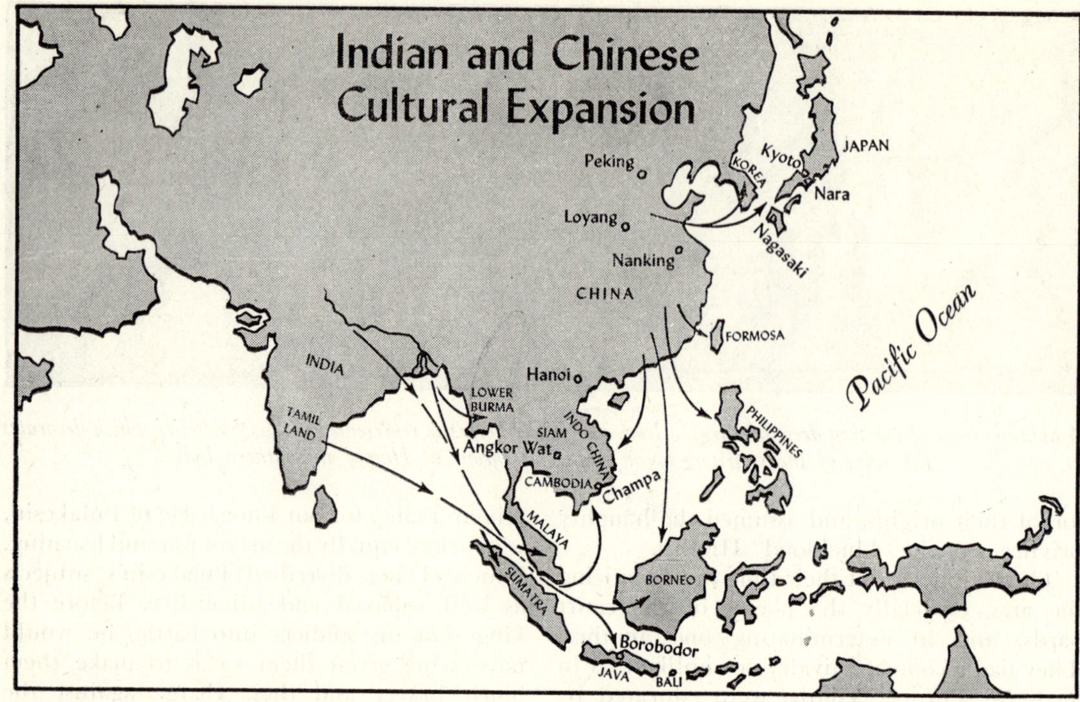

Chola and Vijayanagar. In the tenth century, the Chola kingdom became the greatest power in the far south of India, only to pass in the fourteenth century under the control of what was by that time the greatest of the southern states, Vijayanagar (see map, page 304). Enduring until the mid-sixteenth century, Vijayanagar was the last Hindu state to be conquered by the Moslems, who pillaged and ravished the empire, spending five months in plundering its fabulously wealthy capital alone. Before succumbing to the invaders, the Vijayanagar empire enjoyed great prosperity, built upon both internal and foreign commerce, and a brilliant culture, in which women occupied a noteworthy status. This empire, which represented a synthesis of southern Indian culture, holds a significant place in Indian history. For well-nigh three centuries, "it stood for the older religion and culture of the country and saved these from being engulfed by the rush of new ideas and forces."[5]

Expansion of Indian culture. As was pointed out in the Prologue, "Perspective on Man," one of the most important aspects of history is the recurring process of culture impact and modification. We now come to an outstanding example of this process, the spread of Indian culture throughout southeast Asia and its societies. The adaptation of this culture permanently enriched that wealthy and thickly populated region of the world.

One scholar is convinced that the introduction of the Indian culture pattern into southeast Asia was a gradual process, beginning with the arrival of merchants and unconnected with military conquest or annexation, and that all regions of India contributed to the expansion of Indian influence.[6] Possibly the people of south India, at once commercial and maritime, represented the strongest single influence in such areas as Malaya, Sumatra, Java, and Borneo, while the presence of Gupta influences in the earlier remains of Burma and Siam could indicate that the Asian mainland to the east may have been primarily affected by north Indian impacts. It is generally held that this Indian expansion occurred as a series of cultural waves, beginning about the second century A.D. and continuing until the ninth or tenth.

The resulting cultural impacts were not, of course, equally strong or enduring over all sections of what has been called "Greater India," which has been divided by one scholar, Quaritch Wales, into two segments. The western zone, including Ceylon, Burma, central Siam, and the Malay peninsula, received the full force of Indian colonizing zeal. As a result, it developed a culture which was a colonial imitation of the original. In the eastern zone, which consisted mainly of Java, Cambodia, and Champa (in Indo-China), there was very definite Indianization, but it was not so strong as to prevent the indigenous peoples from responding with their own cultural contributions.

From the second century A.D., we read of kingdoms in "Greater India," established by Indian colonists and ruled by monarchs with Indian names. Some of these kingdoms—whose religion, social manners, and language were all Indian—endured more than a thousand years, and in fact persisted after Hindu rule had come to an end in India itself. Several of these states deserve mention. In what is now Indo-China, we find two powerful kingdoms. Champa comprised at its zenith almost the whole of modern Annam. In existence until the sixteenth century, when it was overrun by Mongol invaders, Champa was covered with splendid Hindu and Buddhist temples. Still more imposing was the Kambuja kingdom which at one time consisted of modern Cambodia, Laos, Siam, and parts of Burma and the Malay peninsula. This kingdom, which maintained its splendor until reduced to a petty principality by invasion in the fifteenth century, was ruled by various Hindu dynasties. One of these around 1100 erected one of the greatest religious edifices of history, the temple of Angkor Wat (see below). Built in long terraces adorned with bas-reliefs of scenes from the Hindu epics, and with its central tower rising over 200 feet, Angkor Wat is surrounded by a stone enclosure measuring half a mile from north to south and two-thirds of a mile from east to west. The kingdom's capital, now known as Angkor Thom, must have been fully as impressive. Square in shape with each side more than two miles in length, and surrounded by a moat more than a hundred yards wide, this city had great avenues running to its center, and a royal terrace some twelve hundred feet long and thirteen feet high sculptured with reliefs of great beauty. Unquestionably there was little, if anything, in Europe to compare with Angkor Thom in its heyday.

Meanwhile another great empire had risen further south. Founded by the Sailendra dynasty in the eighth century, this kingdom extended over the Malay peninsula and nearly all of the Indonesian archipelago. The Sailendra kings lived sumptuously and maintained diplomatic relations with both India and China. They were also Mahayana Buddhists and great builders, the most magnificent of their works being the immense *stupa* of Borobodor in central Java—undoubtedly the most imposing Buddhist shrine in the world. Erected on the top of a hill in nine successive terraces and crowned with a bell-shaped *stupa*, Borobodor is covered with sculptures illustrating Buddhist texts and with images of Gautama executed in the finest Indo-Javanese style. The art of these colonial kingdoms was unmistakably influenced by Indian art, but their finest

AERIAL VIEW OF THE TEMPLE OF ANGKOR WAT

works are far more imposing than anything found in India itself.

The Sailendra kingdom was invaded in the eleventh century, and recovered only temporarily from the attack. Then, toward the close of the thirteenth century, a new royal dynasty founded in Java the kingdom of Madjapahit, which by 1365 comprised almost all of the Malay peninsula and the Indonesian archipelago. However, in the sixteenth century, the Hindu rulers were driven off their throne by Moslems, with the result that Java was converted to Islam. Meanwhile, the former ruling family fled eastward to Bali—which has retained a basically Hindu culture.

Speaking of the medieval expansion of Indian culture into Indo-China, Malaya, and Indonesia, one Indian historian states: "Indian religion, Indian culture, Indian laws and Indian government moulded the lives of the primitive races all over this wide region, and they imbibed a more elevated moral spirit and a higher intellectual taste through the religious art and literature of India. In short, the people were lifted to a higher plane of civilisation.... So long as Hinduism was in full vigour at home, Hinduism in the colonies was also a vital force, but the downfall of the Hindus in India also led to the decay of their colonial supremacy."[7]

The Moslem Conquest of India (1175-1450)

Decline of Hindu culture. What was the cause of the decline in Hindu vigor which, as we have seen, eventually had repercussions as far away as the Indonesian archipelago? We will recall that in the political field, the death of Harsha in 647 left northern India without a strong ruler and in the grip of petty groups whose feuding only weakened and disorganized Hindu society. True, the Hindu kingdoms in southern India were "national" in character and built upon firm economic and military foundations, but elsewhere little effective resistance could be expected in the event of any aggression from the outside.

But the existing weakness was more than political—a decline, in fact, was occurring throughout the fabric of Hindu society. By the tenth century, the last great waves of colonization had subsided. Contact with China diminished, and with this isolation there grew a sense of complacency and superiority. As one contemporary observer recorded: "The Hindus believe that there is no country but theirs, no nation like theirs, no religion like theirs, no sciences like theirs. . . . If they travelled and mixed with other nations they would soon change their mind, for their ancestors were not so narrow-minded as the present generations."[8] As might be expected in such an environment, the caste system became set in a rigid mold and, according to Pandit Nehru, there was a "decline all along the line—intellectual, philosophical, political, in techniques and methods of war, in knowledge of and contacts with the outside world."[9] In short, Hindu India in the eleventh century was no longer in any position to withstand the sustained attacks of a determined foe. And such a foe, implacably opposed to Hinduism and its culture, was already on the northwest frontier.

Spread of Islam. The phenomenally wide and rapid expansion of Moslem civilization is outstanding in the history of the spread of culture. Within a hundred twenty-five years after the Prophet's death in 632, his fanatic followers had carried his message of monotheism, salvation, and simplicity of worship as far as Tours in France (732) and to the Tigris in the east, where they rebuilt Bagdad in 757. We have already seen the cultural heights which Islamic civilization attained in the years which followed. Their civilization stretched from Bagdad to Cordova and produced some of the greatest medieval scientists, doctors, mathematicians, poets, and artists.

The Moslems were accustomed to proselytize among conquered peoples, but not usually to exert stronger pressure. When they arrived in India, however, there was considerable persecution of Hinduism, for that faith, with its countless deities, elaborate ritual, powerful priestcraft, and fondness for images, was the exact opposite of everything which Islam held sacred. The gap between the two religions is so tremendous that there has never been a reconciliation.

Moslem invasions. The Arabs had their first encounter with the Indians in the eighth century, when some of their ships were attacked by Indian pirates. In 711 the Moslems sent a retaliatory expedition to a seaport on the Indus. In a year or two the southern valley of the Indus became a Moslem province. The invaders and the Hindus to the east remained on good terms. In the tenth century, however, more Moslem invaders came sweeping through the northwest passes. The newcomers were Turks. They established a principality in the mountains and then proceeded to engage in a completely successful war with the Rajputs of northern India.

The most famous of these invaders was the Moslem Turk, Mahmud of Ghazni, ruler of a small principality in Afghanistan. This fierce warrior regarded India as a land of infidels and unbelievers, fair prey for the followers of Allah. Mahmud made some spectacular raids, capturing enormous quantities of booty, and as a result of his campaign of 1022, he annexed northwest India (see map below).

Despite destructive forays by various sultans, the Hindu kingdoms of the interior remained independent, and not until the closing years of the twelfth century did the Moslems begin to establish a permanent Indian dominion. Mohammed Ghori was the leader of the successful movement against the kingdoms of the interior. He first overran and conquered the lower Indus valley and the Punjab by 1187. Mohammed Ghori then coveted the rich Hindu kingdoms of the interior, but in 1191 the Hindu rajahs combined against the sultan and defeated him. The next year Mohammed Ghori returned with another army and routed the Hindu confederacy. In the year 1193 the reduction of Hindustan by the Moslems began, for the petty kingdoms fell in quick succession, until finally by 1236 upper India was completely under Moslem control.

The Delhi sultans. In 1206 victorious Mohammed Ghori was assassinated and one of his generals proceeded to make himself sultan of Delhi and ruler of a strong Moslem kingdom covering much of north India. This Delhi sultanate was in existence from 1206 until 1526. During the period of its greatest power—from the former date to 1388—it gave northern India political unity. In the latter part of the fourteenth century, however, it declined and never regained the influence and glory of the first period of its rule. The early Delhi sultans pushed Moslem authority southwards in India. By 1318 the Deccan was conquered from Hindu rulers (see map below) and a few years later practically all Hindu resistance collapsed in the south. In 1336, however, a group of Hindu refugees from Moslem expansion established the state of Vijayanagar which became a prosperous and powerful kingdom. This state was the last flicker of Hindu independence, for after little more than two centuries of existence it succumbed to Moslem arms in 1565.

To return to the Delhi sultans, these rulers who are called Turko-Afghans, were on the whole a cruel, bigoted, and often depraved group of men. Many fierce fanatics delighted in the slaughter of infidel Hindus. As there was no legal machinery of succession to the throne, every death of a sultan was followed by a bloody conflict for power. In addition, many of the sultans were masters of refined debauchery. Yet in spite of these repulsive features, a number of these Moslem potentates, such as Mohammed Tughluk and Ferozshah were patrons of the arts, dilettante scholars, and creators of noble architecture.

Sultan Mohammed Tughluk (1325-1347) was eccentric, cruel, and fanatical. He "acquired the throne by murdering his father, became a great scholar and elegant writer, dabbled in mathematics, physics, and Greek philosophy, surpassed his predecessors in bloodshed and brutality, fed the flesh of a rebel nephew to the rebel's wife and children, ruined the country with reckless inflation, and laid it waste with pillage and murder till the inhabitants fled to the jungle."[10] When Delhi rivaled Bagdad and Cairo in size and wealth, the sultan

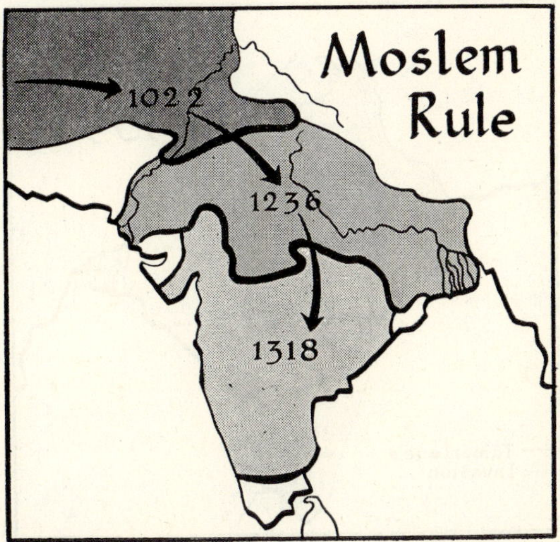

suddenly gave an order demanding immediate evacuation of the whole population within three days to a new capital 600 miles distant.

Ferozshah (1351-1388) may well have been the most enlightened Moslem ruler in India to this time. He assisted in irrigation projects, reduced crime and poverty, abolished tortures for crimes, erected some two hundred towns, forty mosques, thirty colleges, fifty dams, one hundred hospitals, and numerous other projects. Ferozshah, however, like all the other sultans, had a profound hatred for Hinduism and acted with the greatest severity and even barbarity in suppressing it wherever possible.

Tamerlane. The death of Ferozshah threw the country once more into civil war and left it unprotected for a great invasion from the northwest. In 1398, there marched into the Punjab a Barlas Turk who had already conquered central Asia and had now set his heart on acquiring the riches of India—Timur the Lame or, as he is better known to us, Tamerlane. Defeating everything before him, Timur attacked and looted wealthy Delhi, slew perhaps a hundred thousand prisoners in cold blood, and departed for Samarkand, leaving Delhi's few surviving inhabitants to perish of famine or plague. "For two whole months, not a bird moved a wing in the city."

After Timur's terrible visitation all semblance of government was destroyed in north India and it was not until 1450 that the Delhi sultanate was restored. The new rulers, however, never succeeded in restoring the glories of the old Delhi empire. In various parts of India independent Moslem sultans set themselves up as independent rulers in defiance of the ineffectual authority at Delhi. We shall see in Chapter 20 that a new Moslem dynasty, the Mogul, arose in the sixteenth century. For a brief two centuries this dynasty united all of the sub-continent, giving it a period of political unity and cultural creativeness, only rivaled by two previous periods in Indian history—that of the Mauryas and the Guptas.

Effects of Moslem rule. The Moslem conquest of India was unusually ruthless. Hindu forces desperately resisted their Moslem conquerors, yet following their defeat, the Hindus suffered wholesale massacre at the hands of their victors.

After the conquest, however, the Moslem invaders had to organize their governments, stabilize their position, and collect the necessary revenue. While many rich Hindu nobles saw their property and land confiscated, the great mass of the people were largely unaffected. Life in the villages went on undisturbed, treading the path of immemorial custom. All that was demanded was the payment of taxes to the new masters. While the upper classes in particular and the masses in general clung tenaciously to their Hindu faith, a fairly large number was converted to Islam. In some cases it was a choice between Allah or the sword; in others it was a voluntary matter, as low caste Hindus became Moslems to escape their degraded status or as ambitious administrators accepted Islam in order to gain employment in the administrative service of the Delhi sultanate.

The impact of the Hindu and Moslem cultures resulted in a certain amount of mixing and exchanging of ways of life. On the Hindu side the Moslem practice of the seclusion of women was introduced, known as *purdah,* and in addition many aspects of Moslem dress and ceremonial were copied. Islamic religion and thought also made a deep impress, contributing to Hinduism certain liberal and reformist movements that stressed democracy and equalitarianism in religion, rather than the caste principle. As for the Moslem ruling clique, it developed a new language to aid in the administering of its alien subjects. This was Urdu, a combination of Persian and Arabic words utilizing the grammatical construction of the native Hindu. Above all, the Turkish sultans exercised a deep impress upon Hindu architecture. While the traditional Indian forms were retained, new elements, such as the arch, minaret, and dome were introduced, together with a distinctively rich art of decoration, which revolutionized architecture.

The injection of the Islamic way of life into the pattern of Hindu society was to have profound effects upon the historic destiny of the Indian sub-continent. Before the Moslem invasions the many alien streams that had penetrated through the mountain passes of the north had all been assimilated by Hinduism. The Rajputs are a case in point. Islam, however, fiercely proud of its faith and contemptuous of Hinduism, jealously retained its own identity. After 1206, the history and life of India was divided into two cultures, which mingled only superficially and never really united. This division was to have momentous consequences in the twentieth century when India, freed from British rule, split into two nations, India and Pakistan.

China from the Han to the T'ang Dynasties (220-906)

An age of division. In India the transition period between the fall of the Kanishka empire and the rise of the Guptas was relatively short. China, however, was destined to undergo three and a half centuries of disorder and division after the fall of the Hans in 220 A.D. before another great dynasty emerged capable of reuniting the country. Like preceding dynasties, the Han had gradually deteriorated from its primary strength to utter incompetence, until it finally disappeared altogether. The centuries that followed were filled with civil wars, divisions of China into numerous kingdoms which rose only to perish in short order, and external wars between the Chinese and such invaders as the Mongols and the Turks. China became a melting pot of races, customs, creeds, and tongues, but what appeared on the surface to be a civilization in collapse was in reality one in the process of change and assimilation.

After the Hans, there was a period of sixty years when the country split into three kingdoms, all contending for imperial control. In 280, unity was precariously restored. But disaster soon struck from the north, which for years had been threatened by various Turkic, Mongol, and Tungusic peoples, who had not attacked China only because of furious struggles among themselves, a state of affairs assiduously fostered by Chinese policy. But early in the fourth century, the Hsiung-nu (Huns) attacked, and in 317 they captured both the capital, Loyang, and the emperor. For the next two and a half centuries northern China was ruled by a succession of nomadic dynasties. "Unquestionably this was a great period for the Turkic, Hsiung-nu, Mongol, and Tungusic peoples, and one during which they brought both the Chinese and the Roman empires to their knees at virtually the same time. Eastern Asia had both earlier and later counterparts of Attila, chief of the Huns in eastern and central Europe."[11]

During the fifth century, the most powerful state in the Far East was the T'opa, which ruled the whole of north China. This state, which gave great encouragement to Buddhism and is remembered today largely in connection with splendid Buddhist grottoes and sculpture, became increasingly sinified before its disappearance in the sixth century.

Meanwhile, when north China fell to alien rule in 317, a Chin prince fled south to present-day Nanking on the Yangtze, where he established the eastern Chin dynasty (not to be confused with the Ch'in dynasty of the second century B.C., discussed in Chapter 4). This dynasty managed to survive just over a century. Prior to the third century, south China had been sparsely populated and, despite a good climate and the fertility of the Yangtze valley, was of little economic importance. During this period, however, the population was greatly increased by refugees from the Yellow River basin. More land was brought under cultivation, and the non-Chinese elements in the south were assimilated into Chinese culture. The fertile soil and the great estates staked out by the southern landowners enabled them to support a luxurious way of life at the capital, so that between the fourth and sixth centuries south China possibly enjoyed the most refined civilization to be found anywhere in the Far East.

The spread of Chinese civilization southward was not the only important cultural development in the period between the Hans and the T'angs. We will recall that Buddhism had been introduced into China in the earlier part of the Han dynasty. However, it was from the third century onward that Buddhism made important gains in both the north and south. One reason was the activity of Buddhist missionaries who came from abroad with foreign merchants. Another lay in the chaotic internal conditions, the danger from foreign invasion, the prevalence of corruption in high places, and the exploitation of the masses. The conservatism and social rigidity of Confucianism retained its appeal among the upper classes, but Buddhism offered the general population a new faith in these difficult days. It substituted for the old notion of fatalism the doctrine of *karma,* which gave a purpose for right conduct, while its theory of reincarnation not only comforted the downtrodden with the hope of eventual betterment but also held out the promise of immortality. As a result, the country population turned increasingly to Buddhism, a faith also accepted by their alien rulers such as the T'opa. But the process of cultural development did not end there. Scores of Chinese Buddhists made pilgrimages to India and brought back important information about lands and customs outside China. Furthermore, with Buddhism came other Indian culture impacts which enriched Chinese mathematics, medicine, architecture and art, and music.

The Sui dynasty (580-618 A.D.). The last of the northern dynasties was brought to an end by a Chinese, Yang Chien, who founded the Sui dynasty and proceeded to reunite the whole country under Chinese rule again. The new dynasty was short-lived, but it was not without its accomplishments. One of the most far-reaching was a highly ambitious program of canal construction which facilitated transportation and the movement of foodstuffs. A contemporary account shows that literally millions of persons were impressed into this public-works program, whose expense and resultant suffering caused wide-spread popular dissatisfaction, as did the second Sui emperor's personal extravagances. According to the account of a much later Chinese writer, this ruler "shortened the life of his dynasty by a number of years, but benefited posterity into ten thousand generations. He ruled without benevolence, but his rule is to be credited with enduring accomplishments."[12] Military defeat at the hands of the Turks brought on revolt, and in 618 the emperor was assassinated. For five years, China saw various groups contending for power, but by 623 the whole country had been brought under the control of what was destined to be one of China's most splendid dynasties—the T'ang.

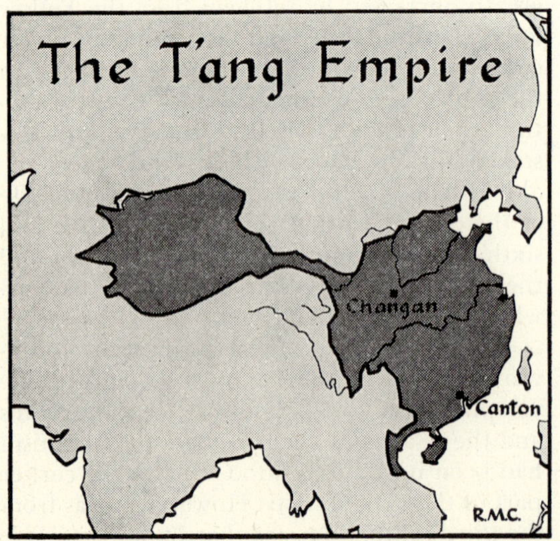

A golden age. As the Gupta empire of medieval India represents the golden age of Hindu culture, so too, the T'ang dynasty represents the golden era of medieval China. So vividly did the T'ang era impress itself upon medieval China that even today many Chinese like to consider themselves not only as "The Sons of Han," but also as "The Men of T'ang."

The first great T'ang ruler of the dynasty was T'ai Tsung (627-650), one of China's outstanding emperors. A great warrior, T'ai Tsung succeeded in overthrowing the eastern Turks in Mongolia in 630. The western Turks, however, situated in Turkestan as part of a great empire stretching across northern Asia, continued to menace China. Taking advantage of internal dissension in Turkestan, T'ai Tsung's expeditionary forces were able to destroy the western Turks and to establish Chinese hegemony over the Tarim basin. Under his son, a successful war was undertaken against Korea, which became an outlying protectorate of the expanding Chinese empire. Medieval China had now reached its zenith of power.

T'ang reforms and government. A statesman as well as a great soldier, T'ai Tsung was energetic in instituting reforms. One of his major reforms was to strengthen the administrative system of the country. Those areas inhabited by non-Chinese were allowed to keep their own princes, who were given Chinese names. Over the rest of his empire, the ruler governed by means of a bureaucracy recruited through a civil-service program, the roots of which (as indicated earlier) went back to the Han period. The empire was divided into provinces, headed by military governors-general, while each province was in turn divided into prefectures. A state secretariat obtained information about economic and political affairs from all parts of the empire and also made necessary decisions.

T'ang reforms also extended to land, because of the government's vital interest in agriculture, the chief source of revenue. Laws were passed in an effort to prevent the growth of large estates and to ensure that the peasants had equitable amounts of land, in return for which they paid taxes and devoted a specified number of days of labor each year to public works. The government tried to be equitable by remitting taxes and services in bad years in accordance with the loss incurred. Merchants in cities paid taxes according to the amount of property held, while those without property were not made to pay. Thus we can see that the tax system in T'ang times was based, at least in large measure, on the theory of ability to pay. The grain used in paying taxes was carried to the capital city, while the government also received revenues accruing from monopolies on the minting of money, iron, copper (later), and salt, as well as from taxes on rice, wine, and tea. Altogether, the reforms instituted by T'ai Tsung worked well in their initial stage, the government was efficiently and vigorously administered, and the people as a whole were contented. Conditions under his rule seem especially remarkable when compared with those of the preceding chaotic centuries.

Economic conditions. The early T'ang period was marked by economic prosperity. The improvements wrought by administrative, land, and tax reforms were partly responsible, as was the more efficient transportation system which the T'ang developed by completing the canal system begun by the Sui dynasty. Another factor contributing to this economic prosperity was a thriving foreign commerce. Caravans arrived constantly from western and central Asia, and merchants made their way from India. Trade also flourished with Japan, which at this time was busy adopting various elements of the Chinese culture pattern, including Buddhism. In addition, a large number of foreign merchants had come by sea and overland alike, so that at the end of the eighth century an estimated four thousand foreign families lived in the capital itself, while others transacted business in inland centers and trading ports. Among the newcomers were the first Jewish and Arabian merchants as well as Nestorian Christians and traders of still other faiths. These merchants bought great quantities of silks and other luxury goods, including pottery and porcelain, which found their way to places as distant as Jerusalem and Cairo.

This is a model in pottery of a two-wheeled oxcart from the T'ang period. The high wheels are evidently designed for traveling on muddy roads and through treacherous streams.

Political expansion and economic prosperity in turn created new social habits and standards. A number of new foods, including pepper, sugar beets, almonds, and dates, made their appearance, while tea, which had still been a luxury in north China as late as the Han period, became available to all classes during the eighth century. There was now a population of some fifty millions; at least one million lived in the capital, Ch'ang-an. As might be expected, with the court and administration located there, Ch'ang-an enjoyed the luxuries and social refinements of a splendid capital, and indeed the cultural and intellectual glories which we associate with the T'ang dynasty centered in this city. Yet it should be pointed out that whereas in Han times all important developments transpired in the capital, now the country's cultural base had been greatly expanded. During the centuries of division be-

This scene from Hsia Kuei's painting, "Ten Thousand Miles of the Yangtze," shows life along the great river and its banks. A precariously perched crew pilots the river boat through the rapids. Two travelers switch their goggle-eyed pack animals away from the stream. The Sung dynasty painting is a detail from a long silk scroll.

tween north and south China, the southern cities had become important in their own right, and they continued to act as local cultural centers. "The institution of governors-general further promoted this decentralization: the governor-general surrounded himself with a little court of his own, drawn from the local gentry and the local intelligentsia. This placed the whole edifice of the empire on a much broader foundation, with lasting results."[13]

T'ang poetry. The eighteenth-century Manchu emperors ordered a collection to be made of T'ang poetry; one anthology consisted of 48,900 poems by 2300 poets. This is the amount that survived nearly a thousand years of turbulent history, so that the literary output of the T'ang era justifies the remark of the critic that "At this age, whoever was a man was a poet." Within the T'ang dynasty itself, the reign of Hsuan Tsung (713-756) probably witnessed the finest flowering of poetry. At his brilliant court were the two greatest Chinese lyric poets, Li Po (701?-762) and Tu Fu (712-770), who have left imperishable glimpses of contemporary life.

In any estimate of Chinese poetry, it must be remembered that the subtlety of meaning of the characters in which the poetry is written renders any adequate translation almost impossible. Again, whereas the translations are usually set forth as free verse, in reality the original is rigid and formalistic in its pattern. Finally, this poetry is restrained and highly allusive, and because the Chinese believe that poetry is a momentary ecstasy and inspiration, their poems are concise and strongly subjective. But the work of the T'ang lyric poets, it has been pointed out, seems more directly accessible because of the universality of its themes. "Perhaps this characteristic is due to the multiple sources from which T'ang lyric poetry is drawn. If we analyse its elements, we find both the great cosmic reverie of ancient Taoism, caused by a wild surge towards the sublime, and Buddhist melancholy, evoked by the universal impermanence of earthly things."[14]

Li Po wrote with humor and elegance, yet he suffused his poetry with a gentle melancholy over the transience of the pleasures of this mortal world. One legend of his death tells of his being carried on a dolphin toward the world of the immortals. Another popular story maintains that he died by falling into a river. While in a state of drunken exaltation, he leaned over the bank to embrace the reflection of the moon.

Though the circumstance of his death is hazy, his poetry is tangible enough. His description of "An Encounter in the Field" helps explain the popularity of Li Po's verse:

Came an amorous rider,
Trampling the fallen flowers of the road.
The dangling end of his crop
Brushes a passing carriage of five-colored clouds.
The jeweled curtain is raised,
A beautiful woman smiles within—
"That is my house," she whispers,
Pointing to a pink house beyond.[15]

Written in another vein is "In the Mountains," whose few lines express the restrained but deep love which the Chinese have for nature:

Why do I live among the green mountains?
I laugh and answer not, my soul is serene:
It dwells in another heaven and earth belonging to no man.
The peach trees are in flower, and the water flows on . . .[16]

Li Po was a highly esteemed court poet until the emperor's favorite, Lady Yang, misinterpreted one of his poems and he was turned out of the palace, to wander from place to place, starving occasionally, drinking frequently, and composing stanzas endlessly. In the following partially quoted poem we catch the nostalgia of the exile:

In the land of Wu the mulberry leaves are green,
And thrice the silkworms have gone to sleep.
In East Luh where my family stay,
I wonder who is sowing those fields of ours.
I cannot be back in time for the spring doings,
Yet I can help nothing, traveling on the river.

The south wind blowing wafts my homesick spirit
And carries it up to the front of our familiar tavern.
There I see a peach tree on the east side of the house
With thick leaves and branches waving in the blue mist.
It is the tree I planted before my parting three years ago.
The peach tree has grown now as tall as the tavern roof,
While I have wandered about without returning.[17]

Li Po has been called the people's poet because of the wide appeal of his work. However, a modern critic maintains that the overwhelming majority of Chinese scholars and poets would consider Tu Fu their greatest poet because as a man he "represents the widest sympathy and the highest ethic principles, while Tu Fu the poet commands the largest variety of artistry and the deepest reality of art."[18] Here is a court excursion as delineated by the poet:

I

How delightful, at sunset, to loosen the boat!
A light wind is slow to raise the waves.
Deep in the bamboo grove, the guests linger;
The lotus-flowers are pure and bright in the cool evening air.
The young nobles stir the ice-water;
The Beautiful Ones wash the lotus-roots, whose fibers are like silk threads.
A layer of clouds above our heads is black.
It will certainly rain, which impels me to write this poem.

II

The rain comes, soaking the mats upon which we are sitting.
A hurrying wind strikes the bow of the boat.
The rose-red rouge of the ladies from Yueh is wet;
The Yen beauties are anxious about their kingfisher-eyebrows.
We throw out a rope and draw in to the sloping bank.
We tie the boat to the willow-trees.
We roll up the curtains and watch the floating wave-flowers.
Our return is different from our setting out.
The wind whistles and blows in great gusts.
By the time we reach the shore, it seems as though the Fifth Month were Autumn.[19]

SILK EMBROIDERY, T'ANG DYNASTY

Scholarly writings. The T'ang period was also outstanding in scholarship. For example, two encyclopedias were compiled to assist students in passing civil examinations, while Buddhist scholars translated hundreds of Sanskrit texts into the vernacular. Before this period, the writing of historical accounts had been the work of individuals, but because the preparation of a standard history for a single epoch was recognized to be beyond the capacity of any one person, the T'ang government inaugurated the practice of employing a corps of scholars to write accounts of the preceding eras. As a result eight histories were brought out. This in turn created an important precedent; each new dynasty wrote a standard history of its predecessor, at the same time gathering data about its own affairs. The account of the Ming dynasty, for example, which was begun in 1679, took fifty-three scholars some forty-six years to complete, and contained one hundred volumes. According to Professor Homer Dubs, this group of standard histories "constitutes the largest single body of historical information anywhere available." Each of the histories also has many volumes of annotations, and he estimates that if all were translated in the same format as the parts of the first two now available in European languages, there would be something like 450 volumes of 500 pages each. More than mere chronicles, they contain treatises on such subjects as law, economics, government administration, anthropological accounts of primitive tribes, and records of astronomical and other scientific phenomena. "The translation and making available to the world of this great set of histories is the greatest single task awaiting occidental humanistic scholarship. More than 99 per cent of these histories remain untranslated. So highly are they esteemed in China that no single deed would give any country greater prestige in China for scholarship and for genuine concern with Chinese interests than the careful translation of these histories."[20]

T'ang art. The T'ang dynasty was the formative period of Chinese painting. The great Wu Tao-tzu, whom the Japanese regard as the father of their painting, furthered the development of a national school independent of foreign influences.

Little remains of T'ang painting. There is evidence of Buddhist influence in the silk embroidery adapted from paintings of the period (compare the illustration on this page with the painting on page 297). The exaggerated scale, with the kneeling figures at the bottom, is typically Indian, as is the flat, broad treatment of the figures. But the manner in which line is used (note the garments on the side figures) is essentially Chinese.

Sculpture in the T'ang period developed along more national lines, but Buddhist subject matter was still used. The Bodhisattva on the opposite page shows that a distinctively Chinese interpretation of these religious figures had developed. Compare this figure with the dancing Shiva (page 295) and with religious sculpture in early medieval Europe (the Chartres figures, page 437). The tools which the artists have used to express their ideas are the same—chisel and stone—but their finished works are essentially different in spirit. The Chartres figures are architectural, while the Bodhisattva, although probably designed for a specific place, is free-standing. In both the artist has composed to bring out the essential features. In the T'ang statue the diagonal line is repeated throughout the drapery to emphasize the graceful curve of the body, whereas the opposite is true in the long, narrow, straight Gothic figures. Comparisons such as these help one to appreciate the manner in which artists express different cultures with the same tools—a block of stone and a chisel, or a brush and ink or paint. Chinese artists were also proficient in other types of sculpture, particularly in the depiction of grotesque mythological dragons and ferocious dogs. Pottery and porcelain were also produced, of so excellent a quality that they are referred to by the poets of the age. Mention should also be made of the famous T'ang figurines made of terra cotta, depicting court ladies, musicians, polo players, and cavalry—reminiscent alike of the splendor of the T'ang court and the epic wars waged against the barbarians in Turkestan.

The invention of printing. In T'ang China printing, one of mankind's most priceless inventions, was developed. At least as far back as the Shang dynasty the writing brush or pencil had been invented, and in the first century A.D. the Chinese invented paper. Buddhism acted as the driving force behind the invention of printing. The Buddhist monks in China felt that they would acquire merit by duplicating passages from their sacred scripture for mass distribution. And so, probably in the first half of the eighth century, block printing was invented—printing from an image cut in a wooden block. The first known block print is from Japan and dates from 770. The invention must have been brought to the islands from China some time before then.

The first printed book, however, came from China itself. It is the famous *Diamond Sutra,* discovered by a mendicant priest in a cave in the far west of China. The *Diamond Sutra* consists of six sheets of text inscribed with a woodcut, pasted together to form a roll some 16 feet long. The sheets are each two and a half feet by almost one foot in size and must have been printed from very large blocks. The Buddhist text was obviously produced as a meritorious act. At the end of the work is written the statement: "Printed on May 11, 868, by Wang Chieh, for free general distribution, in order in deep reverence to perpetuate the memory of his parents."[21]

The Chinese used their new invention not only to print books but also, in the tenth century, to issue paper money on a large scale and to print playing cards. These cards found their way either directly or indirectly from China to Europe in the fourteenth century. Because the Chinese language is made up of separate characters (some 40,000), China found it advantageous to rely principally upon block printing. However, the Chinese were the first to invent movable type, which the Koreans and Japanese used to good advantage later.

CHINESE BODHISATTVA, T'ANG DYNASTY

The T'ang decline. In 751, as the result of a disastrous battle fought with the Arabs—"the first clash between the world of Islam and China"—the latter lost Turkestan. This was swiftly followed by defeats inflicted by the Khitan in the north and Thai in the south. That the people were weary of war and its heavy toll in human lives is told by Li Po:

The Great Wall, which separates China from
the desert,
Winds on into infinity.
On all stretches of the frontier
No towns have been left standing.

Here and there a few scattered human bones
Seem to express their everlasting hatred.
Three hundred and sixty thousand men, dragged from their homes,
Weep as they bid their families farewell.
Since it is the order of the prince, they must obey,
But who is to cultivate the fields?[22]

Meanwhile, Tu Fu was contrasting the luxury and corruption of the royal court with conditions of the masses:

The humble people have no share in the feastings.
But the silk distributed in the royal harem
Was woven by poor women;
The officers beat their husbands
To extort the tribute for the Court. . . .
And we hear too that the golden platters of the palace
Have all gone to the houses of the royally related.
In the central halls there are fair goddesses;
An air of perfume moves with each charming figure.
They clothe their guests with warm furs of sable,
Entertain them with the finest music of pipe and string,
Feed them with the broth of the camel's pad,
With pungent tangerines, and oranges ripened in frost.
Behind the red-lacquered gates, wine is left to sour, meat to rot.
Outside these gates lie the bones of the frozen and the starved.
The flourishing and the withered are just a foot apart–
It rends my heart to ponder on it.[23]

In 755 a revolt broke out under the leadership of a military governor and the emperor was forced to flee, abdicating in favor of his son. The latter, aided by the Turkish Uigurs, recaptured the capital. When the rebellion was finally put down in 763, both the dynasty and China had been shorn of their power and prestige. Trade diminished and the revenue from taxes owed to the central government decreased. Meanwhile the provincial governors became increasingly powerful. Conditions grew progressively difficult for the common people, and the ninth century witnessed various popular uprisings. The most important of these insurrections took place in 874 in the south, led by a peasant, and though it was eventually put down, the T'angs were doomed. The governors of various provinces declared their independence, and in 906 the dynasty came to an end.

Civilization versus Barbarism (906-1368)

The "Five Dynasties." The fall of the T'ang dynasty left China in another of its periodic eras of internal anarchy and external attack. In this particular period, five dynasties followed each other quickly in north China. Meanwhile, various secessionist movements had established ten independent states in the south. At the same time, the Khitan Tatars had made successful attacks in the extreme north and northeast, and the decades ahead saw their progressive territorial aggrandizement at the expense of China.

Despite the political disintegration of this period, important developments occurred in other fields. The extensive use of printing produced Confucian, Buddhist, and Taoist texts and stimulated the spread of education. The small southern states made commercial and cultural advances. It was during this period too, that the crippling custom of binding women's feet was introduced–a fashion to which Chinese women submitted until contemporary times.

The Sung dynasty (960-1368). The period of disorder was followed by the founding of the Sung dynasty, which by 979 had subdued the secessionist states in the south. However, the Khitan still remained in the area north of the Yellow River, where they had established the kingdom of Liao. In the eleventh century, the Sung emperors had adopted the practice of "buying protection" by paying to the Khitan an annual tribute which by 1042 had increased to the sum of 200,000 ounces of silver and goods in kind. In time, the Sungs were also paying tribute to other border kingdoms.

Such payments in themselves represented only a fairly small percentage of the total state revenues. But the economic situation had become serious as a result of the existing monetary inflation and the unprecedented development of large estates whose owners managed to evade paying their proper share of taxation, so that an increasingly heavy burden fell on the small farmers. As a result, there was a fall in revenues and a succession of budget deficits. The emperor turned to one of China's most fascinating statesmen and fiscal reformers, Wang An-shih (1021-1086).

As part of his economic reforms, this prime minister devised many schemes to improve the state of agriculture, which with commerce was the greatest national asset. "His Agricultural Loans Measure was intended not only to relieve the farming class of the intolerable burden of interest which the callous money lenders exacted of them in difficult times, but also to ensure that the work of agriculture should be regularly conducted without such hindrances as lack of capital involved. His irrigation projects, and measures for river control, were designed to ensure an adequate water supply on the one hand, and to prevent flooding on the other. In this way large tracts of land would be reclaimed and brought under the plough."[24] Wang An-shih also regulated commerce by fixing prices so as to destroy speculation and break the strangle hold of monopolist elements. In addition, he is credited with appointing boards in all the districts to regulate wages and with planning pensions for the aged and unemployed. But this energetic minister did not stop with these measures. Dissatisfied with the existing state examination system which emphasized style and memorization of the classics, Wang An-shih instituted reforms so as to put greater emphasis upon practical knowledge.

Corruption, conservatism, opposition from the rich, and the impracticality of some of his projects all combined to defeat Wang An-shih's purpose. Yet it is remarkable to see how modern were the theories of this statesman who lived nine hundred years ago. The concepts of the welfare state and planned economy are apparently not quite so new as we may have supposed.

The Sungs and Chins. During the eleventh century, the Sung rulers attempted by diplomatic methods and the payment of tribute to dissuade the barbarians on their northern frontiers from further aggressive action. In the midst of such maneuvers, a new factor was injected—the appearance at the rear of the Khitan empire of the Jurchen, a Tungus people from what is now northeastern Manchuria. Hoping to improve his position at the expense of the Khitan, the Sung emperor allied himself with the Jurchen, who proceeded in 1114 to destroy the common enemy. Unhappily, the Jurchen presently marched against the Sungs as well, with the result that in 1126 the Sung capital was taken, and the emperor was sent into Jurchen territory in northern Manchuria. From this time on, the Sungs lost control over territory north of the Huai and Yangtze Rivers. A son of the deported emperor established a capital in the south, first at Nanking and then at Hangchow. As a result, China for the next century consisted of two empires (see map below) with the Jurchen having established a dynasty known as the Chin (not to be confused with the fourth century dynasty of the same name).

Sung thought. Though the Sung era was one of political tragedy, it represented great achievements in other fields. Whereas, in the words of one scholar, the T'ang dynasty "had been a time of rapidly extending frontiers, and of contact with the lands of the West, a period of freshness and youth, an era of lyric poetry and religious faith," the Sung dynasty, "shut out from the West by the steadily encroaching nomads, was a time of ripe maturity."[25] For example, Sung philosophers interpreted Confucius anew, adding portions of Buddhist thought. As a result, Confucianism, which hitherto had been largely a code of ethics for everyday living, was now provided

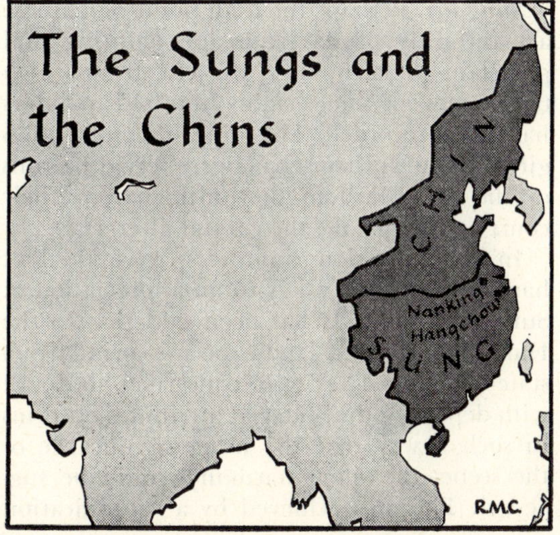

LANDSCAPE WITH BUFFALOES—DETAIL OF A SCROLL BY THE PAINTER CHIANG T'SAN, SUNG DYNASTY

with a metaphysic which taught that the universe was governed by eternal law or reason. The result was a new interpretation called Neo-Confucianism.

The advocates of Neo-Confucianism included some of the outstanding scholars of the day, who wrote influential commentaries on the classics. In addition, two great encyclopedias were compiled, whose value is enhanced because they cite from works which no longer exist. Outstanding among the historical works was that of Ssu-ma Kuang (1084) whose *Comprehensive Mirror of Materials for Government* chronicles events from 403 B.C. to 959 A.D. in 294 chapters. Though paraphrased in Spanish, this work—considered by one scholar as the "best universal history of China"—has never been translated in its entirety.

Sung art. Perhaps the high point of Chinese art—certainly of its landscape painting and porcelain—came in the Sung era, from which the names of some eight hundred painters have been recorded. The Sung emperors, often gifted painters themselves, were fervid patrons of the artists whom they attracted to their court at Hangchow, the capital after 1132.

In the expression "infinite space and silent harmony" we find a key to an appreciation of Sung landscapes. It has been said that to the Hangchow masters landscape was primarily a state of mind. They were concerned above all with depicting the material attributes of forms in such a way that the inner significance of the scene—the silent harmony—could be suggested. This was achieved by a simplification of line and shading, by the softening effects of mist and water, and by creating a feeling of the vastness of nature. The painting above illustrates this approach, where the spacious beauty of nature completely overshadows the status of the individual in the picture. This approach is in striking contrast to the Renaissance interpretation of landscape, as seen for example in the painting "Pastoral Concert," page 503. There human beings are all-important, and nature is subordinated.

Ceramics. Sung pottery and porcelain were also of unsurpassed excellence. The ware reflected the restrained and elegant tastes of the period, which is marked by the creation of different types of porcelain. Perhaps the best-known of the Sung ware is the gray-green porcelain called celadon, of which a graceful example is shown in the illustration on page 315. It has been pointed out that the qualities of Sung ceramic art have directly affected the work of present-day artists.

Genghis Khan. While the brilliant intellectual and esthetic developments centering on the Sung capital of Hangchow were transpiring, a new and terrible enemy was building up his strength to the north. In the twelfth century, one of the groups making up the Chin empire broke away and went into Mongolia, where they joined the Mongols (Tatars). There next arose a leader, Genghis Khan (1162?-1227), who used his formidable talents for uniting the Mongols and obtaining undisputed mastery over Mongolia—which was confirmed in 1206. He now turned his attention to the south. First, his armies campaigned against the Chin empire, and in 1215 its capital, Peking, was sacked and its inhabitants massacred. After that the campaign against the rest of the Chin empire slowed down, but only because Genghis Khan had meanwhile concerned himself with ambitions in the west. As a result, he pillaged central Asia, invaded India, ordered his armies across Persia and Asia Minor, and had them push on as far as the Danube. Between 1237 and 1240 many Russian cities were sacked and ruined. Kiev was one of the last to be pillaged. Now Russia passed under the rule of the Mongol Tatars. This conquest, as we will see in Chapter 16, was to have momentous influence upon the development of modern Russia. Genghis Khan had died in 1227, but his successors succeeded in vanquishing the last remnants of the Chin empire by 1234. Then, after years of fighting and heroic resistance, the Sungs themselves were overthrown by the new Mongol dynasty.

The Yuan, or Mongol, dynasty. When the last Sung pretender was eliminated in 1279, the Mongol dynasty, known as the Yuan, ruled supreme in China. For the first time China had been completely subjugated by foreign conquerors. After 1260 the sprawling Mongol empire had been divided into a suzerain khanate and four vassal khanates, all ruled by descendants of Genghis Khan. Kublai Khan, who held the suzerain khanate comprising China and Mongolia, made his capital at Peking. Because the Mongols constituted only a minority of the population, Kublai Khan enacted legislation to safeguard their dominant position. This legislation failed, however, to prevent the resurgence of Chinese power within a century.

Nor was Kublai Khan successful in adding Japan to the Mongol empire. Failure also attended his attempts at imperial expansion in the direction of Champa, Annam, and Java. But his reign at home was marked by various favorable developments. He improved the imperial roads and constructed canals, while his famous postal system—with stations posted every twenty-five to thirty miles and employing at least 200,000 horses—ensured the swift dispatch of messages throughout the empire. This remarkable ruler also built granaries to store food surpluses against times of scarcity, revised the calendar, aided the sick, orphans, and old scholars through state care, and built a beautiful new capital at old Peking. Kublai realized the cultural superiority of the people he had conquered and ruled wisely, showing tolerance for all religions, including Christianity, and maintaining peace and order throughout his vast empire.

Marco Polo's account. For knowledge of Kublai Khan's reign, we are indebted to Marco Polo, the author of probably the world's outstanding travelog and what has been called the finest European account of Chinese medieval civilization. As a youth, Marco Polo had

OLIVE-GREEN SUNG BOWL WITH CHRYSANTHEMUM PATTERN IN RELIEF

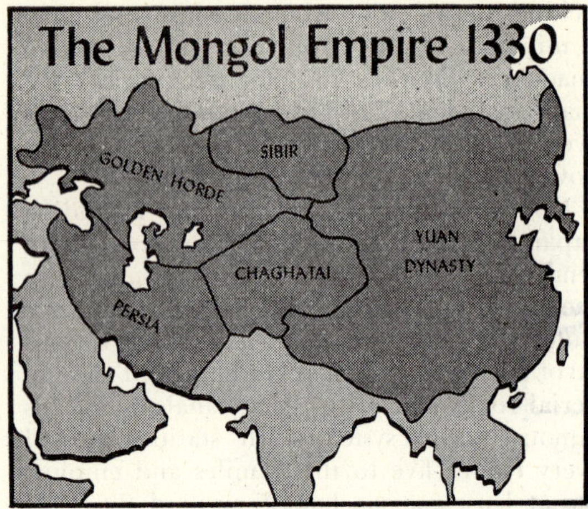

accompanied his father and uncle, two Venetian merchants, eastward to Kublai Khan's court, arriving there around 1275. Received with honor and given posts in the imperial service, they remained some seventeen years in China, during which time Marco traveled throughout the country. In this way he gathered material for the account which he wrote after his return to Italy, thus providing the West with the most detailed information that it had ever received about the Far East. But Marco's contemporaries were so incredulous of the wonders he had seen in China—whose civilization was superior to anything in thirteenth-century Europe—that they dubbed him "Messer Millione" because of his numberless "fables." In such a category they must have placed his account of black stones (coal) for heating purposes, and of the size and magnificence of the capital, Peking, or the old Sung capital, Hangchow—which, according to Marco Polo and other European travelers, may well have been the greatest city in the world at that time, with its large circumference and purported 12,000 stone bridges spanning a network of canals. Marco Polo's account of trade and commerce in silks, rice, sugar, pepper, pearls, and precious stones, and involving central Asia, India, southeast Asia, and Japan must also have seemed exaggerated to his European contemporaries.

Actually, however, these prosperous appearances were largely deceptive. Many peasants were being dispossessed of their land and forced to work for great landowners; the number of taxpayers was diminishing while taxes increased; an unchecked flow of hard currency out of the country was accompanied by the issuance of large amounts of paper money which in turn depreciated. All of this added to the impoverishment of the masses.

The drama and the novel. Kublai Khan and his successors were munificent patrons of the arts. They were also enthusiastic in their attendance at the theater. Consequently, although the drama had its origins in earlier centuries, it was firmly established as an art form in the Mongol period. There are still in existence over a hundred plays written at this time, and many of them possess genuine literary merit. This period was also marked by important advances in the writing of fiction. It has been suggested that the drama inspired the writing of novels, whose plots were similar in character. For a long time, neither the drama nor the novel was recognized as "literature," but the artistic merits of both have since been acknowledged.

Decline of the Mongols. Kublai Khan was succeeded by seven other Yuan emperors before the dynasty was overthrown, but none of them proved adequate rulers. Meanwhile, the peasantry was impoverished, the Mongols had not kept up their armed strength, and their exclusion of Chinese from the imperial administration tended to weaken their hold on their subjects. Finally, as the result of a successful rebellion, an ex-Buddhist monk entered Peking in 1368 and established a new dynasty —the Ming.

Pax Tatarica. We will recall that in the first centuries of the Christian era, the West had been linked by the spice and silk trades with India and China (Chapter 7). Then came hundreds of years of mutual isolation. During the T'ang dynasty the court at Changan attracted such diverse groups as Moslems, Nestorian Christians, followers of Manichaeism, and Persians. Now, thanks to the nomadic Mongols, East and West were again linked together along the ancient silk routes. The resumption of this trade had permanent consequences. The Mongol dynasty, by making safe the trade routes across Asia and by tolerating diverse religions, attracted more Nestorian Christians, Franciscan and Dominican missionaries, and European traders to China.

At the height of its power, the Mongol empire stretched from the Danube to the Pacific. With the unification, however temporary, of almost all Asia and the restoration of roads, the Polos were far from being the only travelers to traverse the great spaces separating East and West. We are told that the Chinese had communities in Moscow and Novgorod, while one Nestorian Christian monk in the thirteenth century traveled as envoy from Peking to Rome, where he saw the Pope, and later met the kings of England and France and visited Sainte Chapelle in Paris. Meanwhile, in the thirteenth century, Rome had sent various missions to the Far East. As a result, in the early fourteenth century there was a Roman Christian community in China which contained several thousand persons, an archbishop, and a number of suffragan bishops. There were also large communities of Arabs and other merchants—some of them Italian—then residing in China.

The cultural exchange between China and India was the result primarily of religion and trade, especially in silk. In the sixth century Mauryan art came to China via the Strait of Malacca. In Nanking examples of this influence remain in the fluted columns and the winged lions. When the Chinese accepted Buddhism, missionaries came from India, and conversely, Chinese pilgrims traveled to shrines in India.

China and the Philippines carried on an active trade and exchange of cultures several centuries before the Spanish conquest of the islands. By the same means China bequeathed Indo-China her science, legal code, Confucian political philosophy, calendar, and governmental titles. As early as the seventh century a constant stream of pilgrims came from Japan, Korea, Burma, Cambodia, the East Indies, central Asia, India, and the environs of the Black and Caspian seas to study Chinese culture. On occasion Chinese naval expeditions sailed to Java and Borneo.

The cultural interchange was considerable. "Chinese block-printing was made known to Europe as a result of the Mongol conquests, especially through the Chinese printed paper currency which aroused so much interest, through playing-cards introduced into Europe by the Tatars, and through religious image-prints made by the Buddhists and probably also by the Nestorians."[26] Meanwhile, as we have seen, the art of paper-making had been introduced into Europe considerably earlier by Arabs, who in turn had learned it from Chinese captives brought to Samarkand in the eighth century. China itself was enriched by the importation of various innovations. One of the most important of these was a new food, sorghum, which was brought to China by way of India in the thirteenth century. By that time the abacus, a familiar sight in Far East shops today, had also made its appearance. Ceramics and bronzes were in turn affected by influences from the west, especially Persia, while the cloisonné technique was undoubtedly borrowed from Byzantine sources.

This interchange of culture factors—and the above are but random examples—certainly enriched East and West alike. Yet, the "profound psychological effect" created in Europe by the accounts of Marco Polo and other travelers was perhaps even more far reaching in the evolution of world history. These accounts had revealed that the Far East not only equaled but exceeded Europe in population, wealth, and luxury—with the result that Latin Europeans now realized that the Mediterranean was neither the central nor the most important area of the world. They had discovered a new world and began to develop new attitudes to fit this knowledge.

The Evolution of Japan

Japanese geography. The Japanese do not use the term "Japan" to designate their native land. Instead they call it *Nippon* or *Yamato,* "the Mountain Portal." The Japanese are fond of the natural beauties of their homeland, although the geographical make-up of the island empire may not deserve such homage. In the archipelago are over four thousand islands of varying size, four of them relatively large and the remainder quite small. The principal one is Honshu, which today contains the main cities of Japan, including the historic capital of the kingdom, Kyoto, and the modern capital, Tokyo. On Honshu also is situated the symbol by which Japan is known all over the world, the holy mountain Fujiyama. Altogether about six hundred islands of the archipelago are inhabited. Today they possess a population of more than 80 million. The support of such a large population on an area whose resources are below the people's needs constitutes Japan's major problem. Only seventeen per cent of the islands' soil is arable. Much of the rice annually consumed has to be imported. Other important crops include rye, soy beans, barley, and wheat. Fish, which abound off the coasts, supply a large portion of the Japanese diet. Japan has few mineral resources and is deficient in iron, coal, and oil deposits, essential to large-scale manufacturing. Added to these deficiencies is the fact that Japan has been subjected to recurring earthquakes, typhoons, and tidal waves. But disaster and want have never prevented the Japanese people from making an annual visit to a grove of cherry trees in blossom; misfortune has not kept them from writing exquisite poetry about the beauties of the chrysanthemums, the trailing wistaria, and the blue lakes.

Origins of the Japanese people. The traditional account of the origins of the Japanese people is highly interesting—and highly fictitious. The first emperor is supposed to have been descended from the Sun Goddess. He is known as Jimmu Tenno, and, according to tradition, became emperor in 660 B.C. Ever since the reign of Jimmu Tenno there has been only one ruling family to preside over the destinies of Nippon. Thus this royal house can claim to have the oldest unbroken line of any in the world.

The historical account of the origins of Nippon is more prosaic but still interesting. Where the Japanese people came from is not definitely known. They are a mixed race. In ancient times the archipelago witnessed many immigrations from the Asiatic mainland and probably from such islands lying to the south as Borneo, Java, and the Philippines. Today there are racial similarities between certain Japanese and people in southern China and Indo-China, while others are akin to the inhabitants of Korea and Manchuria. The most primitive people living in Japan today are an interesting aboriginal group called Ainu. At present they live mainly on the island of Hokkaido, although at one time they inhabited the other principal islands of the archipelago. Ainu artifacts have been found which may be six thousand years old. The Ainu people, now only about twenty thousand in number, are low-statured, hairy, with eyes not almond-shaped like the Japanese, thick nosed, and with rather high cheekbones. These aborigines were a branch of the original population of the Japanese islands whom the invading Japanese either drove from the southern islands or absorbed into their own people. Japan had a Stone Age, for there are artifacts to prove it. The Stone Age in Japan may have persisted as late as 1000 B.C.

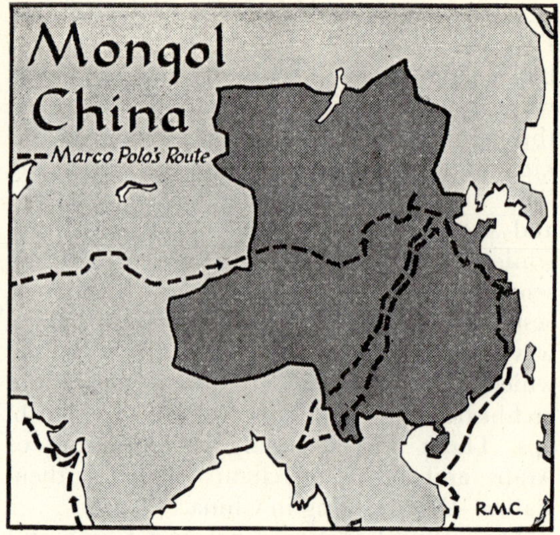

The Chinese influence. It seems certain that during the days of the Chou dynasty in China (1122-249 B.C.) successive immigrations to Japan took place, possibly from northeast Asia by way of Korea. These invaders exterminated the Neolithic inhabitants or drove them into remote districts, and planted their own cul-

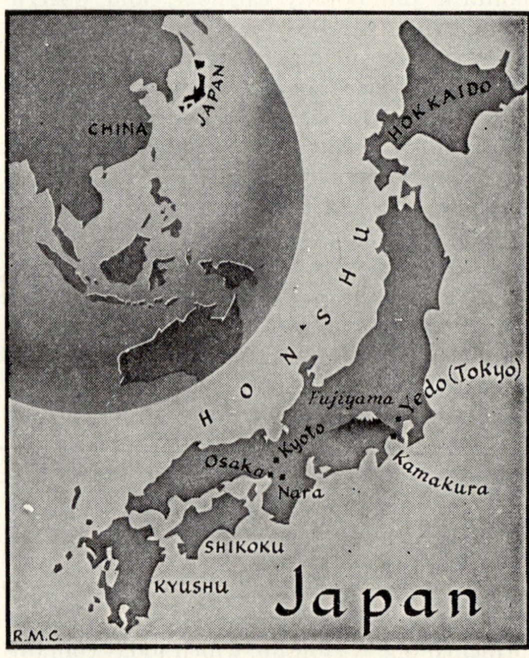

ture. They brought with them the use of metal. Chinese influence probably predominated at this time and became even more powerful as time elapsed. Not later than the first century B.C. there existed a strong outpost of Chinese culture in Korea, and unquestionably traffic existed between that area and the Japanese islands. China's culture at this time ranked with any in the entire world, and the inhabitants of Nippon did not remain unaffected by its splendor.

Although the Japanese profess to trace the history of their ruling house from 660 B.C., we know little or nothing about the island kingdom until the sixth century A.D. Koreans in large numbers were then crossing over from the mainland, and Japan was enriched by the advent of artisans, potters, weavers, painters, and farmers skilled in agriculture and the breeding of silkworms. The educated immigrants, scribes, and accountants brought over the Chinese language with its character script, of inestimable value for Japanese culture. Then in 552 Buddhism came from Korea and in time grew to be the principal faith of the islands (together with native Shintoism).

The spread of Buddhism in Japan was due largely to the propagandizing efforts of Prince Shotoku Taishi, revered today for his humanitarianism and vision. When Shotoku died in 621, the year before Mohammed was forced to make his Hegira from Mecca to Medina, it was said that all people mourned him as though he were a close kinsman. Buddhism stimulated the refinement of manners and morals and at the same time introduced many new artistic ideas from India and China. Early art in Japan was to a great extent stimulated by Chinese art. The T'ang dynasty had commenced its age of enlightenment. Students were journeying westward to learn more about the country of which a Chinese priest said in 622 at the court in Japan: "The land of Great T'ang is a wonderful country, whose laws are complete and fixed. Constant communication should be kept up with it."[27]

Evolution of Japanese government. In 645 an important document in Japanese constitutional history was set forth—the Great Reform. According to its provisions the ruler of Yamato was no longer a weak chieftain with only nominal suzerainty over the heads of the various clans, but the real emperor of Japan who in theory owned every acre of land in his empire. In 702 a law code, the Tai-ho ("Great Treasure") was set forth, founded on Chinese antecedents. Dealing with a multitude of subjects, including duties of officials, services to the gods, the land, taxation, salaries, army and frontier defense, stores of rice and grain, arrest of criminals, funerals and mourning, and other social topics, the Tai-ho stressed that all persons, irrespective of birth or position, owed equal allegiance to the government. This concept of duty was manifest particularly in the Second World War. No sacrifice was too great for a citizen to make for Nippon.

The Nara period (710-794). The period from 710 to 794 is known as the Nara period because the beautiful city of Nara was made the capital of Japan. At Nara can be found the *Daibutsu,* a huge bronze image of Buddha whose casting began in 747. The Daibutsu—"Buddha of Infinite Compassion"—is 53 feet high (the little finger is nearly as long as a man is tall) and required over a million pounds of metal. Travelers from all over the world have visited the great shrine. Buddhism continued to flourish in the Nara period, and poetry was popular. The verse forms in which Nara poetry was couched originally came from China and were used by the refined court people to express moods and attitudes. The favorite pattern was the *tanka,* a rigid and conventional form. These poems made use of puns, double meanings, and classical allusions.

The Heian period (794-1156). In 794 a new capital, the political center until 1869, was built at Kyoto. Kyoto, "City of Peace," is historically perhaps the richest city in all Japan. The period lasting down to 1156 is known as the Heian period. It is an age noted particularly for its literature, owing largely to the invention of two new types of phonetic writing during the eighth and ninth centuries. Syllabic in make-up, both are natural developments of the Chinese character system. Much of the best Heian literature was written by feminine authors, the most famous diary of the age, the *Pillow Book,* being composed by a court lady, Sei Shonagon. Apparently courtiers and ladies wrote poems about trivial matters in their idle hours. They admired the cherry blossoms in the spring, arranged flowers, and concerned themselves with the painstaking details of socially correct color scheme in dress. The common people led no such idyllic life, but instead toiled at raising rice, tea, and cotton. Fishing furnished a livelihood for many of the poorer people, although the influence of Buddhism, which forbids the killing and eating of flesh and fish, must have seriously curtailed the fishing industry.

Social structure of medieval Japan. The populace of medieval Japan was divided into two groups: the free and the non-free. The highest members of the free group were the heads of the great clans, all of whom bore important rank at court. The lesser nobles were not eligible to occupy the state's highest offices, but devoted their talents to the professions, the arts, or warfare. The lowest of the free people were the peasant, small landholders and members of certain guilds, who paid taxes in grain and labor. The guildsmen followed such occupations as smith, armorer, and lacquer-worker. Among the non-free people were both public and private slaves. The public slaves worked on the land, from which they received a food ration, or were engaged in such menial tasks as scavenging and grave-digging. The private slaves belonged to the households of wealthy nobles and could be sold or given away. At this time the slaves, made up in large measure of Korean and Ainu captives as well as political offenders, comprised one tenth to one fifth of the total population.

The shogun. At various times during Japan's early history a virtual military dictatorship was established, with supreme power given to an officer called the *shogun*—"generalissimo." The title was usually bestowed upon some deserving soldier, and only for the duration of the national crisis. But upon one of Japan's greatest statesmen, Yoritomo (1146-1198) the title was conferred for life, and to him also was given the right to name his successor. Yoritomo established a form of government, the *bakufu* (army headquarters), which existed for almost seven hundred years. Henceforth the *shogun* as military commander took over the control of justice, law, and finance. He appointed constables and land stewards over every province to prevent rebellion. Thus the *shogun* became the real ruler of Japan. Although he continued to pay the utmost respect to the emperor and governed at a discreet distance from the imperial court, the principal power in Nippon belonged to him and not to the emperor. This was the state of affairs down to the revolution of 1867.

"The Great Wind." In 1260 Kublai Khan came to the throne of China. Hearing reports about the mythical wealth of Nippon, the Great Khan decided to extend his rule to Japan. He made extensive plans for the invasion, gathering over 100,000 men in 3500 ships. The stoical Japanese prepared to meet a danger fully as great as that faced by Elizabethan England when the Spanish Armada sailed northward. But, as befell the Armada, nature came to the aid of the Japanese. A tempest—thenceforth known as "the Great Wind" —dispersed the ships of the invaders, in 1281. The fleet was scattered and thousands of men perished or were cast on Japanese soil to be captured by the natives as slaves. Yet so great was the danger that the Nipponese never forgot it, and it is said that even in recent times the Japanese mother would ask her crying child, "Do you think the Mogu are coming?"[28]

The Hojo period. The thirteenth century in Japan belongs to what is called the Hojo period, noted for its literature, art, and social customs. Painting continued to be mostly portraiture, concerned with depicting court figures. Caricature appeared, however, and has continued throughout Japanese painting. During the Hojo period official recognition was given the *bushido,* the unwritten code of chivalry and honor as practiced by the *samurai* (warrior nobility). The *bushido* stressed courage, fortitude, composure, benevolence, politeness, and loyalty. It also approved the custom of self-immolation known as *seppuku* (popularly known as *hara-kari*). *Seppuku* was not mere suicide but a ceremonial by which the warrior could expiate crimes, escape disgrace, or prove his loyalty. There is a story that a policeman once committed *seppuku* because he had the misfortune to misdirect an imperial procession through a village street. These customs reveal the stoical indifference to death which the Japanese people possess.

Summary

At the very time when Europe was beset by the tribulations following in the wake of the collapse of the Graeco-Roman world, Asia was being enriched by what were probably its most splendid centuries of cultural development. The first of these centuries saw the emergence of a golden age in India. With the Guptas we reach the apogee of Hindu culture. It produced frescoes and sculpture characterized by dignity and restraint. The Gupta poet Kalidasa wrote dramas which have been compared with those of Shakespeare, while the art and poetry of the Deccan and Tamil Land prove how richly endowed with artistic genius was non-Aryan-speaking India. In science, too, medieval India made valuable contributions. Its astronomy and mathematics were the most advanced of any people to that time, and we are indebted to it for the so-called "Arabic" numerals, the decimal system, and many of the basic elements of algebra. The Hindus of the Gupta age also made valuable discoveries in the fields of industrial chemistry and medicine.

Recurrent in India's history have been the rise and fall of dynasties and kingdoms, and the Gupta age itself was followed by a period of internal dissolution and external invasion, culminating finally in the subjugation of the country by the forces of an uncompromisingly antagonistic religious culture, Islam. The consequences of that impact —which we shall take up in a later chapter—were in our own age to split the Indian subcontinent into two separate states. Nevertheless, despite the political anarchy which has gripped India from earliest to contemporary times, this country's culture pattern has been singularly unified and enduring. The great majority of Indians are Hindus in their faith, and Hinduism still teaches the ancient doctrines of the *Upanishads,* the unity of life, *maya, moksha, karma,* and reincarnation. It has been natural for the Hindu to regard our physical world and its pains and limitations as evils from which to escape—a view certainly strengthened by the unhappy political and economic features of so much of India's history. Again, because the Hindus believe in the social and religious necessity of a caste system, their unique theory of society has endured for three thousand years and has kept Indian social life fixed, though there are present-day indications that the system is undergoing modification. In the period under review, we saw that the basic social and cultural motivations were provided by Hinduism. So powerful was the civilization which reached its zenith in the Gupta period that it succeeded in creating a "Greater India" throughout south and southeast Asia, thereby raising materially the cultural level of a large segment of mankind.

We have in turn reviewed the history of the great and dynamic Chinese people over a period of some twelve centuries. We have seen the rise and fall of numerous dynasties, each with its individual problems and contributions, yet all prolonging the continuous sweep of cultural traits which make Chinese civilization unique. Similarly, we have noticed how various dynasties made themselves outstanding in particular ways. Thus, the T'ang period was marked especially by the rich flowering of poetry, painting, and sculpture, and the invention of printing. The Sungs, despite political chaos and Tatar invasion, contributed to a resurgence of Confucian philosophy and saw painting and pottery reach new artistic heights. The Yuan, or Mongol, dynasty patronized the arts and helped develop the drama and fiction. It is true that the Mongol dynasty was foreign in origin, but its rulers aided rather than retarded the expansion of native culture.

One fact is preëminent when a summation of Chinese civilization is attempted. It is the vitality of Chinese temperament. Even as the Chinese can biologically assimilate other races without losing their own characteristics (and have done so all through their history), so in their culture they assimilate foreign customs without seeming to impair their own. Physically, the Chinese are a strong people who *en masse* appear to be impervious to racial degeneration and who are indisputably among the most productive groups in the world today. They have always lived simple lives close to the soil, which they cherish deeply, and for that reason, if for no other, they are strong traditionalists who desire to perpetuate those cultural habits which have made them enduring as a race. Despite the rise and fall of dynasties and the periodic invasion of barbarian tribes from the west and north the Chinese people until the most recent times have led much the same physical existence and enjoyed the same social customs as their ancestors who died over two thousand years ago. They are deeply conservative, and their conservatism has acted to their disadvantage in an age of change. But they have a priceless heritage of sanity and tradition which may see them through the present years of turmoil.

In this chapter we have learned something, too, about the origins of the people of Japan and their early history. They owed a great debt of gratitude to China for their initial cultural advancements, but had already begun to make their own individual contributions. We shall come back to the subsequent evolution of the island kingdom in a future chapter. At the conclusion of this chapter, Nippon was still static and slumbering. But already her people had been inculcated with such important traits as unswerving loyalty to their emperor, an almost fanatical courage, and a great pride in their indigenous customs and ideals.

Part Four

The panorama of Europe

The Panorama of Europe

THE FOREGOING CHAPTERS have given a picture of the high level of civilization in the Near East and the Far East in medieval times. In the history of world civilization, it was a period when these areas outshone other parts of the world. Bagdad became a metropolis of two million people. Constantinople displayed an architectural magnificence and a superiority in the making of luxurious wares not rivaled anywhere in the West. Hindu culture enjoyed its golden age under the Gupta dynasty. And China during the glorious T'ang period developed printing, subsidized art, and produced the matchless poetry of Tu Fu and Li Po. Passing from the notable achievements in the Near and the Far East, we now consider the course of events in medieval Europe.

The time span for the Middle Ages in western Europe can be thought of as the thousand years separating the fifth from the fifteenth century. So much research in the medieval field has been done in our times that we scarcely need feel obliged to refute the charge that the Middle Ages were devoid of order and learning. This error arose largely out of the false emphasis placed by Renaissance scholars on the culture of ancient Greece and Rome, so that they were unable to appreciate the true significance of the many original contributions of their immediate predecessors. But modern scholars have demonstrated that the medieval mind was just as capable as any other and medieval learning and art just as remarkable. The Middle Ages, however, were motivated by a perspective quite different from what had gone before or was to come after. This perspective has been called "otherworldly." The attention of our medieval ancestors tended to be turned toward a religious goal—one of preparation for the hereafter. The Church was the great arbiter of human destiny.

Although the Middle Ages were in an important sense "otherworldly," they were at the same time peopled with men who were very much concerned with secular interests and who championed the cause of this world. The Middle Ages were a period of transition from the rich classical culture of Greece and Rome to the still more complex culture of modern times, a transition which was marked, at the outset, by several centuries of uncertainty and a lowering of material, moral, and intellectual standards. But by 800 A.D. the process of revival had definitely begun. The fusion of four great elements, Greek, Roman, Christian, and German, was well on its way, and in the next six hundred years the upward trend of civilization was vigorous. After the twelfth century the advance of culture in western Europe was stimulated by contact with the Near East and even the Far East.

WE HAVE ALREADY, in Chapter 8, acquainted ourselves with the difficult centuries of transition from the fifth to the seventh. In the following four chapters, which are titled "The Panorama of Europe," we will first discuss the trend of political history in the early Middle Ages, roughly from the mid-seventh to the end of the eleventh century. On the surface this period might seem to be a barren and confused segment of history, but in reality it was one of tremendous significance, for during this time the basic foundations of modern western culture were laid. By the end of the eleventh century a new Europe had emerged in which the fusion of Greek, Roman, Christian, and German traditions, had taken place in a distinctive culture we term medieval.

After examining the political history of the Middle Ages, we will turn to a survey of medieval life. A study of life in the castle, manor, and town will acquaint us with how men were governed, how food was produced, and how some few commodities were manufactured and sold. Interwoven with the political and economic manifestations of medieval culture were the social habits of the time. We shall see how the lords and ladies lived and dined, how they amused themselves, how the serfs eked out a miserable existence and tried to get a little joy out of life, and what kind of life was led by the burgher in the city. The Middle Ages were far from barren in thought, for we shall see that during this period our modern European languages took form, the Gothic style was evolved, many literary classics were produced, and finally, the university in its modern form was born.

As for the Christian Church, its influence pervaded everywhere, for it gave the medieval scene its dimensions, its main characteristics, its goal, and its inner meaning. All men were born, lived, and died under the protection of the Church, and the Church was stern toward those who tried to reject its ministrations. But there were few indeed who tried, for within the Church was consolation from the harshness and uncertainty of life. The Church provided warmth and color and drama in a society that was often drab and unexciting. Within the Church, too, a career might be made when social stratification outside had stifled the opportunities of all but the wellborn. Finally, the authority of the Church, stemming from the Pope in Rome and filtering down through an hierarchy of archbishops, bishops, and other functionaries to the humble parish priest, provided the nearest approach to effective centralized government in the Middle Ages.

Chronology of events and developments discussed in this chapter

Chapter 12

Expansion of the Slavs: menaced the Germanic tribes and area between Oder and Elbe rivers	500-900
Charles Martel became Mayor of the Palace: united Frankish lands; suppressed the nobles; fortified the borders	714
Moors defeated by Charles Martel in the battle of Tours	732
Pepin the Short: crowned king of the Franks by the Pope	741-768
Donation of Pepin: formed the Papal States	756
Charlemagne: summit of Carolingian and Frankish power	768-814
Charlemagne crowned: missi dominici *acted as royal envoys; defeated Lombards and Moslems*	800
Vikings devastated northwest France and Ireland	800-880
England united against the Danes under Alfred the Great	800-900
Strasbourg Oaths: Louis and Charles united against Lothaire	842
Treaty of Verdun: Carolingian empire broken up; began shaping of modern boundaries	843
Freemen placed under protection of lords: encouraged feudalism	847
Founding of the duchy of Kiev, forerunner of Russia	882
Henry the Fowler: first Saxon king in Germany	919-936
Battle of Lechfeld: Otto the Great halted the Hungarians	955
Otto crowned king of the Lombards: Germany and Italy under one rule	961
Otto II: defeated by the Moslems in Italy	973-983
Hugh Capet crowned: theory of divine kingship	987
Russians converted to Byzantine Christianity	989
Caliphate of Cordova overthrown: separate states emerged in Spain	1031
Norman invasion of England by William the Conqueror	1066
Last Byzantine outpost conquered in Italy by Norman mercenaries	1071
Normans under Robert Guiscard captured Sicily	1094
Mediterranean opened to Christian commerce; Moslems conquered	1100

The dawn of a new Europe

Medieval political history: c. 700 to 1100

We left the history of Europe (Chapter 8) in the seventh century, with the Germans in Italy, the Franks in Gaul, and the papacy exerting a persuasive influence throughout the western world. As this chapter opens, taking up the story from that date, western Europe was beginning to reel under the impact of a new wave of invasions—by Slavs from the east and Moslems from the south. Commerce and cities were destroyed as the Moslems took control of the Mediterranean and cut the vital trade routes between the East and the West. With the destruction of East-West contacts, the cities soon lost their cosmopolitan character. Europe became isolated, self-contained, and predominantly agrarian.

It was under these circumstances that a remarkable Frankish noble house tried to re-create the empire of the Caesars, unifying much of Europe under its law and administration. It was an amazing accomplishment, but we will see that Charlemagne's empire was short lived. After its disintegration came the terrible ninth century with its invasions and melancholy disorders.

European rulers, less ambitious than before, now became more successful in their undertakings. New political divisions began to emerge, such as France, England, and Germany. In England we shall see the rivalries of some seven quarrelsome little kingdoms being resolved in the triumph of a united country under the leadership of the House of Wessex. In France the establishment of stable government was more difficult, because the area involved was much larger and there was much more political fragmentation. In 987, however, the destinies of this land passed into the hands of a remarkable family, the House of Capet, or the Capetians, who were ultimately to make the name of their small duchy, "France," the name of an entire country. In this formative period of European politics, Germany and its monarchy seemed to hold the most promise. We shall follow the heroic figures of Henry the Fowler and Otto the Great, his son, as they curb factionalism and begin the epic eastward movement of the Germans against the Slavs.

Far to the east the impact of doughty Viking traders and adventurers had resulted in the rise of a new state, the duchy of Kiev, on the banks of the Dnieper River. With this state begins the history of Russia. In the eleventh century Kiev was one of the most civilized states in the world, its capital a "second Constantinople," and the Christian "Rus" gave every indication of being in the front ranks of western civilization.

Much of this chapter describes Europeans, under the blows of invasions or the blight of incompetent governments, struggling to maintain some semblance of civilization. But the narrative, as we will see, ends on a note of promise. By the end of the eleventh century western Europeans were strong enough to seize the offensive against the Moors in Spain, to clear the islands and the lairs of the Mediterranean from Moslem pirates (and thus to rebuild the thalassic foundations for European life and trade), and finally, even to undertake an invasion—a Crusade—against the Saracens of the Middle East.

New Empire in the West

Decline of the Merovingians. When last we surveyed the history of western Europe following the Germanic invasions and the overthrow of Roman imperial authority, we noted the all-important role of the Christian Church in helping to conserve civilization and bring about a new fusion of culture made up of the best Germanic and Graeco-Roman elements (page 243). In this task the Church secured the aid of the dynamic Franks by the conversion of their leader, Clovis, to orthodox Roman Catholicism. For the space of two hundred years the history of western Europe is no more than the narrative of the rise, expansion, and decline of the Frankish empire.

Following the death of Clovis in 511, his descendants followed well his example of conquest, extending the Frankish domain so that it soon came to include all of modern France, Belgium, western Germany, and much of central Germany. At the same time, however, the Merovingian royal house began to decay from inner weaknesses. The pernicious practice of dividing the realm among all the sons of a late king resulted in constant strife and civil war. Various members of the royal house plotted murders and became adept at intrigue and treachery. No wonder the Frankish monarchy at this time has been defined as "despotism tempered with assassination."[1] There was also a deterioration in character as the Merovingian princes engaged in all manner of debaucheries, the least unpleasant of which was excessive drinking. It has been well said that "The family affairs of this dipsomaniac house, whose marital troubles were only equalled by their murderous tendencies, make exciting, if not elevating reading...."[2]

These crimes and excesses had their inevitable effect; the Merovingian kings became weaklings and many of them died after only a few years on the throne. Although the Frankish state still retained its unity in theory, for all practical purposes it had broken up into four separate parts. In each of these provinces or divisions, the chief official in the royal household, known as the Mayor of the Palace, became all powerful. As for their royal masters, they were mere puppets and are known as the *rois fainéants* (do-nothing kings). These rulers were still crowned, but as a writer of the time, Einhard, has described them: "Nothing was left the king.... He sat on his throne and played at government, gave audience to envoys, and dismissed them with the answers which he had been schooled, or rather commanded, to give."[3]

New barbarian invasions. It was just at this time of Merovingian decay that a new wave of barbarian invasions threatened to engulf Europe. In the late seventh century the Moslem Arabs, overconfident from their easy triumphs in Syria and Egypt, swept across north Africa and prepared to invade Spain. And from the east a great movement of the Slavic people got underway. The beginnings of these prolific and restless people is largely unknown and only vaguely hinted in ancient legend, but it seems that their original home was in the Pripet Marshes. From this nucleus, the Slavs fanned out in all directions, especially in the centuries between 500 and 900 A.D.

Three main Slavic groups can be identified. The western Slavs moved eastward, filling in the vacuum left by the Germanic tribes as they gave up their lands between the Oder and the Elbe Rivers to push into the Roman empire. By 600 the Slavs had made the Elbe their frontier. As we will read in this and a later chapter, there was incessant fighting between these western Slavs and the Germanic peoples. This is one of the great themes of the Middle Ages, and indeed the struggle of Slav versus Teuton was bequeathed to modern times and has been very much alive after the Second World War. Another great branch of Slavic stock, the southern Slavs, moved to the south toward the Balkans and the magnet of Constantinople. We have already seen in Chapter 9 how these people, together with Asiatic stocks like the Avars and Bulgars, devastated Thrace and Macedonia and became a serious menace to the Byzantine empire.

It was the western Slavs who constituted the most serious danger to the Frankish kingdom, for the fierce Avars, who became masters of these people, had hurled them not only against southern Europe but in the west against the Bavarians, Saxons, Franks, and other Germanic people. As for the eastern Slavs, soon to be known as the Russians, their effective entry upon the western European scene was not to take place for more than one thousand years. During this millenium and more, these Slavs were occupied with the epic challenge of expanding eastward, moving across the empty steppes, filling the vast Eurasian plain, and finally reaching the Pacific.

Enough has already been narrated in this volume to make clear how often history concerns the movement of peoples and the consequent impact of cultures that takes place when a migrant people forces itself into a new area. In this respect notice the difference between the historical wanderings of the Germanic and Slavic stocks. The former, together with the Latin peoples of France, Spain, and the Mediterranean, were crowded into Europe, which is really a relatively small peninsula. When western expansion did occur at the end of the Middle Ages it was transoceanic. Immigrants settled the Americas and colonizers conquered rich tropical areas like India and Java. Slavic expansion, on the other hand, while less spectacular, was able to take advantage of a vast and relatively empty continent conveniently situated on its doorstep.

Charles Martel and the rise of the Carolingians. During these perilous times of effete Merovingian rule and danger from without, the Mayors of the Palace, belonging to what was to become known as the Carolingian family, defeated their rival Mayors in other divisions of the kingdom and seized all power. A new period of history began with the accession to power of Charles Martel, who became Mayor in 714. The Frankish kingdom was in a critical condition. But Charles beat down the rebellious nobles, reunited the Frankish realm, and became in all respects the king. For the time being, however, the Merovingian royal ciphers were kept as a kind of decorative feature at the court.

Charles Martel strengthened the eastern frontier of the Frankish kingdom against the inroads of the western Slavs, but his greatest achievement was victory over the great host of Moslem Arab invaders. As noted in our discussion of Mohammed and the expansion of Islam in Chapter 10, the governor of Moslem north Africa sent his General Tarik and an army of Moors across the strait into Spain in 711. By 718 the weak kingdom of the Visigoths had completely crumbled and its Moslem conquerors looked across the Pyrenees for new lands to conquer. After a number of sorties and feints in which various Frankish cities were raided and pillaged, in 732 the Moslem host under the command of the governor of Spain hurled itself into the Frankish kingdom and stormed Bordeaux. Charles collected his forces and prepared to meet the invader. The encounter took place between Tours and Poitiers, with the Moors attacking with their light cavalry and the Frankish foot soldiers standing on the defensive. All day the battle was engaged and "The Frankish warriors, who in the heat of the fight had formed a hollow

732 Battle of Tours

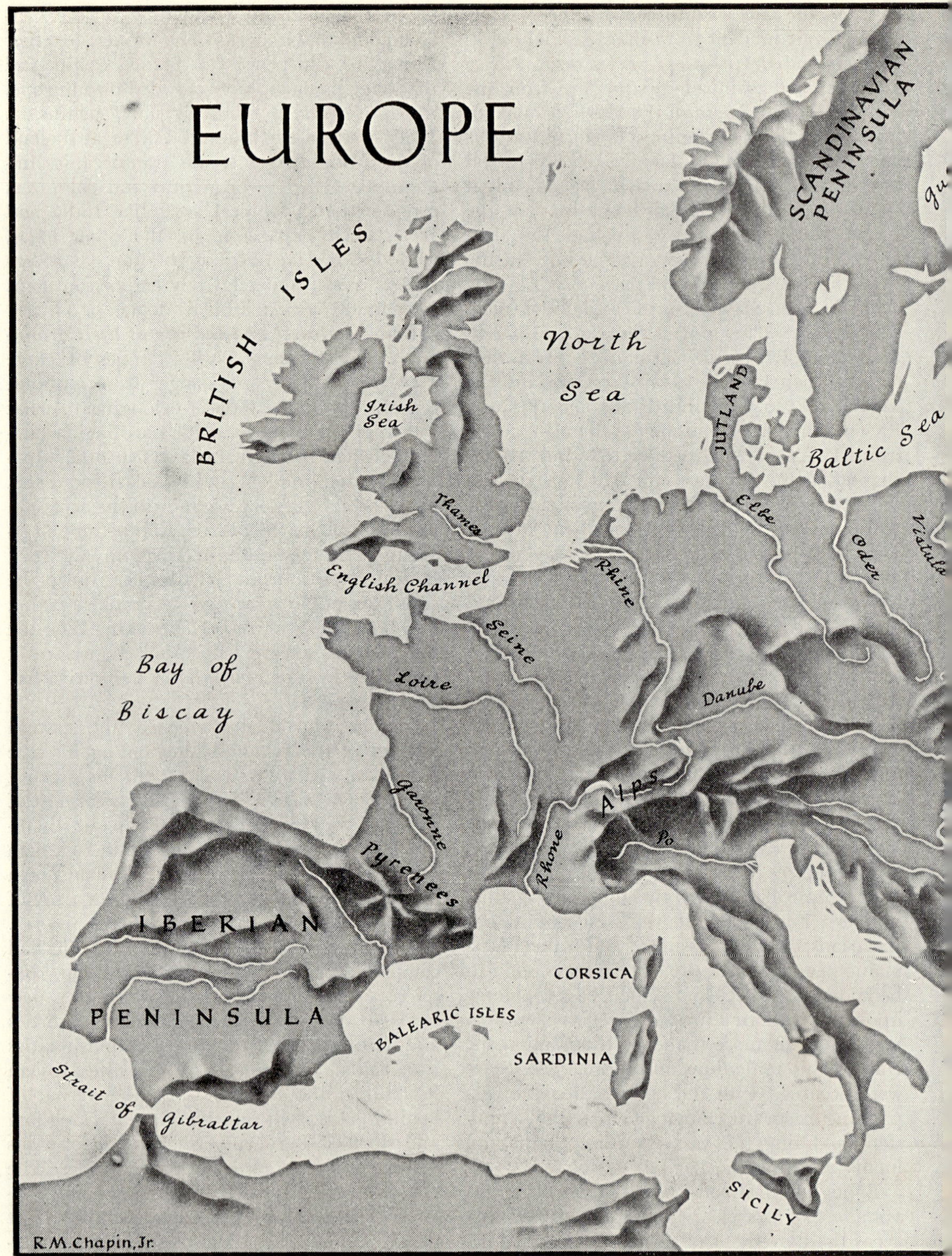

In the history of Europe, natural boundaries such as mountains, rivers, and seas have played an important role. I studying this map closely you can sometimes tell what boundaries were to mark off states and nations as these gre

up in later times. As you study the history of the succeeding centuries, compare other maps with this one to notice how some of the greatest trouble spots have been those where no natural boundaries marked off one state from another.

square, stood shoulder to shoulder, firm as a wall, inflexible as a block of ice...."[4] The Moslem losses were heavy, the Arab commander being killed, and during the night the invaders deserted their tents and retreated back into Spain.

Many historians have regarded Tours as one of the decisive battles in world history. The great eighteenth-century English historian, Edward Gibbon, saw the whole future of western Europe in the balance, with the possibility of mosques in London and Paris and the Koran being used instead of the Bible. The Frankish victory should not be unduly minimized, for undoubtedly it was a great achievement in the eyes of contemporary Europeans and added luster and prestige to the House of Charles Martel. In the long view of history, however, the battle of Tours meant little. Arab expansion was now 1000 miles from the Strait of Gibraltar where it had received its impetus. By the time it reached Tours its strength had been spent; or as modern military experts would say, logistically it had overreached itself. The Moslems continued their raids until 759, when their main base on the French coast was captured, but they never crossed the Pyrenees in force again.

What has been described as the most important military reform in Europe before the introduction of permanent national armies was carried out by Charles Martel. Up to his time the army was a mere levy of foot soldiers called together to protect the realm. In modern parlance we might call this force "militia." At Tours the Frankish leader observed the important role of the quick-striking Moslem cavalry and he determined to build up such a force of professional soldiers. A large amount of land was distributed for this purpose. Each recipient obtained a tenure or a benefice which was sufficient for him to maintain a designated number of war horses plus the essential equipment. It is said of Charles that he "put the medieval knight upon horseback."

Pepin the Short. Pepin, called the Short, son of Charles, was a worthy successor to his great father. Ruling from 741 to 768, he continued to strengthen the Frankish state. To make the position of the Mayor of the Palace fully secure, he requested the Pope at Rome to rule on his royal status. The expected answer came back granting that he who had the actual power should be the legal ruler. In this quiet maneuvering, St. Boniface, the great missionary to the Germans, was the intermediator, and in 751 this church dignitary officially crowned Pepin King of the Franks. As for the last Merovingian do-nothing king, he was quietly shelved in a conveniently secluded monastery.

In 754 the Pope came personally to the Frankish kingdom, and outside the royal villa was met by the newly proclaimed king, who prostrated himself before the head of the Church. Not long afterward the Pope solemnly crowned and annointed Pepin as king. Back of the Pope's mission was a very serious problem and, from his point of view, a menace that threatened not only papal independence but its very existence. At this time Italy was a jumble of rival political units, as it was to remain down to the nineteenth century. In the south the Byzantine empire still controlled the island of Sicily and the heel and toe of the long peninsula. Farther north was the exarchate of Ravenna, also imperial territory located on the east coast, slightly north of Rome. As for the area called the duchy of Rome, the Pope was the actual ruler, but in theory the emperor at Constantinople was his overlord.

Practically all of the peninsula, with the exception of the states we have mentioned, was controlled by the Lombards. These Germanic people had two important duchies in the south and a vigorous, promising kingdom in the north that opened out into the fertile Po valley. The Lombards were eager to expand and gave promise of uniting all Italy under their rule. In 751 their king conquered the exarchate of Ravenna and then proceeded to demand tribute from the Pope. At this critical moment, Pope Stephen could not appeal to the eastern emperor for assistance, for the Byzantine ruler could not spare the resources for a campaign in Italy. Furthermore, even if such help could have been obtained it is extremely unlikely that Pope Stephen would have asked for it. The iconoclastic controversy initiated by Leo III (Chapter 9) had thoroughly alienated the papacy, giving it both the desire of being completely independent and the necessity of securing a strong and new protector.

Pope Stephen's recognition of Pepin as king of the Franks placed the new ruler under obligation to him. Therefore, following the coronation in 754, it was not difficult for the Pope

An idealized study of Charlemagne shows him with the imperial crown and other symbols of authority.

to secure Pepin's promise of armed intervention in Italy and also his pledge to give the papacy the exarchate of Ravenna when once it was conquered. The two parties concerned, with a Frankish army, crossed into Italy in 755 and the Lombard king was compelled to relinquish his conquests. Papal officials prepared to take over the ceded lands, but once the Frankish troops had left Italy, the Lombard king again resorted to arms. Again in 756 Pepin led an army into Italy and forced the wily Lombard to carry out his promises, and to pay an indemnity. Pepin now officially conferred upon the Pope the territory of the exarchate. Known as the "Donation of Pepin," it made the Pope a temporal ruler over a strip of territory that extended from coast to coast, cutting the peninsula in two, and creating what was to become known in history as the Papal States.

These events of the remote eighth century may seem unimportant and no longer significant in terms of understanding the modern world. But the alliance between the Franks and the papacy, initiated by Clovis in 496 and thoroughly sealed by Pepin, not only influenced the character and direction of medieval history but also affected the course of politics and religion down to our own day. This alliance accelerated the separation of Latin Christendom from Greek; it paved the way for the creation of the Holy Roman Empire (shortly to be discussed); it contained the germs of the bitter struggle waged between the temporal and spiritual powers of western Europe, a struggle climaxed in the medieval duel between the empire and the papacy; and for better or worse it created the Papal States, whose existence complicated the full political unification of modern Italy down to 1871.

Charlemagne: the man, his conquests. With Charles the Great (768-814), better known as Charlemagne, the Frankish state and the Carolingian House reached the summit of their power. We have a fine description of Charlemagne from a biography written by Einhard, a member of his court. This slender but precious work shows Charlemagne to have been every inch a true king and leader of men. We know that he was tall, physically very strong, a great horseman, and always in the van of the hunt. This ruler is one of the most outstanding figures in European history. He was not only a successful statesman and administrator, but a lover of learning and a zealous spreader of Christianity, imbued with the ambition of subjugating as many people as possible and at the same time imposing upon them Christian civilization. In this way he carried on the policies of the first Merovingian, Clovis, but on a much grander scale.

Charlemagne in Spain. South of the Frankish state, the Moslem nobles of Spain were feuding. Charlemagne took advantage of this situation by heeding the invitation of three Arab emirs to come to their assistance. In 778, Charlemagne and his army crossed the Pyrenees, and drove the Moslems back across the Ebro River. Further advance southward was halted, however, by stiffened Moslem resistance, and Charlemagne contented himself with setting up a buffer state with Barcelona as its capital. This territory was known as the Spanish March, and extended from the Pyrenees to the Ebro River. As the Frankish army moved back to the north and went through the pass of Roncesvalles, its rear guard was set upon by the wild Basque mountaineers. In the melee, the leader, a gallant Frankish knight named Roland, was killed. The memory of his heroism was to be later enshrined in the great medieval French and Christian epic, the *Chanson de Roland.*

Conquest of Avars and Saxons. Charlemagne's greatest conquest was carried out against the heathen Saxon tribes who lived between the Rhine and the Elbe Rivers. Altogether their subjugation took eighteen campaigns extending over a period of thirty-three years. The method followed was first to send in an army, next beat down resistance, then establish permanent garrisons. The conquered region was then divided into bishoprics, and monasteries and schools were built. Charlemagne was determined that paganism was to be destroyed, and extremely harsh laws were promulgated against any Saxon who refused to be baptized. Eating meat during Lent, cremating the dead (an old pagan practice) and pretending to be baptized were offenses punishable by death. The Church and its priests were the main agents in enforcing these orders, set forth in the Saxon Capitulary (Law).

Charlemagne's coronation in Rome. Like his father before him, Charlemagne intervened in Italian politics. Expansionist ambition had again stirred in the heart of the Lombard king, who prepared to invade the territories of the papacy. At the behest of the Pope, Charlemagne invaded Lombardy in 772, defeated the Lombards, and proclaimed himself King of Lombardy. At the same time he further cemented his father's alliance with the Church by celebrating Easter in Rome and solemnly confirming Pepin's donation of territory to the papacy.

Saxony and north Italy had been conquered, but Charlemagne did not let up on his conquest, for all around his empire's eastern frontier there were fierce and expansionist tribes who continually threatened the peace and stability of his dominions. In particular there were the Avars, an Asiatic people of nomadic horsemen, who had established themselves in the valley of the Danube and who continuously raided their neighbors. Charlemagne carried out six campaigns against the Avars between 788 and 805 and completely exterminated them. The stronghold of the raiders destroyed, the Frankish king set up a military province in the valley of the Danube to guard against any possible future depredations from eastern nomads. This territory was called the East Mark (Ostmark), later to be known as Austria.

The most important event in this momentous reign of Charlemagne took place on Christmas Day in the year 800. The previous year the unruly subjects of the Pope in Rome had revolted and mistreated him. Leo III hurried from his city on the Tiber to the court of Charlemagne to seek assistance. After a conference with the great Carolingian, the Pope returned to Rome and was followed by Charlemagne in November 800. The various charges brought against Leo were examined and dismissed as baseless by the Frankish ruler, and the Pope was restored to his office. Not long afterwards, as Charlemagne was attending service on Christmas Day, kneeling before the altar at St. Peter's, the Pope placed a crown on his head amid the cries of the assembled congregation: "To Charles Augustus crowned of God, great and pacific Emperor of the Romans, long life and victory."[5] This coronation scene, staged amid the rich vestments of the church, with the greatest Christian warrior of western Europe in the title role, has been the favorite theme of many historians. This ceremony demonstrated that the memory of the once great Roman empire still lived as a very vital tradition in the hearts of men in Europe. There was a strong desire to reëstablish the political unity that had existed in the Roman world before the great invasions of the fifth century.

We will see in Chapter 16, on European politics and the origins of modern nations, that this tradition of political unity, of universal empire, persisted throughout the medieval era. Implicit also in this coronation ceremony was another great theme of medieval

history, the struggle between the empire and the papacy. Charlemagne was crowned not only by, but presumably with the consent of, the Pope. He was emperor by the Grace of God, with Heaven and its earthly agency, the Church, on his side. But it was not all gain for the ruler; the Church now had its hold over him and could claim its superiority over emperors and kings. Comments one authority: "...the papal claim of the right to bestow the imperial crown involved the church more than ever before in political affairs. From this time on papal and imperial power stood side by side, each claiming supreme authority over all human affairs and relationships. The future was inevitably to witness a direct collision."[6]

His empire: the governmental system. Men living in the time of Charlemagne must have been awed by the emperor's accomplishments. His territories included all of the western area of the old Roman empire except Africa, Britain, southern Italy, and Spain. In the east the frontier, stretching from the Baltic south, ran along the Elbe and the Saale Rivers, across the mountains of Bohemia, along the Danube to the Adriatic Sea, while in the west the line followed the coast from Denmark south to Spain. As the empire was faced with hostile neighbors, such as the Moors in Spain and the pagan Slavs in the east, defensive provinces, known as marks, were set up. These included the Danish Mark, the East Mark in the Avar country, and the Breton Mark. All of the Carolingian territories were divided into administrative divisions, each under a count, or *Graf.* Charlemagne devised an ingenious method of checking and controlling his officials, especially the counts. By his famous law, or capitulary, of 802 he created the *missi dominici,* the king's envoys and supervisors of the counts. These were itinerant officials who were sent out each year into the counties to see that justice was done to orphans, the poor, the Church, and all the people. The *missi dominici* checked the roads, administered the oath of allegiance, listened to grievances, and sent accused officials back to the king's court for trial. In order to prevent collusion between these traveling justices and the local county officials it was ordered that no envoy could travel in an area where he lived and no two justices could be teamed for more than one year. All things taken into account, Charlemagne's subjects enjoyed a high degree of law, order, and good government—a remarkable achievement when one considers the huge area involved.

Agrarian society. In the early ninth century, western Europe was in the process of forming new social and cultural conditions. The slim links of commerce connecting the West with the eastern Mediterranean and Asia Minor had been snapped by the Moslem conquest of Spain, and with them went naval control of the Mediterranean. The great inland sea, once the thalassic basis for the prosperity and civilization of the classical world, from the early eighth century was at the mercy of Moslem pirates. Oriental products, such as papyrus, spices, and silks, were no longer imported into the West in significant quantities. As inland trade was no longer supported by sea-borne traffic, great ports such as Marseilles shriveled up, urban life almost disappeared, and the middle class sank into insignificance. Without trade there were no market dues for the king's treasury and money almost ceased to circulate. Civilization in western Europe now retrogressed economically to a self-sufficient, purely agricultural system, which has been termed a "closed-house economy."[7] The kings of this time did not live and go from city to city but rather went from "barn to barn." Lack of transport made it difficult for them to live at one permanent palace or court, so the kings lived on their lands, their domains in the country, going from one section to another as their large retinues used up the supplies that had been accumulated on the various farms.

Germs of the manorial system. In this thoroughly agricultural way of life lay the germs of the manorial system which, as we will see in the next chapter, was so distinctive a feature of the medieval economy. Socially and politically, also, a new pattern was evolving. In this dominantly agricultural society two classes were crystallizing: one, the landlords and nobility, who did the ruling and the fighting, and the other, the semifree peasants, called serfs, who tilled the soil and did all the "servile work."

The Carolingian Renaissance. It is to the credit of Charlemagne that he not only created a great empire but also endeavored to foster learning within it. In this field he was so concerned with advancing education and scholarship that historians speak of his efforts as the Carolingian Renaissance. In 789 a royal capitulary decreed "Let every monastery and every abbey have its school, where boys may be taught the psalms, . . . singing, arithmetic, and grammar; and let the books that are given them be free from faults, and let care be taken that the boys do not spoil them either when reading or writing."[8] Charlemagne's most famous educational accomplishment was his Palace School at Aix-la-Chapelle, the Carolingian capital. Here the children of the emperor and his nobles were instructed, and even those of a few commoners were admitted. The head of the school was Alcuin, a great Anglo-Saxon scholar, whose teacher had been a student of the Venerable Bede in north England. The school attracted many famous scholars and became a model for western Europe.

Handwriting reform. The reform of handwriting and the preservation of manuscripts were significant and lasting achievements of the Carolingian revival. The old Merovingian cursive script was unsatisfactory, and Charlemagne's scholars set to work to improve their documents. At this time the English monks, largely indebted to Irish scholars, had reached a high level of calligraphy (handwriting). Large numbers of these Anglo-Saxon and Irish copyists were imported by Charlemagne to rewrite and correct the old texts and to write new ones. Thus it came about that many precious classics were saved for posterity, the originals of which only exist in the copy produced by these scholars. The barbarous writing then in vogue was replaced by a new style of writing, both beautiful and legible, which is known as the Carolingian minuscule. Alcuin made the monastery at Tours the center for diffusing the new writing, which was to influence the whole trend of calligraphy in the Middle Ages. Later, when printing from moveable type was introduced, the Carolingian minuscule became the foundation for the roman type face, which is still widely used.

Relapse in the West

Disintegration of the empire. Aix-la-Chapelle was the center and capital of the Carolingian empire. Here its ruler tried to recapture something of the grandeur and majesty of the Roman Caesars. Marbles and statues were brought from Rome and Ravenna, swimming baths were constructed, and a chapel with octagon dome adorned in gold, silver, and bronze was erected—an edifice that was preserved in the great cathedral of Aix-la-Chapelle (or Aachen, as it is also known) until our own day, when it was destroyed in World War II. Charlemagne's seat of government during most of his reign was itinerant, for he had to live off the land, but toward the end of his rule he tried to reside as frequently as possible at Aix. To this center of government came envoys from distant lands. Although there was some imperial splendor, it was artificial; commerce had to revive and with it flourishing urban life before the courts of kings in the West could approach the magnificence of Roman imperial prosperity. As one historian has said of Charlemagne's court, "It is a strange mixture of vigorous, barbaric life and faded classical culture."[9]

Charlemagne died at Aix in January 814. This personality, so remote in time from our own day, must be considered one of the great constructive statesmen of world history. His accomplishment lay in the extension of Christian civilization throughout central Europe and the erection of effective barriers against the incursions of the Slav and Avar. Furthermore, he gave western Europe a breathing space in which law and order were again enforced, permitting the process of fusion to go on between Germanic, Roman, and Christian elements. The Carolingian empire, however, was no more than a breathing space, for its territories were too vast, its peoples too diverse, to be held together after the dominating character of its creator had passed from the scene. Charlemagne had no standing army, no fleet, and no bureaucratic administrative machine comparable to that of Roman times. With agriculture as the sole base of the economy there could be no taxes levied in money, no fiscal organization, and therefore no real funds for administration. In essence the great empire was a personal achievement that could not last after the death of the man whose genius had created it.

In the centuries that followed, legends grew up about the heroic figure of Charlemagne, the warrior, the law giver, the patron of learning, and defender of the Church. He became the ideal ruler and the perfect soldier and knight. Both Germany and France later claimed him as their hero, and the latter glorified him in the *Chanson de Roland.*

Weak rulers. The greatness of the Carolingian House was the achievement of three strong rulers—Charles Martel, Pepin the Short, and Charlemagne—and was the work of just a century, from 714 to 814. It took only one ruler and barely more than twenty-five years to undo the achievements of the great trio of rulers. The once mighty empire disintegrated amid the impotence of weak rulers, civil wars, and bloody feuds. Before Charlemagne's death he had had Louis, his surviving son, crowned, but three years later the new king had consented to another coronation at the hands of the Pope. Louis was well named the Pious; all his reign he deferred to the clergy and his willingness to be crowned by the Pope gave the Church an additional claim of superiority over secular rulers. Early in his reign Louis the Pious partitioned his realm between three sons. A second marriage, however, produced a fourth male heir, Charles the Bald, and in consequence bitter rivalry and even hostilities broke out involving the brothers and their father. In 840, Louis the Pious died, a tragic and broken-hearted figure.

Strasbourg Oaths and Treaty of Verdun. Meanwhile one of the brothers had died and of the three remaining, Lothaire, the elder, was opposed by the two younger—Louis the German and Charles the Bald. In 842, the younger brothers united their forces and pledged each other mutual aid in the famous Strasbourg Oaths. The text of these oaths is of unusual significance, for one part was in early French, the other in early German. The

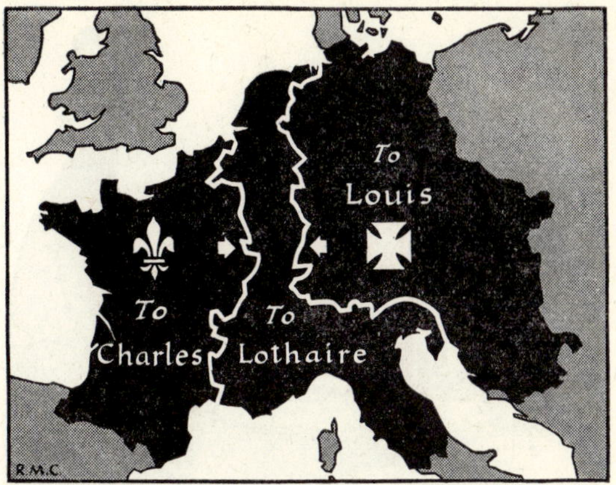

DIVISION BY THE TREATY OF VERDUN

first could be understood by the followers of Charles, who lived mainly west of the Rhine; the other by the followers of Louis the German, who lived east of this river. These oaths show how the Carolingian empire was splitting into two linguistic parts—East Frankland, which was soon to be known as Germany, and West Frankland, which was to be known as France.

In 843 the warring brothers called a halt to their fighting, signed the Treaty of Verdun, and split the Carolingian lands three ways. Charles the Bald obtained the western part, and Louis the German the eastern; but Lothaire, who retained the title of emperor, obtained an illogical middle kingdom comprising both Teutonic and Latin peoples (see map above). This middle strip was a narrow corridor, not more than 150 miles wide, running from central Italy to the North Sea. It had a brief existence, for in 870 it was divided between Charles and Louis.

The emergence of France and Germany. The importance of the Treaty of Verdun is that it began the shaping of the modern European nations, France and Germany, and gave political recognition to the cultural and linguistic division shown in the Strasbourg Oaths. Unfortunately the area north of the Alps, eventually known as Lorraine (Lotharingia), encompassed both French and German cultures, and was never divided in a lasting fashion. It was to be one of the cockpits of Europe, a land drenched with the blood of countless Teutonic and Latin peoples. The House of the Carolingians moved rapidly toward extinction. The last of the line of its East Frankish rulers died in 911; and in West Frankland the nobles

Restored sailing ship of the type used in Viking invasions of the ninth and tenth centuries.

in 887, ignoring the eight-year-old Carolingian prince, had made Odo, the Count of Paris, the king.

New invaders: Moslems and Scandinavians. The Carolingian empire not only decayed internally from fratricidal wars; it was also assailed from without by a new wave of invaders. Slavic tribes, especially the Croats and Moravians, raided eastern Germany, and to these were added the dreaded Hungarians, or Magyars, a ruthless, mounted, nomadic people. In addition, the Moslem Saracens also took the offensive in the Mediterranean, capturing most of the island of Sicily between 827 and 878 and invading southern Italy. The coastal towns farther north were attacked and harried; even Rome and the great monastery at Monte Cassino were pillaged. The Moslem invaders also set up forts along the Corniche (east of Nice on the French Mediterranean coast), whose ruins can still be seen. From these bases, like modern commandos, swift raiding parties penetrated far inland to attack the parties of merchants in the Alpine passes.

The most widespread and destructive raiding waves, however, came from Scandinavia. During the ninth and tenth centuries Swedes, Danes, and Norwegians—collectively known as Vikings—stormed out of their remote and wild forests and fiords with such force as to constitute a veritable ethnographic explosion. The explanation for this expansion is not clear. Some historians stress overpopulation and a surplus of young men; others see a clue

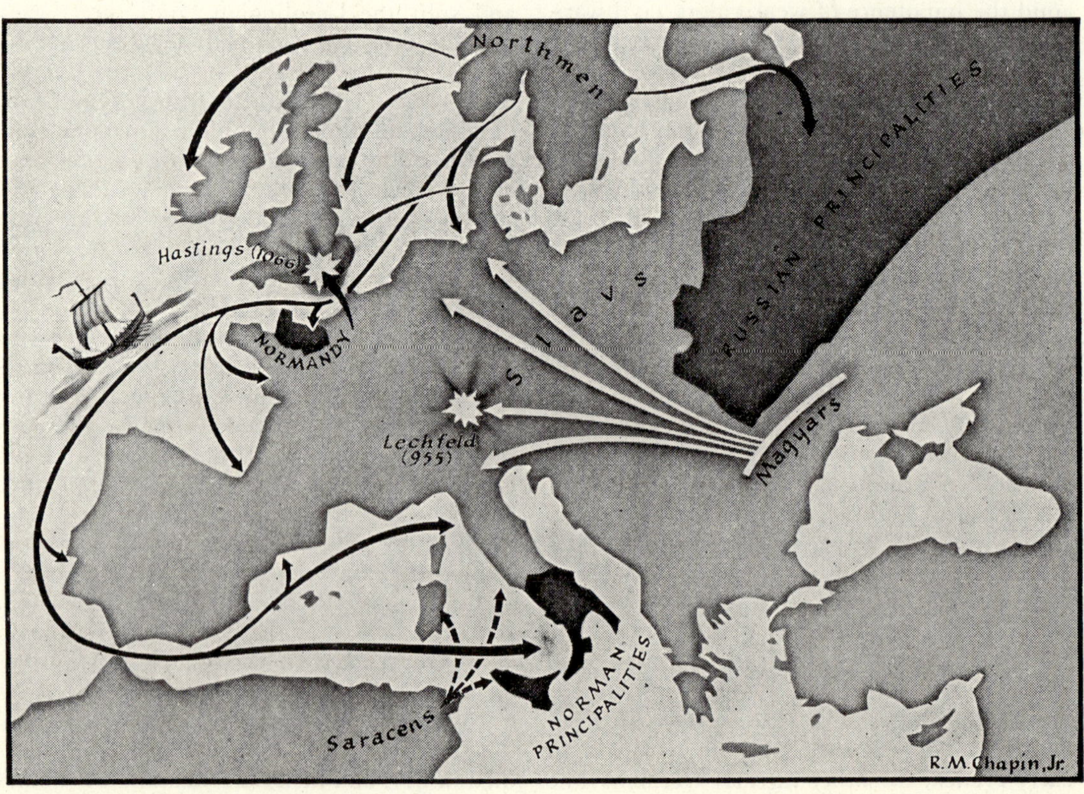

in navigational improvements which enabled the Vikings for the first time to traverse the seas far from land; and there are scholars who believe that Norse expansion was a countermovement of northern paganism against the stern Christian missionary expansion of Charlemagne.

Activity of the Vikings. No matter what the cause, the range of Viking expansion was amazing. They went as far as North America to the west and to the Caspian Sea on the east. These sea raiders attacked the coasts of Brittany, Gascony, and Spain, and robbed and pillaged towns and monasteries in the British Isles. For a century their activities were destructive and the prevailing terror they caused is reflected in an old litany of the Church: "From the fury of the Northmen, O Lord Deliver us." As we will see later in this chapter, there was a second phase of Viking expansion in the tenth century; at that time the sea raiders made permanent settlements in the area of France later known as Normandy, in the British Isles, and in remote Iceland and Greenland. The Vikings, once they had settled down, became law-abiding citizens and good Christians. They showed a genius in government, an avid eagerness to absorb the best in Christian culture, and a remarkable skill in trade plus a capacity to open up new routes for commerce.

Three main Viking routes. During the first century of their expansion, however, the Vikings only plundered and burned. Coming out of their fiords they sailed the seas in fleets having as many as 350 boats. These "dragon boats" were long and narrow, capable of carrying 100 persons, powered by long oars and by a sail when the wind was right. They usually had high prows carved in the form of some fearsome animal, often a dragon. In 1893 an exact model of one of these boats crossed the Atlantic in four weeks.

Three main routes of Viking expansion can be identified. The outer, followed mainly by the Norwegians, swung westward to Ireland and the west coast of Scotland. Ireland in particular was ravaged, and between 800 and 850 the entire island was under invasion. Monasteries, the center of culture, were destroyed, and the golden age of Irish Celtic culture ended. The so-called middle passage was followed by the Danes, who raided the east coast of England and the shores of France and Spain. By the end of the eighth century, yearly Viking raids were carried out against England, and on the continent the dragon boats sailed up such navigable rivers as the Rhine, Scheldt, Seine, and Loire. Once inland, the well-armed Vikings attacked farms and, seizing the horses, galloped through the countryside burning and robbing as they went. Between 840 and 880, the Vikings devastated northwest France, destroying dozens of abbeys and towns. An eye witness of these horrors declared: "The cities are depopulated, the monasteries ruined and burned, the country reduced to solitude. As the first men lived without law or fear of God, abandoned to their passions, so now every man does what seems good in his own eyes, despising laws human and divine and the commands of the Church. The strong oppress the weak; the world is full of violence against the poor and of the plunder of ecclesiastical goods. Men devour one another like the fishes in the sea."[10]

The third route, the eastern line, was followed mainly by the Swedes who, while always willing to engage in a good bout of conquest, came mainly as merchants. Establishing themselves in an important trading station on Lake Ladoga, they ventured down the Volga and the Dnieper, finally reaching the Caspian and the Black Sea. Later in this chapter we will follow the remarkable role these Swedish adventurers played in the rise of the Russian state.

Feudalism rises from chaotic conditions. By the end of the ninth century, civilization in western Europe was at a low ebb and it seemed as if society were in the process of dissolution. Weak central government was unable to carry out its basic functions and people more and more surrendered both their land and their persons to lords for protection. A Carolingian law in 847 ordered every freeman to place himself under a lord, indicating recognition on the part of the central government that it was not able to afford protection to the people of the realm. At the same time the king was forced to grant privileges of immunity to the great landowners, exempting them from the interference of royal officials. Domains in which the king could not intervene grew up throughout the realm. At the same time, the decline of commerce further weakened the small middle class but strengthened the self-sufficient landed aristocracy.

There was also the continuation of a trend already noted in connection with the military reforms of Charles Martel. The primitive military system of levying freemen was dying out in favor of a professional force of heavily armed mounted men, called knights, who received large estates from the king in return for their fighting services. Out of all these elements—the disintegration of central power, the decrease in the class of freemen, the growing need for protection, the rise of a new and largely independent landed aristocracy, and the creation of the mounted knight—a new pattern of society, the feudal and manorial, rapidly took shape in western Europe in the ninth century.

The Carolingian empire disintegrated, the victim of internal weaknesses and external predatory invaders. The perspective of time enables one to see that it was entirely too grandiose and ambitious. Sentimentally it looked back upon the past traditions of the classical world rather than recognizing the limitations imposed by the conditions of the time. To be sure, the genius of Charlemagne gave western Europe a precious interim of order and law, but the economic facts of a dominantly agricultural society made impossible the successful perpetuation of a great imperial government. The only alternative was less ambitious political units directed by feudal monarchs who consciously tried to do less than the successors of Charlemagne, and thus were able to do more in meeting the needs and solving the problems of their own time. We now turn to trace the origins of what we know as the modern states of Germany, France, England, Spain, Italy, and Russia.

Beginnings in Germany

Early Germany. After the collapse of Charlemagne's empire, east of the Rhine the nation now known as Germany seemed to be crystallizing. Here the East Franks as early as 800 were calling themselves Germans and speaking a distinct language which could not be understood by their former kinsmen in France. Germany in the ninth and tenth centuries was a loose political union of five governmental areas, Bavaria, Franconia, Saxony, Swabia, and Lorraine. Each was ruled by a duke who possessed his own army and governmental assembly and was to all intents and purposes a sovereign ruler. Decentralization had not reached the same degree in Germany as in France. Five duchies certainly were preferable to the hodgepodge of feudal fiefs that lay in the way of national consolidation in France. But localism was bad enough in Germany. Numerous linguistic and racial differences, conflicting law codes, and varying customs acted as barriers to unity.

The attachment of the German peoples to their ancient tribal subdivisions—in short, their loyalty to Saxony or to Bavaria rather than to a central government—has colored the history of Germany from the days of Charlemagne to those of Hitler. Until very recent times certain sections, such as Bavaria and Saxony, have tenaciously clung to their old customs and traditions, which go back to tribal times. It is said that in 1914 when Germany was involved in the First World War many Bavarian peasants quite cheerfully went to war believing that they had been called to fight against their traditional enemies, the Prussians.[11]

The Saxon line. In spite of the independence of the great German duchies, there existed, as a holdover from Carolingian days, the tradition of kingship, the kings being chosen by the rulers of the great duchies. But throughout the ninth century monarchy was impotent in the land of the East Franks.

The last Carolingian ruler died in 911 and the nobles elected Conrad of Franconia to be their king. The new ruler was on the throne just eight years and proved quite incapable of reëstablishing strong government in Germany or of successfully meeting the growing menace of the Hungarian raids. In 919 Conrad was succeeded by Henry the Fowler, the first of the famous Saxon dynasty, which ruled Germany until 1024. The House of Saxony began the real history of medieval Germany, successfully repulsed the Hungarian invaders, and effectively built up the power of the royal government. In fact Germany, under the Saxon kings, was the first western nation in Europe to achieve a strong and orderly government at a time when Spain was still under Moslem rule and France and England had just barely moved in the direction of strong statehood. The founda-

The boundaries shown on this map of feudal Europe were constantly in a state of flux. Many of the place names are still familiar today.

tions laid by this Saxon House were to make medieval Germany from the tenth to the twelfth centuries the greatest state in Europe.

Henry the Fowler. Henry pushed back the Danes, occupied the narrow neck of their peninsula and established the Danish Mark as a protective buffer. This occupation began the long rivalry between Dane and German over the area we now know as Schleswig-Holstein, a rivalry which caused a war between Prussia and Denmark as late as 1864. The Hungarians, mounted raiders and kindred of the ancient Huns, had reached the southeast frontier of Germany and in 924 carried out a devastating invasion. The Saxon Germans were especially vulnerable to Hungarian attacks because they lived in open villages without benefit of protective walls. Henry thereupon devised a successful strategy. He set up strongholds throughout the threatened area by erecting log palisades with towers around the convents, monasteries, and villages. These centers of protection were called *Burgwärde,* and every ninth freeman was expected to serve one year in garrison duty. In 933 Henry was able to defeat the Hungarians in open battle.

Advance against the Slavs. Advances were also made against the north Slavs, as Henry led an army across the Elbe in the winter of 928-929. The Slav stronghold of Brunabor was captured and here was set up another defensive mark, called Brandenburg. A little later the Saxon warrior king inflicted a heavy defeat upon the Slavs at the battle of Lenzen. In these areas conquered from the Slavs, Henry made no attempt at colonization, being content to hold the fortified *Burgwärde* he constructed. Further to the east in Bohemia, the Saxon ruler forced the Slavic people, the Czechs, to recognize his overlordship.

Growth of central government: Otto the Great. Henry the Fowler was succeeded in 936 by his son Otto the Great. Henry left a much stronger throne to his son than that which he had received seventeen years earlier. He had, in addition, earned the gratitude of the German people, who remembered him as the defender of their country against the wild invader.

Otto, who, interestingly enough, had married the granddaughter of Alfred the Great of England, set to work immediately to carry on the policies of his father. He was a good administrator, expanding the royal government with obedient and efficient new officials. Otto was resolutely intent upon exalting the status of German kingship. As a beginning—recalling the glory of Charlemagne—he went to Aachen to be crowned. There at a great banquet he was served personally by the great dukes of the realm, a ceremony that was symbolically important as public recognition of German unity. During his reign Otto maintained the authority of his throne, putting down serious revolts engineered by the restless nobles.

Defeat of the Hungarians. Forgetting their defeat at the hands of Henry the Fowler, the Magyars (Hungarians) quite early in Otto's reign recommenced their raids. In 955 the raiders initiated a great invasion which threatened to engulf Germany. Otto managed to rally under his banner a large army in which most of Germany was represented, and he met the invaders at the river Lech. In the great battle that followed (see map, page 338), German arms were completely victorious; only a remnant of the Hungarians escaped. The battle at Lechfeld was likened by the people of the time to the victory of Charles Martel at Tours, and Otto was hailed as the savior of European civilization.

Epic movement of German expansion. In addition to frustrating the incursions of the Hungarians, Otto, like his father, continued German expansion eastward against the Slavs. As he probed into Slavic territory he built many *Burgwärde,* from which Germanic culture was spread and its authority established. For hundreds of years thereafter German colonists, impelled by their desire for land, were to move to the east. This expansion, perhaps the greatest achievement of the medieval Germans, was an epic movement involving both land settlement and the spread of western Christian culture. Had it not been for this eastward expansion modern Germany would have been a narrow strip of land wedged in between the Rhine and the Elbe. In fact, it has been estimated that sixty per cent of German territory before the First World War had been taken from the Slavs.

Otto's intervention in Italy. The most momentous step taken by Otto the Great was his intervention in Italian affairs. The breakdown of the Carolingian empire in the ninth century had resulted in a more stable and defensible kingdom in Germany and, as we will note shortly, in France also. Would Italy become the third strong kingdom to emerge from the Carolingian wreckage? Unfortunately, there was no outstanding noble house and no commanding popular leader who came forth to achieve this desirable end. Italy broke up into warring fragments (see map, page 341) and soon was in a state of virtual anarchy. In the north lay the old Lombard kingdom, whose crown was frequently the object of various rival contenders. To the south were the Papal States, in which the Pope presided in Rome as the vicar of Christ, the Supreme Head of the Christian Church, and also the secular ruler of a central Italian state. In practice, however, the Pope's authority was often flouted by the restless and uncouth nobility. Further south were two Lombard duchies; and, finally, at the extreme tip of the peninsula, there was territory in which the Byzantine empire retained its slim hold upon the Italian mainland. Dotted here and there were rising and dynamic cities, such as Venice. These city-states of the late medieval era became veritable miniature nations, strong and wealthy, and avid patrons of the arts.

Italy in the tenth century, then, was a tempting field for an invader. The country was weak, divided into rival states, and rich. These conditions led Otto to cross the Alps and intervene in Italy in 951, when he conquered Lombardy and took the title of King of the Lombards. On his second visit to Italy, in 961, he was crowned emperor by the Pope. Undoubtedly Otto the Great was excited by the grandiose idea of re-creating the empire which had been established by Charlemagne. Later the new political creation was given the title of Holy Roman Empire (see map, page 341).

Achievements of the later Saxons. After the death of the German king and emperor, succeeding kings of his Saxon line were able, despite some setbacks, to build up the power of royal government and central authority in Germany. When the last Saxon ruler died in 1024, it was fully apparent that this royal line had achieved a dominating prestige in Europe. When Henry the Fowler had died in 936, he was described in the Chronicles as the greatest king in Europe, and his son, Otto the Great, achieved even greater fame. All in all, the Saxon kings had been able to curb the divisive tendencies of the great stem duchies, had utilized the Church as their loyal ally, and had defeated the attempts of the dreaded Hungarians to pillage the German provinces. Economically, too, there was progress. Much of central and eastern Germany was a land of wilderness, and a good start was made in clearing the forests and draining the swamps. In describing the fundamental achievement of the Saxon kings an eminent American historian has written:

"The historical evidence of the material prosperity of Germany during the Saxon epoch is widespread and unanimous. Long before the Norman kings had set England's house in order, long before the monarchy of the Capetians in France had begun to rise above the welter around them, the Saxon kings of Germany not only had established an ordered government in central Europe, but had also extended a firm and masterful hand over northern and central Italy, giving that rich but bleeding land the first taste of substantial peace and prosperity it had enjoyed since the vanishment of the Ostro-gothic Kingdom in the sixth century."[12]

Effects of Saxon involvement in Italy. The success of these Saxon German kings at home is all the more remarkable in view of their commitments and distractions in Italy. After Otto the Great all the Saxon kings were forced to spend considerable time in their southern kingdom. They went on occasion to rescue the Pope, again to be crowned as emperor, or more usually to put down rebellion and assert their authority. Several German armies were destroyed by the dread Italian fever and two Saxon kings themselves succumbed to this disease.

The distracting, even malevolent, effect of the Saxon pursuit of empire in Italy is seen in the case of Otto II (973-983), who felt constrained to go down into southern Italy to repulse the Arab Moslem invaders. His army was completely destroyed in battle in 982, and the German king died of fever before he could get reinforcements from home to recoup his loss. News of the defeat was received with sorrow in Germany, but with jubilation among the many Slavic peoples who had been conquered and colonized in the marks. They rose in rebellion, plundering Hamburg and destroying strong points such as Brandenburg. German eastward expansion was halted for 150 years.

Perhaps the best example of the negative effect of the German pursuit of empire in Italy is demonstrated by the reign of another Otto—the Third. Otto, who became king as a youth of only fourteen, was impatient to be in Rome wearing the imperial crown. He greatly admired the cultured society of Italy, and tended to be contemptuous of his own Germany. Regarding Rome as his real home and capital, he built there a new palace. On one occasion this mystically inclined young emperor journeyed to Aix-la-Chapelle and had the tomb of Charlemagne opened, so that he might gaze upon the body of the great Christian emperor. Notwithstanding Otto's love for Italy and his good intentions, however, the fickle Roman populace turned against him and revolted; and the heartbroken young emperor, only twenty-one, died of grief and bitter remorse.

Some historians contend that Otto the Great was justified in his imperial unification of Germany and Italy.[13] This school argues that Germany profited by its connection with a higher culture that gave it contact with the Mediterranean. More important, the assumption of the imperial crown enabled the German kings to get their hands on the old middle kingdom of Lothaire, notably Burgundy. Italy profited by the stable government buttressed by the German emperors.

The opposition maintains that, no matter what the original justification and no matter what the occasional success, the union of Germany and Italy in the form of the empire was in the long run deeply inimical to the best interests of both countries. Reflecting sadly upon the effect on Germany, a noted European historian has written:

"Her kings exhausted their strength in maintaining the Empire. They were all Germans, but they had no German policy. All their strength lay to the north of the Alps, yet they were continually drawn to Italy. They were destined to wear themselves out in pursuit of their policy. Germany has been the victim of the Empire...."[14] In a later chapter we shall have an opportunity to evaluate the worth of this prophecy.

Early England and France

The Roman occupation. We now turn from the German Saxon kingdom and empire, which loomed so large and appeared so promising, to England and France, neither of which by the mid-tenth century gave indication of the great role it would play in European and, later, world affairs. We have already seen in Chapter 6 that England became part of the Roman empire. The conquest of the Celtic peoples of England by the Romans brought about a fusion of cultures. In the main the less advanced Celtic culture surrendered to the superior civilization of the conqueror. From the Romans the subjected peoples obtained a new religion—Christianity. They came to use Roman pottery and utensils. Small cities sprang up on the sites of Roman garrisons. Everywhere there were splendid Roman roads, whose direction was so well planned that even today many roads in England follow the course of the old Roman highways.

Later invasions. In the fifth century the Roman legions were forced to return home by the threat of Germanic invasions into Italy, and shortly after their withdrawal other invaders—Angles, Saxons, Jutes, and Frisians—entered England. During their occupation of England the Romans gave the people peace and protection, but as soon as they left, bloodshed and pillage stalked the land. Roman villas were destroyed wholesale, and many Celts were put to the sword. Proof of the force with which the invader struck is the fact that there are left almost no traces of Celtic influence in the English language. During the fifth and sixth centuries England was in a chaotic condition. Not only did the Celts wage war on the invaders, but the various Anglo-Saxon tribes carried on war against each other. At one time there were seven distinct little tribal kingdoms, all jealous and hostile.

King Alfred. Finally, in the ninth century, the kingdom of Wessex rose to power, mainly as a result of another wave of invaders, the Danes. In fighting the new menace Wessex assumed leadership and successfully vanquished the enemy. This accomplishment was largely the work of the Wessex king, Alfred the Great, one of England's finest monarchs. The Danes were allowed to remain in England, and, settling in the central part of the island, they developed a prosperous community. The Danes were great traders, and their little towns soon became flourishing centers of commerce. Danes and Saxons soon merged, and all difference between victor and vanquished disappeared.

During the reign of King Alfred other notable developments took place. In the realm of government the king reorganized the army, improved the system of local government, and issued a set of laws. He also did much to advance the intellectual life of the people. Alfred founded a palace school, encouraged the writing of the famous *Anglo-Saxon Chronicle,* the earliest existing vernacular history of any nation, and the translation into Anglo-Saxon of such classics as Boethius' *Consolation of Philosophy* and Bede's *Ecclesiastical History of the English Nation.*

Anglo-Saxon monarchy at its height. The descendants of Alfred were able and great rulers, and the Saxon monarchy reached its height under the rule of Edgar the Peaceful (959-975). But a decline set in immediately after his reign: the power of the central government lagged and with it the ability to keep order at home and repel attacks from without. The impotence of the kingdom is well illustrated in the unhappy reign of Ethelred the Unready (978-1016), who was unable to keep a firm hand on the great nobles and, more important, had no answer to a new attack by the Danes. All that he could do was to impose a heavy tax on his subjects, called the Danegeld, to try to buy off the invader. In the long run, however, the Danes conquered England and their king, Canute, actually ruled it together with his home realm of Denmark and Norway. Canute proved to be a wise and Christian king respecting the rights and customs of his Saxon subjects. But after his death chaos again prevailed until some semblance of order and royal authority was achieved by the return of a king of the old Saxon line in 1042.

The Anglo-Saxons possessed a strong inclina-

A scene from the Bayeux tapestry showing the death of two Britons, presumably King Harold's brothers, in the Battle of Hastings.

tion toward what we today call representative government. They utilized numerous assemblies and courts in which any freeman had the right to participate if he were chosen to do so by his fellows. As we shall see, here was one of the seeds that later flowered into democratic government. The system of local government was so efficient that some of its features have been handed down to us today in England and the United States.

In Saxon England, however, there were serious weaknesses. While the system of local government was efficient, the royal power was fatally weak. The central government was not closely knit, and the king had little power over the great Saxon nobles, the earls. The shock of the Norman conquest in 1066 initiated in England the needed novelty of a strong and efficient central government.

The Norman conquest. The Norman conquest of England really began in the reign of Edward the Confessor (1042-1066). Although he himself was English, Edward spent most of his early life in France, particularly in Normandy (one of the fiefs of the king of France), where he had received his education from Norman monks. When he returned to England and subsequently became king, Edward showed a strong pro-Norman bias in all his actions.

The great need of Anglo-Saxon England in the reign of Edward was a stronger central government, but Edward had no definite policy except one of showering favors on his Norman friends. On his death in 1066 the Witan, council of the kingdom, selected Harold as the new ruler. Immediately William, Duke of Normandy, put forward a claim to the English throne, based on a tenuous hereditary right and on the assertion that Edward had promised him the throne.

William was one of the most outstanding statesmen and soldiers of his time. He had become Duke of Normandy at the age of eight. Following his accession, rebellion broke out in his domain. Three of the young duke's guardians were murdered, and for a few years he was kept under cover by his friends. When late in his teens, William came out of hiding and began to assert his power. He soon proved himself to be one of the best soldiers of his time, a man who showed little mercy to those who stood in his way. By 1047 he had ferreted out the nobles who had hoisted the banner of rebellion and from then on was the absolute master of Normandy.

William's Viking forebears had made their state the best administered, the most strongly unified in Europe. Normandy was far ahead of other European states in the art of governing. Here a strong government had subordinated all contending powers to the law of the duke, while across the Channel in England the powerful earls were continually embarrassing the king.

By the clever use of propaganda, apparently an effective weapon as far back as the eleventh century, William secured the favor of the Pope, which gave to his challenge the flavor of a crusade. He secured a well-equipped army of hard-fighting adventurers, mostly Norman knights, who looked upon the proposed conquest of England as a kind of investment which would pay them rich dividends in the form of lands and serfs.

Conquest of William the Norman. In the whole venture William had extraordinary luck. His neighbors around Normandy, often very quarrelsome, were obligingly tranquil. The cross-channel maneuver was very hazardous, with 5000 men involved and many horses that had to be transported in open boats. For several months the duke had to wait for a favorable breeze, as medieval sailors had not yet learned to sail against the wind. Finally the wind was favorable and the sea fairly calm. Fortunately for William, Harold, the Saxon king, was forced at the critical moment to leave the south coast unguarded and hurry north to meet the invasion of a Norwegian contender to the English throne. After victory in the north, he rushed south with no respite to meet William's challenge.

On October 14, 1066, King Harold with his army of Saxons at Hastings blocked the way of William on his march to London. All day long, masses of heavily armored Norman knights charged the serried ranks of the Saxon king's *housecarls* (picked palace guards) and the poorly equipped militia. By a clever ruse William broke the ranks of untrained levies, and late in the afternoon Harold was killed when an arrow pierced his eye. With their brave leader fallen, the ranks of the regular soldiers broke, and William was master of the field. The defeat spelled the end of Anglo-Saxon rule and the beginning of a new pattern of events in England.

France: political decentralization. In England the Saxon monarchs, at least during the ninth century, had united their country and had achieved a large measure of stable and centralized government. In the case of France, however, the country in the ninth and tenth centuries broke up into a motley group of small and independent states (see map, page 341), and the monarchy just barely kept alive. This process of disintegration took place as the Carolingian House, made so famous by Charlemagne, declined. In 887 the Carolingian heir was ignored (page 337) and during the next hundred years West Frankland, or France, suffered from both civil war and periodic invasions by the dread Magyars. While impotent Carolingian kings tried to retain their precarious grasp on the throne, a new family sought to dislodge them. Founded by Robert the Strong, Count of Paris, this noble family had gained renown when Robert's son, Odo, in 885 successfully defended Paris against the attacks of the Northmen. Three years later Odo was chosen king, but the Carolingians proved too strong and on the hero's death the crown was given by the nobles again to this family. For a century France was wracked by the implacable rivalry between two contending factions, until in 987 Louis v, the last of the Carolingian line, was killed accidentally and the nobles turned to the then Count of Paris, Hugh Capet, descendant of the courageous Odo.

Rise of the Capetians. In the late tenth century, France was merely the name of a small section of territory around Paris (see map, page 341); it did not refer to a country. There was a vague notion of a "kingdom," roughly comparable to, but smaller than, the France we know today. The population of this kingdom was varied, consisting of such peoples as Franks, Normans, Celts, Basques, and Provençals. A noticeable gulf existed between the north and the south. In the north the Germanic element was very strong and the climate, which affected the culture, was similar to that in England or Germany. In the south, the sky was kinder, the climate warmer, and the people Mediterranean and Latin rather than Germanic. One historian has summed up the culture of these two regions by saying that in the north there was a "beer and butter" economy and in the south one based on "oil and wine."[15] It was natural that the people of these two sections had trouble understanding each other and had little use for each other's customs. The backbone of the southern region was Aquitaine, Gascony, and Toulouse; under the last Carolingian monarchs and the first kings of the new royal line begun by Hugh Capet, the south was left pretty much alone and went its own way.

As stated above, France in 987 was not a country but a small feudal duchy, a region twenty-five miles long and a little more wide surrounding Paris, almost surrounded by rivers (hence, perhaps, its name the *Ile de France*). It is said that up to very recent times when a French peasant said he was going to France he really meant that he was going to Paris! This little area, the royal domain of Hugh Capet, was entirely surrounded by what have been called the "great lordships," which made up more than three-quarters of the country. These great independent dukedoms, such as Flanders, Normandy, Anjou, and Poitou, were a law unto themselves, paid little attention to the word of the king in Paris, and were content to tolerate him as a kind of theoretical figurehead of the country.

The Capetian line of kings, founded by Hugh Capet in 987, were to rule France until 1328. Starting out with little power and a limited amount of territory under their direct rule, these monarchs patiently but inexorably extended their control over the great dukedoms. France literally was made by its kings, for ultimately, as we will see in Chapter 16, the royal domain in which the king's word was law came to coincide with the boundaries of the entire country.

What accounts for the expansion of the once puny *Ile de France,* or explains the victory of a weak king over the great dukedoms? The answer lies first in the power of tradition. A tradition of royal authority prevailed which went back to Charlemagne and can be called the myth of kingship. There was a royal ideal which in theory saw the king as the guardian of law and order and the protector of the Church. While all the great nobles were quite independent of their monarch, they were, according to custom and theory, his men and were expected to swear allegiance to him. There was always the opportunity for strong kings to try to make theory coincide with practice.

Hugh Capet on his accession to the throne not only possessed important theoretical rights but as king he was unique, a man above all other men, the servant and symbol of God. Going back to the days of Clovis and Pepin, the coronation ceremony gave the king a sacred character; he had the alliance of the Church and ruled by divine right. What has been called the "moral ascendancy" of the French king was specially imparted in the coronation ritual presided over by the archbishop of Rheims. For example, in 1059 when the young prince who was to become Philip I was associated with his father, King Henry I, in the rule of the country, the following oath was taken in the ceremony:

"I Philip, by Grace of God soon to be king of France, on the day of my ordination promise, in the sight of God and his Saints, that I will maintain inviolate for every one of you and for all the churches under your charge their canonical privileges, their legal rights and their security in justice; that, with the help of God, I will defend you to the utmost as a king must defend every bishop and church in the kingdom committed to him. Further I promise to the people over whom I am given authority that I will use it solely in the execution of the laws which are their right."[16]

It made no difference that the king's claim to be protector of both Church and people did not at all exist in fact. The important thing was that this claim was sound and positive. It lay in the logic of history that the numerous conflicting laws and authorities existing in France be superseded by one all-embracing authority.

The establishment of hereditary monarchy. In the late tenth and throughout the eleventh centuries there was little tangible evidence that the Capetian kings were going to fulfill their destiny. The most important achievement of these early Capetians is that they imperceptibly built up the tradition of hereditary monarchy. The nobles who elected Hugh Capet to the kingship had no thought of giving the Capetian family a monopoly on the royal office. But the Capetians, with the support of the Church, cleverly arranged for the election and coronation of their heir while they were alive. The young prince was designated and crowned by the Church and became "associated" with his father in his rule; then when the king died, his son, the co-ruler, was crowned again. For three hundred years the

House of Capet never lacked a male heir and by the end of the twelfth century the hereditary principle had become so ingrained that French kings no longer took the precaution of crowning their sons during their own lifetime.

Apart from building up this hereditary principle, the first four Capetians, from 987 to 1108, added little territory to the royal domain. Compared to the German kings of this time their power was quite insignificant, but the Capetians quietly bided their time. The day came in the last quarter of the twelfth century when effective measures could be taken by the kings to exalt their authority and expand their royal domain. This they did with superb skill and astounding success.

The Rise of Russia

The Slavic peoples. The most important state in southern Europe and the Balkans, as we have seen, was the Byzantine empire. To the north and northeast of it was a confusing medley of nomadic and largely barbaric peoples, including the West, South, and East Slavs, and other groups like the Khazars, Patzinaks, Bulgars, and Polovtsi. Much of the history of these peoples is the story of migrations, continuous marauding and conflicts, and ephemeral power and influence. Among all these ethnic groups, only the East Slavs—the later Russians—were destined for greatness. We will at this point, therefore, concentrate our attention upon the origin of the Russian state and defer our brief account of the other Slavic nations, in eastern Europe and the Balkans, until Chapter 16. For the time being we will merely note that the Poles set themselves up in the basin of the Vistula, the Wends confronted the Germans along the Elbe, and the Czechs moved into Bohemia and Moravia. All of these peoples are known as the West Slavs. Others pushed southward, occupied the valley of the Danube, moved into the Balkan peninsula, and got as far as Thrace. These South Slavs—partly mixed with Asiatic stocks—were the Bulgars, Serbs, Croats, and Slovenes. As we have already noted in our treatment of the Byzantine empire, the South Slavs were intermittently at war with the eastern empire at Constantinople.

The East Slavs. The East Slavs, or the Russians as they came to be, have a beginning shrouded in vagueness; in fact there are no records of any kind dealing with these people before the ninth century.

The first important historical record is the *Original Chronicle,* written by a monk in the city of Kiev in the eleventh century. It is from this document that the beginnings of Russia have been reconstructed. Along the great rivers and lakes connecting the Baltic and the Black Sea, especially the Dnieper River (see map, pages 330-331), the East Slavs by the seventh and eighth centuries A.D. had established small city-states. Their inhabitants engaged in trade, but were often at war with each other and also suffered from attacks by fierce nomads.

The Varangians. Just at the time when these Slavic settlements were beginning to feel the need for stable government and adequate protection, the Swedish Northmen began to venture down the great waterway from the eastern Baltic south to the Black and Caspian seas (see map, page 349). This was at the moment when their brethren were venturing out in their long boats to attack the British Isles and France and to sail as far west as America. As these Swedes sailed down the Dnieper they engaged in trade with the local Slavs and also were quite ready to take part in any good fight. Some of these traders and adventurers reached Constantinople, where they became mercenary soldiers, members of the Byzantine emperor's famous Varangian Guard, which included soldiers of fortune from all over Europe. The scope of trade of the "Varangians," as all these Swedish adventurers are often called, is indicated by the fact that more than 200,000 Arabic and Byzantine coins have been unearthed in Sweden.

As the Varangians were mighty men of war, the Slavic settlements along the rivers began to hire them as protectors. According to the *Chronicle* one such warrior, Rurik, had been employed by the people of Novgorod. After he left he was urged to return, and about 862 he became the prince of the city. Two of his brothers also established themselves in other cities, one in Kiev. On Rurik's death he was succeeded by a Varangian named Oleg, who was able to unite both Kiev and Novgorod under his rule in 882. It is from this date that one can recognize the foundation of the Russian state. This duchy of Kiev, as it came to be called, was really another Normandy and was established not long before the Northmen set themselves up in a duchy in northern France. It is interesting to note that the word "Rus" was now more and more being applied by the Slavic subjects as the name for their Varangian rulers. This term was first applied to the Varangians by the Finns and apparently was a corruption of the word "Ruotsi," meaning "seafarers."

Kiev: foundation of Russia. The duchy of Kiev ruled over a vast area of connecting lakes and rivers, on which were located many busy trading posts and which served as an important economic link between Scandinavia and Byzantium. Every spring after the ice had melted on the great waterway, down the Dnieper went cargoes of furs, hemp, wax, amber, and slaves in the direction of Constantinople; and from the south came metal and glass wares, silks, spices, and jewelry. The Rus, as we will now call the Swedish Varangians, ruled the rivers and lakes, built forts at strategic points, and protected the trade caravans. On several occasions they attacked Constantinople, but finally in 945 they signed a commercial treaty regulating trade with the Byzantine empire. In the late tenth century Kiev expanded and became a great state, thrusting its authority far to the east into the endless Russian plain. The Scandinavians continued by immigration to reinforce the dynasty that had been founded by Rurik, but during the eleventh century the old Varangian stock was assimilated by the Slavs. The term Rus, however, persisted as the designation for the Slavic people of Kiev.

In keeping with the modern Soviet policy of minimizing all borrowing from outside sources, contemporary Russian scholars now refute the Scandinavian origin of the term Rus, asserting it was already in use 500 years before the coming of the Varangians. According to these historians, the Scandinavians did not bring civilization to Russia but rather they borrowed it from the Slavs and were absorbed by them.

Christianization of Russia. It was under Prince Vladimir, in 989, that the Russians were officially converted to Christianity. According to the Russian *Chronicle,* this prince

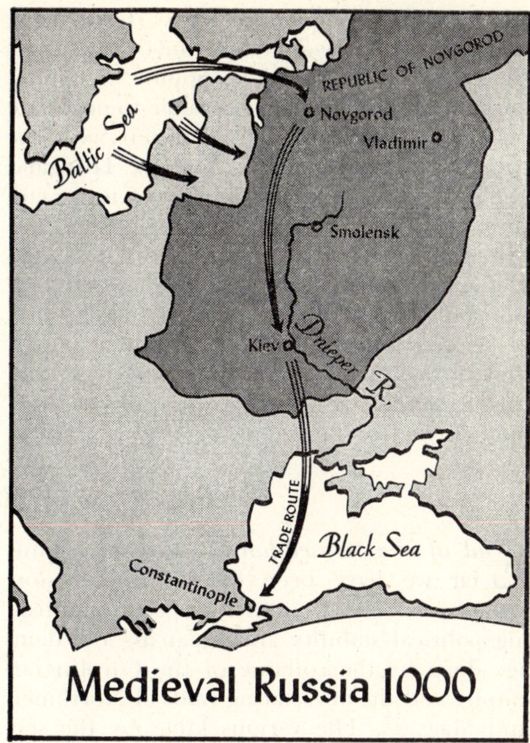

Medieval Russia 1000

of Kiev shopped around before making his choice of religions. Islam was rejected because of its injunctions against the use of strong drink; Judaism because the God of the Jews could not be very strong in allowing them to be ejected from their Holy Land; and Roman Christianity because the Pope entertained dangerous thoughts about his superiority to all secular rulers. There remained the Orthodox Church of the Byzantines, which was presented to Vladimir's subjects without any choice. The people of Kiev were baptized en masse in the Dnieper, idols were demolished, Christian churches erected on their ruins, and the children of influential nobles taken and sent to Greek priests for education. This Christianization of the Rus had important results, as we have noted in our discussion of Byzantine Constantinople as a center of culture diffusion. The music, art, learning, and architecture of an advanced civilization became available, and in many ways Kiev became a cultural reflection of the great metropolis on the Bosporus.

The culture of Kiev. It was in the reign of Yaroslav "the Wise" (1019-1054) that Kievan Russia reached the summit of its prosperity and influence. This monarch was a good scholar, translating Greek works, beautifying Kiev, and building churches, one of which was the cathedral he called St. Sophia. An influential ruler of his day, he was able to negotiate marriage alliances for his children with the royal families of Poland, Norway, Hungary, and France. About the stature of Kievan culture, an American historian has observed: "It must be borne in mind that Russia had in the eleventh century a culture and civilization far superior to that of England, France, or Western Europe generally; that Russia partook of the glories of the Byzantine East; and that Kiev was the greatest capital of Christendom after Constantinople . . . it would seem safe to say that never since has Russia achieved the relatively high status of culture apropos of the other nations that Kiev enjoyed in the age of Yaroslav."[17]

Every sign pointed to a rapid advance in culture and enlightenment among the Rus, indicating that the East Slavs would keep pace with the western Europeans in the development of science, the arts, humanitarianism, and liberal government. But, as we will see in a later chapter, Russia was alienated from western Europe and its civilization was retarded partly by its conquest by the Asiatic Mongols, which blighted its early promise and left a tragic legacy for the modern world.

The West Takes the Offensive

End of the "closed-house" economy. Thus far we have been describing the slow progress made in western Europe in establishing political stability and repairing the damage done by the collapse of the Carolingian empire and the devastating raids of Northmen and Magyars. The various kings by the seventh century had barely made a start in the direction of strong, centralized government. As a makeshift, the landed aristocracy took over much of the responsibility of dispensing justice and giving protection to the average man, thus establishing the basis of medieval feudal society. By the eleventh century western Europe was moving beyond the agricultural economy of feudal times, and commerce was revived as the Mediterranean was cleared of Moslem sea power and extirpating the menace of its piratical strongholds.

The Normans in Italy. One of the most shattering blows struck against the Moslems was the Christian conquest of Sicily. About the year 1000, southern Italy was a battleground between rival Lombard dukes, the Byzantine empire, and the Moslems. The dukes were rulers of several duchies; the eastern empire controlled the "heel and toe" of the peninsula; and across the Strait of Messina the Moslems were secure in the rich and fertile island of Sicily (see map, page 341). Into this cockpit of continual warfare the Normans came in 1016. A group of Norman knights, passing through Lombardy while on a pilgrimage to southern Italy, were urged to return home and bring back knights to help the Lombard cities fight against their overlord, the Byzantine empire. These knights did just that and became mercenary soldiers in south Italy.

Soon the news was brought to Normandy, where there was a surplus of knights, that Italy was a land where a knight could easily acquire an estate, provided he had a sword and a strong right arm. One famous Norman house, that of Tancred of Hauteville, had twelve husky sons whose exploits are amazing, for they took south Italy from the eastern empire, Sicily from Islam, captured Antioch from the Turks on the First Crusade, and threatened the Byzantines. Two Normans of this House of Tancred became especially famous: Robert Guiscard—the "Crafty"—a blond giant renowned for his military prowess, and his brother Roger.

Conquest of Sicily. For a time the Norman knights fought for hire and were not loath to turn to brigandage if the loot were promising. They turned next to organized conquest and carved out for themselves large estates in southern Italy. Out of the confusion of each knight-adventurer working for himself rose the figure of Robert Guiscard, who established his authority over his fellow Normans and by 1071 had extinguished the last Byzantine post in southern Italy. Robert had made his peace with the Pope and become his ally. In return, the papacy recognized Robert as the ruler of southern Italy and of Sicily, still in the hands of the Moslems. Under the leadership of Robert and his brother Roger, the Normans crossed the Strait of Messina at great hazard, in the face of a large Moslem fleet, and gained a footing on the island just a few years before William the Conqueror crossed the Channel to invade England. In 1072 Palermo was captured, and twenty years later the entire island had fallen into Norman hands.

Robert Guiscard died before this conquest had been achieved. This amazing adventurer had taken time off during the Sicilian campaign to launch an audacious attack on the Byzantine empire by invading Greece, but Robert's dream of becoming emperor in Constantinople had little chance of success and the expedition failed. On his death he left for his son, Roger Borsa, a powerful military state closely allied to Sicily, which was to rise to greatness.

In retrospect, the part played in early medieval history by the Normans is nothing short of amazing. Upon the history of France, England, Italy, and Russia, they left a deep impress, not to mention their miscellaneous exploits: fighting in the Holy Land against the Turks, helping the Christians to expel the Moors from Spain, and sailing the western seas thousands of miles from land.

Advances of Venice, Genoa, Pisa. While Europeans had been ejecting the Moslems from Sicily, a similar offensive had been going on in the Mediterranean. The rapidly advancing city of Venice had cleared the Adriatic Sea and in 1002 had won a great naval victory

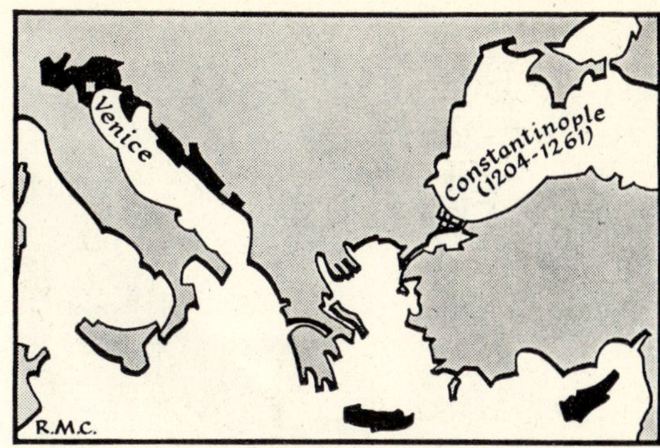

Before feudal Europe had begun to build nations, enterprising Italian towns, led by Venice, were building "empires" to protect their Mediterranean trade.

over a Moslem fleet. Venice then proceeded to consolidate her trade routes and stations in the eastern Mediterranean. During the eleventh century the coastal towns of western Italy made rapid naval and commercial advances. Both trade and religion were motivating factors. Genoa and Pisa, in particular, began to fight the Moslems in the Tyrrhenian Sea, capturing Corsica and Sardinia. Finally, in 1087, the fleets of Genoa and Pisa attacked the Barbary coast of north Africa and burned the main fleet of the Moslem emirs. By 1100 the Mediterranean had been reconquered for Christian commerce.

Moslem Spain

Moslem civilization in Spain. The offensive of the West had cleared the Moslems from the waters of the Mediterranean, but Moslem power remained in Spain. We recall that when the Roman empire crumbled under the barbarian invasions in the fifth century, Visigothic tribes migrated to Spain and settled there, but they never succeeded in establishing a strong government. While Roman Spain had been prosperous and highly civilized, economic life declined under the Visigoths, as it did everywhere after the fall of the empire, and the kingdom became weaker.

Such a state of affairs was an open invitation to conquest. In Chapter 10 we saw how the Moslems came out of the desert of Arabia in the seventh century and swept west across the northern coast of Africa. As we have already seen in connection with our discussion of the Battle of Tours, in 711 the narrow strait separating Africa from Spain was crossed by the Moslem leader Tarik, who subjugated Spain, leaving only a remnant of Christian influence in the mountainous northwestern part of the peninsula.

The lot of the conquered Christians was not especially bad. Christian worship continued, although curtailed, and, generally speaking, tolerance was granted to all people—Christians, Jews, and Moslems. There was much intermarriage, and many of the later Moslem leaders were of Gothic or Roman descent. The government of Spain centered in Damascus until 756 when Moslem Spain became an independent state.

Moslem civilization reached its height in the tenth century. The Caliphate of Cordova, as Moslem Spain was now called, endured brilliantly for a century. During that period Spain saw many economic and cultural advances. Grain growing flourished, water power was harnessed to drive mills, and new crops

GREAT MOSQUE AT CORDOVA

such as rice and sugar were introduced. Wine production and the making of olive oil also flourished. In certain sections of Moslem Spain the country resembled a prosperous garden, with fruit trees, vines, shrubs, and flowers.

Industry prospered. Spanish linens became famous, and Cordova became noted for its silks. Spanish leather goods, weapons, glass, and tapestries were unmatched in Europe. It is said that Cordova in the tenth century was a city of half a million people and that it had three hundred public baths and a library of 400,000 volumes. Cordova was in a sense the intellectual center of the western world. Scholars from Christian Europe came to Moslem Spain to study, and through them much of the learning of the Arabs passed to France and Italy. Cordova had the first paper factory in the West for bookmaking; and chemistry, pharmacy, and mathematics made notable advances.

Despite these accomplishments in the economic and intellectual fields, Moslem Spain was politically weak and disunited. Spain had been conquered by a medley of Arabs, Syrians, Berbers, and Egyptians. The invaders themselves were outnumbered by the original Gothic population. After about the year 1000 the caliphs were a mediocre lot, and revolutions prevailed. In 1031 the Caliphate of Cordova was overthrown and twenty-three separate Moslem kingdoms took its place. This disunity gave the Christians their opportunity.

Christian successes in Spain. During the period of Moslem conquest a few Christian communities survived after they had been driven into the Cantabrian mountains in the northwestern part of the country. The cradle of Christian resistance, according to legend, was the miracle of the Cave of Covadonga. Traditionally a small band of Christians led by a noble named Pelayo in 718 sought refuge in a remote cave-stronghold in the mountains. The cornered band put up a desperate resistance against all attacks and caused the Moslems to withdraw without crushing this last remnant of opposition. This withdrawal was a fatal mistake; one Moorish historian later wrote: "Would to God that the Moslems had then extinguished at once the sparks of a fire that was destined to consume the whole dominions of Islam in those parts."[18]

It was around this nucleus of opposition that the small kingdom of Asturias took shape with a king and a capital at Oviedo. It was about this time that Charlemagne invaded Spain (pages 333-334) and established the buffer territory of the Spanish Mark, a sanctuary for many Christian communities. When the Carolingian empire collapsed, the following Christian states survived in the north of Spain: the county of Barcelona in the east, peopled mainly by the Catalans; in the west, Asturias; and in between, Navarre (peopled mainly by Basque stock) and Aragon.

Slowly gathering power and resolution, these Christian states expanded to the south through the hills, with Asturias leading the way. Leon was reached by 866 and the line of the Douro River by 900, when the Asturian king changed his title to King of Leon. In this new conquered territory many castles were built and it became known as the land of Castile. In the mid-tenth century Castile became strong enough to throw off the rule of the mother country and developed into an independent Christian kingdom. During the height of the power of the Caliphate (912-1002) the expansion of the Christian kingdoms was halted and in some instances severe defeats were inflicted by the Moslems.

Decline of the caliphs. The last strong caliph died in 1002 and his successors were unable to control factionalism. In 1031 the last caliph was deposed and Moslem Spain split up into small states, such as Seville, Toledo, Granada, and Saragossa, each ruled by a so-called king. The collapse of the Caliphate gave the Christian kingdoms their opportunity. Castile made important gains, capturing a large part of what was to become Portugal, pushing her frontier from the Douro to the Tagus River. Apprehensive at this advance, the kings of Seville and Toledo accepted the overlordship of the ruler of Castile.

Start of the Reconquista. For nearly five hundred years more, this reconquest—or the *Reconquista,* as it is known—was to continue, and it will be one of the themes of a later chapter. It is the key to the formative years of the two nations in the Iberian peninsula, a fact acknowledged by Professor Merriman in his classic history, *The Rise of the Spanish Empire,* which opens as follows: "The medieval history of Spain is first and foremost the history of a crusade. For nearly eight centuries the Christians of the North devoted themselves to the task of expelling the Moors from the peninsula."[19]

Summary

This span of 500 years has often been referred to as the Dark Ages. Careful study, however, reveals it as both a dynamic and formative period in which a new Europe was being fashioned. At the outset it seemed as if Carolingian political unity and stability would form the foundation for a new western civilization. However, Charlemagne's empire was ephemeral and subsided into anarchy.

But constructive forces began to gain impetus in the tenth century. Outlines of new kingdoms—later to be Germany, France, England, and Spain—began to be delineated. While central government was weak, individual security and property rights were taken care of by a new political system, feudalism. One historian has seen the years around the critical date of 911 as a historical watershed separating earlier anarchy from the recovery that followed. He points out that in 911 the Northmen settled down in Normandy; that the Saxon House in England won a victory over the Danes, which presaged a united England; and, that the last Carolingian king of Germany died, opening the way for a stronger royal house. Important, too, were the founding in 910 of the monastery at Cluny—destined to initiate a spiritual revival—and, five years later, the ejection of the Moslems from the Italian mainland. "So, while the history of Western Civilization in the ninth century is mainly concerned with destruction and disintegration, in the tenth century there is a cessation of destruction and a revival of order, the construction of a new framework of government...and a renewal of civilization, which was not to be followed again by reaction. The year 911 marks the beginning of the change."[20]

If the great achievement of the tenth century was recovery, that of the eleventh was expansion and offensive action by the forces of western Europe. The Moslems were ejected from Sicily, Corsica, and Sardinia. They lost naval supremacy, and a Christian reconquest was initiated in Spain. In 1096 Christian knights launched an offensive against the Moslem East in the First Crusade. The "closed-house" economy of Europe had come to an end and communications between East and West had been restored. This resulted in the increase of wealth, the growth of cities, the rise of universities, and the tremendous artistic achievements in Gothic art.

Chronology of events and developments discussed in this chapter

Chapter 13

Independence of vassals from the king had spread through France	900
Rise of towns in Italy, Flanders, and southern France	900-1000
Peace of God: Church banned attack on sacred places and noncombatants	990
Towns fostered trade, industry, art, and thought	1000-1200
Venice defeated Moslems: began trade with eastern Mediterranean	1002
Truce of God: limited the time when nobles could fight	1025
Mediterranean routes cleared: Crusades and pilgrims added new commerce	1100
Some Lombard, French, and Flemish towns were chartered communes	1200
Hanseatic League: distributor in northern Europe; controlled Baltic and North seas	1200-1500
Peasants' Revolt: threatened social revolution	1381
Merchant guilds declined when government provided protection	1400
Guild elections controlled by a wealthy clique	1400-1600
Paris: largest city in Christian Europe; population of 300,000	1450

Castle, manor, and town

The feudal age: 843 to 1400

In Chapter 12 we saw how western Europe reorganized its political structure after the fall of the Roman empire. Although the origins of the European state system can be detected in the centuries just described, the outstanding political development was the disappearance of the strong central government that had once radiated from Rome, guaranteeing law and order to all Roman subjects. Economically, the prosperous city life, so important a feature of the Roman empire, practically disappeared in the sixth and seventh centuries. Civilization retrogressed during the so-called Dark Ages, but life still went on. New institutions as well as new political groupings arose to replace those destroyed by the fifth-century Germanic invasions of the Roman empire. Politically, economically, and socially these new agencies were generally crude when compared with those which served society in the days of the Caesars, but even so, they served their purpose of providing the men of medieval times with food and shelter and the means of obtaining at least some form of law and order.

Beside the church, the most characteristic features of medieval European society were feudalism and the manor. While feudalism referred primarily to political organization, the manor constituted the system by which medieval man obtained economic subsistence. Feudalism did not spring up overnight in Europe following the Germanic invasions. In fact, its roots, as we shall see, go back to practices prevailing in the Roman empire and even to certain institutions possessed by the Germanic tribes before they came into the empire. Like so many things in medieval civilization, feudalism was a blend of both Germanic and Roman customs. The essence of feudalism was lack of an effective central government and reliance upon local authorities to carry on governmental functions.

Equally important and perhaps even more basic than feudalism was the manor, for the manorial system was the method by which food and clothing were provided. The manor, as we shall soon discover, was a small area of land peopled mainly by serfs, who constituted the overwhelming majority of the population of Europe in the Middle Ages. Not slave and yet not free, these peasants were bound to the soil which they tilled for their betters, the feudal nobility. Agriculture on the manor was primitive, contact with the outside world was rare, and self-sufficiency was the economic keynote.

For several hundred years, in fact throughout the early centuries of the Middle Ages, feudalism and the manor dominated the medieval scene. But slowly and imperceptibly a new institution gathered its strength and expanded its activities. This was the city. By 1200 flourishing cities existed in many areas of Europe. The revival of city life first began in northern Italy, and about the same time city life began anew in southern France, in Flanders, in a few localities in England, and in the Rhine valley and along the Baltic Sea in Germany. While nourished by medieval civilization, the city soon showed that its spirit was entirely foreign to the organization of medieval life. The cities weaned serfs away from their manors, ended the self-sufficiency of the manors by contributing to the expansion of trade, and combined with the kings to destroy the influence of the feudal aristocracy.

Feudalism

Why feudalism developed. With the collapse of the Roman empire, Europeans were forced to devise some means of protecting themselves from the attacks of foreign invaders. For a while, the Carolingian empire governed most of western Europe, but after its disintegration, the protection that had once been offered by a well-organized and efficiently governed empire no longer existed. By the middle of the ninth century, it was obvious to all that the central government was unable to ward off foreign attacks. As a result, the less powerful men began to seek the protection of the more powerful, and soon every freeman was under a protecting lord. Two main factors then—the disintegration of central power and the growing need for protection—served to create in western Europe a new concept of government—feudalism.

Feudalism defined. Feudalism can be said to have emerged as a well-defined governmental system throughout most of western Europe by the year 900. It was a system of government whose outstanding feature was the distribution, or decentralization, of political authority among a landed aristocracy. In theory this aristocracy was subordinate to the king, but in practice it was a law unto itself. Feudalism was characterized by the following features: (1) the exercise of governmental functions by numerous local authorities, (2) a distinctive form of landholding, (3) an elaborate system of personal relationships, (4) a military system, and (5) certain judicial agencies.

Feudalism was really a transitional political stage, for it was seldom anywhere more than a poor substitute for a closely knit and centralized government. It served as a stopgap following the collapse of a unified political system until a more effective government could be developed.

The origins of feudalism. European feudalism was based upon customs and institutions that came from two main sources, Roman and German. By the fifth century the ability of the emperor to protect his subjects had disappeared and the provinces were at the mercy of marauders. Since individuals needed protection both for themselves and their lands, two practices arose in the later Roman empire. The weak landowner, fearing the loss of everything, gave over his land to a stronger neighbor, who permitted him to cultivate it. However, he no longer owned the land but was now a tenant, and the new owner, although he granted the property to the original owner without rent and usually for no specific time, had the right to take it back at will. This Roman practice was known as the *precarium,* and continued to exist into the Merovingian period. But as the grant of land could be terminated at any time, the tenant often found that his tenure was most "precarious." When the land was granted to the original owner on the condition that he render military service, the practice was called *beneficium,* and when the *beneficium* became hereditary and involved feudal dues other than military service, it was called the fief. There was a second Roman practice for the freeman who owned no land. He went to the strong neighbor and asked for protection and support. This he received, through the practice called the *patrocinium.* In return for various services he was added to the lord's household.

The institution of *comitatus* came from German society, where for a long time the chieftains had chosen picked warriors as a personal retinue. The *comitatus* was a relationship of mutual protection wherein these warriors swore solemnly to aid their chief loyally at all times. In return they were provided by him with food and military equipment. The personal relationship of feudalism arose from the union of the practices of the *patrocinium* and *comitatus,* while the feudal system of land tenure grew out of the *precarium.*

A third practice was the granting of immunity. Through force or favor the landed aristocrat, or noble, as he came to be called, exacted from the king the exemption of his estate from taxes or royal supervision. Thus the lord won the all-important right to govern his own territory as he wished. The lord now had definite political and legal powers and responsibilities, so long as he governed according to his obligations to the king. His immunity was legally recognized in the course of time. By 900 this process of decentralization was completed in France, and it was soon common elsewhere in Europe, though not to such a complete extent.

Relation of lord and vassal. One of the principal elements of feudalism was the personal one, the lord-vassal relationship. The vassal knelt before his lord and promised to be his "man." This ceremony was the act of homage, and it was filled with all the solemnity which the Middle Ages could create. With the lord sitting and the man kneeling before him with head uncovered, the vassal placed both hands in those of the lord and said, "I become your man, to keep faith with you against all others." The lord then helped him to his feet, kissed him on the mouth, and promised to take him as his vassal. The latter then swore upon the Gospel or some other sacred object an oath of eternal fidelity to his lord, called the oath of fealty.

The next rite was that of investing the vassal with the fief by a symbolic act on the part of the lord. A lance, glove, stick, or even a bit of straw was handed the vassal to signify the latter's right of private jurisdiction over a fief (but not ownership of the land). The fief was ordinarily a unit of land, varying in size but always large enough at least to support a knight and his horse. The granting of the fief was called infeudation, or enfeoffment, while the ceremony by which the vassal was symbolically invested with the fief was known as investiture. The fief was like the *beneficium* except that the former was not a life estate but was hereditary, transferred from father to son, with each fulfilling the usual services of vassalage.

The feudal contract thus entered into by lord and vassal was considered sacred and binding upon both parties. Breaking this tie of mutual obligations was considered to be a felony because it violated the feudal code of chivalry by which all knights good and true patterned their lives.

The lord's obligations. Let us now examine the reciprocal feudal contract and see what the obligations of both the lord and his vassal were. The lord was obliged (1) to protect his vassal from his enemies, (2) to ensure him justice at the feudal court, (3) to refrain from corrupting nobles who held land from his vassal (a relationship known as subinfeudation, which will be described on the next page), (4) to build no castles on the fief without the vassal's consent, and (5) to refrain from injuring his vassal's honor by abusing his children or wife. The nonfulfillment of any of these obligations broke the feudal contract and freed the vassal of his fealty and obligations.

The vassal's obligations. The vassal's obligations were more numerous and complex. (1) The primary duty was that of military service. He and his knights and followers were expected to devote forty days' service each year to his lord at no expense to the lord. Beyond that time he did not have to stay and was free to return home or else demand payment for his services. At other times it was usual for the lord to ask for a money payment from his vassals in place of armed knights. The payment was called *scutage* (shield money) and enabled the lord to hire mercenary soldiers. Another military duty was known as castleward service, which consisted of performing garrison duty at the lord's castle or coming to its defense when it was attacked.

(2) The vassal was obliged to assist the lord in his court and often had to devote much time to the judging of disputes between vassal and vassal, for feudal law asserted the right of a noble to be judged only by his peers, or social equals. The vassal was also expected to bring all his own disputes before the lord's court.

(3) The lord had the right to demand at certain times definite money payments which drained his vassal's resources heavily. The payments were customarily called *aids* and could be levied on three occasions: whenever the lord's eldest son was made a knight, whenever the eldest daughter was to be married and a dowry had to be provided for her, and whenever the lord was captured and had to be ransomed.

(4) Another money payment, called the *relief*, was exacted whenever either the lord or the vassal died and his heir succeeded. This "inheritance tax" came as a result of performing homage (which had to be undertaken each time there was a new lord or vassal), and it was a sum often equivalent to the fief's revenues for the first year, a big expense for the vassal.

(5) Another financial obligation dreaded by the vassal was the right of hospitality. By this right the lord and his retinue had to be provided with shelter, food, and entertainment when passing through the territory of his subject. Because a large retinue and a long stay might bankrupt the vassal, the extent of such hospitality came in time to be precisely limited.

Feudal incidents. In addition to the vassal's obligations, the lord had certain privileges regarding the administration of the fief, called feudal incidents. (1) Whenever a vassal died without leaving any legitimate heirs, the fief reverted, or escheated, to the lord. The latter was then free to bestow it upon whomever he wished. (2) If the vassal failed to live up to his feudal obligations, the lord might confiscate his estate. Such a practice was called forfeiture. (3) When a vassal died leaving only a minor heir, the lord enjoyed the right of wardship, that is, the administration of the estate until the boy came of age, meanwhile keeping its yearly revenues for himself as payment for his trouble. (4) If the vassal left no son and a daughter was to inherit the fief, the lord claimed the right to provide her with a suitable husband. He did this because it was essential that the fief be administered by a man who could fight well and be loyal to his suzerain. It was a right which often brought misery to the women, for even girls of ten or less might be compelled to marry men many times older, whom they had never seen before, and whose only virtue lay in their ability to crack skulls with a heavy mace. (5) If the vassal went away on a pilgrimage or crusade, the lord possessed the right to administer the fief during his absence.

Subinfeudation. A great lord often found that the fief which he held from the king was too large for him to administer personally. So, while he kept a certain portion (called the demesne) for his personal use, he subdivided, or subinfeudated, the remainder of his fief to men who thereby became his vassals. Each of these vassals could in turn, if he so desired, subinfeudate his particular fief. Thus if A received a fief from the king, he might subinfeudate part of it to B, who in turn might subinfeudate part of his fief to C.

Meanwhile, in order to add to his small portion of land, B might also have pledged fealty to D, a noble as powerful as A. Now, if A and D should fight one another, to which lord does vassal B owe allegiance? A king might even be the vassal of another king, as in the case of Philip of France and John of England. John was the vassal of Philip for certain French lands, yet John in no manner thought that he was the social inferior of the French monarch. Thus men could be at the same time lords and vassals. It even happened that a lord, desiring a particular bit of land held by one of his own subjects, was actually the vassal of his own vassal. Therefore, while subinfeudation aided feudal management of large fiefs by dividing them into smaller units, the conflict of loyalties was a great defect. In France especially the process of subinfeudation was carried to such a complicated and minute extent that the entire feudal system lacked cohesion.

The feudal hierarchy. In theory feudalism was a vast hierarchy. At the top stood the emperor or king, and all the land in his dominions belonged to him. He kept large areas for his personal use (royal or crown lands) and invested the highest nobles—dukes, counts, and earls—with the remainder. Those nobles holding lands directly from the king were called tenants-in-chief. They in turn parceled out portions of their fiefs to lesser nobles—viscounts and barons. All vassals other than tenants-in-chief were known as mesne tenants. The lowest in the hierarchical scale was the humble knight. His bit of subinfeudated land, sufficient only to support him and maintain his military needs, was called the knight's fee. "The landless knight was known only in Germany and originally he was . . . but a serf doing military service."[1] Thus we see how important land was in the social and economic life of feudalism. However, it is important to keep in mind that the great mass of people fell below the feudal hierarchy, which was made up of the nobility and higher members of the clergy. The common people will be discussed later in connection with the manorial system and the rise of towns.

The Church and feudalism. One of the complicating factors in feudalism was the inclusion of the Church in the system. It so happened that many devout nobles, for the sake of the souls of their ancestors and themselves, would bequeath lands to the Church. The land was often held by feudal tenure, and the local abbot or other church official who obtained the fief would become the vassal of the heir of the deceased noble. The abbot had to perform military service through his representative in secular affairs, the *advocatus*. The fundamental difficulty, as the Church obtained more and more lands held by feudal tenure, was that its officials as churchmen owed their loyalty to the Pope and to the Church, but as vassals holding feudal land they also owed certain secular or governmental obligations to their respective lords. There was a serious clash of loyalties here, which caused a bitter struggle between the head of the feudal system, the king, and the head of the Church, the Pope. Even worse, preoccupation with his worldly duties as a feudal vassal often caused a churchman to neglect his spiritual duties.

Feudal warfare. In practice the feudal hierarchy often worked in sharp contrast to its ideal. Force in the Middle Ages was the final authority. Some of the French nobles had lands greater in extent than those possessed by the kings, and they frequently made war upon their suzerains. The general atmosphere of the feudal system was one of violence. The vassal performed only those services which he could not possibly escape. Warfare for its own sake was often resorted to by the nobility. Although much of the fighting was done for the king in some campaign or other, private warfare was a common occurrence.

There were good reasons for this distressing state of affairs. First of all, land was the only real source of wealth, and the supply of land was limited. Holdings could be increased in only two ways, marriage and war. If the former course proved inconvenient because the noble was already married, the second method was always open. Again, warfare enabled a noble to reward his followers with fiefs, and, if they produced nothing else, forays and raids kept a man in good mettle. To die in battle was the only honorable end for a spirited gentleman; to die in bed was a "cow's death."

It is true that the Church by two institutions both lessened and "Christianized" this evil of warfare. About the year 990 it threatened to curse and ban from the Church all persons who pillaged sacred places or refused to spare noncombatants. This restraint was called the Peace of God. But a far more effective check on knightly pugnacity appeared in the south of France about 1025—the Truce of God. This second restraint represented an attempt to provide certain "closed seasons" by limiting the times when the nobles could fight. Originally the period covered by the truce included only Friday, Saturday, and Sunday of each week. Later the period was lengthened from sunset on Wednesday to sunrise on Monday, and certain seasons, such as the one extending from the beginning of Lent through Whitsuntide, were also observed.

We should be careful not to take an exaggerated view of the extent of medieval private war. Brigandage was a greater menace than private warfare, while "the worst evil of the Middle Ages was its cruelty to enemies, captives, criminals, and heretics."[2]

The function of feudalism. What shall be our general estimate of feudalism? Hegel has stated that it was "a protest of barbarism against barbarism,"[3] and Henri Martin has maintained that "it concealed in its bosom the weapons with which it would be itself one day smitten."[4] That is, feudalism, by maintaining a king at the head of the feudal hierarchy, was really keeping intact the agency of strong monarchy which would gradually reassert itself and thus restore centralized government in Europe at the expense of the feudal nobles. Feudalism was crude and makeshift, but it was perhaps the system best fitted to bring order out of the chaos into which Europe had fallen. It put an end to the political fluctuations of the centuries of barbarian invasions by stabilizing society and creating a system of law and order. It even contributed to democracy, for its principle that feudal law was above the king (as witnessed in *Magna Charta*) was later used by the middle class to curb royal absolutism. Despite its cruelty and high-handed methods, feudal society had instilled into it the ideals of personal honor and reciprocal obligations between individuals; and however much these ideals were honored in the breach, they passed into the mores of our own society.

The Age of Chivalry

Chivalry in feudal society. The members of the feudal hierarchy were aristocrats belonging to either the nobility or the clergy. Medieval society is conventionally thought of as consisting of three quite distinct classes: the clergy, the nobility, and the common toilers. It was often difficult, however, to show where one order left off and the other began. For example, the clergy was recruited from all classes, and serfs in France are known to have become knights—although by the twelfth century knighthood had become a closed class in France. The "three orders" theory of feudal society, furthermore, fails to include a large group whose importance grew with the passing of time—the townsmen. But the feudal social life which we are about to describe affected only the aristocracy. The code of conduct that developed in this society was called chivalry.

Chivalry defined. The word chivalry comes from *chevalier,* meaning horseman, and it refers to a code of etiquette connected with knighthood. It did not appear until quite late in the Middle Ages. It developed from three sources: the German tribal custom of investing adolescent youth with military arms, the Christian religious and moral ideas, and the Saracenic concepts of poesy and heraldry. Chivalry as an institution reached its zenith in the twelfth and thirteenth centuries.

The chivalric code of conduct was strict. It demanded fidelity to one's lord and to one's vows, championship of the Church against her enemies, protection of women, children, and the infirm, generosity, courtesy, reverence toward womanhood, and service to God by warring against the infidel and the heretic. Unfortunately, chivalry was quite different in practice. While he might cloak his motives under high-sounding words, the average knight continued to plunder, fight, and abuse women, especially if they were not of the noble class. With the decline of chivalry, its code became fantastic and even ridiculous. But the ideals of chivalry definitely affected the conduct of later society. They seeped down into middle-class life and today color our own conception of a true "gentleman."

Training for knighthood. Chivalry imposed a rigid training for knighthood. Until the age of seven, a boy was kept in the care of his mother. When he became seven, he was sent by his father to the household of a relative, a friend, or the father's suzerain. There he became a page, attending the ladies and running their errands, learning the rudiments of religion, manners, hawking and hunting, and being instilled with the valuable lesson of obedience. When about fifteen or sixteen, he became a squire. Now the lad prepared himself seriously for the art of war. He learned to keep a knight's equipment in good order, to ride a war horse with dexterity, and to handle the sword, the shield, and the lance correctly. To that end he practiced long hours in the tilting field against other squires or rode at full gallop against the quintain, an object which administered the passing squire a crushing blow unless it was struck fairly with the lance. The youth also waited on his lord and lady at table and learned music and poetry and the popular medieval games of chess and backgammon.

It is from such prints as this one, in which the artist has crowded the whole life of a manorial village, that we get many of our ideas of medieval times. A hunting party is shown in the foreground, the ladies (one of them with a falcon on her wrist) riding behind the knights. The hilltop castle has the typical drawbridge and moat. The houses of the village are surrounded by a "close" with the church in a central place. Note also the mill, the mill race, and what appears to be a wine or cider press. In the upper right corner of the picture can be seen evidence of strip-farming, the serf using the heavy plow common in the north (for economy's sake the artist has shown only two draft animals). The nets were apparently set to catch hares. Below them stands a wayside shrine. Visible on the horizon is an occupied gibbet with buzzards wheeling over it.

The knighting ceremony. If not actually knighted on the battlefield for valor, the squire was usually considered eligible for knighthood when twenty-one. By the twelfth century the Church claimed to have a role in the ceremony. It maintained that the knight was highly privileged because he performed service for God in the secular world. Therefore knighthood was invested with impressive symbolism. The candidate bathed to symbolize purity, an act called the bath of purification, and watched his weapons before the altar in an all-night vigil, confessing and making resolutions to be a worthy knight. This was followed by a solemn Mass, during which his sword was blessed on the altar by the priest or bishop. Then came the ceremony in which he was dubbed knight. Kneeling before his lord, the candidate received a blow on the back of the neck (the accolade), with these words: "In the name of God, Saint Michael, and Saint George I dub thee knight. Be valiant." The new knight was then armed ceremoniously, particular significance being attached to the binding on of his golden spurs, for the horse was the indispensable companion of the knight and represented in itself the symbol of nobility. The knight then sprang to his horse and tilted against the quintain to prove his dexterity at arms. Thus the code of chivalry and the Church combined to impress upon the knight that he must be brave, gentle, and loyal to his God and suzerain.

Heraldry. One of the most fascinating aspects of chivalry was the development of heraldry. Heraldry has to do with the decorative designs worn by all noble families on their armor and helmets. Heraldry goes back to early Mesopotamia and to China, where in the oldest times the five-clawed dragon had become the heraldic device of the empire. In Japan the emperor had his symbol of chrysanthemums, and the Aztec eagle symbol is famous. As the feudal system developed, noble families took great pride in possessing an ancient heraldic device, the symbol for family dignity and honor.

The popularity of heraldry swept through Europe during the Middle Ages, especially when the closed helmet came into vogue, hiding the face of its wearer. At first the distinguishing devices used were simple emblems, but in time the most complex and strange forms and colors were designed. Two hundred eighty-five variations of the simple design of the cross were devised by ingenious feudal artists,[5] while such animals (real and fictitious) as the lion, leopard, griffin, dragon, unicorn, and a host of others could be found in fanciful postures on the shields of noble families. A man's social position was proved by his coat of arms, for by its quarterings, or divisions, could be seen the noble families to which its owner was related.

The castle. The life of the nobles centered about the castle. The earliest of these structures appeared in the ninth century and were mere blockhouses built solely of timber. Stone castles did not appear until the late eleventh century, and even then only the tower (called donjon, or keep) was built of stone. Not until the twelfth and thirteenth centuries, when chivalry was in full bloom, did massive structures of stone appear.

The important part of the castle was the donjon, surrounded by a yard called the bailey. This in turn was encircled by cleverly constructed flanking walls protected by turrets from which arrows, boiling oil, and other refinements of feudal military science might be showered upon the attackers. Surrounding the wall fortifications was the moat, a steep-sided ditch filled with water over which the enemy must cross. The only entrance to the castle lay across the drawbridge, which led to the gate. (Note the castle shown in the print on page 361.) The latter was protected by a heavy iron grating called the portcullis, which could be let down swiftly while the drawbridge was raised, thus interposing an additional barrier. Inside the bailey were storerooms, workshops, and a chapel. The lord at first dwelled in the donjon, but by the thirteenth century he was living in a more spacious apartment in the inner castle.

Medieval castle furniture. Life in the castle was anything but comfortable or romantic. Because it had been built for purposes of defense, the castle possessed no spacious windows but only slits in the thick walls from which archers might shoot down on the attacker. The rooms were therefore dark and gloomy. The stone walls were damp and bare except for occasional pieces of tapestry to break the monotony (and keep the dampness out), and the stairs were steep. The furnishings were meager in the extreme. In the great hall were dining tables set upon trestles; when not in use the boards were laid against the wall and the trestles cleared away. The principal table was set on a raised section called the dais, and here the important personages sat. The seats were generally backless and uncomfortable. In the room was a huge fireplace which afforded the drafty room its only warmth. The floor was covered with rushes which were seldom replaced and which became dirty and evil-smelling, since they contained the bones and scraps of bread and meat which the diners threw over their shoulders to the dogs who roamed about behind the seats while the meal was in progress. The use of carpets was an expensive oriental luxury which slowly won favor only after the crusades.

Besides the hall there were bedrooms, also sparsely furnished, each containing a few chests and bureaus and an enormous bed. The bed was built upon a platform and stood under a large canopy from which hung heavy curtains. The curtains kept away drafts and preserved modesty, for nobody in feudal days wore any night clothes. The bedroom was also unusual in that falcons, hounds, and even barnyard creatures often took up their abode there.

Life in the castle. Life began early in the day, breakfast being served about six o'clock. The riser washed his face and hands—and in passing we might note that medieval civilization was not "a thousand years without a bath," for each castle had its well, and running water was often brought through lead pipes; the larger castles and abbeys also had latrines. Dinner was served at ten in the morning and the last meal at five. Our medieval ancestors

A banquet in a medieval castle is shown in this miniature painting, an illustration for a fourteenth-century work. Note the squires serving the meal, the dog pursuing scraps, the absence of silverware.

were certainly hearty eaters, although the fare was limited. Meat, fish, and fowl were served in great variety and greater quantity, while such vegetables as onions, cabbages, beets, beans, peas, and the popular turnip were in common use, as were such fruits as pears, apples, cherries, plums, and strawberries. One elaborate medieval recipe for "leche lumbard" —a sort of German sausage—ran like this:

"Take pork and pound it in a mortar with eggs; add sugar, salt, raisins, currants, minced dates, powdered pepper, and cloves; put it in a bladder and boil it; then cut it in slices."[6] The sausage was served with a sauce made of raisins, red wine, almond-milk colored with saffron, pepper, cloves, cinnamon, and ginger.

Potatoes were absent from the medieval fare, as were coffee and tea. But there was no lack of beverages. Beer and cider were commonplace drinks, while the noble prided himself upon his knowledge of wines. To the connoisseur a wine should be "clear like the tears of a penitent, so that a man may see distinctly to the bottom of the glass; its color should represent the greenness of a buffalo's horn; when drunk it should descend impetuously like thunder; sweet-tasted as an almond; creeping like a squirrel; leaping like a roebuck; strong like the building of a Cistercian monastery; glittering like a spark of fire; subtle like the logic of the schools of Paris; delicate as fine silk; and colder than crystal."[7]

Table etiquette. Table manners were both interesting and startling. The gentleman cut up the meat with his dagger. Certain dishes were served on plates, but portions of meat were placed on thick slabs of bread, into which the gravy soaked. After the meat was eaten, the bread was thrown to the dogs or deposited in the alms-basket for the poor. Forks were unknown. Food was carried to the mouth by the thumb and two fingers. Men were allowed to wear their hats at table, but etiquette insisted that they should not fill their mouths too full, laugh or talk with the mouth full, wipe their knives on the tablecloth, roll their eyes, or pick their teeth publicly. Also

Scratche not thy head with thy fyngers
  When thou arte at thy meate;
Nor spytte you over the table board;
  See thou doest not this forget.

Pick not thy teeth with thy knyfe
Nor with thy fyngers ende,
But take a stick or some cleane thing,
Then doe you not offende.[8]

In fact, Chaucer informs us that his coy Prioress was a model of deportment because

At table she had been well taught withal,
And never from her lips let morsels fall,
Nor dipped her fingers deep in sauce, but ate
With so much care the food upon her plate
That never driblet fell upon her breast.
In courtesy she had delight and zest,
Her upper lip was always wiped so clean
That in her cup was no iota seen
Of grease, when she had drunk her draught of wine.
Becomingly she reached for meat to dine.[9]

Amusements. The amusements of the nobility were scarcely intellectual. Only those persons who had decided upon a church career had received an education sufficiently sound to enable them to enjoy reading and conversing on such subjects as philosophy or other serious subjects. The average noble derived his pleasures differently. He spent as much time as possible out-of-doors. He considered warfare almost the finest of sports, for he had been trained from birth in military matters. During the monotonous days of peace, however, he found several excellent substitutes. One was mock battle, the joust and tournament. The joust was a conflict between two armed knights, each equipped, usually, with a blunted lance with which he attempted to unseat the other. The tournament was a general mêlée in which groups of knights attacked each other. Often fierce fighting ensued, with frequent casualties.

The nobles were very fond of hunting, and fresh meat was much in demand. This requirement afforded a legitimate excuse for galloping over the countryside. At times some poor peasant's crops might be ruined during the chase, but most hunting was done in the nearby forests. Some great nobles had scores of horses and hounds trained in hunting the stag and wild boar.

Another popular outdoor pastime, which lords, ladies, and even high church dignitaries delighted in, was falconry. Birds were reared with the utmost care, and many an afternoon was spent by large companies of lords and ladies eagerly wagering with one another as to whose falcon would bring down the first victim. In fact the nobles often attended Mass with hooded falcons on their wrists.

Indoor amusements included the universally popular diversions of backgammon, dice, and chess. The long and monotonous nights were sometimes enlivened by the quips of jesters or the recital of passages from the great *Chanson de Roland* by a wandering *jongleur*, or minstrel, glad to entertain his noble hosts in exchange for a bed and place at the table.

The life of the women. There were really two attitudes toward women during medieval times, one put forward by the Church and the other by the code of chivalry. These attitudes were never reconciled. The Church moralists preached that Eve had caused Adam to lose Eden and therefore that women were not only inferior to men but were the surest means by which men lost their souls. But chivalry and the troubadours placed women on a pedestal and maintained that they were worthy of all reverence and loyalty. Was not the blessed Mary Queen of Heaven, and did she not rival even the Holy Trinity in popularity because of her tenderness and compassion? And if Mary was so worthy of devotion, were not all gentlewomen worthy of reverence? Thus argued the troubadours, with the interesting result that in the Middle Ages women were placed either very close to paradise or very, very close to the pit.

In actual practice, however, woman's life was near neither one nor the other. She was legally inferior to man. She had little real choice as to whom she might marry. A rich widow stood the chance of being kidnaped by impulsive suitors. Such a predicament befell Eleanor of Aquitaine, who was pursued by no fewer than five men after she had been divorced from King Louis VII of France. However, very often the lady of the castle was the most influential person there, aiding her husband in its administration and even defending it from attack when her lord was absent. With more men than women leading celibate lives in the Church, not all medieval women could be furnished with husbands, and since it was a man's world, it was difficult for women to find a proper place except as wives. The medieval moralists kept rebuking women constantly for their extravagant dress and fashions. The use of stays to gain slimness, the plucking of eyebrows, the painting of cheeks, and the expensive clothes shocked the male preachers. Listen to Berthold of Regensburg:

"In order that ye may compass men's praise ye spend all your labour on your garments—on your veils and your kirtles. Many of you pay as much to the sempstress as the cost of the cloth itself; it must have shields on the shoulders, it must be flounced and tucked all round the hem; it is not enough for you to show your pride in your very buttonholes, but you must also send your feet to hell by special torments, ye trot this way and that with your fine stitchings. Ye busy yourselves with your veils, ye twitch them hither, ye twitch them thither; ye gild them here and there with gold thread; ye will spend a good six months' work on a single veil. . . . When thou shouldest be busy in the house with something needful for the goodman, or for thyself, or thy children, or thy guests, then art thou busy instead with thy hair; thou art careful whether thy sleeves sit well, or thy veil or thy headdress, wherewith thy whole time is filled."[10]

The Manorial System

The manor and feudalism. We have seen that feudalism was concerned with the life of the landholding class, the nobility. But some ninety per cent of the medieval population was non-noble, living on lands which it did not own. N. S. B. Gras maintains that "The most characteristic institution in the economic history of the Middle Ages, following the fall of Rome, was the manor."[11] Here dwelled the rank and file of the medieval population. The manor was almost a self-sufficient world. It was at once "a structure of society, an economic régime."

We have seen that the land a vassal held from his lord was called a fief. The fief consisted of one or more estates called manors, varying in number from a knight's fief (fee) of one manor to that of a large landholder which might contain hundreds of manors. The fief was a political unit of land; the manor was an economic unit. The manor was the basic unit of production on the fief, and the term "manorial system" refers to the type of economic and social system which was centered around the manor. In studying the manorial system, therefore, we shall consider not only methods of tilling the soil but the people who lived on the manor and the relationships which existed between them, especially between the lord of the manor and the serfs who farmed for him.

Feudalism and the manorial system did not necessarily depend on each other. In fact, the two systems evolved independently, the manorial being established before the end of the ninth century was over, the feudal system taking final shape later than the eleventh. Gras states: "The manor may be said to have four ages. Its growth in England was during the period 800-1200. It was at its height 1200-1300. Decline . . . took place 1300-1500. After 1500 the manor survived only in non-essentials."[12]

However, for the most part medieval feudalism and the manorial system were intimately connected. The feudal system was the means whereby protection was obtained for society, while the manor was the agency which provided the necessary food for the entire feudal system.

Origins of the manor. Like feudalism, the manor seems to have had its origins in both Roman and German institutions, with the former making perhaps the greater contribution. From the Roman villa, or *latifundium* (see page 168) came elements of medieval serfdom. The Roman *colonus,* once a freeman, gradually became a serf bound to the soil, a prisoner for debt, because he could never pay off his arrears of rent through daily toil.

The German contribution is not so clearly traced. Some scholars have maintained that the Germans were originally tribes of freemen living in a free village community, the German *mark.* But after the German invasions of the fifth and sixth centuries into Roman territory, these communities sank into serfdom. Other scholars believe that the great mass of Germans were not free in their own lands and that the unfree village was set up in Roman territory. At any rate, we find that the manor of the Middle Ages was a blending of the Roman villa and the German *mark.*

A typical manor. The medieval manor was an estate that varied in size from one locality to another. A small one might contain only about a dozen households, but as the allotment to each family averaged about thirty acres, even the smallest manor contained at

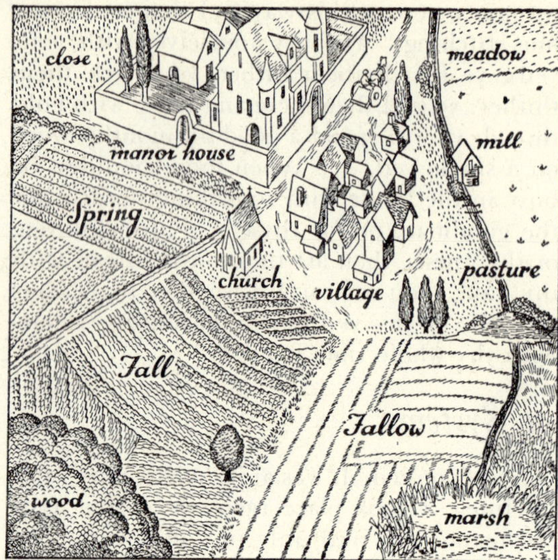

least 350 acres, not counting the meadows, woods, wasteland, and the lord's demesne. A large manor might contain fifty families and a total area of five thousand acres. The feudal saying "No lord without land, no land without a lord" is important here. Kings and monasteries might possess hundreds of manors, a noble might have scores, sometimes scattered over whole kingdoms. Therefore one who possessed but one manor, such as the knight, was at the lowest rung of the feudal social ladder.

The center of the manor was the village. The peasants did not live in scattered farmhouses throughout the manor but grouped together closely in thatched cottages along one street. Around each cottage was a space large enough for a vegetable patch, chicken yard, hayrick, and stable. Running through the manor was the stream from the woods, emptying into a pond which became the village duck pond. The lord's demesne would be nearby and would certainly constitute the finest farming land. If the manor was large, the lord's dwelling might be a castle, with the village built up to its walls; if small, there would be a manor house surmounting a knoll on the demesne. An important feature of the landscape was the village church, together with the priest's house and the burial ground.

The fields stretched out from the village, and along the roads the villagers trudged to work. The arable land was divided into three great sections, "the spring planting ground, the autumn planting ground, and the fallow." If one followed the stream to its source, he came to the woods and the nearby meadowland, areas which were used in common. Altogether the typical manor possessed seven distinct divisions of land:

1. The lord's demesne, owned and used solely by him and cultivated by his serfs.
2. The lord's close, a part of the demesne which he rented out to the villein or tenant cultivators.
3. The tenures of the villagers, scattered in strips among the three fields of arable land.
4. The meadowland, used in common by the peasantry and the lord.
5. The woods, also held in common.
6. The wasteland.
7. The domain of the village priest, or "God's piece." This land was either in one area or scattered in strips, and was cultivated for the priest by the villagers.[13]

Farming on the manor. Agriculture is the most important aspect of the manorial system to be considered. It is dangerous to generalize too sweepingly about agricultural methods, because differences in locality, fertility of soil, crop production, and other factors resulted in a variety of farming methods. But if we study farming as practiced in northwest Europe, we can discover some common factors. Farming techniques were quite primitive, although some advances were made with the passage of time. The implements which the peasants used were extremely crude; the plow was a cumbersome affair with heavy wheels, often drawn by as many as eight draft animals in order to break the heavy soil. There were also crude harrows, sickles, beetles for breaking up clods, and flails for threshing. The farmer knew nothing of the value of nitrogen-yielding plants, artificial fertilizers, and scientific crop rotation and had an inadequate supply of manure, with the result that the soil was soon depleted and the crop return poor. It has been estimated that the average yield per acre was only six to eight bushels of wheat, a fourth of the modern yield.

Cultivated grasses and clovers were not known until the seventeenth century; thus the supply of hay in the meadowland was limited to natural grasses. The shortage of hay meant undernourishment of animals, a condition which, together with an ignorance of the principles of proper breeding, kept the livestock small and weak. The animal most commonly raised on the manor was the pig, which foraged in the forest and devoured the refuse. The peasant often used the ox instead of the horse as a draft animal, for it was cheaper to maintain. The medieval cow was a poor specimen indeed. In the wintertime it was fed on straw and the loppings of trees, a diet which left it so weak that frequently it had to be carried out to pasture in the spring. The supply of milk was small, and the peasants turned most of it into cheese. Sheep were raised, especially in England, while hens, geese, and ducks, as well as bees, were kept by the peasants.

Crop rotation. Bitter experience had long ago taught our ancestors that land devoted exclusively and continually to one crop, such as wheat, oats, rye, or barley, would become exhausted in short order. To counteract such a situation, the Greeks had used a three-field system, while the Romans and Germans had made use of the two-field system, whereby the arable land was divided into two portions, one of which would be sowed and the other left to lie fallow to recover its fertility. But at some undetermined date the Middle Ages learned that wheat or rye could be planted in the autumn as well as in the spring, thus doubling the year's crop. It was also discovered that while a continuation of the same crop soon exhausts the soil the alternation of crops does not bleed the land so quickly. It was possible to divide the land into three fields, with two different crops growing at the same time and the third field lying fallow only once in three years instead of every two years. Here is the plan of rotation:

1st year	Field A—wheat	B—oats	C—fallow
2nd "	" B—wheat	C—oats	A—fallow
3rd "	" C—wheat	A—oats	B—fallow

The advantages of the three-field system over the two-field have been admirably demonstrated by N. S. B. Gras with the following illustration:

"Let us compare the two systems on a manor containing 1800 acres of arable land. In the two-field system we would have:

900 acres (arable plowed once)........ 900
900 acres (fallow plowed twice, to get rid of stubble).................... 1800
Total acres of plowing.............. 2700

In the three-field system we would have:

600 acres (winter grain plowed once)... 600
600 acres (spring grain plowed once)... 600
600 acres (fallow plowed twice, to get rid of stubble).................... 1200
Total acres of plowing.............. 2400

Thus in the two-field system we get only 900 acres of crops for 2700 acres of plowing, whilst in the three-field system we get 1200 acres of crops for 2400 acres of plowing."[14]

The development of the three-field system has been considered the greatest agricultural contribution of the Middle Ages. While it was never universally practiced, owing to mass inertia or ignorance, it revolutionized agriculture in countries such as England, though here, too, the two-field system did not soon die out.

Distribution of the land. From one third to two fifths of the manor was given over to the lord's demesne. The land in the demesne might be sharply set off from the tenures of the villagers, or portions of the demesne might be scattered among the lands of the tenants. The land not held in demesne was allotted among the householders of the village under what is called the open-field system. As we have stated before, the arable land of the manor was divided into three great fields, one for spring planting, the second for fall planting, and the third to be left fallow. The three fields were subdivided into acre strips a furlong in length and four rods wide, or half-acre strips of the same length but only two rods wide. The strips were not individually fenced but were separated from one another by narrow balks of unplowed turf, on which weeds and brambles grew. This unfenced system is called the open-field system.

The peasant's holding varied from place to place, but the average holding was a vir-

A medieval miniature painting shows serfs at work plowing, harvesting, and gathering fruit.

gate, or thirty acres. ("Virgate" was the term used in England.) The villein's holding was not in one distinct area, for the fertility of the soil did not remain constant throughout the manor. The villein had the hereditary right to the produce of thirty acres, but no two strips of his virgate lay side by side; ten acres were scattered throughout each of the three fields. The villeins worked together in these large fields, the lord usually supplying the heavy plow and the villagers bringing the oxen required to move it, together with tools, such as axes, according to the size of their holdings. The open-field system was therefore a combination of individual ownership and cooperative labor.

The open-field system was cumbersome and wasteful because the land was cut up so minutely into strips with innumerable balks intervening. On the other hand, the system represented a cooperative agricultural enterprise in which all the resources of the manor were pooled. A serious attempt was made to give to all villagers equally fertile land to cultivate. The same spirit of cooperation forms the basis of the huge cooperatives which exist today in the Soviet Union and some other countries, but there, of course, the farm is worked as one large unit, and there are no dividing "strips" which hinder efficiency and cut down productivity. A more direct relative of the feudal system is that still persisting in some parts of Europe where, like their ancestors, the peasants till their crops in long strips with balks between. And reminders of the old French manorial system may still be seen along the St. Lawrence River, where traces of the strip system persist.

Pasture, meadow, wood, and waste lands. Each householder was really a shareholder in the village community, a situation which applied not merely to the open-field system but to the pasture, meadow, wood, and waste lands. Each householder had definite rights in all these divisions of manor lands, and his rights were according to the number of acres he held in the open fields. Each could turn a certain number of animals into the common pasture where they were gathered into one herd and guarded by herdsmen. Pigs foraged in the woods, but each shareholder was limited as to the number of these animals which he might turn loose there. The tenants possessed the privilege of gathering dead wood there also, but the cutting down of green wood was prohibited unless sanctioned by the lord, who was then paid for his permission. The amount of hay produced in the Middle Ages was not large. Consequently meadow land, where the hay was grown, was at a premium. Therefore this meadow land was divided into strips to correspond with each villager's rightful share, and plots were often apportioned by drawing lots.

Administration of the manor. Even though the lord lived on the manor, it was administered through certain of his officials. The most important of these were the steward, or seneschal, the bailiff, the reeve, and the beadle. The steward was the highest of the officials. He was general overseer for all his lord's manors, acted as the lord's legal adviser, supervised the business of the manor by seeing that the usual dues were paid and manorial accounts checked, and presided over the manorial court. The court is an important indication of the lord's independence of the world outside his lands.

Through the steward the lord had complete jurisdiction, civil and criminal, over the nonfree inhabitants on his manor. The peasants acted as jurors in the manorial court, but the prestige of the steward gave him ultimate authority. He usually took into account the findings of the peasant jurors. The court treated civil as well as criminal cases, and the custom of a manor was powerful. Justice was severe. Minor offenses brought in fines to the lord, while poaching, arson, murder, and robbery were rewarded with swift and sure hanging. This system of punishment made the steward a much respected and feared person.

Below the steward was the bailiff, who acted as the lord's personal representative on each manor. While the lord had but one steward, who traveled from manor to manor, he had a bailiff on each of his manors to look after his affairs. It was the bailiff's duty to supervise the cultivation of the demesne, to collect rents, dues, and fines, to keep the manor's financial accounts, and to inspect the work done by the peasants.

The reeve was the "foreman" of the villagers, chosen by them and representing their interests. He was responsible to the lord for the services of the tenants and for seeing that the villeins were at the demesne at the proper time for plowing, sowing, and reaping. He also had to bear to the lord the complaints of the peasants against the other officials and had to cooperate with the bailiff in the distribution of arable land among the peasants and its cultivation.

The people of the manor. It is difficult to draw distinctions between some of the various social classes which made up the manor community because they often blurred into one another. But they can be divided roughly into four major categories: the lord and his officials, the free element, the semi-free group, and the small slave class. All classes except the first belonged to the peasantry, for whether free or unfree they were not members of the political feudal society.

Freemen. There were always freemen on the manor, however small a proportion of its population they may have represented. They differed from the servile groups by being free from the services demanded of the villein and by possessing personal freedom. The freeman did not have to work in the lord's fields himself but could send substitutes. He paid a cash rent for his holding and was free to dispose of his land as he pleased, provided the transfer took place in open court in the lord's presence and the new tenant was acceptable to the lord. Aside from these privileges, however, the freeman was little different from the villein. He had to cultivate strips which adjoined those of the servile worker, and he lived in a cottage in the same village. The freeman class was very small in the twelfth century, but from then on it grew rapidly through emancipation of the lower classes.

Serfs. The semi-free persons of the manor are generally referred to as serfs. These people were bound to the soil of the lord and could not leave the manor without his consent. Serfdom was a hereditary status, the children of a serf being likewise attached to the soil. In the event of a marriage between a serf and a freewoman, the children would generally be considered serfs, although in certain instances such a marriage would elevate the children to the status of freemen. The position of the individuals in question depended upon the local custom of the manor.

Among the semi-free class, however, were certain families who enjoyed privileges not possessed by the common serfs. This upper crust of the serf class was made up of the villeins. "In status the villeins were unfree. They might not leave the manor, marry their daughters to men on other manors or to freemen on the same manor, or send their sons to learn a handicraft or to enter the Church; they might not do these things without securing the lord's permission, usually obtained, however, on the payment of a fine."[15]

In England the words "villein" and "serf" meant the same. Elsewhere, however, the serf held a lower social rank. Whereas the villein was in theory free as to his person and "often resembled rather the Roman *colonus*," the serf, "like the Roman *servus*, was the bodily property of a master."[16] The serf was subject to greater exploitation than the villein and had fewer privileges.

Although the status of the common serf was quite low, he was not a slave. The lord of the manor was bound by the force of custom to respect certain rights of his serfs. So long as they paid him certain dues and labor services, serfs could not be evicted from the lands they cultivated. Although a serf could not appear in court against his lord or against a freeman, he could appeal to the manor court against any of his fellows.

Slaves. In the lowest class of manorial society were the slaves. In most regions they represented a very small proportion of the peasant population. The slave was the absolute chattel of the lord and could be bought and sold without reference to his connection with any particular plot of ground. He possessed no legal personality which would permit him to appear in court. The slave class gradually became extinct in the later Middle Ages, being absorbed by and elevated into the lowest rung of serfdom. Just as the slaves were raised to the status of serfs, so as time went on, the classes of villein and serf tended to merge, the former pulling the latter up to his level and both finally attaining the rank of freemen.

The lord and his privileges. The lord of the manor was its proprietor. In other words, whereas the peasants found in the manor their economic, political, legal, and social life, the lord considered it chiefly as the means whereby he received his income. This income came from obligations imposed on the peasantry, which were divided into three main classes: (1) services rendered in the form of the peasant's own labor, (2) dues levied on the peasant, and (3) manorial monopolies.

The most important personal service was

Schilling's Swiss Chronicle contained this picture of a medieval mint. Strips of metal were flattened, trimmed to coin size, and the faces stamped.

week-work, known in France as the *corvée.* The peasant had to donate his services, consisting of two to three days' work each week for the lord. The lord's demesne had prior rights, and nobody on the manor ever dared argue the point. Involved in the week-work might be the task of repairing roads or bridges or carting manure to the fields. Because the lord's demesne "had always to be plowed first, sowed first, and reaped first," during the season of sowing or harvesting, the peasant was forced to perform extra work, in addition to week-work, called boon-work. He did not get paid for either of the services, but during boon-days his meals were generally provided free by the lord. Serfs and villeins had to contribute their services, while the freemen, exempt usually from week-work, had to provide substitutes to work for them on boon-days.

Various payments were made to the lord, either in money or in produce. The *taille* (or *tallage*) was the most common manorial levy. It could be imposed on grain, stock, chickens, and beeswax, and freeman, villein, and serf were thus taxed one or more times a year. The poor serf was taxable to the limit of the lord's mercy (*taillable à merci*), although the *taille* became a fixed sum for freeman and villein. A burdensome tax was often imposed whenever a peasant died. Before the widow or son could inherit the cottage, the lord claimed, as inheritance tax, the best beast or movable possession. Such a tax was known as the *heriot.*

In addition to services, taxes, and dues the lord received, he was the richer for certain monopolies. A toll was collected each time the serf or villein brought his grain to be ground at the lord's mill, baked his bread in the lord's oven, or used the lord's press for his wine and cider. The peasant was prohibited from taking his grain, flour, or fruit elsewhere, for that would deprive his lord of revenue. Further, since no peasant or group of peasants could have afforded, or would have been allowed, to set up mills, ovens, or presses, the lord's control of these essential services was a monopoly of the most rigid kind. The lord also made money by his monopoly of the right to sell wine at certain times in the village.

Money. Following the fall of the Roman empire, commerce and manufacturing rapidly declined. This tended to restrict the use of money. As most manors were self-sufficient and had little economic contact with the outside world, money was hard to get and equally difficult to use. But while restricted in its use, money never entirely died out in the early Middle Ages. The Frankish kings, for example, had a system of coinage based upon that of the Romans. Since money was scarce in Europe, the peasants usually paid most of their taxes to their lord in produce, but as commerce and city life developed, especially after the thirteenth century, the use of money rapidly increased and it became easier for the peasants to obtain it for payments.

Self-sufficiency of the manor. Economically the manor was almost self-sufficient. The food essential to the sustenance of the population, such as the staple grains, wheat, rye, oats, and barley, could be grown at home. Flax was cultivated where rainfall was sufficient. Among the vegetables most common to the manor were turnips, peas, onions, parsley, sage, celery, beans, and cabbage, while the fruits included apples, quinces, plums, cherries, and pears.

Famines were common, warfare and wolves were a constant threat, grasshoppers, locusts, caterpillars, and rats destroyed crops endlessly. There was no adequate protection against animal diseases. Communication with the outside world was extremely limited, because of bad roads and other dangers of travel. Leather for boots was tanned on the manor, clothing was spun at home, and other necessary communal jobs were performed by the village miller, butcher, carpenter, and smith.

The manor lived on a barter economy, but such commodities as salt, iron, and millstones had to be imported and were generally procured from one of the country fairs. Money did exist although "it was not until towns were well developed, feudalism decaying, and nationalism growing strong, that money economy was enthroned on the manor."[17] Journeys outside the community, as well as the arrival of a pilgrim who had traveled to far-away shrines, or a recent bride from another manor, all gave the inhabitants glimpses of the outside world so that they were by no means completely isolated. But the manor remained the center of the peasants' lives. Many of them never left its confines. The manor was not only a relatively self-sufficient economic and social unit but the judicial, administrative, and religious center as well. The parish priest was the spiritual father, and the small church represented the medieval link between the sorrows of this world and the pleasures of the next.

Peasant life. The life of the peasant was not easy. Men and women alike had to toil long hours in the fields, and the crudity of agricultural implements made their tasks much harder. The squalor of the peasant's life was reflected in his cottage. His home had a wooden frame with mud walls, a clay floor, and a thatched roof. The fire was on a hearthstone, flat on the middle of the floor, and unless the peasant was rich enough to afford a chimney, the smoke escaped through a hole in the roof. The windows had no glass and were stuffed with straw in the winter. Furnishings were meager, consisting usually of a table, a bed, a kneading trough for dough, and a cupboard. The bed was often either a heap of straw or a box filled with straw, and it was used by the entire family. Pigs and chickens wandered about the cottage continually, while the stable was frequently under the same roof, next to the family quarters. It is not difficult to imagine the sights, sounds, and smells that must have greeted the visitor as he picked his way down the crooked village street past the pile of refuse and manure that lay in front of each cottage. The Middle Ages were not clean by our standards, but even by the standards of feudal nobility the peasant was filthy.

The peasant's food was coarse and not overplentiful. He seldom obtained fresh meat and usually had salt pork in its stead. Porridge, soups, and cheese comprised most of his meals, washed down with cheap wine, beer, or cider.

The peasant was illiterate and superstitious. Like almost everyone else, he believed in the power of witchcraft and chanted strange doggerel verses to guard against "spells" or to exterminate such pests as caterpillars and rats:

Aius, sanctus,
Cardia cardiani!
Mouse and she-mouse,
Hamster, mole,
Marmot, cony,
Young and old
Leave the land,
I command.
You are banned!
Up above and down below
From the fields get you hence,
  Pestilence!
Go with you, where'er you go,
Afrias, aestrias, palamiasit![18]

Peasant amusements. There was no love lost between the peasantry and nobility. The latter considered that the serf and villein had been born inferior to themselves in every respect and that God had meant it to be so. Hence the noble and peasant did not share in each other's amusements. But the peasant, despite his hard and monotonous life, was not without compensatory pleasures. The churchyard sometimes witnessed communal dances during the many holy days, and the peasants occasionally traveled to the fairs, which they found exciting. Wrestling was exceedingly popular, as were cockfighting and fighting with quarterstaves, in which both of the contestants stood an excellent chance of getting their heads bashed in. Football of a crude type was played, and everyone attended the pageants and entertainments put on by wandering actors and minstrels.

Around the porch of the parish church the peasants would often congregate to dance and sing. The Church preached in vain against

Although these people are somewhat above the peasant class, their home is still bare of adornment and has very little furniture. This picture is from the House Book of the Cerrutti family, fourteenth century.

"ballads and dancings and evil and wanton songs and such-like lures of the Devil." The peasants refused to give up these amusements, which were little compensation for the constant exploitation which they suffered.

However, it is unwise to generalize too broadly when we evaluate the life of the peasants. Some nobles were kind, and some were merciless, and their tenants suffered or prospered accordingly. While it was bad business to treat one's peasants so poorly that they were rendered unfit for labor, the view generally prevailed that the peasantry should spend their lives toiling for the upper classes.

Peasant revolts. Throughout the Middle Ages the peasants generally remained quiet, although they were discontented and often on the point of revolt. On several occasions they did resort to force in an attempt to better their lot. Serious rebellions of serfs took place in England and France in the fourteenth century and later in central Europe in the sixteenth. During the early part of the fourteenth century a large number of village priests incited the peasants in England to rise and sweep away their unjust masters. The most famous was John Ball, the "Mad Priest," who preached to the peasants that things would not be just until all things were shared in common and all distinctions were leveled. The poem *Piers Plowman* aptly summarized the growing criticism of the peasants toward their lords. The medieval rhyme asked:

> When Adam delved and Eve span,
> Who was then the gentleman?

The Peasants' Revolt in 1381 in England was a great upsurge that threatened for a time to bring about a social revolution. The discontent of the English peasants flared into open revolt in June 1381, and led by their leader Wat Tyler the serfs marched through southeastern England pillaging manor houses and even mobbing one royal chief justice. The masses controlled London for a few days, but gradually the nobles gained command of the situation, and in the end the movement was savagely crushed. In France and Germany on the few occasions when the peasants did revolt, the upper classes likewise crushed the movement with great ferocity. The rights of the common man were not to be recognized for over five hundred years.

The manorial system appraised. Yet the manorial system had many admirable aspects. It fostered the development of the most important of all medieval agricultural contributions, the three-field system. It encouraged cooperation in the tilling of the fields, which gave solidarity to peasant society. That solidarity in turn afforded even the lowliest member of the peasantry an economic security which many a modern farmer or worker would envy. The twentieth-century curse of poverty in the midst of plenty was not the curse of the twelfth-century manor. The latter never had much more than a bare subsistence, but its society tended to suffer or prosper together.

The Revival of Towns and Trade

Cities and civilization. The growth of town life is synonymous with a quickening of the tempo of civilization. The history of man proves this fact, whether we examine the civilizations of Egypt, ancient India, Mesopotamia, Greece, Rome, or Byzantium.

Their large cities have been the focal points of civilization in the past. Today civilization has tended to center in such cities as London, New York, Paris, Berlin, Moscow, Buenos Aires, Sydney, Shanghai, Calcutta, and Tokyo. The city, large or small, has always been the center of new ideas, new inventions, new classes of people, new styles of dress, new tastes in food, new schemes in politics and economics, new ventures in trade, and new contacts in culture. Civilization has experienced more radical changes since the era of the Commercial Revolution in the fifteenth and sixteenth centuries than in all preceding years, and since that time life has become predominantly urban. The city has been one of man's chief aids in creating cultural changes. As we are about to discover, the modern city owes its existence to its medieval ancestor, as does the class of society that has controlled and modified our modern social pattern, the bourgeoisie.

The decline of the Roman city. To understand the importance of the revival of town life in the Middle Ages, we must remember that the civilization of the Roman empire was largely concentrated in cities. With the empire's collapse, trade was disrupted, manufacturing languished, and city life became almost extinct. The pleasant Roman town of Bath in England, for example, became completely depopulated. As for Rome herself, her population declined from about a million to less than fifty thousand.

City life is based on economic specialization. City dwellers concentrate upon the production of certain commodities or engage in wholesale and retail selling and are dependent upon the country for raw materials and for food. At the same time, the farming folk obtain their textiles and other goods from the city. The disruption of trade and the general confusion attending the deterioration of the Roman empire destroyed the complementary economy of town and country. So a back-to-the-soil movement began, and the manorial system arose to take care of the people's economic wants, just as the feudal system, in the absence of strong centralized authority, developed to provide for their political needs.

The rise of the medieval city. In the tenth century towns began to spring up throughout Europe, and by the end of the twelfth they had surpassed many of the cities of the Roman empire in size and prosperity. The renewal of town life occurred first in three areas: northern Italy, Flanders, and southern France.

The Italian towns. Venice in northern Italy has a fascinating history. In the fifth century a group of refugees fleeing from the Huns made their way to the northern shores of the Adriatic. They settled in the midst of mud flats and small islands. Stretching as a barrier between the settlements and the sea were many sand dunes which prevented an attack from pirates, while between them and the mainland was a barrier of lagoons and sandbanks. By 1100 Venice consisted of 117 islands connected by 378 bridges. She controlled a vast fleet of merchant vessels and had achieved a prosperity at once the envy and despair of other towns in Europe.

But Venice was not the only town in northern Italy to achieve importance early in the Middle Ages. Milan by 1200 had a population of 12,000, Genoa had become especially active in the trade of the western Mediterranean, and Pisa and Bologna were also becoming flourishing towns. A little to the south was the important manufacturing center of Florence, soon to become a great banking center. In 1281 its population was about 45,000.

French and Flemish towns. If northern Italy was the most important center of town life in the Middle Ages, Flanders was not far behind. In fact, Flanders has been called the Lombardy of northern Europe. Here a number of towns grew up in the early Middle Ages, mainly because of the manufacture of textiles. Lisle from Lille and cambric from Cambrai soon became famous all over Europe. The raw wool for these textiles was obtained from England. It is known that by 1200 Bruges, Ghent, Lille, and Ypres, all Flemish towns, each had populations of many thousands.

Next in importance to the towns of northern Europe were those in southern France. In such towns on the Mediterranean as Marseilles, trade and manufacturing created prosperous urban centers rivaling those in Flanders and northern Italy.

As the Flemish towns increased in population and wealth, trade and industry spread up the Rhine valley and influenced the growth of such towns as Cologne and Basel. Most of these towns, however, had a population of only 5000 even as late as 1300. The northern German ports of Hamburg, Lübeck, and Bremen had a slightly larger population, perhaps 12,000 at the most. In central France such river towns as Paris, Orléans, and Tours were slowly increasing in importance. London, England's largest center, destined to be the world's greatest metropolis, had fewer than 25,000 inhabitants in 1200.

The origin of the medieval town. Generally speaking, town life in western Europe between 500 and 800 was moribund and of little importance. But the next two centuries saw its active revival, and from 1000 to 1200 the town again became an invaluable agency in the growth of trade, the development of manufacturing, and the nurturing of art and thought. How can the revival of urban civilization be explained? The answer to this question, like the answer to questions about many great historical processes, is not a simple one and can best be given by examining certain basic social, geographical, and economic factors. Let us examine these briefly, keeping in mind that town development differed in various localities according to environment, traditions, and local situations.

Social factors. Perhaps the most striking of the social factors was the growth of population. The population of Europe after the fall of Rome is estimated at 30,000,000, whereas it reached 60,000,000 by 1300. France in 1300 had some 20,000,000 inhabitants, Italy 10,000,000, the Low Countries 3,000,000, and England 2,200,000. England had increased its population only 1,000,000 in the two hundred years from 1100 to 1300. The rapid increase in population has not been satisfactorily explained, but some reasons for it might be the stabilization of feudal society with its furtherance of public safety, the ending of large foreign invasions with their bloodshed and confusion, and a general raising of the standard of living for the common people through increased trade. In any case, the growth of population had an important bearing on the growth of town and commercial activities.

Another social factor was the decline of serfdom, a phenomenon we have already alluded to on page 355. The increase in the number of freemen allowed persons to enter new occupations and migrate to scenes of industrial growth.

Geographical factors. Geography played an important role in the revival of town life. It determined the location of certain strategic towns and conditioned very largely the type of commercial activities in which a town would engage. Just as rivers were important in the growth of ancient civilizations, so rivers played an important role in the development of European towns. They were natural highways on which articles of commerce could be easily transported, and many communities arose to take advantage of a site at the confluence of two important streams. Again, some towns arose where a river might be easily crossed by a ford or bridge, Ox-ford, or Cambridge, for example. Situations at a mountain pass, near natural resources, or on a part of the seacoast which afforded good harbors were also desirable. The location of Italian towns on the great water routes of the Mediterranean, by which trade to the Near East and Africa was open to them, proved of inestimable value. And many towns in Europe grew out of small communities that clustered for protection near some castle already built on a strategic site by mountain or river.

Economic factors. The growth of trade and of manufacturing was probably the most important reason why town life revived. It can be said that town and trade had an interacting influence upon each other, so that the revival of one meant the revival of the other. Throughout the eleventh century there were signs of ever-growing commercial activity, especially in the expansion of special trade routes. Venetian merchants in Italy had been in touch with the Near East since the seventh century, but the dominance of Moslem seapower had for a number of years hindered the growth of a lucrative trade with Constantinople and Asia Minor. In 1002 Venice defeated the Moslems and opened up the eastern Mediterranean. Meanwhile the Italians and Normans swept the Saracen pirates from the western end of the Mediterranean and the Normans conquered Sicily. By 1100 the sea routes to the Near East were open to the Italian merchants, while thousands of pilgrims and the various crusades of the next two centuries added to the new commerce.

Another great system of trade routes opened up now that Asia and Europe were linked together. The new routes ran overland by the old Roman highways that crossed the Alps northward from Italy via passes that led on the west to the Rhone and on the east to the Rhine and Danube valleys. Other land routes followed what are now the southern French and Dalmatian seacoasts. A third great system of trade routes was established by the Vikings in the ninth century, when they made settlements in Russia and created the famous and very lucrative Varangian route, through Russia to the Black Sea and Constantinople. Wherever an important trade route existed, towns sprang up along the way to take care of the commerce.

Throughout feudal Europe there were military strongholds which had been built by various lords for purposes of protection. The German word for such an edifice was *burg*, and the Latin word was *burgus*. The military fort, the typical burg of the ninth and tenth centuries, had no real urban features. But during the next two centuries, when the revival of commerce took place, merchants making their way along the trade routes would seek out a stopping place which would be advantageous to commercial activities and at the same time afford them protection. Therefore they would choose a well-situated burg, and as time elapsed, permanent merchant colonies would grow up at such strongholds. In Flanders, Ghent and Ypres are typical examples of this sort of development. In Germany, Magdeburg and other towns grew up in the same way, while England had such *boroughs* (from *burh*) as Bristol. Sometimes a fortified abbey or cathedral could afford protection, like Durham, "half cathedral and half fortress against the Scot."

In time the merchant population grew too big to be housed within the old burg's walls, and so the merchants established a new burg beyond the walls. This new section, called the *faubourg*, was inhabited by merchants and artisans. The old burg still remained the abode of the noble or bishop with his retinue of soldiers and officials. Therefore when we talk about the origins of the town, we refer to the new burg, which came into existence after the eleventh century, and not to the old burg or fortified section. As time went on, the old stronghold failed to grow larger but the new portion, the trade center, developed into the modern town.

The townspeople. The town was composed mainly of two classes, the artisans, or producers, and the merchants. The artisans composed a majority of the urban population. The revival of trade naturally encouraged the growth of industry and the rise of an artisan class. Many serfs escaped from the manors and made their way to the towns, to become artisans or merchants. After living a year and a day in the town a serf was considered a free man. It became possible for a former serf to become a wealthy and influential craftsman or merchant.

The merchant class was a distinct social group by the twelfth century. It was composed of those traders who lived in one place permanently and those who journeyed from place to place selling their wares. But artisans and merchants alike were under the domination of the lord upon whose domain the city stood. Friction soon arose, for manorial customs differed widely from those of the town. The merchants wanted to be free of the market tolls and dues imposed by the lord, for they did not cultivate the soil and therefore felt that they should not be taxed by the lord like peasants. So the townsmen demanded the privileges of making their own laws and governing themselves, administering justice for themselves, levying their own taxes, and issuing their own coinage. Naturally the feudal lord resented the impertinence of the urban upstarts who dared demand the right of self-government. The entire movement was really the struggle of the new burg to free itself from dependence on the old burg.

The towns' struggle for freedom. The townspeople gained their freedom in the following ways. The expansion of trade during the crusades had made the northern Italian cities large and very wealthy. The merchants resented the dominance of the lord, and they created a "businessman's government" by grouping themselves into associations of free citizens. The united strength of these unions enabled them to wrest concessions from the lord and even to win complete autonomy. A self-governing city of this type was called a *commune*. Often the privileges gained and guaranteed by charter had to be won by insurrection, but at other times they were purchased, for the feudal lord was always in need of money. By 1200 the Lombard towns could boast of communal privileges, while many French and Flemish towns were also communes.

In England, central France, and parts of Germany another technique was used to secure urban autonomy. There the royal authority was strong, and so we find the rise of privileged towns. In a charter granted to the town by

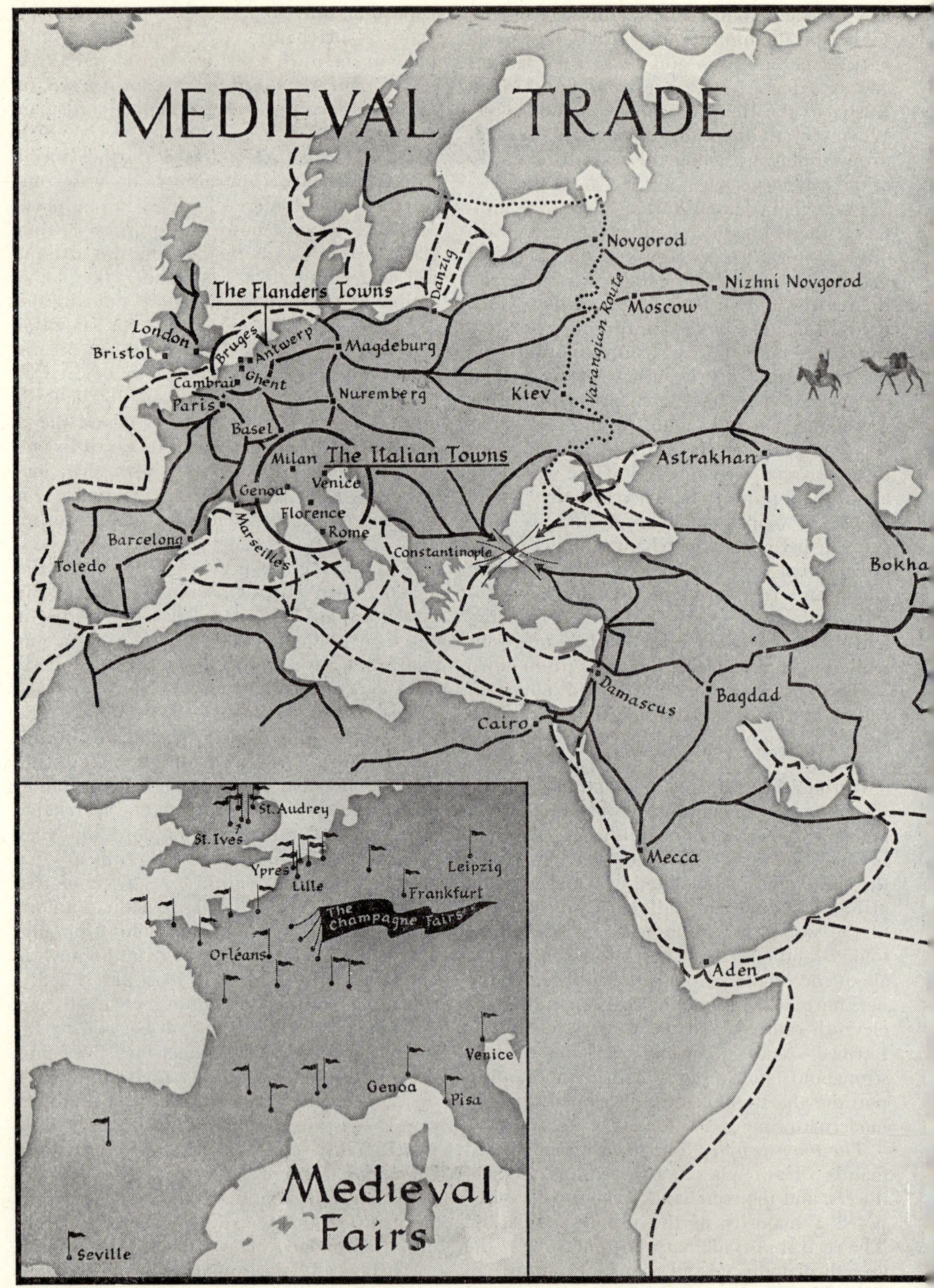

MEDIEVAL TRADE
Novgorod
Nizhni Novgorod
Moscow
Varangian Route
Danzig
The Flanders Towns
London
Bristol
Bruges
Antwerp
Ghent
Cambrai
Paris
Magdeburg
Nuremberg
Kiev
Basel
Milan
The Italian Towns
Venice
Genoa
Florence
Rome
Marseilles
Barcelona
Toledo
Constantinople
Astrakhan
Bokha
Damascus
Bagdad
Cairo
Mecca
Aden
St. Audrey
St. Ives
Ypres
Lille
Leipzig
Frankfurt
The Champagne Fairs
Orléans
Venice
Genoa
Pisa
Seville
Medieval Fairs

The Hanseatic League
Members
Lübeck
Hamburg
Bremen
Danzig
Cologne
SIBERIA
UR-
STAN
MONGOLIA
MANCHURIA
Turfan
Samarkand
Peking
KOREA
NIPPON
MONGOL
CHINA
TIBET
Peshawar
Multan
MOSLEM
INDIA
Canton
China
Sea
MALABAR
CEYLON
Indian
Ocean
EAST
INDIAN ISLANDS
SPICE ISLANDS
R.M.Chapin, Jr.

the monarch the inhabitants won extensive legal and financial powers. The town was given the management of its own fiscal business and paid its taxes in a lump sum to the king. It was also generally given the right to elect its own officials and organize its own guilds. The king often was glad to grant such a charter, for it weakened the power of his nobles and at the same time won the strong support of the townsmen for himself.

Founding new towns was still another way in which people freed themselves of medieval restrictions. By the twelfth century it was obvious that the town was there to stay. Consequently shrewd lords and ecclesiastics, who recognized the increasing importance of cities and the impossibility of checking their development, founded carefully planned centers with well-laid-out streets and open squares. As a means of obtaining inhabitants many inducements were offered in the form of personal privileges and tax limitations. Berlin was such a town.

The triumph of the townsmen in their struggle for greater self-government was significant. It meant that a new class had evolved in Europe, a very powerful, independent, and self-assured class, whose interest in trade instead of warfare was to revolutionize all social and economic history. This class was born of the burg and hence was called burgher or in French, as it is known today, the *bourgeoisie*. The town movement was indeed a people's movement, and with it (if not through it) went the fall of feudalism, the waning of the Middle Ages, and the advent of modern society.

The guilds. We have now seen how the towns won autonomy and how the townsmen emerged as a distinct social class whose prime concern was with commerce and industry. We can logically examine next the means whereby the townsmen organized and administered their own business relations. The association they created for the furtherance of their economic and social interests was called the guild. More important to us than its origins (disputed among scholars) are the economic and social aspects of the medieval guild. The guild was designed to solve all employer-worker problems, regulate prices and wages, govern production and distribution, create a code of fair business practices, protect the individual member as a business associate, and assure the social status of his family.[19] There were two kinds of guilds: merchant and craft.

The merchant guild. The fundamental purpose of the merchant guild was to ensure monopoly of trade within a given locality. Membership was usually limited to merchants of a particular town, although members were sometimes permitted from other places. With a monopoly of the town's import and export trade the guild could enforce its standards as it willed. All alien merchants were supervised closely and made to pay fixed tolls and fees. Weights and measures were also supervised. Disputes among merchants were settled at the guild court according to its own legal code. A standard quality for goods was insisted upon, and a legitimate profit only was allowed by the fixing of a "just price," which should be fair both to the producer and consumer. Three practices in particular were frowned upon, and the guilds did their best to limit their operation; they were forestalling, engrossing, and regrating. The forestaller bought goods on their way to the open market in order to get them more cheaply; the engrosser cornered the market so as to enjoy a monopoly and raise the price; and the regrater bought his commodity wholesale and sold it retail without having made any change in the commodity itself.

The merchant guild was officially separated from the town government, but as the leading members of the guild were generally the officials of the town, the policies of both tended to merge, to the benefit of the guild and sometimes at the expense of the urban populace. The guild performed various social and charitable functions. If a guildsman fell into poverty, he was aided. If he was imprisoned in another town, the guild tried to secure his release, at its own expense. It provided financial assistance in connection with the burial expenses of its members and looked after their dependents. Guildsmen had their own guildhall, where social meetings were held, and each member was expected to attend the feast and "drink the guild" or be fined. The guilds had also a religious side and periodically held processions in honor of their patron saints. They performed such social duties as giving alms to friars and lepers, the poor and sick.

The chief merit of the guild was its emphasis upon fair business practices and its protection to the individual trader, for without the guild he would always have been at the mercy of the local lord. When the guild first grew up, there was no central government adequate to protect merchants as they carried on their trading activities throughout the land. In the absence of national regulation and protection of commerce, the guilds as local agencies had to try to protect their members. Thus if a merchant of a London guild refused to pay a debt owed to a merchant of a guild in Bristol, the merchant guild in the latter town would seize the goods of any London merchant coming to Bristol. Just as political activities were localized in fiefs in the absence of a central government, so the commercial life of a country was decentralized in the hands of the guilds. Thus the fief, the manor, and the guild were all manifestations of one basic characteristic of the Middle Ages —decentralization.

As the Middle Ages drew to a close, when the kings began to assert their power, national regulation of commerce made the guilds less important. By the fifteenth century, when the central government had taken over control of local government and could afford adequate protection, the merchant guild declined to a comparatively unimportant position.

The craft guild. The increase of commerce brought a quickening of industrial life in the towns so that, in the eleventh century especially, an artisan class arose within the city walls. Craftsmen in each of the necessary medieval trades—weaving, cobbling, tanning, and so on—began to organize. The result was the craft guild, which had the same purposes as the merchant guild—the creation of a monopoly and the enforcement of a set of trade rules. But it differed from the merchant guild in that it was limited to one specific trade or craft. Thus the goldsmiths were all together in one guild, the arrow makers in another, and so on with each variety of artisanship. The system created a great deal of specialization, so that a "guild might specialize in a single kind of hat, as the peacock-hatters did." Each guild had a monopoly of a certain article in a particular town, and regulations were enforced to protect the consumer from bad workmanship and inferior materials. Thus articles made at night or in private and out of sight were rightly regarded with suspicion, for as L. F. Salzman points out,

The maker of these larger-than-life thimbles (Nuremberg, fifteenth century) was probably a member of one of the highly-specialized medieval guilds.

"The subtle craft of the London bakers, who, while making up their customers' dough, stole a large portion of the dough under their customers' eyes by means of a little trap-door in the kneading-board and a boy sitting under the counter, was exceptional only in its ingenuity. . . . Cloth was stretched and strained to the utmost and cunningly folded to hide defects; a length of bad cloth would be joined onto a length of superior quality, or a whole cheap cloth substituted for the good cloth which the customers had purchased; inferior leather was faked up to look like the best, and sold at night to the unwary; pots and kettles were made of bad metal which melted when put on the fire; and everything that could be weighed or measured was sold by false measure."[20]

Faulty workmen were fined for the first offense and, if old offenders, were pilloried or banished.

The craft guild had social and religious functions similar to those of the merchant guild. It differed from the merchant guild in that it recognized three distinct classes of workers within its jurisdiction—apprentice, journeyman, and master craftsman. The relationship between the master and his workmen was very personal. The apprentice was a youth who lived at the master's house and was taught the trade thoroughly. Although he received no wages, all his physical needs were supplied. His apprenticeship lasted from three to twelve years, depending upon personal circumstances and the type of craft. When his schooling was finished, the youth became a journeyman, or day worker (from the French *journée* meaning day's work). He was then eligible to receive wages and to be hired by a master for varying periods of service.

When about twenty-three, the journeyman sought admission into the guild as a master. To be accepted, he had to prove his ability and integrity, and in the later Middle Ages some crafts demanded the production of a "master piece," by making, for example, a pair of shoes that the master shoemakers would find acceptable in every way. Unfortunately the master craftsmen in the closing years of the Middle Ages sought to make their rule monopolistic and placed unnecessary restrictions upon the journeymen. Hence the guilds suffered from lack of young blood and new ideas, and rejected journeymen naturally set up their own organizations outside the older guilds. In the fifteenth and sixteenth centuries, the guilds were in the hands of a few wealthy masters who controlled the guild through the election of officials from their own group only. This "top layer" was recognizable by its privilege of wearing the expensive guild dress on festive occasions and hence was called the livery company. Many of these livery companies still exist today as philanthropic groups, and their resplendent medieval dress can still be seen in some of London's civic ceremonies.

The craft guild declined because of its lack of democratic government and because of competition from a new method of production called the domestic system, discussed in a later chapter. But it strove to protect both consumer and producer and prevented the problem with which modern society has been so much afflicted, the conflict between laborer and employer with its bitterness, unrest, strikes, lockouts, and occasional violence.

A typical town. The town usually had three parts, the town proper within its walls, the *faubourgs*, or suburbs, outside the walls, and the *banlieue*, or outer zone, extending for a variable distance on all sides of the town, over which the town had jurisdiction. Within the *banlieue* there were often hamlets under the jurisdiction of town authorities, supplying much of the town's foodstuffs. The early towns had been fortified by walls of wood, but in the twelfth and thirteenth centuries these were replaced with stone structures. The effect of the walls was to constrict the town so much that space was at a premium. Overcrowding prevailed to an extent beyond that of the average modern city, houses were even built on bridges leading into the town (as on the old London Bridge), and buildings were erected to a height of seven or more stories. The houses projected over the street with each additional story so that it was often possible for persons at the tops of houses opposite one another to touch hands.

The streets below were dark and narrow and almost invariably crooked, although they were often designed wide enough "to give passage to a horseman with his lance across his saddle-bows." They were evil smelling because of the refuse that was thrown from the upper balconies into the middle of the lane. To guard the dress of the lady pedestrian her gentleman escort gallantly risked the finery of his own clothes by walking on the outside, a custom that still exists. Likewise men meeting on the street passed one another on the left side in order to give their sword arms free play. When the musket was introduced, it was more natural for men to carry it with the barrel cupped in the left elbow; so the practice arose of passing on the right, a custom which is generally observed except in England.

Because the towns lacked efficient water and sanitation systems, plagues and typhoid fever were constantly carrying off alarming numbers of people. Fire was another perennial curse, sometimes destroying whole towns. The streets were full of discordant sounds—shouts from drivers swearing at pedestrians to step aside (if that was possible) to allow teams of horses and oxen to push through, dogs, pigs, and geese adding their alarms, merchants bawling out their wares, people of every description jostling past one another, and unoiled signs above inns and shops creaking ominously in the wind and constantly threatening to crash down on the skull of some innocent passer-by.

However, some efforts were made in the medieval town to reduce confusion and bad smells. As early as 1388 in England a sanitation act was passed in an attempt to prevent the pollution of streams and ditches. Similarly, an act was passed to cause the removal of the tanning industry to the outermost part of the town because of the stench it created. But complaints were sometimes voiced regarding the effects of the smoke of pit coal. Thus, what is "an urgent problem of the present day was already a subject of complaint some six hundred and fifty years ago, when Queen Eleanor of Provence, the pious but asthmatic wife of Henry III, was driven away from Nottingham by the poisonous fumes of coal fires."[21]

Size of the town. The medieval city was not large by modern standards. It has been estimated that Paris by 1450 had grown to 300,000, which made it the largest city in Christian Europe. Among the leading metropolises was Cordova in Spain. In 1400 London had merely 40,000 inhabitants, while only two cities in Germany, Cologne and Nuremberg, could boast of being above the 20,000 mark. But the medieval city had inhabitants who were intensely loyal and prided themselves upon their civic liberties. Townsmen of various places vied with each other in the erection of beautiful and costly cathedrals (especially in France), and cities came to boast of their new university or a superbly built town hall which housed their civic government. These were justifiable boasts, for the towns quickened the intellectual and political pace of medieval society.

Town government. Municipal government consisted generally of a town council elected by the burghers for one year. The town councils were the first examples of popular representation in western Europe. They performed services in matters of defense, charity, public works, and the regulation of trade and industry.

Amusements. The townspeople did not lack for amusements. On the many holidays the apprentices and youths would play at tilting, wrestling, and other sports in both the neighboring countryside and in the streets themselves. It is amusing to note that in London wrestling had to be forbidden in St. Paul's churchyard, while sports of a raucous nature were prohibited in Westminster when Parliament was in session. Football was an exciting and irresponsible pastime in which huge numbers of ardent souls divided themselves into two sides and attempted to push the ball through the narrow and congested streets, with devastating results.

"Bowls and quoits, played down the streets, doubtless relieved life of its monotony, but also occasionally relieved an unwary pedestrian of his life altogether, and were, therefore, not encouraged in towns. In the winter, when the marshes were covered with ice, the young men would fasten to their feet rough skates made of the leg-bones of animals, and, propelling themselves with iron-shod poles, shoot across the ice, tilting at one another, to the breaking of many heads and limbs."[22]

The townspeople loved pageants and attended mystery and miracle plays held in the streets and open spaces. Masquerades, royal and civic processions, dancing in the open, and drinking bouts were tremendously popular. In fact the city of Nuremberg had a special wagon for picking up inebriates.

Travel in medieval times. The revival of commerce throughout Europe was largely responsible for the revival of town life. Trade was carried on by peddlers and at fairs and markets. If we were to step beyond the city walls and journey into the country to the famous medieval fairs, we should encounter numerous difficulties of travel. The roads were full of ruts and in winter became bogs and quagmires, for the fine system of Roman roads had all but disappeared. Probably we should travel by horseback (if we were nobles) or by foot or cart. Vehicles were clumsy, heavy, and springless. Often there was no bridge at a stream and it became necessary to ford it. If there was a bridge, it was likely to be quite unsafe, unless workmen from some monastery had repaired its foundation. Bridge tolls were high, as one might expect them to be when levied by the rapacious noble through whose domain we should have to pass.

If we had merchandise which we hoped to sell at the fair, we should be wise to attach ourselves to the retinue of a noble traveling in our general direction, for the roads were infested with bandits, runaway slaves and serfs, starving villeins, idle mercenary soldiers, and robber knights whose code of chivalry did not extend down to the peasantry or townspeople. If we decided to journey by river, we should frequently find chains strung across the stream by nobles who levied tolls on all passers-by. If we were crossing from England to the continent, we would very likely confess our sins and offer candles at a seaside shrine, for the ships were unsafe little craft and ran the continual risk of pirates. If the ship should be driven ashore in a storm, we might have our cargo confiscated under the pernicious "law of wreck," which gave the lord upon whose shore we were cast the right to keep all merchandise. Profits encouraged gangs of professional wreckers purposely to change lights on the seacoast to lure vessels to their graves, while the wreckers made certain that no survivor would recount the incident.

The fair. But if the traveler were not too unlucky, he might manage to get safely to the fair. The fair differed from the market, which was a distinctly local affair held about once a week to allow the peasants to dispose of surplus goods from the manor and obtain manufactured goods from the town. The fair was a much more important and elaborate event, held in certain specified areas in each European country only seasonally or annually. To the fairs came products from all over Europe, and these gatherings did much to promote industry and agriculture. Strict regulations governed fair activities—stall locations, the days and hours when certain types of goods might be sold, the acceptable weights, measures, and coinage, and the proper forms which made transactions and contracts valid. Fees and fines were also fixed, and a special tax was paid by the Jews. The regular laws governing the region were set aside when the fair was held, and in their place was substituted a commercial code called the law merchant. Special courts settled all disputes which arose. In England they were called pie-powder courts, from the French *pied-poudré*, dusty foot.

The receipts from the courts, together with the local fees and taxes, went into the coffers of the lord in whose territory the fair was being held. This was a prime reason why the holding of fairs was so encouraged. The most famous fairs in all Europe were held in Champagne in northeastern France, but there were many others: Leipzig and Frankfurt in Germany, Venice and Genoa in Italy, Ypres and Lille in the Low Countries, Seville in Spain, and St. Ives in England. The word "tawdry" is derived from a corruption of the words "St. Audrey," the name of a medieval English fair where cheap goods were often sold.

The fair was of great value. It was a clearing house for both goods and ideas. Men from all over Europe congregated and exchanged information about new methods in industry and transportation. The fairs were largely responsible for the growing use of bills of exchange, letters of credit, and a money economy. They helped break down the provincialism of the manor and the isolation of the town.

The Hanseatic League. The merchants were a new element in the medieval pattern of society. In establishing their rights and seeking privileges in foreign towns they often banded together for mutual benefit and protection. In similar fashion groups of towns occasionally joined forces to establish their merchants in foreign towns and win them preferred treatment. During the thirteenth century such a confederacy, called the Hanseatic League, originated among north German trading cities, including Cologne, Lübeck, Danzig, and Hamburg. As the League grew in strength it began to include other large river towns. It established permanent trading stations in such leading European centers as London and Bruges and in strategic locations like Novgorod, key town for Russian trade. As political authority in Germany was weak, the Hanseatic League built up its own navy to safeguard its commerce from pirates and even waged successful wars against Denmark. It had a representative diet, or assembly, for dealing with trading problems common to all member cities. Its wealth came primarily from its monopoly of the Baltic herring fisheries, its control of Russian trade, and its rich trade with England and the Low Countries. The League controlled trade on the Baltic and North seas and was a great distributor for northern Europe until the fifteenth century.

Summary

The castle, manor, and town represent three great medieval institutions. With the castle we associate feudalism, a political system of decentralization of power which brought a measure of order to the chaos that engulfed Europe after the collapse of the Carolingian empire. The feudal system involved a social and political hierarchy in which there existed lords and vassals according to a complicated system of loyalty and land tenure.

With the castle too we link its lordly inhabitants and the social code known as chivalry. The castle epitomizes the power of the aristocracy.

Evolving independently of feudalism but linked to it economically was the manor. The manor's origins appear to be Roman (the villa) and German (the *mark*). The most important advance in agriculture, the three-field system, was developed on the manor. Most manors were practically self-sufficient. Under the supervision of the lord and his staff, food was raised, clothing was made, and justice was administered. The village priest watched over the welfare of the people. While most of the common people lived in superstition and squalor, their lives were not wholly without gaiety or comfort.

The castle and the manor passed away in time because of the rise of the national state and because of the growth of trade and industry which made possible the introduction of a money economy and the increase of freemen. But the third institution, the town, continued to flourish, until today our culture is more urban than rural. The medieval town lived primarily by its trade and industry. The townsmen had to struggle for their freedom against the feudal lords. Their victory marks the rise of a new class which increasingly dominated the affairs of modern life—the bourgeoisie, or middle class. The townsmen were organized into merchant and craft guilds according to their profession. The guilds regulated trade and industry, maintaining standards and privileges as well. Life in the medieval town was colorful and interesting, much more attractive than the drab existence led by the manorial peasants. In a rather static and stratified society, the townspeople were an alive and changing element.

We seem removed from the medieval castle, manor, and town, perhaps, until we discover that the people who lived there were as human as we. We can feel the resentment of the serf through whose painfully tilled fields the nobles swept in search of sport, and we can laugh at the games of the manor villein and the pranks of the town apprentice. But our bonds with the Middle Ages go much deeper. The code of chivalry, despite its artificiality and limited scope, has lived on in modified form and affected our social behavior. The farm measurements of the manor are the same measurements which we use today. The development of the three-field system made possible an agricultural revolution whose benefits we are still reaping. Finally, the medieval town, with its emphasis upon individual initiative and rights and its shattering of traditions, was the melting pot of revolutionary forces from which the urban civilization which we know has arisen.

Chronology of events and developments discussed in this chapter

Chapter 14

Coronation of Charlemagne by the Pope	800
Religious revival: monasteries; clerical reform; Crusades	900-1100
Holy Roman Empire created: Otto the Great crowned in Rome	962
Gregory VII: enforced clerical celibacy and papal power; fought simony, lay investiture	1025-1085
College of Cardinals created: electors of the Pope; administrators	1059
Gregory VII deposed lay invested clergy	1075
Henry IV: humbled by Gregory at Canossa; papal victory	1077
Council of Clermont: Pope Urban II called the First Crusade	1095
Crusades: Holy Land held by Seljuk Turks; diffusion of Moslem commerce	1096-1291
Cistercian rule founded: monastic reform	1098
Latin kingdom of Jerusalem: established by the First Crusade	1099-1187
Concordat of Worms: settled investiture controversy	1122
Innocent III: height of papal power	1161-1216
Waldensian heresy: objected to wealth and hierarchy of the Church	1173
Lombard League, supported by the Pope, defeated Frederick I	1176
St. Francis: founded the mendicant preaching Franciscan order	1181?-1226
"Crusade of Kings": pilgrims allowed to visit Jerusalem	1189
Fourth Crusade: Venetian mercantile competition destroyed	1198
Dominican order: educators; theologians; led the Inquisition	1206
Crusade against the Albigensian heretics in Toulouse	1208
England under interdict: England returned to King John as a fief	1208
Lateran Council: Otto IV deposed; Frederick II made emperor	1215
Frederick II: ward of Innocent III; resisted later Popes	1220-1250
Last Christian state in the East fell to the Turks	1291

Bishop, priest, and monk

The medieval Church: fifth century to 1300

The Middle Ages have been called the Age of Faith. Nevertheless there were many conflicts of authority and many religious heresies. The fundamental difference between that time and ours is one of perspective. Today science and the affairs of the world in which we live tend to monopolize our attention. In the Middle Ages people were concerned mainly with religion and the life of the world-to-come. Again—and this is important to appreciate—we no longer possess the unity of intellectual purpose which the Middle Ages knew. We now have outstanding thinkers interested in scientific discoveries and outstanding thinkers interested in religious and philosophical problems, and very often there is a definite conflict of opinion and purpose between such men. In the Middle Ages such a situation was virtually impossible. The greatest thinkers were enlisted on the side of the Church. Even as brilliant a scientist as Roger Bacon believed that theology was the science of sciences and that his chief task was to increase its usefulness and to broaden its scope. It would be impossible today to find such an attitude among our best scientists. But the Middle Ages saw no conflict between the Church and learning. With relatively few exceptions, everyone believed that the Church was universal, that its powers were God-given, and that all human knowledge could be reconciled with its creed and dogmas.

We must also realize at the outset that the Christianity in the Middle Ages was not a go-to-church-on-Sunday affair. It was extraordinarily vivid and real. We shall see that the sacraments and services of the Church were considered the most vital aspects of living, for they assured the participant of eternal salvation, and salvation was the goal of everyone. The sermons of the age abounded with vivid descriptions of hell, devils prodding or devouring howling, tortured sinners, and brimstone and smoke rising in clouds out of the seething pit. Descriptions of heaven were as vivid; salvation assured the happy soul of "a splendour that is sevenfold brighter and clearer than the sun." The Church guaranteed our ancestors this destination in return for an acceptance of its teachings. How could our forefathers fail to accept the teachings and the protection of the Church? During the Middle Ages almost every person in western Europe was automatically a member of one Church. He was born into it and he died in it, and membership, in return for an unswerving allegiance to the power and purpose of the Church, assured him the priceless gift of salvation.

It is now our purpose (1) to trace the genesis and growth of the Church as an all-powerful universal organization, (2) to examine the methods by which the Church obtained such complete mastery over the spiritual and secular lives of all Christians, (3) to witness the triumph of the Church as the most powerful temporal institution in medieval Europe, together with its gradual decline, and (4) to appreciate the multitude of ways in which medieval life centered about the universal Church.

How the Church Came to Be Universal

Aspects of Christianity. In Chapter 8 we saw how the Christian religion triumphed throughout the western world, evolving slowly and tortuously from a despised and hunted sect to the state religion of the Roman empire. When we examine medieval Christianity, we should think of it in three distinct aspects: (1) as a religion only, the personal faith in a divine Saviour and the desire to enter into conscious affinity with God, (2) as a Church, an organization, an ecclesiastical system, an actual government based on definite political and religious beliefs, and (3) as theology, an attempt to fit the teachings of Christ into a logical system of beliefs. Without a complex church organization and a definite theology, Christianity as a simple religion could never have endured the chaos and conflict of the centuries immediately following the decline of the Roman empire.

The organization of the Church. The medieval Church was to be found in every hamlet; its influence was felt by every inhabitant. To maintain its universality and power, the Church had a highly organized administrative system. The strength of the Church in the Middle Ages was in large measure the result of its strong personal link with every man, woman, and child under its jurisdiction. This link was forged in the parish, the smallest area of jurisdiction of the Church.

The laity. The largest single group within the medieval Church was the lay population. Every child of Christian parents was automatically born into the Church, just as today he is born into a nation. The Church was official and public, and therefore all the people contributed to its upkeep by taxes. Each person was subject to both its religious and its secular authority, for it was binding upon every ruler to enforce obedience to the one Holy Apostolic Universal Church. Thus the Catholic Church was an all-embracing institution, resting on divine foundation and authority, buttressed by secular powers, and including almost the entire population of western and central Europe.

The parish priest. If we were to walk down the single street of a manorial village, we could not help noticing the parish church at the end of it. The priest's house, close to the church, would be little larger or better constructed than the average serf's cottage. A few weeks' observation would soon make us realize that the parish priest was the most important single character in the manor (often identical with the parish in area), not by reason of rank or social prestige, but because of the service he rendered to the common man.

The priest was generally of humble birth, with little education. Nevertheless he won the respect of his parishioners by the faithful performance of his many duties. He administered the sacraments, had an eye for the moral behavior of his flock, and helped the sick. He was father-confessor, social worker, policeman, and recreational director, all rolled into one. After Sunday service, he often organized games on the village green or judged archery contests. He sometimes felt called upon to threaten with the pains of purgatory a husband who had become known as a wife beater. On occasion he censured a nagging wife whose rasping tongue was sending her husband too frequently to the tavern. Some of the parish priests saw many years of service in the same parish and were loved by their flock as friend and counselor. The ambitious young serf could whisper into the sympathetic ear of the priest his plans to run away to a nearby town to escape from serfdom, or a lovesick lad might unburden his heart and seek advice from the priest as to how he might gain the favor of his sweetheart.

Though some of the parish clergy were guilty of keeping concubines, drinking and gambling, and even selling the sacraments for money, the majority were a credit to their Church. Chaucer's most sympathetic character sketch pertains to the "poure" parson.

Wide was his parish, houses far asunder,
But never did he fail, for rain or thunder,
In sickness, or in sin, or any state,
To visit to the farthest, small and great,
Going afoot, and in his hand a stave.
This fine example to his flock he gave,
That first he wrought and afterwards he
taught;

. . . .

There is nowhere a better priest, I trow.
He had no thirst for pomp or reverence,
Nor made himself a special, spiced conscience,
But Christ's own lore, and His apostles' twelve
He taught, but first he followed it himselve.[1]

The bishop. Leaving the manor with its busy priest, we might then proceed to the nearby town, in which lived the bishop. This official was responsible for the administration of a diocese, a church unit made up of many parishes. A bishop was indeed an exalted person. He was, in fact, a prince of the Church. In the early days, when the church organization was forming, there came to be established in the larger cities the authority of the bishop, consisting of administrative control in religious matters over the area known as the diocese. During the fourth and fifth centuries these bishops were granted judicial power in civil as well as ecclesiastical matters, and in time they displaced the Roman governors in importance. Throughout the Middle Ages the ranks of the bishops were largely recruited from the European aristocracy. The bishops thus tended to side with the conservative nobles, since they were in the same social class. These churchmen even maintained elaborate retinues befitting their high position.

The bishops were great landowners. They held large tracts of land under feudal tenure. This meant, of course, that in addition to his religious duties the average bishop had to carry out the normal activities of a feudal vassal. These activities included liability for military service, and a few churchmen actually fell in battle fighting for their lords. By possessing land, the bishop was part of the secular machinery of the state. As part of the feudal system he was expected to have a lord, possess vassals of his own, and be true to his lord. On the other hand, he was a member of the Church, an organization that demanded his full loyalty. The Middle Ages seemed to forget the New Testament writ that "no man can serve two masters." The conflict of loyalties caused much bitterness between the lay lords and the Church. In the ordinary routine of the feudal system, when a lord died, his heir automatically succeeded to his fief, but a bishop or other churchman holding feudal land had no legal heir, and a new selection was therefore necessary. The chief problem in connection with the selection of this successor was the identity of the person making it, the lay lord or some authority such as the Pope.

Although the bishop did not come into intimate contact with the common people as did his parish priests, he was nevertheless a very busy man. His days were occupied with ordaining priests, visiting abbeys, dedicating new churches, and administering discipline to wayward priests. Towering above the city in which the bishop lived was his church, the cathedral. These great edifices of Romanesque or Gothic architecture were the most imposing buildings in medieval Europe. Not far from the cathedral was the court of the bishop, where canon law, the law of the Church, was enforced. Most cases tried here concerned charges of heresy, misconduct of priests, adultery, and matters pertaining to contracts, wills, and dowries. The bishop also had his cathedral school, the most important educational agency in medieval society until the rise of the universities.

The archbishop. Many miles away from the cathedral town of the bishop was the seat of the archbishop, who administered a province consisting of several bishoprics. In early times the bishops of the larger towns had naturally wielded greater powers than some of their brother bishops. Thus the bishops of these important centers came to have jurisdiction over whole provinces and were placed over each bishop whose diocese lay within their province. The archbishop often had a magnificent cathedral in keeping with his exalted rank. From time to time the king consulted him on important problems. The archbishop was supposed to call an annual provincial council so as to announce papal messages and decrees. In addition he had to consecrate bishops and preside over his court, where cases appealed from the bishop's court were reviewed.

The Pope. Above the archbishops was the supreme head of the Church—the Pope, or Bishop of Rome. Not until the fifth century, when Emperor Valentinian III ordered all bishops to give obedience to the Bishop of Rome, did the headship of the latter originate. But it was logical that the Bishop of Rome should be the Pope. Rome was the greatest city in the empire and had existed for centuries as capital of the Roman world. Perhaps of even greater importance was the famous Petrine theory. According to church teachings, the Apostle Peter was the first Bishop of Rome. Now the Lord had said:

> "And I say also unto thee, That thou art Peter, and upon this rock I will build my church; and the gates of hell shall not prevail against it.
>
> "And I will give unto thee the keys of the kingdom of heaven: and whatsoever thou shalt bind on earth shall be bound in heaven: and whatsoever thou shalt loose on earth shall be loosed in heaven."[2]

The Petrine theory maintained that all subsequent Bishops of Rome, as heirs to Peter (the first Bishop) also possessed this same power which the Lord had given to Peter.

Because of the size of the Church it was imperative that the Pope have a court, called the *Curia,* to assist him. The leading churchmen of the *Curia* were called cardinals, who, sitting together as a College (the body created in 1059), elected the new Pope. By the thirteenth century the *Curia* had developed three important departments. The *Chancery* concerned itself with all judicial matters, including the preparation of papal bulls. (A bull is a solemn letter or promulgation of the Pope to which is always attached an official leaden seal, the *bulla.*) The *Penitentiary* wielded the Church's two great weapons for enforcing obedience, the interdict and excommunication. The third department was the *Camera* (chamber) whose duty it was to collect and disburse papal revenues.

When we reflect that the whole of Europe was divided into a number of great provinces, each administered by a powerful archbishop, we can picture the vast army of Christendom in which the authority of the Pope descended through cardinals, archbishops, bishops, and parish priests and through them was diffused throughout Europe. Political boundaries were no obstacle to the authority of the Church. Every man, whether he was born in England, France, or Italy, was expected to give his first loyalty to the international Church. Such was the Church—with its own courts, with thousands of official workers, and with rich sources of revenue. No wonder that when the kings began to try to increase their power and make their commands absolute within the confines of their countries a struggle was precipitated between the universal Church and the rising national monarchs.

Early monasticism. The clergy we have discussed so far, those who administered the Church's services and teachings among the laity, were known as the secular clergy. But another branch had developed outside the ranks of the ecclesiastical hierarchy. To many of the faithful, the Church's complex administrative powers and the growth of a rigid theology meant a serious departure from the simple teachings of the New Testament. As early as the third and fourth centuries the common charge was that the Church had become as worldly as the rich men whom Christ had condemned. Besides those who wanted simplicity in church matters, there were others who wanted to lead a life of contemplation away from the noise and temptations of the world. The individuals who did so became

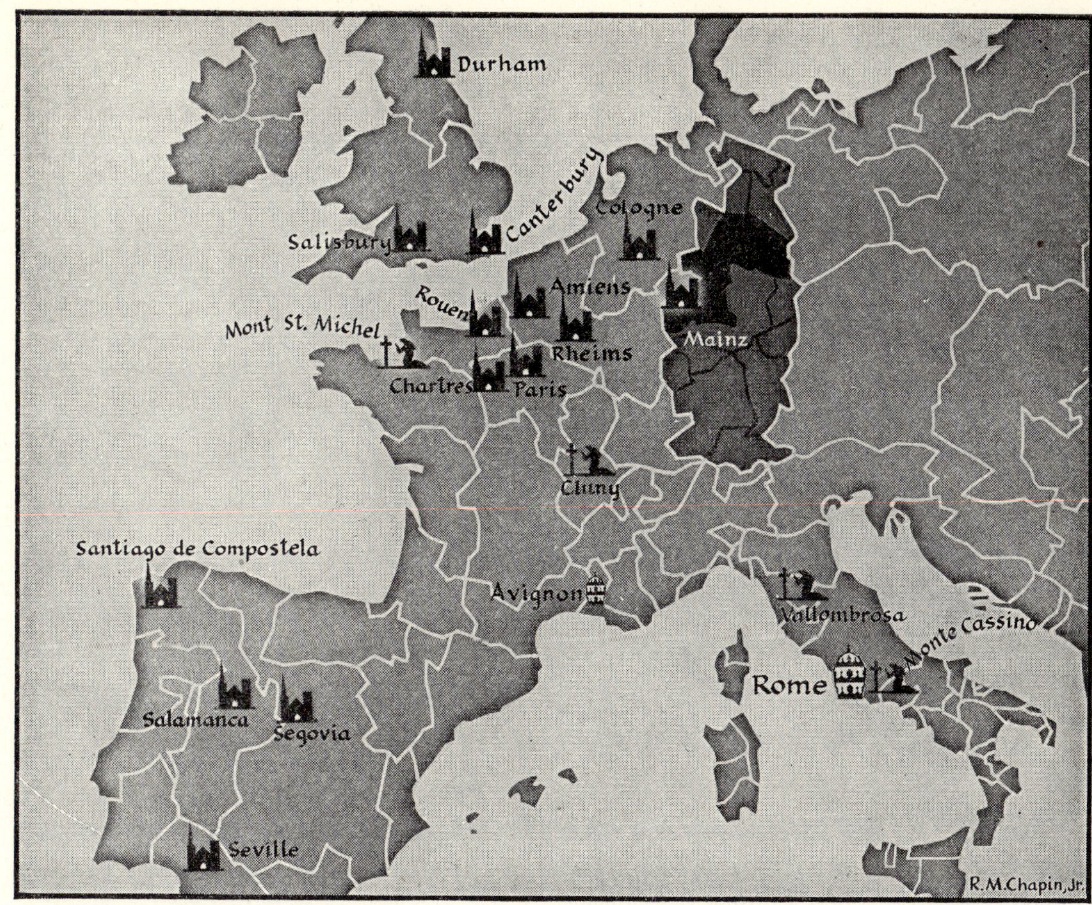

The Church as an all-embracing spiritual organization divided Europe into ecclesiastical provinces as shown on this map. A province was subdivided into dioceses, each administered by a bishop. The province of Mainz (darker area) is shown divided in this manner. The archbishop of Mainz had jurisdiction over all the bishops of the province and in addition administered the black area directly as bishop himself.

known as ascetics and monks. The life of Christ in many ways fitted into such a pattern.

"Alone among all the great religious teachers of the world, He never was married. He was heralded by the Baptist hermit. He spent much of His time in lonely contemplation among the deserts. . . . He told a rich young man who wished to be perfect that he might go, sell everything he had and give to the poor. His teachings are full of exhortations that are admirably appropriate to monks and yet in some cases very hard sayings to those who live in the world."[3]

In the east, where it originated, asceticism took many extreme forms. In third-century Egypt the hermit, or anchorite, would abandon the world entirely, denouncing even beauty as evil, and in the midst of filth would try to starve or torture himself into a state of holiness. In Syria the mania for self-torture took the strange form of dwelling on pillars. The most famous of the pillar saints was St. Simeon Stylites, who dwelt for thirty years on the top of a pillar sixty feet high, braving the utmost rigors of pain and inclement weather. St. Simeon attracted great crowds who came from far away to stare at him.

Regular clergy. However, such extreme asceticism brought about a reaction, and Christians in Egypt developed the monastic life, wherein men seeking a common spiritual goal lived together under a common set of regulations. These monks were known as the regular clergy, because they lived according to a rule (*regula*). St. Basil (about 329-379), a Greek from Asia Minor, is to be remembered for his

Jean Mielot, secretary to Philip the Good, is copying a fine manuscript in his scriptorium. Producing such books as these sometimes required a lifetime of painstaking effort. Most medieval books were made by monks.

splendid pioneering work in the organization of monastic life. He substituted hard labor, works of charity, and a communal life for the asceticism of the hermit. The *Rule* of St. Basil to this day remains the standard life in all the monasteries of the Eastern Church.

Monasticism spread westward to Italy from Egypt and was popular by the close of the fourth century. In the west organized monasticism rather than extreme asceticism won lasting approval. Religion in the Near and Far East has always been more introspective and, one might say, less practical than in the west. The famous organizer in the west was St. Benedict (about 480-543). About 520 he led a band of devoted followers to a hill named Monte Cassino, where they built a monastery. There Benedict composed a set of monastic rules whose effect upon subsequent religious life is incalculable.

The Benedictine Rule. In the Prologue to his *Rule* St. Benedict stated that he was founding "a school for the Lord's service, in the organization of which we trust that we shall ordain nothing severe and nothing burdensome." He admitted that the rule might be at first "a trifle irksome," but its disciplinary measures would insure a proper monastic life and a good preparation for the way of salvation.

The novice desiring entrance to the monastic life had to take the vows of poverty and obedience to the abbot, the head of the monastery. Benedict assumed that as the monk had forever abandoned the life of the world he would remain true to the ideal of chastity. The daily routine of the brothers was carefully worked out in the Benedictine system. Divine worship was the chief duty to be performed, and to that end the monks were to take part in eight daily services or "offices," beginning with Matins "at the eighth hour of the night" (after sunset), followed by Lauds at daybreak, and closing with Complin at dusk.

Thus, something like eight hours of unbroken sleep was allowed to the conscientious performer.

Some excerpts from Benedict's *Rule* throw light on his monastic ideals. A monk "should have absolutely not anything; neither a book, nor tablets, nor a pen—nothing at all. For indeed it is not allowed to the monks to have their own bodies or wills in their power. . . . Indeed we read that wine is not suitable for monks at all. But because in our day it is not possible to persuade the monk of this, let us agree at least as to the fact that we should not drink till we are sated, but sparingly. . . . Idleness is the enemy of the soul. And, therefore, at fixed hours, the brothers ought to be occupied in manual labor; and again at fixed times in sacred reading."[4]

The *Rule* also stressed the value of manual work, six or seven hours of daily labor being required. The daily fare was plain, consisting mainly of a vegetarian diet (except for invalids). The *Rule* insured a simple, virile, and useful life when properly carried out and enabled the monasteries to make innumerable contributions for centuries in the realms of agriculture, animal husbandry, architecture, and learning. The Church recognized the merits of Benedict's *Rule* by endorsing his system as the universal one, a model monastic pattern.

Militant orders of monks. Besides the monks who lived in fixed abodes, there were two other main branches of monastic life. First of all, there were militant orders of monks who organized crusades, bore arms, and tended the holy places connected with the life of Christ. Among these were the Templars, the Hospitallers, and the Teutonic Knights. The latter order undertook to convert the heathen Slavs of eastern Europe and establish themselves as the military rulers of the Prussians.

The begging friars. The second group arose in the thirteenth century, largely as a protest against the growing worldliness and laxity of the medieval Church. The monks in this group were known as the begging friars, or mendicants, because they possessed no fixed abode but wandered through the countryside preaching to the people and depending upon alms for a living.

The two great orders of begging friars are the Franciscan, founded by St. Francis of Assisi (1181?-1226), friend of criminal and leper, and lover of "birds of the air" and "beasts of the field," and the Dominican, whose practical founder, St. Dominic, emphasized the value of preaching. Some of the most brilliant medieval scholars and Popes were members of these two humble orders, Roger Bacon being a Franciscan and St. Thomas Aquinas a Dominican. We shall say more about the two orders later in the chapter, when we discuss the subject of medieval reform.

The Church's Methods of Salvation

The purpose of the Church. Up to this point we have seen how the Church came to be the only religious institution in western Europe and how it developed its complex and all-embracing administration. But for what purpose did it exist?

The Church was the agency of Christ. It alone could interpret and carry out the instructions of its founder. It alone possessed the means necessary for salvation. The individual was helpless and could not secure salvation without belonging to the Church. In a word, the Church was the essential intermediary between God and man.

The Middle Ages had as a primary objective the preparation for an afterlife. To die safely rather than to build up earthly treasures or gain fame was the goal of every true Christian.

According to the Church, salvation was achieved through the performance of certain ceremonies. These were found mainly in the sacramental system. The nature and process of salvation was expounded by an elaborate system of thought known as theology—the evaluation of man's relationship to God, together with the study of the reasons for man's existence. It should be noted that a unified system of theology scarcely took definite shape until the thirteenth century, when canon law, papal administration, and the works of such theologians as Peter Lombard, Albert the Great, and St. Thomas Aquinas established a fairly harmonious system of theology.

Theology. Salvation was the object of living, and therefore the main tenets of medieval theology center about the means of achieving salvation. Man had originally lived in a state of perfection. But Adam and Eve of their own free will fell from the perfect state and so lost Paradise. Furthermore, Adam bequeathed to his children the taint of original sin, and they bequeathed it in turn to their descendants. Thus all the human race was damned from the outset. Jesus, the Son of God, sacrificed Himself upon the cross at Calvary in order that He might atone for the sins of mankind, and through His sacrifice God again gave to man an opportunity to win eternal perfection. But—and this was paramount in the minds of every medieval person—salvation was won only by the grace of God, and salvation came only to the man who believed in redemption through the atonement made on the cross by Christ.

Each man, therefore, had to act if he were not to be damned forever. However, since he could perform no act worthy of salvation without divine grace, how was this to be earned? The theologians taught that God bestowed His grace on man by means of the Church and its officials, for (according to the Petrine theory) the successors of Peter held the very keys of salvation. The Church created definite ceremonies by which men secured grace. These ceremonies are known as sacraments, "the outward and visible signs of invisible grace."

The sacraments. By the twelfth century, these sacraments had been limited to seven, a number made official in the fifteenth century.

As Pope Eugene IV wrote in 1438: "There are seven sacraments under the new law: that is to say, baptism, confirmation, the mass, penance, extreme unction, ordination, and matrimony . . . these our sacraments both contain grace and confer it upon all who receive them worthily."[5]

In *baptism* the taint of original sin was washed away, and the person was given a Christian name (hence "christening"). *Confirmation* took place during the period of adolescence and was intended to strengthen the character of the youth during his formative years. *Penance* was designed to remove personal sins committed after baptism. Penance depended upon three elements. The first was contrition, which involved a turning away from sin and a sense of shame. The second was oral confession, in early times made publicly, but later made to a father confessor. The third element was satisfaction, by which the penitent made restitution for his wrongs in any way which his confessor suggested, such as prayer, fasting, almsgiving, or pilgrimages. For those penalties imposed but not discharged before death, a stay in purgatory was necessary.

The most important sacrament was the *Holy Eucharist*, or Lord's Supper. In the Fourth Lateran Council of 1215, the full teaching of the Church regarding the Eucharist was set forth. The dogma of "the real presence of the incarnate Christ by the process of transubstantiation" was there affirmed. No proper appreciation of the ceremony of the Mass can possibly be obtained unless the significance of transubstantiation is understood. According to this doctrine, when the priest pronounces over the bread and wine the age-old words of Christ, "For this is My body. . . . For this is the chalice of My blood," a miracle takes place. To all outward appearances, the bread and wine appear unchanged, but in "substance" they have been transformed into the very body and blood of the Saviour. The laity used to receive both the wine and bread. However, the spilling of the wine—now become Christ's blood—led to the practice of the priest drinking the wine for them.

Marriage was sanctified by a sacrament. The Church preferred celibacy as an ideal, but without marriage there would soon be no Church at all. Marriage within certain degrees of family relationship was strictly forbidden.

Extreme unction was the sacrament administered at the time of death and was designed to give the Christian comfort as to his chances of salvation, by removing from him the remains of sin, except, of course, those unatoned for, requiring an interval in purgatory.

The seventh sacrament was that of *holy orders*, or the ordination into the priesthood. It was administered by the bishop and gave the priest virtues which made him distinct from secular men. The ordained priest was capable of making possible the miracle of transubstantiation as well as performing the other sacraments. Therefore the clergy (through the sacrament of ordination) became an integral part of the system which insured mankind's salvation.

The religion of the common people. The problems of theology attracted the attention primarily of the intellectuals. The majority of the people then, as today, accepted the beliefs of the world in which they lived without very much questioning. To the unlettered population, the following constituted the essentials of the Christian faith: (1) the Creation and Fall of Adam, (2) the birth and the crucifixion of Christ, (3) the Last Judgment, (4) the horrors of hell, and (5) the eternal bliss of heaven. The sacramental system promised a safe entrance into heaven. Then why worry needlessly over fine points of theology?[6]

How the Church Enforced Its Teachings

The weapons of the Church. The weapons the Church used to implement its teachings and commands were very effective indeed. The principal ones were (1) canon law, (2) excommunication, (3) interdict, and (4) command of vast revenues.

Canon law. Canon law had been developed from the Scriptures, the writings of the Church Fathers, the disciplinary and doctrinal rules made by church councils, and the decrees of the Popes. The collection of these canons resulted in many problems and contradictions. The *Digest* of Justinian's Code was found in the eleventh century, and thus Roman law was studied afresh. In the following century (1140) a monk named Gratian compiled his famous code *Concordia descordantium canonum* (harmony of conflicting canons), known generally as the *Decretum.* Ultimately, the Church issued its official body of canon law, known as the *corpus iuris canonici.* This represents the ecclesiastical counterpart to the Justinian Code, known as the *corpus iuris civilis.*

Canon law protected the clergy from laymen. Every man who had been admitted to the clerical state and could read and write enjoyed what is known as benefit of clergy. This meant that a churchman could be tried only in church courts according to canon law, in spite of the fact that he might have committed a serious crime against a layman. This practice led to serious abuses, for the clergy usually got off with lighter punishments in their own courts.

The Church used canon law to punish such crimes as perjury, blasphemy, sorcery, usury, which the medieval Church denounced, and heresy, the most horrible of all crimes in medieval eyes. A murder was a crime against a fellow man, but disbelief in the teachings of Christ or His Church was a crime against God Himself.

The Inquisition. In the thirteenth century, the Church devised an institution known as the Inquisition to cope with a rising tide of heresy and to bring religious conformity to Europe. These heresies were certain schools of thought which questioned the basic doctrines of the Church or argued that salvation could be attained by methods different from those officially prescribed by the Church. The Inquisition was an elaborate system of inquiry into the beliefs of persons suspected of being heretics. People accused of heresy were tried in the court of the Inquisition. If an accused person confessed and abjured, or renounced, his heresy, he was "reconciled" with the Church on performance of penance. If he did not voluntarily confess, he could be subjected to torture, one of the most commonly used forms being the rack, which wrenched the limbs of the victim. If torture failed to make the prisoner confess, he was declared a heretic and turned over to the secular authorities (unless he abjured in the meantime) to be burned at the stake.

Few scholars have been able to look at the Inquisition objectively. Some have condemned it completely, while others have tended to minimize its errors. It must be kept in mind that Roman law had made use of torture and that Roman emperors often ordered condemned persons to be burned at the stake. Furthermore, to the medieval mind the soul was infinitely more important than the body. Therefore the torturing of a suspected heretic was justifiable if by confession his soul could be saved from certain hellfire. The great French scholar of the Inquisition, Jean Guiraud, has analyzed some 930 inquisitional sentences pronounced between 1308 and 1323. He found that 42 persons, or between four and five per cent of the cases, were sentenced to death; 139 persons (about fifteen per cent) were acquitted. The remainder were either imprisoned or assigned various penances.

Excommunication. But the Church generally made use not of outright physical punishments but of spiritual penalties. The most powerful of these was excommunication, which simply meant exclusion from the Church. If a man would not heed the commands of the Church, he was excommunicated.

It was a very serious penalty, for *extra ecclesiam nulla salus*—outside the Church there is no salvation. Excommunication might vary in its punishment. At its worst it banned the victim from all participation in the ritual of the Church, denied its spiritual help, forbade other Christians to associate with him or help him in any way, freed all his vassals from their oaths of fealty to him, and prevented his burial in consecrated soil. The attending ceremony added solemnity and terror to the punishment. On occasion the bishop appeared, attended by twelve priests, each holding a lighted candle. At the moment when the curse, or anathema, was declared, the candles were dashed to the ground to signify the extinction of the guilty one's soul.

Here are the concluding lines of a thirteenth-century Scottish excommunication directed against enemies of the Church.

"Accursed be all the forenamed persons; cursed be they without and within, from the sole of the foot even to the crown of the head. And may their part and companionship be with Dathan and Abiram whom the earth swallowed quick. May their days be few and their offices let others take; may their children be orphans; and as this light is at this moment extinguished, so may the lights of their lives be extinguished before the face of Him who liveth for ever and ever; and may their souls be plunged in hell unless they repent and amend their ways and make satisfaction. So be it! So be it! Amen! (The candles are extinguished, and a bell is rung.)"[7]

Interdict. Excommunication was directed against single persons; interdict punished whole groups in localities. The interdict has been termed "an ecclesiastical lockout." In the country or territory thus penalized, no church services were held, and all sacraments save baptism, penance, and confirmation were withheld. The interdict was a most powerful weapon, one instrumental, as we shall see later, in bringing King John of England to his knees and forcing him to give his entire kingdom to the Pope, getting it back as a fief.

Church revenues. The main revenues which the Church received were (1) donations, (2) tithes, (3) fees, and (4) feudal dues. For centuries kings and nobles were generous contributors to bishoprics and monasteries. The lands given to the Church were said to have fallen *in mortua manu*, or into the clutch of a dead hand (*mortmain*), because the Church kept perpetually all lands which were donated to her. Kings saw their wealth disappearing alarmingly from such bequests. Finally in England in the reign of Edward I the famous Statute of Mortmain was passed in an attempt to put an end to this loss of wealth.

The tithe, which means one tenth of a man's income, was the regular income of the priest. In the twelfth century Pope Alexander III extended the tithe until it was levied on forests, mills, and even the labor of artisans. The common people came to resent the levying of tithes very much, especially when the taxes went to clergymen who remained absent from their residences among the people.

Fees for the performance of religious services and for the administration of some of the sacraments were another source of wealth. Revenue also came from the payment of feudal dues by vassals to bishops and abbots who were feudal lords and from the payment of manorial dues by peasants to churchmen who possessed manors. We shall see later that the growing wealth of the Church, the greatest landowner in medieval Europe, brought about many abuses and a worldliness among the clergy which weakened the faith of the common people.

The Triumph of the Medieval Church

Two international institutions. At the time when the feudal system was at its fullest strength, Europe believed in the supremacy of two universal institutions, the Holy Roman Church and the Holy Roman Empire. The Holy Roman Empire was, as we noted in Chapter 12, a revival of the tradition of the Roman empire, under which all Europe had been united politically. The Holy Roman Empire was created in 962 when the German king Otto the Great was crowned emperor in Rome. As the legitimate successor of the old Roman empire it claimed universal political authority throughout western Europe, though its actual power was confined to the Germanies and northern Italy.

The powers of both universal Church and Empire were not clearly defined. The first was regarded as the chosen instrument of God in spiritual matters, the second as His chosen political organization. But the Church and the Empire both laid claims to the highest of rights, and neither could exercise full powers without involving the subjection of the other. A conflict between the two was therefore inevitable.

The greatest of the earlier Popes was the sixth-century Gregory I, who defended the Roman Church against the ambitious eastern empire, checked the advance of the Lombards, one of the German tribes that had invaded Italy, converted the Saxon kingdoms, and became virtual sovereign of Rome and its surrounding territory. From his time on, the church leaders organized their work among the Franks and Germans, until, with the coronation of Charlemagne at Rome in 800, the Church had added to its spiritual solidarity a compact political organization.

But Charlemagne's temporal powers constituted a threat to the supremacy of the Pope. There was a danger that the Pope of Rome would fall again under the domination of the emperor of the west, just as the patriarch of Constantinople had gradually fallen into a subservient position under the emperor of the east. However, even though a great empire claiming international power had been created, the Church, in theory, had the upper hand. Charlemagne had received his crown from the Pope, a ceremony which could be interpreted later to signify the supremacy of the Church over the empire. That interpretation lay at hand for the Popes to use as a weapon in any struggle with the empire.[8]

Feudalization of the Church. Although a showdown between emperors and Popes loomed only faintly on the historical horizon, a very real danger to the Church lay in its steadily growing feudalization. As the Church gradually became the greatest landlord in Europe, the feudal lords attempted to bring the Church under their domination. On every possible occasion kings had their younger sons and relatives made bishops and archbishops in order to keep the wealthy church lands in royal possession. Feudal lords tried to control church elections. Even the office of Pope was not free from feudal taint, for the emperors of the Holy Roman Empire, the Italian barons, and the nobility in Rome itself quarreled over papal elections.

The Church was saved from the dangers of feudalism, and the papacy was rescued from becoming a political pawn by two important tenth- and eleventh-century events. These were (1) a great religious revival, and (2) the coming to the papal throne of Gregory VII and his powerful successors.

The religious revival. The religious revival, which began in the tenth century, affected all classes. Among the factors contributing to its force were a realization on the part of officials in the Church that many of the clergy were not fulfilling their duties and a desire to free the church from control by feudal lords. As for the common people, several serious plagues and famines turned them toward religion as a bulwark against death and suffering. The revival took the following forms: In the first place, it resulted in a widespread building of cathedrals throughout Europe. With the construction of churches as community enterprises, Europe for awhile "snowed churches." Secondly, many new monastic orders were founded, including the order of Vallombrosa and the Burgundian order of Cluny. The last, begun at the monastery of Cluny in 910, had the following four policies: (1) to free the papal office from lay control, (2) to enforce clerical celibacy, (3) to establish absolute authority of the Pope over all clerics, and (4) to abolish simony and lay investiture, shortly to be explained.[9] The Cluniac movement was made a part of papal policy—now directed by able and aggressive Popes—and hence was very important to the rising power of the Church. A third form of the religious revival was the attempt of the Church to limit feudal warfare and "humanize" conflict. We saw previously how the Church limited the evils of warfare through the Peace of God and Truce of God. The fourth aspect of the religious revival, the crusades, begun, as we shall see, late in the eleventh century, not only gave the Church a chance to direct the weapons of the nobles away from its own possessions but also furnished a popular outlet for the great religious zeal of the day.

Gregory VII. The second great force of the eleventh century which brought the power of the papacy to an unknown height was Gregory VII. That famous pontiff, born Hildebrand about 1025, had spent his career in papal service and was so well known that, when his predecessor died in 1073, the Roman populace tumultuously shouted for Hildebrand and forcibly placed him on the papal throne.

Of low stature, short-legged, corpulent, of dull complexion, and inclined to stammer, Gregory VII possessed little learning but much zeal and honesty. His magnetic power over men, moreover, was extraordinary. One fanatical follower called him his "holy Satan." Completely convinced of the rightness of the Cluniac policies and seeing all about him kings and princes leading corrupt and unchristian lives, Gregory took as his ideal the establishment of a theocracy—the creation of a world government under the control of God's regent on earth, the Pope.

The pontiff once wrote: "Human pride has created the power of kings; God's mercy has created the power of bishops. The Pope is the master of Emperors. He is rendered holy by the merits of his predecessor, St. Peter. The Roman Church has never erred, and Holy Scripture proves it can never err. To resist it is to resist God."[10]

Gregory's program. For the next twelve years until his death in 1085 Gregory VII devoted his energies to breaking all such "resistance." The task before him was enormous, yet never once did he shrink from it. Gregory took the platform of the Cluniac reformers as his own. A step had been taken in the direction of freeing papal elections in 1059 by the creation of the College of Cardinals to elect the Pope, a duty which the College still performs.

In the later Roman empire the higher clergy had been forbidden to marry. However, the rule had not been strictly kept, and in the tenth and eleventh centuries there were many married priests in various parts of Europe. The same synod, or ecclesiastical council, which created the College of Cardinals in 1059 also declared illegal the marriage of the clergy, and Gregory had this decree made effective. The position of the Church on the much debated point of celibacy can be easily understood. Single priests could be easily transferred from country to country, a process necessary for the functioning of an international institution. Secondly, there was always the temptation for married clergy to alienate church property for the benefit of their children. Thirdly, marriage might distract men from giving full thought and loyalty to their religious duties. Lastly, the medieval mind looked upon celibate life as more spiritual and more in keeping with the personal life of Christ.

The third matter which Gregory undertook to solve, by far the most difficult of all, was the suppression of simony and lay investiture. Selling ecclesiastical offices to the highest bidder or acquiring them by bribery was known as simony (from Simon the magician, who tried to buy the gift of the Holy Spirit from the apostles). Gregory now gave simony an even broader interpretation to make it include all appointments to important church offices made by laymen, even those made by kings and the emperor of the Holy Roman Empire.

The new interpretation involved the problem of lay investiture, the power exercised by kings and feudal lords of "investing" the new incumbent of a bishopric or abbey with his religious office and his fiefs. Many of the church lands had been granted by the kings and nobles to the higher clergy, who became their vassals. The new bishop or abbot had to do them homage for his fief and received from them his ring and staff, the symbols of his religious functions. Furthermore, the nobility were given control over church property during the vacancy between the death of one incumbent and the selection of his successor, which meant that powerful laymen had an important stake in the election to church offices. The feudal lord not only invested the churchman, but also let it be known whom he wanted elected. This practice was particularly obnoxious to a Pope like Gregory, who believed that a lord guilty of bloodshed should never have the right to bestow the spiritual symbols upon the successors of the Apostle Peter, and that lay investiture weakened the temporal authority of the papacy.

The investiture struggle between Empire and papacy. Gregory decided, therefore, to exercise full power in stamping out the practices of simony and lay investiture. In the synod of 1075 he formally deposed all ecclesiastics who had received their investitures from a lay person. Such a drastic act was the same as a declaration of war against the kings of Europe. As the emperor of the Holy Roman Empire was the most powerful monarch, claiming sovereignty over all Christendom in political matters, Gregory first waged war with him, knowing that if he should win a victory against the most powerful of kings his triumph everywhere was assured.

The climax to the famous lay investiture struggle between the papacy and the Empire occurred in the clash involving Pope Gregory VII and the emperor Henry IV. The high lights of this dramatic conflict are very interesting. Gregory accused Henry of simony and immorality and of having appointed the archbishop of Milan, and summoned him to Rome to answer for his conduct. Henry answered by summoning a synod of German clergy in 1076, where he deposed the Pope! "Henry, king not by usurpation but by God's ordinance, to Hildebrand, no longer Pope, but false monk. . . . I, Henry, king by the grace of God, with all of my bishops, say unto thee, 'Come down, come down!' "[11] Gregory excommunicated Henry and deposed him in turn, absolving all his subjects from their oaths of allegiance.

Henry, driven at last by baronial revolt to make his peace with the pontiff, finally appeared before Gregory at Canossa, a castle in the Apennines. Here one of the most dramatic scenes in history was enacted. It was January, 1077. Henry, the temporal ruler of all the Holy Roman Empire, appeared in the forecourt of the castle, dressed in the garb of a penitent, standing barefoot in the snow. Three days he begged for forgiveness until (in the words of Gregory) "finally, won by the persistency of his suit and by the constant supplications of all who were present, we loosed the chain of the anathema and at length received him into the favor of communion and into the lap of the Holy Mother Church."

But while the humiliation of the emperor and the triumph of the Pope were spectacular, contemporary accounts of the incident did not attach much significance to it. Soon after Canossa the struggle between the empire and the papacy broke out again, and before many years Gregory died in exile (1085), his last words (according to one report) being, "I have loved justice and hated iniquity; therefore I die in exile."[12]

Although Gregory's greatest success lay in the imposition of celibacy among the clergy, his other struggles and the masterful manner with which he directed his campaigns tended to increase the power and prestige of the papacy.

The problem of lay investiture was settled in 1122 by the compromise known as the Concordat of Worms. The Church gained the right to choose the man for office. The candidate received the lay investiture as a political and feudal officer from the king and the spiritual investiture as an ecclesiastical officer and pastor, from the Church. After this time the problem of lay investiture never again became so acute.

Frederick Barbarossa's Italian ambitions. Despite this settlement the struggle for supremacy between the Empire and the papacy continued unabated for another century, because the contest between them was still undecided and because the Popes resented the emperors who came down from Germany into Italy to interfere in local politics. In 1152 Frederick I (Barbarossa) of the brilliant Hohenstaufen family came to power with the full intention of recovering his dominions and gaining a firmer hold on them. With this purpose Frederick crossed the Alps from his German kingdom, to bring the prosperous and powerful cities in northern Italy into conformity with his will. But by 1166 they were united in the Lombard League, a coalition determined to maintain its independence and commercial power. Frederick was defeated in 1176 by the League, which received valuable support from the Pope.

It soon became obvious that Italy was not to be united under any single political power. At the same time the failure of the emperor in Italy so weakened his strength in Germany that even there the hope of a strong, centralized government began to diminish rapidly in the thirteenth century. Not until the nineteenth century were the German and Italian states consolidated into nations.

Frederick I married his son Henry VI to Constance, the heiress of the Norman kingdom, which included Sicily and southern Italy. Once more the papacy saw itself threatened by imperial ambitions in Italy, for Henry VI, in his brief reign, formed the plan of consolidating Germany, Italy, and Sicily into a single hereditary rather than an elective monarchy.

Frederick II. This plan failed to materialize, for Henry died in 1197, leaving his possessions to his three-year-old son Frederick. The boy was brought up as the ward of that most powerful of medieval popes, Innocent III, who himself had been elected pope in 1198. The Empire fell on evil ways during the minority of Frederick, for rebellious groups wrought chaos and confusion. In 1211 Frederick was crowned as the German king; in

1220 he was crowned emperor of the Holy Roman Empire. In Innocent's time this ruler appeared to be in full agreement with the papacy's aims and promised to undertake a crusade. But Frederick was probably the most extraordinary monarch of the Middle Ages: a many-sided genius with strong plans as to the political role he should assume. Frederick did not quarrel with Innocent III (1161?-1216), but waged a fierce struggle against later Popes. The emperor wanted powers coequal with those of the Pope, but the latter demanded submission.

The two universal forces fought for supremacy throughout Frederick's reign. Because of their conflicting aims in Italy and Frederick's success in his crusade (wherein he did no fighting but won splendid concessions for Christians from his friend the Moslem sultan of Egypt) Pope Gregory IX excommunicated him twice, tried to depose him, and called him "this scorpion spewing poison from the sting of his tail."[13]

Gregory further branded Frederick a heretic and blasphemer who dared to utter that mankind had been deceived by three liars, Christ, Moses, and Mohammed, and wound up his papal condemnation with the charge, "And Frederick maintains that no man should believe aught but what may be proved by the power and reason of nature."[14]

After Frederick's death in 1250, the empire never regained its power, though it lingered on into early modern times. In the sixteenth century under the emperor Charles V it reached again a short period of apparent power, but the advance of national states steadily reduced it to impotence until Napoleon I of France finally extinguished it in 1806.

The Crusades

The Popes and the crusades. The Popes led the way in organizing one of the best-known movements of the Middle Ages, the crusades. These crusades were pilgrimages whose object was usually the recovery of the Holy Land from the infidel. The word "crusade" is derived from "taking the cross," after the example of Christ, a practice started by the participants in the First Crusade. On the way to the Holy Land the crusader wore a cross of cloth upon his breast. On the journey home he wore the cross on his back. Those who went to these wars were granted extensive indulgences by the Popes and were assured that their previous obligations for penance would be remitted.

Reasons for the crusades. After the death of Mohammed in 632, the Moslem faith had spread along the north coast of Africa and up the eastern and western fringes of the Mediterranean world. The crusades (1096-1291) were Christendom's answer to the threat of Moslem expansion. The original Moslem advance in the Near East had embraced all the provinces of the eastern empire in Asia and Africa except Asia Minor. However, the Moslem governors had been enlightened rulers and had allowed Christians to visit their holy shrines. But in the tenth and eleventh centuries the Seljuk Turks, recent converts to Islam and capturers of the caliphate at Bagdad, came plundering and sweeping westward out of Asia. They sought Constantinople as their goal and in 1071 defeated the eastern emperor at the battle of Manzikert (see page 257). So near did they get to within striking distance of Constantinople that in 1095 the Byzantines appealed to Pope Urban II for assistance.

Meanwhile the Seljuks had captured Jerusalem from their fellow Moslems in 1071, and the fanatical Turks mistreated the Christian pilgrims. When accounts of the mistreatment reached Europe, men's minds became inflamed. In 1095 at the Council of Clermont Pope Urban II preached the need of the first great crusade to rescue both the eastern empire and the Holy Land. In masterful fashion Urban besought the gathering to take up the cross and to strive valiantly for a cause that promised not merely spiritual reward but even physical gain when the Christians should possess the Holy Land that "flowed with milk and honey." At the end of his appealing oration the crowd shouted, "It is the will of God"—the expression which the crusaders later used in battle.

The impetus back of the crusades was undoubtedly religious. There was a real and spontaneous outpouring of religious enthusiasm following Pope Urban's appeal. The devout Christian believed that one crusade would cancel all his sins. The papacy also was of the opinion that the stimulation of religious enthusiasm following in the wake of the crusades would strengthen the power of the papacy.

Nevertheless there were other motives behind the crusades. Nobles saw an opportunity to fight and perhaps to obtain some valuable lands in Syria. The merchants in the Italian city-states were quite happy to support the crusades, since they would create a demand for Italian ships to carry the crusaders and their supplies to the Holy Land. The crusades, therefore, offered an opportunity for profit. Some of the crusaders were little more than riffraff. There were thieves trying to escape justice, debtors who could not meet their creditors, and outright ruffians and cutthroats. Like many historical movements the crusades were compounded of undiluted idealism, enlightened self-interest, and downright skullduggery.

The crusades. From the end of the eleventh century to the end of the thirteenth there were eight distinct crusades as well as other movements of people who went to the Holy Land to try a hand against the Saracen from time to time. The First Crusade, led principally by princes and nobles from Normandy, Toulouse, parts of Germany, and southern Italy, proceeded overland to Constantinople, forced its way through Asia Minor, and succeeded in capturing Jerusalem in 1099. Mingled with the sincere and simple-minded knights in the First Crusade were shrewd Norman adventurers and profiteering merchants and shipowners of Genoa and Pisa. The crusades are full of paradoxes. Even as the cynical and heretical emperor Frederick II was more successful in his crusade than the saintly King Louis, so the materialistic and bargain-hunting Italian merchants achieved more lasting benefits than the devout pilgrims who had been willing to give their lives that the Sepulchre might be rescued from the infidel.

The First Crusade. The First Crusade conquered lands in Syria and Asia Minor and created the feudal Latin kingdom of Jerusalem, which lasted from 1099 to 1187. Yet surprisingly enough, the western culture thus introduced had little or no effect upon the Near East, because the crusaders from western Europe were encountering a people culturally

Crac-de-Chevaliers, a vast fortress high in the Syrian hills, dates from the crusades, when it was the outpost of the Knights of St. John of Jerusalem. It is similar to French castles of the period and is one of the few vestiges of the European feudal kingdoms. The French government helped in its restoration.

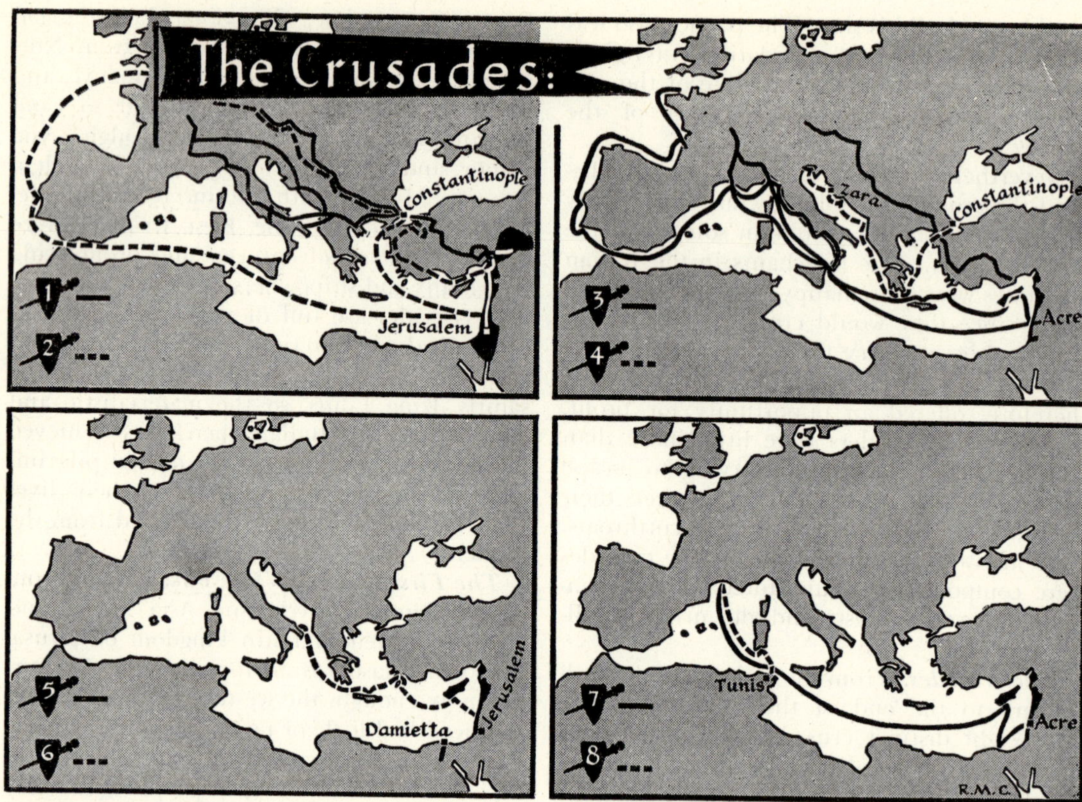

superior to them. As we noted in our discussion of the rise of the town in Chapter 13 (page 374), a most important effect of the crusades was the diffusion of Moslem commerce throughout Europe.

The Second Crusade. When the kingdom of Jerusalem found itself in danger in 1144, Bernard of Clairvaux preached a Second Crusade, and Louis VII of France and the emperor Conrad III joined forces. They met with many misfortunes in getting to the Near East, and the Second Crusade ended when they failed to capture Damascus.

The "Crusade of Kings." The Third Crusade (1189) took place because of the attempts of the brilliant Saladin to end Christian rule in Syria. The "Crusade of Kings" was the answer to Saladin's challenge. The three leading monarchs of Europe, Frederick Barbarossa of the Empire, Richard I of England, and Philip Augustus of France set forth on their holy mission. Frederick was drowned, and after a quarrel with Richard, Philip went home before hostilities were concluded. After Richard and Saladin fought, they agreed to a three-year truce by which Christians were given control of a small strip of coast and pilgrims were allowed to visit Jerusalem. The truce scarcely compensated for the cost of such an expensive crusade.

The Fourth Crusade. The Fourth Crusade is an example of the degradation of a great religious ideal. When Innocent III first issued a call in 1198 for a crusade, no great response was forthcoming. However, some nobles proceeded to Venice, there to take ships to Egypt to make war against the Moslem power. But the Venetian merchants were out to make money. They charged the knights outrageous sums for shipping their retinues, and since the crusaders could not pay the bill, the Venetians persuaded them to pay off the sum by capturing the Christian town of Zara, which had long proved troublesome to Venetian trading interests. Despite excommunication by the Pope, the merchants of Venice now proposed that these Egypt-bound crusaders should attack Constantinople. Although this proposition was really criminal, because the First Crusade had been designed, among other reasons, to preserve the independence of the eastern empire and Eastern Church, the Venetians wanted to wrest the rich trade from the troubled Byzantine empire. In 1204 the city was captured and looted. Soldiers smashed the sacred altar of Saint Sophia to steal the precious stones, and even led in mules and horses to carry away the booty. Illiterate crusaders destroyed priceless Greek manuscripts and other works of art. The Fourth Crusade, despite the infamy of the expedition, transferred the center of Mediterranean trade from the Near East to Venice and thence to western Europe.

Later crusades. The thirteenth century saw other crusades, including the ill-fated Children's Crusade in 1212, in which thousands of youngsters were tricked and sold into slavery by Marseilles merchants. The Fifth Crusade captured Damietta in Egypt in 1219, only to lose it soon and fail altogether. The Sixth Crusade in 1228, organized by Frederick II, differed from previous attempts in that it involved no slaughter, pillage, or robbery. Through Frederick's negotiating skill and tolerance it gained privileges for Christian pilgrims far superior to any gained previously. The Seventh Crusade was begun by Louis IX of France some time after the fall of Jerusalem in 1244, but despite the zeal and devotion of the leader it proved a fiasco from beginning to end. In 1270 Louis attempted another crusade to Tunis but died at Carthage. Then, in swift succession, the feudal states created by the crusaders in the Near East were captured by the Turks, and in 1291 Acre, the last stronghold of the Christians, fell.

Thus two centuries of struggle on the part of the crusaders to keep the infidel out of the Holy Land ended in dismal failure. However, the crusading spirit was by no means destined to die. In Spain the small Christian states ejected the Moors, and in eastern Europe Christians zealously held back the high tide of Moslem invasion in the sixteenth century, while the primary aim of the crusades failed.

A medieval army attacks a fortified town held by Turks in Africa. Heraldic devises (lion, fleur-de-lis) indicate that several armies have encamped together for the seige. The cannons are a new element, supplementing the crossbows. The artist has depicted a typical medieval walled city.

Effects of the crusades on the Church. The cultural results of the crusades will be taken up in a later chapter. At this point let us note their effect on the Church. Outwardly, these great movements at first tended to enhance the prestige of the papacy, especially the first three crusades prior to the pontificate of Innocent III. But the remainder showed all too clearly the mercenary motives of many of the Italian merchants, the European nobles, and some of the Popes. During the thirteenth century the clergy were made to pay a tithe to help the crusades which the papacy often used for their own aims. Moreover, the Popes had begun to make increasing use of the expeditions for their own political interests.

Medieval Reform

Agencies for reform. By the thirteenth century so many evils were apparent in the Church that determined efforts were made to eliminate them. New monastic orders arose to rout Church abuses, and the mendicant orders of Franciscans and Dominicans were founded to bring men back to the truths of Christ and to stamp out heresy.

New monastic orders. New monastic orders were springing up throughout Europe, of both the hermit and the communal type. The most impressive of the former was the Carthusian order, famed for its severe simplicity of life. Another order, known as the Augustinian canons, was designed to remove the laxity in cathedral chapters by making the canons live under a regular discipline. Still another order was the Premonstratensian, founded in 1119. These orders were an answer to the increasing laxity of the older Benedictine groups and even of the reforming Cluniac order. Practically all European monastic orders were based on the precepts of the Benedictine rule. The order of Cluny had been founded to make other orders realize that they had turned away from the ideas of St. Benedict. But the Cluniac order itself began to be lax, and a new order, the Cistercian, came into existence to sound the note of reform. With the rise of the Cistercians, founded in 1098 by St. Robert of Molesme, the second and last movement of Benedictine reform took place. Yet even the Cistercians fell from their founder's high moral purpose. The truth was that monasticism was no longer a practical ideal. Monasticism was based on an agricultural society and a love of solitude; hence it could not cope with the growing secularism and the rise of heresy in the towns. New techniques had to be found to enforce the Church's teachings.

The growth of heresy. Heresy has been defined by the Church as "obstinate adherence to opinions arbitrarily chosen in defiance of accepted ecclesiastical teaching and interpretation." It appeared in the towns because the Church did not answer the problems of the new critical urban mind, and because the exchange of goods between towns also meant an exchange of ideas not always orthodox.

Pierre Abélard, one of the most brilliant intellects of the Middle Ages and a very famous teacher at the schools of Paris, had been persecuted as a heretic, although he was only guilty of possessing an inquiring mind. His pupil Arnold of Brescia lost his life for advocating a return of the Church to simplicity and a reform of the corrupted clergy and cardinals. The two major heretical sects were the Cathari, or Albigensians, in southern France and the Waldensians of Lyons. These sects were generally made up of simple, well-meaning people who sought to return to the life of Christ.

The Albigensians and the Waldensians. The Cathari (The Pure), or Albigensians, believed that this world is the battleground of two opposing forces, Good and Evil. The Albigensians held that Good is represented by Jesus and the teachings of the New Testament. They were utterly heretical, however, in maintaining that Jehovah as represented in the Old Testament was the embodiment of Evil, and their heresy went even further. This world of matter was inherently evil; therefore possessions and the Church with its great organization were likewise evil. So was marriage, for it perpetuated the human species in this sinful world.

The Cathari had a theory of salvation. By utter purity of living, such as strict vegetarianism and chastity, one could attain to the spiritual life. Because few men could live so severe an existence, the Cathari divided their ranks into two groups. The Perfect followed this rigid discipline and so were assured of salvation. The Believers could live quite normal lives otherwise, although they, too, repudiated the Church. Before death, however, they received the *consolamentum*, a sacrament of consolation that ushered them into the ranks of the Perfect. The Cathari were earnest people, but their views were in large measure anti-social. For this reason they were punished by the secular authorities as well as by the Church.

The Waldensians, while just as sincere as the Cathari, possessed none of the latter's dualistic views. The Waldensians derived their name from Peter Waldo, a merchant of Lyons who gave up his possessions in 1173 and founded a lay order called the Poor Men of Lyons. The principal complaint of the Waldensians was directed against the wealth and worldliness of the Church. Their heresy came from their repudiation of the efficacy of the sacraments when not administered by holy priests. As Jean Guiraud has summed it up: "The Waldensians wanted above all to return to evangelical poverty, and they condemned everything in the Church which departed from this, the wealth of the clergy, their princedoms, and their temporal authority. In the ecclesiastical hierarchy they found no longer any sanctifying force; sanctity was in their eyes individual and could be acquired, not by sacraments or by ritual practices, but by personal work."[15]

Because the Waldensians maintained their views steadfastly and said that God would hear a prayer anywhere, or that anyone—man or woman could preach, they have been looked upon by some as forerunners of the Protestant Revolt.

Heresy suppressed. Although southern France was noted for its tolerance, the Church appreciated the dangers to itself from these two groups of heretics. Innocent III tried for ten years to reconvert them, and failing in his purpose, he instigated a crusade in 1208 against the county of Toulouse, where many of the subjects of its ruler, Count Raymond, subscribed to the Albigensian heresy. The crusade began with horrible slaughter. Heretics and protectors of heretics were put to the sword. " 'Kill them all, God will know His own' has reëchoed down the centuries as the slogan of the conflict which ensued . . . massacre followed massacre with all the cruelty which perverted fanaticism could devise."[16] Hundreds of worldly knights flocked to Toulouse to extirpate the heretics, not because they were interested in strengthening the Pope's authority but because they saw in the crusade a good opportunity to become rich by seizing the lands of the Albigenses. In fact, the Pope promised their land to the crusaders. Soon the south of France was the scene of savage fighting, with the original religious motive of the crusade lost in a welter of selfish cross-currents. The crusaders were out after land, the Count of Toulouse was desperately trying to eject the invaders, and on the sidelines the king of France was waiting his chance to step in and incorporate Toulouse into his own domain.

Amid the fighting commerce dwindled and the culture of Toulouse—perhaps the finest in Europe—rapidly declined. The Albigensian heresy was almost completely destroyed by fire and sword, and the lands of the Count of Toulouse were obtained by the king of France, who benefited most of all by the religious fanaticism. It was many years before the splendid culture of Toulouse was able to stage a revival.

Thus the thirteenth-century Church was able to suppress the growing heresies in Europe. But the time came when the Popes could not destroy the work of such reformers as Wycliffe and Hus so easily as they had destroyed the Albigensians.

The mendicant Franciscans. The second important phenomenon of the medieval reformation was the rise of the two great mendicant orders of the thirteenth century, the Franciscans and Dominicans. St. Francis of Assisi (1181?-1226) is one of the noblest figures of history. Like Waldo of Lyons, he rejected riches and spread the gospel of poverty and Christian simplicity. The order he founded was strictly evangelical, for its members were friars (*fratres*), who differed from the monks in that they went about preaching and teaching the gospel to others, whereas the monks lived a sequestered life and were primarily interested in personal salvation. Francis was convinced that his friars must own absolutely nothing of a personal nature. Hence they were begging, or mendicant, brothers. The character of the poetic Francis has been mentioned before. Infinitely lovable, simple, humble, and of great physical and moral bravery, Francis was a fine example of the best of medieval religious idealism.

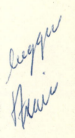

Simplicity of life and humanitarianism were fundamentals in St. Francis' *Rule:*

"I counsel, also warn, and exhort my brethren in our Lord Jesus Christ that they brawl not . . . but that they be meek, peaceable, soft, gentle, and courteous and lowly, honestly speaking and answering to every man as unto them accordeth and belongeth. And they shall not ride, but if they be constrained by evident necessity or else by sickness.

"I command steadfastly and straitly to all the brethren that in nowise they receive any manner of coin or money, but care shall be taken of the sick."[17]

The papacy saw in the zeal and fervor of the Franciscans a great weapon with which to combat the rising tide of heresy. To bring the order more in conformity with its plans, it set aside Francis' will in 1230 (four years after he had died and two years after his canonization as a saint) and saw to it that the Franciscans had an elaborate form of government and possessed property. The order split into two factions: those who accepted the new order, the Moderates or Conventuals, and those who refused to give up the ideals of their founder, the Spirituals or Observants. Nevertheless, the Franciscans did an immense amount of good work both in instructing the common people in matters of faith and in helping the poor. By the beginning of the fourteenth century the Spirituals were being burned at the stake, although they were upholding the ideals of their beloved founder.

The Dominican Friars. St. Dominic (1170-1221) founded his order in 1206. It was confirmed in 1216 and received the name of Friars Preachers, although it is commonly known as the Dominican order. St. Dominic was a practical-minded Spaniard whose zeal for the propagation of the faith knew no bounds. Dominic met St. Francis and his followers once and was so impressed that he knelt before Francis.

"Truly God hath taken care of these saintly little ones and I did not know it. Wherefore I now promise to observe holy evangelistic poverty, and I in God's name utter a malediction against all brethren of my order who in the said order shall presume to have possessions of their own."[18]

Versed in theology, these preachers were skilled in debate and attempted to destroy both clerical and lay ignorance. They were soon occupying the chairs of theology at the universities (whose origin and significance are discussed in the next chapter) and so helped formulate theological doctrines. The Dominicans were also controlled by the papacy, and like the Franciscans they were put in charge of the Inquisition.

Later mendicants. The Dominicans as well as the Franciscans came with the passage of time to own much wealth and thereby to fall from the high purposes of their zealous founder, until we find Chaucer describing Huberd, the wanton friar, thus:

In towns he knew the taverns, every one,
And every good host and each barmaid too—
Better than begging lepers, these he knew.
For unto no such solid man as he
Accorded it, as far as he could see,
To have sick lepers for acquaintances.
There is no honest advantageousness
In dealing with such poverty-stricken curs;
It's with the rich and with big victuallers.
And so, wherever profit might arise,
Courteous he was and humble in men's eyes.[19]

Innocent III and the Zenith of the Church

Innocent III. Innocent III was born in 1161, not far from Rome. We know little of his early life, though he came from a noble family. He studied law at Bologna and theology at Paris, and later entrusted high offices to some of his former teachers. Some of his relatives were cardinals, and he himself earned a thorough knowledge of papal administration. At 29 he was a cardinal, and when only 37 he became Pope. This scholarly, brilliant, and sincere pontiff took the name Innocent. Innocent III, a dignified person at all times, held an exalted view of his office. In his own words:

"The successor of Peter is the Vicar of Christ: he has been established as a mediator between God and man, below God but beyond man; less than God but more than man; who shall judge all and be judged by no one."[20]

Gregory VII had nearly succeeded in fulfilling this ideal in its entirety; Innocent III was to succeed completely. The new Pope told the princes of Europe that the papacy was as the sun, whereas the kings were as the moon:

One should rule the day (men's souls), the other the night (their bodies). Even as the moon derives its light from the sun, so do kings derive their powers from the Pope.

Innocent and the French-English quarrel. Innocent III was not only complete master of the Church in all administrative, judicial, and financial matters but politically powerful outside the Church. His interference in matters pertaining to France and England is of the greatest importance. As we shall see later, the kings of France throughout the Middle Ages had one main objective in foreign policy: to oust the English king as a feudal landowner from France. Richard I of England and Philip Augustus of France were bitter enemies and plotted and fought against each other almost continuously. Innocent persuaded Richard and Philip to sign a five-year truce.

John, who succeeded to the English throne upon Richard's death, soon showed himself to be a miserable ruler. He was probably the worst king England ever had. He arbitrarily interfered in the election of bishops, illegally seized church revenues, and in general browbeat the Church as he did all his subjects. Finally, after the disputed election for the archbishopric of Canterbury, in which Innocent's candidate, Stephen Langton, was elected, relations between the Pope and the king were broken off. When John refused to receive Langton and drove the Canterbury monks into exile, Innocent placed England under interdict in 1208, and John under excommunication in 1209. Although John continued his struggle against clergy and nobles for several years, he finally had to capitulate to Innocent by receiving Langton, compensating the clergy, becoming the vassal of the Pope, receiving England back as a fief, and paying a tribute of one thousand marks a year. Innocent now dealt with Philip Augustus of France, whose power had in the meanwhile increased. While Philip was not forced into the humiliating position of John, he capitulated in 1213 to the Pope's demands that the king should take back as his rightful queen the lovely Ingeborg of Denmark whom he had tried to divorce.

Innocent and the Empire. When Henry VI died in 1197, the Empire did not go at once to his three-year-old son Frederick. Innocent took him as his ward as we have seen, and supported his imperial claims. Meanwhile Otto IV had been elected emperor, and in assuming the title in 1209, had revived Hohenstaufen claims to supremacy in Italy. Innocent hurled against him the anathema of the Church and set about advancing the claims of his ward Frederick, who promised that he would never incorporate his kingdom of Sicily with the northern states.

Innocent's opportunity came when Otto IV became involved in a war with Philip Augustus. King John of England detested and feared Philip of France, while Otto believed that Pope Innocent III might utilize the French king to depose him and substitute Frederick. John organized a strong coalition led by himself and Otto and marched against Paris. In 1214 a splendidly trained French army crushed the forces of Otto and John, leaving Otto helpless. At the Lateran Council in 1215 Innocent III deposed the emperor and confirmed the youthful Frederick as ruler of the Holy Roman Empire. Innocent died in 1216, too soon to find out what kind of ward he had been championing in the interests of the papacy.

The papacy at its height. With John of England the vassal of the Pope, Philip Augustus forced to abide by Innocent's decisions, and the leadership of the Holy Roman Empire dictated from Rome, the papacy had attained its zenith of temporal power. Innocent's ideal of a papal theocracy appeared realized, for the nations of Europe had acknowledged the power of Christ's vicar. True enough, strong-minded monarchs and Popes whose ability in no wise matched that of Innocent III were one day to topple papal supremacy from its throne. But during the pontificate of Innocent III (1198-1216) he could and did "judge all and be judged by no one."

The Church: Center of Medieval Life

Church appeal for common people. Thus far we have considered the Church largely as a universal political and religious organization. Here we shall deal with its appeal to the common people, which did not lie in its Petrine theory, its carefully worked out theology, or its pretentions to universal authority. The appeal had to be much more human and informal in order to hold the allegiance of the simple but devout Christian of the French countryside or English village. The medieval Church was very real in the lives of the people. They were born into it, and they died in its embrace; it was at once their moral guide and their spiritual sustenance; it brought them solace on this earth and assured them salvation in the next life.

Pilgrimages. Chaucer's *Canterbury Tales* can give us clues regarding the "humanness" of medieval religious life. Here were twenty-nine pilgrims "of ful devout courage," wending their way leisurely through the English countryside to worship at the shrine of the martyred St. Thomas à Becket at Canterbury. In addition to the religious benefits to be achieved by pilgrimages, these journeys gave people a chance to travel, to see new sights and customs, and to converse with pilgrims outside their own neighborhood. Thus pilgrimages proved to be social attractions, and that they were anything but dull and solemn can be seen by reading the tales which Chaucer's pilgrims told one another.

Saints and relics. Chaucer also gives us an insight into two more aspects of popular religious practices, the cult of the saints and martyrs, and the belief in the miraculous power of relics. The veneration of saints and martyrs, such as Thomas à Becket, loomed large in medieval religious life. Every medieval group had its patron saint, who could always be relied upon to give heavenly aid in times of war, famine, pestilence, and personal trouble. Frenchmen rode into battle invoking the aid of St. Denis, Englishmen shouted, "St. George for England!" and Scotsmen looked to St. Andrew for help. The Christian of the Middle Ages would address his patron saint with a familiarity and tell stories about the blessed one's personal life in a manner which would shock a religious person today.

Our medieval ancestors relied a great deal on relics. Most people believed implicitly in the power of such a relic as the thigh bone of some obscure saint to stop disease or create better harvests. The manner in which illiterate persons were duped by unscrupulous traffickers in fictitious relics has been vividly recounted by Chaucer when he describes his Pardoner:

Was no such pardoner in any place.
For in his bag he had a pillowcase
The which, he said, was Our True Lady's veil:
He said he had a piece of the very sail
That good Saint Peter had, what time he went
Upon the sea, till Jesus changed his bent.
He had a latten cross set full of stones,
And in a bottle had he some pig's bones.
But with these relics, when he came upon
Some simple parson, then this paragon
In that one day more money stood to gain
Than the poor dupe in two months could attain.
And thus, with flattery and suchlike japes,
He made the parson and the rest his apes.[21]

Yet this reverence of relics stimulated artistic production. Caskets and reliquaries designed to hold these "pigges bones" encouraged craftsmen to create beautiful objects of gold, silver, and enamel, and even churches were built as resting-places for the remains of saints and other venerated objects.

An Italian visitor in 1496 described thus the wealth surrounding the shrine of Becket at Canterbury:

"The magnificence of the tomb of St. Thomas the Martyr, Archbishop of Canterbury, surpasses all belief. This, notwithstanding its great size, is entirely covered over with plates of pure gold; but the gold is scarcely visible from the variety of precious stones with which it is studded, such as sapphires, diamonds, rubies, and emeralds; and on every side that the eye turns, something more beautiful than the other appears. And these beauties of nature are enhanced by human skill, for the gold is carved and engraved in beautiful designs, both large and small, and agates, jaspers, and cornelians set in relief, some of the cameos being of such a size that I dare not mention it. But everything is left far behind by a ruby, not larger than a man's thumb nail, which is set to the right of the altar. The church is rather dark, and particularly so where the shrine is placed, and when we went to see it, the sun was nearly gone down and the weather was cloudy; yet I saw that ruby as well as if I had it in my hand; they say it was the gift of a king of France."[22]

The veneration of Mary. The magnificent Gothic cathedrals of France attest the pride of the common people in showing their faith and reverence. The cathedrals were symbols in stone of the people's concepts of God, the Trinity, heaven and earth, salvation, and

The medieval artist cuts away a wall in doll-house fashion to show us the interior of a church in this miniature painting from the Miracles of Notre Dame. A religious service is in progress.

above all the love and protection of the Virgin Mary. The veneration of Mary was one of the most magnificent and potent forces in medieval religion. In an age when the prospect of hell and eternal damnation loomed perilously close indeed, and when even the most educated person could see in thunderstorms, pestilence, and famines only the evil designs of ever-lurking devils and soul-snatchers, how natural and comforting it was to turn to her who could always be relied upon to protect and comfort. As an earthly mother will supplicate for mercy on behalf of her erring child, so the mother of Christ would always supplicate in heaven for other mothers' children on earth.

Religion in the town. The universality of the Church brought its influence into every home. Approaching a medieval town, one would see above the thick city walls the tapering spires of the cathedral, the largest and most centrally located structure in the community. Entering the city, the modern visitor would be amazed to see the narrow streets filled with ecclesiastics—black- and yellow-cowled monks rubbing shoulders with steel-helmeted soldiers of a lord bishop's retinue, nuns and their charges hurrying past tavern doors to escape coarse comments, pilgrims staring at unfamiliar objects while searching out the local shrine, and perhaps a cavalcade clattering over the uneven road and announcing the arrival of a great papal legate from overseas. Many buildings would be church property. Churches, monasteries, colleges, hospitals, or almshouses would meet the eye, as well as the elegant palace of the bishop. For the Church performed many tasks other than that of religion. It was the one great social organization of the Middle Ages. Monks built bridges and repaired roads; the Church's hospitals and almshouses took care of the lepers and the poor; the schools and colleges of the Church were the sole places of education; its courts had jurisdiction over every Christian's moral and religious acts.

The Church supervised the amusements of the populace, and the church porch was the setting of popular religious dramas, or mystery plays. When one left the city behind, he would see wayside shrines along the highway, parish church steeples everywhere, and the massive buildings of a monastery, whose inmates were engaged (at least during the earlier Middle Ages) in transcribing manuscripts, writing chronicles or local histories, teaching the peasants new methods of farming, tending vineyards, fishing in nearby waters, and making new discoveries in animal husbandry.

The parish church. But the Church came closest home at the parish church. We have already read Chaucer's description of the poor parson who taught his parishioners the message of Christ "but first he folwed it hymselve," and who traveled the length and breadth of his parish in all kinds of weather to minister to the sick and dying and to comfort his spiritual charges. True, the parish priest was often ignorant and even immoral, and he was invariably of low birth, but his lowly origin meant that he was made welcome by the meanest serf on the lord's manor. The Church's popularity depended in the last analysis upon the ability of the parish priest to administer the sacraments, attend the sick, hear confessions, supervise the morals of the parish, and hold the respect of his parishioners.

To peer inside a parish church on a medieval Sunday would be a revelation to the modern mind, for the scene would prove how human and informal yet indispensable religion was to our medieval forebears:

"The conduct at a service would probably astonish the modern; the knight sauntered about with hawk on wrist, his dogs following, and perhaps fighting, behind; the women gathered together and talked (as women do) and laughed and took mental notes of each other's dresses for future imitation or disparagement. It was enumerated among the virtues of St. Louis that he rarely conducted business of State while he was attending service in Church."[23]

Despite the apparent lack of reverence, the congregation gazed with awe and complete faith toward the altar where the priest intoned the age-old words of simplicity and power, and where the solemn mystery of transubstantiation took place.

The parish priest would give his charges their religious instruction mainly during the sermon. He would paint for them the terrors of hell—how the damned are thrust from the flames into icy water so they do not know which is worse, since each state is intolerable, and how, "to increase their pains the loathsome hell-worms, toads, and frogs that eat out their eyes and nostrils, and adders and water-frogs, not like those here, but a hundred times more horrible, sneak in and out of the mouth, ears, eyes, navel, and at the hollow of the breast, as maggots in putrid flesh, ever yet thickest."[24] But heaven was pictured to be just as desirable as hell was hateful, and the Church assured the parishioner of heaven as a reward for his faith. The priest also sermonized on parish topics. He would upbraid the people for their lax attendance at church, their addiction to the joys of the tavern, their squabbling and fighting, their laziness or gluttony. He was their father confessor and moral teacher. He knew every member of the community intimately. He made every person, high or low, supremely aware of the vividness, the omnipresence, and the reality of religion.

Summary

With this picture of how the medieval Church functioned in the lives of every man, high or low, in Christendom, we conclude our discussion of the Age of Faith. We have surveyed the structure of Europe's greatest medieval organization and examined the doctrines to which it adhered. We have seen how the Church enforced its will and how it was involved in the feudal system. We have followed the eras of reform in the Church and seen its power culminating in the magnificent pontificate of Innocent III. Lastly, we have tried to appreciate how real was the influence of the Church in the everyday life of our medieval ancestors.

The Church made rich contributions in the realms of religion, government, and society. Not only did it spread the message of Christianity throughout Europe and give men a sense of security against the fears of the unknown in an age when superstition was rife, but it championed a Christlike code of ethics and morality. As a great international institution which persisted through centuries of political upheaval, the Church possessed the only unified system of law and governmental administration in Europe. It acted as mediator between kings and princes, and gave to the western world perhaps its first glimpse of the value of an international political organization. In the social field it attempted to humanize warfare, fostered the code of chivalry, performed deeds of charity, fulfilled such necessary community tasks as the repairing of bridges and roads, and tried to raise business standards through banning usury and unfair trade practices.

In the following chapter we shall see how the medieval Church also fostered artistic expression and intellectual inquiry. The Middle Ages have been called the Age of Faith, because the people as a whole believed in the Church and her mission to an extent which we, in our age of intellectual criticism and science, do not. But it would be an unfortunate mistake were we to view the Middle Ages as devoid of intellectual interests or scientific achievements.

Chronology of events and developments discussed in this chapter

Chapter 15

Romanesque architecture evolved: rounded arch, barrel and groined vaulting	1000-1150
Abelard: Conceptualism; universal ideas exist only in our minds	1079-1142
Council of Soissons: Realism superseded Nominalism	1092
Twelfth-century Renaissance: translation of Greek and Arabic learning	1100-1200
Hugh the Primate: writer of Goliardic poetry	1140
The Archpoet: satirical Goliardic poet; excellent parody	1160
St. Albertus Magnus: Christian interpretation of Aristotle	1193-1280
Frederick II: encouraged science; stressed observation	1194-1250
Period of excellence in Gothic architecture: pointed arch, flying buttresses	1200-1300
Roger Bacon: inductive reasoning superior to Scholasticism in science	1214-1294
St. Thomas Aquinas: Scholasticism; reconciliation of science and dogma	1225-1274
Sorbonne founded at Paris	1257
Dante: synthesis of classical writers and religion; The Divine Comedy	1265-1321
Petrarch; Italian poet; devised the Petrarchian sonnet form	1304-1374
Chaucer: forerunner of the English Renaissance; Canterbury Tales	1340-1400

University and cathedral

Medieval thought and art: 800 to 1400

In the Seine River at Paris is a small island on which stands a great edifice of weatherbeaten stone. Its towers have been etched against the sky for hundreds of years, and its massive shadow has afforded welcome relief on countless summer days to thoughtful scholars and carefree students. Paris gazes with veneration upon its lovely cathedral dedicated to the glory of Our Lady, a cathedral made famous by poet and painter. This structure and its many rich associations offer a fascinating glimpse into the life and treasures of the Middle Ages. Begun in 1163 and completed in 1235, Notre Dame de Paris was constructed during some of the most exciting and epoch-making decades of the entire medieval period.

While workmen were fashioning the graceful towers which are the pride of the cathedral, supporting its vault with arched flying buttresses, and carefully fitting the many-colored windows into place, churchmen and students lolled on the Petit Pont that led to the Left Bank, where were situated buildings that represented the capital of Europe's learning. True, Abélard was no longer alive to hold eager young minds spellbound with the brilliance of his lectures. But the shadow of the rising cathedral fell on worthy successors, who wrangled over the Trinity on street corners and accused one another of heresy in their lectures. In the new University were sacrilegious students who penned clever blasphemous poems which parodied the sacred liturgy but who were one day to occupy episcopal thrones as sober princes of the Church. On the great throne of St. Peter in Rome sat the mightiest ruler of all Christendom, the Pope who was one day to be regarded as the symbol of the medieval Church at the zenith of its earthly power—Innocent III, who had himself once studied at Paris.

During the Middle Ages the dreaded Mongols rose under the redoubtable Genghis Khan in Asia, the Byzantine capital was scuttled by Venetian pirates and crusading freebooters, a brilliant court flourished in Sicily during the reign of that extraordinary scientist-monarch, Frederick II, and the great new religious orders were founded, one by the gentle humanitarian, Saint Francis of Assisi. All these events took place while scaffolding partly hid the growing beauty of Notre Dame de Paris, a shrine worthy to adorn France's proud capital and a fitting monument to the glory of the Virgin. The townsmen of Paris had dedicated their cathedral to Our Lady and ascribed to her the place of honor in the great rose windows, a significant point, for such was the spirit in which all France's cathedrals were constructed.

We are now to concern ourselves with the thought and art of medieval times. The cathedral of Notre Dame and the University of Paris should forever silence those voices which would maintain that the Middle Ages were devoid of artistic and intellectual splendor. We shall soon discover how keen were medieval minds as they debated intricate points of philosophy, translated classical and Arab treatises into the Latin which they spoke as volubly as their own tongue, and spun complex theological theories in an effort to reconcile faith and reason. We shall notice other men who made valuable advances in the physical sciences and so helped pave the way for the civilization which we possess today. Still other thinkers contributed to the growth of education and created one of the finest medieval institutions, the university. Nor can we forget the rich array of poets, troubadours, and student versifiers who sang of the joys and sorrows of human nature and produced from their numbers such immortals as Dante and Chaucer. Then, having wandered through medieval Europe with these poets, we can retrace our steps to the great Gothic structures that rose above the roof tops of almost every town and hamlet.

A study of the thought and art of the Middle Ages should re-create those centuries for us by making us realize that the twelfth was just as vital a century as the twentieth. It should also completely dispel the old delusion that medieval culture was sterile and backward. The fundamental difference between our ancestors of the Middle Ages and ourselves is not one of character and intelligence but of perspective. If they laid their offerings upon the altar of theology and not upon the altar of science as we do, if they built cathedrals and not skyscrapers, and if their strength was derived from an age of faith instead of an age of steel, they surely are not to be condemned. Their Abélard is worthy to stand beside Einstein and Notre Dame de Paris beside the Empire State Building.

Philosophy

Medieval and Greek philosophy compared. Man has always worried about how he came to be alive, why he is alive, and what will happen to him when he is dead. We have seen how the Greeks tried earnestly to find answers to these eternal questions. The success with which they evolved philosophical theories was due largely to their great freedom of thought. The Greeks stood at the dawn of a new western European civilization. They were free to think as they wished. Socrates, Plato, and Aristotle produced the finest achievements of this intellectual freedom. During the Middle Ages men were just as eager to explain the problems of life, but they labored under handicaps which the Greeks did not have to encounter. Where the Greek philosopher possessed freedom, the medieval philosopher was possessed by authority. Where the former placed his faith in reason, the latter was forced to place his reason in faith.

In the chapter on the medieval Church we described how that vast institution came to control the political and religious life of western Christendom. The theology of the Church was based on certain sources which were considered infallible: (1) the Scriptures, (2) the creed and dogmas as set forth by Church councils, and (3) the writings of such Church Fathers as St. Augustine. Thus the Scriptures were shaped into an authoritative dogma, one which could not be questioned.[1]

Nominalism versus Realism. But problems were bound to arise whenever scholars had to deal with a dogma for which they could not find any rational basis. Berengar of Tours, for example, came to question the doctrine of transubstantiation, while other scholars argued over the eternal problem of free will and predestination. Two schools came into prominence, each maintaining that it could better interpret the so-called "unexplainable" dogmas. The two schools, which came to be called the Realists and the Nominalists, both existed within the jurisdiction of the Church, and both claimed complete allegiance to it. Furthermore, high-ranking ecclesiastics were to be found enrolled in the ranks of each of the rival camps, although the Church, for reasons which we shall soon see, tended to favor the school called Realism.

The Realists and the Nominalists fought over the problem of universal ideas. Let us recall the controversy between Plato and Aristotle over this point. Plato said that reality consists in a hierarchy of general Ideas. Of these the most important was the Idea of the Good. Hence, to Plato, a specific object was real only in so far as it represented the nature of its Idea; Socrates, for example, was real only in so far as he partook of the Idea of Man. Aristotle held a completely opposite view. Individuals exist as individuals; Socrates as such was real. To Aristotle it was not possible that before man was created he existed as an Idea somewhere or that human man was not a real entity but only a reflection of a universal Idea of Man.

In the Middle Ages men were as sharply divided on the point. To the Realists, only universal Ideas could be real and exist independently without any reference to the names given them. To the Nominalists (who were in the minority), abstract concepts such as universal Ideas were only names (*nomina*) and had no real existence. The Realists as a group naturally placed more reliance upon faith than the Nominalists did, because they believed in the existence of universal Ideas. The Realist view was first put forward clearly by Anselm, archbishop of Canterbury, who said man learns in two ways, by faith and reason. While Anselm is famous for his statement "I do not seek to know to the end that I may believe, but I believe that I may know," he nevertheless maintained that reason could be used to prove the existence of God. Anselm himself championed the cause of Realism, asserting that Nominalism "was not only philosophical nonsense, but was incompatible with the dogma of the Trinity."[2] Anselm was here arguing against the views of an outstanding Nominalist, Roscellinus of Compiègne. Roscellinus was held to be guilty of theological heresy. How could a Christian possibly assert that the Church had no real existence apart from the congregation of individual men who worshiped? Roscellinus' position meant that there was no Church but only thousands of separate churches, that the unity of the Trinity could not exist. It meant that he was worshiping three Gods. In 1092 the Council of Soissons condemned this heretical position, and Roscellinus was forced to recant.

Abélard and Conceptualism. What the eleventh-century logicians did not comprehend was that either Realism or Nominalism, carried out to its logical extreme, resulted in a *reductio ad absurdum.* Realism became pantheism (that is, the universe as a whole is God), and Nominalism became materialism (that is, the universe is composed solely of matter), tenets equally abhorrent to the Church. Pierre Abélard (1079-1142) has been traditionally credited with having effected the acceptable compromise known as Conceptualism. A brilliant scholar, lover, poet, dialectician, and exponent of the critical method, Abélard is one of the most fascinating and tragic of all historical characters. Clever to the point of antagonizing his theological masters to acts of dangerous revenge, vain of his excellent poetry and attractiveness to women, and utterly lacking in tact and diplomacy, Abélard nevertheless excites our profound admiration both for his intellectual gifts and the impetus he gave to learning.

Abélard ridiculed his pompous teacher, William of Champeaux, and drove him into an untenable position of extreme Realism. Abélard took the stand that universal terms have no objective existence as such; they exist only as thoughts or concepts in our minds. Thus, he distinguished between a thing itself (*res*) and its name (*nomen*). How do we get the mental concept "chair"? By experience, he would reply. By seeing many chairs and sitting in them, our minds note certain similarities among them all. We see that each has as its purpose the bearing of our weight, that in general each has four legs, is movable, and has a back. From all these similarities, our observation and experience build up a concept "chair." Therefore, there exists in particular things a similarity or identity of qualities, through whose abstraction a concept is formed by a mental act. To that extent, therefore, class terms are objectively valid.

Abélard and St. Bernard. Abélard has been remembered for other matters as well. He had a tragic love affair with the beautiful Héloise, the niece of Canon Fulbert of Notre Dame, and a continuous quarrel with St. Bernard of Clairvaux. Abélard was gifted with an inquiring mind that accepted no authority blindly. Hence he said, "By doubts we are led to inquire; by inquiring we perceive the truth." St. Bernard, more saintly than Abélard, was a devout mystic who relied on unquestioning faith to win the truth for man. He was an ascetic who viewed all pagan writings with severe distrust and, although he allowed manuscripts to be copied, forbade all illumination and ornament. Abélard and St. Bernard had nothing in common save a burning sincerity for the cause which each championed.

Abélard's spirit of inquiry. Perhaps Abélard's greatest significance lies in the challenge he made against the mental habits of his age. He said that we must learn to doubt, for doubting leads us to inquire, and inquiry leads us to the truth. This is the true spirit of inductive science based upon observation, experimentation, and intellectual skepticism. While he himself could never transcend superimposed authority, he did stimulate intellectual curiosity by writing his *Sic et Non* (*Yes and No*). His epoch-making work proposes 158 questions concerning faith and reason, the angels, Adam and Eve, the origin of evil, and other problems. According to the prologue his intention was to compile a list of apparent contradictions which are to be found in the most authoritative writings of the Church. These are typical propositions propounded in *Sic et Non:*

1. That faith is to be supported by human reason, *et contra.*
5. That God is not single, *et contra.*
55. That only Eve, not Adam, was beguiled, *et contra.*
122. That marriage is lawful for all, *et contra.*
141. That works of mercy do not profit those without faith, *et contra.*
154. That a lie is permissible, *et contra.*[3]

In Holy Scripture, of course, there can be no real contradictions; therefore the discrepancies are to be reconciled by rational interpretation. Abélard himself offered no reconciliation, but he undoubtedly believed that it was possible. So did his pupil Peter Lombard, whose *Sentences* (*Opinions*) became immensely popular. What Abélard perhaps did not comprehend was that he had set in motion a system of inquiry which was to bring problems of Biblical criticism in its train.

Greek and Arabic learning. In Abélard's lifetime, in the twelfth century, the west began to undertake a serious study of Greek and Arabic learning. The early Middle Ages had been able to digest only the works of the Latin Church Fathers and such classical science as was contained in Pliny's *Natural History.* In the early Middle Ages, Byzantine and Moslem scholarship was greatly superior to anything in the West. Because of the prevailing ignorance of Greek and Arabic in Europe, western scholars for centuries were virtually ignorant of what was transpiring elsewhere.

In the Norman kingdom of southern Italy and Sicily, in Spain, and in southern France, scholars began to study and translate Greek and Arabic manuscripts. By the end of the twelfth century many important Latin translations of Greek philosophical and scientific works had been made. Western Christendom also learned now of the intellectual contributions of the Moslem world. Subsequent to the thirteenth century, learning in the East had far outshone that in the west. The era of translation tended to change matters, however. The learning of the east became available for scholars in western Europe, the intellectual pulse quickened in the west, and from that time forward the west achieved the greater intellectual results.

The most important of the western translators was Gerard of Cremona, who translated some seventy Arabic works into Latin before his death in 1187. Most of Gerard's translations concern scientific subjects such as astronomy, mathematics, and medicine. "Indeed, more of Arabic science in general passed into western Europe at the hands of Gerard of Cremona than in any other way."[4] The philosophical implications resulting from the opening up of eastern thought were enormous. Aristotle's *Ethics, Poetics,* and *Rhetoric* were translated directly from Greek. When all his logic was brought to the west, it established him there as the master of logic. To the medieval thinker he was in all learning an authority considered second only to the Scriptures. Arabic numerals, the algebra and trigonometry of Al-Khwarizmi, Euclid's *Geometry,* Ptolemy's *Almagest* (which established the geocentric view of the universe until Copernicus refuted it in the sixteenth century), treatises of Hippocrates and Galen in medicine, Avicenna's *Canon of Medicine,* and Arabic works on optics, alchemy, and physics brought into the west a host of ideas which had to be reconciled with existing Church dogmas.

The task of reconciliation. The heroic, if impossible, task of reconciliation resulted in what is known as Scholasticism. Theologians tried to apply Aristotelian logic to the new Greek and Arabic science and philosophy and to harmonize the whole with the Scriptures and Church dogmas in order to show the purpose of God's plan. The problem was exceedingly complicated. A great deal of the new-found knowledge was the product of Aristotle's brain, while further material came from Plato by way of the mystical school of Neo-Platonism. Thus Neo-Platonism and Aristotelianism had to be spliced and the two brought into agreement with the theology of the Church. It was no easy matter to make Christians out of Aristotle and Plato, although the two pagans were treated by medieval scholars with almost as much veneration as though they had been canonized by the Pope.

To the modern reader, the net result is brilliant but scarcely convincing. But the enormity of the task excites our admiration. With mingled devotion and confidence the scholars of the time wrote compendiums of knowledge called *summae* (from the Latin for "sum total") which tried to include systematic treatises on theology and related subjects, such as science.

But the irreconcilable would not be reconciled, even though the cause was highly religious and idealistic. Adelard of Bath, who introduced Arabic science into England in the twelfth century and who believed that reason, not authority, should be the final judge, says as much to his nephew: "It is hard to discuss with you, for I learned one thing from the Arabs under the guidance of reason; you follow another halter, caught by the appearance of authority; for what is authority but a halter?"[5]

In the thirteenth century Scholasticism attained its greatest heights. Both Realists and Nominalists were Scholastics, and the greatest of them lived in the thirteenth century. With such authorities as the Bible, the creeds developed in the Church councils, the writings of the Church Fathers, and the works of Aristotle they sought by deductive reasoning to harmonize theology and reason, sacred and profane learning, science and religion. Two such scholars were St. Albertus Magnus and St. Thomas Aquinas.

St. Albertus Magnus. Albert the Great (1193-1280), a German, the principal master of the Dominicans at Paris, wrote a *Summa Theologiae* of thirty-eight quarto volumes. It is an interpretation of Aristotle in the light of Christian truth. Although his great work was lacking in coherence and symmetry, Albert is remembered for "testing authority by experience." Such a contribution from the thirteenth century is worthy of admiration. In fact, it makes us recognize how false is the generalization that the Middle Ages were devoid of any critical faculty where doctrines were involved.

St. Thomas Aquinas. It remained for Albertus' Italian pupil St. Thomas Aquinas (1225?-1274) to bring Scholasticism to its culminating peak of attainment. Modern critics have called him "the greatest of the schoolmen." Aquinas, for one, wanted to purge Aristotle's works of the heretical views which had come in through translations from the Arabic as well as through commentaries on Aristotle by such great Moslem thinkers as Averröes. Aquinas at last attained the formula which was to be accepted by the Church as the final statement of the relation between philosophy and revelation, reason and faith. In his *Summa Theologiae* the Scholastic did not falter in his task, insurmountable though it seemed. Aquinas refused to hold one conviction on rationalistic principles and the opposite conviction on faith. Therefore, working industriously from the most basic of premises, even from proving the existence of God to his satisfaction, Aquinas built his cathedral of Scholastic philosophy on the twin pillars of authority and Aristotle. He aimed through logic to reconcile all science with the creed of the Church. So successful was Aquinas in his task that his works are today used as basic texts in Catholic schools and colleges. Whether or not one agrees that Aquinas succeeded in reconciling Aristotle with Christianity and reason with faith, everyone must agree that he made a magnificent effort, an effort which exhibits unsurpassed powers of systematization and a gift of lucid presentation. As Henry Osborn Taylor states: "Of all mediaeval men, St. Thomas Aquinas achieved the most organic and comprehensive union of the results of human reasoning and the data of Christian theology. He may be regarded as the final exponent of Scholasticism, perfected in method, universal in scope, and still integral in purpose."[6]

The decline of Scholasticism. But Scholasticism, having reached its zenith, soon began to decline rapidly. Aquinas had maintained that certain doctrines are beyond discovery by the unassisted reason. Two Franciscan thinkers, William of Occam and Duns Scotus, began to argue that if reason confines us to the natural world and divinely revealed truth is not understandable by the human intellect, then what the human reason can hope to attain is so far removed from divine truth as to be quite uncertain. Such a position served to separate philosophy from theology, to reawaken an interest in Nominalism, to justify the growing scientific spirit, and to weaken the unifying authority of the Church. There were other reasons which explain the decay of Scholasticism. It was losing its grasp on life. Philosophy was becoming empty, divorced from the new forces of the age.

Significance of Scholasticism. Men had begun to doubt and to inquire; the truth which they now perceived was not Scholasticism. But too many writers have dismissed medieval philosophy by saying that the Scholastics wasted all their time arguing about how many angels could dance on the point of a pin. That is by no means the whole story. The Middle Ages strove to unify everything. There was one great Church, which encompassed all Christians, one great Holy Roman Empire, whose ideal was to unite all peoples, one feudal, manorial, and guild system, which tried to attain a common denominator for men's social and economic relations. Therefore it was logical for thinkers to try to work out an all-embracing system of thought to reconcile and direct faith, logic, and science. That it failed to impress all men is no fault of the earnest Scholastics. Today we have not successfully reconciled religion and science, nor have we even unified our warring political and economic ideologies.

The controversy between the Nominalists and the Realists has significance today. Realism stood for the old order; its trust was placed in authority, and the group was considered more important than the individual. Nominalism stood for the order which was to come in the modern age; it revolted against authority, and the individual was considered superior to the group. Nominalism stood for inductive science, just as Realism favored deductive philosophy. Roger Bacon, the great thirteenth-century English scientist and Nominalist, indicated this when he said, "One individual is worth more than all the universals in the world. God has not created the world for the sake of the universal man but for the sake of individual persons."[7]

Science in the Middle Ages

Obstacles to science. Many people think that the Middle Ages were completely lacking in any scientific attainments, that its thinkers spent their time debating useless questions, and that they never interested themselves in experimentation. It is true that the early Middle Ages contributed little of genuine importance to scientific advancement, but to believe that this is true of the entire period is erroneous.

Science in the Middle Ages was forced to labor under certain adverse conditions. Emphasis was placed principally on theology and authority, and the findings of science were supposed to illuminate rather than contradict the dogmas of the theologians. Moreover, theology is a deductive study. It reasons from given premises. Science as we know it is inductive. It works through experimentation from particulars to a conclusion. Therefore, the methods of theology and science vary radically, and so long as theology had the power to control the actions of science, the latter could not investigate freely. However, let us point out now that there were numerous occasions in medieval times when experimentation was made use of with excellent results and that theology by no means throttled all scientific investigation.

Perhaps the greatest obstacle facing science in the early Middle Ages was its ignorance of Greek learning. Science had to rely for its knowledge upon such compilations as the *Etymologies* of Isidore of Seville. This extremely popular work embraced medicine, law, the liberal arts, animals, agriculture, ships, the earth, the universe, household utensils, and other subjects. It was a work for credulous readers and was often allegorical. Its inaccuracies can be imagined from the following "facts":

"XI, 3, 23. The race of the Sciopodes is said to live in Ethiopia. They have one leg apiece, and are of a marvellous swiftness, and the Greeks call them Sciopodes from this, that in summertime they lie on the ground on their backs and are shaded by the greatness of their feet.

"XII, 7, 18. The swan (*cygnus*) is so called from singing (*canendo*), because it pours forth sweet song in modulated tones. And it sings sweetly for the reason that it has a long curving neck, and it must needs be that the voice, struggling out by a long and winding way, should utter various notes."[8]

Science advances. When Greek and Arabic works were translated in the twelfth century, the west came into possession of a magnificent legacy of scientific knowledge. In mathematics the Arabic numerals together with the invention of the zero made the decimal system of computation possible. Algebra came from the Arabs. The geometry of Euclid was now accessible, and trigonometry was borrowed from the Moslems. The greatest mathematician of the thirteenth century, Leonard of Pisa, worked out a method of extracting square roots and solving quadratic and cubic equations. In astronomy the geocentric theory of Ptolemy (that the sun revolved about the earth) was generally accepted. Unfortunately for the best interests of science, astronomy was still bound up with astrology, that pseudoscience which maintains that the position of heavenly bodies has an influence upon the destiny of men and nations. Kings and Popes had their private astrologers to forecast the most favorable times for carrying out policies, and even battles were postponed for days so that Mars or Saturn might be in a better position in the heavens to aid the believing general.

Geography. Medieval literature on geography was largely a collection of fables. Rivers were to be found full of boiling water, the giant roc was a bird that could lift two elephants, and oceans were filled with gigantic serpents clad in armor who devoured merchant ships. True enough, medieval geography had been slowly progressing in the science of map-making, but the translation of Ptolemy's *Geography* in 1409, with its erroneous concepts, in some respects proved a handicap. One thing that should be emphasized is that the Middle Ages did not look on the earth as flat. Educated men taught and believed that it was a sphere. The voyages of Christian pilgrims and of European traders to China and India gradually added to geographical knowledge. It is said that "The thirteenth century knew China better than we knew it in the middle of the nineteenth century."[9] Navigation progressed slowly, but as early as the twelfth century some sailors were making use of the magnetic compass.

Physics and chemistry. Physics was based on Aristotle's theory of four elements—earth, water, air, and fire—and on his theories of dynamics, doctrines which it took centuries to prove wrong. Nevertheless, there were thinkers who attacked Aristotelian physics in the fourteenth century, and several very modern hypotheses were put forward concerning dynamics. Chemistry was also based on Aristotle's theory, combined with a mixture of magic, astrology, and alchemy. The medieval alchemist tried in vain to transmute base metals into gold and silver and attempted to purify ordinary mercury to obtain "philosophical mercury," which he thought would act as an elixir that could change anything in the world to whatever the owner of the elixir wished. Not until centuries had elapsed did Christian and Arab doctors give up their pursuit. Yet in their search to transmute one metal into another the alchemists indirectly made important discoveries.

Inventions. That the fourteenth and fifteenth centuries were not lacking in inventive qualities is shown in this partial enumeration of data compiled by Lynn Thorndike:

"We have both practical inventions and the development of scientific instruments. The invention of the mariner's compass in the twelfth century was followed about 1300 by that of the rudder, and by changes in the build of shipping and in masts, spars, and rigging in the fourteenth and fifteenth centuries. Similarly the invention of gunpowder in the thirteenth century was followed in the fourteenth and fifteenth centuries by further developments in fortifications and armor and by the invention of artillery and firearms. The fourteenth century also saw the introduction of the blast furnace and progress in iron-working. Indeed, by 1300 almost all the coal fields of England were being worked, and the iron and textile industries were already in existence; but she did not yet have an empire to which to sell."[10]

Medieval medicine. By the thirteenth century the commentaries by Avicenna and Averroës on Galen, Hippocrates, and Aristotle's biology were translated, and the theories of the Greeks and Arabs continued to dominate medicine up to the Renaissance and even, in northern Europe, up to the seventeenth century.

Too much of an entirely fallacious nature has been written regarding medieval medicine. The surgeons of the fourteenth and fifteenth centuries were not always barbers who performed crude operations but men who systematically studied the dissection of human bodies and who have left us treatises showing their skill in operations and autopsies. Southern France in the fourteenth century saw the invention of an extracting instrument in dentistry. Anesthesia was understood because narcotics were inhaled, although medieval anesthesia was evidently feeble. A great many towns had municipal doctors, and sanitary conditions prevailed to a surprising degree in some of the hospitals.

Leprosy in Europe was virtually stamped out in the fourteenth century, a fact that merits our undying gratitude, and public health received an impetus when Venice instituted quarantine (from *quarantina,* forty days) for contagious diseases in the fourteenth century. One problem which always confronted our medieval ancestors was the prevalence of plagues and epidemics. Ignorant of the germ theory of disease and the means of combatting the spread of epidemics successfully, our ancestors accepted the terrible calamities as visitations from God and tried to propitiate heaven.

While epidemics came often in the Middle Ages, perhaps the most calamitous was the Black Death of 1348. The plague probably came by trade routes across Asia and was carried throughout Europe in the course of time. Akin to the bubonic plague, the Black Death killed from perhaps one third to one half of Europe's population. The pestilence took its name from the dark blotches which appeared on the body of the victim, although there were other symptoms such as swellings in the glands so that lumps arose sometimes the size of hen's eggs. The one stricken often vomited blood or became delirious, and most of the victims died within three days. The terror caused by the Black Death in the fourteenth century was heart-rending. Nor did the terror die out, for the plague cropped up time and again all through the Middle Ages.

Frederick II (1194-1250). Two fascinating scientists of the Middle Ages were the emperor Frederick II and the Franciscan monk Roger Bacon. Frederick II gathered about him in his Sicilian court many notable scholars (irrespective of their religious beliefs) and was accustomed to addressing questions to scholars in distant countries concerning problems in science. He took a keen delight in zoology, and was famed for his large traveling menagerie, which included an elephant on which Frederick would mount Saracen troops when the menagerie traveled. Many experiments are attributed to this brilliant scholar-ruler. One was an attempt to raise children in conditions of absolute silence in order to discover what language they would speak. The attempt never succeeded because the children died. Frederick wrote a remarkable treatise, *On the Art of Hunting with Falcons,* in which he placed higher reliance upon actual observation than on Aristotle—because "Aristotle seldom or never hunted with birds, while we have ever loved and practiced hawking." Frederick's details as to the life and habits of various kinds of hunting birds are still considered largely accurate, and the work is comprehensive in its treatment of ornithology.

Roger Bacon. Perhaps the greatest experimental scientist of the Middle Ages was an English Franciscan, Roger Bacon. Bacon favored the inductive method and steadily criticized the scholastic techniques of the day. In his *Opus Maius* he states:

"There are four principal stumbling blocks to comprehending truth, which hinder wellnigh every scholar: the example of frail and unworthy authority, long-established custom, the sense of the ignorant crowd, and the hiding of one's ignorance under the show of wisdom. In these, every man is involved and every state beset. . . . From these deadly pests come all the evils of the human race; for the noblest and the most useful documents of wisdom are ignored, and the secrets of the arts and sciences. Worse than this, men blinded by the darkness of these four do not see their ignorance but take every care to palliate that for which they do not find the remedy; and, what is the worst, when they are in the densest shades of error, they deem themselves in the full light of truth."[11]

There is an interesting likeness between Roger Bacon's four stumbling blocks and the four "Idols" which were to be put forward three centuries afterward by Francis Bacon (no descendant of Roger). Certainly both men won much of their fame by decrying the limitations of Scholasticism and advocating the employment of inductive techniques in science. Yet they were by no means the first to stress the value of observation and experimentation, for Frederick II and St. Albertus Magnus had already glimpsed the light.

But Roger Bacon is unique in that he gave full rein to his imagination and envisaged a world transformed by the empirical sciences. He not only made important findings in optics, geography, and astronomy (from which he advocated a reform of the existing calendar), but his interest in mechanics enabled him to make the most startling predictions, predictions which have since come true with uncanny accuracy.

"Machines for navigating are possible without rowers, so that great ships suited to river or ocean, guided by one man, may be borne with greater speed than if they were full of men. Likewise cars may be made so that without a draught animal they may be moved *cum impetu inaestimabili,* as we deem the scythed chariots to have been from which antiquity fought. And flying machines are possible, so that a man may sit in the middle turning some device by which artificial wings may beat the air in the manner of a flying bird."[12]

Education and the Rise of the Universities

Education in early medieval times. From the fall of the Roman empire to the ninth century all education and learning were the monopoly of the Church. While secular classical learning was considered "unworthy of the attention of a good Christian," the Church did realize that she had need of an educated clergy. Thus schools were maintained in most of the monasteries and later on in many of the cathedrals.

The old rhetoric schools of Rome had a curriculum of seven liberal arts, consisting of two divisions, a *trivium* of grammar, rhetoric, and dialectic and a *quadrivium* of arithmetic, music, geometry, and astronomy. Whereas Roman education had been designed to prepare youths for public life and to instill in them a love of literature, art, and philosophy, church education was designed to prepare youths for ecclesiastical life and to instill in them a devotion to the Church and her creed. But the seven liberal arts were easily adapted. Grammar was of value in studying Latin, the language of the Church, and in developing a sound style. Rhetoric helped in interpreting the allegories of the Scriptures. Dialectic was chiefly logic and could be used to deduce truths from texts. Arithmetic was needed for computing the movable feast days, such as Easter, in the church calendar. Music was used in the singing of the liturgy. Geometry included the geography of the Holy Lands and heaven. Astronomy was largely neglected, although the Church taught that heaven and earth were created in six days and that the stars were inferior to the earth. Thus, the *trivium* and *quadrivium* served the purposes of the Church.

Monastic schools. Throughout the early Middle Ages the chief centers of learning were the monasteries. While they had as their chief function the chanting of services and not the education of the people (throughout the entire Middle Ages only a very few people could read or write, and these were churchmen who were educated for a specific ecclesiastical purpose), the monastic schools nevertheless performed an invaluable service. As early as the fifth century education had made great progress in Ireland. The Benedictine monasteries became educational centers in the seventh and eighth centuries, producing such famous scholars as the venerable Bede in England.

Cathedral schools. In the eighth century there was a renaissance of culture because of the splendid work of Charlemagne. At his capital in Aix-la-Chapelle he established a palace school, placing the outstanding English scholar Alcuin in charge. The experiment, designed mainly to educate the sons of the nobility, did not continue after the death of its founder. Yet the type of school which Charlemagne established in connection with the cathedrals made advances. Cathedral schools were founded at Paris, Tours, Chartres, Orléans, Rheims, Canterbury, Toledo, and other cathedral towns. "During the eleventh and twelfth centuries the cathedral schools produced the greatest scholars of Europe, far surpassing the monastic schools, though many monks gave their whole lives to learning."[13] In the twelfth century the monastic orders, even including the reforming order of Cluny, which had been founded in 910 and had reached its height in the pontificate of Gregory VII, went into an intellectual decline. The new orders that sprang up in the twelfth century demanded a spiritual rather than an intellectual renaissance and stressed asceticism, not learning. Hence cathedral schools superseded those of the monasteries.

The twelfth-century renaissance. Meanwhile, the "renaissance of the twelfth century" brought students in great numbers to the schools. Western Europe was growing intellectually wealthier all the time. The Justinian Code, lost for six hundred years, had been rediscovered, stimulating the study of law. The Church was emphasizing canon law more now than in earlier centuries, and the monastic and cathedral schools were not prepared to teach this study. Aristotle was becoming known, and his teachings affected logic, theology, and the sciences. Euclid's geometry and a new arithmetic based on Arabic numerals were coming into Europe via Arabic translations. The west was finding out what the Greeks had bequeathed to medicine. The impetus to learning was enormous—a learning which encompassed much more than theology or philosophy. The cathedral and monastic schools, with their limited curriculum of the seven liberal arts, were obviously not capable of teaching the new concepts in mathematics and logic or of coping with professional studies such as law, medicine, and theology. Another educational institution was required to meet the demands of the twelfth-century revival of learning. That institution was the university. The "intellectual revolution" was accompanied by an "institutional revolution."

Origins of the universities. The first universities began to take form in the twelfth century. The word "university" at one time stood for a guild or corporation of sorts. Thus there were universities of barbers, tanners, goldsmiths, and so on. When persons came together to study at a particular place —both students and teachers—they could be addressed as a *universitas*, because the university was at first a guild of learners, composed of teachers and students, patterned along lines similar to guilds of craft, composed of masters and apprentices. So we can say that in the thirteenth century there were only two requisites needed for a university—teachers and students. There were no buildings, campuses, endowments, or university organizations as we know them today.

In the beginning, universities were created by that love of learning which made men want to listen to some outstanding thinker. The whole procedure was informal and unofficial. Later, Popes and kings saw the possibilities of the new educational movement and granted charters which gave legal status to the universities and special rights to the students, such as freedom from military service and the jurisdiction of townspeople.

The two most famous medieval universities were at Bologna and Paris. The Italian university, Bologna, owed its growth to the fame of the great teacher of civil law, Irnerius, who lectured on the *Digest*, as well as to the teaching of Gratian, whose *Decretum* systematized canon law. The French university grew out of the cathedral school of Notre Dame at Paris. This university became the most influential in medieval Europe.

Bologna. The University of Bologna was a paradise for undergraduates. The students organized the university as a means of protection against the rapacious townspeople, who had raised prices of foodstuffs and lodgings for those who flocked into the town to study under the masters of law. Since the individual student was helpless against such profiteering, organization was essential to bring the townspeople to terms. The students therefore threatened to depart as a body, something that could be done quite easily since the university possessed no permanent buildings at first. There is more than one case on record to show that universities did migrate on occasion.

The students not only ruled over the cowed townsmen but also managed to keep the professors under their control. For instance, in the earliest statutes (1317), we read:

". . . that a professor might not be absent without leave, even a single day, and if he desired to leave town he had to make a deposit to insure his return. If he failed to secure an audience of five for a regular lecture, he was fined as if absent—a poor lecture indeed which could not secure five hearers! He must begin with the bell and quit within one minute after the next bell. He was not allowed to skip a chapter in his commentary or postpone a difficulty to the end of the hour, and he was obliged to cover ground systematically, so much in each specific term of the year. No one might spend the whole year on introduction and bibliography!"[14]

The students at Bologna were organized into two student guilds, the cismontane, composed of men from Italy, and the transmontane, composed of men from beyond the Alps. The student guilds controlled all academic matters save the granting of degrees, a prerogative which remained in the hands of the masters.

Paris. Conditions developed in an opposite fashion in Paris, the center of theology and hence the foremost in importance of all European universities. It is said that, when Abélard started teaching, thousands of students poured into Paris, overflowing the island in the Seine and spreading along the left bank of the river, thereby creating (because of the language spoken) the Latin Quarter.

The youths who flocked to Paris were much younger than those who went to study law at Bologna, and the chancellor who had controlled the cathedral school never once allowed the students to take the law into their own hands. The power passed into the hands of the masters' guild, composed of the four faculties of arts, theology, law, and medicine.

The collegiate system. The poor lad who wanted an education and trudged weary miles from home to acquire it at Paris or some other university center labored under decided handicaps. There were fees to pay the instructor. Since only the wealthiest student could afford to buy a text (which had to be copied by hand), the poor student wrote on wax tablets. There were no dormitories; so students had to manage as best they could in cellars or garrets. Sometimes they pooled resources and lived on a cooperative basis.

Out of these meager beginnings arose the collegiate system. A philanthropic patron would donate quarters where indigent scholars might board free of charge. Such a patron was Robert de Sorbon, who endowed a hall at Paris for sixteen needy persons who were working for their doctorates in theology. Thus was founded in 1257 the famous Sorbonne, the oldest of academic colleges. As time elapsed, other colleges were created, not only in Paris but elsewhere, as in England, where the system became extremely popular. With the rise of the collegiate system these centers came to furnish instruction as well as residential quarters. In Oxford and Cambridge today the students live in colleges (Balliol, Magdalene), attend lectures, and make use of the college library. The university is made up of these colleges, and it is the university that confers the degrees.

Papal regulation. With the rise of universities came papal regulations. Innocent III, who had studied at Paris himself, defined the privileges and obligations of the embryonic theologians. Paris received its first code of regulations from him in 1215. A student had to be twenty years old before he could become a master of arts and thirty-five before he could teach theology. The master, who was required to keep a decent appearance, wore a clerical gown of dark color. Each student had to

Henricus De Alemania delivers a lecture to a motley gathering at the University of Bologna. Evidently his words do not impress one student.

attach himself to a master, who had the right to discipline him when necessary.[15]

Student life. Judging from contemporary accounts, the problem of discipline must often have loomed very large. Coulton's *Medieval Garner* recounts an Oxford brawl in 1238 in which the Pope's legate was attacked and nearly killed and his brother slain by an arrow by students who were afterward carried to London in tumbrils, cast into prison, excommunicated, and forced to walk barefoot through the streets and beg humbly for pardon. Members of Parliament in 1422 complained of the "manslaughters, murders, rapes, felonies, robberies, riots, conventicles, and other misdeeds" committed by Oxford students, to be sure—but by Irishmen attending the university, according to the English statesmen.

The largest part of student correspondence in any age is taken up with requests for money. The student had to pay fees, and he was always writing home to his father asking for more money for fees or rent. A doleful request from a scholar at Orléans ends, "Well-beloved father, to ease my debts contracted at the tavern, at the baker's, with the doctor and the bedells [beadles], and to pay my subscriptions to the laundress and the barber, I send you word of greetings and of money."[16] C. H. Haskins gives us further techniques which were used to soften a father's heart and loosen his purse-strings:

"If the father was close-fisted, there were special reasons to be urged: the town was dear—as university towns always are!—the price of living was exceptionally high owing to a hard winter, a threatened siege, a failure of crops, or an unusual number of scholars; the last messenger had been robbed or had absconded with the money; the son could borrow no more of his fellows or of the Jews; he has been ill with the cold and tempted to run away; the cold is so great that he cannot study at night; and so on."[17]

The quiet, scholarly, and well-behaved student is seldom heard of in contemporary accounts for the reason that he was generally neither famous nor infamous enough to catch the chronicler's attention. But Chaucer's picture of the diligent Clerk of Oxford, who "looked holwe . . . and . . . thredbare," whose little money went for the purchasing of books on Aristotle, and who "gladly wolde . . . lerne, and gladly teche,"[18] shows that the most exemplary scholars also attended Paris and Oxford in the Middle Ages.

An average day. The average day of the medieval student was patterned much in this way: He attended as a rule only a class or two a day, but each might be three hours long. The first was at daybreak and might be devoted to a text of Aristotle. The student went into a bleak hall (provided that the university possessed its own buildings), very often without windows and unwarmed. Concern with physical comfort was frowned upon and commonly regarded as effeminate. The professor lectured from a platform, while the students sat on low benches. The only books were manuscripts. These consisted of costly parchment leaves bound together and very often inaccurately copied, which were rented out to those students rich enough to pay for such texts. Later, students bought their own books. After the first lecture, the scholars would have their first meal, at ten or eleven o'clock. Then came recreation, then a second lecture. Supper was at four or five o'clock. Until curfew the students engaged in social activities. Many did not study at night, being unable to afford candles. They had to converse in Latin in the colleges, under threat of punishment.

Curriculum and degrees. The value of a university degree was that it gave its owner the right to teach. However, the bachelor's degree was not considered important and could be obtained after studying the *trivium* from three to five years. In order to gain his master's degree, the student spent almost as much time on the *quadrivium*, with particular emphasis on the works of Aristotle. Many scholars studied for a doctorate in one of the three great professions—theology, medicine, and law. To do this they read texts pertaining especially to their chosen profession. It was no easy matter to get a doctorate from a medieval university. At Paris the requirement for a doctor of theology was fourteen years of study, and when this time had elapsed, the candidate had to defend his thesis publicly for twelve hours. If successful in his defense, he then had to stand the expense of a banquet for the masters. But at last he "arrived" in his profession and had all the rights and privileges of teaching.

The spread of universities. The influence of Bologna and Paris was very marked in the creation of other university centers. The influence of Bologna was strong in Italy, southern France, and Spain. Paris became the model of a group of universities which were founded in Great Britain, Germany, northern France, and the Low Countries. Around 1200 there was a migration from Paris to Oxford, at that time an exceedingly small center of learning. A decade or two later, another group of students migrated from Oxford and founded Cambridge. The University of Prague was founded in 1347; Heidelberg (the first German university), in 1386. By the close of the Middle Ages Europe could boast of about seventy-five universities.

The legacy of the medieval university. Modern universities have large campuses, fine buildings, and wealthy endowments, while the medieval institution had none of these things. But the modern university resembles its venerable alma mater in its main reason for existence, the organization of institutions of learning for the advancement of human knowledge and the training of each new generation of students. It has also received the idea of "a stated curriculum covering a fixed number of years, formal instruction, examinations, and degrees." The gowns and hoods which are to be seen every commencement day are the same kind of attire in which the medieval student was garbed and in the sleeves of which he would store his books or the food which he begged from indulgent townspeople. The college system at Oxford and Cambridge came from the creation of the Sorbonne and the collegiate system at Paris. Our subject matter is different from that of our medieval teachers, but our ideals and purpose are substantially the same.

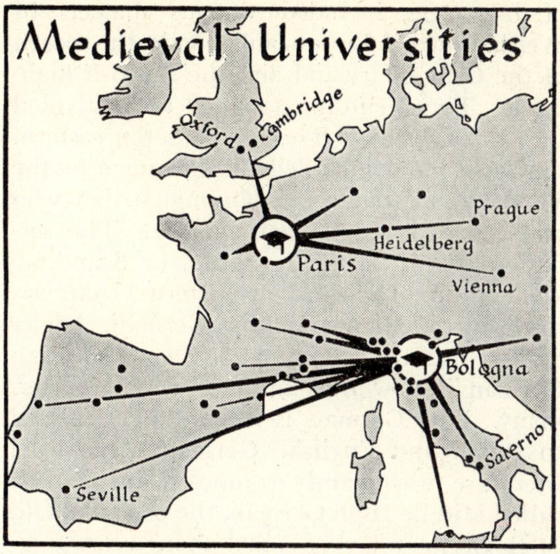

"The two most essential functions which a true university has to perform . . . are to make possible a life of study, whether for a few years or during a whole career, and to bring together during that period face to face in living intercourse, teacher and teacher, teacher and student, student and student."[19]

Medieval Literature

The vernacular. During the Middle Ages the intellectual growth of the western world was stimulated by the flowering of Latin and vernacular literatures. Though the first gradually died out, the second became richer and more universal in the succeeding centuries. Latin was the international language of the educated, who prayed, preached, sang, and wrote in this medium. But the great majority of Europe's population neither spoke nor understood Latin. Their language was vernacular, that is, it pertained to a specific country or locality and was indeed their mother tongue. Therefore any literature written to appeal to the people had to make use of the language of their daily life.

There was a variety of vernacular tongues in use in medieval Europe. The Celtic group of languages included various dialects of Welsh, Cornish, Breton, and Gaelic, the speech of the Celts of Ireland and the Scottish highlands. The Teutonic tongues were divided into three groups. The first was the eastern, or Gothic, and included the language of the Vandals and some other German tribes who had invaded the Roman empire. The second consisted of the northern, or Scandinavian, group. The third, or western, group was made up of High and Low German, Anglo-Saxon, Frisian, Dutch, and Flemish. High German is now the national speech of Germany. Low German is more closely related to Dutch and English. Germany's medieval literature was mainly composed in what is called Middle High German, the period of Old High German having ended about 1100.

Even in the days of Virgil and Cicero two distinct types of Latin were in daily use. The first, and most familiar to us, was the finished and polished product of the finest literary writers. The second was "vulgar Latin," the speech of the people. The two types had many easily distinguishable differences, of course, just as the colloquial speech of modern English differs markedly from formal English. In the provinces the tongue of the common people came to merge with the dialects of the barbarian tribes, and through this process the Romance languages of Italy, France, Portugal, and Spain developed. Dialects grew up in various districts. From the northern dialects in France modern French developed. The southern tongue, known as Provençal, eventually disappeared as a written language, although peasants in certain sections of southern France still speak it.

The literature composed in all these vernacular languages was transmitted orally at first, and sometimes centuries elapsed before it was written down, probably because the men who could read and write did so in Latin and looked with contempt upon literature written in any of the vulgar tongues. But vernacular literature sprang from the people themselves. Its flesh-and-blood quality was more vital and dynamic than the phraseology of the scholars, and so it was natural that by and large it should outstrip Latin literature. This is evident from the fact that the greatest of the medieval poets, Dante, Chaucer, and Villon, composed their greatest works in their vernacular tongues.

Rivalry of Latin and vernacular literature. The Latin tradition of law, language, and literature persisted into medieval times. The eleventh century witnessed the flowering of medieval Latin literature and the rise of its rival, the vernacular. This rivalry has been well expressed by Cesare Foligno of Oxford:

"The new languages were not the foes but became the rivals of Latin, and rivals more deadly than foes; for Latin survived as the language of learning, sometimes as the medium of emotional expression when the writer happened preëminently to be a man of learning; but as a rule it was a language into which the full breath of life was ceasing or had ceased to flow. It is a proof of the tremendous force of tradition that Latin should have survived so long. It would seem gallantly to have kept up a semblance of life until all the new languages had risen to literary rank. Yet one dare not mistake the semblance of life for life itself. Creative literature, the literature of poets in the etymological meaning of the word, found readier means of expression in the Germanic and Romance vernaculars."[20]

Latin retired into the schools, churches, and scriptoria of the learned, there to continue to serve as a language of culture and knowledge. Therein lies much of the strength of the Middle Ages, for Latin possessed a universality of expression which bound all scholarship and knowledge together, a situation we might do well to re-create today, confronted as we are by a plethora of tongues. Furthermore, medieval Latin, although criticized as bad and ungrammatical Latin, was in reality a language which coined new expressions and simplified its syntax in order to meet the demands of an ever-changing environment. While Foligno is correct in stating that the creative spirit of the age turned more and more to those languages which had sprung from the vitality of the people, Latin was still spirited enough to produce some excellent literature.

Latin prose. Medieval Latin prose embraced church and government documents, treatises on law and medicine, and essays on theology and dialectic. Histories of earlier periods, annals, chronicles, biographies, and hagiography (saints' lives) were also written in Latin prose.

One of the glories of Latin is its rich, sonorous tone, and even the formal documents of the Middle Ages are enriched by the dignity and music of Latin phraseology. But undoubtedly the most splendid Latin of the Middle Ages is to be found in the liturgy of the Church, which was chanted rhythmically by the priest.

Three periods of Latin poetry. The Latin poetry of this age shows warmth and richness. The writing of Latin poetry experienced three periods of revival: the Carolingian (the most limited in scope), the eleventh and twelfth centuries, and the age of Petrarch (1304-1374). The poetry of Petrarch's time found itself in hopeless competition with the vernacular tongues. Thus, although Petrarch expected immortal fame from his Latin epic *Africa,* he won it through his Italian sonnets. However, the poetry of the second revival was full of vigor and new ideas. It is true that much of medieval Latin poetry was merely an imitation of ancient models, but contributions were made, especially in the lyrics of the university students and the new religious drama.

Religious verse. A great deal of the Latin poetry of the religious type—and there was a very large quantity of it—was mediocre in quality, but several new developments are worth mentioning. An interesting innovation was the introduction of rhyme. While much of the new rhymed verse was of the jingle variety, some of the effects achieved were excellent. The following lines, taken from a chorus chanted by pilgrims swinging along the dusty roads which led to Rome, are superbly sonorous:

O Roma nobilis, orbis et domina,
Cunctarum urbium excellentissima,
Roseo martyrum sanguine rubea,
Albis et virginum liliis candida,
Salutem dicimus tibi per omnia,
Te benedicimus: salve per secula.[21]

The religious poetry of St. Bernard and Abélard and the writing of great hymns like the *Stabat Mater, De Contemptu Mundi,* and the *Dies Irae* show the genuineness of the religious spirit which permeated the medieval Latin sacred poetry.

Goliardic literature. Far different, however, was the spirit of secular poetry. Abélard, who could write sincere religious lyrics, could just as spontaneously give words to the most sensuous, satirical, and untrammeled thoughts. Nor was Abélard alone in this duality of spirit. A certain paganism pervades the youth in every age, and the Middle Ages were no exception. The hard-worked young scholars who were one day to become priests, bishops, and even grave pontiffs needed an escape from their humdrum existence. And they found it—in town and gown riots, pranks against professors, parodies of the Mass, and a madcap literature that joyously proclaimed the pleasures of wine, women, and song.

One can never hope to appreciate the medieval spirit without taking full account of the student literature. It is known as Goliardic verse because the authors called themselves the disciples of Golias—possibly Goliath the Philistine.

The spirit of these wandering scholars is admirably caught in "A Song of the Open Road":

We in our wandering,
Blithesome and squandering,
  Tara, tantara, teino!

Eat to satiety,
Drink with propriety;
  Tara, tantara, teino!

Laugh till our sides we split,
Rags on our hides we fit;
  Tara, tantara, teino!

Jesting eternally,
Quaffing infernally:
  Tara, tantara, teino!

Craft's in the bone of us,
Fear 'tis unknown of us:
  Tara, tantara, teino!

When we're in neediness,
Thieve we with greediness:
  Tara, tantara, teino![22]

The chief center of the Goliardic poets was in northern France. They were primarily wandering students, and their two greatest poets were Hugh the Primate (about 1140), the deformed and impoverished canon of Orléans, and the Archpoet, whose poetry was written chiefly for Reinald, archbishop of Cologne about 1160. The Archpoet appears to have been of knightly origin and to have had a classical education. He used to solicit openly the bounty of the archbishop, maintaining in the autumn that with winter's approach he had need of warm clothes or that the quality of his verse depended upon the quality of the wine which his patron gave him. His masterpiece is the *Confession of Golias.* Addressed to his patron, the poet's request runs in part as follows:

Prelate, most discreet of priests,
  Grant me absolution!
Dear's the death whereof I die,
  Sweet my dissolution;
For my heart is wounded by
  Beauty's soft suffusion;
All the girls I come not nigh,
  Mine are in illusion.

'Tis most arduous to make
  Nature's self-surrender;
Seeing girls, to blush and be
  Purity's defender!
We young men our longings ne'er
  Shall to stern law render,
Or preserve our fancies from
  Bodies smooth and tender.

In the second place, I own
  To the vice of gaming:
Cold indeed outside I seem,
  Yet my soul is flaming:
But when once the dice-box hath
  Stripped me to my shaming,
Make I songs and verses fit
  For the world's acclaiming.

In the third place, I will speak
  Of the tavern's pleasure;
For I never found nor find
  There the least displeasure;
Nor shall I find it till I greet
  Angels without measure,
Singing requiems for the souls
  In eternal leisure.

. . . .

In the public house to die
  Is my resolution;
Let wine to my lips be nigh
  At life's dissolution:
That will make the angels cry,
  With glad elocution,
"Grant this toper, God on high,
  Grace and absolution!"[23]

The Goliardic poets were brilliant at satire and parody. Versed in classical mythology and possessed of the pagan spirit, they wrote Masses for topers, substituted Venus for the Virgin, and performed other pagan blasphemies. But their satire often hit home, especially the parody called the *Gospel According to the Mark of Silver,* in which the venality of the Roman Curia becomes the object of biting scorn. Yet the disciples of Golias could, and frequently did, pen verses of genuinely serious feeling.

Vernacular epic poetry. The growth of the vernacular Romance languages out of vulgar Latin, together with the growth in northern Europe of the Germanic languages, meant the inevitable emergence of vernacular literatures. The types of medieval vernacular literature are many and varied. Down to the thirteenth century poetry was the commonest means of expression, of which the epic was the earliest form. The Anglo-Saxon *Beowulf,* the German *Hildebrandslied,* and the Norse sagas show literary productiveness as early as the seventh and eighth centuries, that turbulent period almost devoid of Latin literature. Later, around the beginning of the thirteenth century, the German saga was recast into the *Song of the Nibelungs* (*Nibelungenlied*), the stirring tales of Siegfried, Brunhild, and the wars against the Huns, all immortalized in the nineteenth century by four music dramas of Richard Wagner called *Der Ring des Nibelungen.*

The German epic tradition was brought into the French vernacular literature, and in the eleventh and twelfth centuries arose the type of poetry known as *chansons de geste,* songs of heroic deeds, centered principally around Charlemagne and ascribing to him and his knights the chivalric code and religious fervor of the crusades. The most famous of these *chansons* is the *Song of Roland,* which sings of the deeds and death of Roland, Margrave of Brittany, in the Pyrenees while defending the rear of the Frankish army against the Moors.

Altogether some eighty epic *chansons de geste* were written around Charlemagne and his knights and were known as the Carolingian cycle. There were other popular cycles also. One was the great Arthurian cycle concerning the British King Arthur and his Round Table, taken principally from Irish,

Welsh, and Breton sources. A third epic cycle was the tale of Troy. In medieval times both the French and English looked upon themselves as direct descendants of the Trojans. Virgil's *Aeneid* was much more popular than Homer in the Middle Ages (though it is true that many could read Latin but few Greek).

Lyric poetry. In the twelfth and thirteenth centuries, while the poets of northern France were creating the epic *chansons de geste,* the troubadours of southern France were singing a livelier lyric of great excellence and variety. The troubadours, often of noble birth, sang in the feudal courts of the south, and their poems, written in Provençal, dealt with fair and virtuous ladies and a formalized chivalric code of love. The troubadours were an interesting lot. At least half of them were either feudal lords or vassals, and they sang to an audience that was itself aristocratic, refined, and courtly. The first-known troubadour was William IX, Duke of Aquitaine (1071-1126), whose poetry deals with war, love, and numerous licentious and humorous topics.

The Provençal lyrics had intricate rhyme schemes and metrical patterns to fit the many types of subject matter. The *chanson* was an ordinary love song, the *salut d'amor* was composed as a love letter, the *sirventes* dealt with political and moral questions rather than love, the *tenso* debated questions of love, the *alba* warned lovers of the approach of dawn, and the *pastorela* recounted the wooing by the knight of the not over-shy shepherdess.[24]

Provençal poetry was dealt almost a death blow by the Albigensian crusade. But the spirit of the troubadours spread to other countries. In Germany love lyrics were sung by *minnesingers,* the most famous of these being Walther von der Vogelweide. In the thirteenth century courtly literature was further refined in France, where *courtoisie,* poetry in which warfare and chivalrous subjects were all used for the glorification of women, also developed. At the same time the old *chanson de geste* was transformed into the *romance,* a long tale filled with fair ladies, dragons, magicians, and talking animals.

Allegory. To the medieval penchant for parody and satire must be added the predilection for allegory. Ovid, Virgil, and the *Gesta Romanorum* (a series of fantastic tales supposedly based on antiquity) were sermonized and allegorized in order to appeal to the medieval love for storytelling. Allegory reached perhaps its fullest development in the long-winded, elegant compendium known as the *Romance of the Rose,* a poem which influenced the early writings of Chaucer.

Bourgeois poetry. But the *chansons de geste,* Provençal lyrics, romances of the Arthurian type, and the *Romance of the Rose* were primarily for the chivalric aristocracy. The burgher was not overly interested in *courtoisie;* he preferred more practical and shrewd tales. His tastes were gratified in the *fabliaux* —bawdy stories often based on the double assumption that neither wives nor priests could ever be trusted. The bourgeoisie also appreciated fully the collection of animal stories known as the *Romance of Renard.* Renard the Fox is a sharp-witted, unscrupulous creature. The tales were particularly amusing to the burghers by virtue of their many rich parodies of the ideals of the *chanson de geste.*

Literature of the common man. Thus, we can see that a distinct literature was growing up to cater to both the aristocracy and the rising middle class. What of the common people and their literature? It was virtually nonexistent, for the simple reason that the peasants could not write. But there still developed a class of literature which found favor among the common people. The Robin Hood ballads of the fourteenth century disclose the social philosophy of robbing the rich to give to the poor. In the same century the remarkable *Vision of Piers Plowman* was written (probably by William Langland), condemning the injustices of a social system that had brought on the Peasants' Revolt of 1381. The author hurled the most trenchant accusations at an intolerant nobility and clergy and dared attack the feudal caste system.

Geoffrey Chaucer (1340?-1400). Chaucer is one of the greatest figures in medieval literature. His works, especially his *Canterbury Tales,* reveal a cross section of fourteenth-century English life, customs, and thought which cannot be obtained from a perusal of royal charters or laws. Chaucer was associated with the English court and had to travel in various official capacities to France and Italy. It is possible that he may have met Petrarch in Italy. At any rate, Chaucer came back from his foreign travels well versed in the subject matter and poetic techniques of French and Italian literature, and in his earlier writings incorporated much of his foreign learning into his verse. His *Troilus and Criseyde,* an outstanding piece of narrative verse, is modeled after a work of the contemporary Italian Boccaccio.

The Canterbury Tales. But the scene of his masterpiece, *Canterbury Tales,* is laid in England, the England of pilgrimages, pleasant countrysides, sleepy hamlets, and the jocund life of a wayfaring people still blessed with the freshness of living. The twenty-nine pilgrims who assembled in the Tabard Inn in April of the year 1387 were a motley group indeed. The "truly perfect, gentle knight," just back from warring against the "heathen in Turkey," was followed by his son, a young squire who loved so hotly by night that "he slept no more than does a nightingale." Then there was the prioress, coy, neat, and pretty—who "would weep if she but saw a mouse caught in a trap." The rotund monk loved to eat fat swan and to ride good horses. The merchant sat high on his horse and talked always of his profits. The friar knew all the best taverns and all the barmaids in town, but the Oxford student spent his money on books and wore a threadbare coat. The miller had a wart on his nose from which sprang a tuft of hairs "red as the bristles in an old sow's ears," and the doctor prescribed gold for the medicines of his patients. There was also the sailor who told disreputable stories and the rascal who sold pardons for sins and cheated people by substituting pig's for saint's bones and represented a pillow-case as being Our Lady's veil. One of the most delightful characters was the worthy wife of Bath, who had married five times and was now visiting the shrines throughout Christendom in search of husband number six. In a sympathetic manner Chaucer paints for us the character of the poor parson, a credit to his religion, who kept his parish alive spiritually. Likewise the English poet draws a favorable picture of the parson's brother, a plowman, who worked honestly and paid his tithes "fully, fairly, well."[25]

It would be hard to find a more vivid account of characters and situations than Chaucer's description in the Prologue to his *Tales.* An examination of the characters discloses the important fact that the poet, though in court circles himself, speaks of no aristocrat higher than the knight. His people are drawn from the ranks of the clergy and the middle classes, seemingly indicating that Chaucer was well aware both of the importance of the Church and the rising strength of the bourgeoisie in fourteenth-century England.

A tremendous knowledge of the times can be gleaned from the works of this genius. In addition to the brilliance of humor and poetical description which have made the *Canterbury Tales* immortal, the reader learns of religious attitudes of the day, the sources from which Chaucer derived his plots, the prevailing belief in astrology, witchcraft, and relics, and the language of the period. But first and foremost Chaucer deserves fame as a brilliant storyteller.

Significance of Chaucer. Chaucer's use of the Midland dialect helped make it the language of future English literature, just as Dante's use of the Tuscan dialect fixed the Italian tongue. Secondly, Chaucer's use of "high comedy" has never been surpassed. He is always satirizing, but his humor and irony are gentle and sympathetic. Thirdly, because his humor does not preach and because he took such a wholehearted pleasure in the everyday realities of this life, Chaucer stands as a great forerunner of the English Renaissance. If Petrarch and Boccaccio are looked upon as poets of the Italian Renaissance, Chaucer may be regarded as occupying a similar position in the English Renaissance.

Dante Alighieri. Dante Alighieri (1265-1321) has been described as "the medieval synthesis." Exiled from his beloved Florence because of his differences with the papacy, Dante wrote *De Monarchia* to stress the divine importance of the Holy Roman Empire and its ruler. In his *De Vulgari Eloquentia* he defended the use of the vernacular tongue as a literary medium and also as the language needed for a united Italy. But Dante, patriot and innovator, brooded over ideas which had been born of his knowledge of Latin classics, his profound religious sense, his knowledge of the writings of Albertus Magnus, St. Thomas Aquinas, and Peter Lombard, and his appreciation of the mysticism of Dionysius and St. Bernard. The result was the *Divine Comedy.*

The Divine Comedy. The poem is divided into the *Inferno,* where those guilty of the seven deadly sins are forever punished; the *Purgatorio,* where Christians still having to perform penance dwell; and *Paradiso,* where the blessed live. Dante is led through the first two regions by his teacher Virgil, but since the latter is a pagan, Beatrice, the symbol of divine love, guides him through Paradise. Herein Dante shows his allegiance to medieval ideology. Dante was scholar and poet, a rare combination. Both sides of the writer are evident in the *Divine Comedy*. Dante's magnificent descriptive powers are shown in this vivid picture of Lucifer:

Oh, what a marvel it appeared to me,
  When I beheld three faces on his head!
  The one in front, and that vermilion was;
Two were the others, that were joined with this
  Above the middle part of either shoulder,
  And they were joined together at the crest;
And the right-hand one seemed 'twixt white and yellow;
  The left was such to look upon as those
  Who come from where the Nile falls valleyward.
Underneath each came forth two mighty wings,
  Such as befitting were so great a bird;
  Sails of the sea I never saw so large.
No feathers had they, but as of a bat
  Their fashion was; and he was waving them,
  So that three winds proceeded forth therefrom.
Thereby Cocytus wholly was congealed.
  With six eyes did he weep, and down three chins
  Trickled the tear-drops and the bloody drivel.
At every mouth he with his teeth was crunching
  A sinner, in the manner of a brake,
  So that he three of them tormented thus.
To him in front the biting was as naught
  Unto the clawing, for sometimes the spine
  Utterly stripped of all the skin remained.[26]

The drama. Another medieval contribution was to the drama. Out of the choral singing of sacred stories in early times developed the medieval religious plays called mysteries, whose themes dealt with Biblical stories and the lives of the saints. The drama proved of great educational value to men who could not read. The most important festivals in the church calendar, especially Christmas and Easter, lent themselves to a vivid presentation of the stories involved, stories which were beloved and revered.

Other popular themes from the Bible were in time added, and actors rigged out in the medieval conception of Holy Land costume would delight the awe-struck audience with such plays as *The Ten Virgins, The Raising of Lazarus, Adam,* and *Daniel.* At first the plays merely supplemented the regular service and were performed in Latin inside the church proper. With their growth in popularity and originality (many interesting and even profane touches were added by thespians for the delight of their "public") the plays began to be presented either in the church porch or on a separate stage built for the occasion. It came to be the custom to add vernacular phrases to the text, a practice which must have delighted the audience.

In the medieval drama we find some astonishing situations. Like the irreverent verses of the students in the midst of pious Latin poetry, in the midst of serious liturgical drama there came to be a group of irreverent revels. The Feast of the Circumcision (January 1) was presided over by the subdeacons. The custom of celebrating the feast was called the Feast of Fools because of the strange license employed by the subdeacons. While the form of the Mass was retained, interpolation was made in the text, an outlandish ceremonial was included such as a drinking bout, the bringing of an ass into the church at the singing of the Prose of the Ass, and the concluding of various pieces of the liturgy with a bray. The revels of the choir boys on Innocents' Day proved a humorous addition to the drama. On that occasion the choir boys would flout their elders, elect a boy bishop who acted as a ludicrous substitute for the true bishop, and perform in pantomime the Flight into Egypt. Armed men would go through the church seeking Mary and Jesus; they would find the pair (a cleric dressed as a woman holding a baby) sitting on an ass, and then another cleric impersonating Joseph would lead the animal through the church.

Mystery and morality plays. As the drama ceased to have a direct connection with the church service, a type of play known as the morality play developed. The morality play was the allegory in drama. The actors personified virtues and vices, and the plot of the drama usually centered around a conflict between them. *Everyman* is the best-known morality play. The morality plays were not so

ST. APPOLLINARE, EARLY CHRISTIAN BASILICA AT RAVENNA

closely bound up with religion as were the mystery plays, although they often had a religious tinge. The mysteries were based on Bible stories, whereas the moralities had allegorical plots, sometimes of religious significance and sometimes not.

Medieval Art

The cathedral in the Middle Ages. The *Summa theologiae* of St. Thomas Aquinas, the learning of Paris, and the *Divine Comedy* are the intellectual expressions of the medieval spirit which manifested itself outwardly in the Gothic cathedral. These works reveal the continual attempt on the part of medieval people to unify all learning according to a definite theological plan to the end that God might be glorified and man saved. Perhaps the most successful of all was the Gothic cathedral. The artists of the Middle Ages evolved a distinctive style of building—as distinctive and appropriate as the skyscraper in our Age of Steel.

Early medieval churches. The early Christians had used catacombs for their religious services. Later, when they could worship openly, they held their services in Roman buildings. Therefore, when they began building, they imitated the Roman basilica, a rectangle divided into three aisles: a central aisle, or nave, ending in a semicircular apse, and two lower side aisles set off by two arcades of semicircular arches. Wood was generally used for the roof. St. Appollinare at Ravenna (pictured above) shows the apse, decorated with mosaics, the three aisle construction, and the typical wooden roof. The higher middle aisle allowed clerestory windows, a method of obtaining extra light. This same device was used centuries earlier by the Egyptians in their temples and in Roman basilicas.

The Carolingian revival modified the true basilica plan. A transverse aisle called the transept, which extended beyond the side aisles, was added between apse and nave. This gave the church the form of a cross, adding to the symbolism of the structure (though the best-known building of the Carolingian period, perhaps, was the octagonal-shaped cathedral at Aachen). Occasionally the Carolingian builders erected towers, but these graceful additions did not become universal until later. Carolingian buildings were generally constructed of wood, and in the disorders of the ninth and tenth centuries most were destroyed.

Romanesque architecture. In the eleventh century, however, a tremendous architectural revival took place, and in the years 1000-1150 the characteristic features of Romanesque architecture evolved. This revival was largely due to the building program of the Cluniac monks. The characteristics of Romanesque architecture differ greatly according to locality. In France they varied stylistically from the classic in the south to the strongly Byzantine in the center. But the round arch and barrel and groined vaulting appeared throughout. The Romans had made use of stone roofing in the form of a heavy barrel vault, together with the groined vault (see diagram below). Thus the Romanesque style of architecture took from the Romans the basilica plan and the Roman vaulting methods. Although Italy built some early vaulted churches, the full development of Romanesque vaulting came in the north, where lighting was more important. Romanesque churches, such as St. Sernin, illustrated below, were heavy, thick-walled, and dimly lighted. They tended to be solid and gloomy. The builders did not solve the problem of how to have many windows yet strong walls. The vaults were so constructed that heavy outside walls had to support the thrust of the nave vaults. The problem was finally solved by the Gothic builders.

Romanesque sculpture. Romanesque sculpture, like Romanesque architecture, varied according to locality. In the south of France, classic remains influenced such works as the portals of St. Gilles, page 432. This can be seen in the classic decorative motifs, the columns, and the general composition. Note the classic "Greek key" motif above the columns, and compare the decorative foliage with Roman decoration on Trajan's forum, page 183. Almost all Romanesque sculpture was used for architectural purposes.

The Cluniac center in Burgundy produced some of the most beautiful Romanesque sculp-

THE GROINED VAULT *as used by Romanesque builders developed out of the principles involved in the Roman intersecting vaults (see page 181). Arches span the sides of a square, and longer arches span the same square diagonally, concentrating the weight on the four corner piers. The spaces between the arches are filled with rubble or bricks.*

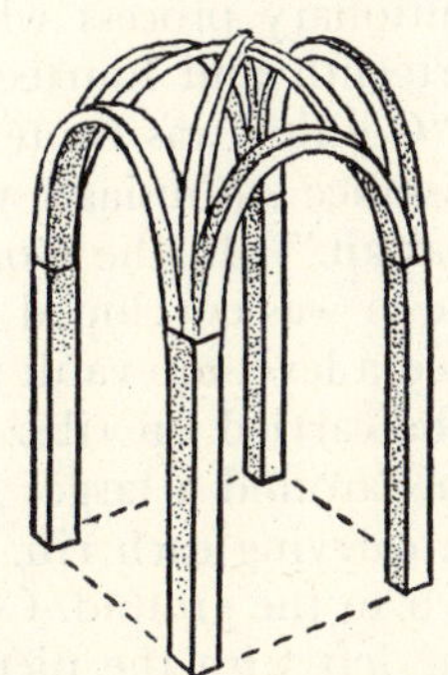

INTERIOR OF ST. SERNIN, TOULOUSE, FRANCE

CLUNY CAPITAL, THIRD TONE PLAIN SONG

PORTALS OF ST. GILLES ABBEY

ture. Little of this work remains, since the large abbey church was blown up in the nineteenth century by profiteers who wanted the stone, but the capitals of the sanctuary still exist. The figures representing the musical tones are skillfully composed and vigorous in conception. The fact that musical subjects were used in the sanctuary of the church shows the importance of this art in the Church.

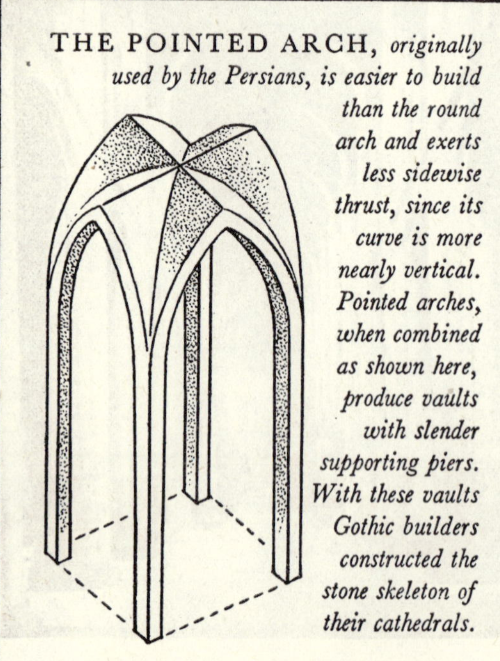
THE POINTED ARCH, *originally used by the Persians, is easier to build than the round arch and exerts less sidewise thrust, since its curve is more nearly vertical. Pointed arches, when combined as shown here, produce vaults with slender supporting piers. With these vaults Gothic builders constructed the stone skeleton of their cathedrals.*

The tympanum over the door at Vézelay (see next page) is an example of sculpture in which the Byzantine influence is strong. Comparison of this low relief with the ivory throne (page 268) will reveal how the later sculptors were influenced by the ivories of Byzantium. This panel was composed so as to fit as many religious stories as possible into the given space. The sculpture on a cathedral was the library of the ordinary man, and through it he learned the stories in the Bible.

Gothic architecture. There is no clearcut cleavage between Romanesque and Gothic. It was a gradual evolutionary process which culminated in the thirteenth and fourteenth centuries. (The term "Gothic" was contemptuously given by Renaissance enthusiasts, who used it to mean "barbarian.") In the Gothic cathedral the pointed arch was developed (see diagram). This produced a level-top vault and allowed the thrust to be carried on ribs. By clustering small columns around a larger one with one small column carrying each rib, the weight was carried down to the ground. Compare the diagram at the left with the picture of the nave of Amiens cathedral, page 434.

TYMPANUM OVER THE DOOR OF THE CATHEDRAL AT VÉZELAY, FRANCE: CHRIST IN MAJESTY

Whereas Romanesque builders had had to make thick walls with a minimum of windows to bear the weight of the roof, in the Gothic ribbed vaulting the small sections of masonry carrying the thrust of the roof arches were supported by flying buttresses on the outside and by the weight of pinnacles (as the view of Notre Dame, Paris, page 434, shows). The important principles of the concentration of thrusts and counter-thrusts had been worked out, and the essential frame of the Gothic structure was a self-supporting, strain-distributed edifice. Walls could now be cut into almost anywhere, and great areas were free to be filled with exquisite stained-glass windows.

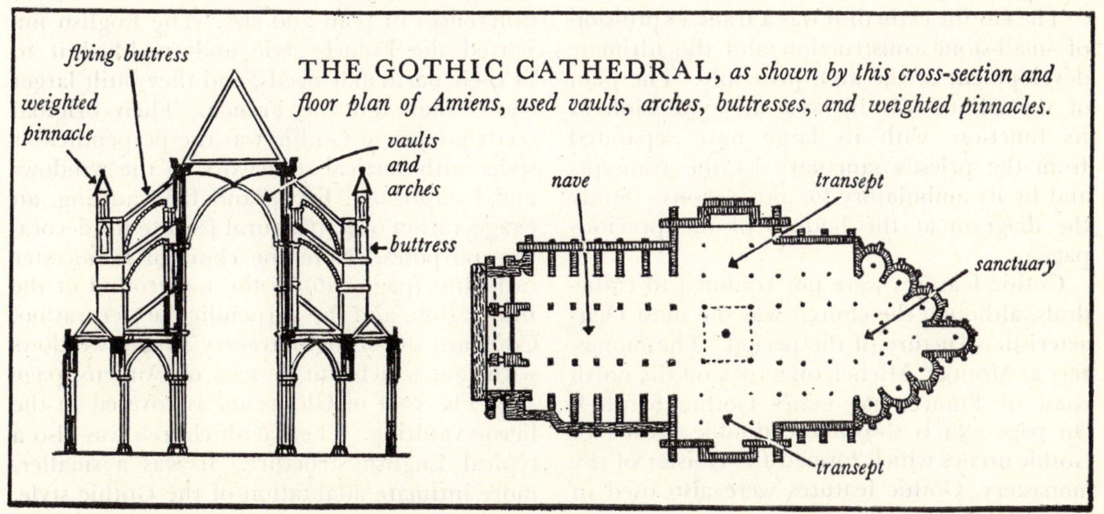

THE GOTHIC CATHEDRAL, *as shown by this cross-section and floor plan of Amiens, used vaults, arches, buttresses, and weighted pinnacles.*

THE NAVE, AMIENS CATHEDRAL

FLYING BUTTRESSES AND PINNACLES, NOTRE DAME, PARIS

The Gothic cathedral was a frank expression of small-stone construction and the ultimate development of the arch principle. The plan of the edifice was likewise an expression of its function, with its large nave separated from the priest's sanctuary by the transepts and by its ambulatory for processions. (Study the diagram at the bottom of the previous page.)

Gothic features were not confined to cathedrals, although the church was the most characteristic structure of the period. The monastery at Mont St. Michel, on a rock off the north coast of France, has many Gothic features. On page 436 is shown the double arcade of Gothic arches which formed the cloister of the monastery. Gothic features were also used in town halls and other secular buildings, as we shall see.

The thirteenth-century architecture was Gothic at its best, and the finest examples are to be found in France. Great cathedrals like Notre Dame of Paris, Amiens, and Chartres are expressions of both the religious feeling and the structural knowledge of the times. Soaring in strength and elasticity, their west portals crowned by two towers, their interiors softened into shadow and colored tints through beautiful stained glass, these cathedrals are the epitome of the Middle Ages.

Regional differences. In England there were differences in plan and size. The English imported the French style and modified it to fit their particular needs, and they built larger choirs than did the French. Their original contribution to Gothic was the perpendicular style, with vertical stonework in the windows and complicated lierne and fan vaulting, an exaggeration of a structural feature for decorative purposes. Note the choir of Gloucester cathedral (page 436) in the foreground of the illustration, and the perpendicular decoration. Compare the straight tracery in the windows with that which can be seen on Amiens, page 435. The roof of Gloucester is covered in the lierne vaulting. The parish church was also a typical English structure. It was a smaller, more intimate adaptation of the Gothic style.

The spire of Amiens, rising out of clustered dwellings to dominate the town, the countryside in fact, breathes the spirit of the Middle Ages. A typical French cathedral, its unmatched towers are proof of the long years spent in its building. Amiens is also typically Gothic with its triple doors, Gothic archings, its plan forming a cross, the sculptural decoration of saints across the façade, and the round rose window dedicated to Our Lady.

INTERIOR OF GLOUCESTER CATHEDRAL

CLOISTER OF THE ABBEY, MONT ST. MICHEL

THE CATHEDRAL AT ROUEN

While the finest Gothic architecture is in France and England, the Spanish cathedrals at Salamanca, Segovia, and Seville are Gothic in style and structure. Distinguishing features of Spanish Gothic are the inclosed choir and the Moorish influence in decoration. Except for the cathedral at Cologne, German Gothic is lacking in France's richness of expression. Much of the Gothic in Germany is greatly influenced by the French style. Italy never took kindly to Gothic, preferring to follow classic traditions and viewing with displeasure the use of great windows, which might be of value in northern climates, but which were drawbacks in Italy. Instead of specializing in stained-glass windows the Italian artists decorated the large wall spaces with murals. Thus geography influenced the arts.

Decorative features. Most of the decorative features of Gothic cathedrals developed from structural or functional beginnings. Thus the tower developed into a decorative feature from the need to place the bells in an openwork structure high enough to sound over the countryside. The pinnacles were used to add weight to the buttresses and later were decorated. The tracery of the windows developed from the original pure structural stone-work to hold the glass, to highly decorative flamboyant tracery.

Gothic art at its best was simple and even ascetic, just as the ideal of spiritual life of the Middle Ages was simplicity and asceticism. In the thirteenth century Gothic architecture reached its apex. Its builders had achieved technical mastery but still believed in simplicity of expression and sincerity of purpose. Their successors wanted to improve on their accomplishments, but their attempts were marred by exaggeration. Cathedrals were covered with unnecessary details, as in the case of Rouen with its flamboyant façade, or they were erected to heights beyond the point of practicality and sometimes came tumbling down. The illustration of Rouen on the opposite page shows how the once purely structural features (pinnacles, gargoyles, tracery, and so on) were used to produce a mass of decoration.

Gothic building and medieval life. The Romanesque church had been built largely by the monastic houses. The Gothic cathedral in France, however, was the creation of the townsmen and bishops. They united in erecting a structure which should at once eclipse the cathedral of a rival town and also express the fervor of their devotion. So the church was built in the center of the town, rising majestically above the low-lying homes of its builders —the social and religious center of all the people.

The archbishop of Rouen wrote to a friend when a French cathedral was in the process of building:

"Who has ever seen? Who has ever heard tell, in times past, that powerful princes of the world, that men brought up in honors and in wealth, that nobles, men and women, have bent their proud and haughty necks to the harness of carts, and that, like beasts of burden, they have dragged to the abode of Christ, these wagons, loaded with wines, grains, oil, stone, timber, and all that is necessary for the construction of a church? . . . They march in such silence that not a murmur is heard. . . . When they halt on the road nothing is heard but confession of sins, and pure and suppliant prayer. . . . When they have reached the church they arrange the wagons about it like a spiritual camp, and during the whole night they celebrate the watch by hymns and canticles. On each wagon they light tapers."[27]

The magnitude of the task of building these huge edifices meant that decades were required to complete a cathedral. Notre Dame at Paris was begun in 1163 but not finished until 1235, while the cathedral at Canterbury took four centuries to build and represents three successive styles.

Gothic sculpture. With the building of the cathedrals grew the arts which were to decorate them. Thirteenth-century Gothic sculpture, as well as the glass of the period, stayed well within the technical limitations and respected its place as a part of one large composition. The central door at Chartres (below) is an excellent example of Gothic architectural sculpture, with the figures distorted in length to fit the door jambs and depicted in a symbolic rather than personal manner. Compare the figures with those of the tympanum at Vézelay (page 433), to see how the use of stylization in the folds of garments remained and was exaggerated at Chartres to emphasize length.

Gothic sculpture gradually developed along more and more realistic and individualized

DETAIL OF CENTRAL DOOR, CHARTRES CATHEDRAL

DECORATIVE SCULPTURE AT CENTRAL DOOR, AMIENS

CLAUS SLUTER: "THE FOUNTAIN OF MOSES," DETAIL

lines. The sculptured figures on the central door at Amiens (left) show an interest in the individual that is absent in the Chartres figures, but the sculptor still respected the architectural setting. Eventually Gothic sculpture became very realistic, like that of Claus Sluter in his Fountain of Moses. Here the saints are faithful depictions of human types, and there is more interest in their personalities than in the whole composition.

Painting. The early Christian paintings on the walls of the catacombs were not really much influenced by Roman painting. Compare the painting "Adam and Eve" (below), a Christian subject, with the pagan subject "Perseus and Andromeda" (page 184). Later, when churches were built, they were decorated with costly and impressive mosaics and Byzantine icons. Mural painting did not appear again until the thirteenth century in Italy. The northern Gothic cathedral did not provide much wall space for painting, other than purely ornamental work on columns and piers.

However, painting was stimulated considerably by the brilliant use of illustration in the adorning of manuscripts. There were no printing facilities in the Middle Ages, and all books had to be copied by hand. The scribes who performed the task were often artists of great ability who took special pride and care in

EARLY CHRISTIAN CATACOMB PAINTING: ADAM AND EVE

fashioning beautifully proportioned letters and enriching the page with exquisite miniature pictures. These illuminated manuscripts (the term is aptly used, for the pages were covered with gold and brilliant color) were psalters and other religious texts. Byzantine stylization and brilliance of color are apparent in these paintings. Illuminations were done in tempera colors, often with gold backgrounds.

Gothic symbolism. One of the most interesting aspects of the Gothic cathedral is its extraordinary symbolism. In addition to religious symbols, animals and flowers appear in the edifice. Statues were erected to the *trivium* and the *quadrivium,* and next to each of the seven figures was often placed a figure of some thinker associated with its progress—geometry and Euclid, astronomy and Ptolemy, and so on. There were also statues of philosophy, the sciences, astrology and alchemy, and architecture and painting. In the French cathedrals were also symbolized the messages of the Old and New Testaments, the great men of antiquity, the history of France, and the surpassing love of the Virgin.

MANUSCRIPT ILLUMINATION, PSALTER OF THE ABBOT OF PETERBOROUGH

Henry Adams in *Mont-Saint-Michel and Chartres* points out that with few exceptions the French cathedrals were dedicated expressly to Our Lady—Notre Dame de Paris, Notre Dame de Chartres, Notre Dame de Rouen, and so on.[29] God the Father was stern and vengeful; God the Son was far removed from this earth; God the Holy Ghost was scarcely understood. But Mary the Mother, who had undergone the joys and tribulations of any other mother, was always present to intercede for saint and sinner alike. Thus arose that interesting phenomenon of the Middle Ages, Mariolatry, the veneration of the Virgin, whose popularity for a time overshadowed that of the Trinity.

The Gothic cathedral was a place where the medieval craftsman could express his feelings without fear or restraint, within the limits of the general plan. While statues of saints and martyrs expressed his reverence, figures of devils in the form of gargoyles were a sort of goliardic touch. A gargoyle's purpose was to carry water clear of the masonry. Some can be seen projecting from the towers on Rouen cathedral (page 436).

MEDIEVAL CASTLE AND WALL, CARCASSONNE

Secular architecture. Secular architecture developed considerably during the Middle

PALACE OF JUSTICE, ROUEN

THE TOWN HALL OF LOUVAIN

Ages, because of the exigencies of the feudal way of living. What the cathedral was to religious life, the castle was to everyday living. Both were havens, and both were built to endure. Development of better methods and machines of siege necessitated more massive castles. By the thirteenth century castle building in Europe reached a high point of development. The towers were rounded, and bastions stood at strategic points along the walls, while the walls themselves were constructed in such a skillful manner that if one section should be taken by attackers it could be isolated from the remaining fortifications and was itself open to strong counterattack from the defenders. So skillfully was the castle of the later Middle Ages constructed that the besiegers had to use all their tactical ingenuity. Whole towns were fortified in the same way, with walls, watch towers, moats, and drawbridges. Carcassonne, still standing, is a dramatic example of the medieval fortified town (page 439). Notice its situation on a hill, the many towers, and the loopholes for archers.

The growth of towns and the rise of the bourgeoisie also stimulated the development of secular architecture. Toward the end of the Middle Ages there was less need for fortified towns and castles. Town and guild halls, the residences of the wealthy classes, and the chateaux of nobles used Gothic decorative features. The Palace of Justice at Rouen has decorated pinnacles and decorative tracery on the windows, taken from Gothic church architecture. In the Low Countries the burghers of the flourishing centers of trade and industry began to construct civic buildings, whose size and richness reflected the growing wealth of the Flemish towns. The town hall of Louvain shows the typically Flemish steep roof and the rich decoration used by Flemish builders.

These secular buildings were hung with large tapestries, presumably to help keep the damp of the walls from the room. The early tapestries are patterned in a decorative manner, with little perspective and conventionalized drawing, as in "The Giving of the Roses," page 441. The shading of the figures is slight and stylized, owing to the difficulty of producing subtle gradations in the weaving.

THE GIVING OF THE ROSES (FRENCH BURGUNDIAN TAPESTRY)

The decorative flower patterns are typical of early Gothic tapestries.

In Italy civic buildings were also erected. Italian town halls were more massive than those in the north, and most of them were capable of being defended. This feature, coupled with the bell tower for ringing alarms, reflects the insecurity of Italian life at that time. The picture on page 497 shows a fortified town hall in the right background and a bell tower at the left.

Stained glass. The making of stained-glass windows was one of the finest medieval arts, one whose excellence we have not duplicated today. Thirteenth-century craftsmen colored the glass in a molten state by adding minerals. Thus the glass was stained, not painted, and was very bright. Details such as hair were painted on later in a very conventionalized manner. This technique was superior to later innovations in which the color was painted on the surface of the glass. The glass of the thirteenth century was fitted as small pieces into patterns held together by leads, with large iron rods crossing the windows to support

A medieval glazier joins small pieces of colored glass with strips of lead to make a large window, using putty or cement to fill in the chinks.

DETAIL OF STAINED-GLASS WINDOW, CHARTRES

them. In the twelfth and thirteenth centuries both the leads of the individual pieces and the iron rods were used to emphasize the design. In the Chartres window on this page notice the use of the leads on the cloak and arm of the left-hand figure.

An interesting feature of many of the windows is the addition of portraits of the donors at the bottom of religious scenes. Often guilds financed windows, and their activities thus portrayed reveal many customs of the day.

The art of making stained glass died out almost completely after the sixteenth century. During the intervening years a lowering of quality came about through the use of large plates of painted glass with the leads arranged in mechanical squares and figures painted on in third dimension, although the decoration, with the light pouring through it, obviously called for flat patterns of color.

Summary

Medieval philosophy was constrained by authority and confined to justifying the creeds, dogmas, and faith of the Church. The process of justification was known as Scholasticism. One of the major problems of medieval philosophy centered about the question of universal Ideas. The Realists, headed by such men as Anselm of Canterbury, believed that these Ideas alone constituted true reality; to the Nominalists, on the other hand, these Ideas were simply names (*nomina*). A compromise was reached in Conceptualism, generally credited to Abélard, who said that, while universal terms have no objective existence as such, particular objects may have similarities which enable us to obtain a mental picture, or concept, of them as a class. The Church inclined toward Realism, with its emphasis upon authority; the new science, aided by Roger Bacon and others, believed in Nominalism because of its stress upon the individual approach and freedom from tradition.

In the twelfth and thirteenth centuries Europe received from Arabic sources not only new scientific discoveries but, more important, the philosophical treatises of Aristotle. Scholasticism attempted to reconcile the new sciences, the new-found Greek philosophy, and the church theology. Great encyclopedias were written, called *summa* (summaries). The most famous Scholastics were St. Albertus Magnus and St. Thomas Aquinas, the latter's *Summa Theologiae* constituting a herculean attempt to reconcile reason and faith, Christianity and paganism, authority and Aristotle, and science and theology. Yet medieval philosophy, despite its failure to affect most modern men, had an admirable ideal, the unification of all knowledge into a logical system of thought.

While theology was of the most importance, some real advances were made in science. Ignorance of proper techniques and of the inductive method of experimentation was a serious handicap, as was the frowning of the Church upon concern with worldly problems.

The contributions of the Greeks and Arabs which became known in the twelfth and thirteenth centuries enlarged European knowledge. Mathematics was enriched by the addition of Arabic numerals, algebra, Euclid's geometry, and trigonometry. Geography and navigation were making slow but sure progress as a result of increased travel and trade as well as the gradual acceptance of the magnetic compass. Alchemy produced many important chemical by-products, while the Arabs' contributions in drugs proved invaluable. Medicine and surgery advanced through the schools founded at Salerno and Bologna, where anatomy, the use of anesthetic, and the value of bathing in mineral waters were understood. Leprosy was all but eliminated in the Middle Ages, and public health advanced with the increasing use of quarantines.

Perhaps the greatest medieval contribution was the university. The Church monopolized education through the early Middle Ages. As learning revived in the twelfth century, it became increasingly obvious that the monastic and cathedral schools could no longer educate the youth in such specialized studies as law and medicine. The curriculum in the new universities consisted of other subjects besides those taught in the *trivium* and *quadrivium.* The universities grew out of the flocking of students to hear some outstanding teacher, and they possessed no buildings or campuses at first. At Bologna the students were largely in charge of affairs; at Paris the masters were in control. These two centers had a tremendous effect on the creation of other universities throughout Europe. We have inherited from these medieval institutions not only our gowns, hoods, degrees, examinations, and concepts of a stated curriculum and formal training but also our ideal of the mission a university should perform—the furtherance of human knowledge and the creation of a "goodly fellowship" of scholars.

Latin was a dynamic language throughout the medieval period. The churchmen did not hesitate to create new words to express new ideas and situations. The business of the Church was carried on in this universal medium, and Latin was also used with striking effects by the Goliardic poets and composers of religious hymns.

But a rival, growing stronger as the Middle Ages passed, rose to dispute with Latin the right to dominate literature—the vernacular languages. Coincident with the gradual rise of the national state, the development of towns, and the growth of trade was the increasing popularity of English, French, German, Italian, and Spanish as literary vehicles. Vernacular poetry developed early in such epics as the Anglo-Saxon *Beowulf* and the stirring sagas of the Germans and the Norse. French literature evolved the *chansons de geste,* tales of heroic deeds. Among the most famous of these poems is the *Song of Roland.* Famous poetic cycles grew and expanded about the deeds of Charlemagne, King Arthur, and the old stories of Troy, Thebes, and Rome. Southern France was meanwhile developing a chivalrous and romantic poetry, called Provençal literature, which was sung in courtly circles by troubadours. All the poetry was aristocratic in content. *Fabliaux* were written to please the bourgeoisie and satirize the stilted concepts of chivalric virtue and nobility, while ballad literature of the Robin Hood type grew up among the common people. Two of the most famous of the medieval poets, both of whom wrote their greatest masterpieces in their native tongues, were Geoffrey Chaucer and Dante Alighieri. Chaucer gave us an unforgettably vivid picture of the lives and thoughts of fourteenth-century Englishmen in his *Canterbury Tales.* Dante's *Divine Comedy* constitutes a complex synthesis of medieval philosophy and ideals.

The greatest artistic achievement of the Middle Ages was the Gothic cathedral, a magnificent structure growing out of Romanesque patterns. The Romanesque building was based on the old Roman basilica, with the round or barrel arch added and a modified floor pattern in the shape of a cross. However, Romanesque architecture had not learned to intersect half-cylinders of different diameters or to create walls which could contain many windows and yet be strong enough to support the heavy weight of a stone roof. The result was that Romanesque churches tended to be low, thick-walled, and gloomy. The solution of the two problems by the introduction of the pointed arch and the flying buttress brought about the slender, soaring Gothic cathedral. Gothic reached its height in France. Spain, England, and Germany utilized the new Gothic, but Italy preferred a modified Romanesque style. The last quarter of the thirteenth century witnessed Gothic at its purest. After that it became overdecorated. It is significant that all the major French cathedrals were dedicated to the Virgin and that the entire Gothic cathedral represents medieval theology and ideals.

With the growth of Gothic came the development of the art of stained-glass windows, while in the churches of southern Europe with their minimum of windows mural painting began to develop. Sculpture was also influenced by the need for decorating these large edifices. Secular architecture in the Middle Ages made advances in building castles and later in erecting town halls and urban dwellings for the bourgeoisie. Painting was a subordinate art, but much artistic work was expended on beautiful illuminated manuscripts.

We can see at once that the cultural attainments of our medieval ancestors were considerable. We must forget, once and for all, the outworn and false views that the Middle Ages were dark and uncivilized. We ought to appreciate the underlying unity of medieval philosophy, science, education, literature, and art, and the one ideal that the *Summa Theologiae* of St. Thomas Aquinas, the curriculum of Paris and Bologna, the *Divine Comedy* of Dante, and the cathedral of Chartres have in common—the unification of human knowledge and the glorification of God.

Part Five

New horizons

New Horizons

THE PANORAMA OF medieval civilization in western Europe, with its manors and fiefs, universities and monasteries, cathedrals, and castles, has been surveyed. Now we enter a period of history in the West roughly from 1100 to 1650, which had momentous consequences for the entire world. This new period was made possible by the remarkable achievements registered in western Europe in the eleventh century. In Chapter 12 we have seen how the revival of commerce, the genesis of well-organized national governments, the securing of Christian control of the Mediterranean, and the renewal of contact with the Near East, made this century a turning point in the upward progress of western Europe. The birth of nations, the amazing fertility in art and thought which we know as the Renaissance, the revolt against the Universal Church, and the discovery of new worlds during the Age of Exploration—these were the four basic movements that brought about the transition to modern times.

During this transitional period, most of the basic medieval characteristics were radically transformed. The idea of political unity was shattered by the rise of nations. We will see that England, France, and Spain are the best examples of centralized nation states, while Germany and Italy are countries where nation-making lamentably failed. In both these lands the forces of fragmentation triumphed over national centralization, bequeathing tragic consequences for Europe in modern times. Nation-making also lagged behind, as we will note, in eastern Europe, especially in Russia, where distinctive circumstances tended to isolate this country from the progressive forces and influence of western Europe. The Protestant Reformation overthrew the hitherto undisputed supremacy of the papacy. The cult of authority and other-worldliness and the subordination of the individual were weakened by the Renaissance. For the first time since the days of classical Greece and Rome, men dared to challenge accepted beliefs and reveled in the beauties and joys of this life. Above all, Renaissance self-confidence showed that the rule of the group over the individual was passing.

In its most correct usage, the term Renaissance refers to the remarkable outpouring of art and literature in Italy from 1300 to 1500. In a much wider sense it is used as a general term descriptive of the age of transition from medieval to modern times. In this sense it includes the rise of nations, the religious revolt, the glorious achievements in art and literature, and the age of geographical exploration.

The economic significance of the Renaissance is important. In the Middle Ages, the landed nobility were literally and figuratively in the saddle, but by the fourteenth century a new class had begun to make its power felt. Composed of merchants and burghers, the middle class, aided by the expansion of trade which accompanied the geographical explorations, rapidly gained in opulence and influence. The middle class forged ahead most rapidly in the city-states of Italy where merchant princes became the patrons of art and scholarship.

Another manifestation of the passing of medieval times was the geographical exploration which expanded the reach and influence of European men until they encompassed the entire world. As early as the twelfth century, contacts with the advanced Moslem civilization stimulated a desire among Europeans to get in touch with other parts of the world. Starting in a halting fashion in the thirteenth century, geographical exploration by the latter part of the fifteenth century had permanently reëstablished East-West contact.

Up to the transitional period in the thirteenth century, the Near East and the Far East had developed civilizations superior in many respects to that in the West. But now the tables were turned, and European culture became the most creative, expansive, and aggressive of any in the world. During the epoch of transition, which rang down the curtain on the medieval panorama, forces were set in motion which explain why the people of practically the entire modern world adopted western culture, or had it thrust upon them. The transfer of dominance from the East to the West is one of the most momentous developments of early modern times.

The Renaissance was not the greatest period in man's history, as so many people believe. But it was an age when man's development was greatly accelerated and when he reasserted his faith in himself. Hence it was a daring age. Imbued with self-reliance and stimulated by new horizons which he saw spreading before his eyes, man turned his telescope on the stars or set sail in frail vessels to explore and acquire the unknown world. He turned his thoughts inward to explore new realms of thinking. The citizens of the Renaissance were irrepressible; they were self-confident to the point of being braggart and arrogant; but they were men of action—and our debt to them is great.

Chronology of events and developments discussed in this chapter

Chapter 16

Capetian rule in France	987-1328
Salian emperors: centralized monarchy in Germany	1024-1125
Collapse of the Caliphate of Cordova: inaugurated the Reconquista	1031
Henry IV: height of German monarchy; Investiture Struggle with Gregory VII	1056-1106
Battle of Hastings: William became king of England	1066
Henry I: curia regis; *used itinerant justices and civil servants*	1100-1135
Louis le Gros: founder of Capetian greatness; suppressed vassals	1108-1137
Roger II: centralized administration of Sicily; controlled vassals; economic growth	1130-1154
Frederick Barbarossa, Holy Roman Emperor: tried to reëstablish control in Italy	1152-1190
Henry II: judicial innovation; Assize of Clarendon	1154-1189
Constitutions of Clarendon: end of benefit of clergy; led to murder of Thomas à Becket	1164
Suzdal defeated Kiev: end of Kievan supremacy	1168
Philip Augustus: attempted control of English lands in France; increased royal domain; strengthened administration	1180-1223
Teutonic Knights founded: settled around the Baltic	1198
Frederick II: Italian policy caused neglect of Germany	1211-1250
Magna Charta: limited royal power; king subordinate to the law	1215
Louis IX: established national courts to circumvent feudal justice	1226-1270
Mongols captured Russian states: became ruling caste; broke with the West	1237
Alexander Nevski ruled Vladimir: victory over the Teutonic Knights	1252-1263
Great Interregnum: rivalry of princely houses in Germany	1254-1273
Edward I: called the first Parliament; envisioned a united Britain	1272-1307
Sicilian Vespers: uprising against Angevin rule	1282
Philip IV: institutional growth; struggle for power with the Pope	1285-1314
Accession of the House of Valois precipitated the Hundred Years' War	1328
Hundred Years' War: English lost all holdings in France except Calais; king dependent on Parliament for funds	1337-1453
Battle of Kulikovo: Mongol defeat marked beginning of Muscovy leadership	1380
Ottoman Turks invaded the southern Balkans	1389
Independence of the Swiss Confederation recognized by the Hapsburgs	1394
Union of Kalmar: Scandinavia under the Danish king	1397
Poles and Lithuanians defeated the Teutonic Knights at Tannenberg	1410
Hapsburg rule of the Holy Roman Empire	1452-1806
Iberian peninsula united by the marriage of Isabella and Ferdinand	1469

Nations in the making

Consolidation of kingdoms: 1100-1500

The emergence of the national state, beginning in earnest in the late Middle Ages and not fully maturing until as recently as the nineteenth century, is perhaps the most outstanding and important political trend in modern history. As a legacy of this development we live today in a world consisting of more than sixty separate, distinct, and independent national states. Each of these units is made up of a group of people accepting the rule of their government, which not only has complete authority over its own citizens but is independent of external control by any other government. The common term used to describe such a political unit is the sovereign state. Often, within one nation the citizens may differ as to religion, language, and race, yet a common attachment to the state provides the cohesive force necessary for effective political unity. This force is usually referred to as nationalism, a word not easily defined and not constant in meaning in modern history. Yet without nationalism—or that spirit among a nation's people which causes them to believe that their common experiences, traditions, culture, and institutions necessitate an independent political unit—the modern state as we know it today would not exist. We shall see the beginnings of nationalism in this chapter, and its manifestation in the early consolidation of kingdoms. But it is in later centuries that we will watch it grow stronger and become a dominant force in world affairs.

World War II and the development of the atomic bomb have demonstrated the serious inadequacies of the national state system in an interdependent world. As a result, the United Nations was set up to maintain peace among national states. Despite the existence of this organization and the efforts of various groups to build it into some form of world government having supreme authority in international affairs, political organization along national lines remains the cardinal feature in modern man's culture pattern. Our lives are strongly influenced by membership in a national state, from the language we speak, the type of government we believe in, and the attitudes we hold, to the opinions we express concerning other human beings living in a nation different from our own. An understanding of our world today, then, demands that we know something about the origin of the national-state system, and its history during the last one thousand years. To begin this story is the purpose of the present chapter.

In Chapter 12, we traced the course of political affairs in western Europe from the sixth to the eleventh century. This narrative dealt with the brilliant achievement of Charlemagne in creating a new empire which promised to restore the unity, law, and order of old Rome. But the Carolingian state was short-lived, and in a few decades it crumbled and split apart. In the absence of effective central governmental institutions, a new political system, feudalism, came into being, in which landed nobles were the pivotal agencies in the numerous feudal states that became the heirs of the Frankish empire.

Due to the inadequacies of feudalism, a new political trend developed, notably at first in tenth century Germany. This is the rise of national monarchs who built strong central governments capable of protecting the weak and restraining the strong, securing the support and loyalty of a large body of people—referred to as citizens—and thus creating what we now know as modern states. While the eleventh century was the decisive period when commerce revived, cities grew, and Europe burst out of the isolation of its "closed-house economy," it is in the fifteenth century that national monarchies gained supremacy in countries like England, France, and Spain, our case studies in the history of nation-making. Italy and Germany were different, for here the forces of faction and division triumphed for centuries longer over those of national unity. In eastern Europe, the numerous Slavic groups established a number of kingdoms of which Russia emerged as the strongest and most centralized state.

As we watch the political process of nation-making, it is worth while to keep in mind the religious and intellectual developments of these centuries, discussed in Chapters 14 and 15. History is a dynamic movement, and the acts of kings can only be properly perceived if the ideas and cultural institutions of their times are set beside them.

The Decline of Feudalism

Inadequacies of feudalism. The thirteenth century may be regarded as the golden age of feudalism with its colorful pattern of chivalry and knighthood, of fief and fealty, all resting on the economic basis of the manor. During the dark days of the ninth and tenth centuries feudalism managed to maintain some semblance of law and order; and, despite many defects, it was much better than no government at all. Giving it its due is not to deny that feudalism was a makeshift order which had to serve until something better could be devised. Between the extremes of a great centralized empire and the localization of the feudal system there was a logical compromise—the national state. Only by merging the dozens of separate feudal units into one unified scheme of government could the lack of a uniform currency be remedied, the many irritating toll and tariff barriers imposed by local barons be removed, and trade advanced. Perhaps the greatest weakness of feudalism was its inability to guarantee law and order. It is true that feudal law was intended to see justice done between man and man, but in the event that the law was defied, there was no certainty that the forces of justice would triumph over those of the law breaker. Amid the welter of hundreds of feudal principalities, each with its own law courts dispensing justice, there was a lack of uniformity in legal codes and judicial procedure, which led to much confusion, inefficiency, and often injustice.

One of the essential prerequisites for good government is that it be in the hands of skilled civil servants, but under a feudal system the units of government were too small and the opportunities for administrative work were on too limited a scale to encourage the development and the support of an efficient staff of civil servants. In any prosperous and well-governed country it is essential to have a group of skilled administrators to map out the right policy of foreign affairs and to plan economic measures for the country as a whole. It is, for example, vital that the main trunk roads used by all the people be maintained in good repair, but without a strong central government any poverty-stricken or indolent noble might refuse to attend to the needs of the main highway which passed through his domain.

In short, the outlook of the feudal baron was too limited. He often lost sight of the welfare of the whole people in his preoccupation with the problems and needs of his petty feudal domain. People can best live in harmony and advance materially when they subscribe to one central government which takes the larger view of their affairs. Under feudalism there were too many conflicting loyalties.

The decline of feudalism. It is impossible to set a fixed date for the decline of feudalism. For example, the growth of royal power in France in the thirteenth and fourteenth centuries curbed feudalism in its political aspects, but its social implications persisted down to the French Revolution. The strength of such English monarchs as Henry II and Edward I handicapped the power of their nobles enormously, while the ruinous Wars of the Roses put an end forever to feudal strength. Yet in Scotland the weakness of the royal family allowed certain nobles virtually to control the kingdom until the sixteenth century, while the lack of national unity in Germany made it possible for feudalism to run unchecked to an even later period.

However, the feudal system finally came to an end (although only recently in eastern and southeastern Europe). We can cite the following reasons for its decline: (1) political: the growth of royal power and the alliance of the new bourgeoisie with the monarchy against the landed aristocracy, making inevitable the establishment of a growing national consciousness, (2) social: the rapid increase of population and the emancipation of serfs during the later Middle Ages, making it impossible for the nobles to control ever increasing numbers of persons who looked elsewhere for their allegiance and protection, (3) economic: the rise of towns and of a new middle class that no longer evaluated wealth in terms of land, the development of trade and industry, which upset the economic localism of the manor, and the introduction of a money economy which made the self-sufficient manor obsolete, (4) military: the effects of such innovations as the longbow and gunpowder, which made infantry superior in striking power to the time-honored steel-clad noble horsemen and rendered obsolete the great stone castles which could not resist the new artillery, and the creation of royal armies equipped with these weapons, which gave monarchs undisputed supremacy over their feudal subjects.

Pioneer nations. From the two dozen or more feudal units that filled the map of Europe in the eleventh century, England, France, and Spain arose as pioneers in national unification. Our main case study in the rise of the national state will be England. Although outdistanced in international affairs by France and Spain until the eighteenth century, England was the first country to achieve a completely organized nationhood. The story of England also merits highlighting because it involves such important developments as the growth of the common law and the genesis of a system of representative government—the Parliament.

The essential pattern of historical development is similar in each of the nations. (1) The king started with serious competitors to his royal authority, usually the Church and the feudal nobility, (2) the competitors were overthrown by building an efficient system of royal government that, above all, gave the people a more efficient standard of justice than they could obtain in the church or feudal courts, (3) wars in which the kings took an active part caused the people to regard the king as their natural leader, and (4) the kings made alliances with the rising middle class in the cities against their common enemy, the landed nobility. The result was approximately the same in the three countries: The king's government expanded to cover the entire country, creating the national state; the old feudal and church courts lost practically all their power; the officials of the king made laws, enforced them, and handed down royal justice without competition from any noble.

Germany and Italy do not fit into this pattern. In Germany brilliant initial achievements toward the creation of a vigorous and united national state were doomed to dismal failure. The failure was to have momentous consequences in modern times, for Germany, achieving her unity late in the nineteenth century, had been left behind by other nations in acquiring a great empire. This fact gave the Germans a sense of grievance and was one of the reasons for international discord in the twentieth century. Italy also did not become unified until the nineteenth century. While England, France, and Spain were becoming national states, Italy remained a collection of small states whose rivalry in commerce and politics prevented their union.

The Genesis of Modern England

Government under William the Conqueror. Our last discussion of England traced the efforts of the west Saxon kings to defend their adopted land from invasion by the Danes and to unify the country under their rule. Building on the remarkable achievements of Alfred the Great, a strong and prosperous monarchy was established in the tenth century, only to decline rapidly in the next (page 344).

At this juncture William, duke of Normandy, asserted his shadowy claim to the English throne, a claim which came through his relation to the mother of the last king, Edward the Confessor. This claim was strengthened by a promise made by Edward when he was shipwrecked in Normandy that William would be his heir. Customarily the king of England was elected by the Witan, the "king's council," but the candidate was expected to be from the reigning family. When the Witan exercised their prerogative and ignored the claims of William, he attacked England, overcoming Harold Godwinson, who was virtually in control of the country. At the battle of Hastings in 1066 William of Normandy made himself king of England.

The task of amalgamating Normans and Saxons faced William. In accomplishing this end he adopted only such Norman customs as would ensure his control of England. From France he imported the feudal system, but maintained a close check on his vassals. Fiefs were distributed so that large holdings were broken up.

No sweeping changes were made in the system of government in England after the coronation of William. Rather the system was infused with a new energy, and old Saxon political institutions were remodeled and their functions redefined and expanded. William the Conqueror believed in utilizing as much as possible the institutions with which the English were familiar. This policy was carried out particularly in the field of local government, where the Saxon shire and another local unit called the hundred were retained as administrative units together with their local courts. The sheriff, the old local Saxon official, was also retained, and his duties and powers expanded to such a degree that he became the most important cog in the Norman system of strong central government.

William's one basic contribution to England was a strong central government. This stern and wrathful man gave England an iron rule and ruthlessly oppressed any opposition to his will, but through the establishment of despotic power he laid the foundation for the erection of a free and well-governed state. The first necessity for the development of a well-ordered state is the removal of civil strife and of rival powers by the creation of one sovereign power. The next step is the development by the supreme authority of an adequate machinery of lawmaking and enforcement. In both of these the sovereign body must exercise its power benevolently; that is, it must not be unjust or capricious. As William certainly brought about the first step and did much to achieve the second, he laid the groundwork for English government as we know it today. Under his vigorous regime the great Saxon earldoms were broken up, the king's commissioners toured the shires, and the sheriffs became the effective fingers on the long arm of royal power.

William's feudal system. William the Conqueror's determination to make his power as king supreme is demonstrated by the way in which he introduced feudalism into England. In Anglo-Saxon England a full-grown feudal system had not developed, although there were tendencies in that direction. William retained the manorial system, advanced political feudalism, and fused the two into a fully developed feudal structure. He exacted homage from all landowners in England, whether or not they were his own immediate vassals. In other words, all nobles, whether tenants-in-chief holding land directly from the king or lesser tenants holding their land as vassals of other nobles, swore loyalty and obedience to the king, their feudal suzerain.

Certain other important modifications were also made in the tentative English version of feudalism. In Anglo-Saxon England lords could not compel their knights to fight for them. The king, therefore, never could rely upon his vassals for troops and armed support. William changed this uncertain situation by demanding that all his vassals and their vassals should provide him with armed knights if the necessity arose. In addition, William did not rely upon feudal levies of knights as the sole basis of his armed forces. Instead he retained the old Anglo-Saxon *fyrd,* militia, in order to give the king a powerful fighting force to overawe any rebellion which might originate among the strong feudal barons.

The Domesday survey. The Domesday survey, conducted in 1085-1086, admirably exemplifies the businesslike, methodical, and strong government which William established in England. The king wished to secure an accurate census of the economic resources of his land and the wealth held by his subjects, as a basis for an equitable tax. Special commissioners sent out by the king collected testimony from special sworn juries. The inventory caused much grumbling and even rioting. Apparently people in the eleventh century had the same aversion to an income tax that their descendants have today. "So narrowly did he cause the survey to be made," grumbles a Saxon chronicler, "that there was not one single hide nor rood of land, nor—it is shameful to tell but he thought it no shame to do—was there an ox, cow, or swine that was not set down in the writ."[1] The original manuscript containing the Domesday survey is still extant—the most valuable document in English history.

Henry I. Namesakes often prove a disappointment, and so it was with William II, who followed his father, darkening his reign by cruelty and capricious government. It remained for Henry I (1100-1135) to carry on the task of developing the strong and efficient government which had been so admirably initiated by his great father. So well did Henry I rule that his contemporaries called him the Lion of Justice. High praise indeed are these words of the Anglo-Saxon chronicler: "A good man he was, and there was great awe of him. No man durst misdo another in his time. He made peace for man and beast."

Henry quelled a serious uprising of rebellious barons who wished to weaken the royal power. Then, having consolidated his position, he turned to the task of improving the structure of government that had been bequeathed him by William I. William's Great Council, made up of the chief nobles, had been the most important agency in advising the king on matters of state. But after the sessions of the Council had been held, the nobles returned to their estates, and it was soon appreciated that there was a real need for the creation of a small but permanent council of advisers to the king which would always be on hand if its services were needed. Such a permanent body, called the *curia regis,* came into being in Henry's reign. In addition, much was done to create a staff of professional civil servants who would bring new efficiency to government. A beginning was also made in the administration of justice through the practice of sending royal judges, known as itinerant justices, out on circuit to all parts of the kingdom.

An interlude of confusion. Henry's achievements in strengthening the monarchy by greater centralization were almost undone by nineteen years of chaos which followed his reign. The king's only surviving child, Matilda, had been married to a French count, the ruler of Anjou, and the barons of England had all faithfully promised to accept her as queen on her father's death. Instead they illegally selected a sovereign more to their liking—an affable and easy-going prince named Stephen of Blois, son of William the Conqueror's daughter. Stephen was chivalrous; his character was pure and his intentions honorable. But he had absolutely no backbone and was equally devoid of any qualities of leadership.

Immediately upon the accession of the new king the great nobles began to pillage and rob and fight among themselves. England became a land where only might made right. To add to the misery, a civil war was carried on between the king and forces that had been raised by Henry I's heir, Matilda.

The accession of Henry II. The anarchy which devastated England for nearly two decades ceased with the accession of Henry II (1154-1189), the son of Matilda and Geoffrey of Anjou. Within five months order had been restored and the illicit fortified castles of the English barons had been demolished. This young king, founder of the Plantagenet (also called Angevin) house, as a result of marriage and inheritance, found himself sovereign at twenty-one of a great empire stretching from Scotland to the Pyrenees (see map opposite). The English holdings in France far exceeded the territory ruled over by the French kings, who from their capital at Paris eyed their vassal rival with fear and jealousy. The year 1154, which witnessed Henry's succession to the English throne and the joining of English and French holdings under the king of England, dates the beginning of the strife between England and France which runs like a red thread through the tapestry of medieval history.

Henry came to the throne well prepared for the profession of king. He had already obtained experience in administering Normandy for his father. He had a passion for efficiency and order and was unusually well educated, perhaps the most learned king of his time, and he had a genius for government.

Contemporary documents give us an interesting and intimate picture of Henry Curtmantle, as he was called. His freckled face, stocky frame, short stout figure, bow legs, and harsh voice do not make a very prepossessing figure. He cared little for royal dignity and never courted popularity. Only after his death did his subjects appreciate the true measure of his worth. Henry was a man of limitless energy, always on the move and ever restless, and his courtiers had little time to relax. It is said that Henry found it particularly hard to sit still during Mass and scandalized some of his subjects by scribbling notes and chatting with his cronies.

Henry's reign was an expression of his restlessness. He was ever improving, changing, copying, and fighting. He fought the feudal nobility, clashed with the Church, warred against the Capetians, quarreled with his rather worthless sons, and had much trouble managing his queen, Eleanor of Aquitaine, who, because of the influence she wielded in the domains of the Plantagenets, has been called the greatest of all Frenchwomen.

Henry II carried on the work of preparing England to be a strong national state, begun by his great grandfather William I and extended by his grandfather Henry I. The methods which Henry II utilized for his work are particularly important, because they have become part of the structure of government in many modern lands. Henry's great contribution to civilization was in the field of law and judicial procedure. The judicial reforms of Henry II cannot be overestimated. As we shall soon see, they constitute the basis for the present law of the British empire and of the United States.

Henry and the judicial system. Stephen, Henry's ineffective predecessor, left him a sorry heritage of corruption in the courts, breakdown in the promising system of governmental administration forged by William the Conqueror and his son Henry I, and a nobility arrogant and strong. The new king, Henry II, was disturbed at the confusion prevailing in England's judicial system. There were royal courts administered by the king's justices, the old Saxon tribunals of the shire and the hundred, baronial courts administered independently by feudal lords, and an aggressive structure of church courts threatening to extend its supremacy over the whole realm.

The Assize of Clarendon. Henry realized that the mere reëstablishment of his grandfather's administrative system was not enough. A more unified, centralized government had to be established, directly dependent upon the king. He began by thoroughly reorganizing the judicial system in a series of decrees called assizes. Most important of these was the Assize of Clarendon in 1166, which laid down the basic features of Henry's new court system. It represents a landmark in English legal history, for (1) it was the first example of a king promulgating laws, in contrast with a mere rewording of traditional custom, (2) it was the first attempt to weaken radically the courts administered by the feudal nobility, (3) it stressed the old Germanic principle of the right and duty of all free men to take part in their own government, preparing the way for self-government in England.

More specifically, the Assize of Clarendon dealt with two judicial agencies, itinerant justices and the jury system, which have exercised considerable influence upon the administration of justice to the present day. Although royal judges had been sent on circuit to dispense justice in the reign of Henry I, it was Henry II's Assize of Clarendon which made this judicial practice a definite and permanent element in the English legal system. And although Henry II did not create the jury, he realized its possibilities, expanded its functions, and started it on its long journey of becoming the most characteristic feature of the judicial system of all English-speaking nations.

The Normans had brought from France the custom of utilizing a group of witnesses to give information under oath to the king's officials. It had been used, we will remember, by William the Conqueror in his Domesday survey. The Assize of Clarendon ordered the king's sheriffs to select a certain number of men who were expected to report all crimes which the witnesses thought should be tried. This ancient jury is the direct ancestor of our modern grand jury. The "presentments" of Henry's juries were turned over to the royal judges on circuit, who then proceeded against the criminals.

Baronial and church courts. Henry not only brought his subjects better justice, but he skillfully diminished the activities of one of his judicial competitors, the courts of the barons. In a series of very important assizes, the king made his courts the protector of the property rights of his people. Against his other legal competitor, the courts of the church, Henry was not so successful. His resolve to prevent rogues from claiming benefit of clergy in the ecclesiastical courts resulted in the murder of Thomas à Becket, archbishop of Canterbury, for which Henry was not really accountable.

Becket was the son of a well-to-do London merchant, who early in life became the boon companion of the king. At that time Becket was not famous for religious zeal or piety. The king made him his chancellor and eventually archbishop of Canterbury. Following his pro-

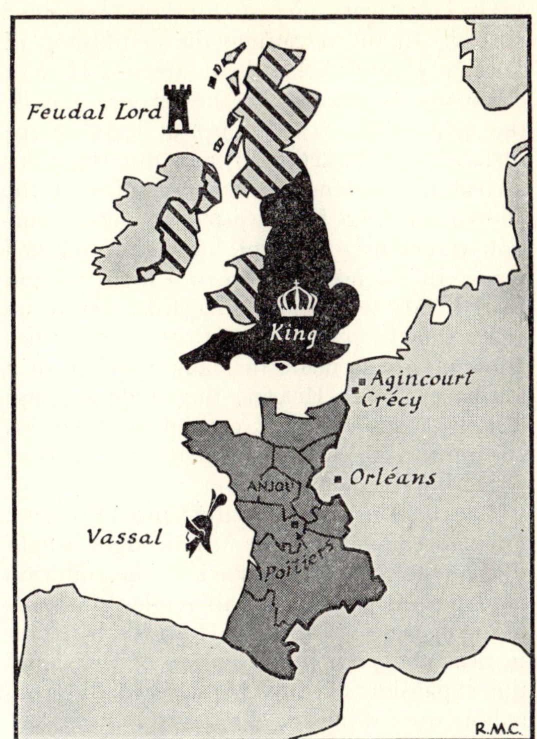

Henry II was king of England and feudal lord of Scotland, Wales, and lands in Ireland and France. Though he held more territory in France than the French king himself, he was vassal to that king for his holdings there. King, vassal, and feudal suzerain, he bequeathed his successors a complicated interest in French territory which was fought out in the Hundred Years' War (see page 465). Crécy, Agincourt, and Poitiers were high points in the war, and the raising of the siege of Orléans by Joan of Arc brought victory to the French.

motion Becket suddenly became passionately attached to the Church, an attachment which Henry found difficult to understand. In 1164 the King issued the Constitutions of Clarendon, which laid down that all church officials accused of any crime should be taken before a royal court. If the royal body thought that a crime had been committed, the culprit was turned over to a church court for trial, and if declared guilty, the man was then sent before a royal court for pronouncement of sentence. It seemed to be a fair solution to the problem of benefit of clergy, but it was repudiated by Becket, who fled to the continent.

For six years the archbishop remained abroad. In the meantime the archbishop of York, at Henry's behest, had crowned Henry's eldest son as successor to the throne. Finally the quarrel was patched up, at least on the surface, and Becket returned. But upon his arrival in England he excommunicated the churchmen who had assisted at the coronation ceremony. News of his action reached Henry in Normandy, who in a fit of passion roared, "My subjects are sluggards, men of no spirit, they keep no faith with their lord, they allow me to be made the laughingstock of a low-born clerk." Hearing the tirade a group of knights slipped away, crossed the Channel, and murdered Becket within the precincts of Canterbury cathedral.

The incident destroyed all chance of reform. For the remainder of the Middle Ages benefit of clergy remained an obstacle to the ambition of the royal government to render the same brand of justice to all men. However, itinerant justices, the jury, the extension of writs, and the expansion of the king's peace did contribute toward uniting the people.

Common law. Out of Henry II's judicial system came the most important contribution in welding the English people together—the common law. Only one other system of law in the entire history of civilization, the Roman, can rival the system which is now used by all English-speaking nations and which owes so much for its existence to England's first Plantagenet king. Unlike its great Roman counterpart, English law is not codified. It is the result of custom, not legislation. Beginning with the reign of Edward I, the important decisions of the royal justices were collected into Year Books, and these legal opinions became the basis for future decisions made in the king's courts. Hence a system of rules and precedents made by the king's judges became the law, "common" to all English people, and superseded the many diverse systems of local justice and custom which had existed in the shires.

Cultural unity under Henry II. Not only was England being welded into a single whole by the governmental agencies of a strong monarchy, but culturally a comparable process took place. The Norman conquest had placed side by side two distinct civilizations, the Norman-French and the Anglo-Saxon. For over two hundred years the former was dominant. In fact, during that period England was only a cultural appendage of France. The language of the ruling class was French. Gothic architecture and the university came from France, as did feudalism, chivalry, and the crusading spirit. The common people continued to speak English, which later was restored as the official language.

The merging of the two peoples, however, proceeded fairly rapidly. Marriages between Saxon and Norman were soon the usual thing. Although the English language maintained an unostentatious existence among the common folk, and French occupied an invulnerable position, quietly the conquerors and the conquered were being merged into a common stock, one in which English elements rather than French were to predominate. The process was completed in the latter part of the fourteenth century. The English language emerged triumphant and was substituted for French in the schools and law courts. This development, whereby English civilization attained its independence and ceased to be a mere offshoot of that of France, was as important in its influences upon the making of national unity as were the legal reforms of Henry II.

With the passing of Henry II, England lost a great king, a man who is regarded by some historians as the greatest of all English sovereigns. His accomplishments in strengthening the royal power at the expense of the feudal nobles, in giving his people prompt and efficient justice, and in initiating a law common to all the realm stamp Henry as one of the greatest architects of the English state.

Henry's successors. It often happens in history that a good beginning made by one generation is marred by the foolish mistakes and lack of intelligence of the next. So it was in early England. The sons and the grandson of Henry were poor successors to the great founder of the Plantagenet line. Richard was a knight-errant. Having no heart for the prosaic tasks of government, he wasted his country's wealth and treasure in military exploits in Europe and the Holy Land. In the Third Crusade Richard earned fame as the peerless knight of his day in his struggle against Saladin, the leader of the Saracens. His brother John was a rogue of whom it has been said, "We search in vain for any good deed, one kindly act to set against his countless offendings."[2] That unworthy ruler became involved in a struggle with Pope Innocent III (discussed in Chapter 14) in which John was forced to make abject surrender to the papacy.

The Magna Charta. The roots of parliaments and representative legislatures can be traced back to medieval England. It was during this time that Englishmen began to transform despotic into limited monarchy, to obtain charters guaranteeing fundamental liberties, and to secure a voice in the government of the country.

The origins of English representative government go back as far as the Saxon era. In the local assemblies of the Anglo-Saxons, called *moots,* there were elected officials. Following the Norman conquest of England in 1066, much of the Anglo-Saxon political tradition was preserved. A little more than one hundred years later another advance in representative government was made during the reign of King John. King John had alienated his barons by trying to collect illegal feudal dues and permitting infractions of feudal law. The king's tyranny brought on civil war in which the nobles were victorious, and in June 1215, John affixed his seal to *Magna Charta,* one of the most important documents in the history of human freedom.

In reality *Magna Charta* did not introduce any new constitutional principles. It was merely an agreement between members of the aristocratic feudal class—the king and his barons. At the time the charter was signed, it did not guarantee trial by jury and taxation only by consent of Parliament. Nor did it initiate representative government. These provisions of the charter, however, were vital:

Clause XII: Taxation or feudal aid except those sanctioned by custom "shall be levied in our kingdom only by the common consent of our kingdom," i.e., by the king's Great Council.
Clause XXXIX: "No free man shall be taken or imprisoned or dispossessed, or outlawed or banished, or in any way destroyed . . . except by the legal judgment of his peers or by the law of the land."
Clause XL: "To no one will we sell, to no one will we deny, or delay right or justice."

These limitations upon the power of the king applied in 1215 only to freemen, that is, to the clergy and the barony. Little or nothing was said about the rights of that five sixths of the population who were serfs. But when the feudal system disappeared, the term "freeman" was interpreted to apply to every Englishman. The guarantees of *Magna Charta,* therefore, became the rights of the many.

Significance of Magna Charta. The importance of *Magna Charta* lies not in its original purpose but in the subsequent use of it. In the struggle against the despotism of the Stuart kings in the seventeenth century, for example, Clause XII of the charter was interpreted to guarantee the principle of no taxation without representation and Clause XXXIX to guarantee trial by jury. G. B. Adams maintains that the importance of *Magna Charta* lies in the fact that potentially it embodied two great principles: (1) that the law is above the king; (2) that if the king breaks customary law he can be compelled by force to obey the law of the land. "It is upon these two principles, henceforth inseparable, . . ." declares Adams, "that the building of the [English] constitution rested. It was through them that *Magna Charta* accomplished its great work for free government in the world."[3] The principle that the power of the crown is limited, that the monarch must obey the law, was relied upon in the fourteenth century in the deposition of two English kings, Edward II and Richard II.

Government under Edward I. John's son, Henry III, although sincerely pious and devout, was a failure as a king. The work of Henry II, however, was not to be left uncompleted. In 1272 Edward I, who ranks as one of England's half dozen really outstanding monarchs, became king. In short order strong government was restored. The governmental reforms initiated by Henry II were continued and advanced. Edward further weakened the powers of the feudal courts. He restricted the power of the Church and built up a fine body of professional civil servants who actually managed the palace. He improved the mode of operation of itinerant justices and gave impetus to a new institution, Parliament, which was to become the most significant governmental agency developed by the English people. These reforms were incorporated in a series of important statutes. In fact so prolific was Edward as a lawmaker that he has been dubbed the English Justinian.

Edward and English unity. Edward was the first king to envision fully a union of the British people—Englishmen, Scots, Welsh, and

Irishmen—under the English crown. Edward's conception of a united Britain was one of the most important elements in his policy, and the steps he took to put it into practice were perhaps his chief work.

Edward was brilliantly successful with the Welsh. After a thorough conquest Wales became part of England in 1284, and in 1301 the oldest surviving son of Edward was given the title of Prince of Wales by his father. It was Edward's cherished ambition to achieve a political union between Scotland and his own country. At the outset of his reign the chances for success appeared bright. But although he obtained recognition of his overlordship from some of the Scots, Edward alienated the Scottish people by his arbitrary actions. A war resulted which postponed the union of Scotland and England for centuries.

English supremacy in Ireland had been asserted by an armed invasion of Norman knights in the reign of Henry II. During the next hundred years, however, little was done by the English rulers to consolidate their conquest, and Edward was so involved with affairs on the continent and in Scotland that he had little time left for Ireland. As we shall see, the modern English state ultimately consisted of a union of four peoples under the leadership of the English, but in the union Ireland was always a rebellious and unwilling partner.

The origins of Parliament. The potential importance of *Magna Charta* would not have been realized without a political institution known as Parliament, which first became important during Edward I's reign. In Anglo-Saxon times the king had had a council of prominent nobles called the Witan. William the Conqueror made this council into a feudal body composed of his tenants-in-chief and called it the Great Council. It acted as a court of trial and as an advisory body in the making of laws.

Parliaments (so-called from the French *parler,* to speak), or assemblies, became common in Europe between 1250 and 1350. The reason is not quite plain. Apparently one important influence was the idea that any exceptional demand for money made by the king should receive the consent of more than just the feudal and official classes convened in the traditional king's council. The growth of assemblies is evidence of the rapidly growing wealth and influence of the bourgeoisie in the towns. As a recognition of the importance of this class and as a means of obtaining another source of revenue, the kings of Europe began the practice of adding representatives of the bourgeoisie to the feudal councils. In the century following the year 1250, *cortes* appeared in Spain, the Estates General were established in France, the Diet in Bohemia, the Diet and *Landtage* in Germany, and Parliament in England. With the exception of the one in England all these assemblies either ceased to exist or remained completely under the tutelage of the monarch.

Under Edward I several significant developments took place in the evolution of the English Parliament. On several occasions Edward summoned representatives of counties and towns to meetings of the Great Council, and in 1295 he called together the "Model Parliament," the most representative group yet convened. Two years later the king agreed that certain taxes could not be levied without the consent of Parliament, a principle which assured that body of being summoned from time to time. From Edward's time on, Parliaments became more and more essential to English government. In calling Parliaments, the English kings had no idea of making any concession to popular government. Their main object was to obtain revenue. The practice of consulting Parliament became so necessary that by the fourteenth century the kings began to realize, too late, the potential danger to their royal prerogatives in this new agency.

Increasing powers of Parliament. Early in the fourteenth century Parliament divided into two houses, the upper, called the House of Lords, representing the barons, and the lower, the House of Commons, composed of the knights and the middle classes. The Commons, main source of financial supply for the king, soon discovered its power. As a result of this "power of the purse," the king was soon forced to agree that no tax should be levied without the consent of Parliament. Later it became the custom for Parliament to withhold its financial grants until the king had redressed certain grievances, attention to which had been directed by petition. Taking advantage of the desperate financial straits of the English kings during the Hundred Years' War, Parliament not only maintained its independence in granting moneys but also acquired the right to direct how revenue should be spent.

Important gains were also made by Parliament in obtaining a voice in actual lawmaking. Originally legislation had been solely a royal function. The Commons, however, began presenting petitions to the king with the request that they be enacted into law. Gradually the right to initiate legislation through petition was obtained; Parliament merely refused to grant revenue if its petitions were not accepted by the king. Often, however, the king tried to thwart the will of the Commons by enacting laws which did not coincide with the original petitions or ones about which the Commons had not been consulted at all.

The Hundred Years' War. It is impossible to follow in detail the complex events which occurred in the development of England from the death of Edward I in 1307 to the coming of the first Tudor king to the throne in 1485. In brief, this span of 178 years embraced the Hundred Years' War with France and the decrease of the power of the English monarchy. For more than one hundred years English kings fatally divided their energies and limited their achievements at home by following the siren call of military glory in France. The object was to regain the large holdings in France which had once in Plantagenet days been subject to the king of England. As long as the English interfered in the affairs of France, the growth of national monarchy was hindered in both countries. It was fortunate, then, that ultimately the English were driven out of France.

Another result of the Hundred Years' War was that kings became financially dependent upon Parliament. This dependence compelled them to grant one petition after another, extending Parliament's powers until, early in the fifteenth century, Parliament became the dominant factor in government. The most important gains made during this period were the guarantee of freedom of debate, the stipulation that money bills must originate in the House of Commons, the rule that statutes should duplicate exactly petitions presented by the Commons, and the right of the House of Commons to determine who should be voters in the country at large.

The Wars of the Roses. The second development after Edward's reign was the decline of the power of the English kings after the reign of Edward I and the recrudescence of the power of the nobles. England became the arena for struggles between selfish baronial cliques who wished to gain control of the monarchy and Parliament, not to insure justice for the mass of the people but in order to feather their own nests. Two years after the end of the Hundred Years' War, in 1453, rivalry between the most powerful baronial groups in England flared into a civil conflict known as the Wars of the Roses, which weakened the feudal system in England. During the civil war Parliament became the tool of whatever noble faction was temporarily in power. England was for thirty years a lawless land.

Tudor rule. A great longing for order, especially among the trading class, brought about the accession in 1485 of Henry VII, first of England's Tudor monarchs. Henry VII and his successors, especially his son Henry VIII, reintroduced strong, almost absolute government into England. The country had now achieved the full status of a national state. Tudor rule was popular because it worked toward the restoration of law and order and the promotion of trade. A single, well-meaning tyrant, the king, was preferred to the many unscrupulous tyrants who had preyed on the land during the Wars of the Roses.

On the surface Parliament received a serious setback, apparently becoming totally subservient—a rubber stamp in the hands of the king. Paradoxically, however, Tudor government eventually made possible a further advance of parliamentary powers, for although the Tudor kings were often highhanded, they always worked through Parliament. This association with the king made the Commons, especially, more conscious of its potential power. Parliamentary procedure became more efficient and standardized. Parliament was willing for a time to follow its strong leader, the king, for fundamentally the two were partners in an alliance against the nobles.

Progress in England. By the end of the fifteenth century Norman and Saxon had merged. A new language had come forth, the old Saxon tongue enriched by the addition of Norman French. A start had been made in the direction of uniting the British Isles, for Wales was now part of England. After a hundred years of struggle the English had learned the bitter lesson that it did not pay to try to conquer France but that it was wise to concentrate on purely English affairs. The lessons of the Hundred Years' War, the achievements of her kings, the development of a new tongue—all of these were forces making for a distinctive English nation. Still another binding element was the common law, which evolved particularly in the reigns of Henry II and Edward I.

The Beginnings of the French National State

The course of French development. In France the process of nation-making followed the same general trend as in England. The accomplishments of great kings were decisive in promoting national unity. The nobles tended to impede the consolidation of the country under royal power and had to be crushed. Townsmen were often supporters of the kings against the nobles. The conflict between the Church and the rising monarchy was dominant in both English and French history. The tragic quarrel between Henry II and his archbishop Thomas à Becket over the judicial supremacy of the king's courts is comparable to the refusal of Philip the Fair to permit the Pope to interfere with the financial affairs of the French kings. By the time of Philip the Fair the kings were strong enough to defy the papacy, and Philip not only defied but actually abused the Pope.

France under the Capetians. As we have already seen, France in the late tenth and early eleventh centuries was not a homogeneous nation administered by one central authority but rather a collection of feudal states. The Capetian counts of Paris at this time enjoyed an empty title—King of France—and exercised effective authority only in their diminutive royal domain which was literally an "island of royalty in a sea of feudalism."[4]

The Capetian line of kings ruled France from 987 to 1328. England as a whole had been united by the conquest of Norman kings, but the Capetians had to build France up bit by bit, as fief after fief was taken from the nobles and added to the royal domain. This explains why France was never so thoroughly unified in the Middle Ages as was England. She had no common law, and each of her provinces, down to the Revolution in 1789, retained its own distinctive customs.

The success of the Capetian kings in creating the kingdom of France may be attributed to the following reasons: (1) The family was extremely fortunate in the matter of succession to the throne. For three hundred years the House of Capet never lacked a male heir. (2) The nobles claimed the right to elect the king (a puppet ruler if they liked), but by having the eldest son elected and consecrated during the reign of the father, the Capetians gradually built up a precedent of hereditary succession. (3) At least in the first stages of national unification, the kings solicited and received the valuable support of the Church and clergy. (4) The Capetians always considered themselves the successors of Charlemagne and inheritors of the royal tradition. The ceremony of coronation and consecration kept alive the idea that an aura of reverence and sanctity adhered to kingship. (5) As supreme overlords of all the nobles in the feudal system, the kings of France had, at least in theory, extensive powers in demanding homage, in enforcing the right of wardship and escheat, and in collecting the usual feudal aids from their vassals. (6) The middle class returned thanks for the royal support given them by tendering the king money and military detachments raised in the cities. (7) As in the growth of the national state in England, the French kings succeeded in creating a system of government and royal tribunals much more efficient and acceptable to the people than that offered by the barons. (8) During the 341 years of Capetian rule France was blessed in having a number of capable kings, several worthy to be classed in their statesmanship alongside such English monarchs as Henry II and Edward I.

Louis le Gros (1108-1137). We saw in Chapter 12 that although progress of royal power under the first four Capetians was almost negligible, they did strengthen the principle of hereditary kingship. It fell to Louis VI (known as *le Gros,* the Fat) to be the founder of Capetian greatness. "He was the first ruler of France since Charlemagne whose conduct was steadily governed by the ideal of a public authority created to maintain public order, with duties toward all and rights over all."[5]

Louis thoroughly suppressed independent and unruly vassals in the royal domain of the Ile de France. Lawless vassals had been in the habit of sallying from their great castles to terrorize and pillage the countryside. By the time of his death Louis had been able to establish the royal power on a firm basis in his own domain.

Philip Augustus (1180-1223). The great expansion of the crown in France took place between 1180, the accession of Philip II, and 1314, the date of the death of Philip IV, when the French king had become the strongest power in Europe. This period covers the reigns of three remarkable rulers: Philip II, who beat down the challenge of his rivals; Louis IX, who ennobled and dignified the office of kingship in France; and Philip IV, who made the government a centralized and efficient despotism. The grandson of Louis VI, Philip II, called Augustus, is as significant in the rise of the French nation as Henry II is in the evolution of England. At the outset of his reign Philip is reported to have said, "I desire that at the end of my reign the monarchy shall be as powerful as in the time of Charlemagne."[6] Certainly Philip did everything possible during his kingship of forty-four years to achieve his goal. Philip's greatest struggle was his effort to wrest from the English Plantagenets the territory they held in France. As the reader will recall, Henry II, England's first Plantagenet ruler, ruled over a large part of France as well as England. Philip's father, Louis VII, stressing the great wealth of Henry II and the meager resources and territory of the French king, said to an English official, "Your Lord, the King, wants nothing—men, horses, gold, silk, diamonds, game, fruits; he has all in abundant plenty. We in France have only bread, wine, and gaiety."[7]

Philip's role was to disrupt the Plantagenet holdings and thus add to the wealth of his royal house. While the redoubtable Henry II lived, Philip made little headway, although he made Henry's life miserable by fomenting plots and encouraging the English king's faithless sons to revolt. During the reigns of Richard the Lion Heart and John, the wily Philip by trickery and warfare gained control of half of the Plantagenet possessions in France. Whereas the puny domain that Philip had inherited was made up of little more than the Ile de France, a state isolated from the sea and hemmed in on all sides by the territories of jealous barons, Philip's accomplishment was to expand his diminutive domain into a middle-sized state (see maps below). Philip not only increased the royal domain threefold but strengthened the royal administrative system. He devised new agencies of centralized government and many new sources of revenue were introduced. At Paris, which had definitely become the royal capital, the king built the fortress of the Louvre to hold his records and moneys. New officials, bailiffs and seneschals, combined the duties of the royal itinerant justices and sheriffs in England. A corps of loyal officials was collected around the king, recruited not from the feudal nobility but from the ranks of lawyers trained in the Roman law and from shrewd burgher businessmen. This class of professional civil servants soon developed into expert governmental advisers and administrators. As in England, the effect of these experts in government is seen in the creation of specialized departments of administration, such as the *parlement*, a supreme court of justice (not to be confused with the English Parliament), the Chamber

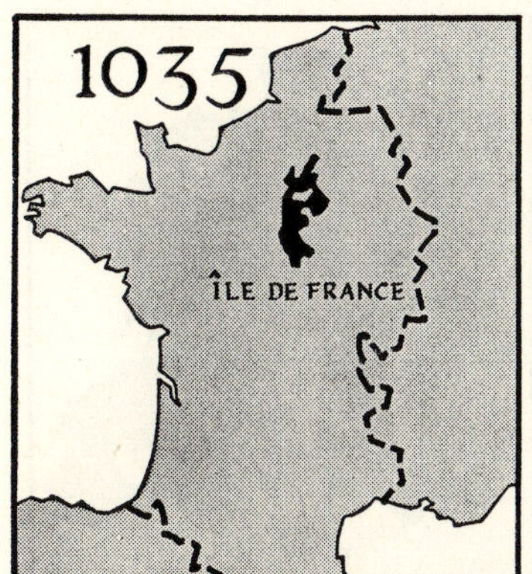

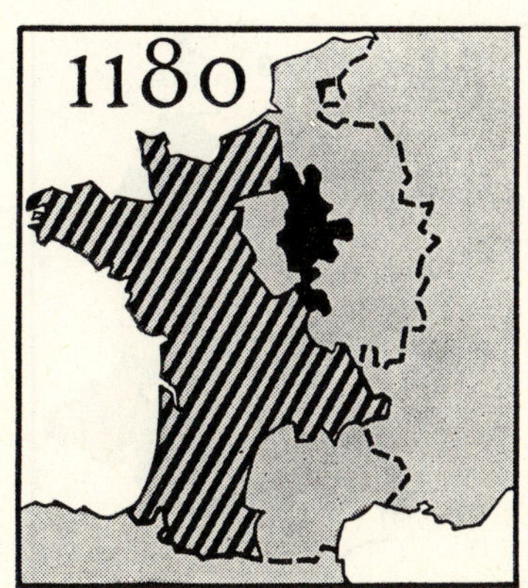

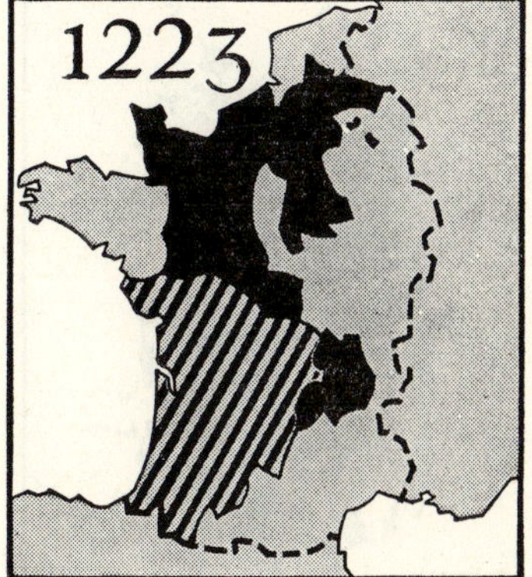

The French royal domain, directly subject to the king, is the black territory on each map. English holdings are diagonally striped. The broken-line boundary represents the extent of the French king's feudal suzerainty.

of Accounts, a financial body, and the Royal, or Privy, Council, a group of advisers who assisted the king in the conduct of the daily business of the state. Like the English monarchs, the Capetian rulers were creating an efficient central government that soon eliminated the competition of feudal lords.

Louis IX (1226-1270). After the brief but strong reign of Louis VIII, Philip's son, France passed under the rule of another monarch, Louis IX, better known as the Saint because the nobility of his character led to his canonization by the Church. Louis, tall and well built, with "the face of an angel and a mien full of grace,"[8] is the perfect example of the true knightly king in the Middle Ages. We possess a splendid picture of this "crowned St. Francis of Assisi, this saint upon the throne," with his sense of moderation, goodness, and justice, in an exceptional biography written by the king's companion, Joinville. It is true that Louis showed what more practical and unscrupulous minds might have called diplomatic naïveté in returning to England certain fiefs that had been annexed by his grandfather, Philip Augustus, but to St. Louis the supreme good was peace and justice, not conquests and diplomatic double-dealing.

Such a viewpoint perhaps slowed up the process of territorial unification initiated by Philip Augustus, for little was added to the royal domain during the reign of St. Louis. But Louis gave to the French monarchy a moral dignity that had heretofore been lacking. In his sympathy for the suffering, in his eagerness for peace, and in his determination to give justice to all, St. Louis convinced the French people that the monarchy was the most important agency for assuring their happiness and well-being.

Louis' passion for justice was reflected in significant developments in the machinery of government. The improvements of Philip Augustus were carried a step further by the employment of officers called *enquêteurs,* who acted as the agents of the king in holding the local officials to a strict responsibility. The most important contribution of St. Louis was the building of a system of royal national courts. So important were Louis' judicial contributions that he is often referred to as the French Justinian. Like Henry II in England, Louis IX forced the nobles to recognize the right of their vassals to appeal to the king for justice in certain cases. He also declared private warfare and judicial duels illegal, and the country now perceived that for justice and protection it must turn to the House of Capet. "For the first time the people felt that the government was not merely a machine designed to oppress them, an instrument of exaction; for the first time the people realized that the power of the Crown was allied with justice, that the king watched over them from afar and had compassion on their misfortunes. The monarchy was becoming popular; it was striking root in the provinces, rallying public opinion, and showing itself to be necessary, indispensable, because beneficent."[9]

Philip IV (1285-1314). The reign of Philip IV, called Philip the Fair, climaxed three centuries of the Capetian line, which became extinct in 1328. Philip was the antithesis of his saintly grandfather. In him the virtues of jus-

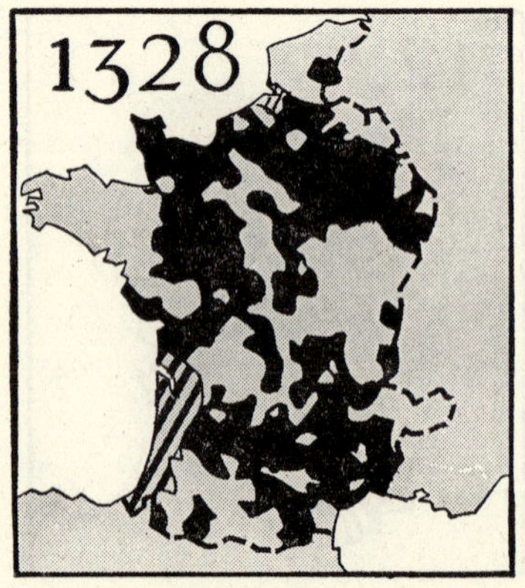

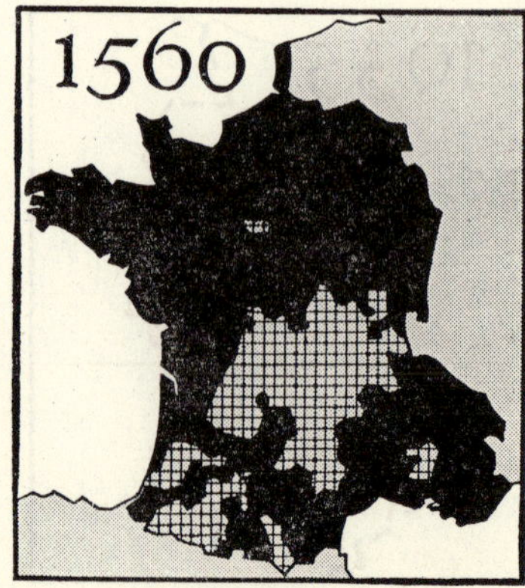

The royal domain was extended bit by bit, not always steadily, and the English were finally driven out. By 1560 only one powerful noble family remained—the Bourbons. Nearly all the checkered lands belonged to them.

This fourteenth-century French manuscript illumination shows an episode in the life of Louis.

tice and honesty were superseded by craft, violence, and deceit. One of the king's harshest acts was the suppression of the wealthy order of the Knights Templars to which the king was heavily in debt. Charges were trumped up, tortures were used to obtain confessions of sundry crimes including heresy, and as many as fifty-four Templars were burned at the stake at one time in Paris. The order's grand master, Jacques de Molay, was one of the last victims; and the story persists that he died saying that his persecutors, the Pope, Philip, and the king's prosecutor, would appear before God for judgment within one year. This prophesy was fulfilled, for within six months all three were dead.

Philip had two objectives, power and wealth, and he was utterly indifferent as to what methods he used to secure these aims. The reign of the last important Capetian monarch is notable for the struggle between the French monarchy and the papacy (see pages 518-519) and, as in the reign of St. Louis, for the institutional growth of the state. There was a tremendous growth of administrative machinery. Agencies became more numerous and specialized. The *parlement,* the court of justice, split into four different judicial bodies and the old feudal justice now rapidly declined before the royal system. As we have noted in our discussion of the origin of the English Parliament, national assemblies were characteristic of thirteenth-century Europe, and France was no exception. On several occasions when Philip wished to arouse public opinion on his behalf he convened the Estates of France. The assembly which he called together in 1302 during his bitter dispute with the Pope, Boniface VIII, is regarded as the first full Estates General, similar to the English Parliament and the Cortes in Spain. The French assembly, however, never developed into a truly representative and powerful legislative body as was the case in England.

Philip extended the practice initiated by Philip Augustus of surrounding himself with astute administrators, mainly recruited from the legal profession, who bent every effort to exalt the prestige and influence of the king at the expense of the nobles. Philip has been called France's first absolute monarch.

No criticism can be leveled at Philip's extension of the policies of his predecessors in improving the royal machinery of justice. In his reign, however, there is strong evidence of a callous indifference to justice and fair dealing, which strikes a new note in the history of the House of Capet. Much later the French people, although appreciating the achievements of their kings in uniting France, came to realize that their absolute monarchy could be as great a menace to the welfare of the state as the uncertainties of feudalism.

The Hundred Years' War. France was now to enter upon one of the most critical periods of her history. Fourteen years after the death of Philip the Fair the Capetian line became extinct, and the House of Valois succeeded to the throne. The succession precipitated a long and bloody war between England and France, waged off and on from 1337 to 1453—the Hundred Years' War already referred to. The English King, Edward III, maintained that through his mother, sister of the late French king, he was the legitimate heir to the French throne. The French nobility, however, maintained that women could not inherit estates or transmit them to a son. The kingship, therefore, was given to a cousin of the last king of the Capetian line. Edward's claim to the French throne was at best a pretext for war. The real cause of the war lay in the fact that Edward and his barons were thirsting for military glory. Another factor was the clash of the economic interests of France and England in Flanders, a region that was coming more and more under French control, to the chagrin of the English wool merchants who sent all their wool to that area.

During the Middle Ages England and France were at war intermittently for four hundred years. Later on there was another period of conflict which began with Louis XIV and ended with Napoleon, another Hundred Years' War. In spite of this legacy of enmity, in modern times Britain and France became for the most part friends and allies.

On such battlefields as Crécy (1346), where yeomen and aristocrats fought together, and Agincourt (1415), when an army of 10,000 fought one three times its size, complete victory was achieved by the English. Naturally these victories stimulated national pride. Time and time again it seemed that the English would entirely undo the work of the Capetians and that the building of a French nation would end in a tragic failure similar to those which took place in Germany and Italy later on.

Joan of Arc. At the critical juncture in this war an amazing thing happened. Impelled by "inward voices," believing that she was divinely inspired, Joan of Arc, a young girl of peasant origin, came to the French king to beg that she be allowed to lead an army to relieve the sorely besieged city of Orléans, whose capture by the English was almost a foregone conclusion. Joan of Arc was permitted to lead an army, to which she imparted a feeling of supreme confidence and a sense of the justice of its cause. Orléans was relieved, and soon the French everywhere were taking the offensive.

The Maid of Orléans met a tragic end. Captured by English soldiers, she suffered a martyr's death at the stake while the French king remained shamefully indifferent. Nevertheless the work of Joan of Arc was done. The weakness of the English had been revealed. By 1453 they had lost every vestige of their holdings except the seaport of Calais. The Hundred Years' War left France impoverished but with a new national consciousness. In the end the monarchy had saved France, and royal power was stronger than it had ever been before. The long struggle with England had all but wiped out the old feudal nobility. The Estates General, a representative body comparable to the English Parliament, had failed to secure the national purse strings as Parliament had done and so held little power over the king.

French consolidation achieved. The process of French consolidation was continued throughout the next century and a half. Louis XI (1461-1483) labored to restore prosperity, to extend the royal domain, and to wreck completely the influence of the few powerful feudal houses that still remained. He loved intrigue and his intricate diplomatic webs resulted in people calling him "the universal spider."[10] On the personal side he was a singularly unpleasant person. Physically he had a spindly body mounted on which was a cadaverous face blighted by a long and sharp nose. Louis had no use for pageantry. He dressed very shabbily and was all business. The end always justified the means, and the king was both unscrupulous and parsimonious. Motivated mainly by self-interest, he had no use for sincerity or altruism.

This calculating, businesslike, and entirely unromantic king successfully carried on the program of statesmanship inaugurated some five hundred years earlier by his Capetian predecessors. His great antagonist in foreign affairs was Charles of Burgundy, whom he foiled and whose territory he seized. The ideals of knighthood and chivalry were becoming old fashioned, especially in the conduct of foreign affairs.

Succeeding kings increased the royal territory bit by bit until by the middle of the sixteenth century only the Bourbon lands and a few other tiny holdings remained outside the royal realm (see map, page 461). These were incorporated in the kingdom when a Bourbon prince came to the throne in 1589. By the end of the sixteenth century, France had become a strong national state, so strong indeed that the ravages of the Hundred Years' War had been completely repaired and the French monarchy was regarded as the strongest in Europe.

The Political Unification of Spain

Conditions in Spain. The unification of Spain was a more complex process than that of France and England. Here in addition to the customary rivalry between the feudal aristocracy and royal authority there was a religious crusade. Unification required the ejection of an alien religion and civilization from Spain. It also involved the union of sev-

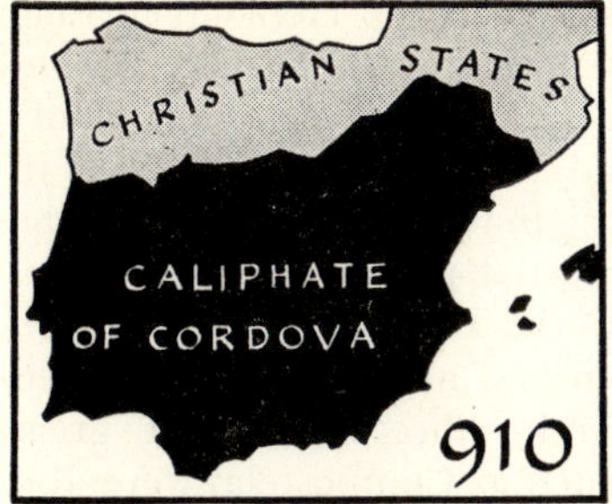

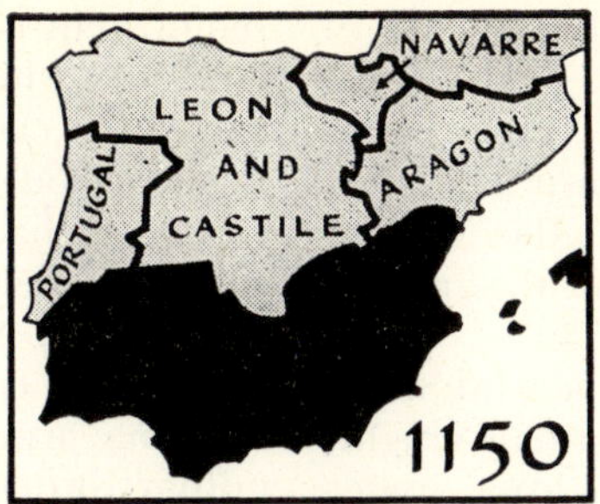

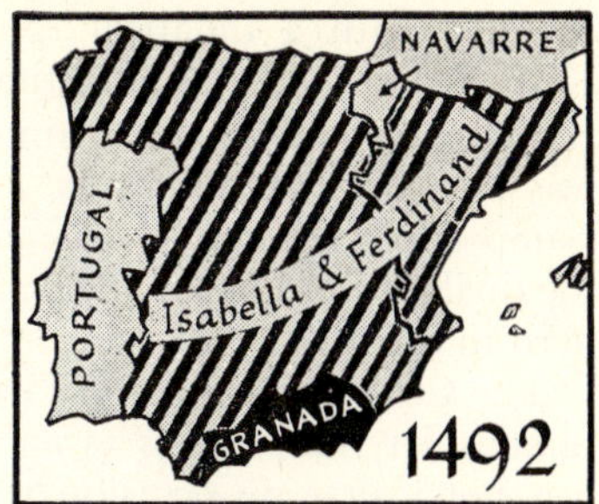

The territory of the Moors (black) gradually diminished as the Christian states slowly pushed them south. United Spain (striped) in 1492 drove the Moors from Spain altogether, in 1515 took over Navarre, in 1580 Portugal.

eral distinct diminutive nations, each possessing its own cultural characteristics.

The Reconquista. The Moslem conquest of Spain has already been recounted (page 278) and we have seen how a few Christian communities managed to survive in the Pyrenees. We saw these small states slowly gathering their strength and expanding southward. The collapse of the Caliphate of Cordova in 1031 inaugurated what is known as the *Reconquista*—the reconquest of the country by the Christian kingdoms. Common fear of the Moslems created in the Christians a sense of unity, the germs of national consciousness, and a deep hatred for the Moslems. The Christian Church played an important part in the offensive against the Caliphate. In the ninth century northern Spain became suffused with a religious zeal. About 835 a bishop is reputed to have found the body of the apostle St. James in the northwestern part of Spain. Soon the site, known as Santiago de Compostela, was known as one of Europe's holiest shrines. Pilgrims by the thousands came to the shrine, and a great cathedral was built in honor of St. James. How better demonstrate one's faith than to drive the Moslems out? The best-known American historian of medieval Spain in speaking of the legend of St. James wrote: "It cemented the alliance of church and state in the sacred duty of reclaiming the peninsula for the faith and of carrying that faith beyond the seas. ...Never was a national legend of deeper and more lasting significance."[11]

The *Reconquista* was, then, a kind of crusade. The clergy did everything possible to encourage the struggle against the Moslems. The battle cry of the Christian soldiers was "Santiago," and banners were consecrated at the shrine. Knights from all over Europe, especially France, flocked to northern Spain to join the Christian forces. The shock troops of the *Reconquista* were the great Spanish military orders, such as Compostela and Calatrava, in which the functions of priest and knight were blended.

In 1085 the important Moslem stronghold of Toledo was captured, and in 1212 a crushing defeat was inflicted upon the Moslems, from which they never recovered. A few years later Cordova and Seville were captured, and by the end of the thirteenth century Moorish influence was confined to Granada. During these struggles a mounting patriotism became

In this seemingly unassailable castle, built to defend Spain against the Moors, Queen Isabella was crowned queen of Castile in 1474. Steep cliffs replace the traditional moat-and-drawbridge protection here.

blended with a fanatical religious spirit. In France, Joan of Arc was the symbol of national reawakening; in Spain the great figure was Rodrigo Diaz de Bivar, known as El Cid Campeador. His exploits against the Moslem foe thrilled Europe, and he became the greatest hero in Spanish literature.

The Cid was a soldier of fortune who, while famous for his prowess as a Castilian knight, was not averse on occasion to fighting under the standard of the Moslem Crescent. Some fifty years after his death, poems began to be written about this incomparable warrior. The most famous is the *Poema del Cid,* in which we see the hero as the perfect Christian knight.

While we have talked of the *Reconquista* as a religious crusade, this statement needs some qualification. It was quite usual when a Moslem area was conquered for its Christian victors to treat their new subjects quite tolerantly, allowing them to enjoy their own religion and laws. It was not uncommon for the Christian kings to protect Moslem traders and businessmen because they realized how valuable they would be from an economic point of view. These rulers often employed Moslem architects and artists and appreciated the cultural refinements of Moslem life. It is said that on one occasion French crusaders left Spain in disgust when they witnessed how tolerantly the Moslems were treated.

Marriage of the monarchs. Following the reduction of Moslem power to the small state of Granada, the process of reconquest halted until the latter part of the fifteenth century. In 1469 Isabella of Castile and Leon married Ferdinand, heir to the kingdom of Aragon. Within a decade both rulers had succeeded to their respective thrones, and by this personal union the Iberian peninsula became united politically, except for the Moslem fragment of Granada, the small state of Navarre, and the kingdom of Portugal (see map, page 465).

Measures for centralization. The keynote of the reign of Ferdinand and Isabella was political centralization. During the long struggles with the Moslems the nobles assumed extensive power, the military brotherhoods became practically independent organizations, and some of the great church officials were difficult to control. The Catholic Sovereigns, as Ferdinand and Isabella came to be called, proceeded with alacrity to establish an effective royal despotism in Spain. Their methods are reminiscent of those used by Henry II in England and Philip Augustus in France. An organization called *La Santa Hermandad* (Holy Brotherhood) had existed for some time in Castile. It had originally been created by the cities for their mutual protection against unruly nobles. Now the Brotherhood was taken over by the crown and made into a combined standing army and police force. The great military orders, such as Compostela, were also brought under the crown. Although Ferdinand and Isabella were devout Catholics, they both believed that the power of the Church should be subordinate to royal government. By tactful negotiation on their part the Pope gave up to them extensive rights in making appointments to the Church in Spain.

During the Middle Ages assemblies known as *cortes* had grown up in the Spanish Christian kingdoms. These bodies resembled the English Parliament and the French Estates General. Spain had its *Magna Charta,* too, in the Ordinances of Leon, issued in 1188. Unlike the course of events in England, however, the early movement toward representative government in Spain lagged in the late Middle Ages and received a death blow from the Catholic Sovereigns in the last years of the fifteenth century. The towns lost their local powers and the *cortes* of the various kingdoms were ignored. In 1480 a Court of Inquisition was set up in Castile. Ferdinand and Isabella as devout Catholics saw in its use a method not only of extirpating heresy but also of increasing royal power. Ferdinand seems to have been especially interested in the prospect of confiscating the fortunes of condemned heretics. Thousands of persons were burned to death and many more lost all their property. For a short time the Inquisition in Spain may have enhanced the power of the crown, but in the long run it caused many talented people to flee the country.

The conquest of Granada. The most dramatic act undertaken by the Catholic Sovereigns was the conquest of Granada. Having made up their minds to wipe out this last Moslem stronghold, Ferdinand and Isabella made their project a great Christian crusade. The king and queen went to the shrine of St. James to invoke divine blessing on the project, and a silver cross sent by the Pope was carried by the Christians. After ten years of hard fighting Granada fell in 1492. Constantinople had fallen to the Moslem Turks in 1453, and now all Europe rejoiced at this squaring of accounts with the followers of the Crescent.

Foundations for greatness. In 1504 Queen Isabella died and the territories of Castile passed under Ferdinand's control. Before his death in 1516 the king was able to seize that part of the kingdom of Navarre which lay south of the Pyrenees. Spain was now a national state. The year Granada fell Columbus discovered the New World and paved the way for Spanish acquisition of a great amount of treasure and for valuable trade.

Ferdinand was an adept diplomat. He married his daughter Joanna to Philip, son of the Hapsburg emperor of the Holy Roman Empire, and a second daughter to Prince Arthur, heir to the English throne. The first of the marriage alliances was to bring Spain great influence in the sixteenth century. Ferdinand, notorious for his cunning and duplicity, promoted Spanish ambitions in Italy to the detriment of France. Machiavelli, in *The Prince,* wrote of Ferdinand, "There is no better instance of a policy of hypocrisy."

Legacies of unification. The particular problems of Spanish unification had some unfortunate results: (1) Geography has had an appreciable effect upon Spanish political development. Just as the mountains of northern Spain cradled and protected the early Christian states, so in spite of the achievement of national unity, the distinct geographical areas into which Spain is divided resulted in a persistent spirit of localism and separatism which has come down to the present day. (2) It has been brought out that the early phase of the *Reconquista* was not fanatical or intolerant. Religious enthusiasm was whipped up as a means to an end, but when victory was achieved the defeated Moslem was treated with courtesy and respect. But in the fourteenth century a tragic change is noticeable as intolerance and hatred took charge of the *Reconquista.* It was especially in the reign of Ferdinand and Isabella that extermination rather than assimilation became the official policy and "What had been a means to an end in the Middle Ages became under Ferdinand and Isabella an end in itself."[12] The sequel was a heritage of religious bigotry and the destruction in a few generations of the spirit of toleration, intellectual curiosity, and lack of fanaticism which was characteristic of Moslem culture in Spain. (3) Centuries of fighting against the Moslems left a legacy of a warlike spirit and inordinate national pride. (4) Contempt for the Moorish unbelievers created a scorn among Spain's ruling classes for those activities in which the Moors engaged—trade, manufacturing, manual labor, and agriculture —a state of mind which was to play an important role in Spanish economic history.

Portugal. Up to 1095 the story of the area which eventually became Portugal was mingled with that of the entire peninsula. About 1050 the king of Castile and Leon, faced with a serious threat of Moslem invasion, appealed to Europe for aid. Count Henry of Burgundy answered the call and did valiant service against the Moslems. As a reward the count was given a Castilian princess for a bride, whose dowry was composed of territory in west Castile. The successors of Count Henry gradually increased their power as counts of Portugal until in the thirteenth century one of them proclaimed himself king of Portugal. During the fourteenth century the rulers of Castile made strenuous attempts to reunite Portugal with their kingdom, but the Portuguese, with the assistance of English troops, defeated a strong Castilian army in 1385, establishing their independence. King John the Great not only won the victory which established his country's independence but inaugurated its overseas expansion. This was to lead to the momentous voyages of Vasco da Gama, the creation of a great empire in India and the Far East, and the establishment of the colony of Brazil. As the sixteenth century dawned Portugal had high hopes of national greatness. Her king could describe himself as "Lord of the conquest, navigation, and commerce of India, Ethiopia, Arabia, and Persia."

The Failure of the National State in Germany and Italy

The Salian emperors (1024-1125). The firm foundation of strong government in Germany was laid by the House of Saxony, founded in 919 by Henry the Fowler, and lasting until 1024. The country was held together by capable rulers and the Saxon German kings enjoyed the leadership of Europe.

These pioneers in nation-making were succeeded in 1024 by a new royal line, the Salian House, which set about with increased vigor to establish a stronger machinery of centralized monarchy. In the next fifty years a trained and loyal body of royal officials was recruited, the lands of the Church brought under the more efficient management of the king's agents, a secure revenue was introduced, and a defensive stronghold for the monarchy was built in a capital in the Harz mountains. Under Henry IV (1056-1106) the German monarchy reached the height of its power and no part of what had once been the Carolingian empire held such promise of a strong and united nation. Yet at the end of 300 years Germany was not unified but only a confused medley of principalities and republics.

Monarchy weakens in conflict with papal power. The first great reverse in the making of a national state in Germany was a direct consequence of the Investiture Struggle. The duel between Gregory VII and Henry IV has been recounted in our discussion of the medieval Church (page 397). This quarrel, involving the right of the king and his nobles to make appointments to church offices, was really only a side issue. What was at stake was the foundation of the strong monarchy in Germany. To Pope Gregory the king was a removable official; he should rule with justice and wisdom, and if he did not, the Pope, as judge, could remove him from his throne. In essence the Pope held that "A good king could still serve the Church; but he was a subordinate serving a master, a warrior using his sword at the pope's behest."[13]

Nobles gain in power as monarchy weakens. The real victors in the Investiture Struggle were the German nobles and princes who at the outset made an alliance with the papacy but continued to wage civil war against their king long after the original issue had been forgotten. Conflict raged not only during the remainder of Henry IV's reign but after his death for nearly another half century, from 1106 to 1152. During this unhappy span of time the kings were quite impotent, with continuous strife between various noble factions, especially the great houses of the Welfs of Bavaria and the Hohenstaufens of Swabia. For the next century there was bitter rivalry between the two families. In Italy a reflected struggle was also waged between these two parties, here called Guelphs and Ghibellines, the first usually being pro-papal and the second antipapal and strongly in favor of the German monarchy's imperial claims in Rome. During the Investiture Struggle in Germany, the city-states of north Italy gained in independence since the German kings were unable to assert their imperial authority.

The outcome of the lamentable disputes and civil wars that plagued Germany from 1075 to 1152 was that the Salian structure of strong monarchy was wrecked. The nobles became independent and a rash of castle building followed—the symbol of defiance to any central authority. Up to this point the nonnoble freeman had been an important feature in German life; now with the growth of localism and uncontrolled feudalism this class practically disappeared. Despite some recovery of royal power later on, as we will shortly note, the evil effects of the period from 1075 to 1152 stemming from the investiture strife were never eradicated. They lingered on until modern times. As an English historian has observed:

"This, in the final analysis, was the outstanding contribution of the Investiture Contest to Germany's future: in the civil wars which it loosed we have to seek the beginnings of the territorial disunity, of the fantastic map of German particularism and of the unlimited sovereignty of the princes, which were the curses of German history from the fourteenth to the nineteenth centuries and which, indurated through long centuries, have perhaps not been entirely obliterated even today."[14]

The kingdom of Naples and Sicily. While rivalries between various noble families and their enmity against the monarchy were transpiring in Germany, Italy was undergoing a period of rapid development and prosperity. It is necessary to interject an account of Italy's activities, especially of the kingdom of Naples and Sicily, inasmuch as the eleventh and twelfth centuries are characterized by German attempts to control and incorporate Italy. We have already noted the exploits of the early Saxon kings toward this same end in the late tenth century.

North Italy, at this time, was becoming notable as a land of prosperous little city republics, but the most promising and brilliant civilization was flourishing in the south of the Italian peninsula and the island of Sicily. We recall the Norman conquests (page 350) in this area which by 1127 had been consolidated into one state—the kingdom of Naples and Sicily (see map, page 487). Under the able rule of Roger II (1130-1154) it became one of the strongest and wealthiest states in Europe. It is interesting that at the time when the Normans were establishing a modern national government in England they were doing the same thing in Sicily. A centralized administration presided over by efficient civil servants was set up. The tax system was particularly just and well administered, and the army was a royal force always ready for service, not an independent feudal levy. There was a remarkable system of royal courts and the king, like his Norman counterparts in England, kept a tight control over all vassals. So advanced was this Norman kingdom of Sicily and Naples that it has been called the first modern state in Europe.

Under the beneficent rule of Roger II there was remarkable economic development; the towns flourished, nourished by busy merchant fleets that plied the Mediterranean, and the income of the great port of Palermo was said to exceed that of the English government. To economic resources there was added the patronage of the arts and a happy toleration for all the diverse cultures that came together in Sicily. Scholars from all over Europe and the East gravitated to Roger's court at Palermo. In fact this center of scholarship ranked next to Spain in the translation of Arabic documents.

Above all, the culture and life of the Sicilian kingdom were amazingly diverse and colorful, made up as they were of Norman, Byzantine, and Arabic elements. Professor LaMonte eloquently paid tribute to this rich diversity when he wrote:

"In every way Palermo reflected the combination of Greek, Arabic, and Latin civilizations, which marked its architecture and art. In material luxury, it partook of the character of an oriental city; in the ceremonial and elaborate costuming of its courtiers it reflected Byzantium; in the military prowess of its nobles and in their distinctive legal genius it was the child of Normandy, while thriving commerce and wealthy bourgeoisie placed it well in the ranks of the Italian towns. Under the Norman kings, Sicily enjoyed almost complete religious toleration; the official clergy were Latin, the monks were mostly Greek, but Moslem cadis touched shoulders with Basilians and Benedictines in the streets, and the call of the muezzin competed with the tolling of the monastic bells."[15]

A fifteenth-century Italian painting pictures the meeting of Frederick III *of Sicily and his bride, Eleanor of Portugal. Such marriages—arranged usually without consulting the bridal pair—were common politics, an accepted part of diplomacy in that day.*

Frederick Barbarossa (1152-1190). Two years before the death of Roger II of Sicily in 1154, there came to the throne in Germany Frederick I of the House of Hohenstaufen, one of the great personalities of his age and a medieval statesman whose policies were to shape decisively not only the political development of his own native land but also that of the numerous city-states of north Italy and the promising kingdom of Naples and Sicily to the south. This great king, known as Frederick Barbarossa, because of his red beard, handsome and powerful in physique, generous and conscientious in spirit, was resolved to play an important role in European affairs. Specifically he was intent upon rectifying the damage done to royal authority by the Investiture Struggle in Germany and reëstablishing his imperial power in Italy. He had an exalted opinion of his imperial office and from the revival of the Roman law that was going on at this time, the king-emperor took the position that his empire was entirely secular, both above and separate from the Church. To strengthen his claims he had Charlemagne canonized and introduced the phrase "Holy Roman Empire" as the official title of the empire. This was done to indicate the divine origin of imperial power, stressing the fact that the emperor did not obtain his authority from the Pope.

Frederick I's Italian expeditions. In attempting to impose Hohenstaufen authority and restore the glory of the empire, Frederick Barbarossa made six expeditions into Italy and spent some twenty-five years in intermittent fighting. In Chapter 14 we followed this struggle with its religious implications and the resolute opposition to Emperor Frederick by the Italian communes and the papacy. The decisive event was the battle of Legnano where Italian burghers, rallying around their symbol of civic liberty—the *corroccio,* an ox-drawn wagon with their flag—completely crushed the German army. At the end of Frederick's reign nothing positive had been achieved by his efforts; some progress had been made in reëstablishing the king's authority in Germany, but in reality Frederick was supreme neither in Italy nor in his homeland.

Before his death this German sovereign had apparently scored a great diplomatic stroke by marrying his eldest son, Henry VI, to Constance, the heiress to the throne of the kingdom of Naples and Sicily. After the death of Frederick I this marriage alliance eventually gave Henry, the new German king and emperor from 1190 to 1197, control of Sicily with its great wealth and well-organized government. There were grave dangers in this acquisition of the southern kingdom however, for the papacy would never reconcile itself to Italy and Sicily being under the same ruler as Germany. The threat of Hohenstaufen encirclement made it vital to the papacy that this royal house be destroyed.

Frederick II in Italy; German interests suffer. It fell to the lot of Frederick's grandson to meet the challenge of the papacy. That grandson was Frederick II (1211-1250), whom we have already met as the ward of Innocent III (page 397), and it is with this ruler that the true results of German kings seeking power and wealth in Italy become manifest. Young Frederick had little or no interest in Germany but was at heart a Mediterranean monarch who much preferred the sunny skies of Italy and the free and easy cosmopolitanism of the court at Palermo to the cold and austerity of castle life in Germany. Frederick II, building on the foundation laid by Roger II, continued to shape Sicily into a modern state, politically and economically, and to foster scholarship and the arts. An excellent fencer, the master of six languages, a diplomat, and, as we have already read in Chapter 15, a scientist, he was in his element as he presided over his brilliant court of scholars and writers. Here the learned men could carry on their disputations, free from all inhibitions, for Frederick II, half-oriental in his outlook and even the possessor of a harem, had little respect for the conventions of his day. His chancellor, reflecting the atmosphere of the court, is supposed to have written:

The life of holy prelates is abominably funny,
Their hearts are full of venom while their
  tongues are dropping honey;
They pipe a pretty melody, and so approach
  discreetly,
And offer you a cordial, mixed with poison,
  very sweetly.[16]

In discussing the medieval papacy in Chapter 14 we noted the relentless struggle between Frederick and the Vatican, between the two forces of the Empire and Papacy. Frederick's attempts to extend his centralized Sicilian administration to the Lombard cities of north Italy met with bitter opposition. Most of his reign was spent in conflict and wars and was an unhappy mixture of papal excommunications and absolutions, of endless campaigns, of victories and defeats.

During his reign Frederick II was continually absent from Germany, and his policy was to surrender whatever the princes demanded just so long as they were quiet. Absorbed in his tangled affairs in Italy, Frederick permitted the nobles and ducal houses in Germany to consolidate their power and render the authority of any central government quite impossible. "The reign of Frederick II was a turning point in German history... when he died in 1250 the political structure of Germany was irrevocably changed."[17]

End of Hohenstaufen rule in Germany and Italy. Frederick II died during one of his interminable campaigns in north Italy. As long as he was alive this brilliant Hohenstaufen was able to hold his empire against his adversaries. On his death, however, the empire he had struggled to maintain quickly disintegrated and in eighteen years his house was annihilated. In 1265 the Pope made an alliance with Charles of Anjou, the brother of the king of France, in which he offered Charles the kingdom of Naples and Sicily as a reward for ridding Italy of the Hohenstaufens. Charles succeeded in defeating them in battle in 1266, and two years later young Conradin, the grandson of Frederick II, invading Italy from Germany to assert his rights, was defeated on the field of Tagliacozzo. Not long afterwards this youth was beheaded in the public square of Naples and thus the Hohenstaufens were extinguished.

How significant was the fall of the House of Hohenstaufen? What importance had the victory of the papacy and its allies, the Italian communes, over the empire? It may be said at the outset that the victory of the papacy was more apparent than real. The extirpation of the Hohenstaufens was a hollow triumph, for in the quest for victory the papacy had lost much of its integrity and prestige. Men had seen the papacy using its spiritual means to achieve earthly ambitions. And it was ironic that the Church really succumbed to the very evil Gregory VII in the Investiture Struggle had attempted to avoid—entanglement in earthly politics and secular ambitions. Popes became more and more like Italian princes, primarily interested in asserting their authority over the restless nobles in the Papal States and in playing the game of alliances in the rough-and-tumble rivalry among the various states in Italy. It is this decay in ideals, this involvement in earthly rivalries that explain the revolt against papal authority that is the theme of the following chapter.

Effects of German pursuit of empire in Italy. What were the consequences for Germany in her attempts to make Italy a part of the Holy Roman Empire? In Chapter 12, we saw how the Saxon emperors, beginning with Otto I in the mid-tenth century, were attracted southward. Historical theories were cited concerning the effects of their pursuit of empire. The imperial policy of the Hohenstaufens raises the same controversy among historians as that of the Saxons.

There are some historians who tend to justify these kings. Frederick Barbarossa's intervention in Italy is stoutly defended on the grounds that only by access to the wealth of the Italian communes could an adequate source of power be secured sufficient to win back royal authority lost by the Salian monarchy during the course and sequel of the Investiture Struggle. Despite some truth in this contention, in the long run the objectives pursued by the German kings in Italy were unattainable. The combined opposition of the communes and papacy was too strong.

Factionalism follows the fall of the monarchy. Following the death of Frederick II, all the forces of localism and factionalism ran riot in Germany. From 1254 to 1273—a period known as the Great Interregnum—the country was tormented by the rivalry of princely houses. The question raised at the outset of Frederick Barbarossa's reign had now been answered; royal power had not been revived, it had actually been further diminished. In speaking of the early promise of both constitutional government and a strong centralized royal administration in the tenth century, an American authority on medieval Germany has cogently observed:

"What defeated both issues in Germany was the untoward, even disastrous, fact that the destiny of the German nation by an ill freak of fortune was tied up with the history of Italy and the Empire. This made Germany's problem an infinitely complex one, whereas that of France and England was a relatively simple one. The German kings as emperors... wasted untold blood and treasure of the German people beyond the Alps under the malign tyranny of the idea of medieval imperialism. The end spelled the ruin of feudal Germany. But for this medieval Germany would have won through... to a great and strong national monarchy."[18]

The decline of the empire. After the fall of the Hohenstaufens, Germany lapsed more and more into political disunity. The country in the later Middle Ages was characterized by interminable civil wars, lawlessness, and private warfare. The Holy Roman Empire never again achieved the brilliance it had enjoyed in the reign of Frederick Barbarossa. The emperors usually did not try to interfere in Italian affairs. In fact, the practice of going to Rome to receive the imperial crown from the Pope died out. The last German king to carry out the tradition was Frederick III in the fifteenth century. Even in German affairs the emperors no longer tried to assert their word over the noble families, which were becoming more and more powerful. To all intents the Holy Roman Empire was dead, and the contrast between the empire in theory and in practice became more and more manifest.

The early Hapsburgs. In 1273, at the end of the Great Interregnum, the imperial crown was revived and given to Count Rudolf of the House of Hapsburg. This family played a prominent part in European history. Rudolf's ancestors had gained control of a small domain in northern Switzerland. Toward the end of the eleventh century the family built a castle which was called Habichtsburg (Castle of the Hawk); hence the word Hapsburg. During the late Middle Ages and in the early modern times the House of Hapsburg had amazing luck in adding to the ancestral lands. In the thirteenth century it acquired Austria, with its important city of Vienna, and in the sixteenth century it obtained Bohemia and much of Hungary. The Hapsburgs presided over their Austrian empire from Vienna. It was an empire only because the Hapsburg ruler, archduke of Austria, was at the same time emperor of the Holy Roman Empire.

The Golden Bull. Germany in the fourteenth century was more a confederation of strong feudal states than a centralized, monarchal, national state. The Golden Bull of 1356, a document which served as the political

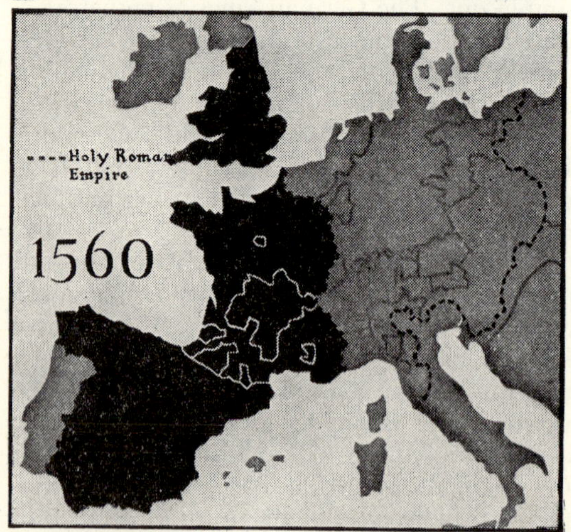

In 1560 England, Spain, and France were maturing national states. Italy and Germany were still collections of small states and cities. The Holy Roman Empire was largely a fiction.

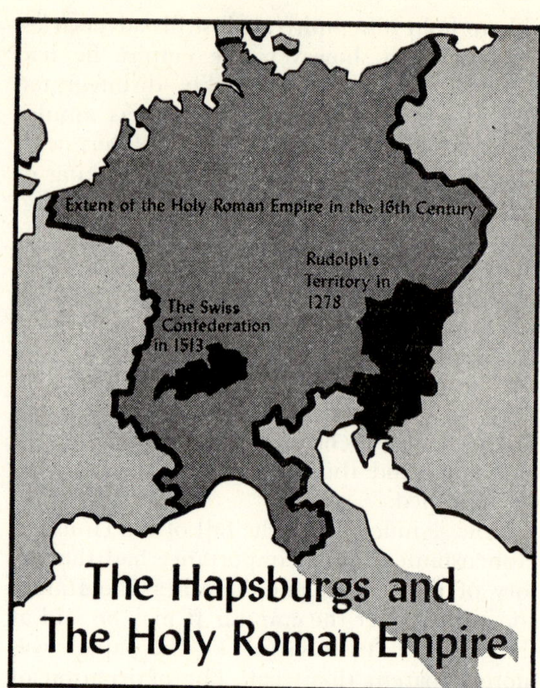

constitution of Germany until 1806, laid down the procedure for election of the emperor by seven German princes. These great nobles, such as the king of Bohemia and the duke of Saxony, were given rights that made them virtually independent rulers. The emperor could no longer tax in the empire; independent princes could even issue their own coinage. An imperial Diet, or legislature, gave some semblance of governmental unity. But it met infrequently and had little authority. It became more and more common to speak of the Germanies, not Germany. By the fifteenth century Germany was a welter of archduchies, margravates, counties, duchies, and free cities.

The Golden Bull crystallized political disunity. Unification under a single all-powerful government was not to be achieved in Germany proper for over five hundred years after the promulgation of the Golden Bull in 1356.

Movements for reform. In the fifteenth century the German imperial crown came again into the possession of the Hapsburgs, after having been held by members of the House of Luxemburg from 1347 to 1437. Frederick of Hapsburg was made emperor in 1452, and from this time until 1806, when the Holy Roman Empire disappeared, this house held the imperial crown almost without a break. During the fifteenth century there was a strong demand from many quarters in the empire for some kind of political reform, the purpose being the creation of an effectual authority. In 1439 a citizen of Mainz wrote: "We have a good constitution, good laws, and good traditionary customs. What we want is power to carry out those laws in the supreme and lower courts. We also want a permanent army under the guidance of leaders who, brave and zealous for right, will ever be ready to see that the law is upheld and its sentences executed without flinching; and the robber barons rooted out of the land.... As long as the Emperor is dependent on the caprices of the princes, and is without an army and sufficient revenue to carry out his government, neither right nor justice can prevail."[19]

During the reign of Maximilian I (1493-1519) a serious attempt at reform was made. In 1495 the Diet of Worms outlawed private warfare. An imperial court was set up in order to settle the many feuds, and steps were taken to insure the annual meeting of the imperial Diet, but the Diet failed to enforce its will.

The Hapsburgs and the Germanies. The Hapsburgs obtained little comfort from being the head of the Holy Roman Empire. More and more this dynasty concentrated on the increase of its family possessions and its own power. The marriage of Maximilian to Mary of Burgundy added the rich possession of the Netherlands to the Hapsburg domain and helped make this family the most potent force in political affairs in sixteenth-century Europe. As Germany approached early modern times, she was at a great disadvantage in comparison with such relatively unified states as England, France, and Spain. In early medieval times such rulers as Henry the Fowler and Otto the Great had started Germany on her way to becoming the strongest state in Europe in the eleventh and twelfth centuries. But early promise was not fulfilled, and in 1500 the area was not Germany but several states collectively known as the Germanies.

Rise of the Swiss state. An interesting feature of the medieval German empire was the emergence of Switzerland, which became a national state in the fifteenth century. During the time of the emperor Frederick II, two peasant communities high on the Alps were permitted to become self-governing cantons subject to the overlordship of the emperor. A little over fifty years later these little cantons were hard put to maintain their rights against the Hapsburg emperors. In 1291 three cantons agreed to a Perpetual Compact, directed against Rudolf of Hapsburg.

But the Hapsburg leaders were determined to bring the Swiss peasants to heel and in 1315 led an army against their puny antagonists. The aroused mountain men gave a good account of themselves, hurled heavy boulders down the passes against the knights in the Hapsburg army, and thoroughly defeated it. The success of the three cantons caused other communities to join the little political union, a Confederation whose members kept their local institutions but were pledged to joint action for defense against a common foe.

In 1394 the independence of the Swiss Confederation was virtually recognized by the Hapsburgs. While the struggle for independence had been going on, the spirit of nationalism had been growing in the cantons. An inspiring story developed, at first sung in ballad form, which told of the bravery of William Tell and his great skill with the bow. Perhaps it is only a legendary tale, but to the Swiss people William Tell became the symbol of their pride of nationality. Another Swiss hero was Arnold von Winkelried, who is supposed to have hurled himself against the lances of the Hapsburgs, thus opening a way for the charge of the Swiss soldiers. Legend relates the exploit in these words:

> "Make way for liberty," he cried,
> "Make way for liberty," and died.

In the fifteenth century the Confederation increased to thirteen cantons, and the Emperor Maximilian renounced all sovereignty over them in the Treaty of Basel (1499). It was not until the Peace of Westphalia in 1648, however, that Switzerland was formally recognized as an independent state.

Failure of a national state to rise in Italy. In Italy as in Germany the effect of the imperial program of the Hohenstaufens was the same: the lack of any national unity or government. In the south, the Norman-founded kingdom of Naples and Sicily might have proved to be what Italy most needed, for it was an efficient centralized government in the hands of benevolent, cultured kings. The kingdom might have developed for Italy what the Normans had achieved in England, a single national monarchy, but this was not to be, for (as we have seen earlier in this chapter) at the Pope's invitation the count of Anjou seized the kingdom.

Angevin and Spanish rule. Angevin rule was very unpopular in the southern kingdom. In Sicily, especially, the people had little use for the counts of Anjou with their alien French officials, and in 1282 at Palermo, the Sicilians, at the hour of vespers, rose up and murdered every Frenchman they could lay hands on. The massacre has gone down in history as the Sicilian Vespers. As a result of the uprising the Sicilian throne went to Peter of Aragon, who had married into the Hohenstaufen line of Frederick II. The two kingdoms were now separate, one in Sicily and one in southern Italy. In 1443 Naples was conquered by Alfonso of Aragon, who again united the kingdoms of Sicily and Naples. The reunion brought little respite to the unhappy kingdom, for Spaniards representing the House of Aragon and Frenchmen representing the Angevins struggled intermittently for its possession for another century. Under Aragon and Angevin rule, south Italy and Sicily precipitously declined amid official corruption, a decadent feudal reaction, and at times horrible cruelty.

The Italian city-states. In contrast to the general decline in the south, in north Italy the elimination of the influence of German kings in the eleventh century left the numerous city-states of Lombardy and Tuscany free to follow their own devices. Milan, Venice, Genoa, Florence, and Pisa especially benefited from the crusades and the opening up of the Mediterranean. They grew opulent and became dynamic centers of culture. These cities were entering upon their golden age, made possible by thriving industry and the lucrative trade from the East. Their rich commercial houses handled the revenues of the Popes, aided bankrupt kings, and financed wars. These city-states exhibited amazing vitality and exuberance. Apart from their achievements in commerce they successfully ousted the feudal control of the nobles in their midst, they were ingenious and prolific in drafting various types of constitutions, and they produced artists and writers whose work remains one of the glories of creative achievement.

The Italian city-states were similar to those of ancient Greece. The once small towns gradually spread out, gained control over surrounding territory, and in certain cases even ruled other towns. The prevailing spirit among these little states was of extreme political individualism. Each city was intensely self-conscious, viewing its neighbors with a jealousy that often flared into open war.

Within each city there was much feuding. Unlike the situation in northern Europe, where nobles lived in the country and the middle class or bourgeoisie in the towns, the Italian nobility not only had their castles in the country but also built their towered houses in the cities. These nobles were always quarreling, for commerce had no attraction for them. In some cities arcaded streets were built so that the merchants and townsmen could go about their mundane business errands and appointments safe from the arrows that were flying from the towers across the street. The middle class fought to control these restless nobles and finally succeeded in enforcing their will. Factionalism, however, continued as rivalries and even fighting were carried on by various groups and cliques. In the old days of the fight against the German emperors, the pro-imperial party in the cities was called Ghibelline and the pro-papal and anti-imperial party the Guelph. These party names, however, were still used by the quarrelsome factions in the city-states long after the original issues had been forgotten.

Governmental structure of the cities. Up to the end of the thirteenth century the prevailing political trend in the cities was toward republicanism and representative government. In the many cities, or communes, civic patriotism and a desire for liberty rapidly advanced. The citizens elected their own magistrates, levied taxes, and kept the revenue. There was much trial and error in the art of government. One authority lists "single and plural executive, direct and indirect election, electoral qualifications and universal suffrage, class representation, long term and short term in office, rotation in offices" as experiments in governmental structure.[20] Two city-state republics were of unusual interest. Venice—"Pearl of the Adriatic" and city of the lagoons—was one of the richest cities of its time, carrying much of Europe's sea trade in its great fleets and controlling an empire of ports and islands in the eastern Mediterranean. It is said that there were six fleets in operation, all standardized as to design, so that spare parts could be kept at the various ports used by the Venetians. The government of this rich republic first resided in a *doge* (duke) together with a people's assembly. The rich merchants, however, gradually took the reins of power into their hands, the main governmental agency being the all-powerful Council of Ten. The Venetian system allowed a rich oligarchy to rule. In the main it gave the people good government and unlike other city-states resolutely prevented strife and factionalism.

Florence was another famous city-state republic. It was the center of a thriving industry in wool, leather, and silk, and its merchants and bankers were among the most prosperous in Europe. Their gold florin circulated as a standard coin in many lands. The Florentine constitution was amazingly complicated, providing for all kinds of checks and counterchecks, election, selection by lot, and short terms of office. The head of the cabinet held office only for two months and all laws needed a two-thirds majority in five different committees or assemblies. Although Florence was in theory a democracy, the real political power was wielded by the rich merchants.

Despotism replaces republicanism. In the fourteenth century there was a rapid decline in republicanism in the Italian city-states. Apparently representative institutions had been premature, for majority rule was never trusted by minorities and there was no art of compromise in the practice of government. Then too, many cities felt the need of a resolute leader who would extirpate factionalism and defend them from external rivals.

In spite of the forms of government that existed in theory, the actual power in the city-states more and more gravitated in the direction of one-man rule. Prominent families came to power in most of the cities and provided the political bosses or despots that ran the government. Behind the scenes rival families carried on bitter duels for power, accompanied by poisonings, stabbing forays, and civil war. In many of these struggles, both within the cities and between the communes, mercenary soldiers were used under the command of leaders called *condottieri.* These adventurers came from all over Europe, selling their swords to the highest bidder. One of the most famous was an Englishman, Sir John de Hawkwood, whose army, called the White Company, played an important part in Italian politics in the latter part of the fourteenth century. The feuds both within and between cities apparently did little to hinder commercial progress. Mercenaries saw to it that the petty wars were not too destructive.

Milan was the best example of the Italian city-state ruled by a suave despot, who was unscrupulous in politics and a patron of the arts. For many years the state was ruled by the Visconti family, the most famous member being Gian Galeazzo who was called the "Viper of Milan." Rising to power by the murder of his uncle, this ruler is an excellent prototype of the Renaissance despot. Gian Galeazzo was the dominant figure in Italian politics from 1385 to 1402, combining ruthlessness against his rivals and complete unscrupulousness in his diplomacy with benevolent and efficient rule which provided Milan's citizens with fine buildings, many public improvements, and a new university.

While Florence retained the form of her republican institutions but in reality came under the control of the famous Medici family, and while Venice maintained the benevolent oligarchy of her merchants under the figurehead of the *Doge,* practically all of the other city-states came under the rule of despots, an amazing group of capable and ruthless men who were lovers of luxury and the fine art of living. "They were brutal, unscrupulous, ambitious men, who were at the same time patrons of the arts and letters; men who murdered an enemy, applauded a poet or orator, or seduced a pretty woman with equal ease and pleasure. They hung pictures on their walls and enemies on their gibbets; wrote poetry and plotted treason; built churches and burned villages; excelled in courtly etiquette and inhuman tortures; lived lustily and died violently."[21]

Age of the Despots: city-states at their peak. The prosperity, lusty combativeness, and creative achievement of the Italian city-states reached its height in the Age of the Despots in the fifteenth century, the *Quattrocento* (see map, page 487). Wars and rivalries continued between the city-states, the most important being the duel between Venice and Milan, in which Florence was also involved, lasting most of the century. Foreign affairs were carried on with complete disregard for pledges or integrity. "In fifteenth century Italy it was every state for itself, and devil take the honest or weak."[22] Despite these internecine wars there was little interference with normal life—the carrying on of business and the enjoyment of the arts. All the great mercenary captains were now Italian, professional soldiers who carried on their fighting with the minimum of bloodshed. "They would try to win, because defeat would lower their market value, but they did not want to beat the enemy too much. He was in the same trade, and cut-throat competition was bad for everyone in the long run. Besides, a war ended too soon might mean unemployment for a long spell."[23] There were, therefore, always degrees of victory and limits to defeat. The grim all-out fighting methods of the north Europeans were regarded as barbarous.

At the close of the fifteenth century Italy was the envy of her neighbors with her wealth, refinement, and art. During this time the peninsula had been left alone by other non-Italian powers but this happy circumstance was now to end, and invasion and foreign rule would destroy wealth and retard culture for four hundred years. The Italian political scene for more than a century had been characterized by instability, lack of national unity, and military backwardness. These weaknesses made her an easy prey to invasion and brought her first would-be conqueror from France in 1494.

Eastern and southern Europe and Russia

Scandinavia. Before following the course of history in eastern and southern Europe, a few words may be said about Scandinavia. These beautiful but harsh northern lands, whose people are so poorly endowed with the resources that give nations power and prestige, have experienced two periods of greatness. We have already followed the truly remarkable expansion of the Norsemen in the Viking Age (page 338) and in the seventeenth century we shall see another age of influence and vigor when Sweden becomes a first-class power. But between these periods Scandinavian importance was relatively meager.

Three separate kingdoms – Denmark, Sweden, and Norway—had developed about the same time during the course of the ninth and tenth centuries. Some progress was made toward national development, but the political history in the main is confusing and unimportant. The kingdoms were united and separated from time to time in a bewildering fashion. The land was not rich, and as late as 1400 the people in all three states numbered only one and a half million. In 1397 an important event occurred, the Union of Kalmar, which united the three crowns under the sovereign of Denmark. This attempt to impose Danish control over the two other states led to much controversy with Sweden, as will be seen in Chapter 19.

The Slavic peoples in political history. In Chapter 12, we merely cited the migrations of the many groups referred to as the West and South Slavs, and concentrated instead on the East Slavs and the origin of the Russian state. The reason for this method lies in the historical significance of one Slavic group as compared to another. Of all the peoples included within the generic term Slavic, only the East Slavs in Russia were destined to play a significant role in modern world affairs.

In the case of the West and South Slavs, their civilization was characterized by strife and instability. National frontiers seldom remained fixed nor were the national groups ever clearly distinguishable. The history of eastern and southern Europe concerns the fate of many diverse nationalities, migrations of various folk groups, the rise and fall of ephemeral kingdoms, and the shrinking and expanding of disputed frontiers. Such manifold activities and movements of these peoples indicate why a study of eastern Europe is often confusing. Although a detailed narrative of the West and South Slavs is inappropriate in a general history, a knowledge of certain events and fundamental trends is all important in casting light upon some of our contemporary problems in eastern Europe.

Renewal of German eastward expansion. During medieval times migrations and conquests caused extensive transplantation of such groups as the Germans, Wends, Poles, Lithuanians, and Prussians along the shores of the central and eastern Baltic and in the immediate hinterland. We have described the conquests of the early Saxon kings (page 344), Henry the Fowler and Otto the Great, over the Slavs and the establishment of Germanic authority in Slavic territory. German eastward expansion was violently halted as a result of Slavic rebellion against German colonization during the reign of Otto II in the late tenth century.

But two hundred years after this setback, the Germans renewed their eastward drive. They pushed back the Slavic frontier from the Elbe to the Vistula. On many occasions the more backward Slavs, such as the Baltic Wends, were exterminated; the German colonists then took over the empty land, cleared and drained it, and built hundreds of prosperous villages. This expansion and clearing of primitive land has been likened to our westward movement in the United States.

Further expansion under the Teutonic Knights. Shortly after 1200 there was a new development in German eastward expansion against the Slav. The Teutonic Knights, a military-religious order for Germans, founded at the time of the Third Crusade (1198), transferred its activities to the conquest of pagan Prussia. This land between the Vistula and the Niemen Rivers and bordering the central coast of the Baltic Sea was conquered, important cities such as Königsberg and Memel were founded, and the Knights even pressed forward into the fringes of north Russia. The conquest of Prussia effectively cut off the Polish kingdom from the Baltic.

Directly northeast of Prussia was the land of the Lithuanians, who had managed to survive in the swamps and woods near the Niemen River. These people preserved their pagan and primitive form of life longer than any other group in Europe and have been compared to the Laplanders. The Teutonic Knights, having conquered the Prussians, gave up their religious character and settled down as a landed nobility; they then turned against their neighbors—the Lithuanians. The excuse was a religious crusade but the motive was greed. The Teutonic Knights reached the zenith of their power in the fourteenth century.

Poland and Lithuania. To the south of Prussia, which as we have just seen, was conquered by the Teutonic Knights, lay Poland. The Polish nation, as a result of military pressure from the Germans on the west, the Bohemians and Hungarians on the south, and the Prussians on the north, was welded into a strong military state in the middle of the tenth century. During this time, Poland was converted to Christianity, a factor which later linked her to western European culture.

The Teutonic Knights

In the eleventh century, the Poles attempted to establish an empire embracing a large bulk of the Western Slavs. This empire was short lived; a major cause of its disintegration lay in dynastic competition and the power of the nobility and clergy against royal rule. During the twelfth and thirteenth centuries, Poland steadily weakened, and only the corresponding weakness of neighboring states prevented her destruction. The Teutonic Knights added

Poland 1000

to Poland's weakness in the early thirteenth century, by conquering Prussia, thereby preventing Polish access to the Baltic Sea. During the middle part of this same century, the country was devastated by the Mongol invasions, although Mongol domination was avoided. Poland lapsed into anarchy and did not become an important state again until the fourteenth century.

The Lithuanians, once helpless and heathen primitives, had gained outstanding leaders in the fourteenth century who initiated a remarkable program of conquest, mainly to the southeast. A huge state was created, stretching from the Baltic to the Black Sea, much of it well inside the western confines of modern Russia. In 1386 Lithuania and Poland were united under a common sovereign, a Lithuanian prince who, as a result of the union, was converted to Catholic Christianity. The expanded state became the largest in Europe.

The Teutonic Knights, as we have seen, had penetrated into Poland and Lithuania in the fourteenth century, and built towns and settled districts. Regarding the Knights as the common enemy, the Poles, supported by the Lithuanians, waged war against what they considered an interloper in their lands. In 1410 the Knights suffered a crushing defeat at Tannenberg; in 1466 a peace was arranged that turned over west Prussia to the Poles while east Prussia, under the Teutonic Knights, retained its autonomy as a vassal state of Poland. The peace was a great blow to German expansion, for the Poles obtained

control of the Vistula River and access to the Baltic Sea through the important port of Danzig. East Prussia was now cut off from the rest of Germany. The port of Danzig, which is strategically located between Poland and Germany and when under Polish control, divides east and west Prussia by a narrow corridor on the northern coast, plays, as we shall see, an important role in the political history of modern Europe.

Poland and Lithuania, after several trial unions, were permanently united at the end of the fifteenth century, the former absorbing the latter. This huge state had the potentialities of a brilliant future, but its boundaries were purely artificial, its governmental system lamentably inefficient, and its ruling class impervious to change. Above all it faced a struggle with a great power, Russia, who shook off its Mongol rulers in the fifteenth century and began to expand energetically in the next. Russian rulers were resolved to shake loose the many Ukrainians and White Russians (people closely related to the main Great Russian stock) from Polish control. The claims of Russia over certain Slavic groups in Poland, her many attempts to incorporate Polish territory, and her success in partitioning Poland in the eighteenth century, provide the background for understanding the bitter enmity between Pole and Russian that has come down to our own time.

Bohemia. Almost in the center of the European continent were the Bohemians, the most westerly branch of the West Slavs. They had established themselves in between Germany and Poland and behind two protective chains of mountains in about the fifth century. During the ninth and tenth centuries, the Czechs, who were the most important member of this Slavic group, established a kingdom on the Bohemian plain. The Czechs, nearly surrounded by Teutonic peoples, have struggled for a thousand years against the menace of German domination. In 1471 the Bohemian nobles elected a Polish prince as their king, and in 1490 this same ruler also became the king of Hungary. Since he maintained his seat of government at Budapest, the Hungarian capital, Bohemia passed very largely under foreign influence. Another change in political fortunes came in 1526, when the king of Bohemia was killed in battle against the Turks. Terrified at the prospect of Moslem rule, the Czechs offered their vacant throne to a Hapsburg prince. Although the Czechs retained their local institutions, their government for nearly four hundred years was centered in Vienna.

Hungary. To the southeast of Bohemia, situated in the wide and fertile plain known as Hungary, were an Asiatic people called the Magyars. These Hungarians were for many years the terror of eastern Europe, harrying their neighbors by wild and brutal raids. In 955, however, they were defeated by the German king Otto I (page 342), and from that time, gradually hemmed in by powerful neighboring states, the Magyars began to adopt a settled mode of life. Under their king St. Stephen I (997-1038), a statesman with great ability and vision, Hungary made great progress in bettering her governmental system, improving agriculture, and advancing culture. Above all, she became Christian.

The Magyars, ruled for a time by capable and conscientious men, might have become a nation had it not been for the nobility, which was sufficiently influential to block a centralized government. The state was further weakened by the conquest and inclusion of unruly racial elements—Croats, Slovaks, and Rumanians. Hungary received her most serious setback when, in 1526, her king—also ruler of Bohemia—fell in battle against the Turks. The nation was now carved into three portions: one ruled by the Turkish sultan, a small segment by a native prince, and the third by the archduke of Austria. This intertwining of the fortunes of Austria, Bohemia, and Hungary explains how, at the time the Turks were ejected from much of southeastern Europe in early modern times, the Hapsburgs at Vienna came to rule over a polyglot empire of Bohemian, Hungarian, and Austrian peoples.

The South Slavs in the Balkans. In the Balkan peninsula about 1000 A.D. there existed only confusion, racial diversity, and intermittent warfare. Bulgarians, Serbs, and Croats—to name the most important Balkan peoples—created ephemeral states, and although some rulers, especially in Bulgaria, dreamed of uniting the diverse Balkan peoples into one great nation, their efforts were fruitless. The multiplicity of small countries in the Balkans in modern times is a legacy of their failure, and the tensions and conflicts resulting from that state of affairs were to make of the Balkan

peninsula "a danger zone of Europe," a source of constant worry to European diplomats, and, as in 1914, the direct or indirect cause of conflict.

The fall of the Byzantine empire. The outstanding political development in southeastern Europe at the close of the Middle Ages was the disappearance of the Byzantine empire and the emergence of a great Moslem state which not only became heir to the lands formerly ruled by the Christian emperors at Constantinople but also to the whole Balkan area. The fortunes of this new power had been laid by a young Turkish chieftain named Osman, who ruled from 1326 to 1359. His followers called themselves *Osmanli* (sons of Osman) a term we have changed to Ottoman. Driving north in 1354, the Turks crossed the Bosporus into Europe. Serbs opposed them but were routed in a bloody battle in 1389. The southern Balkans fell to the Turks.

Constantinople, last remnant of Byzantine power, held out until 1453, when it too succumbed. St. Sophia, once the glory of eastern Christendom, became a Moslem mosque. The close of the fifteenth century saw the Ottoman Turks in complete control of the Balkans and pushing on toward Vienna. A great new empire with its center at Constantinople, comparable to that created by Justinian in the sixth century, was now ruled by the Ottoman sultans. It was in no sense a national state but a bewildering mixture of Turks, Serbs, Hungarians, Bulgarians, Rumanians, Armenians, and Jews. The imposition of Turkish rule upon southeastern Europe delayed the rise of national states in the Balkan area until the nineteenth century.

Russia: decline of Kiev, rise of small states. In Chapter 12 we described Kievan Russia, noting its liberal government and enlightened culture in science and the arts. Under Yaroslav the Wise (1019-1054) the early promise of Kievan civilization reached its height. Unfortunately this culture rapidly declined in the eleventh century as Kiev suffered from the raids of destructive nomads who cut off her trade routes, retarded her civilization, and alienated her from western Europe.

In the eleventh century, Russia consisted of a number of principalities. Various princes, who had set up rival principalities, fought each other for control of Kiev, thereby adding to its decline.

Among these new states was Suzdal, with its main city of Vladimir, near the Volga River (in the area later to be known as the Grand Duchy of Muscovy). It was the ruler of this principality who attacked Kiev in 1168 and sacked it, thus bringing to an end the Kievan period of Russian history. In 1240 Mongol invaders again pillaged this area and Kiev never regained its leadership.

The princes of Suzdal attained supremacy ruling at the new capital of Vladimir for about a century and then their state became a victim of internal feuds. At this time several other small states gained prominence, including Smolensk, Novgorod, and Galicia. Novgorod became the most important commercial center in Russia, the entrepôt for commerce passing between Siberia, eastern Russia, and the Baltic. Galicia, in the southwest on Russia's frontier with the East Slavs, in the early thirteenth century became the most wealthy in Russia with a prosperous commercial and agricultural economy supporting fifty towns. It would have been a worthy successor to Kiev, the nucleus perhaps for a new Russia that would have been oriented to western Europe in its culture. This opportunity never materialized, for the state suffered from constant attacks from its neighbors—Lithuanians, Poles, and Hungarians, was invaded by the Mongols who destroyed its prosperity, and finally was incorporated into Poland in the first part of the fourteenth century.

In early Russia there was a strong republican tradition, especially in Kiev and in commercial cities like Novgorod which were influenced by the institutions of the free German towns along the Baltic belonging to the Hanseatic League. As in western Europe during this medieval period there was a trend toward representative institutions based upon the old Russian assembly known as the *Vieche.* This body, made up of the free men of the towns,

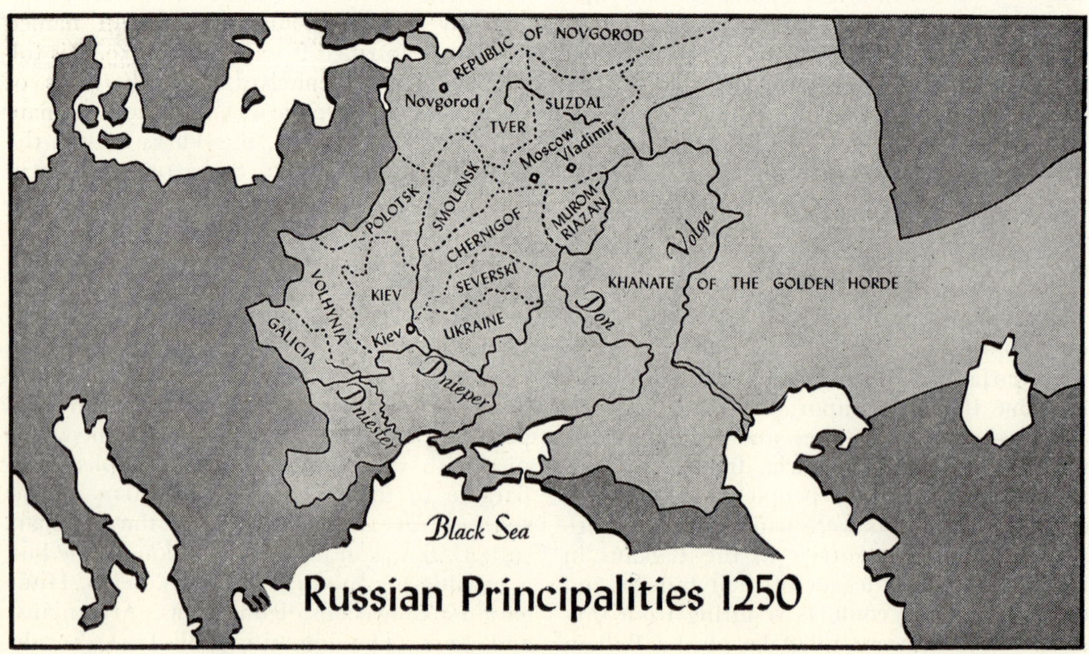

Russian Principalities 1250

was a primitive method of ascertaining the wishes of the people. Attendance was not compulsory, meetings were held in the open, voting was by voice, and most decisions had to be unanimous. As the political center of Russia moved away from the Baltic and from the old culture of Kiev into the remote center of the great Russian plain there was a tendency to discard republican traditions and to substitute instead strong and despotic government.

The Mongol conquest. The Mongol or Tatar conquest descended upon Russia during this formative period. In studying medieval China we have followed the amazing career of Genghis Khan (page 314), who united the unruly tribesmen of Mongolia and then launched them like a thunderbolt on a campaign of world conquest. The distances covered by these Mongols as they carried out their raids were almost unbelievable and their tactics of terror were indescribable. One of Genghis Khan's generals invaded eastern Europe in 1223; southern Russia lay open to conquest, but this raid was more of a reconnaissance than an attempt at conquest and the Mongol army returned to their base in eastern Asia.

This Mongol expedition of 1223 opened the eyes of the Mongol leaders to the defenselessness of Russia and eastern Europe and in 1237 they again turned west. The various Russian principalities, including Suzdal, were conquered and in 1241 the exultant Mongols invaded Poland and Hungary. None of the armies was able to cope with the rapid mobility of these Asiatic tribesmen and the sheer mass of their disciplined battalions, numbering at times as many as 150,000 horsemen. Brutal warfare in which captured cities were completely gutted and all living things slaughtered took the will to fight out of their enemies. The Mongols penetrated to the outskirts of Vienna, but just at a time when western Europe seemed theirs for the taking, the news of the death of the great Khan caused the quick return of the Tatar armies so that their leader could hurry to eastern Asia to take part in the election of a new khan.

Mongol control of Russia. Europe was not molested again but the Mongols established themselves as a ruling caste in Russia, governing the vast plains from their capital at Sarai on the Volga not far from the modern city of Stalingrad, north of the Caspian Sea. The various Russian principalities were allowed to govern themselves as long as they paid their tribute to the Golden Horde as the Tatars in Russia were called. The Khanate of the Golden Horde was only one of the Mongol states, for the successors of Genghis Khan, including Kublai Khan in China, ruled an empire stretching from Korea on the east to Poland on the west and to the south ran along a line that included much of Asia Minor, Persia, and Afghanistan and then ran eastward along the north slopes of the Himalayas, north of what is now India and Burma, to the South China Sea (see map, page 316). Only after the Second World War did an empire arise, that of Soviet Russia and her satellites, which could rival the vast expanse of contiguous territory controlled by the Mongols. In fact the Russian empire not only rivaled but nearly duplicated that of the Mongol khanates.

Influence of the Mongol conquest on Russia. The consequences of Mongol conquest in their vast empire were not altogether negative. After the utterly ruthless extermination of resistance, the Mongols ruled their subjects tolerantly, respecting their religion and customs. In fact the Mongols often exhibited an eager desire to take over the civilization of their subjects, as in the case of Kublai Khan who accepted Buddhism and for all intents settled down as a Chinese emperor.

In Russia, however, any positive effect of Mongol conquest such as the setting up of trade routes with the Far East was completely overshadowed by the tragic effect upon the course of historical development. Mongol domination changed the whole course of Russian history; it completed the break between Russia and western European civilization that had been initiated by the decline of Kiev. There was considerable Asiaticizing, for the status of women was lowered as they accepted the veil and oriental seclusion, and there was much mixing of Mongol and Russian blood. Hence the saying—"Scratch a Russian and you will find a Tatar." The late Bernard Pares, a noted English authority on Russia, says that the Mongol conquest was "a wholesale calamity." He stresses the cutting off of Russia from Europe and the fact that a new Russia far to the east of Kiev began to develop, whose nucleus was to be the despotic state, the Grand Duchy of Muscovy, where "civilization had been completely thrown back, learning was almost lost, and art in decline."[24]

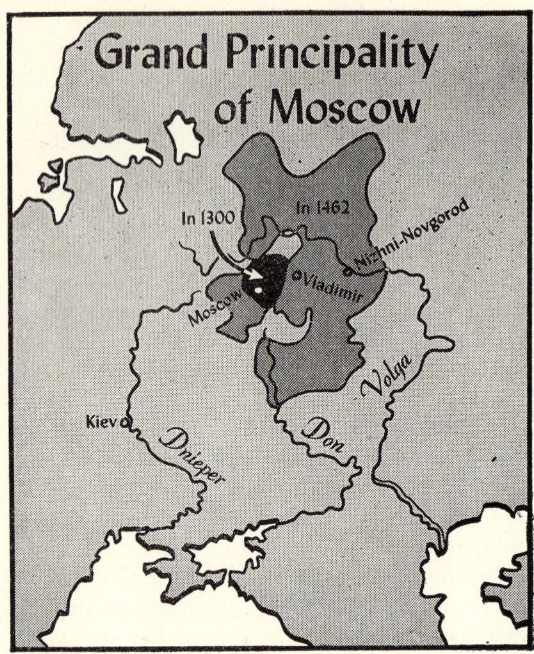

Alexander Nevski: pioneer of Russian greatness. The most important leader of the Russians following the Mongol conquest was Prince Alexander Nevski, the ruler of the principality of Vladimir from 1252 to 1263. This doughty warrior won great victories over the Swedes, Finns, and Lithuanians who, hoping to profit from the Russian collapse under the Mongol impact, began to try to annex territory. Nevski not only repulsed these aggressors but also won a great victory over the Teutonic Knights in 1242 in the famous "Battle of the Ice," at Lake Peipus. With determined craftiness Nevski accepted the regime of the Tatars and strove to prevent insurrection against their rule. In effect he became their main agent or deputy in Russia. In return he obtained their protection and assistance in fighting the invasions launched by the Swedes and Lithuanians and at the same time built up his strength for the day when his successors would be strong enough to challenge Tatar rule.

Muscovy: challenge to Tatar rule. It was the youngest son of Nevski, Daniel, who by founding the Grand Duchy of Muscovy, created the instrument that was to carry out the intentions of his famous father of building a state powerful enough to expel the Tatars from Russia. Moscow is first mentioned in historical records as early as 1147 and this city, well situated in the central river system of Russia, surrounded by protective forests and marshes, advanced rapidly in population and power. At first only a vassal and part of the parent state of Vladimir, it soon absorbed its parent. Following the policy of cooperation with their Mongol overlords, the rulers of Muscovy secured from the Mongol khans the permanent appointment of deputy or Grand Prince, an office carrying with it the right to collect from the various Russian cities and principalities all the tribute annually paid to the Mongols. Early in the fourteenth century the Grand Prince Ivan I, known appropriately as "Moneybag," used to good advantage this economic power in advancing his primacy over rival Russian princes. His sons added to the power of Muscovy by obtaining the right of acting as arbiter in the quarrels and rivalries of the various small principalities. Another factor enhancing Muscovy's prestige was that it became the center of the Russian Orthodox Church. Its head, the Metropolitan, had fled from Kiev to Vladimir in 1299 and a few years later had established the permanent headquarters of the Church in Moscow.

In the middle of the fourteenth century it became evident that the power of the Tatars was declining and the Grand Princes now felt strong enough to scrap the old policy of subservience for one of openly setting forth to rid the country of the Mongol yoke. Following the Russian reduction of the amount paid in tribute, the khan, in 1380, determined to assert his authority and formed a large army for this purpose. The Grand Prince of Moscow rallied a large force in opposition and met the Mongol host on the field of Kulikovo where the soldiers of the khan were defeated. Kulikovo was the first important step in the removal of alien Tatar rule and the Grand Princes of Muscovy were now regarded as the leaders in this national emancipation.

During the first half of the fifteenth century Muscovite territory grew to 15,000 square miles; a century before it had been barely 500. In this process of ridding the land of Tatar rule and at the same time establishing Muscovite supremacy the princes perforce resorted to ruthlessness and cunning. The only path to success was the one of absolute centralized government; the only way to survive was the harsh concentration of political power. Any chance of the growth of a democratic movement evolving out of the old town assembly was thus blighted. The political center of Russia in the fifteenth century was the Grand Duchy of Muscovy, a position she never lost. By ridding the country of its Mongol rulers and by exercising absolute control over their own principality, the princes of Muscovy set the foundations for the eventual rule of the Tsars in Moscow.

Summary

Following the collapse of Charlemagne's empire, the disjointed political system of feudalism endeavored to carry on the essential functions of government. Although better than no government at all, feudalism was weak. A new political organization was needed. Beginning in the twelfth century, the establishment of independent units called national states provided Europe with a new political framework.

The architects of these national states were efficient and aggressive monarchs. At first often overshadowed by powerful nobles, the kings established efficient governments consisting of (1) a professional civil service, (2) a standing army which made the ruler independent of feudal barons for troops, (3) a well-organized treasury department, and, above all, (4) a national system of courts. Assisting the kings in their struggle against the feudal barons was the growing dependence of the people upon the crown for protection. As the king's influence spread, the people developed an attachment to the crown and identified themselves with the nation. The making of nation states brought with it the seeds of modern nationalism.

England and France are especially good examples of the process of nation-making. In England the achievements of William the Conqueror, Henry II, and Edward I strengthened the power of the monarchy; in France, territorial consolidation and administrative centralization were accomplished by Louis le Gros, St. Louis, and Philip Augustus. Spanish unification took on the distinctive aspect of a religious crusade, which culminated in the union of the country in the reign of Ferdinand and Isabella.

Whereas in England, France, Portugal, Spain, and the Scandinavian peninsula, the monarchs succeeded in making themselves supreme over united states, in Italy and Germany efforts to create a national state were a failure. The most important single factor explaining this result was the ill-fated ambition of the German kings to re-create a great empire reminiscent of Charlemagne's. The efforts of Otto the Great, Frederick Barbarossa, and Frederick II failed in the face of resistance from the Italian cities, treachery of the German nobles, and the opposition of the papacy. Unlike England and France, Germany and Italy at the end of the Middle Ages were disunited. Eastern Europe was also the scene of nation-making, although only one state, Russia, developed sufficient power and centralization to influence present-day European history.

By the end of the fifteenth century the national state had become a reality in Europe, despite opposition from feudal nobles and the international institution of the Church, with whose collective interests the state clashed. The end of the fifteenth century represents a new era in European political organization. The nation-state is now the crucial unit in international politics; hereafter the efforts of kings and their subjects are more and more directed toward aggrandizing the strength and prestige of the state.

Chapter 17

Chronology of events and developments discussed in this chapter

Cimabue: beginning of modeled forms	1240-1302
Duccio: human forms replaced symbols; conventional techniques	1260-1320
Giotto: portrayed human qualities in frescoes	1266-1337
Petrarch: gave Humanism its first big impetus; Italian sonnets	1304-1374
Boccaccio: satirized feudalism; source for later writers; Decameron	1313-1375
Brunelleschi: architect; used Roman style; dome of the cathedral of Florence	1377-1446
Ghiberti: experimented with light and shade	1378-1455
Donatello: sculptor; advanced knowledge of anatomy	1386-1466
Fra Angelico: religious painter; essentially medieval	1387-1455
Gozzoli: influence of earlier experimentation; studies of town life	1420-1497
Botticelli: linked religious and pagan themes imaginatively	1444-1510
Savonarola: averted French invasion of Florence; wanted reform of the Popes	1452-1498
Leonardo da Vinci: peak of Renaissance innovation	1452-1519
Gutenberg: used movable type for printing	1454
Erasmus: rationalist; advocated tolerance; In Praise of Folly	1466-1536
Lorenzo de' Medici: patron of Michelangelo	1469-1492
Dürer: German painter; emphasized details and character	1471-1528
Michelangelo: human form given strength and dynamics	1475-1564
Titian: sensuous love of color and atmosphere; oil glaze technique	1477-1576
Sir Thomas More: conjectured an ideal state in Utopia	1478-1535
Raphael: fluent style of painting	1483-1520
Margaret of Navarre: French patroness	1492-1549
Invasion of Italy resulted in Humanistic ideas spreading north	1494
Rabelais: attacked hypocrisy; descriptions of his own age; Gargantua	1495-1553
Holbein: incisive drawing	1497-1543
High Renaissance: classical influence; importance of the individual; experimentation	1500-1530
Palestrina: wrote polyphonic religious music	1525-1594
Montaigne: leading French Humanist; saw the importance of human problems	1533-1592
Cervantes: created Don Quixote; satire on medieval ideals	1547-1616
Francis Bacon: tried to free science from Scholasticism and authority	1561-1626
Shakespeare: great English playwright; broke with tradition; patriotism	1564-1616

Man is the measure

Renaissance thought and art: 1300 to 1600

The term "Renaissance" means literally rebirth. Until recent times, men have looked upon the age which bears the name as a "sudden turning on of the light after some centuries of darkness." Today we know that the Middle Ages were anything but "dark ages" because, as we have seen, medieval thought and art made rich contributions to our modern culture. Furthermore, most scholars of this period have come to feel that there was no revolutionary change in the development of European culture from the fourteenth to the sixteenth centuries. Rather, these centuries witnessed a gradual shift from a purely medieval viewpoint to a modern one and saw the quickening of human interest in nearly every phase of worldly life.

In a narrow sense, the Renaissance was a new and intense interest in the art and learning of Greece and Rome, to the disparagement of the Middle Ages. The Renaissance scholars, called Humanists, imitated things classical, loved the past, "were less interested in the present, and not at all in the future." This phase of the Renaissance was regressive, for it looked backward in history toward antiquity. But the Renaissance in its broader aspects was a stimulation of interest in discoveries by explorers and scientists, a new urban culture of the rising middle class, advances in statecraft and the growth of the national states, new concepts in literature and art, and a lively interest in secular affairs as contrasted with the otherworldliness of the Middle Ages. In its broad sense the Renaissance was progressive, for, in breaking away from medieval restrictions, it laid the foundations of our modern civilization.

The Renaissance was an age of transition, a transition from medievalism with its emphasis on Scholasticism, church authority, and asceticism to modernism with its emphasis on science, skepticism, and individualism. The Renaissance was also a transition from a relatively static to a dynamic culture, from a society based on feudal, rural, and monastic ideals to one based on an individualistic, urban, and secular pattern. The Middle Ages tended to look upon the world as sinful and human nature as destined to be repressed; the modern age looks upon the world as vital and invites human nature to be expressed. In the Renaissance we find an intermingling of the two ideals. The common people remained illiterate and clung to the ways of their forefathers; the relatively few who had acquired education and the new culture revolted from medievalism. In this chapter we shall deal almost entirely with the latter group, for they heralded the modern world.

The Early Renaissance in Italy (1300-1500)

The waning of the Middle Ages. The Middle Ages were waning throughout Europe in the fourteenth century. The Church was split with schism and heresy; its international power was slowly but surely giving way before the rise of powerful monarchies. Trade was increasing among Mediterranean seaports and along the rivers of central Europe, bringing with it the rise of towns and growing wealth, new business methods, and an increasing interest in secular activities. Feudalism was declining before the mixed forces of the new middle class, which sided with the national monarchs, and the invention of gunpowder, which made useless the battle-ax of the steel-coated knight. Scholasticism was unable to satisfy the growing interest in science, travel, and commerce. Medieval art had exhausted its originality, and its particular expression of religious themes no longer captured the taste of a generation which had turned away from the ideal of asceticism. Even the great Gothic architectural forms had degenerated into exaggerated and flamboyant shapes, and the Italian architects were already looking about for more suitable modes of expression. Religious subject matter in literature was losing its appeal. Themes of love and satires against chivalric ideals were proving more engaging to the sophisticated northern Italian cities.

Why the Renaissance came first to Italy. The reason the Renaissance came first to Italy is not difficult to appreciate. The growth of town life in the prosperous city-states of Tuscany and Lombardy stimulated a strong secular spirit and a concern with practical affairs. Prosperity came in great measure from the brisk trade which such cities as Venice and Genoa enjoyed with the Near East. Florence had also built up substantial industries and an extensive banking system. There were many among the well-to-do who could and did spend their money for pictures, books, and fine goods of all kinds. Trade had brought about the importation of a variegated Greek culture from the Byzantine empire. Within the towns themselves there existed a strong civic pride which brooked little interference from either Pope or emperor. The despots who controlled the city-states were as a rule patrons of the new learning who tended to foster the arts. They helped rather than hindered the Renaissance in Italy.

Humanism defined. Of primary importance in the early Renaissance was the movement known as Humanism. In its narrower sense, Humanism was a reawakening of interest in the literature and philosophy of Greece and Rome. In its broader sense, it was a revival of interest in the affairs of this world and in the importance of the role of men here on earth. In the early Renaissance the spirit of Humanism centered mainly about the veneration of classical thought and literature, but the seeds of a broader ideology were already taking root. In the later Renaissance Humanism took on a more positive character. It manifested itself in new intellectual, social, political, and economic activity. In its broadest and best sense, then, Humanism represented a rebirth of interest in the activities of the everyday world and as such prompted men to make the discoveries and inventions which gave the Renaissance its dazzling quality.

The classic revival. The classical tradition had never died out during the Middle Ages.

Virgil, Cicero, and Caesar had always been popular; Aristotle had been venerated as though he were a Christian saint; and Roman law had been of inestimable help in the formation of canon doctrines. But the classical writers had been interpreted in the Middle Ages along purely religious lines and were cited as authorities to strengthen Christian dogmas. Early Humanism, on the other hand, was the enthusiastic appreciation of the classics not for the sake of Christianity but for the sake of the pagan civilizations of Greece and Rome. In the past the true nature of the classical world had been obscured and misjudged. Churchmen made a practice of allegorizing pagan literature for the uses of Christian theology. Moreover, early Christian scholars were not able to study the manuscripts of antiquity accurately enough to assign to them their proper place in history. The result was that

the classical world always remained inexact and fanciful to scholars, while the Church tended to shun it because it was pagan and disturbing.

In fourteenth-century Italy, however, a new perspective was attained. The remains of Rome's imperial glory were to be found all over the peninsula, and Greek remains could be seen in southern Italy and Sicily. From the University of Bologna came an increasing desire to discover more about Roman legal practices. The struggle of Italian cities against feudal, papal, and Hohenstaufen control recalled the achievements of Rome as a free republic. By the end of the fifteenth century the Popes had recovered their temporal powers in central Italy and were engaging in secular activities to the detriment of their spiritual mission. These Renaissance Popes vied with the rulers of other Italian states to increase their prestige, and it became the fashion for them to act as patrons of scholars. Humanism spread through the land, bringing with it a veneration of ancient civilization and a desire to make over the arts, the literature, the language, and the modes of living according to classical models.

Petrarch (1304-1374). One of the earliest of the Humanists was Petrarch. As a youth he had resented his father's ambition to have him become a lawyer, and he turned to reading Virgil and Cicero for consolation. The story goes that his father once hurled the copies of the two classical writers into the flames, but the wail set up by the anguished boy caused the father to snatch the writings from the fire. From 1323 to 1326 Petrarch studied law at Bologna, but he dreamed always of the glories of the classical age. In 1327 he met the lady Laura, and inspired by his love of her, Petrarch wrote sonnets which made him one of the greatest lyric poets of all time. Because he had composed his poetry in Tuscan Italian, he was influential along with Dante in making the vernacular tongue the prevailing literary medium.

Petrarch's portrayal of Laura is exceedingly significant. Earlier poets had woven about their heroines an air of courtly love and religious idealization which made them quite unreal. Petrarch's Laura was a "flesh-and-blood" creature whom all readers could recognize as being as real and human as themselves.

In his *Secret* Petrarch has an imaginary conversation with St. Augustine, and here the conflict between new and startling ideas and those of medieval times is forcibly brought out. He comes to the conclusion that despite the possible importance of the world-to-come this world has many delights which should not be shunned.

Petrarch felt that he had to return to the study of antiquity, for the ancients also sang of the joys of this world. From youth he had collected the works of classical writers. He now began to compose in Latin and wrote an epic called *Africa*, in which he glorified the deeds of Scipio Africanus and by which he hoped to gain literary immortality. In this poem and his *Familiar Letters* (he was in the habit of addressing his thoughts to such men as Livy, Ovid, Virgil, and Seneca) he showed his passion for the departed glory of Rome, and he hoped through these works to reëstablish classical thought in his own age. Ironically, however, Petrarch gained immortality as a writer not from his Latin *Africa* but from his Italian sonnets to Laura.

Petrarch was unable to carry out his ambition to learn Greek, and he was not a careful scholar. But his interests were very broad. He was a great traveler; he loved nature, good Latin, the poets of antiquity, and the beauties of the world in which he lived. He was an enemy of medieval traditionalism and of those who sought to stifle an age of new attitudes. For all these reasons, along with his many personal gifts, including a love of music and gardening, Petrarch's influence upon his contemporaries was enormous. He gave Humanism its first great impetus.

Boccaccio (1313-1375). Another important early Humanist was Giovanni Boccaccio. Sent early in life to work in Naples for the banking house of Bardi, Boccaccio witnessed there the actions of a gay and immoral court. In 1330 he saw a beautiful lady whom he immortalized in his writings as Fiammetta. Encouraged by her interest in him he wrote three romances: *Filocolo, Filostrato* (which deals with the tragic story of Troilus and Criseyde), and *Teseide* (an account of the rivalry of Palamon and Arcite over the lady Emilia). Chaucer got inspiration for his immortal *Troilus and Criseyde* and *The Knight's Tale* from Boccaccio's *Filostrato* and *Teseide.* In fact, it is possible that Chaucer may have met both Boccaccio and Petrarch in Italy.

Boccaccio's greatest work is the *Decameron*, a selection of one hundred bawdy and irreverent tales which are supposed to have been recounted by three young men and seven young women who had gone to a villa to escape the Black Death in 1348. Ten tales are recounted each day, tales based on the old *fabliaux* and chivalric accounts. Now, however, the spirit has changed. This time the tales are told by townsmen, and they satirize the follies of knights and other medieval characters. The contempt which so many of the townsmen had developed toward the old and outworn ideals of feudalism is clearly portrayed. The *Decameron* is highly indecent by present standards, but the stories are told with brilliant color.

When Boccaccio met Petrarch in 1350, Humanism was given a fresh impetus, for Boccaccio now received an insight into the values of antiquity. He attempted to learn Greek, wrote an encyclopedia of classical mythology, and went off to monasteries in search of manuscripts. By the time Petrarch and Boccaccio died, the study of classical literature and learning was in full swing in Italy.

The search for manuscripts. The search after ancient manuscripts became a Renaissance mania. Monastic libraries were known to be treasure houses, and agents of the Popes and other patrons carried out a diligent search. Before the middle of the fifteenth century, works by most of the important Latin authors were discovered.

About the time of Boccaccio's death the accumulation of Greek manuscripts and their study was enthusiastically undertaken. Italians journeyed to Constantinople and brought back rich materials. Greeks traveled west, and one of them in particular, Bessarion, became the leader of Greek studies in Rome, translating many Greek manuscripts into Latin for the use of those who did not know Greek. Another important Greek scholar, Chrysoloras, lectured in Florence. During the fifteenth century many eager Italian scholars journeyed to Constantinople to learn Greek and acquire precious manuscripts. By 1515 the most important Greek works in all fields were readily available.

The reading of Latin and Greek literature led to a more careful study of ancient ruins and other works of art. From such study the Humanists came to understand the classical world in a truer historical perspective. For example, whereas the Middle Ages had thought of the soldiers of Alexander the Great as knights, the Renaissance historians no longer made this naïve mistake. On the other hand, so intent were the Humanists on getting back to antiquity that they resented the centuries between ancient Rome and themselves. This resentment resulted in their condemning or forgetting the best that the Middle Ages had produced.

Shortcomings of Humanism. The cult of classical letters had other serious defects. The scholars and intellectuals became so dominated by Roman and Greek forms that they tended to imitate rather than create for themselves. Their passion for Ciceronian Latin became pernicious; their writings were rich in form and barren in content. Furthermore, in their denial of medieval values the Humanists lost perspective toward their own social relationships. They were prone to engage in gambling, debauchery, gluttony, drinking, and other excesses.

Classical learning showed men that great civilizations had existed outside Christianity, and to that extent it broadened religious views. But, because the Greeks and Romans had said little about natural science, the Humanists scoffed at the scientific advances of their own day.

Lynn Thorndike maintains that Humanism "did very little to further the growth of natural or mathematical science," while it by no means put an end to Scholasticism. "The Humanists themselves continued to indulge in debates and disputations, only they argued whether Hannibal or Scipio was the greater man, instead of whether universals were real. . . . In short, Scholasticism continued almost unabated until Descartes or later, and the making of many commentaries on the *Sentences* of Peter Lombard and the *Metaphysics* of Aristotle was still going on merrily in the eighteenth century."[1]

The growth of individuality. A highly important characteristic of the Renaissance was its emphasis upon the freedom and dignity of man as an individual. The history of the Renaissance is in a sense the history of the revival of the individual expressing himself brilliantly and often tempestuously in art, literature, science, geographical discovery, and religion. Furthermore, in Italy man as an individual began to free himself from the control of the medieval guild, the commune, and the authority of an age-old religious hierarchy.

The Greeks had been staunch supporters of individuality, even to the extent that Greek cities refused to sink their differences in the interest of the common good. The early Romans had also been individualistic, but the growth of the empire and compulsory stratification of society in later centuries broke down the ideal. The Middle Ages tended to be antagonistic to individuality in most ways. Medieval Christianity preached self-abnegation and demanded obedience. To the degree that Abélard was an individualist, he was persecuted as a nonconformist.

PISANO: PRESENTATION AND FLIGHT TO EGYPT

DUCCIO: THE BETRAYAL OF JUDAS (TEMPERA)

The crusades had much to do with the revival of individuality by giving to people a passion for travel and a knowledge of other lands. The contact with Moslem culture, the new observation of nature, the hearkening back to classical ideals, the rise of vernacular languages at the expense of medieval Latin, the desire of artists to be untrammeled by medieval patterns, and the political jealousy and suspicion existing among the individual Italian cities—these and other factors were instrumental in fostering the ideal of individuality among men.

Of course the cult of individuality had its drawbacks, for some carried it to excess. The lawlessness and political confusion of the Italian Renaissance was due in no small measure to the prevailing view that every man was a law unto himself.

The transition in art. While the Humanists were often guilty of mere imitation, the artists of the Renaissance were richly original. But these artists, like those of any period, did not break completely with the art that preceded them. They took from the Greeks an interest in the individual and in the beauties of the human form. The Renaissance artists, while striving for greater secular expression, found in the Church their greatest patron. But the support of the Renaissance Church was given to individual artists, whereas the medieval Church employed countless craftsmen who remained nameless. Building churches, sculpturing saints and madonnas, and painting religious murals continued throughout the Renaissance. But artists also found other subjects in classical mythology and in the life around them.

Transitional sculpture. Sculpture had been developed with much skill in the Middle Ages, as we have noticed in a previous chapter. In the thirteenth century such sculptors as Niccolo Pisano produced works which revealed both classic and medieval influences. Pisano's work is an interesting mixture of the Gothic, the classic, and a certain realistic vigor. His famous pulpit at Siena illustrates the work of the new school, which adopted certain features of classic sculpture but made of it something different. In the detail shown on the preceding page, the drapery, many of the faces, and the Roman decorative motifs at top and bottom show the classic influence. The realism of some of the faces shows the new Humanist influence, while the arrangement of the figures is typically medieval.

Transitional painting. The transition from the Gothic to the Renaissance can be seen in painting in the works of such men as Cimabue, Giotto, and Duccio. The mere fact that there are individuals known by name shows a change to individualism in contrast to medieval anonymity. Cimabue (1240?-1302), whose madonnas appear very medieval at first glance, had actually begun to search for fresh types of expression. He continued the medieval craft with his gold backgrounds and still painted altar panels in tempera as the medieval painters had done, but his madonnas vary slightly; they show the beginning of modeled forms when compared to the Byzantine flat patterns. The madonna shown here is patterned in the typical medieval manner. Note the stilted angle of the heads, the flat, round halos, the symmetry of pattern, and the Byzantine technique of scratching lines in the garments through the paint to the gold. But the figures of the child and some of the angels look round and real. The small figures at the bottom are a typical oriental device to make the central figure important.

The Sienese painter Duccio (1260?-1320?), shows again the mixture of medieval and Renaissance characteristic of the transitional painters. His compositions have much of the Byzantine about them. He took many of them from Byzantine icons and painted in the minute tempera technique of the medieval period. His use of such conventions as flat halos, scratched lines, brilliant color, and gold is distinctly Byzantine. But his painting shows interest in the narrative, as "The Betrayal of Judas" (opposite) discloses, and his figures are not merely symbols for saints but real human beings with individual characteristics. Notice the different ways in which the figures are reacting to the kiss of Judas—some fearful, some angry, and the Christ calm and sad. These are no longer mere symbols for people. Duccio's intense religious mysticism is, of course, very medieval. In Siena Duccio and others developed painting along conventional religious lines, while in Florence experimentation brought forth the painting of the Renaissance.

Giotto (1266?-1337), a friend of Dante, gave the new school the greatest impetus. His work reveals a change in technique which was of great importance in developing Renaissance painting. At this time, owing mainly to the influence of the Franciscan order, there was great activity in building. The buildings had large wall spaces to be decorated, and mosaic was expensive and slow. Fresco was cheaper and faster. The technique of fresco painting requires a freedom of style not possible in tempera. Because fresco is painted directly into wet plaster, the painter has only a few hours in which to work on each plastered section. This naturally results in greater freedom of style. Giotto used fresco to decorate whole churches. He shows the Renaissance interest in the individual by painting human emotions and the gestures which express them. Note

CIMABUE: MADONNA AND CHILD (TEMPERA)

St. Francis' expression of tenderness while preaching to the birds. Although there is a good deal of realism in his use of shading to create depth and roundness, the simplified manner in which Giotto treats such details as the tree in the painting below indicates that he is not yet completely of the Renaissance.

Early Renaissance art. The most characteristic developments of early Renaissance art took place in Florence, but changes were going on all over Italy as well, in such cities as Pisa, Venice, and Rome. In Florence the influences of classicism, Humanism, scientific experiment, and the patronage of the Medici rulers brought forth a large group of artists, too numerous to mention by name, who experimented in various techniques and types of expression. The interest in the classic wakened the artists to the use of the human body as a means of expression, while the increased knowledge of science directed them to study anatomy, light and shade, and perspective. That the classic influence was of great importance is not to be denied, but the art of this period was not a mere imitation of the classic ideals, but an expression of the brilliant and dramatic era which produced Renaissance work.

GIOTTO: ST. FRANCIS PREACHING TO THE BIRDS (FRESCO)

Renaissance patrons. In the Italian cities continually growing trade and industry produced a moneyed class of traders, bankers, and manufacturers, many of whom displayed their wealth and bolstered their social importance by patronizing artists and scholars. Nearly all the art of the period was made possible by the patronage of wealthy businessmen, ruling families, and Popes. The leadership of Florence in the development of Renaissance art can be traced in great part to the patronage of the ruling house of Medici. The Medici were wealthy bankers and brilliant rulers, controlling the government of Florence throughout the fifteenth century and fostering the arts with enthusiasm. Cosimo, who controlled the destinies of the family from 1429 to 1464, for example, ably managed the affairs of Florence, gave commissions to Fra Angelico and Fra Filippo Lippi, collected manuscripts, and created the Platonic Academy, which stimulated the reading of Plato in opposition to the medieval reliance upon Aristotle.

Cosimo's grandson, Lorenzo de' Medici ("the Magnificent"), first citizen of Florence from 1469 until his death in 1492, not only carried on the family's proud traditions but gave it additional luster. He bestowed patronage and good advice upon painters, scholars, sculptors, and poets. Lorenzo himself was an able writer of verse. During his lifetime and under his patronage and guidance Florence reached its highest degree of artistic and intellectual perfection. Lorenzo not only gave commissions to Botticelli and Verrocchio, he also encouraged a young lad with a broken nose who was working with stone in his gardens at Florence. Lorenzo had not erred in his discernment of genius; the lad was Michelangelo.

Other princes, ruling despots of city-states, also patronized the arts—the Sforzas in Milan, the Gonzagas in Mantua, the Estes in Ferrara, the Montefeltros in Urbino, the court of Naples, and the Popes. The Popes were temporal as well as spiritual rulers, since they were political heads of the territory known as the Papal States. They were as eager as the other Italian princes to patronize the arts, and some of them were themselves scholars of ability. Their projects for the beautification of Rome included the Sistine chapel, commissions to Michelangelo, da Vinci, Raphael, and Cellini, and the costly cathedral of St. Peter's.

In the sixteenth century the Popes resembled the other secular rulers and even outdid them in the splendors of their court. Such a Pope as Alexander VI (1492-1503), in fact, gave the religious critics of the age something to cry against. He was the father of the unscrupulous Cesare and Lucrezia Borgia and devoted more time and thought to furthering the fortunes of his family than he did to religious matters. Wealthy families came to consider the office of Pope a desirable plum, and the Medici succeeded in achieving the office for two of their members, Leo X (1513-1521), son of Lorenzo, and Clement VII (1523-1534), nephew of Leo. Leo was a Humanist of brilliant endowments, and his pontificate was one of great activity in the arts and learning in Rome. But religious thinkers objected to his Humanism, and indeed the situation of the Renaissance Popes as patrons of Humanist scholars was an anomaly, for Humanism implied the negation of the authority of the Church.

Renaissance artists. The artists of the period were fine craftsmen and were also businessmen. Some of them ran studios with many assistants, and filled commissions as a shop would fill orders. The patrons allowed the artists a great deal of artistic freedom, but nevertheless the patron must be flattered occasionally and his commissions followed carefully. The Renaissance artist worked almost exclusively on commission, with a definite place in mind for the finished work. This situation provides an interesting contrast with later periods, when artists painted when and as they wished and then attempted to sell the work to anyone who would buy it.

Early Renaissance architecture. In architecture the influence of the Church continued, but there was also a great deal of interest in Florence in secular buildings such as palaces. The Pitti palace (below), owned at one time by the Medici family, is an example of early palace architecture, with its impressive, heavy façade, a dwelling capable of being used as a fortress when intrigues and conspiracies became dangerous. A comparison of this Brunelleschi design with the later Farnese palace by Michelangelo (page 499) will show not only the change in general type but the later elaboration of detail, as life became more sumptuous.

Filippo Brunelleschi (1377-1446) marked the beginning of the new architecture. The fact that we know the names of individual architects is significant in showing the change from the group building of the Middle Ages to the individualistic work of the Renaissance. As a youth Brunelleschi visited Rome, where he studied the construction of ancient edifices.

THE FAÇADE OF PITTI PALACE IN FLORENCE

GHIBERTI: ADAM AND EVE (BRONZE RELIEF)

His buildings in Florence were not just copies of Roman models, although the Roman influence is everywhere. His most famous creation was the dome of the cathedral at Florence (visible at the far left of the picture on page 497). More characteristic were buildings with arcades of round Roman arches, Roman pediments above the windows, and Roman decorative motifs.

Early Renaissance sculpture. In Florence Lorenzo Ghiberti (1378-1455) was advancing further in the direction of a new type of sculpture. Ghiberti was trained to be a goldsmith, which gave him proficiency in creating delicate figures. When he completed the bronze east doors of the baptistry in Florence, his workmanship was so superb that Michelangelo declared his doors worthy to be the gates of Paradise. His attempt to produce atmosphere and perspective in a bronze relief, however, was perhaps not the best use of a material which in itself is three-dimensional. In "Adam and Eve" (left), one of the panels of the baptistry doors, perspective is used in the distant figures of the angels to create, on an almost flat surface, an impression of atmosphere and space. Ghiberti's experiments were of great importance in their influence on the painters. In this period sculpture led painting in experiments with anatomy and light and shade.

Another sculptor living in Florence at this time was Donatello (1386?-1466), a man who was influenced by classical models to a great extent. His work shows an advanced knowledge of anatomy, which he used in a lifelike manner. His bronze equestrian statue of Gattamelata the *condottiere* (professional soldier) is realistic in detail. The casting of these huge bronze statues, twice life size, was an achievement in itself. The statue of Colleoni by Verrocchio, sketched on the map on page 487, is another example of the Renaissance equestrian statue. Verrocchio's horse has one foreleg unsupported, a difficult achievement with the casting facilities of the time. In that time the figures were first modeled in clay on wood frames, then cast in a mold made from the clay.

DONATELLO: STATUE OF GATTAMELATA

Early Renaissance painting. In Florence there were two trends in painting. On one hand were the scientific painters, who were constantly searching for new techniques and means of expression, and on the other were those painters who made use of their contemporaries' discoveries for self-expression without contributing technical knowledge of their own. An example of the first trend was the brilliant young Masaccio, whose work gave impetus to painting. Although he painted traditional subjects, he introduced a note of realism which influenced later painters as Donatello influenced sculptors. Compare the "Expulsion of Adam and Eve" (page 495) with the Cimabue madonna (page 491) to see the new treatment. The figures of Adam and Eve show Masaccio's more realistic portrayal of anatomy and his use of perspective and modeling of figures in light and shade.

Domenico Veneziano (d. 1461) introduced the technique of oil glazing, an innovation of great importance. In his profile portraits Veneziano used tempera "underpainting" for his hard, precise drawing, and then laid over it thin "glazes" of oil paint. In this way he could get a softness of shading not possible in the more linear tempera technique. Oil glazing came to be very popular with later artists, because it could produce depth and atmosphere more realistically. Compare Duccio's tempera painting "The Betrayal of Judas" (page 490) with the much later oil-glazed painting "Virgin of the Rocks" (page 501). Oil glazing had already developed in Flanders, and through Venetian contacts there Veneziano brought the technique to Venice and from there to Florence.

An example of the less scientific painter is Fra Angelico (1387-1455), a contemporary of Masaccio really only in time, for the two artists represent completely different ages. Fra Angelico painted religious scenes of surpassing beauty and reverence, but although he was himself influenced by Masaccio to the point of incorporating the latter's realism into his backgrounds and settings, the spirit of his work remained essentially medieval.

Benozzo Gozzoli (1420-1497) and Sandro Botticelli (1444-1510) were other painters who did not experiment in science as applied to art but showed the influence of the experimenters

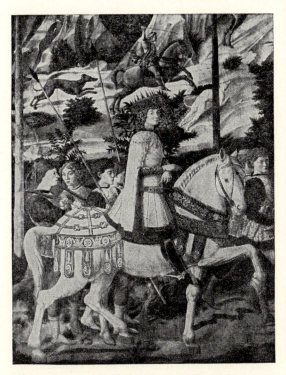

GOZZOLI: JOURNEY OF THE MAGI

MASACCIO: EXPULSION OF ADAM AND EVE

BOTTICELLI: THREE GRACES (DETAIL OF "SPRING")

of the day. Gozzoli pleased the townsmen of Florence by painting interesting secular studies of city life. His decorations in the Medici chapel of the Riccardi palace show the procession which took place when the patriarch of Constantinople visited Florence. The procession is entitled "Journey of the Magi," but in reality it is full of portraits of important people of the day. As such it is interesting reportorial work. The detail shown on page 495 is a portrait of Lorenzo de' Medici, represented as one of the three kings.

Botticelli used a nervous and sensitive line. Observe the fluttering line in the garments in the detail of the Three Graces from "Spring," opposite. The movement and patterning of hair and garments in his paintings are particularly distinctive. He painted in an imaginative and unrealistic manner and linked both pagan and Christian subject matter. After painting many such classically inspired pictures, Botticelli was influenced by the Dominican preacher Savonarola and thereafter became intensely religious in his subject matter, even to the extent of destroying some of his earlier works.

The High Renaissance (1500-1530)

Political change in Italy. In April, 1492, Lorenzo the Magnificent, ruler of Florence, was dying in his villa outside the city. Suddenly he sent for the Dominican preacher Savonarola, whose words and zeal in preaching had been taking all Florence by storm and who had prophesied that the Church was to be scourged and regenerated. He came to the dying Lorenzo, told him that he must have faith in the mercy of God, restore all ill-gotten gains to the city, and give back to Florence its freedom from Medicean rule. Lorenzo agreed to the first two stipulations, but he regarded the ascetic Savonarola in stern silence upon hearing his third request. No true son of the Medici could think of giving up control of Florence. Lorenzo turned his face to the wall, while Savonarola waited in vain for an answer. Lorenzo died without giving back to Florence her lost liberty.

Lorenzo died in an era of great change. A new day was at hand for Italy, though not exactly the kind which Savonarola had anticipated. Three years after Lorenzo's death Charles VIII of France came down to conquer Italy. We are not here concerned with tracing the details of political events. It will suffice to say that from 1495 to 1559 the Italian states were the pawns of foreign powers. French and Spanish armies fought on Italian soil. Battles were fought over boundaries. All Europe became involved in the struggle for supremacy between rival Hapsburg and French kings. Strangely enough, it was in the midst of this political turmoil that the Italian Renaissance reached its zenith. In fact, the very turbulence of conditions was in a sense an expression of Renaissance individuality.

Savonarola (1452-1498). When Charles VIII of France was invited by the Duke of Milan to seize the kingdom of Naples, there was one man who welcomed the invasion of the foreigner—Savonarola, the Florentine preacher and reformer, who had long been prophesying the coming of such a man as the scourge of God. Savonarola's influence upon his own times was enormous. When the discredited Medici fled before Charles, the Dominican zealot organized the city as a republic and managed to keep the French from sacking

The martyrdom of Savonarola in the public square of Florence is pictured in this contemporary painting.

Florence on their way to Naples. Meanwhile he attacked the iniquities of the Borgia Pope, Alexander VI, and he was such a master of oratory that he persuaded the wealthy and pleasure-loving Florentines, for a while, to make bonfires of their luxuries and jewels. Savonarola was later hailed by Luther and the Protestants as a forerunner of their movement. Actually he was trying to bring the papacy back to its tradition of simple living and high thinking and thus avert the Protestant Revolt.

But Savonarola did not possess the power to enforce his dictates. On May 23, 1498, publicly humiliated in the great square of Florence by having his Dominican garb torn from him, Savonarola with two companions was hanged and burned, a victim of political intrigue.

Machiavelli's political theories. The rise of powerful states during the Renaissance, discussed in Chapter 16, was accompanied by new political theories. The most famous exposition of the methods of state diplomacy of the day was *The Prince* of the Florentine Niccolo Machiavelli, which we shall examine in Chapter 19. *The Prince* is a brilliant exposition of the low state of morality during the Renaissance. Machiavelli has been soundly criticized for his lack of morality; but we must remember that he was a product of his age and with extraordinary objectivity simply wrote down what appeared to him the most valid means of ensuring success in the administration of a state.

High Renaissance art. In the Italy of a martyred Savonarola, an invading French army, a secularized papacy, and a calculating Machiavelli, Renaissance art achieved a high state of brilliance. We may wonder how art could flower in so much political turmoil. For one thing, Renaissance warfare was conducted by professional armies and involved comparatively few people, so that most people could continue with their daily tasks without much interference. Another reason lay in the spirit abroad. The age pulsated with activity and new ideas, and the artists of the period were probably influenced by the new ideas and enthusiasms of others. Still another reason, one which we have mentioned earlier, was the existence of so many genuine patrons of the arts. These wealthy men were constantly carrying on war with one another, but they appreciated the value of the artist in society, and took special pains to see not only that he would not be harmed but on the contrary that he be allowed to grace their courts and receive particular favor.

A great deal of the artistic activity of the High Renaissance was carried on in Rome.

Rome had patrons who could give more money and opportunities to artists. The Popes of the period had become the most art conscious and lavish of all patrons, as the pontificates of Leo X, Clement VII, and others attest. The greatest artists of the period worked in the Vatican at one time or another. It was full of secular luxuries. It did not seem inconsistent to Popes and artists to include representations of mythological figures in the decorations of the sacred palace.

Architecture in the High Renaissance. Some of the period developments in architecture can be seen in the cathedral of St. Peter's in Rome (illustrated on the next page). This building was the work of many famous Renaissance architects. It shows the lavish decoration so popular in these times. By this time no more building was done in the Gothic style and in its place arose a style which took inspiration from the buildings of classical times. The vogue of borrowing styles of architecture from former periods was begun in the Renaissance. Not until recently have architects become interested in developing new structural methods instead of borrowing styles from other periods. Renaissance architects made no structural innovations; in fact, they often had to use iron rods to support their beautiful but badly built arches. Their contribution was in decoration and in decorative features, such as the balustrade, arcade, and cornice. The balustrade usually served the purpose of a guard rail. The one on the top of the façade of St. Peter's is almost as high as a man, and although this makes it more noticeable as a decoration, it is useless as a guard rail. The cornice was used in the interior of St. Peter's between the columns and the vault of the roof, as can be seen in the illustration. It served no purpose but that of decoration. The interior of St. Peter's shows a lack of scale. The structure itself, the decoration, and even the figure sculpture is so large that it is impossible in such a picture as this to see how huge it is. A man is not much taller than the bases of the columns in the nave.

The architect Bramante (1444?-1514) was most influential in fixing the stamp of old Rome indelibly on the products of the new "Roman school." He is especially remembered for his plans for the construction of St. Peter's, in which he visualized an edifice built in the form of a Greek cross. Bramante died before the church was finished, and it was left to the artist Michelangelo to complete the work with an impressive dome (see map on page 487).

Renaissance architects also made advances in the construction of palaces and other secular buildings. Examples of these are to be found in Rome, Venice, and the smaller cities. The Palazzo Farnese in Rome was the work of the architects Sangallo and Michelangelo. It illustrates the new use of classical details applied to Renaissance compositions. The pediments over the windows, the engaged columns, and the decorative details all show classical inspiration made into something new. The palaces of this period did not have to be fortresses, too, and, compared with the earlier palaces, they are more decorative and refined. From the height of the Renaissance onward, all Europe began to take to the new architecture, which appealed to the bourgeoisie, the lovers of secularism and luxury, and the devotees of antiquity.

Sculpture. Sculpture in the High Renaissance reached its peak in the work of Michelangelo Buonarroti (1475-1564). The glorification of the nude, particularly the male body, was a characteristic of Michelangelo's art. The Middle Ages had looked upon nudity as indecent and alien to the philosophy of despising everything human as sinful and evil. Michelangelo was a fitting follower of Phidias the Greek in his portrayal of the male body. But there is none of the classic left in Michelangelo's use of the human form. He has idealized the body and given it a strength and force which lift it to superhumanness. Even the thoughtful figure of Lorenzo (p. 500) and the reposing figures below him are full of strength. In his great compositions such as the Medici tombs can be seen Michelangelo's free, sweeping composition, which contained the seeds of the later baroque style.

Perhaps the finest of the sculptors after Michelangelo was Benvenuto Cellini (1500-1572). However, Cellini was a greater craftsman than artist. As a goldsmith he was extremely skillful, and the objects which he created show an extraordinary ability with detail. The salt cellar of Francis I is a *tour de force* in luxurious gold craftsmanship, but it exhibits a Renaissance interest in ornamentation rather than utility.

High Renaissance painting. Painters of the period extended the technical experiments of

INTERIOR VIEW OF ST. PETER'S CATHEDRAL IN ROME, FROM THE MAIN DOOR

the fifteenth-century artists and used the new techniques in creating art which was a true expression of the age which produced it. In their work there is no trace of the medieval, and they went far beyond the earlier classic influences. The great technical facility which permitted them to embody their ideas in works of art was made possible by earlier experiments in light and shade, perspective, and representation of anatomy. But although these men were great technicians, they did not allow workmanship to outweigh content in their work but maintained a balance between the two.

***Leonardo da Vinci* (*1452-1519*).** The little information we have concerning the life of Leonardo the Florentine comes in large measure from the colorful but often inaccurate account by Vasari, a contemporary artist. According to Vasari:

"The radiance of his countenance, which was splendidly beautiful, brought cheerfulness to the heart of the most melancholy . . . he possessed so great a degree of physical strength, that he was capable of restraining the most impetuous violence, and was able to bend one of the iron rings used for the knocker of doors, or a horseshoe, as if it were lead . . . he extended shelter and hospitality to every friend,

COURTYARD OF FARNESE PALACE IN ROME

MICHELANGELO: TOMB OF LORENZO DE' MEDICI

rich or poor...and as the city of Florence received a great gift in the birth of Leonardo, so did it suffer a more than grievous loss at his death."[2]

We know that Leonardo was an extraordinarily versatile man, proficient in as wide a variety of subjects as Aristotle: mathematics, architecture, geology, botany, physiology, anatomy, sculpture, painting, music, and poetry. He was always experimenting. The result was that he finished very little that he began. To quote Vasari again: "Leonardo, with his profound intelligence of art, commenced various undertakings, many of which he never completed, because it appeared to him that the hand could never give its due perfection to the object or purpose which he had in his thoughts, or beheld in his imagination."[3]

BENVENUTO CELLINI: SALT CELLAR OF FRANCIS I

In painting, Leonardo was a superb draughtsman and a master of soft modeling in full light and shade. He went about his placement of figures scientifically and created groups perfectly balanced in the given space. He was particularly fond of a pyramidical composition such as that in the "Virgin of the Rocks." Yet his is not a mere mechanical formula repeated again and again.

One of Leonardo's most famous paintings is the "Mona Lisa." Another is "The Last Supper," a deep psychological study of the moment when Christ tells His twelve disciples that one will betray Him. Unfortunately it has been practically obliterated by climate. Leonardo was experimenting with the use of an oil medium combined with plaster when he painted this picture on the walls of the refectory of Santa Maria della Grazie in Milan. It was an unsuccessful experiment, and the painting is rapidly disappearing.

Leonardo da Vinci was really the last of the great Florentine painters, the one who developed the science of the earlier painters to its highest point. In the "Virgin of the Rocks" (page 501) can be seen the realistic perspective and light and shade which he developed. Meantime painters in Rome were executing the commissions of Popes, and the center of artistic activity moved to Rome.

Raphael. Raphael Sanzio (1483-1520) was wealthy, courted, praised, and imitated throughout his brief but brilliant career. Not only was he the special favorite of Leo x, but he was idealized for the next three and a half centuries as having all the qualities of a great artist. Although a brilliant painter, Raphael was guilty of a certain superficiality and sentimentalism. He was himself aware of these faults when he saw some of Michelangelo's work, for he attempted, rather unsuccessfully, to incorporate into his own eclectic style his rival's achievement of dynamic strength and virility. Raphael was not very successful in his attempt, but his fluent style is pleasing in its own way. The mural "The School of Athens" shows Raphael as an able composer, while his portraits show an insight into character. A comparison of the way in which Raphael decorated a wall (page 502) with the treatment of the same problem by an Egyptian (page 53), and Giotto (page 492) will reveal striking differences. Raphael used perspective, creating the illusion of depth in the wall.

Michelangelo as a painter. Excelling as a sculptor, poet, engineer, and architect, Michelangelo was also a painter of the highest caliber. Michelangelo looked upon sculpture as his first love. When he turned to painting the Sistine Chapel at the command of Julius II, he grumbled at the enormous task and said he was a sculptor, not a painter. The gigantic task of painting the ten thousand square feet of ceiling took him four years and included one hundred forty-five pictures. Most of this work he did absolutely alone on high scaffolds, lying on his back. In painting as in sculpture he made use of the male nude figure, and his knowledge of anatomy and the movement of the human body is remarkable. To conceive of these figures as one unified composition required a vast store of knowledge and an almost incredible skill. The figures in the Sistine Chapel are pagan in the extreme, with Christ "like a Hercules." "The Creation of Adam" (below) is a detail from the Sistine Chapel paintings. Notice the way in which the long, relaxed lines of Adam's body contrast with the tense, active lines of the group supporting the Creator.

LEONARDO DA VINCI: VIRGIN OF THE ROCKS

MICHELANGELO: THE CREATION OF ADAM (FRESCO)

RAPHAEL: THE SCHOOL OF ATHENS (FRESCO)

One of those versatile geniuses who were the idols of Renaissance society, Michelangelo in addition to being an artist and engineer was also a creditable poet and politician. Writing as an old man, he shows a thin-edged humor in his description of himself: "I live alone, confined like the pith in a tree. My teeth rattle like the keys of a musical instrument; my face is a scarecrow; in one ear a spider spins its web; in the other a cricket chirps all night; my catarrh rattles in my throat and will not let me sleep. This is the end to which art, which proves my glory, has brought me."[4]

The decline of Roman and Florentine painting. It was next to impossible to expect that Renaissance painting could have continued to maintain the standard of quality which had been set by such artists as da Vinci, Michelangelo, and Raphael. Painting was bound to decline in the hands of successors who had the technical facility but lacked the imagination of the masters, and who tried to hide their deficiencies by exaggeration and sentimentalism. Where, for example, the madonnas of da Vinci and Raphael had been marked by restraint of feeling and poise of feature, the madonnas of lesser artists were depicted with tears rolling down their cheeks or gazing at the onlooker with simpering smiles.

The Venetian school. In Venice, however, painting continued on a high level. The Renaissance came later there than elsewhere. It was an appropriate setting for the development of a lavish art. The beautiful colors and clear atmosphere of Venice led painters to be interested in rich color and the effect of air and space, rather than in the more solid form of the other Italian schools. Its wealthy middle-class merchant princes were willing to play the role of patron. A Venetian school of artists now arose under the most favorable circumstances, given great impetus by the painting of Giovanni Bellini (1430-1516), who was the first to depart from the rather sculptural art of other parts of Italy.

Venetian art was the final expression of the secularization of painting. While the artists sometimes painted exquisite madonnas, they were imbued with the Venetian spirit of wealth, civic pride, and love of splendor and color. Wealthy merchants and proud doges commissioned pictures of themselves rigged out in rich brocades and gold chains and grouped with beautiful young women who scarcely looked like madonnas. There is sensuality in Venetian painting evident in the artists' love of decoration, rich costumes, and striking nude figures.

The Venetian painters excelled in *chiaroscuro* (the technique of employing full light and shade). Compare such paintings as "Pope Paul" and the Florentine "Virgin of the Rocks" with Duccio's "Betrayal of Judas" and Giotto's "St. Francis" to see this development. They used the technique of tempera and oil glaze in a characteristic manner, applying a thick tempera underpainting which produced a rich color and light with oil glazing.

Giorgione (1478-1511) was strongly affected by Humanism. His indebtedness to antiquity is shown in his subject matter by his use of classical themes and idyllic landscapes. In this respect Giorgione was like Botticelli, who also delighted in pagan subject matter. But unlike Botticelli, who made his mythological figures imaginative and unrealistic, Giorgione's muses and Venuses were quite obviously lovely Venetian models. The figures in the "Pastoral Concert" (above) show this complete worldliness.

Titian (1477?-1576) made particularly brilliant use of the oil-glaze technique. In his active life of ninety-nine years (it took a plague to carry him off) he painted prolifically. Deft in his handling of figures and color, he painted in a completely secular fashion, and even his religious pictures are concerned with sensuous beauties of color and atmosphere. His portraits show the same love of color and texture of rich fabrics, but these are always subordinated to the portrayal of the sitter's character. This love of rich fabrics and delight in textures can be seen in Titian's portrait of Pope Paul III (right), but the clothes and background are treated as large masses which do not detract from the face.

Paolo Veronese (1528-1588) and Tintoretto (1518-1592) are two other important Venetian painters. Tintoretto used strong light and shade quite dramatically. Later we shall find his influence in the work of El Greco in Spain.

Music in the Renaissance. Music made great advances at this time. Polyphonic music came into existence, with its combination of various voice parts. Such new instruments as the

GIORGIONE: PASTORAL CONCERT

violin, spinet, and harpsichord were developed. The greatest of the masters of polyphonic music was Giovanni da Palestrina (1525-1594), who gave expression to his own deep piety with religious music that is today as much admired by music lovers as it ever was. In 1594 the first opera was produced. But the greatest composers were yet unborn.

The rise of secular drama. The Renaissance also witnessed the rise of secular drama. During classical times the drama was free both in

TITIAN: PORTRAIT OF POPE PAUL III

expression and subject matter. The decline of the Roman empire was accompanied by decline in the drama and the use of theaters. However, as we saw earlier, the drama arose again during the later Middle Ages, although it began as an agent of the Church and was at first used simply for purposes of visual education. Thus grew up the miracle and morality plays, which drew the townsmen eagerly to the church porch or an adjacent stage to witness the enactment of scenes which they all knew and loved. Certain rather naïve secular elements were introduced into these plays, but a complete divorce of the Church and stage did not occur until the Renaissance.

The new plays were written in the vernacular, and their themes were often taken from classical sources. In time there developed a type of comedy, called the *commedia del arte,* which reflected the everyday life of the Renaissance. As secular dramas grew in popularity, theaters were again built as a permanent setting for their presentation. The stage had walls on the side and back, with five entrances.

Poetry and prose. Epic poetry was extremely popular. The best known epic was Ariosto's *Orlando Furioso,* written in 1515. Poetry with pastoral motifs also won attention at this time. Novels and lampoons attracted interest. The most notorious of the lampoonists was Pietro Aretino (1492-1556), whose blackmail of famous contemporaries won him both a large fortune and a notorious reputation and gave to him the title Scourge of Princes.

Manners. Manners became more refined in the Renaissance. Giovanni della Casa (d. 1556) wrote a *Galateo of Manners and Behaviours,* stating what the socially correct lady and gentleman should (and should not) do:

"It is also an unmannerly part for a man to lay his nose upon the cup where another must drink; or upon the meat that another must eat, to the end to smell unto it; but rather I would wish he should not smell at all, no, not to that which he himself should eat and drink because it might chance there might fall some drop from his nose. . . . Neither, by my advice, shalt thou reach to any man that cup of wine whereof thy self hast drunk and tasted, without he be more than a familiar friend unto thee. And much less must thou give any part of the pear or the fruit which thou hast bitten in thy mouth before."[5]

The most famous book dealing with Renaissance manners, written by Baldassare Castiglione (1478-1529), is called *The Courtier.* According to Castiglione the best courtier is likely to be of noble birth, but his true worth is created "by character and intellect rather than by birth."[6]

In his *Autobiography* Cellini has given us a remarkable insight into the manners and morals of that vivid period of history and at the same time demonstrated that he possessed that prime characteristic of the Renaissance—*virtu.* *Virtu* is not to be confused with virtue. The two words had no connection with each other; in fact, a man possessing *virtu* often appeared to be conspicuously deficient in virtue, as did Cellini himself. *Virtu* meant the gifts of natural ability and tremendous vitality, culminating in genuine achievement. To possess *virtu* and to be a universal man (*uomo universale*)—these constituted the Renaissance ideal of a great man. While Cellini approximated the ideal closely, it was achieved completely by such geniuses as da Vinci and Michelangelo. If in our eyes Cellini appears immoral, it is because his age was immoral. If he astounds us with his violence and turbulence, it is because the High Renaissance was violent and turbulent. If he amazes us with his vitality and rich imagination, it is partly because his age was strong and unruly and lavish in its creativeness.

Women in Renaissance society. Renaissance women enjoyed a much higher social position than they had known in the Middle Ages. Some of them were extremely intellectual and well educated. To women who took an active part in public affairs (and possessed much *virtu*) the name virago was given. Catherine Sforza, who carried on warfare as ably as any man, is a celebrated example of the virago.

The Renaissance throughout Europe

Spread of the Renaissance. The Renaissance developed first in Italy, for reasons we have already examined. Presently the stimulating ideas current in Italy began to spread beyond the Alps and combine with indigenous developments to produce a French Renaissance, an English Renaissance, and so on. In each country thought and art, while influenced profoundly by Italy, developed in distinctive ways. The Renaissance outside Italy was not merely a copying or adaptation of Italian modes and forms; it was a movement which arose in each country in part out of the same conditions that produced it in Italy.

Remaining feudal and monastic much longer than Italy, the northern countries gradually came to life while Italy was at the zenith of her wealth and influence. The great discoveries which began at the end of the fifteenth century brought great changes in European life. The Italian trade monopoly was broken by the discovery of new routes to the east. The increase of trade which developed in northern Europe, especially with the influx of precious metals from the New World, brought more and more people to the towns and made wealthy burghers of many tradesmen, bankers, and craftsmen. The towns had their own life —their own laws and customs and atmosphere. Urban life was sophisticated as compared with life on the manor, and townsmen were eager for entertainment, interesting ideas, and means of showing their wealth and enhancing their social prestige. At the same time, the new towns of northern Europe entered into greater commercial activities with Italian cities, and thus Italian ideas traversed the routes of trade northward over the Alps.

As in Italy, wealthy burghers played patron to artists and scholars, both native and Italian. The rulers of the rising nations also added brilliance to their courts by importing artists from Italy or sponsoring their own countrymen.

The development of printing. Printing was an important element in the diffusion of the Italian Renaissance and in the exchange of ideas between men of all countries. Two elements were essential to this invention, paper and movable type. The Greeks and Romans had written on papyrus. The Middle Ages made use of parchment, the dressed skins of such animals as sheep. Both papyrus and parchment were unwieldy, costly, and not easily adaptable to printing. As early as the second century the Chinese had been making paper from silk. In the eighth century the Moslems had created a cotton paper, which, upon being introduced into Spain, resulted in the thirteenth century in the substitution there of a linen texture. The new linen paper (*paper* is from papyrus) spread throughout Europe and proved to be a proper medium for taking the impression of movable type.

We saw earlier that the Chinese first invented type that was non-movable, consisting of a whole group of characters cut together. They were also the first to invent movable type, a method used in Europe as early as 1448. Associated with the earliest European development of printing is the name of John Gutenberg, who used movable type in his printing shop at Mainz to produce papal documents and the first printed version of the Bible in 1454.

The new invention was a tremendously important medium for culture diffusion. It is difficult to overestimate the effects of printing in the quickening of Europe's intellectual life. At once knowledge could reach a thousand times more people, and there was a genuine incentive to learn to read. By 1500 all the chief countries of Europe possessed the means for printing books. It is said that prices of books soon sank to one eighth of their former cost, thus placing books within the reach of a multitude of people who formerly were unable to buy them. Learning was no longer the private domain of the Church or of those few people wealthy enough to own hand-copied volumes. At first the Church tried to use printing to further its own ends and also to control what was printed. But such a censorship was futile, and knowledge became the heritage of anyone who could learn to read instead of an advantage enjoyed by merely a small group of intellectuals. It was now possible and profitable to cater to the tastes of the common people, and pamphlets and controversial tracts soon became common.

Humanism comes to France. In addition to the invention of printing, the invasion of Italy by Charles VIII in 1494 was instrumental in bringing many of the Humanistic ideas of the south to France. French scholars had visited Italy prior to the invasion, but the Sorbonne in Paris had so far remained the stronghold of church orthodoxy. The greatest of the early French Humanists was Guillaume Budé (1467-1540). He studied law at Orléans, translated Plutarch, and, sent as royal ambassador to Italy, investigated Roman law and coinage as a means of gaining a greater insight into the daily life of the ancients. Budé was the principal agent in the establishment of the Collège de France and of a great library which

A Flemish artist paints the building of a highway between two walled towns in the fifteenth century. Ax and rope men are chopping and pulling down trees to clear the path for the pavers, who sit on stools. The road surface is to be of heavy block stone. Note the construction of the arched bridge.

later became the Bibliothèque Nationale. Two other scholars, named Estienne, father and son, were publishers by trade.

Francis I (1515-1547) desired to make his court a center of enlightenment. He was not able to do so until after he had fought two costly wars with the great Charles V of Spain from 1522 to 1529. But after the signing of the Treaty of Cambrai (1529) Francis cultivated Renaissance studies at his court. He sponsored Budé in the establishment of the Collège and the French library. Francis had a sister even more brilliant than himself, Margaret of Navarre (1492-1549). This intelligent and attractive queen was versed in current religious thought, classical philosophy, and Italian literature. Margaret wrote poetry herself, as well as a series of stories known as the *Heptameron.* This work, written in imitation of Boccaccio's *Decameron,* contains both spiritual and lascivious themes and includes some of the most advanced thought of the time. The talented queen is to be remembered even more, however, for the influence which she exerted on the people of her own era.

Rabelais (1495?-1553). Among the friends of Margaret of Navarre was the fascinating French Humanist François Rabelais. He was a monk who lived as no true follower of the Benedictine rule should live. But his brilliant, if scurrilous, attack upon all hypocrisy and his vivid descriptions of his own age have made delightful and informative reading down through the years.

Rabelais learned medical science, read with insatiable appetite in the classics, yet used his native French in a manner which the most humble person could enjoy. In 1532 he finished that extraordinary work later known as *The Inestimable Life of the Great Gargantua, Father of Pantagruel.* The work relates the adventures of Gargantua, a giant of French folklore, of tremendous stature and appetite, to whom the French peasants ascribed the most marvelous feats, and his son Pantagruel. In the course of the narrative Rabelais gives his views on educational reform and the monastic system and makes pungent attacks upon the abuses of the papacy, the schoolmen, the monks, and the magistrates.

Rabelais himself drank in all knowledge, and hence to him there was nothing repugnant about anything which was part of life and man's natural activities. Human nature was to Rabelais a manifestation of God's purpose and therefore good, and the less trammeled and thwarted it was, the better. What Rabelais could not stomach was hypocrisy and repression. For those who were guilty of these tendencies, he reserved his choicest invective and obscenities. He attacked the monks with peculiar pleasure—he called them a "rabble of squint-minded fellows, dissembling and counterfeit saints, demure lookers, hypocrites, pretended zealots, tough friars, buskin-monks, and other such sects of men, who disguise themselves like masquers to deceive the world. . . . Fly from these men, abhor and hate them as much as I do, and upon my faith you will find yourself the better for it. And if you desire to be good Pantagruelists, that is to say, *to live in peace, joy, health, making yourselves always merry,* never trust those men that always peep out through a little hole."[7]

Such a quotation illustrates Rabelais' impetuous style of writing, and it sums up his Humanistic philosophy.

Montaigne. When Rabelais died in 1553, Michel de Montaigne was twenty years old. Until his death in 1592 this polished, urbane essayist was France's leading Humanist. His *Essays* condemned the pedantry of the day (into which Humanism had largely degenerated) and showed the need of educating children so that they might understand what they are learning. "To know by rote is no knowledge and signifies no more but only to retain what one had intrusted to our memories." Montaigne was a forerunner of our modern psychology of education, originator of the modern essay, and a thinker who saw that the problems of human life are more important to solve than the syntax of an obscure sentence from Horace.

The northern Humanists. The discoveries and literature of the Italian Humanists were also disseminated throughout northern Europe by means of the new printed books. Another reason for the spread of Italian thought was the close political connection between the German and Italian states. Because of this fact, as early as Petrarch's times the Humanism of the south crossed the Alps. Because the northern universities were still hidebound by tradition and conservatism, many German students journeyed to Italian schools and returned with the new concepts which were transforming Italian thought. Humanism began to flourish with especial vigor in many of the wealthier trading centers such as Augsburg.

Erasmus (1466?-1536). Among the northern Humanists, the most influential and cosmopolitan in thought was Erasmus, a contemporary of Rabelais. Born in Rotterdam, he passed most of his long life elsewhere—in Germany, France, England, Italy, and Switzerland. At Basel in Switzerland the scholar *par excellence* lived out his last years in comfortable safety, content that Basel was free from national wars and free to print his books. Erasmus was eminently balanced and moderate. He was a doctor of sacred theology, yet he delighted in poking fun at unimaginative theologians. His Greek text of the New Testament was scholarly and accurate, yet he flayed those pedants who split hairs endlessly in their studies. He believed in complete tolerance, yet was himself intolerant of bigotry.

There are some geniuses who dominate the intellectual life of the ages in which they live —Petrarch in the fourteenth century and Voltaire in the eighteenth. The first half of the sixteenth century was dominated by Erasmus. His influence was felt in intellectual circles everywhere. He corresponded with practically every prominent writer in Europe. He knew personally such men as the English Humanists, John Colet and Sir Thomas More, Budé in France, the Medicean Pope Leo x, the emperor of the Holy Roman Empire, and the kings of England and France. He was the scholar of Europe. His writings were read eagerly everywhere.

In Praise of Folly. Perhaps his most famous and influential work was *In Praise of Folly*, a satire written in 1511 at the house of Sir Thomas More. The book concerns a female character called Folly, Erasmus' conception of human nature.

"At first the book makes kindly and approving fun of the ways of action and the foibles and weaknesses of mankind. It is not mordant, only amused. But gradually from fools innocent and natural and undebased, it passes to those whose illusions are vicious in their setting and results. Such are stultified grammarians, scribblers, sophisters; such are passionate dicers; and then those addicted to the marvellous and incredible, gaping fools, greedy of strange tales, who ascribe virtue to shrines and images, and to vows made to saints. Worse than such are they who rely on rotten pardons, and think to measure . . . the ages, years, months, days, which they have knocked off from Purgatory. Priests promote these evil follies, and reap gain from them. Now the satire becomes mordant; it ridicules, it lashes the fool-vices, their panders and their votaries; the fool-sophisters, scotists, dabblers in split hairs and things incomprehensible, and the like-minded theologians, with their impossible fool-questions; and then the Monks! These are well scourged. As to kings, allowance is made for the blinding effect of their exalted station; but their courtiers are handled roughly. The discourse pounces upon Popes and Cardinals and bishops; the lashing becomes merciless. Luther might lay on more violently but not more deftly."[8]

A Flemish miniature shows the various steps in glass-making: sand is mixed with alkali and deposited in the furnace; the blower shapes his gather of molten glass on a slab; the finished pieces are shelved.

Analysis of *In Praise of Folly* yields the significant revelation that only a relatively few scholars and thinkers were enlightened. Superstition and blind reliance on authority were as prevalent then among many scholars as in the earlier centuries. Again, we can see from *In Praise of Folly* that Erasmus was unconsciously preparing the mind of Europe for religious reformation. But he was not one of the leaders of the Protestant revolt. Erasmus was a rationalist, and he saw about him only passions; he was tolerant, and Europe was bleeding from bigotry; and he saw no conflict between secular and religious truth. Erasmus was religious, but "reasonable." He preferred the pen of the scholar to the cross of the martyr.

Spanish thought. The Renaissance produced in Spain two outstanding thinkers—Juan Luis Vives (d.1540) and Miguel de Cervantes Saavedra (1547-1616). Vives was a social thinker as well as a Humanist scholar. He declared that the towns should look after the poor in an efficient manner, since the monasteries and clergy neglected their duty. Among his views in the educational field was the belief that girls as well as boys should be given training, especially along moral lines.

Cervantes is remembered because he created two immortal characters, the eccentric but chivalric Don Quixote and the practical but much less gallant Sancho Panza. Tilting at windmills, mistaking serving wenches for high-born ladies, and inns for castles, and lamenting the invention of gunpowder as depriving gallant knights of a chance of winning immortality, Don Quixote is one of the most lovable characters in literature. But more than that, he is the foil by which Cervantes satirizes the bankrupt medieval ideology which still held Spain in its grip.

Don Quixote was much more than an amusing novel. It represented a great ideological change, a change from the outworn ideals of the Middle Ages to the newer concepts of modern times. There was something futile in the attempt of the old knight to keep alive the chivalric code in which he was brought up but in which nobody else appeared to take any interest. The world had entered upon a new way of living, one which no longer required horsemen to gallop across the countryside redressing wrongs, one which was infinitely more complex and practical.

A third literary figure of the Spanish Renaissance was the dramatist Lope de Vega. This prolific genius turned out, by his own count, over 2000 plays, most of them comedies written to order for production in the theaters of his time. He once said that "more than a hundred of my comedies have taken only twenty-four hours to pass from my brain to the boards of the theatre." Writing to amuse his audiences rather than to instruct them, de Vega was a master of plot and often a skillful delineator of character types, to whom he gave appropriate speech and costumes, an innovation in his day. Because he wrote to please a public drawn from all classes of people, he ignored the classical styles then popular and championed the use of the language of the people. Much of his material was taken from Spanish history and from everyday life in the Spain of his day. Lionized and honored during his lifetime, Lope de Vega was the most important influence in the development of a native Spanish drama.

Early Humanism in England. King Henry VII of England (1485-1509) had little time to play the role of patron, so busy was he consolidating his kingdom after the long-drawn-out Wars of the Roses. The bourgeoisie and a group of Oxford scholars were mainly responsible for the entrance of the Renaissance into England. Thomas Linacre (1460?-1524) taught Greek at Oxford upon his return from Italy, but in addition he brought back the latest medical knowledge, translated Galen's works, and founded the London College of Physicians. The greatest of the early English Humanists was John Colet (1467?-1519), who lectured at Oxford on the literal sense of the Biblical texts. Later he reëstablished, along Humanistic lines, the famous old school attached to St. Paul's Cathedral in London, including Ciceronian Latin and Greek in the curriculum. The popularity of the new ideas resulted in the formation of a group of men known as the Oxford Reformers. Although Henry VII had been too deeply interested in statecraft to be a Humanist patron, his son Henry VIII (1509-1547) encouraged the work of Colet and his friends, and England's Renaissance began.

Sir Thomas More (1478-1535). Sir Thomas More, the famous humanistic friend of Erasmus in England, has in recent years been canonized for his saintly life and for his martyrdom in opposing Henry VIII's divorce and break with the Church of Rome. But he is better known for his *Utopia,* the first important book since Plato's *Republic,* describing conditions necessary for an ideal state.

In his epoch-making work More criticized the harshness of existing laws and, like Erasmus and Rabelais, denounced the folly of warfare. The second book of *Utopia* attracts our attention particularly, for in it is given a description of Amaurote, the ideal city in the state of Utopia (The Land of Nowhere). The model capital was surprisingly modern. Each dwelling had glass windows and a garden. The city maintained a water supply; the streets were broad (twenty feet, impressively wide for the day); filth was not permitted either in foodstuffs or family dwellings, and everybody had to move every ten years by lot. People worked diligently and planned their day so that they labored only six hours, slept eight hours, and passed their leisure "in some proper exercise according to their various inclinations, which is for the most part reading." A fine international spirit was fostered by the citizens of Utopia, and war was justified only in defense "or in compassion to assist an oppressed nation in shaking off the yoke of tyranny."

In economic matters, according to More, happiness cannot come while money is the "standard of all other things." Precious metals caused so much internal strife elsewhere that the Utopians showed their contempt for gold and silver by making their pots and kettles out of these metals and by fastening their criminals with gold chains. Finally, the state's goods were distributed equally to every citizen, for More believed the most unworthy tend to obtain the greatest share of wealth.

Undoubtedly *Utopia* was influenced by Plato's *Republic,* for as a Humanist More read Plato avidly and must have been attracted to the idea of putting forward philosophical and sociological principles of an ideal state by means of fiction. In turn, More gave to Francis Bacon and many later writers the incentive to write about ideal societies in fictional form. The word "Utopia" has passed into the language, signifying an ideal society

POL DE LIMBOURG: DECEMBER

VAN EYCK: DONOR, DETAIL OF BRUGES MADONNA

not likely to be achieved, or, as the adjective "Utopian," it means "visionary."

English poetry. The English Renaissance of the sixteenth century was notable for its rich and musical poetry. Sir Thomas Wyatt and the Earl of Surrey introduced the Petrarchian sonnet. Sir Philip Sidney wrote the pastoral romance *Arcadia* and a critical *Defense of Poesy.* Edmund Spenser is chiefly famous for his *Faerie Queene,* in which the best classical and Humanist influences are interwoven with Arthurian romantic elements. The whole poem is an artistic appeal to the patriotic feelings of sixteenth-century Englishmen.

Early Elizabethan drama. The most splendid development of Elizabethan literature was in its drama. A majority of the earlier plays conformed to the classical doctrine of the unities of place, time, and action. Among these were the comedies *Ralph Roister Doister* and *Gammer Gurton's Needle* and the tragedy *Gorboduc,* written in 1561.

The reign of Elizabeth witnessed the production of *The Spanish Tragedy* by Thomas Kyd; *The Jew of Malta, Doctor Faustus,* and *Tamburlaine* by the brilliant but erratic Christopher Marlowe, and *Every Man in His Humor* and other plays by the famous Ben Jonson, who is today remembered as a poet, dramatist, and critic.

William Shakespeare (1564-1616). The greatest writer of all Elizabethan literature—perhaps of all literature—was William Shakespeare. He broke with the classical tradition by violating the doctrine of the unities of time, place, and action and striking out in new and daring concepts. His historical plays reflect the patriotism Englishmen increasingly felt as their country grew stronger and more prosperous. In the following lines we get an insight into the Elizabethan love of country:

This royal throne of kings, this scepter'd isle,
This earth of majesty, this seat of Mars,
This other Eden, demi-paradise;
This fortress built by Nature for herself
Against infection and the hand of war;
This happy breed of men, this little world,
This precious stone set in the silver sea,
Which serves it in the office of a wall,
Or as a moat defensive to a house,
Against the envy of less happier lands;
This blessed plot, this earth, this realm, this
England.[9]

Shakespeare's comedies are played today to enthusiastic audiences—*A Comedy of Errors, As You Like It, The Taming of the Shrew, All's Well That Ends Well,* and *The Merchant of Venice,* to mention but a few. In his tragedies—*Hamlet, Othello, King Lear,* and *Macbeth*—the master dramatist-poet runs the gamut of human emotions and experience. The rich vocabulary and poetic imagery are matched only by his turbulent imagination. Shakespeare showed typical Renaissance interest in man and the world about him. His plays are concerned first of all with man's personality, passions, and problems. The problems of love and sex are studied from many angles in such works as *Romeo and Juliet, Twelfth Night, Measure for Measure,* and *Troilus and Cressida.* The passion of jealousy is analyzed in *Othello,* ambition in *Macbeth, Richard III,* and *Julius Caesar,* family relationships in *King Lear,* and man's struggle with his environment and circumstances in *Hamlet.* The extraordinary ability of the dramatist to give to every concrete fact or action a universal truth makes the observations of Shakespeare as applicable today as when they were first presented in the Globe Theater.

Sir Francis Bacon (1561-1626). A notable contemporary of Shakespeare was Sir Francis Bacon. Like his predecessor Roger Bacon, Francis aimed at divorcing science from authority and Scholasticism; like Montaigne he wrote brilliant essays about everyday matters; and like Sir Thomas More he described a Utopian form of society. His book, known as *The New Atlantis,* resembles *Utopia* in so far as both pretend to give a description of island civilizations. But whereas More concentrated on the sociological aspects of society, Bacon specialized in the technological advances and showed the importance of science in the new cultural plan. "The end of our foundation is the knowledge of causes, and secret motions of things, and the enlarging of the bounds of human empire, to the effecting of all things possible."

Sir Francis Bacon, like Roger, anticipated flying machines, submarines, and many of the later improvements in medicine, surgery, meteorology, and mechanical contrivances. In his ideal society chief interest centered around Solomon's House, the "College of the Six Days Works," which supervises experimentation and inventions.

Painting in the Low Countries. Even as Italian Humanism gradually permeated the intellectual life of northern Europe, so the art of the southern peninsula in time crossed the

ALBRECHT DÜRER: HIERONYMUS HOLZSCHUHER

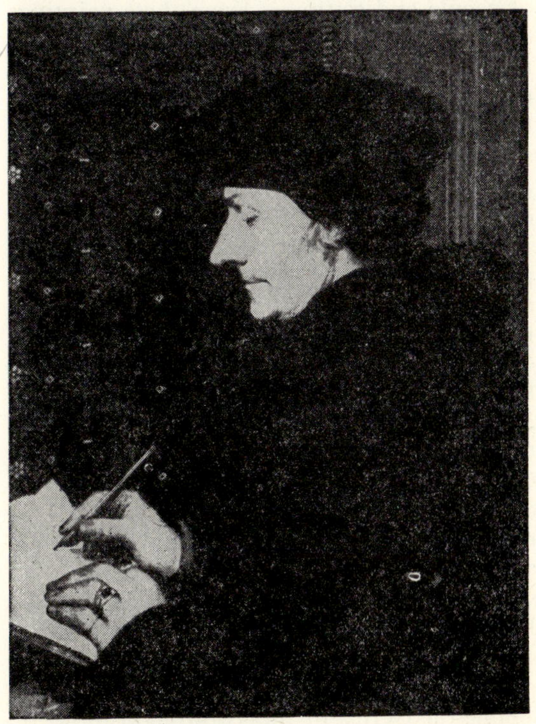

HANS HOLBEIN: ERASMUS OF ROTTERDAM

Alps. But certain native departures from medieval methods and conventions preceded the Italian influence.

In the Low Countries in the fourteenth century there had been a final burst of Gothic manuscript painting. Of this the work of Pol de Limbourg is outstanding. "December," shown on page 510, is an example. His technical excellence was great, and his figures show the beginning of the Renaissance interest in people. Much of the Gothic style remains, such as the use of a hedge of trees in the background instead of a landscape in perspective.

In the fifteenth century there was a culmination of medieval painting. Among the many painters the brothers Van Eyck were particularly important. They perfected the oil-glaze technique which was taken to Italy and there used with thick tempera underpainting which gave a very different effect from the enamel-like surface of the Van Eyck painting. Compare the Van Eyck painting at the bottom of page 510 with Titian's portrait of Pope Paul III shown on page 503. The fifteenth-century painters flourished under the patronage of wealthy burghers and the dukes of Burgundy. They painted in a detailed, realistic manner, and their paintings reveal many Flemish types of people and costumes. From these paintings can be constructed an accurate picture of the times. Their themes were still mainly conventional medieval ones, however, except that to the figure of the Virgin or saint was often added the portrait of the donor (see the Van Eyck detail on page 510) and perhaps, too, that of the donor's wife.

Dürer (1471-1528). The first great German painter to be influenced deeply by Italian art was Albrecht Dürer of Nuremberg. He made more than one journey to Italy, where he could not help being impressed by the excellence of the art. However, he did not entirely lose many of the medieval qualities of his native environment, partly because the bourgeois Germans who gave him commissions were still demanding traditional religious subjects. The result was that his work is a blend of the old and the new in art. Dürer received aid from such notables as the emperor of the Holy Roman Empire and Erasmus, and he gained a great reputation with his paintings and even more with his engravings and woodcuts. He among the German painters did most to break away from the prevailing medieval standards of his homeland and incorporate the ideas of Italy. "Hieronymus Holzschuher" (page 511) shows the German medieval approach in the careful, rather labored painting of details such as the hair and beard, but his interest in the portrayal of individual character was a departure from the work of his contemporaries.

Holbein (1497-1543). The greatest German painter after Dürer was Hans Holbein the Younger. He traveled extensively, doing some of his greatest work in Switzerland and England. He achieved an enviable record as a draftsman, a painter, and a designer of jewelry, glass windows, and woodcuts. In his work the typical northern linear quality was softened to a great extent, but his drawing was still incisive and sharp.

Holbein was less imaginative than Dürer, but whereas Dürer lived in Germany and interpreted its spirit, the younger painter worked abroad, and his work was not quite so national in character. His portrait of Erasmus (page 511), with its strong pattern of light and dark, is still northern in its reserve and sharp detail. Compare the Dürer and Holbein portraits with Titian's (page 503).

The Flemish school gradually fell under the permeating influences of the Italian masters and lost its northern individuality of technique. It became a poor imitation of the art of the south in attempting to copy the Venetian lavishness and love of large, showy paintings.

Breughel (1525?-1569). There was one artist, Peter Breughel, who was not influenced by southern tastes but painted with fidelity the faces and scenes of his native land. Breughel painted the life which delighted him the most —village squares, skating scenes, and marriage festivals—and when he painted religious pictures, he did them in the same everyday manner and interpreted Bible stories in terms of life in the Flemish towns. A painting showing the hearty peasant life is "The Wedding Dance," page 514. Notice the patterning of the white blouses and kerchiefs. The style depicting everyday scenes in realistic fashion is known as *genre* painting, and the Flemish painters excelled in it.

French and English painting. It took longer for the Renaissance in painting and sculpture to reach France, England, and Spain. Painters from foreign countries were imported for fashionable courts. Francis I invited to his court such Italian masters as Leonardo da Vinci. English artists were also inferior. As a result, foreign masters like Hans Holbein were employed by the worldly and sophisticated king, Henry VIII.

Spread of Renaissance architecture. The architecture of the Italian Renaissance made particular headway in France during the reign of Francis I. At this time part of the palace of the Louvre was constructed, embodying many Italian ideas. Philip II of Spain built the magnificent royal palace, the Escorial, between 1563 and 1584; it likewise shows Italian innovations. In Germany Renaissance architects excelled in the construction of town halls and private city dwellings. At the same time England slowly began to incorporate the new architectural pattern.

Summary

In the Middle Ages man had thought of himself primarily as part of a universal order of things, such as the Church and the Holy Roman Empire. But gradually, for a variety of reasons, he began to discover himself and the world about him. This change in attitude, the period in which it occurred, and the ways in which it manifested itself in art, literature, and learning, we call the Renaissance. The change took place earliest in Italy, and first expressed itself in the great intellectual movement—Humanism.

Humanism was in its early stages a revival of the learning of classical times. It became the fashion in Italy to study Greek and to imitate the Latin of Cicero's day, while wealthy patrons brought scholars to their courts and sponsored the search for ancient manuscripts. The reverence for antiquity led to the copying of literary and artistic forms and fashions from ancient Rome and Greece. The homes of the well-to-do became museums for classics of all kinds.

In so far as Humanism was merely an imitation of the manners and fashions of Greece and Rome, it was sterile and produced little of real value. But there were artists and writers who were stimulated by their study of the classics or were indirectly encouraged by the subtle change in outlook among the scholars of the day to create works of art and literature which broke with the medieval tradition yet did not simply imitate classical compositions. It is impossible to ascribe the new developments in art and literature solely to the influence of the revival of learning, but the study of classical times did help to achieve the following effects: It encouraged men to seek subject matter outside the Church and furnished many new ideas for subjects. It encouraged a certain amount of realism in art in contrast to medieval convention and symbolism. It was one factor behind the new individualism. The medieval emphasis on otherworldliness—the idea that life in this world was only a preparation at best for heaven in the next world—slowly gave way, among the wealthier and better educated, at least, to a new interest in the world of here and now and the life of the present.

Changes in the economic and political aspects of life likewise brought about distinct changes in man's outlook. The growing concern of the city dweller with affairs of trade and manufacturing undermined the Church's authority, for when church doctrine clashed with material benefit, the new burgher class was apt to disregard censure in favor of making money. The medieval Church concepts of the just price and its ban on usury conflicted with the new urban commercial practices that involved banking and moneylending. As we shall see later, a capitalistic society was taking form at this time.

PETER BREUGHEL THE ELDER: THE WEDDING DANCE

This new individualistic and realistic attitude manifested itself in various ways, and produced changes of importance in many fields of expression. In literature, stories of flesh-and-blood people supplanted allegories and ideal and unearthly love. Petrarch's *Laura* was a real person, and Boccaccio's *Decameron* was anything but devout. In painting, artists were interested in creating depth and form instead of flat surfaces, developing perspective and the science of light and shade to achieve realistic effects. Oil glaze was used over tempera to give soft and natural modeling. Artists painted mythical scenes and the life around them as much as they did religious pictures, and even religious decorations in churches were often sensuous and worldly. Sculptors and painters portrayed the nude figure and studied anatomy, procedures foreign to the medieval mind.

In architecture the Renaissance contribution was less original. Innovations were in detail and decoration rather than in structural principles. The medieval style was shunned, and much was borrowed from the classic style. The classic, however, was used in a manner that made it typically Renaissance. In the Renaissance, architects who were primarily designers and not engineers made elaborate buildings which were occasionally structural absurdities.

In political theory, the medieval ideal of a universal state ruled by the twin powers of emperor and Pope gave way to the opportunistic individualism expounded by Machiavelli, whose writings were a reflection of what he saw going on around him in Italy. Manners and morals were likewise affected by the new interest in the present. Individuality became a cult, occasionally carried to excesses of self-expression.

Outside Italy the Renaissance in art and literature was partly indigenous and partly an expression of Italian influences. In France it was largely imitative in art, but such literary figures as Rabelais and Montaigne wrote originally and fathered the modern essay. In England Wyatt and Surrey imported Italian forms, but a great native drama developed under the aegis of Shakespeare and lesser writers. In the Low Countries art, before it declined to a mere imitation of Italian models, reflected the rich burgher life. In Germany, as we shall see, the break with medieval tradition took the form of speculative thought and religious criticism, although there were rich developments in the other arts as well.

In all countries the Renaissance of the fifteenth and sixteenth centuries was mainly the property of a few people. While countless works of art were available to everyone—decorations for churches, statues in public squares, and buildings on city streets—the new learning and the new attitudes were almost entirely confined to the upper social classes. They, in fact, sponsored much of the whole movement. Their wealth supplied the artist with his materials, his place to work, and often his subject, and they directed the scholars in their researches and literary productions.

The creations of Renaissance artists and writers were a reflection of the changing attitudes, the enthusiasms, and the lavishness of the age. Though there were many facets to the pattern of developments, and though many different and occasionally conflicting influences were at work, there was common to all creations of the period a new attitude of individuality.

Chapter 18

Chronology of events and developments discussed in this chapter

Papal bull: Boniface VIII forbade clerical taxation without papal consent	1296
Babylonian Captivity: papal headquarters in Avignon under French influence	1309-1376
Wycliffe: church should be subordinate to state; individual salvation	1320-1384
Statute of Provisors: invalidated papal appointments in England	1351
Statute of Praemunire: illegal to take cases to the papal court	1352
Hus: Bohemian martyr; burned at the stake	1369-1415
Great Schism: two Popes, each claimed universal control; Church lost prestige	1378-1417
Council of Constance: solution to the Great Schism; voted on national basis	1414
Zwingli: gave impetus to Protestantism in Switzerland	1484-1531
Calvin: predestination; established a new branch of Protestantism	1509-1564
Luther posted the ninety-five propositions; instigated the Protestant Revolt	1517
Peasants' War: revolt against the nobles; Luther lost peasant support	1524-1525
Imperial Diet ruled Catholic and Lutheran activities coexistant	1529
Act of Supremacy under Henry VIII: king should be head of the English church	1534
Jesuit order founded: part of the Catholic reformation; emphasized education	1534
Monastic houses disbanded in England	1539
Council of Trent: peak of Catholic reformation	1545-1563
Schmalkaldic Wars: Lutheran princes revolted against suppression of heresy	1546-1555
Catholic Mary: unsuccessful return to Catholicism in England	1553-1558
Peace of Augsburg: ended Schmalkaldic Wars; local religious autonomy; beginning of state religion	1555
Elizabeth: Protestantism firmly reëstablished; revised prayer book obligatory	1558-1603

The Ninety-Five Theses

The religious revolt: 1300 to 1650

On October 31, 1517, a professor of theology by the name of Martin Luther nailed some papers on the door of the Castle Church in Wittenberg. Why he nailed those papers where and when he did and what happened as a result are the story of this chapter. It was the custom of the day to act thus when a man wanted to engage in a scholastic debate with another; in this respect Luther's action was by no means unusual. Yet the forces set in operation by that event in 1517 altered the entire religious and intellectual pattern of the western world. For they launched a great religious revolt that split Christendom from its former basis of unity into innumerable factions and sects. To this day the unity of Christendom has not been restored.

The present chapter, then, is one fraught with significance from the standpoint of religious changes. We have already seen how men of the Renaissance rebelled ceaselessly against the feudalism, Scholasticism, arts, and otherworldliness of the Middle Ages. During the Renaissance, too, the ideal of a universal state was shattered by the rise of aggressive national states. Now, the greatest of all medieval institutions, the universal, all-powerful Church, was to be stripped of its supremacy. The Roman Church had not ceased to act as a great religious and historical force; but the medieval ideal of unity had fallen before the onslaught of Renaissance individualism. Henceforth the Roman Church had to share its influence, both spiritual and political, with other churches, built upon different beliefs and goals.

When Luther and his followers came to believe in doctrines contrary to those held by the Roman Church, they did not try to reform Catholicism but broke away entirely and established their own Church. This movement has often been called the Reformation, but that term is not quite accurate. There had been periods of "reform" in the Church before, as we have seen, and another was to occur as a result of the forces released by Luther. But the significant action of Luther and his followers was more than reformation; it was a religious revolt. Those who agreed with Luther set up their own churches, denying the exclusive right of the Pope to direct all religious affairs.

The Protestant movement, striking at the very roots of the Church, fostered in turn a Catholic revival, and the two movements fought for supremacy throughout the sixteenth century. The bitter and passionate rivalries engulfed the Renaissance spirit of humanism and tolerance; instead persecution, bigotry, and bloodshed were common wherever Protestant and Catholic clashed. The religious upheaval and conflicts it engendered left their mark on nearly every phase of life. In particular they served the political ends of rulers anxious for power at home and abroad, who utilized them, as we shall later see, to write some of the most unhappy pages of history.

The Decline of the Medieval Church

Dangers facing the papacy. In our discussion of the role of the Church in western Europe in the Middle Ages we saw how that great organization dominated the life of the time. Of all forces shaping the form of medieval culture there can be no doubt that the Church was the most influential. In the thirteenth century the Church seemed unassailable in its prestige, dignity, and power. During the pontificate of Innocent III especially, it appeared completely triumphant. But its strength was already waning.

Papal centralization was harassed by four main forces: (1) the growing national states which rose to take the place of the dying Holy Roman Empire as opponents of the Church's temporal pretensions, (2) the local clergy, who joined with the princes in opposing papal interference in internal matters and who favored the establishment of general church councils to curb the powers of the Pope, (3) reformers who had seen the medieval reformation and the crusades transformed from their original high purposes to suit the ambitions of the pontiffs at Rome, and (4) the growing opposition of the middle classes throughout Europe, whose attitudes toward life had been undergoing some severe changes because of the growth of trade, the exchange of more and more ideas among all classes of people, and a growing feeling of national patriotism and religious self-reliance. The fact was that church domination of the medieval world depended on the continuance of the medieval world order, and forces were at work which were slowly undermining every aspect of that order. The fourteenth and fifteenth centuries witnessed the collapse of papal supremacy.

Boniface VIII and temporal rulers. In the pontificate of the proud Boniface VIII (1294-1303) the papacy was unable to compel such states as England and France to bow down before its commands. The struggle, involving Edward I of England and Philip IV of France, was over the right of the kings to tax the Church for the support of the war they were about to wage with one another. When the Cistercian order in France protested to the Pope about Philip's laying special state taxes upon them, Boniface answered in 1296 with his famous bull *Clericis laicos* (papal bulls are named from the words with which they begin), which forbade the kings to tax the clergy without Rome's consent. Edward retaliated by outlawing all clergy who would not support him. Philip forbade the exporting of all French moneys to Rome, thus jeopardizing the papal financial structure.

Trouble soon broke out again between Boniface and Philip over the right of a secular court to try a member of the clergy, in this instance a bishop. Philip had treated the bishop in a high-handed manner, and the Pope was furiously threatening to correct and even depose the "impious king." Philip in turn stirred up public opinion against Boniface's "great fatuousness." When Philip was defeated in a battle against the Flemish, the

Pope issued his famous bull *Unam Sanctum* in which he maintained that in order to obtain salvation every human creature must be subject to the pontiff of Rome.[1] But his bold assertion had come too late.

Philip now decided to take the advice of his shrewd legal adviser William Nogaret to summon a general council, depose the pontiff, and call a new papal election. Meanwhile, to make Boniface a prisoner of Philip, Nogaret and some accomplices went to the home of Boniface and broke into his palace. But kidnaping failed, and the Pope was taken safely to Rome by his friends, only to die in October of the same year.

The Avignon papacy. The success of the French monarchy was as complete as if Boniface had been dragged before Philip. In the election which eventually followed, a French archbishop was chosen Pope. Taking the title of Clement v, he acted according to the wishes of Philip iv, even to the point of taking up his residence at Avignon, where he was subject to French influence, instead of at Rome. From 1309 to 1376 the Popes remained at Avignon. This period has been called the Babylonian Captivity of the Church. The loss to papal prestige was enormous. The Romans resented the lack of the court and the revenues, the English justifiably accused the Popes of favoring the French kings, the Germans resented the claims of the Pope to temporal power over the emperor of the Holy Roman Empire, and all Christendom believed that Rome was the only rightful capital for the Church.

The Avignon papacy had the following general effects: (1) its shortcomings gave men the opportunity to attack church corruption, papal temporal pretensions, and the spiritual authority of the Roman hierarchy, (2) it alienated the obedience and support of England and the Holy Roman Empire, (3) it stimulated questioning, especially by John Wycliffe in England, about the divinity of the papal office and the sacramental system, bringing on much heresy, and (4) it produced a cry from such writers as William of Occam and Marsiglio of Padua for reformation by church councils.

The Great Schism. The sad state of papal conditions in Italy prompted Gregory xi to return to Rome in 1377. A betterment of conditions seemed at hand, but Gregory died the following year. The Roman multitude demanded in loud voice that an Italian Pope be elected, and their demand was met with the election of Urban vi. However, the French cardinals maintained that the election was invalid because of outside pressure on the voters, and, retiring to Avignon once again, they elected a Frenchman who took the title of Clement vii.

The Church was now in an even worse state than it had been during the Babylonian Captivity. There were two Popes, each claiming universal sovereignty, each with his college of cardinals and capital, each sending forth papal administrators and taxing Christendom, and each excommunicating the other as the "anti-Christ." The nations of Europe, of course, gave allegiance as their individual political interests prompted them. France supported Clement, as did Scotland, Navarre, Castile, and Aragon. Urban found his strength in Italy, England, Portugal, Flanders, and most of northern, central, and eastern Europe. But in order to keep the allegiance of the various countries, the rival Popes had to make concessions, such as abandoning to a large extent the practice of interfering in national politics.

Religious life also suffered. The Great Schism, as the split in the papacy was called, had become an international disgrace.

"Christendom looked upon the scandal helpless and depressed, and yet impotent to remove it. With two sections of Christendom each declaring the other lost, each cursing and denouncing the other, men soberly asked who was saved. The longer the schism lasted, the more difficult did it seem to heal it, and yet people generally felt that for that very reason positive action was all the more necessary. The very sublimity of papal pretensions made earthly jurisdiction and compulsory abdication seem very difficult. Still the fact stared Europe in the face that the schism itself, with the cupidity, selfishness, and meanness accompanying it, had shattered the sanctity of papal claims in breaking up the unity of Christendom."[2]

The Conciliar Movement. Positive action came in the form of the Conciliar Movement. In 1395 the doctors of the University of Paris (as Europe's chief theologians) suggested that if the two claimants to the papal throne would not abdicate, a general council of all the Church should be held. The Popes would not abdicate nor arbitrate their differences. So in 1409 a majority of the cardinals of both camps met at the Council of Pisa, deposed both pontiffs, and elected a third man. But neither of the two deposed Popes would give up his office, and the papal throne now had three claimants.

Such an intolerable situation necessitated the calling of other church councils. In 1414 Emperor Sigismund assembled at the Council of Constance the most impressive church gathering ever known. For the first time voting was done on the basis of four nations—French, English, Italian, and German. This was highly significant as an indication that the new tendency toward nationalistic alignments was being recognized by the Church. Finally, through the deposition of the line of Popes started by the Council of Pisa, and of the Avignon Pope, the Roman Popes succeeded, in the election of Martin v in 1417, to a virtually uncontested supremacy in the Church once more. The Great Schism was ended.

Aeneas Sylvius Piccolomini sets out for the Council of Basel. Later, as Pope Pius II, *the most versatile and brilliant of all the "literary" Popes, he became a strong foe of Conciliar reform.*

Heresy: Wycliffe and Hus. Other great problems facing the Church had not been solved, however. The growth of heresy had been very great in the fourteenth century. The *Vision of Piers Plowman* in England mercilessly upbraided in verse the corruption, ignorance, and worldliness of the clergy. During the Avignon papacy there had also appeared in England a master of Oxford by the name of John Wycliffe (1320?-1384) who assailed not only church abuses but, what was more dangerous, church doctrines. Briefly, he believed that the Church should be subordinate to the state, that salvation was primarily an individual matter between man and God, that transubstantiation as taught by the Church was false, and that outward rituals and veneration of relics were idolatrous. Wycliffe was really the dawn-star of the Protestant revolt. He formed bands of poor priests, called Lollards, who taught his views, and he translated the Bible into English, a great service to literature and the common people.

Wycliffe's ideas were taken up especially in Bohemia by Bohemian students who had heard him at Oxford. The greatest of the Bohemian heretics was John Hus (1369?-1415), a patriot, ardent preacher, and propagator of Wycliffe's radical views. So popular did his doctrines become and so great was his influence that the Church decided to take him in hand. He was given a safe-conduct to the Council of Constance (which had as its purpose not only the healing of the schism but also the stamping out of heresy and reform of the papacy), but because Hus did not recant from his position, the Council condemned him, and he was burned at the stake in spite of his safe-conduct. But heresy was not stamped out by such action. On the contrary, it served only to make Hus a martyr and to strengthen the doctrines for which he had died. Hus was burned in 1415, but the faggots which had cost him his life were kept burning by his heresies for a century and set ablaze in Luther's declarations of 1517 a conflagration which was to consume all Europe.

The failure of internal reform. The Church had demonstrated by the Council of Constance that it possessed in the Conciliar Movement the means of reforming itself. But the movement was not to endure. There was a fundamental conflict between church councils and church Popes, for both claimed supreme power. With Martin v's resumption of headship of all the Church, together with the inability of the Conciliar Movement to bring about much-needed reforms at the councils of Pavia and Basel, the Popes managed by 1450 to discredit the Conciliar Movement entirely.

The Popes refused to reform themselves and forbade the calling of a council to attempt the job. Therefore, no great council was called until 1550, when the Council of Trent was summoned to reform a Church which had already irreparably lost many countries to Protestantism. The Conciliar Movement represented a reforming and democratizing influence in the Church. It aimed at transforming the papacy into something like a limited monarchy. If it could not find expression inside the Catholic Church, it would find expression outside that body. A break was inevitable, especially as the Popes now busied themselves not in reform but in Italian politics and devoted their time to becoming patrons of the arts in the Italian Renaissance.

Reasons for Church decline. Having related the decline of the Church from 1300 to about 1500, we can logically ask what were the major causes for the decline of the once all-powerful institution. Alexander Clarence Flick, a noted church historian, in *The Decline of the Medieval Church* has divided these into causes that existed within the church structure itself and those which were weakening it from the outside. In the first category can be placed (1) the growing formal nature of much of the church worship, (2) the failure of the Church to keep pace with intellectual developments taking place in the outside world, (3) the immorality of many of the clergy, (4) the concentration of all power over the Church in the hands of the Pope. In the second category can be listed (1) the rise of skepticism, (2) the development of nationalism and the growing reluctance of national monarchs to obey any alien institution, even the Church, (3) the intellectual results of printing, which hastened the spread of the new secular spirit of the Renaissance, and (4) the revolutionary changes in the economic field, such as the rise of capitalism, the growth of the middle class, and the expansion of Europe, forces that were bound to undermine the power of the Church.[3] All of these factors blended into a complex pattern of causes to bring about what is usually known as the Religious Revolt, by which the unchallenged authority of the once universal Church was destroyed.

New attitudes. Internal causes explain much of the Church's loss of prestige; loss of its universal power came largely from the other factors mentioned. The spirit of the Middle Ages was one of faith, devotion to institutions—the feudal order, the guild, and the Church—and denial of the importance of the individual. It was this spirit which fed the universal strength of the Church. The Renaissance changed the spirit. Man became conscious of his own importance. He became assertive. He came to revolt against all institutions which prevented him from acting as he wished. So he broke away from feudalism in order that he might become an urban merchant. Later he preferred to be a free businessman rather than a member of a merchant guild. And finally he created his own politically independent national state rather than be subordinated to an Empire.

He was finding himself quite out of sympathy with the Church's economic concepts of the "just price" and anti-usury statutes, for they conflicted with the new capitalism, while the Church's spiritual dictates demanded complete obedience and self-abnegation. Furthermore, the Church at this time presented a dangerous contradiction. In dogma it was medieval, yet its highest officials, including even the Popes, were patrons of a Renaissance culture deriving its inspiration from pagan Greece and Rome.

Thus it was not simply that the Church stood in need of correcting its financial and moral abuses. The Church's ideals no longer commanded the same respect and allegiance among all the population. A soldier who had fought in the Hundred Years' War could not fail to realize that the names England and France had a new meaning for him, the merchant whose ships traveled to newly discovered lands and the banker whose loans made those journeys possible could not help rejoicing in their new economic independence, and the reader of books just off the recently invented printing press was going to have his traditional views challenged from new quarters. The ideal of the Middle Ages was otherworldliness; the ideal of the Renaissance was presentworldliness. The Church favored the first ideal. The rise of some leader with a religious message more compatible with the spirit of the new age was inevitable. It was also inevitable that when he arose he should use as his weapon not the incongruity of the Church's ideology, for that was a philosophical problem of which few were conscious, but rather the financial and moral abuses of the Church, of which almost everyone was aware. As we are about to see, the leader with the new message did arise, and he won his converts with the weapon which we have described.

The Religious Revolt

The revolt in Germany. The religious revolt began in Germany. Scholastic philosophy and the traditional faith were more firmly entrenched among the Germans than among the Italians. The burgher piously read his *Imitation of Christ,* written by a German mystic, Thomas à Kempis. He resented deeply the corrupt financial and moral abuses of the papacy. The invention of printing in the north had stimulated reading and critical scholarship among educated German people, with the result that they began to study the Scriptures very carefully and at the same time to criticize the ignorance of the German clergy.

The political situation in the German states also had a bearing on the religious question. Germany was divided into hundreds of states, lacking unity except for the nominal rule of the weak, elective emperor of the Holy Roman Empire. Therefore patriots could be expected to make use of a German religious revolt to further the cause of German nationalism at the expense of imperial power and an Italian-controlled Church. Nor must economic factors be overlooked. Trade and banking flourished in the fast-growing Rhenish towns. The Hanseatic League was prospering. The German burgher found no conflict between piety and profits. On the other hand, his piety and profits were both affected by the draining of German revenues by the Roman Church, especially when unscrupulous means were used to gather them. Germany was ripe for religious changes.

Martin Luther. On November 10, 1483, a poor German couple became the parents of a son, later baptized Martin Luther. In 1491 Hans, the father, joined a firm of copper miners. Twenty years later by virtue of thrift and hard work Hans Luther was a petty capitalist.

Martin was often given the rod that he might not be spoiled. He was also given a sound education which included university studies. He accepted as a matter of course the beliefs prevalent among the common people regarding witchcraft and other superstitions, with the result that to the end of his life Luther believed vividly in the existence of devils and witches. Indeed, the story goes that he once threw an ink pot at the devil, whom he thought he saw leering at him. In 1505 he became a member of the mendicant order of Augustinian monks, at first much to the disgust of his practical-minded father, who nearly disowned him. In 1508 he was given a temporary lectureship at the recently founded University of Wittenberg. Within a few years he had become professor of theology.

The next few years were epochal, not only in Luther's own life but also in the history of religious thought. He began to probe deeply the problem of eternal salvation. As we have seen in a previous chapter, the Church taught that salvation could not be gained without the good works prescribed by it. Luther felt that man was so depraved in God's sight that no amount of good works could possibly save him. One day, while contemplating the words of St. Paul's Epistle to the Romans, Luther found these words: "For therein is the righteousness of God revealed from faith to faith: as it is written, The just shall live by faith."[4] He felt that his problem was solved. Man was saved only by his faith in the validity of Christ's sacrifice, which alone could wash away sin. Luther had come to his famous doctrine of "justification by faith" as opposed to the Roman Church's "justification by sacraments and works."

The implications of his radical doctrine were enormous. If salvation could come only through a personal belief in Christ's sacrifice, then an interceding priesthood became superfluous, for each man would then be his own priest. But Luther himself had no idea as yet what his views meant or where they would eventually lead him and half of Christendom. It required a financial abuse of the Church, not a theological subtlety, to bring on the religious revolt.

Tetzel and the indulgences. Leo x, a cultured scion of the Medici family, "who would have made an excellent Pope if he had only been a little religious," wanted to complete the magnificent new Cathedral of St. Peter's in Rome. But money for the costly enterprise was lacking. Several papal agents were sent out to dispose of indulgences as a means of raising money. One of these agents, by the name of Tetzel, discharged his mission "in the German archbishopric of Mainz in a manner which would be recognized in America today as high-pressure salesmanship."[5]

The position of the Church in regard to indulgences has been much misunderstood. An indulgence never permitted a person to sin. Rather, it was a promise of remission of part or the whole of the penalty which a person must receive after death on account of his sins. The indulgence demanded that the sinner repent of his deeds and do some form of penance. The penitent had to perform good works by saying prayers, visiting shrines, or donating money for worthy ecclesiastical purposes.

The common people held a wrong view of the practice. Most of them could not read the language of the indulgence, and they thought that a payment of money was all that was required to escape both the temporal and eternal penalties of sin. Because Tetzel did nothing to enlighten the populace as to the true nature of indulgences but rather exhorted them to give liberally for themselves and for their dead relatives in purgatory who were "crying to them for help," Luther angrily questioned the validity of the whole system of indulgences.

Luther's ideas developed. In October, 1517, Luther, following a university custom, posted ninety-five propositions (theses) on the subject of indulgences on the church door at Wittenberg, at the same time challenging anyone to debate them with him. In so acting Luther was not just protesting the unscrupulous methods of Tetzel; he was questioning the whole philosophy of good works. Here are some of the more important theses:

"11. The erroneous opinion that canonical penance and punishment in purgatory are the same assuredly seems to be a tare sown while the bishops were asleep.

"21. Therefore those preachers of indulgences err who say that a papal pardon frees a man from all penalty and assures his salvation.

A woodcut depicts the issuing of letters of indulgence at a German market place in Martin Luther's time.

"28. It is certain that avarice is fostered by the money chinking in the chest, but to answer the prayers of the Church is in the power of God alone.

"43. Christians are to be taught that he who gives to the poor or lends to one in need does better than he who buys indulgences."[6]

The ninety-five theses were originally written in Latin. They were soon translated into the common tongue and by March, 1518, were quite well known throughout Germany. The Church at Rome did not seriously trouble itself at first. Heresy was anything but new, as the history of the Waldensians, Albigensians, Wycliffe, and Hus showed. But this particular "squabble among monks" (as Leo x dismissed the matter) did not subside. In 1519 Luther debated with an eminent Catholic theologian, Johann Eck, and conceded there that he believed a man could possess a direct relationship with God without the need of the Church's mediation. It was the same view for which Hus had been burned by the Council of Constance.

Luther now found himself propelled by circumstances and the implications of his philosophy to a position far removed from that of the Church. In 1520 he separated himself completely by publishing three pamphlets. In *An Address to the Nobility of the German Nation* he maintained that the priesthood was not sacred and that the nobles should free Germany from Roman control and take over the wealth and lands of the Church for themselves. *On the Babylonian Captivity* attacked

Martin Luther defies the Pope's decree by burning the papal bull while students and townsfolk applaud.

both the papacy and the sacramental system. A third pamphlet, *On the Freedom of a Christian Man,* set forth Luther's new views on salvation.

In June, 1520, the Pope issued the bull *Exsurge Domine,* which gave Luther sixty days to cease from his heretical course. If at the end of that time he had not confessed his errors, he was to be cut off from the Church and handed over to secular authorities for punishment. In December, 1520, Luther publicly burned the bull amid the applause of students and townsmen. The eyes of all the German people now turned in the direction of a man who had been suddenly transformed from an obscure monk into a prominent reformer and political figure.

Events of momentous importance now occurred in quick succession. On January 3, 1521, Leo x issued a bull of excommunication, and four months later the Diet of the Holy Roman Empire declared Luther an outlaw. Luther, however, was given protection by Frederick, elector of Saxony, at whose castle the reformer translated the New Testament into German, a literary feat of outstanding importance in the development of the German language.

Spread of Lutheranism in Germany. Very quickly the teachings of Luther swept through central and northern Germany. Pious persons who wanted the Church reformed saw good in the cause. Worldly individuals wanted to appropriate church lands and therefore aided the movement. Patriots who saw in the movement a chance to unite Germany backed Luther. Emperor Charles v, a Catholic, was too deeply involved in a war with Francis I of France to stamp out the new heresy. Finally, Luther's pamphleteering and active direction of his party led to a Lutheran triumph.[7]

The Peasants' War. In 1524, encouraged by Luther's movement, the German peasants revolted. Ground down by the nobles and wealthier classes, they demanded abolition of serfdom, payment in wages, and other improvements of their lot. Their grievances were legitimate and their demands reasonable. While the Catholic clergy appeared to be a main object of their wrath, Luther supported the peasants. However, when he saw that they were rising also against lay lords, many of whom were now espousing the principles of Luther, the reformer turned savagely on them and asked the princes to put down the peasants' revolt. "Therefore let every one who can, strike, strangle, stab secretly or in public, and let him remember that nothing can be more poisonous, harmful, or devilish than a man in rebellion."[8]

The revolt was stamped out in 1525 at a cost of about fifty thousand lives, and the lot of the German peasant for the next two centuries was probably the worst in Europe. Luther had become a false prophet to these serfs, and Lutheranism received a serious check. The conservatism of Luther, who felt that the equality of all men before God applied in spiritual but not in secular matters, made aliens of the peasants but allies of the princes.

Measures of the imperial Diet. The Diet of the Empire was composed of the seven electors, the lesser princes, and representatives of the free cities. The emperor was not supposed to do anything affecting the various states in the Empire without the approval of the body. At its meeting in 1526 the princes of Germany were divided into a Lutheran and a Catholic party. The legal status of the Lutherans was not settled at the meeting, but the Diet ordered that "each prince should so conduct himself as he could answer for his behavior to God and to the emperor."[9] In 1529 the Diet was told by the emperor that heresy must be uprooted. The Mass was not to be interfered with anywhere. This meant that, while Lutheran activities were restricted, those of the Catholics could be carried on even in Lutheran areas. The Lutheran leaders naturally dissented, drawing up a protest which said that they would adhere only to the law of 1526.

From such a protest arose the word Protestant.

The Diet, meeting in 1530 at Augsburg, was presented by Philip Melanchthon, the scholarly colleague of Luther, with a "reformed confession," called the Augsburg Confession. His document was a statement of Christian doctrine from the Lutheran viewpoint and was designed to conciliate the two parties. The Diet did not accept the confession, but it became the creed of the new faith.

Schmalkaldic Wars and the Peace of Augsburg. The emperor now made public his intention to crush the growing heresy. In defense the Lutheran princes banded together in the League of Schmalkalden in 1531, and from 1546 to 1555 sporadic civil war resulted. Finally in 1555 a compromise was reached through the Peace of Augsburg. This allowed each prince to decide the religion of his subjects, gave Protestants the right to keep all church property appropriated prior to 1552, forbade all sects of Protestantism other than Lutheranism, and ordered all Catholic bishops to give up their property if they turned Lutheran.

The implications of the provisions were great. For the first time in Christian history religious opinions became the private property of princes. The theories of political absolutism and the divine right of kings were thus given a strong impetus. Again, the Peace of Augsburg established Lutheranism as a state religion in large portions of Germany. Lastly, the new Protestantism did not bestow political or religious liberty on the individual. The individual had to believe what his prince wanted him to believe, be it Lutheranism or Catholicism. The Peace of Augsburg marks the real beginning of state religion, the natural ally of the new national political state now ripe for development throughout Europe.

The reference to Catholic property in the settlement was important, for it had been the cause of much bitterness. Following Luther's religious revolt many nobles accepted his teachings not because they necessarily believed them but because it gave them an excuse to seize the Church's property. Wholesale plundering of church lands enriched many a noble, and there was little prospect of peace until some arrangement suitable to both sides had been worked out. It was realized in the agreement of 1555, for the Protestant princes retained their hold on the lands they had already seized, while at the same time the Church was promised that the seizures would be discontinued.

The death of Luther. Meanwhile, the founder of the new faith died in 1546. Martin Luther had been a born leader, genius, bigot, and zealot. As Preserved Smith says, "His grandest quality was sincerity. Priest and public man as he was, there was not a line of hypocrisy or cant in his whole being."[10] His life was molded by the belief that he was absolutely right in his acts, which explains both his driving power and his intolerance. He put his trust in faith and not in the "harlot" reason. In this respect Luther represents a step backward in intellectual history to medievalism, a step far different from the one taken by such Humanists as Erasmus.

In closing our account of Luther and the gigantic movement which he set on foot, it is of interest to point out an irony of history. The money which was gathered for the purpose of creating for the universal Church a fitting capital in St. Peter's at Rome was the same money which destroyed the Church's universality. It is a strange capital which is built to glorify its own destruction. Only the Palace of Versailles, the symbol of absolutism in France, can equal this circumstance.

Lutheranism in Scandinavia. Lutheranism affected all the regions about the Empire. However, it established itself permanently only in Scandinavia. By 1560 Denmark established a national Church. The Augsburg Confession was adopted, the Bible was translated into Danish, and Catholic and Protestant dissenters of other sects were suppressed. Norway was at this time part of Denmark, and Lutheranism triumphed there also. Sweden, under Gustavus Vasa, rebelled against the union of the Scandinavian countries, and in 1523 Vasa became king of Sweden. During his rule (1523-1560) Protestantism was introduced; the religious change was interwoven with the nationalist cause. More than once it appeared possible during the sixteenth century that Catholicism might win back its lost power in Sweden, but Lutheranism triumphed. In 1593 the Confession of Augsburg was officially adopted by the Swedish Church, and in 1604 Catholics lost their property and offices.

Background of the English Revolt. The religious revolt in Germany arose principally because numbers of people were shocked by the moral and financial evils of the Catholic Church and because they were led by a fanatically religious leader. Therefore in Germany the revolt was primarily religious in nature, although it possessed political implications. In England the situation was reversed. True, there was an ecclesiastical revolt, but the leader was a king, not a commoner. Furthermore, he did not consider himself a Protestant but was proud of his title "Defender of the Faith"—that is, of Catholicism. Basically, moreover, the revolt was political in nature, with the religious implications of a secondary value.

The Anglican (English) revolt had its basis in the very history of the kingdom. England had lately gone through a bitter civil conflict, the Wars of the Roses. In 1485 a strong leader of the Tudor family mounted the throne, taking the title Henry VII. The king had a double aim: to make his family's position on the throne secure and to make England a strong national state. He was successful in his double aim for the following reasons: England was no longer a simple agricultural country. Lands were being enclosed for the purpose of sheep raising; at the same time, towns were springing up, and in them the wool from the sheep was made into cloth. Shipping developed as a logical sequence, for traders found a ready market on the continent for this growing export. Thus the bourgeoisie became increasingly stronger and wealthier. The landowners also became wealthy and sought to obtain by one means or another the rich lands which the Church had acquired through centuries of gifts and expansion. The Tudors, a new family looked down on by the old aristocrats, saw the future of England's power in the townsmen and landowners. Henry VII encouraged trade and peaceful pursuits, curbed the restless nobility, and thus became very popular with the bourgeoisie.

A national state must sooner or later clash with an international Church when the Church claims the right to interfere in the temporal affairs of the state. The brilliant and much-married Henry VIII, son of the first Tudor, embarked upon a policy designed to place the Church under the direct control of the monarch. In England there had been signs for several centuries that the English government as well as the people were getting more and more restive at papal control. We recall the quarrel of Henry II in the twelfth century with his archbishop, Thomas à Becket, over the jurisdiction of the royal courts over clerics who had committed crimes. Then in the reign of Edward I the famous Statute of Mortmain was designed to protect the interests of the overlord when land was alienated from the Church. The so-called provisor system especially irked the English people. It was an arrangement by which the Pope demanded the right to fill clerical positions in England with his own appointees, usually from Italy. One Pope demanded that three hundred positions be reserved for appointees selected from leading Roman families. Many of the papal appointees never even came to England but had substitutes, usually Englishmen, who did all the work, while they remained in Italy enjoying the revenues of their office.

Agitation against the papacy reached a high pitch in the fourteenth century. In 1351 the Statute of Provisors declared invalid all papal appointments to English church benefices, and the following year the Statute of Praemunire made illegal the carrying of suits to foreign courts. The papal court was not mentioned, but the statute was directly aimed against the practice of taking cases to that court. The Church seemed to be able to evade many of these restrictions. It continued to get more and more land. Its income was said to be greater in England alone than that of the English king, and all church officers were expected to send to Rome a payment called annates, which was equivalent to the income of their office the first year they held their post.

The religious revolt in England, then, was not a sudden growth but a movement that had been maturing for several hundred years. By the time Henry VIII came to the throne, the smallest happening could precipitate a crisis between the monarchy and the papacy. It is idle to discuss whether the Tudor king really deliberately planned the break from the Church. In the early phases of the revolt in England it seems likely that Henry had no intention of breaking from the Church if he could have his way on the divorce question we shall shortly discuss. Unlike the revolt in Germany, that in England had at its inception no quarrel with the doctrines of the Church. The Anglican revolt threw off the supremacy of the Pope without adopting the Protestant faith. The elements of Protestantism in the new Anglican Church crept in after the break with

Rome. The revolt centers about the private ambitions and amours of Henry VIII.

Henry VIII's quarrel with Rome. In his youth Henry was handsome and athletic, and his joviality made him beloved of the people. He was the second son of Henry VII, his older brother Arthur being the heir apparent. The crafty and miserly Henry VII had engaged Arthur to Catherine, the daughter of Ferdinand and Isabella of Spain. A large dowry was to be paid the Tudors with the marriage. Unfortunately Arthur died in 1502, shortly after his marriage to Catherine, and part of the dowry was left unpaid. Henry VII, wishing both the dowry and the alliance with Spain, then married Henry to Catherine. To this union six children were born, of whom only one, Mary, survived.

Then came the conflict in Henry VIII's mind. First of all, although legally Henry did not need a male heir, one was desirable if the newly established Tudors were to endure as a dynasty and England was to be spared another bloody War of the Roses. Thoughts may have assailed him that he had never properly been married to Catherine. She was the widow of his brother, and since the Church forbade a man to marry his brother's widow, a special papal dispensation for Henry's marriage had been required. Therefore, he may have feared that God in his displeasure had denied him a son. There was another reason for conflict in Henry's mind, a much more tangible reason. A young attendant in the queen's suite by the name of Anne Boleyn had attracted Henry, and it was not long before he sought her as his wife.

Henry asked Pope Clement VII to revoke the dispensation which had allowed him to marry Catherine. The Pope would gladly have acquiesced to Henry's wishes, for Henry had been a staunch supporter of the old faith in England. He had personally written a *Defense of the Seven Sacraments* (1521) in answer to Luther's pamphlet *On the Babylonian Captivity.* A fierce war of words had been waged between Luther and the king's supporters, Luther calling Henry "a damnable and rotten worm, a snivelling, drivelling swine of a sophist,"[11] and Sir Thomas More, representing Henry, complaining of the language of "this apostate, this open incestuous lecher, this plain limb of the devil and manifest messenger of hell."[12] At any rate, Henry's devotion to the Catholic faith had won him the title "Defender of the Faith," a title which the English kings still possess. But now the Pope, much as he wished, could not support Henry's desires for two reasons: It might be dangerous for one Pope to reverse the judgments of a predecessor, and, second, the emperor Charles V, the most powerful monarch in Europe, was a nephew of Catherine and threatened the Pope severely if he declared the marriage null and void. Clement decided to wait awhile before giving his answer, hoping in the meantime that events would take care of themselves.

Henry would not wait. His chief advisor, Cardinal Thomas Wolsey, who had served his king well for years, had now failed to obtain the all-important consent of the Pope. Angrily Henry vented his wrath upon the hapless official. Deprived of his office and disgraced, Wolsey died in 1530, barely escaping the headsman's ax. In 1531 he fined the English clergy a large sum of money on a mere technicality, compelling them to acknowledge the king as "their singular protector, only and supreme lord, and, as the law of Christ allows, even Supreme Head." He next had his Parliament cease sending annates to Rome and give him the power to appoint bishops in England without the Pope's permission. Henry now went further. He appointed as archbishop of Canterbury a willing tool named Thomas Cranmer, who was sure to do his master's bidding. Cranmer pronounced Henry's marriage to Catherine invalid. Immediately afterward Henry's marriage to Anne Boleyn was declared legal. Clement VII, at last goaded into action, excommunicated Henry and maintained that Catherine alone was the king's true wife.

Henry completely severed all connections with Rome in 1534. The *Act of Supremacy* stated that the king "justly and rightfully is and ought to be supreme head of the Church of England." Two of England's most gifted men, Sir Thomas More (author of the famous *Utopia)* and the saintly bishop John Fisher, were beheaded because they could not approve of Henry's assumption of so much authority over the Church. To gain popular approval, Henry suppressed the rich monasteries, giving much of the land to the willing landowners for their sheep raising, making them fellow conspirators. By 1539 all monastic houses were dissolved. That same year Parliament passed the *Six Articles,* which reaffirmed the main points of Catholic theology, and the Catholic who denied the supremacy of the king and the Protestant who denied the validity of transubstantiation were alike punished severely.

In all this development, Parliament took a leading role, enacting the several necessary laws.

Protestantism under succeeding rulers. After Henry's death in 1547 his frail son mounted the throne as Edward VI. During this reign England advanced toward a more definite Protestantism. The *Six Articles* were repealed. Through the efforts of Cranmer the *Book of Common Prayer* translated the old Latin service into English. Priests were no longer held to their vows of celibacy. Many religious works of art were destroyed. In 1553 the *Forty-Two Articles* defined the faith of the Church of England along Protestant lines. Under the devoutly Catholic Mary (1553-1558), the unfortunate daughter of the still more unfortunate Catherine of Aragon, England experienced a Catholic reaction, and hundreds of heretics, including Archbishop Cranmer, were put to death.

But with the accession to the throne of Anne Boleyn's red-headed and fiery-tempered daughter, Elizabeth (1558-1603), Protestantism was firmly and permanently reëstablished in England. Elizabeth astutely took the title "Supreme Governor" of the Anglican Church. Her *Act of Uniformity* (1559) made the acceptance of the revised Prayer Book obligatory. The *Thirty-Nine Articles* (three of the *Forty-Two Articles* passed in Edward's reign were deleted) stamped Protestantism upon the Anglican Church in their emphasis upon the Scriptures as the source of authority. To this day the *Thirty-Nine Articles* have remained the authoritative statement of Anglican theology. Elizabeth did not really care what her subjects believed inwardly, but they had to conform outwardly.

Calvinism. The most famous sixteenth-century Protestant leader next to Luther was John Calvin (1509-1564). A Frenchman of the middle class, Calvin studied theology and law at Paris, where he became interested in Luther's teachings. About 1533 he had what he called a "conversion," whereby he deserted Catholicism. When Francis I decided to persecute heretics, Calvin fled to Switzerland, finally taking up his abode at Geneva. There he spent the remainder of his life, acquiring complete political power by means of a constitution which made him the real ruler of the city. His constitution created a theocratic republic in which the administration of religion and politics were blended into one organization.

In 1536 he published his great work, the *Institutes of the Christian Religion*, unquestionably one of the most important books on systematic theology ever written. The definitive edition of 1559 contained his mature views on theology, the most famous being his theory of predestination. According to Calvin, God is omnipotent; He knows the past, present, and future. Therefore He must always know what men are to be saved by Him and what men are to be damned eternally. "And His act was purely arbitrary; He foreknew and predestined the fate of every man from the beginning; He damned and saved irrespective of foreseen merit."[13] Calvin maintained that the outward sign of a man's election to grace is his moral behavior. Therefore when Calvin came to dictatorial power in Geneva, he saw to it that every man's moral acts were judged vigorously. The city's 16,000 inhabitants were spied upon and punished for acts considered heretical or immoral by Calvin and the elders. During the years 1542-1546 the little town witnessed fifty-eight executions and seventy-six banishments. The theater was banned as immoral, bright colors in dress were forbidden, swearing and dancing were punished, and nobody was allowed to sit up in the inns after nine o'clock at night except spies. As Preserved Smith says, "Calvin also pronounced on the best sort of stoves and got servants for his friends. In fact, there was never such a busybody in a position of high authority before or since."[14]

Calvin punished with ferocity those holding religious views other than his own. One man wrote "all rubbish" on one of Calvin's tracts and was put on the rack twice a day, morning and evening, for a whole month. When Servetus, a scholarly Unitarian, fled to Geneva as a place of refuge, Calvin prosecuted him for heresy, saying that his defense was "no better than the braying of an ass, and that the prisoner was like a villainous cur wiping his muzzle."[15] Servetus was sentenced to be burned.

Yet despite his bigotry and self-righteousness Calvin possessed an austerity of spirit and power of mind which could not fail to influence religious thought. Calvinism made many converts in France, especially among the bour-

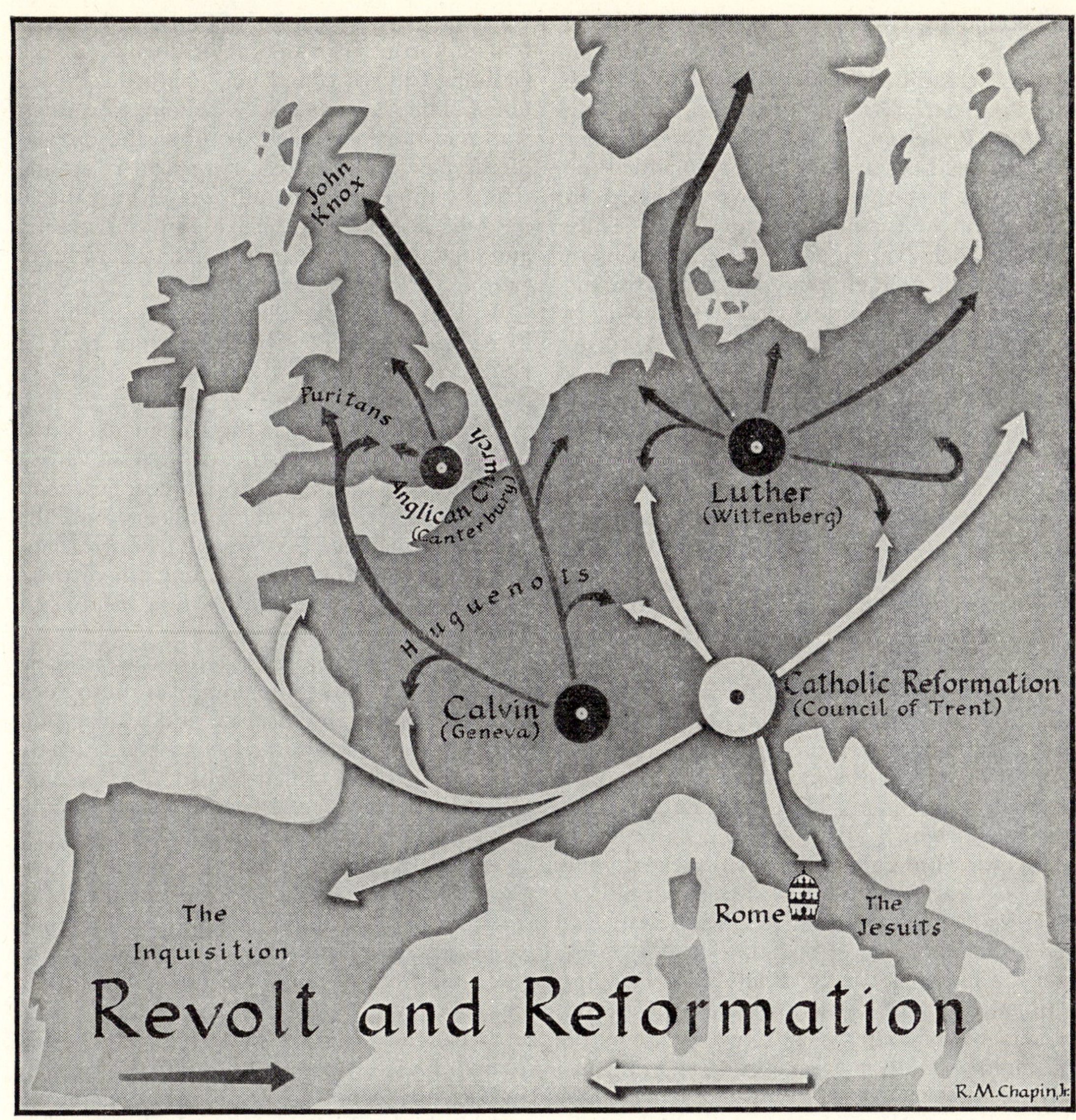

geoisie. The French Calvinists were known as Huguenots and comprised about three to five per cent of the total population. Later we shall see how the Huguenots became involved in French religious wars.

The spread of Calvinism. The teaching of Calvin came down the Rhine River to the northern Netherlands, where it was known as the Dutch Reformed religion. The fact that the Dutch fought for their independence against a Catholic king of Spain helped establish Protestantism in their country. Meanwhile in Scotland the authority of the old Church had been challenged. This was the work of John Knox, a zealous reformer who had made the acquaintance of Calvin in Geneva. He returned to Scotland and became leader of the Lords of the Congregation, a movement of Protestant nobles who desired to overthrow the established faith. In 1560 Knox drew up the Articles of the Presbyterian Church and, with the help of English troops, effected a religious revolution. In 1561 the beautiful but ill-fated Mary Stuart returned from France to her bleak kingdom, which was already alienated from her own Catholic views. Although she showed amazing skill and logic in her arguments with Knox, the fiery reformer carried the realm with him in his denunciation of the queen. By the time Mary had been defeated in battle and, after fleeing to England, had been executed by Elizabeth in 1587, Scotland had been won over to Calvinistic Presbyterianism.

Other Protestant sects. There were other men besides Luther and Calvin who aided the Protestant revolt. Calvin was preceded in Switzerland by a scholarly and sincere leader named Ulrich Zwingli (1484-1531). Even more than Luther, Zwingli placed his faith in the authority of the Scriptures alone. At the heart of the Swiss reformer's teaching was the principle that the Lord's Supper does not contain the miracle of transubstantiation but is merely a symbolic ceremony. In 1531 trouble broke out between the Catholics and the adherents of Zwingli, and in the civil conflict which ensued Zwingli and many of his followers were slain. But he had given an initial impetus to Protestantism in Switzerland.

There were other Protestant sects. An evangelical form of Protestantism known as Anabaptism flourished for a while in parts of Germany, Bohemia, and Holland. The Anabaptists believed that adults alone should receive baptism. They also favored social reforms and were involved in the Peasants' War. Some of them believed in a kind of primitive communism in which all governments would be swept away. In England Robert Browne (about 1550-1633) preached that Christians should be organized into individual democratic congregations for the purpose of following the Christian life more effectively. Thus arose Congregationalism. Meanwhile, owing to the efforts of Servetus (1511-1553) and two members of the Italian family Sozzini, the tenets of Unitarianism (in which the divinity of Christ and the reality of the Trinity were challenged) came to be spread abroad. While these various sects were never large in the number of their adherents, their effect on later religious thought was great.

The Catholic reformation. All the while the new movements were spreading, the Roman Catholic Church was on the defensive in the face of the growth of Lutheranism, Anglicanism, Calvinism, and the independent sects. But with the accession of Paul III to the papal throne in 1534 the ancient Church began to institute reforms, a policy which continued under the leadership of a group of earnest and able Popes. This Catholic reformation came to a peak in the Council of Trent (1545-1563). There a clear enunciation of Catholic doctrines was set forth. In no point of dogma did the Catholic Church compromise with the Protestants. The successors of St. Thomas Aquinas. who had done so much to shape the dogmas of the medieval Church, were firm in stating that the Bible and the traditions of the Church must be accepted as the basis of Christianity and that only the Church had the right to interpret these vital elements.

As proof of the fact that the Catholic Church in no wise departed from its age-old body of beliefs, the following reaffirms the validity of the sacramental system:

"If any one saith that the sacraments of the new law were not all instituted by Jesus Christ, our Lord; or that they are more or less than seven, to wit, baptism, confirmation, the eucharist, penance, extreme unction, orders, and matrimony; or even that any one of these seven is not truly and properly a sacrament; let him be anathema."[16]

At the same time drastic reforms were made in Church discipline and administration. Such evils as simony, absenteeism, and secular pursuits on the part of the clergy were strictly forbidden. The Council forbade prelates and other holders of ecclesiastical offices to aid their kinsmen at the expense of the Church:

"It strictly forbids them . . . to strive to enrich their own kindred or domestics out of the revenues of the Church; seeing that even the canons of the apostles forbid them to give to their kindred the property of the Church, which belongs to God; . . . yea, this holy Council, with the utmost earnestness, admonishes them completely to lay aside all this human and carnal affection towards brothers, nephews, and kindred, which is the seed plot of many evils in the Church."[17]

The Vulgate, the Latin Bible, was reissued in a new edition. A list of heretical and immoral books was prepared, known as the *Index*. The Inquisition, the court which tried heresy, was given fresh life in Italy and Spain.

The Jesuit order. Meanwhile a Spanish ex-soldier, Ignatius Loyola (1491-1556), founded an order in 1534 which had much to do with the revival of Catholicism in the latter half of the sixteenth century. The order, known as the Company of Jesus, took in addition to the three vows of chastity, obedience, and poverty a special vow of allegiance to the Pope. It was the Jesuits' purpose, by means of preaching and education, to win back converts to the Roman Church. They succeeded remarkably well. They recovered most of Poland, maintained Catholicism in Bavaria, the southern Netherlands (now Belgium), and Ireland, and performed excellent missionary work in North and South America, China, and India. Owing to their efforts and to the weight always lent by tradition, Italy, Spain, and Portugal remained loyally Catholic, France saw Protestantism checked, and Ireland, Poland, and Austria remained predominantly Catholic.

Effects of the Religious Upheaval

The religious division of Europe. Prior to 1500 there had been two religious divisions in Christendom—Greek Orthodox and Catholic (see map, page 260). Now in 1550 Christendom was composed of three divisions—Orthodox, Catholic, and Protestant. Protestantism had become uppermost in northern Europe, while Catholicism held sway in the south, as the map below shows, and in the Spanish and Portuguese possessions in the Americas and the Philippines. This great religious division had struck a mortal blow at medieval unity. The Catholics placed their faith in the infallibility of the Pope and the need of a mediatory priesthood. The Protestants placed their faith in the infallibility of the Bible and the ability of every Christian to win salvation with no mediation. The Protestants differed among themselves in their interpretation of the Bible and the methods of church organization; thus in time hundreds of Protestant sects arose, each claiming to possess the one and only true interpretation and logical administration.

The return to faith. Although the religious upheaval irreparably split the unity of Christendom and in so doing fostered the religious diversity of modern times, it also represented in many ways a return to medievalism. It was a great religious revival, a renewal of faith. After the Renaissance era of free and secular thought, of individualism and humanism, men's thoughts were turned again to salvation and the life hereafter. Free thought gave way once more to authority—for Protestants the Bible, for Catholics the Church. The Renaissance movement, having fostered doubt and criticism of medieval values, was now engulfed in a return to those values. Freethinkers were persecuted by both sides, and talented writers and thinkers who in Renaissance times might have followed the prevailing pattern of individualism and secularism now devoted their abilities to arguing one side or another of the burning conflict of the day.

Renaissance art was likewise affected. While Catholic churches were sometimes made more beautiful and sumptuous than ever in an effort to attract worshipers, in Protestant churches paintings and sculpture were banned as smacking of idolatry, and the elaborately beautiful Catholic musical service was replaced by the singing of simple hymns—often of great beauty in themselves.

Thus, temporarily at least, the Renaissance spirit was stifled. But it was to prove stronger than this intense return to medievalism and in the end to profit by the passing of the universal Church.

Achievement of reform. In addition to renewing the medieval ideal of faith, the religious upheaval brought about a great deal of genuine religious reform. In the new Protestant churches, born of the reform movement, abuses that had crept into the old Church were eliminated by simply eliminating the Church, with its hierarchy of officials and elaborate system of duties and rituals. The service of worship was simplified in an effort to return to the purity of early Christian times. Strict attention was given to conduct and morals. Within the Catholic Church a similar reform movement took place in answer to the Prot-

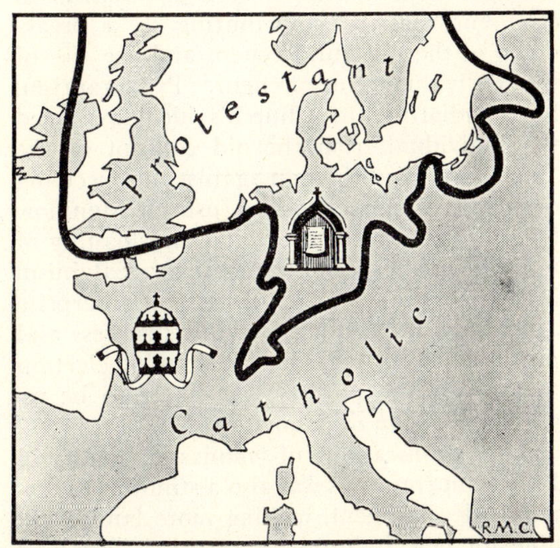

estant challenge, beginning, as we have seen, with the accession of Pope Paul III and culminating in the decrees of the Council of Trent. This movement changed neither doctrine nor organization but aimed at reaffirming and purifying both. In both Protestant and Catholic movements the revival of religious enthusiasm, raised to fever pitch by the conflicts between them, operated to restore religion to the all-pervading position it had held in medieval times.

Education stimulated. A by-product of the religious upheaval was a new interest in education. Each faith was concerned that its youth should be properly trained in its teachings. In particular the Jesuit order acted as a stimulus to education, developing, as part of its campaign to win Protestants back to the fold, a school system so superior and so attractive that many Protestant as well as Catholic youths attended. Protestant churches of the period developed nothing to compare with the Jesuit colleges and universities, but one feature of Protestantism did act eventually as a stimulus to education. This was its tenet that the one source of religious truth is the Bible. To find truth, therefore, one had to learn to read. This eventually acted as a stimulus for universal training in reading, which was to become one of the basic features of modern education.

Protestantism and capitalism. While religious developments in many ways fostered a return to medieval attitudes, in the economic sphere the opposite was true. We have noted earlier (page 489) that the Renaissance encouraged a new attitude of individualism in economic matters, contributing to a breakdown of the old guild system and the rise of the individual entrepreneur. Protestantism, by repudiating the Church's ideology, freed the individual from the old concept of the "just price" and the ban against the receiving of interest on money loaned (usury). Men now felt that investment of capital and loaning of money were respectable practices. Calvinism in particular encouraged thrift and enterprise as virtues, and among Calvinists success and prosperity were regarded as signs of election to grace, while poverty was likely to be regarded as a sign of damnation.

The confiscation of monastic lands in Protestant countries was also a stimulus to economic development, making more land available for new industrial enterprises. England in particular benefited from the use of former monastic lands and in the sixteenth century experienced rapid economic development. We have noted earlier that the business classes were among those who encouraged the revolt from Rome. We can now see that they were also among those who benefited by it most.

Growth of national churches. The religious division of Christendom was underlined by political division into Catholic and Protestant states. We have already seen how the English king assumed the headship of the Church in his kingdom, binding national church and national state together under a single head. Likewise in Germany the Peace of Augsburg gave the ruler of each state the right to decide the faith of his subjects, thus controlling the church in his realm. Similarly rulers of other countries, both Catholic and Protestant, developed national churches, so that Europe was divided religiously into an Anglican church, a French (Gallican) church, a Swedish church, a Spanish church, a church for each German state, and so on.

In many countries one effect of such division was to strengthen the hand of the king in building a unified state. The authority and prestige of the Protestant monarch was increased as he became the spiritual as well as political ruler of his subjects. Even in Catholic countries, though the Pope remained the spiritual ruler, the church became national in organization and sentiment, and it was the king rather than the Pope who enforced religious conformity among his subjects. On the other hand, in countries where the split between Protestants and Catholics was severe, as in the Empire, the effect was to limit the power of the ruler and impede national unity.

Persecution of minorities. Freedom of religion was as yet as far from reality as in the days before the Protestant Revolt. Church and state were firmly bound together and there was—ideally—but one church in a state. Protestants were persecuted in Catholic countries and Catholics in Protestant states. This was partly because of the intolerance engendered by the clash between faiths but even more because religious uniformity was the ideal of the rulers of the rising national states. Just as he sought to create a uniform system of law and justice throughout his realm, so the strong monarch endeavored to establish a single faith to which his subjects owed obedience. The ideal was aptly phrased by a French ruler of a later period—"One king, one law, one faith." An incidental result of this policy—often having important consequences—was the emigration of religious minorities to areas of religious freedom, particularly to the New World.

Influence of the national state. We can see, then, that the religious upheaval was intimately related to the outstanding political development of the period. The national state had made the international Church an anachronism. The day of the Pope as supreme arbiter of Europe was over. Instead he was forced to seek the aid of kings in waging his fight against the great Protestant heresy.

The "religious wars." Political and religious developments continued to be closely related throughout the sixteenth and early seventeenth centuries. In a series of "religious wars" political duels were superimposed on religious quarrels, resulting in some of the bloodiest and most prolonged warfare in human history. The founder of the Christian religion had given as a primary command, "Thou shalt love thy neighbor as thyself." But there was no brotherhood between Catholic and Protestant nor between political rivals who played on religious antagonisms to serve their own ends. The story of this sorry record of politico-religious warfare will be told in the next chapter.

Summary

Within the space of a few decades the religious unity of western Christendom, having endured almost unchallenged for centuries, was irreparably split by the Lutheran revolt and succeeding Protestant movements. The essence of the new movements was a denial of the need for church mediation as necessary for salvation (except in England) and repudiation of the Pope as head of the Church. The challenge thus flung at Catholicism was caught up by a new Catholic brotherhood, the Jesuits, whose militant proselytism recovered much of Europe for the Catholic fold. Also, under Pope Paul III and his successors the Church energetically combatted the Protestant movement.

There was no hope, however, of reuniting Europe within the Catholic fold. Protestants and Catholics clashed, with bitterness, passion, and bloodshed. In addition, religious issues became entangled with political quarrels and were often used as spiritual justification for worldly and sometimes unworthy causes. After the Reformation the church became national in organization and outlook, enhancing royal power and national unity wherever one faith was triumphant. Thus national state triumphed over international church. Within the state there was but one legal faith, and dissenters were persecuted relentlessly.

After the Renaissance era of tolerance and freedom of action and thought, Europe was plunged into an epoch of intolerance and bigotry from which she emerged only slowly, when after prolonged and bloody struggle it became apparent that no one faith could exterminate the others. But if the clock was thus set back in some ways for a time, in many ways the religious upheaval furthered the transition from a medieval to a modern pattern of life. The revolt from the universal Church shattered the medieval pattern of unity and gave us the religious diversity of the modern world. The challenge to authority implicit in that revolt, while dormant through a long period of conflict, eventually strengthened the Renaissance spirit of doubt and questioning and encouraged the development of tolerance and reason. The impetus to capitalism furthered a potent force in the shaping of modern economic life, while the strengthening of the national state contributed to what is perhaps the most characteristic institution of modern times.

Chapter 19

Chronology of events and developments discussed in this chapter

Spanish tolerance subsided; replaced by the Inquisition	1450
Wars of the Roses: Henry VII, first Tudor king	1455-1485
Italian Wars: first phase; rise of power politics; French evicted from Italy	1494-1514
Epitome of Venetian power; Italy not unified	1500
Charles V: vast holdings were neither compact nor unified	1500-1558
League of Cambrai: the Pope, Spain, Holy Roman Empire, and France defeated Venice	1508
Holy League: Pope, Venice, Spain, Switzerland, Holy Roman Empire, and England against France	1511
Italian Wars: second phase; Francis I defeated	1521-1544
Sweden under Vasa gained independence from Denmark	1523
Battle of Pavia: French army routed	1525
Rule of Philip II: aims: absolute power, suppression of heresy, extension of Spanish influence	1556-1598
Civil war in France: political and religious motivation	1562-1595
Eighty Years' War: Dutch won independence from Spain	1568-1648
Ottoman sea power defeated at Lepanto	1571
Portugal came under the rule of Spain	1580
Defeat of the Spanish Armada: indicative of decline of Spanish power	1588
Treaty of Vervins: settlement between England and Spain in French civil war	1598
Edict of Nantes: more than one religion could exist in a state	1598
James I: arbitrary taxation and Catholic sentiments led to English revolt	1603-1625
Thirty Years' War: religious, political, and property issues; Peace of Westphalia	1618-1648
Petition of Right: Parliamentary consent to tax; no imprisonment without cause	1628
English civil wars	1642-1660
Puritans (Roundheads) defeated the king's forces	1642-1646
Charles I executed; England a Commonwealth under Cromwell	1649
Commonwealth replaced by Instrument of Government; *Cromwell still ruled*	1653
Peace of the Pyrenees: French triumph over Spain	1659
Restoration of the exiled Stuart; king had to act through Parliament	1660

Powers and power politics emerge in the West

The political revolt: 1500 to 1650

With the religious movements initiated by such leaders as Luther, Calvin, and Henry VIII, the pattern that had characterized the Middle Ages came to an end. Gone was the religious unity of the western world with its obedience to the Pope and to the Church Universal. Religious unity gave way to bitter rivalries, and the Pope, no longer head of a universal Church, saw the heads of states—kings and princes—assume the headship of state churches. At the same time, and usually intimately connected with the struggle between Protestantism and Catholicism, momentous changes were taking place in the field of European politics. Thus the dissolution of *religious* unity was enmeshed with that institution which shattered the tradition of *political* unity—the national state.

In Chapter 16 we saw that the growth of national states began as early as the eleventh century, and that by the end of the fifteenth century strong dynastic states had been created in England, France, Portugal, Spain, and elsewhere. These budding nations—ancestors of the modern nation-state—differed from their own feudal ancestors in three fundamental features: a strong and effective central government, increasing national consciousness among the people, and sovereignty, that is, the claim of a state to possess supreme power limited by no other authority. The appearance of these strong sovereign states produced an essentially new political system. The feudal system was giving way to the national state system.

The century and a half following 1500 constitutes a period of crucial importance in the development of international relations. As a few strong sovereign states replaced the innumerable weak feudal units, these new states had to work out some kind of power relationship among themselves. Would one state be able to dominate all the rest? Would there be wide differences in the power exercised by various states without any one becoming all-powerful? Would the various independent and sovereign states be able to work out some pattern of cooperation, thereby insuring a goodly measure of peace and political amity in the western world? Now that the Religious Revolt had ended the role of the Church as a universal agency with power and authority in every phase of life, the Church could no longer pose as the arbiter of right and justice in disputes between secular rulers. The sovereign state was now untrammeled. Its rulers were completely free and uncontrolled in the arena of politics. Would they exercise some kind of restraint and develop among themselves some moral basis for the conduct of statecraft? These were some of the fundamental questions that were answered by the unfolding of history from 1500 to 1650. And the way in which they were answered in that period has set the pattern of international relations from that day to this.

As the narrative of this chapter will show, these questions were not argued by reason or cooperative good will but rather by bloodshed and force. The hundred and fifty years following 1500 are among the bloodiest in European history. They form an era often referred to as the period of the Religious Wars, for the religious issues which flamed forth from the Protestant upheaval colored every political conflict. Sometimes the alliance between religious and political factions was genuine and well-intentioned. Often, however, religion was a convenient device used by ambitious rulers to hide their desires for more territory, for dynastic glory, or for destroying the power of their rivals. Aristocratic nobles and solid members of the middle class also engaged in many a so-called religious struggle merely to seize wealth and land from some well-to-do neighbor.

All of this is not to say that the Religious Wars were without religious significance, for there were many men who fought and died for their faith. But such men were often the unconscious tools of leaders who pulled the strings of history for their own selfish interests. In some of the early wars of this period religion and politics were closely entwined. As the period played its course, however, the final struggle—the Thirty Years' War—ended with some contestants openly fighting for political and economic advantage.

Out of these conflicts emerged the political fabric of modern Europe. An understanding of how this came about requires a careful survey of the following wars: the struggle between the French royal house and the Spanish-Austrian Hapsburgs for control of Italy, the Schmalkaldic Wars between Protestant and Catholic factions in Germany, the struggle for Dutch independence, Elizabethan England's conflict with Spain, the struggle waged by western Europeans against the Ottoman Turks, the French Wars of Religion, the Thirty Years' War, and the English civil wars.

Much of the material we are now to consider has to do with battles, alliances, and treaties—in a word, drum-and-trumpet history. We may well raise the question: What has this to do with the development of our modern civilization? The answer is that the way men have managed their political affairs has had tremendous effects on the culture of mankind. It is not too much to say that the supreme challenge of the twentieth century lies within the realm of politics—how not to duplicate the tragedy of two world wars

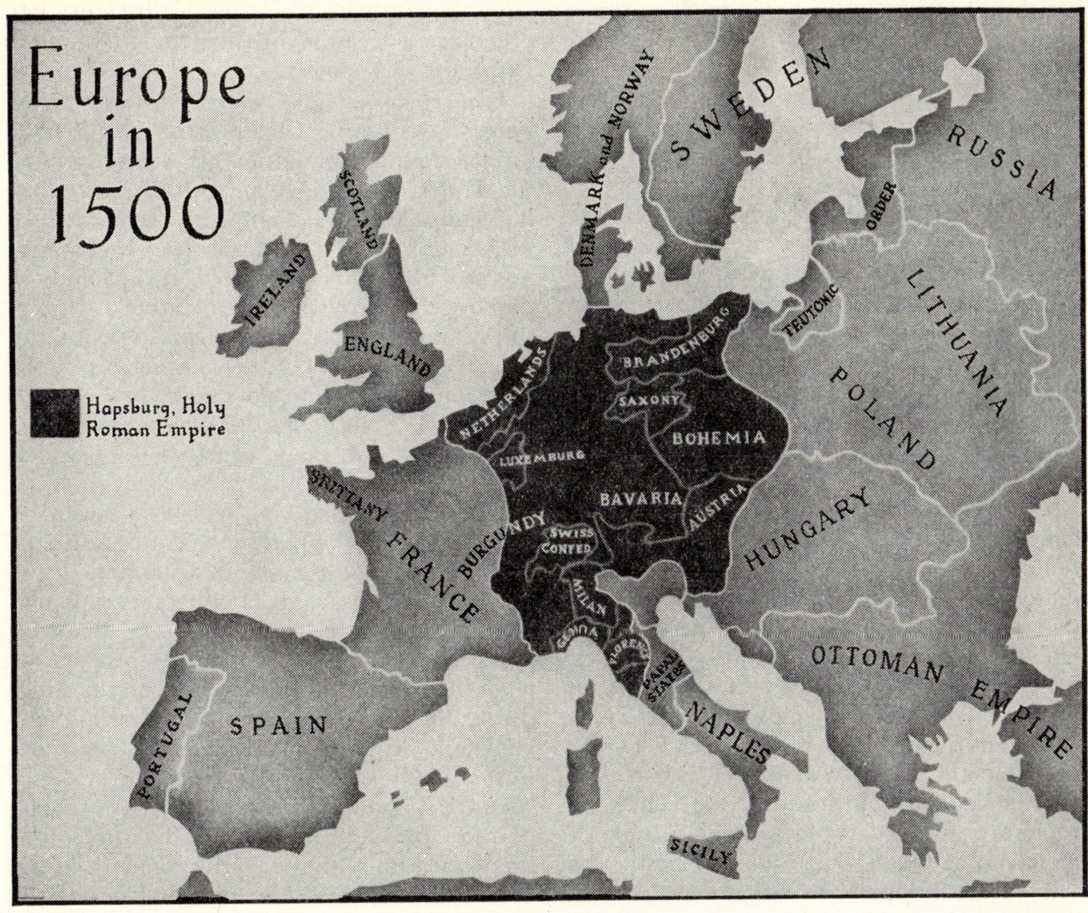

within a single generation; and how, rather, to insure cooperation and harmony among the peoples of the world.

Perhaps one of the best ways of studying this political challenge of our own generation is to go back to the period when present-day diplomatic practices were born, when rulers first began to play the modern game of the "balance of power," and when statecraft began consciously to follow the maxims of the cynical Italian diplomat, Machiavelli.

The Sovereign State and Power Politics

Before we consider the nature of European politics in the period from 1500 to 1648 it is necessary to have a bird's-eye view of sixteenth-century Europe—to discover what dynasties were ruling in the various countries and how far their kings had succeeded in building up strong, national monarchies.

England under Tudor rule. As the fifteenth century closed, England had just emerged from the Wars of the Roses, which had kept the country in intermittent turmoil from 1455 to 1485 (Chapter 16). What the people now wanted above all was order, peace, and a strong government. The words which Shakespeare gives to Henry Tudor following his victory on the battlefield of Bosworth express the nation's deep desire for tranquility:

Abate the edge of traitors, gracious Lord,
That would reduce these bloody days again,
And make poor England weep in streams of
blood!

Let them not live to taste this land's increase
That would with treason wound this fair
land's peace!
Now civil wounds are stopp'd, peace lives
again:
That she may long live here, God say amen![1]

Victory at Bosworth had secured the throne for Henry VII and inaugurated the rule of the Tudors in England. This dynasty, in its century-long rule, was to give the nation efficient centralized government, break away from the papacy and establish a new national Anglican Church (Chapter 18), found English colonial and maritime enterprise (Chapter 20), and defy successfully the strongest power in Europe—Spain.

It was the solid, if uninspiring and unromantic, work of Henry VII that laid the foundation for Tudor greatness. Henry made himself powerful. His benevolent tyranny was supported by the people because his strong hand was directed against the nobles. Henry made the Court of Star Chamber an instrument to crush rebellious barons. This court put the nobility in the power of the king, for the trials were secret, swift, and without benefit of juries. Because Henry restored law and order and promoted trade at home and abroad, the Tudor dynasty was built primarily upon the support of the middle class. Henry VII and his successors were careful to work through Parliament, and thus their strong, almost absolute rule met with little opposition.

In foreign as in domestic affairs Henry VII set precedents for his successors, following a policy of shrewd diplomacy. He desired above all to secure international recognition for his dynasty. To that end he secured an alliance with powerful Spain, marrying his eldest son Arthur to Catherine, the daughter of Ferdinand and Isabella. (It was Catherine of Spain who, becoming the wife of Henry VIII after Arthur's early death, was the center of the divorce question which precipitated the English break from the Roman Church [Chapter 18].) Henry also married his daughter Margaret to James IV, the Scottish king, a marriage that led ultimately—in 1707—to the union of the two kingdoms of Scotland and England.

The first Tudor was niggardly in his expenditures and managed to exact large sums from the rich barons. At his death Henry left "the richest treasury in Christendom"—and a rising national power.

France, growing in territory and royal power. Across the Channel the kingdom of France was consolidating her strength after the Hundred Years' War with England that had ended in 1453. France had achieved victory in this long struggle largely because power had been concentrated in the hands of the king; the French representative assembly, the Estates-General, had lost prestige, for the people had obtained their leadership from the monarchy. Even more than in England, the king in France presided over a centralized government, the main instrument of which was his Council. During the struggle with England the French king had been given the right to levy an important tax, the *taille,* to provide revenue to maintain a standing army. Following the peace this tax became a permanent arrangement, giving the king financial independence. Within France proper all lands had come under the rule of the king, the most recent important territorial gain being the acquisition of the important province of Brittany in 1491.

On the frontiers, however, the strategic position could be improved. To the south, French territory did not quite come up to the Pyrenees, the best mountain frontier in Europe. In the north and east the frontier did not coincide with "natural boundaries" and in certain cases came too close to the French capital for safety. France was to fight many wars in early modern times to improve these boundaries for her own strategic advantage.

All in all, France, under the Valois dynasty, entered the modern period a strong and compact state. Her population was relatively large—sixteen million as compared with England's four and a half million. And although industry was as yet undeveloped compared to that in the Netherlands and in Italy, France had a rich soil and produced immense quantities of grain and wine. Economic prosperity and political unity were to enable France to play an important role in European politics.

Absolutism in Spain. In an earlier chapter (Chapter 16) we surveyed the Christians' gradual reconquest (the *Reconquista*) of Spain from the Moors. Until the middle of the fifteenth century there had been much tolerance and love of liberty among the Spaniards. The people prided themselves upon their local assemblies, the *cortes.* The *cortes* of Castile possessed large powers in finance and lawmaking, while that of Aragon was even more independent of the royal government, for in it the nobles had the right of renouncing their allegiance to the crown and no laws were valid without the sanction of the *cortes.* The independent spirit of the nobles in Aragon is well shown by their oath of allegiance to the king:

"We, who are as good as you, swear to you, who are no better than we, to accept you as our king and sovereign lord, provided you observe all our liberties and laws; but if not, not."[2]

But much of the easy-going tolerance and love of liberty had declined after 1450. An absolute and centralized monarchy ruthlessly enforcing religious orthodoxy took their place. There were several reasons for this fundamental change. The people felt a national pride in the monarchy that had united their land, helped to discover the New World, and finally conquered the Moors. The long struggle of seven hundred years ending with the conquest of Granada did much to stimulate religious fanaticism and racial intolerance.

For centuries there had been a great deal of crime and disorder in the country. The people turned to Ferdinand and Isabella, the first monarchs of a united Spain, for strong government, just as Englishmen looked to the Tudors for order and tranquility. The Spanish monarchs, therefore, did not find it difficult to erect the most absolute government in Europe. Monarchical power was based upon a competent system of councils staffed by a well-trained civil service, an army that had no equal in Europe, and the Inquisition, an agency that was used both to enforce religious orthodoxy and to strengthen the power of the king. It may be noted that any wealth of a convicted heretic was divided between the government and the inquisitors of the Church, two thirds to the former and one third to the latter. Ferdinand's zeal in persecuting heretics was undoubtedly influenced by economic greed, and the Pope at one time protested against his harsh treatment of Jews, declaring that the King was moved "by ambition and greed for earthly possessions"[3] rather than Christian zeal.

It was this strong royal absolutism, plus the acquisition of territories, such as the Netherlands, Portugal, and Naples, that was to make Spain in the sixteenth century the strongest power in Europe.

Portuguese independence endangered by Spain. The glory of Portugal belonged mainly to the first half of the sixteenth century. The monarchy had gained great renown from its patronage of geographical exploration, and its East Indian possessions brought much wealth to Lisbon. Portugal, however, was too small to exploit these overseas possessions. It was the aim of her kings to gain the Spanish throne through matrimonial alliances and thus unite the Iberian peninsula under the leadership of the Portuguese ruling house. Such marriages were made, but the outcome was that the Spanish monarchy claimed and gained Portugal in 1580.

Cities flourish in the Low Countries. On the continent, just north of France fronting the North Sea, were the Low Countries, an area that today consists of Holland, Belgium, and the Grand Duchy of Luxemburg. Much of the land level of what is now Holland was below sea level, and as far back as 1000 A.D. continuous efforts had been made to build dikes, pump out the salt water, and reclaim the land. This battle of the dikes has well been called the "conquest of the water."

In the seventeen provinces of the Low Countries town life had reached a level unrivaled in its day. Commerce and industry supported such cities as Ghent, Bruges, Ypres, Antwerp, Brussels, Haarlem, and Rotterdam. These cities were among the richest in the world, for there opulent burghers managed their thriving businesses, helped to build civic buildings of great beauty, and patronized the arts.

The rise and fall of Burgundy. During the Middle Ages the dukes and counts of the various small states in the Low Countries had become practically independent. Early in the fifteenth century, however, nearly all the small political units were brought under the rule of Philip the Good, duke of Burgundy—the first time they had been united. Philip, a statesman of far vision, established his residence in Brussels, which became the capital of the unified Low Countries. In this city he supported one of the most brilliant courts of his day, even excelling that of the king of France.

Duke Philip patronized the arts, and the University of Louvain, the first in this region, became famous for its advances in science. Important reforms were made in governmental administration—a uniform system of justice was introduced, the currency was reformed, and a standing army was supported. It appeared likely that a flourishing middle kingdom between France and Germany might be erected by the dukes of Burgundy.

All hope in this direction was blasted by the impetuosity of Charles the Bold, sometimes called the Rash. The ambition of this ruler was boundless and in his mind loomed the grandiose plan of establishing a middle state from the North Sea to the Mediterranean. Charles was a brave soldier but a poor general and statesman. He wasted the riches left by his father and made himself hateful to his subjects because of his tyranny. At the crest of his power he suffered a series of defeats at the hands of the Swiss and finally lost his life on the battlefield in 1477. The Duchy of Burgundy then came into the possession of the French king, the rival of the Burgundians. Thus began the rupture of the unified Low Countries.

The history of the Low Countries is of special importance in the sixteenth century, for it came to play a pivotal part in the rivalries of European diplomacy. Furthermore, the failure of the dukes of Burgundy to set up a strong middle kingdom that might have acted as a buffer between France and Germany was to have important consequences from the sixteenth century down to the present.

Autonomous Switzerland. Little Switzerland was a mountainous oasis of sturdy independence in central Europe. The mountaineers of this little land had successfully defied their overlords, the Hapsburgs, and had formed a loose league of autonomous cantons. The population was only half a million. Agriculture was carried on only with difficulty and industry was of little importance. Swiss towns in consequence were of secondary significance, Basel and Zurich being the most important urban centers. The Swiss had a surplus of men and developed the profitable trade of supplying hardy soldiers as mercenaries to various European rulers.

Sweden wins independence. The Scandinavian peoples were on the fringe of Europe's economic activities. Raw materials were exported and in return manufactured products were imported. In general, however, the middle class was not so wealthy or influential as in France, Italy, England, or the Low Countries. The total population of Norway, Denmark, and Sweden was only one and a half million.

The Scandinavians were closely related to each other in ancestry and culture but were never effectively united. To be sure, the three kingdoms had been joined in 1397 in the Union of Calmar under a common Danish monarch, but this union was not popular.

The Swedes in particular were restless, and when the Danish king tried to make their country really subject to Denmark, revolt followed. In 1520 resistance was strengthened by the Massacre of Stockholm, an incident in which the Danish king executed eighty-two Swedish patriots. The struggle against Denmark was sparked by a courageous leader named Gustavus Vasa, who was elected king of Sweden in 1523. The new national leader was able to expel all Danish political influence from his country. Gustavus Vasa is an excellent example of the strong monarch who was appearing in such countries as England, France, and Spain. To help meet the government's financial needs, Gustavus confiscated the lands of the Catholic Church, introduced Lutheran doctrine, and placed the new Lutheran Church under the state.

Denmark continued to rule Norway down to the nineteenth century and might have been the leading power in Scandinavia. It was Sweden, however, which, led by its brilliant ruling family—the Vasas—was to play an important part in early modern European history. In fact, for a brief space in the seventeenth century Sweden was to be a first-class military power.

Italy divided. Italy at the close of the fifteenth century was the home of one of the most remarkable cultural developments in the history of the western world—the Renaissance. Her painters, architects, and humanists amazed and inspired men throughout Europe. Italian cities were among the most advanced in Europe; a flourishing urban culture was supported by flourishing commerce and industry. Italy had one of the largest populations in Europe, her people totaling about thirteen million. Yet despite these great advantages,

Italy during the next three centuries was to be the victim of European power politics, her land frequently invaded, her people ruled by the foreigner.

The reason for this sad state of affairs was the political disunity of the Italian people. While well-organized national states were developing in other parts of Europe, the Italian peninsula remained divided into a number of separate and often antagonistic city-states. Five of these states were of special importance.

Venice, a little republic known as "the Queen of the Adriatic," was at the height of her power about 1500. The most powerful city-state in Italy, long the possessor of the best fleet in Europe, Venice was approaching the days of her decline. Geographical explorations were opening up new trade routes to the Indies, thus weakening the Venetian predominance in trade with the East. And in a war waged against the Turks from 1463 to 1479 the Venetians had lost their control of the eastern Mediterranean.

Milan, next in wealth to Venice, was located in the fertile plain of Lombardy. To the north were the important passes of Brenner, Splügen, and St. Gothard, through which went a steady stream of goods to northern Europe. Milan was famous for her manufactured wares, especially silks, woolens, velvets, and weapons. The population of this city state was approximately one million, about half that of Venice.

Florence was regarded as the center of Italian art and culture. This city-state of three-quarters of a million people was famous for her rich bankers and for the manufacture of silks and brocades. While some of the Italian city-states, such as Milan, were ruled rather harshly by soldier-despots, in Florence the people were kept in hand more subtly by the money and diplomacy of the Medici family, who were the "political bosses" of the city.

The Papal States extended from fifty miles south of the mouth of the Tiber to the northeast across Italy as far as the mouth of the Po River. This political unit, ruled by the Pope, was poorly organized. Hampered by lack of hereditary rule, the Popes found it difficult to force their will upon various petty despots who ruled over small subject states and defied the political authority of the Popes. In the sixteenth century the Popes made an aggressive attempt to reëstablish their authority. Although the head of a great spiritual organization, the Pope at the same time was the secular ruler of a political unit in central Italy. As such the various Popes felt obliged to participate in Italian politics, to make treaties, hire armies, and wage wars. Where Italian politics was concerned the Popes acted little differently from the rulers of the other city-states.

The kingdom of Naples covered the southern half of the Italian peninsula. Once this kingdom had included the island of Sicily, but in the fifteenth century this connection was broken, Naples going to a branch of the house of Aragon and Sicily and Sardinia to Ferdinand of Aragon, ruler of all Spain. The Neapolitan kingdom differed from the rest of Italy, for its industry was insignificant and most of its towns were unimportant. The nobles were rebellious and brigandage was rampant. The social and economic backwardness of Naples, in contrast to north and central Italy, was to last even into modern times.

Phantom power of the Holy Roman Empire. As in Italy, political development in the Holy Roman Empire ran counter to the trend toward national unification. The Empire had long been the symbol of peace and unity in Europe, but by 1500 its power was a pathetic pretense. More than half of Europe was outside its borders, and within the Empire the emperors had little power over the many duchies, counties, baronies, and free cities of which it was composed. The Empire had no imperial treasury, no effective central administration, and no standing army.

Since 1273 the imperial crown had usually been held by the Hapsburgs (as we have seen in Chapter 16), who secured their power not from the empty imperial title but by virtue of holdings in eastern Europe. Commenting on his position as emperor of the Holy Roman Empire, Maximilian of Hapsburg once jokingly declared:

> "I am a king of kings, for no one regards himself bound to obey me; while the King of Spain is a king of men, since men, though they raise objections, render him obedience; and the King of France is like a king over animals, for no one ventures to dispute his authority."[4]

We shall see later, however, that the Hapsburgs had unusual success with marriage diplomacy, a series of matrimonial alliances giving them control over a number of important territories, such as Bohemia, Hungary, and the Netherlands.

The disunity of the Holy Roman Empire did not prevent some of its constituent political parts from developing strong, centralized governments. Since the Empire could not give unity and efficient administration to the Germanies, the rulers of various small states, such as Brandenburg, Bavaria, and Saxony, administered law and order to their own subjects. Far in the future, Brandenburg was to become the nucleus of the state of Prussia, which was ultimately to unite the Germanies. Thus a part of the Empire was to weld the whole into a strong union.

Royal power declines in eastern Europe. Generally speaking, the political trend in eastern Europe was also opposite to that we have observed in countries like France and England. In Bohemia, Hungary, and Poland the monarchy declined in power, hampered by its elective character and by powerful nobles who were too much interested in maintaining their own powers and quarreling among themselves to perceive the advantages of a strong monarchy and a cohesive state. In eastern Europe the middle class was relatively weak; urban culture was far behind that of Italy, France, and the Netherlands; and commerce and industry were backward. Under an unrestrained nobility the peasants in these countries were even more oppressed than their contemporaries in western Europe.

The discontent of the peasantry and the ineffectiveness of the central government in these countries offered the Ottoman Turks an invitation to conquest in the sixteenth century. As the fifteenth century closed, the Turks were under the aggressive and capable Sultan Selim. This Turkish ruler defeated Persia, conquered both Syria and Egypt, and at his death was planning an attack on the strategic island of Rhodes. Led by Suleiman, the Turks, as we shall see later in this chapter, played an important part in European affairs in the sixteenth century.

Russia was culturally isolated from western Europe until the seventeenth century (see Volume II). Politically and economically she was backward, under the tempestuous rule of tsars more tyrannical than any of their contemporary rulers.

The formative period of international relations. While certain areas, such as Germany, Italy, and eastern Europe, lagged behind England, France, and Spain, well-organized national governments were by 1500 becoming a feature of European politics. And having consolidated their power at home, rulers were in a position to interest themselves in foreign affairs. The sixteenth century was the formative period for the behavior pattern of the modern nation in international affairs. We must now turn to Italy for a prophetic idea of how the nascent nations were to act toward each other.

As the fifteenth century drew to a close Italy was generally peaceful. Her city-states were in rough political balance, with Milan, Florence, and Naples on one side and Venice and the Papal States on the other. While insuring peace at home, this political balance did not give protection from invasion by outside powers. The first to seize the opportunity was France.

The Italian Wars begin. Charles VIII came to the French throne in 1483. His predecessors, especially Louis XI, had done their work well; France was a powerful, well-organized state. Charles was really a rather insignificant figure but he had grandiose notions of imitating the exploits of Alexander the Great, Hannibal, and Charlemagne. Though there was still much to do at home in promoting industry and improving the system of government, Charles thought of these matters as too mundane and dull.

Italy was rich and defenseless, and the prospect of little fighting and much loot was too great a temptation. To make his project look somewhat respectable, the French king talked about restoring the liberties of Florence and, in turn, those of the people of Naples. To this role of self-chosen Italian liberator, Charles added hints of a plan to lead a great crusade against the Ottoman Turks in Constantinople.

Claiming to be the rightful ruler of the kingdom of Naples, the French king made plans for his invasion of Italy. The neutrality of England was insured by payment of a large sum to Henry VII, the parsimonious Tudor king, while the emperor of the Holy Roman Empire was persuaded to look the other way by the cession of districts seized by Louis XI from the House of Burgundy. King Ferdi-

In this illustration by Erhard Schoen of a sixteenth-century camp is shown the casual, homey character of warfare.

nand of Spain agreed not to interfere in Charles' Italian plans in return for the cession of two small but valuable territories on the eastern side of the Pyrenees.

Believing his diplomatic fences to be intact, Charles crossed the Alps into Italy with much fanfare in the fall of 1494. At first the expedition was little more than a holiday. Charles was at the head of thirty thousand well-trained troops, and his mounted French knights, Swiss pikemen, and new light, quick-firing cannon could not be matched by any force in Italy. In Florence the Medici fled before Charles and his army, and in their wake was set up the republic of Savonarola, which we noted in Chapter 17. With little opposition the French army then marched on to Naples and took possession of the kingdom.

This easy conquest, however, alarmed other rulers in Europe. Ferdinand of Spain suspected that Charles might next try to conquer Sicily, and the emperor of the Holy Roman Empire was uneasy at the prospect of French dominance in Italy. Venice feared for her independence. The consequence was the formation of a league, the members of which were Venice, the Papal States, the Holy Roman Empire, and Spain. Ferdinand and the emperor had no compunctions over repudiating their promises to Charles VIII. This new league threatened to cut the French army off from its base of supplies at home. A hard battle had to be fought in northern Italy against the league's army before Charles was able to get back to France. Despite a brilliant beginning, Charles, to quote a contemporary observer, had gained only "glory and smoke" in Italy.

Following the death of Charles VIII in 1498, his successor, Louis XII, proceeded to claim both Naples and the Duchy of Milan. Louis paved the way for another Italian adventure by making an alliance with the papacy and Venice and renewing treaties with England and Spain. In 1499 French troops again crossed the Alps and occupied Milan.

Ferdinand of Spain thereupon proposed to Louis that their joint forces should attack the kingdom of Naples. Against this coalition there was little resistance, and Naples was conquered. But the victors quarreled over the spoils. In the fighting that followed, the French were defeated and Ferdinand took possession of Naples. For the time being, however, the French king held on to Milan.

The League of Cambrai formed against Venice. Venice was the next victim in what was becoming ruthless statecraft. This city-state was envied by its neighbors for its power and wealth. In addition, the Pope desired to regain some of the lands formerly part of the Papal States that had been conquered and seized by the Venetians.

In December 1508 the League of Cambrai was formed to wage war on Venice. It was supported by Pope Julius II, Ferdinand of Spain, the Emperor Maximilian, and Louis XII of France. The true purpose of the League was at first disguised by the promise of a general crusade against the Turks in the name of Christianity. Pope Julius initiated the war against Venice by declaring that the republic had committed treason against God. From Milan a French army marched south and had little difficulty conquering the mainland possessions of Venice.

The Holy League formed against the French. The Pope was now quite satisfied. Venetian power had been reduced; there was no longer any reason for French troops in Italy. In 1510 the League of Cambrai broke up and Pope Julius, after having made peace with Venice, formed the Holy League in 1511 for the purpose of driving Louis XII out of Italy. This new coalition consisted of the papacy, Venice, Spain, Switzerland, the Holy Roman Empire, and England. Fighting began the end of 1511 and the French suffered defeats everywhere. The Swiss defeated French forces in the lands of Milan, the English enjoyed victory in northern France, and Ferdinand of Spain seized the French territory of Navarre. When peace was agreed upon in 1514 the French were no longer in Italy.

The new diplomacy. Thus the first phase of the Italian wars came to an end, though peace for Italy was not to last for long. By the time Louis XII was finally defeated, it was apparent that the new sovereign states were frequently going to engage in unscrupulous diplomacy; no holds were to be barred in the arena of international rivalry. Ferdinand of Spain in particular is a good example of the duplicity and treachery of his day. He betrayed Charles VIII by violating his promises and joining Charles' enemies. Later he helped Louis XII to conquer Naples, then tricked his ally out of the spoils of war. A few years later he again betrayed Louis by deserting the League of Cambrai for the Pope's Holy League directed against France. It is no wonder that Louis XII accused Ferdinand of cheating him on at least two occasions. Ferdinand, hearing this, scoffed, "The drunkard! He lies! I have cheated him ten times."

Young Henry VIII of England, now married to Catherine of Aragon, was also a catspaw in Ferdinand's diplomacy, for his father-in-law persuaded him to join the Pope's Holy League. The English army Henry sent to France was used by Ferdinand as a screen to seize Navarre from France. Then, quite satisfied, the Spanish monarch made peace with France and left Henry to extricate himself as best he could from this difficult situation. By such bitter experience Henry learned the crafty and treacherous ways of the mature diplomat of his day.

The end of the tradition of European unity. The first phase of the struggle for Italy has an important significance in the development of modern international relations. In the Italian wars are revealed the earliest answers to the question of what kind of mutual relations the rising sovereign states were going to develop. Dynastic rivalries unfettered by any concept of European unity set the keynote of international relations; gains in territory and prestige outweighed moral or religious considerations.

The Italian wars highlighted the passing of the ideal of European unity. In medieval times, as we have seen, western Europeans had generally considered themselves members of one great Christian commonwealth. All men, and even governments, owed obedience to the Universal Church. On many occasions the Pope had acted as arbiter between disputing kings. In 1298, for example, the Pope intervened in a quarrel between Philip IV of France and Edward I, the English sovereign. We observed in Chapter 14 the spectacular triumph of Pope Innocent III over King John, when the latter was forced to do homage for England and Ireland as fiefs of the papacy.

In politics as in religion the ideal of unity

had held an important place. Over a large part of medieval Europe the belief was held that one international organization, the Holy Roman Empire, should be supreme. Lamenting the passing of its power, Dante maintained in his *De Monarchia* (1309): "Whole heaven is regulated by a single ruler—God. It follows that the human race is at its best state when it is ruled by a single prince and one law. So it is evidently necessary for the welfare of the world that there should be a single monarchy or princedom, which men call the Empire."[5] In the mind of Dante, the basis of human welfare was a system of politics consisting of "divine governance, universal empire, perpetual peace, eternal justice and the general reign of law."[6]

This hope for European unity and perpetual peace was vain. The tradition of political and religious unity was destroyed by the rise of national states and by the successful Protestant Revolt from Rome. No longer was there one Church and one empire; no longer was the Pope the sole interpreter of God's truth or the supreme arbiter of right and justice in political quarrels. Instead of heeding the appeal of Dante, kings and princes followed the advice of a later Italian, Machiavelli.

Machiavelli and Machiavellian politics. This Italian diplomat was one of the most important influences in the development of modern politics. Born in Florence in 1469 of an ancient and distinguished family that had long been in government service, Machiavelli grew up during the time of Lorenzo de' Medici. After the French troops of Charles VIII had ousted the Medici, Machiavelli found employment as a diplomatic agent in the Florentine Republic. He was sent on numerous missions and gained wide knowledge about the politics of his day.

In 1512 the Republic was overthrown and the Medici were restored. And so at the age of forty-three the ambitious Machiavelli lost his position, soon was implicated in a plot, and was arrested and tortured by the new Florentine government. Following his release from prison Machiavelli retired to the country, where he lived on a small farm. There he whiled away the time writing stories, poems, and plays. More important, he wrote several books on politics: *The Prince, The Art of War,* and *The History of Florence.*

It is upon *The Prince* that the fame and influence of Machiavelli rests. For some time he had been saddened and outraged by the cavalier manner in which foreign invaders, such as Louis XII, had forced their way into Italy. Machiavelli described his native land as "more captive than the Jews, more enslaved than the Persians, more divided than the Athenians, without a head, without discipline, bruised, despoiled, lacerated, ravaged, and subjected to every kind of affliction." Machiavelli desired to see his country powerful and united under the leadership of Florence. So he set about writing a manual of politics for a leader who would end Italian disunity and foreign intervention. The result was *The Prince.*

Machiavelli's wide acquaintance with the unprincipled politics of the early Italian Wars and his own bitter personal frustration combined to give him a completely cynical, realistic, and ruthless attitude toward mankind in general and politics in particular. He wrote: "When the entire safety of our country is at stake, no consideration of what is just or unjust, merciful or cruel, praiseworthy or shameful, must intervene. On the contrary, every other consideration being set aside, that course alone must be taken which preserves the existence of the country and maintains its independence."

The Prince argues that no state can stand still. It must either expand and grow more powerful or contract and be conquered. "Nothing is so natural or so common," says Machiavelli, "as the thirst for conquest, and when men can satisfy it, they deserve praise rather than censure. But when they are not equal to the enterprise, disgrace is the inevitable consequence."

Machiavelli gives his Prince many suggestions as to how he can survive and conquer in this anarchic and brutal world of unrestrained power. "Let the prince, then, determine to conquer and maintain his state; the means employed by him will always be deemed honorable." "It is not necessary for a prince to have piety, faith, humanity, integrity, and religion, but it is necessary to seem to have them." That Machiavelli was a subtle psychologist is attested by the following statement: "The usurper of a State should commit all the cruelties which his safety renders necessary at once, that he may never have cause to repeat them . . . for when time is allowed for resentment, the wound is not so deep; but benefits should be frugally dispensed, and by little at a time, that they may be the better relished."

Machiavelli did not, of course, invent in *The Prince* the precepts of ruthlessness in relations between states. Rulers were breaking treaties, assassinating their opponents, and using brute force to attain their ends before *The Prince* was written. What Machiavelli did was to accept the world of politics as he saw it, rid it of all idealism, and lay down the essential rules for success.

He accomplished his task so well that *The Prince* was translated into all the languages of Europe. Famous rulers carefully studied its maxims and Machiavellian methods became an indispensable element in the politics of Europe. Nor was his influence confined to the sixteenth century. Napoleon read Machiavelli, and King Victor Emmanuel, under whose rule Italy was united in the nineteenth century, slept with Machiavelli's *Prince* beneath his pillow. The ideology of *Mein Kampf* of the twentieth century bears a striking resemblance to that of *The Prince.*

Sovereignty and power politics. So it was that the rising national rulers disdained the authority of the Holy Roman Empire and the Church and claimed to be the supreme and sole judges of their actions and hence a law unto themselves. This characteristic of independence, termed sovereignty, came to be regarded as the very heart of the rising dynastic system.

The exercise of dynastic sovereignty inaugurated the practice of what is termed power politics. More and more the idea of a unified cooperative European commonwealth faded away in favor of a new political system in which dynastic states competed against each other for land, commerce, and power without restraint and with few scruples or none.

Although war of a somewhat limited kind had been common in the Middle Ages, the smallness of feudal states and the existence of a powerful international agency, the Church (to which all men belonged) had tended to reduce the possibilities and the extent of armed conflict. The conflicts of the Middle Ages were usually such that "men could stop over the week-end, and all go home for the harvest."[7] With the rise of power politics, which may be dated from the first phase of the Italian Wars, which we have just surveyed, war became the conscious and deliberate tool of dynastic policy. Egged on by a rising spirit of dynastic competition and a craving for glory and conquest, rulers initiated an era of undisguised power politics in which might made right and war was the chief measure of national power.

The Age of Charles V: European Empire or Sovereign States?

The manner in which the rulers of Europe practiced power politics and followed the dictums laid down by Machiavelli is admirably illustrated by the course of international politics in Europe during the first half of the sixteenth century, a period often referred to as the Age of Charles v.

Charles V and the challenge of a European empire. Born in 1500, this scion of the house of Hapsburg soon enjoyed a position no ruler had possessed since Charlemagne. His grandfather, Maximilian I, was Archduke of Austria and Emperor of the Holy Roman Empire (1493-1519), and had added to his domain by marrying Mary of Burgundy, heiress of the Netherlands. The son of this marriage, Philip, became the husband of Joanna, daughter of Ferdinand and Isabella of Spain; and thus, by a calculated policy of dynastic marriages, the Austrian Hapsburgs extended their interests to the Netherlands and Spain. This success in matrimonial alliances was expressed in a Latin couplet that read: "Let others make war. Thou, happy Austria, marry, for Venus gives thee those realms which on others Mars bestows."

Charles, son of Philip and Joanna, became ruler of the Netherlands following his father's death in 1506; and in 1516 the death of his grandfather Ferdinand gave him the Spanish realm together with the southern half of Italy. In 1519 the death of his other grandfather, Maximilian, left the throne of the Holy Roman Empire vacant. A spirited contest for the imperial title followed, in which Henry VIII of England and Francis I of France were candidates. Charles won out, however, and in 1520 became Emperor Charles v. Never had a monarch so many possessions. Ruler of the Netherlands, wearer of the crowns

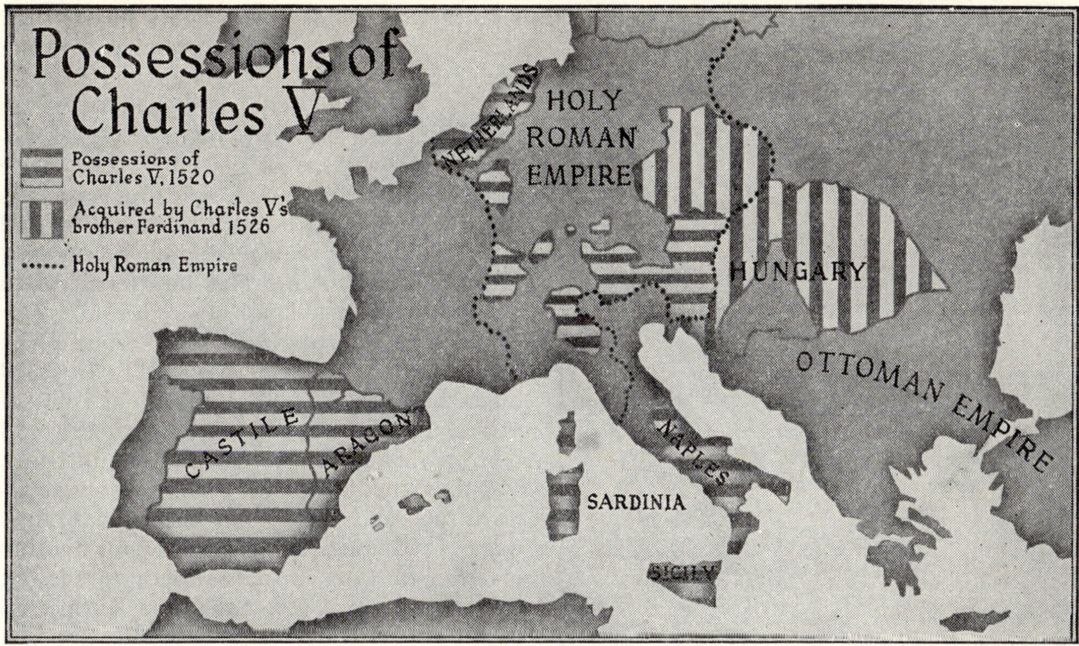

of Castile and Aragon, together with those of Naples, Sicily, and Sardinia, emperor of the Holy Roman Empire, possessor of the hereditary Hapsburg states in eastern Europe, and master of a vast colonial empire, he made it appear in 1520 as if Hapsburg power might dominate all of Europe. There was a chance that the growth of sovereign and usually jealous nation states might be halted and that Dante's dream of a universal empire in Europe could be achieved.

The nation state in the long run, however, was to thwart this Hapsburg dream of universal empire. The power of Charles v was deceptive. His empire was not a compact state and was united only in the sense that it had a common personal ruler. Moreover, as we shall see, Charles had too many irons in the European fire. This ruler was intelligent, conscientious, and hard-working; but the very extent of his power gave him too many problems. All his reign he was forced to rush from one part of his realm to another, frustrating plots, putting down rebellions, or meeting invasions from his foes.

The problems of Charles v were inextricably connected with the activities of three of his contemporaries: Francis I of France, Henry VIII of England, and Suleiman, Sultan of the Ottoman Empire. It was out of the interplay of the rivalries of these rulers that the nation states, especially France, were able to prevent Hapsburg domination of Europe.

Rivalry between Charles and Francis I. There were numerous reasons for enmity between Charles and Francis. The latter was an impetuous, frivolous, and glory-seeking young man. In his youth he had read many courtly romances and had become an excellent athlete, proficient in hunting, tennis, and jousting. Despite the sorry conclusion of the Italian adventures of his two predecessors, Charles VIII and Louis XII, Francis decided to seek glory in Italy. Invading northern Italy, he won a decisive victory at Marignano over forces defending Milan, and French troops occupied Milan. The victory was swift and easy, and the fame of Francis spread throughout Europe.

In addition to conquering Milan, a duchy that Charles v considered a fief of his empire, Francis revived the French claim to Naples, and also had his eyes on the little Spanish kingdom of Navarre. For his part Charles was anxious to regain the Duchy of Burgundy which had been added to the French realm by the wily Louis XI.

In addition to these territorial rivalries, Francis was personally jealous of Charles and was embittered over his unsuccessful bid for the imperial title in 1520. Taking precedence over all other causes of Franco-Hapsburg ri-

A barber washes the hair of a customer in this Nuremberg woodcut (about 1550). Notice the tap consisting of a kettle suspended from a crane.

valry, however, was the fact that the empire of Charles threatened the very independence of France. Hapsburg lands encircled the realm of Francis to the north, east, and south. Only by war could the power of Charles be checked and perhaps reduced, and the balance of power be maintained in Europe.

Henry VIII plans to maintain the balance of power. Across the Channel the strong-willed Henry VIII, who believed in himself and in England, decided to take a hand in the duel between Charles and Francis. Acting on the advice of Cardinal Wolsey, Henry aimed to use his power as a makeweight in the Franco-Hapsburg rivalry, shifting it from side to side in such a way that neither of the rivals would be in a position to dominate Europe. Naturally, both Francis and Charles wooed Henry. In 1520 the French and English kings met on the famous "field of the cloth of gold." Thousands of ornately decorated tents were set up, many graceful ceremonies were held, and knights pitted their skill against each other in the tourney. Henry and Francis were very gracious and friendly as they discussed matters of state. "It was rubbing noses, but rubbing noses very politely, with a pane of glass between." The English king had already sized up Francis as being militarily stronger than Charles, and so, shortly after these elaborate ceremonies, became an ally of the Hapsburg emperor in the interest of a balance of power.

Francis' defeat in Italy. The second phase of the Italian Wars began in 1521. Imperial forces of Charles V drove the French out of Milan. In 1523 it appeared that France would be overwhelmed by forces from Spain, Italy, and England, and this peril was only narrowly averted. The following year Francis was able to muster a strong army for another invasion of Italy. Milan was captured, but the following year (1525) the French army was disastrously defeated at Pavia by the imperial forces. Francis was taken prisoner and wrote his mother, "Nothing in the world is left me except my honor and my life."

The "balance of power." It was now quite obvious that England had miscalculated, and had backed the stronger rather than the weaker of the two rivals on the continent. Following the battle of Pavia a defensive alliance was created to check the growing Hapsburg power. This Holy League of Cognac was made up of France, the Papal States, Rome, and Venice, together with other less important Italian powers. England executed a sudden *volte-face,* deserting her ally Charles and supporting the new League. This use of English power and prestige to equalize the power of the continental rivals was one of the earliest instances of what came to be a familiar feature of modern international politics. Time and again in modern history, when a single country or dynasty has become too powerful, other countries have united to check-mate it and restore equilibrium. This phenomenon is known as "the balance of power."

Francis was released from captivity in 1526 and set about working with the Holy League of Cognac for the ruination of Charles. The Hapsburg emperor had little chance to exploit the great opportunity gained on the battlefield of Pavia, for other serious matters engaged his attention.

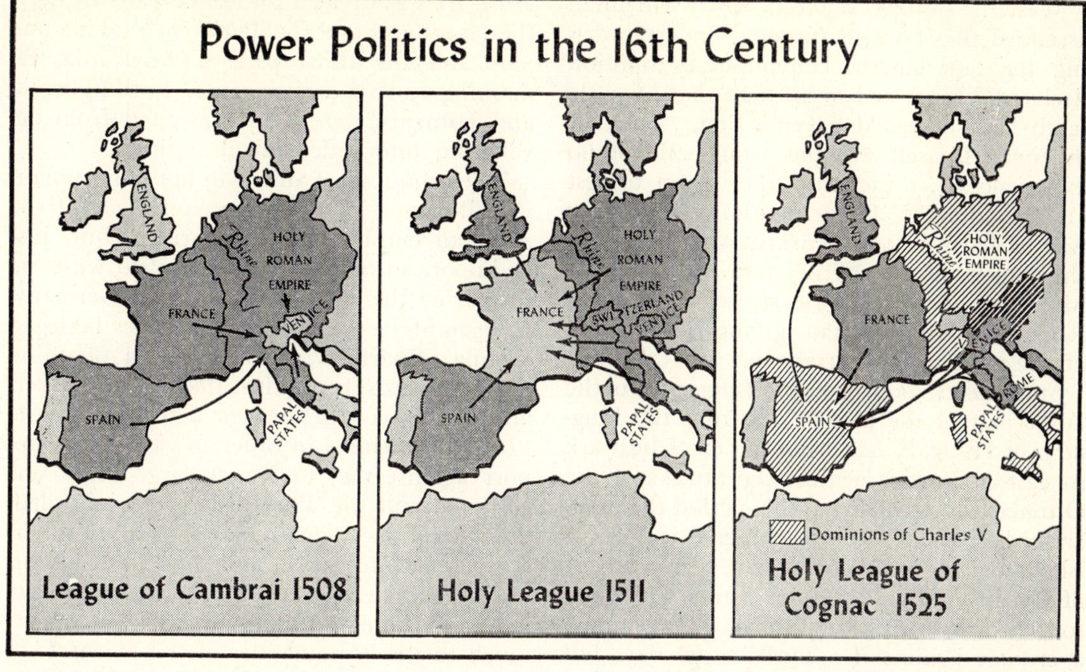

A country which became too powerful was subject to attack from a coalition, or league, of enemies. This system was used to maintain the balance of power. In 1508 Venice was the objective of the League of Cambrai. The Holy League was organized in 1511 to drive Louis XII *out of Italy. The Holy League of Cognac was formed to check the vast holdings of Charles* V.

Lutheran princes form the League of Schmalkalden. While the conflict with Francis I was at its height, Charles was seriously embarrassed by the Protestant Revolt in the Empire. War with the French and the menace of the Turks had prevented Charles from initiating a serious attempt to crush all heresy in his empire until after it had reached formidable proportions. Now, in 1531, the Lutheran Princes formed the Schmalkaldic League for self-defense. Though open civil war between the Schmalkaldic League and the Catholics led by Charles did not develop until 1546, as we have seen (Chapter 18), continual controversy diverted Charles' attention from his quarrels with the French king.

Charles hampered by the Turkish menace. The very year Charles became emperor of the Holy Roman Empire (1520) there ascended the throne in Constantinople a young Turk who was to play an important role in the political and religious affairs of Europe. The new sultan was Suleiman, known in Turkish history as "the Magnificent" and "the Legislator." Inheriting a full treasury, a well-governed empire, and a disciplined army from his father, Suleiman planned to extend his empire and strengthen its organization.

Even more than the Protestant Revolt, the menace of the Turk prevented Charles from delivering a knockout blow against Francis I. The German states on several occasions were seriously alarmed over the advances of Suleiman's armies. And, as we shall see shortly, Francis I, despite his title of the Most Christian King, had no compunctions over making a close military alliance with the Infidel Turk.

Suleiman the Magnificent is known best in history as a military conqueror. He led an army ten times into Europe and three times into Asia, while his fleets sailed as far as Morocco and India. During a lifetime of almost continuous war he annexed Tunis, Algeria, Tripoli, the Yemen, Mesopotamia, and part of Hungary. His governmental reforms at home were as important as these conquests, however, for in spite of feeble leadership, the Ottoman empire left by Suleiman endured with little change for three hundred years.

Western Europe rejoiced when Suleiman ascended the Turkish throne. Underestimating the new sultan, contemporary opinion declared, "It seemed to all men that a gentle lamb had succeeded a fierce lion, . . . since Suleiman himself was but young and of no experience . . . and altogether given to rest and quietness."[8] This equanimity soon gave way to alarm when a Turkish army captured the important city of Belgrade in 1521 and when, the next year, the strategic island of Rhodes fell to Suleiman, giving him control of the eastern Mediterranean.

Suleiman strikes against Hungary. In the latter half of the fifteenth century the kingdom of Hungary had been the chief bulwark in eastern Europe against the attacks of the Ottoman Turks. During this period the monarchy had been strong, commerce had flourished, and the king's court had been a center of Renaissance culture. For a time Hungary, so sure of its own strength, had even planned a crusade against the Turks. Evil days fell upon the monarchy, however, in the opening years of the sixteenth century. The king was lamentably weak, royal power declined, and the nobles quarreled continually among themselves.

Suleiman knew the situation well and resolved to strike a decisive blow against Hungary and bring it under the rule of the Crescent. At the head of his troops the sultan met the army of the Hungarian king on the plain of Mohacs (1526). The battle was decided in one hour and a half, with the Hungarians completely routed and their king drowned while fleeing the field. Mohacs has been called "the tomb of the Hungarian nation." Perhaps as many as 25,000 Hungarian troops were killed, including the leaders of the nobility.

A Hapsburg king in Bohemia and Hungary. The Christian king who perished at Mohacs had been the ruler of both Hungary and Bohemia. We have already had occasion to mention the effects of the Turkish victory and the death of the Christian king (Chapter 16). After Suleiman returned home, taking with him a tremendous booty and over 100,000 captives, nobles in each of these kingdoms elected as their king Ferdinand of Hapsburg, brother of Charles v. It was the victory of the Turk, therefore, that placed the destiny of the Czechs of Bohemia in the Hapsburg empire. Hungary was divided into three parts in 1547, the Hapsburgs and the Turks each taking one part and the third part, Transylvania, remaining under a native prince. Both Bohemia and Hungary were thus prevented from developing into independent nations.

The conquests of Suleiman not only explain why Bohemia and Hungary were part of the Austrian empire in modern times, but, just as important, they had much to do with the success of the Protestant cause in Germany. In 1529 and 1532 Suleiman's armies besieged Vienna. Charles v, who had been planning energetic measures against the heretic Lutherans, was forced to arrange a truce with the Protestant princes in order to gain their support against the Turks. A large army was collected and the Turkish danger was foiled. The threat of Suleiman had given the Lutherans a breathing space, and thus "it is indeed one of the strangest ironies of fate that the cause of Protestantism should have owed so much to the 'Commander of the Faithful.' "[9]

Francis I and Suleiman allies. Meanwhile the war between Francis I and Charles v continued. Following the disastrous defeat at Pavia, Francis decided upon desperate measures—he would seek an alliance with the Turkish Sultan Suleiman. There is something ironic in the implacable foe of Christianity, Suleiman, assuring Francis, the Most Christian King: "There is nothing wonderful in emperors being defeated and made prisoners. Take courage then, and be not dismayed. Our glorious predecessors and our illustrious ancestors (may God light up their tombs!) have never ceased to make war to repel the foe and conquer his lands."[10] Power politics had precedence over religion in Constantinople as well as in Paris.

Turkish successes in the Mediterranean. After Suleiman's unsuccessful thrusts against Vienna in 1529 and 1532, Turkish pressure was diverted from eastern Europe to the Mediterranean. In this theater of conflict French and Moslem fleets combined to attack Italian towns, and Francis handed over the port of Toulon for use by the Turkish fleet. Much of the strength that Charles might have built up to crush the French monarchy was diverted to the Mediterranean. In 1535 Charles sent a great fleet of 400 ships and 30,000 men to recapture Tunis from the Moslem forces. During the entire reign of Charles much of the north African coast was controlled by Turkish pirates known as corsairs. From strongholds such as Algiers these pirates preyed upon Christian shipping and harried the coasts of Sicily and Italy. In 1541 Charles sent a great fleet against the corsair lair at Algiers, but the attack failed with a loss of 150 ships and some 12,000 men. After this expedition Charles ceased active warfare against the corsairs in the Mediterranean. By the mid-sixteenth century Turkish sea power was at its height; corsairs began to venture into the Atlantic to prey upon Portuguese and Spanish shipping.

Charles recognizes Lutheranism. A truce in 1544 called a halt to the French-Hapsburg struggle. Charles' efforts were again centered in the German states, where in 1546 the Lutheran struggle flared out into civil war. The Schmalkaldic Wars ended in 1555 with the compromise Peace of Augsburg, which, as we have seen, officially sanctioned the Lutheran faith in the Empire. Thus Charles was thwarted in his cherished aim of restoring religious unity throughout his far-flung dominions. Politically the Augsburg settlement further entrenched the power of the princes, thwarting the revival of a strong imperial government and reinforcing the decentralization of the Germanies.

Charles' abdication. Francis I of France died in 1547 and in 1552 his son and successor, Henry II, renewed the war against Charles. By that time the emperor was thoroughly worn out. In 1555 he turned over the rule of the Netherlands to his son, Philip, and the following year he gave up to Philip his royal responsibilities in Spain. To Ferdinand, his younger brother, he turned over his sovereignty of the Hapsburg Austrian lands and also the imperial authority. Charles retired to a monastery to spend the remaining few years of his life. A legend has it that he spent much time trying to make several clocks keep exactly the same time—obviously an allegory suggesting that he was faced with so many problems he was never able to settle all of them at any time.

Charles died in 1558. He had been a ruler who did not realize what seemed to be his destiny. Napoleon once remarked that he was surprised that Charles had not been able to master the world. After thirty-five years' rule as the greatest monarch in the western world, at his death Charles was a failure; for French resistance to the House of Hapsburg was stronger than ever, religious unity had not been secured in the Germanies, and Suleiman the Turk was still a menace to Christian Europe.

What explains the virtual failure of this conscientious, brave, and well-meaning monarch? The most important reason was the existence of too many problems in too many places. The very extent of his power was often a drawback. He was fated to be continually on the move, fighting battles, making truces or treaties, combatting heresy, or stamping out rebellion. Also, throughout his reign he was faced with the continual hostility of France and the menace of the Ottoman empire.

Significance for modern times. The rather complicated political narrative that revolved around the ambitions and plans of four monarchs—Charles v, Henry VIII, Francis I, and Suleiman the Magnificent—is significant because it helped to lay down much of the political and religious foundation of modern Europe:

(1) During the reign of Charles v the balance of power was maintained. It was decided by force of arms that no single state was to unify all of Europe. The growth of nations proved to be too far advanced to permit of the revival of a single European empire.

(2) The general course of events during the Age of Charles v was fatal to the fortunes of German and Italian national growth. The armies of France and Austria had invaded and weakened Italy. When peace was finally arranged between the sons of Charles and Francis at Cateau-Cambrésis in 1559, much of Italy was left in the hands of the Hapsburgs, France surrendering all her Italian holdings. As for the Germanies, Charles was unable to create an effective and centralized German government. The Schmalkaldic Wars and the Peace of Augsburg accentuated the political and religious separatism of Germany.

(3) Charles' rivalry with Francis I and the French king's alliance with Suleiman played an important part in reducing the pressure that might have been applied by the emperor against the Lutheran movement. Francis himself, although a Catholic, sent aid to the German Protestants in order to embarrass their ruler. As a result of such diversions, the Protestant movement gained so firm a foot-

hold that the religious unity of Europe was irreparably destroyed. Thus Charles failed to maintain the unity of Christendom as he failed to create a single European empire.

(4) The failure of Christian Europe to present a common front against the advance of the Ottoman power meant that Turkish control over the Balkans was handed down to later European statesmen as an explosive legacy. The alliance of France with Turkey became an enduring, though irregular, factor in European diplomacy.

(5) The history of the first half of the sixteenth century made it quite clear that diplomacy *à la* Machiavelli was to be the order of the day. Deceit, treachery, surprise attacks, and broken promises—all these are part of the record. It is apparent that no moral scruples were to be allowed to stand in the way of the interests of any nation state.

The Golden Age of Spain

Philip II faces a promising future. In 1556 the son of Charles V became Philip II of Spain. Conditions developed most auspiciously for the new ruler. All danger from France was removed when that country plunged in 1562 into a long series of horrible civil wars. Following the death of Suleiman the Magnificent in 1566, Turkey fell into the hands of incompetent rulers. Just before assuming his royal duties in Spain, Philip had married Mary Tudor, queen of England. This gave Philip a strong ally. Perhaps the most important development was that Philip was relieved of the complications of the German problem, for his uncle Ferdinand had inherited the Hapsburg Austrian lands together with the imperial crown of the Holy Roman Empire. And if Philip II was rid of the thankless task of ruling the Germanies, he had inherited a new empire overseas, one more easily administered and much more lucrative. During the reign of Charles V, Cortes had conquered Mexico, Pizarro had vanquished the Incas of Peru, and various other settlements and conquests had been made from the Strait of Magellan to Mexico (Chapter 20). From these lands of the New World came huge quantities of treasure to enrich the Hapsburg coffers at Madrid.

In addition to the riches of the Americas and the possessions of Spain in Europe—the Netherlands, Naples, Sicily, and Milan—Philip had the best soldiers in Europe. In training and discipline the Spanish infantry were rivaled only by the Turkish janissaries. The code of the Spanish soldier was "to obey orders, to aid a comrade even when he is a personal enemy, to keep one's place unshaken, to step into the place of a dead soldier, to stand firm and to charge home."[11] So richly endowed was Spain with all these assets of military power, extensive territory, and treasure, that it was natural for a Spanish historian to write, "The Sun never set on the dominions of the King of Spain and at the slightest movement of that nation the whole earth trembled."[12] In spite of these many advantages, however, Philip was fated, like his father, to suffer frustration and failure.

During his long reign from 1556 to 1598 Philip sought three basic goals: to make his royal power absolute, to combat heresy and strengthen Catholicism, and to extend the influence of Spain.

Building on the foundations of absolutism laid by his grandparents Ferdinand and Isabella, Philip erected a centralized system of government in which every decision rested with the king and in which all agencies of government were subordinate to his will. Philip read all the documents and burdened himself with a vast amount of paper work. Many of these papers, in fact, with marginal notations of the king, can still be seen in the Spanish archives. One letter from the king's ambassador in London, for example, described a new kind of insect he had seen crawling on his window panes; upon this Philip solemnly scribbled, "Probably fleas."

Philip was devoted to the Catholic Church. In fact, it is often said that he subordinated the interests of Spain to those of Catholicism. Once Philip wrote the Pope, "I would lose all my States and a hundred lives if I had them rather than be lord of heretics."

Actually, no religious scruples were permitted to interfere with the interests of the Spanish state. Fear of France and desire for the friendship of England led Philip to try to restrain Catholic Mary Tudor from persecuting her Protestant subjects. The same fear of France explains why Philip did his best to support Queen Elizabeth when she first came to the English throne. The Spanish king actually waged war against Pope Paul IV, and at home he controlled and utilized the Church for the political interests of the state. The Spanish Inquisition ferreted out heretics but at the same time Philip used it to strengthen royal power. It was convenient for Philip that his duties to the old Church seemed to coincide with those of the new Spain. By championing Catholicism he was able to justify his interference in England and France and his attempt to extirpate local nationalism in the Netherlands.

Much controversy has raged around the nature of Philip's character. To loyal Catholics all over Europe and to his own faithful subjects he was the main foe of the Protestant Revolt, a staunch defender of the faith, and a relentless foe of heresy. To most Englishmen, Scotsmen, Dutch, Scandinavians, and German Lutherans, he was a bigoted, ruthless, and intolerant fanatic. It so happens that the actions of Philip have most often been recounted from the standpoint of England, France, and Holland. In consequence the Spanish king is singled out as a detestable example of trickery, cruelty, and religious intolerance. The truth is that Philip did not equal Elizabeth of England when it came to diplomatic duplicity, and in the sixteenth century practically all the rulers in Europe considered the relentless persecution of nonconformists as essential to the welfare of the state. The failures of Philip, therefore, that we are now to recount were not due to unusual bigotry or cruelty in his character; it was rather that he was not so skillful as his opponents in the game of power politics. Also Philip unwittingly pitted himself against certain historic forces, mainly nationalism, that were bound to win out in the long run.

Philip annexes Portugal and defeats the Turks. In the first part of his reign Philip scored several notable successes. In 1578 the direct line of the Portuguese royal family became extinct. For two years the throne was held by the uncle of the late king, an old man without children. Brushing aside the claims of a Portuguese prince who was next in line to succeed to the throne, Philip, who had the next best hereditary claim, seized the throne for himself. After uniting Portugal to Spain in 1580 Philip made every effort to placate his new subjects by respecting their institutions. The annexation of Portugal and with it a great colonial empire brought considerable new revenue from Brazil, Africa, and the East Indies.

After the death of Charles V, Christian Europe turned to Philip as the one monarch who might block the expansion of the Turks in the Mediterranean. Suleiman was trying to destroy completely Christian defenses in this area. In 1561 the Turks raided the Balearic Islands and in 1562 Turkish corsairs preyed upon shipping in the Atlantic. In the spring of 1565 Suleiman struck at the island of Malta, one of the keys to control of the Mediterranean, with a fleet made up of 200 ships carrying 30,000 soldiers. Malta was held by the Knights of St. John of Jerusalem, who for more than three months, under the courageous leadership of the Grand Master Jean de La Valette, held off the Turkish attacks. Finally, reinforcements sent by Philip forced Suleiman's army to withdraw after losing 20,000 men.

Six years after the Turkish repulse at Malta, Christian Europe was able to strike a more deadly blow against Ottoman power. In 1571 a great Christian armada, organized by Spain, Venice, and the papacy and commanded by Don John, half brother of Philip, met the main Turkish fleet at Lepanto, on the western side of Greece. Ottoman sea power was decisively defeated, never to be completely restored in the Mediterranean. No wonder Pope Pius, when he heard the glorious news of Lepanto, declared, "There was a man sent from God whose name was John."

Philip in the Netherlands. The conquest of Portugal and the defeat of the Turks were signal victories for the Spanish monarchy, but in the Netherlands it met with decisive defeat, which influenced for the worse the whole of Spanish foreign policy. The seventeen provinces of the Low Countries had been restive in the reign of Charles V. Philip's father had imposed heavy taxes to help finance his wars, made the people support large contingents of Spanish troops, and introduced the Inquisition. In spite of these unpopular acts, Charles, who had been born in the city of Ghent, continued to enjoy the confidence of the Netherlanders, who regarded him as one of themselves. It was not so with Philip. He was first and last a Spaniard and could not even speak the Dutch language. From the very first, the people of the Netherlands distrusted Philip. Their new sovereign placed Spanish officials over them, disregarding their own nobles, continued to maintain a Spanish army of occupation, and speeded up the persecution of heretics.

In spite of the Inquisition, however, Protestantism spread in the Netherlands, and in 1566 a group of the leading burghers and nobles petitioned Philip to abolish the Inquisition and other grievances. The story goes that when Philip's regent at first expressed alarm at the petition, which warned of revolt if grievances were not redressed, an adviser turned to him and said, "What? Is Your Highness afraid of these beggars?" At any rate, the party of resistance to Philip in the Netherlands assumed the name of Beggars.

Nothing was done to rectify the evils from which the people suffered, and in 1566 a series of violent riots took place. Philip's answer was to send his best general, the Duke of Alva, to quell the revolt. This stern soldier's program was to create a state in which the authority of the Spanish crown should be unquestioned and in which there should be only one Church. It is said that when Alva arrived in the Netherlands he announced, "I have tamed men of iron and I shall soon have done with these men of butter."

A court called "the Council of Troubles," soon dubbed by the people "the Council of Blood," was set up to stamp out disloyalty. On an average fifty to seventy victims were executed every day, and it has been estimated that during Alva's reign of terror eight thousand people were executed (including some of the highest nobles), thirty thousand were deprived of their lands and property, and one hundred thousand fled the country.

The Dutch war for independence. In 1568 the Eighty Years' War (1568-1648) broke out against Spain. The Dutch, as the people of the northern Netherlands came to be called, were resolved to fight tyranny, for the Duke of Alva had antagonized the growing nationalism and religious sentiments of the people, and his heavy taxation had created widespread enmity among the wealthy burghers.

From the perspective of the twentieth century the Netherlands revolt constitutes one of the first chapters in the narrative of the origin and development of modern democratic government. The Dutch of the sixteenth century had only the vaguest perception of what we know as democracy. They believed they were fighting for freedom, but it was freedom to maintain their rather aristocratic institutions, their machinery of local self-government. There were, however, certain modern democratic principles back of the struggle against Spain. When the Eighty Years' War commenced, the Dutch leader William the Silent of the House of Orange declared, "The privileges are not free grants of the sovereign to his subjects, but form contracts binding both prince and people." From time to time other leaders stressed that the people had certain rights which never could be taken away from them by their rulers. At all times there was a strong feeling for religious toleration in the Netherlands.

In the first years of the war the Duke of Alva was victorious, and the puny forces commanded by the tenacious William the Silent were dispersed again and again. In 1569, however, the Netherlanders turned to the sea and began to outfit privateers to prey on Spanish shipping. Much loot was captured, and from then on the patriots gained ground. The struggle went on, and in 1576 the terrible event known in history as "the Spanish Fury" occurred. In that year the Spanish soldiery rebelled because their pay and food were not forthcoming, marched upon the rich city of Antwerp, and sacked the town with indescribable ferocity. News of the atrocity ended some of the differences that had existed in the patriotic party, and in 1576 the Pacification of Ghent was signed by representatives of all seventeen provinces. This agreement declared that all Spanish soldiers must be expelled from the land, after which a representative Estates-General should be called to govern the country. Both Protestants and Catholics were to enjoy toleration. While Philip was to be the nominal overlord of the provinces, the actual ruler was to be William the Silent.

The seventeen provinces did not long continue the unity manifested in the Pacification of Ghent. The Spaniards were able to create discord between the northern provinces, mainly Protestant, and those in the south, where there were many complaints against Spanish political measures but few against Philip's religious policy, since the people there were mostly Catholic. In 1579 the people of

Peter Breughel made this copper engraving of skaters on the Canal of Antwerp. It is full of rough good humor (the fallen skater, the laughing onlookers, the jokester in the foreground).

the Netherlands came to the parting of the ways, for the southern leaders declared in favor of reconciliation with Philip II, while the northern provinces declared that they would not rest until Spanish tyranny had been crushed and complete freedom achieved. In 1581 the Estates General of the United Provinces, as the country came to be known, formally repudiated its sovereign Philip in an announcement that can be regarded as the Dutch Declaration of Independence. One of its provisions stated, "The people were not created by God for the sake of the Prince . . . but, on the contrary, the Prince was made for the good of the people."[13] This declaration of 1581 set the model for later declarations justifying revolution in England, France, and the United States.

The cause of Dutch freedom was placed in serious jeopardy in 1584 when William the Silent was assassinated and the Spanish renewed efforts to crush Dutch independence. At this critical moment valuable military assistance was rendered the cause of Dutch freedom by Queen Elizabeth of England. The queen's motive in sending assistance, however, as we shall see shortly, was not primarily sympathy for the Dutch cause; rather, defeat for Philip in the Netherlands fitted the national interests of England.

The Dutch struggle against Spain continued, and in 1597 the patriots won a decisive land battle against Philip's army. This victory was a sign of the decline of Spanish power. In 1609 a Twelve Years' Truce put an end to sporadic fighting, but the conflict was renewed in 1621 during the Thirty Years' War. Not until 1648 did the Dutch gain a formal recognition of their independence.

As for the southern provinces, they remained for more than two hundred years in the hands of the Hapsburgs, first as the Spanish Netherlands and then as the Austrian Netherlands. Early in the nineteenth century, following a brief and unsatisfactory union with "Holland," as the northern provinces were popularly called, the southern provinces were to obtain their independence and enter the family of nations as Belgium.

Reasons for Dutch success. Philip II's plans for intervention in France and England, shortly to be discussed, depended for their success on the failure of the Dutch revolt. Victory was vital for Philip; yet he failed. There are several reasons why the Dutch were able, ultimately, to foil the attempts of Philip to crush them. The existence of canals enabled them to flood out their enemies on several occasions. The Dutch proved to be fine sailors, while the Spanish authorities never appreciated the importance of sea power. Again and again Dutch sailors brought needed help to their beleaguered armies. William was a patient and cautious general, who refused to fight decisive battles when the Spanish armies were too strong but chose to play a waiting game that wore out his adversaries. Privateering activities and growing commerce gave the Dutch funds to hire mercenary soldiers. The Dutch received much help from the friends of Protestantism, especially England. Finally, the people of the northern provinces displayed a steadfastness and resoluteness without which victory could never have been achieved. The Dutch people are rightly proud of their royal coat of arms with its motto *Je maintiendrai* ("I shall persist").

Spain threatens England. During the reign of Philip II it seemed on more than one occasion that England would come under the domination of Spain. The first period was during the rule of Mary Tudor, who, as Philip's adoring wife, was strongly influenced by him. Mary died after a brief reign of six years, and her half sister Elizabeth assumed the throne. Elizabeth's disputed succession provided the second occasion on which it seemed possible that Spain would dominate England. Daughter of Anne Boleyn, whose marriage to Henry had touched off the English revolt from the papacy, Elizabeth was considered illegitimate and hence no true queen by Catholics, who recognized only Henry's first marriage as valid. In the eyes of Catholic Europe the heir to the English throne was the Catholic Queen Mary Stuart, great-granddaughter of Henry VII.

Brought up in the Catholic faith in France, Mary in 1558 married Francis, heir to the French throne, who became king in 1559. The fact that Mary Stuart was a queen in France and Scotland, that her mother governed Scotland for her with the aid of French troops, and that she had a strong claim to the crown in London, seemed to indicate that a political union of France, Scotland, and England might be possible. Such a combination could mean the end of Protestantism in England and the control of that country by France. Further, it would mean to Philip of Spain a strong rival that could challenge his leadership in Europe.

Philip offers alliance to Elizabeth. For the moment the interests of England and Spain ran parallel, and in 1559 Philip, the foremost Catholic sovereign in Europe, actually offered his hand in marriage to the Protestant Queen Elizabeth in order to thwart Mary Stuart. The French danger was removed in 1559, however, by the outbreak of a Protestant national revolt in Scotland. Led by John Knox, a Calvinist patriot, the movement abolished Catholicism and ousted French influence. English soldiers were sent to Scotland by Elizabeth, who had much to gain by the removal of the French from Edinburgh, the Scottish capital.

While the nationalist Protestant revolt was being staged in Scotland, Francis II died after a reign of little more than a year, and the dynastic connection between Scotland and France was broken. Mary returned to Scotland in 1561 to rule her kingdom. A year after Mary returned home, civil war between rival Protestant and Catholic factions broke out in France. Any prospect of France's becoming too strong for Spain and dominating Europe had now been removed.

Philip supports Mary Stuart. Mary Queen of Scots came back to Scotland a widow of eighteen famous for her charm, beauty, and grace. She proceeded to alienate her subjects by a series of blunders. Mary was too frivolous for her strait-laced Calvinistic subjects, she was unsuccessful in concealing her pro-Catholic sympathies, and finally, she was accused of being involved in the sordid murder of her husband, Lord Darnley. The Scottish people revolted against this crime, and Mary in 1568 fled the country and threw herself upon the mercy of Elizabeth.

Now that Mary's connection with the ruling house of France had been severed, Philip of Spain had no compunctions about plotting to place Mary on the throne of England. Philip's ambassador in London became the center of a web of intrigue against Elizabeth, and on several occasions serious conspiracies were uncovered by the English government barely in time to prevent disaster.

Rivalry between England and Spain. After 1570 Philip emerged as the chief enemy of Protestant England, and at the same time Elizabeth gradually became the chief obstacle to the expansion of Spanish influence in Europe. Unlike her cousin Mary Stuart, who was impetuous and often the blind instrument of her emotions, Elizabeth was realistic, calculating, and thoroughly Machiavellian in her foreign politics. In Elizabeth personal desires and interests were always subordinated to the interests of the state.

In her duel with Philip of Spain, Elizabeth resorted to every subterfuge and trick available to her. Using her sex as a diplomatic weapon, she carried on long flirtations with the brothers of the French king, thereby helping to prevent a Franco-Spanish alliance. At the same time she secretly sent assistance to the Dutch, realizing that their rebellion was sapping the strength of Spain.

While nominally at peace with Philip, Elizabeth secretly encouraged her sea captains to prey upon Spanish shipping. The most famous of the Elizabethan "Sea Dogs," Sir Francis Drake, attacked the rich Spanish settlements on the Isthmus of Panama in 1572. In 1577 *El Draque* (The Dragon), as the Spaniards called Drake, sailed into the Pacific, plundering wherever he went, and, after circumnavigating the globe, arrived in England with a hold full of silver and gold. Elizabeth knighted Drake for this exploit. Again in 1585 Drake raided the West Indies. Elizabeth disclaimed any responsibility for these acts of piracy, and her sea captains knew full well that, if they were captured, their queen would not lift a hand to save them. Philip knew what the queen was up to, but it suited these monarchs to pretend to accept each other's assurances until the convenient time arrived for the inevitable showdown. It is no wonder that the Spanish ambassador wrote to Philip:

"Your lordship will see what a pretty business it is to treat with this woman who I think must have a hundred thousand devils in her body, notwithstanding that she is forever telling me that she yearns to be a nun and to pass her life in prayer."[14]

By the assassination of Elizabeth, Philip hoped to place Catholic Mary on the throne and thus avoid the necessity of waging war on England. In 1586 a serious plot against the life of the English queen was discovered, a plot in which Mary was implicated. Parliament came to believe that as long as Mary lived, even as a prisoner in England, Elizabeth's life would be endangered; in 1587 Mary was executed.

Philip and Elizabeth at war. Realizing that the time for a decisive test of arms had arrived, Elizabeth sought to embarrass Philip by openly sending arms and soldiers to the Netherlands, by aiding the cause of Protestantism in France, and by authorizing Drake to raid Cadiz and Lisbon in order to destroy Spanish shipping—exploits described as "singeing the King of Spain's beard." By 1587 Philip had made up his mind to send a great Armada against England.

Just as Spanish oppression had stimulated Dutch nationalism, so threat of invasion raised English patriotism to a high pitch. The queen herself gave her people an example of courage and resoluteness. Appearing before her land forces, she rode bareheaded through their ranks declaring: "I am come among you at this time being resolved . . . to lay down for my God, and for my Kingdom, and for my people, my honour and my blood, even in the dust. I know that I have but the body of a feeble woman, but I have the heart of a King and a King of England too."[15]

England defeats the Spanish Armada. Spanish strategy was to have the Armada make a juncture with a large Spanish army in the Netherlands and then land this force on the English coast. This plan was endangered in the beginning of its execution by the activities of the Dutch, who helped to block the main ports in the Low Countries. The English then completely wrecked Spanish plans by thoroughly disorganizing the Armada in a number of savage naval engagements in the English Channel. Unfortunately for Philip, his bulky galleons were outmaneuvered by the small but fast ships of Sir Francis Drake and John Hawkins. At the same time a severe storm completed the debacle. A few Spanish vessels fleeing into the North Sea managed to return to Spain by sailing around the northern coast of Scotland.

The defeat of the Armada meant that Eng-

A CONTEMPORARY WOODCUT SHOWING THE MASSACRE OF ST. BARTHOLOMEW'S DAY

land was to remain Protestant, that Holland was eventually to secure its independence, that modern English sea power was born, and that Spanish power was now in decline.

Civil war in France. In the complicated seesaw of European sixteenth-century diplomacy the French Wars of Religion played their part. Though Francis I encouraged the Lutherans to revolt against their emperor Charles V, his motto at home in France was *"Un roi, une foi, une loi"* ("One king, one faith, one law"). The French Protestants, therefore, were persecuted; but in spite of the government's measures the "Huguenots," as they were called, constantly multiplied, so that by 1560 they numbered 400,000.

Henry II of the French house of Valois, successor to Francis, died in 1559 following an injury received in a tournament. He left behind three sons. The first, Francis II, a boy of fifteen on his accession, and husband of Mary Queen of Scots, died after only seventeen months on the throne. His brothers, who followed him, were Charles IX (1560-1574), a nervous and perhaps mad prince, and Henry III (1574-1589), a degenerate.

With the reign of Charles IX it became obvious that the royal line would become extinct, for the weakling sons of Henry II would not leave behind them any heirs. This led to ruthless factional rivalry between two important noble houses in France, both of which aspired to the throne. The Bourbons, who espoused Protestantism, traced their descent from St. Louis, a French king of the thirteenth century. The Guises, descendants of the powerful duke of Lorraine and champions of Catholicism, were determined to block the ambitions of the House of Bourbon in order to gain the throne themselves.

Thus a civil war was brewing, partly religious as Catholics and Huguenots reviled one another, partly political as the Guises and Bourbons plotted for royal power. Actual fighting began in 1562 and a succession of eight bitterly fought wars followed. Until her death in 1589 the most powerful individual in France was Catherine de' Medici, the queen mother of France. She was determined to maintain the power of her sons, to try to steer a middle course between the extreme Protestant and Catholic factions. Catherine, like her contemporary in London, Queen Elizabeth, was utterly cynical and ruthless when it came to statecraft. It is said that her youngest son referred to her as "Madame la Serpente." No weapon, no matter how cruel or base, was beneath her attention; one of Catherine's political weapons was "a flying squadron of beautiful but unprincipled ladies whose charms were employed to seduce the leaders of the opposition."[16] The terrible Massacre of St. Bartholomew's Day is blamed on Catherine. This horrible exhibition of religious fanaticism and political ruthlessness began at dawn on August 24, 1572, with a signal from the bell of the Palace of Justice in Paris. The Catholic party fell upon their Protestant rivals and before the day was done 10,000 were killed (see picture, page 558).

England and Spain intervene. The massacre did not destroy Huguenot power and the conflict went on. A new phase of the struggle began in 1585 when Philip of Spain joined with the Catholic party of the house of Guise to extirpate the Bourbon party. Following the assassination of Henry III in 1589, Henry of Navarre, a Bourbon prince and a Protestant, by right of succession became king of France as Henry IV. Philip II determined to crush the new king before he could consolidate his power. At this critical moment Queen Elizabeth, openly at war with Spain, sent 5000 English and Scottish troops to aid Henry of Navarre. The tide turned, civil war ended in France in 1595, and peace was made between France and Spain in the Treaty of Vervins in 1598.

The Edict of Nantes. Henry IV, realizing that the majority of his subjects were Catholic, changed his faith to that of Rome. He is supposed to have observed, "Paris is worth a mass." At the same time he sought to protect the liberties of the Huguenot minority in the Edict of Nantes (1598), a notable document in the history of civilization. It was the first important recognition by a major power that more than one religion can be maintained in a state. The Edict insured freedom of religion to the Huguenots in many cities, and by granting them other privileges saved Protestantism in France.

Spain's political and cultural dominance. Despite Philip's failures in the Netherlands, France, and England, Spain still enjoyed the reputation of being the first power in Europe. Her soldiers were considered the best trained on the continent, and in the arts of peace her writers, scholars, and painters were on a par with those found in any other country. In fact, the last half of the sixteenth century and the first decades of the seventeenth are usually regarded as the Golden Age of Spain.

During this period there were twenty-nine universities filled with students. Spanish scholars produced important works in history, geography, and mathematics. Painting flourished in the hands of such great artists as El Greco, Velásquez, and Murillo. Rubens was Flemish and lived in the Netherlands, but he was assisted and honored by Spanish governors of the territory. In the field of literature Cervantes with his immortal *Don Quixote* made the most important single Spanish contribution to world literature in this period; and the prolific and popular Lope de Vega began a distinctively Spanish drama (Chapter 17).

During the Golden Age of Spain the Iberian peninsula not only dominated Europe politically and produced masterpieces in scholarship and art, but it also diffused its language, religion, and culture from Patagonia to California in the New World as well as to the Philippines and colonial areas elsewhere.

Notwithstanding this expansive energy, political power, and cultural creativeness, Spanish culture and dominance began to decline early in the seventeenth century. The last of the so-called religious conflicts, the Thirty Years' War, accelerated this decline.

Spain in Decline: European War in the Germanies

An interlude of peace. Early in the seventeenth century, Europe, it seemed, was to have a respite from war. In England, King James I was a sincere lover of peace and was pro-Spanish in his foreign policy. France was having internal troubles and was in no position to renew the French-Hapsburg quarrel. A truce was arranged between Spain and Holland in 1609, bringing to a halt hostilities that had begun in 1568. Prospects for a long period of peace were illusory, however, for the most terrible of all the religious wars broke out in 1618.

The issues of the Thirty Years' War. The Peace of Augsburg in 1555 (Chapter 18) had failed to bring about a satisfactory religious settlement in the Germanies. By the so-called "ecclesiastical reservation" the Peace had endeavored to prevent the loss by the Catholic Church of the lands of churchmen who gave up their adherence to Rome and embraced Protestantism. It was specifically stated: "Where an Archbishop, Bishop, or other priest of our old religion shall abandon the same, his archbishopric etc. and other benefices shall be abandoned by him. The chapters and such as are entitled to it by common law shall elect a person espousing the old religion who may enter on the possession of all the rights and incomes of the place."[17] Contrary to this agreement many of the clergy who accepted Protestantism secularized and retained the lands they had held as Catholic prelates. Protestant princes claimed the right to take over lands of the Catholic Church within their states, while Catholics maintained that the Peace of Augsburg had laid down the rule that no further secularization of Church property might take place after 1552.

Another cause of dispute was that the Peace of Augsburg had recognized only the Lutheran and Catholic religions. It was declared: "All such as do not belong to the two above-named religions shall not be included in the present peace but shall be totally excluded from it."[18] There was no recognition of Calvinism, a faith that had spread rapidly in the latter part of the sixteenth century.

Although religious toleration was an issue in the case of the German Calvinists, the basic issues concerned property rights and political power that stemmed from them. In addition to questions of religion and property rights, political rivalries played an important part in bringing about the Thirty Years' War. The inevitable political rivalries among the numerous petty princes were sharpened by religious differences among them. To this was added rivalry between the emperor and many of the German princes. The emperor wanted a united and subservient Empire to strengthen his position in Europe, an ambition opposed by princes whose own power was stronger when Germany was divided and the emperor weak. Not all the princes were opponents of the emperor, however. As a Catholic leader in the continuing fights against Protestantism the emperor had a considerable following among the Catholic princes, and an occasional Protestant prince sided with him for the sake of temporary political advantage. The numerous different and sometimes conflicting issues in the Germanies created an atmosphere of tension in which one slight incident was enough to upset the precarious peace. A prelude to the contest of arms was the formation of a Protestant League of German princes in 1608 and a Catholic League, 1609. The rival parties had begun to muster their strength.

The war begins in Bohemia. The spark that ignited the new conflagration came in eastern Europe. The Bohemians, then preponderantly Protestant, had until 1618 enjoyed a large measure of toleration even under Catholic kings. Ferdinand of Hapsburg (who was to become emperor in 1619), a thoroughgoing Catholic, withdrew that measure of tolerance when he mounted the throne of Bohemia in 1617, and so precipitated the "defenestration" incident of 1618. In Prague, the capital of Bohemia, a number of Czech nobles entered the castle where the king's officials were quartered, dragged them to an open window, and hurled them into space. The two officials and their secretary dropped fifty feet but seemingly by a miracle escaped unharmed. The Catholics declared their escape was divine providence; the Czechs scoffingly retorted that the officials had landed on a soft dunghill.

The rebellious Bohemians invited Protestant Elector Frederick v of the Palatinate, a large German province along the Rhine, to rule them. The Thirty Years' War thus began. By 1620 the Catholic forces of the deposed King Ferdinand had defeated the Bohemians and their new ruler Frederick, called derisively the "Winter King." Protestantism was banned in Bohemia and Austria, and the Palatinate was turned over to Catholic Bavaria.

Renewal of the Dutch War. With the expiration of the Twelve Years' Truce in 1621, the Spanish Hapsburg monarch Philip iv decided that the time was ripe for an attack on

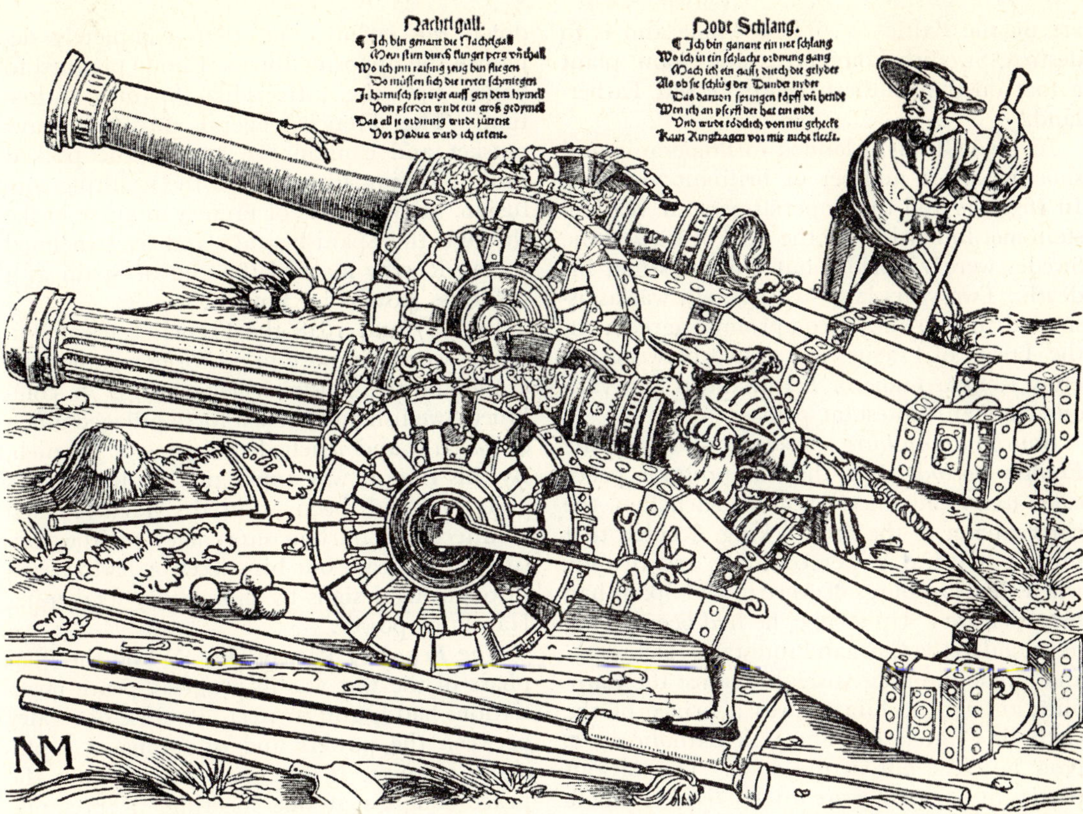

A CANNON OF ABOUT THE YEAR 1600, ILLUSTRATED BY ERHARD SCHOEN

Holland. Perhaps this rich land might be reconquered. And the defeat of Holland, added to the Hapsburg successes in the Bohemian War, might restore the Hapsburgs to European dominance and most of Europe to the Catholic fold. France and England assisted the Dutch in holding off the Spanish threat.

Hapsburgs continue victorious in the Danish period. The Bohemian revolt was the first phase of the war; the Danish period was the second. Christian IV (1588-1648) of Denmark and Norway now entered the fray, not only to champion hard-pressed Protestantism but to gain further control over North Sea ports and to thwart Hapsburg ambitions. Invading Germany in 1625, Christian was forced to fight against imperial forces led by the brilliant soldier of fortune Wallenstein, whose mercenary army composed of Protestants and Catholics alike and soldiers from all over Europe was interested primarily in booty. Christian was defeated and peace was made in 1629.

The Swedish period ends in compromise. The success of the Catholic cause drew the leading Lutheran power, Sweden, into the fray. The king of Sweden, Gustavus Adolphus, was brilliant in the arts of both peace and war. This ruler, one of the most capable statesmen in modern times, had been carefully trained by his parents. He was a good linguist, having at least a smattering of ten languages. At the age of ten he had begun to attend the council meetings of his father's advisers. As a successful administrator, he had improved Sweden's finances, courts, and schools. As a soldier, he had waged successful wars against Russia, Poland, and Denmark, and he founded a new technique of warfare based on the use of cavalry and greater mobility of armies. With his day the dominance of the foot soldier in Europe began to decline.

The Swedish king was sincerely sympathetic with the Protestant cause in Germany. Even stronger was his desire to protect Swedish national interests; he was fearful that the emperor would seize Baltic ports and threaten Sweden's sea power. Before leading his expedition to Germany, the Swedish king declared, "This is a war for the defense of our Fatherland. Denmark is used up. The Papists are on the Baltic . . . Their whole aim is to destroy Swedish commerce, and soon plant a foot on the southern shores of our Fatherland."

In 1630 Gustavus landed in Pomerania and shortly won a number of brilliant victories. In 1632, he and the imperial general Wallenstein met in battle. On the field of Lützen the Swedes were victorious but Gustavus met his death. Two years later Wallenstein was assassinated, and in 1635 a compromise agreement, the Treaty of Prague, was signed between the Holy Roman Emperor Ferdinand II and various German Protestant princes.

Bourbon-Hapsburg rivalries during the French period. But the compromise peace came to an end when Cardinal Richelieu, the chief adviser of the French king, decided that French political power could be secure only when the Hapsburgs of Austria and Spain had been defeated. Up to 1635 he had been giving secret aid to the German Protestants, Denmark, and Sweden in their struggle against the Catholics, though he himself was a prince of the Catholic Church and France a Catholic state. Now he came out in the open. The various parties in Germany were utterly tired of bloodshed, but Richelieu's game of French power politics lengthened the conflict by thirteen years. Religious issues had now largely disappeared from the war. The struggle was primarily a contest between Bourbons and Hapsburgs for the mastery of Europe.

France was in a strong position. She knew that the Protestants in Germany would keep the imperial Hapsburg armies busy while French arms could be concentrated against the Spanish Hapsburgs. The Spanish King, Philip IV, had to give up his notions of conquering Holland and was forced to meet French attacks in Burgundy, in the Spanish Netherlands, in Italy, and in Spain itself. The French army of some 200,000 men at first lacked experience in the field, but it soon developed into an effective, battle-hardened force under the command of two brilliant generals, Condé and Turenne.

Condé dealt a crushing blow to Spain's military power and reputation at the battle of Rocroy. For a century the Spanish military supremacy had been based on "hedgehog" tactics in which pikemen were wedged in a solid formation. The Spanish infantry were thus able to hold off cavalry attacks, wear down the enemy, and then completely demolish the opposing forces. Condé planned to "open up" the fortress-like Spanish formation. The French general directed heavy musket and cannon fire against the packed ranks. Taking advantage of the resulting confusion, mobile units of French infantry broke through the Spanish ranks and overwhelmed them. Rocroy marked the end of Spain as a first-class power in Europe.

In 1647 and 1648 the French general Turenne scored important victories against the armies of the Austrian Hapsburgs. A combined Swedish and French force pillaged much of Bavaria and reached the gates of Munich. By this time it was apparent that Richelieu's objective had been secured. That French architect of Bourbon supremacy on the continent was dead, but his successor had carried through his designs by thoroughly weakening Hapsburg power.

The Peace of Westphalia. While the final phase of the war was in progress, peace negotiations had begun in 1644. Because of rivalry between the powers and questions of diplomatic etiquette it was impossible to have the peace congress at one meeting. Representatives of the Catholic powers met at Münster and representatives of the Protestant states gathered at Osnabrück. The envoys of France were at both meetings.

A series of treaties, collectively known as the Peace of Westphalia, were agreed to and finally signed in October 1648. Switzerland and Holland were recognized as independent states. Sweden gained part of Pomerania and the bishoprics of Bremen and Verden. This peace marked the height of Sweden's influence in European politics. For a short time she was recognized as a first-class power. France obtained possession of Alsace together with the bishoprics of Metz, Toul, and Verdun. The rising Protestant state of Brandenburg, which later became Brandenburg-Prussia, made important gains.

The Peace of Westphalia also dealt a heavy blow to the Holy Roman Empire. The old imperial machinery of emperor, electors, and diet remained but with only a shadow of power. According to a German historian of the seventeenth century, "the imperial office had become a mummy; the constitution a monstrosity."[19] German princes were now sovereign, with the right to coin money, make war, maintain armies, and send diplomatic representatives to foreign courts.

The Peace of Westphalia likewise contained important religious provisions. Calvinists received legal recognition. Any piece of Church property was to be held by the Protestants or the Catholics who had held it in 1624. An equal number of Catholic and Protestant judges were to be provided for the Imperial courts.

France victorious over the Hapsburgs. The settlements made at Osnabrück and Münster brought no peace to harried Spain. The Austrian Hapsburgs made peace without their Spanish relatives. In consequence, Philip IV carried on the war against France for another eleven years. The French were now on the offensive and after 1657 had an alliance with England which brought 6000 of the crack troops of the famous English general Oliver Cromwell to Europe to fight against Spain.

The Peace of the Pyrenees between Spain and France was finally signed in 1659. Spain ceded to France a province in the Pyrenees region as well as a southern strip of the Spanish Netherlands. The Spanish king also consented to the marriage of his daughter to Louis XIV, the Bourbon king of France.

Thus the struggle against Hapsburg dominance begun by Francis I in the second decade of the sixteenth century was concluded successfully by France in the Peace of Westphalia and the Peace of the Pyrenees. We recall that Philip II had acknowledged his failure to conquer France in the Peace of Vervins (1598). Philip IV in 1659 was forced to sign a peace that acknowledged the end of his country's political dominance.

The English Civil Wars

The English civil wars (1642-1660) were in many respects quite different from the other religious wars. Like most of the wars on the continent, the English conflict was a complex blend of politics and religion. But unlike the Thirty Years' War, which saw the Germanies as a battleground for conflicting ambitions of various nations, the English political struggle was a domestic duel. And unlike the other wars, the English conflict carried with it a traditional English movement, the growth of representative government. Indeed, although the religious implications of the English civil wars were important, they were overshadowed by the constitutional results.

King Henry VII, gaining the throne after the Wars of the Roses, had established what might be called a popular despotism and restored law and order (Chapter 16). In order to secure speedy results, Henry VII had made his Parliaments subservient to his wishes and created a machinery of despotism which hunted down and imprisoned any malefactor who opposed the king's will. In breaking with the Church of Rome, Henry VIII, as we have seen (Chapter 18), had acted in the main with the approval of the English people. For hundreds of years there had been strong feeling manifested in England against what was felt to be unwarranted interference in domestic affairs by the Pope. The fact that the religious revolt in England had popular support, although its prime mover was a despotic king, reflected the essential nature of Tudor rule. The strong Tudor government, whether in the hands of Henry VII or his granddaughter Elizabeth, was accepted by the English people.

From 1485 to 1603, therefore, the forward march of English constitutional progress was halted. After the defeat of the Armada in 1588, however, a new spirit began to manifest itself in England. After more than a century of benevolent despotism, the English people were ready to resume the development of representative government.

James I and Parliament. Elizabeth's successor in 1603 was James Stuart, king of Scotland, who was imported from Edinburgh to reside in London. Scotland and England, though not united, now had a common king. It was of supreme importance that James I appreciate the temper of his new subjects, but this the new monarch did not do. From the outset of his reign he made it plain that he meant to be an absolute monarch. Dubbed "the wisest fool in Christendom" because of his immense book-learning and his lack of political tact, James believed in the divine right of kings.

The religious issue. As the constitutional issue of king against Parliament crystallized, it became complicated by religious issues. We remember that the religious changes brought about by Henry VIII were not basically a doctrinal revolt. Henry became head of the English Church, and independence from Rome was declared, but much of the old theology and ceremony was retained. During the reigns of Edward VI and Queen Elizabeth there was a decided trend toward Protestant changes in doctrine and ceremony. When James came to the throne, some Englishmen were content with the English church as it then stood; some, while not actually wishing to return to papal control, did wish to reintroduce much of the old ritual and some of the tenets of the Catholic Church; and some took an extreme Protestant position.

The extreme Protestants were called Puritans, because they wished to purify the Anglican Church still further, simplify the ritual, and lessen the authority of the bishops chosen by the king. The ranks of the Puritans were made up largely of men engaged in trade and commerce—the middle class living in the cities. These businessmen resented very much the growing tendency of James to resort to illegal and arbitrary taxation. The middle class was interested in influencing government in order to avoid useless and expensive wars and to secure laws to protect and expand the commercial interests of the nation. Also in the Puritan ranks were the lawyers, who supplied the middle class with historical precedents as ammunition against the growing absolutism of the Stuarts.

James's policy and its effects. James's arbitrary taxation, his evident sympathy with the pro-Catholic, or High Church, movement, and his insistence upon the royal prerogatives were the first steps leading to civil war. James quarreled with Parliament over taxation and bluntly told its members to mind their own business and not discuss church matters. This led the House of Commons to draw up and pass what it called an *Apology,* in reality a statement of its parliamentary rights. The Commons especially claimed the right "that in Parliament they may speak freely their consciences without check and controlment." In retaliation, James ruled the country practically without Parliament from 1611 to 1621.

In the latter part of King James's reign England was confronted by the Thirty Years' War. The Puritans sided with the German Protestants and were quite willing to enter the struggle. James, however, was not only pacifistic but pro-Spanish as well. Because of James's ambition to marry his son Charles to one of the daughters of the king of Spain, the Spanish ambassador at London was able to twist him in any direction he wished. James's foreign policy infuriated the Puritans, to whom Catholic Spain was anathema.

Charles I and Parliament. At the death of James I in 1625 his son Charles I inherited the English throne. The mistakes of the father were repeated by the son, to an even greater degree. Charles was well-meaning and his private life was irreproachable, but he too insisted on absolute royal power. The new reign began with stormy debate between king and Parliament. Three years later, in order to obtain revenue from Parliament, the king agreed to the famous Petition of Rights—a parliamentary declaration that ranks with *Magna Charta* as one of the great documents in the development of representative government. The most important provisions of the petition denied the right of the king to tax without parliamentary consent or to imprison a freeman without cause.

Little immediate good came of this petition, however, for Charles soon broke its provisions and ruled England from 1629 to 1640 without calling Parliament. During this period the king resorted to methods of taxation which the supporters of Parliament considered illegal. He supported the High Church party and punished those, mainly Puritans, who refused to fall in line with his religious beliefs. Several outstanding Puritan leaders of the House of Commons were imprisoned for their political and religious views. The king's taxes fell heavily upon the shoulders of the wealthy —often Puritan merchants and shopkeepers.

Charles's personal rule was terminated in 1640. When he attempted to force his brand of High Church Anglican religion on the Presbyterian Scots, they promptly took up arms against the king. Faced by a hostile army and without sufficient funds to put forces of his own into the field, Charles was forced to convene Parliament. When Parliament refused to vote any money until Charles had redressed certain grievances, Charles promptly dissolved it. But riots in England and a Scottish invasion compelled him to recall Parliament. This session became known as the "Long Parliament" because it lasted nearly twenty years. Sensing the weakness in the king's position, Parliament immediately

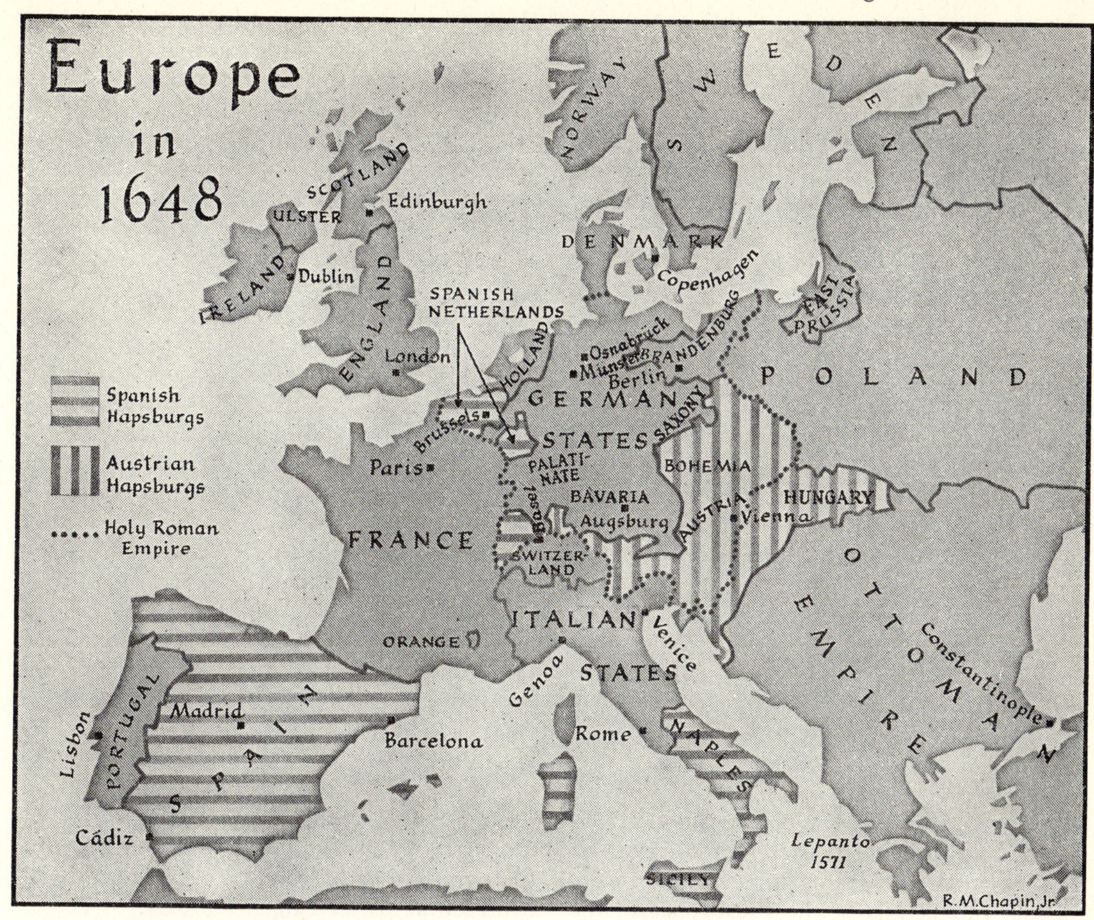

set to work to make its powers at least co-equal with those of the king. Its reforms represented a great victory for Parliament.

Trouble also arose over the question of religion. Few wanted a High Church system, but there was no unanimity as to what form of Protestantism should take its place. Out of this stalemate there quickly developed two bitterly antagonistic parties. The parliamentary, or "Roundhead," faction, was composed largely of the middle class, and won the support of the Puritans. The Puritans were divided between Independents and Presbyterians, who differed over questions of church government but agreed in holding generally to a Calvinistic system of religion and demanding even further reduction in the politico-religious prerogatives of the king. The Royalist party was called the "Cavaliers." It was supported by a great many of the landowning nobles, who opposed extreme Protestantism and, although one with the Puritans in opposing royal despotism, were unwilling to see the monarchy stripped of all its powers.

The war. Civil war broke out in 1642. In the end, control of the sea, possession of greater economic resources, superior generalship, and alliance with the Scots enabled the Roundheads to defeat the king's armies, the fighting coming to an end in 1646. For two years there was an interlude in which Charles tried to play his enemies—the Scots, the Presbyterians dominant in Parliament, and the Independents dominant in the army—against each other. He actually succeeded in splitting Parliament and making a secret alliance with the Scots. The upshot was the rise of fierce resentment against the king in the ranks of the Independent army, and in 1648 a second civil war broke out. The allies of the king were defeated, and in December 1648, all Presbyterian members of the House of Commons were excluded from that body by the victorious Independent army. Following a brief trial, King Charles was executed in January 1649.

The Commonwealth and Cromwell. The next month the House of Commons abolished the House of Lords and declared the office of king unnecessary. In May 1649, England was proclaimed a Commonwealth. The main figure in the new republican government was the Independent leader Oliver Cromwell, whose military genius had been largely responsible for defeating the king's cavalier armies. Cromwell, adopting the tactics of Gustavus Adolphus, had drilled the parliamentary forces into crack regiments of God-fearing soldiers who fought as well as they prayed.

In 1653 the Puritan army, still distrusting Parliament, overthrew the Commonwealth and set up a new form of government based on a written constitution called *The Instrument of Government.* This document, one of the earliest written constitutions of modern times, was to become influential in the later European constitutional movement. Cromwell was given supreme power as Lord Protector for life, assisted by a council and Parliament.

Now virtual dictator of England, Cromwell endeavored to achieve a religious settlement for the nation, favoring a rather tolerant religious system. But it was impossible to reconcile the Independents, the Presbyterians, the High Church party, and other religious factions, and the last three years of Cromwell's life were filled with disappointment and trouble. Although he did not favor it, his more extreme Puritan colleagues foisted on a pleasure-loving folk a series of hateful prohibitions which closed the theaters, muzzled the press, and stamped out many wholesome as well as unwholesome amusements of the people.

The Restoration. Cromwell died in 1658 and was succeeded by Richard Cromwell, his son. A man of blameless character and high ideals but without any qualities of leadership, Richard found it difficult to carry on his father's work and resigned in less than a year (1659). The restoration of the monarchy seemed the only solution to most men. Arrangements were made for Charles, the son of the late king, to return to England to become Charles II. In 1660, amid wild excitement and enthusiasm, the exiled Stuart returned to London as the legal king. But civil war and revolution had not been for nought. When Charles II became king of England it was with the explicit understanding that he should not emulate his father and grandfather but should rule through Parliament. Thus the monarchy of England was made responsible to a representative body, in contrast to the continental pattern of absolutism.

Summary

The period surveyed in this chapter witnessed the passing and disintegration of many of the outstanding features of the medieval design in western Europe. What unity the western world had possessed in the Holy Roman Empire and the Universal Church gave way before the rising national states and the Protestant Revolt. The new states, created by able and aggressive dynasties, were perhaps the dominant feature in shaping the transition from medieval to modern times. Among the new states England, France, and Spain, under the rule of ambitious dynasts, played leading roles in European politics in the sixteenth and seventeenth centuries. Areas in which effective nation states were not established became the prey of the centralized governments of other states. Italy, rich in wealth and culture, was impotent politically because disunited and became one of the cockpits of international conflict in the sixteenth century. The disunited Germanies became the battleground of European politics in the Thirty Years' War. In eastern Europe weak Bohemia and Hungary passed under alien rule.

The period we have just reviewed, roughly from 1500 to 1648, also saw the emergence of a new system in international affairs. As the influence of the Empire and the papacy declined, Europe became the battleground for the rivalries of a number of ambitious and sovereign nation states. In their relations to each other the nations practiced what has become known as "power politics," a system that was given classical exposition by the Italian diplomat Machiavelli. In this initial phase of power politics in modern Europe the implacable rivalry between the French monarchy and the Hapsburgs overshadowed all else. During this period the "balance of power" in international relations came into play on a large scale, especially in the French-Hapsburg conflict culminating in the Thirty Years' War. England was also one of the earliest powers to pursue deliberately the balance of power. Beginning with Henry VIII and his adviser Wolsey, England sought to be the main weight in maintaining the balance of power on the continent.

After 1500 Europe experienced a number of Religious Wars, so-called, that did not cease until the Peace of Westphalia in 1648. Just what was religion and what politics in these wars is often difficult to determine exactly. In fact, religion was largely politics and politics was largely religion. It is, however, undeniable that in all these wars the contestants often used religion as a cloak for selfish designs. Elizabeth fought the Armada and aided the Dutch in the name of Protestantism, but she was concerned mainly with preventing Spanish domination of Europe and interference with English maritime expansion. With Philip II of Spain, the staunch defender of Catholicism, religious conviction appropriately coincided with Spanish national interests. To champion the Catholic Church was, in Philip's mind, to build a strong Spain and to support the winning cause. When making choices, few statesmen subordinated national interests to religious principles. Witness Francis I's alliance with the Turks, Richelieu's support of the German Protestants, and Philip's early support of Elizabeth against Mary Stuart.

The Peace of Westphalia was the last set of diplomatic negotiations in which the Pope took a prominent part as an international power. When the peace was finally concluded, Pope Innocent X condemned it as "null, void, invalid, iniquitous, unjust, damnable, reprobate, inane, empty of meaning and effect for all time."[20] As was to be expected, the rulers of the time paid little attention to this denunciation.

Among the motives behind the many Wars of Religion were the ambitions of monarchs to gain territory and international influence and also the desire to strengthen their thrones at home and to add to royal prestige. The sixteenth century was the formative period of political absolutism in Europe. The seventeenth century was to be its Golden Age. Only in England did absolutism in a first-class power receive a decisive setback, which paved the way for the ultimate triumph of constitutional government.

In conclusion, it should be said that the emphasis upon wars and power politics in this chapter does not imply that history, as one famous English historian put it, "is past politics." History is much more than this, but like technology, science, religion, and the arts, politics has always had an important influence on the course of human events. A knowledge of the trend of politics from 1500 to 1648 helps to explain the governmental pattern of modern Europe. It also offers an opportunity for acquaintance with the behavior of nation states in international affairs. The cavalier manner in which sixteenth-century states broke treaties, deserted alliances, and invaded their neighbors is a good introduction to realistic thinking about power politics in our own century.

Chronology of events and developments discussed in this chapter

Chapter 20

Ming dynasty: contact with Portuguese, Jesuits, and Japanese	1368-1644
Ashikaga period in Japan: excellence in literature and architecture	1392-1568
Henry the Navigator: encouraged science and exploration	1394-1460
Columbus: discovered the New World by reaching the West Indies	1446-1506
Da Gama: sailed to the west coast of India	1469-1524
Pizarro: conquered the Incas in Peru	1471-1541
Magellan: circumnavigated the world	1480-1521
Cortes: captured the Aztecs and their tremendous wealth	1485-1547
Diaz rounded the Cape of Good Hope	1486
Rule of Babur: founded the Mogul empire in India	1494-1530
Cabot established the English claim to North America	1497
Cabral sighted land in South America	1500
Albuquerque captured Socotra; Portuguese control of the Red Sea	1506
Portuguese conquered Malacca; step toward trade with China	1511
Balboa reached the Pacific via the Americas	1513
Cartier explored the St. Lawrence River; established French claim to North America	1534-1541
Portuguese Inquisition in India	1540
Akbar: extended the Mogul empire; unsuccessful campaign in the Deccan	1542-1605
England chartered the East India Company; established posts at trading points	1600
United East India Company formed; Dutch replaced the Portuguese in eastern trade	1602
French colony founded at Nova Scotia	1604
Champlain planted a colony in Quebec	1608
Shah Jahan: Deccan added to the empire; height of Mogul power	1627-1666
Alien teachers expelled from Japan	1639
French East India Company set up; trade centered in India	1664

To the ends of the earth

Exploration; the New World; the Orient: 1400-1650

Moved by a love of adventure, of braving the unknown and its lurking danger, and of seeking fame and fortune, hardy souls have pitted their strength against their environment, until in the twentieth century they have set foot on every continent and traversed the seas from pole to pole. The same motives prompted ancient Chinese traders to brave the wastes of the Gobi Desert, Phoenician sailors to skirt the north coast of Africa and venture beyond the Pillars of Hercules out into the unmapped depths of the ocean beyond, Viking privateers to pick their way gingerly among the ice floes of the north until they had reached North America, and Mohammedan pilgrims to penetrate the arid interior of Arabia. And, as we are about to discover, a stout heart and a burning desire to explore the unknown and discover new lands for the sake of "gospel, gold, and glory" made possible the exploits of Columbus, Da Gama, Magellan, and a host of lesser luminaries. While we are reading about some of these epoch-making journeys, let us not forget the dangers which the mariners had to face daily.

They were plunging into uncharted seas whose vastness they generally knew nothing about and whose winds, currents, and shoals they had to discover by bitter experience. The vessels in which the explorers had to place their trust were unbelievably small and fragile. Whereas some of our modern liners are 80,000 tons, the two vessels which Vasco da Gama used in his voyage to India were each 120 tons, the three ships of Columbus' first voyage were one hundred, fifty, and forty tons, respectively, and the *Squirrel,* one of two ships used to found the first colony in Newfoundland, was only ten tons. Such a ship as the *Squirrel* could not have been much larger than a good-sized modern lifeboat, yet it crossed the Atlantic. These vessels had to carry as large crews as possible because skirmishes with enemy ships and hostile natives depleted the ranks, while the dreaded disease, scurvy, caused by a lack of fresh vegetables and the continued use of salt meat, often carried off half the crew. We can scarcely imagine the ignorance and superstition rampant in those centuries. The tales of travelers were replete with descriptions of strange and awful birds like the roc (which could fly away holding an elephant), mammoth sea serpents that lay in wait to devour ships, treacherous whirlpools that sucked down vessels, and great waterspouts that blew them skyward. The average sailor believed with the Hellenistic scientist Ptolemy that nobody could pass through the torrid zone and return alive, and was firmly convinced that if one sailed far enough he would come to the edge of the flat earth and even plunge over its side.

With this background in mind we should be able to obtain a clearer perspective of the daring spirit with which the Renaissance explorations were accomplished. Few leaders of such expeditions were altruistic and saintly. They were often avaricious, cruel, and unscrupulous, and the pain and degradation which they inflicted upon the peoples with whom they came in contact fill some of the darkest pages of history. But they were fearless and resourceful, and these qualities enabled them—a mere handful of Europeans—to conquer and colonize North, South, and Central America and later Australia and New Zealand, and to obtain rich concessions in Africa and Asia. It is due most of all to the deeds of the men whom we shall meet in this chapter that the civilization of western Europe became, and has remained, the dominating influence in world culture.

Geographical Discoveries

Limitations of classical knowledge. The farther one went from the Mediterranean basin, the less accurate the data became. Western Europe, the eastern Mediterranean countries, north Africa, the Red Sea region, Persia, and that part of central Asia reaching to western India were fairly well known in classical times, but the rest of the world stretched north, south, east, and west into uncharted and mysterious regions concerning which there existed the most extraordinary legends. To explain the lands and seas about which no accurate data was known was the self-assigned job of the most influential of all classical geographers, Ptolemy, whom we met in Chapter 6.

Ptolemy (about 130 A.D.). Having to rely for much of his information upon sailors' tales, legends, and hearsay remarks, Ptolemy constructed a map of the world that was in many respects fantastic. Yet two mistakes which he made proved of great value to later generations of explorers. He constructed his map according to a system of latitude and longitude, but as his calculations were inaccurate, he made the degree too long. Furthermore, his circumference of the world was 5000 miles short. The result was that he exaggerated the length and especially the width of the known inhabited world, so that the interval between western Europe and eastern Asia looked very much smaller than it really is. Because men of the fifteenth century accepted Ptolemy as the chief geographical authority, Columbus accepted his calculations concerning the distance which would have to be traversed and so was encouraged to sail west from Spain in search of the Asiatic coast. Had Columbus known the exact distance between Europe and Asia, he would unquestionably never have attempted the almost impossible journey.

Another important error of Ptolemy's map was the inclusion of a strip of land which extended from Africa to Asia, making the Indian Ocean an inland sea. Explorers were encouraged by Ptolemy's map to search the southern seas for the fictitious territory, known as "terra australis incognita." Finally explorers stumbled upon Australia; so Ptolemy's wrong guess was in a sense actually confirmed.

However, Ptolemy made other serious errors which hindered the progress of exploration for more than a thousand years. One of them was his belief that the habitable world of the north temperate zone was separated from the south temperate zone by a middle zone of heat so deadly that it was impossible to cross from the north to the south.

Medieval geography. During the Middle Ages geography became a handmaiden of theology in the hands of devout cartographers. In *Christian Topography,* written about 547 by Cosmas the Alexandrian traveler, the earth was made flat, with Jerusalem in the center, paradise in the east, and the Pillars of Hercules in the west. St. Beatus' eighth-century map follows a similar pattern. Such early medieval maps were documents of curiosity rather than fact, with lands drawn in which no man had ever seen, fabulous monsters depicted in choice localities, and the blanks filled in with elephants for towns. However, during the later Middle Ages books on astronomy taught that the earth was a sphere, and "sufficient records remain to reveal the middle of the fourteenth century to us as an age of globetrotters and world-wide adventurers."

Norse discoveries. Somewhere around 982 the son of a Norwegian noble by the name of Eric the Red, banished from Iceland, sailed west and discovered Greenland. Four years later settlers arrived and two towns were established. A colony existed in Greenland until the fifteenth century.

In 1002 Leif, the son of Eric the Red, voyaged to America. He probably arrived first at Labrador, then journeyed southward, where he saw land containing trees, wild grain, and grapevines, a region either in Nova Scotia or New England. Leif called the country Vineland. Other voyages were made by the Norse, who sailed Arctic waters in open boats with neither chart nor compass five hundred years before Columbus dared the crossing in warmer waters. But monumental though these voyages were, they apparently added little or nothing to the geographical knowledge of contemporary Europeans.

Medieval travelers. In the thirteenth and fourteenth centuries a number of Europeans, many of them Christian missionaries, journeyed to the Far East. The most famous of the travelers was Marco Polo. But the exploits of the fourteenth century had little permanent effect because of certain political changes that came in the last decades of that century. The Mongol dynasty in China, which had been friendly to European missionaries and merchants, was overthrown, and the succeeding Mings proved anti-foreign. Meanwhile the Turks with their fanatical Islamic religion had overrun western Asia. These two developments put an end to further European penetration into the Orient. Travel was stopped, but trade continued at certain terminals which the Moslems controlled.

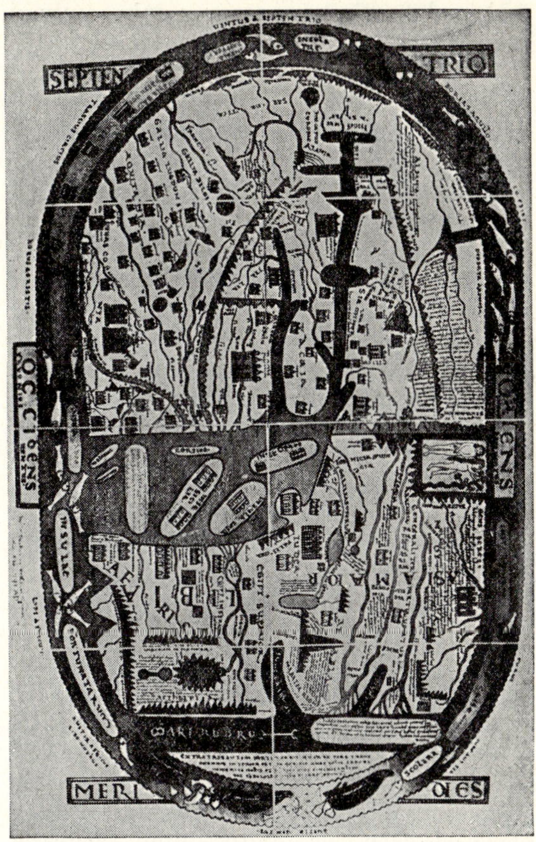

St. Beatus drew this map depicting a flat world in a Spanish monastery in the eighth century. Judea and a paradise for Adam and Eve occupy the center. Discernible are the Mediterranean, Europe, Africa, and Asia Minor.

Far Eastern trade routes. There were three major routes by which the rich commerce flowed from the Far East to Europe (see map, pages 202-203.) The northern one cut across central Asia to the Caspian and Black seas, the middle route passed through the Persian Gulf and the Euphrates valley to termini in

Syria and the Black Sea coast, and the southern route struck up the Red Sea and over to the Nile and northern Egypt. The commerce which flowed through these routes was rich indeed, especially after the impetus given it by the crusades.

The search for new routes. During the fifteenth century, however, certain European nations were seeking new routes to the east. One reason lay in the numerous difficulties which commerce had to undergo on its long and dangerous journey from the Orient to Europe, together with the payment of many heavy tolls and duties en route. But an even more important reason is to be found in conditions in Europe itself. The Mediterranean carrying trade was in the hands of the Italian city-states, who thus wielded a complete and rich monopoly. Hence the merchants of northern and western Europe were garnering but little of the huge profits of the expanding trade with the east. High prices and low profits were scarcely palatable to the merchants and rulers of the countries along the Atlantic seaboard, and they determined to do something about the matter.

Furthermore, they were in a position to do something. We will recall that because of Ptolemy's mistaken views on the distance between Europe and Asia many mariners believed firmly that contact could be made directly between the two continents by sailing westward. Still other sailors were of the opinion that if Africa could be circumnavigated, a route lay east to India and Cathay. Fifteenth-century political conditions also favored the Atlantic seaboard countries. Southeastern Europe was being harried by the Turks, while the Italian city-states were weakening each other by bitter commercial quarrels. But the situation on the Iberian peninsula had a positive aspect. The Moors were being driven slowly but surely out of Spain, while the zealous Spaniards were eager to expand their territory to the south. Meanwhile Portugal, being poor in land and resources, was anxious to explore the Atlantic to the south in order to gain more territory and wage war against the infidel.

Prince Henry the Navigator. The real driving force behind the new and brilliant Portuguese achievements in exploration and discovery was Prince Henry, known in history as Henry the Navigator. Born in 1394, the third son of King John of Portugal, Prince Henry the Navigator devoted his life to scientific exploration and the extension of Portugal's empire and commerce. For over forty years Henry pored over maps and sent forth expedition after expedition to unravel the secrets of the coastline of Africa. Prince Henry gathered about him skilled cartographers and navigators to construct accurate maps and eradicate errors, so that his sailors were the best equipped mariners of their time. He took pains to create the finest vessel for long voyages, and thus the caravel, which contemporaries called the best sailing ship afloat, was developed.

It was much easier now to send ships off great distances with a fair hope that they would return safely. As early as the twelfth century a crude form of the compass was in use, a magnetic needle floating on a straw in water. This device, employed in China as early as the first century, had been improved by the fourteenth century so that it was now a needle which pivoted on a card showing the points of the compass. During the fifteenth century another great aid to navigation came into general use—the astrolabe, a graduated brass circle by which the altitude of stars could be estimated and latitudes more accurately measured.

The African voyages. Henry's mariners did not fail him, although he died before any of the numerous expeditions he sent forth had explored the length of Africa. However, in 1486 Bartholomew Diaz succeeded in rounding the Cape of Good Hope. Diaz noticed that the African coast now swung to the northeast, but he was forced to turn back at the insistence of his disgruntled crew, and once more rounding the great cape, which he named *Cabo Tormentoso*, or Cape of Storms, he sailed back to Lisbon. Pleased with the prospect of soon finding a direct sea route to India, King John II of Portugal renamed the Cape of Storms with the less forbidding title Good Hope.

Vasco da Gama (1469?-1524). The final stage in the African voyages was reached by Vasco da Gama. He commanded the African expedition of 1497, on which he proved himself a splendid navigator and a firm leader of men. His resourcefulness was demonstrated after his four ships had arrived at the Cape Verde Islands. Instead of hugging the coastline as his predecessors had done, da Gama struck

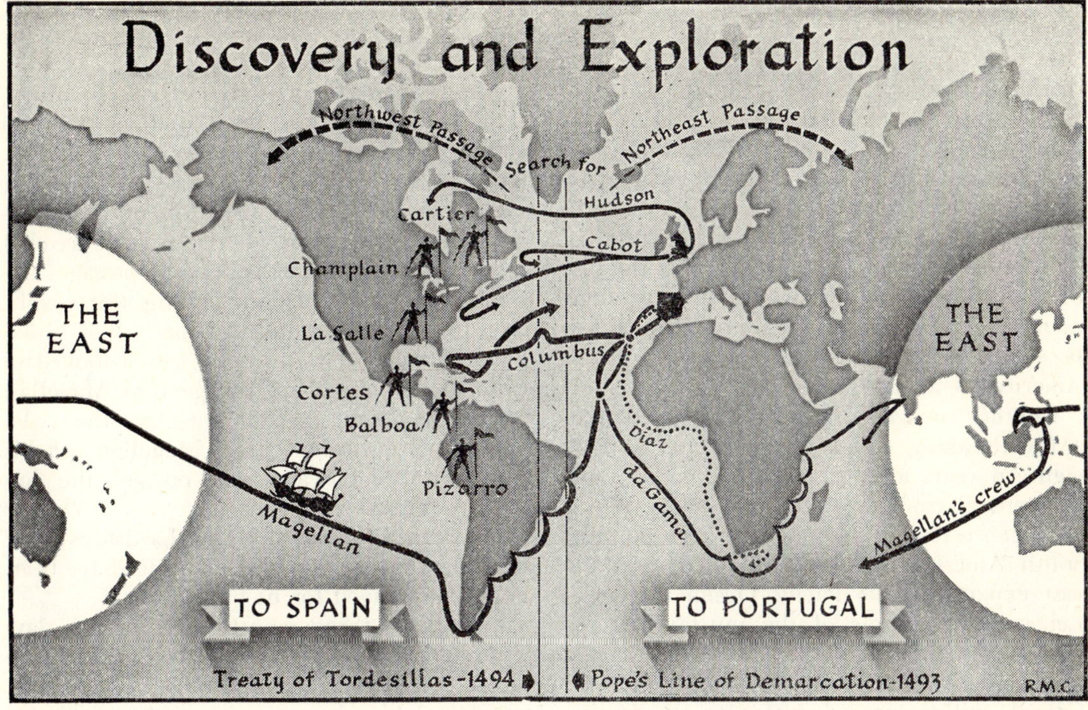

bravely out into the Atlantic and sailed for ninety-three days in a direct course toward the Cape of Good Hope. Rounding the Cape, he pushed northward into Arab waters. Finally he procured an Arab pilot who brought him, after a sail of twenty-three days across the Indian Ocean, to the west coast of India. It is amusing to read that the Portuguese mistook the Hindus for Christians (because they were not Moslems) and even reverently attended a service. "They were, however, somewhat amazed that the figures painted on the walls, which they assumed to be those of saints, had teeth protruding an inch from their mouths and possessed four or five arms."[1]

The Portuguese incurred the enmity of the Arabs, whose Indian trading monopoly they had thus broken, and difficulties were put in the way of the Europeans' home voyage. Not until July of 1499 did da Gama drop anchor at Lisbon, after having lost half his ships and two thirds of his men through scurvy and other misfortunes. But the cargo which da Gama brought home was worth sixty times the cost of the expedition, and da Gama was rewarded fittingly, for the King of Portugal could now assume the mighty title "Lord of the Conquest, Navigation, and Commerce of Ethiopia, Arabia, Persia, and China."

***Columbus* (*1446?-1506*).** Meanwhile another Atlantic power had not been idle. The Spaniards, proud of their powerful new state, were anxious to enjoy the riches and prestige of a colonial empire. Their ambition was realized mainly through the exploits of an Italian sailor called Christopher Columbus.

Columbus' expedition left Spain in August 1492. Proceeding westward into uncharted waters, Columbus sailed thirty-three days before land was sighted. At length he set foot on a small island in the West Indies. After traveling for three months among the islands, he sailed home, arriving at Spain in March 1493.

Although he made three other voyages to the New World in a vain attempt to find a direct opening to the mainland of Asia, Columbus by his first voyage had already revolutionized history, though he did not know it. A new world had been discovered, the old geographical views concerning the earth and its size had been shattered, and Europe was soon to colonize and fight over the new lands. The voyage had immediate repercussions. The monopoly of Portugal on discovery was broken, and some sort of compromise had to be worked out regarding the respective geographical spheres of both the Portuguese and the Spanish. By a papal bull issued in 1493 a line of demarcation was drawn on the map (see page 573). All lands lying to the west of this meridian belonged to Spain, while all new discoveries made to the east were to become the rightful property of Portugal. But the latter country felt that the Pope's arrangement would keep its operations too close to the African coast. Consequently the Treaty of Tordesillas with Spain a year later set the line of demarcation farther west. This arrangement later allowed Portugal to claim Brazil because of Cabral's accidental voyage to South America, as we shall see.

Cabral's voyage to Brazil. We now come to a breath-taking epoch of discovery. Within eighteen years after Columbus died in 1506, the general configuration of the New World had been revealed, the most southern point of South America had been rounded, and the vast expanse of the Pacific Ocean traversed. Let us review some of the outstanding explorers and their deeds.

In 1500 a Portuguese commander named Cabral, sailing around Africa to the Indies, was blown far off his course. He sighted land in South America. This territory was acquired for Portugal, and that is why today the people of Brazil speak the Portuguese language.

Balboa. Explorers kept looking for a passage through the new lands which would lead them to Asia, voyaging along the coasts of Central America and the northern portion of South America. A settlement was made on the isthmus of Darien, and here a youthful Spaniard, Vasco Núñez de Balboa, heard tales from the Indians of a great ocean but a short distance to the west. In 1513 Balboa with a handful of soldiers set eyes upon the Pacific Ocean—and Europe was ready to explore a new realm of conquest.

Magellan (1480?-1521). In 1519 a Portuguese navigator in the service of Spain found the passage that led into the Pacific. He was Ferdinand Magellan, whose remarkable achievements entitle him to equal rank with Columbus and Vasco da Gama. Columbus made Europe acquainted with the New World; da Gama showed the way to the Far East; Magellan now linked the two areas by circumnavigating the world. He had for some time believed that it was possible to sail around South America just as Diaz had rounded Africa. The Spanish king fitted him out with a fleet of five small ships which were "very old and patched up" and ordered Magellan to make straightway for the Spice Islands.

We have an excellent account of the voyage, thanks to the Italian Antonio Pigafetta, who accompanied Magellan and kept a diary. Toward the end of August 1520, Magellan made his memorable discovery of the strait which bears his name. Between huge ice-clad mountains and through tortuous passages the small ships made their way, taking thirty-eight days to journey 320 miles. Finally they sailed out upon the western ocean, which looked so calm after the stormy voyage that Magellan termed it Pacific. After hugging the coast northward for some time, Magellan set his course northwestward and crossed the unknown expanse of the Pacific.

Pigafetta's account. The hardships that Magellan and his men had to suffer have been vividly portrayed for us by Pigafetta:

"We were three months and twenty days without getting any kind of fresh food. We ate biscuit, which was no longer biscuit, but powder of biscuits swarming with worms, for they had eaten the food. It stank strongly of the urine of rats. We drank yellow water that had been putrid for many days. We also ate some ox hides that covered the top of the main yard to prevent the yard from chafing the shrouds, and which had become exceedingly hard because of the sun, rain, and wind. We left them in the sea for four or five days and then placed them for a few moments on top of the embers, and so ate them; and often we ate sawdust from boards. Rats were sold for one-half ducado apiece, and even then we could not get them. But above all the other misfortunes the following was the worst: The gums of both the lower and upper teeth of some of our men swelled, so that they could not eat under any circumstances and therefore died. . . . We sailed about four thousand leagues during those three months and twenty days through an open stretch in that Pacific Sea. In truth it was very pacific, for during that time we did not suffer any storm. . . . Had not God and His blessed Mother given us so good weather, we would all have died of hunger in that exceeding vast sea. Of a verity I believe no such voyage will ever be made [again]."[2]

The end of the voyage. In March 1521, Magellan came to islands that he mistook for the Spice Islands, which were in reality the Philippines. At one of these islands the intrepid explorer was slain during a skirmish with natives. After numerous adventures his crew in a single vessel, the *Victoria,* crossed the Indian Ocean, rounded the Cape of Good Hope, and dropped anchor in a Spanish harbor in September 1522. Practically three years to the day had been required to circumnavigate the globe.

Cortes in Mexico. Meanwhile the Spaniards were making valuable land discoveries in the interior of the New World. In 1519, the year Magellan set forth, a youthful adventurer by the name of Hernando Cortes (1485-1547) led an expedition to Mexico, whence had come rumors of great riches and a high native civilization. Montezuma, ruler of the native Aztecs, had thousands of warriors, while Cortes had a mere handful. But the Spaniards possessed horses, iron armor, and gunpowder, all unknown to the Aztecs. Two other factors aided the Europeans—the discontent of many native tribes, who chafed under the stern rule of the Aztecs and who were willing to join Cortes, and an ancient legend in Mexico that the Aztecs would one day be visited and destroyed by strange, white-skinned gods.

The superstitious Montezuma sent many embassies bearing rich gifts to Cortes with the order to leave the country. A helmet was brought filled with gold dust to the brim. But such lavish gifts had the opposite effect, for instead of persuading the Spaniards to depart, they excited the gold-mad adventurers to push on to Tenochtitlan, the Aztec capital city. After various exploits, Cortes eventually captured Tenochtitlan in 1521. With this defeat the Aztecs soon lost their entire empire to the Spanish conqueror, or *conquistador,* and it was not long before the Spanish had explored most of Central America and California.

Pizarro in Peru. Other *conquistadores* now emulated the success of Cortes. Tales had come to Darien that a mighty empire lay to the south, of such boundless riches that a cattle raiser by the name of Francisco Pizarro (1471?-1541) decided to explore and conquer the fabulous kingdom of Peru.

The civilization which Pizarro was searching for was that of the Incas, the most advanced people in the western world, whose far-flung empire stretched along the western

Cortes, in western armor and apparently aided by other Indian tribes, does battle with the Aztecs in this illustration from a contemporary manuscript.

coast (see map, page 580). Pizarro managed to meet the emperor, whom he treacherously seized. To win his freedom the emperor promised to pay the following ransom: He would have a room twenty-two feet long and seventeen feet wide filled halfway up the walls with jars and other objects of gold and also have it filled twice over with silver. One may expect that the impoverished Pizarro and his men accepted the offer. Magnificent golden treasures of art poured in from the empire, such as "fountains designed to emit sparkling jets of gold," and golden trees, plants, animals, birds, and fruits. But the Christians were not art connoisseurs, with the result that the priceless treasures were all melted down into simple but solid bullion.

Despite the ransom the Spanish did not release the emperor but on trumped-up accusations sentenced him to be burned to death. However, because the ruler turned Christian, he was merely strangled to death. In 1533 Pizarro entered the Inca capital, where he reaped further treasure. Later he built a new city, Lima, the "City of Kings." It took many years to subjugate the infuriated Incas elsewhere, but eventually most of South America (with the exception of Brazil) passed into Spanish control.

Spaniards in North America. Meanwhile the Spanish had not been inactive in exploring North America. During the sixteenth century various intrepid Spanish explorers opened up the interior, thereby giving Spain the right to claim a huge area in North America, stretching from Florida to California.

English exploration. While Portuguese and Spaniards were making discoveries and establishing empires, other European powers had not been idle. France, England, and Holland were embarking upon significant geographical schemes. Naturally the division of the overseas world between Spain and Portugal as set forth by the Bull of Demarcation of 1493 and the treaty of 1494 was scarcely calculated to arouse enthusiasm among other European powers, and it was not long before France and England encroached on the private preserves of both Portugal and Spain.

In 1497 an Italian mariner in the employ of England, John Cabot by name, sailed across the north Atlantic in a small ship manned by only eighteen men. Although close-fisted Henry VII had contributed no money to the defraying of expenses, he granted Cabot the right to enlist English sailors and sail west to Cathay in the name of the king of England. After six weeks of turbulent sailing the ship arrived off the northern coast of the New World. Cabot's main discovery was an extensive fishing ground, but he was disappointed in not reaching at least Japan and the Spice Islands. When he returned home, he was made Grand Admiral and given £10 by Henry VII with the right to make another voyage. He made his second voyage in 1498, coasting along the eastern shore in a vain attempt to find a passage to the orient.

Cabot was the first European after the hardy Northmen to land on the continent of North America, and, what was most important, his discovery laid the foundation for England's claim to the whole rich continent. Thus for £10 and a title England eventually won all of Canada, Newfoundland, Labrador, and even thirteen unruly colonies along the Atlantic coast—certainly an excellent business transaction.

For the next hundred years England tried to get to China by means of the famous "northwest passage." It was believed that such a passage must exist north of Canada. Explorers like Henry Hudson lost their lives in a vain attempt to discover this route. Meanwhile, an attempt to reach Cathay via a "northeast passage" above Russia also ended in disaster.

Certain other English explorers distinguished themselves in various ways. Sir Francis Drake circled the globe in 1577-1580, plundering Spanish galleons en route and bringing his ship *Golden Hind* home to Elizabeth laden with booty. Still later, in the eighteenth century, Captain Cook explored Australia and other lands in the south Pacific.

French exploration. Between 1534 and 1541 Jacques Cartier tried to find the northwest passage. As a result he discovered much about the St. Lawrence, and so gave France its claim to sovereignty over eastern North America.

France followed up this initial work by founding a colony in Nova Scotia in 1604. Then in 1608 an adventurous soldier called Samuel de Champlain (b. 1567) founded at Quebec the first permanent French settlement in America (the English had already established a colony in Virginia the year before). In later years this vigorous explorer and administrator journeyed through the lake which bears his name and went westward to the Great Lakes.

Other Frenchmen continued the task of opening up the interior of North America. The great explorer of the Mississippi was La Salle. In 1681 he sailed down the Mississippi to the Gulf of Mexico, taking possession of the entire territory and naming it Louisiana. He encountered frightful privations at times, his expedition more than once having to eat crocodiles in lieu of better food. La Salle himself nearly died from fever which racked his body for forty days. Thanks to La Salle more than to any other man, France was able later to claim the entire Mississippi valley.

Old Civilizations in the New World

The Spanish colonial empire. Spanish exploration had won for Spain most of the New World—the southern portion of North America, all Central America, and the greater part of South America, as well as various groups of islands in the Pacific. Whereas the eastern hemisphere proved to be of little colonizing value to Portugal, Spain found the opposite to be true in the western hemisphere. The New World was sparsely populated, and the native peoples were no match for the superior arms and organization of the invaders. The *conquistadores* soon learned that important fact and ruthlessly began to exploit and subjugate the natives. How the highly civilized peoples of Mexico and Peru were largely tricked into subjugation by Cortes and Pizarro has been discussed earlier. The Spaniards subjected the Indians to slavery, pillaged them of their wealth, and often exterminated them.

Spanish colonial affairs were administered along absolutist lines. The king made all laws for Spanish America, and his agency was the Royal and Supreme Council of the Indies. This council nominated and the crown appointed the most important official, the viceroy. Each viceroy had his own advisory council. While the administrative system was designed to act fairly, difficulties of communication in the New World and the prevalence of graft in the highest administrative circles made it possible for the entire setup to become corrupt, cumbersome, and oppressive.

The commercial policy was one that came to be called mercantilism, a system in vogue in all the European countries in early modern times in which the ruler and his government rigidly supervised trade and all commercial activity, to the end that the mother country would be able to use her colonies, if she had any, for her own enrichment. It was believed that by exporting more goods than were imported a favorable trade balance would build up a constantly growing reserve of gold and silver. The king exercised a royal monopoly through the establishment of the *Casa de Contratación*, or House of Trade. It regulated commerce, furnished licenses, granted trading rights, and controlled emigration and immigration. Until the middle of the seventeenth century it was a crime punishable by death or lifelong servitude in the mines for a foreign shipmaster to enter Spanish-American waters. Later, smuggling did not cease on that account, while political losses by Spain in Europe finally brought about a liberalizing of trade policy overseas.

Yet despite the great wealth of the New World—its fabulous mines, of which the Spanish king enjoyed a "royal fifth" of all gold, silver, and precious stones, and its extensive farming and lucrative stock raising—Spain nevertheless lost her great colonial empire. Her colonial policy was harmful; mercantilism proved an artificial barrier to trade, and smuggling by other countries increased. The brutality of the colonists toward the natives, who were little used to such hard work as was now imposed on them, together with such innovations of European civilization as smallpox and cheap intoxicating liquors, wiped out a terrible percentage of the native population. This state of affairs was not properly corrected by the government. The loss of native help brought about a loss of productivity, and the introduction of Negro slaves to replace the Indians created more social problems. From the seventeenth century onward Spain gradually declined from a first- to a second-class power, losing her South American colonies in the early nineteenth century and Cuba and the Philippines in the last decade of the same century.

The real "American tragedy." "The only good Indian is a dead Indian" was the simple creed of the American frontier as the plainsmen drove back and exterminated the original inhabitants of the continent. Not only the Spanish and Portuguese but the English, French, and Yankees looked with contempt upon the Indian, considering him little more than a savage and his possessions and lands fit prey for Europeans. Today, after we have taken away his continents and destroyed most of his ancient heritage, after we have ruined his physical constitution with alcohol, tuberculosis, and smallpox and almost exterminated his race as we exterminated the buffalo, we realize the tragic injustice which we inflicted upon that proud individual, whose chief sin was that his way of living interfered with the territorial ambitions of those who came before us.

Today, when in many instances it is too late to remedy the situation, we are beginning to appreciate the Indian not only as a human being but also as the creator of cultures as complex and advanced as those which we studied in Egypt, Mesopotamia, and ancient India. It is true that we had much to offer besides "firewater" which would better the Amerind (American Indian). But he, too, had lessons to teach us, lessons which were admirably expressed in an answer delivered to the Virginia Commission in 1744 when that worthy body offered to educate six Indian youths at William and Mary:

"Several of our young people were formerly brought up at Colleges of the Northern Provinces; they were instructed in all your sciences; but when they came back to us, they were bad runners, ignorant of every means of living in the woods, unable to bear either cold or hunger, knew neither how to build a cabin, take a deer, or kill an enemy, spoke our language imperfectly, were therefore neither fit for hunters, warriors, or counsellors; they were totally good for nothing. We are, however, not the less obliged by your kind offer, though we decline accepting it; and to show our grateful Sense of it, if the Gentlemen of Virginia will send us a Dozen of their Sons we will take great care of their Education, instruct them in all we know, and make Men of them."

When the Europeans first came to the western hemisphere, North and South America contained numerous peoples, each having distinctive patterns of living. Four civilizations stand out in particular: the Pueblo culture in the southwest, the Aztec in the valleys and highlands of Mexico, the Maya in the Yucatan peninsula of Mexico, and the Inca in South America. These four outstanding cultures evolved to such a complex level that they can be properly compared with those found in Egypt, Mesopotamia, and the Indus valley.

The Pueblo culture. In a high mesa land in the southwest there developed in prehistoric times probably the highest culture in North America, that of the Pueblo Indians. These peoples built two kinds of pueblos, or communal villages. The Mesa Verde people constructed their pueblos in caves usually located a short distance beneath the rim rocks of canyons and hence were true cliff dwellers. The picture shows a typical cliff pueblo. The other type was built on the floor of a canyon. At Chaco Canyon the sites of forty or more such settlements have been found. A few of the largest have been excavated and reveal the great advancement which these early peoples had made before they abandoned the area altogether. In Asia, in Africa along the Nile, and in Mexico and Central America the architecture of temples and palaces was far superior to anything built by the Pueblo Indians, but in architecture evolved for actual living and family needs, Pueblo residential buildings were the equal of anything found in the most advanced ancient cultures. The Pueblo Indians were unique among the Indians of North America in their use of masonry for permanent buildings, in contrast to the relatively temporary structures of the more nomadic tribes.

The people of Chaco Canyon were agriculturalists, intensively cultivating numerous small plots of ground on the floor of the canyon, ranging from a few square feet to a few acres in area. Their crops consisted of corn, squash, beans, and a few other vegetables. They used no metals for farming, and their tools were made of wood and stone. The Pueblos were the only North American Indians to cultivate cotton for making textiles and to domesticate the turkey. They were also unique in that the men instead of the women did the weaving and the cultivating of the crops. Other interesting features of their culture were snake dances, rain ceremonies, and corn dances. Not knowing anything about the wheel, they had no kind of vehicle for hauling stone or logs. They made fine pottery, bone awls, and other implements and tools needed for living. The Pueblo Indian was exceptionally gifted in the making of pottery. No other tribe north of Mexico could rival the variety, form, and decoration of the Pueblo wares.

Of all the Indians of the North American continent, the Pueblo people were the only group to come near the excellence of the very advanced civilizations of the ancient Maya and Aztec Indians. The governing body in the pueblo was a council presided over by a chief, who was in no sense an arbitrary ruler but was duly chosen by the people. Some anthropologists assert that pueblo representative government is one of the oldest republican governments in world history.

The Aztecs. Twelve to fifteen hundred miles to the southeast of the Pueblo area, two other advanced cultures originated and developed, comparable in many respects to the highest civilizations found in the Nile, Mesopotamian, and Indus valleys. The Aztecs were the dominant people in the highlands of Mexico just prior to the coming of Columbus to the western continent. The rise of the Aztecs to power came about in this way. About the first century A.D. a people called the Toltecs swept down from the north and took possession of the Mexican plateau. Coming in contact with the Mayas, the Toltecs absorbed much of the Mayan culture and themselves built splendid cities. By the twelfth century the Toltecs and allied peoples created a sizable empire. Soon

A PUEBLO CLIFF DWELLING AT MESA VERDE

thereafter the Aztecs swept down from the northwest. About 1325 they founded a lake settlement called Tenochtitlan on the site of the present Mexico City. Then, allying themselves with two other tribes, the Aztecs created a confederacy which in the fifteenth century ruled an empire extending across Mexico from the Gulf of Mexico to the Pacific Ocean. Aztec domination, however, lasted less than a century, for the arrival of Cortes in 1520 brought about its collapse.

Aztec religion. The Aztecs, like the Mayas, were devoted sun worshipers. They were fiercely religious, so much so that the form and function of their great state might be called a democratic theocracy. In every city of their large domain great pyramids were built, and on top of them were erected their temples to the sun. In the temples stone altars were set up, on which were sacrificed thousands of victims in ceremonies dedicated to Huitzilopochtli, the war and sun god, a bloodthirsty deity whom tradition credited with having need of human blood to sustain him in his daily task. Captives, including men, women, and children, were led up to the summit of the pyramid, where, stretched out on the sacrificial stone, they had their hearts torn out by the priests as an offering to the god. The ever-present problem was a sufficient supply of victims for these sacrifices. One method of getting them was to send emissaries among the neighboring tribes to stir up trouble so that an excuse for warfare could be found. Aztecan superiority usually enabled them to capture large numbers of their nomad neighbors.

Fortunately there was a more benign god whose influence was in the direction of tolerance—Quetzalcohuatl, the gentle god of the winds and heavens, to whom no blood sacrifices were offered. This deity is symbolized in their art as a feathered serpent, a being with the combined qualities of a bird—the feathers—and a serpent—fangs, tongue, and scales on the body. This composite creature symbolized the earth as mother and the sky as father of all. The Aztecs were thus worshipers of both the earth and the sun. Although Huitzilopochtli, the war god, had the strongest influence, Quetzalcohuatl was associated with law, order, and enlightenment. Their belief in Quetzalcohuatl made for what refinement and virtue the Aztecs possessed. They also had some conception of an abstract god, who is referred to in their poems and other literary in-

In a book of Indian folklore appeared this picture of an Aztec orchestra. A drum made from a tree trunk, sea snail shells, and rattlers are shown. The Aztecs also played clay pipes and flutes.

ventions as the "Cause of All." The Aztecs believed in a life after death with future rewards and punishments, baptism as a means of getting rid of innate sin, and confession to do away with sins committed after birth.

Culture advances. The Aztecs developed efficient systems of irrigation and agriculture and had a very complicated form of government under Montezuma II at the time of the coming of Cortes. They also constructed a very accurate calendar and an interesting pictographic system of writing. Architecture, sculpture, pottery, and weaving were highly developed. Their religion influenced their social structure, their form of government, their agriculture, and their art. Quetzalcohuatl, the feathered serpent, furnished the motif of much of their artistic endeavors, which combined complex decoration and simplified figures.

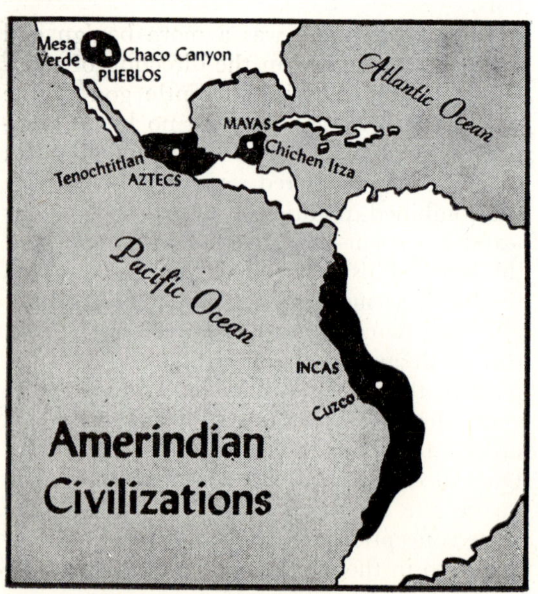

Among some writers there are differences of opinion as to the form of government of the Aztec peoples. Earlier writers looked upon it as an empire, and the ruler was thought of as an absolute king. The present tendency in interpreting their governmental development is to look upon it as essentially a democracy. All men except the rather large priesthood were soldiers. Schools were maintained for both groups, the priests and the warriors. Rank was determined mainly by success in war. Common warriors were classed in one rank; those who had distinguished themselves, in another, higher rank. Chiefs were elected from powerful families and could be removed. Sons or brothers of chieftains succeeded chiefs if they were fit.

The Mayas. More than a thousand years before the birth of Christ a group of Indians called Mayas migrated into northern Central America. It is estimated by some scholars that Mayan civilization had an even longer history before the beginning of the Christian era, for their calendrical system was in working order at least six hundred years B.C. Gradually evolving their culture, by about 600 A.D. the Mayas had built wonderful cities in the southern part of their territory. Later, these southern cities sank into decay, and a new empire flourished in the northern lowlands, where thriving cities were erected. From about 980 to 1200 a confederacy of city-states held sway, and during that period there was a splendid Mayan renaissance, with advances in architecture, art, and drama. Mayan civilization at its height was much more advanced than any other on the western continents. The new empire, however, fell prey to internal strife, with petty chieftains fighting for supremacy. Added to civil war were the inroads made by Toltec and Aztec invaders, so that Mayan population and culture declined. When the *conquistadores* came upon the scene, the country was in chaos, and the Spaniards found it a simple matter to annex the Mayan peoples.

Mayan society. The Mayan political system, like that of the Greeks, was based upon independent city-states. Each city-state had perhaps 25,000 inhabitants and was protected by stone walls. Within the city-state there was strict social stratification. The highest classes consisted of the priests and nobles. Below them were the farmers, craftsmen, and merchants. Then came the lowest freemen, while the bottom rank was the slaves. The lot of the slaves was anything but advantageous, for until the arrival of the Spaniards there were no beasts of burden or wheeled vehicles in North America, and the slaves were made to perform all tasks of drudgery. Clothing was scanty, but the upper classes wore a great deal of jewelry, and tattooing was much in vogue. Daily bathing was practiced by all classes; the Mayans enjoyed a reputation for cleanliness in both person and dress.

The successful conquest of rich agricultural lands made possible the achievement of a civilization ranking in many respects with the highest of the Old World. Less militant and warlike than the Aztecs, the Mayas were able to devote much more time to the development of the arts and sciences, philosophy and literature.

Mayan art. In architecture and sculpture they produced work of the highest quality. Their principal structures were built around courts or plazas, a plan which carried with it the idea of a civic center. In the court or plaza was built a terraced mound or pyramid. Temples built on top of the pyramids were generally one story in height, but in palaces two and three stories were common. The Mayas applied their sense of design to architecture with fine success. They had not invented the true arch with a keystone but used a type of corbeled arch. This meant that the rooms were narrow. Limestone abounds in nearly all parts of the Mayan area; it was burned into lime from which they made concrete mortar. Their buildings were to a great extent made of rubble mixed with mortar and veneered with stone or stucco. The architectural composition emphasized horizontal lines and showed a fine sense of proportion, as the Temple of the Warriors on page 583 proves. Compare the temple

This is the Aztec god Quetzalcohuatl, looking not so kindly as one might expect but smoking a peace pipe. He is surrounded by feathered serpents.

In this Mayan village the inhabitants are seen fishing, tilling the soil, cooking, and playing games. Notice the motif of the plumed serpent, perhaps pictured as guarding over the village, in the upper right corner. This picture was an illustration for a Mayan manuscript.

with the ziggurat of Sargon's palace in Assyria (page 73). At Chichen Itza are the ruins of the city which was the center of the golden age of Mayan art.

Much of their sculpture was architectural in use, decorating the terraces of the temple pyramids. The art of the Mayas was almost completely religious in inspiration, and used for motifs the deities and the animals connected with the deities—frogs, snakes, jaguars, and hummingbirds. At the time of the decorations at Chichen Itza the portrayals of gods and animals were highly stylized. Walls and sculptured figures were brilliantly painted, but no real mural paintings remain. Monuments, called stelae, were usually large limestone monoliths with four sides, ranging in height from three to twenty-seven feet. On them are carved dates and messages commemorating important events and accounts of the founding of cities. The sculpture on them was in many cases done in a flat relief and was again very stylized and decorative in treatment. Mayan sculptors had nothing but stone tools with which to do the carving; no metal tools have been found in archaeological sites.

Minor arts were highly developed also. Weaving, jade sculpture, ceramics, and gold and silver work were all outstanding. These arts again testify to the extremely sophisticated sense of design and decoration typical of the Mayas. Their work compares favorably with the best of Egyptian design in its understanding of spacing and pattern.

Mayan religion. Like the Aztecs, the Mayas were sun worshipers. In the temples on top of the truncated pyramids there was always an altar on which human sacrifice was made to the sun. Their victims of sacrifice were not so numerous as those of the Aztecs, but probably their ceremonies were more complex and refined. Numerous gods and deities were worshiped, the most important of which corresponded to the Aztec Quetzalcohuatl. Religion was a very important part of their total life pattern. Its influence permeated all phases of social activity. Their government was a form of theocracy, dominated by a powerful priesthood. The priests were the only persons who could decipher the hieroglyphics and carve, or have carved, the inscriptions on stelae, lintels, and building façades. Evidently the observatories and all public buildings were erected and maintained under the supervision of the priesthood and therefore had important religious bearings in the life of the people.

Mayan science and education. The Mayas gave much attention to dates and solar events and to keeping accurate account of important days for religious ceremonies. Their progress in measuring time by observing the movements of heavenly bodies amazes the most learned scientists of today. Using these precise observations, they were able to construct the most accurate calendar yet known, more accurate, in fact, than that of the ancient Egyptians and possibly fully as refined in calculation as our own calendar. To accomplish this they had several astronomical observatories. At one of these, two stelae were raised on opposite sides of the valley, establishing a line which runs within 9° north of west. Investigations have indicated that the sun sets behind the western stone twice a year, shortly after the vernal and autumnal equinoxes.

Accurate calculations and observations were made possible through the type of number system which the Mayas used. They invented the zero, which no other peoples on the western continent were able to do. Their number system, like that of the Aztecs, was based upon twenty, and they represented their notation by dots and bars. One dot represented one, two dots two, three dots three, and so on up to five, which was represented by a bar. A bar with one dot over it stood for six, a bar and two dots seven, and so on. Two bars stood for ten, three indicated fifteen, and so forth. The highest number in their notation system was in the hundred billion. Both the Aztecs and the Mayas used approximately the same calendar, though they employed different words or names for days and dates and had a different system of notation. No Rosetta Stone has yet been discovered to give us a key to the inscriptions either on stelae or on building façades. The greatest use of hieroglyphic writing was in inscribing stone monuments in the earlier period of Mayan history; at a later time the writing was confined to books.

The Mayas wrote many books in symbolic and pictographic form, whose meaning has likewise not yet been deciphered. They used phonetic symbols rather than individual alphabetic letters. Most of the original Mayan books were destroyed by the Spanish *conquistadores.* Only three books, known as codices, have so far come to light. These copies reached Europe, it has been said, through some of the soldiers of Cortes and other military leaders. Most of their literature was burned by the priests and religious leaders who accompanied the Spanish occupation.

The Mayas had schools, primarily for the education of the priesthood, and a nunnery for girls of a religious caste. It is not known how extensive the training in these schools was, but it probably included all materials and habits related to religious ritual. The Mayas were more religious than warlike,

RUINS OF THE TEMPLE OF THE WARRIORS AT CHICHEN ITZA

and therefore most of their efforts at education were directed toward religion. Like all early peoples, they had some vocational education, for they were an agricultural people and had to become familiar with the cultivation of plants and breeding of animals. They also had a soldiery which had to be educated in the art of defense.

Mayan economy. Economically the Mayas were an agricultural people and devoted most of their efforts to producing food and clothing. Clearing away jungles and preparing ground for cultivation consumed much of their energy. They raised maize, squash, pumpkins, chili peppers, and many cereals and vegetables in their rich soil. They also developed irrigation to a high degree. Their agricultural efforts must have been very successful, for they supported a large population.

Aztecs and Mayas, Greeks and Romans. A fair analogy may be drawn between the Mayas and the Aztecs in the New World on the one hand and the ancient Greeks and Romans in the Old World on the other. Similarities may be found in the character, achievements, and general advancement in government, in art, and in philosophy, and in their general intellectual and artistic development. The Mayas were more artistic and intellectual than were the Aztecs, as is indicated by their sculpture, painting, architecture, science, and astronomy. Likewise the Greeks were more artistic and philosophical than were the Romans. Politically both Greeks and Mayas were divided into small states, and there was constant bickering and quarreling between petty sovereignties. Both had a number of temporary leagues composed of certain cities, and both were scarcely ever united except in the presence of a common enemy. Culturally both Mayas and Greeks were respectively one people with numerous linguistic dialectical differences. They both had a common religion and calendar. There is this difference: the Mayas were far more barbaric than the reason-loving Greeks.

Both the Aztecs and the Romans were brusque and warlike and built an advanced culture on the ruins of an earlier people's civilization which decayed or fell before their onslaught of arms. The Toltecs preceded the Aztecs in their power and cultural development, just as the Etruscans were forerunners of the Romans. Both the Etruscans and the Toltecs created a culture, and the Romans and the Aztecs profited by these predecessors to rise to a greatness far surpassing them.

The Incas of Peru. South of the equator in Peru another very advanced culture and civilization flourished, reaching its highest development in the Peruvian highlands. All along the Pacific coast of South America are scattered archaeological sites, which indicate a large population and a complex culture scattered over a wide territory. Some anthropologists have estimated that the Inca population numbered ten million at the time of the Spanish conquest in the sixteenth century. Even today the bulk of the population on the Peruvian coast and highlands is from Inca stock. The Incas developed the highest culture in Peru, although the peoples who preceded them gave good account of their ability.

The history of the origins of the Peruvians is extremely indefinite because they left no form of script, even of a pictographic kind. However, there appear to have been three successive Indian civilizations in Peru. Up to about the ninth century an agricultural people inhabited the region, raising potatoes, corn, and peanuts. Then appeared a more civilized group, who built a great stone city thirteen thousand feet above sea level, a marvel of palaces, fortresses, and huge, perfectly carved monoliths. Then about the eleventh century some peoples calling themselves Incas, "children of the sun," settled in the fertile valley of Cuzco, and that center became the capital of the Inca empire, which extended for some 2700 miles at the time of the coming of Pizarro. The empire was consolidated in a thorough, Roman-like manner by the construction of fortresses at strategic points, the establishment of colonies of peasants in conquered areas, and the creation of a splendid system of roads and trails radiating from Cuzco to every part of the Inca dominions.

Among the Incas' many achievements, three in particular stand out. One was the erection of huge stone structures built either as temples or as forts. The second is their remarkable irrigation system. The third is the creation of a great empire under one ruler and the efficiency, absolutism, and organization of one of the most despotic forms of state socialism known to history.

Architecture. While the Mayas were proficient in carving delicate hieroglyphics, the Incas and their predecessors excelled in carving out immense stone slabs from the mountain sides and transporting them for miles over mountains. Most impressive is the size of the huge stone blocks and the accuracy in cutting them at the quarry to fit into a definite place in a temple or fortress wall. All the work, of course, was done with stone tools. The transportation of the massive stone blocks is a mystery, for they had no wheeled vehicles, and there were no draught animals to be had in the whole of South America.

Irrigation. No less important than the extensive building of temples and fortresses are the immense irrigation systems. Whole mountain sides of some sections of the Andes were put under cultivation by building stone walls three to six feet high. Behind the walls earth and loam from the small river valleys were carried up in baskets by slaves. On the edge of the narrow, winding strips of artificially prepared garden plots, small irrigation ditches were built, and in them water was conducted long distances to furnish the necessary moisture in that very arid country. In the lowlands were numerous narrow valleys made by small rivers flowing rapidly down to the Pacific. Intensive cultivation of the valleys and the irrigation plots scattered over the vast empire made the Inca land a wealthy agricultural area.

Government. Neither the extensive stone building nor the intensive agriculture could have been possible without the despotic form of government which the Incas developed. It was a hereditary absolute monarchy, or rather theocracy—for they, too, were sun worshipers and believed the Inca rulers were royal offspring from the sun. The deep religious devotion of the population made it possible, in part at least, for the Inca ruler himself to exercise the power of life and death over any individual in the empire. His power was further increased through the excellent military organization the Incas developed.

The Inca ruler had control over all food in all districts. If any district should produce more than was needed for that area, the ruler had the surplus stored for future use. If other districts through ill luck or drought failed to produce enough food, a sufficient quantity was transferred from the storehouse to the district needing it. The Incas had no money, but a perfect barter system of trade was in operation.

Every young man was required to marry by the age of twenty-four, and if he did not marry of his own accord, he was united to someone selected for him. Once a year marriage ceremonies were enforced on all who had reached the age limit. Girls married at eighteen.

Origin of the American Indian. It is generally agreed that man did not originate in the Americas, for no bones of early man antedating *Homo sapiens* have been found there. The ancestors of our American Indians, therefore, must have migrated from African or west Asian areas. Four theories have been advanced to explain how these wanderers came to our western world: (1) they crossed the Pacific by raft or some form of boat, (2) the continents were much closer in prehistoric times, thereby making a crossing comparatively easy, (3) at one time there was a chain of islands between the Americas and Africa enabling migrants to cross on this Atlantis bridge, and (4) man crossed over (from Asia to Alaska) by boat or on a land bridge now sunk in the ocean in the area of the Bering Strait. Most authorities deem the fourth theory the most plausible, inasmuch as the stream of migrants has never completely ceased and interchanges of population still exist between the American and Asiatic continents at this point.

The Amerinds probably first came in little bands or groups. Some traveled down the west coast of North America by both land and sea, while others cut across the Canadian northwest, filtering into the western plains and the Mississippi basin. In the beginning probably all were nomadic, but as some tribes developed agriculture, they established a more settled way of life.

When the Indians came to the Americas is even more a mystery than how they came. Until recently it was thought that the Indians had come to our hemisphere not more than three thousand years ago but startling archaeological discoveries have revolutionized the estimate of man's existence in the Americas. In 1926 the Colorado Museum of Natural History discovered the Folsom culture in New Mexico. An arrow or dart was found embedded in the ribs of a fossil bison. Other arrows were found in the next few years. Although scholars disagreed over the age and significance of these artifacts, the age of this Folsom culture is now generally admitted to be about 20,000 B.C. In the 1930's a Harvard University geologist unearthed flints, animal bones, and pottery 25,000 years old in a cave in the Sandia Mountains between Santa Fe and Albuquerque. Another important find was unearthed in 1931 in the gravel bed of an ancient glacial lake—the skeleton of an Indian girl, the so-called Minnesota Man, claimed to be more than 20,000 years old.

These discoveries completely upset the traditional ideas of the chronology of the Indian in America. But more startling developments came early in 1953 when Dr. George Carter of Johns Hopkins University announced that he had discovered evidence showing that man existed in America more than 100,000 years ago and perhaps as long as 400,000. While exploring the ancient gravel beds of several rivers in the vicinity of San Diego, California, he found a number of crude, but definitely chipped flakes of rock designed for cutting and stabbing. It is believed that the gravel in which the artifacts were found was deposited before the fourth and last glacier, more than 100,000 years ago. In fact, Dr. Carter suggests it is feasible that the length of human habitation may be the same in both Europe and the Americas.

Another theory of the early wanderings of the American Indians was in part substantiated when a dramatic voyage was made in 1947 to show that the Polynesians, living on a chain of islands stretching from New Zealand to Easter Island, originally migrated from Peru. Six men pushed off from the Peruvian coast on a balsa log raft built with materials known only to pre-Columbian Indians. This crude craft slowly drifted with the ocean currents and after 101 days was beached on an atoll in the Polynesian Tuamotu Islands. This achievement proved it was possible for men in such rafts to voyage westward from South America to the Pacific islands. Whether this was actually done is another matter but the arguments in favor of oceanic migration may be read in Thor Heyerdahl's *American Indians in the Pacific: The Theory Behind the Kon-Tiki Expedition,* or in *Kon-Tiki,* the popular account of the expedition.

Contributions of the Amerinds. The Amerinds, or American Indians, have contributed immeasurably to the world's culture. Their contributions have been chiefly in place names, foods, utensils, tools, weapons, modes of transportation, and methods and products of agriculture. The Amerind has not added much directly to our literature, science, or philosophy.

But his great skill in art and architecture show that he is in no way inferior mentally to any other peoples. Bringing with him little from his Asiatic home, he carved out a distinctive culture on this continent. So far as is known he brought few, if any, seeds of vegetables or grain with him. Nor did he bring methods of agriculture, patterns of pottery or architecture, house types, dress, or religion. These developed mainly on his adopted soil. His architecture, pottery, and other crafts are certainly the most distinctly American arts yet produced on the western continent.

Another of the native Americans' contributions to our culture is a variety of foods, fruits, medicines, and drinks. Irish potatoes, sweet potatoes, tomatoes, corn, pumpkins, peanuts, and numerous fruits were raised. Root crops are likewise an important legacy. Probably the variety of native fruits which the Amerinds taught us to use is greater than that of any other food product. The Amerinds also developed native perfumes, drugs, and medicines. Tobacco is a widely used product originated by the natives of America.

A few utensils, tools, and weapons from the Amerind enrich our culture, and though some of them in varying forms were known by other peoples in Europe, the types which the Indians used have modified our notions and use of them. The bow and arrow, the crossbow, the atlatl (throwing stick), the tomahawk, canoes, baskets, certain types of pottery, blankets, and various forms of clothing are to be accredited to the Indian.

The origin of traits of culture. The study of culture—how its traits originate, how it grows, and how it has become disseminated over the earth—is one of the most difficult problems that social sciences have to solve. For example, the Egyptians developed writing and built pyramids, the Phoenicians invented the alphabet, the Hindus probably invented the zero, the Mesopotamians devised the keystone arch. The Mayas of Central America likewise invented the zero, wrote books (without an alphabet, however), and built pyramids. The Mayas, Aztecs, Incas, the Plains Indians, and other American tribes were sun worshipers; so were the Egyptians. The Incas had a form of mummification of the dead, as did the Egyptians. Generally most American tribes used some form of the bow and arrow; so did our early European ancestors.

Parallel invention. How is it that the Egyptians and the Mayas, peoples living ten thousand miles apart, with the vast and dangerous Atlantic Ocean between, developed similar cultural elements? Did the Egyptians first invent these traits and ideas and lend them to the Mayas of Central America, or did the Mayas invent them and lend them to Egypt, or did each people invent the ideas, practices, or items independently? Most anthropologists hold that neither the Egyptians nor the Mayas had any contact with each other at any time in the past and that each one developed all the items, ideas, and practices of its own culture independently.

Borrowing and modification. The spread and practice of some useful ideas, materials, and arts cannot be explained by the principle of parallel invention. The seven-day week, which originated in Babylonia and spread to the Mediterranean basin and then into Europe, and the alphabet, which was first formulated by the Phoenicians, next improved and enlarged by the Greeks, and from the latter taken over in a modified form by the Romans, are examples of the borrowing and improvement of culture traits. The invention of the keystone arch by the brick-making Babylonians and its improvement by the Etruscans and later European peoples is still another example of the spread of culture through borrowing and modification. So is the origin of the use of tobacco and the pipe by the Amerinds on the eastern coast of the United States, their spread to Europe and the whole civilized world, and their ultimate return to America by way of Asia to the Eskimo, thus completing the circuit around the earth.

Degrees of civilization. Why some tribes developed a very complex civilization, while others almost adjoining them did not, is a question that remains as yet wholly unanswered. Authorities generally agree that none of the migrants from Asia brought their ideas and culture with them but that every tribe developed its own independent culture after arriving on the western continent.

To what extent the cultures of the peoples of the northwest coast, the Pueblos, the Mayas, the Aztecs, the Incas, and others would have evolved had the Europeans never discovered the western continent will always remain an interesting conjecture. Some scholars assert that a cultural level almost equal to that of Europe at the time of discovery might have resulted. Others hold that cultural disintegration had already set in and that probably a state of primitive savagery in most parts of the continent would have resulted.

Europe Invades the East

East versus West. Whereas the Spaniards found the New World sparsely populated and relatively undeveloped, the Portuguese found in India and the Far East civilizations that were in some ways superior and more mature than those in Europe. The cultures of the East, however, had already passed their zenith. They were only superficially brilliant and prosperous. On the downgrade these cultures were static and after 1500 they progressively lagged behind the dynamic West.

The Indians of the New World looked upon Columbus and his men as great white gods; the Indians of the eastern world recognized Vasco da Gama and his cohorts as strong and well-armed pirates. The eastern civilizations, proud of their past contributions to world culture, naturally resisted European domination. At the same time they refused to imitate the developments in the West that were making Europe unrivaled in scientific, economic, and political power. The inevitable result, as we shall see in Volume II, was the conquest of much of the East by the West.

Motives of the Portuguese. Prince Henry the Navigator had a double purpose in sending his Portuguese mariners down the uncharted coast of Africa. He wanted to add new lands to the domain of Portugal, and he earnestly sought to bring Christianity to those peoples who had not yet heard of the faith. So closely interwoven were these ambitions that the struggle for foreign conquest assumed a religious fervor which seemed to sanctify even the most predatory acts.

Yet underlying the Portuguese voyages was an even stronger motive—the desire for trade and wealth. The year after Da Gama returned to Lisbon bearing from India a cargo worth sixty times the cost of the expedition, another expedition set sail for India under the command of Cabral. Completely self-reliant, the Portuguese invaded Indian waters, and the newcomers soon established a monopoly over trade in the Indian Ocean.

Albuquerque's strategy in the East. In 1509 the most famous of Portuguese governors, Afonso de Albuquerque, was sent to India. Resolved to consolidate Portuguese supremacy in the East, he realistically saw that his countrymen could maintain such a position only by force of arms. His plan was to establish fortified centers at strategic sites, which would dominate the trade routes and protect Portuguese interests on land. Possession of Aden, for example, could close the mouth of the Red Sea and thereby divert trade to the Persian Gulf, commanded by the Portuguese city of Ormuz.

Albuquerque failed to capture Aden, but possession of the island of Socotra, gained in 1506, gave the Portuguese control of the Red Sea trade. Albuquerque made Goa the center of Portuguese operations in the East. In 1511 he sailed to Malacca, a large trading center in the Malay archipelago. After a week of bitter street fighting, Malacca fell to the invaders and Portuguese control was established.

Extension of the Portuguese empire. The capture of Malacca was of inestimable value. It was a logical jump from here to the rich Moluccas, whence came the finest spices, nutmeg, and cloves. The occupation of Malacca also opened the way to Portuguese participation in the rich trade with China. The first Portuguese ship to invade Chinese waters docked at Canton in 1516. From that time on, except for periods of nonintercourse, the Chinese and the Europeans carried on an expanding trade. In 1557 the Portuguese were granted the right to establish a settlement near Canton, which grew into Macao.

The Portuguese early established control over Ceylon, dominating points about the coast which gave them the control of the wealthy cinnamon-growing regions of the island. By controlling Ceylon on the west and the Malay archipelago on the east, the Portuguese also commanded the coastal trade of the Bay of Bengal.

Portuguese colonial government. During the sixteenth century Portugal enjoyed almost undisputed sovereignty of the eastern sea routes. In Goa, the capital of the empire, lived the viceroy of India, who was sent out from Portugal for a term of three years.

Under the viceroy at Goa were numerous civil and legal officers, while *capitans* had charge of subordinate governments at other centers. Unfortunately for Portugal's interests, her governmental organization both at home and abroad was inefficient and corrupt.

Decline of the Portuguese empire. There is no denying the richness of Portugal's commercial empire. She had royal monopolies of pepper, nutmeg, cloves, mace, silk, and lace, and monopolies over trade both between India and Europe and between different ports in India. Turkish traders were virtually cut off from Indian commerce, while Venice and Genoa also suffered seriously. But Portugal's star was destined to set for many reasons. One was governmental corruption. Another lay in the heavy mortality resulting from the great risks of trading in those days. By 1538 difficulty had arisen in procuring the necessary quota of men from Portugal's small population. The quality of stock declined as time elapsed, and the morale of Goa and other centers steadily deteriorated owing to the influx of banished criminals, the easy acquisition of riches, and the debilitating climate.

Still another important reason for Portugal's decline in the East was the cruel intolerance displayed by the Portuguese everywhere they journeyed. At first the Portuguese were content to harry and slay only the Moslems whom they encountered, asking no mercy and giving none, while treating the Hindus with some measure of tolerance. But after 1540 the Church ordered that Hindus in Goa could not practice the rites of their faith, and their temples were demolished. The Inquisition had now made its appearance in India, and relapsed converts and heretics filled the prisons. Hindu merchants, refusing to dwell in Portuguese territory under such conditions, left it in huge numbers. The loss of their trade seriously impaired the economic life in Goa and other European held centers.

Dutch inroads in the East. The Portuguese decline was accelerated by a new and serious thrust from a European neighbor—Holland. Two political events in sixteenth-century Europe helped create this new danger to Portuguese imperial power. One of them was the Netherlands revolt against Spanish rule. The other was the Spanish acquisition of the crown of Portugal. After the Dutch had declared themselves free of Spanish domination (1579), they looked upon Spain's trade and colonies as fit prey for their ships. With the union of Portugal with Spain, the colonial possessions of both countries were administered as one. The Dutch now felt free to attack Portuguese territory in eastern waters, because it was part of the empire of their deadly enemy, Spain. Furthermore, the rich carrying trade which the Dutch had enjoyed, distributing throughout northern Europe the eastern goods brought to Lisbon, ceased when Spain took control of Portuguese ports. If Dutch trade was even to exist, the Hollanders had to go out and capture it at the expense of Spain.

This they did. In the 1590's various Dutch trading groups sailed for the Malay archipelago, preferring that region to western India, where the Portuguese were in greater force. But the competing trading companies lowered one another's rate of profit. In 1602, therefore, they amalgamated into the United East India Company. The Dutch government gave this powerful body the right to trade and rule from the Cape of Good Hope eastward to the Strait of Magellan. The Dutch East India Company broke the power of the Portuguese in the islands of the Malay archipelago.

The Dutch East Indies empire. In 1609 the Dutch established the office of governor general. This official, with a council of seven (later nine) members, had final authority over all matters concerning trade, war, justice, and administration in each Dutch settlement. In time the governor general came to have supreme authority in the East Indies. In 1618 a governor general was appointed who might be called the Albuquerque of the Dutch. J. P. Coen was the administrator who laid the firm foundations of the East Indies empire. Coen believed that his countrymen must possess the productive areas if they were to control them, whereas Albuquerque had felt that it was sufficient to occupy strategic, fortified sites which commanded maritime trade routes. Coen built a fortified trading station at Batavia in Java, a site which eventually became the capital of the Netherlands East Indies. From the extremely wealthy island of Java Dutch ships carried back to Europe such sought-after products as coffee, tea, spices, indigo, sugar, mace, nutmeg, camphor, and cloves. The Dutch gradually extended their control over the entire island, while its strategic situation in the center of the Malay archipelago enabled them in time to take over Sumatra to the west and the rich Spice Islands (Moluccas) to the east.

Meanwhile the Portuguese power in India and Ceylon fell before the onslaughts of the Dutch. By 1658 the Portuguese had been driven from Ceylon, and the Dutch had captured the lucrative cinnamon trade. They also coveted the pepper trade along the western coast of India. Despite the peace made in 1661 between Portugal (now independent of Spain again) and Holland, the Dutch in India used illegal pretexts to wrest from their Portuguese rivals such wealthy centers as Cochin.

By the latter half of the seventeenth century the Dutch were the supreme European power in the east. The Portuguese had fallen before their attacks, and Portugal's trade had dwindled. Portugal still held Goa and Diu in India and Macao in China, but they were no longer significant factors in Asiatic affairs. The Dutch, however, did not try to monopolize all trade east of the Cape of Good Hope, as the Portuguese had tried in vain to do. Rather they concentrated on holding the rich East Indies. The vast subcontinent of India was thus left open to control by another invader—England.

The English in India. In 1600 Queen Elizabeth incorporated the East India Company, granting it a monopoly of trade from the Cape of Good Hope eastward to the Strait of Magellan. This rich and famous company, which was at times the most powerful political force in India, quickly saw the value of establishing posts at the important points of trade. The Company established numerous outposts scattered at strategic points in India, the islands of the Malay archipelago, and even in Japan. It put the Portuguese posts on the Persian Gulf out of business in 1622, acquired Madras in 1639 and Bombay in 1668, and founded Calcutta in 1690. The Company pushed forward in India by means of political stratagems, presents, bribes, diplomacy, compulsion over weak native rulers, and downright hard work on the part of English merchants and administrators. The Company failed to obtain a permanent foothold either in the East Indies, where the Dutch were too powerful, or in Japan, but it found India rich enough. Whereas in 1601 it could send out only four second-hand vessels, in 1801 it owned 122 ships, some of them weighing 1400 tons, large ships for those days.

GREENLAND
ICELAND
Hudson Bay
LABRADOR
NEWFOUNDLAND
Quebec
NOVA SCOTIA
COLONIAL EMPIRES
LOUISIANA
VIRGINIA
AZORES
CANARY IS.
MEXICO
Mexico City
CUBA
WEST INDIES
CAPE VERDE IS.
GUIANA
GUINEA
DARIEN
PERU
Lima
BRAZIL
Rio de Janeiro
Santiago
CHILE
Buenos Aires
Strait of Magellan
British
French
Spanish
Portuguese
Dutch

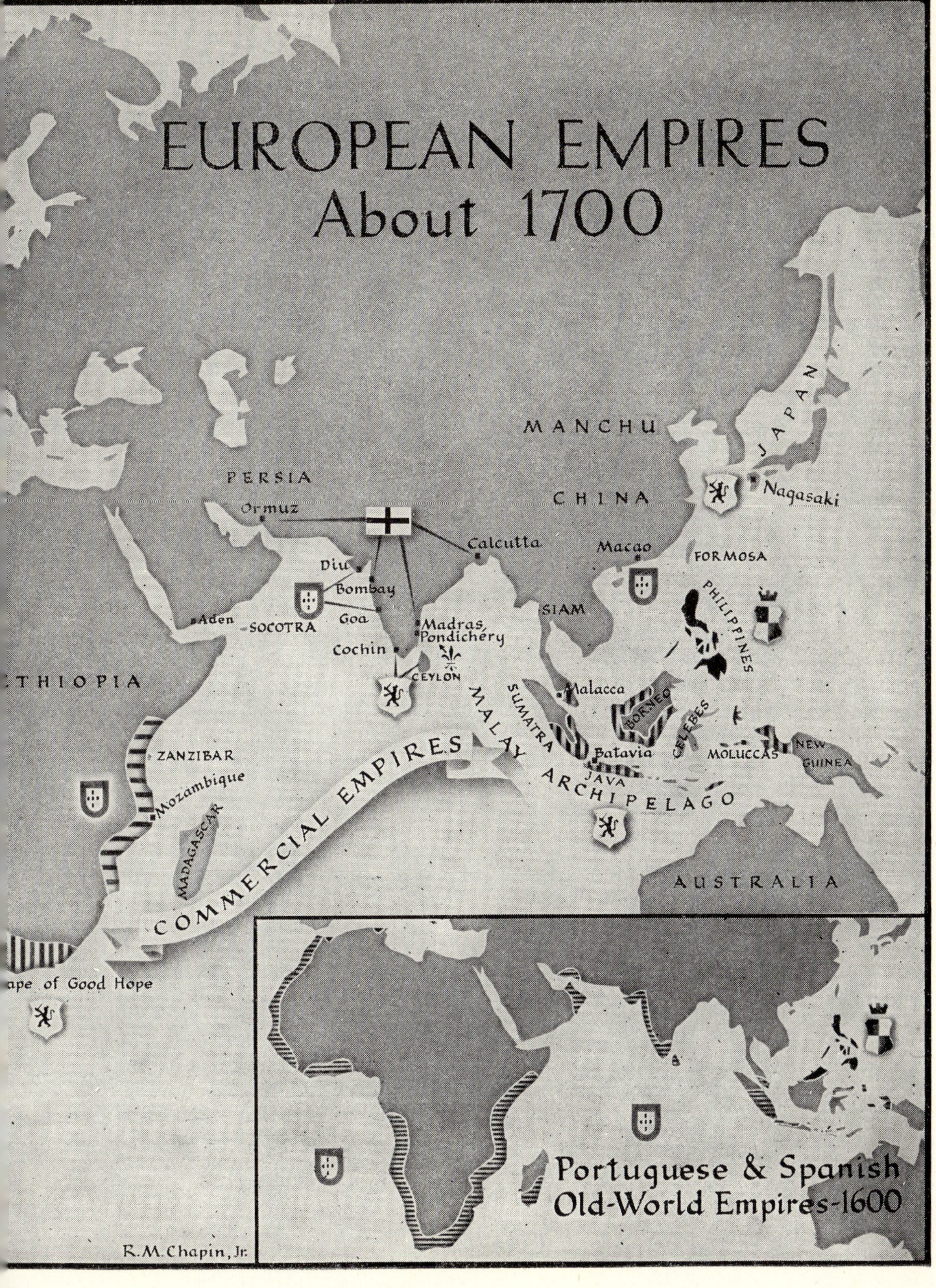
EUROPEAN EMPIRES
About 1700
MANCHU
CHINA
JAPAN
Nagasaki
PERSIA
Ormuz
Calcutta
Macao
FORMOSA
Diu
Bombay
Goa
SIAM
PHILIPPINES
Aden
SOCOTRA
Madras
Pondichéry
Cochin
CEYLON
THIOPIA
Malacca
SUMATRA
MALAY
BORNEO
CELEBES
ZANZIBAR
Mozambique
COMMERCIAL EMPIRES
Batavia
MOLUCCAS
NEW GUINEA
JAVA
ARCHIPELAGO
MADAGASCAR
AUSTRALIA
ape of Good Hope
Portuguese & Spanish
Old-World Empires-1600
R.M.Chapin, Jr.

The French in India. Meanwhile the French had not been unconcerned over the profits wrung from the east by their Dutch and English rivals. However, the French mercantile classes occupied a smaller proportion of their country's population than did the mercantile classes of Holland and England, and their influence accordingly was much smaller. Nevertheless Louis XIV, acting on the advice of his economic adviser, Colbert, began to build up France's mercantile power by establishing a French East India Company in 1664. This body was financed in large measure by the state and was always subject to governmental regulation. Despite opposition from the Dutch and English on the scene, the French succeeded in 1674 in establishing a center at Pondichéry on the southeast coast of India. The Company established other posts along the Indian coasts, but fared none too well.

After 1700, however, the French grew stronger in India. The Portuguese had controlled the east during the 1500's, gradually losing out to the Dutch, who in turn during the 1600's garnered most of the profits in the east. Gradually the Dutch concentrated more and more on the East Indies, while the English East India Company built up a commercial stronghold in India. After 1700, while Holland's profits remained large in her own sphere, they did not increase at the enormous rate enjoyed by the English in India. The great rivals of the English were the French. The rapid betterment of France's position in India in the eighteenth century was due largely to the work of an able administrator named Dupleix. That astute statesman went out to India in 1720, where he amassed a fortune and learned much about native politics. In 1741 he became governor of Pondichéry.

At this time the Mogul empire was quite effete. Certain rulers (nabobs) of large regions in the empire, such as the Deccan and Bengal, had become semi-independent princes. Dupleix used this lack of national unity to advance his own interests. The next few years were to see a sharp struggle between France and England in India.

The Mogul Empire in India

Commercial empires in the east. The European empires created in Asia were commercial rather than colonial. They were areas possessing fortified trading sites and commercial concessions rather than regions populated by European emigrants. Whereas the New World soon had a preponderance of Europeans who transplanted their own customs and institutions to North and South America, Asia continued to enjoy its indigenous cultures, in India, China, and Japan, and European civilization was found only in scattered settlements belonging to a number of foreign powers.

Babur, founder of the Mogul empire. In 1494, two years after Columbus had sailed westward toward India, a descendant of Tamerlane and Genghis Khan mounted the throne of a little principality in Turkestan. The youthful ruler was Zahir-ud-din Muhammad, surnamed Babur (the Tiger). Babur was the founder of the great Mogul empire. An able general with the strength of a giant, Babur spent his early years in gaining the throne of a city on the highway to India. Babur says in his memoirs that he used to think ceaselessly of the capture of Hindustan. At length, in 1524 he set out with an army of no more than 12,000 men to achieve his goal. He defeated the large forces belonging to the sultan of Delhi, who then ruled all Hindustan, and in 1526 Babur made himself sultan. In 1527 he defeated the Rajputs, who were trying to bring back Hindu supremacy in northern India.

The submission of the Rajputs placed the Mogul dynasty securely on the Delhi throne. The name "mogul" is a corruption of "mongol," a word much dreaded in India because of its association with Tamerlane. It has been suggested that "mongol" was converted into "mogul" through either a common mispronunciation or a wish on the part of the Indians to cover the fact that the Moguls were in truth Mongols.

Babur himself did not live long to enjoy the fruits of his victory. He died in 1530, worn out by his campaigns and adventures.

Akbar's empire. Babur's grandson was named Muhammad, but he is known as Akbar, meaning "Very Great." Until he was eighteen, his kingdom was administered by a regent. In 1560 Akbar took over full control himself. His empire at that time consisted of an eighth of India, a strip of territory some three hundred

Akbar receives ambassadors to celebrate the submission of Bayram Khan. Note the Persian influence in faces, the canopy, and the trappings of the horse.

miles wide extending from the northwest frontier eastward to Bengal. By 1576, although only thirty-four years old, he had made himself ruler of all northern India from the Indus to the mouth of the Ganges and from the Himalayas to the Vindhya mountains. In 1593 Akbar decided to annex the Deccan. The campaign was unwise, for the Vindhya mountains constitute the natural boundary of Hindustan, and the Deccan war later proved to be the downfall of the Mogul empire. When Akbar died in 1605, his dominions exceeded those of any previous Indian monarch.

Akbar's administrative measures. Akbar's greatness is not to be measured by his military conquests only, but rather by his governmental, cultural, and religious contributions. As an administrator he had few equals. He divided his empire into twelve provinces (later increased to fifteen), ruled by royal or noble governors. Each province was divided in turn into districts, and each district into yet smaller units. Thus the problem of administration was very thoroughly handled. The emperor made all appointments to the higher posts himself, and the officials received monthly salaries from the imperial treasury. He kept a strict check on bribery and embezzlement and left a rich surplus in the treasury when he died. Taxation was somewhat more lenient.

Law was ably administered. The headman in each village was responsible for keeping law and order, while special officials were responsible in the larger cities. The emperor himself constantly acted as judge, for everyone in his domains had the right to appeal personally to the ruler. He forbade child marriage and suttee, permitted widows to remarry, prohibited such practices as trial by ordeal, and allowed perfect freedom of religious belief. As in contemporary Europe, the use of various tortures (such as impalement, amputation, and death by elephant dragging) was allowed. However, Akbar probably had the most enlightened code in existence in the sixteenth century.

Akbar's patronage. Akbar as a boy had refused to do his lessons, so that until his dying day he could neither read nor write. But he possessed an insatiable love of learning and constantly had all types of literature read to him. Because of this practice, Akbar may have been actually the "best read" man of his age. He paid enormous sums to artists and penmen to design and transcribe books, and he collected a valuable library of 24,000 volumes. Like his grandfather Babur, Akbar had a poetic nature, and he therefore liberally patronized poets, painters, and architects. Music, painting, and architecture advanced rapidly owing to his liberal patronage. Largely because of Akbar's sympathy for both Moslem and Hindu cultures, the architecture of his period interwove Persian and Indian styles. Manuscript illumination was highly developed, and brilliant, jewel-colored paintings decorated Indian books. One of these miniature paintings, with its oriental flat pattern and lack of perspective, is illustrated on this page.

Religious tolerance of Akbar. Religion is taken very seriously in India, and tolerance among faiths has never been the rule. Buddhism was undoubtedly the most tolerant of all the major religions, yet its own gentleness only made it easier for fanatical Brahmans to drive it out of India. The history of Hindu-Moslem relations has always been a bloody one. During Akbar's time the Hindus were the object of endless persecution by their Moslem conquerors. Because Akbar realized that religious strife made for political disintegration, he came to favor complete tolerance of belief. But his views were not based simply on political grounds; his own temperament was the chief reason for his amazingly liberal policy.

Akbar felt that every faith had something of truth to offer but that all were untrue when they denied each other's sincerity of purpose. Every Thursday in his Hall of Worship he held religious debates which often lasted until dawn, to which Moslems, Brahmans, Jains, and Zoroastrians were invited. Hearing of the arrival of Jesuits in India, he had them stay at his court for periods of several years. He treated them with every courtesy, and they built a chapel and translated the Gospel into Persian. Akbar even attended Mass, wore a medallion with the image of the Virgin, and walked in public with one of the Jesuit fathers.

But the sultan could never accept any one religion completely, and the Jesuits had to admit ruefully that "the Emperor is not a Muhammedan, but is doubtful as to all forms of faith and holds firmly that there is no divinely accredited form of faith, because he finds in all something to offend his reason and intelligence, for he thinks everything can be grasped by reason."[4] Instead he created his own religion, promulgating a new faith called *Din Ilahi*, the Divine Faith, which incorporated what he considered the best features of the other existing religions. By it he hoped to bring all India into common agreement on religious matters. But traditional bigotry was too strongly intrenched in the older faiths. When Akbar died his religious theories died with him.

Akbar's grandson, Shah Jahan. Shah Jahan, who came to the throne in 1627, held none of Akbar's views on religious toleration. He returned India to the Moslem faith, persecuted the Christians, and destroyed Hindu temples wholesale. We will recall that Akbar had tried to conquer the Deccan; in 1630 Shah Jahan attempted the same conquest. He eventually subjugated it and divided the territory into four provinces. In 1657 his health began to fail, and a ruinous civil war broke out among his four sons, each of whom was practically an independent ruler. When Shah Jahan died at the age of seventy-four in 1666, his son Aurangzeb succeeded him as emperor.

The reign of Shah Jahan marks the height of power for the Mogul empire. The emperor amassed a huge treasure at Agra. His hobby being costly and beautiful buildings, he tore down the red sandstone buildings of Akbar at Delhi and raised a huge capital of marble containing fifty-two palaces. The famous Hall of Private Audience had ceilings of solid silver and gold and a Peacock Throne encrusted with costly gems. On the walls still can be seen the inscription by a Moslem poet, "If anywhere on earth there is a Paradise, it is here, it is here, it is here." Besides making Delhi a site of unrivaled splendor, Shah Jahan erected a magnificent fort at Agra. Here stood the famous Pearl Mosque, while across the river rose the slender minarets of the Taj Mahal, the marble mausoleum built as a final resting place for Shah Jahan and his favorite wife. Twenty-two thousand workmen labored twenty-two years to complete the enormously costly structure. It shows the influence of the Moslems in the general composition and particularly in the beauty and elegance of decoration (see the Mosque of Kazennain on page 289).

Decline of the Mogul empire. Lavishness of building and wealth of treasury such as existed in the days of Shah Jahan endured only at a terrible price, the grinding of the emperor's subjects to exploit every possible source of income. The Mogul empire under Shah Jahan

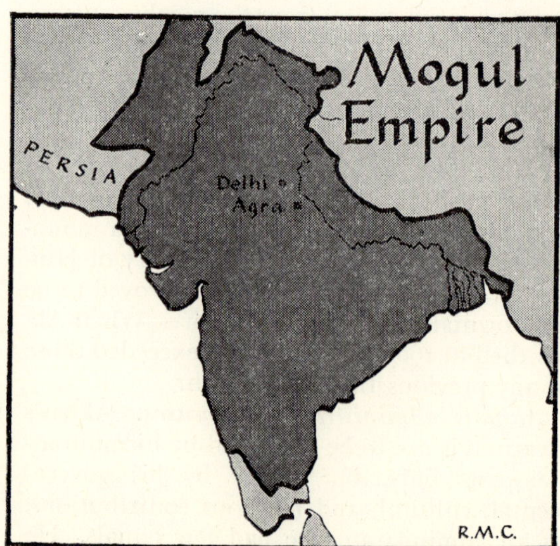

All symmetry and formality is the jewellike Taj Mahal with its gleaming dome, its precise gardens with their neat, clipped hedges. The Moslem influence is evident in the arches, the domes, the decoration, and the minarets.

was still powerful. But the misery of its people, the oppression of non-Moslem faiths, and the lack of wisdom of its rulers had sown the seeds of its final destruction.

The Advent of Modern China (1368-1644)

E***stablishment of the Ming dynasty.*** For thousands of years prior to the entrance of Portuguese ships into Canton harbor, China had enjoyed a rich and largely indigenous culture. In our last chapter on the evolution of the Chinese people, we noted especially the great advances made during the T'ang and Sung dynasties in literature and art. This was the age of Li Po and Tu Fu, the delightful poets, the artist Chiang T'san and the printing of the Buddhist book, the *Diamond Sutra.* But like other dynasties, the T'ang and Sung crumbled away, leaving China in a weakened state. Finally, groups of tribes calling themselves Mongols overran China, establishing the dynasty which bore their name, headed by the renowned emperor Kublai Khan. The Mongol dynasty adopted the superior Chinese civilization and so reigned tolerantly and well. But weak rulers and the gradual assimilation of the Mongols by the numerically superior Chinese led to the overthrow of the dynasty. Rebellion broke out, and in 1368 an ex-Buddhist monk captured the capital city, Peking, and established the Ming dynasty.

The ex-Buddhist monk who captured the imperial throne and established the Ming dynasty took the reigning title Hung Wu. He made himself popular by eradicating all traces of Mongol rule and reëstablishing such Chinese traditions as the "scholar rule," with which the Mongols had dispensed. He aided education and had a law code compiled known as the Code of the Great Ming. His reign of thirty years was marked by prosperity, but his successors were not all so fortunate. However, nearly all patronized art and public works.

The Portuguese in China. During the Ming dynasty three important foreign contacts were established. Earlier in the chapter we noted that in 1516 the first Portuguese ships arrived at Canton. The story of the coming of the Europeans to China is another example of gross misbehavior on the part of the invaders, who did not appreciate the customs of the people they met and treated the "heathen" with arrogance and cruelty. The mutual suspicion and hostility which marked Sino-European relations in the nineteenth and early twentieth centuries stem from this period.

When the Portuguese first arrived in China, the government afforded them the same privileges which Persian and Arab merchants had enjoyed for centuries. Unfortunately, the Portuguese carried into China their misguided viewpoint that non-Christian property was valid booty under any circumstances. A typical case of violence was one Portuguese captain's activity at Canton. This braggart sailor built a small fort, erected a gallows, and, scandalizing the Chinese, proceeded to hang one of his own men. He was discovered buying Chinese boys and girls who had been kidnaped. To climax his violent acts, he refused to leave port when ordered, but waged a bloody skirmish in the streets of Canton, where several Portuguese sailors were slain. Tales which Chinese officials had heard from merchants returning from India, the Persian coast, and the Spice Islands were now confirmed: The Portuguese come first to a new land in the guise of peaceful traders, but, as soon as they gain a foothold, they pillage and establish their own authority. The upshot of the incidents was the banning of the foreigners from Chinese waters.

In 1542, however, the Portuguese reappeared, at a coastal town whose officials either had forgotten events twenty years earlier or else risked safety for the sake of profitable trading. At first all went well, and hundreds of Portuguese flocked to the city. But when the foreigners felt themselves powerful enough, they fell back into their old practices and began to pillage and murder. The embittered city officials raised a force which attacked the Portuguese fort and slew all who could not make their escape. It is little wonder that westerners earned at this time the nickname "ocean devils." However, because trade was mutually profitable to Chinese and foreign merchants, in 1557 the Portuguese were granted the right to trade at Macao, a peninsula in the Canton estuary. Here, under close surveillance and subject to many strict regulations, the "ocean devils" were allowed to trade.

Jesuit missionaries in China. The second foreign contact was the coming of Jesuit missionaries. The Jesuit leader Francis Xavier did signal work in converting people in Goa, Malacca, and Japan. But he died in 1552 on a small island near Macao before he could reach the mainland of China itself. Some of his followers carried on the work, converting many persons of importance at the imperial court and in the provinces, who protected the Christians by their influence.

Japanese encroachment on China. A third incursion from across the sea was the attempt of Japan to conquer Korea and China. In the latter part of the sixteenth century the powerful Japanese leader Hideyoshi warned the Koreans that he was planning to take all China. The Koreans replied that such a plan was like "a bee trying to sting a tortoise through its shell" or like "measuring the ocean in a cockleshell." Excellent Japanese armies landed in Korea, however, and won many battles against Korean and Chinese armies. Unlike the Sino-Japanese conflict of the twentieth century, the Japanese at that time did not control the sea lanes. Therefore, when the Korean sailors

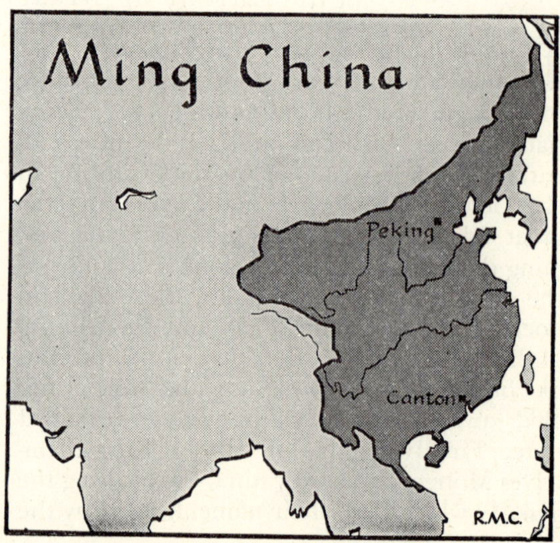

This is the hall of the throne in the Forbidden City at Peking. The carved stairway at the center of this palace, dating from the Ming dynasty, is a spirit staircase. An ordinary mortal must use the steps at the side.

routed their fleets, using ironclad vessels, the Japanese were finally forced to withdraw.

Fall of the Ming dynasty. Although China and its Korean vassals under the Mings successfully withstood the Japanese invasion from the east, the Middle Kingdom fell victim to a new horde of invaders, the Manchus, who broke through the Great Wall in the north. Matters had become critical for the Mings when revolution broke out, and in 1644 a rebel leader had defeated the emperor's armies and captured Peking. The rebel leader soon fell a victim to the stronger Manchus, however, who in 1644 established their dynasty.

Ming scholarship and art. Ming means "brilliant," a word appropriate to the literary and artistic accomplishments of the period. Stimulus was given to scholarship when the traditional competitive examination system, which existed until 1905, was reëstablished. Given every three years, these examinations were based upon a thorough knowledge of the classics, and their form and style followed rigid rules. The examination system has preserved Chinese traditions remarkably, but it has kept China excessively conservative and intellectually sterile.

Ming craftsmen produced many works, but few as original as those of some earlier dynasties. They tried to duplicate the standards of the classic Sung pottery, but instead of emphasizing the beauty of the form of the vessel, they were more interested in brilliant coloring and elegant decoration. The Ming age is outstanding for its glazes and enamels, and for its blue and white "eggshell" porcelains. Cloisonné ware, an art popular during Byzantine days in the Near East, was popular in China during the Ming period. The art of the Ming dynasty is the best known of Chinese art but is by no means of so high a standard as earlier art. It turns to elegance and technical facility as opposed to simplicity and proportion.

The Forbidden City at Peking was constructed in the early part (1403-1424) of the Ming dynasty. With its series of courtyards, its brilliant colored lacquer work, its tile, marble, and alabaster decorations, it is typical of a period of richly decorated architecture. In the throne hall, illustrated opposite, notice the popular pagoda form and the beauty of proportion. The beauties of detail and color must be seen for a true appreciation of the richness of the building.

Japan's Voluntary Semi-Isolation (1542-1639)

European discovery of Japan. In a previous chapter the origins and evolution of the Japanese people through medieval times were briefly considered. Outstanding in that period of Nippon's development were its comparative isolation and sleepiness. Receiving its initial cultural impetus from China, the island kingdom continued along a path of comparatively little change. The same royal house ruled (and still heads the State today), the country remained free from foreign attack except when the Mongols twice unsuccessfully attempted to conquer it, and generation after generation kept much the same social pattern.

But Nippon was destined to have its complacent culture shaken by the coming of the foreigner. About 1542 three Portuguese sailors were driven off their course while sailing south from Macao to Siam, and came to one of the southern Japanese islands. It was not long before others visited the islands and began trading. The great Jesuit missionary, Francis Xavier, hearing about Japan after he had sailed from Lisbon in 1541, went there and started to convert the inhabitants. After Xavier's death, the work he inaugurated was carried on by successors. Within thirty years of Xavier's departure Japanese converts to Christianity numbered around 150,000.

Medieval Japanese arts. The period known as the Ashikaga (1392-1568) is famous for its arts and for its feudal system. A type of literature developed during the Ashikaga era was the classical drama known as *No*, in which masks of a highly decorative quality were used. The elaborately ornamented architecture of this period had lost the qualities of beauty and proportion characteristic of the earlier periods. Pictorial art flourished under the influence of China. Early in this period the famous color prints were developed. Many minor arts reached a high state of excellence after many centuries of development. The casting of bronze bells and mirrors, the making of porcelain, and the fashioning of bows, saddles, and swords were popular.

Japanese society. At this time people in Japan lived in one of two extremes in society. The majority of the people lived in squalor and misery as a result of numerous civil wars, but the noble class whiled away its time following complex rituals for eating, drinking, dressing, and fighting. The tea ceremony was especially unusual, with its aim to instill in the devotee "urbanity, courtesy, purity, and imperturbability." Even soldiers were noted "teaists," and, as the scholar Nitobe points out, to be an "a-teaist" was as unforgivable then in Japan as to be an "a-theist" in England. It was an age in which militarists, not the emperor, controlled the empire. The head of a family was a *daimyo*, who gathered about him the *samurai*, "sworded men," who were supposed to live according to the chivalric *bushido*. A soldier who had no master became a *ronin*, or knight-errant, who fought for himself.

Japanese expulsion of foreigners. One of the greatest Japanese soldiers and statesmen was Hideyoshi (d. 1598). He put down brigandage, encouraged the arts, stimulated trade

A Kamakura Buddhist monk has removed his shoes to sit in contemplation at his writing table. Notice the writing brush in his hand and the ink vessel.

with China, and built splendid edifices in Kyoto and elsewhere. The dictator, himself of humble origin, rose to the top and was quite willing to employ commoners in his government if they possessed the requisite ability. Hideyoshi had few religious interests, but when told that Christian soldiers appeared after Christian missionaries, Hideyoshi persecuted the Jesuits and their converts.

Suspicion on the part of the Japanese rulers that Christianity was merely a cloak for political usurpation, the bigotry shown by many Christians where they had the upper hand in certain communities, and economic exploitation on the part of various unscrupulous Portuguese merchants, all combined to cause the Japanese to banish the Christians from their country. Christianity was formally disallowed by an edict in 1614, and all foreign teachers were ordered deported. In 1639 the final expulsion was ordered in the edict: "For the future, let none, so long as the Sun illuminates the world, presume to sail to Japan, not even in the quality of ambassadors, and this declaration is never to be revoked on pain of death."[5] Except for a small, closely watched Dutch post at Nagasaki, the island was closed to intercourse with the West until 1853.

Renewal of East-West Contact

Contact in the classical world. The remarkable series of geographical discoveries which began in the fifteenth century and carried intrepid European soldiers, traders, explorers, and missionaries to the ends of the earth recalls a similar movement a thousand years ago (see Chapter 7), when not only Europeans, but Hindus and Chinese traveled widely exchanging trade goods and items of culture. It was in the second and third centuries A.D. that rich cultural contacts in commerce, religion, art, philosophy, and language existed among three intercommunicating empires—the Graeco-Roman, the Indian, and the Chinese. Cultural diffusion from these empires spanned the Atlantic and Pacific oceans.

Truly the possibilities of peaceful diffusion of culture and the growth of an intercommunicating global culture seemed bright in the second century A.D. Unfortunately this promise was not realized. The fourth century witnessed the decline of Rome and the depredations of the Arabs and Abyssinians on the trade routes. Other factors (discussed in Chapter 7) weakened the lines of contact between the three great centers of civilization and ultimately destroyed them. For nearly a thousand years there was little exchange or communication between East and West.

Contact in the modern world. At the end of the fifteenth century, however, came the amazing expansion of Europe described in this chapter. Western Europe in the late Middle Ages began to experience an astonishing resurgence of creative power which was reflected in the movement known as the Renaissance, in the rise of powerful and well-administered nations, and in the growing importance of the middle class. But while Europe was pulsating with insatiable energy, the once powerful centers of flourishing empires in the East, such as India and China, were becoming decadent culturally and impotent politically. The ruling classes adopted a false pose of cultural superiority; following a policy of isolation, they failed to learn from what was going on in Europe. When contact between East and West was renewed, therefore, in the fifteenth century, it was not made between equals. The discrepancy in effective political organization, in disciplined armies, in energy and ambition prevented the resumption of East-West cultural contact on the same basis as that of a thousand years earlier. Thus there is an unfortunate, even tragic, aspect to the manner in which Europe's geographical expansion was carried out.

The natural result of this impact of the strong upon the weak was that the former took advantage of the latter; the East became the servant of the West. In the following volume the opening chapters will show how European power became irresistible as the commercial, scientific, political, and industrial revolutions thoroughly transformed and energized the culture of the West. This modern expansion of Europe and its mastery of much of the world's people—especially in the East—is generally referred to as Imperialism. The conflicts and tensions in modern world politics find their source to a large degree in the imperial policies of the West.

Summary

This chapter has briefly surveyed the great era of geographical expansion, which shifted Europe's axis from the Mediterranean to the Atlantic and saw such nations as Portugal, Spain, Holland, France, and England rise to power. To the New World these powers transplanted European culture, and great colonial empires were established.

European expansion eastward around Africa and into Asia proved just as important, but the results were not the same. The empires which Portugal, Holland, France, and England carved out were not based primarily on colonization, for Asia was far more populous than Europe. Rather, western domination of the East was secured by the establishment of strongly fortified settlements located at strategic sites, whence the better equipped Europeans could maintain economic and political control. The Europeans could not substitute their culture for the civilizations in India, China, and Japan because these lands had an ancient and proud history. In fact sixteenth-century India under Akbar was a brilliant age, and when the Portuguese dropped anchor at Canton, China was flourishing under the urbane rule of the Mings. But the East by this time had ceased to be dynamic. Showing little interest in the forces that were rapidly transforming and modernizing the European nations it became relatively more and more backward in technology and political power. The inevitable result was the domination of the East by the West.

Bibliography and acknowledgments

Prologue: Perspective on man

SPECIFIC REFERENCES

1. *World Economic Report, 1950-1951* (New York: United Nations, 1952)
2. Frederick Lewis Allen, *The Big Change, America Transforms Itself, 1900-1950* (New York: Harper & Brothers, 1952), p. 8
3. R. G. Collingwood, *The Idea of History* (Oxford: Clarendon Press, 1949), p. 10
4. Caroline F. Ware, "Introduction," *The Cultural Approach to History* (New York: Columbia University Press, 1940)
5. Arnold J. Toynbee, *Civilization on Trial* (New York: Oxford University Press, 1948), p. 11
6. Herbert Butterfield, *Christianity and History* (New York: Charles Scribner's Sons, 1950), p. 132
7. Thomas Carlyle, *On Heroes, Hero-Worship and The Heroic in History* (New York: Oxford University Press, 1946), p. 1
8. Oswald Spengler, *The Decline of the West* (London: George Allen & Unwin Ltd., 1926), p. 21
9. H. A. L. Fisher, *A History of Europe* (Boston: Houghton Mifflin Company, 1949), p. v
10. Samuel Eliot Morison, "Faith of a Historian," *The American Historical Review,* LVI, no. 2 (January 1951), pp. 261, 264
11. Collingwood, p. 332
12. Arnold J. Toynbee, *The World and the West* (New York: Oxford University Press, 1953), p. 71
13. William Howells, *Mankind So Far* (New York: Doubleday & Company, Inc., 1952), p 312

1. Toward civilization

SPECIFIC REFERENCES

1. *Frontiers in Space,* Official Publication of the Mount Wilson and Palomar Observatories (n. p., n.d.)
2. H. H. Newman, ed., *The Nature of the World and of Man* (Chicago: University of Chicago Press, 1926), p. 30
3. L. F. Richardson, quoted by George Gamov, "Turbulence in Space," *Scientific American,* vol. 186, no. 6 (June 1952), p. 27
4. Ernest A. Hooton, *Up from the Ape* (New York: The Macmillan Company, 1931), p. 314
5. John Grahame Clark, *From Savagery to Civilization* (London: Cobbett Press, Ltd., 1946), p. 71
6. J. T. Shotwell, *The History of History* (New York: Columbia University Press, 1939), p. 63

GENERAL REFERENCES

For the nature of the universe and geologic processes: Charles Schuchert and Carl O. Dunbar, *A Textbook of Geology* (John Wiley and Sons, 1933); William C. Krumbein and C. G. Croneis, *Down to Earth* (University of Chicago Press, 1936); H. H. Newman, ed., *The Nature of the World and of Man* (University of Chicago Press, 1926); *Frontiers in Space* (publication of the Mount Wilson and Palomar Observatories). There is much material available in H. G. Wells, *The Outline of History,* 4 vols. (The Macmillan Company, 1924) . For early man the authors relied mainly on the following standard works: George Grant MacCurdy, *Human Origins* (D. Appleton-Century Company, 1924); M. C. Burkitt, *Our Early Ancestors* (The Macmillan Company, 1929); H. F. Osborn, *Men of the Old Stone Age* (Charles Scribner's Sons, 1923); Ernest A. Hooton, *Up from the Ape* (The Macmillan Company, 1931); Sir Arthur Keith, *The Antiquity of Man* (J. B. Lippincott Company, 1925). On the nature and significance of culture and cultural processes in history, much helpful information was found in: John Grahame Clark, *From Savagery to Civilization* (Cobbett Press, Ltd., 1946); William Howells, *Mankind So Far* (Doubleday & Company, Inc., 1952); V. Gordon Childe, *Man Makes Himself* (New American Library of World Literature, Inc., 1951); Wilson D. Wallis, *Culture and Progress* (McGraw-Hill Book Company, Inc., 1930); James H. S. Bossard, ed., *Man and His World* (Harper & Brothers, 1932); Clark Wissler, *Man and Culture* (Thomas Y. Crowell Company, 1923). The discussion of primitive society owes much to Dr. Diedrich Westermann, *The African Today and Tomorrow* (Oxford University Press, 1939); G. G. Brown and A. M. Hutt, *Anthropology in Action* (Oxford University Press, 1935); Alexander Goldenweiser, *Anthropology* (F. S. Crofts & Co., 1937).

2. The Nile, the Tigris, and the Euphrates

SPECIFIC REFERENCES

1. Stanley Casson, *Progress of Archaeology* (New York: Whittlesey House, McGraw-Hill Book Company, Inc., 1934), p. 28
2. Adolf Erman, *Life in Ancient Egypt* (New York: The Macmillan Company, 1894), p. 389
3. Albert T. Trever, *History of Ancient Civilization* (New York: Harcourt, Brace & Company, 1936), I, p. 50
4. James H. Breasted, *A History of Egypt* (New York: Charles Scribner's Sons, 1924), p. 173
5. Quoted by James H. Breasted, *The Development of Religion and Thought in Ancient Egypt* (New York: Charles Scribner's Sons, 1912), p. 324, 326. Reprinted by permission of the publishers
6. Quoted by Trever, p. 24
7. Quoted by G. A. Dorsey, *Man's Own Show: Civilization* (New York: Halcyon House, Blue Ribbon Books, 1937), p. 328. Reprinted by permission of Harper & Brothers
8. Quotations from Hammurabic code are taken from Robert Francis Harper, *The Code of Hammurabi* (Chicago: University of Chicago Press, 1904)
9. Quoted by Samuel N. Kramer, "The Oldest Laws," *Scientific American,* vol. 188, no. 1 (January 1953), p. 28
10. M. I. Rostovtzeff, *A History of the Ancient World,* 2nd ed. (Oxford: Clarendon Press, 1936), p. 132
11. *Ecclesiastes* 12:1-7
12. Quoted by W. E. Caldwell, *The Ancient World* (New York: Farrar & Rinehart, 1937), p. 105
13. Quoted by Dorsey, p. 333. Reprinted by permission of Harper & Brothers
14. James A. Breasted, *Ancient Times,* 2nd ed. (Boston: Ginn & Company, 1935), p. 204
15. *Ibid.,* p. 277
16. John Grahame Clark, *From Savagery to Civilization* (London: Cobbett Press, Ltd., 1946), p. 103

GENERAL REFERENCES

The following works have been of great assistance in writing this chapter: C. E. Van Sickle, *A Political and Cultural History of the Ancient World* (Houghton Mifflin Company, 1947); Henri Frankfort, *The Birth of Civilization in the Near East* (Williams and Norgate, 1951); W. E. Caldwell, *The Ancient World* (Farrar & Rinehart, 1937); Albert A. Trever, *History of Ancient Civilization* (Harcourt, Brace & Company, Inc., 1936); James H. Breasted, *Ancient Times* (Ginn and Company, 1935). All the above covered the area of both the Nile and Mesopotamia. On Egypt, J. H. Breasted, *A History of Egypt* (Charles Scribner's Sons, 1924) was indispensable. Excellent material may also be found in George Steindorff and Keith C. Seele, *When Egypt Ruled the East* (University of Chicago Press, 1942), and John A. Wilson, *The Burden of Egypt* (University of Chicago Press, 1951). For Mesopotamia the authors are indebted to H. R. Hall, *The Ancient History of the Near East* (Methuen & Co., Ltd., 1932); Charles L. Woolley, *The Sumerians* (Oxford University Press, 1928); A. T. E. Olmstead, *History of Assyria* (Charles Scribner's Sons, 1923). For an overall interpretation of historical developments in Egypt and Mesopotamia, the authors relied heavily on M. I. Rostovtzeff, *A History of the Ancient World,* I, (Clarendon Press, 1936).

3. The Indus and the Ganges

SPECIFIC REFERENCES

1. Ananda Coomaraswamy, *The Dance of Shiva* (Bombay: Asia Publishing House, 1948), p. 22
2. Sir John Marshall, ed., *Mohenjo-daro and the Indus Civilization* (London: Arthur Probsthain, 1931), I, p. 106
3. *Ibid.,* p. 112
4. See Stanley Rice, *Hindu Customs and Their Origin* (London: George Allen and Unwin, Ltd., 1937), pp. 35-132
5. J. Takakusu, trans., *Buddhist Religion* (New York: Oxford University Press, 1896), p. 182
6. Quoted by M. A. Mehendale, "Language and Literature," *The History and Culture of the Indian People,* R. C. Majumdar and A. D. Pusalker, eds. (London: George Allen and Unwin, Ltd., 1951), I, *The Vedic Age,* pp. 469, 470
7. S. Radhakrishnan, ed. and trans., *The Bhagavadgita* (London: George Allen and Unwin, Ltd., 1948), p. 14
8. *Ibid.,* pp. 103, 108; chap. II, verses 12, 22
9. F. Max Müller, *Chips from a German Workshop* (New York: Charles Scribner's Sons, 1872), I, pp. 76-77

10. See F. Max Müller, ed., *The Sacred Books of the East* (Oxford: Clarendon Press, 1881), XI, pp. 96-114
11. Radha Kumud Mookerji, *Hindu Civilization* (London: Longmans, Green & Company, Inc., 1936), p. 249
12. Junjiro Takakusu, "Buddhism as a Philosophy of 'Thusness,'" *Philosophy—East and West,* Charles A. Moore, ed. (Princeton: Princeton University Press, 1944), p. 73
13. *Ibid.,* p. 83
14. Nalinaksha Dutt, "Religion and Philosophy," *The History and Culture of the Indian People,* R. C. Majumdar and A. D. Pusalker, eds. (Bombay: Bharatiya Vidya Bhavan, 1951), II, *The Age of Imperial Unity,* p. 371
15. *Ibid.,* p. 377

GENERAL REFERENCES

Among the books consulted for the general background of this chapter were Vincent Arthur Smith, *Early History of India* (Clarendon Press, 1925); V. A. Smith, *The Oxford History of India,* 2nd ed. (Clarendon Press, 1923); John Allan, *The Cambridge Shorter History of India* (The Macmillan Company, 1934). Indian scholars have recently inaugurated a valuable series, *The History and Culture of the Indian People,* R. C. Majumdar and A. D. Pusalker, eds. The authors extensively consulted vol. I, *The Vedic Age* (George Allen and Unwin, Ltd., 1951) in particular the chapters on "The Indus Valley Civilization" by A. D. Pusalker, "Religion and Philosophy" and "Social and Economic Conditions" by V. M. Apte, and "Language and Literature" by M. A. Mehendale. The most authoritative study of the unearthing of the Indus valley civilization was found in the work edited by Sir John Marshall, *Mohenjo-daro and the Indus Civilization,* 3 vols. (Arthur Probsthain, 1931). An excellent treatment of the early Indo-Aryan peoples was found in Radha Kumud Mookerji's *Hindu Civilization* (Longmans, Green & Company, Inc., 1936). An excellent reference embodying the latest research on the Indus civilization is Sir Mortimer Wheeler, *The Indus Civilization,* a supplementary volume to *The Cambridge History of India* (Cambridge University Press, 1953). N. K. Sidhanta, *The Heroic Age of India* (Alfred A. Knopf, 1930) pointed out similarities in the Indian and Greek heroic ages, while Gilbert Slater was invaluable for indicating *The Dravidian Element in Indian Culture* (Ernest Benn, 1924). For an analysis of India's cultural contributions, the authors made extensive use of Hugh George Rawlinson, *India, A Short Cultural History* (D. Appleton-Century Company, 1938), and also consulted René Grousset, *The Civilization of India,* C. A. Phillips, trans. (Tudor Publishing House, 1939). Arthur Berriedale Keith, *The Religion and Philosophy of the Veda and Upanishads,* 2 vols. (Harvard University Press, 1925), and the essays of F. Max Müller, *Chips from a German Workshop,* I (Charles Scribner's Sons, 1872). Of genuine help in the intellectual, literary, and artistic fields was *The Legacy of India,* Geoffrey T. Garratt, ed. (Clarendon Press, 1937). An authoritative modern study of *The Bhagavadgita* is found in the work by that name by the Indian scholar, Sir S. Radhakrishnan (George Allen and Unwin, Ltd., 1948), while the authors also consulted his essays on *The Hindu View of Life* (George Allen and Unwin, Ltd., 1948). The second volume of Majumdar and Pusalker, *The Age of Imperial Unity* (Bharatiya Vidya Bhavan, 1951) was consulted for its study of the Buddha, found in "Religion and Philosophy" by Nalinaksha Dutt. Mookerji, *op.cit.,* was also valuable in this field.

4. The Wei and the Hwang Ho

SPECIFIC REFERENCES

1. L. Carrington Goodrich, *A Short History of the Chinese People* (New York: Harper & Brothers, 1943), p. 1
2. Wolfram Eberhard, *A History of China* (London: Routledge & Kegan Paul, Ltd., 1950), p. 13
3. Herrlee Glessner Creel, *The Birth of China* (London: Jonathan Cape, Ltd., 1936), p. 24
4. Eberhard, p. 21
5. Ch'en Meng-chia, "The Greatness of Chou (ca. 1027-ca. 221 B.C.)," Harley F. MacNair, ed., *China* (Berkeley: University of California Press, 1946), p. 60
6. C. P. Fitzgerald, *China, A Short Cultural History,* rev. ed. (London: Cresset Press, Ltd., 1950), p. 59
7. *Ibid.,* p. 60
8. Ch'en Meng-chia, pp. 61-62
9. Kenneth S. Latourette, *The Chinese, Their History and Culture,* 3rd rev. ed., 2 vols. in one (New York: The Macmillan Company, 1951), p. 58
10. Fitzgerald, pp. 60-61
11. René Grousset, *The Rise and Splendour of the Chinese Empire* (London: Geoffrey Bles, Ltd., 1952), p.26
12. Wu Ching-ch'ao, "Economic Development," Harley F. MacNair, ed., *China* (Berkeley: University of California Press, 1946), p. 456
13. Ch'ao-ting Chi, *Key Economic Areas in Chinese History* (London: George Allen and Unwin, Ltd., 1936), p. 62
14. Quoted by Wu Ching-ch'ao, p. 456
15. L. Carrington Goodrich, p. 23

16. Fung Yu-Lan, *A History of Chinese Philosophy* (Peiping: Henri Vetch, 1937), I, p. 3
17. W. E. Soothill, *The Three Religions of China,* 2nd ed. (London: Oxford University Press, 1923), p. 31
18. Leonard Shihlien Hsü, *The Political Philosophy of Confucianism* (New York: E. P. Dutton & Co., Inc., 1932), pp. 87-88
19. Quotations found in Chan Wing-tsit, "The Story of Chinese Philosophy," Charles A. Moore, ed., *Philosophy–East and West* (Princeton: Princeton University Press, 1946), p. 28
20. Eberhard, p. 42
21. Fung Yu-Lan, I, p. 113
22. *Ibid.* Quoted on p. 177
23. Quoted by C. P. Fitzgerald, *China, A Short Cultural History* (New York: D. Appleton-Century Company, 1938), p. 84
24. See *ibid.*, pp. 121-132, for a discussion of jade art and its significance
25. From *Book of Odes,* quoted by Will Durant, *The Story of Civilization* (New York: Simon and Schuster, 1935), I, p. 648
26. Helen Waddell, ed. and trans., *Lyrics from the Chinese* (London: Constable and Company, 1913)
27. Herrlee Glessner Creel, *Studies in Early Chinese Culture* (Baltimore: Waverly Press, 1937), p. 254

GENERAL REFERENCES

For the preparation of this chapter on ancient China, the authors are indebted to Wolfram Eberhard, *A History of China* (Routledge & Kegan Paul, Ltd., 1950), invaluable for the light which it threw on the early sociological developments of the Chinese people and its bibliographical notes; Carl Whiting Bishop, *Origin of the Far Eastern Civilizations* (The Smithsonian Institution, 1942); Marcel Granet, *Chinese Civilization* (Alfred A. Knopf, 1930); L. Carrington Goodrich, *A Short History of the Chinese People* (Harper & Brothers, 1943); C. P. Fitzgerald, *China, A Short Cultural History,* rev. ed. (Cresset Press, 1950); Kenneth S. Latourette, *The Chinese, Their History and Culture,* 3rd rev. ed., 2 vols. in one (The Macmillan Company, 1951); Richard Wilhelm, *A Short History of Chinese Civilization* (The Viking Press, 1929); and René Grousset, *The Rise and Splendour of the Chinese Empire* (Geoffrey Bles, Ltd., 1952). George Babcock Cressey, *China's Geographic Foundations, a Survey of the Land and its People* (McGraw-Hill Book Company, Inc., 1933) has a full account of the physical characteristics of China. Among the works consulted on the pre-Shang and Shang periods were Herrlee Glessner Creel, *The Birth of China* (Jonathan Cape, Ltd., 1936) and his *Studies in Early Chinese Culture* (Waverly Press, 1937); Johan Gunnar Andersson, *Children of the Yellow Earth; Studies in Prehistoric China* (The Macmillan Company, 1934); James M. Menzies, "The Culture of the Shang Dynasty," *Annual Report of the Smithsonian Institution* (Smithsonian Institution, 1931), pp. 549-558; William Charles White, "Some Revelations of Recent Excavations," *China,* Harley F. MacNair, ed. (University of California Press, 1951). The material for the Chou period was augmented by Ch'en Meng-chia, "The Greatness of Chou (ca. 1027-ca. 221 B. C.)," and Wu Ching-ch'ao, "Economic Development," both found in MacNair, *op. cit.;* Ch'ao-ting Chi, *Key Economic Areas in Chinese History* (George Allen and Unwin, Ltd., 1936); Fung Yu-Lan, *A History of Chinese Philosophy,* I, *The Period of the Philosophers (from the Beginnings to ca. 100* B.C.) (Henri Vetch, 1937); W. E. Soothill, *The Three Religions of China,* 2nd ed. (Oxford University Press, 1923); Leonard Shihlien Hsü, *The Political Philosophy of Confucianism* (E. P. Dutton & Co., Inc., 1932). For material on early Chinese art, George Soulié de Morant, *A History of Chinese Art from Ancient Times to the Present Day,* G. C. Wheeler, trans. (Robert O. Ballou, Publisher, 1931) and Grousset, *op. cit.* were among the works consulted. Arthur Waley, *The Way and its Power* (George Allen and Unwin, Ltd., 1934) provides a good interpretation of Lao-Tzu's work.

5. The Greek achievement

SPECIFIC REFERENCES

1. Quoted by M. Cary, *The Geographic Background of Greek and Roman History* (Oxford: Clarendon Press, 1949), p. 310 n. See also M. P. Nilsson, *Homer and Mycenae* (London: Methuen & Co., Ltd., 1933), p. 113
2. Harry R. Hall, *The Civilization of Greece in the Bronze Age* (London: Methuen & Co., Ltd., 1928), p. 272
3. *Ibid.*, p. 114
4. Cary, pp. 47, 57
5. M. Rostovtzeff, *A History of the Ancient World* (Oxford: Clarendon Press, 1926), I, p. 206
6. George W. Botsford and Charles A. Robinson, *Hellenic History* (New York: The Macmillan Company, 1929), p. 157
7. Thucydides, *History of the Peloponnesian War,* 2nd rev. ed., trans. and ed. by B. Jowett (Oxford: Clarendon Press, 1900), I, pp. 127-128
8. Rostovtzeff, I, p. 210
9. Arnold J. Toynbee, *Civilization on Trial* (New York: Oxford University Press, 1948), p. 59
10. Thucydides, I, p. 139

11. *Ibid.*, I, pp. 16-17
12. Reported in Jules Toutain, *The Economic Life of the Ancient World* (London: Kegan Paul, Trench, Trubner and Company, 1930), p. 53
13. Thucydides, I, p. 129
14. Quoted by M. Cary and T. J. Haarhoff, *Life and Thought in the Greek and Roman World* (London: Methuen & Co., Ltd., 1951), p. 200
15. *Ibid.* Quoted on p. 192
16. W. W. Tarn and G. T. Griffith, *Hellenistic Civilization,* 3rd ed. (London: Edward Arnold & Co., 1952), p. 185
17. Tarn and Griffith, p. 271

GENERAL REFERENCES

In the preparation of this chapter the authors found of inestimable help: Botsford and Robinson, *Hellenic History* (The Macmillan Company, 1939); Wallace E. Caldwell, *The Ancient World* (Farrar & Rinehart, 1937); J. B. Bury, *A History of Greece to the Death of Alexander the Great* (The Macmillan Company, 1913); James Henry Breasted, *The Conquest of Civilization* (Harper & Brothers, 1938); M. Cary, *The Geographic Background of Greek and Roman History* (Clarendon Press, 1949); Harry R. Hall, *The Civilization of Greece in the Bronze Age* (Methuen & Co., Ltd., 1928); M. Rostovtzeff, *A History of the Ancient World,* I (Clarendon Press, 1926); Mason Hammond, *City-State and World State in Greek and Roman Political Theory until Augustus* (Harvard University Press, 1951); Jules Toutain, *The Economic Life of the Ancient World* (Kegan Paul, Trench, Trubner and Company, 1930); J. Oliver Thomson, *History of Ancient Geography* (Cambridge University Press, 1938). Their chief sources for the Hellenistic period were: W. W. Tarn, *Hellenistic Civilization* (Longmans, Green & Company, Inc., 1930); M. Cary, *The Legacy of Alexander: A History of the Greek World from 323 to 146* B.C. (Methuen & Co., Ltd., 1932); M. Rostovtzeff, *The Social and Economic History of the Hellenistic World,* 2 vols. (Oxford University Press, 1941); W. W. Tarn and G. T. Griffith, *Hellenistic Civilization,* 3rd ed. (Edward Arnold and Company, 1952). The social aspects of Greece were discussed thoroughly in Gustave Glotz, *Ancient Greece at Work* (Alfred A. Knopf, 1926). The economic side was clarified by G. M. Calhoun, *The Business Life of Ancient Athens* (University of Chicago Press, 1926). Thucydides' classic, *History of the Peloponnesian War,* trans. and ed. by B. Jowett, 2nd rev. ed. (Clarendon Press, 1900) was quoted often in connection with both the Peloponnesian War and the Age of Pericles. In the section on the culture of Greece and of Hellenistic times, the following works were consulted: Arnold J. Toynbee, *A Study of History,* abridged version (Oxford University Press, 1947); Sir William Dampier, *A History of Science and Its Relations with Philosophy and Religion,* 3rd ed. (The Macmillan Company, 1942), pp. 10-64; B. A. G. Fuller, *A History of Philosophy,* I (Henry Holt & Co., Inc., 1938); R. W. Livingstone, ed., *The Legacy of Greece* (Clarendon Press, 1928); "The Hellenic Age," *Universal World History,* J. A. Hammerton, ed. (Wm. H. Wise & Company, 1939); Percy Gardner, *The Principles of Greek Art* (The Macmillan Company, 1936); Sir Banister Fletcher, *A History of Architecture,* 7th ed. (Charles Scribner's Sons, 1924).

6. The ascendancy of Rome

SPECIFIC REFERENCES

1. M. Rostovtzeff, *A History of the Ancient World* (Oxford: Clarendon Press, 1927), II, p. 23
2. M. Cary, *The Geographic Background of Greek and Roman History* (Oxford: Clarendon Press, 1949), p. 133
3. James H. Breasted, *Ancient Times* (Boston: Ginn and Company, 1935), p. 611
4. David Magie, *Roman Rule in Asia Minor to the End of the Third Century after Christ* (Princeton: Princeton University Press, 1950), I, p. 378
5. Mason Hammond, *City-State and World State in Greek and Roman Political Theory until Augustus* (Cambridge: Harvard University Press, 1951), p. 153
6. W. Stearns Davis, *A Day in Old Rome* (New York: Allyn and Bacon, 1925), p. 2
7. Rostovtzeff, II, p. 291
8. C. H. V. Sutherland, "Greece in Rome," *The Root of Europe—Studies in the Diffusion of Greek Culture* (London: *The Geographical Magazine,* 1952), pp. 30-31
9. Hammond, p. 165
10. M. Cary and T. J. Haarhoff, *Life and Thought in the Greek and Roman World* (London: Methuen & Co., Ltd., 1951), p. 262
11. R. G. Collingwood, *The Idea of History* (Oxford: Clarendon Press, 1949), p. 36

GENERAL REFERENCES

In the preparation of the chapters dealing with Roman civilization, its rise and fall, the general ancient histories already cited were of much assistance: Wallace E. Caldwell, *The Ancient World* (Farrar & Rinehart, 1937); Albert A. Trever, *History of Ancient Civilization* (Harcourt, Brace & Company, Inc., 1936); James H. Breasted, *Ancient Times* (Ginn and Company, 1935); M. Rostovtzeff, *A History of the Ancient World* (Oxford University Press, 1927); Francis S. Marvin, ed., *The Unity of*

Western Civilization, 2nd ed. (Oxford University Press, 1922); F. de Zulueta, "Rome As the World's Law-Giver," *Universal World History.* H. A. L. Fisher, *A History of Europe* (Edward Arnold & Co., 1937) and David Magie, *Roman Rule in Asia Minor to the End of the Third Century after Christ* offered valuable suggestions on the political history. Mason Hammond, *City-State and World State: In Greek and Roman Political Theory until Augustus* provides interesting parallels between Greek times and our own, while M. Cary, *The Geographic Background of Greek and Roman History* (Clarendon Press, 1949) is excellent in this aspect of the history. M. Cary and T. J. Haarhoff, *Life and Thought in the Greek and Roman World* (Methuen & Co., Ltd., 1951) is a concise reference work for cultural developments in the classical period. R. G. Collingwood, *The Idea of History* (Clarendon Press, 1949) is valuable for his studies in historiography.

7. The world in classical times

SPECIFIC REFERENCES

1. Quoted by Eva M. Sanford, *The Mediterranean World in Ancient Times* (New York: The Ronald Press Company, 1938), p. 473
2. Quoted by David Magie, *Roman Rule in Asia Minor to the End of the Third Century after Christ* (Princeton: Princeton University Press, 1950), I, p. 629
3. W. F. Oakeshott, *Commerce and Society, A Short History of Trade and its Effects on Civilization* (Oxford: Clarendon Press, 1936), p. 31
4. Quoted by M. P. Charlesworth, *Trade-routes and Commerce of the Roman Empire,* 2nd rev. ed. (New York: Cambridge University Press, 1926), p. 224
5. W. W. Tarn, "Macedon and the East," *The Root of Europe: Studies in the Diffusion of Greek Culture* (London: The Geographical Magazine, 1952), p. 18
6. John P. Mahaffy, *The Progress of Hellenism in Alexander's Empire* (Chicago: University of Chicago Press, 1905), pp. 40-41
7. On this subject, and for the conflicting views of authorities, see J. Oliver Thomson, *History of Ancient Geography* (New York: Cambridge University Press, 1948), p. 176
8. Quoted by H. G. Rawlinson, *India, A Short Cultural History* (New York: D. Appleton-Century Company, 1937), p. 72. The description of Pataliputra and Chandragupta Maurya are also from this work, pp. 66-75. For further material on Pataliputra and Chandragupta, see also V. A. Smith, *Oxford History of India* (London: Oxford University Press, 1923), pp. 74-92; and R. C. Majumdar, H. C. Raychaudhuri, Kalikinkar Datta, *An Advanced History of India,* 2nd ed. (London: Macmillan & Company, Ltd., 1946), pp. 113-114, 197-198, 97-102
9. Majumdar, Raychaudhuri, Datta, *An advanced History of India,* p. 135
10. Quoted by Rawlinson, *Intercourse between India and the Western World from the Earliest Times to the Fall of Rome,* 2nd ed. (New York: Cambridge University Press, 1926), p. 39
11. V. A. Smith, ed., *The Edicts of Asoka* (London: Essex House Press, 1909), pp. 7-8
12. R. K. Mookerji, "Asoka, the Great," *The History and Culture of the Indian People,* R. C. Majumdar, ed. (Bombay: Bharatiya Vidya Bhavan, 1951), II, *The Age of Imperial Unity,* p. 92
13. W. W. Tarn, "Macedon and the East," p. 20
14. Ananda Coomaraswamy, *The Dance of Shiva* (Bombay: Asia Publishing House, 1948), p. 79
15. H. G. Rawlinson, *Intercourse Between India and the Western World* (New York: Cambridge University Press, 1916), p. 109. Consult this work also for a more detailed account of Tamil-Roman relations, chapters 6, 7; see also E. H. Warmington, *The Commerce Between the Roman Empire and India* (New York: Cambridge University Press, 1951), p. 138
16. Martin P. Charlesworth, "Roman Trade with India: a Resurvey," *Studies in Roman Economic and Social History in Honor of Allan Chester Johnson,* P. R. Coleman-Norton, ed. (Princeton: Princeton University Press, 1951), p. 138
17. John K. Shryock, *The Origin and Development of the State Cult of Confucius* (New York: D. Appleton-Century Company, 1932), p. 229
18. René Grousset, *The Rise and Splendour of the Chinese Empire* (London: Geoffrey Bles, Inc., 1952), p. 60
19. W. F. Oakeshott, p. 31
20. Frederick J. Teggart, *Rome and China, A Study in Correlations in Historical Events* (Berkeley: University of California Press, 1939), pp. ix, 243
21. H. H. Gowen and J. W. Hall, *An Outline History of China* (New York: D. Appleton-Century Company, 1926), p. 101
22. Translated by Hu Shih, *Symposium on Chinese Culture,* Sophia H. Chen Zen, ed. (Shanghai: Institute of Pacific Relations, 1931), p. 44; L. Carrington Goodrich, *A Short History of the Chinese People* (New York: Harper & Brothers, 1943), p. 46
23. G. F. Hudson, *Europe and China* (London: Edward Arnold & Co., 1931), pp. 99-100
24. Max Cary and E. H. Warmington, *The Ancient*

Explorers (New York: Dodd, Mead & Co., 1929), p. 184

25. Quoted by H. G. Rawlinson, "The Eastward Spread of Hellenism," *Universal History of the World.* J. A. Hammerton, ed. (London: The Amalgamated Press, Ltd., n.d.), III, pp. 1503-1504
26. R. C. Majumdar, "India and the Western World," *The History and Culture of the Indian People,* II, pp. 631, 633

GENERAL REFERENCES

For the section dealing with the Graeco-Roman world, attention was directed toward such works as: Eva M. Sanford, *The Mediterranean World in Ancient Times* (The Ronald Press, 1938); M. Rostovtzeff, *The Social and Economic History of the Hellenistic World,* 2 vols (Oxford University Press, 1941), as well as his *A History of the Ancient World,* II (Clarendon Press, 1927); and Albert A. Trever, *History of Ancient Civilization,* II (Harcourt, Brace & Company, Inc., 1936). Studies consulted on the diffusion of Graeco-Roman culture eastward included: John P. Mahaffy, *The Progress of Hellenism in Alexander's Empire* (University of Chicago Press, 1905); W. W. Tarn, "Macedon and the East," *The Root of Europe, Studies in the Diffusion of Greek Culture* (The Geographical Magazine, 1952); W. W. Tarn, *The Greeks in Bactria and India* (Cambridge University Press, 1938); "The Successors of Alexander the Great," *The Cambridge History of India,* E. J. Rapson, ed., I, chap. 22 (The Macmillan Company, 1922); and H. G. Rawlinson, "The Eastward Spread of Hellenism," *Universal World History,* J. A. Hammerton, ed. (Wm. H. Wise & Company, 1937). For geographical data, the authors made use of materials found in Max Cary and E. H. Warmington, *The Ancient Explorers* (Dodd, Mead & Co., 1929); J. Oliver Thomson, *History of Ancient Geography* (Cambridge University Press, 1948). On the subject of trade between East and West, they found the following works of value: H. G. Rawlinson, *Intercourse between India and the Western World from the Earliest Times to the Fall of Rome,* 2nd ed. (Cambridge University Press, 1926); E. H. Warmington, *The Commerce Between the Roman Empire and India* (Cambridge University Press, 1928); W. F. Oakeshott, *Commerce and Society, A Short History of Trade and its Effects on Civilization* (Clarendon Press, 1936); M. P. Charlesworth, *Trade-routes and Commerce of the Roman Empire,* 2nd rev. ed. (Cambridge University Press, 1926); and by the same author, "Roman Trade with India: a Resurvey," P. R. Coleman-Norton, ed., *Studies in Roman Economic and Social History in Honor of Allan Chester Johnson* (Princeton University Press, 1951). On contemporary India they used various works, including: H. G. Rawlinson, *India, A Short Cultural History (D.* Appleton-Century Company, 1937); R. C. Majumdar, H. C. Raychaudhuri, Kalikinkar Datta, *An Advanced History of India,* 2nd ed. (Macmillan & Company, Ltd., 1946); R. C. Majumdar, "India and the Western World," Majumdar, ed., *The History and Culture of the Indian People,* II, *The Age of Imperial Unity* (Bharatiya Vidya Bhavan, 1951), while in this same volume was also found R. K. Mookerji, "Asoka the Great." Among the books consulted on contemporary China were Wolfram Eberhard, *A History of China* (Routledge and Kegan Paul, 1950); René Grousset, *The Rise and Splendour of the Chinese Empire* (Geoffrey Bles, Ltd., 1952); C. P. Fitzgerald, *China, A Short Cultural History,* rev. ed. (Cresset Press, 1950); and Hu Shih, *Symposium on Chinese Culture,* Sophia H. Chen Zen, ed. (Institute of Pacific Relations, 1931). Two interesting works depicting the interplay of forces between the Roman Empire and China were G. F. Hudson, *Europe and China* (Edward Arnold & Company, 1931); and Frederick J. Teggart, *Rome and China, A Study in Correlations in Historical Events* (University of California Press, 1939).

8. Interval in the West

SPECIFIC REFERENCES

1. M. I. Rostovtzeff, *A History of the Ancient World* (Oxford: Clarendon Press, 1927), II, p. 309
2. Quoted by F. Lot, *The End of the Ancient World* (Oxford: Clarendon Press, 1927), II, p. (New York: Alfred A. Knopf, 1931), p. 70
3. M. I. Rostovtzeff, *Social and Economic History of the Roman Empire* (Oxford: Clarendon Press, 1926), p. 460
4. *The Works of Tacitus,* The Oxford Translation (New York: Harper & Brothers, 1889), p. 309
5. *Ibid.,* pp. 310-311
6. Sydney M. Brown, *Medieval Europe* (New York: Harcourt, Brace & Company, Inc., 1932), p. 29
7. Rostovtzeff, *A History of the Ancient World,* II, p. 366
8. Gregory of Tours, *History of the Franks,* O. M. Dalton, ed. (Oxford: Clarendon Press, 1927), I, p. 2
9. Cited by Christopher Dawson, *The Making of Europe* (London: Sheed & Ward, 1932), pp. 88-89
10. This phrase is attributed to Fustel de Coulanges; cited by Dawson, p. 84

11. J. W. Thompson, *Economic and Social History of the Middle Ages, 300-1300* (New York: D. Appleton-Century Company, 1928), p. 132
12. *Ibid.*, p. 611
13. Quoted by Dawson, p. 94
14. Henri Pirenne, *Mohammed and Charlemagne* (New York: Norton & Company, Inc., 1939), p. 116

GENERAL REFERENCES

For various aspects of the Roman narrative: Frank F. Abbott, *Roman Politics* (Marshall Jones Company, 1923); Ferdinand Lot, *The End of the Ancient World and the Beginnings of the Middle Ages* (Alfred A. Knopf, 1931); J. W. Thompson, *Economic and Social History of the Middle Ages, 300-1300* (D. Appleton-Century Company, 1928). The rise of Christianity was briefly but admirably discussed by: E. M. Hulme, *The Middle Ages* (Henry Holt & Co., Inc., 1938); R. W. Collins, *A History of Medieval Civilization* (Ginn and Company, 1936). An excellent reference for the early Christian Church was A. C. Flick, *The Rise of the Medieval Church* (G. P. Putnam's Sons, 1909), which proved invaluable.

The discussion of the early Middle Ages is indebted to: Hulme, Thompson, and Collins, *op. cit.;* for interpretation especially; G. B. Adams, *Civilization During the Middle Ages* (Charles Scribner's Sons, 1914). W. O. Ault, *Europe in the Middle Ages* (D. C. Heath and Company, 1937) was referred to for the discussion of the rise of the Franks. For general political history of the Middle Ages see: Z. N. Brooke, *A History of Europe, 911-1198,* 2nd ed. (Methuen & Co., Ltd., 1947); R. B. Merriman, *The Rise of the Spanish Empire in the Old World and in the New,* I (The Macmillan Company, 1918); Christopher Dawson, *The Making of Europe* (Sheed & Ward, 1932); Henri Pirenne, *Mohammed and Charlemagne* (Norton & Company, Inc., 1939). See the General References for chap. 12 for a more extensive bibliography on medieval political history.

9. Crossroads of the world

SPECIFIC REFERENCES

1. See Charles Diehl, *History of the Byzantine Empire,* trans. from French by George B. Ives (Princeton: Princeton University Press, 1925), pp. 156-167
2. See F. H. Marshall, "Byzantinism in Its Varied Aspects," *Universal World History,* J. A. Hammerton, ed. (New York: Wm. H. Wise & Co., 1937), V, pp. 1481-1482
3. See Robert Byron, *The Byzantine Achievement* (New York: Alfred A. Knopf, 1929), pp. 223-229, for a fuller account of Byzantine court splendor
4. Norman H. Baynes, *The Byzantine Empire* (New York: Henry Holt and Company, 1926), p. 31, and Toronto, Oxford University Press
5. Henry B. Dewing, trans., *Procopius,* 6 vols. (London: William Heinemann, 1914), I, pp. 231-233
6. See Harry E. Barnes, *The History of Western Civilization* (New York: Harcourt, Brace and Company, 1935), I, pp. 505-509, for a good brief study of Byzantine social life and institutions
7. See Prosper Boissonnade, *Life and Work in Medieval Europe* (New York: Alfred A. Knopf, 1927), pp. 48-50
8. Referred to by Marshall, p. 1476
9. Barnes, p. 502. Compare Baynes, pp. 207-220
10. Quoted by A. A. Vasiliev, *History of the Byzantine Empire,* II (University of Wisconsin Studies in the Social Sciences and History, no. 14, 1929), p. 151
11. *Ibid.* Quoted on p. 152
12. *Ibid.* Quoted on p. 152
13. Diehl, p. 96
14. Diehl, p. 31
15. Quoted by Barnes, p. 511
16. Sheldon Cheney, *A World History of Art* (New York: The Viking Press, 1937), p. 336

GENERAL REFERENCES

A detailed political account of the early Byzantine empire was found in J. B. Bury, *A History of the Eastern Roman Empire,* 2 vols. (The Macmillan Company, 1912). Two brief but worth-while accounts of the principal historical events were: Charles Diehl, *History of the Byzantine Empire* (Princeton University Press, 1925); N. H. Baynes, *The Byzantine Empire* (Henry Holt and Company and Oxford University Press, 1926). Charles Diehl, *Byzantine Portraits* (Alfred A. Knopf, 1927), was consulted especially for two essays: "Life of a Byzantine Empress" and "Theodora." Robert Byron, *The Byzantine Achievement* (Alfred A. Knopf, 1929), gave a vivid account of life in the Byzantine empire, as did Steven Runciman, *Byzantine Civilization* (Longmans, Green and Company, 1933). The economic aspects were set forth in: Prosper Boissonnade, *Life and Work in Medieval Europe,* chaps. 3, 4, 5, 11 (Alfred A. Knopf, 1927); H. E. Barnes, *A History of Western Civilization,* I, chap. 14 (Harcourt, Brace and Company, 1935); A. A.

Vasiliev, *History of the Byzantine Empire,* II, University of Wisconsin Studies in the Social Sciences and History, no. 14, 1929. A detailed account of some aspects of political administration was procured from the work of A. E. R. Boak and J. E. Dunlap, *Two Studies in Later Roman and Byzantine Administration* (The Macmillan Company, 1924). Regarding art and architecture, the authors consulted Sir T. G. Jackson, *Byzantine and Romanesque Architecture,* 2 vols., 2nd ed. (University of Chicago Press, 1920), a work copiously illustrated.

10. The triumph of Islam

SPECIFIC REFERENCES

1. See Robert Ernest Hume, *The World's Living Religions* (New York: Charles Scribner's Sons, 1931), p. 220
2. Quoted by Carl Stephenson, *Mediaeval History* (New York: Harper & Brothers, 1935), p. 137
3. *Ibid.,* p. 137
4. From *The Bible of the World,* ed. by Robert O. Ballou (New York: The Viking Press, 1939), p. 1294
5. Philip K. Hitti, *The Arabs, A Short History* (London: Macmillan & Company, Ltd., 1950), p. 21
6. Hume, pp. 225-228
7. Edward W. Lane, *Selections from the Koran* (London: J. Madden and Company, 1843)
8. Hume, pp. 228-229
9. Quoted by Hitti, p. 32
10. Diedrich Westermann, *The African Today and Tomorrow* (London: Oxford University Press, 1939), p. 275
11. See Stephenson, pp. 146-147, regarding reasons for the spread of Islam
12. H. A. R. Gibb, *Mohammedanism, An Historical Survey* (London: Oxford University Press, 1949), p. 4
13. Hitti, p. 1
14. Quoted by David de Santillana, "Law and Society," *Legacy of Islam,* ed. by Sir Thomas Arnold and Alfred Guillaume (Oxford: Clarendon Press, 1931), p. 304
15. Stanley Lane-Poole, *A History of Egypt in the Middle Ages* (London: Methuen & Co., Ltd., 1901), p. 145
16. Quoted by E. H. Palmer, *Haroun Alraschid, Caliph of Bagdad* (London: Marcus Ward and Company, 1881), p. 76
17. See G. Le Strange, *Baghdad During the Abbasid Caliphate* (Oxford: Clarendon Press, 1900), pp. 242-300, for a fuller description of the magnificence of life in the Abbasid palaces
18. D. S. Margoliouth, *Mohammedanism* (London: Williams and Norgate, n.d.), pp. 123-124
19. J. H. Kramers, "Geography and Commerce," *Legacy of Islam,* p. 100
20. See Harry E. Barnes, *History of Western Civilization* (New York: Harcourt, Brace & Company, Inc., 1935), I, pp. 535-536, for a brief summary of reasons for the adoption of Hellenic and Indian learning by Islam
21. Philip K. Hitti, trans., *An Arab-Assyrian Gentleman and Warrior in the Period of the Crusades,* Memoirs of Usamah Ibn-Munqidh (New York: Columbia University Press, 1929), p. 162
22. The résumé of Islamic science is based largely on two essays in the *Legacy of Islam:* Max Meyerhof, "Science and Medicine," and Carra de Vaux, "Astronomy and Mathematics."
23. Edward FitzGerald, trans., *Rubáiyát of Omar Khayyam* (Boston: Thomas B. Mosher, 1899), pp. 24, 26, 27

GENERAL REFERENCES

Valuable in the preparation of this chapter were D. S. Margoliouth, *Mohammed and the Rise of Islam,* 4th ed. (G. P. Putnam's Sons, 1927), and by the same author, *The Early Development of Mohammedanism* (Charles Scribner's Sons, 1914). The authors are indebted in large measure also to: Carl Stephenson, *Mediaeval History* (Harper & Brothers, 1935); H. E. Barnes, *The History of Western Civilization,* I (Harcourt, Brace & Co., Inc., 1935). The tenets of the Moslem religion were discussed in Robert E. Hume, *The World's Living Religions* (Charles Scribner's Sons, 1931). For the political development of Islam the authors consulted: Sir T. W. Arnold, *The Caliphate* (Clarendon Press, 1924); P. K. Hitti, *The Origins of the Islamic State* (Longmans, Green & Company, Inc., 1916); Moslem science was analyzed in E. G. Browne, *Arabian Medicine* (The Macmillan Company, 1921); Max Meyerhoff, "Science and Medicine," and Carra de Vaux, "Astronomy and Mathematics," Sir Thomas Arnold and Alfred Guillaume, eds., *The Legacy of Islam* (Clarendon Press, 1931). This last-named work was helpful also in gathering data concerning Islamic commerce, geography, architecture, and art. Selections from the Koran were taken principally from Stephenson, *op. cit.;* Robert O. Ballou, ed., *The Bible of the World* (The Viking Press, 1939). A vivid and fascinating account of the Fatimid caliphs was provided by Stanley Lane-Poole, *A History of Egypt in the Middle Ages* (Methuen & Co., Ltd., 1901).

11. The Guptas and the T'angs: two golden ages

SPECIFIC REFERENCES

1. Quoted by R. C. Majumdar, H. C. Raychaudhuri, Kalikinkar Datta, *An Advanced History of India,* 2nd ed. (London: Macmillan & Company, Ltd., 1950), p. 197
2. Ananda Coomaraswamy, *The Dance of Shiva* (Bombay: Asia Publishing House, 1948), p. 27
3. Arthur W. Ryder, trans., *The Little Clay Cart,* Harvard Oriental Series, IX, 1905, p. 62. Reprinted by permission of Harvard University Press.
4. Coomaraswamy, p. 25
5. Majumdar, Raychaudhuri, Datta, p. 366
6. Georges Coedès, *Les États Hindouisés d'Indochine et d'Indonésie* (Paris: E. de Boccard, 1948), p. 61
7. Majumdar, Raychaudhuri, Datta, p. 222
8. Quoted in K. M. Panikkar, *A Survey of Indian History* (London: Meridian Books, Ltd., 1948), p. 130
9. Jawaharlal Nehru, *The Discovery of India* (New York: The John Day Company, 1946), p. 221
10. Will Durant, *The Story of Civilization* (New York: Simon and Schuster, 1935), I, p. 461
11. L. Carrington Goodrich, *A Short History of the Chinese People* (New York: Harper & Brothers, 1943), p. 82
12. Chi Ch'ao-ting, trans., *Key Economic Areas in Chinese History* (London: George Allen and Unwin, Ltd., 1936), p. 122
13. Wolfram Eberhard, *A History of China* (London: Routledge and Kegan Paul, Ltd., 1950), p. 189
14. Quoted by René Grousset, *The Rise and Splendour of the Chinese Empire* (London: Geoffrey Bles, Ltd., 1952), p. 152
15. From the book *The Works of Li Po.* Shigeyoshi Obata, trans., 1928. Published by E. P. Dutton & Co., Inc., p. 66
16. *Ibid.,* p. 71
17. *Ibid.,* p. 97
18. William Hung, *Tu Fu, China's Greatest Poet* (Cambridge: Harvard University Press), pp. 1-2. Copyright 1952 by the President and Fellows of Harvard College.
19. Amy Lowell and Florence Ayscough, trans., "The Excursion," *Fir-Flower Tablets* (Boston: Houghton Mifflin Company, 1921), pp. 107-108
20. Homer H. Dubs, *China, the Land of Humanistic Scholarship* (Oxford: Clarendon Press, 1949), pp. 17-18
21. Thomas Francis Carter, *The Invention of Printing in China and Its Spread Westward,* rev. ed. (New York: Columbia University Press, 1931), p. 41
22. Grousset, pp. 161-162
23. Hung, p. 88
24. H. R. Williamson, *Wang An Shih* (London: Arthur Probsthain, 1937), II, pp. 166-167
25. Carter, p. 55
26. G. F. Hudson, *Europe and China* (London: Edward Arnold & Co., 1931), p. 166. See also Carter, pp. 139-144 on playing cards as a factor in the westward movement of printing.
27. Quoted by Herbert H. Gowen, *An Outline History of Japan* (New York: D. Appleton-Century Company, 1927), p. 91
28. *Ibid.,* p. 158

GENERAL REFERENCES

In preparing the materials on India, the authors consulted: H. G. Rawlinson, *India, A Short Cultural History* (D. Appleton-Century Company, 1937); R. C. Majumdar, H. C. Raychaudhuri, Kalikinkar Datta, *An Advanced History of India,* 2nd ed. (Macmillan & Company, Ltd., 1946); and K. M. Panikkar, *A Survey of Indian History* (Meridian Books, Ltd., 1948). Essays on Indian thought, art, and science with emphasis upon the Gupta period were found in Geoffrey T. Garratt, ed. *The Legacy of India* (Clarendon Press, 1937). The authors consulted A. C. Bouquet, *Hinduism* (Hutchinson's University Library, 1949) for its discussion of Hinduism during the medieval period; Ananda Coomaraswamy, *The Dance of Shiva* (Asia Publishing House, 1948) for his contribution to the study of Indian esthetics; R. Mookerji, *The Foundations of Indian Economics* (Longmans, Green & Company, Inc., 1916) for an analysis of economic life. In connection with the expansion of Indian culture into southeast Asia, the authors are indebted to H. G. Quaritch Wales, *The Making of Greater India* (Bernard Quaritch, Ltd., 1951); and to Georges Coedès, *Les États Hindouisés d'Indochine et d'Indonésie* (E. de Boccard, 1948).

On medieval China, the authors wish to acknowledge their appreciation of C. P. Fitzgerald, *China, A Short Cultural History,* rev. ed. (Cresset Press, 1950); Wolfram Eberhard, *A History of China* (Routledge and Kegan Paul, Ltd., 1950); L. Carrington Goodrich, *A Short History of the Chinese People* (Harper & Brothers, 1943); Marcel Granet, *Chinese Civilization* (Alfred A. Knopf, 1930). Other informative works included John K. Shryock, *The Origin and Development of the State Cult of Confucius* (D. Appleton-Century Company, 1932); Thomas Francis Carter, *The Invention of Printing in China and Its Spread Westward,* rev. ed. (Columbia University Press, 1931). The authors derived valuable information from H. R. Williamson's study of the Sung statesman and reformer, *Wang An Shih,* 2 vols. (Arthur Probsthain, 1937). Excellent translations of two T'ang poets are found in Shigeyoshi Obata, *The Works of Li Po* (E. P. Dutton & Co., Inc., 1928); and William Hung, *Tu Fu, China's Greatest Poet* (Harvard University Press, 1952). The authors used Leigh Ashton and Basil Gray, *Chinese Art* (Faber and Faber, Ltd., 1945), and G. F. Hudson, *Europe and China* (Edward Arnold & Co., 1931) in connection with East-West culture contacts during the Mongol period.

The basis of the short treatment of Japanese history is chiefly to be found in George B. Sansom, *Japan, A Short Cultural History* (D. Appleton-Century Company, 1931); and Herbert H. Gowen, *An Outline History of Japan* (D. Appleton-Century Company, 1927), while the authors went to Inazo Ota Nitobé, *Bushido, the Soul of Japan* (G. P. Putnam's Sons, 1905), for an explanation of Japanese feudal ethics and chivalric code.

12. The dawn of a new Europe

SPECIFIC REFERENCES

1. Quoted by John L. LaMonte, *The World of the Middle Ages* (New York: Appleton-Century-Crofts, Inc., 1949), p. 47
2. *Ibid.*, pp. 46-47
3. Quoted by H. A. L. Fisher, *A History of Europe,* rev. ed. (Boston: Houghton Mifflin Company, 1939), p. 150
4. Philip K. Hitti, *The Arabs, a Short History* (Princeton: Princeton University Press, 1949), p. 74
5. Cited in Henry St. L. B. Moss, *The Birth of the Middle Ages, 395-814* (London: Oxford University Press, 1935), p. 222
6. Edward Maslin Hulme, *The Middle Ages,* rev. ed. (New York: Henry Holt and Company, 1938), pp. 272-273
7. Moss, p. 244
8. Cited in Ross William Collins, *A History of Medieval Civilization in Europe* (Boston: Ginn and Company, 1936), p. 200
9. Moss, p. 238
10. Cited in Christopher Dawson, *The Making of Europe* (London: Sheed & Ward, 1932), pp. 266-267
11. Noted in J. W. Thompson and E. N. Johnson, *An Introduction to Medieval Europe, 300-1500* (New York: W. W. Norton & Company, Inc., 1937), p. 353
12. J. W. Thompson, *An Economic and Social History of the Middle Ages* (New York: The Century Company, 1928), p. 296
13. Barraclough and to a lesser extent LaMonte.
14. Henri Pirenne, *A History of Europe* (London: George Allen and Unwin, Ltd., 1939), p. 140
15. See Warren O. Ault, *Europe in the Middle Ages,* rev. ed. (New York: D. C. Heath and Company, 1937), p. 261
16. Ch. Petit-Dutaillis, *La Monarchie Féodale en France et en Angleterre, Xe-XIIIe siècle* (Paris: La Renaissance du Livre, 1933), p. 23
17. LaMonte, p. 149
18. Cited in Roger Bigelow Merriman, *The Rise of the Spanish Empire in the Old World and the New* (New York: The Macmillan Company, 1918), I, pp. 56-57
19. *Ibid.*, p. 53
20. Z. N. Brooke, *A History of Europe from 911 to 1198* (London: Methuen & Co., Ltd., 1938), p. 14

GENERAL REFERENCES

John L. LaMonte, *The World of the Middle Ages* (Appleton-Century-Crofts, Inc., 1949); Sidney Painter, *The Rise of the Feudal Monarchies* (Cornell University Press, 1951) and *A History of the Middle Ages* (Alfred A. Knopf, 1953); C. W. Previté-Orton, *Shorter Cambridge Medieval History,* 2 vols, (Cambridge University Press, 1952), and *A History of Europe, 1198-1378* (Methuen & Co., Ltd., 1943); W. T. Waugh, *History of Europe from 1378-1494* (G. P. Putnam's Sons, 1932); Henri Pirenne, *A History of Europe from the Invasions to the XVI Century* (George Allen and Unwin, Ltd., 1949); James Westfall Thompson, *Feudal Germany* (University of Chicago Press, 1928); Ch. Petit-Dutaillis, *La Monarchie Féodale en France et en Angleterre, Xe-XIIIe siècle* (La Renaissance du Livre, 1933); G. Barraclough, *The Origins of Modern Germany* (Basil Blackwell, 1946); Anatole G. Mazour, *Russia Past and Present* (D. Van Nostrand Company, Inc., 1951). For other medieval political studies see the general references for chap. 8.

13. Castle, manor, and town

SPECIFIC REFERENCES

1. James W. Thompson, *An Economic and Social History of the Middle Ages, 300-1300* (New York: D. Appleton-Century Company, 1928), p. 708
2. *Ibid.*, p. 717
3. Quoted by George Burton Adams, *Civilization During the Middle Ages,* rev. ed. (New York: Charles Scribner's Sons, 1914), p. 222
4. *Ibid.*, p. 222
5. Sydney M. Brown, *Medieval Europe,* rev. ed.

(New York: Harcourt, Brace and Company, 1935), p. 307

6. L. F. Salzman, *English Life in the Middle Ages* (London: Oxford University Press, 1926), p. 96
7. Quoted by Brown, p. 312
8. Quoted by Salzman, p. 139
9. Geoffrey Chaucer, *The Canterbury Tales,* J. U. Nicolson, trans., p. 5. Copyright 1933 by Covici-Friede. Used by permission of Crown Publishers, Inc.
10. Quoted by Salzman, p. 261
11. N. S. B. Gras, *A History of Agriculture in Europe and America* (New York: F. S. Crofts & Co., 1925), p. 78
12. *Ibid.*, p. 94
13. Thompson, p. 738
14. Gras, p. 48
15. *Ibid.*, p. 87
16. Carl Stephenson, *Mediaeval History* (New York: Harper & Brothers, 1935), p. 268.
17. Gras, p. 92
18. Thompson, p. 760
19. *Ibid.*, p. 790
20. L. F. Salzman, *English Industries of the Middle Ages* (Oxford: Clarendon Press, 1923), pp. 309-310
21. Salzman, *English Life in the Middle Ages,* p. 87
22. *Ibid.*, p. 83

GENERAL REFERENCES

The authors are primarily indebted for the framework and data of this chapter to James Westfall Thompson's splendid study, *An Economic and Social History of the Middle Ages, 300-1300* (D. Appleton-Century Company, 1928). Other books which proved of value and deserve recognition are: Carl Stephenson, *Mediaeval History* (Harper & Brothers, 1935); G. B. Adams, *Civilization During the Middle Ages,* rev. ed. (Charles Scribner's Sons, 1914); H. E. Barnes, *A History of Western Civilization* (Harcourt, Brace and Company, 1935). Light was thrown on the various aspects of feudalism by: Charles Seignobos, *The Feudal Régime* (Henry Holt and Company, 1902); Achille Luchaire, *Social France in the Time of Philip Augustus* (Henry Holt and Company, 1912); Sir Paul G. Vinogradoff, "Customary Law," *The Legacy of the Middle Ages,* G. C. Crump and E. F. Jacob, eds., (Clarendon Press, 1927). Of special help in the discussion of the manorial system were: F. A. Ogg and W. R. Sharp, *The Economic Development of Modern Europe* (The Macmillan Company, 1926); Prosper Boissonnade, *Life and Work in Medieval Europe* (Alfred A. Knopf, 1927); Sir P. G. Vinogradoff, *The Growth of the Manor,* 2nd ed. (The Macmillan Company, 1911), a rich and detailed study of the origins of the manor. Life on the manor was vividly discussed in G. G. Coulton, *The Medieval Village* (The Macmillan Company, 1925). The origins of the town were set forth in: H. Pirenne, *Mediaeval Cities,* trans. from French (Princeton University Press, 1925); Carl Stephenson's more technical *Borough and Town* (Medieval Academy of America, 1933).

Trade and industry were discussed in: Herbert Heaton, *Economic History of Europe* (Harper & Brothers, 1936); L. F. Salzman, *English Industries of the Middle Ages* (Clarendon Press, 1923); N. S. B. Gras, "The Economic Activity of Towns," *The Legacy of the Middle Ages;* essays appearing in *Universal World History,* J. A. Hammerton, ed. (Wm. H. Wise & Co., 1939). Some delightful sketches of medieval social life in the country and city were furnished by J. J. Jusserand, *English Wayfaring Life in the Middle Ages* (G. P. Putnam's Sons, 1889), and L. F. Salzman, *English Life in the Middle Ages* (Oxford University Press, 1926).

14. Bishop, priest, and monk

SPECIFIC REFERENCES

1. Geoffrey Chaucer, *The Canterbury Tales,* J. U. Nicolson, trans., p. 5. © 1933 by Covici-Friede. By permission of Crown Publishers, Inc.
2. *Matthew* 16:18-19
3. Ian C. Hannah, *Christian Monasticism* (New York: The Macmillan Company, 1925), p. 13
4. *Ibid.* Quoted on pp. 79, 80, 81
5. J. H. Robinson, *Readings in European History* (Boston: Ginn and Company, 1906), p. 159
6. J. W. Thompson and E. N. Johnson, *An Introduction to Medieval Europe, 300-1500* (New York: W. W. Norton & Company, Inc., 1937), p. 682
7. David Patrick, ed., *Statutes of the Scottish Church, 1225-1559* (Edinburgh: Edinburgh University Press, 1907), p. 4
8. See G. B. Adams, *Civilization During the Middle Ages* (New York: Charles Scribner's Sons, 1914), chap. 10
9. Warren O. Ault, *Europe in the Middle Ages* (Boston: D. C. Heath and Company, 1937), pp. 314-318
10. T. F. Tout, *The Empire and the Papacy, 918-1273,* 8th ed. (London: Rivingtons), p. 126
11. *Ibid.*, p. 128
12. Carl Stephenson, *Mediaevel History* (New York: Harper & Brothers, 1935), p. 317
13. Ault, p. 412
14. *Ibid.*, p. 412
15. Jean Guiraud, *The Medieval Inquisition,* E. C.

Messenger, trans. (London: Burns Oates and Washbourne, 1929), p. 133

16. Sidney R. Packard, *Europe and the Church under Innocent* III (New York: Henry Holt and Company, 1927), p. 79
17. Hannah, p. 158
18. *Ibid.,* pp. 161-162
19. Chaucer, p. 8
20. Quoted by Packard, p. 15
21. Chaucer, p. 21
22. Quoted by L. F. Salzman, *English Life in the Middle Ages* (London: Oxford University Press, 1927), p. 278
23. Sydney M. Brown, *Medieval Europe* (New York: Harcourt, Brace & Company, Inc., 1935), pp. 386-387
24. *Ibid.,* pp. 382-383

GENERAL REFERENCES

Of valuable assistance in the preparation of this chapter was the work of J. W. Thompson and E. N. Johnson, *An Introduction to Medieval Europe, 300-1500* (W. W. Norton and Company, 1937). Other sources consulted included: Carl Stephenson, *Mediaeval History* (Harper & Brothers, 1935); Warren O. Ault, *Europe in the Middle Ages* (D. C. Heath and Company, 1937); Sydney M. Brown, *Medieval Europe* (Harcourt, Brace & Company, Inc., 1935); G. B. Adams, *Civilization During the Middle Ages* (Charles Scribner's Sons, 1914). Two works by A. C. Flick whose value cannot be overestimated were *The Rise of the Medieval Church* (G. P. Putnam's Sons, 1909), and especially *The Decline of the Medieval Church,* 2 vols. (Alfred A. Knopf, 1930). Ian C. Hannah, *Christian Monasticism* (The Macmillan Company, 1925), was most useful in preparing material pertaining to this phase of church history; the Albigensian Crusades and the origin of the Inquisition were admirably summarized in Jean Guiraud, *The Medieval Inquisition,* E. C. Messenger, trans. (Burns Oates and Washbourne, 1929). A work found helpful in the study of the pontificate of Innocent III was Sidney R. Packard, *Europe and the Church under Innocent* III (Henry Holt and Company, 1927).

Helpful also were G. G. Coulton, *Five Centuries of Religion,* II (Cambridge University Press, 1927) and Gabriel le Bras, "Canon Law," *The Legacy of the Middle Ages,* G. C. Crump and E. F. Jacob, eds. (Clarendon Press, 1927).

15. University and cathedral

SPECIFIC REFERENCES

1. Henry Osborn Taylor, *The Mediaeval Mind,* 4th ed. (Cambridge: Harvard University Press, 1938), II, p. 327
2. Quoted by Carl Stephenson, *Mediaeval History,* (New York: Harper & Brothers, 1935), p. 420
3. Quoted by Charles Homer Haskins, *The Renaissance of the Twelfth Century (*Cambridge: Harvard University Press, 1927), pp. 354-355
4. *Ibid.,* p. 287
5. Quoted by C. H. Haskins, *Studies in the History of Mediaeval Science* (1927), p. 40
6. Taylor, II, p. 514
7. Quoted by Warren O. Ault, *Europe in the Middle Ages* (Boston: D. C. Heath and Company, 1937), p. 499
8. Trans. by E. Brehaut, *An Encyclopedist of the Dark Ages* (New York: Columbia University Press, 1912)
9. Quoted by Lynn Thorndike, *Science and Thought in the Fifteenth Century* (New York: Columbia University Press, 1927), pp. 20-21
10. *Ibid.,* p. 19
11. Quoted by Taylor, II, p. 524
12. Quoted by Taylor, II, p. 538
13. Ault, p. 495
14. C. H. Haskins, *The Rise of the Universities* (New York: Henry Holt and Company, 1923), p. 15
15. Stephenson, p. 438
16. C. H. Haskins, *Studies in Mediaeval Culture* (Oxford: Clarendon Press, 1929), pp. 11-12
17. Haskins, *The Rise of the Universities,* p. 105
18. Geoffrey Chaucer, *The Canterbury Tales,* J. U. Nicolson, trans., p. 10. Copyright 1933 by Covici-Friede. Used by permission of Crown Publishers, Inc.
19. Quoted by Ault, p. 504
20. Cesare Foligno, *Latin Thought During the Middle Ages* (Oxford: Clarendon Press, 1929), pp. 96-97
21. Quoted by Stephenson, p. 446
22. John Addington Symonds, *Wine, Women, and Song* (London: Chatto and Windus, 1931), pp. 61-62
23. *Ibid.,* pp. 67-69
24. This material is skillfully handled in Thompson and Johnson, *An Introduction to Medieval Europe, 300-1500* (New York: W. W. Norton and Company, 1937), pp. 770-774. For a longer study of troubadour forms, see Joseph Anglade, *Historie Sommaire de la Littérature Méridionale au Moyen Age* (Paris, 1921).
25. The Chaucerian phrases are the translation of Nicolson, pp. 3, 4, 5, 17, and 18
26. Henry W. Longfellow, trans., "Inferno," *The Divine Comedy of Dante Alighieri* (Boston: Houghton Mifflin Company, 1886), IX, canto xxxiv, pp. 174-175
27. James Westfall Thompson, *An Economic and*

Social History of the Middle Ages, 300-1300 (New York: D. Appleton-Century Company, 1928), p. 672

GENERAL REFERENCES

The scholar to whom the authors feel most indebted in the preparation of this chapter is Charles Homer Haskins. They acknowledge their debt to this eminent medievalist for: *The Rise of the Universities* (Henry Holt and Company, 1923); *The Renaissance of the Twelfth Century* (Harvard University Press, 1927); *Studies in the History of Mediaeval Science* (Harvard University Press, 1927); *Studies in Mediaeval Culture* (Clarendon Press, 1929). Thanks are tendered also to J. W. Thompson and E. N. Johnson for the assistance derived from their *Introduction to Medieval Europe, 300-1500* (W. W. Norton and Company, 1937). In the preparation of general background, the authors also drew on: Sydney M. Brown, *Medieval Europe* (Harcourt, Brace and Company, 1932); Warren O. Ault, *Europe in the Middle Ages* (D. C. Heath and Company, 1937); H. E. Barnes, *A History of Western Civilization* (Harcourt, Brace and Company, 1935). In regard to medieval philosophy, by far the most important source used was Henry Osborn Taylor, *The Mediaeval Mind,* 2 vols., 4th ed. (Harvard University Press, 1938); and an excellent biography was Joseph McCabe, *Peter Abélard* (G. P. Putnam's Sons, 1901). Besides using Haskins extensively in compiling data for the rise of the medieval universities and their life, recourse was also made to Gabriel Compayre, *Abélard, and the Origin and Early History of Universities* (Charles Scribner's Sons, 1901); H. Rashdall, *The Universities of Europe in the Middle Ages,* 2 vols. (The Macmillan Company, 1895); Robert S. Rait, *Life in the Medieval University* (Cambridge University Press, 1931). H. E. Barnes, *A History of Historical Writing* (University of Oklahoma Press, 1937), was consulted in regard to medieval historiography. In the section on literature use was made of Helen Waddell, *The Wandering Scholars* (Houghton Mifflin Company, 1927); J. A. Symonds, *Wine, Women, and Song* (Chatto and Windus, 1931); Cesare Foligno, *Latin Thought During the Middle Ages* (Clarendon Press, 1929); essays by Claude Jenkins and Cesare Foligno in *The Legacy of the Middle Ages,* G. C. Crump and E. F. Jacob, eds. (Clarendon Press, 1927). Lynn Thorndike, *Science and Thought in the Fifteenth Century* (Columbia University Press, 1929), was useful on medieval science. Three works were important in the writing of the section on medieval art and esthetics: Elie Faure, *History of Art,* 4 vols., II (Harper & Brothers, 1921-1924); E. Male, *Religious Art in France, Thirteenth Century* (E. P. Dutton and Company, 1913) on the symbolism in Gothic art; and Henry Adams, *Mont-Saint-Michel and Chartres* (Houghton Mifflin Company, 1924) on the spirit which motivated the building of the great Gothic cathedrals of France. Mention should also be made of Paul Vitry's analysis of medieval sculpture in *The Legacy of the Middle Ages.*

16. Nations in the making

SPECIFIC REFERENCES

1. Quoted by Walter Phelps Hall and Robert G. Albion, *A History of England and the British Empire* (Boston: Ginn and Company, 1937), p. 70
2. Quoted by A. L. Cross, *A Shorter History of England and Greater Britain* (New York: The Macmillan Company, 1939), p. 89
3. G. B. Adams, *Constitutional History of England* (New York: Henry Holt and Company, 1934), p. 130
4. Sydney M. Brown, *Medieval Europe* (New York: Harcourt, Brace & Company, Inc., 1932), p. 219
5. Paul Van Dyke, *The Story of France from Julius Caesar to Napoleon* III (New York: Charles Scribner's Sons, 1928), p. 101
6. Quoted by F. Funck-Brentano, *The Middle Ages* (New York: G. P. Putnam's Sons, 1923), p. 250
7. Quoted by H. A. L. Fisher, *A History of Europe* (London: Edward Arnold & Co., 1937), p. 294
8. George G. Coulton, *From St. Francis to Dante* (London: David Nutt, 1906), p. 140
9. Henri Pirenne, *A History of Europe from the Invasions to the* XVI *Century* (London: George Allen & Unwin, Ltd., 1939), pp. 338-339
10. W. T. Waugh, *History of Europe from 1378 to 1494* (New York: G. P. Putnam's Sons, 1932) p. 241
11. Roger Bigelow Merriman, *The Rise of the Spanish Empire in the Old World and the New* (New York: The Macmillan Company, 1918), I, p. 60
12. *Ibid.,* pp. 88-89
13. G. Barraclough, *The Origins of Modern Germany* (Oxford: Basil Blackwell, 1946), p. 115
14. *Ibid.,* pp. 146-147
15. John L. LaMonte, *The World of the Middle Ages* (New York: Appleton-Century-Crofts, Inc., 1949), p. 282
16. Quoted by H. D. Sedgwick, *Italy in the Thirteenth Century* (Boston: Houghton Mifflin Company, 1912), I, p. 119
17. Barraclough, p. 233
18. James Westfall Thompson, *Feudal Germany*

(Chicago: University of Chicago Press, 1928), xviii

19. Quoted by J. Janssen, *History of the German People at the Close of the Middle Ages* (St. Louis: B. Herder Book Company, n.d.), II, pp. 156-157
20. J. W. Thompson, *An Economic and Social History of the Middle Ages, 300-1300* (New York: D. Appleton-Century Company, 1928), p. 783
21. LaMonte, p. 710
22. Waugh, p. 447
23. Waugh, p. 448
24. Bernard Pares, *A History of Russia* (New York: Alfred A. Knopf, 1941) p. 73

GENERAL REFERENCES

For the general narrative of European political history frequent reference has been made to the following works: Ross William Collins, *A History of Medieval Civilization* (Ginn and Company, 1936); E. M. Hulme, *The Middle Ages* (Henry Holt and Company, 1938); Warren O. Ault, *Europe in the Middle Ages* (D. C. Heath and Company, 1937); G. B. Adams, *Civilization During the Middle Ages* (Charles Scribner's Sons 1914); H. A. L. Fisher, *A History of Europe* (Edward Arnold and Company, 1937). The following works were relied upon for medieval English history: G. M. Trevelyan, *History of England* (Longmans, Green and Company, 1927); A. L. Cross, *A Shorter History of England and Greater Britain* (The Macmillan Company, 1939); F. C. Dietz, *A Political and Social History of England,* rev. ed. (The Macmillan Company, 1932). William E. Lunt, *History of England* (Harper & Brothers, 1928), was especially helpful on constitutional developments, as were Albert B. White, *Making of the English Constitution,* 2nd ed. rev. (G. P. Putnam's Sons, 1925); W. A. Morris, *Constitutional History of England to 1216* (The Macmillan Company, 1930). George B. Adams, *Constitutional History of England* (Henry Holt and Company, 1934), was especially valuable in preparing the discussion on *Magna Charta.* The treatment of the growth of the French monarchy is chiefly indebted to J. W. Thompson and E. N. Johnson, *An Introduction to Medieval Europe, 300-1500* (W. W. Norton and Company, 1937); G. B. Adams, *The Growth of the French Nation* (The Macmillan Company, 1919); Paul Van Dyke, *The Story of France from Julius Caesar to Napoleon* III (Charles Scribner's Sons, 1928); George W. Kitchin, *History of France,* 3 vols. (London: Oxford University Press, 1873-1887); Robert B. Mowat, *The Later Middle Ages* (London: Oxford University Press, 1917). Other sources valuable for the political development of Italy, Spain, Russia, and Germany were: H. D. Sedgwick, *A Short History of Italy* (Houghton Mifflin Company, 1905); and M. W. Williams, *The People and Politics of Latin America* (Ginn and Company, 1930), for a résumé of Iberian political history; C. E. Chapman, *A History of Spain* (The Macmillan Company, 1922); J. W. Thompson, *Feudal Germany* (University of Chicago Press, 1928); Bernard Pares, *A History of Russia* (Alfred A. Knopf, 1941). Suggestions and interpretations on medieval Italy and Germany were also obtained from Sydney M. Brown, *Medieval Europe* (Harcourt, Brace and Company, 1932).

17. Man is the measure

SPECIFIC REFERENCES

1. Lynn Thorndike, *Science and Thought in the Fifteenth Century* (New York: Columbia University Press, 1929), pp. 12-13
2. Taken from Giorgio Vasari, *Lives of Seventy of the Most Eminent Painters, Sculptors, and Architects,* 4 vols., ed. and annotated by E. H. and E. U. Blashfield and A. A. Hopkins (New York: Charles Scribner's Sons, 1926), II, p. 404
3. *Ibid.,* II, p. 376
4. Quoted by Thomas Craven, *Men of Art* (New York: Simon and Schuster, 1931), p. 158
5. Quoted by Henry S. Lucas, *The Renaissance and the Reformation* (New York: Harper & Brothers, 1934), p. 335
6. *Ibid.,* p. 335.
7. Quoted by Henry Osborn Taylor, *Thought and Expression in the Sixteenth Century* (New York: The Macmillan Company, 1920), I, pp. 328-329
8. *Ibid.,* I, p. 175
9. *Richard* II, Act II, Scene 1, 40-50

GENERAL REFERENCES

In the preparation of this chapter, much reliance was placed upon Henry S. Lucas, *The Renaissance and the Reformation* (Harper & Brothers, 1934), both for data and structure. Among other sources of a general nature consulted were: J. Huizinga, *The Waning of the Middle Ages* (Longmans, Green and Company, 1924); W. T. Waugh, *History of Europe from 1378 to 1494* (G. P. Putnam's Sons, 1932); E. M. Hulme, *The Renaissance, the Protestant Revolution and the Catholic Reformation in Continental Europe* (D. Appleton-Century Company, 1914); C. J. H. Hayes, *A Political and Cultural History of Modern Europe,* I (The Macmillan Company, 1933); H. E. Barnes, *The History of Western Civilization,* I, chaps. 31-32 (Harcourt, Brace and Company, 1935); J. W.

Thompson and others, *The Civilization of the Renaissance,* Florence Clement, ed. (University of Chicago Press, 1929). Data for the intellectual aspects of the Renaissance was procured from: H. O. Taylor, *Thought and Expression in the Sixteenth Century,* I, chaps. 1-4, 6-7, 11-13 (The Macmillan Company, 1920); J. H. Randall, *The Making of the Modern Mind,* Book II (Houghton Mifflin Company, 926); besides direct reference to Machiavelli's *Prince,* W. K. Marriott, trans. (E. P. Dutton and Company, 1908); More's *Utopia,* William D. Armes, ed. (The Macmillan Company, 1912); Erasmus' *In Praise of Folly* (Oxford University Press, 1925); Francis Bacon's *New Atlantis* (Oxford University Press, 1915). Supplementing the fascinating accounts of the lives and works of the Renaissance artists found in Giorgio Vasari, *The Lives of Seventy of the Most Eminent Painters, Sculptors, and Architects,* ed. and annotated by E. H. and E. U. Blashfield and A. A. Hopkins, II (Charles Scribner's Sons, 1926), were the works by: Thomas Craven, *Men of Art* (Simon and Schuster, 1931); Sheldon Cheney, *A World History of Art,* chaps. 15-19 (The Viking Press, 1937); F. J. Mather, *A History of Italian Painting* (Henry Holt and Company, 1923). A better insight into the scope of Renaissance letters was gained from the *Cambridge History of English Literature,* III, A. W. Ward and A. R. Waller, eds. (G. P. Putnam's Sons, 1911); Arthur Tilley, *The Literature of the French Renaissance,* 2 vols. (The Macmillan Company, 1904). Benvenuto Cellini, *Autobiography,* J. A. Symonds, trans. (Garden City Publishing Company, 1927), also affords insight into the Renaissance.

18. The Ninety-Five Theses

SPECIFIC REFERENCES

1. Alexander C. Flick, *Decline of the Medieval Church* (New York: Alfred A. Knopf, 1930), I, pp. 26, 27
2. Quoted in *ibid.,* p. 293
3. *Ibid.* Summarized by H. E. Barnes, *The History of Western Civilization* (New York: Harcourt, Brace and Company, 1935), I, p. 710
4. *Romans* 1:17
5. Quoted by Carlton Hayes, *A Political and Cultural History of Modern Europe* (New York: The Macmillan Company, 1933), I, p. 154
6. Quoted by Preserved Smith, *The Life and Letters of Martin Luther* (New York: Houghton Mifflin Company, 1911), p. 41
7. Hayes, I, pp. 156-157
8. Henry S. Lucas, *The Renaissance and the Reformation* (New York: Harper & Brothers, 1934), p. 457
9. Quoted by Hayes, I, p. 158
10. Preserved Smith, *The Age of the Reformation* (New York: Henry Holt and Company, 1920), p. 124
11. Quoted in *ibid.,* p. 285
12. Quoted in *ibid.,* p. 185
13. *Ibid.,* p. 164
14. *Ibid.,* p. 174
15. *Ibid.,* p. 178
16. James H. Robinson, *Readings in European History* (Boston: Ginn and Company, 1906), II, p. 159
17. *Ibid.,* pp. 160-161

GENERAL REFERENCES

Acknowledgment for the material found in this chapter should be made principally to Alexander C. Flick, *Decline of the Medieval Church,* 2 vols. (Alfred A. Knopf, 1930); Preserved Smith, *The Age of the Reformation* (Henry Holt and Company, 1920); T. M. Lindsay, *History of the Reformation,* 2 vols. (Charles Scribner's Sons, 1928); Charles Beard, *The Reformation of the Sixteenth Century in Its Relation to Modern Thought and Knowledge* (Constable and Company, 1927). General sources used were: Henry S. Lucas, *The Renaissance and the Reformation* (Harper & Brothers, 1934); Carlton J. H. Hayes, *A Political and Cultural History of Modern Europe,* I (The Macmillan Company, 1933); H. E. Barnes, *The History of Western Civilization,* I, chap. 23 (Harcourt, Brace and Company, 1935); essays in *Universal World History,* VII, J. A. Hammerton, ed. (Wm. H. Wise & Company, 1939); George M. Trevelyan, *History of England,* Book II (Longmans, Green and Company, 1937). The economic aspects of the Religious Revolt were admirably put forward in R. H. Tawney, *Religion and the Rise of Capitalism* (Harcourt, Brace and Company, 1926). Preserved Smith, *The Life and Letters of Martin Luther* (Houghton Mifflin Company, 1914) is useful, as is G. E. Harkness for *John Calvin: the Man and His Ethics* (Henry Holt and Company, 1931).

19. Powers and power politics emerge in the West

SPECIFIC REFERENCES

1. William Shakespeare, *King Richard* III, Act V, Scene 5.
2. Quoted by A. J. Grant, *A History of Europe from 1494 to 1610* (New York: G. P. Putnam's Sons, 1932), p. 28
3. Quoted by Robert Ergang, *Europe from the*

Renaissance to Waterloo (Boston: D. C. Heath and Company, 1939), p. 18

4. Quoted by D. J. Hill, *A History of Diplomacy in the International Development of Europe* (New York: Longmans, Green and Company, Inc., 1914), II, p. 321
5. Quoted by Frederick L. Schuman, *International Politics: An Introduction to the Western State System* (New York: McGraw-Hill Book Company, Inc., 3rd ed., 1937), p. 33
6. Quoted in *Encyclopaedia of the Social Sciences,* Edwin R. A. Seligman, ed. (New York: The Macmillan Company, 1933), I, p. 90
7. John H. Randall, *The Making of the Modern Mind* (Boston: Houghton Mifflin Company, 1940), p. 175
8. Roger B. Merriman, *Suleiman the Magnificent* (Cambridge: Harvard University Press, 1944), p. 37
9. *Ibid.,* p. 115
10. Quoted in *ibid.,* p. 130
11. Grant, p. 374
12. R. T. Davies, *The Golden Century of Spain* (New York: The Macmillan Company, 1937), p. 117
13. Quoted in Ergang, p. 296
14. Quoted in *ibid.,* p. 246
15. Quoted in Arthur L. Cross, *A Shorter History of England and Greater Britain* (New York: The Macmillan Company, 1920), p. 260
16. Warren O. Ault, *Europe in Modern Times* (Boston: D. C. Heath and Company, 1946), p. 134
17. Quoted in Grant, p. 177
18. Quoted in *ibid.,* p. 176
19. Quoted in *Encyclopaedia of the Social Sciences,* III, p. 426
20. Quoted by C. V. Wedgwood, *The Thirty Years' War* (New Haven: Yale University Press, 1939), p. 526

GENERAL REFERENCES

In the preparation of this chapter frequent reference has been made to the following works: G. M. Trevelyan, *England Under the Stuarts* (G. P. Putnam's Sons, 1925); A. J. Grant, *A History of Europe from 1494 to 1610* (G. P. Putnam's Sons, 1932); W. T. Waugh, *History of Europe from 1378 to 1494* (G. P. Putnam's Sons, 1932); Arthur H. Johnson, *Europe in the Sixteenth Century, 1494-1598* (The Macmillan Company, 1928); and Robert Ergang, *Europe from the Renaissance to Waterloo* (D. C. Heath and Company, 1939). Many helpful suggestions were gleaned from the late Professor H. A. L. Fisher's *A History of Europe* (Houghton Mifflin Company, 1939), which is brilliantly written as well as being the product of profound scholarship. An interesting interpretation of the period was found in Sir Charles Oman's *The Sixteenth Century* (E. P. Dutton and Company, 1937), and by the same author, *History of the Art of War in the Sixteenth Century* (E. P. Dutton and Company, 1937). Chapters in Esme Wingfield-Stratford's *The History of British Civilization* (Harcourt, Brace and Company, 1930), dealing with early modern times in England, were most helpful. For the English scene the following works were also useful: C. H. Firth, *Oliver Cromwell and the Rule of the Puritans in England* (G. P. Putnam's Sons, 1906); Conyers Read, *The Tudors: Personalities and Practical Politics in Sixteenth Century England* (Henry Holt and Company, 1936); J. E. Neale, *Queen Elizabeth* (Harcourt, Brace and Company, 1934); and Francis Hackett, *Henry the Eighth* (Horace Liveright, 1929). The most valuable survey of international relations in western Europe in the first half of the seventeenth century was found in C. V. Wedgwood's *The Thirty Years' War* (Yale University Press, 1939). Other works of special importance were: R. T. Davies, *The Golden Century of Spain* (The Macmillan Company, 1937); Roger B. Merriman, *The Rise of the Spanish Empire,* especially vol. IV (The Macmillan Company, 1934); William L. McElwee, *The Reign of Charles* v, *1516-1558* (The Macmillan Company, 1936); Pieter Geyl, *Revolt of the Netherlands against Spain, 1555-1609* (Williams and Norgate, 1932); and Albert H. Lybyer, *Government of the Ottoman Empire in the Time of Suleiman the Magnificent* (Harvard University Press, 1913).

20. To the ends of the earth

SPECIFIC REFERENCES

1. J. E. Gillespie, *A History of Geographical Discovery, 1400-1800* (New York: Henry Holt and Company, 1933), p. 22
2. Quoted by Gillespie, pp. 36-37
3. Quoted by H. G. Rawlinson, *India, A Short Cultural History* (New York: D. Appleton-Century Company, 1938), p. 262
4. Quoted by Rawlinson, p. 313
5. Quoted by Herbert H. Gowen, *An Outline History of Japan* (New York: D. Appleton-Century Company, 1927), p. 255

GENERAL REFERENCES

The section of this chapter devoted to exploration was based largely on: J. N. L. Baker, *History of Geography and Exploration* (Houghton Mifflin Company, 1932); J. E. Gillespie, *A History of Geographical Discovery, 1400-1800* (Henry Holt and Company, 1933); J. K. Wright, *The Geographical Basis of European History* (Henry Holt and Company, 1928); W. C. Abbott, *The Expansion of Europe,* 2 vols. (Henry Holt and Company, 1924). Data for the New World civilizations is based in large part on: Edgar Hewett, *Ancient Life in the American Southwest* (The Bobbs-Merrill Company, Inc., 1930); H. E. Bolton and T. M. Marshall, *Colonization of North America, 1492-1783* (The Macmillan Company, 1920); Herbert J. Spinden, *Ancient Civilizations of Mexico and Central America,* 2nd ed. rev. (American Museum of Natural History, 1922); Thomas A. Joyce, "The America of Aztec and Inca," *Universal World History,* ed. by J. A. Hammerton, VII, chap. 119 (Wm. H. Wise & Co., 1939). Important in the gathering of data for the European invasion of Asia were: R. S. Whiteway, *The Rise of Portuguese Power in India, 1497-1550* (Constable and Company, 1899); K. G. Jayne, *Vasco Da Gama and His Successors, 1460-1580* (Methuen and Company, 1910); Clive Day, *The Policy and Administration of the Dutch in Java* (The Macmillan Company, 1904); Edward Thompson and G. T. Garratt, *Rise and Fulfillment of British Rule in India* (The Macmillan Company, 1934); Arnold Wright, *Early English Adventures in the East* (E. P. Dutton & Co., 1917). Civilization under the Moguls was traced through help derived from: H. G. Rawlinson, *India, A Short Cultural History* (D. Appleton-Century Company, 1938); V. A. Smith, *Akbar, the Great Mogul* (Oxford University Press, 1919); George B. Malleson, *Akbar and the Rise of the Mughal Empire* (Clarendon Press, 1908); René Grousset, *The Civilization of India,* trans. from French by C. A. Phillips (Tudor Publishing House, 1939); two works by William Harrison Moreland, *From Akbar to Aurangzeb: A Study in Indian Economic History* (The Macmillan Company, 1923), and *India at the Death of Akbar: An Economic Study* (The Macmillan Company, 1920). The study of China under the Mings was derived largely from C. P. Fitzgerald, *China, A Short Cultural History* (D. Appleton-Century Company, 1938); Gowen and Hall, *Outline History of China* (D. Appleton-Century Company, 1939); Lionel Giles, "China Under the Ming Dynasty." *Universal World History,* J. A. Hammerton, ed., VII, chap. 123 (Wm. H. Wise & Co., 1939). The growth of Japan at this time is told well in: George B. Sansom, *Japan, A Short Cultural History* (D. Appleton-Century Company, 1931); Herbert H. Gowen, *An Outline History of Japan* (D. Appleton-Century Company, 1927), on which the authors relied heavily. Another important work to be acknowledged is Inazo Nitobe, *Bushido, the Soul of Japan* (G. P. Putnam's Sons, 1905).

List of illustrations

1. Toward civilization

2. The Nile, the Tigris, and the Euphrates

3. The Indus and the Ganges

4. The Wei and the Hwang Ho

5. The Greek achievement

6. The ascendancy of Rome

7. The world in classical times

8. Interval in the West

9. Crossroads of the world

10. The triumph of Islam

11. The Guptas and the T'angs: two golden ages

12. The dawn of a new Europe

13. Castle, manor, and town

14. Bishop, priest, and monk

15. University and cathedral

16. Nations in the making

17. Man is the measure

18. The Ninety-Five Theses

19. Powers and power politics emerge in the West

20. To the ends of the earth

General index

A

C

D

E

H

I

J

M

P

Q

R

S

T

U

V

4 5 6 7 8 9 10 11 12 13 14 15 16 17 18 19 20 21 22 23 24 25 64 63 62 61 60 59 58 57 56

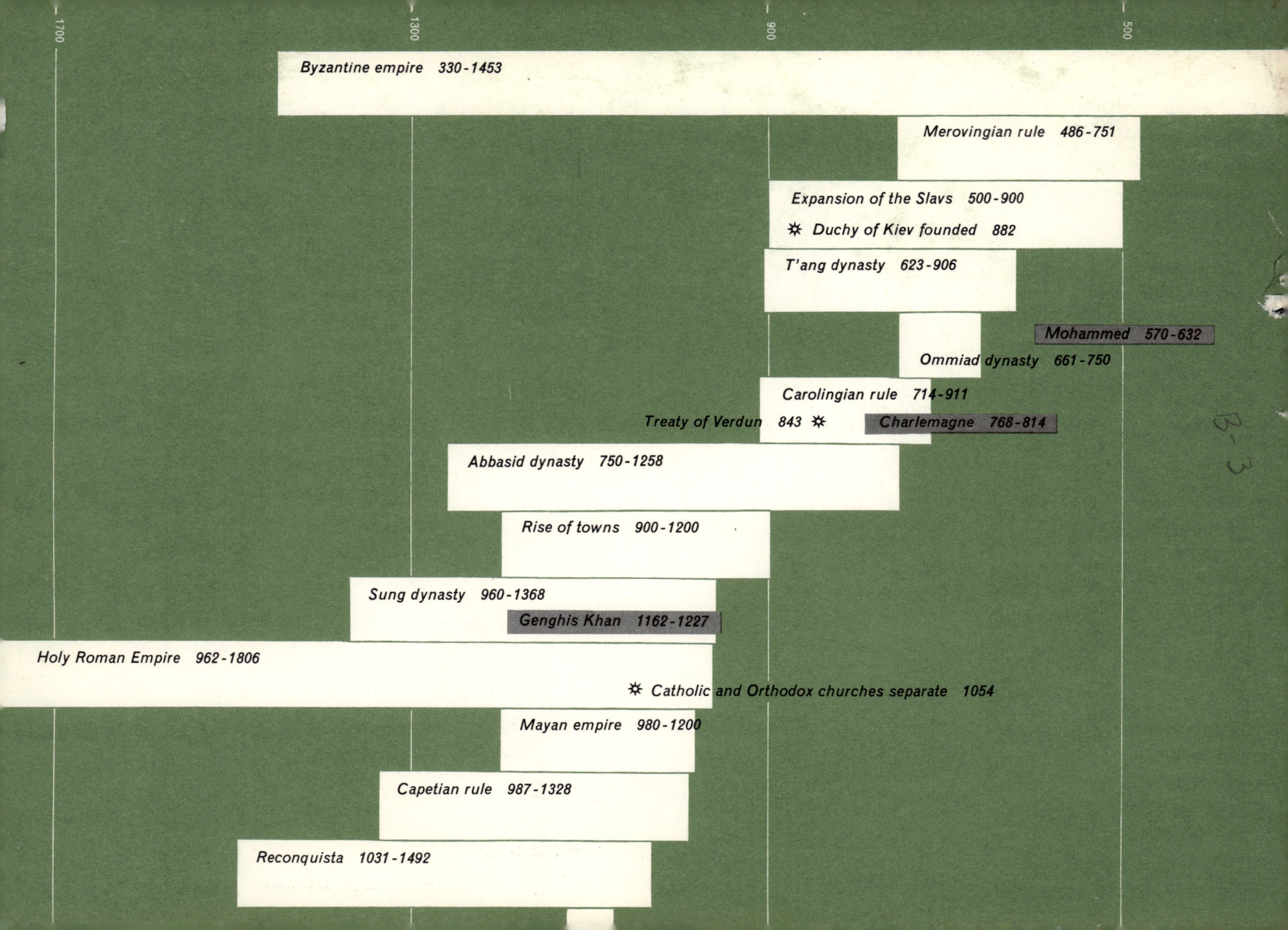

1700 1300 900 500

Byzantine empire 330-1453

Merovingian rule 486-751

Expansion of the Slavs 500-900

✲ *Duchy of Kiev founded 882*

T'ang dynasty 623-906

Mohammed 570-632

Ommiad dynasty 661-750

Carolingian rule 714-911

Treaty of Verdun 843 ✲

Charlemagne 768-814

Abbasid dynasty 750-1258

Rise of towns 900-1200

Sung dynasty 960-1368

Genghis Khan 1162-1227

Holy Roman Empire 962-1806

✲ *Catholic and Orthodox churches separate 1054*

Mayan empire 980-1200

Capetian rule 987-1328

Reconquista 1031-1492

B-3